LIBRARY ASSOCIATION
LONDON AND HOME COUNTIES BRANCH
KENT SUB-BRANCH

THE KENT BIBLIOGRAPHY

A finding list of Kent material in the
Public Libraries of the County and of
the adjoining London Boroughs

Compiled by the late George Bennett

Hon. Editors: Wyn Bergess and Carleton Earl

LIBRARY ASSOCIATION
LONDON AND HOME COUNTIES BRANCH
1977

+
016.94223
B439

8109141

To past and present members of the Kent
Sub-Branch on the occasion of the Centenary
of the Library Association, 1877-1977

ISBN 0 902119 20 6

Printed and bound in England by
STAPLES PRINTERS LIMITED
at The Stanhope Press, Rochester, Kent.

The publication of this list of books on Kent provides what many librarians in the area have felt would be a desirable aid to their work in providing local historical information to the public.

It is my pleasant duty, as Chairman of the Sub-Committee formed to bring this endeavour to fruition, to thank all those who have worked so hard to bring about this very comprehensive result.

The greatest possible thanks go to the late George Bennett, former Librarian of Sevenoaks, who laboured so long and so hard in gathering and collating the information supplied to him by the librarians who participated in this work.

Tribute must be paid to those Reference Librarians who spent so much time recording their Local History Collections and to their Chief Librarians for allowing them to do so.

Thanks are also due to the Honorary Editors, Wyn Bergess and Carleton Earl for the final collation and preparation of the material for printing.

In conclusion, I must thank the other members of my Sub-Committee, George Lawrence of Sevenoaks Library and the late Kenneth Chatfield of Sittingbourne Library, for the time and thought which they brought to this task.

A. Joyce
Former Borough Librarian of Maidstone

ERRATA

Please note 178 should be followed by 182 then by
179, 180, 181 and 183.

CONTENTS

The material listed in this Bibliography was collected by George Bennett and is inclusive to the end of March, 1973. Acquisitions which have been notified by the participating librarians since that date will be presented in a supplement.

In general, three categories of material have been excluded from the Bibliography:-

1. Newspapers and Periodicals - These have been listed in the "Kent Union List of Periodicals", compiled by Brian Bishop and Carleton Earl (London and Home Counties Branch of the Library Association). A new edition is projected.

2. Electoral Registers, Poll Books and Directories are included in "Kent Directories Located", compiled by W.F. Bergess and B.R.M. Riddell (Kent County Library). A new edition is in preparation.

3. Maps - A bibliography of maps and plans relating to Kent is at present being compiled through a Sub-Committee of the Kent Sub-Branch of the Library Association.

The Bibliography is arranged in one alphabetical sequence of places and subjects, and, within each such section, alphabetically by author, title, publisher, etc.

Added entries have been made for items with multiple content wherever feasible. If the subject matter relates to Kent in general, the item appears under the subject heading only; if a specific place is also mentioned, then the entry appears under both subject and place headings.

> e.g. A Flora of Kent   - Natural History
>
> A Flora of Maidstone - Natural History and Maidstone

In some cases an assessment of author or date has been made from sources available; this is indicated by brackets in the case of an author, e.g. (BLACK, William Henry) and by brackets, "circa" or a questionmark in reference to a date, e.g. (1901), c.1900, 1901? Brackets may also be used to indicate an assumption in part of a title, but those used in relation to a note, extract, etc., are enclosing information. Abbreviations are few and may easily be discerned, e.g., n.d. = not dated, pseud. = pseudonym.

The Index links authors, titles (where not indicative of content), publishers, etc., with the main place and subject arrangement.

The Editors apologise for any duplication, irregularities and discrepancies in content and format which may remain in the Bibliography. The lack of uniformity in the form and depth of the information supplied on the notification slips has added to the complexity of their task.

They would like to thank Mrs. Lynda Baldwin, not only for her efficient typing, but for her patience and for her understanding of the work to be done.

Wyn Bergess and Carleton Earl
Honorary Editors

LIST OF REPOSITORIES

1. London Borough of BEXLEY: Local Studies Centre.
    Hall Place, Bourne Road, Bexley, Kent, DA5 1PQ.
    Tel: Crayford 26574   Telex: 896119

2. London Borough of BROMLEY: Local Studies Department.
    Central Library, High Street, Bromley, Kent, BR1 1EX.
    Tel: 01-460-9955   Telex: 896712

    Note: It is advisable to contact the library before
          making a visit.

3. CANTERBURY Library.
    The Beaney Institute, High Street, Canterbury, Kent, CT1 2JP.
    Tel: Canterbury 63608

4. CHATHAM Library.
    Riverside, Chatham, Kent, ME4 4HL.
    Tel: Medway 43589

5. DARTFORD Library.
    Central Park, Dartford, Kent, DA1 1EU.
    Tel: Dartford 21133

6. DOVER Library.
    Maison Dieu House, Dover, Kent, CT16 1DW.
    Tel: Dover 204201

7. FOLKESTONE Library.
    Grace Hill, Folkestone, Kent, CT20 1HD.
    Tel: Folkestone 55228

8. GILLINGHAM Library.
    High Street, Gillingham, Kent, ME7 1BG.
    Tel: Medway 51066

9. GRAVESEND Library.
    Windmill Street, Gravesend, Kent, DA12 1AQ.
    Tel: Gravesend 2758

10. HYTHE Library.
    Stade Street, Hythe, Kent.
    Tel: Hythe 67111

11. KENT COUNTY LIBRARY HEADQUARTERS.
    Springfield, Maidstone, Kent, ME14 2LH.
    Tel: Maidstone 671411   Telex: 965212

    Note: This location represents the Local History
          collections of the libraries in the County
          system prior to the Local Government
          Reorganisation of April, 1974.

12. MAIDSTONE Library.
    St. Faith's Street, Maidstone, Kent, ME14 1LH.
    Tel: Maidstone 52344

13. MARGATE Library.
    Cecil Square, Margate, Kent, CT9 1RE.
    Tel: Thanet 23626   Telex: 96289

14. RAMSGATE Library.
    Guildford Lawn, Ramsgate, Kent.
    Tel: Thanet 53532

15. ROCHESTER Library.
    Northgate, Rochester, Kent, ME1 1LS.
    Tel: Medway 43837

16. SEVENOAKS Library.
    The Drive, Sevenoaks, Kent, TN13 3AB.
    Tel: Sevenoaks 53118

17. London Borough of GREENWICH: Local Studies Centre.
    Woodlands, Mycenae Road, London, SE2.
    Tel: 01-858-4631

18. London Borough of LEWISHAM: Manor House Library.
    Old Road, London, SE13 5SY.
    Tel: 01-852-5050

19. TUNBRIDGE WELLS Library.
    Mount Pleasant, Tunbridge Wells, Kent, TN1 1NS.
    Tel: Tunbridge Wells 30214

20. SITTINGBOURNE Library.
    Central Avenue, Sittingbourne, Kent, ME10 4AH.
    Tel: Sittingbourne 3465

21. WYE COLLEGE (UNIVERSITY OF LONDON).
    The Library, Wye College, Wye, Ashford, Kent.
    Tel: Wye 812401

ABBEY WOOD

Abbey Wood Alphabetical Directory, 1912.
Thomas Jenkins.
17

Abbey Wood Estate, 1854 - Sales catalogue.
Reform Freehold Land and Building Society.
17

DURKIN, M.K.
Field meeting at Abbey Wood and Swanscombe, Kent by
M.K. Durkin and S.A. Baldwin (offprint from Proceedings of
the Geologists' Association, Vol. 79, Pt. 2, 1968).
Geologists' Association. 1968.
5

EPPS, F.J.
Field meeting at Abbey Wood, Kent by F.J. Epps and S. Priest
(reprinted from Proceedings of Geologists' Association, Vol.
XLIV, Pt. 4).
Geologists' Association. 1933.
5

ACRISE

BROWN, John Howard.
A history and description of St. Martin's Church, Acrise.
(Typescript).
195-.
3,7

(Particulars and plan of)...Freehold, residential, sporting
and agricultural estate...Acrise Manor, Elham...in all about
57 acres. The agricultural portion of the estate includes
five compact farms...a total area of about 983 acres...to
be offered to auction...on 25th July, 1929.
Nicholas in conjunction with H.F. Finn-Kelcey. 1929.
7

ADDINGTON

ALEXANDER, John.
The excavation of the Chestnuts megalithic tomb at
Addington, Kent.
(Reprint from Archaeologia Cantiana). (1961).
11,17

GRIFFIN, Ralph.
Kentish items: Elham, Preston-next-Faversham, Addington.
n.d.
7

MADDAN, James Gracie.
Material for a history of Addington. (MS.).
1939 onwards.
11

ADISHAM

REGIS, B.
A sermon preached on the fast-day the 18th December, 1745 at
Adisham and at Staple the 22nd.
Canterbury J. Abree. 1746.
3

AGRICULTURE AND HORTICULTURE

ACWORTH, Robert William Harrison.
Hop-pickers' tokens, No. 2. Overprinted from The Journal
of the South-Eastern Agricultural College, Wye, No. 44,
July, 1939.
11,21

ACWORTH, Robert William Harrison.
Hop tokens in Kent.
K.C.S.S. 1938.
1,2,7,8,11,12,13

AGRICULTURE AND FISHERIES, Ministry of.
Hops.
H.M.S.O. 1947.
8

AGRICULTURE AND FISHERIES, Ministry of.
Hops marketing scheme.
H.M.S.O. 1965.
8

AGRICULTURE AND FISHERIES, Ministry of.
Land drainage and improvement of land. Kent River Board
Order, 1964.
H.M.S.O. 1964.
8

Agriculture in Kent, Summer, 1948 (photostat).
1948.
1,4,11,12,15

ALLANSON, G.
Kent or Romney Marsh sheep.
Wye College. 1961.
4,7;9,11,12,21

B., E.
Through the light remaining. (Short essays including
hops and cherries).
Mitre Press. n.d.
12

BAGENAL, Nicholas Beauchamp.
Fruit growing areas on the Hastings Beds in Kent, by
N.B. Bagenal and B.S. Furneaux.
1949.
4,6,8,11,13,19

BAKER, Dennis.
The marketing of corn in the first half of the 18th
century: North East Kent.
British Agricultural History Society. 1970.
11

BANE, W.A.
Fruit growing areas on the Lower Greensand in Kent, by
W.A. Bane and G. Jones.
Ministry of Agriculture and Fisheries. n.d.
6,11

BEST, Robin Hewitson.
The changing location of intensive crops, by R.H. Best
and R.M. Gasson.
Wye College. 1966.
2,7,11,12

BEST, Robin Hewitson.
The major land uses of Great Britain: an evaluation of
the conflicting records and estimates of land utilization
since 1900, by Robin H. Best.
Wye College. 1959.
12

BODDINGTON, M.A.B.
Pig production in Kent.
Wye College. 1970.
2

BOYS, J.
General view of the agriculture of the County of Kent
with observations on the means of its improvement.
London, for G. Nicol. 1796.
1,3,4,5,6,7,8,11,13,17,21

BOYS, J.
General view of the agriculture of the County of Kent
with observations on the means of its improvement.
2nd edition.
London, for G. Nicol. 1805.
21

BRADE-BIRKS, S.G.
Soil profiles in Kent: reprinted from the Journal of
the South Eastern Agricultural College, Wye, Kent, No.
25, July, 1928, by S.G. Brade-Birks and B.S. Furneaux.
3

BRISTOL UNIVERSITY - DEPARTMENT OF ECONOMICS.
Fruit growing industry in Kent.
11

BROWNLOW, Margaret Eileen.
The delights of herb growing.
Seal, The Herb Farm. 1965.
1,4,11,12,19

BROWNLOW, Margaret Eileen.
Herbs and the fragrant garden.
Seal, The Herb Farm. 1957.
12,15,16

BUCKLAND, G.
On the farming of Kent (Royal Agricultural Society
Journal).
Royal Agricultural Society.
11

BUNYARD, George AND CO. LTD.
The house of Bunyard, 1796-1919.
Alabaster Passmore and Sons. 1919.
12

BURGESS, Abraham Hale.
Hops.
L. Hill. 1964.
3,19

CHATER, G.P.
Report on hop picking by machine, by G.P. Chater and Miss
C.L. Jary.
Wye College. 1955.
12

CLINCH, George.
English hops - history of cultivation and preparation for the
market from its earliest times.
McCorquodale and Co. 1919.
3,4,6,7,12

COLE, Helen Margaret.
Year round cauliflower production in Lincolnshire, Kent and
Cornwall.
University of Exeter. 1971.
9

CRONK, Anthony.
English hops glossary; edited by A. Cronk.
West Malling, Cronk. 1959.
1,4,8,11,12

DORLING, M.J.
East Kent Horticulture, by M.J. Dorling and R.R.W. Folley.
Wye College. 1957.
3,8,11,21

EAST KENT CHAMBER OF AGRICULTURE.
Laws and constitution, annual reports, etc. 1884-5, 1886-7.
17

EAST MALLING RESEARCH STATION.
Abstracts and index to the annual research reports, 1954-1961.
East Malling Research Station. 1963.
12

EAST MALLING RESEARCH STATION.
Annual reports.
1(1955,1964,1966) 4(1954-58,1968-71) 6(1953-56) 7(1952-57)
8(1958) 12(1951 in progress) 15(1958) 19(1964)

EAST MALLING RESEARCH STATION.
East Malling Research Station...general development and
activities.
East Malling Research Station. (c.1948).
1

EAST MALLING RESEARCH STATION.
Subject index of papers published from East Malling Research
Station...between 1913 and 1953.
East Malling Research Station. 1957.
1

ELEY, W.
The agricultural labourer (an address given at the third
meeting of the Rochester Farmers' Club, January 27th, 1880).
W.T. Wildish. 1880.
15

EVERSHED, H.
The farming of Kent, Sussex and Surrey.
Clowes. 1871.
11

FARLEY, James George Wilson.
Pull no more poles.
Faith Press. 1962.
3,4,7,11,12,15

"FARMER IN KENT", pseud.
An address to the landowners and farmers of Great Britain,
delineating the extent, cause and relief of our present
agricultural depression, by A Farmer in Kent.
Printed for J. Ridgeway. 1823.
11

Farmers Household Accounts Book, 1686-89 (Handwritten).
1689.
5

FELTONS, CATTLEY AND CO.
Hops: an alphabetical arrangement of those parishes
in the County of Kent in which hops are cultivated.
1868.
7

FINN, Arthur.
A history of Kent or Romney Marsh sheep.
Country Life. 1924.
7,11

FOLLEY, Roger Roland Westwell.
Some orchard costs, 1950-59.
Wye College.
1,11

FOLLEY, Roger Roland Westwell.
Ten years' yields of apples and pears, 1948-1957.
Wye College.
4,11,12

FOLLEY, Roger Roland Westwell.
Investment in orchards, by R.R.W. Folley and K.C.
Yates.
Wye College. 1960.
3,7,12

From Hay-Time to Hopping, by the author of "Our Farm of
Four Acres".
Chapman and Hall. 1860.
11

GARRAD, G.H.
A survey of the agriculture of Kent. (County
agricultural surveys, No. 1).
London, R.A.S.E. 1954.
1,2,3,4,5,6,7,8,9,11,12,14,15,17,19,20,21

GASSON, H.M.
Comparative advantages and agricultural land use with
particular reference to Kent. (Microfilm copy of
University of London Thesis).
1965.
8

GASSON, Ruth.
Influence of urbanisation on farm ownership and practice.
Wye College. 1966.
11

GEYELIN, George Kennedy.
Poultry breeding in a commercial point of view as carried
out by the National Poultry Company Ltd., Bromley, Kent.
Simpkin and Marshall. 1865.
2

GREAT BRITAIN. Parliament.
Hops. Various returns, 1852, 1856, 1859, 1861, 1862.
8

GREAT BRITAIN. Parliament. Select Committee on the
Hop Industry.
Report from the Select Committee...together with
proceedings of the Committee, minutes of evidence and
appendix.
Eyre and Spottiswoode. 1890.
11

GREAT BRITAIN. Parliament. Select Committee on the
Hop Industry.
Report. 1908.
17

HAGGAR, R.J.
Kent wild white clover: the growth and management of
wild white clover with special reference to seed
production, by R.J. Haggar and W. Holmes.
Wye College. 1963.
4,11

HALL, Sir Alfred Daniel.
Report upon a chemical and physical study of the soils
of Kent and Surrey (Kent edition).
Kent County Council. 1902.
2,3,5,6,9,11,15

HALL, Sir Alfred Daniel.
Report on the agriculture and soils of Kent, Surrey and
Sussex, by Sir A.D. Hall and Sir E.J. Russell.
H.M.S.O. 1911.
1,2,3,4,5,8,11,12,19,20

HENNELL, Thomas.
Change in the farm. Includes numerous Kentish references.
Cambridge University Press. 1934.
11

HENNELL, Thomas.
Change in the farm, 2nd edition. Includes numerous Kentish
references.
Cambridge University Press. 1936.
11

Scenes in Hop Gardens.
Smith Elder. 1838.
11

Hop Planter's Assistant.
Maidstone, J. Blake. n.d.
11

Hop Trade: A Bill.
1866.
12

HOPS MARKETING SCHEME.
The hops marketing scheme, 1932 (a): (as amended by the
Hops Marketing Scheme (amendment) Orders, 1934, 1939, 1945,
1948, 1949 and 1950).
H.M.S.O. 1950.
4

HUNT, A.R.
The cherry situation, by A.R. Hunt and R.R.W. Folley.
Wye College. 1964.
11,12

INDERWICK, F.A.
Taxes on agriculture: the extraordinary tithes on hops,
fruit and market gardens.
National Press Agency. 1880.
11

"IOTA", pseud.
The labour dispute in Kent.
1878.
3,17

JACKSON, Arthur Percy.
Jackson allotments scheme.
1896.
17

JOHN OF CANTERBURY.
False impressions; or, the rick burners.
London, Lacey's Juvenile Library. 183-?
3,11

JONES, Daniel.
Sheep farming in Romney Marsh in the 18th century.
Wye College. 1956.
3,11

KENT COUNTY ALLOTMENTS AND GARDENS COUNCIL.
Garden of England Year Book.
Kent County Allotments and Gardens Council.
1(1959 and 1964) 4(1958-59 and 1966).

KENT COUNTY ALLOTMENTS AND GARDENS COUNCIL.
Handbook, 1971.
Kent County Allotments and Gardens Council. 1971.
8

KENT AND ROMNEY MARSH SHEEP-BREEDERS' ASSOCIATION.
Flock books, 1951-1967.
1(1951) 4(1959-1967) 8(1952-1967) 11(1952-1967) 12(1966)

KENT BEE-KEEPERS' ASSOCIATION.
Year Book.
Kent Bee-Keepers' Association. 1963.
11(1963 and 1971-72)

KENT COUNTY AGRICULTURAL SOCIETY.
Catalogue of horses, cattle, sheep...at the sixteenth
annual show, 1938.
Kent County Agricultural Society. 1938.
7

KENT COUNTY AGRICULTURAL SOCIETY.
Catalogue of...the eighteenth show...1947.
Kent County Agricultural Society. 1947.
7

KENT COUNTY COUNCIL - TECHNICAL EDUCATION DEPARTMENT.
Cold stored, dried and evaporated orchard and garden
produce.
Caddel and Son. 1897.
9

KENT COUNTY COUNCIL - TECHNICAL EDUCATION COMMITTEE.
First report of experiments on pasture land with
farmers, conducted by H.J. Monson.
Maidstone, Dickinson. 1894.
11

KENT COUNTY COUNCIL - TECHNICAL EDUCATION COMMITTEE.
First report of the Technical Education Committee of
Kent and Surrey, on the chemical and physical study of
the soils of Kent and Surrey, by A.D. Hall and F.J.
Plymen.
Kentish Express. 1902.
5,11

KENT EDUCATION COMMITTEE.
Agricultural education in Kent, 1933-38.
Kent Education Committee. (1939).
8

KENT EDUCATION COMMITTEE.
Clean milk in Kent.
Kent Education Committee. 1924.
11

KENT MILK RECORDING SOCIETY.
Official handbook, 1923.
Kent Milk Recording Society. 1923.
3,12

KNIGHT, Charles J.
Essay on hop picking: MSS.
16

KNIGHT, J.Y.
Hops: an alphabetical arrangement of those parishes...
in which hops are cultivated.
Cattley, Gridley and Co. 1876, etc.
11

LAIRD, A. Bonnet.
My part of the country.
Jenkins. 1925.
1

LAIRD, A. Bonnet.
This way to Arcady.
Jenkins. 1926.
4,11

LANCE, E.J.
The hop farmer...
Ridgway. 1838.
1,11

LEVY, Mary L.S.
How we fight nature on a Kentish fruit farm (Rochester
Naturalist).
1907.
7

MALCOLM, James.
A compendium of modern husbandry, principally written
during a survey of Surrey...illustrative also of the
best practices in the neighbouring counties, Kent etc...
3 vols.
1805.
4,12

MANWARING, H.M.
A treatise on the cultivation of hops...
Privately Printed. 1855.
11,12

MARKHAM, Gervase.
The inrichment of the Weald of Kent, edited by G. Markham..
1,4,5,6,7,11,12,15,17,19,21
For details of editions see under Weald.

MARSH, John B.
Hops and hopping...
Simpkin, Marshall. 1892.
7,14,17

MARSHALL, W.
Rural economy of the southern counties...2 vols.
Nicol. 1798.
1,11,12,17

MASSEE, A.M.
The pests of fruits and hops.
Crosby Lockwood. 1937.
12

MASSEE, A.M.
The pests of fruits and hops, 2nd edition.
Crosby Lockwood. 1946.
12

MELLING, Elizabeth.
Aspects of agriculture and industry...edited by E. Melling.
Kent County Council Archives. 1961.
1,2,3,4,5,6,7,8,9,11,12,14,15,16,18,19,20,21

ORWELL, George.
George Orwell in Kent - hop-picking.
Bridge Books. 1970.
2,4,5,9,11,21

PARKER, Hubert H.
The hop industry.
London, King. 1934.
4,12

PATTENDEN, Ann.
Market gardening in North-West Kent (typescript thesis).
1965.
5

PETTMAN, William Robert.
A letter to Arthur Young Esq., on the situation of the growers
of corn in Great Britain, by William Pettman of Ham in the
County of Kent.
Printed by James Saffery. 1815.
11

PLANT PROTECTION LTD.
Common farm weeds, illustrated.
Butterworth. 1952.
12

PLATT, Bryan.
Farming in the South-East.
David Rendel Ltd. 1967 and 1968.
2,5,6,7,12,14

POCOCK, D.C.D.
England's diminished hop acreage...
Wye College: Department of Hop Research. 1958.
11

POCOCK, D.C.D.
England's diminished hop acreage.
"Geography". 1959.
11

POCOCK, D.C.D.
Fluctuation in hop cultivation in South-Eastern England.
Wye College. n.d.
9,11

REID, Ian G.
Small farms on heavy land.
Wye College. 1958.
11,12

The Rickburners: A tale from the Present Time.
Canterbury, Cowtan and Brown. 1830.
3

ROYAL COMMISSION ON AGRICULTURE.
England. Reports...on the Andover district of Hampshire
and the Maidstone district of Kent.
H.M.S.O. 1894.
8

ROMNEY SHEEP BREEDERS' SOCIETY.
The flock books, 1968 in progress.
4(1968 in progress) 11(1968 in progress)

RUSSELL, RUSSELL AND WILLMOTT.
Catalogue of garden, grass and flower seeds.
1800.
17

SACKVILLE-WEST, Victoria.
The Women's Land Army.
Joseph. 1944.
12

SALMON, E.S.
Notes on the hop mildew (Sphaerotheca humuli (DC)
Burr).
From Journal of Agricultural Science, Vol. 11, Pt. 3,
1907.
3

SARGENT, Miles.
Saint Francis of the hop-fields.
Philip Allan. 1933.
8,11

SCOT, Reynolde.
A perfite platforme of a Hoppe Garden...
Denham. 1578.
11

SHINDLER, Robert.
Mission work among the hop-pickers in the Weald of
Kent.
Morgan and Scott. n.d.
11,12,13,17

SMITH, George Walter.
Enterprise (Market gardening and farming in Kent).
Stockwell. 1953.
12

STRATTON, John Young.
Hops and hop-pickers.
S.P.C.K. 1883.
1,3,4,11,12,13

SYKES, Joseph Donald.
Economic aspects of grain maize production in East Kent
and East Suffolk in 1970. A grower's report by J.D.
Sykes, Ashford: Wye College School of Rural Economic
and Related Studies.
(For the) Wye College Maize Unit. 1971.
8

SYKES, Joseph Donald.
Farm business statistics for South-East England.
Wye College.
1,5 and 7(1960) 8(1969-70) 11(1959-60 in progress)
12(1969-70) 14(1960)

SYKES, Joseph Donald.
Profits and problems of farming in South-East England,
by J.D. Sykes and G.P. Wibberley.
Wye College. 1956.
12

SYKES, Joseph Donald.
The recession in farm profits in South- East England:
a study of success and failure in the business of
farming in Kent, Surrey and Sussex since 1955 (by J.D.
Sykes).
Wye College. 1958.
11,12

The Teston System of Farming, together with the Courland
Method of Making Clover...
Maidstone, W. Wildash. 1816.
15

THEOBALD, Frederick V.
Attack of...larvae, etc. Report in Vol. 1 of South-
East Agricultural College at Wye. Report of experiments
in Woodchurch, Romney Marsh, Ashford.
Reprint. 1925.
17

THEOBALD, Frederick V.
Potatoe disease new to Kent...
1928.
17

TORRINGTON, Viscount.
On farm buildings; with a few observations on the state of
agriculture in the County of Kent.
London, Ridgway. 1845.
21

A VOICE FROM KENT, pseud.
Observations on tithes: showing their oppressive operation
on the cultivation of the land.
Welsh. 1834.
12

WAUGH, Mary.
Fruit and hop farming in Kent (written for children).
Oxford University Press. 1962.
1,2,5,6,7,8,11,15

WEST KENT FEDERATION OF WOMEN'S INSTITUTES.
Old days in the Kent hop gardens, edited by M. Lewis.
West Kent Federation of Women's Institutes, Tonbridge, 1962.
1,2,3,4,5,6,7,8,9,11,15,19

WHITEHEAD, Sir Charles
Fruit growing in Kent.
Wilson. 1881.
12

WHITEHEAD, Sir Charles
Hop cultivation.
John Murray. 1893.
11

WHITEHEAD, Sir Charles.
Hops: from the sets to the sky-lights.
Effingham Wilson. 1881.
11

WHITEHEAD, Sir Charles.
Retrospections.
Maidstone, Thorpe. 1908.
1, 11, 15

WHITEHEAD, Sir Charles.
A sketch of the agriculture of Kent.
Spottiswoode. 1899.
1,2,5,7,8,9,11,12,14

WIGAN, RICHARDSON AND CO.
Hop report.
Wigan, Richardson.
1(1952 in progress) 8(1955-65, 1968 and 1969)

WORMALD, H.
Diseases of fruit and hops.
Crosby Lockwood. 1939.
12

WYE COLLEGE.
The changing location of intensive crops: an analysis of
their spatial distribution in Kent and the implications
for land-use planning.
1966.
4,5,19

WYE COLLEGE.
East Kent horticulture (results from 6 holdings for 1953-55).
Wye College. 1957.
3,12,19

WYE COLLEGE.
The journal of the South-Eastern Agricultural College, Wye,
Kent. No. 19.
Ashford, Headley. 1910.
8

WYE COLLEGE.
Management aspects of horticultural production under
glass.
Wye College. n.d.
12

WYE COLLEGE.
Market gardening in East Kent. Results for 1950,
1951 and 1952 crops.
Wye College. 1954.
7

WYE COLLEGE.
Pig production in Kent, 1967-1969: results for a small
sample of farms.
Wye College. 1970.
8,9

WYE COLLEGE.
Ten years of market gardening.
Wye College. 1963.
12

WYE COLLEGE.
Wheat production on part of the North Downs...results
of the 1954 harvest.
Wye College. 1956.
11

WYLLIE, James.
National Farm Survey: results of some investigations
on the Wye province.
Wye College. 1945.
11

ALDINGTON

ELLISTON-ERWOOD, Frank Charles.
Notes on the architecture of Aldington Church, Kent...
Archaeologia Cantiana. n.d.
11,17

HUGHSON, D. pseud.
...Elizabeth Barton, the Holy Maid of Kent.
1814
17

LONG, G.S.
Church of St. Martin, Aldington.
1935
3,11

LONG, G.S.
A short life of Erasmus, formerly Rector of Aldington.
1929.
12

(MOULTON, W.R.)
The story of Elizabeth Barton.
F.J. Parsons. c.1927.
7

NEAME, Alan.
The Holy Maid of Kent: the life of Elizabeth Barton,
1506-1534.
Hodder and Stoughton. 1971.
3,4,7,8,11

SAMPSON, Aylwin.
The church of St. Martin, Aldington, Kent.
Southampton, Shirley Press. 195-?
7,11

ALKHAM

GILL, Walter.
Geographical survey of the Alkham and Upper Dour Valleys.
Typescript. n.d.
11

GOUGH, G.H.
A geographical study of the Alkham valley.
MSS. 1956.
6

ALLHALLOWS (HOO)

BUDGEN, T.
Terrier of the parish of Allhallows in the County of
Kent, surveyed in the year 1804. MS.
8

ALLHALLOWS (HOO) Cont'd

DUNCAN, Leland Lewis.
The Church of Allhallows, Hoo.
n.d.
12

HAMMOND, F.J.
Church of Allhallows, Hoo.
K.A.S. 1926.
11,12,15,16

HAMMOND, F.J.
Story of an outpost parish - All Hallows, Hoo.
S.P.C.K. 1928.
1,3,4,6,7,8,9,11,12,15,16,17

ALLINGTON

CONWAY, William Martin. 1st Baron Conway of Allington.
Autobiography of a mountain climber.
Cape. 1933.
12

CONWAY, William Martin. 1st Baron Conway of Allington.
Episodes in a varied life.
Country Life. n.d.
12

EVANS, Joan.
The Conways: a history of three generations.
Museum Press. 1966.
4,11,12

THOMSON, Patricia.
Sir Thomas Wyatt and his background.
Routledge-Kegan Paul. 1964.
12

ANESLEY

JOBSON, A.
South London sepia (memories of childhood and youth in
Anesley - Typescript).
(1967).
2

APPLEDORE

Papers and printed documents relating to Appledore bequeathed
to the National Trust by Miss D.E. Johnstone, to be
preserved at Hallhouse Farm, Appledore...A preliminary
list made at the University Library, Canterbury, September,
1969.
Typescript. 1969.
7

COCK, F. William.
Notes on Appledore Church, by F.W. Cock and G.W. Humphry.
Ashford, Headley. 1927 etc.
7,11,13

COCK, F. William.
Notes from the transcript and registers of Appledore, Kent.
1927.
1,12

SOTHEBY AND CO. Auctioneers.
Catalogue of the interesting and extensive Appledore library
...of the late Dr. F.W. Cock of The Well House, Appledore,
Kent.
Sotheby and Co. 1944.
1,7,11

ARCHAEOLOGY - See HISTORY AND ARCHAEOLOGY

ARCHITECTURE

ARCHIBALD, John.
Kentish architecture as influenced by geology.
Ramsgate, Monastery Press. 1934.
1,2,3,4,5,7,8,9,11,12,13,14,15,17,18,19

ARNOLD, George Matthews.
The ruined chapels and chantries of Kent.
William Andrews and Co. n.d.
9

BAINES, John Manwaring.
Wealden Firebacks.
Hastings Museum. 1958.
1,3,5,11,12,19

BEATTIE, William.
The castles and abbeys of England, Vol. 1.
George Virtue. 183-?
8

BRADE-BRIKS, Stanley Graham.
Flintwork in Kent. 2 page typescript. Also "Kentish
flint work", offprint of article written from these
typescript notes.
1958.
3

BUCK, Samuel.
Twenty-four views of castles and abbeys in Kent, by
S.and N. Buck.
S. and N. Buck. 1736.
11

COWPER, H.S.
Two Headcorn cloth halls.
n.d.
12,17

CULMER, George G.
Architecture and architectural history of the church.
n.d.
11

DAVIES, John.
Kentish barns and their prototypes. Woolwich and
District Antiquarian Society. Annual Report, 1899-90.
Woolwich and District Antiquarian Society. 1899.
17

DAWBER, E. Guy.
Old cottages and farmhouses in Kent and Sussex, by E.G.
Dawber and W.G. Davie.
Batsford. 1900.
1,2,3,4,5,6,7,8,10,11,12,13,15,17,18,19,20

ESAM, Frank.
The manors and farmhouses of Kent...
Maidstone South-East Gazette. (1906).
1,2,5,6,8,11,12

FEA, Allan.
Old English houses.
Secker. 1910.
12

FEA, Allan.
Picturesque old houses.
Bonsfield. 1902.
1,3,7

FEA, Allan.
Secret chambers and hiding places, 3rd edition.
Methuen. 1908.
15

GODFREY, Walter Hindes.
The English almshouse, with some account of its
predecessor, the medieval hospital.
Faber. 1955.
11

GRAVETT, Kenneth.
Timber and brick buildings in Kent: a selection from
the J. Fremlyn Streatfeild Collection.
Phillimore, for the Kent Archaeological Society Records
Branch, 1971.
3,4,8,9,11,21

HARVEY, John H.
Henry Yevele.
London, Batsford. 1944.
3

HOGG, Warrington.
The book of old sundials and their mottoes.
Foulis. 1914.
7

HOLME, C.
Old English country cottages, edited by C. Holme.
1906.
17

HOPKINS, R. Thurston.
Old English mills and inns (includes some Kentish).
Cecil Palmer. 1927.
4,5

HOMERSHAM, Samuel Collett.
Report on the supply of water to Ashford.
Ashford, Elliott. 1852.
11

IGGLESDEN, Sir Charles.
Ashford Church.
Ashford, "Kentish Express". 1901, etc.
1,3,4,6,7,8,11,12,14,15,17,18,20,21(1908)

IGGLESDEN, Sir Charles.
The demon eleven, etc.
Simpkin, Marshall, Hamilton. 1901.
6

KENT COUNTY COUNCIL - PLANNING DEPARTMENT.
Expansion at Ashford.
Kent County Council. 1967.
1,2,3,4,6,7,9,11,12

"KENTISH EXPRESS". Publisher.
Guide and directory to Greater Ashford.
Ashford, "Kentish Express". n.d.
11

"KENTISH EXPRESS". Publisher.
Guide and directory to Ashford, Romney Marsh, Tenterden and
district...
Ashford, "Kentish Express". 1911.
1

LICHFIELD, Nathaniel and Associates.
Ashford expansion, 2 Vols.
N. Lichfield and Associates. 1967-68.
2,4,7,11,21

Master of Hounds; being the life story of Harry Buckland
of Ashford.
Faber. 1931.
1,7,11

MILLS, Mark.
Dr. George Wilks, 1840-1919.
Privately Printed. (1970).
11

Particulars...of sale of the Bockhanger estate, Ashford...
including "Bybrook", Little Bybrook, Kingsmead, Bockhanger,
Oak Farms, Ashford Golf Links, Parsonage Barn land, Ashford,
to be sold on 1st October, 1912.
A.J. Burrows. 1912.
7

PEARMAN, Augustus John.
Ashford.
Ashford, Thompson. 1886.
1,3,6,8,11,12,15,17,19

PEARMAN, Augustus John.
History of Ashford.
Ashford, Igglesden. 1968.
1,7,11,12

Residential attraction of Ashford.
Ashford, Geering. 1926.
11

RICE, John.
The Stour Centre, Ashford: a feasibility study
commissioned by Ashford Urban District Council (and others),
by John Rice and D.S. Roberts.
London, the Authors. n.d.
21

ROCHARD, J.
Ashford, illustrated and historical: being a concise and
comprehensive account of this picturesque and interesting
neighbourhood.
Gravesend, J. Rochard. 1897?
11

SCOTT, Ernest.
Annotated list of Lepidoptera (macro and micro) occurring
in the neighbourhood of Ashford, Kent. Revised by Dr. E.
Scott.
Kent Field Club. 1964.
4,7

SCOTT, Ernest.
List of butterflies and moths (Macro Lepidoptera)
occurring in the neighbourhood of Ashford.
Ashford, Headley. 1936.
4(1950) 7,8,11,15

SHARP, Nevill Maurice Granville.
St. Mary's Church, Ashford, Kent.
(1966).
4

SMITH, Herbert L.
Notes of brasses formerly existing in Dover Castle,
Maidstone and Ashford Churches.
n.d.
17

SOUTHERN RAILWAY COMPANY.
Ashford works Centenary, 1847-1947.
Southern Railway Co. 1947.
3,4,6,7,8,11

WARREN, William.
Some account of the Church College (now the Vicarage
House), Free School, etc. of Ashford.
Ashford, Thompson. 1895.
3,11,12,15

ASHURST

WHITE, A.C.
Notes on the history of Ashurst, Kent, by A.C. White
and others.
Tunbridge Wells, Courier Co. 1955.
7,11,19

ASHWELL

ORDISH, George.
The living house.
Hart-Davis. 1960.
8,12,15

AYLESFORD

AINSWORTH, William Harrison.
Old Court: a novel.
Chapman and Hall. 1867.
12

ANDERSON, H.J.
Kit's Coty, by H.J. Anderson and Frederick Evans.
Lincoln, Williams. n.d.
6

Aylesford Estate: plan.
1884.
12

AYLESFORD PARISH COUNCIL.
Official guide to the parish.
Home Publishing Co. 1960.
11,12

BENNETT, F.J.
Upper and lower Kit's Coty.
South Eastern Gazette. 1907.
17

BENNETT, F.J.
The White Horse Stone. (Kit's Coty).
1907.
1,7,11,17

BOYS, William.
Observations on Kit's Coty House.
1792.
4,11

BROMLEY, Francis E.
Manuscript notes on the View of Frankpledge in the Manor
of Aylesford. In Latin with some English translation.
3

CLEEVES, Janet D.
Guide to The Friars, Aylesford.
Maidstone, British Legion Press. 1954.
2(1960) 7,15

COLEMAN, Donald Cuthbert.
Sir John Banks, baronet and businessman.
Oxford, Clarendon Press. 1963.
8,11,12

DENNE, Samuel.
Inscription on a barn door near Preston Hall, Aylesford,
1796.
Royal Society of Antiquaries.
11

EVANS, Arthur John.
On a late Celtic urn-field at Aylesford, Kent.
Royal Society of Antiquaries. 1890.
1,11,12

FIELDING, Edwina.
Courage to build anew: the story of the rebuilding of
The Friars, Aylesford...
Burns Oates. 1968.
4,11,19

GOODRICH, Alec T.
Aylesford parish church: an illustrated guide.
Sidcup, Sparta Press. 1968.
11

GRIFFIN, Ralph.
Kentish items: Aylesford, Pluckley, Stourmouth, Faversham,
Sittingbourne, Wouldham, Chatham.
n.d.
7

Illustrated guide and history of The Friars...
Maidstone, British Legion Press. 1965.
11

KIMBERLEY-CLARK LTD.
This is Kimberley-Clark.
Kimberley-Clark. 1963.
12

LE DESPENCER, Thomas, Lord and others v.s. EVELEIGH,
William.
Report of the proceedings of the trial between Lord
Despencer, Thomas Edmeads and Charles Lewis, plaintiffs,
and William Eveleigh.
Wickham and Cutbush. 1815.
12

KENT COUNTY COUNCIL - PLANNING DEPARTMENT.
Aylesford: conservation study.
Kent County Council. 1972.
11

LUFF, S.G.A.
The first monks and hermits.
Aylesford, St. Albert's Press. 1958.
4,15

McCRERIE, Alan.
Knowing Aylesford.
Hadlow, John Hilton. 1965?
1,2,3,4,7,8,11,15,19

MOULD, Daphne Desiree Charlotte Pochin.
The resurrection of Aylesford.
Aylesford, The Friary. 1956.
1,2,8,11

PEAKE, W. Brian.
Kit's Coty House.
Ohio, United Printing Co. 1936.
5

REED PAPER GROUP.
A tour of the Aylesford paper mills and associated
factories.
n.d.
8

RIGOLD, S.E.
Two Kentish Carmelite houses - Aylesford and Sandwich.
Ashford, Headley. 1965.
11

Round about Kit's Coty House.
Bell and Daldy. 1861.
1,3,4,6,11,15,17

SEWELL, Brocard.
A Carmelite library. (Article in "The Private Library",
Vol. 3, No. 3, July, 1960).
"The Private Library". 1960.
12

SEWELL, Brocard.
My dear times waste.
Aylesford, St. Albert's Press. 1966.
4,12

STAFFORD, Ann.
Blossoming rod. (Fiction based on facts - History of
The Friars).
Hodder and Stoughton. 1955.
12

The story of Kit's Coty House.
London, R.G. Thomas and Co. 1907.
3,11,17

WALLS, Raymond William.
A short description of the church of St. Peter in
Aylesford.
Maidstone, British Legion Press. 194-? etc.
4,8,11,12

WRIGHT, Thomas.
Wanderings of an antiquary...VII. The valley of
Maidstone - Kit's Coty House and the cromlechs around.
1852.
4,11

BADFORD (SIC) - See BAYFORD

BAPCHILD

LORD, Hugh F.
Short history of the parish of Bapchild, Kent, and its
church.
Canterbury, Gibbs. 1926.
1,3,4,6,7,8,11,12,14,15,20

READ, C.H.
(Horse trappings). From the Proceedings of the
Society of Antiquaries, February 25th, 1904. (Includes
account of a flat bronze enamelled ring round at
Bapchild).
8

BARFRESTON

BONNER, Stephen.
Early Norman secular musicians of the church of
Barfreston in Kent.
Bois de Boulogne. 1969.
7,11

BOYER, P.J.
The altar of St. Nicholas, Barfrestone.
Printed by W.E. Giraud. 1928.
3,7,11

CLARKE, Charles.
An attempt to ascertain the age of the church at
Barfreston.
(1812).
8,11

DOWSE, A.W.E.
Barfreston Church, compiled by A.W.E. Dowse.
Dover, Dover Express. 1911.
7,11,12,15

GOODSALL, Robert Harold.
The church of St. Mary, Barfreston.
S.P.C.K. 19--?
11

HUSSEY, Richard C.
Barfreston Church in A.D. 1840.
Mitchell and Hughes. 1885.
11,17

BARFRESTON Cont'd

WORSFOLD, Frederick Henry.
A guide to Barfreston Church and its world-famous carvings.
Canterbury, "Kentish Gazette". 1951 etc.
3,4,6,7,8,11,12,15

BARHAM

BARHAM WOMEN'S INSTITUTE.
History of Barham. Duplicated typescript.
Barham Women's Institute. 1960.
3

CARRE, Meyrick H.
The new heaven of Thomas Digges. (Article from History
Today, Vol. XI, No. 11, November, 1961).
3

CONYNGHAM, Lord A.
An account of the opening and examination of a considerable
number of tumuli on Breach Downs, Kent, by Lord Conyngham
and J.Y. Akerman.
1843.
6,7,17

EDWARDS, Frank.
Dear old Barham.
Page Bros. 1960.
3,12

GRIFFIN, Ralph.
Brasses in Barham Church.
Archaeologia Cantiana. 1928.
3,11,17

JELL, James.
What Broome is and isn't. (History of Broome House).
1953?
3

KENT COUNTY CREMATORIUM LTD.
The Barham Crematorium and garden of remembrance.
Kent County Council. 1957.
3

LANE, William G.
A new letter and poem by Thomas Ingoldsby.
Boston Public Library Quarterly, Vol. 5, No. 4. 1953.
3

MALLORIE, Rev. W.T.
The parish church of Barham: St. John the Baptist.
Canterbury, Gibbs and Son. 1932.
3

OXENDEN, Sir Henry.
Henry Oxenden's notebook.
n.d.
3

OXENDEN, Sir Henry.
The Oxenden letters, 1607-1642.
Constable. 1933.
1,3,6,8,11,14,19

OXENDEN, Sir Henry.
The Oxenden letters, 1642-1670.
Sheldon. 1937.
1,3

OXENDEN, Sir Henry.
Recollections of the late Sir Henry Oxenden Bt. of Broome
Park...
Canterbury, Ward. 1862.
7,11

The parish church of Barham, St. John the Baptist.
George Snell. n.d.
3,12

Particulars...of sale of..."The Little Manor", Barham...
and Wingmore Court Farm, Elham...also 2 Beech Villas, High
Street, Elham, which Messrs. P.R. and B.J. Coltman will
sell by auction...on Saturday, 18th July, 1959.
P.R. and B.J. Coltman. 1959.
7

Particulars, plan, photographs and conditions of sale in
the delightful old-fashioned freehold residential property
distinguished as "The Lawn", Barham.
London, A.H. Turner. 1904.
3

Particularas, plan and conditions of sale of Broome
Park near Canterbury...comprising...Elizabethan mansion
...garden and grounds...extending in area to about 650
acres...Messrs. Geering and Colyer...are instructed to
sell by auction...at...Canterbury...on Saturday, 17th
July, 1937.
Geering and Colyer. 1937.
3,7,11

Particulars, plans and conditions of sale of the Barham
Court Estate...comprising Barham Court, three farms,
small-holdings and cottages, extending to about 930
acres...which will be offered by auction in lots on...
13th July, 1911...by Messrs. Knight, Frank and Rutley...
Knight, Frank and Rutley. 1911.
3,7

Particulars, views, plans and conditions of sale of the
...residential, sporting, agricultural and manorial
domain of 5,408 acres...known as The Broome Park Estate,
comprising a stately XVII century mansion house, a
picturesque dower house, 24 farms and small-holdings...
to be offered for sale by auction by Messrs. Wriford,
Dixon and Winder...on...23rd September, 1908...
Wriford, Dixon and Winder. 1908.
7

Recollections of the late Sir Henry Oxenden Bt., of
Broome Park...by a late steward.
Canterbury, Ward. 1862.
12

BARMING

CHARE, F.K.
A brief history of St. Andrew's Church, Barming Heath,
Maidstone.
Chare. 1965 and c.1960.
12

BAYFORD

Badford and Goodnestone manor rolls, 1721-1863.
(Badford believed to be Bayford).
11

BEAKESBOURNE

Beakesbourne: the Old Palace. Illustrated sale
catalogue.
Hampton and Jon, Auctioneers. 1930.
3

BEARSTED

Holy Cross Church: a short account.
Maidstone, Kent Messenger. 1955.
3,11

Milgate Park, Bearsted: catalogue of the contents.
Wood and Co., Auctioneers. 1966.
11

ORCZY, Baroness Enuska.
Links in the chain of life.
Hutchinson. n.d.
12

The thought of the month: a noble Rosicrucian
apologist Dr. Robert Fludd by the Imperator. (Born
in Bearsted, buried there).
Included in "Rosicrucian Digest", Vol. XXXIV, No. 4,
1956.
3

BECKENHAM

BEAN, James.
The aspects and duties of the times (A sermon
preached in the parish church of Beckenham...on 7th
March, 1798).
F. and C. Rivington. 1798.
2

BECKENHAM BOROUGH COUNCIL.
Official Guides, 1955,1957,1962.
Pyramid Press.
2,11(1960)

BECKENHAM URBAN DISTRICT COUNCIL.
Official Guide, 1920.
2

BECKENHAM URBAN DISTRICT COUNCIL.
Official Guide, 1933.
17

BEYNON, V.C.
The "gazebo". (Typescript).
n.d.
2

BORROWMAN, Robert.
Beckenham past and present.
Beckenham, Thornton. 1910.
1,2,7,8,11,12,17,18

BORROWMAN, Robert.
The bells of Beckenham Parish Church.
Beckenham, T.W. Thornton - printer. 1905.
2

BORROWMAN, Robert.
A short description of the parish church of Beckenham, Kent.
Beckenham, Thornton. 1906.
2,5,12

BRABY, B.E.
Development of Beckenham, 1660-1900 (photocopy of MS. thesis).
(1963).
2

CHRISTIE-MURRAY, David.
Heraldry in the churches of Beckenham.
Europa. 1954.
1,2,4,8,11,12,17

CLARK, Frank J.
Story of Christ Church, Beckenham, 1876-1926.
Chatham, Diocesan Chronicle. 1926.
11,18

COLLETT, Sydney W.
1872-1972 Centenary of Beckenham Hospital.
Bromley Group Hospital Management Committee. 1972.
2

COMPTON, Doreen.
Alfred Wright, 1848-1924. Bank Manager and public figure, Beckenham and Bromley.
The Author. (1970).
2

COPELAND, H. Robert.
From village to borough: a brief outline of the history of Old Beckenham.
Privately Printed. 1916.
2,11

COPELAND, H. Robert.
Manors and estates of Old Beckenham.
The Author. 1967.
2

COPELAND, H. Robert.
The village of Old Beckenham.
Privately Printed. 1970.
2,4,7(1971) 11

CROYDON NATURAL HISTORY AND SCIENTIFIC SOCIETY.
Regional survey atlas of Croydon and district. (Surrey area including Beckenham, Penge, Shortlands, West Wickham).
The Society. 1936 in progress.
2

DAVIS, A.G.
On the Blackheath Beds at Beckenham. (Reprint from Proceedings of the Croydon Natural History and Scientific Society).
Roffey and Clark. 1927.
2

FRY, John.
Profiles of disease. (Note: based on general practice in Beckenham).
E. and S. Livingston. 1966.
2

GROTE, Mrs. Harriet.
The personal life of George Grote (of Beckenham). Grote was a master at Sevenoaks School.
Murray. 1873.
2,16

HARDING, Rev. John.
Fourteen annual addresses to the congregation and parishioners, 1884-97, compiled by J. Harding.
Beckenham, Thornton. n.d.
11

HARDING, Rev. John.
Fourteen annual addresses to the congregation...of Christ Church, Beckenham, compiled by J. Harding.
n.d.
11

HARDING, Rev. John.
Ten annual addresses to the congregation...of Christ Church, Beckenham, compiled by J. Harding.
n.d.
11

HARRIS, C.W.J.
Beckenham volunteer fire brigade, 1869-1886. (Typescript).
1972.
2

HOUSING AND LOCAL GOVERNMENT, Minstry of.
The Beckenham Sewage Order.
H.M.S.O. 1961.
8

KENT PUBLISHING COMPANY. Publishers.
Buying a house in Beckenham.
Kent Publishing Co. 1969.
2

LOCAL GOVERNMENT BOUNDARY COMMISSION.
Minutes of proceedings of a consultation...Bromley and Beckenham.
1947.
2

NICHOLS, W.J.
Recent discoveries at Toot Hill Wood near Beckenham.
Extract from: Society of Antiquaries, Proceedings 2nd series, Vol. 23, 1889.
1889.
2

Parish church of St. Barnabas, Beckenham; dedication of the extension, 1933.
1933.
12

Proceedings, etc. of the Vestry of Beckenham relating to the question of drainage.
Printed by Strong. 1871.
11

ROCHARD, J.
Bromley, Beckenham and Christchurch.
J. Rochard. c.1893.
2

TOOKEY, G.W.
The chapel of St. Agatha at Kelsey, Beckenham. (Typescript).
1969.
2

TOOKEY, G.W.
List of negatives relating to Beckenham and neighbourho in the possession of G.W. Tookey. (Typescript).
1968.
2

TROLLOPE, Constance A.N.
Beckenham in the olden times, 1538-1660.
Beckenham, Thornton. 1898.
1,2,11

BEDGEBURY

FORESTRY COMMISSION.
Bedgebury Pinetum and forest plots.
H.M.S.O. 1961.
4,5,7,8,11,12,19

FORESTRY COMMISSION.
Bedgebury Pinetum and forest plots, 4th edition, edited by A.F. Mitchell and A.W. Westall.
H.M.S.O. 1972.
11

BEDGEBURY Cont'd

FORESTRY COMMISSION.
Guide to the National Pinetum and forest plots at
Bedgebury.
H.M.S.O. 1951, etc.
1,3,8,11(and 1955)

FORESTRY COMMISSION.
Short guide to Bedgebury Pinetum and forest plots.
H.M.S.O. 1962.
8

GREAT BRITAIN: LAWS, etc. STATUTORY INSTRUMENTS.
The Bedgebury Pinetum byelaws, 1969.
H.M.S.O. 1969.
12

MITCHELL, A.F.
Short guide to Bedgebury Pinetum and forest plots.
H.M.S.O. 1969.
2,8,9,11

BEKESBOURNE

BRENT, John Junior.
Ancient sepulchral shaft at Bekesbourne. A paper which
appeared in Archaeologia Cantiana, Vol. 2, 1859.
1859.
4

GRIFFIN, Ralph.
Kentish items. West Malling, Hythe, Denton, Allington,
Elham, Bekesbourne.
7

HASELOFF, G.
Fragments of a hanging-bowl from Bekesbourne.
Reprint from Medieval Archaeology Vol. II, 1958.
3

JENNER, S. (A Clergyman, pseud. - Vicar of Bekesbourne).
Steepleton...
Longmans. 1847.
12

Particulars and conditions of sale of the very interesting
and charming small freehold country residence known as The
Old Palace (otherwise Bekesbourne House), Bekesbourne...
to be offered for sale by S. Hampton and Sons on 3rd June,
1930.
Hampton and Sons. 1930.
7

PYPER, R.B.
Notes on the history of Bekesbourne.
Canterbury, Gibbs. n.d.
1

BELTRING

WHITBREAD AND CO. LTD.
A souvenir of your visit to Whitbread's hop garden at
Beltring, Paddock Wood.
c.195-?
4

BELVEDERE

CALLENDER'S CABLE AND CONSTRUCTION CO. LTD.
The story of Callender's, 1882-1932.
Callender's Cable and Construction Co. Ltd. 1932.
1

SCRIBE, E.
The history of the Saye and Sele R.A. Chapter No. 1973,
1885-1935.
Saye and Sele R.A. Chapter. 1935.
7

BENENDEN

CRAN, Marion.
The story of my ruin. The author's account of how she
discovered a cottage and a garden in a village near
Tenterden.
Jenkins. (1924).
4,11

DAUBENEY, Giles.
Reminiscences of a country parson.
n.d.
3,11

CATHORNE-HARDY, Gathorne. 1st Earl of Cranbrook.
The past history of Benenden.
Hawkhurst, Williams. 1883.
11

HARDY, Charles Frederick.
Benenden letters. London, country and abroad, 1753-
1821, edited by C.F. Hardy.
Dent. 1901.
1,3,4,11,12,17

HASLEWOOD, Francis.
Parish of Benenden...also a reprint of..."This
Winter's Wonders", dated 1673.
Privately Printed. 1889.
1,3,4,6,8,11,12,14,15,17

LEBON, Cicely.
St. George's Church, Benenden, by C. Lebon and M. Price.
Courier Co. Ltd. n.d.
12

St. Margaret, East End, Benenden, Kent.
Benenden Chest Hospital. 197-?
11

BETHERSDEN

PEARMAN, Augustus John.
Kentish family of Lovelace.
Archaeologia Cantiana. 1876.
11,17

BETTESHANGER

BRETT, Thomas.
Sermon on the remission of sins.
1712.
17

BRETT, Thomas.
True moderation: a sermon.
London, Wyat. 1714.
11

In memorium: Walter Charles, Lord Northbourne of
Betteshanger..
Canterbury, Gibbs and Son. 1893.
3

Life through young eyes: a collection of children's
work. (Work of the children of Betteshanger School
1942-1959).
Dolphin Publishing Co. 1960.
12

BEULT, RIVER

MILLS, Halford L.
The river Beult and ponds of the Weald.
South-Eastern Gazette. 1930.
11

BEXLEY

BEXLEY BOROUGH COUNCIL.
Official guide, illustrated.
Burrow, Cheltenham. 1959 etc.
1,4,11,12,15,17(1953) 19

BEXLEY, London Borough of.
The London Borough of Bexley book, 1970-71.
Regency Publicity. 1970.
11

BEXLEY PUBLIC LIBRARY.
Hall Place, historical study (first draft). (Duplicated
typescript).
Bexley Libraries and Museums Department. 1969.
2

Bexley tracts, 1832, by the Vicar of that parish.
Richmond, F.H. Wall. 1832.
1,11

BRETT v SAWRIDGE and others.
Nathaniel Wilkins Brett, Appellant, Jacob Sawbridge and
others, respondents. (Lawsuit re: Sir E. Brett's will).
1736.
11

BUCKLAND, Frank.
Bexley: an historical sketch of the borough.
(Typescript). n.d.
1

The church of St, Michael, East Wickham, Welling, Kent
(historical notes).
1964.
4

A copy of the inscriptions upon the vaults and tablets
erected to the memory of the Ord family in Bexley Parish
Church, Kent.
n.d.
11

CRANE, Maurice A.
A thesis on the history of Bexley. (Typescript).
n.d.
1

DU BOULAY, Francis Robin H.
Medieval Bexley.
Bexley Public Libraries. 1961.
1,2,4,5,7,8,11,12,17,18,19

ENVIRONMENT, Department of.
Report on the collision that occurred on 12th November,
1970 at Bexley station.
H.M.S.O. 1972.
8

GREAT BRITAIN: LAWS, etc. (QUEEN ANNE)
An Act for vesting the inheritance of the Mannor of Court
at Weeke...in the county of Kent.
n.d.
11

GREAT BRITAIN: LAWS, etc. (GEO. III).
An Act for inclosing lands in the parish of Bexley.
1814.
11

HAZAEL, Patricia H.
Sir Hiram Maxim, 1840-1916: a biography (Typescript).
Bexley, Kent. 1960.
5

HOGG, A.H.A.
Earthworks in Joydens Wood, Bexley, Kent.
Kent Archaeological Society. 1940.
5,17

JOHNSTON, Charles.
Sonnets, original and translated.
John Murray. 1823.
6

KENT PAEDIATRIC SOCIETY.
A study in the epidermiology of health...schoolchildren
in Bexley.
1954.
8,19

LEVY, L.A.
Education in Bexley: a history in the area of the London
Borough to 1970, by L.A. and L.M. Levy.
London Borough of Bexley Libraries and Museums Department.
1971.
11

MORRIS, P.E.
Hall Place, Bexley.
London Borough of Bexley Libraries and Museums Department.
1970.
2,3,8,11

NEWMAN, Leonard Hugh.
Butterfly farmer.
Phoenix House. 1953.
5,12,15,17

ROBERTSON, William Archibald Scott.
Bexley: the church, Hall Place and Blendon.
Mitchell, Hughes, London. 1889.
5,17

TESTER, Peter J.
Hall Place, Bexley. (Reprinted from Archaeologia Cantiana).
Ashford, Headley. 1957.
1,17

TESTER, Peter J.
Medieval buildings in the Joydens Wood square earthwork
(Reprinted from Archaeologia Cantiana), by P.J. Tester
and J.E. Caiger.
Ashford, Headley. 1958.
1,5,9,17

BEXLEYHEATH

CASTELLS, Francis dePaula.
Bexleyheath and Welling.
Bexleyheath, Jenkins. 1910.
1,2,5,8,11,12,17,18

GIROUARD, Mark.
Red House, Bexleyheath, Kent.
1960.
17

HIGGS, Lionel F.
The story of "Trinity" Bexleyheath; produced for the
centenary year of the Trinity Baptist Church,
Bexleyheath, 1868-1968.
Trinity Baptist Church. 1968.
11,12

MILLER, R.R.
St. Peter, Bexleyheath, Kent: a record of the first
21 years, 1930-1951.
Charles Thorn. 1952.
12

NOYES, Alfred.
William Morris. (Resident at Bexleyheath).
Macmillan. 1908.
12

SUNDERLAND, Oliver.
Bexleyheath considered with regard to health.
1894.
17

THOMPSON, Paul.
The work of William Morris (who lived at Bexleyheath).
Heinemann. 1967.
12

BIBLIOGRAPHY

LIBRARY ASSOCIATION - KENT SUB-BRANCH.
List of pamphlets and other ephemeral material relating
to Kent.
1957(58,59).
3,9

UPCOTT, William.
Bibliographical account of the principal works relating
to English topography; Kent section.
Taylor. 1818.
1

BICKLEY

BRAIN, Mrs. M.
Extract from a paper on...Charles Newnham, 1799-1970.
(Note: includes notes on work of Sir Robert Smirke at
Bickley Hall).
Typescript. 1960.
2

KENT COUNTY COUNCIL - ARCHIVES OFFICE.
Bickley parish records.
1964.
2

MOORE, Walter.
Bromley and Bickley.
London Suburban and Provincial Development Association.
1908.
2

REID, D.A.G.
Bickley Park Cricket Club centenary year 1967, compiled
by D.A.G. Reid.
The Club. 1967.
2

BICKLEY Cont'd

SLEVIN, Bernard.
Pioneer missionaries: a short history of the Holy Ghost
Fathers. (Note: provincial residence established in
Bickley, 1947).
The Paraclete Press. (1966).
2

BIDBOROUGH

Printstile Place - Sale catalogue.
1966.
12

SKINNER, Frederick A.
Bidborough - a parish history.
Reverend F.A. Skinner, Rectory, Bidborough. 1969.
4,7,8,11,19

BIDDENDEN

Birchwood farmhouse, Biddenden - Sale catalogue.
1967.
12

Iborden Park, Biddenden - Sale catalogue.
1967.
12

BIDDENDEN LOCAL HISTORY SOCIETY.
Story of Biddenden.
1953, etc.
1,3,11,18,19

CHILLINGWORTH, P.C.H.
The Biddenden fault, near Tenterden, Kent. (Reprinted from
the Proceedings of the Geologists' Association, Vol. 81,
Pt. 1).
1970.
11

HAMMON, George.
A discovery of the latitude of the loss of earthly paradise
by original sin: occasioned by a disputation betwixt Mr.
Matthias Ruxton, Minister of Boughton Monchelsea and George
Hammon, Pastor...Biddenden.
Ibbitson. 1655.
12

JONES, A.J.
Biddenden Church and its history.
1928.
12

JONES, H. Gordon.
Biddenden Church and its history (new edition).
1957.
2

JONES, H. Gordon.
A short guide to the church of All Saints, Biddenden,
Canterbury.
Gibbs and Son. 1963.
15

KEMP, John.
Memoir of John Kemp.
C.J. Farnscombe. 1933.
12

KENT COUNTY COUNCIL - PLANNING DEPARTMENT.
Biddenden: village study.
Kent County Council. 1969.
2,11

A short and concise account of Eliza and Mary Chulkhurst, who
were joined together by the hips and shoulders in (Sic) the
year of our Lord 1100 at Biddenden in the county of Kent.
Tenterden, W. Thomson. n.d.
3,11

WOOLNER, Anne.
The story of Biddenden, compiled by A. Woolner.
Biddenden Local History Society. 1953.
7

BIGGIN HILL

ANTHONY, Jane.
The story of Foal Farm, Biggin Hill.
Robert Hale. 1966.
2,12

AVIATION, Ministry of.
Civil aircraft accident: report on the accident to
Auster Mk. VG-ANHO at Biggin Hill aerodrome on 9th May,
1964.
H.M.S.O. 1965.
8

AVIATION, Ministry of.
Civil Aviation Order. Manston.
H.M.S.O. 1964.
8

Boundaries of the district of St. Mark, Biggin Hill...
copied from Order in Council...7th May, 1928.
(Typescript).
1928.
2

KENT COUNTY COUNCIL - PLANNING DEPARTMENT.
Kent development plan (part A). Biggin Hill town map
...report on the survey and written statements.
Kent County Council. 1964.
2

PAINE, William James.
Hopping around. (Photocopy, unpublished local biography
of Biggin Hill resident).
(1965).
2

SMITH, Gilbert Arthur.
Biggin Hill guide.
Biggin Hill, G. Smith. (1964).
1,2,4

SMITH, Gilbert Arthur.
Biggin Hill and Leaves Green guide.
Biggin Hill, G. Smith. 1965.
2,12

SYMONS, Vivian.
The Moving Church.
Jenkins. 1956.
2,5,11,12

WALLACE, Graham.
R.A.F. Biggin Hill.
Putnam 1957.
1,2,8,9,11,19

WALLACE, Graham.
R.A.F. Biggin Hill.
Tandem. 1969.
7,11

BILSINGTON

COLLEY, W.W.
The churches of Bonnington, Bilsington and Hurst.
Quick Service Press. 1939.
11

NEILSON, N.
The cartulary and the terrier of the Priory of Bilsington
Kent, edited by N. Neilson.
Oxford University Press. 1928.
3,7,11

SAMPSON, Aylwin.
The parishes of Bonnington, Bilsington and Hurst.
Kent Messenger. 1957.
1,3,4,7,11,12,15

BIOGRAPHY

ABBE, Truman.
Robert Colegate, the immigrant, by T. Abbe and H.A.
Howson.
1941.
16

AIRY, Sir George B.
Autobiography of Sir George Airy.
Cambridge University Press. 1896.
17

ALEXANDER, Herbert.
Boyd Alexander's last journey, with a memoir.
Arnold. 1912.
12

ALLAN, D.G.C.
William Shipley: founder of the Royal Society of Arts.
Hutchinson. 1968.
12

ALLAN, Mea.
The Tradescants, their plants, gardens and Museum, 1570-
1662.
Joseph. 1964.
9,11

ALLEN, B.M.
Gordon in China.
MacMillan. 1933.
12

ALLEN, Charles H.
The life of "Chinese" Gordon, R.E.C.B.
Abraham Kingdon and Co. 1884.
9

ALLEN, Grant.
Charles Darwin.
Longmans, Green. 1885.
12

ALMEDINGEN, Edith Martha.
Ellen.
Oxford University Press. 1971.
11

ALMEDINGEN, Edith Martha.
Life of many colours: the story of Grandmother Ellen.
Hutchinson. 1958.
3

ASPINALL, A.
Cornwallis in Bengal.
Manchester University Press. 1931.
12

AUSTEN-LEIGH, Mary Augusta.
Personal aspects of Jane Austen.
Murray. 1920.
3

AUSTEN-LEIGH, R.A.
Austen papers, 1704-1856, edited by R.A. Austen.
Privately Printed at Colchester by Spottiswoode, Ballantyne
and Co. 1942.
3

AYLESFORD REVIEW.
Frederick Rolfe and others.
The Friars, Aylesford. 1961.
12

BALSTON, Thomas.
James Whatham: father and son.
Methuen. 1957.
4,5,11,12,15

BALSTON, Thomas.
William Balston, papermaker, 1759-1849.
Methuen. 1954.
1,4,8,11,12,18

BANKS, Charles Edward.
Edward Godfrey, 1584-1664.
Riverside Press. 1887.
11

BARHAM, Richard Harris Dalton.
The life and letters of Rev. Richard Harris Barham.
Bentley. 1880.
1,6,8,12

BAVINGTON-JONES, T.
Kent at the opening of the twentieth century. Contemporary
biographies, edited by T. Bavington-Jones and W.T. Pike.
Pike and Co. 1904.
1,4,5,7,8,11,14,15,17,18,19

BAX, Arthur Newsham.
A Bax family of East Kent.
1950?
3,11

Baily of Ightham Place and Nepicar House, Wrotham, County of
Kent.
n.d.
12

BAILEY, William
Memoirs of William Drawbridge and his widow.
Thorne. 1847.
12

BEHRENS, Lillian Boys.
Love, smugglers and naval heroes.
Palmer. 1929.
7,11,13

BEHRENS, Lillian Boys.
Under thirty-seven kings: legends of Kent and records
of the family of Boys.
1926.
1,2,3,4,6,7,11,12,13,14

BICKERSTETH, Samuel.
Morris Bickersteth, 1891-1916. (Born at Belvedere).
Cambridge University Press. 1931.
11

BLADES, William.
The biography and typography of William Caxton,
England's first printer.
Trubner. 1882.
12

BLAKE, N.F.
Caxton and his world.
A. Deutsch. 1969.
12

BLOOM, Ursula.
The house of Kent.
Hale. 1969.
12

BOYCE, Charles.
The Boys family in Virginia.
In The Genealogists' Magazine, Vol. 3, Dec., 1927, No
3

BOYS, Edward.
Narrative of a captivity and adventures in France and
Flanders, 1803-09, 2nd edition.
London, J.F. Dove. 1831.
6

BRIGGS, Alice Jane.
The fortunes of Sir Richard de Thorn, Knight of Kent:
a story of the 15th century.
Robert Culley. (1899).
11

BROOKE, Jocelyn.
The dog at Clambercrown.
J. Lane. 1955.
3,12

BRYDGES, Sir Samuel Egerton.
Autobiography.
1834.
3,11,12,17

BRYDGES, Sir Samuel Egerton.
The autobiography, times...of Sir Egerton Brydges, 2
vols.
n.d.
11

BURNET, Gilbert.
Lives, characters and an address to posterity.
Duncan. 1833.
12

CAIGER, Nesta D.
F.C.J. Spurrell, Kentish antiquary and archaeologist.
Bexley Antiquarian Society. 1971.
2,5

CARTER, Mrs. Elizabeth.
Letters from Mrs. Elizabeth Carter to Mrs. Vesey,
1763-1787.
1809.
11,17

CARTER, Mrs. Elizabeth.
Letters to Mrs. Montague, 1755-1800, 3 vols.
1817.
17

CARTER, Mrs. Elizabeth.
Memoirs of the life of...with her poems and miscellaneous
essays in prose, by Montague Pennington.
n.d.
17

CARTER, Mrs. Elizabeth.
Series of letters between Mrs. Elizabeth Carter and Miss
Catherine Talbot, 1741-1770.
1809.
11,17

CHAMBERS, F.
The Fair Maid of Kent: an historical and biographical
sketch.
n.d.
13

CHAPMAN, Herbert Turlay.
Reminiscences of a highway surveyor, 1886-1932.
Maidstone, Alabaster Press. 1932.
1,2,5,11,12,13,15

CHURCH, Richard.
Kent's contribution.
Adams and Dart. 1972.
11

COCK, F. William.
Kentish men at the University of Padua.
1928.
7,11,17

COLTHUP, William.
A man of Kent at home and abroad.
Colthup. 1953.
12

CORNHILL MAGAZINE.
A Kentish Boswell. "The Cornhill Magazine", April, 1886.
11

CORNWALLIS, Charles. 1st Marquess.
Correspondence of Charles, 1st Marquess Cornwallis, edited
by C.H. Ross, 3 vols.
Murray. 1859.
12

COWTAN, Robert. ("Man of Kent", pseud).
Passages from the autobiography of a "Man of Kent",
together with a few rough pen-and-ink sketches...of some of
the people he has met, etc., 1817-1865.
Whittingham and Wilkins. 1866.
1,3,4,6,7,8,11,12,13,15,17,19

COX, Horace.
Who's who in Kent, Surrey and Sussex.
Cox. 1911.
2,5,8,9,11,12,13,15,18

DAY, James Wentworth.
H.R.H. Princess Marina, Duchess of Kent: the first
authentic life story.
Hale. 1962.
15

DUFF, David.
Edward of Kent: the life story of Queen Victoria's father.
Stanley Paul and Co. 1938.
12

East Kent Times Portrait Gallery, No. 1
East Kent Times. 1898.
14

EELES, Henry Wanston.
Lord Chancellor Camden and his family.
London, P. Allan. 1934.
3

ELLIS, Clarence.
Hubert de Burgh: a study in constancy.
London, Phoenix House. 1952.
3,6

ELLIS, William Smith.
Notices of the Elleses of Franch (from the time of
Charlemagne) and of England (from the Conquest to the
present day).
E. Tucker, London. n.d.
15

ELLISON, Grace.
The authorised life story of Princess Marina.
Heinemann. 1934.
9

Evering family.
n.d.
11

FITZMAURICE, Edmond.
The life of Granville George Leveson Gower, 1815-91,
2 vols.
Longmans, Green. 1905.
6

FRY, George S.
The "Taylor Papers".
Privately Printed. 1923.
3,11

GARDINER, Mrs. Dorothy.
Thomas Cockes, the diarist.
Archaeologia Cantiana, Vol. LVI. n.d.
3,17

GARDINER, Mrs. Dorothy.
The Tradescants and their times. (Reprint from Journal
of Royal Horticultural Society, Vol. LIII, Pt. 2).
1928.
3

GATHORNE-HARDY, Alfred A.
Gathorne-Hardy, first Earl of Cranbrook: a memoir, with
extracts from his diary and correspondence, 2 vols,
edited by A.E. Gathorne-Hardy.
Longmans, Green. 1910.
4,12,15

GILLINGHAM PUBLIC LIBRARY.
Saints connected with Kent.
Typescript. n.d.
8

GOUGH, John Bartholomew.
Autobiography.
Morgan and Scott. 1858, etc.
7,11,17

HASTED, Edward.
Letters of Edward Hasted to Thomas Astle. (Reprinted
from Archaeologia Cantiana).
Hughes and Clarke. 1905.
1

HIGGS, William Miller.
A history of the Higges, or Higgs family of South Stoke
(of Kent interest...Orpington, Ramsgate, Chiselhurst and
Faversham).
Adlard. 1933.
7,14

JELF, Mrs. Katherine Frances.
George Edward Jelf.
Skeffington . 1909.
17

Kent, historical, biographical and pictorial.
Baxter. 1907.
1,5,11,12,14,19

KENT MESSENGER.
Marriage of Duke and Duchess of Kent.
Kent Messenger. 1934.
3

KENT MESSENGER.
Newspaper cuttings taken from Kent Messenger, April
16th, 1954 relating to notable Kentish personalities.
Kent Messenger. 1954.
3

KING, Stella.
Princess Marina: her life and times.
Cassell. 1969.
12

KITTON, Frederic G.
"Phiz" (Hablot Knight Browne): a memoir.
1882.
4

KNATCHBULL-HUGESSEN, _Sir_ Hughe.
Diplomat in peace and war.
Murray. 1949.
3,7,8,12

KNATCHBULL-HUGESSEN, _Sir_ Hughe.
Kentish family.
Methuen. 1960.
1,3,4,5,7,8,11,12,14,15,17,18,21

LANGTON, Robert.
The late Charles Roach Smith, F.S.A.
The Manchester Examiner. 1891.
4

LOCKER-LAMPSON, F.
My confidence.
Smith, Elder. 1896.
17

MacKAIL, J.W.
Life and letters of George Wyndham by J.W. MacKail and
Guy Wyndham, 2 vols.
Hutchinson. n.d.
6

MASTERS, John Neve.
Amusing reminescences of Victorian times and of today.
Rye, Masters. 1921.
6,7,11,12

MASTERS, John Neve.
The second book of reminiscences.
Rye, Masters. n.d.
6,12

MATTHEW, _Sir_ Tobie.
The life of Lady Lucy Knatchbull.
Sheed and Ward. 1931.
11

Memorials of the family of Sankey, 1207-1880, printed from
the genealogical collection of Clement Sankey Best-Gardner
of Eaglesbush, Neath.
Privately Printed, Swansea. 1880.
3

MILLS, Mary C.S.
Edith Davidson of Lambeth.
London, Murray. 1938.
3

NEAME, _Sir_ Philip.
Playing with strife: autobiography of a soldier.
London, Harrap. 1947.
3

Memoirs of the families of Sir Edward Knatchbull Bart and
Filmer Honeywood, Esq.
Printed at Gravesend by R. Pocock. 1802.
9

Memorials of the family of Tufton Earls of Thanet.
Gravesend, Pocock. 1800.
1,3,6,9,11,12,13,15,17

PUBLIC CHARACTERS OF 1805.
(Includes Egerton Brydges, John Jeffreys-Pratt, 2nd Earl
Camden, Lord Charles Whitworth, Charles Marsham, Earl of
Romney).
Phillips. 1805.
11

SASSOON, Siegfried.
The weald of youth.
Faber. 1942.
11

SHEARS, Sarah.
Tapioca for tea: memories of a Kentish childhood.
Elek. 1971.
8,11

SIMSON, James.
Eminent men of Kent.
Elliot Stock. 1893.
1,2,4,5,6,7,8,9,11,12,13,14,15,17,18,19

SMITH, Gill.
Genuine history of the life of Gill Smith.
1738.
17

SMITH, Logan Pearsall.
Life and letters of Sir Henry Wotton.
Oxford, Clarendon Press. 1907.
11

SMITH, Thomas.
Vita. cl. Gulielmi Camden, et illustrium virorum ad G.
Camdenum epistolae.
Chiswell. 1691.
12

SMITH, _Sir_ William Sidney.
The life of the gallant Sir Sydney Smith (was educated at
Tonbridge School. M.P. for Rochester, 1802).
1803?
4

SPRIGGE, Elizabeth.
Sybil Thorndike Casson.
Victor Gollancz. 1971.
4

SUCKLING, Florence H.
A forgotten past: being notes of the families of
Tyssen, Baker, etc.
Bell. 1898.
1,3,7,8,11,12,18

TASSEL, J.S.
"Tassel": members of the French family who came to
England as Huguenots.
Typescript MS. 1962.
11

TERRY, William H.
Life and times of John, Lord Finch, Speaker of the House
of Lords.
Simpkin, Marshall. 1936.
3,11

THOMSON, Arthur Alexander.
Great men of Kent.
Bodley Head. 1955.
2,3,5,7,8,11,15,19

THORNDIKE, Russell.
Sybil Thorndike.
Rockliff. 1950.
4

TREWIN, J.C.
Sybil Thorndike. (Youth spent in Rochester).
15

TRITTON, Jospeh Herbert.
Tritton: the place and the family.
London, A.L. Humphreys. 1907.
4,8

True history of a Kentish lawyer.
n.d.
11

TWYMAN, Frank.
An East Kent Family.
Twyman. 1956.
1,3,4,6,7,8,11,14,15,17

"Upper Ten Thousand, for 1877" - handbook of the titled
and official classes.
3rd Annual Edition. 1877.
18

WATERS, Henry S.
Notes on the Manning family of County Kent.
Boston (Mass). 1897.
11

WHETMORE, S.A.H.
Some further notes on Thomas Simon. (Reprinted from
British Numismatic Journal, Vol. 30).
British Numismatic Society. 1961.
12

Who's who in Kent.
Worcester, Baylis. 1935.
1,2,3,4,5,6,7,8,9,11,12,14,15,17,18

WINGFIELD-STRATFORD, Esme.
This was a man: the biography of the Hon. Edward Vesey Bligh.
London, Robert Hale. 1949.
1,3,4,8,15,19

WINNIFRITH, Alfred.
Men of Kent and Kentish men: biographical notices of 680
worthies.
Folkestone, Parson. 1913.
1,2,3,4,5,6,7,8,9,11,12,13,14,15,17,18,19

WINNIFRITH, Alfred.
The fair maids of Kent.
Folkestone, Parsons. 1921.
1,3,4,5,6,7,8,11,12,13,14,15,18,19

WOODGATE, Gordon.
A history of the Woodgates of Stonewall Park and of Summerhill
in Kent, by G. Woodgate and M.G. Giles.
Privately Printed. 1910?
11

BIRCHINGTON

BARRETT, J.P.
History of the Ville of Birchington, Thanet.
Ramsgate, Keble. 1893, etc.
1,3,4,7,8,11,12,13,14,15

BIRCHINGTON PUBLICITY COMMITTEE.
Birchington in Thanet: official guide.
Chatham, Printed by Wood and Co.
11(192-?) 13(1935)

BIRCHINGTON PUBLICITY COMMITTEE.
The Birchington Post.
1938
13

BIRCHINGTON PUBLICITY COMMITTEE.
Sunny Birchington-on-Sea, 1962,1964,1969.
Margate, Central Press.
11

BIRCHINGTON PUBLICITY COMMITTEE.
Why not come to Birchington?
1947.
13

CLARKE, M. Dudley.
Birchington.
Homeland Association. n.d.
11,13

COLES, Cyril A.G.
Some notes concerning All Saints Church, Birchington.
Margate, Cooper. 1945.
11,12,13

COOKE, H.B.S.
The Powell-Cotton Museum of African Fauna and Ethnology,
Kent, England. (Reprint from South African Museums
Association Bulletin, Vol. 6, No. 11, Sept. 1957), by H.B.S.
Cooke and L.R. Barton.
3

CRISP, Frederick Arthur.
Collections relating to the family of Crispe. (No. 46 of 50
copies).
Privately Printed. 1897.
13

CRISP, Frederick Arthur.
Monumental inscription in the church at Birchington.
Privately Printed. 1899.
12

Day account of building ye workhouse at Birchington, 1792-
1794. Accompts of charges on enlarging ye workhouse, 1794-
1795...with day account of money received and paid for the
use of ye workhouse of Birchington, 1796-1822 (MS.) n.d.
13

Margate, Birchington, Westgate-on-Sea.
1936.
13

Margate and Westgate with Birchington.
1903/4.
13

POWELL-COTTON MUSEUM, BIRCHINGTON.
Guide to the big game park in the Powell-Cotton Museum,
Quex Park, Birchington, Kent.
Birchington, Jones. 1954.
3

The scheme, etc., for the regulation and management of
Crispe's charity, for the benefit of the Parish of
Birchington and Ville of Acole, in the County of Kent.
Printed in pursuance of a resolution, passed at a special
meeting of the Trustees, held at Birchington on 25th July
1862.
1862.
13

SERRES, H.A.
A short guide to the parish church of All Saints,
Birchington.
1904.
13

SERRES, H.A.
Short guide to the parish church of All Saints, Birchington, 2nd edition.
1913.
3,13,15

WALKER, Alfred T.
A guide to the parish church of All Saints, Birchington.
Westwood. 1967.
11,13

WORSFOLD, Frederick Henry.
A report on the late Bronze Age site excavated at Minnis
Bay, Birchington, Kent, 1938-40. (Reprinted from
Proceedings of the Prehistoric Society).
1943.
3

BIRLING

All Saints Church, Birling.
1961.
11

BISHOPSBOURNE

CASTLE, Alice.
Church of St. Mary, Bishopsbourne.
Canterbury, Gibbs. 1961.
1,3,11

Charlton Park, Bishopsbourne, nr. Canterbury, Kent...
official guide.
English Life. 1971.
3

BLACKHEATH

BAKER, Gerard L.
Blackheath: the story of the Royal Hundred.
Morden Society. 1925.
1,11,12,17,18

BAKER, L.A.J.
House and its occupiers: Park House, now know as
St. Mary's Presbytery, Cresswell Park.
Privately Printed. 1957?
4,11

BAKER, L.A.J.
Pictures from the past: reprinted from the Blackheath
Local Guide.
n.d.
4,11,17,18

BINGHAM, Frederik.
The "Borough" pocket guide to Blackheath, Kent.
Ed. J. Burrow. 1909.
17

Blackheath local guide. Boung volumes, 1911, 1924-25,
1946-47, 1948, 1949.
17

BLACKHEATH RUGBY FOOTBALL CLUB.
The Blackheath Rugby Football Club records, 1862-1898.
Blackheath Rugby Football Club. n.d.
1,12,18

BUTTS, Robert.
Historical guide to Lewisham, Ladywell, Lee, Blackheath
and Eltham.
1878.
17,18

CRASK, C.W.
The Blackheath cavern.
1948.
18

DARWIN, Bernard.
The Royal Blackheath Golf Club.
Golf Clubs Association. 1954.
1

A descriptive account of Lewisham, Lee, Blackheath and Catford.
1894.
18

DIXSON, Owen.
Blackheath since the war: the continued story of Blackheath
Football Club.
O. Dixson. 1971.
11

DOWRICK, C.E.J.
The heavy minerals of the Blackheath Bed. (Reprinted from
Proceedings, Croydon Natural History and Scientific Society).
The Society. 1965.
2

FULFORD, Roger.
George the Fourth. (References to Queen Caroline, resident
at Blackheath).
1935.
18

FULFORD, Roger.
The trial of Queen Caroline.
Batsford. 1967.
17

GREAT BRITAIN: LAWS, etc. (WILLIAM IV).
An Act for the amendment of three several Acts passed...
for the recovery of small debts within the hundreds of
Blackheath etc.
1836.
11

GREEN, T. Frank.
Morden College, Blackheath.
London Survey Committee. 1916. (Survey of London No. 10).
1,11,17,18

Greenwich and Blackheath: a handy guide.
Fisher, Unwin.
11,17,18

Greenwich and Blackheath, with rambles in the district.
Marshall Jupp. 1881.
1

GREENWICH AND LEWISHAM ANTIQUARIAN SOCIETY.
Catalogue of the paintings, prints, photographs, etc.
exhibited in All Saints Hall, Tranquil Vale, Blackheath,
S.E.3, November 12th-19th, 1955.
1955.
4

GREENWICH NATURAL HISTORY CLUB.
The fauna of Blackheath and its vicinity, Part 1.
Clowes. 1859.
11

HARVEY, A.E. Martin.
Sir John Morden and his College.
Blackheath, Morden Society. 1925.
17,18

HUGHES, W.E.
Chronicles of Blackheath golfers...edited by W.E. Hughes.
Chapman and Hall. 1897.
1,17,18

HUSSEY, Christopher.
"Colonnade House, Blackheath" (article in "Country Life").
Country Life. 1950.
18

Indication of houses of historical interest in London,
Part 27. (Macartney House, Blackheath).
18

KIRBY, John William.
History of the Blackheath Proprietary School.
Blackheath Press. 1933.
11,18

KIRBY, John William.
The Royal Subsidy of 1641 and the levy of 1644 on...
Blackheath.
Greenwich and Lewisham Antiquarian Society, Vol. 6. 1963.
17,18

MALIM, Mary Charlotte.
Book of the Blackheath High School, by M.C. Malim and
H.C. Escreet.
Blackheath Press. 1927.
1,17

MARSH, T.
Blackheath golfing lays.
1872.
18

Memioirs of the life and exploits of George Wilson, the
celebrated pedestrian. (Note: record performance at
Blackheath).
Dean and Munday. 1815.
2,18

Morden College: a brief guide and handbook.
Blackheath, Morden College.
4,11

A narrative of the proceedings of the Magistrates
against G. Wilson, the Blackheath pedestrian, October
5th, 1815.
Elizabeth Delahoy. 1815.
11

NEALE, J.M.
Letters of J.M. Neale.
Longmans Green. 1910.
12

NOBLE, T.
Blackheath: a poem in 5 cantos.
Cowthorpe. 1808.
2,6,17,13

NUNN, F.W.
Antiquariana. An episode on Blackheath in 1815.
(George Wilson, pedestrian).
c.1910?
2,18

ORD, Hubert William.
The adventures of a schoolmaster...with some account of
the Blackheath Proprietary School.
Simpkin, Marshall. 1936.
1,12,17,18

ORD, Hubert William.
The story of Greenwich as a port and Blackheath in times
of war, 2nd edition.
Blackheath Press. 1916.
1,17,18

Greenwich and Blackheath souvenir.
Perkins and Son. n.d.
17

Quizzical Quorum...(Broadsheet). (1815, George Wilson,
the Blackheath walker).
18

RHIND, Neil.
Blackheath centenary, 1871-1971: a short history of
Blackheath from earliest times.
Greater London Council. 1971.
2,4,11

ROW, John.
Brief memoir of Hephzibah Row.
Bartlett. 1864.
11

SINCLAIR, W.B.
The Black Heath...(article in the Journal of the London Society).
1955.
18

A sketch of the life of George Wilson, the Blackheath pedestrian.
1815.
18

SMITH, W.H.
Rough notes towards a memoir of Sir John Morden Bart, founder of Morden College, Blackheath.
Blackheath, Smith. 1867.
12,17

WHITEFIELD, George.
Journals, 1738-47. (Local references to Blackheath, etc.). (Enlarged edition).
1960.
18

BLEAN

BLEAN UNION AND RURAL DISTRICT COUNCIL.
List of members of Council, etc., 1899-1900.
17

BLEAN WOMEN'S INSTITUTE.
Blean, 1965: scrapbook of Blean Women's Institute.
1965.
3

Tyler Hill, Blean near Canterbury: particulars and conditions of sale of capital freehold properties including "Tyler Hill House". Truscott and Co. will offer for sale by auction, at the Rose Hotel, Canterbury on Saturday, 4th August, 1917 at 3.00 p.m.
Canterbury, Kentish Observer Printing Works. n.d.
3

WOODRUFF, Charles Everleigh.
The hill in the Blean.
1902.
17

BOBBING

Parish of Bobbing, Kent: Vicarage building fund.
1911.
12

WHATMORE, Leonard E.
A pioneer recusant family: the Greenes of Bobbing, Kent. (Included in "The Southwark Record", Vol. XXXIII, No. 377, Jan. 1959).
3

BONNINGTON

COLLEY, W.W.
The churches of Bonnington, Bilsington and Hurst.
Sellindge, Quick Service Press. 1939.
11

SAMPSON, Aylwin.
The parishes of Bonnington, Bilsington and Hurst.
Maidstone, Kent Messenger. 1957.
1,3,4,7,11,12,15

BORDEN

St. Peter and St. Paul, Borden, Kent.
Church Publications. 1966.
1,8,11,12

BOROUGH GREEN

BOROUGH GREEN WOMEN'S INSTITUTE.
Scrapbook, 1965. MS. Copy.
1965.
11

PIKE, Leslie Edgar.
Wrotham, Borough Green and district.
Home Publishing Co.
1

BORSTAL

BARNES, C.H.
Shorts aircraft since 1900.
Putnam. 1967.
4

BLAW KNOW LTD.
General catalogue, Blaw Knox construction equipment, (196-?) (loose-leaf).
4

LESLIE, Shane.
Sir Evelyn Ruggles-Brise: a memoir of the founder of Borstal, compiled by S. Leslie.
1938.
4

POOLMAN, Kenneth.
Flying boat: the story of the "Sunderland".
Kimber. 1962.
15

SHORT BROTHERS (ROCHESTER AND BEDFORD) LTD.
Pamphlets describing aircraft and history of the firm.
c.1920-1945.
4

TANNAHILL, Thomas F.
The influenza epidemic of 1890 at H.M. Convict Prison, Borstal, Rochester.
Glasgow Medical Journal. 1890.
15

BOSTALL HEATH

PRIEST, Simeon.
Excursion to Plumstead and Bostall Heath and excursion to Cobham and Strood.
1924.
5

BOUGHTON ALUPH

Boughton Aluph Church, leaflet appealing for funds, giving short description of church.
(1959).
3

BOUGHTON ALUPH CHURCH REPAIR FUND.
Four pennyworth of shoeleather and Boughton Aluph Church: urgent repairs.
Boughton Aluph Church Repair Fund. (1952).
3

COUNCER, C.R.
The medieval painted glass of Boughton Aluph.
Kent Archaeological Society. 1938.
11,17

GARDINER, Mrs. Dorothy.
Manor of Boughton Aluph.
Archaeologia Cantiana. n.d.
3,11

GARDINER, Mrs. Dorothy.
Manor of Boughton Aluph and Sir Thomas de Aldon.
n.d.
3,11,17

BOUGHTON MALHERBE

Boughton Place, Boughton Malherbe - Sale catalogue.
1937.
12

CAVENAGH, W.O.
Colonel Daniel O'Neill, circa 1612-1664. (Reprinted from the Journal of the Proceedings of the Royal Society of Antiquaries of Ireland, Pt. 3, Vol. XXXVIII, 4th Qrt., December, 1908).
3

WOTTON, Thomas.
Thomas Wotton's letter-book, 1574-1586, edited by G. Eland.
Oxford University Press. 1960.
11

BOUGHTON MONCHELSEA

Coombe Bank, Boughton Monchelsea - Sale catalogue.
1968.
12

Guide to Boughton Monchelsea Place, near Maidstone.
n.d.
2,12

HAMMON, George.
A discovery of the latitude of the loss of the earthly
paradise by original sin: occasioned by a disputation
betwixt Mr. Matthias Ruxton, Minister of Boughton Monchelsea
and George Hammon, Pastor, Biddenden.
Ibbitson. 1655.
12

HEAD, Sir John.
Sermon preached in the parish church of Boughton Monchelsea
in Kent...on occasion of the first muster of volunteers for
the general defence of the country.
Shaw. 1803.
11

STRANGEWAYS, J.G.V.
The church of St. Peter, Boughton Monchelsea: a revised
guide.
n.d.
12

WARREN, Joseph Henry.
St. Peter's Church, Boughton Monchelsea.
Sittingbourne, Parrett. 1957.
4,8,11,12,15

Weirton Place, Boughton Monchelsea - Sale catalogue.
1967.
12

BOUGHTON-UNDER-BLEAN

BOODLE, John Adolphus.
Boughton under the Blean. (Reprinted from Archaeologia
Cantiana).
Mitchell and Hughes. 1895.
3,7

COLLINS, I.
Notes on the geology of Boughton-under-Blean...by I. Collins
and D.M.C. Gill.
n.d.
11

BOXLEY

CAVE-BROWN, John.
The Abbots of Boxley.
n.d.
4,11

CAVE-BROWN, John.
History of Boxley parish.
Maidstone, Dickinson. 1892.
1,3,4,6,8,11,12,15,18

CAVE-BROWN, John.
Notes about Boxley, its Abbey and Church.
Maidstone, Wickham. 1870.
1,6,12,15

CAVE-BROWN, John.
The seals of Boxley Abbey. In Leeds, Kent, its priory
church and Parish.
British Archaeological Association. (189-.).
4

EDWARDS, J.W.F.
The geology of Boxley Hill, Kent. (Turonian). Typescript
MS. of a thesis.
11

Indenture made 13th November, 1669 between Edwin Wyatt and
Dame Margaret Wyatt...Sir Robert Wiseman... in respect of
Upper Grange, Boxley.
12

MOORE, C.
Parish church of St. Mary the Virgin, Boxley.
Billing and Sons, Printers. c.1939.
2

RICHARDS, Frederick J.
Notes about Boxley.
Maidstone, Wickham. 1870.
3,8,11,17

(ROBERTS, Barre Charles).
Tracts, etc. Notes on Boxley Abbey.
(1807).
17

ST. ANDREW'S COLLEGE, BOXLEY.
Prospectus. 1963.
8

St. Mary and All Saints, Boxley.
Ramsgate, Church Publications. 1963.
11

Saint Mary and All Saints, Boxley: a short history.
Printed by Westwood Press. 1965.

BOXTED

PAYNE, George.
Account of the discovery of the foundations of Roman
buildings at Boxted, Kent. (Reprinted from Proceedings
of the Antiquarian Society, 1883).
17

BRABOURNE

HIGENBOTTAM, Frank.
Shorthand two hundred years ago: the manuscript short-
hand diary of the Rev. Joseph Price, Vicar of Brabourne.
Included in, I.P.S. Journal, Vol. XVIII (new series),
No.7, October, 1960.
3

SAMPSON, Aylwin.
The church of St. Mary the Virgin, Brabourne.
Canterbury, Cross and Jackman. 1954.
3,7(1958) 11,12

SCOTT, F. Douglas.
History of the church of St. Mary the Virgin, Brabourne.
(Typescript).
1963.
3

SCOTT, Sir G. Gilbert.
Brabourne Church: substance of an address, 30th July,
1874.
Mitchell and Hughes. 1875.
11,17

SCOTT, James Renat.
The Scott monuments in Brabourne Church. (Reprint from
Archaeologia Cantiana, Vol. 10).
1876.
4

BRADBOURNE

CONWAY, William Martin. 1st Baron Conway of Allington.
Bradbourne, Kent: the seat of Sir John R. Twisden, Bt.
Ashford, Headley. 1918.
4,11,12

MANNINGHAM, John.
Diary of John Manningham, 1602-1603, edited by John
Bruce.
Nichols. 1868.
1,11,12,15,17

PHILLIPS, Charles J.
Bradbourne, Sevenoaks.
1916.
11

BRANDS HATCH

JONES, Ken.
Brands sixty two: a personal review of the 1962 motor
cycle racing.
Court Studio, Eltham. n.d.
5

JONES, Ken.
Brands sixty three: recollection of the 1963 motor
cycle racing at Brands Hatch.
Court Studio, Eltham. n.d.
5

BRASTED

Brasted and district guide.
Croydon, Home Publishing Co. 1953.
1,11

CAVE-BROWN, John.
History of Brasted, its manor, parish and church.
Westerham, Jewell. 1874.
1,2,3,6,11,12,13,15,17,18

PYM, Horace N.
Odds and ends at Foxwold.
Ballantyne, Hanson. 1887.
6,8,11

South Bank, Brasted.
1966.
12

BRASTED CHART

Wildwoods, Brasted Chart - Sale catalogue.
1967.
12

BREDGAR

The parish church of St. John the Baptist, Bredgar: a
short guide.
1964.
8,12

BREDHURST

ANDREWS, Rev. Thomas.
Letter to W. Norwood, Charing solicitor, suggesting a
parochial meeting of Bredhurst landowners for the purpose
of making an agreement regarding the compulsory commutation
of tithes. MS.
1836.
4

BRENCHLEY

All Saints, Brenchley, Kent.
1932.
8

Brenchley Old Vicarage - Sale catalogue.
1967.
12

FEAR, William H.
Church of All Saints, Brenchley.
Paddock Wood, Turner. 1953.
2,11

HOARE, Edward.
Sermons and memorials of Francis Stort, Vicar of Brenchley,
by E. Hoare and W. May.
1888.
17

KENT COUNTY COUNCIL - PLANNING DEPARTMENT.
Brenchley.
Kent County Council. 1967.
2,7,11,12

Minnows from Brenchley brook.
Barrett. 1861.
12

BRIDGE

Bridge and district.
Barron. n.d.
12

PINHORN, Malcolm.
Exhibition of family portraits and papers, at Bridge Place,
near Canterbury, Kent. Catalogue edited by Malcolm Pinhorn.
Phillimore. 1963.
4

BRIDGES

JERVOISE, E.
The ancient bridges of the South of England.
Architectural Press. 1930.
3,8,12,15,18,19

BROADSTAIRS

All about Ramsgate and Broadstairs, 1864, 1870.
W. Kent and Co.
13,14

BARLOW, P.W. Junior.
Broadstairs past and present.
Broadstairs, Parsons. 1882.
11,14

Breezy Broadstairs.
Broadstairs, James Simson, Weekly News Office. 1897.
3

BRIGGS, Enid Semple.
Horses and donkeys in retirement: true story of "The
Ranch", Broadstairs.
Exmouth, Raleigh Press. 1955.
11,13

BRIGGS, Enid Semple.
"The Ranch", a paradise for horses. ("The Ranch" is a
home for retired horses at Broadstairs).
Warne. 1946.
8,11,14

Broadstairs, 1836-1859, during the time of Charles
Dickens.
Broadstairs, Ward and Sons. 193-?
2

Broadstairs and neighbourhood: historical and illustrative of that fashionable place...
Margate, Denne. 1832?
11

BROADSTAIRS AND ST. PETER'S URBAN DISTRICT COUNCIL.
Official guide.
Broadstairs and St. Peter's Urban District Council.
c.1924?
11

BROADSTAIRS AND ST. PETER'S URBAN DISTRICT COUNCIL.
Official guide.
Broadstairs and St. Peter's Urban District Council.
1956, etc.
1,4,11,12

BROADSTAIRS AND ST. PETER'S URBAN DISTRICT COUNCIL.
Souvenir programme to commemorate the landing of the
Danish Viking ship...1949.
1949.
11

Broadstairs during the time of Charles Dickens, 1836-
1859.
Ramsgate, "East Kent Times". 1949.
4,11

Broadstairs illustrated.
Gravesend, Rochard. 1900?
11

BURROW, E.J. AND CO. LTD. Publishers.
The "Borough" guide to Broadstairs.
E.J. Burrow and Co. Ltd. c.1923?
4

CALLAM, Gertrude Marion Norwood.
The Norwoods, 2 vols.
1963-65.
3,7,11,13

Charles Dickens and his Bleak House.
Canterbury, Gibbs. c.1960.
1,2,4,6,8,11,12,15,19

COMMISSIONERS OF BROADSTAIRS PIER AND HARBOUR.
Copy of Deeds, 1571-1616. (Typewritten copy).
13

THE DICKENSIAN.
The Dickensian: a magazine for Dickens lovers...
special Broadstairs number, Vol. IV, No. 6, June, 1908.
Dickens Fellowship.
3

GARDNER, Peter G.A.
St. Peter's village community: a selection of documents,
c.1700-c.1900, compiled by P.G.A. Gardner and P.J. Hills.
1972.
11

GREAT BRITAIN: LAWS, etc. (GEO. III).
An act for repairing or rebuilding the pier adjoining
to the harbour of Broadstairs.
1792.
11

GREAT BRITAIN: LAWS, etc. (GEO. III).
An Act for amending an Act...for the repairing...of the
pier adjoining to the harbour of Broadstairs.
1805.
11

HEYWOOD, John. Publisher.
Illustrated guide to Broadstairs.
Manchester, Heywood. n.d.
11,14

HILLS, Peter J.
Dane Court, St. Peter's-in-Thanet: a Kentish manor and
its families.
Printed by G.W. Belton. 1972.
11

HILLS, Peter J.
The parish church of St. Peter's-in-Thanet, Broadstairs:
an introductory history and guide.
Printed by G.W. Belton. 1970.
2,4,11,12

HURD, Howard.
Some notes on recent archaeological discoveries at
Broadstairs.
Broadstairs and St. Peter's Archaeological Society. 1913.
8,11,13

JOHNSON, H.C.
Sunny Broadstairs, edited by H.C. Johnson.
Broadstairs and St. Peter's Advancement Association.
c.1910?

LAPTHORNE, William H.
A broad place: an historical account of Broadstairs from
1500 A.D. to the present; illustrated with old views.
Thanet Antiquarian Book Club. 1971.
8,11

LAPTHORNE, William H.
Smuggler's Broadstairs: an historical guide to the
smuggling annals of the ancient town of Bradstow;
illustrated with old views, 2nd edition revised.
Thanet Antiquarian Book Club. 1971.
11

MAY, George W.
Broadstairs, edited by G.W. May.
n.d.
11

MAY, George W.
Broadstairs and St. Peter's, edited by G.W. May.
Health Resorts Association. 1906.
11

MOCKETT, John.
An address to the inhabitants and parishoners of St. Peter's,
Thanet, containing an account of the proceedings of the
Parish Officers...
1822.
13

The parish church of St. Peter the Apostle in Thanet...
Canterbury, Gibbs and Son. n.d.
8,12

Photographic views of Broadstairs.
Idiens. n.d.
12

Picture of Broadstairs and neighbourhood...
1832.
13

Picturesque Broadstairs: a collection of hand-coloured
prints with descriptive sketch.
1913.
13

ROWLAND, J.
Calamity in Kent: novel about Broadgate (?Broadstairs?).
Jenkins. 1950.
12

St. Peter (in Thanet) church history.
c. 195-?
12

SMITH, Charles Roach.
On a Roman villa near Broadstairs.
Mitchell and Hughes. 1876.
1

Twenty-four views of Broadstairs and neighbourhood.
J.S. and Co. c.1870-80.
13

BROCKLEY

BUTYAERS, E.
Brockley in pre-reformation times.
1920.
18

BROMFIELD

CAVE-BROWNE, John.
In and about Leeds and Bromfield parishes, Kent.
1894.
1,4,11,15

BROMLEY

ADAMS, HOLDEN AND PEARSON.
Bromley and District Hospital: report on future
development. (Typescript).
Adams, Holden and Pearson. 1946.
2

BALDWIN, S.J.
The bee-keepers instructor, with a complete catalogue of
appliances manufactured by S.J. Baldwin.
Bromley, "The Apiary". c.1894.
2

Ballad - on Bromley surgeons.
1824.
2

BASKCOMB, G.H.
The arborist: practical treatise on moving and
replanting large...trees.
Bromley, E. Strong. 1865.
2

BAXTER, William.
History of Bromley (diary concerning the compilation of
Horsburgh's history...).
(Manuscript). 1926-1932.
2

BAXTER, William.
Itinery of Bromley.
(Manuscript). 1922.
2

BAXTER, William.
Short account of Bromley College.
Bromley College Trustees. 1926.
2

BECKLEY, William. Publisher.
History, antiquities, etc. of the parish of Bromley,
Kent.
W. Beckley. 1832.
18

BEEBY, Walter Thomas.
Bromley Church. (The copy at Bromley Library has extra
annotations and illustrations).
Bromley, E. Strong. 1872.
1,2,6,11,12,15,17

BEHRENS, Lillian Boys.
Echoes of the good and fallen angels de Cawston,
Norfolk (also Cawstons at Bromley, Orpington).
Battle, The Author. 1956.
2,3

BEHRENS, Lillian Boys.
Echoes of a turbulent Victorian family. (Cawston
family, Bromley Hill).
Privately Printed. 1953?
2

BEHRENS, Lillian Boys.
Legends and echoes of Bromley, Kent.
n.d.
1,2,8,11

BENHAM, D.
Notes illustrative of an ancient inscription on a brass
plate in Bromley Church, compiled by D. Benham.
Bromley, E. Strong. 1861.
2

BENJAMIN, J.
Bromley looks at youth. (Extract from Youth Review, No.
7, November, 1966).
1966.
2

BIRTHWHISTLE, N.A.
Milestones: story of Bromley High Street Methodist Church.
Bromley Methodist Church. 1965.
2

BISSMIRE, A.S.
History of Bromley Football Club, 1892-1938, edited by
A.S. Bissmire.
Bromley Football Club. 1938.
2

BOND, John Arthington Walpole.
The birds of Bromley, Kent, and its neighbourhood.
Bromley, S. Bush. 1901.
1,2

BOY SCOUTS.
50 years of scouting...5th Bromley (St Luke's) Group.
The Group. 1962.
2

BRITISH MARKET RESEARCH BUREAU LTD.
Shopping in suburbia...reactions to supermarket shopping.
(Note: Bromley, Kent one of the 7 areas surveyed).
J. Walter Thompson Co. 1963.
2

BROMLEY, John.
History of Bromley Chapel, Kent.
Whittaker. 1837.
2,11,12

Bromley, Beckenham and district: a handbook...of educational
facilities.
Century Publications. 1956?
11

BROMLEY AND DISTRICT CONSUMERS' GROUP.
Bromley pubs.
Bromley and District Consumers' Group.1967.
2,12

BROMLEY AND DISTRICT CONSUMERS' GROUP.
Footpaths survey.
Bromley and District Consumers' Group. 1968.
2,12

BROMLEY AND DISTRICT CONSUMERS' GROUP.
Footpaths survey, No. 2. Keston to Hawleys Corner.
Bromley and District Consumers' Group. 1968.
2

BROMLEY AND DISTRICT CONSUMERS' GROUP.
Halls for hire: a survey...Spring, 1968.
Bromley and District Consumers' Group. 1969.
11

BROMLEY AND WEST KENT TELEGRAPH.
The ghost of Keston Common. (Broadsheet reprinted from
Bromley and West Kent Telegraph).
c.1880-1895.
2

BROMLEY BOROUGH COUNCIL.
1951 Festival of Britain official programme (greater part
consists of outline history of Bromley).
Bromley Borough Council. 1951.
2

BROMLEY BOROUGH COUNCIL.
Official guide.
E.J. Burrow and Co. Various dates.
1,2,4,8,11,15,19

The Bromley Case: statements of...circumstances which have
led to the separation from Bromley Chapel of certain
individuals.
J.W. Madox, Printer. 1837.
2

BROMLEY CENTRAL HALL.
By the highway-side. (Note: Wesleyan Mission...).
Central Hall, Bromley. 1928.
2

BROMLEY CHAMBER OF COMMERCE.
Golden Jubilee...year book (includes histories of Bromley
and of the Chamber of Commerce).
Bromley Chamber of Commerce. 1966.
2

BROMLEY CHAMBER OF COMMERCE.
Year book and directory, 1963-4 (classified).
Bromley Chamber of Commerce. 1963.
2

BROMLEY COLLEGE.
Papers: (on the state of Bromley College, 1738; rules and
orders for the good government...1672).
MS.
2

BROMLEY COLLEGE.
Sermons preached at Bromley College, 1863-1882.
MS. (Duplicated).
2

BROMLEY COLLEGE.
Some impressions of life in Bromley College, Kent.
W. Lewis for Private Circulation. 1943.
2

BROMLEY COLLEGE.
The state of Bromley College in Kent. (Broadsheet).
1738.
2

BROMLEY COLLEGE: RESIDENTS
Some impressions of life in Bromley College.
Privately Printed. 1943.
2

BROMLEY COMMUNIST PARTY.
The Bromley we want: a discussion pamphlet.
Bromley Communist Party. 1946.
2

BROMLEY CONGREGATIONAL CHURCH.
Manuals, 1885-1906 (some gaps).
2

BROMLEY CONGREGATIONAL CHURCH.
New Congregational Chapel and Schools. (4 page appeal
with outline of history). 1880.
2

BROMLEY DESIGN GROUP.
Town centre study, 1966.
Bromley Design Group. 1966.
2

BROMLEY FEMALE FRIENDLY SOCIETY.
Articles and tables.
Bromley, J. Dunkin, Printer. 1821.
2

BROMLEY FOOTBALL CLUB.
Official handbook, 1958/9-1961/2.
Sports Publications.
2

BROMLEY GRAMMAR SCHOOL FOR BOYS.
Jubilee brochure, 1911-1961. (Includes history of the
school).
Bromley Grammar School for Boys. 1961.
2

BROMLEY HIGH SCHOOL.
Jubilee record, 1883-1933.
Bromley Printing Co. 1933.
2

BROMLEY HIGH SCHOOL.
75th Jubilee, 1958. (History and memoirs, etc.).
Bromley High School. 1958.
2

BROMLEY LITERARY INSTITUTE.
Catalogues, 1851, 1877, 1888 (and supplements, various
dates).
Bromley Literary Institute.
2

BROMLEY LITERARY INSTITUTE.
General information...(4 page brochure).
n.d.
2

BROMLEY LITERARY INSTITUTE.
List of members.
Bromley, E. Strong, Printers. 1895.
2

BROMLEY LITERARY INSTITUTE.
Rules and byelaws (1846)...reports (1846-1909, 1910-14,
1934). 3 vols. and separate reports.
Bromley Literary Institute.
2

BROMLEY LOCAL BOARD.
Plan showing position of oil lamps. (Manuscript in
sheets).
c.1890.
2

BROMLEY: LONDON BOROUGH COUNCIL.
London Borough of Bromley.
London Borough of Bromley. 1965.
1,2,4,5,8,11,19

The Bromley Magazine, conducted by the pupils of
Mr. Raw's academy.
Beckley. 1845.
12

BROMLEY NATURALISTS SOCIETY.
Flora and fauna of the Bromley district, i.e. lists 1-4:
Mammalia...mollusca...macio-lepidoptera and flowering plants.
Bromley Naturalists Society. 1895-98.
2

BROMLEY NATURALISTS SOCIETY.
Flowering plants of the Bromley district (list 4).
Bromley Naturalists Society. 1898.
2

BROMLEY NATURALISTS SOCIETY.
Mollusca and algae of the Bromley district (list 2).
Bromley Naturalists Society. 1894?
2

Bromley newspapers: various local papers filed dating
respectively from 1858,1878,1891,1919, etc.
2

BROMLEY PRIMITIVE METHODIST CHURCH.
Jubilee souvenir, 1924 (with extra annotations by Baxter).
Bromley Primitive Methodist Church. 1924.
2

BROMLEY PUBLIC LIBRARY.
Hand-list of selected recent additions to the home reading
and reference departments.
Library Committee. 1904.
2

BROMLEY PUBLIC LIBRARY.
London Borough of Bromley public libraries: a directory.
1964.
2

BROMLEY RURAL DEANERY.
List of roads with parishes in the rural deanery...
excluding Biggin Hill.
(Typescript). c.1966.
2

BROMLEY: ST. LUKE'S.
Some facts about St. Luke's. (Single leaf from St. Luke's
Parochial Magazine).
(After 1910).
7

BROMLEY TECHNICAL COLLEGE - ADVANCED COMMERCIAL GROUP.
A short account of the Rookery Estate and its owners.
Duplicated Typescript. 1961.
2

BROMLEY UNION.
Provisional Committee...to visit orphans...(handbook).
Bromley Local Offices. 1894.
2

BROWN, E.E.S.
An unusual "pipe" in the Blackheath Beds at Bromley Hill...
(Reprint from Proceedings, Geologists' Association, Vol. XL,
1929, P.P. 70-76), by E.E.S. Brown and F.A. Edmonds.
Geologists' Association. 1929.
2

BURCH, Brian.
Bibliography of printed material relating to Bromley, Hayes
and Keston in the county of Kent.
Bromley Public Library. 1964.
1,2,3,4,5,7,8,11,12,15,16,17,18

BYFORD, C.W.
The story of the parish of St. Augustine's, Bromley Common.
(From Parish Magazine). 1958.
12

Called home: Bromley.
n.d.
2

Census, 1801. Number of persons...(with names).
Manuscript. 1801.
2

CENTRAL BROMLEY COUNCIL OF YOUTH.
21st anniversary year, 1946-1967. (Including account of
activities from 1946).
Central Bromley Council of Youth. 1967.
2

CLARK, A.R.
Church of St. Augustine, Bromley Common.
The Church. 1970.
2

CLARK, David B.
Survey of Anglicans and Methodists in 4 towns. (Bromley
included in this survey).
Epworth. 1965.
2

CLARKE, Amanda.
10th Bromley Guides, '21-'51, 50 years jubilee.
(Duplicated Typescript). Compiled by A. Clarke and
E. Acton. 1971.
2

CLINCH, George.
Antiquarian jottings relating to Bromley, Hayes, Keston
and West Wickham. (Copy at Bromley Library has
additional material).
Edinburgh, Turnbull. 1889.
1,2,4,5,7,8,11,12,14,15,17,18

CLINCH, George.
Bromley and the Bromley district.
Homeland Association. 1902.
1,2,5,7,17,18

COLLETT, Sydney W.
Centenary of Bromley Hospital, 1869-1969.
Bromley Hospital. 1969.
2

COLTMAN, R.I.
Stray leaves, poems, essays, etc. (Includes essay,
In and around Bromley...).
King and Jarrett. 1915.
2

COMPTON, Doreen.
Alfred Wright, 1848-1924.
Beckenham. n.d.
2

COOK, Charles T.
Bromley Baptist Church...1863-1963.
Bromley Baptist Church. 1963.
2

COX, E.W.
Some XVI century panelling...extract from Sussex County
Magazine, Vol. 24 (references to panelling from the Grete
House, Bromley).
2

COXALL, J.N.
The Westminster Bank in Bromley.
(Typescript. 1967.
2

CRESSWELL, D'Arcy.
Margaret McMillan: a memoir. (M. McMillan lived in
Bromley, 1902-1913).
Hutchinson. 1948.
2,18

CUMBERLAND, George.
Bromley Hill, the seat of the Right Hon. Charles Long,
M.P.: a sketch.
Printed by W. Bulmer for W. Miller. 1811.
11

CUMBERLAND, George.
Bromley Hill, the seat of the Right Hon. Charles Long,
M.P.
Triphook. 1816.
1,2,11,12

DAVIES, R. Gwynne.
Aspects of married-female employment in Cray Valley
industry, Bromley Borough (photocopy of M.A. thesis).
1968.
2

DELSIGNORE, J.
Development of hospital service in Bromley...to 1919.
(Teacher training course study - Typescript).
1970.
2

DE SALVO, Brian.
Bromley Repertory Company...anecdote and opinion to celebrate
the thirteenth birthday of the New Theatre, Bromley, edited
by B. De Salvo.
1960.
2

DUGARD, Donald.
Brief history of the Methodist Church in Bromley...to 1958.
(Note: includes Beckenham, Farnborough, Keston, West
Wickham).
(The Author. 1958).
2

DUNKIN, John.
Outlines of the history and antiquities of Bromley. (Copy
at Bromley Library has additional material).
Bromley, Dunkin. 1815.
1,2,4,5,11,12,17

EAMES, Geoffrey Leonard.
Bromley Cricket Club, 1820-1970.
G.L. Eames. 1970.
11

EAMES, Geoffrey Leonard.
History of Bromley Hockey Club, 1888-1963.
1963.
2,8,11

EAMES, Geoffrey Leonard.
Joseph Wells, father of "H.G." and of Bromley Cricket Club.
(Typescript). 1970.
2

EARLE. Publisher.
Photographic album of Bromley and district.
Earle. c.1895.
2

EMMETT, William.
Diary of an 18th century J.P., edited by L. Vance. (Extract
from "The Countryman", Vol. 40, No. 2).
1949.
2

FREEMAN, Charles.
History, antiquities, improvements, etc., of the parish of
Bromley.
Bromley, Beckley. 1832.
1,2,3

GARCIA, Ray.
15th Bromley (Bickley and Widmore) Scout Group, 1919-1969,
edited by R. Garcia.
1969.
2

Gaumont, Bromley, Kent: souvenir of the opening...Nov. 23rd.,
1936. (Note: including account of building and equipment).
Cook's Publicity Service Ltd. 1936.
2

GENTLEMAN'S MAGAZINE.
Bromley: notes from the Gentleman's Magazine, 1731-1841.
(Manuscript extracts, mainly obituaries).
2

GEOLOGICAL SURVEY OF ENGLAND AND WALES.
Geology of the London district. (Note: includes whole of
Bromley area).
H.M.S.O. 1909.
2

GIBB, George D.
The oyster conglomerate bed at Bromley. (Reprinted from
"The Geologist").
1858.
2,17

GREAT BRITAIN: LAWS , etc. (GEO. III).
An Act for extinguishing the Right of Common...upon certain
commonable lands, grounds within the manor and parish of
Bromley.
1764.
2

GREAT BRITAIN: LAWS, etc. (GEO. IV).
An Act for inclosing lands in the parish of Bromley.
(Photocopy).
1821.
2

GREAT BRITAIN: LAWS, etc. (ELIZ. II).
Bromley Corporation Act.
H.M.S.O. 1953.
2

GREAT BRITAIN, Parliament.
Bromley Corporation Bill - addenda.
1906?
2

GREATER LONDON COUNCIL - RESEARCH AND INTELLIGENCE UNIT.
Interim demographic population projection (quinquennial
table, Bromley, 1966-1986).
Greater London Council. 1968.
2

HAMPTON, H.B.
New Theatre, Bromley. Index. (Productions, 1947-1958).
Compiled by H.B. Hampton.
n.d.
2

HARRIS, C.W.J.
History of Bromley Public Library, 1892-1965.
(Typescript essay for course in librarianship).
1969.
2

HASSARD-SHORT, F.W.
St. Luke's Church, Bromley Green, 1887-1937.
1937.
12

HAYES, John.
Bromley's New Theatre (pamphlet).
New Theatre Press Office. 1969.
2

HEALTH, Ministry of.
Bromley, Kent - planning scheme, No. 1
H.M.S.O. 1938.
2

HEATH, Arthur George.
Letters...with memoir by Gilbert Murray. (Heath's
home was at Bromley. He was a Lieutenant in 6th Batt.,
Royal West Kent Regt. Killed in France,1915).
1917.
4

HELLICAR, Arthur Gresley.
Letter to the parishioners of Bromley (concerning
proposed new church).
Bromley, E. Strong. 1871.
2

HELLICAR, Arthur Gresley.
Notes on the parish church of Bromley.
Bush. 1893.
2

HILL, J.M.
The development of education in Bromley from 1860-
1920. (Typescript thesis, Stockwell College of
Education).
1967.
2

A history of Bromley in Kent and the surrounding
neighbourhood...
Bromley, E. Strong. 1858.
2,12

HODGSON, Sir Gerald.
Coats of arms in Bromley College Chapel. (Reprinted
from Coat of Arms, July, 1969 - July, 1971).
1971.
2

HOLLOWAY, John.
A London childhood. (Norwood, Anerley Elmers End,
1920-1929).
Routledge. 1966.
2

HOLWORTHY, Richard.
Monumental inscriptions in the church and churchyard of
Bromley, transcribed by R. Holworthy.
Mitchell, Hughes and Clarke. 1922.
2,11,12

HORSBURGH, Edward Lee Stuart.
Bromley, Kent...(extra illustrated and annotated copy,
2 vols. at Bromley Library).
1929.
2,17

HORSBURGH, Edward Lee Stuart.
Bromley, Kent...with a chapter on the manor and palace by
Philip Norman.
Hodder and Stoughton. 1929.
1,2,7,8,11,12,16,18

HORSBURGH, Edward Lee Stuart.
Bromley, Kent; from the earliest times to the present
century.
S.R. Publishers Ltd. 1929. (Republished, 1971).
2,4,5,

HOUSING AND LOCAL GOVERNMENT, Ministry of.
Provisional list of buildings of architectural or historic
interest...(list for London Borough of Bromley area).
(Duplicated Typescript).
1952.
2

HOYS, Frank Dudley. (L.D.V. pseud.).
The Bromley Home Guard.
Sun Engraving Co. Printers. 1945.
2

HUGHES, M.
Short history of Bromley Parish Church.
British Publishing Co. 1971.
2,4

IMPERIAL WAR GRAVES COMMISSION.
Civilian war dead, 1939-45. Roll of honour...(facsimile
pages for the London Borough of Bromley).
Imperial War Graves Commission. 1954.
2,18

Inscriptions in Bromley Church and churchyard.
n.d.
17

INSTITUTION OF MUNICIPAL ENGINEERS.
Proceedings, Vol. 78, 1951-2. (Containing articles on
Bromley and road developments in Kent).
1951-2.
2

INSTITUTION OF MUNICIPAL ENGINEERS.
78th Annual General Meeting and Conference, 1951. (Containing
account of work of Bromley Borough Engineer's Department,
1926-1951).
1951.
2

INTERNATIONAL COMPUTERS AND TABULATIONS.
Local Government Magazine, No. 13, Oct. 1967. (Containing
"A total approach to the computer - by Bromley" and "The
computer as an aid to secondary school allocation in Kent").
1967.
2

JACKSON, Arthur Percy.
St. Luke's parish, Bromley Common. Some account of its
church, schools, etc.
1896.
2

JENNINGS, James.
Ornithologia , or, the birds: a poem (containing local
references, Lewisham and Bromley).
Poole and Edwards. 1828.
2

KENT COUNTY COUNCIL - ARCHIVES OFFICE.
Bromley, St. Luke's parish records, 1880-1959.
1968.
2

KENT COUNTY COUNCIL - EDUCATION COMMITTEE.
Arts and music (Beckenham and Penge Association for
cultural recreation). 16 Vols. MSS. records, programmes,
newscuttings.
1945/6-1960/1.
2

KENT COUNTY COUNCIL - EDUCATION COMMITTEE.
Schools of Bromley, Beckenham and district.
Century Press. 1954.
2

KENT COUNTY COUNCIL - EDUCATION COMMITTEE.
Stockwell College: prospectus, 1962-3.
Kent Education Committee. 1962.
2,11

KENT PUBLISHING CO. Publishers.
Buying a house in Bromley.
Kent Publishing Co. 1968.
2

KROPOTKIN, Prince Peter.
Memoirs of a revolutionist. (Resident, Bromley,
1895-1907).
Gloucester, Massachusetts, Peter Smith. 1967.
2

LA CHARD. Theresa.
A sailor hat in the House of the Lord. (Note:
childhood in Bromley).
Allen and Unwin. 1967.
2

LANGLEY PARK SCHOOL FOR BOYS.
Dedication. (Note: includes short history and
architect's description).
Bromley, London Borough Council. 1969.
2

LITTLEWOOD, Kathleen. D.B.
Brief account of the founding of Bromley High School.
G.P.D.S.T. 1950.
2

LOCAL GOVERNMENT BOUNDARY COMMISSION.
Minutes of proceedings of a consultation...Bromley and..
Beckenham...proposal to unite Bromley and Beckenham
as a County Borough.
Bannerman. 1947.
2

McMILLAN, Margaret.
Life of Rachel McMillan. (R. McMillan resident in
Bromley, 1895-1913).
Dent. 1927.
2,18

MANN, Sidney L.
My Bromley days...(Typescript).
(1966).
2

MANSBRIDGE, Albert.
Margaret McMillan, prophet and pioneer. (M. McMillan
resident in Bromley, 1902-13).
Dent. 1932.
2

MARTINDALE, T.D.
Beckenham and Penge Grammar School, 1901-1968, compiled
by T.D. Martindale.
Beckenham and Penge Grammar School. 1968.
2

MATTHEWS, Pat.
The third aim. (Note: aims of the Bromley Youth
Service). Typescript.
1967.
2

MEDHURST, F. LTD.
A brief history of F. Medhurst Ltd., Bromley.
(Typescript).
c.1964.
2

MOORE, Walter.
Bromley and Bickley. (Corporation guide lines).
London Suburban and Provincial Development Association, 1908.
2

MURRAY, George. (Bishop of Rochester).
In commemoration of the consecration of the new church on
Bromley Common.
1842.
17

NATIONAL UNION OF TEACHERS - BOROUGH OF BROMLEY TEACHERS'
ASSOCIATION.
The importance of education. (Note: analysis of expenditure
with particular reference to Bromley).
Borough of Bromley Teachers' Association. 1969.
2

NEW, Vincent.
Sketches of Bromley and district...reproduced from "The
Bromley and Kentish Times".
Sevenoaks, Vincent New.(1932).
2

NORMAN, George Warde.
Memoranda regarding Bromley and its neighbourhood during the
residence of the family there (photocopy of typescript).
c.1857-1880.
2

NORMAN, Philip.
Notes on Bromley and the neighbourhood. (Reprint from
Archaeologia Cantiana, Vol. 24).
Mitchell and Hughes. 1899.
2,17

NORMAN, Philip.
The palace or manor-house of the bishops of Rochester, at
Bromley, Kent...(Reprint from Archaeological Journal, 2nd
series, Vol. 27).
Royal Archaeological Institution. 1920.
2

OFFORD, A.G.
The first fifty years (1904-1954): a history of Westcombe
Park Rugby Football Club, edited by A.G. Offord.
The Orpington Press. 1953.
2

ORDNANCE SURVEY.
Book of reference to the plan of the parish of Bromley...
(acreage and description of plots on 25" sheets).
Ordnance Survey. 1862.
2

ORDNANCE SURVEY.
Book of reference to the plan of the parish of Bromley...
(Note: acreage of plots on 25" sheets).
Ordnance Survey. 1871.
2

OWEN, Mrs. Julia.
Treat yourself for your rheumatic or arthritic disease...
(medicated bee venom clinic in Bromley...to 1966).
Mrs. J. Owen. 1963.
2

PATHFINDER, pseud.
Wayfaring round London. Field paths and woodland rambles
in the Home Counties (includes Bromley and district).
Warne. 1915.
2,18

PEILE, Diana.
Bromley: a genetic description of a Kentish borough.
(Photocopy of geography thesis).
1962.
2

Platinotype processes. (Note: process invented by William
Willis of Bromley), in the Photominiature, Vol. 1, No. 7.
New York, Tennant and Ward. 1899.
2

POWELL, L.H.
Our heritage: a history of the first 21 years of Lodge No.
5572, Bromley.
Heritage Lodge. 1956.
7

QUINEY, Anthony.
2 Bickley Road, Widmore. (Typescript report, G.L.C.
Department of Architecture and Civic Design, Historic
Buildings Division).
1969.
2

RACHEL McMILLAN TRAINING COLLEGE.
Margaret McMillan, 1860-1931 (resident in Bromley,
1902-13).
Rachel McMillan Training College.(195-).
2

RAMSEY, Vic A.
New life story (Work for drug addicts and hostel in
Bromley).
New Life Foundation.(1968).
2

RANDALL, Simon.
Drugs in your town.(A review of drug abuse...in...
Bromley).
Bromley Council of Social Services. 1969.
2

REYNOLDS, Thomas.
Some experiments on the chalybeat water...near the
Palace...at Bromley in Kent.
J. Payne. 1756.
2

ROCHARD, J.
Bromley, Beckenham and Chislehurst (with professional
and commercial appendices).
J. Rochard. c.1893.
2

ROSEVEARE, Helen.
Doctor among the Congo rebels. (Autobiography - local
resident).
Lutterworth. 1965.
2

ROSEVEARE, Helen.
Doctor returns to Congo. (Autobiography - local
resident).
Lutterworth. 1967.
2

ROSEVEARE, Helen.
Give me this mountain. (Autobiography - local
resident).
Inter-Varsity Fellowship. 1966.
2

Round Bromley and Keston: a handy guide to rambles in
the district.
Fisher, Unwin. n.d.
2,11

ST. PETER AND ST. PAUL'S CHURCH, BROMLEY.
List of records deposited at the public library.
(Typescript).
1961.
2

ST. PETER AND ST. PAUL'S CHURCH, BROMLEY.
List of records kept...in the church. (Typescript).
1961.
2

ST. PETER AND ST. PAUL'S CHURCH, BROMLEY.
Report and statement of accounts, 1903.
Bromley, E. Strong and Sons, Printers. 1904.
2

ST. PETER AND ST. PAUL'S CHURCH, BROMLEY.
Some more particulars referring to brasses, memorials
in church and churchyard. (Typescript).
1933.
2

ST. PETER AND ST. PAUL'S CHURCH, BROMLEY.
Yearbooks, 1909, 1911.
1910, 1912.
2

SALE CATALOGUE.
(Note: a selection of Sale Catalogues held for area of
London Borough of Bromley).
2

SANTER, J.R.
Bromley Co-operative Society Ltd: a brief history, 1882-
1903.
Bromley Co-operative Society Ltd. 1903.
2

SCOTT, Thomas.
Bromley bewailing her lost bishop...and On the consecration...
of a burial ground to Bromley churchyard...(poems).
T. Cockett, Printer. 1845.
2

Short history of Bromley Parish Church (St. Peter and St. Paul).
British Publishing Co. 1959.
2,4,8,12

SIMPSON, Janet.
Bromley, reproductions of etchings...
S. Bush and Son. 1916, 1929.
2

SINDALL, H.W.
Bromley Boy Scouts: a record of war-time service.
Scout Association. 1946.
2

SMITH, G.W.
Notes on Bromley for Mr. Norman's new history. (Transcribed
from a pencilled notebook). (Typescript).
1908.
2

SOUTHERN, J.A.
Rustic rambles through Kentish orchards...neighbourhood of
Bromley.
E.J. Larby. n.d.
2,18

SPENCE, G.M.
Bromley and District Hospital, 1869-1941. (Typescript).
(1942).
2

STEER, Francis W.
Relics of a bishop (photocopy). In Chichester Cathedral
Journal, 1959. (Includes reference to Tudor panels from
"The Grete House", Bromley).
1959.
2

(STRONG, Edward).
History of Bromley in Kent.
Bromley, E. Strong. 1858.
1,2,11,17

SURRIDGE, R.G.
British Public Library Scene. (Russian text). In "Anglia
30", No. 2, 1969. Features Bromley Public Library.
(Translation available).
Central Office of Information. 1969.
2

SWAN, Sir Kenneth Raydon.
In the days of my youth. (1883-1894 in Bromley).
Sir Kenneth R. Swan. 1964.
2

SWAN, Mary Edwards.
Sir Joseph Wilson Swan, F.R.S., inventor and scientist.
(Reprint with added appendix - Note: Swan family lived in
Bromley, 1883-1894), by M.E. and K.R. Swan.
Oriel. 1968.
2

TAYLOR, Bessie. (Sister Mary Baptist).
Bromley, Beckenham and Penge, Kent since 1750. Comparative
study of the changing geography. (Photocopy of Ph. D. Thesi
1965.
2

TOWN AND COUNTRY PLANNING, Ministry of.
List of buildings of special architectural and
historical interst...(section covering London Borough
of Bromley). (Typescript).
(1961).
2

TURNER, J.W.
Bromley, Kent with particular reference to the past 25
years. In Proceedings of the Institute of Municipal
Engineers, Vol. 78, 1951-52.
2

Views of Bromley. (12 engravings).
Rock and Co. c.1866.
2

WARD, Edward.
The merry travellers: or, a trip upon ten-toes from
Moorfield to Bromley. A humorous poem.
W. Downing, Printers. 1721.
2

WHITFIELD, O.G.
Memories and memories. (Photocopy of series from
Bromley Congregational Church Record, May-November,
1952).
1952.
2

WILLS, W. David.
A place like home: a hostel for disturbed adolescents.
(Reynolds House, Bromley).
Allen and Unwin. 1970.
2

WILSON, Thomas.
An accurate description of Bromley.
Hamilton. 1797.
1,2,6,11,12,17

WILTON, Eric.
Centre crew. A memory of the Royal Observer Corps.
(Centre at Bromley).
Privately Printed. 1946.
2

WOOLWICH DISTRICT ANTIQUARIAN SOCIETY.
Visit to Bromley, September 6th, 1902. (Photocopy of
extract from Annual Report, 1902-3).
1903.
2

BROMPTON

Diary of an unknown lady visiting relatives in Brompton,
2 vols., the second in code). (Manuscript).
1860, 1862.
4

GUMMER, Selwyn.
Brompton centenary story. 1948.
8

HARRIS, Edwin.
The history of Old Brompton. (In bound volume of the
Eastgate series).
11,15

INSTITUTE OF ROYAL ENGINEERS.
Catalogue of the...library. 1929.
8

ORDNANCE, Board of.
Plan of Chatham Lines showing their state in the year
1786. Scale: 1 inch=100 (Sic i.e. 300) feet.
(Photocopy of copy of original).
1786.
4

ORDNANCE, Board of.
Plan of the new barracks within the Lines at Chatham
with part of the town of Brompton, 1763. Copied by
Henry Mercier...(Photocopy slightly reduced from
original scale of 130 feet to 1 inch).
4

BROOK

BRADE-BRIKS, Stanley Graham.
A short history of Brook in Kent: a talk. (Typescript).
n.d.
3

KERNEY, M.P.
The late-glacial and post-glacial history of the chalk
escarpment near Brook, Kent, by M.P. Kerney and others.
Philosophical Transactions of Royal Society, Vol.248, 1964.
21

TRISTRAM, Ernest William.
The roof-painting at Dadesjo, Sweden. (Includes an account
and an illustration of the wall-painting at Brook Church,
Kent).
Article in "Burlington Magazine For Connoisseurs", Vol.
XXXI, July-December, 1917.
3

BROOKLAND

DRUCE, George.
Font in Brookland Church.
British Archaeological Association. 1924.
3,7

Notes on St. Augustine's Church, Brookland.
Ashford, Geerings. 1926.
1

The Religion of a Lawyer, crazy tale (in four cantos);
analytical of the Kentish story of Brookland steeple.
Printed for J. Walker. 1786.
1,11

ROPER, Anne.
Church of St. Augustine, Brookland.
Ashford, Geerings. 1936, etc.
2,7,11,13,14,15

ROPER, Anne.
The church of St. Augustine, Brookland, 12th edition.
Geerings. 1953.
11

ROPER, Anne.
The church of St. Augustine, Brookland, 21st edition.
Rye, Printed by Adams. 1971.
8,11

St. Augustine's Church, Brookland: a pamphlet and a print.
n.d.
13

BROOMHILL

CHRISTIE, C.J.
Poorbook of Broomhill. (Tonbridge School Local History
Researches).
1961.
11

PARKES, James.
The story of three David Salomons at Broomhill.
Constable. n.d.
11,19

BUCKLAND-IN-DOVER

HILL, Derek Ingram.
From Saxon times to the present day: a history of the
parish church of St. Andrew, Buckland-in-Dover.
A.R. Adams and Son. 1938.
6,12

The parish of St. Andrew, Buckland-in-Dover: Christian
stewardship campaign.
Buckland Press. 1962.
12

ROOKWOOD, O.M.
Buckland-in-Dover, 1852-1952.
Buckland Press. 1952.
6,19

BURHAM

MARTIN, Alan R.
The church of St. Mary at Burham, Kent.
British Archaeological Association. 1928.
12

PAYNE, George.
Burham: from Proceedings of Society of Antiquaries,
March, 12th, 1896.
8

BURNT ASH - See LEWISHAM

BURWASH

ROPER, Anne.
Church of All Saints, Burwash.
Ashford, Geerings. 1967.
8,11

CANALS AND WATERWAYS

GREAT BRITAIN: LAWS, etc. (GEO. III).
An Act for making and maintaining a navigable canal from
the River Thames to the River Medway.
1800.
9

GREAT BRITAIN: LAWS, etc. (GEO. III).
An Act for making and maintaining a navigable canal from
the River Thames to the River Medway.
1800.
9

GREAT BRITAIN: LAWS, etc. (GEO. III).
An Act for enabling the company of proprietors of the
Thames and Medway Canal to vary the line of the said
canal.
1804.
9

GREAT BRITAIN: LAWS, etc. (GEO. III).
An Act for enabling the company of proprietors of the
Thames and Medway Canal to vary the line of the said
canal.
1810.
9

GREAT BRITAIN: LAWS, etc. (GEO. III).
An Act for enabling the company of proprietors of the
Thames and Medway Canal to raise a further sum of money.
1818.
9

GREAT BRITAIN: LAWS, etc. (GEO. III).
An Act for enabling the Thames and Medway Canal Company
to raise a further sum of money.
1824.
9

GREAT BRITAIN: LAWS, etc. (GEO. III).
An Act for maintaining and preserving a military canal
and road, made from Shorncliffe, Kent to Cliff End,
Sussex.
1807.
7

GREAT BRITAIN: LAWS, etc. (GEO. III).
An Act for making a harbour and wet dock at or near
St. Nicholas Bay. (See under Thanet).
1811.
3,11,12

GREAT BRITAIN: LAWS, etc. (VIC.).
An Act to confirm a provisional order made by the Board
of Trade under the Railway and Canal Traffic Act, 1888,
containing the classification of merchandise traffic, and
the schedule of maximum tolls and charges applicable
thereto, for the River Ancholme navigation and certain
other canals.
1894.
9

HADFIELD, Charles.
The canals of Southern England.
Phoenix House. 1955, etc.
2,3,7,18

JAMES, O.S.
The Croydon Canal (MSS.).
1944.
18

RAILWAY AND CANAL HISTORICAL SOCIETY - LONDON GROUP.
Historical notes and itinery for tour of Thames and
Medway Canal, 7th September, 1963.
(Duplicated).
9

VINE, Paul Ashley Laurence.
The Royal Military Canal.
David and Charles. 1972.
3,11

CANTERBURY

"Abbot's Barton" - Sale catalogue.
Canterbury, Cooper and Wacher. 1923.
3

"Abbot's Mill" - Sale catalogue. (Particulars, plan and
conditions of sale...of Abbot's and Dean's water mills.
Chinnock, Galsworthy and Chinnock, Auctioneers. 1891.
3

ADLER, Michael.
Jews of Canterbury.
Ballantyne. 1911?
3,11

ADLER, Michael.
Jews of medieval England.
Published for the Jewish Historical Society of England by
E. Goldston. 1939.
3

Abstract of the statutes of Jesus Hospital in Northgate,
Canterbury.
c.1778.
3

AITKEN, George A.
Defoe's "Apparition of Mrs. Veal". (Photocopy of article
appearing in "The Nineteenth Century", Vol. XXXVII, 1895).
1895.
3

AKERMAN, John Yonge.
Account of...an ancient British barrow in...Canterbury, 1842.
1842.
11

AKERMAN, John Yonge.
Account of the opening of an ancient British barrow in Iffins
Wood, near Canterbury.
Nichols. 1843.
11,17

The album of Canterbury views.
Germany. n.d.
3

"ALIQUIS" (pamphlet).
New Canterbury guide...
1848.
17

ALLEN, Derek F.
A remarkable Celtic coin from Canterbury. (Reprinted from
The British Numismatic Journal, Vol. 28, 1958).
British Numismatic Journal. 1958.
3

ALLEN, Derek F.
Three ancient British coins. (Reprinted from The British
Numismatic Journal, Vol. 27, 1955).
British Numismatic Journal. 1955.
3

ANCIENT ORDER OF FORESTERS - CANTERBURY.
Annual Report, 1887, 1888.
17

ANCIENT ORDER OF FORESTERS - CANTERBURY (pamphlet).
Rules and regulations of Court "Victoria", No. 1895 at
George and Dragon, Canterbury.
1863.
17

An ancient prophecy; commenced by the Chaldean astrologer,
Naboch Abekur, concluded by Typho Rameses...translated by
Tydus Pooh Pooh...with a preface, critical remarks,
explanatory notes and a complete key; the whole being
dedicated without permission to the ruler of the City and the
Council thereof.
Canterbury, R. Smithson. 1838.
3

ANDREW, DOUGLAS LTD.
Hand looms for home weaving...bench built by Canterbury
craftsmen...(pamphlet).
Harbledown, Canterbury. Andrews. c.1949.
3

ANSTRUTHER, Robert.
Epistolae Herserti de Losinga, Orberti de Clara, et
Elmeri, Prioris Cantuariensis.
1846.
17

ARCHER PRINTING CO.
The Archer guide to Canterbury; written by G. Manus-
Wright.
Archer. 1905?
3

THE ARCHER'S REGISTER.
Extract from "The Archer's Register for 1895-96",
edited by Fred. T. Follett. (Typescript copy of pages
66-68 relating to the Canterbury Archery Club).
Horace Cox. 1896.
3

ATKINSON, Frank.
'Knur and spell' and allied games. (Reprinted from
"Folk Life", Vol. 1, 1963). (Includes bat and trap).
Folk Life. 1963.
3

AUSTEN, B.
The vanished gates of the City of Canterbury.
1900.
3,6,11,14

AUSTEN. Publisher.
Handbook of Canterbury and Cathedral.
n.d.
3,11,14

AUXILIARY BRITISH AND FOREIGN BIBLE SOCIETY - CANTERBURY.
Sixty-fifth annual report, 1878. Sixty-seventh annual
report, 1880.
17

AVELING, Henry F. Compiler.
Monumental inscriptions in the churchyard of St.
Mildred's, Canterbury, copied by Henry F. Aveling.
(Typescript).
1926.
3

BAILEY, Henry.
Twenty-five years at St. Augustines College, Canterbury.
Hyde. 1873.
1,3,11,17

BAILEY, Henry.
A letter to a secretary of a missionary studentship
association.
Canterbury, Bailey. 1867.
3

BAILEY, Melville K.
Through a franciscan window: the mother house of the
Grey Friars at Canterbury.
Church Mission Publishing Co. 1926.
3,4,11

BAINE, Rodney M.
The apparition of Mrs. Veal: a neglected account.
(Photocopy of article appearing in Proceedings of the
Modern Languages Association, Vol. LXIX 1954).
Modern Languages Association. 1954.
3

BAINE, Rodney M.
Defoe and Mrs. Bargrave's story. (Photocopy of article
in the "Philological Quarterly", XXXIII, IV, October,
1954.
Philological Quarterly. 1954.
3

Baker's Hotel, 1634-1934.
1934.
3

BALLARD, Adolphus.
An eleventh-century inquisition of St. Augustines,
Canterbury
Oxford University Press. 1920.
3,11

BAMFORD, Alfred Bennett.
Sketches in Canterbury.
1895.
3,11,18

BAMFORD, Francis and BANKES, Viola.
Vicious circle.
Parrish. 1965.
3

BARHAM, Richard Harris.
"A son of Canterbury", "the wittiest of English poets".
The Rev. Richard Harris Barham, suggested memorial.
n.d.
3

BARNES, Ernest.
A concise guide to Black Friars Monastery. (Antient
Blakefrerys Canterbury, Dominican Priory notes).
n.d.
13

BARNES, Ernest.
A concise guide to Mother City. (Antient Blakefrerys
Canterbury, directions easily followed).
n.d.
13

BARRIE, E.A.
Canterbury's architecture. In "The Municipal Journal",
June 5th, 1953, pp 1191-1204, by E.A. Barrie and L.H.C. Jennings.
Municipal Journal. 1953.
3

BARWICK, John.
Harmonia cantica divina, or, the Kentish divine harmonist:
being a new set of psalm tunes and anthems.
T. Skillern. 1796.
3

BARWICK, John.
A set of psalm tunes and anthems, 74 leaves. (Manuscript
with no title page).
3

BAXTER, Dudley.
Cardinal Pole: a memoir.
Art and Book Co. 1901.
3

BAXTER, Dudley.
The Holy Road: a paper read at the International Catholic
Congress, Munich, September, 1900.
Art and Book Co. 1901.
3

BAYNTON, Alfred.
Canterbury: ancient and modern. In "The Rotarian", October,
1922.
Rotarian. 1922.
3

BEECHAM, Thomas Publisher.
Beecham's photo-folio: 24 choice photographic views,
Canterbury, Deal and Walmer.
n.d.

BELL, G. and Sons. Publishers.
Canterbury and Rochester with Minster-in-Sheppey.
1929.
17

BENNETT-GOLDNEY, Francis.
Canterbury: the official guide.
Canterbury and District Chamber of Trade. 1912.
8

BENNETT-GOLDNEY, Francis.
Canterbury: the official guide, 7th edition, 1909; 10th
edition, 1911, 1912; 11th edition, 1913, by F. Bennett-
Goldney and S. Evans.
Canterbury and District Chamber of Trade. 1909, etc.
3,13

BENNETT-GOLDNEY, Francis.
Chief events in the history of Canterbury - 6p.
Dickinson, Maidstone. 1901?
7

BENNETT-GOLDNEY, Francis.
L' ancienne et royale cite de Cantonbery guide officiel.
n.d.
11

BENNETT-GOLDNEY, Francis.
Antiquities of the bronze, Roman and Saxon periods,
found near Canterbury. (From The Proceedings of the
Society of Antiquaries, March 14th, 1901).
3

BENNET-GOLDNEY, Francis.
The Royal and ancient City of Canterbury: official
guide.
n.d.
11

BENNETT-GOLDNEY, Francis.
The west gate, walls and castle of Canterbury.
Gibbs. 1914.
3,11

BENNETT-GOLDNEY, Francis and OTHERS.
Official guide to the west gate, Canterbury.
Canterbury Corporation. 1906.
1,3,7 (1906 and 1920), 11,13,15

BENNETT-GOLDNEY, Francis.
History of Westgate.
Canterbury Corporation. 2nd edition, 1910 and 1951
3,11

BENNETT-GOLDNEY, Francis.
The story of the west gate.
Jennings. 1937.
14

BENNETT-GOLDNEY, Francis.
The story of the west gate.
Canterbury and District Chamber of Trade at the request
of the Canterbury Corporation. 1951.
3

BENTWICH, Norman.
A Jewish corner of Kent. (From The Jewish Chronicle,
26th September, 1952).
3

BERBIERS, John L.
Canterbury: reconstruction in the central area. In
Journal of The Town Planning Institute, Vol. XLVII,
No. 2, February, 1961.
3

BERESFORD-JONES, A.B.
The Kent and Canterbury Hospital, 1790-1940.
(Reprinted from "The Medical Press and Circular", April
23rd, 1941, Vol. CCV, No. 5320).
S. Temple. 1941.
3

BING, F.G.
Book of Canterbury verse, edited by F.G. Bing.
Canterbury, Gibbs. 1932.
3,6,11

BING, F.G.
The world's pedlar, and other verse.
Canterbury, Printed by Gibbs. 1935.
3

BLACK, ADAM AND CHARLES LTD. Publishers.
Black's guide to Canterbury and East Kent.
(See East Kent).

BLACK, ADAM AND CHARLES LTD. Publishers.
Black's guide to Canterbury and Rochester.
Black. 1893.
7

The black and white concise Canterbury and cathedral
guide.
Canterbury, Stevens. 195-.
3

Blackfriars Monastery, Canterbury. Sale catalogue.
1913.
3

BOGGIS, Robert James Edmund.
History of St. Augustine's College, Canterbury.
Cross and Jackman. 1907.
3,6,11,15,17

BOGGIS, Robert James Edmund.
History of St. Augustine's Monastery, Canterbury.
Cross and Jackman, Canterbury. 1901.
1,3,4,6,7,8,11,12,13,17

BOGGIS, Robert James Edmund.
I remember.
Exeter, W.V. Cole. 1947.
3

Book of ordinances of Jesus Hospital in the parish of Saint
Mary, Northgate...39 Eliz. A.D. 1596. (Manuscript copy).
3

The book of the Chronicles. (Containing the history of the
Jews with a few hints concerning the Samaritans by an old
woman, Yanbutnerc).
Canterbury, Sold by John Atkins. 1806.
3

Booke of the lost beauty: automatic script received by R.
Thomas and E. Oram.
Tyndall Ely. 1925.
11

BOWLER, E.
Canterbury.
1896.
11

BOWMAN, W.
Royal and ancient City of Canterbury, edited by W. Bowman.
S.E. and C. Rly. 1922.
7,11

BOYLE, John.
Canterbury's illustrious story: "the first English city to
become Christian". (Article in The Municipal Review, Vol.
35, No. 410, February, 1964).
3

BRADE-BIRKS, Stanley Graham.
A short history of the church of St. Peter, Canterbury.
Canterbury, Printed by Gibbs. 1955.
3

BRAITHWAITE, Lewis.
Canterbury: historic town or write-off? (Article in The
Architectural Review, Vol. 142, No. 848, October, 1967).
3

BRENT, John.
Canterbury in the olden time.
Ginder, Canterbury. 1860, 1879.
1,2,3,4,6,7,8,11,12,13,15,17,18,19,20

BRENT, John.
The Egyptian, Grecian, Roman and Anglo-Saxon antiquities in
the museum at Canterbury.
1875.
3,11,14

BRENT, John Junior.
On glass beads with a chevron pattern. (From Archaeologia
Vol. XLV).
1879.
3

BRETHERTON, Ralph Harold.
The apparition of Mrs. Veal. (Article in The Gentleman's
Magazine, December, 1901).
3

A brief outline of the Canterbury Reform Festival, September
4th, 1832.
Canterbury, Elizabeth Wood. 1832.
3

BRITISH ARCHAEOLOGICAL ASSOCIATION.
Proceedings of the congress at Canterbury, July 13th to 18th,
1914. (Reprinted from the Journal of the British Archaeological Association).
British Archaeological Association. 1914.
3,6

BRITISH ARCHAEOLOGICAL ASSOCIATION.
Report of...British Archaeological Association at the 1st
general meeting at Canterbury.
1844.
3,4,6,7,11,12,14,17

BRITISH ASSOCIATION FOR THE ADVANCEMENT OF SCIENCE.
Handbook to the City of Canterbury.
Dover "Observer". 1899.
3,6,11

BRITISH WORKMAN (periodical).
Lord Chief Justice, Tenterden: how a barber's boy
became Lord Chief Justice of England. (Article in
"The British Workman", No. 61, January, 1860).
1860.
3

BROCK, E.P. Loftus.
Christianity in Britain in Roman times with reference
to recent discoveries at Canterbury.
n.d.
11,17

BROCKINGTON, C. Fraser.
Medical Officers of Health, 1848 to 1855: an essay in
local history (about Thomas Sankey Cooper).
Hodgetts. 1957.
3

BROMLEY, Francis E.
Sir Egerton Brydges and the "Lee Priory Press".
(Typescript).
19--.
3

BROOKS, Charles S.
Roundabout to Canterbury.
Harcourt Brase. 1926.
4

BROWN, John.
Memoir of Mrs. Parnell of Canterbury. (Article
extracted from the Wesleyan Methodist Magazine",
July, 1858, Vol. IV - fifth series.
1858.
3

BRUCE, C.R.
Translation of the several charters...granted to the
citizens of Canterbury.
Canterbury, Grove. 1791.
11

BRYDGES, Ann Mary.
Diary of (?) Ann Mary Brydges, March-June, 1828,
transcribed by Robert H. Goodsell. (Typescript).
3

BUCHANAN, COLIN AND PARTNERS.
Canterbury traffic study - final report.
Buchanan. 1970.
2,8,11

BULTEEL, John.
A relation of the troubles of the three forraign
churches in Kent caused by the injunction of William
Laud, Archbishop of Canterbury. The Walloons in
Canterbury; the Dutch in Sandwich and Maidstone.
Enderbie. 1645.
12

BUNCE, Cyprian Rondeau.
Abridgment of the Court of Burghmote, 1542-1793.
(Manuscript).
3

BUNCE, Cyprian Rondeau.
Ancient Canterbury.
1924.
1,11,12

Canterbury guide: or traveller's companion.
Canterbury, Cowtan. 1803.
3,11

CANTERBURY HANDWEAVER AND SPINNER.
1951-1953.
Canterbury Handweaver and Spinner.
3

CANTERBURY HOUSE OF COMMONS.
Constitution and standing orders.
1888.
17

Canterbury in Roman times.
192-?
4

Canterbury martyrs...in the Martyr's Field, 1555-1558.
1890.
17

The Canterbury martyr's memorial: influential meeting at
the Guildhall, Canterbury. Speeches by the Mayor, Dean
Farrar and Lord Northbourne. (Reprinted from the "Kentish
Gazette" and "Canterbury Press" of February 5th, 1898).
3

Canterbury mayoral quincentenary.
1948.
3,12

CANTERBURY PHILOSOPHICAL AND LITERARY INSTITUTION.
Annual reports, 1827-1834.
3

CANTERBURY PHILOSOPHICAL AND LITERARY INSTITUTION.
Annual reports, Vol. I, Vol. III, 1828-1834. Catalogues of
library, paintings, museum.
17

CANTERBURY PHILOSOPHICAL AND LITERARY INSTITUTION.
Rules and regulations.
Canterbury, G. Wood. 1826.
3

CANTERBURY PHILOSOPHICAL AND LITERARY INSTITUTION.
Synopsis of the museum of the...Institution.
Canterbury, G. Wood. 1826.
3

CANTERBURY RAGGED SCHOOLS.
27th annual report of Sabbath School...10th...weekday.
1870.
17

CANTERBURY SOCIETY.
Canterbury: conservation and traffic in Canterbury.
Canterbury Society. 1969.
11

The Canterbury seal. 5 page typescript.
(1960).
3

Canterbury Synagogue, King Street: reconsecration of
Canterbury Synagogue.
1889.
17

Canterbury tale of fifty years ago: extraordinary career of
Sir William Courtenay.
Canterbury, Cross and Jackman. 1888.
3,6,11,12,17(1882), 19

Canterbury town planning scheme: 1st period – development of
central area.
Canterbury, J.A. Jennings. 1947.
3

Canterbury Waterworks: set of plans.
3

CANTERBURY WATLING STREET CONGREGATIONAL CHAPEL.
Annual reports, 1883, 1888, 1889 – manual, 1891.
17

Canterbury weavers.
Dent. 1901.
11

Canterbury wells: the mineral waters lately discovered .
Baldwin. 1702.
11

CARLETON, Mary.
Memoirs of Mary Carleton, commonly styled, the German
Princess.
1673.
17

CARPENTER, R. Herbert.
History of the church of St. Alphege, Canterbury.
Canterbury, Gibbs. 1888.
11,15

CASWALL, Henry.
A pilgrimage to Canterbury in 1852.
Rivington. 1852.
3,11

Cathedral rhymes.
1847.
17

CHARITY COMMISSIONERS.
Scheme relating to King's School, Canterbury, 1878.
Canterbury, Kent Herald. 1878.
3

CHENEY, Christopher Robert.
William Lyndwood's Provinciale.
School of Canon Law Catholic University of America.(196-).
11

CHILDS, D. Rigby.
Canterbury. In The Architect's Journal, April 24th,
1952, by D.R. Childs and D.A.C. Boyne.
3

CHIP, Will.
Village politics. ("Circulated by the East Kent and
Canterbury Association").
Canterbury, Printed by Simmons, Kirkby and Jones. n.d.
3

CHURCH, Richard.
A portrait of Canterbury.
Hutchinson. 1953.
1,2,3,4,5,6,8,11,12,13,14,15,17,18,20,21

"A CITIZEN".
A translation of the several charters, etc., granted...
to the citizens of Canterbury...
Canterbury, J. Grove (Printer). 1791.
1,17

CLAPHAM, Sir Alfred William.
St. Augustine's Abbey, Canterbury, Kent.
H.M.S.O. 1955.
1,3,4,8,11,12

CLARK, Thomas Arranger.
The Union harmonist: a selection of sacred music,
consisting of original and standard pieces, anthems,
etc. Suitable for use in Sunday Schools, congregations
and musical societies arranged by Thomas Clark of
Canterbury.
London Sunday School Union. n.d.
3

CLAY, Rotha Mary.
The medieval hospitals of England.
Methuen. 1909.
3

CLIFFORD, Henry.
Account of two cases of controverted elections...of the
City of Canterbury...oath of supremacy to Catholics.
1797.
17

COCK, F.William.
The Kentish Post or the Canterbury Newsletter.
Moring. 1913.
3,12

Collection of nine programmes of "The Old Stagers and Old Faces" from Canterbury cricket week, 1870-1898.
11

Collection of programmes and epilogues of "The Old Stagers" from Canterbury cricket week, from 1927 to 1957 (some missing).
3

Collection of tracts relating to the City of Canterbury and the Eastern division of the County of Kent.
Canterbury, Ward. 1836.
3,11,15

Collection of twenty pamphlets relating to Canterbury,
11

COLLIER, Richard.
Origins of the English inn, 2: The Secular Inn. In "A Monthly Bulletin", Vol. 26, No. 2, February, 1956.
3

A complete and correct biographical history of the late Sir W. Courtenay.
Canterbury, S. Prentice. 1838.
3

A concise history of Canterbury...by an inhabitant.
Canterbury, Printed by R. Colegate. 1825.
3

COOLE, Albert.
The Dominican Monastery, Canterbury.
n.d.
3

COOLE, Albert.
St. Martin's Church, Canterbury.
Canterbury, Jennings. n.d.
3

COOPER, Thomas Sidney Painter of Canterbury.
My life.
Bentley. 1890.
3,15

COOPER, Thomas Sidney.
Views in Canterbury and its environs, drawn from nature, and on stone. (Portfolio of six engravings).
Westmead Press. 1972.
3

COTTERELL, Howard Herschel.
Pewter church vessels from the old church of St. Mary, Northgate, Canterbury. In "The Connoisseur", October, 1923, Vol LXVII, No. 266.
3

COTTON, Charles.
A brief history of St. Margaret's Church, Canterbury. (Reprinted from "The Canterbury Press").
Canterbury, Kentish Gazette.(1932).
3

COTTON, Charles.
The Canterbury chantries and hospitals in 1546, edited by C. Cotton.
Kent Archaeological Society. 1934.
3,5,11,12,17,18

COTTON, Charles.
Churchwardens' accounts of parish of St. Andrew, Canterbury, 1485-1685.
1916.
14

COTTON, Charles.
The Greyfriars of Canterbury, 1224 to 1538.
Manchester University Press. 1924.
1,3,4,6,7,8,11,12,14,15,17

COURTENAY, Sir William P.H. pseud of John Nichols Tom.
The eccentric and singular productions of Sir. W. Courtenay, K.M. alias Mr. Tom.
Canterbury, Henry Ward. n.d.
3,11,14

COURTENAY, Sir William P.H.
An essay on the character of Sir. W. Courtenay.
Canterbury, Henry Ward. 183-, etc.
3,6,14,17

COWPER, Joseph Meadows.
Accounts of the churchwardens of St. Dunstan's, Canterbury, A.D. 1484-1580.
Mitchell and Hughes. 1885.
3,11,15,17 (1887)

COWPER, Joseph Meadows.
Ginder's handbook for Canterbury and Canterbury Cathedral
Canterbury, Ginder. 1886.
3,11,17

COWPER, Joseph Meadows.
Intrantes: a list of persons admitted to live and trade within the City of Canterbury, from 1392 to 1592.
Canterbury, Cross and Jackman. 1904.
1,3,11,12

COWPER, Joseph Meadows.
Our parish books and what they tell us: Holy Cross, Westgate, Canterbury.
Canterbury, Cross and Jackman. 1884-5.
1,3,6,11,12,17,18

COX, John Charles.
Canterbury.
Methuen. 1905.
1,2,3,4,6,7,8,10,11,12,13,14,15,16,17,18,20

COZENS, Walter.
Canterbury in the Roman times.
Canterbury, Kentish Gazette. n.d.
3,11

COZENS, Walter.
Old Canterbury.
Canterbury, Cross and Jackman. 1900.
1,3,4,6,8,11,12,13,14,15

Craftsmen of Kent exhibition, July 18th-27th, held in the Slater Art Gallery, Canterbury. (Explanatory booklet).
Whitstable, Caxton Printing Works. 1963.
3

CRAIG, Henry.
The poor man's plaster: thoughts addressed to the working men of Kent.
Canterbury, Printed for Author by C. Marten. 1849.
3

CROSS, Francis W.
History of the Walloon and Huguenot Church at Canterbury.
London, Huguenot Society. 1898.
1,3,11,12

CROSS, Francis W.
History of the Walloon and Huguenot Church at Canterbury.
Kraus Reprints. 1969.
11

CROSS, Francis W.
Rambles round old Canterbury, by F.W. Cross and J. Hall.
Simpkin and Marshall. 1882.
1,3,4,6,7,8,11,12,13,15,17,18

CROSS, Francis W.
The Walloon Church of the crypt at Canterbury in the sixteenth century. (Typescript).
Huguenot Society. 1896.
3

CROSS AND JACKMAN. Publishers.
Brief sketch of freemasonry in Canterbury, 1730-1880.
"Canterbury Press". 1880.
17

CROUCH, Marcus.
Canterbury.
Longman. 1970.
6,7,11,21

CUTTS, Edward L.
Augustine of Canterbury.
Methuen. 1895.
11,12

DANKS, W.
Canterbury. ("Beautiful England" series).
Blackie. 1910.
1,4,6,7,8,11,12,14,15,20

DAVIES, William.
Brief memorials of the late Mrs. William Davies.
1842.
11

DAVIES, Walter Goodwin.
The ancestry of Mary Isaac, c.1549-1613.
Privately Printed for Author. 1955.
3

DAWSON, Ralph.
The living past: guide to exhibits at 17 Burgate, Canterbury.
1954.
3,11

DEANESLY, Margaret.
Augustine of Canterbury.
Nelson. 1964.
1,3,6,8,11,12,15

DEANESLY, Margaret.
The pre-conquest church in England.
Nelson, 2nd edition. 1964.
3

DEANESLY, Margaret.
The Canterbury edition of the Answers of Pope Gregory I to
St. Augustine, by M. Deanesly and P. Grosjean. In the Journal
of Ecclesiastical History, Vol. X, No. 1, April, 1959.
3

Declaration of many thousands of the City of Canterbury...
concerning the late tumult.
1647.
11

DEFOE, Daniel.
A true revelation of the apparition of one Mrs. Veal...at
Canterbury, the 8th September, 1705.
10th edition.
3

Description of the moat, near Canterbury. (Bibliotheca
Topog. Britannica).
11

Descriptive account of Canterbury. (Illustrated).
Brighton, W.T. Pike. 1895.
3

DILNOT, Frank.
Neame of Kent.
Brentano. 1928.
6,7,8,11,12

DODWELL, Chas Reginald.
The Canterbury School of Illumination, 1066-1200.
Cambridge University Press. 195-.
1,3,4,11,12,18

DONALDSON, Christopher.
A short history and guide of St. Martin's Church, Canterbury.
1966, etc.
3,4,12

DONALDSON, Christopher.
A short history and guide of St. Paul's Church, Canterbury.
Ramsgate, Church Publishing. 1964.
1,3,4,8,11,12

Dover, Canterbury, Deal, Walmer and Sandwich by camera and
pen.
Brighton, W.T. Pike. 1904-5.
6

Dover, Deal, Canterbury, Sandwich and Walmer.
Brighton, Pike. n.d.
11

DOVER STANDARD.
The "Standard" picture guide to Dover, Canterbury and Deal.
Dover Standard Office. 1899.
3,17

DOWKER, G.
Roman remains at Canterbury. (Pamphlet - 4p).
1887?
7,17

DOWNTON, H.M.
St. Augustine of Canterbury: an ecclesiastical and
historical play.
Mowbray. 1902.
3

DU BLES, Charles.
La dernier ressource due peuple de Dieu contre les
jugemens due ciel...17th February, 1758. (Sermon by
Pastor of Walloon Church at Canterbury).
Canterbury, Jacques Abree. 1758.
3

DU BOULAY, Francis Robin H.
The Lordship of Canterbury: an essay on medieval
society.
Nelson. 1966.
1,3,4,6,7,11,15

DUCKETT, Eleanor Shipley.
St. Dunstan of Canterbury: a study of monastic reform
in the tenth century.
Collins. 1955.
3,4,8,12

DUGGAN, Alfred.
God and my right.
Faber. 1955
3

DUNCOMBE, John.
The Civil War between the Israelites and Benjamites...
a sermon preached in the parish church of St. Andrew,
Canterbury on Friday, February 27th, 1778.
Canterbury, Printed by T. Smith. 1778.
3

DUNCOMBE, John.
The history and antiquities of...St. Nicholas at
Harbledown, St. Johns, Northgate and St. Thomas of
Eastbridge, by J. Duncombe and Nicholas Battely.
1785.
1,3,6,11

DUNCOMBE. John.
History and antiquities of the three Archiepiscopal
Hospitals at and near Canterbury.
Printed for J. Nichols. 1785.
11

DUNKIN, Alfred John.
Nundinae cantianae.
Smith. 1842.
5,6,12,18

DUNN-PATTISON, R.P.
The Black Prince.
Methuen. 1910.
3

EAST KENT AGRICULTURAL SOCIETY.
Catalogue of horses, cattle, etc. at first annual show,
Canterbury, July, 1895.
1895.
17

EAST KENT ART SOCIETY.
Catalogues of 17th exhibition, 1925; 21st exhibition,
1929; 25th exhibition, 1933; 43rd exhibition, 1957.
3

EAST KENT CLUB.
Rules and regulations of East Kent Club, St. George's
Street, Canterbury.
Printed at Kentish Observer Office. 1861.
3

EATON, Kenneth J.
Newspapers and politics in Canterbury and Maidstone,
1815-1850. (MA. thesis U.K.C. - bound typescript).
Not Published. 1972.
3

EDWARDS, Anthony J.
The library of Christ Church College, Canterbury. In
Kent News Letter, Vol. 15, No. 5, October, 1964.
3

EDWARDS, Anthony J.
A new College of Education library. In Education Libraries
Bulletin, No. 24. 1965.
3

EDWARDS, David Lawrence.
A history of King's School, Canterbury.
London, Faber and Faber. 1957.
3,4,6,8,11,14,15,21

EDWARDS, David Lawrence.
Kings and Queens at Canterbury.
Canterbury, Canterbury Cathedral Appeal Fund. 1946.
3

Eighteen views of Canterbury.
London, Newan and Co. 1871.
3

Election Commission at Canterbury. (Extracts from 17 fol.).
1880.
3

ELLIS, S.J.
Electricity undertaking, 1899-1948.
Canterbury Corporation.
3

ELLIS, S.M.
Richard Harris Barham - "Thomas Ingoldsby". (Article included
in "The Bookman", January, 1917).
1917.
3

EMANUEL, Manly.
Brief memoir of the life of Benjamin Wanstall...particulars
of Mary Wanstall (his daughter)...full report of the trial of
Mrs. Levi Manly Emanuel, Mary Emanuel and Benjamin Wanstall.
Canterbury, Henry Ward. 1831.
3

EMDEN, Alfred Brotherston.
Donors of books to St. Augustin's Abbey, Canterbury. (Oxford
Bibliographical Society Occasional Papers, No. 4).
Oxford Bibliographical Society. 1968.
4,11

EMSLIE, John Philipps.
New Canterbury tales.
London, Griffith, Farran, Redan, Welsh. 1887.
3

ENDERBY, H.M.
House of Jacob the Jew of Canterbury: notes on the history
of the County Hotel, Canterbury.
Printed by J.A. Jennings. 1953.
3

ENDERBY, H.M.
The inns of Canterbury; parts 1 and 2, lectures delivered
to Canterbury Archaeological Society, 9th March, 1950 and
8th March, 1952.
1950 and 1952.
3

ENDERBY, H.M.
The Norman Keep, Canterbury Castle: lecture delivered to
Canterbury Archaeological Society, 19th November, 1932.
1932.
3

ENDERBY, H.M.
Town planning scheme: final report.
Canterbury, J.A. Jennings. 1945.
3

ENGLISH, John.
New guide to the Elham Valley and Canterbury.
English. (1892).
7,11

ERASMUS, Desiderius.
Pilgrimages to Saint Mary of Walsingham and St. Thomas of
Canterbury,
Nichols. 1849.
1,3,11,12,17

ERWOOD, Guy R.
Panorama of Canterbury: the ancient and modern city.
Sidcup, Lambarde Press. 1963.
1,2,3,4,5,6,7,8,10,11,12,15,17,20

EVANS, John.
Importance of educating the poor: a sermon preached
July 17th, 1808 at Black Friars, Canterbury on behalf of
Royal Free School recently established there.
Canterbury, Bristow and Cowtan. 1808.
3

EVANS, Sebastian.
A bugle call to the men of Kent, by S. Evans and Francis
Bennet-Goldney.
Dover, Dover and County Chronicle Ltd. 1900.
3

EVANS, Sebastian.
Canterbury: mother city of the Anglo Saxon race,
edited by S. Evans and Francis Bennett-Goldney.
Canterbury Chamber of Trade. 1903.
3,4,12,17

EVANS, Sebastian.
Canterbury: mother city of the Anglo Saxon race,
edited by S. Evans and Francis Bennett-Goldney.
Canterbury Chamber of Trade. 1906?
4

EVANS, Sebastian.
Canterbury: the official guide, by Francis Bennett-
Goldney and Sebastian Evans.
Canterbury, Cross and Jackman. 1912.
3

EVANS, Sebastian.
Handbook to the City of Canterbury. British Association
for the Advancement of Science, Dover meeting, 1899,
edited by S. Evans and Francis Bennett-Goldney.
Dover, Observer. 1899.
1,3,7,11,17

EVANS, Sebastian.
The penny guide to the ancient City of Canterbury and
its historic port - Fordwich, 1904, 1905, 1906, 1907,
1908, 1909, 10th edition, n.d., 1913.
Canterbury, Cross and Jackman. (Dates, see above).
3,7,11

EVERSHED, W.
The Messengers mission: a sermon preached at Canterbury
July 29th, 1783.
Brown. 1783.
12

EWELL, Robert.
Guide to St. Augustine's Monastery and Missionary
College, Canterbury.
1902.
17

EWELL, Robert.
A short account of the history of St. Augustine's
Monastery.
n.d.
11

Examination of a book entitled "A brief account of many
of the prosecutions of the people called Quakers...so
far as the clergy of diocese of Canterbury are concerned
in it".
London, Roberts. 1742.
3

Excerpta E compoto thesaurarae monasterii sancti
Augustini extra muros cantuariae, A.D. 1432, with
accounts for 1395,1396 and 1397 (Custodian, William
Cherr.
Mitchell and Hughes. 1881.
11,17

Exhibition of Crown Jewels (replicas) from Eastgate
House Museum, Kent in Royal Museum, Canterbury.
1952.
3

FARQUHARSON AND MILLARD. Auctioneers.
Sale catalogue of Gouldens, 39/40 High Street,
Canterbury.
1960.
3

FAUSSET, T.G. Godfrey.
Canterbury till Domesday.
Archaeological Journal.
11

Featherstones, 1901-1951. (Calendar, 1952).
Featherstones Ltd.
3

FELTOE, Charles Lett.
Three Canterbury kalendars.
11

FIELD, Thomas.
Canterbury: official guide to the Cathedral Church and
handbook to the City, by T. Field and C.F. Routledge.
Canterbury, Crow. 190-?
3,8,11,12,17 (1895)

Fifty years of St. Edmund's School, Canterbury, 1855-1905.
Gibb. 1905.
1

FIRTH, Sir Charles H.
Defoe's true relation of the apparition of Mrs. Veal.
(Reprinted from "Review of English Studies", Vol. VII, No. 25,
January, 1931).
London, Sidgwick and Jackson. 1931.
3

"The Fleur-de-Lis Hotel": a tariff of the hotel and souvenir
of Canterbury.
n.d.
3

FORAN, E.A.
Notes on the lives of the English Augustinian martyrs.
London, Foran and Perry. 1922.
3

Four telegrams from Secretary Admiralty; Supt. Chatham
Dockyard; Naval Commander in Chief, Sheerness; and O/C
Chatham to the Mayor of Canterbury, September 9th, 1872
(offering help to fight Cathedral fire).
3

FOWLER, Frank.
Dottings of a lounger.
Routledge. 1859.
11

FRANCE, Walter Frederick.
St. Augustine's, Canterbury: a story of enduring life.
S.P.C.K. 1952.
1,3,8,11

FREMANTLE, W.H.
Christianity and liberal politics - address delivered as
President of Liberal Association, Canterbury, Thursday October
1st, 1885 in support of canditature of Dr. Aubrey.
London, National Press Agency Ltd. for Liberal Central
Association. 1885.
3

FRENCH, Katharine.
The house of the Grey Friars, Canterbury.
Tunbridge Wells Courier. 1932 and 1950.
1,3,7,11,12,14

FRERE, Sheppard.
Canterbury excavations, 1944-1948. (Reprinted from Antiquity,
Vol. XXIII, pp 153-160.
1949.
3

FRERE, Sheppard.
Roman Canterbury.
Medici. 1947, etc.
1,2,3,4,6,7,8,11,12

FRERE, Sheppard.
Roman Canterbury: an account of the excavations at the Rose
Lane sites, Summer, 1946. (Reprinted from Arch. Cant.).
Canterbury Excavation Committee. 1955.
2,3,4,6

FRERE, Sheppard.
Roman Canterbury, No. 4. No. 1, Butchery Lane, 1945 and 1946.
6

FRERE, Sheppard.
Roman Canterbury, 1945-57.
Canterbury, J.A. Jennings. 1957.
3,6

FRERE, Sheppard.
Roman Canterbury, the city of Durovernum: an illustrated
non-technical summary, 2nd edition.
Canterbury, Jennings. 1957?
4,8

FRERE, Sheppard.
Roman Canterbury, the city of Durovernum: an illustrated
non-technical summary, 3rd edition.
Canterbury, Jennings. 1962.
4,6

FRERE, Sheppard.
Roman Canterbury, the city of Durovernum, 4th edition.
Canterbury Excavation Committee. 1965.
12

FRERE, Sheppard.
The Roman theatre at Canterbury. (Reprinted from
Britannia, Vol. 1, 1970).
2,3,4,11

FRITH, Francis Photographer.
Canterbury, photographed by F. Frith.
Canterbury, H. Drury. n.d.
1

FRITH, Francis.
Frith's photo-pictures, Canterbury.
n.d.
3

Front line school: the war-time story of the Simon
Langton Boy's School, Canterbury, as told by masters
and boys of the school.
Canterbury, J.A. Jennings. (1946).
3

The Gamesters: a poem addressed to the Mayor of
Canterbury: uter est insanior horum.
London, Printed for Lewis and Bew. 1774, 2nd edition.
3

GARDINER, Mrs. Dorothy.
The Berkeleys of Canterbury. (Reprinted from Archaeologia
Cantiana, Vol. LXIX, 1955).
3,17

GARDINER, Mrs. Dorothy.
Canterbury.
Sheldon Press. 1933.
1,2,(1923), 3,4,6,7,8,11,12,15

GARDINER, Mrs. Dorothy.
Canterbury lyrics.
Canterbury, Gibbs. 1943?
3,8,11,17

GARDINER, Mrs. Dorothy.
Commonwealth Canterbury.
Canterbury Archaeological Society. 1956.
1,2,3,11,12,18,19

GARDINER, Mrs. Dorothy.
English girlhood at school.
London, Oxford University Press, Humphrey Milford. 1929.
3

GARDINER, Mrs. Dorothy.
"The home of seven centuries": history of Cogan House,
Canterbury.
Canterbury, Elvy. 1955.
3,11

GARDINER, Mrs. Dorothy.
Letter to Mayor of Canterbury on Putting Lane.
3

GARDINER, Mrs. Dorothy.
The literary traditions of Canterbury.
Canterbury, Gibbs and Son. 1930 and 1952.
3,11

GARDINER, Mrs. Dorothy.
A Mayor of Canterbury: William Watmer, the children's friend.
Ashford, Headby. n.d.
11,17

GARDINER, Mrs. Dorothy.
The Mayor's insignia of the City of Canterbury.
Canterbury, Gibbs. n.d.
3,11

GARDINER, Mrs. Dorothy.
Notes on an ancient house in Church Lane, Canterbury.
Archaeologia Cantiana. n.d.
3,11,17

GARDINER, Mrs. Dorothy.
The Oxinden letters, 1607-1642, being the correspondence of
Henry Oxinden of Barham and his circle, edited by Mrs. D.
Gardiner.
Constable. 1933.
8,11,13,21

GARDINER, Mrs. Dorothy.
The Oxinden and Peyton letters, edited by Mrs. D. Gardiner.
Sheldon. 1937.
3,12

GARDINER, Mrs. Dorothy.
St. Margaret's Church, Canterbury.
Canterbury. 1952.
3

GARDINER, Mrs. Dorothy.
Six little scenes from Canterbury history.
Canterbury, Cross and Jackman. 1929.
3

GARDINER, Mrs. Dorothy.
Some notes on petitions concerning Canterbury monastic
houses in the Court of Chancery.
Archaeologia Cantiana, Vol. XLIII. n.d.
3,17

GARDINER, Mrs. Dorothy.
Story of Canterbury Castle.
Canterbury, Jennings. 1932, 1957.
3,11

GARDINER, Mrs. Dorothy.
Story of St. Margaret's and its worshippers through the
centuries.
Canterbury, Elvy Bros. 1955.
3

GARDINER, Mrs. Dorothy.
What Canterbury knew of Mrs. Veal and her friends.
Sidgwick and Jackson.(1931).
3,12

GARNIER , Rev. A.J.
The Huguenots in Britain with special reference to their
settlements in Canterbury.
Canterbury, Gibbs and Son. 1965.
3

GASQUET, A. Cardinal.
Mission of St. Augustine.
London, C. Bell. 1954.
3

GATES, Henry.
The Canterbury tale. (Article in "Courier", Vol. 23, No. 6,
December, 1954).
3

GENTLEMAN'S JOURNAL.
Cathedral cities of England: Canterbury. (Article in
Gentleman's Journal, May 4th, 1907).
3

GILBERT, George, 1796-1874.
Reminiscences.
Privately Printed. 1938.
3,11

GILBERT, R.G.
St. Augustine's College, Canterbury: a brief guide, by R.G.
Gilbert and F.H. Maycock.
Canterbury, Printed by A.J. Snowden. 1971.
11

GINDER. Publisher.
Ginder's handbook for Canterbury and Canterbury
Cathedral.
Canterbury, Ginders, St. George's Hall. n.d.
3

GOODRICH, Harold S.
Thomas Field: Headmaster of King's School, Canterbury.
S.P.C.K. 1937.
3,11

GOODSALL, Robert Harold.
Canterbury.
Canterbury, Cross and Jackman. 1935.
2,3,11

GOSTLING, William.
A walk in and about the City of Canterbury, various
editions.
Simmons and Kirkby. 1774, etc.
1,2,3,4,5,6,7,8,9,10,11,12,13,14,15,17,18

GOULDEN, A.T.
The Gouldens of Canterbury.
Courier. 1948.
3,19

GOULDEN, C. Publisher.
Canterbury guide.
Canterbury, Goulden. n.d.
3,7,11,12,15,17,19

GOULDEN, C. Publisher.
Handbook and guide through Canterbury.
c.1850.
17

GOULDEN, C. Publisher.
Selected views of Canterbury and its neighbourhood.
Canterbury, Goulden. n.d.
3

GOULDEN, H.J. LTD. Publisher.
The authentic guide to the cathedral and City of
Canterbury.
Canterbury, Goulden. 1911.
3

GOULDEN, H.J. LTD. Publisher.
Guide to Canterbury and the cathedral.
Canterbury, Goulden. 1848, etc.
3,8,17

GOULDEN, H.J. LTD. Publisher.
Kent almanack and the Canterbury calendar for 1895,
1896, 1897, 1898, 1899, 1900, 1901, 1902.
Canterbury, Goulden. (Dates - see above).
3,17 (1899 only)

GOULDER, Laurance.
Canterbury.
Guild of Our Lady of Ransom. 1954.
3,12

GOULDER, Laurance.
Canterbury.
Guild of Our Lady of Ramsom. 1962
3,11

GRANVILLE-BAKER, B.
Canterbury pilgrims. (Article in "Tourist", Vol. 5,
February, 1930).
3

GREAT BRITAIN: LAWS etc. (GEO.I).
An Act for erecting a work-house and for lighting the
streets. (In the City of Canterbury).
1727-8.
17

GREAT BRITAIN: LAWS etc. (GEO.II).
An Act for erecting a workhouse in the City of
Canterbury.
1728.
3,8,11

GREAT BRITAIN: LAWS etc (GEO.II).
An Act for...speedy recovery of small debts within the
City and County of the City of Canterbury.
1752.
3,11

GREAT BRITAIN: LAWS etc. (GOE.III).
An Act for paving the streets, lanes in the City of
Canterbury...1787.
3,11

GREAT BRITAIN: LAWS etc. (GEO.III).
An Act for altering, amending and rendering more effectual
an Act of the first year of King George the Second for
erecting a workhouse...54 Geo.III - Sess. 1814.
3

GREAT BRITAIN: LAWS etc. STATUTORY INSTRUMENTS.
The Canterbury and District Water Order.
H.M.S.O. 1961.
4,8

GREAT BRITAIN: LAWS etc. STATUTORY INSTRUMENTS.
Mid Kent Water (Canterbury) Order, 1968.
H.M.S.O. 1968.
12

GREENFIELD, Lilian.
Grimsby's freemen: contrasted with the freemen of other
towns.
Grimsby, Gait. Albert. 1950.
3

GREGORY, C.W.
Canterbury weavers, past and present.
Press Printers. 1905.
3,11

GRIERSON, Elizabeth.
Canterbury.
Black. 1910.
1

Guide to St. Augustine's Monastery and Missionary College by
the Manciple.
Canterbury, Cross and Jackman. 1902.
3

A guide to the Canterbury museums.
(1967).
4,11

GUNNIS, Erhart.
A first series of the chronicles of Canterbury.
London, Richard Bentley. 1840.
3

HACKETT, Benedict.
Blessed John Stone: Austin Friar martyr.
London, Office of the Vice Postulation.
3,11

Hackington Church, Canterbury: a pamphlet and a print.
W. Lefevre Ltd. n.d.
13

Hales Place, Canterbury - Sale catalogue.
1880.
3

HALL, Hubert.
Manorial accounts of the Priory of Canterbury, 1260-1420, by
H. Hall and F. Nicholas. (Bulletin: Institute of History
Research).
Institute of History Research. 1931.
11

Handy guide to Canterbury.
Canterbury, Canterbury Register. 1899 and 1900.
3

HARMER, F.E.
Selected English historical documents of the ninth and tenth
centuries, edited by F.E. Harmer.
Cambridge University Press. 1914.
3

HART, Henry.
Representation of Canterbury, meeting at the Forester's Hall
c.1881.
17

HARTHOORN, P.A.
Hollandse gebrandschilderde vamen te Canterbury. (The
Dutch painted and stained window on staircase of Royal
Museum, Canterbury). (3 articles in Gens Nostra). n.d.
3

HARVEY, Wallace.
A son of Canterbury: Thomas Clark.
n.d.
3

HASSELL, Christopher.
Bell Harry and other poems.
London, Longmans. 1963.
3

HASTED, Edward.
Canterbury guide.
Bristow, Canterbury. 1803.
3,17

HASTED, Edward.
The Canterbury guide.
Canterbury, W. Bristow and Cowtan. 1807, 3rd edition.
3

HASTED, Edward.
Canterbury guide.
Canterbury, Cowtan and Colegate. 1809, 5th edition.
3

HASTED, Edward.
History of the ancient and metropolitan City of
Canterbury.
Canterbury, Simmons and Kirkby. 1799, etc.
3,6,7,11,12,15

HASTINGS, T.
Vestiges of antiquity.
1813.
1,3,4,11,12,17

HASTINGS AND THANET BUILDING SOCIETY.
Then and now (a history of) Mercery Lane, Canterbury.
Hastings and Thanet Building Society. 1965.
3,4,11

Headley's short guide to St. Augustine's, Canterbury.
Headley. 1922.
7

Headlight: Canterbury, St. Edmund's School.
1966.
3

HEDLEY, John Cuthbert.
Apostle of England. (Re: St. Augustine).
London, Art and Book Co. 1897.
3

HENFREY, Henry W.
The Canterbury coins of Edward I,II,III. (Article in
Antiquary No. 1, Vol. 1, January, 1880).
3

HIGENBOTTAM, Frank.
Apparition of Mrs. Veal to Mrs. Bargrave at Canterbury.
(Reprinted from Archaeologia Cantiana, Vol. LXXIII, 1959)
3,17

HIGENBOTTAM, Frank.
Canterbury Royal Museum and Public Library. (Article in
Kent Newsletter, Vol. 3, No. 2, 1951).
3

HILL, Derek Ingram.
The ancient hospitals and almshouses of Canterbury.
Canterbury Archaeological Society. 1969.
2,4,6,11,12

HINSCLIFF, M.W.
King John and the Abbott of Canterbury.
London, Routledge. n.d.
3

History of Berry Bolaine the Canterbury miser (containing an account of her avarice and wonderful escapes
from matrimony).
Rochester, Caddell. 1828?
3,8

HOBSON, John Morrison.
Some early and late houses of pity.
London, Routledge. 1926.

HOLLAND, Edward Lancelot.
The Canterbury chantries and hospitals...in 1546.
K.A.S. 1934.
1,2,3,5,11,12,15,18

CANTERBURY Cont'd

HOLLAND, Mary Sibylla.
Additional letters of Mary Sibylla.
Edinbrugh, R. and R. Clark. 1899.
3

HOLLAND, Mary Sibylla.
Letters of Mary Sibylla.
London, Edward Arnold. 1898.
3

HOME, Gordon.
Canterbury.
1911.
1,3,6,8,12,13,14,15,16,17

HOME, Gordon.
Canterbury of our grandfathers and of today.
Homeland Association. 1927.
1,4,6,11,15,17

HOME, Gordon.
Canterbury of our grandfathers and of today.
Homeland Association. 1948.
3

HOME, Gordon.
The threat to Canterbury's ancient buildings. (Article in
"Illustrated London News", No. 4911, June 3rd, 1933).
3

"Homecrafts" national handweaving exhibition.
Canterbury, Dane John Press. 1955.
3

HOOKER HERALD.
No. 13. 1963.
3

HOOKER - School history.
n.d.
3

HOPE, Sir William Henry St. John.
Excavation at St. Austin's Abbey, Canterbury.
Mitchell and Hughes. 1902.
11,17

HOPE, Sir William Henry St. John.
On the English medieval drinking bowls called mazers
(includes the mazers of St. John's Hospital Canterbury and
Harbledown Hospital).
Westminster Society of Antiquaries. 1887.
3

HOPE, Sir William Henry St. John.
Recent discoveries in the abbey church of St. Austin at
Canterbury. (Reprinted from Archaeologia Cantiana, 1916).
3,8,17,21

House of the Greyfriars, Canterbury.
Tunbridge Wells, Courier Co. Ltd. n.d.
3

HOW, Harry.
Illustrated interviews, 31 Mr. T.Sidney Cooper.
London, Strand Magazine. n.d.
3

HOWORTH, Sir Henry H.
Saint Augustine of Canterbury.
Murray. 1913.
1,3,6,11,12

HUNTER (of The Queen's Bays Regiment). "Rusticus" pseud.
Ball-room votaries: or Canterbury and its vicinity.
London, Printed for Henry Colburn. 1810.
3,11,17

HUSSEY, Arthur.
Parish churches of Canterbury.
Kentish Gazette Off Prints.
3

HUXLEY, T. Scott.
A handy guide for visitors to Canterbury by an old inhabitant.
Canterbury, Crow. 1893.
15

HUXLEY, T. Scott.
A handy guide for visitors to Canterbury and the Cathedral.
Printed by Gibbs and Sons. 1895.
3

HYDE, S. Publisher.
New Canterbury guide. 1870.
3,11,12,17

HYDE, S. Publisher.
The new illustrated Canterbury guide.
n.d. (after 1846).
7

Hymns, occasionally sung at the parish churches of St.
Alphage and St. Mary, Northgate. (Tracts No. 4).
Canterbury, Henry Ward. n.d.
3

ILOT, Charles Henry.
Men of the trees: report on pictorial exhibition held
at County Hotel, Canterbury, May 1959.
Canterbury. 1959.
3

INDEPENDENT ORDER OF ANCIENT DRUIDS, CANTERBURY.
General laws.
1883.
17

INGLIS, K.S.
Hospital and the community...Melbourne. (Including
information on the work of Dr. J.G. Beaney).
Melbourne University Press. 1958.
3

Ingoldsby, 2 Watling Street, Canterbury - Sale catalogue
of contents.
1930.
3

"AN INHABITANT".
Canterbury guide.
n.d.
17

"AN INHABITANT".
Strangers'and visitors'companion and guide to Canterbury.
18th century.
17

"AN INHABITANT".
Strangers' and visitors' guide to Canterbury.
1849.
17

IRVING, Laurence.
Henry Irving: the actor and his world.
London, Faber. 1951.
3

The Isle of Thanet and Canterbury Review.
n.d.
JACKSON, Esther.
Art of the Anglo Saxon age. (Includes chapter on
Canterbury).
Peterborough, Richard R. Smith. 1964.
3

JACKSON, Katharine Frances.
St. Augustine of Canterbury.
Junior Auxiliary Publishing Co. 1897.
11

JACOBS, J.
Narrative of the erection of the new synagogue at
Canterbury.
Canterbury, Hebrew Congregation, Births, Marriages and
Deaths. 1830-1861.
3

JACQUES, Edward Tyrrell.
The pilgrim from Chicago. (Chaps. 3-7 cover Reculver,
Fordwich and Canterbury).
Longmans and Green. 1913.

JAMES, G.P.R.
History of the life of Edward the Black Prince, 2
vols.
London, Longman. 1836.
3

JAMES, Montague Rhodes.
The ancient libraries of Canterbury and Dover.
Cambridge University Press. 1903.
1,2,3,6,7,11,12,15,17

JENKINS, Frank.
Roman Canterbury: an account of the excavations at No. 5,
Watling Street, 1947.
Canterbury Excavation Committee. 1953.
1,2,3,4,6,11

JENKINS, Frank.
Roman Canterbury: an account of the excavations in Burgate
in 1946-48.
Medici Society. 1951.
1,2,3,5,8,11,12

JENKINS, Frank.
A Roman tilery and two pottery kilns at Durovernum,
Canterbury. (Reprinted from The Antiquarians Journal, Vol.
XXXVI, 1956).
3

JENKINS, Frank.
St. Martin's Church at Canterbury. (Reprinted from Medieval
Archaeology, Vol. IX, 1965).
3

JENKINS, Frank.
St. Martin's Church at Canterbury.
Headley Bros. 1966.
15

JENKINS, Robert Charles.
Canterbury.
Society for Promoting Christian Knowledge. 1880.
1,2,3,6,7,8,9,11,12,17,18

JENNINGS, W. Publisher.
The new Canterbury guide.
n.d.
3,7,17

JENNINGS, W. Publisher.
New Canterbury guide book.
1850, 1856.
17

JESSUP, Ronald F.
Canterbury (Information sheet No. 60).
1948.
3

JOHN OF SALISBURY.
Letters, Vol. 1.
Nelson. 1955.
12

JOHNSON, Isaac.
Sermon preached at the parish churches of Swalecliffe and St.
Paul's, Canterbury.
1739.

JOHNSTON, James.
The finding of St. Augustine's chair.
Cornish Bros. 1898.
3,12

JOINT EDUCATION COMMITTEE - KENT AND CANTERBURY.
Frank Hooker Secondary School official opening.
Canterbury, Kentish Gazette. 1956.
3

JOINT EDUCATION COMMITTEE - KENT AND CANTERBURY.
List of schools and their head teachers.
1956.
3

JOINT EDUCATION COMMITTEE - KENT AND CANTERBURY.
Report, 1948-1951.
3

JOINT EDUCATION COMMITTEE - KENT AND CANTERBURY.
Youth Employment Service annual reports, 1955,1956,1958,1959.
(Dates, see above).
3

JONES, Dora M.
The Duke's ward: a romance of old Kent.
Edinburgh, Oliphant. 1896.
11

JONES, Ira.
King of air fighters.
Chivers. 1970.
3

KAEHLER, Richard D.
The rectors of St. Margaret's Church, Canterbury,
compiled by R. Kaehler. n.d.
3

KAEHLER, Richard D.
St. Alphege Church, Canterbury.
1942?
3

KAEHLER, Richard D.
St. Andrew's Church, St. Mary Bredman's Church, etc.
1939?
3

KAEHLER, Richard D.
St. Margaret's Church, Canterbury.
1942?
3

KEESEY, Walter M.
Canterbury.
Black. 1915.
1,3,5,6,11,12,17,18

KEMP, Ethelbert Thomas.
A Canterbury apprentice's notebook. MS.
1835.
3

KENT, Douglas H.
Flora of bombed sites in Canterbury.
Arbroath Buncle. 1951.
3,4,11

KENT AND CANTERBURY HOSPITAL.
Ceremony of opening the new hospital by H.R.H. the Duke
of Kent, accompanied by H.R.H. the Duchess...July 14th,
1937.
Printed by A. Jennings. 1937.
11

KENT AND CANTERBURY HOSPITAL.
Laws and byelaws.
1891.
17

Kent and Canterbury illustrated family almanac for 1865.
Jennings. 1865.
3

KENT ARCHAEOLOGICAL SOCIETY.
The Canterbury chantries and hospitals, together with
some others in the neighbourhood in 1546. (Kent Records,
Vol. 12, supplement, 1934).
1934.
4,8,17,18

KENT ARCHAEOLOGICAL SOCIETY - RECORDS BRANCH.
Meeting held at Canterbury...celebrate the 21st
anniversary of its foundation.
Ashford, Headley Bros. 1934.
3,11

Kent College, 1885-1935.
Kent County Newspapers Ltd. 1937.
4,7,11,19

KENT COUNTY COUNCIL - PLANNING DEPARTMENT.
Kent development plan (part A). County map, University
site.
Maidstone, K.C.C. 1962.
3

KENT COUNTY PHOTOGRAPHIC ASSOCIATION.
Fifteenth annual exhibition...presented by Canterbury
Camera Club at the Slater Art Gallery. 1965.
3

Kent County war memorial. (Folder with short
description and illustration of the memorial).
3

KENT MESSENGER.
Canterbury looks back over seven centuries.
December 1st, 1934.
3

KENT SOCIETY FOR THE ENCOURAGEMENT OF AGRICULTURE AND
INDUSTRY, CANTERBURY.
Rules, orders and premiums. 1804.
17

KENTISH GAZETTE.
The bombing of Canterbury, Page 4, October 28th.
Kentish Gazette. 1944.
3

KENTISH GAZETTE.
A friar was hanged. (Leaflet to illustrate the exhinition
of Canterbury archives in the Slater Art Gallery -
Reprinted from Kentish Gazette, July 27th, 1951).
3

KENTISH GAZETTE AND CANTERBURY PRESS.
Mrs. Veal's apparition. (Reprinted from Kentish Gazette and
Canterbury Press, May 19th, 1931).
3

KENTISH OBSERVER.
The City suicidal   (Reprinted from Kentish Observer, March
20th, 1902).
3

KENTISH OBSERVER AND CANTERBURY TIMES.
Twenty years after. (An account of the bombing of Canterbury
on June 1st. 1942).
Kentish Observer and Canterbury Times. June 5th, 1962.
3

KERSHAW. S.
Canterbury's ancient coinage.
British Archaeological Association. 1902.
3,7,11

KETTLE, L.D.
Canterbury national school-girls register, 1814-1845.
(Included in University of London Institute of Education
Bulletin, Spring Term, 1964).
3

King George V Silver Jubilee celebrations - Monday 6th May,
1935.
Canterbury. 1935.
3

King John and the Abbot of Canterbury (poem).
Bristol, Printed by Henry Hill Ltd. n.d.
3

KING'S SCHOOL, CANTERBURY.
Books given by W. Somerset Maugham.
King's School. (1966).
3

KING'S SCHOOL, CANTERBURY.
Catalogue of the Hugh Walpole collection.
King's School. n.d.
3

KING'S SCHOOL, CANTERBURY.
Great Hall, King's School, Canterbury. (Article in "The
Builder", Jan 10th, 1958).
3

KING'S SCHOOL, CANTERBURY.
The King's School, Canterbury founded in VIIth century,
reconstituted by King Henry VIII in 1541.
King's School. 192-?
11

KING'S SCHOOL, CANTERBURY.
Oldest public school in England.
c.1910.
17

KING'S SCHOOL, CANTERBURY.
Register, 1859-1931.
O.K.S. Association. 1932.
3,11

KING'S SCHOOL, CANTERBURY.
Register, 1931-1970 with alphabetical index.
O.K.S. Association. 1971.
3

KING'S SCHOOL, CANTERBURY.
Reports, 1879, 1880, 1886.
17

KING'S SCHOOL, CANTERBURY.
School songs.
n.d.
17

KINGSFORD, Felix.
Poetry: a memoir of Felix Kingsford, edited by his
father.
Canterbury, Kentish Observer. 1876.
3,17

KINGSFORD, Thomas.
Canterbury in the modern time.
Canterbury. 1873.
3,17

KNIGHT, Charles.
Handbook to Canterbury, Dover, Isle of Thanet...
Nattali and Bond. 1853.
1,13,14

LADD, G.P. Publisher.
Visitors' handbook to Canterbury.
1859.
17

The land we live in: Canterbury. (Extracted from a
larger work).
n.d.
3

The Langtonian, Vol. 15, No. 4.
1929.
3

LAWLER, Alan.
The parish church of St. Dunstan, Canterbury.
Gloucester British Publishing Co. 1959, etc.
1,3,4,6,11,12,15

LEACH, Arthur Francis.
The schools of medieval England.
London, Methuen. 1915.
3

LEE, Sophia.
Canterbury tales, by Sophia and Harriet Lee.
Colburn and Bentley. 1832.
12

LE FEVRE, WILLIAM LTD.
Celebrating our 75th anniversary.
Canterbury, Le Fevre Ltd. 1950.
3

The legend of Bab's Oak, "Will O' the Wisp".
Canterbury, Cross and Jackman. 1884.
3

Life of Sir William Courtenay. (Article in the Penny
Satirist, No. 60, June 9th, 1838).
3

LINCOLN, Edward Frank.
Story of Canterbury.
Staples Press. 1955.
1,3,4,5,7,8,11,12,15,18

"THE LION".
Eccentric and singular production of Sir, W. Courtenay.
K.M. alias Mr. Tom.
Canterbury, Henry Ward. n.d.
3

A list of the mayors of the City of Canterbury from the
year 1449 until 1825. MS.
14

Literary tradition of Canterbury from Chaucer to Conrad .
Cambridge University Press. 1930.
11

LIVETT, Grevile Mairs.
Manuscript notes on the Royal Mint situated at 37 High
Street, Canterbury.
3

LOCAL GOVERNMENT BOARD.
Canterbury Union. (Regulations for accounts).
1881.
3

LONGHAYE, LE. R.P.G.
Les Lecons d l'exil...du College Sainte-Marie de
Canterbery.
1881.
17

LOUGHBOROUGH, George W.
Short history of St. Alphege and St. Peter's Church and
Eastbridge Hospital, compiled by F.W. Loughborough and H.J.
Small.
Ramsgate Church Publishing Co. 1963.
3,11

LOVERING, J. Publisher.
A souvenir of Canterbury.
London, Lovering and Co. 1907.
3

LOW, Ernest W.
The Canterbury riding establishment.
The Windsor Magazine. 1896.
3

LUKYN, I.
Manuscript letter of I. Lukyn to her aunt dated October 9th,
1705 giving an account of the apparition of Mrs. Veal to
Mrs. Bargrave.
3

LYLE, Laurence.
Canterbury.
Norwich, Jarrold. 1966.
1,3,6,

LYLE, Laurance.
Show yourself around Canterbury.
Jarrold. 1966.
12

MS. collection of news cuttings and photographs of Canterbury
men (contemp.).
1900
3

M'BEAN, James.
Testimonials of Mr. James M'Bean for the office of
Superintendent of Police for Canterbury.
1884.
17

McCLEMENT, Rev. F Kerr.
The lives of Blessed Robert Wilcox, Blessed Edward Campion,
Blessed Christopher Buxton, Blessed Robert Widmerpool,Cant.
1st October, 1588. (Typescript from lives of English
martyrs, 2nd series, Vol. 1, 1583-88, edited by E.H. Burton
and J.H. Pollen, 1914).
3

McCULLOCH, William.
The Simon Langton Boy's School.
1954.
3

MACKENZIE, Norman
The battle of Canterbury: the problem of rebuilding its
blitzed areas.
Picture Post, Vol. 29, No. 8, November, 1945.
3

MACKENZIE, P.A.
A day in Canterbury.
1951.
3

MACLEAR, George Frederick.
St. Augustine's, Canterbury.
Well Gardner Darton. 1888.
1,3,4,6,11,12,15

MAJOR, M.B.
Man of mystery or exploits of the King of Jerusalem in verse.
Printed in Canterbury. 1833.
3

MANNOCK, Edward.
The personal diary of Major Edward 'Mick' Mannock.
London, Spearman. 1966.
3

MARSHALL, Emma.
In the service of Rachel Lady Russell: a story.
London, Seeley and Co. 1893.
3,17

(MARSHALL, Jane).
Tour of Canterbury and Rochester.
Oxford University Press. 1954.
3,11

MARSTON, John.
Sermon preached at St. Margaret's in Westminster on
Sunday the sixth of February last...by John Marston,
Master of Arts, and Rector of the parish church of St.
Mary Magdelen in Canterbury.
London. 1642.
3

MARTIN, Alan R.
The Dominican Priory at Canterbury. (Reprinted from
Archaeological Journal, Vol. LXXXVI).
London, The Institute. 1930.
3

MARTIN, Norah Baldwin.
Canterbury.
Blackie. 1951.
1,3,8,11,12

Mary Carleton. (Single-leaf extract, together with
engraved portrait)...(adventuress, daughter of a
musician at Canterbury, executed, 1672).
3

MASON, Arthur James.
Canterbury sonnets.
1919.
3,6,11,12

MASON, Arthur James.
The mission of St. Augustine to England according to the
original documents, edited by A.J. Mason.
Cambridge University Press. 1897.
3,11,12,14

MAUGHAN, William Somerset.
The merry-go-round. (Author was pupil at King's School,
Canterbury).
Heinemann. 1905.
3

MEAD, Henry Thomas.
Some treasurers in the Royal Museum. (Typescript of
articles appearing in the Kent Herald during 1927).
1927.
3

MEE, Arthur.
Canterbury.
Hodder and Stoughton. 1949.
1,3,4,7,8,11,12,15

A meeting of the inhabitants of...Canterbury...for
relieving the poor...in 1840.
17

Memorials of T.G. Godfrey-Faussett.
Parker. 1878.
11

MERCER, William John.
Exerpts from sundry works relative to the family of
Bunce, compiled by W.J. Mercer.
3

MERCER, William John.
Extracts from various works relating to the family of
OAKSHOTT, compiled by W.J. Mercer.
1910?
3

Mercery Lane: presented on the opening of new premises,
May, 1913 by J. Hunt and Sons.
3

MERRIOTT, Jack. Illustrator.
Canterbury: with eight plates in colour from paintings
by Jack Merriott.
London, Blackie. 1951.
3

MILLER, Amos.
A gift for 1838...the Cook's plain English guide and
economical assistant. (Cook at Wright's Fountain Hotel,
Canterbury).
Canterbury, Ward. 1838.
3

MILLER, E.A.
A short history of the parish church of St. Dunstan's,
Canterbury, compiled by E.A. Miller.
British Publishing Co. (1936).
3,11

MODERS, Mary alias STEDMAN (Defendant).
Trial of Mary Moders, alias Stedman styled the German
Princess, at the Old Bailey for bigamy. 15 Charles II,
A.D. 1663. (Extracted from Cobbett's (Howell's) State
Trials, 1810 - she was alledged to be from parish of St.
Mildred's, Canterbury).
3

MOLESWORTH, Sir Guilford Lindsey, 1828-1925.
Life of Sir Guilford L. Molesworth (son of Rev. J.E.N.
Molesworth, Vicar of St. Martin's and Rector of St. Paul's,
Canterbury).
London, Spon. 1922.
3

MOLONY, Eileen.
Portraits of towns, edited by E. Molony. "Canterbury", by
William Townsend, Page 47.
London, Dobson. 1952.
3

MONK, Captain. d.1700
Photostat copy of a letter entitled "the fatal century" or
"the double duel". A memorial of North Holmes, Canterbury,
Part 1, A.D. 1600, Part 2, A.D. 1700. (Captain Monk fought
Major C. Neville in a duel).
3

MORRIS, John.
On a wall painting in St. Anselm's Chapel in Canterbury
Cathedral Church.
Westminster, Nichols and Sons. 1891.
3

MORTON, Henry Canova Vellan.
I saw two Englands. Chap. 3 describes Canterbury (under
Kent).
Methuen. 1942.

MUNICIPAL JOURNAL.
Canterbury appoints architect - planner. (Article from
Municipal Journal No. 3,594, 5th January, 1962).
3

MURPHY, Leonard.
On Mr. Beaney and his urological writings and experiences.
Sydney Australasian Medical Publishing Co. Ltd. 1960.
3

MUSEUMS ASSOCIATION.
Report of proceedings with papers read at the eleventh
annual general meeting held in Canterbury, July 9th-12th,
1900.
London, Dulan and Co. 1900.
3

NAIRN, Ian.
Canterbury: the happy City. (Included in The Listener,
Vol. LXIV, No. 1639, August 15th, 1960).
3

NASONS (CANTERBURY) LTD.
A Canterbury enterprise.
Canterbury, Jennings. 1960.
3

NATIONAL SOCIETY FOR THE PREVENTION OF CRUELTY TO CHILDREN.
Canterbury and East Mid-Kent Branch 3rd annual report, 1896,
4th annual report, 1897.
17

The new Canterbury guide.
Hyde. 1870.
3,11,12

New Canterbury guide.
Canterbury, Jennings. n.d.
3,7

OFFICIAL ARCHITECTURE AND PLANNING.
Canterbury: development and planning. (Article in Official
Architecture and Planning, Vol. 25, No. 10, October, 1962).
3

OFFICIAL ARCHITECTURE AND PLANNING.
Museums improvements at Canterbury.
Official Architecture and Planning, Vol. 25, No. 3 , 1962.
3

Old Canterbury: a description of a timber-build house...
in Station Road West.
Cross and Jackman. 1906.
12

"AN OLD INHABITANT".
Handy guide for visitors to Canterbury.
1893.
17

Old Trade Bills of Canterbury. (Collection of 5 Bills).
Canterbury, Simmons, Kirkby and Jones. 1792.
3

OLDCASTLE, Geoffrey.
The Canterbury Magazine, Vol. 1, July-December, 1834.
Kentish Observer. 1834.
3(also Vol. 2, Jan-April, 1835), 12,17

O'NEILL, Sibyl.
Views of the King's School, Canterbury. (Sketched in pen
and ink).
Austen. 1910.
3,11

ORGER, E.R.
Life of Henry Bailey, D.D. Honorary Canon of Canterbury,
sometime Warden of St. Augustine's College and Rector
of West Tarring.
London, Hugh Rees Ltd. 1912.
3

Original and whimsical poetical fancies dedicated (by
permission) to Captain H.R. Benson, 17th Lancers,
Canterbury.
Canterbury, Henry Chivers. 1846.
3

OUGHTON, Frederick.
Ace with one eye: life and combats of Major Edward
Mannock, by F. Oughton and V. Smythe.
London, Muller. 1963.
3

"OUT-PATIENT".
Dialogue in rhyme between Benevolus and Eugenis, relative
to the Kent and Canterbury Hospital.
1825.
17

OUTLINE, Oliver.
New Canterbury tales, 2nd edition.
Colburn. 1811.
1,3,11,14

Oxinden portraits, Lot 172 etc. - Sale catalogue of
"Ingoldsby", 2 Watling Street, Canterbury.
Canterbury, Amos and Dawton. 1930.
3

PAINTER, Kenneth S.
A Roman silver treasure from Canterbury. (Reprinted from
Journal of the Archaeological Association, Vol. XXVIII,
1965).
3

PALMER, James L.
The Cornish Chough through the ages. Marazion (Cornwall)
Printed for the Old Cornwall Societies by Worden
(Printers) Ltd. 1954.
3

PARKER, Michael St. John.
Christian Canterbury: city of pilgrims.
Pitkin. 1970.
8,11

Particulars and conditions of sale of the desirable
freehold semi-detached residence. Wickham Lodge, 47
St. Augustine's Road, Canterbury.
1949.

PEARCE, Rev. E.H.
English Christianity in its beginnings.
London, S.P.C.K. 1908.
3

PENNELL, Elizabeth Robins.
The life and letters of Joseph Pennell.
London, Benn. 1930.
3

PENNY MAGAZINE.
Canterbury: monthly supplement of the Society for the
Diffusion of Useful Knowledge, Jan 31st-February, 28th, 1834.
3

The Penny Sunday Reader, edited by the Rev. J.E.N.
Molesworth.
Canterbury, Kentish Observer. 1833,1835,1837.
3

PERCY, Edward.
The enduring stones: a miming pageant for St. Augustine's
Monastery. Canterbury festival, 1951 A.D.
3

PERRAULT, Charles.
Tales of passed times written for children...and newly
decorated by John Austen. (Artist was a master at
Canterbury School of Art, 1939).
London, Selwyn and Blount. 1922.
3

PERRONET, Edward.
Correspondence and typescript relating to Edward Perronet.
1962.
3

PHOTOGRAPHIC ALLIANCE.
Inter-federation competition and exhibition of pictorial
photography...catalogue.
1954.
3

PILBROW, James.
Discoveries made during excavations at Canterbury in 1868.
Society of Antiqities of London. 1871.
1

PINNOCK, Kenneth.
Canterbury.
1958.
3,8,11,12

Plan and estimates for improving and extending the
navigation of the River Stour.
(Under - Stour, River).
17

PLOMER, Henry Robert.
James Abree a printer and bookseller of Canterbury.
(Reprinted from "The Library", January, 1913).
3

PLOMER, Henry Robert.
Manuscript cards of Canterbury printed books in the
Bodleian Library, Oxford.
n.d.
3

PLOMER, Henry Robert.
Names of persons implicated in Falconbridge's rebellion,
1471. (Transcribed from the archives of the City of
Canterbury, 1914).
3

PLOMER, Henry Robert.
Short account of the records of Canterbury.
Canterbury, Cross and Jackson. 1892.
1,3,11,17

PLOWMAN, Allan W.
Canterbury: the Newdigate prize poem, 1935.
Oxford, Blackwell. 1935.
3

POPE, Sydney.
Freemasonry in Canterbury and Provincial Grand Lodge, 1785-1809.
and Dr. Perfect, Provincial Grand Master of Kent, 1795-1809.
Margate, Parrett. 1941.
3

POTTS, R.U.
The Abbey of St. Augustine, Canterbury.
S.P.C.K. n.d.
11

POTTS, R.U.
Plan of St. Austin's Abbey, Canterbury.
St. Augustine's College. 1934.
1,3,11,17

POWELL, A.H.
Canterbury: a series of impressions.
n.d.
17

Practicability...of navigating the River Stour through
Canterbury.
(Under - Stour, River).
17

PRAGNELL, D.
St. Dunstan of Canterbury. (Article in Thanet Catholic
Review, Vol. XIII, No. 3, 1955).
3

PRENTICE. Publisher.
Canterbury guide.
Canterbury, Prentice. 1843.
3,11,17 (1844)

PRESTWICH, Joseph.
On some swallow holes on the chalk hills near Canterbury.
(From the Quarterly Journal of the Geological Society,
May, 1854).
Geological Society. 1854.
7

Provident institution, or saving's bank of the City of
Canterbury and of the Home and Wingham divisions of the
County of Kent - rules.
Canterbury, Goulden. n.d.
3

Provisional proposals for a measure of "poor law reform".
Deputation (including Councillor J.G.B. Stone), March
9th, 1926. Verbatim report.
London, W.G. Lewis. 1926.
3

PUCKLE, J.
Ecclesiastical sketches from the past and present of
St. Augustine's, Canterbury.
Rivington. 1849.
1,3,6 (1899),11,17

PULLE, John. (Bellman of Canterbury).
Your loyal pullman. (Bound volume of broadsides).
1745, 1748, 1749, 1750, 1751, 1752, 1754, 1755, 1756,
1757, 1758, 1759, 1760, 1761, 1762, 1765, 1767.
Canterbury.
3

PURDIE, A.B.
A pilgrim - walk in Canterbury.
London, Catholic Truth Society. 1910.
3

R.S.P.Q.
Canterbury in Roman times.
Eastes.
8,12

RAMSAY, Michael.
Canterbury described by Michael Ramsay.
c.1951.
3

REDIFFUSION TELEVISION LTD.
A tale of Canterbury with John Betjeman, script by J.
Betjeman and Peter Hunt. Broadcast on Christmas Day, 1967.
London, Rediffusion Television Ltd. 1967.
3,11

REGAL PUBLICITY SERVICE LTD.
Canterbury: what's on.
London, Regal Publicity Service Ltd., July, 1958 to date.
3

Remarks on the incidental ambiguities and false imports
attendant on the use of the auxiliary signs in the
English language.
Canterbury, Cowtan and Colegate. 1814.
3

THE REVIEW.
Parish magazine of St. Gregory the Great, Canterbury.
Kentish Gazette, January, 1948 to date.
3

RHODES.
Book of words of Mr. Rhodes, 23rd annual concert,
Canterbury. 1885.
17

RICHARDSON, Olive.
Canterbury.
Jarrold. 1962.
1,3,11

RIDGEWAY, W.
The origin and evolution of the brooch, by W. Ridgeway and
Reginald A. Smith. (Page 17, Canterbury brooches).
From the Proceedings of the Society of Antiquaries, March
22nd, 1906).
3

RIGDEN, Brian.
Canterbury weather, 1884-1897. Tables printed in the
"Canterbury Press" and "Kentish Observer".
3

RIGDEN, George.
Vital statistics of Canterbury.
Maidstone, W.H. Vale (Printer). 1858.
3

RIGG, J.M.
St. Anslem of Canterbury: a chapter in the history of
religion.
1896.
3,4,12

RILEY, Peter.
The Canterbury experimental weekend.
A.R.C. 1971.
8

ROBERTS, H.V. Molesworth.
"Anglo-Saxon zone", Canterbury. Drawing showing Anglo-Saxon
sites.
"The Builder", No. 5875, September 9th, 1955.
3

ROBINSON, C.H.
Short account of St. Augustine's Manastery, now St.
Augustine's Missionary College.
n.d.
17

(ROCH, Thomas).
Charters destructive to liberty and property demonstrated
by the principles and practices of Corporation patriots.
London, Sold by Crowder. 1776.
3

ROCH, Thomas.
Proceedings of the Corporation of Canterbury showing the
abuse of Corporation Government...printed for the author
and sold by R. Stevens, bookseller, London.
1760.
3

ROGERS, Philip George.
Battle in Bossenden Wood: the strange story of Sir
William Courtenay.
Oxford University Press. 1961.
1,3,4,5,6,7,8,11,12,15,17,18,20.

ROGERS, Tom.
The village coquette, or an Irishman's stratagem...brought
out at the Canterbury Theatre Royal, 18th and 19th June,
1884, by Tom Rogers and C. Marland Gann.
Canterbury, Cross and Jackman. 1884.
3

ROSENFELD, Sybil Marion.
A project for an iron theatre (for Canterbury). (Article in
Theatre Notebook, Vol. II, No. 1, October- December, 1956).
3

ROTH, Cecil.
The rise of provincial Jewry. (Article in The Jewish
Monthly, Vol. 2, No. 5, August, 1948).
3

ROUTLEDGE, Charles Francis.
Excavations at St. Austin's Abbey, Canterbury. II The
Church of St. Peter and St. Paul. (Reprinted from
Archaeologia Cantiana).
London, Mitchell and Hughes. 1902.
3

ROUTLEDGE, Charles Francis.
The history of St. Martin's Church, Canterbury.
1891, etc.
1,2,3,4,5,6,7,8,11,12,13,14,15,17,18

ROUTLEDGE, Charles Francis.
Roman foundations at St. Pancras, Canterbury.
n.d.
11

ROUTLEDGE, Charles Francis.
St. Augustine's Abbey and St. Martin's Church.
Canterbury Chamber of Trade. n.d.
11

ROWSELL, T. Norman.
Historic Canterbury.
S.P.C.K. 1899.
1,3,8,11,14

Royal album of Canterbury views.
Printed in Germany. n.d.
3

ROYAL ARCHAEOLOGICAL INSTITUTE OF GREAT BRITAIN AND
IRELAND.
Descriptive programme of the summer meeting, 1929 at
Canterbury.
1929.
3,7,11

ROYAL AUTOMOBILE CLUB.
What to see in Canterbury (and the surrounding country) -
a handy guide for motorists.
R.A.C. 1947?
4

ROYAL COMMISSION ON HISTORICAL MANUSCRIPTS.
Reports, 1st-9th, 1870-1884. 24th- 1960-1962.
H.M.S.O. (Dates - see above).
3

ROYAL INSTITUTE OF BRITISH ARCHITECTS.
Handbook of the British Architects' Conference,
Canterbury and Folkestone, 10th-18th June, 1953.
Canterbury, W. Heffer. 1953.
3

The Royal Museum, Canterbury.
(Article in "Folklore", Vol. 73, Autumn, 1962).
3

RULE, Martin.
The Missal of St. Augustine's Abbey, Canterbury, edited
by M. Rule.
n.d.
1,3,11,12,14,17

Saint Augustine's College.
1858.
17

ST. AUGUSTINE'S COLLEGE.
Central College of the Anglican Communion. (Prospectus
and brief history).
Church Army Press. 195-?
2

ST. AUGUSTINE'S COLLEGE.
Circulars, occasional papers.
17

ST. AUGUSTINE'S COLLEGE.
Occasional papers. Nos. 1-100 + 2 extra numbers.
233,247-9, 257, 261-8, 270-359, 361-388, 391-401,
404-5.
1853-1949.
3

ST. AUGUSTINE'S COLLEGE.
Plan and short account of the discoveries, 1913-1915.
College Occasional Papers. 1916?
8

ST. AUGUSTINE'S GAOL.
Rules, orders and regulations for the management of the
new gaol.
Canterbury, Printed Cowtan and Colegate. 1812.
3

ST. AUGUSTINE'S MISSIONARY STUDENTSHIP ASSOCIATION.
Reports, etc. for year 1887-8.
17

ST. EDMUNDS'S SCHOOL CHRONICLE.
Vol. XXIX, No. 7, Jan. 1951. Vol. XXIX, No. 7, April,
1951. Vol. XXIX, No. 9, Sept. 1951. Vol. XXXV, No. 3,
Oct. 1962. Vol. XXXVI, No. 1. Vol. XXXVI, No. 2.
Vol. XXXVI, No. 3. Vol. XXXVII, No. 4. Vol. XXXVII,
No. 5.
Canterbury.
3

ST. EDMUND'S SCHOOL.
Natural History Society reports, 1945-49.
Printed by Gibbs. (1949).
11

St. Martin's Church, Canterbury.
Northgate Press. 194-?
1,2,11

St. Martin's Church, Canterbury.
Northgate Press (Printers). 195-?
11

ST. MARTIN AND ST. PAUL'S PARISH GUIDE, CANTERBURY.
Plain manual for...Guild of the Work of Jesus Glorified.
1889.
17

St. Martin's Priory - Sale catalogue.
Folkestone, Smith-Woolley. 1960.
3

ST. MARY'S COLLEGE, CANTERBURY.
Programmes of Xmas tree entertainment, 1884.
1884.
17

St. Mildred's Church, Canterbury.
Canterbury, Printed Austen. 191-?
3,11,12

ST. STEPHEN'S COMMUNITY ASSOCIATION, CANTERBURY.
Newsletter.
March, 1967 to date.
3

St. Thomas's Church, Canterbury, 1170-1970.
Church Publishers. (1969).
11

SALTER, Emma Gurney.
Some Canterbury letters. (Extract from Contemporary Review,
May, 1951).
1951.
11

SANDYS, Charles.
An enquiry into the liability of the Corporation of
Canterbury to maintain the gaol of the City.
Canterbury, Colegate. 1828.
1,3,11,17

SANDYS, Charles.
A letter of Messrs. Kingsford Sons and Wightwick,
Solicitors, Canterbury.
1848.
1,3,11

Scheme for the management and regulation of the municipal
charities of the City and Borough of Canterbury and the
application of the income thereof; approved by order of the
High Court of Justice (Chancery Division), dated 1st Nov.,
1887.
3

SCOTT, Elizabeth.
Canterbury, the home of handweaving (leaflet).
n.d.
3

SCOTT-MONCRIEFF, Joanne.
Portrait of a city - Canterbury. (Copy of script for B.B.C.
programme).
1948.
3

SCOUTEN, Arthur H.
An early printed report on the apparition of Mrs. Veal.
(Photocopy of article in "Review of English Studies", July,
1955).
3

SCOUTEN, Arthur H.
At that moment of time: Defoe and the early accounts of the
apparition of Mistress Veal.
"Forum", Vol. II, No. 2, Winter, 1961-62.
3

SCOUTEN, Arthur H.
"The Loyal Post", a rare Queen Anne newspaper and Daniel
Defoe. (Article in Bulletin of the New York Public Library,
April, 1955, Vol. 59, No. 4).
3

SECORD, Arthur W.
A September day in Canterbury: the Veal-Bargrave story.
(Reprinted from Journal of English and Germanic
Philology, Vol. LIV, No. 4, October, 1955).
3

SENDELL. Publisher.
Canterbury almanack, 1887-92, 6 vols.
17

SHEPPARD, J. Brigstocke.
The records of Canterbury.
1882?
11

SHORT, W. Teignmonth.
Canterbury.
Black. 1907.
1,3,4,12,15,17,18

Short account of the history of St. Augustine's
Monastery and guide to St. Augustine's Missionary
College.
Canterbury, Cross and Jackman. 1893.
11

Short history and guide of St. Paul's-without-the-walls.
Church Publisher. 1964.
8

SIDEBOTHAM, J.S.
Memorials of the King's School, Canterbury.
Canterbury, Ginder. 1865.
1,3,11,17

SIDNEY COOPER SCHOOL OF ART.
Channel port: a short history of Dover.
Canterbury, College of Art Press. 1966.
3

SIDNEY COOPER SCHOOL OF ART.
Prospectus, 1893-4, 1896, 1898. Rules and byelaws,
annual report, etc., 1882-3. 1884-5, 1885-6.
17

SIDNEY COOPER SCHOOL OF (SCIENCE AND) ART.
Report, 1888-9.
17

SIMON LANGTON HIGH SCHOOL FOR GIRLS, CANTERBURY.
Prospectus and yearbook.
1894, 1896.
17

SMALL, E. Milton.
Canterbury cricket week.
1,3,6,11,17

(SMALL, E. Milton).
The Canterbury pilgrim's guide.
Canterbury, Gibbs and Son, 2nd edition. n.d.
3,17

SMALL, E. Milton.
An hour or two in old Canterbury.
Canterbury, Gibbs. 1890.
1,3

SMALL, E. Milton.
Ye Canterbury pilgrim. Ys guyde booke yu, through,
and arounde ye auncient citie.
Canterbury, Gibbs and Sons. 1889?
3,17

SMILES, Samuel.
The Huguenots, their settlements, churches in England.
(Refs. Canterbury, Greenwich).
1880.
3(1895), 18

SMITH, Charles Roach.
Roman leaden coffin discovered at Canterbury.
n.d.
11

SMITH, Reginald Anthony Lendon.
Collected papers: essays on monastic places (including
Canterbury).
London, Longmans, Green and Co. 1947.
3

SMITH, Reginald Anthony Lendon.
Early Anglo-Saxon weights. (Contains 1 page on those found
at Canterbury). (Reprinted from Antiquarian Journal, Vol.
III, No. 2, April, 1923).
3

SOMNER, William.
The antiquities of Canterbury, or a survey of that ancient
citie.
Thrale. 1640.
3(1661), 6,7,8,11,14,15,19

SOMNER, William.
The antiquities of Canterbury in two parts. The first part:
the antiquities of Canterbury...2nd edition reviewed and
enlarged by Nicolas Battely.
1703.
1,3,4,6,7,11,17

SORRELL, Alan.
Canterbury as it was in Roman times: a reconstruction of
Durovernum in the 2nd century A.D., based on excavations
made possible by the blitz of 1942. (Drawings in Illust.
London News, December 27th, 1952).
3

Souvenir album of the City of Canterbury.
Aldershot, Gale and P. 190-?
11

SPILLETT, H.C.
Rainfall for the past 20 years taken at 10 London Road,
Canterbury. (Typescript).
1954.
3

SPILLETT, P.J.
A pottery kiln site at Tyler Hill, near Canterbury, by P.J.
Spillett and others. (From Arch. Cant., Vol. 55).
Ashford, Headley. 1943?
3,11,17

The standard picture guide to Canterbury.
Dover, R. Turner. 1900.
3

Standard picture guide to Herne Bay and Canterbury.
1907.

STANLEY, Arthur Penrhyn.
Historical memorials of Canterbury.
John Murray. 1857 and other editions.
1,2,3,4,5,6,7,8,11,12,13,14,15,16,17,18,19,21

Statement of the plan and operations of Canterbury Model
Schools.
1840.
17

STORR, Francis.
Canterbury chimes, by F. Storr and Hawes Turner.
Kegan Paul. 1878.
6

Story of St. Margaret's Church, Canterbury and its
worshippers through the centuries.
Elvy. 1958.
11,12

Stranger's and visitor's companion and guide to Canterbury
and environs.
Canterbury, Goulden. 1848.
11,13

The stranger's Canterbury guide.
Canterbury, J.H. Goulden. 1888.
3

SUMMERLY, Felix.
Handbook for the City of Canterbury.
Bell. 1843.
3,8,11,17

SUMMERLY, Felix.
Felix Summerly's handbook for Canterbury with additions by
John Brent.
Canterbury, Ginder. 1860.
1,11,17

SWANN, Edward.
An artist in old Canterbury.
Charles Skilton. 1970.
4,6,7,8,11

TAYLOR, Arthur F.
The free churches of Canterbury: a sketch of their
history and of their relations to one another.
1929.
3

TAYLOR, G.R. Stirling.
The story of Canterbury.
Dent. 1912.
3,5,11,12,13,18

TAYLOR, Joseph C.
Handbook and guide to the minerals, rocks and fossils
in the Royal Museum, Canterbury.
Canterbury, Royal Museum Commission. 1947.
3

TEMPLE LODGE. NO. 558.
The Temple Lodge, No. 558 Centenary festival, 29th
January, 1949.
(1949).
7

THOMAS, Edward.
The booke of the lost beauty, by E. Thomas and E. Oram.
Minster Press. 1925.
3,11

THOMAS, Edward.
Our beautiful homeland: Canterbury, etc., by E. Thomas
and others.
1913?
4,8

THOMAS, OF ELMHAM.
Historia monasterii St. Augustini Cantuariensis, by
Thomas of Elham, formerly monk and treasurer of that
foundation.
Longmans. 1858.
3,11,12

THORNE, William.
Chronicle of St. Augustine's Abbey, Canterbury.
(Rendered into English by A.H. Davis).
Basil Blackwell. 1934.
1,3,7,11,12,13,14,17,18

THORNTON, W. Pugin.
Descriptive catalogue of two old Dutch painted and
stained windows in the Royal Museum, Canterbury.
Cross and Jackman. 1899.
12,17

THORNTON, W. Pugin.
The mangement of the Home Military Hospitals –
Canterbury Military Hospital. (Reprinted from "The
Lancet", March 30th, 1901).
3

TOC, H. (Canterbury Branch).
40th birthday celebration.
1962.
3

TONKS, Rev. Charles Frederick.
The parish church of St. George the Martyr, Canterbury.
Canterbury, Gibbs and Son. n.d.
3

TOUCHEFEU-MEYNIER, Odette.
Le grand date la sirene-poisson? (Article includes
discussion and photographs of Roman lamp in Royal
Museum). (Article in Bulletin de L'Association
Guillaume Bude, December, 1962).
3

Tower House – Sale catalogue of contents.
1936.
3

TOWN PLANNING INSTITUTE.
37th annual conference, 1963. (Includes supplement on
Canterbury with articles by John Boyle and J.L. Berbiers).
London, Town Planning Institute. 1963.
3

TOWNSEND, George.
A word of caution (or advice) against the socinian
poison of William Frend. Addressed to the inhabitants
of Canterbury.
Canterbury, Simmons and Kirkby. 1789.
3

TOWNSEND, William.
Canterbury.
Batsford. 1950.
1,2,3,4,8,9,11,12,15,18,20

TRAILL, John.
Canterbury, by John and Joan Traill.
Cheltenham, Shentons. 1955.
3,4,8

A translation of the several charters granted by Edward IV,
Henry VII, James I and Charles II to the citizens of
Canterbury.
Grove. 1791.
11,17

Translation of transcription of receiption to the Right
Worshipful the Mayor of Canterbury in the Mayor's parlour,
Rheims on Saturday, 29th March, 1958.
3

TUCKER, Alfred G.
The Quakers and their meeting houses in Canterbury.
(Reprinted from Kentish Gazette, March 23rd, 1956).
3

TURNER, G.J.
The register of St. Augustin's Abbey, Canterbury - commonly
called the black book, edited by R.J. Turner and H.E.
Salter.
n.d.
1,11,17

Twenty-four views of Canterbury and neighbourhood.
A.J. Goulden. n.d.
3

Twenty-four views of Canterbury and neighbourhood.
Matthews. c.1875.
13

UNITED KENTISH BRITONS FRIENDLY SOCIETY - CANTERBURY.
Rules, 1865.
1865.
17

UNIVERSITY OF KENT AT CANTERBURY.
Canterbury guide for the disabled.
Canterbury, University of Kent. 1971-2.
4

UNIVERSITY OF KENT AT CANTERBURY.
Canterbury campus.
New Education. 1965.
11

UNIVERSITY OF KENT AT CANTERBURY.
Foundation fund appeal (brochure).
1965.
3

UNIVERSITY OF KENT AT CANTERBURY.
Gazette, No. 2, February, 1968. (Includes presentation of
honorary M.A. degree to Frank Jenkins).
Canterbury, University of Kent.
3

UNIVERSITY OF KENT AT CANTERBURY.
Library handbook, 1966-67.
Canterbury, University of Kent. 1966.
3

UNIVERSITY OF KENT AT CANTERBURY.
Prospectus, 1965-.
3,8,12

UNIVERSITY OF KENT AT CANTERBURY.
University of Kent.
Arch. Review. 1965.
11

UNIVERSITY OF KENT.
University of Kent at Canterbury. (Kent Messenger, 11th
June, 1965).
Kent Messenger. 1965.
8

UNIVERSITY OF KENT.
University of Kent at Canterbury - handbook, 1965.
Canterbury, University of Kent. 1965.
7,14

UNIVERSITY OF KENT.
Unjustified. (Magazine of the University).
Canterbury, University of Kent. 1966.
3

URRY, William.
Boots, Mercery Lane, Canterbury.
1950?
3

URRY, William.
The buttermarket. (Typescript).
(1948).
3

(URRY, William).
Canterbury and the Crown: a companion to a walk round
the exhibition held in the Royal Museum, Canterbury in
Coronation Year, 1953.
Canterbury Corporation.
3

URRY, William.
Canterbury au temps de Saint Thomas Becket. (Article
in Archaeologia Tresors des Ages, October, 1966).
3

URRY, William.
Canterbury in the first Elizabeth period (guide to
exhibition in Royal Museum, 14th July-20th September,
1952).
Canterbury Corporation. 1952.
3

URRY, William.
Canterbury mayoral quincentenary, text by William Urry,
edited by Frank Higenbottam.
Canterbury, Jennings. 1948.
3

URRY, William.
Canterbury under the Angevin Kings.
Athlone Press. 1967.
1,2,3,4,7,11,12,15

URRY, William.
The Normans in Canterbury.
Canterbury Archaeological Society. 1959.
1,2,3,4,6,7,8,11

URRY, William.
The Normans in Canterbury. Substantially a paper read
at the Anglo-French Historical Conference, Caen, July
1957.
Annales De Normandie, 8 Annee, No. 2, May, 1958.
3

URRY, William.
Pictorial guide to Canterbury Cathedral.
Willett. 1950.
7,11

VALENTINE AND SONS LTD. Publishers.
Grand photographic view album of Canterbury.
Valentine. 19--?
11

The vanished gates of Canterbury. (Illustrations only).
n.d.
4

VICKERS, John A.
The story of Canterbury Methodism, 1750-1961.
Canterbury, Holme. 1961.
3,4,6(1970),7,11,12

Victoria coronation festival. Report of the proceedings
of a dinner held at the Castle Tavern, Canterbury on
Wednesday, July 25th, 1838.
Canterbury, C. Marten. 1838.
3

Views of ancient buildings selected by the Museum
Committee. (Volume of photographs of Canterbury).
1886.
3

Views of Canterbury.
John Secra, Bookseller. n.d.
3

Volume of engravings and cuttings relating to Canterbury.
3

WACHER, Harold.
A medical history of the City of Canterbury being a thesis
for the degree of M.D. of Cambridge University.
1928.
3

WADDAMS, Herbert Montague.
The pictorial history of Canterbury.
Pitkin Pictorials. 1968.
1,3,8,11

WADDAMS, Herbert Montague.
The pictorial history of Canterbury (new edition).
Pitkin Pictorials. 1971.
11

WALCOTT, Mackenzie E.C.
Memorials of Canterbury.
Canterbury, Drury. 1868.
1,3,11,12,17

WALCOTT, Mackenzie E.C.
Vestiges of St. Augustine's Abbey.
1879.
3

WALL, J. Charles.
The four shrines of St. Thomas at Canterbury.
Talbot. 1932.
1

WANSTALL, Benjamin.
A brief memoir of the life of Benjamin Wanstall who was
tried at St. Augustines, on Wednesday, 29th June, 1831 on a
charge of stealing furniture from Mrs. Frances Still Dower
at St. Thomas' Hill, Canterbury.
Canterbury, Henry Ward. 1831.
3

WARD, Henry Publisher.
Ward's Canterbury guide.
6(1843), 17(1841)

WARD, Henry Publisher.
Ward's Canterbury guide. (Containing a concise account of
whatever is curious or worthy of observation in and about
that ancient City and its suburbs, 10th edition).
Henry Ward. 1847.
11,17

WARD, Henry Publisher.
Canterbury guide, 12th edition.
Henry Ward. c.1850.
6,13

WARWICK, P.H.
Canterbury - some town planning problems. (Article in
Journal of the Town Planning Institute, Vol. XI, No. 12, 1925).
3

WATSON, Francis.
Daniel Defoe.
London, Longmans, Green. 1952.
3

WATSON, R.J.
Presbyterian Canterbury. (Article in Journal of the
Presbyterian Historical Society of England, Vol. XIII, No. 4,
May, 1967).
3

"Weavers" House, A.D. 1500. King's Bridge, Canterbury.
3

WEBSTER, Graham.
A Roman pottery kiln at Canterbury, by G. Webster and others.
Ashford, Headley. 194-?
11,17

WELBY, Mrs.
Canterbury Catch Club: a description copied from a
manuscript by Mr. Welby, 1875. In The Music Student,
edited by Percy S. Scholes.
Vol. XII, No. 8, pp. 468-469. 1920.
3

WEST, Rebecca.
St. Augustine.
Davies. 1933.
12

WEST, Richard.
Canterbury. (Article in Time and Tide, 22nd June, 1961).
3

Westgate Prison: a Canterbury story.
1773.
17

WETHERELT, Alexander.
Churches round Canterbury, compiled by A. Wetherelt in
1883. (Collection of mounted photographs).
3

WETHERELT, Alexander.
Maisons around Canterbury, compiled by A. Wetherelt
in 1883. (Collection of mounted photographs).
3

WHATMORE, Leonard E.
The sermon against the holy maid of Kent and her
adherents, delivered at St. Paul's Cross and Canterbury,
1533, edited by L.E. Whatmore. (Article in The English
Historical Review, Vol. LVIII, No. 232, October, 1943).
3

WHEELER, Clifford.
The light of the world, or the complete paradise
regained.
Canterbury, 13 St. Peter's Street, Canterbury. 1924.
8

THE WHIM.
A periodical paper by a society of gentlemen, Nos. 1-11,
Monday, December 31st, 1810 - Monday, May 20th, 1811.
Canterbury, Rouse, Kirkby and Lawrence.
3

WHITING, William.
A Roman cemetry at St. Martin's Hill, Canterbury, by
W. Whiting and H.T. Mead. (Reprinted from Archaeologia
Cantiana, Vol. 140).
Maison Dieu Museum, Faversham.
3,12,17

The Wilderness - Sale catalogue.
Folkestone, Smith-Woolley.
3

(WILKINSON, John Eric).
St. Martin's Church, Canterbury.
Canterbury, Northgate Press. 1948?
3

WILLETT, Charles.
See Canterbury in a day.
Cinque Ports.
3,8,11

WILLIAM OF MALMESBURY.
The Historia Novella, Canterbury.
Nelson. 1955.
12

William Somerset Maugham, with a list of his works.
London, Heinemann. 1954.
3

WILLIAMS, Audrey.
An account of excavations...September-October, 1944.
(Roman Canterbury No. 2 - Reprinted from Archaeologia
Cantiana, Vol. 59,1946).
Medici. 1947.
2,3,6,17

WILLIAMS, Audrey.
An account of the excavations...during 1945. (Roman
Canterbury No. 3 - Reprinted from Archaeologia Cantiana,
Vol. 60, 1947).
Medici. 1948.
2,3,6,17

WILLIAMS, Audrey.
Roman Canterbury. (Reprinted from Archaeologia Cantiana).
Medici Society. 1944.
1,11

WILLIAMS Audrey.
Roman Canterbury: an account of excavations in Butchery
Lane, Christmas, 1945 and Easter, 1946 - No. 4, by A.
Williams and S. Frere. (Reprinted from Archaeologia
Cantiana).
London, Medici Society. 1949.
1,2,3,6,11,17,21

WILLIAMSON, Catherine Ellis.
Though the streets burn (Canterbury).
Headley. 1949.
1,3,4,6,7,11,12,17

WILSON, S. Gordon.
The pageant book of Canterbury through the ages.
Canterbury, Kent Herald. 1930.
3

WILSON, S. Gordon.
Short history...of the old Pilgrims' Hospital of St. Thomas
the Martyr, Eastbridge, Canterbury.
S.P.C.K. n.d.
3,7,11

WINTER, William.
Shakespeare's England. A glimpse of Canterbury. In
"Shakespeare's England", page 234 by the above.
London, Foulis. 1923.
3

WOOD, Elizabeth.
Brief outline of the Canterbury reform festival.
1832.
17

WOOD, Susan.
English monasteries and their patrons in the thirteenth
century. (Includes Canterbury).
London, Oxford University Press. 1955.
3

WOODCOCK, Audrey M.
Cartulary of the Priory of St. Gregory, Canterbury, edited
for the Royal Historical Society by Audrey M. Woodcock.
Royal Historical Society. 1956.
3,4,8,11,12,18

WOODRUFF, Charles Everleigh.
The register and chartulary of the hospital of St. Lawrence,
Canterbury. (Reprinted from Archaeologia Cantiana, Vol. 1).
Ashford, Headley Bros. n.d.
3

WOODRUFF, Charles Everleigh.
Schola regia Cantuariensis, by C.E. Woodruff and H.J. Cape.
King's School, Canterbury. 1908.
1,3,4,6,8,11,12,14,17

WOTTON, Sir Henry.
The characters of Robert Devereux and George Villiers, Duke
of Buckingham.
Kent, Printed at the Private Press of Lee Priory. 1814.
18

WRIGHT, Thomas.
The archaeological album, or museum of national antiquities,
edited by T. Wright. (Contains an account of a meeting at
Canterbury).
Chapman and Hall. 1845.
3,12

WRIGHT, Thomas.
The life of Daniel Defoe.
London, Cassell. 1894.
3

WRIGHT, Thomas.
Observations on the municipal archives of the City of
Canterbury. (From Archaeologia, Vol. XXXI).
London, Printed by J.B. Nichols and Son. 1844.
3,17

YOUNG WOMEN'S CHRISTIAN ASSOCIATION.
Queen Elizabeth Club for Girls, 22 St. George's Street,
Canterbury. Annual report, 1927-8.
Kentish Gazette. 1928.
3

YOUNGMAN, E. Publisher.
Drawings of St. Martin's Church, Canterbury.
Canterbury, Youngman and Son. 192-?
2,3

YOUNGMAN, E.
St. Martin's Church, Canterbury.
Canterbury, Stevens. n.d.
11,14

CANTERBURY CATHEDRAL

An accurate description and history of the Metropolitan
and Cathedral churches of Canterbury and York, from their
first foundation to the present year.
W. Sandby. 1755.
1,11,13,15

ALFORD, Henry.
Life journals and letters of Henry Alford, late Dean
of Canterbury, edited by his widow.
Rivington, 2nd edition. 1873.
3

"ALL THE YEAR ROUND" (Extract).
English Cathedrals: Canterbury.
1865.
17

ASSOCIATION OF MEN OF KENT AND KENTISH MENT.
An illustrated souvenir for the occasion of the placing
of the battle-torn flags of H.M.S. 'Kent' in Canterbury
Cathedral, 1st July, 1916.
Association of Men of Kent and Kentish Men.
9

BABINGTON, Margaret Agnes.
Canterbury Cathedral, illustrated.
Toronto, Dent. 1933, etc.
1,3,5,6,8,10,11,12,14,15

BABINGTON, Margaret Agnes.
The romance of Canterbury Cathedral.
Canterbury, Tuck. 1932, etc.
1,2,3,4,5,6(1945), 7,8,11,12,13,14,15,17

BAILEY, Derrick Sherwin.
Thomas Bacon and the reformation of the church in
England. (Bacon was a Canon of Canterbury Cathedral).
Oliver and Boyd. 1952.
3

BAKER, John.
English stained glass.
Thames and Hudson. 1960.
3

BARTLETT, Thomas.
Sermon preached in the Cathedral Church of Canterbury,
1832.
Canterbury, Ward. 1832.
11

BEAZELEY, M.
The Canterbury bones.
Headley Bros. n.d.
1,3,6

BEAZELEY, M.
History of the chapter library of Canterbury Cathedral.
Beazeley. 1907.
3,12

BEAZELEY, M.
"On certain human remains found in the crypt of
Canterbury Cathedral Church and supposed by some to be
those of Archbishop Becket". (From the Proceedings of
Society of Antiquaries, 25 XXII, 15. December 5th,
1907).
Society of Antiquaries. 1907.
3

BECCATELLI, Lodovico. Archbishop of Ragusa.
The life of Cardinal Reginald Pole...translated into
English to which is added an appendix, by the Rev.
Benjamin Pye.
Bathurst. 1766.
3

BELL, GEORGE AND SONS. Publishers.
The Cathedral Church of Canterbury.
Bell. 1896.
8

BERKELEY, George. Vice-Dean of Canterbury.
The danger of violent innovations in the state...a
sermon preached at the Cathedral and Metropolitical
Church of Christ, Canterbury on Monday, January 31st,
1785.
Canterbury, Printed and Sold by Simmons and Kirkby.
1785.
3

(BIBLIOTHECA TOPOGRAPHICA BIRTANNICA).
List of the manorial houses which formerly belonged to the
see of Canterbury.
(Printed by J. Nichols). 1787.
11

BINYON, Laurence.
The young King: a play. Acting edition arranged by
Eileen Thorndike for presentation in the Chapter House,
Canterbury Cathedral, 9th to 16th June, 1934.
Canterbury, Goulden. 1934.
3

BISHOP, Terence Alan Martyn.
Facsimiles of English Royal Writs to A.D. 1100 presented to
Vivian Hunter Galbraith, edited by T.A.M. Bishop and P.
Chaplas.
Oxford University Press. 1957.
3

The black and white concise Canterbury and Cathedral guide.
(Under Canterbury).
Stevens. 195-?
3

BLAKE, Philip Haslewood.
Christ Church Gate, Canterbury Cathedral.
Phillimore. 1965.
3,4,6,8,11,12

BLORE, W.P.
Recent discoveries in the archives of Canterbury Cathedral.
In Archaeologia Cantiana, Vol. 58, 1945.
17

BORENIUS, Tancred.
The iconography of St. Thomas of Canterbury.
Society of Antiquaries. 1929.
12

BORENIUS, Tancred.
St. Thomas Becket in art.
Methuen. 1932.
3,6,12

BOX, Ernest George.
Donations of manors to Christ Church, Canterbury.
1932.
16,17

Brief account of Cathedral and Collegiate Schools,
(Canterbury)with an abstract of their statutes and
endowments.
1824.
17

BRIGHT, William.
Chapters of early English church history.
Oxford University Press. 1878.
3

BRITISH RECORD SOCIETY.
Index to the Act books of the Archbishops of Canterbury,
1663-1859.
British Record Society. n.d.
11

BRITTON, John.
History and antiquities of the Metropolitan Church of
Canterbury.
1821, etc.
1,3,4,6,8,11,12,14,15,17

BROMLEY, Francis E.
Note on the corona of St. Thomas of Canterbury. In
Archaeologia Cantiana, Vol. 46, 1934.
17

BROMLEY, Francis E.
History of Canterbury Cathedral. MS. notes.
3

The building of Canterbury Cathedral. (Article from the
English Illustrated Magazine).
English Illustrated Magazine. n.d.
3

BUMPUS, Thomas Francis.
Canterbury Cathedral.
Laurie. n.d.
11,17 (1910)

BURNBY, John.
An historical description of the Metropolitical Church
of Christ, Canterbury.
Simmons and Kirkby. 1783.
1,3(1772), 8,11,17

Canterbury: 19th annual conference of clergy and
laity, 1894.
Canterbury, Gibbs.
11

Canterbury: the case of the minor canons...particularly
with reference to Canterbury.
Canterbury, Ward. 1839.
3,11

Canterbury Cathedral: extracts from ancient documents
relating to the Cathedral and precincts of Canterbury.
Mitchell and Hughes. 1887.
3,11,17

Canterbury Cathedral: an historical description of the
Cathedral and Metropolitan Church of Christ, Canterbury.
Canterbury, Smith. 1772.
11

Canterbury - Cathedral Church of Christ. The statutes
and other documents.
Privately Printed. 1925.
1,11

Canterbury Cathedral festival of commemoration, 7th-
14th June, 1930. Catalogue of the exhibition of
treasures in the Cathedral library.
Printed, Butler and Tanner.(1930).
1,3

CANTERBURY CATHEDRAL.
Guide.
Thanet Advertiser. n.d.
11

CANTERBURY CATHEDRAL.
Guide.
Jennings, Printers. c.1860.
2

CANTERBURY CATHEDRAL.
Guide.
Margate, Central Press. 1931.
11

CANTERBURY CATHEDRAL.
Illustrated views.
Canterbury, Ward. 1836.
10

Canterbury Cathedral Old Choristers' Association, 1st-
5th annual reports, 1911-1915.
3(3rd. 1913 only), 11

Canterbury Diocesan Calendar.
Church Printing Co.
3(1869-1927 incomplete), 7(1899-1904), 11(1895), 12(1866-
1923)

Canterbury Diocesan Choral Union - canticles etc.,
for festivals.
1862-1889.
17

Canterbury Diocesan Church. Building and Endowment
Society, annual reports for 1887 (23) and 1889 (25).
17

Canterbury Diocesan Clergy - list and church calendar,
1895-1900, 6 vols.
Church Printing Co. 1895-1900.
12

Canterbury Diocesan Clergy - list and directory for
1938-9(11), 1946-7(7).

Canterbury Diocesan Directory.
1847-48 (8)
1931-32 (3)
1936-37 (3)
1947-48 (3,11)
1948-49 (3,7,11)
1949-50 (3,11)
1950-51 (3,7,11)
1951-52 (3,6,11)
1952-53 (3,6,7,8)
1953-54 (3,6,7,8)
1954-57 (3,4,6,7,11)
1957-60 (4,7,8,11,12)
1960-61 (7,12)
1963-66 (12)
1966-69 (4,7,12)
1971-72 (4,11)
1972-73 (3,11)

Canterbury Diocesan Directory - Supplement.
1956-57 (11)
1958-59 (3)
1959-60 (3,7,8)
1960-61 (3)
1962-63 (3,7,11,12)
1964-65 (3)
1967-68 (3,11,12)
1968-69 (7,11,12)
1969-70 (11)
1970-71 (11)

Canterbury Diocesan Handbook (1962).
(1962).
3,7

Canterbury Diocesan Yearbook, 1937.
Canterbury Gibbs. 1938.
11

Canterbury Diocesan Yearbook, 1951.
Canterbury, Gibbs. 1952?
8

The Canterbury Psalter, with an introduction by M.R. James.
(Printed for the Friends of Canterbury Cathedral by
P. Lund Humphries and Co., London. 1935).
3,11,13

Canterbury rhymes, suggested by passages in the liturgy
and lessons.
E. Churton. 1847.
3

CAROE, William Douglas.
Canterbury Cathedral.
Oxford University Press. 1925.
3,8,11

CAROE, William Douglas.
Canterbury Cathedral choir during the commonwealth and
after. (From Archaeologia, Vol. LXII).
Oxford Society of Antiquaries. 1911.
1,3

CAROE, William Douglas.
Wall paintings in the Infirmary Chapel, Canterbury
Cathedral. (From Archaeologia, Vol. LXIII).
Oxford Society of Antiquaries. 1912.
3

CAROE, William Douglas.
The water tower. (Reprinted from "Report of Friends of
Canterbury Cathedral", 1929).
Cambridge. 1929.
1,3,4,14

The Cathedral and Metropolitan Church of Canterbury - a
handbook for pilgrims.
Gibbs, 1938, etc.
1,3,4,7,8,11,12

The Cathedral and Metropolitan Church of Christ,
Canterbury.
Central Press. 1931.
11

Cathedral and Metropolitan Church of Christ, Canterbury.
Kent Messenger. 1931, etc.
6,8,11,12

Cathedral Church of Canterbury.
Bell. 1896.
11,18

Canterbury Church of Christ, Canterbury: notes on
the cloister shields.
1936.
4

Cathedral Church of Christ, Canterbury: notes on the
old glass.
Gibbs. 1931.
4,12

CAVE, C.J.P.
The roof bosses of the Cathedral Church of Christ,
Canterbury. (Canterbury Papers No. 4).
Friends of Canterbury Cathedral. 1934.
1,3,4,11,12

CHALKLIN, Christopher William.
Compton census of 1676...the Dioceses of Rochester and
Canterbury.
K.A.S. 1960.
11

CHAPPELOW, Eric Barry Wilfred.
Mater angliae - poem.
British Authors Press. (1947).
3,17

CHARTRAIRE, E.
The Cathedral of Sens: Sens and Canterbury.
(Translated from French by Mme. Monthaye-Bremonde).
Paris, Henri Laurens. 1926.
3

Christ Church or Holy Trinity Cathedral and Monastery of
Benedictines in Canterbury. (pp 81-152 of unidentified
volume).
n.d.
3

Christ Church Gateway, Canterbury.
Canterbury, Printed by J.A. Jennings. 1931.
3

CHRIST CHURCH MONASTERY LIBRARY.
Catalogue of the books, both manuscript and printed, which
are preserved in the library of Christ Church, Canterbury.
1802.
1

CHURCH INFORMATION OFFICE.
The Archbishop of Canterbury's enthronement: background
notes on Canterbury Cathedral service, June 26th, 1961.
(Typescript).
3

CHURCH OF ENGLAND LITERARY ASSOCIATION.
The laws relating to the Institution with a catalogue...
of the library.
Canterbury, Church of England Literary Assocation. 1856.
3

CHURCHILL, Irene Josephine.
Canterbury administration.
S.P.C.K. 1933.
1,11,17

CLAY, Rotha Mary.
The hermits and archorites of England.
Methuen. 1914.
3

COCKS, Thomas.
The diary of Thomas Cocks, March 25th, 1607 to December 31st,
1610, edited by J. Meadows Cowper (auditor to Dean and
Chapter).
Canterbury, Cross and Jackman. 1901.
3,11

COLBOURNE, A.F. Photographer.
Deans of Canterbury.
Colbourne. c.1895.
3

COLE, James.
The ichnography or plan of the Cathedral Church of
Canterbury.
1726.
3

A collection of anthems performed in the Cathedral of
Canterbury.
Canterbury, Printed by Rouse, Kirkby and Lawrence. 1823.
3

COOK, George Henry.
Portrait of Canterbury Cathedral.
Phoenix House. 1949.
1,3,4,5,6,7,9,11,12,14

COOK, George Henry.
Mediaeval chantries and chantry chapels.
Phoenix House. 1948.
3

CORNER, John.
Canterbury Cathedral: a book of pictures. (Editor, John
Corner - photographs, John Moody).
Canterbury, Dean and Chapter. 1948.
3

CORNWALLIS, James Dean of Canterbury.
A sermon preached in the Cathedral and Metropolitan Church
of Christ, Friday, February 4th, 1780.
Canterbury, Printed by Simmons and Kirkby. 1780.
3

CORYN, M.
The Black Prince, 1330-1376.
Arthur Barker. 1934.
3

COTTON, Charles.
Notes on the documents in the Cathedral Library at
Canterbury relating to the Grey Friars.
c.1922.
3

COTTON, Charles.
Of the burning and repair of the church of Canterbury,
1174, from the Latin of Gervase, edited by C. Cotton.
(Canterbury Papers No. 3).
Cambridge University Press. 1930.
7

COTTON, Charles.
The Saxon Cathedral at Canterbury and the Saxon Saints
buried therein.
Manchester University Press. 1929.
1,3,4,6,7,8,11,12,13,14,15,17

COWLES, Frederick.
Dust of years. (Chapter 3, The Road to Canterbury).
Sands. 1933.
3

COWPER, Joseph Meadows.
Colonel Frederick Mackeson. (Extracted from "Memorial
inscriptions in Canterbury Cathedral", by W. Pugin
Thornton).
3

COWPER, Joseph Meadows.
The lives of the Deans of Canterbury, 1541-1900.
Canterbury, Cross and Jackman. 1900.
1,3,4,6,8,11,12,15

COWPER, Joseph Meadows.
The memorial inscriptions of the Cathedral Church of
Canterbury, edited by J.M. Cowper.
Canterbury, **Priva**tely Printed. 1897.
3,11,12

C.(rum), J.M.C.
Notes on the old glass of the Canterbury Church of Christ,
Canterbury.
Canterbury, Gibbs. 1931.
1,3,4,11

CULMER, Richard - the elder.
Dean and chapter newes from Canterbury.
Cotes. 1649.
11

CULMER, Richard - the younger.
Cathedral newes from Canterbury.
Cotes. 1644.
3,7

CULMER, Richard - the younger.
A parish looking-glasses for persecutors of ministers.
Printed for Abraham Miller. 1657.
11

DANKS, William.
The gospel of consolation: University and Cathedral
sermons.
Longmans, Green. 1917.
3

DART, James.
History and antiquities of the Cathedral Church of
Canterbury.
1726, etc.
1,3,4,7,8,11,12,14,15,17

DAVIES, N.J.
Canterbury Cathedral: history of the bells. In"Bells
and Bellringing", Vol. 1, No. 1, May, 1966.
3,4

DENMAN, John L.
Canterbury Cathedral Library: ac**coun**t of the building.
Friends of Canterbury Cathedral. 1954.
4,8,11

Descriptive account of the Cathedral Church of Canterbury
Canterbury, Ward. 1839, etc.
1,3,6,7,11,12,13

DICKINSON, Patric.
A durable fire: a play.
Chatto and Windus. 1962.
3

DONKIN, J.
The capitals in the crypt of Canterbury Cathedral.
Published by Author. 189-?
11

DOUGLAS, David C.
Domesday Monachorum of Christ Church, Canterbury, edited ⟩
D.C. Douglas.
Royal Historical Society. 1944.
1,2,3,8,11,12

DOWSE, I.R.
The pilgrim shrines of England.
The Faith Press. 1963.
15

DUNCOMBE, John.
An elegy written in Canterbury Cathedral.
Dodsley. 1778.
3,6,11·

DUNCOMBE, John.
An historical description of the Metropolitan Church of
Christ, Canterbury.
1783.
3,11,12

DUNKIN, Alfred John.
Canterbury Cathedral, edited by A.J. Dunkin.
Smith. 1851.
12

DUNKIN, Alfred John.
The monk Gervase's account of the descruction and rebuildi⟩
of Canterbury Cathedral, A.D. 1174, edited by A.J. Dunkin
J. Russell-Smith, Soho. 1851.
5

ELHAM, Charles C.
Medieval mason's marks. In Stone Trades Journal, Vol.
XLIX, No. 5. 1929.
3

ERASMUS, Desiderius.
The adages of Erasmus.
C.J.P. 1964.
12

ERASMUS, Desiderius.
Twenty select colloquies.
Chapmann, Dodd. n.d.
12

Extracts from ancient documents relating to the Cathedral
and precincts of Canterbury.
London, Mitchell and Hughes. 1881.
3

FAIRBAIRNS, Arnold.
Portfolio of English Cathedrals with historical and
architectural notes - Canterbury.
Review of Reviews Office.·n.d.
3,15

FAIRBAIRNS, Arnold.
Sketch of Canterbury Cathedral. n.d.
11

FAIRBAIRNS, W.H.
Canterbury. (Notes on the Cathedral series).
S.P.C.K. n.d.
11

FARRAR, Frederic William.
The Cathedral (Canterbury).
Canterbury Chamber of Trade. 1906?
1,4,11

FARRAR, Reginald.
The life of Frederic William Farrar, sometime Dean of
Canterbury.
London, James Nisbet. 1904.
4,12

FELLOWS, Edward.
Correspondence between the very Rev. Henry Alford...
and the Rev. Edward(Teaswso). In pamphlets relating
to Canterbury.
17

FELTON, Herbert.
Canterbury Cathedral.
Jarrold. n.d.
1,3,11

FIELD, Thomas.
Canterbury: the Cathedral Church of Christ, by T.
Field and C. Routledge.
Canterbury, Crow. 1893.
1,3,8,11,12,13,17

FOX, John.
Acts and monuments of matters special and memorial,
happening in the Church; with a universal history of
the same.
London, Printed for Stationers Company. 1684.
3

FOX, John.
The book of martyrs...with notes and an appendix by the
Rev. William Bramley-Moore.
London, Cassell, Petter and Galpin. (1867).
3

FREMANTLE, W.H.
Canterbury Cathedral.
Isbister and Co. 1897.
3,8,11,13,17

FRIENDS OF CANTERBURY CATHEDRAL.
Annual Reports.
1 (1928-32,1933-37,1938-44,1945-47,Index 1945-49,
    1967,1968,1971,1972 - in progress)
4 (1928 - in progress)
8 (1928 - in progress)
10 (Current copy only)
11 (1971)
12 (1928 - in progress: 1967,1973 missing)
16 (1932-36)

FRIENDS OF CANTERBURY CATHEDRAL.
Chough: a magazine for youth members. No. 1, 1961-
No. 13, 1967.
Canterbury, Friends of Canterbury Cathedral. 1961-67.
4

FRIENDS OF CANTERBURY CATHEDRAL.
Record of the Royal visit on 11th July, 1946, festival
day of The Friends.
Canterbury, Friends of Canterbury Cathedral. 1946.
4,11

FRITH, Francis. _Photographer_.
Photo-pictures (of Canterbury Cathedral) selected from
the Universal series.
17

FRY, Christopher.
Curtmantle.
London, Oxford University Press. 1961.
3

FRY, Christopher.
Thor: with angels...acting edition for the Festival of
The Friends of Canterbury Cathedral.
Canterbury, Goulden Ltd. 1948.
3

GARDINER, _Mrs_. Dorothy.
Cathedral and Metropolitan Church of Christ, Canterbury.
Maidstone, Kent Messenger Office. 1931.
3

GARDINER, _Mrs_. Dorothy.
Recent discoveries in the archives of Canterbury
Cathedral. (Reprinted from Archaeologia Cantiana).
Ashford, Headley.
11,17

GEM, R.H.D.
The Anglo-Saxon Cathedral Church at Canterbury - a
further contribution. (Reprinted from The Archaeological
Journal).
Royal Archaeological Institution. 1971.
4

GERVASE, _of Canterbury_.
Of the burning and repair of the Church of Canterbury, 1174.
Cambridge University Press. 1937.
1,3(1851), 4,11

GILBERT, E.C.
The date of the late Saxon Cathedral at Canterbury.
(Reprinted from The Archaeological Journal).
Royal Archaeological Institution. 1971.
4

GITTINGS, Robert.
Makers of violence: a play in two acts, commissioned by
Friends of Canterbury Cathedral for the festival of 1951.
London, Heinemann. 1951.
3,17

GRIFFIN, Ralph.
The heraldry in the cloisters of the Cathedral Church of
Christ at Canterbury. (From Archaeologia, Vol. LXVI).
1915.
3,7

HADFIELD, Charles.
On the history of the rebuilding of the choir of Canterbury
Cathedral.
1877.
3

Handbook to the Cathedrals of England: Southern division,
Part II, Canterbury, Rochester, etc.
J. Murray. 1876.
1,12(1861)

HARDCASTLE, Edward Hoare.
Memories of a mediocrity.
Canterbury, Gibbs. n.d.
3,11

HARRISON, Benjamin.
Patient waiting: sermons preached in Canterbury Cathedral.
London, Rivingstone. 1889.
3

HARVEY, Sidney W.
The organs of Canterbury Cathedral. (Article in "The Organ",
No. 9, Vol. III, July, 1923).
3

HARVEY, Sidney W.
A short history of the organs of Canterbury Cathedral.
London, Novello. 1916.
3,11

HASSELL, Christopher.
Christ's comet: play produced at 1938 Cathedral Festival.
London, Heinemann. 1937.
3

HAYNES, Dagmar.
Ervin Bossanyi: the splendour of stained glass.
Canterbury, Friends of Canterbury Cathedral. 1965.
3,4,21

HEATH, Sidney.
Our homeland cathedrals, Vol. II. The cathedrals of the
South, East and West of England, by S. Heath and P. Rons.
Homeland Association. n.d.
8

HENDERSON, Arthur E.
Canterbury Cathedral then and now.
S.P.C.K. 1938.
1,3,4,8,11,12,13,15

HER MAJESTY'S COMMISSIONER FOR INQUIRING INTO THE
CONDITION OF CATHEDRAL CHURCHES IN ENGLAND AND WALES.
Report...upon the Cathedral...of Canterbury...
Eyre and Spottiswoode for H.M.S.O. 1884.
8

HESELTINE, W.
Tenant's statement of the conduct of the Dean and Chapter
of Canterbury.
1839.
17

HIGENBOTTAM, Frank.
The heraldry of Christ Church gateway (notes).
3

HILDYARD, J. _Publisher_.
An accurate description and history of the churches of
Canterbury and York.
1755.
17

HILL, Derek Ingram.
Stained glass of Canterbury Cathedral.
Canterbury, Friends of Canterbury Cathedral. 1963.
3,4,8,11,12,15,19

HOLE, Christina.
English shrines and sanctuaries.
London, Batsford. 1954.
3

HOPE, Sir William Henry St. John.
(Vetusta monumenta, Vol. 7, Part 1). On the tomb of an
archbishop recently opened in the Cathedral Church of
Canterbury. (Society of Antiquaries).
Nichols. 1893.
1,11

HORNE, Dr. George. (Dean of Canterbury).
Character of true wisdom and the means of attaining it, a
sermon.
Oxford, Princes Cooke. 1784.
3

HORNE, Dr. George. (Dean of Canterbury).
Sunday schools.
Oxford, Clarendon Press. 1786.
3

HUMPHERY-SMITH, Cecil Raymond.
The Christ Church gateway. (Article in "The Coat of Arms",
Vol. IV, No. 27, July, 1956).
3

HUMPHERY-SMITH, Cecil Raymond.
Heraldry in Canterbury Cathedral.
Canterbury, Friends of Canterbury Cathedral. 1961.
1,3,4,8,11,12

HUMPHERY-SMITH, Cecil Raymond.
Studies in the heraldry of Canterbury Cathedral.
East Knoyle Heraldry Society. (1954).
3,12,21

Illustrative views of the Metropolitan Cathedral Church of
Canterbury.
Canterbury, Ward. 1835.
1,6

IRVING, Laurence.
The Canterbury adventure: an account of the inception and
growth of The Friends of Canterbury Cathedral, 1928-1959.
(Canterbury papers 10).
Canterbury, Friends of Canterbury Cathedral. 1959.
2,3,4,8,11,12,21

JACOB, Ernest Fraser.
The Archbishop's testamentary jurisdiction, 1960. (In
Canterbury Abps of Mediaeval records of the Archbishops
of Canterbury, 1962).
4

JACOB, Ernest Fraser.
The medieval register of Canterbury and York.
St. Anthony's Press. 1953.
1,3,4,8,11

JACOB, Ernest Fraser.
Register of Henry Chichele, 1414-1443, 4 vols.
Canterbury and York Society. 1937-1947.
1,3,11

JAMES, John.
The survey and demand for dilapidations in the archiepiscopal
see of Canterbury justified.
1717.
14,17

JASPER, Ronald Claud Dudley.
George Bell, Bishop of Chichester. (Dean of Canterbury)
London, Oxford University Press. 1967.
3

JENNER, Sir Herbert.
Sentence pronounced by the Judge, Sir Herbert Jenner in 1836
in a cause of John Batnes against Louisa Mansel.
Clowes. 1836.
12

JENNINGS, W. Publisher.
Guide to Canterbury Cathedral.
1858.
17

KENT ARCHAEOLOGICAL SOCIETY.
Calendar of institutions by the chapter of Canterbury sede
vacante. (Kent Records, Vol. 8).
Canterbury, Gibbs. 1924.
4,8,10,17,18

KENTISH GAZETTE AND CANTERBURY PRESS.
Interesting military ceremony at Canterbury Cathedral.
The Buffs colours deposited in the Warrior's Chapel.
(Reprinted from Kentish Gazette and Canterbury Press,
October 15th, 1892).
3

KENTISH GAZETTE AND CANTERBURY PRESS.
Map of the bombing of Canterbury Cathedral...compiled
to 30th September, 1944.
Kentish Gazette and Canterbury Press. 1944.
3

KERSHAW, S. Wayland.
Refugee inscriptions in Cathedral and churches of
Canterbury.
1892.
7

KING, Richard John.
Handbook to the Cathedrals of England. Southern
division, Parts 1 and 2. (Under Rochester Cathedral).
1876.
8

LEE, Laurie.
Peasants' priest: a play. Acting edition for the
festival of The Friends of Canterbury Cathedral, 1947.
Canterbury, H.J. Goulden. 1952.
1

LEGG, J. Wickham.
Inventories of Christchurch, Canterbury, edited by
J.W. Legg and W.H. St. John Hope.
Constable. 1902.
1,3,4,8,11,12,15,17

LOFTIE, W.J.
Memorials of J.G. Godfrey-Faussett.
London, Parker and Co. 1878.
3

LOFTIE, W.J.
Notes on the early glass in Canterbury Cathedral.
Headley. 1871.
12

LORD, Mrs. Freisen.
Tales from Canterbury Cathedral - told to the children.
Sampson, Low. 1897.
1,3,7,8,11,15,17

LYALL, William Rowe.
Short account of life of the very Rev. W.R. Lyall,
Dean of Canterbury.
1857.
17

MACLEAR, George Frederick.
An introduction to the Articles of the Church of
England.
London, Macmillan and Co. 1895.
3

MANN, Sir James.
The funeral achievements of Edward the Black Prince,
3rd edition, revised.
(1951).
4

MASON, Arthur James.
A guide to the ancient glass in Canterbury Cathedral.
Canterbury, Goulden. 1925.
1,2,3,4,6,8,11,12

MASON, Arthur James.
What became of the bones of St. Thomas?
Cambridge University Press. 1920
1,3,6,11,14,15

MAYNE, William.
Cathedral Wednesday.
London, Oxford University Press. 1960.
3

MAYNE, William.
Chorister's cake. (Author was a master at Cathedral
Choir School).
London, Oxford University Press. 1956.
3

Medieval records of the Archbishops of Canterbury: a course
of public lectures, 1960 by I.J. Churchill, E.W. Kemp, E.F.
Jacob, F.R.H. Du Boulay. (Lambeth lectures).
Faith Press. 1962.
4

Memorial of the registrars of the registrars of the courts
of the several diocese in the province of Canterbury.
London, S. Sweet. 1833.
3

MESSENGER, A.W.B.
The heraldry of Canterbury Cathedral, Vol. 1. The great
cloister vault.
Canterbury, Friends of Canterbury Cathedral. 1947.
1,3(1939), 4,6,7,8,11,19,21

MILLS, Dorothy.
Edward, the Black Prince: a short history by D. Mills and
his funeral achievements by Sir James Mann.
Canterbury Cathedral Gifts. 1972.
11

MITCHINSON, John.
Cathedral school.
1862.
17

MOLESWORTH, J.E.N.
The danger of a divided house - a sermon.
Rivington. 1830.
11

MOLESWORTH, J.E.N.
A sermon preached in the Cathedral Church of Canterbury,
August 9th, 1832.
Rivington. 1832.
11

MORRIS, John.
Canterbury: a guide for Catholics.
Canterbury, Crow. 1891.
3,17,19

MORRIS, John.
Canterbury: our old metropolis.
Canterbury, Crow. 1889.
1,3,8,15

(MOULE, Thomas).
(Canterbury Cathedral). Extract from "Winkles" Architectural
and Picturesque Illustrations of the Cathedral Churches of
England and Wales.
(Bogue)(1836-42).
11

(MOULE, Thomas).
Descriptive account of the Cathedral Church of Canterbury,
illustrated with ten engravings.
H. Ward. 1839.
11

(MOULE, Thomas).
Descriptive account of the Cathedral Church of Canterbury,
illustrated with ten engravings.
H. Ward. 1842.
11

(MOULE, Thomas).
Descriptive account of the Cathedral Church of Canterbury,
with a short description of St. Augustine's Monastery.
H. Ward. 1846.
11

MOULE, Thomas.
Illustrations of the Cathedral Church of Canterbury.
1835.
15

NICHOLS, Beverley.
A pilgrim's progress. (Chapter 2 "Canterbury Bells" is an
attack upon Dr. Hewlett Johnson, Communist Dean of Canterbury.
London, Cape. 1952.
3

NISBETT, Marjorie.
The storied undercroft. (Article in "The Lady", Vol. CLIV,
No. 3993, October, 1961).
3

Notes on the painted glass in Canterbury Cathedral.
Aberdeen University Press. 1897.
1,11,17

OWEN, Walter Tallant.
Bits of Canterbury Cathedral.
New York, Camstock. 1891.
8,11,17

(PARKER, Matthew).
De antiquitate Britannicae ecclesiae...(Cantuariensis).
1605.
17

(PARKER, K. Bewster).
Canterbury Cathedral: a history in verse.
Canterbury, Cross and Jackman. 1929.
3,11

PARKES, M.B.
A fifteenth-century scribe - Henry Mere. (Article in
Bodleian Library Record, Vol. VI, No. 6, September, 1961)
3

PASKE, Dr.
The copy of a letter sent to an honourable Lord by Dr.
Paske, Sub-Dean of Canterbury.
London. September, 9th, 1642.
3

PELLEW, Rev. George.
A sermon preached at the Cathedral, Sunday, June XII,
MDCCCXXV.
London, Rivington. 1825.
3

PHILLIPS, Charles Stanley.
Canterbury Cathedral in the Middle Ages.
S.P.C.K. 1949.
3,6(1969), 8,11,12

Photographs of Canterbury Cathedral and other places of
interest in Canterbury.
3

PINNOCK. K.A.T.
Mother of England. (Included in "Everybody's", 1944).
3

POLLEN, John Hungerford.
King Henry VIII and St. Thomas Becket, being a history
of the burning of the saint's bones and the reports
thereon by Thomas Derby, William Thomas and P.
Crisestone Henriquez. (Reprinted from The Month,
February and April, 1912).
3

PROTHERO, Rowland E.
The life and correspondence of Arthur Pewlyn Stanley,
D.D. Late Dean of Westminster.
London, Murray. 1893.
3

PURFIELD, N.K.
Canterbury Cathedral Church of Christ. Catalogue of
the Frampton Papers in the Chapter Library (MS.),
compiled by N.K. Purfield.
n.d.
7,11

RACKHAM, Bernard.
The ancient glass of Canterbury Cathedral.
Printed for Friends of Canterbury Cathedral by Lund
Humphries and Co., London, 1949.
1,2,3,4,6,8,11,18

RACKHAM, Bernard.
Stained glass windows of Canterbury Cathedral.
S.P.C.K. 1957.
3,4,7,11

RAIT, Robert Sangster.
English episcopal palaces, Part I. (Province of
Canterbury), edited by R.S. Rait.
Constable. 1910.
4,12

RAMSEY, Arthur Michael. (Archbishop of Canterbury).
Canterbury essays and addresses.
London, S.P.C.K. 1964.
3

RATCLIFFE, F.E.
The Royal Maundy: a brief outline of its history and
ceremonial.
London, Royal Almonry Office. 1963.
3

RENSSELAER, M.G. Van.
Canterbury Cathedral. (Article in "The Century Magazine",
Vol. XXXIII, April, 1887).
3

ROBERTS, R. Ellis.
H.R.L. Sheppard: life and letters.
London, Murray. 1942.
3

ROBERTSON, William Archibald Scott.
The crypt of Canterbury Cathedral.
Mitchell and Hughes. 1880.
1,3,6,8,11,12,17

ROUTLEDGE, Charles Francis.
First report of the Committee appointed 'to make an
antiquarian investigation of the Cathedral', by Routledge
and others.
Canterbury, Crow. 1888.
1,17

ROYAL EAST KENT REGIMENT - THE BUFFS.
A service of remembrance for all ranks of The Buffs, 9th
August, 1959...the Cathedral Church of Christ, Canterbury...
the order of service.
1959.
4

S., E.
Our children's visit to Canterbury Cathedral.
1876.
17

S., G.
Chronological history of Canterbury Cathedral.
H.S. Claris, "Kent Herald". 1883.
1,3,6,12,13,17

SANCROFT, William. Archbishop of Canterbury, defendant.
The proceedings and trial in the case of the most Rev. Father
of God, William Lord Archbishop of Canterbury and the Right
Rev. Fathers in God...1688.
London. 1739.
12

SANDYS, Charles.
A critical dissertation on Prof. Willis's "Architectural
History of Canterbury Cathedral".
J.R. Smith. 1846.
1,3,6,11,15

SANDYS, Charles.
The memorial and case of the clerici-laici or layclerks of
Canterbury Cathedral.
J.R. Smith. 1848.
11,17

SAYERS, Dorothy Leigh.
The Devil to pay. (Acting edition for the festival of The
Friends of Canterbury Cathedral, 1939).
Canterbury, H.J. Goulden. 1939.
1

SAYERS, Dorothy Leigh.
The zeal of thy house (written for the Canterbury festival,
June, 1937).
London, Gollantz. 1937.
3

SEAGER, S. Hurst.
Canterbury Cathedral.
Simpkin, Marshall. 1910?
3,11

SEARLE, William George.
Christ Church, Canterbury. 1. The chronicle of John Stone,
monk, 1415-71. 2. List of the Deans etc. of Canterbury
Cathedral Monastery, 1902, edited by W.R. Searle.
n.d.
1,11,12

SHEPPARD, J. Brigstocke.
Christ Church letters, edited by J.B. Sheppard.
London, Camden Society. 1877.
3

SHEPPARD, J. Brigstocke.
The letter books of the Monastery at Christ Church,
Canterbury, edited by J.B. Sheppard.
H.M.S.O. 1887-89.
11,12

SHEPPARD, J. Brigstocke.
A notice of some MSS. selected from the archives of the
Dean and Chapter of Canterbury.
1875?
11

SHIRLEY, J.
Pictorial history of Canterbury Cathedral.
Pitken. 1952, etc.
1,2,3,6 (1967), 8,11,12,19

SMITH, G.
Complete guide to Canterbury Cathedral, revised edition.
Austens.(1930).
11

SMITH, G.
Complete guide to Canterbury Cathedral.
Canterbury, Austen. 1933.
11

SMITH, Reginald Anthony.
Canterbury Cathedral Priory.
Cambridge University Press. 1943.
1,3,7,8,11,15,18,21

Some notes on the cloister shields.
W. and H. Ltd. 1936.
4,11

STANLEY, Arthur Penrhyn.
Sermons preached mostly in Canterbury Cathedral.
Murray. 1859.
12

The statutes of the Cathedral.
Privately Printed for Dean and Chapter. 1925.
3

STEVENS AND SON. Publishers.
Concise Canterbury and Cathedral guide.
Stevens. c.1947.
2

STORER, J.
The history and antiquities of the Cathedral Church of
Canterbury.
Rivingtons. 1814?
6,9,11

SYKES, Norman.
Canterbury Cathedral Library.
n.d.
8,11

SYKES, Norman.
Canterbury Cathedral Library: lecture delivered on
the opening day, July 18th, 1954.
Canterbury, Friends of Canterbury Cathedral. 1954.
(Canterbury Papers No. 9).
1,4,8,11,21

TAYLOR, H.M.
The Anglo-Saxon Cathedral Church at Canterbury.
(Reprinted from The Archaeological Journal, Vol. CXXVI).
1970.
4

TENISON, Edward. Archdeacon.
True copies of some letters occasioned by the demand
for dilapidations in the See of Canterbury.
1716.
17

THOMPSON, E. Margaret.
Registrum Matthei: Parker, Diocesis Cantuariensis.
A.D. 1559-1595.
Canterbury and York Society. 1928-33.
11

THOMSON, Gladys Scott.
Medieval pilgrimages.
London, Longmans. 1962.
3

THORNTON, W. Pugin.
Report on a human skeleton found in the crypt of Canterbury
Cathedral, supposed to be Thomas a Becket's.
Canterbury, Crow. 1888.
1,17

THORNTON, W. Pugin.
Becket's bones.
Cross and Jackman. 1901.
7,12,13,14

The times of Edward the Black Prince; replicas of his
achievements; Knights of the Garter, past and present.
(Canterbury Papers No. 8).
Canterbury, Friends of Canterbury Cathedral. 1954.
1,4,11,21

TODD, Henry John.
Catalogue of the books, both manuscript and printed which are
preserved in the library of Christ Church, Canterbury.
Clerkenwell, Bye and Law. 1802.
3

TODD, Henry John.
Some account of the Deans of Canterbury.
Canterbury, Simmons. 1793.
1,3,6,8,11,12,15,17

TOMLINSON, F.W.
The Warriors' Chapel and The Buffs; The Ship's Bell of
H.M.S. "Canterbury".
(Canterbury Papers No. 2).
Canterbury, Friends of Canterbury Cathedral. 1936.
11,21

Translation of the Monk Gervase's tract on the burning and
reparation of the Church of Canterbury. (Latin text).
London, Smith. 1851.
10

TRISTRAM, Ernest William.
The paintings of Canterbury Cathedral.
(Canterbury Papers No. 6).
Canterbury, Friends of Canterbury Cathedral. 1935, etc.
1,2(1960), 3,4,11,12,21(1960)

VALLANCE, Aymer.
The tapestries from Canterbury Cathedral. (Reprinted from
Archaeologia Cantiana, Vol. 44).
Ashford, Headley. 1930.
3,11,17

WALKER, Colin W.
The stone of Canterbury Cathedral.
n.d.
3

WALKER, Colin W.
The woodwork of Canterbury Cathedral.
n.d.
3

WARD. H. Snowden.
The Canterbury pilgrimages.
Black, 1904, etc.
1,3,4,5,6,7,8,9,11,12,13,15,17,19

WARD, Henry. Publisher.
Descriptive account of the Cathedral Church of Canterbury.
1840.
17

WARNER, S.A.
Canterbury Cathedral.
S.P.C.K. 1923.
1,3,6,8,11,12,15,18,21

WETHERELT, Alexander.
Collection of photographs of Canterbury Cathedral, compiled
by A. Wetherlet.
1870.
3

WHATMORE, Leonard E.
Catholic Record Society, London. Archdeacon Harpsfield's
visitation, 1557, Vol. 1, by W. Sharp and L.E. Whatmore.
1950.
6,8

WHATMORE, Leonard E.
Catholic Record Soceity, London. Archdeacon Harpsfield's
visitation, 1557, Vol. 2, 1556 and 1558, notes by Rev.
Whatmore.
1951.
6,8

WHITE, Joseph William Gleeson.
The Cathedral Church of Canterbury, edited by J.W.G.
White.
Bell. 1896, etc.
1,3,4,6,7,9,11,12,13,17,18,20

WILD, Charles.
Twelve perspective views of the exterior and interior
parts of the Metropolitan Church of Canterbury
accompanied by two ichonographic plates and an historical
account.
The Author. 1807.
3,4,7,17

WILLEMENT, Thomas.
Heraldic notices of Canterbury Cathedral.
1827.
3,4,6,7,8,11,12,17

WILLETT, Charles.
Pictorial guide to Canterbury Cathedral, edited by C.
Willett.
Margate, Willett. 195-?
3,11

WILLIAMS, Emily.
Notes on the painted glass in Canterbury Cathedral.
Aberdeen University Press. 1897.
3

WILLIAMSON, Hugh Ross.
Canterbury Cathedral.
"Country Life". 1953.
1,3,4,8,11,12,18

WILLIAMSON, Hugh Ross.
This eminence of England: a play in two acts. (Play
on the life of Cardinal Pole (?) performed at Canterbury
festival.
London, Heinemann. 1953.
3

WILLIS, Robert.
Architectural history of Canterbury Cathedral.
Longman. 1845.
1,3,6,7,8,11,12,15

WILLIS, Robert.
The architectural history of the conventual buildings
of the Monastery of Christ Church in Canterbury.
K.A.S. 1869.
1,3,6,11,15,17

WOODCOCK, Brian Lindsay.
Medieval ecclesiastical courts in the Diocese of
Canterbury.
Oxford University Press. 1952.
1,2,3,4,6,7,11,13

WOODRUFF, Charles Everleigh.
Calendar of institutions by the Chapter of Canterbury,
sede vacante, edited by C.E. Woodruff and I.J.
Churchill.
K.A.S. 1924.
1,3,4,8,11,12,15,18

WOODRUFF, Charles Everleigh.
Catalogue of the MS. books in the library of Christ
Church, Canterbury.
Canterbury, Cross and Jackman. 1911.
11

(WOODRUFF, Charles Everleigh).
A list of the Archdeacons of Canterbury.
Privately Printed. 1928.
11

WOODRUFF, Charles Everleigh.
Memorials of the Cathedral and Priory of Christ in
Canterbury, by C.E. Woodruff and W. Danks.
Chapman and Hall. 1912.
1,3,4,6,7,8,11,12,13,14,15,19

WOODRUFF, Charles Everleigh.
A monastic chronicle lately discovered at Christ Church,
Canterbury.
1911.
11

WOOLLEY, R.M.
The Canterbury Benedictional, edited by E.M. Woolley.
(H.B. Society Publications, Vol. 51).
Henry Bradshaw Soc. 1917.
11

WOOLNOTH, William.
A graphical illustration of the Metropolitan Cathedral
Church of Canterbury.
Cadell and Davies. 1816.
1,3,6,7,8,11,12,15,16

WOOLNOTH, William. (Drawings by T. Hastings).
Illustrative views of the Metropolitan Cathedral Church of
Canterbury.
Henry Ward. 1836.
6

CANTERBURY CATHEDRAL - ARCHBISHOPS

(B., A).
Life, or the ecclesiastical historie of St. Thomas,
Archbishop of Canterbury.
1639.
17

BARTH, Karl.
Anselm: fides quaerens intellectum.
S.C.M. Press. 1960.
12

BAXTER, Dudley.
Cardinal Pole, legate and primate. (Reprinted from "The
Month", December, 1900).
"The Month". 1900.
3

BECKET, Thomas. Saint, Archbishop of Canterbury.
The prophecie of Thomas Becket...concerning the wars
betwixt England, France and Holland.
G. Freeman. 1666.
3

BELL, G.K.A. Bishop of Chichester.
Randall Davidson, Archbishop of Canterbury, 2 vols. 1st ed.
Oxford University Press. 1935.
3,4,5,12

BELLOC, Hilaire.
Becket: St. Thomas of Canterbury.
Catholic Truth Society. 1933.
3

BELLOC, Hilaire.
Cranmer.
Cassell. 1931.
12

BENEDICT. Abbot of Peterborough.
The life and miracles of Saint Thomas of Canterbury.
Caxton Society. 1850.
3

BENHAM, William.
Catharine and Cranfurd Tait, wife and son of Archbishop
Campbell, Archbishop of Canterbury - a memoir.
1879.
4

BENSON, Arthur Christopher.
The life of Edward White Benson, sometime Archbishop of
Canterbury, 2 vol.
Macmillan. 1899, etc. 1900 (abridged) 1901.
3,4

BENSON, Robert Hugh.
The holy blissful martyr Saint Thomas of Canterbury.
MacDonald and Evans. 1908.
3

BENSON, Robert Hugh.
Saint Thomas of Canterbury.
MacDonald and Evans. 1908.
1

BEVAN, Gladys Mary.
Portraits of the Archbishop of Canterbury, edited by
G.M. Bevan.
Mowbray. 1908.
1,2,3,6,8,11,12,15,19

BING, Harold F.
St. Augustine of Canterbury and the Saxon Church in
Kent. In Archaeologia Cantiana, Vol. 62, 1949.
17

BOURGCHIER, Thomas. Cardinal Archbishop of Canterbury.
Registrum Thome Bourgchier, Cantuariensis Archiepiscopi,
1454-6.
n.d.
11

BOYCE, Charles.
The family of William Sancroft, Archbishop of Canterbury.
(Reprinted from the Proceedings Suffolk Institute of
Archaeology and Natural History, Vol. XX, Part 2, 1929).
3

BROMILEY, G.W.
Thomas Cranmer, Archbishop and martyr.
Church Book Room. 1956.
3,12

BROMILEY, G.W.
Thomas Cranmer, theologian.
Lutterworth. 1956.
12

BROOK, Victor John Knight.
Life of Archbishop Parker.
Oxford University Press. 1962.
3,12

BROU, Father.
Saint Augustine of Canterbury and his companions.
Art and Book Co. 1897.
3,12

BUSHELL, W.D.
Saint Thomas of Canterbury. Extracts from the
biographies, translated into English with explanatory
notes.
Macmillan and Bowes. 1896.
11

THE CANTERBURY AND YORK SOCIETY.
Diocesis Roffensis, registrum Hormonis Hethe, pars
prima.
Canterbury and York Society. 1914, 1915.
7,8

THE CANTERBURY AND YORK SOCIETY.
Registrum Johannis Pecham. The register of John
Peckham, Archbishop of Canterbury, 1278-1294.
Canterbury and York Society. 1908-1910.
11

CARPENTER, Edward.
Cantuas: the Archbishops in their office.
Cassell. 1971.
4,11

CAVE-BROWNE, John.
Lambeth Palace and its associations.
Blackwood. 1882.
12,17

CHENEY, Christopher Robert.
Hubert Walter.
Nelson. 1967.
3

CHICHELE, Henry. Archbishop.
Register of Henry Chichele, Archbishop of Canterbury,
1414-1443.
Canterbury and York Society. n.d.
1,3,11

CHRISTOPHER, Richard A.
George Abbot, Archbishop of Canterbury: a bibliography.
Charlottsville, University Press of Virginia. 1966.
3

CHURCH, R.W.
Saint Anselm.
Macmillan. 1870.
12

CHURCHILL, Irene Josephine.
Medieval records of the Archbishops of Canterbury: a course
of public lectures delivered in Lambeth Palace Library in
1960, by I.J. Churchill and others.
The Faith Press. 1962.
4,11,12,15,19

COMPTON, Piers.
The turbulent priest: a life of St. Thomas of Canterbury.
Staples. 1957.
4,12

CONGRES INTERNATIONAL DU IXe CENTENAIRE DE L'ARRIVEE
D'ANSELME AU BEC.
Spicilegium Beccense. (Contains "Saint Anselm and his cult
at Canterbury", by William Urry).
Paris, J. Vrin. 1959.
3

COOLE, Albert.
The life of Thomas Becket.
Eastes. n.d.
3

DAHMUS, Joseph.
William Courtenay, Archbishop of Canterbury, 1381-1396.
Pensylvania State University Press. 1966.
3,12

DANT, Charles H.
Archbishop Temple.
Walter Scott Publishing Co. 1903.
12

DARK, Sidney.
Archbishop Davidson and the English church.
P. Allen. 1929.
3,12

DARK, Sidney.
St. Thomas of Canterbury.
Macmillan. 1927.
7,11,12

DARK, Sidney.
Seven Archbishops.
Eyre and Son. 1944.
1

DAVIDSON, Randall Thomas.
Life of Archibald Campbell Tait, Archbishop of Canterbury, 2
vols., by R.T. Davidson and W. Benham.
Macmillan. 1891.
3,4

DAWLEY, Powel Mills.
John Whitgift and the Reformation.
Black. 1955.
4

DE PARAVICINI, Frances.
Life of St. Edmund of Abingdon, Archbishop of Canterbury.
(Photocopy of edition published by Burns Oates, 1898).
University Microfilms. 1962.
12

DERING, Sir Edward.
Fovre speeches made by Sir Edward Deering in the High Court
of Parliament - concerning the Archbishop and divers other
grievances.
Francis Coles. 1641.
11

DE VERE, Aubrey Thomas.
St. Thomas of Canterbury (poem).
King. 1876.
11,17

DOUIE, D.L.
Archbishop Peckam.
Oxford University Press. 1952.
3,12

DU BOULAY, Francis Robin H.
The Archbishop as territorial magnate, 1960.
(In Canterbury Archbishops of Mediaeval records of the
Archbishops of Canterbury, 1962).
4

DUCK, Arthur.
The life of Henry Chichele, Archbishop of Canterbury.
Chiswell. 1699.
12,17

DUGGAN, Alfred.
Thomas Becket of Canterbury.
Faber. 1952, etc.
1,3,5,12,21

DUNCAN-JONES, A.S.
Archbishop Laud.
Macmillan. 1927.
3

DUNKIN, Edwin Hadlow Wise.
Index to tne Act books of the Archbishops of Canterbury,
1663-1859, compiled by E.H.W. Dunkin.
British Record Society. n.d.
3,11

DWYER, J.J.
Saint Thomas of Canterbury, 1118-1170.
Catholic Truth Society, Revised Edition, 1948.
3

EADMER.
Saint Anselm and his biographer: study of monastic life
and thought, 1059-1130.
Cambridge University Press. 1963.
3

EADMER.
Vita sancti Anselmi, archiepiscopi canturiensis.
The life of St. Anselm, Archbishop of Canterbury, with
introductory notes and translation by R.W. Southern.
London, Nelson. 1963.
3

ELIOT, Thomas Stearns.
Film of "Murder in the Cathedral", by T.S. Eliot and
George Hoellering.
London, Faber. 1952.
3

ELIOT, Thomas Stearns.
Murder in the Cathedral.
London, Faber and Faber.(1935).
3,6

ELIOT, Thomas Stearns.
Murder in the Cathedral: a screen play (programme).
London, Westminster Press. 1951.
3

ELIOT, Thomas Stearns.
Murder in the Cathedral.(television) camera script.
1964.
3

EVANS, John.
Coins of Archbishop Jaenberht and Acthilheard.
London, Numismatic Society. 1865.
3

First day covers (philatelic), celebrating meeting of
Archbishop of Canterbury with the Pope, 2nd December,
1960.
Issued by Private Firm Without Authority of the Vatican.
3

FISHER, Geoffrey. Archbishop of Canterbury.
Christmas sermon (corrected by the Archbishop in his own
handwriting). 3 fol.
1953.
3

FITZSTEPHEN, William.
The life and death of Thomas Becket.
Folio Society. 1961.
3,4,11

FOREVILLE, Raymonde.
Le Jubile de Saint Thomas Becket du XIIIe au XVe siecle.
Paris, Imprimeries Oberthur. 1959.
3

FOWLER, Montagu.
Some notable Archbishops of Canterbury.
S.P.C.K. 1895.
1,11

GARDINER, Mrs. Dorothy.
Henry Oxinden's authorship. (Reprinted from Archaeologia
Cantiana, Vol.LVII. n.d.)
3,17

GARDINER, Mrs. Dorothy.
John Kempe of Olantigh, Cardinal and Archbishop.
Ashford, Geerings. 1949.
3,11

GARROW, D.W.
The history and antiquities of Croydon...(and)... the life of
John Whitgift, Archbishop of Canterbury. 1818.
18

GILES, J.A.
Life and letters of Thomas a Becket, 2 vols.
London, Whittaker and Co. 1846.
3,17

GRAHAM, Rose.
Registrum Roberti Winchelsey, Cantuariensis Archiepiscopi,
A.D., 1294-1313, edited by R. Graham.
Canterbury and York Society. 1952-5.
11

GREENAWAY, George.
Life and death of Thomas Becket: based on the account of
William Fitzstephen, his clerk, edited by G. Greenaway.
Folio Society. 1961.
3,4,11

HALL, D.J.
English medieval pilgrimage. (Chapter 6: St. Thomas Becket).
1965 (i.e. 1966).
4

HARRISON. Archdeacon.
Records of Archbishop Howley.
1893.
17

HERBERT, Charles.
Twenty-five years as Archbishop of Canterbury. (Randall T.
Davidson).
Wells, Gardner, Darton. n.d.
3,8,11,12,17

HEYLYN, P.
Cyprianus Anglicus. (Concerns Archbishop Laud).
Seile. 1668.
12

HOBSON, John Morrison.
Some notes on the Old Palace of the Archbishops of Canterbury
at Croydon. (Article in Reliquary and Illustrated
Archaeologist, October. 1909).
3

HOOK, Walter Farquhar.
Lives of the Archbishops of Canterbury, 12 vols.
Bentley. 1860-84.
1,3,4(vols. 1-6), 6,7,11,12,17

HUTTON, William Holden.
Saint Thomas of Canterbury...from contemporary biographers
and other chroniclers.
London, D. Nutt. 1899.
3

HUTTON, William Holden.
Thomas Becket, Archbishop of Canterbury.
London, Pitman and Sons. 1910.
3,6(1926)

IREMONGER, F.A.
William Temple, Archbishop of Canterbury.
Oxford University Press. 1948.
4,8,12

JACOB, Ernest Fraser.
Archbishop Henry Chichele.
Nelson. 1967.
3,11,12

JACOB, Ernest Fraser.
Henry Chichele and the ecclesiastical politics of his
age.
U.L.P. 1952.
12

JENKINS, Claude.
Index to the Act books of the Archbishops of Canterbury,
1663-1859, Vol. 1, A-K, edited by C. Jenkins and C.A.
Fry.
n.d.
11

JENKINS, Claude.
Index to the Act books of the Archbishops of Canterbury,
1663-1859, Vol. 2, L-Z, edited by C. Jenkins.
n.d.
11

JENKINS, Claude.
Life and times of Cranmer.
Canterbury, Jennings. 1936.
1,3,11

KEMP, E.W.
The Archbishop in Convocation, 1960. (In (Canterbury,
Archbishops of) Medieval records of the Archbishops of
Canterbury, 1962).
1960.
4

KENTISH GAZETTE.
Enthronement of the Most Reverent Edward White Benson
D.D.,Lord Archbishop of Canterbury Cathedral. (Reprinted
from Kentish Gazette, April 3rd, 1883).
3

KERSHAW, S. Wayland.
The Archbishops' manors in Sussex. (Reprinted from
Journal of British Archaeological Association, June,
1914).
3

KNOWLES, Dom. David.
Archbishop Thomas Becket. (From the Proceedings of The
British Academy, Vol. 35).
London, Oxford University Press. 1949.
3

KNOWLES, Dom. David.
The episcopal colleagues of Archbishop Thomas Becket.
Cambridge University Press. 1951.
3

KNOWLES, Dom. David.
Thomas Becket.
Adam and Charles Black. 1970.
12

LAMB, John William.
The Archbishopric of Canterbury, from its foundation
to the Norman Conquest: with a foreword by the
Archbishop of Canterbury.
Faith Press. 1971.
3,4,11

LANFRANC. Archbishop of Canterbury.
Decreta Lanfranci...The monastic constitutions of
Lanfranc.
Nelson. 1951.
3,12

LANGHAM, Simon. Cardinal Archbishop of Canterbury.
Registrum Simonis Langham, A.D. 1366-1368.
Canterbury and York Society. n.d.
11

LANGTON, Stephen. Cardinal Archbishop of Canterbury.
Acta Stephani Langton, 1207-1228.
Canterbury and York Society. n.d.
11

LAUD, William.
The history of the troubles and tryal of William Laud.
Chiswell. 1695.
12

LAUD, William.
A relation of the conference betweene William Laud (Land) and Mr. Fisher the Jesuite.
n.d.
12

LAWLER, Ray.
A breach in the wall: play about tomb of Becket in village church.
William Doran. 1971.
3

LAWSON, John Parker.
The life and times of William Laud, D.D., Lord Archbishop of Canterbury, 2 vols.
Rivington. 1829.
12

LE BAS, Charles Webb.
The life of Archbishop Laud.
Rivington. 1836.
12

LEE, Frederick George.
Reginald Pole, Cardinal Archbishop of Canterbury.
Nimms. 1888.
12

LEEMING, J.R.
Stephen Langton.
Skeffington. 1915.
12

LOANE, Marcus Lawrence.
Archbishop Mowll.
London, Hodder and Stoughton. 1960.
3,6

LOCKHART, J.G.
Cosmo Gordon Lang.
Hodder and Stoughton. 1949.
3,4,12

McKilliam, A.E.
A chronicle of the Archbishops of Canterbury.
Clarke. 1913.
1,3,4,8,11,12

MAJOR, Kathleen.
Acta Stephani Langton, 1207-1228, edited by K. Major.
Canterbury and York Society. 1950.
11

MARCEL, Jean-Marie. Photographer.
I'Abbaye du Bec-Hellovin, text by La Varende. (Includes plaques commemorating 11th and 12th Archbishops of Canterbury - also Abbaye du Bec).
Paris, Libraire Plon. 1951.
3

MASON, Arthur James.
Thomas Cranmer.
Methuen. 1898.
12

MAYNARD, Theodore.
The life of Thomas Cranmer.
Staples. 1956.
4

Memorials of St. Dunstan, Archbishop of Canterbury.
H.M.S.O. 1874. (Reprinted Kraus, 1965).
8

MILLS, Dorothy.
Stephen Langton, Archbishop of Canterbury, 1207-1228.
Canterbury, Friends of Canterbury Cathedral. 1961.
3,4,11,12

MILLS, Dorothy.
Thomas Becket, 1118-1170, Archbishop of Canterbury.
Canterbury, Friends of Canterbury Cathedral. 1960.
3,4,7,11,19

MORRIS, John.
The relics of St. Thomas of Canterbury.
n.d.
1,3,11,15,17

MORRIS, John.
Tombs of the Archbishops in Canterbury Cathedral.
Canterbury, Crow. 1890.
1,6,11,15,17

MYDANS, Sheila.
Thomas: a novel of the life of Becket.
London, Collins. 1965.
3

OWEN, D.M.
A catalogue of Lambeth manuscripts 889 to 901 (Carte antique et miscellannee).
Lambeth, Palace Library. 1968.
3

PAIN, Nesta.
Thomas Becket: B.B.C. TV. camera script.
1968.
3

PATCH, Rev. John D.H.
Guide to the parish church of St. Thomas the Martyr, Winchelsea.
Rye, Adam and Son. 1933, Revised Edition.
3,15 (1913)

POWICKE, F.M.
Stephen Langton.
Merlin Press. 1965.
3,12

PURCELL, William Ernest.
Fisher of Lambeth.
Hodder and Stoughton. 1969.
3

RIDLEY, Jasper.
Thomas Cranmer.
Oxford University Press. 1962.
3,12

ROBERTSON, James C.
Becket, Archbishop of Canterbury.
Murray. 1859.
12,17

ROBERTSON, James C.
Materials for the history of Thomas Becket, Archbishop of Canterbury.
London, Longman and Co. 1875.
3,17

ROBERTSON, William Archibald Scott.
Archbishop Hubert Walter and his tomb in Canterbury Cathedral Church.
Printed by Bemrose and Sons.(1890).
11,17

ROBERTSON, William Archibald Scott.
Tombs of the Archbishop of Canterbury.
1890.
17

ROUTLEDGE, Charles Francis.
Short summary of the controversy as to "Becket's bones".
Canterbury, Crow. 1888.
1

ROUTLEDGE, Charles Francis.
Survey of the "Becket bones", controversy, by C. Routledge and others.
1888.
17.

ROUTLEDGE, J.M.
Saint Dunstan.
Catholic Truth Society.(1921).
11

RULE, Martin.
The life and times of St. Anselm, 2 vols.
Kegan, Paul. 1883.
12

SALTMAN, Avrom.
Theobald, Archbishop of Canterbury.
Athlone. 1956.
3,12,15

SANDFORD, E.G.
The Exeter episcopate of Archbishop Temple, 1869-1885.
Macmillan. 1907.
12

SANDFORD, E.G.
Frederick Temple: an appreciation.
Macmillan. 1907.
3,12

SANDFORD, E.G.
Memoirs of Archbishop Temple by seven friends, 2 vols.
Macmillan. 1906.
12

SCHENK, Wilhelm.
Reginald Pole, Cardinal of England. (Afterwards Archbishop
of Canterbury).
London, Longmans, Green. 1950.
3

SCOTT, Patrick.
Thomas a Beckett and other poems.
1853.
17

SEARLE, William George.
Anglo-Saxon bishops, kings and nobles.
Cambridge University Press. 1899.
3

SIMPKINSON, C.H.
Life and times of William Laud, Archbishop of Canterbury.
London, Murray. 1894.
3,17

SIMPSON, James B.
The hundredth Archbishop of Canterbury.
New York, Harper. 1962.
3

SIMPSON, W. Sparrow.
On the head of Simon of Sudbury, Archbishop of Canterbury,
a relic preserved in the Church of St. Gregory, Sudbury,
Suffolk. 1895.
3

SNELL, F.J.
Early associations of Archbishop Temple: a record of
Blundell's School and its neighbourhood.
Hutchinson. 1904.
12

SOUTHERN, Richard William.
Saint Anselm and his biographer.
Cambridge, Cambridge University Press. 1963.
3

SPEAIGHT, Robert.
Thomas Becket.
Longmans. 1949.
3(1938) 4,12

STALEY, Vernon.
The life and times of Gilbert Sheldon.
Gardner, Darton.(1913).
12

STRYPE, John.
The life and acts of John Whitgift.
Horne. 1718.
12

STRYPE, John.
Life and acts of Matthew Parker, the first Archbishop of
Canterbury.
London, Printed for John Wyat. 1711.
3,17

STRYPE, John.
Memorials of Thomas Cranmer.
Chiswell. 1694.
3(1812 Oxford University Press) 12

STUBBS, William.
Memorials of Saint Dunstan, Archbishop of Canterbury.
Longman. 1874.
3,12

SYKES, Norman.
William Wake, Archbishop of Canterbury, 1657-1737.
Cambridge University Press. 1957.
12

TENNYSON, Alfred. 1st Baron Tennyson.
Becket: a play.
London, Macmillan. 1884.
3(also 1888 and 1933 editions) 11(1932)

TENNYSON, Alfred. 1st Baron Tennyson.
Souvenir of Becket...first presented at the Lyceum
Theatre, 6th Feburary, 1893 by Henry Irving.
London, Black and White. 1893.
3

TREVOR-ROPER, Hugh R.
Archbishop Laud, 1573-1645.
Macmillan. 1962.
12

THOMPSON, Robert Anchor.
Thomas Becket: martyr patriot.
London, Kegan, Paul, Trench and Co. 1889.
3

TILLOTSON, John. Archbishop of Canterbury 1630-1694.
The golden book of Tillotson: selections from the
writings of the Rev. John Tillotson, D.D. Archbishop
of Canterbury, edited with a sketch of his life by
James Moffatt.
London, Hodder and Stoughton. 1926.
3

TOUT, Thomas Frederick.
The place of St. Thomas of Canterbury in history.
(Reprinted from the collected papers of Thomas Frederick
Tout, Vol. III).
Manchester University Press. 1934.
3

URRY, William.
Saint Anselm and his cult at Canterbury. (Article
from Spicileguim Becceuse).
Paris,Librarie Philosophique, J. Vrin. 1959.
3

URRY, William.
Two notes on Guernes de Pont Sainte Maxence: vie
de Saint Thomas. (Reprinted from Archaeologia Cantiana
Vol. LXVI).
3,17

Vita et processus S. Thomae.
1495-6.
17

WARD, Bernard.
St. Edmund, Archbishop of Canterbury: his life as
told by old English writers, edited by B. Ward.
Sands and Co. 1903.
3,12

WARREN, W.L.
A reappraisal of Simon Sudbury, Bishop of London, 1361-
75 and Archbishop of Canterbury, 1375-81. (Included in
Journal of Ecclesiastical History, Vol. X, No. 2,
October, 1959).
3

WELSBY, Paul Anthony.
George Abbott, the unwanted Archbishop, 1562-1633.
London, S.P.C.K. 1962.
3

WHITEBROOK, J.C.
The consecration of the most Reverend Matthew Parker,
Archbishop of Canterbury.
Mowbray. 1945.
12

WILLIAMS, Charles.
Cranmer of Canterbury.
Goulden. 1936.
3

WILLIAMS, Charles.
Thomas Cranmer of Canterbury: (a play written for
Canterbury Festival, June, 1936).
Oxford University Press. 1936.
3

WILLIAMSON, Hugh Ross.
The arrow and the sword...being an enquiry into the
nature of the deaths of William Rufus and Thomas Becket.
London, Faber, 1955.
3

WINSTON, Richard.
Thomas Becket.
Constable. 1967.
1,5,12

WOOD, A.C.
Registrum Simonis Langham, 1366-1368, edited by A.C. Wood.
Canterbury and York Society. 1956.
11

WOODGATE, Mildred Violet.
Thomas Becket, 1118-1170.
St. Paul Publishers. 1971.
11

WOODHOUSE, Reginald Illingworth.
The life of John Morton, Archbishop of Canterbury.
London, Longmans. 1895.
3

CAPEL-le-FERNE

Capel Church Farm - Sale catalogue.
1874.
12

The Cliffs Estate, overlooking The Warren, Folkestone. Third
sale...120 plots of splendidly situated freehold land,
comprising the third portion of the estate to be sold by
auction on 10th July, 1901. (Vendor, Mr. Joseph Henry
Retallack-Moloney - Auctioneers, Messrs. Protheroe and
Morris). Comprises 60 acres in Capel-le-Ferne.
Protheroe and Morris. 1901.
7

The Cliffs Estate, overlooking The Warren, Folkestone,
eleventh sale...137 plots of freehold building land,
comprising the eleventh portion of the estate, to be sold
by auction on May 13th, 1902. (Vendor, Mr. Joseph Henry
Retallack-Moloney - Auctioneers, Messrs. Protheroe and
Morris).
Protheroe and Morris. 1902.
7

The Cliffs Estate - particulars and conditions of sale of the
plots available, September, 1906.
Protheroe and Morris. 1906.
7

Particulars of sale of the noted dairy, sheep and potatoe
farm known as Capel Church Farm, Capel (by direction of Messrs.
W. Miller and Sons).
Finn-Kelsey and Ashenden. (1955).
7

Particulars, plans and conditions of sale of the important
country estate known as Hockley Sole, comprising an imposing
residence and valuable mixed farm lands...about 434 acres.
To be sold by auction as a whole on 26th June. 1946.
A. Savill and Sons. 1946.
7

CATFORD

ALLDER, Joshua T.
Souvenir of old Catford, 1877-1928.
J.T. Allder and Co.
18

A descriptive account of Lewisham, Lee, Blackheath and Catford.
1844.
18

SOUTHCOTT, E.J.
First fifty years of the Catford Cycling Club, edited by E.J.
Southcott.
1939.
18

CENSUS

The Domesday Book for the county of Kent: portion of a return
of owners of land, 1873.
Lewes, "Sussex Express". 1877.
1,2,5,6,11,12,14,15,17,18,20
Eyre and Spotiswoode for H.M.S.O. 1875.
8,11

Ecclesiastical Census - census of Gt. Britain, 1851. Places
of worship in...Charlton, Deptford, etc.
Public Records Office. n.d.
18

GENERAL REGISTER OFFICE.
Census of Kent, 1801, 1811, 1821,1831, 1941.
H.M.S.O. n.d.
15

GENERAL REGISTER OFFICE.
Abstract of the population census of 1841.
Fullarton. n.d.
3

GENERAL REGISTER OFFICE.
Census, 1861 - Bromley.
2

GENERAL REGISTER OFFICE.
Census, 1881, Vol. 2.
Eyre and Spotiswoode for H.M.S.O. 1883.
8

The Census of 1891.
Graham.
12

GENERAL REGISTER OFFICE.
Census of England and Wales, 1901: County of Kent.
H.M.S.O. 1902.
2,11,17

GENERAL REGISTER OFFICE.
Census, 1911 - Kent.
H.M.S.O. 1914.
2,8,17

GENERAL REGISTER OFFICE.
Census of England and Wales, 1921 - County of Kent.
H.M.S.O. 1923.
1,2,7,9,11

GENERAL REGISTER OFFICE.
Census of England and Wales, 1931 - County of Kent, 2
vols.
H.M.S.O. Vol. 1, 1932, Vol. 2, 1935.
1,2,3,7,9,11,17(Part 1 only)

GENERAL REGISTER OFFICE.
Census, 1951 - Kent.
H.M.S.O. 1954.
1,2,3,4,5,7,8,9,11,12,13,14,15,17,19,20

GENERAL REGISTER OFFICE.
Census, 1961 - Kent.
H.M.S.O. 1963.
1,2,3,4,5,8,11,12,14,15,17,18,19,20

GENERAL REGISTER OFFICE.
Census, 1961 - occupation, industry socio-economic
groups, Kent.
H.M.S.O. 1965.
1,2,3,4,5,7,9,11,12,15,18,19,20

GENERAL REGISTER OFFICE.
Census, 1961 - populations, dwellings, households -
Kent and Surrey.
H.M.S.O. 1963.
4,5,8,9,20

GENERAL REGISTER OFFICE.
Sample census, 1966 - Kent.
H.M.S.O. 1967-8.
1,2,3,4,5,8,9,11,12,17,18,19,20

GENERAL REGISTER OFFICE.
Sample census, 1966 - county report, Greater London,
(i.e. includes Bexley, Bromley, Greenwich, Lewisham).
H.M.S.O. 1967.
2

GENERAL REGISTER OFFICE.
Sample census, 1966 - England and Wales: economic
activity county leaflet, Kent.
H.M.S.O. 1968.
2,7,9,11,14

GENERAL REGISTER OFFICE.
Sample census, 1966 - migration, South Eastern Region.
H.M.S.O. 1968.
2

GENERAL REGISTER OFFICE.
Population projection for the South East, by Eric J.
Thompson.
H.M.S.O. 1967
2,3

GREATER LONDON COUNCIL - RESEARCH AND INTELLIGENCE UNIT.
Interim demographic population projections (quinquennial
table, Bromley, 1966-1986).
Greater London Council. 1968.
2

LOCAL GOVERNMENT BOARD.
Return of owners of land, Kent. Extract from England and
Wales (inclusive of the Metropolis) Return of owners of
land, 1873, Vol. I counties.
H.M.S.O. 1875.
2,11

OFFICE OF POPULATION CENSUSES AND SURVEYS.
Census, 1971, England and Wales, advance analysis - Kent.
H.M.S.O. 1972.
3,4,9,11

CHALK

Chalk Parish Church and illustrated guide.
Solus Arts Advertising Service. 1951.
8,9,11

CLARKE, Charles.
Observations on episcopal chairs and stone seats, as also
to piscinas and other appendages to altars still remaining
in chancels, with a description of Chalk Church, Rochester.
Royal Society of Antiquaries.(1793).
11

JOHNSTON, D.E.
Ministry of Works excavations at Chalk, near Gravesend.
Provisional report. (Typescript).
1961.
9

PERKINS, Rev. Malcolm B.
A guide to Chalk Parish Church.
Solas Arts Advertising Service. 1951.
4,9,12

CHALLOCK

St. Cosmos and St. Damion, Challock.
n.d.
12

CHANNEL TUNNEL

ABEL, Deryck.
Channel underground.
Pall Mall Press. 1961.
1,6,7,11,12,18

BATEMAN, John Frederic.
Channel railroad: description of a proposed cast-iron
tube for carrying a railway across the channel, by J.F.
Bateman and J.J. Revy.
Vacher. 1869.
7

BERNEY, Thomas.
The Battle of the Channel Tunnel and Dover Castle and forts.
(1882),etc.
7,12

BOWDLER, Henry.
The highway implications of the Channel Tunnel. (Photocopy
of paper and discussions from Journal of the Institution
of Highway Engineers, June, 1968).
June, 1968.
4

BRADLAUGH, Charles.
The Channel Tunnel: ought the democracy to oppose or
support it?
Bonner. 1887.
1,4,7

BROWN, A.G.
Channel Tunnel bibliography.
Channel Tunnel Association. 1969.
6,7

BUTLER, Sir. William Francis.
Channel Tunnel, by Sir. W. Butler and others.
Channel Tunnel Company. 1907.
7,9

CHALMERS, James.
The Channel railway connecting England and France.
Spon. 1867.
7(1861) 11,17(1861)

THE CHANNEL BRIDGE AND RAILWAY CO. LTD.
Le pont sur la Manche.
Siege Social. 1892.
7

The Channel Tunnel: a few notable opinions in support.
c.1907.
3

CHANNEL TUNNEL ASSOCIATION.
Bulletin, No. 1, January, 1964. (Typescript).
3

CHANNEL TUNNEL COMPANY.
The Channel Tunnel and the World War.
Channel Tunnel Company. 1917.
3,6,9

CHANNEL TUNNEL STUDY GROUP.
The Channel Tunnel: the facts.
Channel Tunnel Study Group. 1964.
6,7

CHANNEL TUNNEL STUDY GROUP.
Report, March, 1960.
Channel Tunnel Study Group. 1960.
6

COLLARD, William.
Proposed London and Paris Railway.
(Under Railways).
Clowes. 1928.
1,4,6,7,8,11,12

FOX, Sir. Francis.
Geographical aspects of the Channel Tunnel. (In
Geographical Journal, Vol. L, No. 2, August, 1917).
12

GAIN, Paul-Henry.
La question du tunnel sous la Manche.
Rousseau.(1932).
7

GIBBONS, Gavin.
Trains under the Channel.
Advertiser Press.(1970).
4,6,7

GREAT BRITAIN, Parliament.
Channel Tunnel Committee report.
H.M.S.O. 1930.
11

GREAT BRITAIN, Parliament.
Report from the Joint Select Committee on the Channel
Tunnel.
Hansard. 1883.
11

GRIP.
How John Bull lost London or, the capture of the
Channel Tunnel.
1882.
6

GULLIVER, Diogenes. pseud.
Great suspension bridge from Dover to Calais.
J. Johnson, Dover (Printers). n.d.
1

HARRINGTON, J.L.
The Channel Tunnel and Ferry.
Oakwood Press. 1949.
1,7,8,11,12,15

INSTITUTE OF GEOLOGICAL SCIENCES.
Geological results of the Channel Tunnel site investig-
ation, 1964-65, by J.P. Destombes and E.R. Shephard-
Thorn.
H.M.S.O. 1971.
4

KATSCHER, Ludwig.
Eine Eisenbahn unter dem Meere (In Vomfels sum Meer,
February, 1883).
7

KENT COUNTY COUNCIL - PLANNING DEPARTMENT.
The Channel Tunnel: a discussion of terminal requirements
on the British side, and the possible locations for terminal
facilities in Kent.
Kent County Council. 1968.
2,6,11,12,21

KNOWLES, James.
The Channel Tunnel and public opinion, compiled by J.
Knowles.
Kegan, Paul, French and Co. 1883.
12

LEROI, David.
The Channel Tunnel.
Clifton Books. 1969.
7,12

LUCAS, J.
Hydrogeology of the Dover Basin...Channel Tunnel ..coalfield.
c.1900.
6

MARSHALL, Horace and Son. Publishers.
By tube to France.
Horace Marshall and Son. c.1914.
7

A MILITARY RAILWAY EXPERT. pseud.
The Channel Tunnel.
London. 1907.
3

NEW DOVER GROUP.
The effect of the Channel Tunnel on the town and port of
Dover.
New Dover Group. 1966.
6

PEQUIGNOT, C.A.
Channel Tunnel: everyman's guide to the technicalities of
building a channel tunnel.
C.R. Books Ltd. 1965.
1,6,7

PERKINS, W. Turner.
Channel Tunnel: deputation to the Prime Minister; full
details of the present scheme - military, engineering,
financial, edited by W.T. Perkins.
Channel Tunnel Company. 1913.
7,11,21

PERKINS, W. Turner.
Channel Tunnel: reports by British and French engineers.
1907.
3 (1913) 6 (1913) 9,12

PRESTWICH, Joseph.
On the geological conditions affecting the construction of a
tunnel between England and France.
Clowes. 1874.
11

ROYAL UNITED SERVICE INSTITUTION.
The Channel Tunnel: important discussion, February 13th.
Royal United Service Institution. 1907.
3,9

SLATER, Humphrey.
The Channel Tunnel by H. Slater and C. Barnett.
Wingate. 1958.
6,7,12

SOUTH EASTERN RAILWAY.
Channel Tunnel: minutes, correspondence and Chairman's
observations.
South Eastern Railway. 1875.
11

SWINBORNE, Frederick W.P.
Our island England. Twenty sonnets giving reasons why we
should not make the Channel Tunnel.
J.A. Dodds. 1907.
7

SYDENHAM OF COMBE, GEORGE SYDENHAM CLARKE, Baron.
The Channel Tunnel: military aspect of the question.
Printed by A. and E. Walter. 1914.
3,6,11,12

TRANSPORT, Ministry of.
Proposals for a fixed Channel link.
H.M.S.O. 1963.
1,4,6,7,8,11,12

TRAVIS, Anthony Stewart.
Channel Tunnel, 1802-1968.
Peter Davis. 1967.
1,2,4,5,6,7,8,11

WHITESIDE, Thomas.
The tunnel under the Channel.
Hart-Davis. 1962.
1,5,6,7,11,12

WOOD, Alan Marshall M.
The Channel Tunnel story. (In Project No. 9, Spring,
1969).
6

CHARING

Charing Church and parish.
Charing, Newton, Clark.(1946 or later).
3,12

Charing Church barn, built 1956-8.
Charing, Newton, Clark. 1958.
11

Charing guide and yearbook, 1953.
Charing, Newton, Clark. 1953?
11

CHARING PLAYING FIELD COMMITTEE.
Charing Tudor May Fayre, 27th May, 1967.
Charing Playing Field Committee. 1967.
11

COCKRANE, Carola.
Two acres unlimited.
Crosby Lockward. 1954.
8,11,12

FOTHERINGHAM, David Ross.
Guide to Charing, with a description of the
archiepiscopal palace.
Charing, Moody. 1915.
1,11

FOTHERINGHAM, David Ross.
Historic Charing.
Charing, Moody. 1927.
3

HALL, G.H.
The forgotten footboy.
S.E.E. Board Magazine. 1963.
12

KENT COUNTY CREMATORIUM LTD.
Kent County Crematorium, Newcourt Wood, Charing, Kent:
a brief description with scale of charges.
Maidstone, Kent County Crematorium Ltd. 196-.
3

RACKETT, Thomas.
A description of Otterden Place and Church, and of the
archiepiscopal palace at Charing.
Nichols. 1832.
1,11,12

CHARITIES

Charities in the County of Kent, 1818-1837, by
commissioner appointed to continue inquiries concerning
charities (also general index).
1840.
17

COMMISSIONERS FOR INQUIRING CONCERNING CHARITIES.
The charities of the County of Kent.
1839.
1,6,11.

COMMISSIONERS FOR INQUIRING CONCERNING CHARITIES.
The report relating to the County of Kent, 1819-1837.
Gray. n.d.
1,3,11

COMMITTEE APPOINTED TO INSPECT AND CONSIDER THE RETURNS MADE
BY MINISTERS AND CHURCH WARDENS, RELATIVE TO THE CHARITABLE
DONATIONS FOR THE BENEFIT OF POOR PERSONS.
Abstract of the returns, 1786-88. (Original copy of Kent
returns).
1816.
8

Draft scheme for the administration of the charity of
Symond Potyn. St. Catherine's Hospital, Rochester and other
charities.
(Typescript). 1959.
15

GREAT BRITAIN, Parliament.
Abstract of the returns of charitable donations, 1786-88 -
County of Kent. n.d.
8

GREAT BRITAIN, Parliament.
Endowed charities - County of Kent.
1868.
8,11

HEATH, Sidney.
Old English houses of alms: a pictorial record.
London, Francis Griffiths. 1910.
4

LANSDELL, Henry.
Princess Aelfrida's Charity, 3 vols.
1911-16.
11,17,18

PEYTON, H.N.
Some curious charities and bequests in the County of Kent,
compiled by H.N. Peyton.
n.d.
11

CHARLTON

The Church, the Bishop, or Corah, - which? Two sermons
preached in Charlton Church by the Rector.
1838.
6

Country homes and gardens - Charlton House, Kent, seat of
Sir Spencer P. Maryon-Wilson.
1909.
17

ELLISTON-ERWOOD, Frank Charles.
The earthworks at Charlton.
(1916).
1

GREAT BRITAIN: LAWS, etc. (GEO. III).
An Act for vesting in trustees certain lands at Charlton.
1803.
11

GREAT BRITAIN: LAWS, etc. (GEO. III).
An Act for making compensation to the proprietors of certain
lands situated in Woolwich and Charlton.
1804.
11

MARTIN, Alan R.
Charlton House, Kent: an historical and architectural
guide.
Blackheath Press. 1929.
1,12(1919) 18

MAY, Leonard Morgan.
Charlton, near Woolwich, Kent: full and complete copies of
all the inscriptions in the old parish church and churchyard.
Charles North. 1908.
1,11,15,17,18

CHARTHAM

BROWNE, Andrew R.G.
A history of St. Mary's Church, Chartham, by A.R.G.
Browne and Marjory K. McClintock.
Mackay. 1954.
3,8,11

Chartham Paper Mills: a short history, 1738-1907.
(Reprinted from "The Stationery World", 1907).
3

FIELD, E.J.
Guide to St. Mary's Church, Chartham.
Canterbury, Gibbs. 1964.
11,12

HOWARD, WILLIAM AND SON LTD.
Chartham enterprise: a paper mill and its story.
London, Wiggins Teape Group. 1963?
4

RANDOLPH, Selina.
Chartham in the days of old.
Ashford, Kentish Express. 1911.
1,3,4,11,12

RANDOLPH, Selina.
Chartham Parish Church.
Canterbury, W.G. Austen. 1914.
3

SOMNER, William.
Chartham news.
n.d.
4,11

CHARTHAM HATCH

Hatch farm house - Sale catalogue.
1967.
12

CHARTWELL - SEE WESTERHAM

CHATHAM

Album of Chatham and Rochester views.
C. Reynolds. n.d.
12

ANCIENT ORDER OF FORESTERS.
Souvenir of the High Court at Chatham.
August, 1938.
4

ARNOLD, A.A.
History of Sir John Hawkins' Hospital at Chatham.
Parrett and Neves. 1916.
15

A.R.P. Chatham: monthly journal, Nos. 1-8.
1939-40.
4

BALDWIN, Charles.
Tender for street lighting in Chatham, for the winter of
1809-10, addressed to the Gentlemen Commissioners. On
the same sheet an invitation to tender dated 15th
August, 1810. MS.
4

BARNABY, H.
Historic notes of Chatham and Rochester in bygone days.
1899.
4,15,17

BARRY, John Wolfe.
Railways and locomotives: lectures delivered at the
School of Military Engineering at Chatham in 1877, by
J.W. Barry and F.J. Bramwell.
Longmans. 1882.
4

BELL, J.A.B.
Trial of John Any Bird.
Bell (Under Maidstone). 1831.
12

BELSEY, F.F.
Centenary of Ebenezer Sunday Schools, Chatham, 1799-1899, by
F.F. Belsey and W. Dunstall.
Chatham, Mackay. 1899.
11,15

BENSON, G.
4 letters to Alexander Bruce, army agent, Pall Mall, about
a claim (possibly fraudulent) for a soldier's clothing
supplied at Chatham in 1801.
1811 MS.
4

CALLENDER, Geoffrey.
The portrait of Peter Pett and the Sovereign of the Seas.
Yelf Bros. 1930.
4,15

Candid remarks on a sermon, preached by Mr. Joseph Hart, at
the Tabernacle at Chatham, 1765. In a letter to a friend.
1765.
4

CAZENEUVE, John and WITHERIDGE, William. Protagonists.
A true story of the case relative to the dispute about the
parish register-book of Chatham in Kent. To which is added,
an answer to a very disingenuous and calumnious charge made
against the late church-wardens, in a pamphlet lately
published by the Minister.
London, Printed for John Townson, Bookseller at Chatham. 1766.
4

CHATHAM BOROUGH COUNCIL.
Annual report, 1960 - in progress.
8,12(1964-5)

CHATHAM BOROUGH COUNCIL.
Chatham, Kent: the official guide, 193-? edition.
E.J. Burrow.
11

CHATHAM BOROUGH COUNCIL.
Guide to Chatham.
Vickery, Kyrle. 1930?
4

CHATHAM BOROUGH COUNCIL.
Borough of Chatham: official guide.
Mowbray. 1958, etc.
1,4,5,8,9,11,12,19

CHATHAM BOROUGH COUNCIL.
Car parking and traffic management proposals.
n.d.
8

CHATHAM BOROUGH COUNCIL.
Central Hall, Chatham.
1968.
4

CHATHAM BOROUGH COUNCIL.
Chatham, Kent.
Cheltenham, Burrow. 1953.
4,11

CHATHAM BOROUGH COUNCIL.
Chatham (including Gillingham): official guide.
1909?
4

CHATHAM BOROUGH COUNCIL.
Chatham Star, 1962 - in progress.
8

CHATHAM BOROUGH COUNCIL.
Council minutes, 1953 - in progress.
8

CHATHAM BOROUGH COUNCIL.
A short description and war service of ships in the Royal
Navy named "Chatham" from the year 1690 to 1912, with a brief
description of Chatham Dockyard, etc.
Parrett, Neves. 1912.
4

CHATHAM BOROUGH COUNCIL.
Souvenir of the local government exhibition held at
Chatham, 2nd-9th October, 1946.
Mackay. 1946.
8

CHATHAM BOROUGH COUNCIL.
Visit of H.R.H. the Princess Christian on February 2nd,
1898.
8

CHATHAM BOROUGH COUNCIL - BOROUGH ENGINEER AND SURVEYOR.
Specification for new Junior Boy's School, Luton Road.
(Typescript).
1930.
4

CHATHAM BOROUGH COUNCIL - BOROUGH ENGINEER AND SURVEYOR.
Specification for new Senior Boy's School, Ordnance
Place.
October, 1938.
4

CHATHAM BOROUGH COUNCIL - PUBLIC LIBRARIES.
Official opening of the new Central Library, 19th
January, 1971 by Miss Christina Foyle.
1971.
4

CHATHAM BOROUGH COUNCIL - PUBLICITY AND ENTERTAINMENT
DEPARTMENT.
River Medway Dutch Week, 1967.
4

CHATHAM MEMORIAL SYNAGOGUE.
Centenary, 1865-1965 (5625-5725), Sunday, 24th October,
1965. The Centenary Service (souvenir booklet with
historical notes).
1965.
4

CHATHAM OLD PEOPLE'S WELFARE COMMITTEE.
The Riverside Magazine, Summer/Autumn, 1971.
1971.
4

CHATHAM OBSERVER.
Illustrated almanac and yearbook.
1904, 1915, 1918.
4

CHATHAM YOUNG MEN'S SOCIETY.
Constitution and rules. Also programme of meetings,
May-August, 1852.
1852.
4

CLAYTON, Charles.
Parochial sermons preached at Chatham and Rochester.
Jackson, J. 1846.
15

COAD, J.G.
Chatham Ropeyard. (Reprinted from Post-Mediaeval
Archaeology).
1969.
4

CULL, Frederick.
Chatham - the Hill House. (Reprinted from Archaeologia
Cantiana, Vol. LXXVII, 1962).
Ashford, Headley Bros. 1962.
8,17

CUNDILL, John.
Folly reproved, or an admonition for the Rev. William
Giles, occasioned by his pamphlet entitled, "Truth
vindicated, and error exposed".
C. and W. Townson. 1818.
4

CUNDILL, John.
An address to the Rev. W. Giles, containing remarks
on his creed, which he professed to believe.
Rochester, W. Epps. n.d.
4

DARTNELL, George Russell.
Notes of Queen Victoria's visit to Fort Pitt and Chatham,
November 28th, 1855, Part 2 only. (Typescript).
4

DAVIS ESTATE RATEPAYERS' ASSOCIATION.
Members' Magazine, Summer. 1967.
1967.
4

DUNGEY, Henry.
Tender for street lighting in Chatham, addressed to the
Committee of Lighting, September 9th, 1809.
1809. MS.
4

DURNFORD, A.W.
A petition to the Right Honourable Sir Henry Hardinge, K.C.B.
(The petitioner was barrack-master at Chatham from 1821-1839,
and is appealing against his removal from the post).
Chatham, James Burrill. 1839?
4

EBENEZER CONGREGATIONAL CHURCH, CHATHAM.
Yearbook, 1956, 1957, 1968.
4

ELY, John.
Brief memorials of the Rev. J. Slatterie: forty-three years
Pastor of the Congregational Church in...Ebenezer Chapel,
Chatham.
Chatham, James Burrill. 1838.
15

Fifteen views of Chatham, Rochester and neighbourhood.
(Drawings).
Iverhowe. c.1861-1884.
4

FRANCIS ILES GALLERIES, CHATHAM.
Leighton-Jones, an exhibition of paintings, 6th March-27th
March, 1971. (Catalogue).
1971.
4

GREAT BRITAIN: LAWS, etc. (GEO. II)
An Act for making compensation to the proprietors of such
lands and hereditaments as have been purchased for the
better securing His Majesty's docks, ships and stores at
Chatham.
1759.
4

GREAT BRITAIN: LAWS, etc. (GEO. III).
An Act for the better paving..., streets and lanes in the
town and parish of Chatham.
1772.
4,8,11

GREAT BRITAIN: LAWS, etc. (GEO. III).
An Act to explain and amend an Act...for paving...the
streets and lanes of Chatham.
1776.
4,8

GREAT BRITAIN: LAWS, etc. (GEO. III).
An Act for improving the funds of the chest at Chatham and
for transferring the administration of the same to
Greenwich Hospital.
1803.
4,11

GREAT BRITAIN: LAWS, etc. (GEO. III).
An Act for making compensation to the proprietors of such
lands...as have been purchased for better securing His
Majesty's docks at Chatham.
1806.
4,11

GRIFFIN, Ralph.
Kentish items: Aylesford, Pluckley, Stourmouth, Faversham,
Sittingbourne, Wouldham, Chatham.
n.d.
7

HAMERTON, C.
Proposal and terms to do the paving in Chatham. To the
Commissioners for Paving...March 8th, 1821. MS.
4

HAMERTON, C.
Tender for paving the streets of Chatham for three
years, 10th March, 1821. (Photocopy of MS. letter).
4

HARKER, Rev. George.
New Church, Chatnam. (A reprint of three addresses...
showing that the repairs (etc.) of the church (i.e.
St. John's) were by law intended to be a charge on the
parish church rate).
Rochester, Wildash.(1825).
4

HARRIS, Edwin.
Abridged account of the first great fire which happened
at Chatham on 30th June, 1800.
Rochester, Harris. 1914. (Eastgate Series No. 20)
1,11

HARRIS, Edwin.
Abridged account of the second great fire which happened
at Chatham on 3rd March, 1820.
Rochester, Harris. 1914. (Eastgate Series No. 21).
1,11,15

HARRIS, Edwin.
Chatham inns and signs (past and present).
Rochester, Harris. 1914.(Eastgate Series No. 22).
1,11

HARRIS, Edwin.
Description of Chatham in the year 1838.
Rochester, Harris. 1915. (Eastgate Series No. 24).
1,11

HARRIS, Edwin.
Dickensian Chatham.
Rochester, Harris. 1911. (Eastgate Series No. 13).
4,11

HARRIS, Edwin.
Guide to Chatham (up-to-date).
Rochester, Harris. 1912. (Eastgate Series No. 15).
1,11

HARRIS, Edwin.
History of Chatham.
Rochester, Harris. 1912.(Eastgate Series No. 17).
1,11,15

HARRIS, Edwin.
History of St. Mary's Church, Chatham.
Rochester, Harris. 1913.(Eastgate Series No. 18)
1,11,15

HARRIS, Edwin.
History of the Chatham Chest and Sir John Hawkins'
Hospital.
Rochester, Harris. 1915. (Eastgate Series No. 23).
1

HARRIS, Edwin.
Reminiscences of Chatham.
Rochester, Harris. 1916. (Eastgate Series No. 25).
1,11,15

HARRIS, Edwin.
Roman Chatham. (Eastgate series).
Rochester, Harris. 1912.(Eastgate Series No. 16).
1,11,15

HARRIS, Edwin.
The second great fire at Chatham, 1820. (Eastgate
series).
E. Harris. n.d.
15

HEARNDEN, Isaac.
Blower's ghost: a legend of Kent.
Chatham, Gale. 1880.
3,8,11,12,15

Hearth Tax Register - Chatham section. (Typescript).
1665.
4,8

History of Sir John Hawkins' Hospital at Chatham.
Parrett, Neves. 1916.
4

HOGG, P. Fitzgerald.
Chatham. (A MS. notebook listing streets as they existed in
1938; inns and signs, 1938; defunct inns; farms within
Chatham boundaries; woods in the vicinity of Chatham).
4

The Holcombeian: magazine of the Technical School for Boys,
Chatham. New series, Nos. 1-3.
1956-9?
4

Home words for heart and hearth, 7 vols. (Included are the
parish magazines of St. Paul's, Chatham).
1883, etc.
4

HOUSING AND LOCAL GOVERNMENT, Minstry of.
List of buildings of special architectural or historic
interest. Borough of Chatham, 29th October, 1952 and
supplementary list.
1952.
4

IMPERIAL WAR GRAVES COMMISSION.
Memorials to the naval ranks and ratings of the Empire who
fell in the Great War and have no other grave than the sea.
The register of the names inscribed on the memorial at the
Port of Chatham, 5 parts and introduction to the registers.
1924.
4

IMPERIAL WAR GRAVES COMMISSION.
The war dead of the British Commonwealth and Empire, No. 1
Chatham naval memorial.
1952.
4,8

INDUSTRIAL DISPUTES TRIBUNAL.
Award No. 1256. Terms and conditions of employment of
certain workers at specified cinemas at Chatham and Norwich.
1959.
4

JAMES, Harold A.
Chatham in 1765. (Written for the bi-centenary of the
launching of H.M.S. "Victory" - duplicated).
1965.
4

JAMES, Harold A.
The development of Chatham: notes compiled to form the
basis of an item in the "International History of City
Development" being produced by the University of Pennsylvania.
(Typescript).
1964.
4

JEFFERYS, William.
An account of the fire which happened at Chatham, 1800.
Chatham, Etherington. 1801.
11,12,15

JEFFERYS, William.
An account of the dreadful fire of Chatham which happened on
Friday, 3rd March, 1820.
Chatham, Townson. 1821.
4,12,17

LAMBERT, Jeffrey Maurice.
Portraits and silver of the Royal Engineer's H.Q. Mess, Chatham.
Chatham, Institute of Royal Engineer's. 1963.
2,4,8,11,15

LYNN, Rev. James.
A sermon preached at Chatham Church, October 19th, 1803 on
the day appointed for a general fast by the Rev. James Lynn
M.A., Curate of Chatham.
Chatham, C. Townson. 1803.
4

MACKAY, W.J. AND CO. LTD. Publishers.
Type for books: a designer's manual.
Mackay. 1959.
12

MEDWAY COMMERCIAL SHIPPING COMPANY.
Prospectus and minutes of meeting of the shareholders at
Chest Arms, Chatham, 15th September, 1837.
1837.
4

MEDWAY TECHNICAL HIGH SCHOOL FOR GIRLS.
Endeavour, Summer. 1967 (Prose, poetry, drawings).
4,11 (1968)

MEDWAY TOWNS COUNCIL OF CHURCHES.
"Whither Britain?". Exhibition...Town Hall, Chatham,
October 10th to 15th, (1960): souvenir handbook and
guide.
(1960).
4

NEWMAN, J.S.
A plain tract for plain people.
n.d.
11

ORDNANCE, Board of.
A plan of the lands belonging to the Parish of Chatham
for the use of His Majesty's Board of Ordnance. Scale:
1.2 ins.=50 rods. (Photocopy).
c.1760.
4

ORR, William S. AND CO. Publishers.
The pictorial guide to Chatham: a handbook for residents
and visitors (SIC).
1847.
3,4,11,17

PHILOMATH, James Almond.
A plot of part of Chatham street and of several houses,
etc., being now the Estate of Mr. John Maudesley of
Chatham, February, 1600. (Copy of original in County
Archives Office).
1600.
4

PINN, W.
Commonplace book of W. Pinn of Chatham.(Containing press-
cuttings, handbills and letters).
c.1803-1817.
4

PRESNAIL, James.
Chatham: the story of a dockyard town and birthplace
of the British Navy.
Chatham Corporation. 1952.
1,2,4,5,7,8,9,11,12,14,15,17,18

PROTEUS, Professor, pseud.
Some untoward remarks on the first annual report of the
Philosophical and Literary Institution, Chatham.
W. Epps. c.1828.
15

RANGER, William.
Report to the General Board of Health on a preliminary
inquiry into the sewerage, drainage and supply of water
and the sanitary condition of the inhabitants of the town
of Chatham.
W. Clowes. 1849.
4

Report on the (Parliamentary) Borough of Chatham, with
a description of the proposed boundary.
1831-2.
4

ROWE, John Tetley.
Some notes on Chatham Parish Church.
c.1906?
4

ROWE, John Tetley.
Upon a briefe. (An appeal for funds to rebuild Chatham
Parish Church, with notes on its history and treasures).
London, Skeffington. (18--).
4

ROYAL NAVAL BENEVOLENT TRUST - CHATHAM LOCAL COMMITTEE.
Annual report for the year ended 30th June, 1957.
4

ROYAL SOCIETY FOR THE PREVENTION OF CRUELTY TO ANIMALS -
CHATHAM BRANCH.
Annual report, 1969, 1970.
1970, 1972.
4

ST. JOHN FISHER R.C. COUNTY SECONDARY SCHOOL, CHATHAM.
Imprint '70.
1970.
4

ST. JOSEPH'S CONVENT SCHOOL, CHATHAM.
Prospectus, 1963.
St. Joseph's Convent School, Chatham. 1963.
8

ST. MARY'S CHURCH.
A Medway millenium, 947-1947 (the festival yearbook of the
Church of St. Mary the Virgin).
1947.
4,8

ST. MARY'S CHURCH.
Miscellaneous programmes and service sheets, 1925-72.
1925-72.
4

ST. MARY'S CHURCH.
Parish magazine.
January, 1896-December, 1907.
4

ST. PAUL'S CHURCH.
Home Words: the Parish magazine.
1896, 1897, 1899.
4

SANDEMAN, Aernold Eric Noble.
Notes on the military history of Chatham. (2 photocopies of
notes intended for eventual publication).
c.196-.
4

SANDERS, Frederick W.T.
A business history of Chatham High Street - mainly from the
year 1838 to the year 1961 (with recordings and notes prior
to 1838 to the year of 1750) 4 vols. (Typescript).
1963.
4

SCAMMELL, S.D.
Chatham long ago and now.
Chatham, Mackay. 1893?
1,3,4,6 and 7(1903) 8,11,12,15,17

SOUTH EASTERN AND CHATHAM RAILWAY - ENGINEER'S OFFICE.
Chatham Station. Drawn from actual survey. Scale: 30
feet=1 inch.
1917.
4

STEPHENS, J.A.
Some interesting coleoptera from the Chatham district.
T. Buncle and Co. 1943.
8

SUMMERS, D.L.
H.M.S. Ganges, 1866-1966: one hundred years of training
boys for the Royal Navy. (Ganges training ship spent several
years at Chatham).
1966.
4

TURNER, John.
On an early palaeolithic workshop site at Stonecross, Luton,
Chatham. (Extracted from the Proceedings of the Prehistoric
Society of East Anglia, Vol. 5, Part 3).
1928.
4

TURNER, Sydney K.
The story of Luton, Chatham. (Typescript).
1952.
4,8,15

Twenty-four views of Chatham.
Mullinger. c.1800.
15

WARD, B.R.
The School of Military Engineering, 1812-1909, Chatham.
R.E. Institute. 1909.
15

WHYMAN, Herbert Francis.
History of the "Royal Kent Lodge of Antiquity", No.
20, Chatham.
Maidstone, Dickinson. 1910.
4,8

WICKHAM, Humphrey.
Roman remains from Luton, Chatham.
1873.
13

YORKSHIRE GEOLOGICAL SOCIETY.
Catalogue of Polyzoa found in the Chatham chalk.
T. Woolley. 1892.
15

YOUNG ENTERPRISE, CHATHAM.
Trade fair, 1968. Old Road, Chatham, April 27th to May
4th.
1968.
4

CHATHAM DOCKYARD

ADMIRALTY.
Navy (trial of coal) for the return of all experiments
made by the Admiralty on coal and patent fuel. (Contain
reports from Chatham and Sheerness Dockyards).
H.M.S.O. 1877.
8

ADMIRALTY.
Queen Anne's Navy: documents, 1702-1714, edited by
R.D. Merriman.
Navy Records Society. 1961.
4,15

ADMIRALTY.
Return showing the principal particulars of the
original legends of the"Rodney, "Howe", "Camperdown"
and "Anson".
H.M.S.O. 1888.
8

ADMIRALTY.
Royal Naval Warrant Officers' manual, 1910.
H.M.S.O. 1910.
8

BOULTER, L.
A diary of the life of H.M.S. "Victory". Chatham
Dockyard Management Training Centre.
1965.
8

BUGLER, Arthur.
H.M.S. "Victory": building, restoration and repair.
(Vol.with plans in accompanying box).
H.M.S.O. 1966.
4

CAPPER, Henry D.
Royal Naval Warrant Officers' manual, 1910, compiled by
H.D. Capper.
Naval Warrant Officers Journal. 1910?
8

CHATHAM DOCKYARD.
Launch of H.M.S. "Ocelot" by Lady Sanders, 5th May,
1962 - programme.
Portsmouth Printing Office. 1962.
4

CHATHAM DOCKYARD.
Periscope, October 29th, 1965 - in progress.
8

The Church of St. George, Royal Naval Barracks, Chatham.
195-?
4

COMMITTEE APPOINTED TO INQUIRE INTO THE CONDITIONS UNDER
WHICH CONTRACTS ARE INVITED FOR THE BUILDING AND
REPAIRING OF SHIPS.
Report.
Eyre and Spottiswood. 1884.
8

Copies of all the minutes and proceedings taken at and upon the several tryals of Captain George Burrish (and others) respecively, before the court martial lately held at Chatham. 1746.
4

CRACE, Sir John Gregory. *Admiral*.
Some notes on the history of Chatham Dockyard.
Privately Printed. 1946?
4,8,11,15

CRAWSHAW, J.D.
History of Chatham Dockyard School (Typescript).
1955.
8

CULL, Frederick.
Chatham Dockyard. (Reprinted from Archaeologia Cantiana Vol. LXXIII, 1959).
Ashford, Headley Bros. 1959.
8

DAILY TELEGRAPH.
The most famous warship in history. (Extract from The Daily Telegraph Weekend Supplement). n.d.
12

DENNE, Samuel.
Extracts from a MS..."The life of Mr. Phineas Pette, one of the master shipwrights to King James the First".
1796.
18

DODD, R.
The Royal Dockyard at Chatham...view taken from the banks of the River Medway, near Upnor Castle. 25½ x 16 ins. (Photograph of drawing in the Royal Engineer's Museum).
1789.
4

ENGHOLM, Frederick Waldeman.
The story of H.M.S. "Victory".
Drummond. 1944.
4,8

EXCHEQUER AND AUDIT DEPARTMENT.
Navy dockyard and production accounts, 1937.
H.M.S.O. 1939.
8

EXCHEQUER AND AUDIT DEPARTMENT.
Navy dockyard and production accounts, 1959-60.
H.M.S.O. 1961.
8

EXCHEQUER AND AUDIT DEPARTMENT.
Navy dockyard and production accounts, 1960-61.
H.M.S.O. 1962.
8

EXCHEQUER AND AUDIT DEPARTMENT.
Navy dockyard and production accounts, 1961-62.
H.M.S.O. 1963.
8

EXCHEQUER AND AUDIT DEPARTMENT.
Navy dockyard and production accounts, 1962-63.
H.M.S.O. 1964.
8

EXCHEQUER AND AUDIT DEPARTMENT.
Navy dockyard and production accounts, 1963-64.
H.M.S.O. 1965.
8

FENWICK, Kenneth.
H.M.S. "Victory".
Cassell. 1959.
4,8

FIELD, C.
Old times afloat, compiled by C. Field.
Melrose. 1932.
8

GORST, Sir John.
Dockyard administration: speech by Sir John Gorst Q.C., M.P. for Chatham in House of Commons, 1886.
Southwark, McCorquodale. 1886.
15

GRACE, J.G.
Some notes on the history of Chatham Dockyard.
1946?
11

GREAT BRITAIN: LAWS, etc. (GEO. III).
An Act to vest certain messuages...for the better securing His Majesty's docks at Chatham.
1780.
4,11,12

GREAT BRITAIN: LAWS, etc. (GEO. III).
An Act to vest certain messuages, lands, tenements and hereditaments in trustees for the better securing His Majesty's docks, ships and stores at Portsmouth and Chatham.
1782.
4

GREAT BRITAIN: LAWS, etc. (GEO. III).
An Act for extinguishing the right of way...leading across the exercising ground in front of Chatham Lines.
1808.
4,8,11

GREAT BRITAIN: LAWS, etc. (GEO. III).
An Act to vest certain messuages in trustees for better securing His Majesty's docks at Chatham and Woolwich.
1804.
4,11

GREAT BRITAIN: LAWS, etc. (GEO. III).
An Act for the purchase of certain lands at Sheerness and Chatham for the use of the navy.
1816.
4,11

GREAT BRITAIN: LAWS, etc. (ELIZ. II).
Harbours, docks, piers and ferries. The dockyard port of Chatham.
H.M.S.O. 1965.
8

GREAT BRITAIN: LAWS, etc. STATUTORY INSTRUMENTS.
The Dockyard Port of Chatham Order, 1964. Made 26th Feb. 1964. Coming into operation 6th April, 1964. (S.I. 1964 No. 264).
H.M.S.O. 1964.
4

H.M. DOCKYARD - MANAGEMENT TRAINING CENTRE.
Chatham in 1765. (Typescript).
Chatham Dockyard. 1965.
8

H.M. DOCKYARD - MANAGEMENT TRAINING CENTRE.
A diary of the life of H.M.S. "Victory". (Typescript).
1965.
8

H.M. DOCKYARD - MANAGEMENT TRAINING CENTRE.
H.M. Dockyard, Chatham.
1965.
4,8

HARRIS, Edwin.
History of H.M. Dockyard, Chatham.
Rochester, Harris. 1911. (Eastgate Series No. 14).
1,11,15

HOBBES, Robert George.
Reminiscences and notes of seventy years' life.
(Under Sheerness).
Stock. 1893-95.
4,11

KELLY, Edward. *Rear-Admiral*.
Death and funeral of Admiral Kelly. (Reprinted from the Chatham and Rochester News, January 23rd, 1892). (Admiral Kelly was Adm. Supt. of Chatham Dockyard at his death).
1892.
4

LEFRANCQ, Paul.
La carriere Mouvementee de Louis Alexandre de Marolles, ingenieur francais.
Valenciennes, Cercle Arch. et Historique. 1963.
11

LEMPRIERE, C.
A plan of His Majesty's dockyard and ordnance wharf at
Chatham. (Photograph of MS. in Royal Engineer's Museum).
1719.
4

LONGRIDGE, C. Nepean.
The anatomy of Nelson's ships, revised edition.
1961.
4

ORDNANCE, Board of.
An exact survey of the piece of land compriz'd in Mr.
Goateley's lease, demand'd by the Office of Ordnance to
enlarge the Gun Wharf at Chatham.   Sclae: 1inch=50 feet.
(Photograph of copy of original).
1725.
4

ORDNANCE, Board of.
Instruction for the issue of stores to Chatham Dockyard for
the year 1742. 6th March, 1741/2. (Manuscript).
4

ORDNANCE, Board of.
Plan of the intrenchment inclosing His Majesty's dockyard
and ordnance wharfe at Chatham. Scale: 1 inch=400 feet.
(Photograph of original).
1756.
4

ORDNANCE, Board of.
Plan of the road from the Dockyard Gate to Chatham. June,
1759. Scale: 1 inch=150 feet. (Photograph of copy of
original).
1759.
4

GREAT BRITAIN - PRIVY COUNCIL.
Harbours, docks, piers and ferries. The Dockyard Port of
Chatham Order, 1964.
H.M.S.O. 1964.
8

ROBINSON, Alan Wellwood Wade.
Notes on the history of Chatham Dockyard: a talk given by
Surgeon-Commander, A.W.W. Robinson at the Dockyard Technical
College. (Typescript).
(1958).
4

The Royal Dockyard Church, Chatham.
1969.
4

ROYAL NAVAL BARRACKS, CHATHAM.
View album.
n.d.
8

SANDERS, Frederick.
The Chatham Dockyard diary, edited, re-written in the
original, with additional notes and comments by Frederick
Sanders. (Typescript, bound).
1964.
4,8

Scheme of prizes for performing shipwrights' work done by
job (at Chatham Yard).
1815.
17

CHAUCER, GEOFFREY

CAWLEY, A.C.
Chaucer's mind and art, edited by A.C. Cawley.
Oliver and Boyd. 1969.
12

CHAUCER, Geoffrey.
Canterbury chimes or Chaucer's Canterbury Tales, retold for
children by Francis Storr and Hawes Turner.
Kegan, Paul. 1878.
6

CHAUCER, Geoffrey.
The Canterbury pilgrims, retold by J.W. McSpadden.
Harrap. n.d.
6

CHAUCER, Geoffrey.
Canterbury Tales, rendered into modern English by
J.U. Nicolson with illustrations by Rockwell Kent.
W.H. Allen. 1934.
3

CHAUCER, Geoffrey.
The Canterbury Tales, translated into modern English
by Nevill Coghill.
Penguin. 1951.
3

CHAUCER, Geoffrey.
The Canterbury Tales, translated into modern English
by Nevill Coghill, Woodcuts by Edna Whyte, 2 vols.
Folio Society. 1957.
3

CHAUCER, Geoffrey.
The Canterbury Tales of Chaucer to which are added an
essay on his language with notes and a glossary by the
late Thomas Tyrwhitt, 2 vols.
Oxford, Clarendon Press. 2nd Edition. 1798.
3

CHAUCER, Geoffrey.
Chaucer: the minor poems, edited by W.W. Skeat.
Oxford University Press. 1896.
12

CHAUCER, Geoffrey.
The tale of Beryn with a prologue of the merry adventure
of the pardoner with a tapster at Canterbury, re-edited
from the Duke of Northumberland's unique MS. by Frederick
J. Furnivall and Walter G. Stone, Parts 1 and 2.
N. Trubner. 1876, 1887.
3

CHAUCER, Geoffrey.
The works of Geoffrey Chaucer: a facsimile of the
William Morris Kelmscott Chaucer, with the original
87 illus. by Edward Burne-Jones and a glossary for the
modern reader.
Cleveland, World Publishing Co. 1958.
3

CHESTERTON, G.K.
Chaucer.
Faber. 1948.
12

CHUTE, Marchette.
Geoffrey Chaucer of England.
Hale. 1951.
12

CROW, Martin Michael.
Chaucer life-records, edited by M.M. Crow and C.C.
Olson. (Includes Ch. 12, Chaucer as guardian of two
'Kentish heirs, etc.).
Oxford, Clarendon Press. 1966.
11

ENGEL, Hildegard.
Structure and plot in Chaucer's Canterbury Tales.
Bonn, L. Nenendorff. 1931.
3

GRIFFITH, Dudley David.
A bibliography of Chaucer, compiled by D.D. Griffith.
Washington University. 1926.
3

HUSSEY, Maurice.
Chaucer's world.
Cambridge University Press. 1967.
3

LOOMIS, Roger Sherman.
A mirror of Chaucer's world.
Princeton University Press. 1965.
3

SPEIRS, John.
Chaucer the maker.
Faber. 2nd revised edition, 1960.
12

CHIDDINGSTONE Cont'd

STAGG, Frank Noel.
Short history of the parish of Chiddingstone. (MSS.).
n.d.
16

Stonewell Park Estate, Chiddingstone - Sale catalogue.
1967.
12

CHILHAM

BOLTON, Arthur Thomas.
Chilham Castle.
Privately Printed. 1912.
1

BRADE-BIRKS, Stanley Graham.
Looking back into Chilham's history. (Article in St. Mary's,
Chilham, Parish Magazine, February, March, April, 1961).
3

CHAMPION, Sir Reginald.
Parish church of St. Mary, Chilham, edited by Sir. R.
Champion.
Hereford, Printed by Jakemans. 1962.
3

Chilham Castle, Kent: its history and guide to the ancient
castle and keep.
Printed by Thompsons, Ashford. 1953 and 1969.
11

CURTIS, Lillian Pitt.
Chilham by its chimneys.
Chilham, Mrs. Curtis. 1960.
1,2,3,4,8,11,12,15

East Stour Farm, Chilham - Sale catalogue.
1967.
2

H(ARDY), C(harles Frederick).
Chilham Castle, 56 B.C.-A.D. 1916, with some notes on Chilham
Church.
Lund Humphries. 1916?
1,3,11,12

HARDY, Charles Frederick.
Records of Chilham.
Hardy. 1906.
12

HUSSEY, Christopher.
The Keep, Chilham Castle, Kent.
From Country Life. 1924.
17

JESSUP, Frank William.
Court Rolls of the Manor of Chilham, 1654-56, edited by
F.W. Jessup.
Kent Archaeological Society. 1960.
11

JESSUP, Ronald Frank.
Excavations at Julliberrie's grave, Chilham. (Reprinted from
The Antiquaries Journal, Vol. XVII, 1937).
3

JESSUP, Ronald Frank.
Further excavations at Julliberrie's grave, Chilham.
(Reprinted from The Antiquaries Journal, July, 1939).
9

McCLINTOCK, Mrs. Marjorie K.
Story of Chilham Castle.
1954.
11

OSWALD, Allan.
Some brief notes on the history and practice of hawking.
Chilham Castle Hawking Centre. 1970.
11

OSWALD, Allan.
Brief notes on the history and practice of falconry, 2nd
edition, revised.
Chilham Castle Hawking Centre. 1971.
11

Parish Church of St. Mary, Chilham.
Hereford, Jakemans. 1960.
11

PHILLIPPS, Sir Thomas.
Charters relative to the Priory of Trulegh in Kent.
"Archaeologia". 1833.
11

Pilgrims, Chilham - Sale catalogue.
1966.
12

WILKIN, W.H.
Loud notes, compiled by W.H. Wilkin. (Loud family at
Chilham). (Typescript).
n.d.
3

WYATT, Sir Stanley Charles.
Cheneys and Wyatts.
Carey and Claridge. 1960.
11

YATES, Elizabeth.
The next fine day: a novel (about Chilham).
New York, John Day Co. 1962.
3

CHIPSTEAD

PERKINS, Frederick.
Sale catalogue of the library of Frederick Perkins of
Chipstead.
1889.
17

CHISLEHURST

Account of the murder of Mr. and Mrs. Bonar of Camden
Place, Chislehurst by Philip Nicholson. (Extract from
Knapp and Baldwin - The Newgate Calendar, 1824-28).
2

ATTENBOROUGH, John.
The first fifty years: a history of the Camden Place
Lodge, No. 3042, 1904-54.
Camden Place Lodge. 1954.
7

AUBRY, Octave.
L'imperatrice Eugenie (P.343-381: Chislehurst).
Paris, Fayard. 1931.
2

BUSHELL, T.A.
Centenary of the arrival in Chislehurst of the imperial
family of France in September, 1870: short history and
programme.
Chislehurst Imperial Centenary Committee. 1970.
1,2,7,11

BUSHELL, T.A.
Chislehurst parish church.
1957.
2

BUSHELL, T.A.
Chislehurst parish church.
Bath, Bawson and Goodall. 1963.
11

BUSHELL, T.A.
Old Chislehurst. (A series of 30 articles - news
cuttings).
1959-60.
2

A catalogue of the Sydney collection at Frognal,
Chislehurst.
Knight, Frank and Rutley. 1915.
4,12,17

CHAPMAN, Hester W.
Eugenie: an historical romance. (P.399-495:
Chislehurst).
Cape. 1961.
2

Charity, still a Christian virtue, or an impartial
account of the tryle of Rev. Mr. Hendley at Chisselhurst.
1719.
11

CHISLEHURST AND NOTTINGHAM CHAMBER OF COMMERCE.
Brochure, 1948-49. (Note: includes brief histories of
Chislehurst and Nottingham).
1948.
2

CHISLEHURST AND ST. PAUL'S CRAY COMMONS CONSERVATORS.
Chislehurst and St. Paul's Cray commons.
Chislehurst and St. Paul's Cray Commons Conservators.
1970.
2,4,11

CHISLEHURST METHODIST CHURCH.
A hundred years of Methodism in Chislehurst, 1870-1970.
Chislehurst Methodist Church. 1970.
2

Chislehurst parish church.
1960.
11

CHISLEHURST URBAN DISTRICT COUNCIL.
Chislehurst and Sidcup: the official guide.
Cheltenham, Burrow. 1954, etc.
1,2,4,5,11

CLUTTON, Margaret M.
Memories of my childhood, 1874-1885 (at Chislehurst).
(Typescript). 193-?
2

CORLEY, T.A.B.
Democratic despot: a life of Napoleon II. (Note: last
chapter refers to Chislehurst).
Barrie and Rockliff. 1961.
2

DE LA CHAPELLE, A. COMTE. Editor.
Oeuvres posthudres...de Napoleon III, edited by A. De La
Chapelle. (Note: photocopy of extracts relating to
residence of Napoleon III in Chislehurst).
Paris, E. Lachaud. 1873.
2

DEFOE, Daniel.
Charity, still a Christian virtue: an impartial account of
the tryal and conviction of the Rev. Mr. Hendley for
preaching a charity sermon at Chislehurst, 1719.
1719.
17

DUNCAN, Leland Lewis.
History of Chislehurst, its churches, manors and parishes,
by L.L. Duncan and others.
1899.
18

Exhibition of fine arts and industry, Chislehurst, 1890-
July 8th-26th.
Eden, Fisher and Co. 1890.
2

FORSTER, T.E.
Chislehurst caves, by T.E. Forster. (Transcribed from
Journal of British Archaeological Association, new series,
Vol. 10, August, 1904).
2

GREAT BRITAIN: LAWS, etc. (VIC.).
An Act to confirm certain provisional orders made by the
Board of Trade under the Electric Lighting Acts, 1882 and
1888 relating to Chislehurst, Gravesend.
1898.
9

GREAT BRITAIN: LAWS, etc. (VIC.).
Metropolitan commons (Chislehurst and St. Paul's Cray)
Supplementary Act, 1888.
1888.
2

GUEST, Ivor.
Napoleon III in England. (Section on exile in Chislehurst).
British Technical and General Press. 1952.
2

The Home Guard in Chislehurst (duplicated typescript).
1945?
2

HUSSEY, Rev. William.
The magistrate's charge for the people's safetie.
n.d.
11

List of flowers and plants, Frognal (Photocopy of
MS. notebook). Frognal was once in Chislehurst, now
in Sidcup).
1814-1820?
2

McCALL, Dorothy.
Patchwork of the history of Chislehurst.
Winchester, Warner. 1963.
1,2,5,11,15,17,18

MARRIOTT, J.W.
Short history of Chislehurst.
Chislehurst, Waters. 1912.
1,2

MURRAY, F.H.
A few words of explanation addressed to his parishioners.
(Author was Rector of Chislehurst).
Baynes and Carpenter. 1877.
2

NICHOLS, W.J.
Chislehurst caves and deneholes.
Bedford Press. 1903.
1,2,4,5,9,11,17,18,21

NICHOLS, W.J.
The Chislehurst caves and deneholes (second paper).
(Extract from Journal of British Archaeological
Association, new series, Vol. 10, 1904).
1904.
2

O'BEIRNE, T.P.
A short history of St. Mary's, Chislehurst. (Cover
title: The Wood on the Stony Hill).
(1967).
2

PARKER, E.N.
Christ Church, Chislehurst, 1872-1972.
Christ Church, Chislehurst. 1972.
2

PIGGOTT, Stuart.
William Camden and the Britannia. (Reprinted from
Proceedings, British Academy, Vol. 37 - Camden was a
resident of Chislehurst).
G. Cumberlege. 1951.
2

REINHARDT, E.A.
Napoleon and Eugenie (last section deals with exile in
Chislehurst).
Hutchinson. 1932.
2

ROCHARD, J.
Bromley, Beckenham and Chislehurst.
J. Rochard. c.1893.
2

SAVOIE-CARIGNAN, C.E. de, Count de Soissons.
The true story of the Empress Eugenie.
Lane. 1921.
2

SOUTH EASTERN RAILWAY CO.
Illustrated tourist guide - Chislehurst, Sevenoaks,
Tunbridge Wells.
Morton. n.d.
11

STEVENSON, R. Scott.
Famous illnesses in history (2nd chapter on Darwin and
Napoleon III).
(Under Downe).
Eyre and Spottiswoode. 1962.
2

TISDALL, E.E.D.
The Prince Imperial. (Ref. St. Mary's Church,
Chislehurst).
1959.
18

TONNET, Pierre.
L'imperatrice Eugenie exitee en Angleterre, 1870-1920.
Bibliotheque des Amis de Napoleon III, 1967.
2

Views of Chislehurst.
Rock and Co. n.d.
13

WEBB, Edward Alfred.
A guide to the ancient parish church of St. Nicholas,
Chislehurst, with a short account of the church of the
Annunciation, the church of St. John the Baptist and Christ
Church.
G. Allen. 1901.
1,2,7,11,12,15,17,18

WEBB, Edward Alfred.
History of Chislehurst.
1899.
1,2,4,6,8,11,12,15,16,17,18

WOLLASTON, Francis. Rector of Chislehurst.
A country parson's address to his flock to caution them
against being misled by the wolf in sheep's clothing, or
receiving Jacobin teachers of sedition.
Printed for G. Wilkie. 1799.
2,11

CHISLET

COOPER, J.E.
The mollusca of Chislet marshes.
n.d.
11

HASLEWOOD, Rev. Francis.
The parish of Chislet.
Privately Printed. 1887.
1,3,4,6,7,8,11,12,15,17

CHURCHES

ASSOCIATION OF FRIENDS OF KENT VILLAGE CHURCHES.
Exhibition of treasures from Kent churches, St. Augustine's
College, Canterbury, July 21st-28th, 1951.
1951.
3,11

BOORMAN, Henry Ray P.
Kent churches.
Kent Messenger. 1954.
1,2,3,4,5,6,7,8,9,11,14,15,17,18,19,20

COUNCER, C.R.
A book of church notes by John Philpot, Somerset Herald.
K.A.S. 1960.
11

CULMER, George G.
Architecture and architectural history of the church.
n.d.
11

DENNE, Samuel.
Further remarks on stone seats in the chancels of churches.
"Archaeologia". 1790.
11

DOVE, Ronald Hammerton.
Bellringer's guide to the church bells of Britain and ringing
peals of the world, compiled by R.H. Dove.
1956.
2,4,5,11

DOVE, Ronald Hammerton.
Bell ringer's guide to the church bells of Britain, compiled
by R.H. Dove.
Aldershot, Gale and Polden. 1962.
5,6,11

DUCAREL, Andrew Coltee.
A repertory of the endowments of vicarages in the dioceses of
Canterbury and Rochester.
Nichols. 1782.
1,2,3,6,7,11,12,14,15,17 (and 1763)

DUNCAN, Leland Lewis.
Parish churches of West Kent.
n.d.
1,2,8,11,15,18 (1895)

ECTON, John.
The saurus verum ecclesiasticarum: being an account
of the valuations of all the ecclesiastical benefices in
in the several dioceses in England and Wales, compiled
by J. Ecton.
London, Printed for D. Browne. 1742.
3,5

ELLISTON-ERWOOD, Frank Charles.
The apse in Kentish church architecture.
n.d.
11,17,18

ESDAILE, Mrs. Katharine Ada.
English church monuments.
London and Malvern Wells, Batsford. (1946).
3

ESDAILE, Mrs. Katharine Ada.
Notes on three monumental drawings from Sir Edward
Dering's collections.
Archaeologia Cantiana. n.d.
11

FISHER, Thomas.
Drawings of brasses in some Kentish churches.
J. Bale. 1913.
1

FLETCHER, Sir E.
Early Kentish churches.
Headley Bros. 1966.
5,15

FOSTER, Joseph.
Index ecclesiasticus, edited by J. Foster, Part I, 1800-
1840.
Oxford, Parker and Co. 1890.
3

FRAMPTON, Thomas S.
Church plate in Kent - Dover deanery.
Mitchell and Hughes. 1903.
6

FRAMPTON, Thomas S.
Early presentations to Kentish benefices.
1893?
11

FRERE, Walter Howard.
Registrum Matthei: Parker, diocesis Cantuariensis, A.D.
1559-1575.
Canterbury and York Society. n.d.
11

GLYNNE, Sir Stephen R.
Notes on the churches of Kent.
Murray. 1877.
1,2,3,4,5,6,7,8,9,10,11,12,13,14,15,16,17,18,19,21

GRAYLING, Francis.
County churches: Kent, 2 vols.
G. Allen. 1913.
1,2,3,4,5,6,7,8,9,10,11,12,13,14,15,16,17,18,19

GRAYLING, Francis.
A lecture on glass painting and staining.
1882.
20

GRIFFIN, Ralph.
Drawings of brasses in some Kentish churches.
Bale. 1914.
2,3,7,11,12

HUSSEY, Arthur.
Chapels and hospitals in Kent.
Mitchell, Hughes and Clarke. 1911.
11,17

HUSSEY, Arthur.
Kent chantries, edited by A. Hussey.
K.A.S. n.d.
1,2,3,5,7,11,12,15,17

HUSSEY, Arthur.
Notes on the churches in Kent, Surrey and Sussex
mentioned in the Domesday Book.
London, John Russell Smith. 1852.
1,2,3,4,5,6,7,8,11,12,13,15,17,18,19,20

KENT COUNTY ASSOCIATION OF CHANGE RINGERS.
Fifty-eighth annual report, 1938.
1938.
7

Kent parish churches - miscellaneous pamphlets.
17

MAXWELL, Donald.
Adventures among churches.
Faith Press. 1928.
3,6,9,12

MAXWELL, Donald.
More adventures among churches.
Faith Press.
3,6,12,15

ORPINGTON DEANERY SYNOD.
Deanery resources. Report by a Committee set up by the
Deanery Synod. (Duplicated).
1972.
2

ORPINGTON RURAL DEANERY.
List of parishes, alphabetical list of streets. (Typescript).
1967.
2

OYLER, Thomas H.
The parish churches of the diocese of Canterbury, with
descriptive notes.
London, Hunter and Longhurst. 1910.
1,3,4,6,7,11,12,13,14,17,18,19,21

PARSONS, Philip.
The monuments of painted glass of upwards of 100 churches,
chiefly in the Eastern part of Kent.
Canterbury, Simmons, Kirkby, etc. 1794.
1,3,6,7,11,21

ROBERTSON, William Archibald Scott.
Church plate in Kent.
Mitchell and Hughes. 1886.
2,6,8,11,17

ROBSON, Edward.
Churches visited by Edward Robson. Manuscript, Vol. 1 only
with notes on Beckenham, Bromley, Hayes, Keston, West
Wickham, Sydenham.
(1847-53).
2

ROE, Frederick.
Ancient church chests and chairs in the Home Counties round
Greater London.
Batsford. 1929.
12

ST. PAUL'S ECCLESIOLOGICAL SOCIETY.
Transactions, Vol. III. The parish churches of West Kent.
St. Paul's Ecclesiological Society. 1895.
8

SANDERS, Frederick.
Kentish (Wealden) churchyards.
1936.
4

Seven churches on the Rivey Cray.
Gilbert and Rivington. 1830.
1,5,11,17

SMETHAM, Henry.
Rambles round churches, 4 vols.
Chatham, Parrett and Neves. 1925-29.
1,2,3,4,5,6(vols. 1,2 and 3) 7,8,9,11,12,13,15,17,18 (vol 4
only).

SMETHAM, Henry.
Rambles round churches in the land of Dickens. (Scrapbook
of articles from Chatham, Rochester and Gillingham News). n.d.
8

STAHLSCHMIDT, J.C.L.
Church bells of Kent.
Elliot Stock. 1887.
1,2,3,4,5,6,7,8,11,12,13,15,16,17,18,19,21

TRISTRAM, Ernest William.
English wall painting of the fourteenth century.
London, Kegan Paul. 1955.
3

WALCOTT, Mackenzie E.C.
Parish church goods in Kent, A.D. 1552 (Edward VI):
inventories, Part 1, edited by the Rev. Mackenzie E.C.
Walcott and the Rev. W.A. Scott Robertson.
London, Printed by Taylor and Co. 1872.
3

WILLIS, Browne.
Parochiale Anglicanum - churches and chapels with the
dioceses of Canterbury, Rochester, London and others.
For R. Gosling at the Mitre and Crown. 1733.
2

WOODRUFF, Charles Everleigh.
Church plate in Kent: Deanery of Sandwich. (Reprinted
from Archaeologia Cantiana).
Mitchell and Hughes. 1908.
1,17

CHURCHILL, SIR WINSTON S.

JAMES, Robert Rhodes.
Churchill: a study in failure, 1900-1939.
Weidenfeld and Nicholson. 1970.
12

KRAUS, Rene.
Winston Churchill: a biography, 2nd edition.
J.B. Lippincott. 1941.
12

"LIFE MAGAZINE".
The unforgettable Winston Churchill: giant of the
century.
Life Magazine. 1965.
12

SCOTT, A.M.
Winston Churchill in peace and war.
Newnes. 1916.
12

SENCOURT, Robert.
Winston Churchill.
Faber. 1940.
12

SIMS, Victor.
Churchill the great, edited by V. Sims.
Daily Mirror Publishers Ltd. 1962.
12

STEWART, H.L.
Sir Winston Churchill as writer and speaker.
Sidgwick and Jackson. 1954.
12

SYKES, Adam.
The wit of Sir Winston, edited by A. Sykes and J.
Sproat.
Frewin. 1965.
12

TAYLOR, A.J.P.
Churchill: four faces and the man, by A.J.P. Taylor
and others.
Allen Lane. 1969.
12

THOMPSON, Carlos.
The assassination of Winston Churchill.
Colin Smythe. 1969.
12

THOMPSON, Reginald William.
The Yankee Marlborough.
Allen and Unwin. 1963.
12

THOMPSON, W.H.
Sixty minutes with Winston Churchill.
Johnson. 1953.
12

THOMSON, Malcolm.
Churchill - his life and times.
Odhams. 1965.
12

"THE TIMES".
The Churchill years, 1874-1965.
Heinemann. 1965.
12

URQUHART, Frederick.
Winston S. Churchill: a cartoon biography, edited by
F. Urquhart.
Cassell. 1955.
12

WHEELER-BENNETT, Sir John.
Action this day: working with Churchill, edited by Sir J.
Wheeler-Bennett.
Macmillan. 1968.
12

WINGFIELD-STRATFORD, Esme.
Churchill.
Gollancz. 1942.
12

WOODS, Frederick.
A bibliography of the works of Sir Winston Churchill.
Nicholas Vane. 1963.
12

WOODS, Frederick.
A bibliography of the works of Winston Churchill, 2nd
revised edition.
Kaye and Ward. 1969.
12

YOUNG, Kenneth.
Churchill and Beaverbrook.
Eyre and Spottiswoode. 1966.
12

CINQUE PORTS

ADAMS, Joseph.
The cinque ports.
n.d.
7,11

BAINES, John Mainwaring.
The cinque ports and coronation services.
Hastings Museum. 1968.
11

BLACK, William H.J.
Memoranda of a journey to the cinque ports, etc. on the
business of the Ramsgate Harbour Trustees, October, 1855 also
researches made about Minster. Transcribed and edited by
Charles Cotton. (Printed extracts from Pullen's Kent Argus,
from January 24th, 1920).
3

BRADLEY, Arthur Granville.
England's outpost: the country of the Kentish cinque ports.
Scott. 1921, 1924.
1,2,3,4,5,6,7,8,9,10,11,12,13,14,15,17,18,19

BRADLEY, Arthur Granville.
An old gate of England: Rye, Romney Marsh and the Western
cinque ports.
Scott. 1918, 1920, etc.
1,2,3,4,5,6,7,8,9,10,11,12,13,14,15,17,18,19,21

BRADLEY, Arthur Granville.
Story of the cinque ports.
Rye, Deacon. n.d.
6,11,13

BRAYLEY, Edward Wedlake.
Delineations - Isle of Thanet and the cinque ports.
W. Marshall. 1830.
1,7,11,12,13,14,15

BRENTNALL, Margaret.
The cinque ports and Romney Marsh.
Gifford. 1972.
11

BRETON, Frederick.
God save England.
Grant Richards. 1899.
6

BROOKS, F.W.
The English naval forces, 1199-1272.
Brown. n.d.
7

BURROWS, Montague.
Cinque ports.
Longmans, Green. 1888, etc.
1,2,3,4,6,7,8,9,10,11,12,13,14,15,17,18

CAPPER, Douglas P.
Famous sailing ships of the world.
Muller. 1957.
6

CINQUE PORTS.
Brotherhood and Guestling at Hastings, 24th July, 1901.
Grigg. 1901.
13

CINQUE PORTS.
Brotherhood and Guestling at Dover, 11th October, 1911.
Grigg. 1911.
13

CINQUE PORTS.
Brotherhood and Guestling at Sandwich, 19th May, 1920.
Grigg. 1920.
13

CINQUE PORTS.
Brotherhood and Guestling at Dover, 16th September, 1925.
Grigg. 1925.
13

CINQUE PORTS.
Courts of Brotherhood and Guestling at Romney, 1937.
Dover, Grigg.
6,11

CINQUE PORTS.
Grand Court of Shepway held at Shepway Cross on 4th
August, 1923 for the unveiling and dedication of a
Memorial Cross.
Deal. 1923.
13

CINQUE PORTS.
The great and ancient charter of the Cinque Ports and
its members, from the first granted by King Edward 1st.
to the last charter granted by Charles 2nd. (Printed
from an old copy dated 1668).
C. Mate. 1807.
7,14

The Cinque Ports and how are they affected by the
Municipal Corporation Act?
Ramsgate, Printed by Burgess and Hunt. 1836.
3

CINQUE PORTS AUXILIARY BIBLE SOCIETY.
3rd annual report, 1815, with a list of subscribers and
benefactors.
Printed, G. Ledger. 1816.
6

Cinque Ports letter guide: Hastings and St. Leonards.
Morgate, Agnes Press. n.d.
3

Clark's guide and history of Rye.
Rye, M.P. Clark. 1861.
6

COOPER, William Durrant.
History of Winchelsea.
Smith. 1850.
1,6,8,11

DAWSON, Charles.
The services of the Barons of the Cinque Ports at the
coronation of the Kings and Queens of England.
1901.
11,13

DEACON, J.L.
Ancient Rye.
n.d.
1,11

DEEBLE, William. Illustrator.
Delineations, historical and topographical of the Isle
of Thanet and the cinque ports, Vols. 1 and 2. (Text by
E.W. Brayley).
Sherwood, Neely and Sons. 1817/18.
8

DOVER CHRONICLE.
Dover, Folkestone, Deal and Cinque Ports, appendix and
almanack for 1870 containing a short history of Dover.
1870.
7

DYMOND, Thomas Southall.
Memoirs of a Mayor of Hastings, 1926-27.
Hastings. 1928.
13

An ENTIRE and complete history, political and personal, of
the boroughs of Great Britain, together with the Cinque Ports,
in three volumes.
1792.
4(Vol.3), 10(Vol.2), 11

Festival at Dover, 26th June, 1897. (Her Majesty's Diamond
Jubilee, 1897).
Rye. 1897.
13

FORD, Ford Madox. (Title page: HUEFFER, F.M.).
The Cinque Ports.
Blackwood. 1900.
1,2,4,6,7,8,10,11,12,13,14,15,17,21

GILBERT, W.G.L.
Rye reformed.
Rye Museum. 1958.
8

GRANT, L.
Chronicle of Rye.
London? 1926 and 1927.
1,3(1926), 11,13,19

Great and ancient charter of the Cinque Ports and its
members, 1668.
Dover, C. Mate. 1807.
1,7,8,11,12

GREAT BRITAIN: LAWS, etc. (GEO. IV).
An Act to empower the Deputy Warden of the Cinque Ports to
act for the Lord Warden during the indisposition of the
present Lord Warden.
1828.
11,18

GREAT BRITAIN: LAWS, etc. (GEO. IV).
An Act to amend an Act for preventing depredations within
the jurisdiction of the Cinque Ports.
1828.
11,18

GREAT BRITAIN, Parliament.
Report from the Select Committee on Cinque Port Pilots.
House of Commons. 1833.
3

HASTINGS BOROUGH COUNCIL.
Document with seal of the Cinque Port of Hastings, wherein
it states that the Grange at Gillingham is a limb of the said
Cinque Port.
1866.
8

HOLLOWAY, William.
History and antiquities of ancient town and port of Rye.
London, John Russell Smith. 1847.
3,6

HUDDLESTONE, John.
Cinque Ports country.
Grenville Publishing Co. 195-?
3,4,7,8,11,14,15

HULL, Felix.
A calendar of the White and Black Books of the Cinque Ports,
1432-1955, edited by F. Hull.
H.M.S.O. 1966.
1,2,3,4,6,7,8,10,11,12,13,14,15

HUNT, Wray.
The Mayor of Rye.
Sheldon Press. 1932.
11

Indexes of the Great White Book and of the Black Book
of the Cinque Ports.
Elliot Stock. 1905.
1,3,4,6,7,10,11,12,13,14,17

AN INHABITANT.
The Hastings guide, 3rd edition.
London, James Barry. 1804.
6

Installation of Lord Dufferin as the Lord Warden of
the Cinque Ports, June 22nd, 1892.
"Standard Office". 1892.
11

Installation of Lord Salisbury as Lord Warden of the
Cinque Ports, 1896.
Dover, Standard Office. 1896.
11

Installation of Earl Beauchamp as Lord Warden of the
Cinque Ports at Dover, 18th July, 1914.
Dover, Express Typo. 1914.
13

Installation of the Most Honourable the Marquess of
Reading as Lord Warden of the Cinque Ports at Dover, 1934
Dover Express. 1934.
6,7,13

Installation of the Most Honourable the Marquess of
Willingdon as Lord Warden of the Cinque Ports at Dover,
1936.
1936.
6,7,13

Installation of the Rt. Hon. Winston Leonard Spencer
Churchill as Lord Warden of the Cinque Ports, 1946.
1946.
6

JEAKE, Samuel.
Charters of the Cinque Ports.
Lintot. 1728.
6,7,11,13,17

JESSUP, Ronald Frank.
The Cinque Ports, by R.F. Jessup and F.W. Jessup.
Batsford. 1952.
1,2,3,4,6,7,8,10,11,12,13,14,15,16,18

JONES, John Bavington.
Cinque Ports.
Dover Express. 1903, etc.
1,6,7,11,19

KNOCKER, Edward.
A paper on the ancient connection between the Cinque
Ports and the Borough of Great Yarmouth and some matters
in relation thereto.
Bound Manuscript. 1876.
6

KNOCKER, Edward.
An account of the Grand Court of Shepway, 1861.
1862.
1,3,4,6,7,8,10,11,12,13,14,15,17

KNOCKER, Sir Wollaston.
Coronation of their Majesties King Edward VII and Queen
Alexandra - proceedings of the Barons of the Cinque
Ports.
Dover, Turner. 1902.
1,4,6,7,11,12,13

List of the names of the Knights, Citizens, Burgesses
and Barons of the Cinque Ports.
1679.
11

List of the names of the Knights, Citizens of the Cinque
Ports.
1680-81.
11

MAIS, Stuart Petre Brodie.
Land of the Cinque Ports.
Johnson. 1949.
1,2,3,4,5,6,7,8,11,12,13,14,15,18,19

MANTELL, Sir Thomas.
Coronation ceremonies and customs relating to Barons of the
Cinque Ports.
Dover, Ledger. 1820.
1,6,11

MANTELL, Sir Thomas.
New editions of tracts relative to Cinque Ports and
coronations...from 1771-1828.
Dover, Warren. 1828.
1,6,8

MARSHALL, M.A.N.
Hastings saga.
St. Catherine Press. 1953.
6

MARTIN, Kenneth Beacham.
Oral traditions of the Cinque Ports.
Harding. 1832.
1,11,13,14,17

MUNICIPAL CORPORATION COMMISSIONERS.
Copy of the report...on the Cinque Ports...generally...
Faversham, S. Ratcliffe. 1835.
11

MURRAY, K.M. Elizabeth.
The constitutional history of the Cinque Ports.
Manchester University Press. 1935.
1,2,3,4,6,7,8,11,12,13,14,15,17,18,19

MURRAY, K.M. Elizabeth.
Faversham and the Cinque Ports.
Royal Historical Society. 1935.
3,11

OSWALD, Arthur.
Rye: the story of an historic town.
Country Life. 1955.
8

PHILIPOTT, John.
Roll of the Constables of Dover Castle and Lord Wardens of
the Cinque Ports, 1627.
Bell. 1956.
1,2,3,4,6,7,8,9,11,12,13,14,17,18,20

Photocopies of 87 documents relating to the Hamlet of Grange
when a limb of the Cinque Ports of Hastings.
n.d.
8

RAWSON, Maud Stepney.
Tales of Rye town.
Rye, Deacons. 1913.
6

RUSSELL, James.
The ancient liberties and privileges of the Cinque Ports and
ancient towns...
1809.
1,6,7,8,11,12,17

RYE MUSEUM. Publisher.
A prospect of Rye, 1574-1934.
Rye Museum. (1958).
8

SOUTHERN, L.W.
The odd Cinque Port...Brightlingsea.
Printed by A. Quick and Co. Ltd., Clacton. 1955.
6

TEICHMAN-DERVILLE, Max.
New Romney and Cinque Port records. (From Archaeologia
Cantiana).
Ashford, Headley. n.d.
11,17

TEICHMAN-DERVILLE, Max.
Report and classification of the Cinque Port records at
New Romney.
Ashford, Headley. 1931.
7,11,13

To the King's most excellent majesty...address sent by the
Cinque Ports to His Majesty King George V on the 25th
anniversary of his accession to the throne. (Photocopy).
1935.
13

TRISTAM, W.O.
Cinque Ports. (From "Illustrated London News",
22nd August, 1891).
17

VIDLER, Leopold Amon.
A new history of Rye...Hove.
Combridges. 1934.
3,6

WILKS, George.
Baron of the Cinque Ports.
Folkestone, J. English. 1892?
1,2,3,4,6,7,8,11,12,14,15,17

WILKS, George.
The Brotherhood and Guestling of the Cinque Ports, with
an account of their "canopy service" at the coronation
of George IV...
Folkestone, J. English. c.1887.
1,6,7,13,17

WILLIAMS, Geoffrey.
The heraldry of the Cinque Ports.
Newton Abbot, David and Charles. 1971.
3,4,6,7,8,11,21

CLIFFE—at—HOO

Cliffe parish almanack, 1870-1880.
n.d.
9

HARRIS, Edwin.
The history of Cliffe—at—Hoo.
Rochester, Harris. 1925. (Eastgate Series No. 34).
11,15

KENT COUNTY COUNCIL - PLANNING DEPARTMENT.
The search for a site for a third London airport. Pt. 1,
background information concerning Sheppey and Cliffe.
Kent County Council. n.d.
9,11

MARTIN, Alan R.
The church of Cliffe—at—Hoo. (Reprinted from
Archaeologia Cantiana, Vol. 41).
1928.
4,17

SMITH, J.J.
The story of Cliffe—at—Hoo, or Cloveshoo.
197-?
11

CLIFTONVILLE - SEE MARGATE

COAL

ARBER, E.A. Newell.
Geology of the Kent coalfield. (Extract from
Transactions of the Institution of Mining Engineers, Vol.
47).
Institution of Mining Engineers. 1914.
7,12,17

BOLTON, Herbert.
The fauna and stratigraphy of the Kent coalfield.
Institution of Mining Engineers. 1915.
12

BRADY, F.
Dover coal boring.
1892.
7

BRADY, F.
The Kent coalfield, by F. Brady and others.
n.d.
6,11

BURR, Arthur.
The development of the South Eastern coalfield.
1908.
11

BURR, Malcolm.
The South Eastern coalfield.
Kent Coal Concessions Ltd. 1906.
6,7,11,17

COAL Cont'd

CROCKALL, R.
The fossil flora of the Kent coalfield. In Geological
Survey of Great Britain, 1932, Part II.
6

DAWKINS, W. Boyd.
The discovery of coal near Dover.
1890.
6,17

DINES, H.G.
Sequence and structure of the Kent coalfield. In Geological
Survey of Great Britain, 1932, Part II.
6

DOVER STANDARD.
Kent coal concessions and allied companies. Opening out of
the Beresford seam.
1913.
17

England's new coalfield.
Dover. c.1914.
13

FUEL AND POWER, Ministry of.
Kent coalfield: regional survey report.
H.M.S.O. 1945.
1,6,8,11

GALLOWAY, W.
A report on Tilmanstone Colliery.
1913.
6

GEOLOGICAL SURVEY AND MUSEUM.
Contributions to the geology of the Kent coalfields. In
Summary of Progress of the Geological Survey, 1932.
H.M.S.O. 1932.
7,17

GEOLOGICAL SURVEY AND MUSEUM.
On the mesozoic rocks in some of the coal explorations in
Kent, by G. Lamplugh and F. Kitchin.
H.M.S.O. 1911.
11,15

HARRISON, Norman.
Once a miner.
Oxford University Press. 1954.
1,5,6

HARRISON, W.J.
On the search for coal in the South East of England.
Hudson. 1894.
12

JOINT STOCK COMPANIES' JOURNAL.
Kent coal concessions: a series of articles reprinted from
Joint Stock Companies' Journal, October 12th–November 9th,
1910.
St. Clemant's Press. 1910.
7,11

KENT CUTTER.
Newspaper about mining, No. 1, No. 3.
Ministry of Fuel and Power. 1946.
3

LUCAS, J.
Hydrogeology of the Dover basin...Channell Tunnel...
coalfield.
c.1900.
6

RITCHIE, A.E.
The Kent coalfield.
1919.
1,3,6,7,8,11,12,13,15,17,19

STEED, Wickham.
England's industrial future – visit to the East Kent
coalfield.
1929.
17

STRAHAM, A.
On boring far coal at Ebbsfleet near Ramsgate.
1912.
17

STUBBLEFIELD, C.J.
Notes on the fauna of the coal measures of Kent. In
Geological Survey of Great Britain, 1932.
6

WHITAKER, William.
Coal in the South East of England, by W. Whitaker and
others.
1890.
17

COASTAL DEFENCES

BUSHE-FOX, Jocelyn P.
Some notes on Roman coast defences.
Journal of Roman Studies. 1932.
8

CLINCH, George.
English coast defences from Roman times to the early
years of the nineteenth century.
Bell. 1915.
2,3,6,7,8,12,14

COTTRELL, Leonard.
The Roman forst of the Saxon shore.
H.M.S.O. 1964.
3,6,8,11,12

FOX, George.
The Roman coast fortresses of Kent.
London, Harrison. 1896.
15

GREAT BRITAIN: LAWS, etc. (GEO. III).
An Act for vesting certain messuages...in trustees, for
the better securing His Majesty's batteries and other
works in the counties of Kent and Devon.
1794.
11

GREAT BRITAIN: LAWS, etc. (GEO. III).
An Act for making compensation to the proprietors of
certain lands...purchased...for better securing His
Majesty's batteries and other works in the counties of
Kent and Devon.
Eyre and Strahan. 1798
12

HINTON, D.R.
The Maunsell Forts – Thames estuary. (Extracted from
"The Gunner", November, 1957). (Photocopy).
4

HORSLEY, Victor.
Roman defences of South East Britain.
Royal Institution. 1900.
12

LANAWAY, H.
The nine fortresses on the Saxon shore. (Antiquarian
pamphlets).
Eastbourne, Swinfield. 192-?
1,3,4,5,6,7,11,12,14,15,19

O'WERT, John
Ramparts of steel...permanent coast, militia and an
army reserve.
1825.
17

PECK, F.
Coast artillery, Dover.
1958.
6

ROSE, J. Holland.
Dumouriez and the defence of England against Napoleon,
by J.H. Rose and A.M. Broadley.
Bodley Head. 1909.
1

THORN, Roland Berkeley.
The design of sea defence works.
Butterworth. 1960.
8,12

COASTAL DEFENCES Cont'd

WILSON, J.D.
Later nineteenth century defences of the Thames, including
Grain Fort. (Extracted from The Journal of the Society for
Army Historical Research). 2 Parts.
1962.
4,9

COASTAL WATERS

BAYLEY, George Bethel.
Seamen of the Downs: a retrospective sketch of the historic
roadstead, and a sequel to"Treanor's Heroes of the Goodwin
Sands", by G.B. Bayley and William Adams.
Blackwood. 1929.
1,3,4,6,7,13,14

BENHAM, Harvey.
Down tops'l: the story of the East coast sailing-barges...
with additional material...
Harrap. 1951.
3,4,15

BLANDFORD, Percy William.
South Eastern England. (Regional sailing guides - 1).
Constable. 1971.
3,7

BOUQUET, Michael.
South Eastern sail, from the Medway to the Solent, 1840-1940.
David Charles. 1972.
4,11

BOWEN, Frank Charles.
His Majesty's Coastguard.
1928.
13,14

BOWEN, J.P.
British lighthouses.
Longmans. 1947.
18

BRADFORD, Ernle.
Wall of England: the channel's 2000 years of history.
Country Life. 1966.
6,7,8

BREWSTER, G.B.
My channel-swimming adventures.
Bale. 1935.
7

CAPPER, Douglas P.
Moat defensive: a history of the waters of the Nore
Command, 55 B.C. to 1961.
Barker. 1963.
4,8,12,15

COLES, K. Adlard.
Pilot to the South coast harbours.
Faber. 1962.
15

COMMISSIONERS TO INQUIRE INTO THE MOST ELIGIBLE SITUATION
FOR CHOOSING A HARBOUR - IN THE CHANNEL.
Report on the subject of harbours of refuge.
1845.
11

COWPER, Frank.
Sailing tours: Part III, the coasts of Kent, etc.
Upcott, Gill. 1909.
1,11

DESSIOU, Joseph.
Laurie and Whittle's new sailing directions, by J. Dessiou
and others.
1813.
15

GARRETT, Richard.
Cross-channel - transport across channel, sea, air and
discusses Channel Tunnel.
Hutchinson. 1972.
11

GENERAL STEAM NAVIGATION CO. LTD.
The way of the Eagles: an illustrated guide of the river
trip from Greenwich to Ramsgate.
Gale and Polden. c.1923.
9

GREAT BRITAIN: LAWS, etc. (GEO. I).
An Act for the better regulating of pilots...ships...
from Dover, Deal and the Isle of Thanet up the River
Thames and Medway.
1717.
8,9,11

GREAT BRITAIN: LAWS, etc. (GEO. I).
An Act for the further regulating the pilots of Dover,
Deal and the Isle of Thanet.
1721.
11

GREAT BRITAIN: LAWS, etc. (GEO. II).
An Act to continue several laws...for the better
regulation...of seamen..., for regulating of pilots of
Dover, Deal and the Isle of Thanet.
1735.
11

GREAT BRITAIN: LAWS, etc. (GEO. II).
An Act to continue several laws for the better
regulating of pilots for the conducting of ships from
Dover, Deal and the Isle of Thanet.
1750.
9,11

GREAT BRITAIN: LAWS, etc. (GEO. III).
An Act to continue several laws for the better regulation
of pilots...from Dover, Deal, etc.
Mark Baskett. 1764.
11

GREAT BRITAIN: LAWS, etc. (GEO. IV).
An Act for the amendment of the law respecting pilots...
and also for the better preservation of floating lights.
1825.
11

GREAT BRITAIN: LAWS, etc. (GEO. IV).
An Act for the amendment...pilots and pilotage...beacons.
Trinity House. 1826.
6

HALL, James S.
Sea surgeon. (Kentish coast and Goodwin Sands).
Kimber. 1961.
8,12

HARGREAVES, Reginald.
The narros seas.
London, Sidgwick and Jackson. 1959.
3

HAY, David.
The Downs from the sea: Langstone Harbour to the Pool
of London, by David and Joan Hay.
Stanford. 1972.
11

HEATHER, William. Publisher.
The new British Channel pilot: containing sailing
directions from London and Yarmouth to Liverpool,
3rd edition.
W. Heather. 1803.
13

MOREY, George.
The English Channel.
Muller. 1966.
6

The Nore Command and Chatham area official directory,
April, 1939.
8

PEARS, Cha(rle)s.
Yachting on the sunshine coast: a volume of information.
Southern Railway Co. 1932.
4,12

PURDY, John.
The new sailing directory for the English Channel.
n.d.
12

ROBERTS, A.W.
Coasting bargemaster.
1949.
4,15

COASTAL WATERS Cont'd

ROCKET, Sam.
It's cold in the Channel.
Hutchinson. 1956.
6,7

SCOTT, Peter.
The battle of the narrow seas, 1939-45.
Country Life. 1946.
6

SPENCE, Graeme.
Chart of the Channel from the Downs to Ramsgate Harbour.
1795.
14

STANTON, William.
Journal of William Stanton, pilot of Deal.
Simpkin, Marshall. n.d.
6,11,12

TEMPLE, Peter.
English Channel.
Hodder and Stoughton. 1952.
8

TRIPP, H. Alker. ('Leigh Hoe').
Shoalwater and fairway. The casual explorations of a
sailing man in the shoal waters of Essex and Kent.
1924.
6,13

VEALE, Ernest William Partington.
Gateway to the Continent: a history of cross-channel
travel.
Ian Allan. 1955.
1,6,7,8,12

WILLIAMSON, J.A.
The English Channel.
Collins. 1959.
6,7,14

WILSON, William Eric.
Pilot's guide to the English Channel, compiled by W.E.
and W.T. Wilson.
Imray Laurie. 1968.
1,5

WYLLIE, W.L.
London to the Nore, by W.L. and M.A. Wyllie.
Black. 1905.
1,4,5,8,9,11,12,15

COASTLINE

DOWKER, George.
Coast erosion (10p).
(1899).
7

DUGDALE, William.
The history of imbarking and draining of divers fens and
marshes.
W. Owen. 1772.
15

DU-PLAT-TAYLOR, M.
A sea wall in Kent. (A paper read to the British section of
the Societa des Ingenieurs Civils de France, 14th April, 1932).
Societa des Ingenieurs Civils de France.
7

Eyre's shilling guide to the seaside and visiting resorts of
Kent.
Eyre. 1878.
1,13

FUSSELL, L.
Journey round the coast of Kent.
Baldwin, Craddock and Joy. 1818.
1,3,4,5,6,7,8,11,12,13,15,18,19

GILPIN, William.
Observations on the coast of Hampshire, Sussex and Kent.
A. Strahan. 1804.
1,4,6,8,11,12,17

Handbook of travel round the Southern coast of England.
1849.
14

HARPER, Charles George.
The Kentish coast.
Chapman and Hall. 1914.
1,2,3,4,5,6,7,8,9,11,12,13,14,15,17,18,19,20

Harwood's scenery of the Southern coast.
1841.
13

HOLLAND, Clive.
From the North Foreland to Penzance.
Chatto and W. 1908.
4,14

JANSON, Hank.
Britain's great flood disaster (Feburary, 1953).
New Fiction Press. 1953?
4

The Kent coast, 3rd edition.
Ward, Lock. 1968.
6,11

LACY, Joseph Melville.
"Littoral drift along the North East coast of Kent".
Institute of Civil Engineers. 1929.
11

LEE, John.
Tour from Northamptonshire to London, down the River
Thames to the Isle of Thanet.
1827.
13

LEWIS, Arthur D.
The Kent coast.
Fisher Unwin. 1911.
1,2,3,4,5,6,8,9,11,12,13,14,15,17,18

MARGATE PIER AND HARBOUR CO. and COMMISSIONERS OF
PAVEMENTS.
Refuge harbours and coast defence.
Margate Pier and Harbour Co. 1853.
11

MARTIN, Kenneth Beacham.
On the necessity for harbours of refuge...in that part
of the British Channel called "The Narrows".
n.d.
11,14

NATIONAL PARKS COMMISSION.
The coasts of Kent and Sussex: report of the Regional
Coastal Conference held in London on May 27th, 1966.
H.M.S.O. 1967.
1,2,3,4,5,6,8,11,12,17,18,19

PALMER, Henry R.
Observations on the motions of shingle beaches on the
sea coast.
1834.
7

A practical guide to the watering and sea-bathing
places on the coasts of Kent, Sussex and Hampshire,
including the Isle of Wight, etc.
London, Craddock and Co. 1845.
3,13

ROBINSON, Adrian H.W.
Coastal evolution in Sandwich Bay, by A.H.W. Robinson
and R.L. Cloet.
Geological Association. 1953.
1,6,11

ROWE, Arthur Walton.
The zones of the white chalk of the English coast.
1. Kent and Sussex.
Geologists' Association. 1900.
8,11

RUSKIN, John.
The harbours of England.
1856.
13,14

(Seaside watering places: being a guide to strangers
in search of a suitable place in which to spend their
holidays).
L. Upcott Gill. 1885.
11

SHARPE, Henry.
Britain B.C....and an attempt to ascertain the ancient
coastline of Kent and East Sussex.
Williams and Norgate. 1910.
11

SMITH, Baker Peter.
A journal of an excursion round the South Eastern coast of
England.
Rivington. 1834.
7,17

SMITH, W.
A new, picturesque steam-boat companion, in an excursion
to Greenhithe, Northfleet, Gravesend, The Nore and Herne
Bay, with a trip up the River Medway to Rochester Bridge,
2 editions.
E. Wilson and others. c.1835.
9,15(1839)

The Southern coast of England: a picturesque, antiquarian
and topographical description of the scenery, towns and
ancient remains.
Nattali. 1849.
12

STANTON, Frederick W.S.
Erosions of the coast and its prevention.
St. Bride's Press Ltd. 1909.
8

The steam-boat companion from London to Gravesend, Southend,
Margate and Ramsgate.
Margate, Brown. 1830.
9,13,14

The steam packet companion to Gravesend, Sheerness and
Herne Bay, with a picturesque description of each of the
above places.
1834.
13

STEERS, James Alfred.
The coast of England and Wales in pictures.
Cambridge University Press. 1960.
5,11

STEERS, James Alfred.
The coastline of England and Wales.
London, Cambridge University Press. 1964.
3

STEERS, James Alfred.
The sea coast.
Collins. 1953.
5,11

STOKES, H.G.
The very first history of the English seaside.
1947.
13,14

THORPE, Teresa.
The development of the coast-line between Hampton Pier and
Reculver at Herne Bay. (Photocopy of thesis).
1970.
11

"A VALETUDINARIAN".
Sea-side reminiscences: a collection of odd thoughts.
Sheffield, Kidd.(1840).
11,13

WALCOTT, Mackenzie E.C.
Guide to the coast of Kent.
Stanford. 1854.
1,4,8,11,12,15,17

WALCOTT, Mackenzie E.C.
Guide to the South coast of England.
Stanford. 1859.
1,6,7,11,13,17

WATTS, R.B.
Aquatic itinerary, or an excursion from London to Margate.
1819.
13

WATTS, R.B.
The Gravesend itinerary.
J. Mallet, Printer. 1821.
9

WATTS, R.B.
The Margate steam yachts' guide, 2nd edition.
1820.
1,13

WATTS, R.B.
A topographical description of the coast between London,
Margate and Dover.
Mallett. 1828.
6,12

WHEELER, W.H.
The sea coast: destruction, littoral drift, protection.
Longmans, Green. 1902.
11

COBHAM

ARNOLD, A.A.
Cobham and its manors.
Mitchell, Hughes and Clarke. 1905.
7,12,17

ARNOLD, A.A.
Cobham College. 48p. (Reprinted from Arch. Cant.).
Mitchell, Hughes and Clarke. 1905.
7,9,17

ARNOLD, Ralph.
Cobham Hall: notes on the house, its owners, the gardens
1951?
8,19

BAKER, T.H.
History of the Cobham Cricket Club, 1850-1898.
Wildish. 1899.
12

BROOKE, F.C.
Cobham memorials.
1874.
9

CHANDLER, Raymond H.
Tertiary section at Shorne Wood, Cobham.
1922.
17

Cobham. (Boxed material).
n.d.
9

Cobham Church, Kent.
Chatham, Mackays. 195-?
5,8,11

Cobham Church, Kent: the brasses.
Rochester, Mackays. 1958?
5,8,11,19

Cobham Church and parochial accounts in the XVIIth
and XVIIIth centuries.
John Higgins. n.d.
12

COBHAM COLLEGE.
So much of the rules and ordinances made for the new
College of Cobham in the county of Kent.
n.d.
9

Cobham Hall. (English Homes, No. XVI, Illustrated
London News, October 27th, 1888, P. 489-495).
Illustrated London News. 1888.
9

GRAHAM, John.
A sermon preached in the parish church of Cobham, Kent
on Tuesday, February 24th, 1835 at the funeral of the
Right Honourable, The Earl of Darnley.
Rochester, John Wildish. 1835.
9

COBHAM Cont'd

HARRIS, Edwin.
Cobham Church and its brasses.
Rochester, Harris. 1909. (Eastgate Series No. 2).
2,9,11,15

HARRIS, Edwin.
Cobham College.
Rochester, Harris. 1909. (Eastgate Series No. 3).
1,4,5,9,11,15

HARRIS, Edwin,
Cobham Hall.
Rochester, Harris. 1909. (Eastgate Series No. 4).
1,11,12,15

HARRIS, Edwin.
Cobham park and estate.
Rochester, Harris. 1910. (Eastgate Series No. 5).
1,4,9,11

HARRIS, Edwin.
The owners of Cobham Hall from the 12th to the 20th century.
Rochester, Harris. 1910. (Eastgate Series No. 6).
1,11,15

History of the parish church of Cobham.
Cobham P.C.C. 1970.
9

HOWELL, George O.
Invitation to Cobham.
1905.
17

HUMPAGE, E. Caroline.
The Darnley Quadrilles and Neva Waltz.
London, D'Almaine and Co. n.d.
9

KENT COUNTY COUNCIL - PLANNING DEPARTMENT.
Cobham: village study.
Kent County Council. 1970.
2,4,7,8,9,11

KNOOP, D.
Some building activities of John, Lord Cobham, by D. Knoop,
G.P. Jones and N.B. Lewis.
(1932).
3,4

ORR, William S. AND CO. Publishers.
The pictorial guide to Cobham.
Orr. 1845.
1,9,17

The parish church of St. Mary Magdalene, Cobham, Kent.
1971.
11

PRIEST, Simeon.
Excursion to Plumstead and Bostall Heath and excursion to
Cobham and Strood.
1924.
5

PUREY-CUST, Arthur Percival.
Edward Vesey Bligh: a memoir, compiled by A.P. Purey-Cust.
Leeds, Jackson. 1908.
4,11,12

Six walks from Cobham.
Meopham Guide Committee. (1970).
11

SUMMERLY, Felix.
Day's excursion out of London to Erith, Rochester and
Cobham in Kent.
G. Bell. 1843.
8,17

VALLANCE, Aymer.
Cobham Collegiate Church. (Reprint from Archaeologia Cantiana,
Vol. 43).
Ashford, Headley. 1929.
11,17

WALLER, John G.
The Lords of Cobham: their monuments and the church.
(Reprint from Archaeologia Cantiana, Vol. XI).
London, Mitchell and Hughes. 1877.
4,17

WINGFIELD-STRATFORD, Esme.
The Lords of Cobham Hall.
Cassell. 1959.
1,5,7,9,11,12

COINS AND TOKENS

BOYNE, William.
18th century tokens relating to...Kent from Atkins'
"Token coinage of 18th century" with MS. additions and
illustrations.
1902.
17

BOYNE, William.
Tokens issued in the 17th century. (Cover title:
"Kent Tokens").
1858.
5 (1889-91), 11

BRITISH NUMISMATIC SOCIETY.
Found 1955: the Dover hoard.
Dover. 1956.
6

CARSON, R.A.G.
Springhead, Gravesend, Roman imperial treasure trove.
1965.
4

CLARK, E.H.
Kentish hop tokens and their issuers.
n.d.
3,11,13

DOLLEY, Michael.
Anglo-Saxon pennies.
British Museum. 1964.
3

DOLLEY, Michael.
The Norman Conquest and the English coinage.
Spink. 1966.
3

EVANS, John. Numismatist.
Coin of Archbishops Jaenbeorht and Aethelheard.
London, Numismatic Society. 1865.
3

HANFREY, Henry W.
The Canterbury coins of Edward I,II,III.
In Antiquary. 1880.
3

KENT NUMISMATIC SOCIETY.
Bulletin, 1959-60.
Maidstone, Kent Numismatic Society. 1960.
3(1955/6), 11,12

KERSHAW, S. Wayland.
Canterbury's ancient coinage.
British Archaeological Association. 1902.
3,7,11

NORTH, George.
Remarks on some conjectures relative to an ancient
piece of money.
W. Sandby. 1752.
12

PEGGE, Samuel.
An assembly of coins fabricated by authority of the
Archbishop of Canterbury.
1772.
3,11

ROLFE, H.W.
Kentish tokens of the 17th century.
n.d.
6,11,17

COLLIER STREET

Consecration of the new church at Collier Street,
Yalding, Wednesday, August 16th, 1848. (Typescript).
12

COLNE, RIVER

SOUTHERN, L.W.
Stories of the Colne.
1849.
6

COMMONS - SEE FOOTPATHS AND COMMONS

CONRAD, JOSEPH

ALLEN, Terry.
The sea years of Joseph Conrad.
Methuen. 1967.
12

BAINES, Jocelyn.
Joseph Conrad: a critical biography.
Weidenfeld and Nicolson. 1960.
6,12

CONRAD, Mrs. Joseph (Jessie).
Did Joseph Conrad return as a spirit?
Webster, Groves, Missouri. International Mark Twain
Society. 1932.
3

CONRAD, Mrs. Joseph (Jessie).
Joseph Conrad and his circle.
Jarrolds. 1935.
3

CURLE, Richard.
The last twelve years of Joseph Conrad.
S. Low, Marston. 1928.
3

GRAVER, Lawrence.
Conrad's short fiction.
University of California Press. 1969.
12

HORNSEY PUBLIC LIBRARY.
Joseph Conrad...centenary booklist.
Hornsey Public Libraries. 1957.
3

JEAN-AUBRY, Gerard.
Joseph Conrad: life and letters.
London, Heinemann. 1927.
3

JEAN-AUBRY, Gerard.
The sea dreamer. (Joseph Conrad).
London, Allen and Unwin. 1957.
3

Joseph Conrad centenary, 3rd December, 1857-1957:
biographical notes...and the houses in which he lived and
wrote.
Aldine Press. 1957.
3

MOSER, Thomas.
Joseph Conrad.
Oxford University Press. 1951.
12

COOLING

COBHAM, Eleanor M.
Siege of Cooling.
Smither Bros. 1896.
9

HARRIS, Edwin.
The history of Cooling Castle.
Rochester, Harris. 1910. (Eastgate Series No. 7).
1,9,11,15

COWDEN

The parish church of St. Mary Magdalene, Cowden, 2nd
edition.
Church Publishers, G. Cumming. 1961.
2 (1965), 4,8

DUNCAN, Leland Lewis.
The Rectory and Rector of Cowden, Kent. (Pamphlet
reprint for Archaeologia Cantiana).
1895.
17,18

EWING, Guy.
History of Cowden.
Tunbridge Wells Courier. 1926.
1,2,3,4,6,11,12,16,19

EWING, Guy.
St. Mary Magdalene, Cowden.
1927.
19

St. Mary Magdalene, Cowden.
Ramsgate, Cumming.(1961).
12

COXHEATH

Coxheath camp.
Fielding. 1779.
12

GREAT BRITAIN: LAWS, etc. (GEO. III).
An Act for inclosing Coxheath.
1814.
12

CRANBROOK

ASHLEY-BROWN, W.
Memory be green: an autobiography by the Venerable
Arch-Deacon. (Rector of Cranbrook).
Hutchinson. 1957.
12

BELL, William.
A memoir of the Rev. William Eddye, M.A., Vicar of
Cranbrook, 1591-1616.
W.T. Simmons. 1902.
11

BRETT, Thomas.
The life of the late Rev. John Johnson, A.M., Vicar of
Cranbrook...with three of Mr. Johnson's posthumous
tracts.
Charles Hitch and William Russell. 1748.
1,11,12

Brief historical account of Cranbrook.
Cranbrook, Waters. 1904.
11

CAROE, William Douglas.
St. Dunstan's Church, Cranbrook: architectural notes.
n.d.
1

CARR, T.A.
A paper on Cranbrook Church, read before the Kent
Archaeological Society.
1873.
3,13,15

CAVE-BROWNE, John.
Cranbrook Church.
n.d.
17

Cranbrook - views of picturesque Cranbrook and
neighbourhood as seen through the camera, 3 vols.
Simmons. n.d.
11

CRANBROOK AND SISSINGHURST LOCAL HISTORY SOCIETY.
Cranbrook notes and records, Nos. 1-8, by C.C.R. Pile.
Bound in one. 1951-1955.
1951-1955.
4,12,17,19

Cranbrook's loyal and patriotic welcome to the 6th
Enniskillen Dragoons on Monday, 28th July, 1856, by A
Townsman.
Printed by G. Waters. 1856.
11

DAVISON, Ian.
Chimes of Cranbrook.
Cranbrook, Eagle Printing Works. 1938.
1,4,11,16,19

DUNCAN, Leland Lewis.
Note on the early history of Cranbrook School (4 page
leaflet inserted in "Weald of Kent", by T.D.W. Dearn).
1923.
17,18

Early history of the Roberts family. (Reprinted from an
ancient book).
Chatford House Press. n.d.
11

EVANS, John.
A sermon preached May 23rd, 1808, at the opening of the new
General-Baptist meeting-house, Cranbrook in Kent.
Printed by C. Stower. 1808.
11

An examination of a discourse or sermon published by Daniel
Dobel of Cranbrook in Kent, on the subject of water-baptism,
by one of the people called Quakers.
T. Sowle Raylton and Luke Hinde. 1744.
1

GANDY, Herbert S.
Cranbrook: the official publication.
Granbrook Parish Council. 1923.
1,17

Golford House, Cranbrook - Sale catalogue.
1967.
12

HUDSON, Alfred W.
Short history of St. Dunstan's Church, Cranbrook.
Cranbrook, Simmons. 1922.
11,12,17,19

LEGG, Michael Arthur.
Short history of the bells of Cranbrook Church.
Hadlow, Hilton Press. 1965.
1,4,8,11,12,19

MARTIN, W. Stanley.
A glimpse of Cranbrook: the town of the Kentish Weald,
2nd edition.
W.T. Simmons. 1902?
1,3,4,7,8,11,12,13,15,18

NAYES, Robert.
Nehemiah's advice to the Jews...a sermon...preached at
Cranbrook, 1755.
1756.
11

PILE, Cecil Charles Relf.
Brief history of Cranbrook.
Cranbrook Local History Society. 1961.
1,2,4,8,11,12

PILE, Cecil Charles Relf.
The Chapel of Holy Trinity, Milkhouse. (Cranbrook notes
and records).
Cranbrook Local History Society. 1951.
1,4,7,8,11,19

PILE, Cecil Charles Relf
Charities of Cranbrook.
Cranbrook Local History Society. 1955.
1,4,7,8,11,19

PILE, Cecil Charles Relf.
Cranbrook: a Wealden town.
Cranbrook Local History Society. 1955.
1,2,3,7,8,11,12,15,18,19

PILE, Cecil Charles Relf.
Cranbrook broadcloth and cloth makers.
Cranbrook Local History Society. 1951.
1,4,7,11,18,19

PILE, Cecil Charles Relf.
Cranbrook broadcloth and the clothiers.
Cranbrook Local History Society. 1967.
7

PILE, Cecil Charles Relf.
Dissenting congregations in Cranbrook.
Cranbrook Local History Society. 1953.
1,4,7,8,11,19

PILE, Cecil Charles Relf.
The inns of Cranbrook.
Cranbrook Local History Society. 1953.
1,4,7,8,11,19

PILE, Cecil Charles Relf.
The parish church of St. Dunstan, Cranbrook.
Cranbrook Local History Society. 1952.
1,2,4,7,8,11,12,19

PILE, Cecil Charles Relf.
Watermills and windmills of Cranbrook.
Cranbrook Local History Society. 1954.
1,4,7,8,11,12,19

ROBINSON, Duncan H.
Cranbrook School: a brief history.
Cranbrook Local History Society. 1971.
11

SIMMONS, W.T. Publisher.
Cranbrook almanac, or Weald of Kent compendium for
1904-05.
Cranbrook, Simmons.
1

Tales of old inns: The George at Cranbrook (pamphlet).
n.d.
19

TARBUTT, William.
The ancient cloth trade of Cranbrook. (Reprinted from
Archaeologia Cantiana, Vol. IX).
n.d.
3

TARBUTT, William.
The annals of Cranbrook Church.
Cranbrook, Dennett. 1875.
1,4,7,11,12,15,17,19

TARBUTT, William.
An historical account of Dence's School and schoolmaster
from 1568-1865.
Cranbrook, Dennett. 1866.
1,11

Tooth family: history.
Bideford, Gazette Printing Service. n.d.
11

TURNER, C.F.
A short account of the Vestry Hall, Cranbrook.
Cranbrook Local History Society. 1959.
7

TYRO-CARMINE, pseud.
Cranbrook.
Cranbrook, Reader. 1819.
1,3,11

Union Hall, Cranbrook, Kent. Appeal for funds for
maintenance.
Chelsea, Printed for the Curwen Press. 1955.
3

Water's Cranbrook almanack for 1871.
Cranbrook, Waters. 1870.
11

CRAY, RIVER

CHANDLER, Raymond H.
Implements of Les Eyzies-Type and a working floor on the
River Cray valley.
1915.
5,11,17

Cray valley notebook (a record compiled by class 13 of
the Midfield Junior School, St. Paul's Cray).
(Typescript). 1958.
2,11

Cray valley paper mills.
W. Nash Ltd.(1958).
2

DOWNIE, S.C.
North West Kent: the Darenth and Cray valleys.
1966.
2,5

MIDFIELD JUNIOR SCHOOL.
The Cray Valley notebooks. (Typescript - 3 years' school projects).
1958-60.
2

Seven churches on the River Cray.
Gilbert and Rivington. 1830.
1,5,11,17

CRAYFORD

CARR, William.
The spot that is called Crayford.
Crayford Urban District Council. 1951, etc.
1,2,4,5,7,8,11,12,15,17,18

CHANDLER, Raymond H.
Excursion of Geologists' Association to...(near) Crayford, by R.H. Chandler and A.L. Leach.
Geologists' Association. 1916.
17

CHANDLER, Raymond H.
Excursion to Crayford and Dartford Heath, 11th May, 1907, by R.H. Chandler and A.L. Leach. (Reprinted from Proceedings, Geologists' Association).
1907.
5,17

CHANDLER, Raymond H.
The implements and caves of Crayford.
1915-16.
17

CHANDLER, Raymond H.
The pleistocene deposits of Crayford. (Taken from Proceedings of Geologists' Association, Pt. 1, 1914).
1913.
5,17

Crayford: official guide.
1930.
17

CRAYFORD URBAN DISTRICT COUNCIL.
Crayford, Kent: official guide.
Homeland Association. 1938, etc.
1,4(1962), 11,15(1956)

CRAYFORD URBAN DISTRICT COUNCIL.
Official handbook. (1957 edition).
Crayford Urban District Council. (1957).
11

DARTFORD UNION GUARDIANS.
Byelaws...with respect to house refuse...in...Crayford and East Wickham.
1885.
5

HAMMANT, Walter.
Crayford: the fortress in Joyden's Wood; deneholes; the last stand of the Britons in Kent.
Privately Printed. 1911.
1,17

HOUGHTON, Charles.
Hundred years short history of Crayford Baptist Church, 1810-1910.
n.d.
5

JACKSON, Richard J.
Crayford.
Woolwich Antiquarian Society. 1896-7.
17

PERKINS, J.B. Ward.
An early Iron Age site at Crayford, Kent. (Reprinted from Prehistoric Society Proceedings, Jan-July, 1938).
n.d.
5

RHODES, Alfred.
Marden Lane, Crayford and others.
Woolwich Antiquarian Society. 1900-1.
17

SCOTT, John Dick.
Vickers: a history.
Weidenfeld and Nicolson. 1963.
1,5

SPURRELL, F.C.J.
On the discovery of paleolithic implements at Crayford. (Reprinted from Quarterly Journal of the Geologists' Society, Nov. 1880).
Geological Society. 1880.
5

STEBBING, W.P.D.
Howbury moated Manor House, Crayford. In Four Miscellaneous Notes.
Ashford, Headley. n.d.
11

CRICKET

AMES, Leslie.
Close of play.
S. Paul. 1953.
3,4,8,15

ARROWSMITH, Robert Langford.
Kent. (History of County Cricket Series).
Barker. 1971.
3,4,5,6,7,8,9,11,19,21

ASHLEY-COOPER, F.S.
Kent cricket records, (1719-1929).
Canterbury, Kent Herald. 1929.
3

ASSOCIATION OF KENT CRICKET CLUBS.
Cricket in Kent, 1954.
Association of Kent Cricket Clubs. 1954.
3,6

ASSOCIATION OF KENT CRICKET CLUBS.
Cricket in Kent: official handbook, 1955.
Association of Kent Cricket Clubs. 1955.
2,4,6,11

ASSOCIATION OF KENT CRICKET CLUBS.
Cricket in Kent, 1956.
Association of Kent Cricket Clubs. 1956.
1,3,6,11

BAX, Clifford.
W.G. Grace. (Resident of Mottingham and Sydenham).
Phoenix House. 1952.
2

BUTLER, Derek R.
One hundred years of Sturry cricket.
Kentish Gazette. (1963).
3,7

CAMPBELL, Barry.
Portrait of a cricket club - Kent transmission B.B.C. Home Service, Wednesday, 7th August, 1963. (Broadcasting script).
n.d.
3

The Canterbury Cricket Week.
Canterbury, Davey. 1865.
1,3,4,11

COWDREY, Michael Colin.
Cricket today.
Barker. 1961.
5,11

COWDREY, Michael Colin.
Time for reflection.
Muller. 1962.
8,12,15

DREW, Bernard.
A hundred years of Farningham cricket.
1957.
1,2,4,5,8,11

EVANS, Godfrey.
Action in cricket.
Hodder and Stoughton. 1956.
8

EVANS, Godfrey.
Behind the stumps.
Hodder and Stoughton. 1951.
1,3,5,6

EVANS, Godfrey.
The gloves are off.
Hodder and Stoughton. 1960.
3,15

FAGG, Arthur.
A photographic collection of past Kent County Cricket Club
teams under all captains for 47 years, 1904-1950, compiled
by A. Fagg.
Fagg. (1951).
1

FEAR, Herbert.
"The W.K.W.C.C.": something of its story. (1856-1955).
(West Kent Wanderers Cricket Club).
Blackheath Press Ltd. (1955).
2,4,18

Felix on the bat.
Baily. 1845.
12

FOSTER, Denis.
Know your cricket county: Kent.
Findon Publications. 1949.
1,15

GILLETTE Cup final, 1971: Kent cricketers' souvenir.
programme.
1971.
9

GOULSTONE, John.
Cricket in Kent; (compiled by John Goulstone). Limited
edition of 50 copies.
International Research Publications. 1972.
11

GOULSTONE, John.
Early Kent cricketers.
International Research Publications. 1971.
11

HAIGH, F.H.
The cricketing career (1906-1927) of Frank Woolley.
1928.
6

HARRIS, George Robert Canning. 4th Baron.
A few short runs.
Murray. 1921.
3,12

HARRIS, George Robert Canning. 4th Baron.
History of Kent County Cricket, edited by G.R.C. Harris.
Eyre and Spottiswoode. 1907.
1,2,3,4,5,6,7,8,11,12,13,15,16,17,19,20

HARRIS, George Robert Canning. 4th Baron.
The history of Kent County Cricket, Appendix F, 1910-23.
Gibbs. 1924.
6,12

HARRIS, George Robert Canning. 4th Baron.
The history of Kent County Cricket, Appendix G, 1924-45.
Geerings. 1949.
3,6

HARRIS, George Robert Canning. 4th Baron.
The history of Kent County Cricket, Appendix H, 1946-63.
Canterbury, Kent County Cricket Club. 1964.
3

HARRIS, George Robert Canning. 4th Baron.
Kent cricket matches, 1719-1880, edited by G.R.C. Harris
and F.S. Ashley-Cooper.
Gibbs and Son. 1929.
1,4,7,11,12,13,16,19

I Zingari: origin-rise-progress-results.
London, Harrison. 1865.
3

IGGLESDEN, Sir Charles.
Sixty-six years' memories of Kent cricket.
Kentish Express. 1947.
1,3,4,5,7,8,11,15,19

KENT COUNTY CRICKET CLUB.
Annual.
1933(11)
1947(1,3,4,6,8,11,12,15)
1952 and 1953(11)
1955(11,12)
1956 and 1957(11)
1958,1959 and 1960(11,12)
1961-1969(11)
1971(3)
1972(11)

KENT COUNTY CRICKET CLUB.
Fixtures, 1946.
Caffyns Ltd. 1946.
3

KENT COUNTY CRICKET CLUB.
Fixtures, 1955.
n.d.
4

KENT COUNTY CRICKET CLUB.
History of County Cricket , 1946-1963.
Canterbury, Kent County Cricket Club. 1964.
1,2,3,4,5,11

KENT COUNTY CRICKET CLUB.
Kent County Cricket Club, 1894.
Canterbury, Cross and Jackman. n.d.
15

KENT COUNTY CRICKET CLUB.
One hundred years of Kent cricket, 1870-1970.
Kent County Cricket Club. 1970.
9,11

KENT COUNTY CRICKET CLUB.
Rules, list of subscribers, matches played, etc.
1877-1899 (20 vols.). (3,17)
1887-1945 (with gaps). (12)
1897-1915(1)
1911-1912(2)
1933,1935,1937(11)
1934(2)
1948-51(3)
1949-50(4)
1949-51(11)

KNOTT, Alan.
Stumper's view.
Paul. 1972.
3

MARRIOTT, Charles Stowel.
Charles Stowel Marriott: obituary notice from "Old
Alleynian".
1967.
12

MORRAH, Patrick.
Alfred Mynn and the cricketers of his time.
Eyre and Spottiswoode. n.d.
1,3,4,8,11,12

NORMAN, Philip.
Scores and annals of the West Kent Cricket Club...
compiled by P. Norman.
Eyre and Spottiswoode. 1897.
1,2(with author's extra annotations) 3,4,5,8,11,12,15,18

PEEBLES, Ian.
Woolley - the pride of Kent.
Hutchinson. 1969.
6,8,12

PYCROFT, James.
The cricket field.
St. James Press. 1922.
12

CRICKET Cont'd

REID, D.A.G.
Bickley Park Cricket Club Centenary Year, 1967, compiled
by D.A.G. Reid.
Bickley Park Cricket Club. 1967.
2

(SUGDEN, A.N.B.).
W.G. Grace...to mark the 50th anniversary of his death...
(Note: W.G. Grace lived in Sydenham and Mottingham).
The Author. 1965.
2

TASSELL, Bryan.
Band of Brothers, 1858-1958.
Privately Printed. 1958.
4,11,15

TAYLOR, A.D.
The story of a cricket picture.
Emery. 1923.
4(1972) 12

WAGHORN, H.T.
Cricket scores, notes, etc., from 1750-1775; written as
reported in the different newspapers; to which are added
two poems, with remarks - published in 1773. On Kent v
Surrey; also rules of the game when betting was permitted,
compiled by H.T. Waghorn.
Edinburgh and London, William Blackwood and Sons. 1899.
3,17

WARNER, Oliver.
Frank Woolley.
Phoenix House. 1952.
1,3,8

WARNER, P.F.
Cricket reminiscences.
Richards. 1920.
12

WEIR, W.R.
A peep into the past: a cricket souvenir.
London, F.H. Ayres. 1902.
3

WOOLLEY, Frank.
The King of games.
S. Paul. 1935.
3,12

CRIME

KENT COUNTY CONSTABULARY.
Analysis of crime in 1964.
Maidstone, Kent County Constabulary. 1965.
11

KENT COUNTY CONSTABULARY.
Analysis of crime in 1965.
Maidstone, Kent County Constabulary. 1966.
11

MELLING, Elizabeth.
Crime and punishment: a collection of examples from
original sources in the Kent Archives Office, from the
16th to the 19th century, edited by Elizabeth Melling.
Kent County Council. 1969.
2,4,5,6,7,8,9,11,12,16,17,18

CROCKENHILL

PRIEST, Simeon.
Excursion to Crockenhill, Saturday, April 1st, 1916.
Geologists' Association. 1916.
5,11,17

CROUCH

Crouch, Winfield Farm - Sale catalogue.
1967.
12

CRYSTAL PALACE

ALDRIDGE, W.
Gossip on the wild birds of Norwood and Crystal Palace
district.
Burdett and Co., Printers. 1885.
2

ART Journal - illustrated catalogue: the industry of
all nations, 1851. (Crystal Palace collection).
G. Virtue. (1851).
2

BEAVER, Patrick.
The Crystal Palace, 1851-1936: a portrait of Victorian
enterprise.
Hugh Evelyn. 1970.
2,4

BERLYN, P.
The Crystal Palace...architectural history, by P.
Berlyn and C. Fowler.
J. Gilbert. 1851.
2

CLARK, W.M. Publisher.
Crystal Palace and its contents...
Clark. 1852.
2

CRUIKSHANK, P.
What is to be done with the Crystal Palace? (14
cartoons in continuous folded strip).
J. Clayton. c.1852.
2

The Crystal Palace. (Auction catalogue giving detailed
history).
Knight, Frank and Rutley, Auctioneers. 1911
8

CRYSTAL PALACE - Exhibition of the works of industry of
all nations, 1851. Reports by the Juries on...the thirty
classes into which the exhibition was divided, 1852 -
Vols. I,II,III.
Royal Commission. 1851, 1852.
18

CRYSTAL PALACE - Great Exhibition of the works of
industry of all nations, 1851. Official...catalogue.
In three vols. (Vols. I and III only).
n.d.
18

CRYSTAL PALACE.
An essay, descriptive and critical.
Walton and Maberly. 1854.
2

CRYSTAL PALACE.
Guide book, 2 vols.
Nelson. (185-?).
2

CRYSTAL PALACE.
Guide to the palace and park. (Official guide).
C. Dickens and Evans. 1885,1888,1893.
2

CRYSTAL PALACE - 1851 and 1854 (coloured engravings).
Read and Co. (1854).
2

CRYSTAL PALACE - 1854-1904. History, souvenir and
programme of Jubilee Concert...
Crystal Palace Co. 1904.
2

Crystal Palace, Sydenham - Sale catalogue.
Knight, Frank and Rutley, Auctioneers. 1911.
2,18

Crystal Palace and the Great Exhibition - historical
account of the building...synopsis of its contents.
H.G. Clarke. 1851.
2

Crystal Palace: district annual, 1885-6.
Burdett. (1885).
2

CRYSTAL PALACE.
Penny guide.
R.K. Burt. (1866).
2

"The Crystal Palace Story" - Exhibition...illustrating
the history of the Crystal Palace at Norwood...and an
indication of its future...Norwood Society, May 2-May 12,
1962. (Catalogue of Exhibition).
18

Crystal Palace that Fox built. A pyramid of rhyme...
D. Bogue. 1851.
2

CYGNUS, pseud.
Crystals from Sydenham; or, what modern authors say of
the Palace.
Hope and Co. 1855.
2

DENARIUS, pseud. (i.e. Sir Henry Cole).
Shall we keep the Crystal Palace...riding and walking...
flowers-fountains-and sculpture?
Murray. 1851.
2

(DUNCAN, Mrs. Isabella).
Geological monsters of pre-Adamite times, as restored at
the Palace Gardens of Sydenham...(Crystal Palace).
Nisbet. 1867.
2

Exhibition of the works of industry of all nations, 1851.
Reports by the Juries...(Crystal Palace).
W. Clowes. 1852.
2,18

Fine Arts Courts in the Crystal Palace (2nd series).
Bradbury and Evans. 1854.
2,18

Fireside facts from the Great Exhibition. (Crystal Palace).
Boulston and Stonedian. (1851).
2

GIBBS-SMITH, C.H.
Great Exhibition of 1851 - commemorative album, compiled
by C.H. Gibbs-Smith.
1950.
18

GIROUARD, Mark.
Crystal Palace - statue from. In article "Faringdon House,
Berkshire".
Country Life, 12th June, 1966.
18

GREAT BRITAIN: LAWS, etc. (GEO. V).
Crystal Palace Act 1914. (4, George V, Chapter 5).
Kings Printer. 1914.
2

GREAT BRITAIN: LAWS, etc. (GEO. VI).
London County Council (Crystal Palace) Act.
H.M.S.O. 1951.
2

GRIFFIN, Frederick.
The world under glass (Crystal Palace).
Trubner. 1879.
2

HOBHOUSE, Christopher.
1851 and the Crystal Palace...the Great Exhibition...Sir
Joseph Paxton and the erection...and destruction of his
masterpiece.
Murray. 1937, 1950.
2,18

The Illustrated Exhibition...sketch...of the principle
objects in the Great Exhibition.
1851.
18

Industrial directory of the Crystal Palace.
Bradbury and Evans. 1854.
2

KAMM, Josephine.
Joseph Paxton and the Crystal Palace.
Methuen. 1967.
2

Knight's pictorial gallery of art...Vol. 1. Useful arts
(Crystal Palace).
London Printing and Publishing Co. 1859.
2

LANGDON-DAVIES, John.
The Great Exhibition, 1851...contemporary documents
(Jackdaw series), compiled by J. Langdon-Davies.
Cape. 1968.
2

LE BLOND, Robert.
The Crystal Palace, ought it to be open on Sunday?
A lecture...April 3rd, 1858.
J. Watson for the Tower Hamlets Literary Institution.
1858.
2

LONDON COUNTY COUNCIL.
Crystal Palace National Recreation Centre.
London County Council. 1964.
2

McDERMOTT, Edward.
Routledge's guide to the Crystal Palace and Park...
Routledge. 1854.
2

MARKHAM, Violet R.
Paxton and the bachelor Duke (Crystal Palace).
Hodder and Stoughton. 1935.
2,18

MARSH, Catherine.
English hearts and English hands: or, the railway and
the trenches...(Note: mission to workmen building
Crystal Palace).
J. Nisbet. 1858.
2

MEASOM, George.
Official illustrated guide to Brighton and South Coast
railways...and to the Crystal Palace.
H.G. Collins. c.1854.
2

MUDDOCK, J.E. Preston.
The romance and history of the Crystal Palace.
L. Upcott Gill. 1911.
2

O'RORKE, L.E.
Life and friendships of Catherine Marsh.
Longmans. 1917.
2

The Palace and Park: its natural history and its
portrait gallery (Crystal Palace).
Bradbury and Evans. 1854.
2

PEVSNER, Nikolaus.
High Victorian design: a study of the exhibits of 1851
(Crystal Palace collection).
Architectural Press. 1951.
2

PHILLIPS, Samuel.
Guide to the Crystal Palace...(various editions and
variant copies).
Bradbury and Evans. 1854 to 1857.
2,18

PLATT, J. Printers.
Handbook to the Crystal Palace district and guide to
walks and drives...
J. Platt. 1888.
2

ROUTLEDGE, George AND CO. Publishers.
Guide to the Great Exhibition...plan...(of) the
Crystal Palace.
Routledge. 1851.
2

SCHARF, George.
Pompeian court in the Crystal Palace.
Bradbury and Evans. 1854.
2

SHENTON, F.K.J.
General guide to the Crystal Palace and...park... compiled by
F.K.J. Shenton.
Crystal Palace Co. 1884, 1873.
2

SKETCHLEY, Arthur, pseud. (i.e. George Rose).
Mrs. Brown at the Crystal Palace.
Routledge. 1875.
2

Statuary of the Crystal Palace. (Cover title).
Bradbury and Evans. 1854.
2

STEAD, W.T.
Our fairy palace and the wonders inside, a child's guide to
the Crystal Palace.
Stead's Publishing House. 1911.
2

The Sydenham Crystal Palace expositor...
Virtue. 185-?
2

The Sydenham Sinbad: a narrative of his journeys to
wonderland...(Children's book on Crystal Palace).
J. and C. Brown. n.d.
2

TALLIS, John and Co. Publishers.
History and description of the Crystal Palace and the
Exhibition...1851.
Tallis. 1852?
2

The ten chief courts of the Sydenham Palace.
Routledge. 1854.
2

TOMLINSON, Charles.
Introductiory essay on the Great Exhibition...1851. (Extract
from Cyclopaedia of Useful Arts, Vol. 1), edited by Charles
Tomlinson.
Virtue. (1851).
2

VICTORIA AND ABLERT MUSEUM.
The Great Exhibition of 1851: a commemorative album.
H.M.S.O. 1950.
2

WARREN, Samuel.
The lily and the bee: an apologue of the Crystal Palace.
Blackwood. 1851.
2

WURTEMBERG STUFFED ANIMALS CO. LTD.
Official handbook to the collection of animals...(Crystal
Palace).
1873
2

WYATT, M. Digby.
The industrial arts of the nineteenth century. A series of
illustrations of the choicest specimens...at the Great
Exhibition...1851.
Day and Son. 1851 (i.e. 1853).
2

WYATT, M. Digby.
Views of the Crystal Palace and Park, Sydenham...1st series.
Day and Son. 1854.
2

WYATT, M. Digby.
The Byzantine and Romanesque Court in the Crystal Palace, by
M.D. Wyatt and J.B. Waring.
Bradbury and Evens. 1854.
2,18

WYATT, M. Digby.
The Italian Court in the Crystal Palace, by M.D. Wyatt and
J.B. Waring.
Bradbury and Evans. 1854.
2,18

WYATT, M. Digby.
The Mediaeval Court in the Crystal Palace, by M.D. Wyatt and
J.B. Waring.
Bradbury and Evans. 1854.
2,18

WYATT, M. Digby.
The Renaissance Court in the Crystal Palace, by M.D.
Wyatt and J.B. Waring.
Bradbury and Evans. 1854.
2,18

YGLESIAS, J.R.C.
London life and the Great Exhibition, 1851. (Then and
there series).
Longmans. 1964.
2

CUDHAM

AVIATION, Ministry of.
Civil aircraft accident: report on the accident to
Druine D31 Turbulent G-APKZ...on 6th December, 1960
at Snag Lane, Cudham...
H.M.S.O. 1961.
8

PEARMAN, R.G.
Early history of Cudham and its church. ..(Typescript),
compiled by R.G. Pearman.
n.d.
2

ST. PETER AND ST. PAUL'S CHURCH, CUDHAM.
Illustrated guide.
Orpington Press. 1961.
2

STEINMAN, G. Steinman.
Some account of the manor of Apuldrefield, in the parish
of Cudham, Kent.
Nichols. 1851.
2,4,8,11

CUSTOMS

BROMLEY, Francis E.
(Kentish) traditions. (Typescript).
(193-).
3

HARRIS, Edwin.
Curious Kentish customs.
Rochester, Harris. 1899.
1,8,11,12

HUNT, Cecil.
British customs and ceremonies.
Benn. 1954.
1,2,5,11,18,19

Jack of Dover: his quest of inquirie...
Percy Society. 1842.
6,12

KENT COUNCIL OF SOCIAL SERVICE.
Kentish recipes.
n.d.
11

KENT COUNCIL OF SOCIAL SERVICE.
Old Kentish recipes.
Deal, Hockley. n.d.
11,19

KENT MESSENGER.
Customs of Kent. (Typescript).
Kent Messenger. 1968.
12

LAMBETH, Minnie.
The golden dolly... corn dollies through the ages.
Fulborn, Cornucopia Press. 1963.
3

LAMBETH, Minnie.
A new golden dolly...revised and enlarged edition.
Fulborn, Cornucopia Press. 1966.
3

MAYLAM, Percy.
The hooden horse, an East Kent Christmas custom.
Canterbury. 1909.
3,4,6,7,8,11,12,13,15,21

SPARVEL-BAYLY, J.A.
More Kentish proverbs, Part 2; and Higham Priory.
Walford's Antiquarian and Bibliographical Review. 1887.
5

CUXTON

CUXTON WOMEN'S INSTITUTE.
Cuxton: a survey undertaken for the "Countryside in the 70's". (Typescript).
c.1960.
12

DANBURY

NARES, Edward.
Letter to the Rev. Francis Stone, in reply to his sermon at the visitation at Danbury.
1807.
17

DANSON - See BEXLEY

DARENT, RIVER

CRAIG, D.M.
Development of the paper industry in Dartford and along the river Darent up to 1933.
Dartford. n.d.
5

Darenth Valley illustrated almanack, 1898.
South Darenth, H.L.B. Press. 1898.
5,17

DOCHERTY, J.
A contribution to the quaternary history of the lower Darent basin Kent. (Bound typescript thesis).
1966.
5

DOWNIE, S.C.
North-West Kent: the Darenth and Cray Valleys. (Bound typescript thesis).
1966.
2,5

GREENFIELD, Ernest.
Darent Valley - archaeological research, 1947-48, by E. Greenfield and others.
n.d.
17

HASSALL, J.M.
Aspects of settlement from the first to the 11th centuries, A.D. (Darent Valley). (Dissertation: University of Southampton).
Typescript. 1970.
5

TAYLOR, J. Paul.
Fly fishing on the Darenth.
n.d.
11

WAYTH, C.
Trout fishing, or The River Darent: a rural poeum.
Simpkin, Marshall. 1845.
1,11

DARENTH

BALLS, Horace J.
Guide to St. Margaret's, Darenth.
H.J. Balls. 1968.
5

BIDDEN, J.
Roman remains at Darenth.
Woolwich Antiquarian Society. 1895-6.
17

CAIGER, John E.L.
Darenth Wood: its earthworks and antiquities. (Reprinted from Archaeologia Cantiana, Vol. 79, 1964).
1,5

CHANDLER, Raymond H.
Excursion of the Geologists' Association to Otford and Darent Valley, by R.H. Chandler and A.L. Leach.
1909.
17

COLLINS, A.H.
The inconography of Darenth font. (Reprinted from Archaeologia Cantiana, Vol. 66, 1944).
5

ELLISTON-ERWOOD, Frank Charles.
The architectural history of the parish church of St. Margaret, Darenth, Kent; together with some notes on the desecrated parish church of St. Botolph, Ruxley. Proceedings of the Woolwich Antiquarian Society. 1912.
5,7

GEDNEY, Charles William.
Angling holidays in pursuit of salmon, trout and pike. (Includes sections on rivers Darenth and Stour).
Bromley Telegraph. 1896.
2

METROPOLITAN ASYLUMS BOARD.
Darenth Asylum: industrial colony - report.
n.d.
5

PAYNE, George.
Experiences at Darenth.
Rochester, Parrett and Neves. n.d.
5,11,15

PAYNE, George.
The old Roman Villa, Darenth.
n.d.
1,5,11,12

PAYNE, George.
Roman Villa, Darenth, Kent: and, lecture on Villa.
n.d.
5,17

PRESTWICH, Joseph.
On the age, formation and successive drift-stages of the valley of the Darent.
Geological Society. 1891.
17

ROGERS, Philip George.
A vale in Kent: a historical guide to the Darenth Valley.
Welling, Erwood. 1955.
1,2,4,5,7,8,9,11,12,15,17

Roman Villa, Darenth, Kent. (Press extracts).
1895?
9,12

TAYLOR, Edmund Seyfang ("Walker Miles", pseud.).
Down by the Darent.
1896.
5,11

DARTFORD

ALBEMARLE, George Monk. 1st Duke.
To...Charles II...humble address of officers of several regiments under command of...Monk as it was presented by them to His Majesty at Dartford Heath.
London, Temple, John Playford. 1660.
5

BAKER, Frank Vidler.
The architectural history of Dartford church.
Snowden Bros. 1918.
1,5,12,17

Baldwyns, Dartford - Sale catalogue.
1874.
12

BECK, P.M.
A study of Dartford Market. (MSS.).
1970.
5

BERRY, W.T.
Augustus Applegarth: some notes and references. (Lived in Dartford).
Oxford University Press. 1966.
5,12

BETTERIDGE, V.I.
Dartford and district: a regional study, 2 vols, text and maps. (Bound typescript thesis).
1962.
5

BOTTEN, Arthur H.
Scenes from the history of Dartford.
Dartford, Chronicle Printing Works. c.1951.
5

BRIDGES, Joseph S.
Dartford Grammar School Song.
J.S. Bridges. 1937.
11

BROOK, Cyril A.
Deneholes - Dartford district: observations taken
August 3rd-12th, 1935, by C.A. Brook and S. Priest.
(Typescript).
5

BUTLER, John Walter.
Some researches into public elementary education in
Dartford in second half of the 19th century. (Bound
typescript thesis).
1957.
5

CHANDLER, Raymond H.
Dartford Heath gravel and a palaeolithic implement factory,
by R.H. Chandler and A.L. Leach.
Geologists' Association. 1912.
17

CHANDLER, Raymond H.
Excursion to Crayford and Dartford Heath, by R.H. Chandler
and A.L. Leach.
Crayford. n.d.
17

CHANDLER, Raymond H.
Excursion...to Dartford Heath, by R.H. Chandler and A.L.
Leach.
Geologists' Association. 1911.
17

CHANDLER, Raymond H.
Note on some prehistoric pottery from Dartford Heath.
Woolwich Antiquarian Society. 1910.
17

CLAPHAM, Sir Alfred William.
The Priory of Dartford and the Manor House of Henry VIII.
Royal Archaeological Institute. 1929.
1,5,8,12,17

COLLINS, P.C.
The story of St. Alban the Martyr, Dartford, 1800-1952.
1952.
5

CRAIG, D.M.
The development of the paper industry in Dartford and along
the river Darent up to 1933. (Bound typescript thesis).
1967.
5

DANIELS, Q.R.A.
History of Heath Street County Primary School, 1877-1895.
1954.
5

Dartford, etc. Directory: giving a complete alphabetical
list of all the principal inhabitants...(1850 edition).
J. Williams. 1850.
11

DARTFORD AMATEUR OPERATIC AND DRAMATIC SOCIETY.
Diamond jubilee, 1906-1966.
1966.
5

DARTFORD AND DISTRICT CHAMBER OF COMMERCE.
Dartford shoppers' annual and local guide.
Dartford and District Chamber of Commerce. 1935.
1,5

Dartford and district directory of commerce and trade,
1965-67.
Regency Publicity. 1965.
5

The Dartford and district directory of commerce and trade,
1968/69: the reference book of the resources of the area...
and voluntary organisations, 2nd edition.
Regency Publicity. 1968.
11

Dartford and neighbourhood photographic views.
Dartford, Snowden. 189-?
11

DARTFORD BOROUGH COUNCIL.
Building byelaws made under the Public Health Act, 1936.
1954.
5

DARTFORD BOROUGH COUNCIL.
Byelaws...(current 1961).
1961.
5

DARTFORD BOROUGH COUNCIL.
Copy of charter creating the Municipal Borough of
Dartford...
1933.
5

DARTFORD BOROUGH COUNCIL.
Dartford, Kent: the official guide.
Croydon, Home Publishing Co. Various Editions.
1,4,5,6,9,11,12,15

DARTFORD BOROUGH COUNCIL
DEPARTMENT.
Draft town centre plan.
1966.
5

DARTFORD BOROUGH COUNCIL.
Minutes and reports, May, 1968-April, 1969.
Dartford Borough Council. 1969.
5

DARTFORD BOROUGH COUNCIL.
Minutes and reports, May, 1969-April, 1970.
Dartford Borough Council. 1970.
5

DARTFORD BOROUGH COUNCIL.
Town centre plan: written statement.
Dartford Borough Council. 1969.
5

DARTFORD BOROUGH COUNCIL.
Yearbook, 1936 to date.
1936 +
5

DARTFORD BURIAL BOARD.
Burial ground regulations...
1856.
5

Dartford charities, with supplementary notes, showing
their present state in 1875.
1860.
15

DARTFORD DISTRICT ANTIQUARIAN SOCIETY.
Library catalogue.
Dartford District Antiquarian Society. 1924.
1

DARTFORD DISTRICT ANTIQUARIAN SOCIETY.
Report, balance sheet and list of members.
Dartford District Antiquarian Society. n.d.
1

DARTFORD DISTRICT LIGHT RAILWAYS.
Plans and sections.
1897.
5

DARTFORD INDEPENDENT CHAPEL.
Dartford (Lowfield Street): a register of births and
baptisms, 1797-1837. (Photocopy).
W. Hardcastle. n.d.
5

Dartford Light Railway Order, 1902.
1902.
5

DARTFORD NATURALISTS' FIELD CLUB.
Occasional papers.
1918-1920.
17

DARTFORD LIBERAL ASSOCIATION.
The Liberal link, Vols. 3-7.
1962-69.
5

DARTFORD PARISH CHURCH.
An account of receipts and disbursements of the churchwardens, 1833-34, 1843-48.
1850.
5

DARTFORD PARISH CHURCH.
The Church Monthly, 3 vols.
1889-91.
5

DARTFORD PARISH CHURCH.
Churchwardens' accounts, 1642-1714.
1934.
5

DARTFORD PARISH CHURCH.
Dartford Parish Home Visitor, Nos. 25-48, January, 1878-
December, 1879 inclusive.
Dartford, A. Perry.
5

Dartford Priory: a history of the English Dominicanesses
by the Dominican Nuns of Headington.
Oxford, Blackfriars Publications. 1945 and 1947.
5

DARTFORD SCHOOL BOARD.
Byelaws.
1895.
5

DARTFORD URBAN DISTRICT COUNCIL.
Byelaws...with respect to new streets and buildings...
1901, 1930.
5

DARTFORD URBAN DISTRICT COUNCIL.
Light railways.
1905.
5

DARTFORD URBAN DISTRICT COUNCIL.
Souvenir of the incorporation of Dartford as a municipal
borough.
1933.
11

DARTFORD YOUNG LIBERAL ASSOCIATION.
The Liberal leader, Vols. 1 and 2.
1950-62.
5

The Dartfordian: magazine of the Dartford Grammar School,
new series, Nos. 32-36, 1966-70.
Dartford Grammar School.
5

DAVIS, William J.
The birds of the Dartford district.
J. and W. Davis. 1904.
5,12,15,17

DAVIS, William J.
An illustrated guide to Dartford.
J. and W. Davis. 1902.
15

DEWEY, Henry.
The geology of the country around Dartford, by H. Dewey and
others.
1924.
1,4,5,8,9,11,12,15,17,18,19

DUNKIN, John, of Bromley.
The history and antiquities of Dartford.
1844, etc.
1,2,5,6,8,9,11,12,15,17,18

GILLHAM, Christopher.
History of the Independent Sect and Congregational Church in
Dartford, 1818-1968: a thesis.
1968.
5

GLUNTZ, J.W.
Dartford: town or suburb? (Typescript).
1960.
5

GREAT BRITAIN: LAWS, etc. (GEO. III).
An Act for lighting, watching and improving the town
of Dartford...
1814.
5,11

GREAT BRITAIN: LAWS, etc. (EDW. VII).
Dartford Improvement Act, 1902. (2, Edw. VII, Ch. 54).
1902.
5

GREAT BRITAIN: LAWS, etc. STATUTORY INSTRUMENTS.
London Traffic (parking places) (Dartford) Regulations,
1965. (1965, No. 842).
H.M.S.O. 1965.
5

GUENTHER, John.
Sidney Keyes.
London Magazine. 1967.
12

HALL, J. AND E. LTD.
150th anniversary...of J. and E. Hall Ltd. of Dartford.
1935.
17

HALL, J. AND E. LTD.
The Hallford Magazine, Vol. I, 1951-56, Vol. II, 1957-
61, 1961-67.
Dartford, H.G. Ellis and Son. n.d.
5

HEADINGTON, Dominican Nuns of.
(See Dartford Priory).

HEALTH, General Board of.
Report...on a preliminary inquiry into the sewerage,
drainage and water supply...of the town of Dartford.
1849.
5

HESKETH, Everard.
J. and E. Hall Ltd., 1785 to 1935.
Glasgow University Press. 1935.
1,5,9,11,15,17

HOUSING AND LOCAL GOVERNMENT, Ministry of.
Local Government, England and Wales. Alteration of
areas, the Dartford (Extension) Order, 1957.
1957.
5

HUDSON, Ronald Loftus.
History of Dartford Grammar School.
Simmond and Co. 1966.
1,4,5,9,11,12

HUNT, T.J.
The life story of T.J. Hunt.
T.J. Hunt Ltd. 1936.
5

JAMES, David.
An address to the inhabitants of Dartford.
Chatham, C. and W. Townson. 1818.
5

JAMES, H.E.
This and that: poems (local author).
Ilfracombe, Arthur H. Stockwell. c.1910.
5

JAMES, R.W.
Sludge digestion works, Long Reach, Dartford - souvenir
of inauguration, Saturday, 6th July, 1935.
Bromley Printing Co. n.d.
5

JOHNSON, Theo.
The flora of Dartford, 2 vols. (Handwritten and drawn),
compiled by T. Johnson.
1913
5

KEITH, Sir Arthur.
A description of the Dartford skull discovered by W.M.
Newton.
1910.
5

KENT COUNTY COUNCIL - ARCHIVES COMMITTEE.
Dartford parish records, 1363-1946.
1961.
5

Kent's new College of Technology (North-West Kent College
of Technology, Dartford).
B.I.C.C. Bulletin. 1957.
12

KEYES, Sidney Kilworth.
Dartford: further historical notes.
Dartford, Perry, Son and Lack. 1938.
1,2,5,7,8,9,11,12,13,15,16,17,18

KEYES, Sidney Kilworth.
Dartford: some historical notes.
Dartford, Perry, Son and Lack. 1933.
1,2,5,6,7,8,9,11,12,13,15,16,17,18

KILEY, A.V.
A survey of Dartford.
1948.
5

KIRBY, John William.
History of the Roan School (the Greycoat School) and its
founder.
Blackheath Press. 1929.
5,17,18

KIRBY, John William.
The manor house of Henry VIII at Dartford. (Typescript).
1959.
5

KNIGHT, Roy.
A bibliography of printed material relating to Dartford
in the County of Kent, 2 vols. (Typescript).
1969.
5

LACAILLE, A.D.
Palaeolithic implements manufactured in naturally holed
flints from Rossington, Yorks., and Dartford, Kent.
Doncaster Art Gallery and Museum. 1945.
5

LANDALE, John.
A collection...of material...and benefactions to...Dartford.
J. Hearne. 1829.
1,3,5,11,12,15,17

LEACH, Arthur L.
Buried channels on the Dartford Heath gravel...with...
report of an excursion to Dartford Heath.
1915.
17

LONDON UNIVERSITY - UNIVERSITY COLLEGE. CONSERVATION COURSE.
Dartford Heath: habitat survey and management.
London, University College. 1970.
5

MAIR, Harold.
"Fairer by time". (Story of Dartford).
H. Mair. 1945, 1946?
1,5,9,11,12

MAIR, Harold.
The XVth mile stage, by Harold Mair, with "The Kingdom of
Kent by Gordon Mair.
Dartford, H. Mair. 1953.
1,2,4,5,8,9,11,12,15,17,18,19,20

MARTIN, Sidney.
Dartford Wesleyan Boy's School. Centenary souvenir booklet,
1839-1939.
Dartford, H.G. Ellis. 1939.
5

MATHEW, George.
The trials and supports of Christ's ministers in times
of religious difficulty and danger.
Rivington. 1819.
11

MAXIM, Sir Hiram S.
My life.
Methuen. 1915.
5

MAY, Jonathan.
The contribution of Madame Bergman Osterberg to the
development of British education. (Bound typescript
thesis).
1967.
5

Monumenta Anglicana: inscriptions on the Dartford
Martyr's monument.
Dunkin. 1851.
12

MORLEY, M.M.
Economic change in 18th century Dartford. (Typescript
thesis).
1964.
5

PAINE, Norman.
Dartford historical pageant, edited by N. Paine.
(Typescript).1951.
5

PALMER, C.F.R.
History of the Priory of Dartford in Kent.
n.d.
17

The parish church of Holy Trinity, Dartford.
British Publishing Co. n.d.
12

PORTEUS, G.H.
A church, a town (text of the illuminated pageant,
Dartford Parish Church).
G.H. Porteus. 1970.
5

PORTEUS, G.H.
Guide to Dartford Parish Church of Holy Trinity .
Dartford, Perry, Son and Lack. 1961?
1,2(1962,1966) 4,5,8(1965) 11,12

PORTEUS, G.H.
An outline of the history of the parish church of the
Holy Trinity, Dartford. (Bound typescript thesis).
1963.
5

PRATT, H.M.
Flowering plants observed in the Dartford area of
Kent in the year 1947-1954. (Typescript).
(1955).
5

PRIEST, Simeon.
The geology of Dartford district. (MSS. notes -
incomplete - pages 1-33 only).
1930.
5

PRIEST, Simeon.
The Heath Lane ancient brick kiln.
1913.
5

READ, Thomas C.
Memoir of Richard Trevithick and his inventions.
Dartford, T.C. Read. 1931.
5

REDSHAW, Charles J.
Dartford and neighbourhood.
Dartford, Snowden. 1911?
1,5,11,15,17

RITSON, J.V.
A gazetteer of Roman remains in and around Dartford.
(Typescript), edited by J.V. Ritson.
1964.
5

ROBSON, George.
A sermon preached at Dartford at the visitation of the
Right Reverend, the Lord Bishop of Rochester...1800, by
George Robson, Rector of Snodland.
James Robson. 1800.
15

ROLT, L.T.C.
The Cornish giant: the story of Richard Trevithick, father
of the steam locomotive.
Lutterworth Press. 1960.
5

SHARPE, Annie.
Dartford Priory...by A. Sharpe and others.
Woolwich Antiquarian Society. 1902.
17

SHOARD, D.E.
The role played by communications in the growth of Dartford:
special study in geography: James Graham College of
Education, Leeds.
(Typescript). 1968.
5

SIMPSON, Dorothy.
Some records of Dartford. (Typescript).
1960.
5

SNOWDEN. Publishers.
Dartford illustrated almanac and directory, 1889-1914.
Dartford, Snowden. n.d.
5

SPARVEL-BAYLY, J.A.
New studies in old subjects. (Dartford Priory).
London, Elliot Stock. 1889.
5

SPARVEL-BAYLY, J.A.
Some historical notes of Dartford and its neighbourhood.
Dartford, Perry, Son and Lack. 1876.
2,5,9,11,12,17

SPURRELL, F.C.J.
Dartford antiquities: notes on British, Roman and Saxon
remains found there.
Mitchell and Hughes. 1889.
5,17

The story of St. Alban the Martyr, Dartford.
n.d.
5

TAGG, A.C.
The early history of papermaking in Dartford. (Typescript).
1929.
5

TAIT, G.A.
The church and vicars of Dartford.
Dartford, Snowden. 1909.
1,2,5,7,11,12,14,15,18

The Temple Hill link (Dartford). April, 1962-March, 1968.
St. Edmund's Parish Church. n.d.
5

WATTS, Alan H.
Guide to Dartford Parish Church.
Dartford, Snowden. c.1900.
1,5,7,12,17

WEEKES, Brian.
The change from Liberal to Labour in Dartford, 1900-1920.
(Bound typescript).
Privately Printed. 1964.
5

WEST KENT ADVERTISER.
"Market Street" (Dartford)...
1926.
17

Wide-Awake Dartford: Dartford Borough Journal, July-
December, 1932, January-December, 1933, January-April,
1934.
5

WIGGINS TEAPE.
Dartford paper mills: issued to commemorate their
opening.
Wiggins Teape. (1958).
1,4,7,8,12,17

DARTFORD TUNNEL

DARTFORD TUNNEL JOINT COMMITTEE.
Byelaws, 1963.
Dartford Tunnel Joint Committee. 1963.
5

DARTFORD TUNNEL JOINT COMMITTEE.
General Manager's report, 1964.
Dartford Tunnel Joint Committee. 1965.
4,6,7,12

DARTFORD TUNNEL JOINT COMMITTEE.
General Manager's report, 1965.
Dartford Tunnel Joint Committee. 1966.
4,6,7,12

DARTFORD TUNNEL JOINT COMMITTEE.
General Manager's report, 1966.
Dartford Tunnel Joint Committee. 1967.
4,6,7,8,12,15

DARTFORD TUNNEL JOINT COMMITTEE.
General Manager's report for period...to December, 1967,
to December, 1968.
Dartford Tunnel Joint Committee. 1968-69.
4

DARTFORD TUNNEL JOINT COMMITTEE.
General Manager's report, 1967-69, 1970.
Dartford Tunnel Joint Committee. 1968-70.
9

DARTFORD TUNNEL JOINT COMMITTEE.
General Manager's report for period 1st January-31st
December, 1969.
Dartford Tunnel Joint Committee. 1970.
12

DARTFORD TUNNEL JOINT COMMITTEE.
General Manager's report for period...to December, 1969,
to December, 1970.
Dartford Tunnel Joint Committee. 1970-71.
4

DARTFORD TUNNEL JOINT COMMITTEE.
General Manager's report for period 1st January to 31st
December, 1971.
Kent County Council, Supplies Department. 1972.
4,11

DARTFORD TUNNEL JOINT COMMITTEE.
A new Thames Tunnel.
Dartford Tunnel Joint Committee. 1964. Printed by Kent
County Council Supplies Department.
1,2,4,5,6,8,11,19

GREAT BRITAIN: LAWS, etc. (GEO. V).
An Act to authorise the construction of a tunnel under
the river Thames between Dartford...and Purfleet...
1930. (Reprinted 1956).
5,8

GREAT BRITAIN: LAWS, etc. (GEO. VI).
An Act to authorise a variation of the works authorised
by the Dartford Tunnel Act, 1930...
1937. (Reprinted 1956).
5,8

GREAT BRITAIN: LAWS, etc. (ELIZ. II).
An Act to amend the Dartford Tunnel Acts, 1930 to 1957,
with respect to tolls and charges...1961.
H.M.S.O. 1961.
12

GREAT BRITAIN: LAWS, etc. (ELIZ. II).
Dartford Tunnel Bill, 1957.
H.M.S.O. 1957.
5

GREAT BRITAIN: LAWS, etc. (ELIZ. II).
Dartford Tunnel Act, 1961.
H.M.S.O. 1961.
4,5,8,12

GREAT BRITAIN: LAWS, etc. (ELIZ. II).
Dartford Tunnel Act, 1962.(10 and 11, Eliz. II, ch. xl.).
H.M.S.O. 1962.
4

GREAT BRITAIN: LAWS, etc. (ELIZ. II).
Dartford Tunnel Act, 1967.
H.M.S.O. 1967.
1,4,8

KENT MESSENGER.
Dartford-Purfleet Tunnel - special supplement, November 15th,
1963.
Kent Messenger. 1963.
2

DARWIN, CHARLES

BETTANY, G.T.
Life of Charles Darwin.
Scott. 1887.
2,4,12

BRITISH ASSOCIATION FOR THE ADVANCEMENT OF SCIENCE.
Down House: the home of Darwin.
n.d.
2,17

BRITISH ASSOCIATION FOR THE ADVANCEMENT OF SCIENCE.
Historical and descriptive catalogue of the Darwin Memorial
at Down House.
British Association for the Advancement of Science. (1945?).
2

CARRECK, J.N.
Field meeting at Keston, Downe, Kent and visit to Darwin
Memorial Rooms at Downe House, by J.N. Carreck and M.P.
Kerney. (From Proceedings of the Geologists' Association).
1954.
5

CHEESMAN, Evelyn.
Charles Darwin and his problems.
Bell. 1953.
2,12

CRELLIN, J.K.
Darwin and evolution, compiled by J.K. Crellin. (Jackdaw
Series).
Cape. 1968.
2

DARLINGTON, C.D.
Darwin's place in history.
Blackwell. 1959.
12

DARWIN, Charles.
Autobiography. (Resident at Downe).
Watts. 1937.
2

(DARWIN, Charles).
Charles Darwin and the voyage of the "Beagle", edited by
N. Barlow. (with some biography).
Pilor Press. 1945.
2

DARWIN, Charles.
Life and letters, including autobiographical chapter, 2nd
edition. (Note: Darwin lived at Downe).
Murray. 1887.
2

Down House (Downe). (Extract from Proceedings of the
British Association for the Advancement of Science -
Report of the 96th meeting...1928 - photocopy of 6th
page).
Birtish Association for the Advancement of Science. 1929.
2

FREEMAN, R.B.
Works of Charles Darwin: an annotated bibliographical
handlist.
Dawsons. 1965.
2

GREGOR, Arthur S.
Charles Darwin.
Augus and Robertson. 1967.
2

HUXLEY, Sir Julian.
Charles Darwin and his world, by Sir J. Huxley and
H.B.D. Kettlewell.
Thames and Hudson. 1965.
2

LINNEAN SOCIETY OF LONDON.
The Darwin-Wallace celebration...1st July, 1908.
Linnean Society of London. 1908.
2

MOORE, Ruth.
Charles Darwin.
Hutchinson. 1957.
12

MOOREHEAD, Alan.
Darwin and the Beagle.
Hamish Hamilton. 1969.
12

ROYAL COLLEGE OF SURGEONS OF ENGLAND.
Charles Darwin and Down House.
Livingstone. 1959.
2

ROYAL COLLEGE OF SURGEONS OF ENGLAND.
Historical and descriptive catalogue of the Darwin
Memorial at Down House (Downe).
Royal College of Surgeons of England. 1957?
2

ROYAL SOCIETY OF LONDON.
Notes and records, Vol. 14, No. 1. (Includes some
Darwin letters and bibliography of published Darwin
letters).
Royal Society of London. 1959.
2

SEWARD, A.C.
Darwin and modern science, edited by A.C. Seward.
Cambridge University Press. 1909.
12

STEVENSON, R. Scott.
Famous illnesses in history. (Note: includes chapter
on Darwin and Napoleon III).
Eyre and Spottiswoode. 1962.
2

DAVINGTON

Account of the church and priory of St. Mary Magdalene,
Davington.
Faversham, Monk. 1852.
3,7,11

COLLIER, Carus Vale.
Coats of arms in Kent churches.
Faversham. n.d.
17

COLLIER, Carus Vale.
Davington Priory.
Kent Archaeological Association - in Archaeologia
Cantiana, Vol. 22. 1897.
17

CULMER, George G.
Davington Church and Priory.
Faversham, Elvy. 1932?
3,7,11

Davington Priory and Nos. 3-8 Davington Hill, Faversham,
Kent, for sale by auction...on...6th April, 1972...
Auctioneers, Burrows.
1972.
11

(A history of the parish of Davingron, Davington Priory
and Davington Court, together with an account of the
neigbouring parish of Preston). MSS. volume.
n.d.
15

SMITH, C. Roach.
Catalogue of the first portion of the library of Thomas
Willement Esq. (Lived at Davington, nr. Faversham), compiled
by C.R. Smith.
n.d.
11

WILLEMENT, Thomas.
Historical sketch of the parish of Davington...
Pickering. 1862.
1,3,4,6,8,11,12,13,15,17

DEAL

Album of Deal and Walmer views.
Charles Reynolds. n.d.
1,11

ANDERSON, A.E.
A guide to Deal Parish Church.
Deal, Pain and Son. 195-?
12

APPLETON, G.
Deal Luggers. In "The Mariners' Mirror", Vol. 45, No. 2,
May, 1959, pp. 145-153.
6

BAKER, Alan R.H.
Field system of an East Kent parish (Deal). In Archaeologia
Cantiana, Vol. 78, 1963).
17

BAKER, A.W.J. Publisher.
Deal at one view, and a glance at Walmer.
c.1842.
11

BEECHAM, Thomas. Publisher.
Beecham's photo-folio: 24 choice photographic views:
Canterbury, Deal and Walmer.
St. Helens, Beecham. n.d.
3

Bucket urns found near Deal. (Reprinted from the Antiquaries'
Journal, 1937).
11

BURROW, Edward J. AND CO. LTD. Publishers.
Walmer and Deal. (Borough guides).
Cheltenham, Burrow. c.1909.
11,13

CARDWELL, E.
Landing place of Julius Caesar in Britain. In Archaeologia
Cantiana, Vol. 3, 1860.
17

CARTER, Mrs. Elizabeth.
A series of letters between Mrs. Elizabeth Carter and
Miss Catherine Talbot, edited by Montague Pennington...
1809.
17

CARTER, Mrs. Elizabeth.
Letters from Mrs. Elizabeth Carter to Mr. Montague, 1755-1800.
Vols. 1-3 n.d., edited by Montague Pennington.
17

CARTER, Nicholas.
Letter to the Mayor and Corporation of Deale...in relation
to their opinion upon the Trinity.
1752.
11

CARTER, Nicholas.
A sermon preached in the Chapel at Deal...August 9th, 1752.
Cave. 1752.
12

CARTER, Nicholas.
A sermon preached in the Chapel at Deal in Kent on the
11th of February, 1757...
R. Griffiths. n.d.
3

CHAPMAN, Henry Stephen.
Deal past and present.
Reeves and Turner. 1890.
1,3,4,6,11,12,15,17

CHAPMAN, Henry Stephen.
A peep at olde Deale.
Deal, T. Pain. 1916
11

CHAPMAN, Henry Stephen.
The story of Dola, Julius Caesar's landing place.
Newnes. 1921.
1,2,3,4,5,6,8,11,12,13,14,18

(CLARK, E.W.).
Reminiscences of old Deal.
Deal, T. Pain. (1950).
7,11

COLLINS, Barbara.
Discovering Deal.
Deal Entertainments and Publicity Committee. 1969.
4,6,8,11

COLLINS, Barbara.
1716-1966: a short history of the Civic Church of St.
George-the-Martyr, Deal, Kent.
East Kent Mercury. 1966.
6

DANIELS, William Edward.
The church of St. George-the-Martry, Deal.
1920?
11

DANIELS, William Edward.
"Those were the days": some reminiscences.
Deal, T. Pain. 1954.
11

DAVIS, John. Publisher.
Deal and Dover illustrated visitors' guide.
J. Davis. n.n.
3(c.1880) 6(c.1895) 7(c.1900)

Deal: a collection of photographs.
Giraud. 190-?
11

Deal, Kent: religious controversy, 1750-1753.
n.d.
11

Deal, Walmer and Sandwich: their attractions as sea-
side and holiday resorts.
n.d.
11

Deal, Walmer and Sandwich illustrated.
Gravesend, Rochard. n.d.
11

DEAL AND DISTRICT LOCAL HISTORY SOCIETY.
Annual reports, 1936-1938, 3 vols.
11

DEAL AND WALMER LOCAL HISTORY SOCIETY.
Exhibition - Summer, 1966.
Deal and Walmer Local History Society. 1966.
3

DEAL BOROUGH COUNCIL.
Abstract of accounts, 1953, 1954.
Deal Borough Council.
11

DEAL BOROUGH COUNCIL
Deal: official guide.
Deal Borough Council. 1961, etc.
1,4,11,12

DEAL BOROUGH COUNCIL.
Deal, Kent, England: the holiday town for all the family.
Borough of Deal Publicity Department. (1971).
11

DEAL BOROUGH COUNCIL.
Opening of Deal Pier, 1957. (Official programme).
Deal Borough Council. 1957.
11

Deal's historic pageant, 1949. (A collection of
photographs...).
n.d.
11

Dover, Canterbury, Deal, Walmer and Sandwich by camera and
pen, 1904-5.
Brighton, W.T. Pike. 1904.
6

Dover, Folkestone and Deal local railway guide.
1898.
17

"DOVER CHRONICLE". Publisher.
Dover, Folkestone, Deal and Cinque Ports appendix and
almanack for 1870, containing a short history of Dover.
Dover Chronicle. 1870.
7

"DOVER CHRONICLE". Publisher.
The Dover, Folkestone, Deal guide appendix and almanack -
rewritten, revised, corrected and enlarged for 1873.
Dover Chronicle. 1873.
7

DOVER STANDARD.
The "Standard" picture guide to Dover, Canterbury and Deal.
Dover Standard Office. 1899.
3,17

DOWKER, George.
Deal and its environs. In Archaeologia Cantiana, Vol. 24,
1900.
17

FELLS, J.M.
The origin of the Deal and Walmer Carter Institute.
Deal, Giraud. 1921.
11

FRANKLIN, W.H. Publisher.
New view album of Deal and Walmer.
W.H. Franklin. (19--).
11

GEDGE, T.E. Publisher.
New guide to Deal and district.
Deal, Gedge. c.1900.
1,11

GERALD, Sydney.
Deal beach. (Extracts from Pall Mall Magazine, 1893).
11

GIBBS. W.
Legal opposition: the case of Mr. John Gibbs, the Deal
pilot...compiled by W. Gibbs.
W. Gibbs. 1840.
11

GOLDRING, Douglas.
Home ground.
Macdonald. 1949.
3,12

GOULDEN, C. Publisher.
Dover, Deal and district, descriptive and pictorial.
Dover, Goulden. c.1890.
6,11

GREAT BRITAIN: LAWS, etc. (GEO. III).
An Act for the more easy and speedy recovery of small
debts within the town and borough of Deal...
1786.
11

GREAT BRITAIN: LAWS, etc. (VIC.).
An Act for confirming...certain provisional orders...
under the General Pier and Harbour Act, 1861...
relating to Carrickfergus, Deal...
Printed by Eyre and Spottiswoode. 1862.
11

Guide to sea angling, Folkestone, Deal, Dover.
Robert McGregor, Angling Association Ltd. 1971.
7

GWINNETT, Ambrose.
The life and unparalleled voyages and adventures of
Ambrose Gwinnett.
Catnach. c.1730.
3(1770?) 12,17

HARDMAN, Frederick William.
Sea valley of Deal. In Archaeologia Cantiana, Vol. 50,
1938.
17

HERSSENS, Leon.
Our stay in Deal and Walmer, 1914-1915, by a Belgian.
Deal, T. Pain. 1915.
6,7,11

HORN, J. AND ALLARD. Publishers.
Dover and Deal directory and guide.
Dover, J. Horn and Allard. 1792.
6,11,17

HOUSING AND LOCAL GOVERNMENT, Ministry of.
The Deal Water Order.
H.M.S.O. 1962, etc.
4,8

Imperial album of Deal views.
Newman and Co. n.d.
11

KENT COUNTY COUNCIL - PLANNING DEPARTMENT.
Deal: a plan for the town centre, by J.S. Allen.
Kent County Council. 1964 and 1966.
11

KENT COUNTY COUNCIL - PLANNING DEPARTMENT.
Deal: draft town plan.
Kent County Council. 1971.
7,8,11

KENT COUNTY COUNCIL - PLANNING DEPARTMENT.
Deal: Middle Street conservation area: an architectural
re-appraisal.
Kent County Council. 1971.
7,8,11

LAKER, John.
History of Deal.
1917, etc.
1,2,3,4,6,7,8,11,12,15,18

MAY, George W.
Deal, edited by G.W. May.
Health Resorts Association. 1903, etc.
11,13

Minerva railway guide and visitors' handbook for Deal,
Walmer, Sandwich and district.
1906.
17

New handbook to the Downs neighbourhood...Deal, Walmer,
Sandwich...
Deal, Hayward. 18--?
1,11,14

O'NEIL, Bryan Hugh St. John.
Deal Castle.
H.M.S.O.
1 (1966)
2 (1953,1966)
3 (1953,1966)
4 (1953,1966)
6 (1953,1966)
7 (1966)
8 (1966)
11 (1953,1966,1971)
12 (1953,1966)

PAIN, E.C.
Deal and the Downs in the war of liberation, 1939-1945.
Deal, T.F. Pain. 1948.
1,8,11,14

PAIN, E.C.
History of Deal (1914-1953).
Deal, T.F. Pain. 1953.
1,3,4,6,7,8,11,12,13,15

PAIN, Harold W.
Deal, Walmer and Kingsdown. (Sketches).
Deal, T.F. Pain. 1919.
11

PENNINGTON, Montague.
Memoirs of Mrs. Elizabeth Carter...2 vols.
1808.
17

POST, Beale.
On the place of Caesar's landing in Britain.
1844.
17

Post Roman pottery from Worth and Deal. (Reprinted from
the Antiquaries' Journal, 1937).
11

PRITCHARD, Stephen.
The history of Deal and its neighbourhood, from the invasion
of Britain, on the shore of Deal, by Julius Caesar, B.C. 55,
to the present time.
Edward Hayward. 1864.
1,4,6,7,11,12,14,15,17

RENNELL.
Concerning the place where Julius Caesar landed in Britain.
1826.
11

ROGER, John Lewis.
Sketches of Deal, Walmer and Sandwich.
Longmans. 1911.
1,3,4,6,11,12,15,17,18

SAUNDERS, A.D.
Deal and Walmer Castles.
H.M.S.O. 1963.
1,2,3,4,6,7,8,11,12,15,19

SHADWELL, Charles.
The fair Quaker of Deal.
1792.
11,12

SHELVEY, Leslie H.
Deal Charter Year, 1699-1949.
Deal Charter Committee. 1949.
11

SHELVEY, Leslie H.
Some early chapters from the story of Deal...
(1949).
2

SHELVEY, Leslie H.
Story of Deal since incorporation, 1699-1949.
1964.
11

SMITH, Charles Roach.
On a hoard of coins found at Deal.
n.d.
11

SPARKE, John.
The old Deal Pier.
Deal, T. Pain. 1917.
6,11,12

STANTON, William.
The journal of William Stanton, pilot, of Deal, 1811-1867.
Portsmouth, Barrell. 1929.
1

STANTON, William.
Journal of William Stanton, pilot of Deal.
Simpkin Marshall. n.d.
6,11,12

STEBBING, W.P.D.
Court Leet and Court Baron record for the Manor of
Deal Prebend in 1708. In Four Miscellaneous Notes.
(Under Speldhurst).
Ashford, Headley. n.d.
11

STEBBING, W.P.D.
Deal and Walmer, 1699, Church and State...
Ashford, Headley. n.d.
11,12

STEBBING, W.P.D.
The Friends of old Deal and its ancient manor.
n.d.
3

STEBBING, W.P.D.
The invader's shore: some observations on the
physiography, archaeology, history and sociology of
Deal and Walmer.
Deal, Howe. 1937.
3,4,6,7,8,11,12

STEBBING, W.P.D.
Some aspects of bygone parish life: lecture delivered
to Deal Literary Club (examples from Deal).
1919.
17

STEBBING, W.P.D.
202 Beacon Street, Deal. (Reprinted from Archaeologia
Cantiana, Vol. 47, 1935).
11

(TAYLOR, Thomas).
The Muggletonian principles prevailing, being an answer
in full to a scandalous and malicious pamphlet (by J.
Williams, Bishop of Chichester) entitled "A true
representation of the absurd and mischievous principles
of the sect called Muggletonians...
Deal, Hayward. 1822.
11

TOPOGRAPHICAL ASSOCIATION OF GREAT BRITAIN. Publishers.
The "holiday handbook" to Deal and Walmer.
Topographical Association of Great Britain. n.d.
11

Views of Deal and neighbourhood (Twenty-four).
Deal, Cook. 187-?
11

Views of Deal and neighbourhood.
Newman. 187-?
11

VIPOND, W.
The doctrines and mode of worship of the Methodists...
sermons preached at the opening of the Ebenezer Chapel,
Deal, 1806.
Cordenx. 1815.
11

WOLLASTON, Sir Gerald Woods.
St. Leonard's, Deal. (Reprinted from Archaeologia
Cantiana, Vol. 49), by Sir G.W. Wollaston and others.
Ashford, Headley. n.d.
11,17

DEER PARKS

SHIRLEY, E.P.
Some account of English deer parks.
Murray. 1867.
3,12

WHITAKER, Joseph.
A descriptive list of the deer parks and paddocks of
England.
Ballantyne. 1892.
12

DENT-DE-LION

PROBY, Mrs. Charles J.
The Dennes of Daundelyon, 3 vols.
1859.
13

DENTON

ARNOLD, George Matthews.
Denton near Gravesend.
Gravesend, Caddel. 1902.
1,3,4,5,7,8,9,11,12,15

GRIFFIN, Ralph.
Kentish items: West Malling, Hythe, Denton, Allington,
Elham, Bekesbourne.
n.d.
7

POCOCK, Robert. Printer.
A chronology of the most remarkable events...of Gravesend,
Milton and Denton.
1790.
9,11

Short history of St. Mary Magdalene Church, Denton near
Canterbury.
(Typescript). n.d.
12

DEPTFORD

ARROW, Frederick.
The Corporation of Trinity House of Deptford Strand: a
memoir...(2 copies).
1868.
18

ASHFORD, Frederick.
The monuments and gravestones in the churches and chapels
of Deptford, Kent.
(MSS.) n.d.
18

ASHFORD, Frederick.
Records of old Deptford, 1439-1870, compiled by F. Ashford.
n.d.
18

BAKER, L.D.J.
List of places of worship in the boroughs of Deptford,
Lewisham, Greenwich and Woolwich...compiled by L.D.J. Baker.
1961.
1,2,5,8,11,12,17,18

BARRETT, C.R.B.
The Trinity House of Deptford Strand.
Lawrance and Bullen. 1893.
17,18

BARROW, J.
Life of Peter the Great. (Photocopy of Chapter IV)
(At Deptford Shipyard).
1887.
18

COTTON, Joseph.
Memoir on the origin and incorporation of the Trinity House
of Deptford Strand.
Darling. 1818.
11,12,18

DALEY, P.D.J.
History of Deptford. (Advanced history thesis, 1947-1949).
(MSS.).

DEPTFORD BOROUGH COUNCIL.
The Metropolitan Borough of Deptford: official guide.
Burrow. n.d.
1(7th edition only).

DEPTFORD BOROUGH COUNCIL.
Official guide to Deptford.
1928.
17

Deptford charities - historical details. (Prepared by
Ernest Field, Town Clerk).
1953.
18

Deptford Charters. Royal Charter of Confirmation...to the
Trinity House, Deptford Strand. (In the reign of James II).
1685.
1,11,17,18

Deptford past and present.
Deptford Borough Council. 1928.
17,18

DEWS, Nathan.
Historic Deptford...
Deptford, J.D. Smith. 1937.
17,18

DEWS, Nathan.
The history of Deptford.
Simpkin and Marshall. 1884.
1,2(1883) 4,8,11,12,13,16,17(1887) 18(1883)

DEWS, Nathan.
The history of Deptford, 2nd edition, revised and
enlarged. (Thamesmead histories).
Conway Maritime Press. 1884. (Reprinted 1971).
4,7,11

DEWS, Nathan.
A muster roll of old Deptford worthies.
1888.
17,18

Dockyards - first report from the Select Committee on.
(References to Deptford statistics).
House of Commons. 1864.
18

DUNKIN, Alfred John.
History of Deptford: Hundred of Blackheath, etc.
(Limited edition).
1854 (Re-issued 1922).
17,18

DUNKIN, Alfred John.
History of the County of Kent - Deptford topographical
survey...of...Lathes and Hundreds in the County...
1855.
5,18

ELLIS, Sir Henry.
History of the boat which gave Peter the Great...first
thought of building...fleet. (Letter to President of
British Museum).
1856.
18

F., J.R.
The story of St. Nicholas, Deptford.
1938.
18

FIRTH, Charles H.
Naval songs and ballads. (References to Deptford),
edited by C.H. Firth.
Navy Records Society. 1908.
18

FRASER, Alan C.
A Deptford estate in the mid-eighteenth century.
n.d.
18

GRAHAM, Stephen.
Peter the Great: a life...
Benn. 1950.
18

GRANT, Mary.
Parish Church of St. Paul, Deptford. (Pamphlet).
1907.
18

GRANVILLE, Augustus K.B.
Deptford worthies: a lecture delivered on...February
15th, 1854, in the hall of the Deptford Institution.
Printed by W. Flashman. 1854.
11

GREAT BRITAIN: LAWS, etc. (GEO. II).
An Act for providing a maintenance for the minister of...
St. Nicholas, Deptford...
1730.
11

GREAT BRITAIN: LAWS, etc. (GEO. II).
An Act for the better regulation...of pilots licensed by
the Corporation of Trinity House of Deptford Strand...
1732.
9,11

DICKENS, Charles.
Charles Dickens: a "Bookman" extra number.
Hodder and Stoughton. 1914.
12

DICKENS, Charles.
Charles Dickens as editor: being letters written by him
to William Henry Wills, his sub-editor.
Smith, Elder and Co. 1912.
4

DICKENS, Charles.
Dickens dictionary of London, 1879.
All The Year Round. 1879.
8

DICKENS, Charles.
Dickens memento, with introduction by Francis Phillimore...
1870.
15

DICKENS, Charles.
The letters of Charles Dickens.
Clarendon Press. 1965.
15

DICKENS, Charles.
The love and romance of Charles Dickens.
Argonaut Press. 1936.
15

DICKENS, Charles.
Mr. and Mrs. Charles Dickens: his letters to her.
Constable. 1935.
8

DICKENS, Charles.
The mystery of Edwin Drood.
Chapman and Hall. 1870.
8

DICKENS, Charles.
The personal history of David Copperfield.
Bradbury and Evans. 1850.
8

DICKENS, Charles.
The speeches of Charles Dickens.
M. Joseph. n.d.
15

DICKENS, Charles.
The unpublished letters of Charles Dickens to Mark Lemon.
Halton and Truscott Smith. 1927.
15

Dickens souvenir of 1912, edited by Dion Clayton Calthrop
and Max Pemberton. (1912).
Chapman and Hall. (1912).
8

DICKENS, Charles.
All the year round, Vols. 11,12,19 and 20, edited by C.
Dickens.
1864-1868.
8

DICKENS, Charles.
All the year round, new series, 1869-1874, edited by C.
Dickens.
n.d.
8

DICKENS, Charles.
Household words, a weekly journal (2 vols.), edited by C.
Dickens.
Bradbury and Evans. 1881-1882.
8,15

DICKENS, Mamie.
My father as I recall him.
The Roxburghe Press. 1897.
15

Dickens Festival Pageant...Rochester, 1951: souvenir
programme.
1951.
4,11,15

DOLBY, George.
Charles Dickens as I knew him: the story of the reading
tours in Great Britain and America (1866-1870).
Unwin. 1885, 1887 etc.
4,6,8,12

DONORAN, Frank.
The children of Charles Dickens.
Frewin. 1969.
12

DU CANN, Charles Garfield Lott.
The love-lives of Charles Dickens.
Muller. 1961.
15

ELSNA, Hebe, pseud. (D.P. Ansle).
Unwanted wife: a defence of Mrs. Charles Dickens.
Jarrolds. 1963.
15

ENGEL, Monroe.
The maturity of Dickens.
Cambridge, Massachusets, Harvard University Press. 1959.
4

FAWCETT, F. Dubrez.
Dickens the dramatist on stage, screen and radio...
W.H. Allen. 1952.
4

FIDO, Martin.
Charles Dickens.
Routledge, Kegan Paul. 1968.
12

FIELDING, K.J.
Charles Dickens.
Longmans. 1953 etc.
4(1953) 8

FIELDING, K.J.
Charles Whitehead and Charles Dickens. (Reprint from
The Review of English Studies, April. 1952).
4

FITZGERALD, Percy.
Boz and Bath: his account of the gay city...
1904.
4

FITZGERALD, Percy.
Bozland, Dickens' places and people.
Downey and Co. 1895.
4,8

FITZGERALD, Percy.
The history of Pickwick: an account of its characters,
localities, allusions and illustrations.
1891.
4

FITZGERALD, Percy.
The life of Charles Dickens as revealed in his writings.
1905.
4,19

FITZGERALD, Percy.
Memories of Charles Dickens, with an account of
"Household Words" and "All the Year Round"...
Bristol, J. Arrowsmith. 1913.
4

FITZGERALD, Percy.
Pickwickian studies.
1899.
4

FITZGERALD, S.J. Adair.
Dickens and the drama: being an account of Charles
Dickens' connection with the stage and the stage's
connection with him.
1910.
4

FLETCHER, Geoffrey.
The London Dickens knew.
Hutchinson. 1970.
12

FORSTER, John.
The life of Charles Dickens, Vols. 1 and 2.
Chapman and Hall. 1872.
8

FORSTER, John.
The life of Charles Dickens...new edition, with notes and an
index by A.J. Hoppe and additional author's footnotes, 2 vols.
1966.
4

FROST, Thomas.
In Kent with Charles Dickens.
Tinsley Bros. 1880.
1,2,3,4,6,8,11,12,15,17,18

FYFE, Thomas Alexander.
Charles Dickens and the law.
1910.
4

GARIS, Robert.
The Dickens theatre: a reassessment of the novels.
1965.
4

GISSING, George.
Charles Dickens: a critical study.
Gresham. 1904.
4

GRAVES, Charles.
Smatterbook, No. 20: 100 facts on Charles Dickens, edited
by C. Graves.
London, Naldrett Press. (1951?).
4

GREEN, Frank.
London homes of Dickens...with an introduction by Walter
Dexter.
Chambers. (194-?).
4

GROSS, J.
Dickens and the twentieth century, by J. Gross, G. Pearson
and others.
Routledge. 1962.
4,8

HAMMERTON, J.A.
The Dickens companion: a book of anecdote and reference.
c.1910?
4

HAMMERTON, J.A.
The Dickens picture book.
1910.
4,8

HARDWICK, Michael John.
The Charles Dickens companion, by M. and M. Hardwick.
Murray. 1965.
3,4,8,15

HARDWICK, Michael John.
Dickens' England.
Dent. 1970.
8

HARPER, Charles George.
Mr. Pickwick's second time on earth. With drawings by
Paul Hardy.
1927.
4

HARRIS, Edwin.
Gad's Hill Place and Charles Dickens.
E. Harris and Son. 1910.
1,4,6,12,15

HARRIS, Edwin.
John Jasper's gatehouse: a sequel to the unfinished novel,
"The Mystery of Edwin Drood", by Charles Dickens.
MacKays. 1931.
4,8,12,15

HARRIS, Edwin.
Houses in which Dickens lived.
Cheltenham, E. Harris and Sons. (1912).
4

HARRISON, Michael.
Charles Dickens: a sentimental journey in search of an
unvarnished portrait.
Cassell. 1953.
1,4,5,15

HATTON, Thomas.
A bibliography of the periodical works of Charles
Dickens: bibliographical, analytical and statistical,
by T. Hatton and A.H. Cleaver.
Chapman and Hall. 1933.
4

HAYWARD, Arthur L.
The Dickens encyclopaedia: an alphabetical dictionary
of references to every character and place mentioned in
the works of fiction, with explanatory notes...
Routledge. 1924.
4,12(1969)

HIBBERT, Christopher.
The making of Charles Dickens.
Longmans. 1967.
4,8

HOLLIDAY, A.C.
Where Dickens walked.
Chatham, Solus Arts Advertising Service. 1951.
2,4,6,8,9,15,19

HOPKINS, Albert A.
A Dickens atlas, by A.A. Hopkins and N.F. Read.
London, Spurr and Swift. 1923.
4,15

HOTTEN, John Camden.
Charles Dickens: the story of his life.
J.C. Hotten. (1870).
4

HOUSE, Humphrey.
The Dickens world.
1941, etc.
4,8

HUTCHINGS, Richard J.
Dickens at Winterbourne, Bonchurch.
1964.
4

JOHNSON, Edgar.
Charles Dickens: his tragedy and triumph.
Gollancz. 1953.
4,15

JONES, Charles Sheridan.
The country of Charles Dickens. Illustrated by Ernest
Coffin.
(1923?).
3,4,6

KITTON, Frederic G.
Charles Dickens, his life, writings and personality.
1902.
4

KITTON, Frederic G.
Dickens and his illustrators: Cruikshank, Seymour
(etc.)...with 22 portraits and facsimilies of 70
drawings...2nd edition.
London, George Redway. 1899.
4

KITTON, Frederic G.
The minor writings of Charles Dickens: a bibliography
and sketch.
London, Elliot Stock. 1900.
4

LANG, Andrew.
A mystery of Dickens (i.e. Edwin Drood). In Blackwood's
Magazine, May, 1911.
4

LANG, Andrew.
The puzzle of Dickens' last plot.
London, Chapman and Hall. 1905.
4,15

LANGSTAFF, John Brett.
David Copperfield's library, with prologue by Sir
Owen Seaman and epilogue by Alfred Noyes.
1924.
4

LANGTON, Robert.
The childhood and youth of Charles Dickens.
Hutchinson. 1891.
1,4,5(1883 and 1912) 15,17

LEACOCK, Stephen.
Charles Dickens: his life and work.
Peter Davies. 1933.
4,15

LEAVIS, F.R.
Dickens the novelist, by F.R. and Q.D. Leavis.
Chatto and Windus. 1970.
12

LEWIS, Bernard.
About "The Olde Curiosity Shop": a short account of the
quaint old shop immortalised...as the home of Little Nell...
195 7.
4 ,12(1959)

LEY, J.W.T.
The Dickens circle: a narrative of the novelist's
friendships.
1918.
4,15

LIGHTWOOD, James T.
Charles Dickens and music.
1912.
4

LINCOLN, Victoria.
Charles (a novel inspired by certain events in the life of
Charles Dickens).
1962.
4,15

LINDSAY, Jack.
Charles Dickens: a biographical and critical study.
1950.
4

LOCKWOOD, Frank.
The law and lawyers of Pickwick: a lecture, with an original
drawing of "Mr. Serjeant Buzfuz".
(189-?).
4

LUCAS, John.
The melancholy man: a study of Dickens' novels.
Methuen. 1970.
12

McHUGH, Stuart.
Dickens and disease: (a discussion of the ailments and
diseases of Dickens and of his characters). (Extracts from
Nursing Mirror, 2,9,16,23 February, 1962).
4

MANNING, John.
Dickens on education.
University of Toronto Press. 1959.
4

MARZIALS, Frank T.
Life of Charles Dickens.
London, Walter Scott. 1887.
4,15

MATZ, B.W.
Charles Dickens: story of his life...
(1902).
17

MAUROIS, Andre.
Dickens. Translated by Hamish Miles.
1934.
4,15

MILTOUN, Francis.
Dickens' London.
London, Eveleigh Nash. 1904.
4

MONTEFIORE, Eade.
Dickensiana. One hundred illustrations...kindly loaned by
Messrs. Chapman and Hall, the original publishers...(for
the Charles Dickens Centenary Festival) , compiled by E.
Montefiore.
(1912).
4

MORELAND, Arthur.
Dickens landmarks in London.
Cassell. 1931.
4

"A NATIVE" (? E. DALE).
Recollections of Charles Dickens at Folkestone in 1855...
Folkestone, Arthur Stace and Sons. 1907.
7

NEALE, C.M.
An index to "Pickwick".
London, The Author. 1897.
4

NICOLL, Sir William Robertson.
Dickens' own story: sidelights of his life and
personality.
1923.
4

NICOLL, W(illiam) Robertson.
The problem of "Edwin Drood": a study in the methods
of Dickens.
London, Hodder and Stoughton. (1912).
4

NONESUCH PRESS. Publishers.
Retrospectus and prospectus. (Cover title: Nonesuch
Dickensiana).
Nonesuch Press. 1937.
4

OSBORNE, E. Allen.
The facts about "A Christmas Carol".
1937.
4

OVERS, John.
Evenings of a working man, being the occupation of his
scanty leisure...with a preface...by Charles Dickens.
London, T.C. Newby. 1844.
4

PASCOE, Charles Eyre.
Dickens in Yorkshire.
(1912).
4

PAYNE, Edward F.
The charity of Charles Dickens: his interest in the Home
for Fallen Women and a history of the strange case of
Caroline Maynard Thompson, by E.F. Payne and H.H.
Harper.
Boston, Privately Printed for Charles E. Goodspeed. 1929.
4,15

PEARCE, Catherine Owens.
Charles Dickens: his life.
Dobson. 1962.
15

PEARSON, Hesketh.
Dickens: his character, comedy and career.
Methuen. 1949.
4,8,15

PEMBERTON, T. Edgar.
Charles Dickens and the stage: a record of his
connection with the drama as playwright, actor and
critic.
1888.
4

PERTWEE, Guy.
Scenes from Dickens for drawing room and platform acting.
n.d.
4

PHILIP, Alexander John.
Dickens and Gravesend.
(Manuscript).1946.
9

PHILIP, Alexander John.
A Dickens dictionary, 2nd edition, by A. J. Philip and
W.L. Gadd.
Gravesend, The Librarian. 1928.
4,8

PHILIP, Alexander John.
Dickens' honeymoon and where he spent it.
Chapman and Hall. 1912.
4,6,9,11

PICCADILLY FOUNTAIN PRESS. Publisher.
Particulars of the Piccadilly Fountain Press issue of
Pickwick: to be completed in 20 fortnightly parts...
n.d.
4

PIERCE, Gilbert A.
The Dickens dictionary, a key to the characters and principal
incidents in the tales of Charles Dickens...with additions
by William A. Wheeler.
Chapman and Hall. 1878.
4

POPE-HENNESSEY, Una.
Charles Dickens, 1812-1870, 2nd edition.
London, Reprint Society. 1947.
4,15

PRIESTLEY, John Boynton.
Charles Dickens: a pictorial biography.
1961.
4,8,15

PRIESTLEY, John Boynton.
Charles Dickens and his world.
Thames and Hudson. 1961.
12

PROCTOR, Richard A.
Watched by the dead: a loving study of Dickens' half-told.
tale (The Mystery of Edwin Drood).
Allen. 1887.
4

PUGH, Edwin.
The Charles Dickens originals.
1913.
4,15

QUILLER-COUCH, Sir Arthur.
Charles Dickens and other Victorians...
Cambridge University Press. 1925.
4

REYNOLDS, George W.M.
Pickwick abroad; or, the tour in France.
London, Willoughby and Co. (1839).
4

RIDEAL, Charles F.
Charles Dickens' heroines and women-folk: some thoughts
concerning them. A lecture, 2nd revised edition.
Westminster, Roxburgh Press. (1894?).
4

RIMMER, Alfred.
About England with Dickens.
Chatto and Windus. 1899.
1,12

Rochester Dickens Fellowship Magazine: conference number,
May, 1914.
Dickens Fellowship. 1914.
12

ROCHESTER DICKENS FESTIVAL PAGEANT COMMITTEE.
Dickens Festival Pageant: souvenir programme, 1951.
8,15

SALA, George Augustus.
Charles Dickens.
Routledge. (1870).
4

SAUNDERS, Montagu.
The mystery of the Drood family.
Cambridge University Press. 1914.
4

SAWYER, Charles J. Editor.
Dickens v Barabbas, Forster intervening: a study based upon
some hitherto unpublished letters, by C.J. Sawyer and F.J.H.
Darton.
London, Charles J. Sawyer. 1930.
4

SEYMOUR, Robert. ("Alfred Crowquill", pseud.).
Humerous sketches.
Bohn. 1872.
12

(SHEPHERD, Richard Herne).
The bibliography of Dickens.
Stock. (1880).
6,12

SHORE, W. Teignmouth.
Charles Dickens and his friends.
1909.
4,6,12,17

SHORE, W. Teignmouth.
Dickens.
George Bell. 1904.
4

SLATER, Michael.
Dickens, 1970, edited by M. Slater.
Chapman and Hall. 1970.
12

SMITH, F. Hopkinson.
In Dickens' London.
Smith, Elder and Co. 1914.
12

Some notes on the writings and life of Charles Dickens.
Chapman and Hall. n.d.
12

SPILKA, Mark.
Dickens and Kafka.
Dobson. 1963.
12

STAPLES, Leslie C.
The Dickens ancestry: some new discoveries. (Reprinted
from The Dickensian).
London, The Author. 1951.
4

STONE, Phyllis.
Dramatic readings from Dickens: Oliver Twist, The Old
Curiosity Shop, arranged by P. Stone.
Nelson. 1927.
12

STONEHOUSE, John Harrison.
Catalogue of the library of Charles Dickens from
Gadshill. (Reprinted from Sotheran's Prices Current
of Literature, Nos. 154 and 155).
Piccadilly Fountain Press. 1935.
12

STONEHOUSE, John Harrison.
Green leaves: new chapters in the life of Charles
Dickens.
1931.
4

STOREY, Gladys.
Dickens and daughter.
Muller. 1939.
4,12

STRACHAN, C. Gordon.
The medical knowledge of Charles Dickens. (Reprinted
from The British Medical Journal, October 25th, 1924).
4

STRAUS, Ralph.
Dickens: a portrait in pencil.
Gollanz. 1928.
8,12

STRAUS, Ralph.
Dickens, the man and the book.
1936.
4

STRAUS, Ralph.
A portrait of Dickens.
Dent. 1938.
4

SUZANNET, Comte de.
Catalogue of a further portion of the well-known library,
the property of the Comte de Suzannet, La Petite Chardiere,
Lansanne, comprising...material concerning Charles Dickens...
Field and Turner. (1870).
12

SWINBURNE, Algernon Charles.
Charles Dickens.
Chatto. 1913.
4

SYMONS, Julian.
Charles Dickens.
1951.
4

SYMONS, Julian.
Charles Dickens.
Arthur Barker. 1969.
12

THOMSON, W.R.
In Dickens street.
Chapman and Hall. 1912.
12

TOMLIN, E.W.F.
Charles Dickens, 1812-1870: a centenary volume, edited by
E.W.F. Tomlin.
Weidenfeld and Nicolson. 1969.
8,12

TOWER HAMLETS LIBRARIES.
Charles Dickens, 1812-1870: a selected reading list.
Tower Hamlets Libraries. 1870.
12

TRUMBLE, Alfred.
In jail with Charles Dickens.
Suckling and Galloway. 1896.
4

WAGENKNECHT, Edward.
The man Charles Dickens: a Victorian portrait.
Constable. 1929.
4,12

WALTERS, J. Cumings.
Phases of Dickens: the man, his message and his mission.
Chapman and Hall. 1911.
4

WARD, Adolphus William.
Dickens.
Macmillan. 1882.
4(2nd edition) 12

WARD, H. Snowden.
The real Dickens land, with an outline of Dickens' life,
by H. S. and C.W.B. Ward.
Chapman and Hall. 1904.
1,4,5,11,12,15

WELLS, George.
The tale of Charles Dickens.
Rochester, Journal Co. Ltd. 1906.
4,8,15

WILKINS, Willian Glyde.
Charles Dickens in America, compiled and edited by W.G. Wilkins.
Chapman and Hall. 1911.
12

WILSON, S. Gordon.
Canterbury and Charles Dickens.
Canterbury Chamber of Commerce. 1927.
1,3,6,15

WING, George.
Dickens.
Oliver and Boyd. 1969.
8

DITTON

AGRICULTURAL RESEARCH COUNCIL - DITTON AND COVENT GARDEN
LABORATORIES.
Annual reports.
H.M.S.O.
4(1964,1965,1966,1967,1968)
12(1963,1964,1966,1968)

BRITISH LEGION.
The British Legion Village, Maidstone, Kent: souvenir
brochure.
British Legion Press. n.d.
11,12

CLINCH, V.
Parish of Ditton.
Kent Messenger. 1966.
12

Ditton Court Estate - Sale catalogue.
1914.
12

Ditton Place - Sale catalogue.
1903.
12

INGLE, Joy.
Preston Hall: history and legend.
British Legion Press. 1962 etc.
11

DODDINGTON

ASHBY, Roy.
Our pets: the true story of an abiding friendship, by
R. Ashby, Jim Babbington and Ken Parfitt. (Doddington
Youth Hostel).
Stansfield Association. 1962.
11

CROFT, Sir John.
Papers and extracts relating to public services rendered
by Sir John Croft...
1842.
15

DODE

ARNOLD, George Matthews.
Dode, in Kent, with some account of its little Norman
church and of its early extinguishment.
Caddel and Son. 1905.
1,4,6,9,11,12,15,17

ARNOLD, George Matthews.
Dode Church: author's scrapbook for his publication on
Dode Church.
n.d.
12

Dode Church.
(c.1954).
12

DONNINGTON

GROOMBRIDGE, Garth.
The history of Chapel House, Donnington.
Sidcup, Groombridge. n.d.
5

DOUR, RIVER

GILL, Walter.
Geographical surveys of the Alkham and Upper Dour
Valleys.
n.d.
11

REYNOLDS, Donald Hugh Baillie.
Movement of water in the middle and lower chalk of the
river Dour catchment. In Journal of the Institute of
Civil Engineers.
1947.
7

DOVER

A., P.
Ancient churches and religious houses of Dover. Being
an extract from "The Home Friend"
1853.
13

ADMIRALTY.
Dover harbour: reports and plans...and breakwater in Dover Bay.
Hansard. 1848.
11

ADMIRALTY.
Report on the harbour of refuge to be constructed in Dover Bay.
H.M.S.O. 1846.
11

An account of the towns of Dover and Tunbridge Wells in 1804.
1804.
19

Album of Dover views.
c.1863.
6

AMOS, E.G.J.
The Saxon shore at Dover, by E.G.J. Amos and R.E.M. Wheeler.
In The Archaeological Journal, Vol. LXXXVI, 2nd series, Vol. XXXVI for the year 1929, pp. 48-58.
Royal Archaeological Society. 1929.
13

AMOS, E.G.J.
The Saxon shore fortress at Dover and the Roman lighthouse, by E.G.J. Amos and R.E.M. Wheeler.
1930.
6

AMOS, J. Publisher.
Amos' guide to Dover and its vicinity.
Amos. n.d.
7

AMOS, J. Publisher.
Visitors' guide to Dover.
Amos. n.d.
17

"ANCIENT FREEMAN", pseud. (Robert P. Keys).
Dover: a reminiscence of its history, past and present, by an Ancient Freeman.
1(1904) 5(1904) 11(1904) 12(1903) 17(1904)

ARMSTRONG, Thomas.
Dover Harbour.
1949.
6

ASPINALL-OGLANDER, Cecil.
Roger Keyes.
Hogarth. 1951.
6

AUDEN, W.H.
Dover. In New Verse, November, 1937.
6

BACON, Sir Reginald H.
The concise story of the Dover Patrol.
Hutchinson. 1932.
4,6,12

BACON, Sir Reginald H.
The Dover Patrol, 1915-1917, 2 vols.
Doran. 1919.
4,6,7,12

BAKER, W.J.
The church of St. Mary the Virgin, Dover.
Dover Printing and Publishing Co. c.1900.
6

BATCHELLER, W. Publisher.
A descriptive picture of Dover.
Dover, W. Batcheller. 1843, etc.
6,11,12,14,15

BATCHELLER, W. Publisher.
New history of Dover and a description of the villages near Dover.
Dover, W. Batcheller. 1828.
1,6,7,11,12,13

BATCHELLER, W. Publisher.
The new Dover guide.
Dover, W. Batcheller. 1836, etc.
1,6,11,12,18

BATCHELLER, W. Publisher.
A short historical sketch of the town of Dover...5th edition.
Dover, W. Batcheller. 1823.
6,12

BATCHELLER, W. AND RIGDEN. Publishers.
List of useful information for the year 1824 to Dover and neighbourhood.
Dover, W. Batcheller and Rigden. 1824.
6

BECKER, Charles Norris.
The true history of the life and times of C.N. Becker, town crier for Dover.
Dover Express. 1912.
6

BENNETT, J.J. ('Jackstaff', pseud.).
The Dover Patrol.
Richards. 1918.
12

BINFIELD, E.J.
Our heritage. Dover Congregational Church, 1644-1959.
Donald S. Martell. 1959.
6

BOARD OF TRADE.
Copy of the recent reports on Dover Harbour.
H.M.S.O. 1877.
17

BONYTHON, William. Publisher.
Dover guide...
Dover, Bonython. 1823.
1,6,7

BOUNDARY COMMISSION.
Report on the town and port of Dover.
H.M.S.O. n.d.
12

BOWEN-ROWLANDS, Ernest.
72 years at the Bar: a memoir. (Writer appeared for the Crown in the "Franconia Case" - "Franconia" collided with "Strathclyde" in Dover Bay, 1876).
Macmillan. 1924.
6

BRADY, Francis.
Dover coal boring, by Francis Brady and others.
1892.
7

BRADY, Francis.
Dover coalfield: papers and reports by Francis Brady, Victor Watteyne, James McMurtrie and M.R. Zeiller.
(1897).
6,11

BRAITHWAITE, Lewis.
Dover Grand Shaft. (Reprinted from the Architectural Review, September, 1967).
6

BRITISH ASSOCIATION FOR THE ADVANCEMENT OF SCIENCE.
Dover Harbour works.
Waterlow Bros. 1899.
6

BRITISH ASSOCIATION FOR THE ADVANCEMENT OF SCIENCE.
Handbook to Dover.
Dover Standard. 1899.
6

BRITISH LEGION - DOVER BRANCH.
Loyalty and service: yearbook and souvenir, 1950.
British Legion. 1950.
6

BRITISH TRAVEL AND HOLIDAYS ASSOCIATION.
Dover Castle.
British Travel and Holidays Association. 1951.
12

BRITTAIN, F.
Saint Radegund, patroness of Jesus College, Cambridge.
Cambridge, Bowes and Bowes. 1925.
6

BROUGHAM, Henry Peter. Baron Brougham and Vaux.
Speech at the Dover Festival proposing the health of
Duke of Wellington.
n.d,
6

BROWN, Reginald Allen.
Dover Castle.
H.M.S.O. 1966.
1,2(and 1967) 3,4,6,7,8(and 1967) 11(and 1967)

BRYANT, Arthur.
Letters, speeches and declaration of Charles II: contains
a section on the Treaty of Dover, edited by A. Bryant.
Cassell. 1935.
6

BUCKINGHAM, Christopher.
Catholic Dover: a book to celebrate the centennial
anniversary of St. Paul's Church.
Thomas Becket Books. 1968.
2,4,6,11,12

BURGESS, W.
Dover Castle.
1847.
6

BURT, Nathaniell.
Mayor and Magistrates of Dover.
1649.
11

CALLCUT AND BEAVIS. Publishers.
Thirty-two photographic views of Dover and neighbourhood.
Callant and Beevis. c.1900.
6

CALVER, Edward Killwick.
Remarks on the proposed national harbour at Dover.
P.S. King. 1875.
6,7

CAMPBELL, R.R.
The history of Westcliffe Church, Dover, compiled by R.R.
Campbell.
1938.
11

Channel Port: a short history and account of the Port of
Dover.
Canterbury, College of Art Press. 1966.
6

"Christ or the Pope": a sermon preached at Christ Church,
Dover on Empire Day, 1925.
1925.
6

CHRISTIAN, Edgar.
Unflinching. (A local author).
Murray. 1937.
6

CHURCHILL, Charles.
Poem, 3 vols in 1 and the life of the author.
J. Wilkes. 1772.
6

CLARK, G.T.
Dover Castle.
Architectural Journal. n.d.
6,11

CLARK, Ronald (William).
Six great mountaineers (including A.F. Mummery who was born
in Dover).
Hamilton. 1956.
6

COGHLAN, Francis.
A new guide to Ramsgate, Margate and Dover.
1837.
14

COLLINS, Charles.
Green leaves; or, lays of boyhood.
W.E. Painter. 1844.
6

COLVIN, H.M.
An Iron-Age fort at Dover. (An article in "Antiquity",
Vol. 33, No. 130, June, 1959).
6

COMMISSIONERS ON MUNICIPAL CORPORATIONS.
Reports on the Borough of Dover, 1833 and 1861.
n.d.
6

CONNELL, Charles.
The world's greatest seiges. (Local author).
Odhams. 1967.
6

CONNELL, Charles.
Meet me at Philippi.
Jenkins. n.d.
6

Courts of Brotherhood and Guestling.
1925?
11

COXERE, Edward.
Adventures by sea, edited by E.H.W. Mayerstein. (Edward
Coxere came from Dover).
Clarendon Press. 1945.
4

COXON, S.W.
Dover during the dark days, by a "Dug-out".
John Lane. 1919.
7,8,12

CRAIK, Mrs. (Formerly Diana Mulock).
Miss Tommy, 4th edition. (A novel set in Dover).
Macmillan. 1886.
6

CROMWELL, Archibald.
In Dover Bay.
Hazel, Watson and Viney. n.d.
6

CUFF BROTHERS. Publishers.
Visitors' guide to Dover, its history and antiquities...
Dover, Cuff Bros.
3(1899)
6(1884 and 1897)
11(1884)
12(1899)
17(1875 and 1880)

CUMING, H. Syer.
On some ancient relics preserved in the Keep of Dover
Castle.
British Archaeological Society. 1870.
11

CUMING, H. Syer.
On some antiquities in the possession of the Corporation
of Dover.
British Archaeological Society. 1871.
11

DARE, M.P.
An inscribed Roman altar discovered at Napchester,
near Dover. In Archaeologia Cantiana, Vol. 62, 1949.
17

DARELL, William.
History of Dover Castle...
1786, etc.
1,6,7,8,11,12,14,15,17,18

DAVIES, Samuel J.
Dover.
Provost. 1869.
1,6

DAVIS, John. Publisher.
Deal and Dover, illustrated visitors' guide.
3(c.1880) 6(c.1895) 7(c.1900)

A day's ramble round Dover Castle.
Dover, W. Brett. 1851.
3,11

DELL, John, of Dover.
Poetical effusions of the heart.
Privately Printed. 1783.
6

DEMPSTER, Derek.
The narrow margin, by D. Dempster and D. Wood.
Hutchinson. 1961.
6

DIBDIN, Thomas Frognall.
The history and antiquities of Dover.
Reprinted for Private Distribution. n.d.
6

Dick and Sal; or, Jack and Joanses Fair.
Dover, Warren. 1830.
3,11

DIGGES, Thomas.
A briefe discourse declaring how honorable and profitable...
the making of Douer haven shall be,... Communicated by T.W.
Wrighte, from the papers bequeathed to the Society of
Antiquaries of London by the late John Thorpe.
1792.
6,11

DIVING, A.D.
Dunkirk.
Faber. 1945.
6

DOLLEY, R.H.M.
"The Dover hoard". (From the Journal of the British
Numismatic Society, 1955).
6,17

DORRICOTT, Rev. J.
Some olden time Methodists: being memorial sketches of the
Russell and Barnsley-Smith families.
London, Robert Bryant. 1904.
6

Dover: photographic views.
Domestic Bazaar. c.1900.
12

Dover: view album.
Dover, Chaplin. n.d.
11

Dover and the European War, 1914-18.
Dover Express. 1919.
1,3,7,11

Dover and the War, 1914-1918.
Dover Express. 1923.
11

Dover, Canterbury, Deal, Walmer and Sandwich by camera and
pen.
Brighton, W.T. Pike. 1904-5.
6,11

Dover, Folkestone and Deal local railway guide.
1898.
17

"DOVER AND COUNTY CHRONICLE". Publishers.
Dover guide and appendix.
Dover and County Chronicle. 1881.
17

DOVER BOROUGH COUNCIL.
Annual report of Minister of Health, 1937, 1938, 1945-to date.
6

DOVER BOROUGH COUNCIL.
Borough of Dover, 1939-1946.
Dover Borough Council. 1946.
6

DOVER BOROUGH COUNCIL.
Byelaws, rules and regulations, 1851-78.
Dover Borough Council. 1851-78.
6

DOVER BOROUGH COUNCIL.
Ceremony of the admission of the Right Hon. W.L.S. Churchill,
O.M., C.H. as an honorary freeman.
Dover Borough Council. 1951.
6

DOVER BOROUGH COUNCIL.
Commemorative volume presented to Alderman and Mrs.
Martyn Mowll, illustrative of events during 1901-2.
Dover Borough Council. n.d.
6

DOVER BOROUGH COUNCIL.
Dover Corporation records.
Dover Borough Council. 1916.
6

DOVER BOROUGH COUNCIL.
The Maison Dieu at Dover.
Dover Borough Council. 1960.
4,8,12

DOVER BOROUGH COUNCIL.
Metreological reports, 1924-34 (except for 1926).
Dover Borough Council. n.d.
6

DOVER BOROUGH COUNCIL.
Official guide - the Gateway of England.
Dover Borough Council.
3(n.d.)
4(1958 etc.)
6(1925,1926,1927,1930,1933,1934,1935,1936,1937,1947,
1949,1950,1951,1952,1953,1956,1957,1958,1959,1961,1962,
1963,1964,1966,1967)
11(1971)
12(1949)
15(1958 etc.)
17(1930)

DOVER BOROUGH COUNCIL.
Official guide and concise catalogue of the Dover
Museum.
Dover Borough Council. 1913, etc.
6,11,13

DOVER BOROUGH COUNCIL.
An original pen-and-ink drawing of the badge of office
presented to Dover by S.H. Poland, c.1898.
6

DOVER BOROUGH COUNCIL.
Standing Orders of Council and Committees.
Dover Borough Council. 1910.
6

DOVER BOROUGH COUNCIL.
Yearbook, 1892-3, 1896-7, 1915, 1916, 1917, 1919-1940,
1945 to date.
6,17(1884 and 1887).

DOVER BOROUGH COUNCIL - EDUCATION COMMITTEE.
Astor Avenue Girl's School, Logbook, April, 1929-July,
1948. (Manuscript).
6

DOVER BOROUGH COUNCIL - EDUCATION COMMITTEE.
Aston Avenue Girl's School, Logbook, October, 1941-
August, 1945. (Manuscript).
6

DOVER BOROUGH COUNCIL - EDUCATION COMMITTEE.
Astor Avenue Senior Girl's School, Logbook, June, 1940-
November, 1943. (Manuscript).
6

DOVER BOROUGH COUNCIL - EDUCATION COMMITTEE.
Barton Road Boy's School, Logbooks, January, 1918-
July, 1930 and July, 1930-July, 1948. (Manuscript).
6

DOVER BOROUGH COUNCIL - EDUCATION COMMITTEE.
Christ's Church Girl's School, Logbook, February, 1920-
March, 1929. (Manuscript).
6

DOVER BOROUGH COUNCIL.
School Logbooks: December, 1567-July, 1881, August,
1881-December, 1904, January, 1905-December, 1917.
(Manuscript).
6

DOVER BOROUGH COUNCIL - ENTERTAINMENT COMMITTEE.
Guide book and itinerary of Dover.
Dover Borough Council. c.1923.
7(c.1923) 11(1906 and 1922)

DOVER BOROUGH COUNCIL - PUBLIC LIBRARY.
Dover past and present: an exhibition of local history...
1965.
Dover Borough Council. 1965.
11

DOVER CHAMBER OF COMMERCE.
Guide book and itinerary of Dover.
1896.
7

"DOVER CHRONICLE". Publisher.
Dover almanack for 1863.
Dover Chronicle. 1863.
7

"DOVER CHRONICLE". Publisher.
Dover, Folkestone, Deal and Cinque Ports appendix and
almanack for 1870 containing a short history of Dover.
Dover Chronicle. 1870.
7

"DOVER CHRONICLE". Publisher.
The Dover, Folkestone, Deal guide appendix and almanack -
rewritten, revised, corrected and enlarged for 1873.
Dover Chronicle. (1873).
7,17

DOVER COLLEGE.
Class lists, 1887-92.
n.d.
6

DOVER COLLEGE.
Register, 1871-99, 2nd edition, edited by W.S. Lee.
Dover G.W. Grigg and Son. 1899.
6,7,11

DOVER COLLEGE.
Register from 1871 to 1910, 3rd edition.
Dover, G.W. Grigg and Son. 1910.
6,11

DOVER COLLEGE.
Register from 1871-1924, 4th edition, edited by C.L. Evans.
Dover, G.W. Grigg and Son. 1924.
6

DOVER COLLEGE.
War services: Roll of Honour and Honours and Awards, 1914-
1918.
St. George's Press, Printer. (1919).
7

"DOVER EXPRESS". Publisher.
Across the Straits - Channel swims.
Dover Express. (1951).
6(1956) 7

DOVER HARBOUR BOARD.
Port statistics, 1958.
n.d.
8

DOVER HARBOUR BOARD. Publisher.
The Port of Dover.
Faversham, Printed by Causton. 1931.
6,11

DOVER HARBOUR BOARD. Publisher.
The Port of Dover.
Cheltenham, Printed by Burrow. 1953.
6,11

Dover illustrated.
Gravesend, Rochard. 189-?
6,11

Dover in the front line (contained in the Dover Express
and East Kent News, 30th June, 1949-20th January, 1950).
6

Dover Naval Harbour (supplement to the "Sphere").
1909.
17

The Dover Railway Centenary: celebration of the opening, on
February 7th, 1844 of the last section of the South Eastern
Railway main line to Dover. (Reprinted from "The Railway
Gazette", 1944).
11

"DOVER STANDARD". Publisher.
The "Dover Standard" Coronation souvenir (1902).
Dover Standard Office. n.d.
6,11,12

"DOVER STANDARD". Publisher.
The "Standard" picture guide to Dover, Canterbury and
Deal.
Dover Standard Office. 1899.
3,17

ELLEY, Richard.
Dover's ghost garrison. Cutting from "The Soldier",
Vol. 9, No. 1, March, 1953.
6

ELVINS, S.W.G.
Invicta.
1953.
6,11

EMBRY, Sir Basil.
Mission completed.
Methuen. 1957.
6

EMDEN, Walter.
Dover: England's gate.
Hentschel. c.1900.
1,6,11,12,18

EVANS, Sebastian.
Handbook to Dover, edited by S. Evans and F. Bennett-
Goldney.
Dover Standard Office. 1899.
7,11,12,13

EVERARD, Ethel M.
A faithful sower, edited by E.M. Everard. (Rev. George
Everard M.A.).
Nisbett and Co. 1902.
6

EVERARD, Rev. George.
Day by day.
Nisbett and Co. n.d.
6

EVISON, Vera Ivy.
The Dover ring-sword and other sword rings and beads.
(Reprinted from "Archaeologia", Vol 101, 1967).
4,6

Expose of mismanagement and abuses practised for many
years by the Agents...holding shares in two Dover steam
vessels.
n.d.
11

FINESTEIN, Israel.
Sir George Jessel, 1824-83. (Reprinted from Transactions
of Jewish Historical Society, 1955). (M.P. for Dover).
6

FIRTH, John B.
Dover and the Great War.
Dover, Leney. 1919.
1,2,3,4,6,7,8,11,12,14,15

FLASHMAN, W.E.
Some in the hundred; or, short notes on a few changes
in seventy of one hundred years.
c.1880.
6

FLOYDD, W.
Handbook of the Channel Swimming Association, edited
by W. Floydd and W.R. Hickingbotham.
Channel Swimming Association. 1957.
6

FOSTER, Reginald.
Dover front.
Secker and Warburg. 1941.
6,7,8,11,12

FOWLER, Frank.
Dottings of a lounger.
Routledge. 1859.
11

FREELING, Arthur.
Picturesque excursions...edited by A. Freeling. (Includes Margate, Tunbridge Wells and Dover).
Orr. 1840.
2,6,8(1839) 11,12,13

GATTY, Charles T.
George Wyndham.
John Murray. 1917.
6

GENERAL BAPTIST AND LOVER OF PEACE, pseud.
The Taverner's ghost - poems. (Captain Samuel Taverner, imprisoned in Dover Castle, 1670).
London, Stower. 1806.
6

GLOVER, Frederick Robert Augustus.
Harbours of refuge.
John Ollivier. 1846.
6

GLOVER, Frederick Robert Augustus.
What is Queen Anne's bounty?
Simpkin, Marshall and Co. 1840.
6

GOULDEN, C. Publisher.
Dover, Deal and district descriptive and pictorial.
Dover, Goulden. c.1890.
6,11

GOULDEN, C. Publisher.
New guide to Dover, forming a complete handbook to the town...
Dover, Goulden. 1884 and 1895.
6,11

GRAHAM, Rose.
An interdict on Dover, 1298-99. (Reprinted from the Archaeological Journal, 1921).
6

GREAT BRITAIN: LAWS, etc.
Acts of Parliament for Dover Harbour, 1828-1913.
6

GREAT BRITAIN: LAWS, etc. (CHARLES II).
An Act for repairing of Dover Harbour.
London, John Bill and Chris Barker. 1662.
6

GREAT BRITAIN: LAWS, etc. (WILL. III).
An Act for the repair of Dover Harbour.
Printed by Charles Bill. 1700.
11

GREAT BRITAIN: LAWS, etc. (GEO. I).
An Act for completing the repairs of the Harbour of Dover... and for restoring the Harbour of Rye...
1723.
6,8,11

GREAT BRITAIN: LAWS, etc. (GEO. I).
An Act for enlarging the term of years granted...for the repair of Dover Harbour.
n.d.
11

GREAT BRITAIN: LAWS, etc. (GEO. II).
An Act for continuing the term of...for repairing the Harbour of Dover...
1738.
6,11

GREAT BRITAIN: LAWS, etc. (GEO. III).
An Act for better paving, cleansing, lighting and watching the streets...of Dover...1778.
1778.
6,12

GREAT BRITAIN: LAWS, etc. (GEO. III).
An Act for the better regulating of the Harbour of Dover, in the County of Kent (11th June, 1794).
Printed by Eyre and Strahan. 1794.
6,11

GREAT BRITAIN: LAWS, etc. (GEO. III).
An Act for enlarging the terms of several Acts of Parliament for the repair of Dover Harbour.
1796.
11

GREAT BRITAIN: LAWS, etc. (GEO. III).
An Act for the more easy and speedy recovery of small debts within the town and port of Dover, and the parishes of Charlton, Buckland, River, Ewell, Lydden, Coldred, East Langdon, Ringwould, St. Margarets-at-Cliffe Whitfield, Guston, Hougham, otherwise Huffham, Caple-le-Fern and Alkham and also the Liberty of Dover Castle.
Printed by Eyre and Strahan. 1784.
6,11

GREAT BRITAIN: LAWS, etc. (GEO. III).
An Act to amend an act...for paving, cleansing, lighting and watching the town of Dover...1810.
1810.
12

GREAT BRITAIN: LAWS, etc. (GEO. III).
An Act to vest certain messuages...in trustees for better securing...and for extending the lines and works at Dover.
1806.
6,11

GREAT BRITAIN: LAWS, etc. (WILL. IV).
An Act to alter and amend several Acts for paving, cleansing and improving the town of Dover...1835.
1835.
12

GREAT BRITAIN: LAWS, etc. (WILL. IV).
An Act to amend two Acts...for paving, cleansing, lighting and watching...Dover...1830.
1830.
12

GREAT BRITAIN: LAWS, etc. (WILL. IV).
An Act to amend three several Acts for paving, cleansing and improving...Dover...1835.
1835.
12

GREAT BRITAIN: LAWS, etc. (GEO. VI).
Dover Corporation Act, 1950.
H.M.S.O. 1950.
6

GREAT BRITAIN: LAWS, etc. (GEO. V).
Dover Harbour Act, 1913.
6

GREAT BRITAIN: LAWS, etc. (GEO. V).
Dover Harbour Act, 1949.
H.M.S.O. n.d.
6

GREAT BRITAIN: LAWS, etc. (ELIZ. II).
Dover Harbour Act, 1953.
H.M.S.O. 1953.
6,8

GREAT BRITAIN: LAWS, etc. (ELIZ. II).
Dover Harbour Consolidation Act, 1954.
6

GREAT BRITAIN: LAWS, etc. (ELIZ. II).
Dover Harbour Act, 1963.
H.M.S.O. 1963.
4,6,8

GREAT BRITAIN, Parliament.
Report from the Committee to whom the petitions concerning the Harbours of Rye and Dover were referred...
1756.
11

GREAT BRITAIN, Parliament.
Report from the Select Committee on Dover Harbour.
Hansard. 1836.
11

GREAT BRITAIN, Parliament.
Report from the Select Committee on Dover Pier and Harbour Bill.
1875.
11

GREAT BRITAIN, Parliament.
Report upon the Dover Harbour Consolidation Bill.
H.M.S.O. 1954.
6

GRIFFIN, Ralph.
Monumental brasses in Kent: St. James (old church) Dover
and Northfleet.
Mitchell Hughes and Clarke. 1916.
2,12

GRIGG, G.W. AND SON. Publishers.
A guide book and itinerary of Dover.
Dover, G.W. Grigg and Son.
6(1908) 12(1909) 17(1914)

A guide to Dover.
Borough Guides. 1909.
13

Guide to sea angling, Folkestone, Deal, Dover.
Robert McGregor, Angling Association Ltd. 1971.
7

A guide to the parish church of St. Mary-the-Virgin, Dover.
1950, etc.
6,7,11,12

H., M.
Some memories of old Dover.
Dover, C. Goulden. n.d.
12

HAINES, Charles Reginald.
Dover Priory.
Cambridge University Press. 1930.
1,4,6,7,8,11,12,13,17

HAINES, Charles Reginald.
The library of Dover Priory: its catalogue and extant
volumes.
n.d.
6,12

HANNAVY, J.L.
The libraries of Dover and Folkestone.
University Microfilms Ltd. 1968.
7

HARBOUR, Henry.
Dover, with its surroundings.
Warne. 1908.
1,6,7,8,11,13,15,17,18

HARDMAN, Frederick William.
Castleguard service of Dover Castle. In Archaeologia
Cantiana, Vol. 49, 1937.
17

HARRIS, George.
The life of Lord Chancellor Hardwicke with selections...
and judgements, 3 vols.
1847.
6

HARTSHORN, Albert.
Dover Castle. In "The Architect", March 27th, 1869.
6

HARVEY, Thomas.
Visitors' guide to Dover.
1880.
17

HARVEY AND HEMMIN. Publishers.
Guide to Dover.
Harvey and Hemmin. (1875).
17

HARWOOD, J.
Views of Dover.
1845.
6,11

HAYDON, Walter T.
Catalogue of the flowering plants found in Dover and its
neighbourhood.
1890.
6,7

HAYDON, Walter T.
What to find on Dover beach.
1926.
6

HAYNES, Alfred Henry.
This is Dover.
1967.
2,3,6,7,8,11,19

HAYNES, R.C.
The municipal tenants' handbook...Dover.
Gloucester, British Publishing Co. Ltd. c.1949.
6

HEATH, William.
Sketches of in and about Dover.
Dover, Rigden. n.d.
12

HERRING, T.S.
Dover, a poem.
London, Richard and J. Edward Taylor. 1841.
6

HODGKIN, L.V. (Mrs. John Huldsworth).
The shoemaker of Dover - Luke Howard, 1621-99.
London, Friends Book Centre. Gloucester, Bellows. 1943.
4,6

HOLLIS, Gertrude.
Tow Dover boys.
Blackie. 1911.
6

HOLYOAK, Walter.
Dover baptists.
Dover Express Office. 1914.
3

HORN, J. AND ALLARD. Publishers.
Description of Dover...
Dover, Horn and Allard. 1819.
4(1817) 6(1817) 11,12,13,17(1807)

HORN, J. AND ALLARD. Publishers.
Dover and Deal directory and guide.
Dover, Horn and Allard. 1792.
6,11,17

HORN, John Vivian.
The story of the Dover Corporation tramways, 1897-1936.
Light Railway Tramways League. 1955.
1,3,4,6,7,8,11,12

HORSLEY, M.
Dover market place then and now.
Dover and County Chronicle. n.d.
6,17

HORSLEY, M.
Old Dover and its churches.
1914.
6

HORSLEY, M.
St. Mary's, Dover, 903-1903.
n.d.
6

H(ORSLEY), M.
Some memories of old Dover.
Dover, C. Goulden. 1892.
6,11,17

HORSLEY, M.
Some memories of old Dover.
Dover, C. Goulden. n.d.
6,12,17

HORSLEY, M.
Something about the Mayor of Dover.
1902.
6,17

HOSEASON, John Cochrane.
The new harbour at Dover...
Stanford. 1874.
11

HOSEASON, John Cochrane.
Remarks on the Channel passage...warfare.
Stanford. 1873.
6

HOWARD, Luke.
Love and truth in plainness manifested...
T. Sowle. 1704.
6,11

"Hughenden, 12 Maison Dieu Road, Dover: a catalogue of...
furniture...of old Dover prints and engravings...of 2,000
volumes, etc.
Worsfold and Hayward. 1921.
4

HUNDLEY, V.A.
History of Dover Castle, A.D. 43-A.D.-1925, compiled by V.A.
Hundley.
Dover, G.W. Grigg and Son. 1925?
6,7,11

HURD, Sir Archibald S.
The National Harbour at Dover.
1903.
11

Illustrated particulars of St. Radegunds Abbey estate
comprising house, buildings, remains of Abbey, cottages,
land, etc...324 acres.
Ashford, Hollett, Creery and Co. n.d.
7

IRON, John.
Keeper of the gate.
Low Marston. c.1936.
6,12

JACKSON, Robert.
Case for the prosecution (biography of Sir Archibald Bodkin).
Barker. 1962.
6

JAMES, Montague Rhodes.
The ancient libraries of Canterbury and Dover.
Cambridge University Press. 1903.
1,2,3,6,7,11,12,15,17

JERROLD, Walter.
Folkestone and Dover, paintings by G.W. Haslehurst.
Blackie. n.d.
1,6,7,8,11,17

JODRELL, Sir Richard Paul.
Dover, ancient and modern.
Longman. 1841.
6,8,17

JONES, John Bavington.
Annals of Dover...
Dover Express. 1916, etc.
1(1938) 2(1938) 6(1938) 7,11,12

JONES, John Bavington.
Dover...
Dover Express. 1907.
1,4,6,7,11,12,13

JONES, John Bavington.
History of Dover Harbour.
Dover Express. 1892.
1,3,6

JONES, John Bavington.
Mayors of Dover, 1559-1890.
Dover Express. 1890.
6,17

JONES, John Bavington.
Public places of Dover.
Dover Express. c.1880.
6

JONES, John Bavington.
Records of Dover...
Dover Express. 1920.
1,6,7,11,19

JONES, John Bavington.
Report on Dover Corporation records.
Dover Express. 1915.
6

JONES, John Bavington.
Town and Port, 1887. (Concerning Dover Harbour Bill).
J. Bavington Jones. 1887.
6

JONES, O.G. Bavington.
Dover and the War, 1914-18.
Dover Express. n.d.
6

Kendall's guide to Dover Castle.
J.B. Jones. n.d.
6(1879) 17(1881)

KENT, Alfred.
Two odes, written upon the occasion of the Cinque Ports
Festival held at Dover...on Friday, August 30th, 1839.
Dover, A. Kent. 1839.
1,6

KENT COUNTY COUNCIL - PLANNING DEPARTMENT.
Town and County Planning Act, 1947 - Development Plan,
Part A, Dover. Programme to accompany map 6"=1 mile
(also the map).
Kent County Council. 1958.
6

The Kentish conspiracy; or, an order and narration
declaring the late plot for the surprizing of Dover
Castle: and the setting on foot of a commission of array
in the County of Kent. Taken and extracted out of the
examination of several conspirators.
Printed by R. Cotes for Michael Spark. 1645.
6,11

KERSHAW, Alister.
A bibliography of the works of Richard Aldington, 1915-
1948.
Quadrant Press. 1949.
6

Key to Dover: a visitors' guide.
Dover, J.B. Jones. n.d.
17

KEYES, Sir Roger.
Adventures ashore and afloat.
Harrap. 1939.
6

KEYES, Sir Roger.
Naval memoirs, Vol. 2. Scapa Flow to Dover Straits,
1916-18.
Thornton Butterworth. 1935.
6

KNIGHT, Charles.
Handbook to Canterbury, Dover, Isle of Thanet...
Nuttal and Bond. 1855.
1,13,14

KNOCKER, Edward.
The church of St. James.
British Archaeological Association. 1884.
6

KNOCKER, Edward.
A lecture on the archives...of Dover...1877.
Dover Standard Office. 1879.
1,6,11

KNOCKER, Edward.
On the antiquities of Dover.
Dover, Batcheller. 1858.
1,4,6,8

KNOCKER, Sir E. Wollaston.
An account of the (Dover) Corporation insignia, seals
and plate, with list of Mayors, Borough Officers, etc.
1898.
1,6,11,12,17

KNOCKER, Frederic.
Illustrated official guide to the Dover Corporation
Museum.
Dover, G.W. Grigg and Son. 1932.
1,7,11

LABARGE, Margaret Wade.
A Baronial household of the thirteenth century. (Plates
of, and references to, Dover Castle).
Eyre and Spottiswoode. 1965.
4,6

LAMBERT, Audrey.
A pilgrim in Dover.
Dover, Buckland Press. 1946.
6

LEARMONT, James S.
Master in sail.
Dover, Johnson. 1950.
6

LEASK, William, of Dover.
Our era.
Dover, Johnson. 1845.
6

LEASK, William, of Dover.
Philisophical lectures.
Percival Marshall. 1846.
6

LEDGER, G. Publisher.
A short historical sketch of the town of Dover and its
neighbourhood.
Dover, G. Ledger.
6(1799,1807,1815)
11(1807,1828)
17(1807)

LESTER, H.F.
The taking of Dover (a draft for an essay on "the best means
to gain possession of a strongly fortified position in a
neighbouring country").
J.W. Arrowsmith. 1888.
15

LEWIS, J.H.
Guide to Dover.
Dover, Batcheller. 1848.
6

LEWIS, J.H.
The illustrated guide to Dover.
Dover, J.H. Lewis. 1848.
6

LIGHT, W.E.
Twenty-four sermons preached at St. James Church, Dover.
Nisbet. 1865.
6

Light through a century: a brief history of Christ Church,
Dover. (Typescript).
1944.
12

LILLYWHITE, Nigel Graham.
One man's wars...Geoffery Lillywhite (cyclostyled).
Privately Printed in Dover by the Author. 1965.
6

LORD MAYOR'S NATIONAL AIR RAID DISTRESS FUND.
Final survey...to 13th January, 1954.
Lord Mayor's National Air Raid Distress Fund, Mansion House,
London. 1955.
6

LOWNDES, Thomas.
Tracts in prose and verse, 2 vols.
Dover, Bonython. 1825.
6

LUCAS, J.
Hydrogeology of the Dover Basin...Channel Tunnel...coalfield.
c.1900.
6

Lucilla Hartley; or, Discipline, by the author of "Happy
Hours with Mother". (Fiction probably based on Dover).
P. Dixon Hardy. 1844.
6

LYON, John.
An account of several new...phenomena discovered in examining
the bodies of a man and four horses...near Dover...
Phillips. 1796.
6,11

LYON, John.
The history and antiquities of Saint Radigund's, or
Bradsole Abbey, near Dover. (Bibliotheca topographica
Britannica No. XLII).
Society of Antiquaries of London. 1787.
7,8,11

LYON, John.
History of Dover, 1787-1823 and 1842-1880.
17

LYON, John.
History of Dover Castle.
1787.
17

LYON, John.
History of the town and port of Dover...2 vols.
Ledge and Shaw. 1813-14.
3,6,7,8,11,12,14,15,17

M., G.
Notes on the Roman Pharos and the church of St. Mary-
in-the-Castle.
1890.
17

McDAKIN, S. Gordon.
Coast erosion. Dover cliffs: a paper read before the
British Association.
Dover, Printed at the Standard Office. 1899.
7

McDAKIN, S. Gordon.
Geological excursion, East Cliffs, Dover to St.
Margaret's.
(Dover Natural History Society). 189-?
7

McDAKIN, S. Gordon.
Geological excursion, West Cliff, Dover.
(Natural History Society, Dover). (189-).
7

MACKIE, S.J.
Thoughts on Dover cliffs. (Reprinted from "The
Geologist", August, 1863).
Lovell Reeve. 1863.
6,7,17

MacQUEEN, John. Minister of St. Mary's.
An essay on honour.
Privately Printed. 1711.
6

MANNERING, John.
First time across. (An article from Yachting Monthly,
January, 1959).
6

MASTERS, W.
Hortus Duroverni: being a catalogue...of roots, trees
and shrubs.
Longman. 1831.
6

MAYNE, Frederick.
On the landing of Her Majesty the Queen at Dover, June
5th, 1820.
Dover, Mate. 1870.
11

Message...concerning the seizing of Dover Castle, 1648.
n.d.
6

Military handbook of the Dover Garrison, No. 187, July,
1939.
n.d.
6

MILLER, Alice Duer.
The white cliffs. (A novel).
1941.
4,15

MINET, James.
Diary, 1807-1885, edited by Susan Minet.
Frome, Butler, Tanner (50 copies). 1958?
6

DOVER Cont'd

MINET, William.
Extracts from the letter-book of a Dover merchant, 1737-
1741.
Kent Archaeological Association. 1917.
7,11,17

MINET, William.
The fourth foreign church at Dover, 1685-1731, edited by
W. Minet.
Lymington, C.T. King. 1892.
1,6,11

MINET, William.
Some account of the Huguenot family of Minet, from their
coming out of France at the revocation of the Edict of
Nantes, 1686.
Privately Printed by Spottiswoode. 1892.
6,11

MINET, William.
Some unpublished plans of Dover Harbour...
Society of Antiquaries. 1922.
1,6,7,11

MITCHELL, Elizabeth Harcourt.
Her Majesty's bear. (A novel set in Dover).
Masters. 1884.
6

MORRIS, Henry A.
Twelve views of Dover.
Dover, Morris. 1864.
11

MOUCHEL, L.G. AND CO.
New...viaduct at Dover...
1922.
17

MOWLL, John H.
Dover-"August, 1914".
Privately Printed. 1934.
1,6

MOWLL, John H.
Royal visitors at Dover.
Dover, St. George's Press. 1937.
6,7,8,11,12

MUNFORD, William A.
3,000 books for a public library. (Borough Librarian,
1934-45).
Grafton. 1939.
6

MYNARD, D.C.
A group of post-medieval pottery from Dover Castle.
(Reprinted from Post Medieval Archaeology, Vol. 3, 1969).
4

"A NAVAL OFFICER", pseud.
A brief history of Dover and Ramsgate Harbours.
Ramsgate, Brewer. 1837.
1

NEILL, Robert.
Hangman's cliff. (A novel).
Doubleday. 1956.
6

NELSON, T. AND SONS. Publishers.
Dover and its neighbourhood. (Pictorial guide).
T. Nelson. c.1871.
6

NELSON, T. AND SONS. Publishers.
Views of Dover.
T. Nelson. c.1870.
6

NEW DOVER GROUP.
The effect of the Channel Tunnel on the town and port of
Dover.
New Dover Group. 1966.
6

NEW DOVER GROUP.
Report and recommendations on the River Dour, May, 1971, by
the Planning Committee.
New Dover Group. 1971.
6

New Dover guide or visitors' assistant...a concise
account of Dover Castle...
Dover, Warren. 1830.
11

NORTH, Roger.
Lives of the Rt. Hon. Francis North, Baron Guilford,
the Hon. Sir Dudley North, the Hon. and Rev. John North,
3 vols.
Henry Colburn. 1826.
6

OAKELEY, Edward Murray.
The life of Sir Herbert Stanley Oakeley.
Allen. 1904.
6

OMAN, Carda.
Mary of Modena.
Hodder and Stoughton. 1962.
6

PAGE, Sir Thomas Hyde.
Considerations upon the state of Dover Harbour, with
its relative consequence to the navy of Great Britain...
Canterbury, Simmons and Kirkby. 1784.
6,11,17

PAPILLON, Alexander F.W.
Memoirs of Thomas Papillon of London, merchant, 1623-
1702.
Reading, Beecroft. 1887.
6

PARKER, Louis N.
The Dover Pageant, July, 1908.
Dover, G.W. Grigg. 1908.
3,6,7,11,12,17

PARKER GALLERY.
The British Isles: catalogue of views (section on
Dover).
Parker. n.d.
6

PARKINSON, James.
Remarks on the fossils...Mr. Phillips...Dover...
Folkestone.
London, W. Phillips. 1819.
6

PARSONS, Charles, of Dover.
Dover as a health resort...
John Churchill. 1868.
6,17

PASKE, C.T.
Dover as a sea angling centre, edited by Miss Hill.
Dover, Goulden. 1900.
6

PASKE, C.T.
Sunny Dover, then and now.
Dover, Goulden. 1894.
1,6,7,11,12,15

PATERSON, J.D.
By Dover and Calais from early times to the present
day.
Dover, "Kings Arms". 1894.
1,6

PAYNE, Nicholas, of Dover.
A true relation...brave exploit...Captain Richard
Dawks...
Printed by L. Norton and J. Field. 1642.
6

PECK, F.
Coast artillery, Dover. (Typewritten).
1958.
6

PENTON, Howard.
Dover, England's gate (28 period sketches).
c.1907.
6

PERRY, John.
An account of the stopping of Daggenham Breach: with the accidents that have attended the same from the first undertaking, containing also proper rules for performing any the like work, and proposals for rendering the ports of Dover and Dublin (which the author has been employed to survey) commodious for entertaining large ships; to which is prefixed a plan of the levels which were overflowed by the Breach.
Printed for Benjamine Tooke at the Middle Temple Gate in Fleet Street and sold by J. Peele at Lock's Head in Pater Noster Row. 1721.
6

PERRY, John Tavenor.
An account of the Priory of St. Martin, Dover.
Oxford, Parker. 1871.
6,11,17

PETTIT, W.J., of Dover.
The management of bees, 2nd edition.
Dover, Printed by W. Brett. c.1868.
6

PEVERLEY, J.R.
Brick cliffs of Dover (Western heights). (Article in Architectural Review, Vol. CXXV, No. 746, March, 1959).
3,6

PHILIPOTT, John.
Roll of the Constables of Dover Castle and Lord Wardens of the Cinque Ports, 1627...
Bell. 1956.
1,2,3,4,6,7,8,9,11,12,13,14,17,18,20

PHILLIPS, William.
Remarks on the chalk cliffs near Dover.
W. Phillips. 1818.
6

PHILPOTT, D.R.E.
Dover: the historical geography of the town and port since 1750. (M.A. thesis).
University of London. 1965.
6,8

The picturesque companion to Dover.
c.1831.
13

PITT, Barrie.
Zee brugge: St. George's Day, 1918.
Cassell. 1958.
6

PLUMPTRE, F.C.
Some account of the remains of the Priory of St. Martins' and the church of St. Martins'-le-grand at Dover.
n.d.
6,11,17

PLUNKETT, G.T.
The development of the fortifications of Dover Castle.
1884.
6

Proceedings on the claim of Mr. Ledger, Town Clerk of Dover...Treasury...appeal.
Printed by Osborn Hendrey. 1839.
6

PUBLIC BUILDINGS AND WORKS, Ministry of.
Le Chateau de Douvres.
H.M.S.O. 1962.
6,8,11(1970)

PUCKLE, John.
The church and fortress of Dover Castle.
John Henry and James Parker. 1864.
1,3,4,6,7,8,11,12,14,15,16,17,19

PUCKLE, John.
The church and fortress of Dover Castle.
Dover, Terson. 1880.
11,15,18

PUCKLE, John.
Four sermons preached at St. Mary the Virgin...Dover...
Advent, 1856.
Rivington. 1857.
6

PUCKLE, John.
Holyday and occasional sermons...St. Mary...Dover, Vol. 4, Parochial Sermons.
Rivington. 1861.
6

PUCKLE, John.
Parochial sermons preached in the parish church of St. Mary the Virgin, Dover.
Rivington. 1847.
6(1,2 and 4) 12

PUNTON-SMITH, S.P.
A short history of the buildings of the Priory of St. Mary and St. Martin (Newark) Dover, now the site of Dover College.
Printed for Private Circulation. n.d.
3,6

R.N.V.R.
Anti-aircraft corps., Royal Naval Volunteer Reserve - member's manual.
Dover, W.E. Giraud, Printer. 1916.
6

RADFORD, C.A. Ralegh.
Dover Castle.
H.M.S.O.
1(1950)
2(1953)
3(1953)
4(1959 and 1962)
6(1959)
7(1959 and 1962)
8(1950)
11(1950 and 1953)
12(1950)

RADFORD, C.A. Ralegh.
Maison Dieu.
H.M.S.O. 1958.
3,6

RAGGETT, G.F.
Saint George the Martyr.
c.1925.
6

Rambling recollections of the neighbourhood of Dover...
Dover, T. Ryder. 1848.
6,11

RAWLEIGH, Sir Walter.
A discourse of seaports...Dover.
London, Printed by John Nott. 1700.
6

RAWLINSON, Robert.
Report to the General Board of Health...Dover.
H.M.S.O. 1849.
6

READING, John, of Dover.
Eight sermons delivered in Saint Marie's Church at Dover, 1636.
Printed for Robert Allot. 1636.
6

READING, John, of Dover.
A faire warning...sickness and health...sermons...
Dover, 1621.
Printed by Bernard Alsop for John Hodgetts. 1621.
6

RENN, Derek Frank.
Norman castles in Britain.
Baker. 1968.
6

Report on the harbour of refuge to be constructed in Dover Bay (bound with) Reports and plans for the construction of a harbour of refuge and brakewater in Dover Bay...1848 (and) Captain Warlington's last report on the harbour at Newhaven, 1847.
H.M.SO. 1846.
7,14

RIGDEN, T. Publisher.
Book of views: Dover and district.
Dover, T. Rigden. (1847/8)
6

RIGDEN, T. Publisher.
Illustrated guide to Dover...
Dover, T. Rigden. c.1850.
6

RIGDEN, T. Publisher.
New guide to Dover...
Dover, T. Rigden. n.d.
17

RIGDEN, T. Publisher.
Panoramic view of Dover.
Dover, T. Rigden. 1836.
6

RIGDEN, T. Publisher.
A short historical sketch of Dover and its environs.
Dover, T. Rigden. 1844.
6,17

RIGDEN, T. Publisher.
Twelve new views of Dover.
Dover, T. Rigden. n.d.
6

RIGDEN, T. Publisher.
The wild flowers of Dover and its neighbourhood, with indices
of their English and Latin names.
Dover, T. Rigden. c.1855.
6,7,11

RIGOLD, S.E.
The Roman haven of Dover. (Reprinted from the Archaeological
Journal, Vol. CXXVI, 1970).
4

RIX, M.M.
Excavation of a medieval garderobe in Snargate Street, Dover
in 1945, by M.M. Rix and G.C. Fleming.
Ashford, Headley. 1955.
11,17

ROBERTSON, William Archibald Scott.
The old church of St. Martin at Dover.
Mitchell and Hughes. 1893.
6,17

ROBERTSON, William Archibald Scott.
Richard Ingworth, first Bishop of Dover.
n.d.
6

ROBERTSON, William Archibald Scott.
Richard Thornden, the second Bishop of Dover.
n.d.
1,6

ROCK AND CO. LTD. Publishers.
Six views of Dover.
London, Rock and Co. Ltd. n.d.
6

Royal cabinet album of Dover.
Dover, J. Amos and Pointer. n.d.
6

Royal cabinet album of Dover.
London, R.B. and P. n.d.
6

Royal cabinet album of Dover.
London, Rock and Co. Ltd. n.d.
17

ROYAL VICTORIA HOSPITAL.
Laws and byelaws of the Royal Victoria Hospital, Dover.
1938.
7

ROYAL VICTORIA HOSPITAL.
Reports, Vol. 1, 1829-46, Vol. 2, 1847-67, Vol. 3, 1868-80,
Vol. 4, 1881-89, Vol. 5, 1890-97, Vol. 6, 1898-1905, Vol. 7,
1906-13, Vol. 8, 1914-25, Vol. 9, 1926-34, Vol. 19, 1935-47-
6

ROYAL VICTORIA HOSPITAL.
Revised rules and regulations...1920.
1920.
7

RUDD, Lewis C.
Duke of York's Royal Military School, 1801-1934...
Dover, St. George's Press. 1935.
11

RUDKIN, Mable S.
Inside Dover, 1914-1918.
Elliot Stock. 1933.
3,6,7,8,11,15

St. Peter and St. Paul, Charlton-in-Dover, 1291-1894.
n.d.
12

SCOTT, Rivers.
Gateway of England.
Dover Harbour Board. 1957.
4,7,8,11,12

SCOTT, Rivers.
The gateway of England: the story of Dover Harbour,
2nd edition.
Dover Harbour Board. 1965.
6,11

Sermons preached in Dover and Rochester. (Four sermons
bound together).
n.d.
6

SHEPSTONE, Harold J.
Building the Dover Harbour. (Pall Mall Magazine, 1905).
6

SMEATON, John.
The report of John Smeaton, engineer, upon the Harbour
of Dover.
London, J. Hughs. 1769.
6,11

SMITH, Herbert L.
Notes of brasses formerly existing in Dover Castle,
Maidstone and Ashford churches.
n.d.
17

SMITH, Percy.
At my door. (Poems, of which two are about Dover, by
a local poet).
Ilfracombe, Stockwell. 1959.
6

SMITH, W.H. AND SON. Publishers.
Environs of Dover and the watering places of Kent
(c.1865-70).
W.H. Smith and Son. n.d.
11

SOUTHEY, H.J.
Congregational church history in Dover, 1600-1925.
c.1925.
6

STATHAM, Samuel Percy Hammond.
Dover archives...commonalty of Dover (press cuttings).
n.d.
6

STATHAM, Samuel Percy Hammond.
Dover Charters and other documents in the possession of
the Corporation of Dover, edited by S.P.H. Statham.
Dent. 1902.
1,3,4,6,8,11,12,15

STATHAM, Samuel Percy Hammond.
History of the castle, town and port of Dover.
Longmans, Green. 1899.
1,2,3,4,6,7,8,11,12,18

STATHAM, Samuel Percy Hammond.
The parish church of St. Mary-in-the-Castle, Dover.
Dover, Parsons. 1897, etc.
6,11,12,13

The swan lake and other poems...for the benefit of the
girl's ragged school.
Emily Faithfull. 1862.
6

TANNER, Terence Edmund.
Saint Edmund's Chapel, Dover and its restoration.
T.E. Tanner. (1968)
2,3,4,6,7,8,11,12

TARRANT, H.P.
A comic history of Dover during the Great War.
Dover Express. n.d.
11

TARRANT, H.P.
Near Dover and other verses.
Dover, Neild. n.d.
6,11

TAYLOR, H.J.
The Dover Pageant, 27th July-1st August, 1908...the book
of the music (words chiefly written by James Rhoades...and
music composed by H.J. Taylor).
London, Weekes and Co. 1908.
3,6

THORPE, John.
A brief discourse...on the making of Dover Harbour.
1792.
12

TOPHAM, John.
Description of an antient picture in Windsor Castle...
embarkation of Henry VIII at Dover, May 31st, 1520.
J. Nichols, Printer. 1781.
6

TRAVELLERS' MISCELLANY.
Watering places of England, No. 3, Dover. (From the
Travellers' Miscellany, 1847).
6

The trial of Mr. Savill.
Savill, Printed by A. Young. 1800.
6

TUKER, Sir Francis.
Chronicle of Pte. Henry Metcalfe...Lt. John Edmonstone...
1858, edited by Sir F. Tuker. (Contains report of festivities
in Dover in 1859 on return of the regiment).
Cassell. 1953.
6

TURNER, B.V.
Two poems, by B.V. Turner and J.R. Cackett. (One poem of
Dover interest).
Ilfracombe, Stockwell. 1968.
6

UNSWORTH, Walter.
Tiger in the snow. (On A.F. Mummery who lived at Dover).
Gollancz. 1967.
6

Views of Dover (scrapbook).
n.d.
6

WALKER, James.
Reports and plans for a proposed harbour in Dover bay, by
James Walker and others.
Clowes for H.M.S.O. 1845.
11

WARREN. Publisher.
A short historical sketch of the town of Dover...6th edition.
Dover, Warren. 1828.
6

WARREN. Publisher.
Short history of Dover Castle from the earliest period.
Dover, Warren. 1828.
12

THE WEBB MEMORIAL FUND COMMITTEE.
National memorial to Captain Matthew Webb: programme of
unvailing ceremony at Clarence Lawn, Dover, June 8th, 1910.
London, Hanbury, Tomsett and Co. 1910.
3

Wellington banquet at Dover, Friday, August 30th,
1839.
W.E. Painter, 342, Strand. c.1840.
6

WHEELER, R.E.M.
The Roman lighthouse at Dover. (Reprinted from the
Archaeological Journal, 1930).
1,6

Where to buy at Dover.
Brighton, Robinson. c.1891.
6

WILLIAM, of Poictou.
Dover in 1066 from the Gesta Guilletmi Ducis Normannorum
(From Archaeologia Cantiana, 1948).
17

WILLS, William.
Grace triumphant. (The author was a living member of the
Church of God in Dover).
Rev. W. Aldridge, Printed by Henry Teape. 1790.
6

WORSFOLDE, E.M.
Walks near Dover.
Dover Express. n.d.
6

WORTHINGTON, B.
Proposed plan for improving Dover Harbour...
Dover, Batcheller. 1838.
1,6,7,11,12,17

YONGE, Charlotte Mary.
The Constables' tower or the times of Magna Carta.
(Fiction - Dover Castle).
National Society's Depository. (1890).
6

YORKE, Philip C.
Life and correspondence of Philip Yorke...Earl of
Hardwicke.
Cambridge University Press. 1913.
6

DOWN(E)

Downe House scrapbook, 1907-1957. (Note: Downe House
School at Downe, Kent from 1907-1922).
Berkshire, Downe House School. 1957.
2

HOWARTH, O.J.R.
Down House: pamphlet.
n.d.
16

HOWARTH, O.J.R.
History of Darwin's parish - Downe, Kent, by O.J.R.
and E.K. Howarth.
Russell. 1933.
2,3,11,13,15,18

KENT COUNTY COUNCIL - ARCHIVES OFFICE.
Downe parish records.
1961.
2

RAVERAT, Gwen.
Period piece. (Part describes visits to Down House,
Downe).
Faber. 1952.
2

RIDLER, Anne.
Olive Willis and Downe House: an adventure in education.
Murray. 1967.
2,8,12

St. Mary the Virgin's Church, Downe.
The Orpington Press. 195-?
2

TESTER, M.
High Elms, Downe and note...of the family portraits.
(Photocopy of typescript).
(1965).
2

DRAINAGE

GREAT BRITAIN: LAWS, etc. (GEO. III).
An Act to enable the Commissioners of Sewers for several
limits in the Eastern parts...of Kent, more effectively
to drain and improve the lands within the general vallies.
1776.
11,12

GREAT BRITAIN: LAWS, etc. (GEO. III).
An Act for amending...Acts passed...relating to the execution
of the Commission of Sewers...from East Mouldsey in Surrey
to Ravensbourne in Kent.
1813.
11

GREAT BRITAIN: LAWS, etc. STATUTORY INSTRUMENTS.
Ministry of Housing and Local Government Provisional Order
Confirmation (West Kent Main Sewerage District) Act, 1968.
(1968, Ch. XXIII). H.M.S.O.
4

SURREY AND KENT SEWER COMMISSION.
Court Minutes, Vol. I comprising the Minutes of the first
two Commissions...1569 to 1579.
London County Council. 1909.
2,11

DULWICH

ALEXANDER, M.B.
History of Honor Oak Cricket...Club.
1965.
18

DARBY, W.
Dulwich discovered.
The Author. 1966.
2,18

DULWICH MILLENNIUM CELEBRATIONS COMMITTEE.
967-1967 A.D., Dulwich...souvenir programme (includes
historical notes).
Parcener Press, Printers. 1967.
2

DUMPTON

The hermit of Dumpton cave...Joseph Croome Petit, of Dumpton,
near Ramsgate.
J.G. Strutt. 1823.
1,13,14,17

DUNGENESS

CENTRAL ELECTRICITY GENERATING BOARD.
Dungeness nuclear power station site: photogrammetric
survey from air photographs taken June, 1959. Scale 1:500.
11 sheets. (Made to record the shingle ridges about to
disappear).
(1960).
4

DUNGENESS BIRD OBSERVATORY.
Annual reports, 1957 (onwards).
1957 etc.
3,7(1961-1968) 11,15

DUNGENESS BIRD OBSERVATORY.
Dungeness Bird Observatory.
1964.
7

GELL, Francis. Publisher.
Dungeness: the protection of the roadstead...
F. Gell. 1889.
11,12

The loss of the ship "Northfleet" with photographs of the
vessel, Romney Church, Captain and Mrs. Knowles...
Waterlow. 1873.
6,7,9,11,12

DUNKIRK

Short memoir of David Ferguson...who has attained the great
age of 123 years.
Cowtan and Colegate. 1817.
11

DUNTON GREEN

DUNTON GREEN PARISH COUNCIL.
Dunton Green, Kent.
Croydon, Home Publishing Co. 1965.
11

DYMCHURCH

CHARITY COMMISSIONERS.
In the matter of Beding Field's Charity for the benefit
of the parishes of Lyminge, Dymchurch and Smeeth.
1924.
7

DYMCHURCH AND DISTRICT CHAMBER OF TRADE.
Dymchurch and St. Mary's Bay...
Adams. 1954.
15

EDINGER, J.H.
The parish church of St. Peter and St. Paul, Dymchurch.
(A short guide).
n.d.
4,12

EAST FARLEIGH

ADAMS, Matthew Arnold.
Report on the chemical and bacterological analyses of the
Farleigh water supply, by M.A. Adams and J.W. Washbourne
Maidstone, Vivish. 1897.
12

The Priory (East Farleigh) - Sale catalogue, 1936.
1936.
12

WALTER, S.
Short history of East Farleigh Almshouse Charity.
Maidstone, Vivish. 1901.
11

EAST HOATHLY

TURNER, Thomas.
Diary of Thomas Turner of East Hoathly (1754-1765).
Bodley Head. 1925.
11

EAST LANGDON

St. Augustine, East Langdon.
1966.
12

EAST MALLING

BUCKLAND, Walter E.
Notes on East Malling Church, 19p.
West Malling, J.J. Alexander. 1907.
7

EAST MALLING AND LARKFIELD PARISH COUNCIL.
Official handbook to East Malling and Larkfield, Kent,
July, 1962.
11

EAST MALLING RESEARCH STATION.
(See under Agriculture).

JESSUP, Frank William.
Sir Roger Twysden, 1597-1672.
Cresset Press. 1965.
1,2,3,4,6,7,8,11,12,15,17

HATTON, Ronald G.
Notes on the family of Twysden and Twisden, by R.G.
Hatton and Christopher H. Hatton.
Printed by Headley Bros. 1945.
11,17

MERCER, Richard C.H.
The parish church of St. James, East Malling.
1966.
12

STONARD, John.
A sermon preached at East Malling Church, the ninth of
October, 1814.
Wickham and Cutbush. (1814).
12

EAST MALLING Cont'd

TWISDEN, Sir John Ramskill.
The family of Twysden and Twisden: their history and archives from an original by Sir John Ramskill Twisden - completed by C.H. Dudley Ward.
London, Murray. 1939.
3,4,11,12,21

EAST PECKHAM

The Arnold Car. (Magazine article). (W. Arnold and Sons Ltd., East Peckham, Kent - makers of the Arnold Car).
Old Motor and Vintage Commercial. 1965.
12

COOK, A.R.
A manor through four centuries. (East Peckham).
Oxford University Press. 1938.
1,3,4,5,6,8,11,12,15,19,20

DUMBRECK, William V.
A history of East Peckham.
East Peckham Coronation Committee. n.d.
11

EAST PECKHAM CORONATION COMMITTEE.
Celebrations at East Peckham to commemorate the Coronation of H.M. Queen Elizabeth II.
1953.
8,11

SERGEANT, John Middlemore.
History of East Peckham, by J.M. Sergeant and others.
Hadlow, Hilton. 1964.
2,4,7,11,15,19

EAST SUTTON

CAVE-BROWN, John.
Sutton Valence and East Sutton.
Dickinson. 1898.
1,6,10,11,12,15,17

FILMER, Sir Robert.
Patriarcha; or, the natural power of kings.
Walter Davis. 1680.
3,11

OYLER, Thomas H.
East Sutton Church.
Kentish Express Ltd. 1898.
1,4,6,11,12,15,17

SHAW, Otto L.
Maladjusted boys.
Allen and Unwin. 1965.
12

EAST WICKHAM - See also PLUMSTEAD

BAKER, Herbert Arthur.
Excursion to East Wickham and Plumstead, by H.A. Baker and S. Priest. (From Proceedings of Geologists' Association, Vol. XXX, 1919).
5

DARTFORD UNION GUARDIANS.
Byelaws...with respect to house refuse...in...Crayford and East Wickham.
1885.
5

EASTCHURCH

All Saints Church, Eastchurch.
n.d.
12

EASTRY

A guide to the church of St. Mary the Virgin, Eastry, 2nd edition.
Eastry Parochial Church Council. 1965.
12

Guide to the parish church, Eastry.
Sandwich, Pain. n.d.
11

LAMPEN, C. Dudley.
Church schools: a sermon...preached at St. Mary's, Eastry, October 11th, 1903.
12

SHAW, William Francis.
Liber Estriae; or, memorials of the Royal Ville and parish of Eastry.
J.R. Smith. 1870.
1,3,4,6,7,8,11,12,13,14,15,17

EASTWELL

Eastwell Park - Sale catalogue, 1921.
1921.
12

I'ANSON, Bryan.
History of the Finch family.
Janson. 1933.
3,7,11

PARKIN, E.W.
Lake House, Eastwell. (Reprinted from Archaeologia Cantiana, Vol. LXXXIII, 1968).
11

EBBSFLEET

St. Augustine's Cross, near Ebbsfleet.
1884.
13

STRAHAN, A.
On boring for coal at Ebbsfleet, near Ramsgate.
1912.
17

EDENBRIDGE

Blackmoor Lodge - Sale catalogue, 1967.
1967.
12

Church and parish of Edenbridge.
Ramsgate, Church Publishers. 1965.
8,11

CROFT-COOKE, Rupert.
The gardens of Camelot.
Putnam. 1958.
12

Edenbridge - assessment to a subsidy granted to Charles I.
1628.
16

Edenbridge - assessments from 1650 to 1656 for the support of the armed forces of Parliament and Commonwealth.
n.d.
16

EDENBRIDGE PARISH COUNCIL.
Edenbridge, Kent: the official guide.
Croydon, Home Publishing Co. 1952 etc.
1,4,11,12,15,19

HUNTER, D.M.
The Great Stone Bridge at Edenbridge. (Tonbridge School Local History Researches).
1963.
11

IRWIN, John.
The church and the parish of Edenbridge, Kent, by J. Irwin and others.
Ramsgate, Church Publishers. 1966.
2,4,12

IRWIN, John.
Place names of Edenbridge.
Edenbridge, Historical Society. 1964.
1,2,3,4,7,8,11,12,15,19

JEFFERY, John.
A short and concise account of the Lord's gracious dealings with Mr. John Jeffery, tanner and fellmonger of Edenbridge...
1818.
11

KENT COUNTY COUNCIL - PLANNING DEPARTMENT.
Kent development plan (1967 revision): Edenbridge: a
local plan for the control of the future development of the
town.
Kent County Council. 1971.
11

The Mill House - Sale catalogue, 1966.
1966.
12

PAYTON, George.
Some account of the life and experience of George Payton,
Minister of the Gospel, Edenbridge.
Edembridge, Payton. 1819.
11

PIKE, Leslie Elgar.
Official guide to the parish of Edenbridge, Kent.
Home Publishing Co. n.d.
1

SOMERS-COCKS, Henry L.
Edenbridge, by H.L. Somers-Cocks and V.F. Bayson.
Edenbridge, Edenbridge Chronicle. 1912.
1,2,4,6,8,11,12,15,16,18,19

Stanborough Castle Hotel and Castle Farm - Sale catalogue.
1967.
12

EDUCATION

ARNOLD, George Mathews.
Some account of the work of education under Kent Technical
Education Committee set up 6th April, 1903.
Spottiswoode for Kent County Council. 1903.
1,5,11

BOARD OF EDUCATION.
Administrative County of Kent endowed charities (elementary
education): report on endowments.
1907.
17

BOARD OF EDUCATION.
Reports on schools recognised as non-provided public
elementary schools - County of Kent.
1906.
17

BUTLER, John Walter.
Some researches in public elementary education in Dartford
in the second half of the 19th century.
Dartford. n.d.
5

CANTERBURY DIOCESAN BOARD OF EDUCATION.
Annual reports, 1872-1877.
Canterbury, Gibbs. 1873 etc.
11

CANTERBURY DIOCESAN BOARD OF EDUCATION.
Report of quarterly meeting, August, 1870.
1870.
17

CARLISLE, Nicholas.
A concise description of the endowed grammar schools in
England and Wales, Vol. 1.
Baldwin. 1818.
12

CARNEGIE UNITED KINGDOM TRUST.
Educational broadcasting: report of the special investigation
in...Kent, during the year 1927.
Carnegie United Kingdom Trust. 1928.
3,8,11,12,17

COMMISSIONERS ON THE EDUCATION OF THE POOR.
Reports on the County of Kent, 1st and 2nd reports.
1818-19.
3,12,18(1st report)

Educational facilities in the County of Kent.
British Isles Publicity Ltd. 1939.
13

Independent schools of Kent.
Morley. 1965.
19

INSTITUTE OF HANDICRAFT TEACHERS AND COLLEGE OF
HANDICRAFT.
Conference handbook (1962) - Kent Branch of the
Institute.
1962.
11

INTERNATIONAL COMPUTER AND TABULATORS.
Local Government Magazine, No. 13, October, 1967.
(Containing "A total approach to the computer by
Bromley" and "The computer as an aid to secondary
school allocation in Kent".
2

KENT ASSOCIATION OF TEACHERS OF RURAL SCIENCE.
Fruit plots for secondary schools...
Kent Education Committee. 1958.
12

KENT COUNTY ASSOCIATION OF TEACHERS.
Yearbook.
n.d.
11(1959-60 and 1963 in progress).

KENT COUNTY COUNCIL - ARCHIVES OFFICE.
Records of Education Committees, 1903-1948.
Kent County Council. 1961.
11

KENT COUNTY COUNCIL - EDUCATION DEPARTMENT.

Adult education in Kent: report of the Adult Education
Committee, October, 1945.
Kent Education Committee. 1945.
8,11(1945 and 1949)

Aids and suggestions for the teaching of local history
with special reference to...rural schools in Kent, by
H.W. Saunders.
Kent County Council. 1922.
1,6,8,11

Annual Reports: Kent Education Department.
2 (1919-1920, 1920-1923)
17 (Nos. 1-14, 1904-1923)

Annual Reports (higher section)
3 (1906-7, 1907-8, 1909-10, 1911-12, 1914)

Day continuation school.
1920.
17

Development plan for primary and secondary education.
Kent Education Committee. 1946.
1,6,8

Development plan for primary and secondary education
as approved by the Minister of Education...revised
edition.
Kent County Council. 1949.
3,5,6,9,11,12

Directory for higher education, 1910-11. Handbook
for higher education in rural districts, 1912-13-14.
Higher education, scholarships handbook, 1912-13, 1914.
17

Draft scheme of education for Kent under the Education
Act, 1918.
London, Charles and Son. 1921.
2,3,9,11,15

Education Act, 1944: outline of educational policy.
Kent Education Committee. 1944.
8,11

Education in Kent.
Kent Education Committee.
1923-28 (1,2,3,5,7,8,11,12,14,15,17)
1928-33 (1,2,3,5,6,7,8,11,12,13,14,15,17,21)
1933-38 (1,2,3,5,6;7,8,11,13,14,15,17,19,21)
1938-48 (1,2,3,4,5,8,11,15,16)
1948-53 (1,2,3,4,5,6,8,10,11,13,15,17,19,21)
1953-58 (1,2,3,4,5,6,7,8,10,11,12,14,15,17,19)
1958-63 (1,2,3,4,5,6,7,8,9,11,12,15,17,21)
1963-68 (6,7,9,11,20)

Further education scheme.
Kent Education Committee. 1954.
3,12

Further education scheme and County college plan.
Kent Education Committee. 1948.
1,2,3,4,5,8,15,19

Higher education...
Kent Education Committee. 1919 etc.
17

How to become a teacher in Kent.
Kent Education Committee. 1832,34,35.
17

Kent summer school for teachers: prospectus.
1932,36,38.
17

Kent summer school for teachers, 1935.
Kent Education Committee. n.d.
17

Memorandum on the Education Act, 1918.
Kent Education Committee. 1919.
3,17

Playing fields.
Kent Education Committee. 1925.
17

Quarterly reports, 1903-37.
Kent Education Committee. 1903-37.
11(1903-37) 17 Nos. 1-70 (1903 etc.).

Report on the special committee appointed by the County
Council on 20th November, 1907 to consider and report as to
what delegation, if any, of the Education Committee's
powers in the administration of elementary education is
advisable...number of the Education Committee's present staff.
Kent County Council. 1909.
11

Review of the work of the vocational guidance and juvenile
welfare...for the years ended 31st July, 1924,1925,1926,
1927,1928,1937-38.
Kent Education Committee.
3,12(1937-38) 17

Scheme for the exercise of powers.
Kent County Council. 1935.
5

Second triennial report on higher education in the County of
Kent.
London, Kent Education Committee. 1910.
2,3,11

Secondary education: general information.
Maidstone, Kent Education Committee. 1954.
3,7

Special report on higher education in the County of Kent.
London, Kent Education Committee. 1906.
1,2,3,11,17

To teach in Kent: an invitation.
Kent Education Committee. 1961.
11,12

The training of teachers.
Kent Education Committee. 1925.
3

Youth Employment Service - Annual Reports.
Kent Education Committee.
6,8,11 (1945/46-1954/55)
8,11 (1955/56-1964/65)
1,3,5,6,9,12 (some during period 1955/56-1964/65)
2(1958-1961, 1963/64)
11(1966/67, 1971)

Youth Employment Service - Maidstone Division.
Annual Report, 1966.
Maidstone Youth Employment Bureau, 1966.
12

KENT EDUCATION DEPARTMENT - ADVISORY COMMITTEE OF TEACHERS.
Schools and the community: a report...prepared for the
Kent Education Committee.
Kent County Council. 1969.
11

KENT FEDERATION OF HEAD TEACHERS' ASSOCIATIONS.
Yearbooks, 1963-64 and 1972.
Kent Federation of Head Teachers' Associations.
11

KENT MUSIC SCHOOL.
Annual report, 1969/71.
Kent Music School. (1972).
11

KENT TECHNICAL EDUCATION COMMITTEE.
42nd report.
1902.
3

KNOX, Vicesimus.
Remarks on the tendency of certain clauses in a Bill
now pending in Parliament to degrade grammar schools,
with cursory strictures on the national importance of
preserving inviolate the classical discipline prescribed
by their founders.
Printed for J. Mawman. 1821.
11

MORGAN, D.R.
The scholastic forge: the autobiography of a schoolmaster.(Author was employed as a teacher by Kent
Education Committee from 1926 to 1938 and several
chapters cover his experiences with the County education
system).
Beck. 1955.
8

MORRIS, Joyce M.
Reading in the primary school.
Newnes Educational. 1959.
1,5

POULTER, Molly.
Playgroups in Kent, compiled by M. Poulter.
Kent Pre-School Playgroups Association. 1971.
3,4,8,9

PRINGLE, M.L. Kellmer.
Remedial education - an experiment: an account of two
years' work by a remedial unit for maladjusted and
deprived children at the Caldecott Community, by M.L.K.
Pringle and B. Sutcliffe.
Caldecott Community and the Department of Child Study,
University of Birmingham Institute of Education. 1960.
4,8,12

Schools of Folkestone, Dover and district.
Century Publications. 1954.
12

Schools of Kent - a handbook.
Directory Publications. 1964.
11,12

Schools of Kent and Sussex...
Directory Publications. 1968.
1,2,5,19

Schools of West Kent.
Century Publications. 1959.
1

Thames-side at work. (Cover title - Thames-side at
school).
Kent Education Committee, Thames-side Division. 1951.
9

EDWARD, THE BLACK PRINCE

HEWITT, Herbert James.
The Black Prince's expedition of 1355-1357.
Manchester, Manchester University Press. 1958.
3

HOPE, Sir William Henry St. John.
The achievements of Edward, Prince of Wales.
Westminster Society of Antiquaries. 1895.
3

MILLS, Dorothy.
Edward, the Black Prince: a short history.
Canterbury, Friends of Canterbury Cathedral. 1963.
4

EGERTON

BAND, Cecil Frank.
Church of St. James, Egerton.
Egerton, Peregrine Press. 1958.
11,12,15

SCULL, Gideon Delaplaine.
Dorothea Scott, otherwise Gotherson and Hogben, of Egerton
House, Kent, 1611-1680: a new and enlarged edition by
G.D. Scull.
Printed for Private Circulation by Parker. 1883.
1,11,12

ELECTIONS   (For Electeral Registers, etc. - See BERGESS, W.F.
              and RIDDELL, B.R.M. "Kent Directories Located").

BARNETT, James.
Proceedings of a Select Committee on the House of Commons
on the petition against the return of James Barnett (M.P.
for Rochester).
1808.
15

CAVE-BROWN, John.
Knights of the Shire for Kent from A.D. 1275 to A.D. 1831.
Mitchell and Hughes. 1894.
12,17

COMMISSIONERS OF MUNICIPAL CORPORATION BOUNDARIES (ENGLAND
AND WALES).
Report on the proposed division of the County of Kent, 1831.
(With maps).
11

COWPER, Joseph Meadows.
The Roll of the Freemen of the City of Canterbury from
A.D. 1392 to 1800.
Canterbury, Cross and Jackman. 1903.
3,11,12,19

COX, H.
Antient parliamentary elections.
n.d.
11

DOVER, Borough of.
The list of the Freemen of the Borough of Dover.
Rigden. c.1860.
6

Election Commission at Canterbury, extracts from.
1880.
3

Freemen of Maidstone, residing outside Maidstone.
1825.
12

Freemen and electors of Sandwich, Deal and Walmer.
1832.
11

GREAT BRITAIN: LAWS, etc. (VIC.).
Redistribution of Seats Act...County of Kent.
1885.
8

GREAT BRITAIN: LAWS, etc. STATUTORY INSTRUMENTS.
Local Government, England and Wales. Local Government areas:-
County of Kent. (Electoral Divisions) Order, 1964, No. 1839.
H.M.S.O. 1964.
8,12

GREAT BRITAIN: LAWS, etc. STATUTORY INSTRUMENTS.
Redistribution of Seats. The Parliamentary Constituencies (Rochester, Chatham and Gravesend) Order, 1964...
H.M.S.O. 1964. (S.1, 1964 No. 277).
4,8

GREAT BRITAIN: LAWS, etc. STATUTORY INSTRUMENTS.
Representation of the people. The County of Kent
(Date of Postponed Election) Order, 1964.
H.M.S.O. 1964.
8

History of Parliament. Poll Books. Draft list covering
Kent. (Typescript).
1954.
17

KENT COUNTY COUNCIL.
Report of the review of electoral divisions with the
proposals which the County Council considers desirable.
Kent County Council. 1936.
2

A list of the Poll Books for the County of Kent.
(Typescript - taken from Institute of Historical
Research information).
1953.
13

Maidstone election petition...enquiry by Justices
Grantham and Lawrence, 2nd edition.
Kent Messenger. 1906.
12,17

Maidstone election petition, 1866. (Newspaper cuttings).
1866.
12

Maidstone election petition, 1901.
Boorman. 1901.
12

Maidstone election petition, 1901. Full report of the
enquiry by Justices Kennedy and Channell.
Kent Messenger. 1901.
12

(The Kentish Conspiracy; or, an order and narration
declaring the late plot for the surprising of Dover
Castle, 1645). Bound with Minutes of a Select Committee
appointed to...determine the merits of the petition of
John Amherst Esq.,...complaining of an undue election
and return for the County of Kent, 1797.
1645.
6

Minutes of the Select Committee appointed to try the
merits of the petition of John Amherst Esq., and others
complaining of an undue election and return for the
County of Kent.
Bristow. 1797.
6,12

Petitions against the return of John M. Fector as
Member of Parliament for...Maidstone.
1838.
12

SEEWELL, James, pseud.
Report of the commissioners appointed to inquire into
the existence of corrupt practices at the last election
of Members to serve in Parliament for the Borough of
Maidstone, together with the minutes of evidence taken
before them, by J. Seewell and others.
1866.
12

TELESCOPE, Thomas, pseud.
Sir Brook Bridges, M.P. for East Kent and his supporters,
their principles and practices...at the General Election,
1852.
n.d.
17

VANE-TEMPEST-STEWART, Charles Stuart Henry, <u>7th Marquess of Londonderry, Defendant</u>.
Maidstone election petition trial, May 8th-16th, 1906.
Maidstone and Kentish Journal. 1906.
8,12,17

ELHAM

Catalogue of Mr. Lee Warly's library bequethed by him to the parish of Elham in 1809, restored by public subscription 1843.
Printed by W. Congreve. 1845.
7,11

ENGLISH, John.
New guide to the Elham Valley and Canterbury.
English. (1892).
7,11

GRIFFIN, Ralph.
Kentish items: Elham, Preston-next-Faversham, Addington.
n.d.
7

GRIFFIN, Ralph.
Kentish items: West Malling, Hythe, Denton, Allington, Elham, Bekesbourne.
n.d.
7

HOPKINS, R. Thurston.
Moated houses of England.
Country Life. 1935.
5,11,15,18

MILLAR, Christine Flora.
Short history of the Manor of Elham.
n.d.
7,11

MILLAR, Christine Flora.
The story of the Abbot's fireside.
Folkestone, Parsons. 1938.
7,11

PARKIN, E.W.
Elham: a village study.
C.P.R.K. n.d.
7,11,14,21

Particulars of the sale of...the Little Manor, Barham...(and) Wigmore Court Farm, Elham...also 2 Beech Villas, High Street, Elham, which Messrs. P.R. and B.J. Coltman will sell by auction ...on Saturday, 18th July, 1959.
P.R. and B.J. Coltman. 1959.
7

ROBERTSON, Rev. William Archibald Scott.
St. Mary's Church, Elham.
London, Mitchell and Hughes. 1876.
3,17

WILLIAMS, R.H. Isaac.
A short history of Elham and its parish church.
Maidstone, Kent Messenger. 1959.
3,4,7

ELMSTEAD

ANOTHER OLD PAST MASTER.
The history of the "Saye and Sele" Lodge, No. 1973, Part II. 1912-1932.
Saye and Sele Lodge. 1932.
7

ELMSTONE

SPURLING, Cuthbert T.
Historical notes, Elmstone Church.
C.T. Spurling. 1969.
4,8

ELTHAM

ANDERSON, E.
Eltham in past times.
North. n.d.
12

ANDERSON, E.
Eltham in past times.
1910.
17,18

BROOK, Roy.
Story of Eltham Palace.
Harrap. 1960.
1,2,3,4,5,8,9,11,12,15,17,18

BUCKLER, John Chessell.
An historical and descriptive account of the Royal Palace at Eltham.
Nichols. 1828.
1,2,4,6,8,11,12,15,17,18

BUTTS, Robert.
Historical guide to Lewisham, Ladywell, Lee, Blackheath and Eltham.
1878.
17,18

COURSE, Edwin A.
Notes on the development of Eltham (with special reference to transport).
1952.
17

COURTAULD, S.L.
Eltham Palace.
Hazell, Watson and Viney, Printers. (1937).
2,17

CROSLAND, Newton.
The Eltham tragedy reviewed, new edition.
F. Farrah. 1871.
11

DILLENIUS, John James.
Hortus Elthamensis...
1732.
1,17

DUNNAGE, H.
Plans...of the Great Hall...Eltham, by H. Dunnage and C. Laver.
Taylor. 1828.
1,8,11,12,17,18

ELIZABETH (I), <u>Queen of England</u>.
Letters patent...granting...offices, etc at Eltham to Christopher Hatton, Esq., 27th July, 1586.
n.d.
17

ELLISTON-ERWOOD, Frank Charles.
Eltham.
n.d.
12

ELLISTON-ERWOOD, Frank Charles.
The end of the House of Roper.
Woolwich Antiquarian Society. 1935.
11

ELLISTON-ERWOOD, Frank Charles.
Well Hall...
1936.
1,2(3rd edition, 1947) 5(3rd edition, 1947) 11,13,18

Eltham. Extract from notes...(MSS. notebook compiled c.1796-1800).
2

Eltham Palace. (Extract from Castles and Abbeys of England, Vol. 1).
1937.
12,13

ELTHAM SOCIETY.
Looking at Eltham.
Eltham Society. 1970.
2

GODFREY, Walter Hines.
New light on old subject: VI - The Royal Palace at Eltham (pamphlet).
n.d.
18

GREAT BRITAIN: LAWS, etc.   (HENRY VIII).
Statutes of Eltham (1526).
17

GREGORY, R.R.C.
Story of Royal Eltham.
Eltham, Kentish District Times. 1909.
1,2,3,5,6,8,11,12,15,16,17,18

Industry illustrated: a memoir of Thomas Jackson of Eltham
Park, Kent.
Privately Printed. 1884.
1

JENKINS, Claude.
Sir Thomas More: a commemoration lecture (Canterbury
Papers No. 5).
Jennings. 1935.
1,3,4,11,12

KING, David.
General observations on records of Eltham Church, 1066-1855.
1855.
17

KING, David.
Subterranean passages at Eltham Palace, by D. King and A.
Clayton.
Greenwich, Helyer. 1834.
11,12,17

LOFTIE, W.J.
Royal Palaces - Eltham and Greenwich.
Art Journal. 1890.
17

MANNING, Anne.
The household of Sir Thomas More, with Roper's life of More.
Dent. 1906.
3,12

MILNE, A.G.
Eltham in past times.
Mackheath Press. 1910.
1,11

MORE, Margaret, 1505-1544.
The household of Sir Thomas More or, diary of his family
circle, written by his daughter Margaret.
London, Hall, Virtue and Co. 3rd Edition. n.d.
3

ORR, William S. AND SON. Publisher.
Pictorial guide to Eltham Palace by way of Charlton and
Shooters Hill...
W.S. Orr and Son. 1845.
1,17

PAUL, Leslie.
Sir Thomas More.
Faber. 1953.
12

REYNOLDS, Ernest Edwin.
Margaret Roper, eldest daughter of Sir Thomas More.
London, Burns and Oates. 1960 and 1963.
3

RIVERS, Elphinstone.
Some records of Eltham, 1060-1903.
Turner and Robinson. (1908).
1,2,6,11,12,17(1903) 18

ROBERTS, Llwyd.
Old Eltham...sketches by L.R., 1875-1940.
Eltham and Kentish Times. 1967.
18

St. Barnabas Church (Well Hall, Eltham) Review.
1957.
11,17

STRONG, D.E.
Eltham Palace, Kent. (Ministry of Works - Ancient
Monuments Series).
H.M.S.O. 1958.
1,2,4,5,8,11,12,17,18

(SUTTON, Frederick).
Life and career of Col. North. (Resident Eltham and
rebuilt Avery Hill).
Kentish District Times. (1896).
2

THOMSON, J.S.M.
The founder of Eltham Palace (Anthony Bek). (Reprinted
from Army Education, December, 1950).
Gale and Polden. 1950.
2

WITTING, Clifford.
The glory of the sons - a history of Eltham College
School for the sons of missionaries, edited by C.
Witting.
Eltham College Governors. 1952.
1,2,11,17,18

ERITH

ARMSTRONG, C.J.
Guide to Erith Parish Church.
1911.
1,11,12

BALL, W.E.
De Luci the Loyal (Chief Justiciar of England and
founder of Lesnes Abbey): a paper read before the
Society, 11th November, 1891.
Lewisham Antiquarian Society. 1891.
3

CHANDLER, Raymond H.
Report...(on)...lower tertiary section and pleistocene
river drifts near Erith, by R.H. Chandler and A.L.
Leach.
1912.
17

CLAPHAM, Sir Alfred W.
The history and remains of the Augustinian Abbey of
Lesnes.
Harrison and Sons. 1911.
12

CLAPHAM, Sir Alfred W.
Lesnes Abbey in the parish of Erith, Kent: being the
complete report of the investigations...1909-1913.
London, Cassio Press. 1915 for Woolwich Antiquarian
Society.
1,2,4,5,6,8,11,12,15,17,18

CLARKE, Frank.
Three papers on Erith, by F. Clarke and others.
Erith, North Kent Argus. n.d.
5,11

DAVIES, William James Keith.
Parish's loam quarries, Erith...being the chronicles
of a typical quarry line.
Narrow Gauge Rly Society. 1959.
1,2,8,11,12

DUNKIN, Alfred John.
History of Kent: Erith.
1856.
18

ELLISTON-ERWOOD, Frank Charles.
A brief account of Lesnes Abbey in the parish of Erith,
Kent.
London, Cassio Press. 1918.
5,17,18

ERITH BOROUGH COUNCIL.
Erith, Kent: the official handbook.
Cheltenham, Burrow. 1955 etc.
1,4,5,11,12,15,17,19

ERITH EDUCATION COMMITTEE.
Education week, June 22nd-27th, 1925.
1925.
17

ERITH GRAMMAR SCHOOL.
Erith Grammar School, 1905-55.
n.d.
1,11

ERITH URBAN DISTRICT COUNCIL.
Erith: the official guide.
1926.
17

EVANS, F.
The geographical position of Erith.
n.d.
11

GREATER LONDON COUNCIL.
Lesnes Abbey: a short history and guide.
1968.
2,11

A guide to Erith Parish Church.
Church Publisher. 1963.
12

HARRIS, John.
The parish of Erith in ancient and modern times.
Mitchell and Hughes. 1885.
1,3,4,5,6,8,11,12,15,17,18

HEWETT, G.W.
Lesnes Abbey and Newington-next-Sittingbourne...
Woolwich, Pryce. 1911.
4,11,17

HIND, H.
Old world Erith.
n.d.
11

HUDD, A.G.
A short guide to Erith Museum.
Erith Borough Treasurer's Department. 1953.
12

LONDON COUNTY COUNCIL.
Lesnes Abbey...
London County Council. 1961.
1,11,12,17

MARRIOTT, St. John.
British woodlands as illustrated by Lessness Abbey woods.
(Typescript). 1925 and supplement published by G. Routledge
and Sons, 1928.
5,12

ORR, Williams S. AND SON. Publisher.
The pictorial guide to Erith and Greenhythe...
W.S. Orr and Son. 1846.
1,12

"Our village"; or, a history of Erith and its neighbourhood.
1855.
17

ROBINSON, Robert Henry.
Erith through the ages.
Randell Press. 1931.
1,2,4,5,8,9,11,12,17,18

SMITH, Charles John.
Erith.
Spalding Virtue. 1873.
1,2,5,6,8,11,12,15,17

SPURRELL, F.C.J.
Sketch of the ancient architecture of Erith Church, Kent.
Mitchell and Hughes. 1885.
5,17(1886)

SQUIRES, A.W.
Erith and District Hospital Centenary Handbook, 1871-1971,
compiled for the Woolwich Group Hospital Management
Committee.
Forward Publicity Ltd. 1971.
4,8

STEELE, E.
Collections for Earith in Kent.
1740.
17

SUMMERLY, Felix.
Day's excursion out of London to Erith, Rochester and
Cobham in Kent.
G. Bell. 1843.
8,17

VINCENT, William Thomas.
Parsonage Farm, Beadonwell, Erith.
Woolwich Antiquarian Society. 1912.
17

WILKINSON, John J.
History of Erith...
1879.
5,11

WOOLWICH AND DISTRICT ANTIQUARIAN SOCIETY.
A brief guide to Lesnes Abbey.
Woolwich Antiquarian Society. 1950.
1,8,11,12,18

WOOLWICH AND DISTRICT ANTIQUARIAN SOCIETY.
The Canon from Lesnes Abbey Missal, c.1200 A.D....
Woolwich Antiquarian Society. 1925.
1,5,8,11,12,17,18

WOOLWICH AND DISTRICT ANTIQUARIAN SOCIETY.
Report on explorations at Lesnes Abbey, 1909-10.
Woolwich and District Antiquarian Society. 1910.
1,7,11

EVELYN, JOHN

ELLIS, Booksellers.
John Evelyn: books illustrating his life and interests.
1932.
18

ESDAILE, Arundell.
Evelyn's diaries. (Extract from the Quarterly Review,
1958).
18

EVELYN, Helen.
...History of the Evelyn family. (References to
Deptford).
Nash. 1915.
18

EVELYN, John.
Diary, 1641 to 1705-6, edited by W. Bray. (Includes
references to Sayes Court, Deptford).
Gibbings. 1890.
2,18

EVELYN, John.
Many editions of diary, correspondence and works,
including:-
1. Directions for the gardiner at Sayes Court...
edited by G. Keynes.
2. ...(his) plan of his...garden at Sayes Court,
Deptford...and his own description of the lay-out of
Sayes Court.
1. Nonesuch Press. 1932. 2. Extract from Illustrated
London News (2 sheets). 1952.
18

HINGELEY, John.
John Evelyn: an appreciation (pamphlet).
1933.
18

HISCOCK, W.G.
John Evelyn and his family circle.
1955.
18

HISCOCK, W.G.
Evelyn and the Royal Society.
Country Life. 1960.
18

KEYNES, Geoffrey.
John Evelyn...
Cambridge University Press. 1937.
18

EYNSFORD

BASSETT, Herbert H.
Village of Eynsford.
Simpkin Marshall. 1909.
1,3,4,5,11,17

COLE, Herbert.
Village of Eynsford, by H. Cole and F. Adcock.
n.d.
4,11,16

Cottages and land (Eynesford) - Sale catalogue, 1911.
12

CURNOW, W.I.
Eynsford: a story through the ages.
Eynsford Village Society. 1953.
1,2(1935) 4,5,8,11,12,16,17

DRUCE, George C.
Sybill Arms at Little Mote. In Archaeologia Cantiana, Vol.
128, 1909.
17

DUNKIN, Alfred John.
History of Eynsford. (Bound extract from Dunkin's History).
n.d.
9

DUNKIN, Alfred John.
History of Eynsford with an architectural account of the
castle, by Edward Cresy.
1856.
11,18

DUNKIN, Alfred John.
William de Eynsford the excommunicator.
n.d.
11

EYNSFORD MILLS, KENT.
Three-hundred years of paper making. (Reprinted from
"Jobbing Printer", May, 1950).
9

Eynsford Mount Estate, Eynsford, Kent - Sale catalogue.
Ibbett, Mosely, Card and Co. (Auctioneers). 1936.
5

Eynsford: short history of the Baptist Church.
South Darenth, Little Boys' Press, 1937.
5

HAMMERTON, Sir John.
Child of wonder: an intimate biography of Arthur Mee.
Hodder and Stoughton. 1946.
5

HARVEY, C.
St. Martin's Church, Eynsford.
Lund Humphries. 1964.
12

HILL, R.H. Ernest.
Little Mote, Eynsford, with a pedigree of the Sybill family.
In Archaeologia Cantiana, Vol. 26, Vol. 28, 1903, 1904, 1906.
5(1903) 17

KIDD, E.R.
Eynsford: a study of the parish. (Bound typescript).
1965.
5

MOORE, E.N.
Hand-made papers and their production at the Eynsford Paper
Mill, Kent. (Typescript).
19--?
9

Park House Farm, (Eynsford) - Sale catalogue, 1966.
1966.
12

RIGOLD, S.E.
Eynsford Castle, Kent.
H.M.S.O. 1963.
1,2,4,5,6,7,11,12,15

The village of Eynsford - illustrated.
Kent, Simpkin Hamilton. n.d.
3,10

EYTHORNE

GILES, John.
A brief sketch of the life and characters of the Rev.
John Giles, late Pastor of the particular Baptist Church
at Eythorne, Kent, who departed this life November 15th,
1827...with numerous extracts from his diary and
correspondence.
(182-?).
11

MILLER, A.C.
Eythorne: the story of a village Baptist Church.
Baptist Union Publications Department. 1924.
1,3,4,6,7,11,12

FARNBOROUGH

BARNARD, Alfred.
Oak Brewery, Farnborough. (Photocopy extract from The
Noted Breweries of Great Britain and Ireland...4 vols.).
Joseph Causton and Sons. 1891.
2

BLANDFORD, J. Harland.
Farnborough and its surroundings.
Bromley, Clarke. 1914.
1,2,11

BOND, M.F.
Farnborough Manor in the 17th and 18th centuries. In
Archaeologia Cantiana, Vol. 59, 1946.
17

FARNBOROUGH WOMEN'S INSTITUTE.
Scrapbook of (photocopy of MS.) Farnborough.
1955.
2

HUTCHINSON, Horace Gordon.
Life of Sir John Lubbock, Lord Avebury.
Macmillan. 1914.
12

TESTER, M.
Deeds of Tubbendens in Farnborough, 1527-1929. (Notes -
typescript), compiled by M. Tester.
(1966).
2

WATERS, S.C.
Farnborough. (Lecture notes - typescript).
(196-?).
2

(WEBB, David B.).
Guide to the parish church of St. Giles, Farnborough,
Kent.
British Publishing Co. 1971.
2,4,11(1969)

FARNINGHAM

Clevelands (Farningham) - Sale catalogue, 1966.
1966.
12

DAPLYN, Edgar.
The Farningham Boy's House. (Extract from "The Quiver",
1907).
11

DREW, Bernard.
Farningham against Hitler: the story of six years of war
in a Kentish village amid barrage. (Photocopy).
Bromley, Kentish District Times Co. 1946.
5,11

DREW, Bernard.
A hundred years of Farningham cricket.
1957.
1,2,4,5,8,11

FARNINGHAM, Marianne.
A working woman's life.
J. Clarke. 1907.
11

FARNINGHAM WOMEN'S INSTITUTE.
Farningham, 1965: a village scrapbook prepared by the
members of the Farningham Women's Institute.
1965.
5

KENT COUNTY COUNCIL - PLANNING DEPARTMENT.
Farningham: village study.
Kent County Council. (1967).
2,3,5,7,11,12

A short guide to the church of St. Peter and St. Paul,
Farningham, Kent.
(195-).
11

SMITH, Frank William.
A short account of the parish church of Farningham, Kent...
Printed by Cassio Press. 1913.
1,11,15,17

FAVERSHAM

ANDREWS, John H.
The trade of the port of Faversham, 1650-1750.
Kent Archaeological Society. In Archaeologia Cantiana, Vol.
69, 1955.
17

Arden of Faversham: a tragedy, reprinted from the edition of
1592, with an introduction by A.H. Bullen.
J.W. Jarvis. 1887.
3,17

BOROUGH DIRECTORIES LTD.
Business and residential directory for Faversham and
Sittingbourne.
Borough Directories Ltd. 1963.
4,5,7,8

BOROUGH DIRECTORIES LTD.
Business and residential directory of Faversham, Sittingbourne
and Milton.
Borough Directories Ltd. 1965.
20

BOROUGH DIRECTORIES LTD.
Business and residential directory of the borough of
Faversham...1963.
Borough Directories Ltd. 1966.
4,8,12,19

BYWATER, Francis.
Inns and taverns of Faversham. (Faversham Papers No. 3).
Faversham Historical Society. 1967.
1,2,4,6,8,11,12

CADMAN, John.
Faversham history trails.
Faversham Historical Society. 1970.
2,4,6,11

CIVIC TRUST.
Conservation areas. (Reprinted from The Architects' Journal,
1967 - case history on Abbey Street, Faversham, p.200-1).
3

COLLIER, Canis Vale.
Coats of arms in Kent churches - Faversham and Davington.
Kent Archaeological Society. In Archaeologia Cantiana, Vols.
22-23, 1897-8.
17

COOKE, Rev. Shadrach.
Legal obedience the duty of a subject (sermon) - Vicar of
Faversham.
London, Knaplock. 1718.
11

COWPER, Joseph Meadows.
Notes from the records of Faversham.
n.d.
11

CULMER, George G.
History of the "Lodge of Harmony", No. 133 Faversham,
1763 to 1936.
Faversham, Voile and Roberson. 1936.
7,11

CULMER, George G.
Queen Elizabeth's Grammar School, Faversham.
Kent Archaeological Society. In Archaeologia Cantiana,
Vol. 47, 1935.
17

CUST, Lionel.
Arden of Feversham.
Mitchell, Hughes and Clarke. 1920.
12,17

DANE, Herbert.
Hundred years of Faversham history, 1854-1954, compiled
by H. Dane.
Faversham Historical Society. 1954.
11

DANE, Herbert.
The Mayoralty of Faversham. (Typescript). (Faversham
Papers No. 1).
Faversham Society. 1964 etc.
1(1968) 2,3,4,7,8,11(1968)

DANE, Herbert.
The story of a thousand years: a chronology of
Faversham's history, compiled by H. Dane.
Faversham Historical Society. 1968.
2,6,11,12

DANE, Herbert.
The War years, 1939-1945 in Faversham and district...
compiled by H. Dane.
Austin. (195-?).
4,11

DODD, C.E.
An essay on the tragedy of "Arden of Faversham"...
n.d.
11

DONNE, C.E.
An essay on the tragedy of "Arden of Faversham"...
Faversham, Russell Smith. 1873.
6,11

Examination, confession, trial and execution of Joane
Williford, Joan Cariden and Jane Hutt who were executed
at Faversham in Kent for being witches, Monday, 29th
September, 1645...
London, Printed for J.G. 1645.
3,11

Extracts from wills and other documents containing
benefactions to the town of Faversham...
Faversham, S. Ratcliffe. 1844.
12

Faversham: a copy of the return of the charitable funds,
etc. of the Corporation of Faversham.
Faversham, Printed by S. Ratcliffe. 1833.
1

Faversham: scheme for the management...of the several
charities in Faversham.
Roworth. 1856.
1,11,17

Faversham: two schemes relating to Faversham Grammar
School and other charities.
1876.
11

Faversham, Kent (being pp.105-112, Vol. III, No. 35
from unidentified book or diary).
n.d.
3

FAVERSHAM BOOK SOCIETY.
Minute Book, 1791-1802. (MS.).
n.d.
11

FAVERSHAM AND DISTRICT CHAMBER OF COMMERCE.
Faversham and district directory, 1926.
Faversham, Voile and Roberson. 1926.
15

FAVERSHAM AND DISTRICT CHAMBER OF COMMERCE.
Official guide to Faversham.
195-?
11,12,15

FAVERSHAM AND DISTRICT CHAMBER OF TRADE.
Official guide to Faversham.
1951(?)
11

FAVERSHAM BOROUGH COUNCIL.
Faversham, Kent: official guide.
Croydon, Home Publishing Co. 1959 etc.
1,3,4,5,11,19

FAVERSHAM BOROUGH COUNCIL.
Photostats of old MS. records of the Faversham Oyster
Fishery Company...22 sheets.
n.d.
3

FAVERSHAM BOROUGH COUNCIL.
Town and port of Faversham, 1252-1952.
Chatham, Mackay. 1952.
3,11,12

Faversham Borough Annual, Directory (including street
directory) and Guide to Faversham.
Faversham, F. Austin. 1908.
3

Faversham Church. (Extract from The Mirror, pp.153-4
illustrated).
n.d.
3

FAVERSHAM DISTRICT NATIONAL SCHOOLS.
Report, 1857-1865 (Vol.1) - 1867-1873 (Vol. II).
n.d.
11

FAVERSHAM INSTITUTE.
Library catalogue and rules.
1923.
11

FAVERSHAM SOCIETY.
Faversham: ancient town and port.
Faversham Society. (1967).
4,11

FAVERSHAM SOCIETY.
Faversham Abbey and its last Abbot, John Caslock, by W.
Telfer. (Faversham Papers No. 2).
Faversham Society. 1965.
4,15

FAVERSHAM SOCIETY.
Open house and garden scheme, 1970.
Faversham Society. 1970.
4,11

FRIED, Erick.
(Arden must die) - Arden muss sterben. Libretto.
Schott and Co. 1967.
12

GIRAUD, Francis F.
Catalogue of the books...in the library of the Free
Grammar School...in Faversham, compiled by F.F. Giraud.
Borough of Faversham. 1895.
11,12

GIRAUD, Francis F.
Extracts from Faversham town accounts in the reigns of
Edward I and Henry VIII.
n.d.
11

GIRAUD, Francis F.
Extracts from wills...relating to...Faversham District
National Schools, compiled by F.F. Giraud.
Faversham. 1867?
3,11

GIRAUD, Francis F.
Faversham town charters...
n.d.
11

GIRAUD, Francis F.
Fremasonry in Faversham, 1763-1899, edited by F.F.
Giraud.
Margate, Keebles Gazette. 1900.
3,11

GIRAUD, Francis F.
Municipal archives of Faversham, A.D. 1304-24. In
Archaeologia Cantiana, Vol. 14, 1882.
17

GIRAUD, Francis F.
On goods and ornaments at Faversham Church, A.D. 1512.
In Archaeologia Cantiana, Vol. 18, 1889.
11,17

GIRAUD, Francis F.
On the insignia of the Corporation of the town, port
and Borough of Faversham.
Faversham, F. Austin. 1897.
3,11

GIRAUD, Francis F.
On the parish clerks and sexton of Faversham, A.D.
1500-1593. In Archaeologia Cantiana, Vol. 20, 1893.
17

GIRAUD, Francis F.
The parish church of St. Mary of Charity, Faversham.
Church Reading Society. 1901.
7,15

GIRAUD, Francis F.
The service of shipping of the Barons of Faversham.
Faversham, Mitchell and Hughes. 1895.
11,17

GIRAUD, Francis F.
Visitor's guide to Faversham, by F.F. Giraud and C.E.
Donne.
Faversham, James Higham. 1876.
1,6,11,12,15,17,20

GREAT BRITAIN: LAWS, etc. (GEO. III).
An Act for the more easy and speedy recovery of small
debts within the town and port of Faversham and
Boughton...
Printed by Eyre and Strahan. 1785.
1,11

GREAT BRITAIN: LAWS, etc. (GEO. III).
An Act for the better paving, repairing, cleansing,
lighting and watching the highways, streets, lanes and
other public passages and places within the town and
liberty of Faversham in the County of Kent and also
certain places near and adjoining thereto and for
removing and preventing incroachments, obstructions,
nuisances and annoyances therein.
Printed by Eyre and Strahan. 1785.
11

GREAT BRITAIN: LAWS, etc. (GEO. III).
An Act for making compensation to the proprietors of
such lands...as have been purchased for more safe
working...gunpowder works...near Faversham.
1786.
11

GREENSTED, Frances.
Fugitive pieces.
Maidstone, Chalmers. 1796.
11

GRIFFIN, Ralph.
Kentish items: Aylesford, Pluckley, Stourmouth,
Faversham, Sittingbourne, Wouldham, Chatham.
n.d.
7

A guide to the ancient Borough of Faversham. (Text by G.G. Culmer).
Faversham, Wyards Printing Works Ltd. 1936.
11,21

HASTED, Edward.
(The parish and town of Faversham).
Faversham Society. 1969.
4,8,11

HILLS, William H.
Catalogue of the...library of...Mr. William H. Hills.
1912.
17

HILLS, William H.
Dialogue between a creditor and a member of Faversham Oyster Company.
1842.
17

HOLT, Anita.
Arden of Faversham.
Faversham Society. 1970.
11

HONYWOOD, Frances. Lady.
Memorial of the Hon. Lady Honywood.
Gosnell. 1812.
11

IRVINE, J.T.
Remains of the Saxon or early Norman work in the church of Stone-juxta-Faversham.
n.d.
11,15

JACOB, Edward.
History of the town and port of Faversham...
London, J. March. 1774.
1,3,4,6,7,8,11,12,14,15,17

JACOB, Edward.
Plantae Favershamienses.
n.d.
1,6,11,14,15,17

JEFFERY, William Henry, of Faversham.
Regeneration; or, The New Birth. (MS. of a sermon)...
n.d.
11

KENT COUNTY COUNCIL - PLANNING DEPARTMENT.
Faversham: its history, its present role and the pattern for its future.
Kent County Council. 1969.
11

LAITHWAITE, Michael.
A ship-master's house at Faversham, Kent. (Reprinted from Post-Medieval Archaeology, 1968).
4

LAMBARDE, Fane F.
The Easter Sepulchre in Faversham Church (with note by the editor Aymer Vallance). (Reprinted from Archaeologia Cantiana, Vol. 41, 1929).
4,12,17

The lamentable and true tragedies of M. Arden of Faversham.
White. 1770.
12

LEWIS, John.
History and antiquities of the Abbey and Church of Faversham...
1727.
1,3,4,8,11,12,14,17

LILLO, George.
Arden of Faversham: historical tragedy in five acts.
n.d.
3

MUNDEN, Alan Frederick.
Eight centuries of education in Faversham.
Faversham Society. 1972.
11

MURRAY, K.M. Elizabeth.
Faversham and the Cinque Ports (a paper).
Royal Historical Society. 1935.
3,11

PERCIVAL, Arthur.
The Faversham gunpowder industry and its developments.
Faversham Society. 1967.   (Faversham Papers No. 4).
1,2,3,4,6,7,8(1969) 9,11(and 1969) 19,20

PERKS, R.H.
A history of Faversham sailing barges.
Society for Spritsail Barge Research. 1967.
2,3,4,7(1968) 8,9,11,12,18,19,20

PHILLIPS, Frederick Wallace.
A guide to Faversham Parish Church.
Gloucester, British Publishing Co. 1957.
3,8,11

PHILP, Brian J.
Excavations at Faversham, 1965: the Royal Abbey, Roman Villa and Belgic farmstead...
Kent Archaeological Research Groups. 1968.
1,2,3,4,6,7,8,9,11,12,15,19,20

SELBY, Prideaux George.
Faversham Farmers' Club and its members.
Canterbury, Gibbs. 1927.
1,3,7,11,12,15,21

SHEPHERD NEAME LTD.
Shepherd Neame Ltd., brewers, Faversham.
n.d.
15

SMITH, Charles Roach.
Catalogue of Anglo-Saxon and other antiquities discovered at Faversham...
Chapman and Hall. 1871.
6,11,14,17

SOUTHOUSE, Thomas.
Monastican Favershamiense in agro Cantiano...
1671.
1,4,6,11,12,14,17

SWAINE, Anthony.
Faversham: its history, its present role and the pattern of its future.
Faversham Borough Council - Kent County Council. 1969.
2,4(1970) 7(1970) 8(1970) 21

SWALE FOOTPATHS GROUP.
Ten walks around Faversham, by G.H.J. Champion.
(Faversham Papers No. 8).
Faversham Society. 1971.
3,8,11

TELFER, William.
Faversham Abbey and its last Abbot, John Caslook...
Faversham Society. 1965. (Faversham Papers No. 2).
1,2,3,4,8,11,15

VALLANCE, Aymer.
Notes on an old house, West Street, Faversham.
(Reprinted from Archaeologia Cantiana, Vol. 30).
Mitchell, Hughes and Clarke. 1913.
11,17

WAINMAN, Paul, psued of Mrs. Sylvia MacDougall.
Let's light the candle: memoirs.
Methuen. 1944.
11

WILSON, Sydney.
Faversham.
Faversham, Carmelite Press. 1963.
7,11

FAVERSHAM Cont'd

WILSON, Sydney.
Guide to the town and port of Faversham...
Faversham, Voile and Roberson. 1936.
3,4,7,11,15

FAWKHAM

PROUDFOOT, W.F.
Fawkham.
Barker. 1951.
1,3,4,5,8,9,11,12,13,17,18,19,20

FINGLESHAM

STEBBING, W.P.D.
Iron Age hearth at Finglesham, near Eastry. (Reprinted from Archaeologia Cantiana, Vol. 41).
Ashford, Headley. n.d.
11,17

STEBBING, W.P.D.
Jutish cemetery near Finglesham. (Reprinted from Archaeologia Cantiana).
Ashford, Headley, 1929.
11,17

FLAMSTEAD

BULLARD, I. Vincent.
Flamstead: its church and history, etc.
1902.
17

FLIGHT

AVIATION, Ministry of.
Civil aircraft accident: report on the accident to Percival Proctor, 5A E1-AMV on 16th October, 1963 at Dundas Park Farm.
H.M.S.O. 1964.
8

BURNABY, Fred.
A ride across the Channel, and other adventures in the air.
Sampson. 1882.
7

FOLKESTONE

Album of Folkestone, Sandgate and Hythe views.
Charles Reynolds. n.d.
1

THE AMATEUR ANGLER, pseud.
Days in clover.
Sampson Low. 1892.
7

ARDLEY, Susan P.
William Harvey: a symposium. In Guy's Hospital Gazette, Vol. 71, No. 1799, 1957.
7

ARTHUR BROUGH PLAYERS.
Silver Jubilee souvenir programme, 1929-1954.
Leas Pavilion. 1954.
7

ATKINSON, Ernest G.
Catalogue of Folkestone Borough records.
Folkestone Borough Council. 1904.
7,11

(BARLOW, L).
Folkestone Town Football Club history.
(1950).
7

BILLINGS, B.R.
Folkestone through the ages.
Printed by Sumner. 1929.
7

BRITISH TRAVEL ASSOCIATION.
Visitors to Folkestone, Summer, 1965.
British Travel Association. 1966.
7

BRITISH VETERINARY ASSOCIATION.
Congress, August 30th-September 5th, 1959, Folkestone.
Pfizer. (1959).
7

BROMLEY, Francis E.
The parish church of St. Mary and St. Eanswythe, Folkestone. (Manuscript).
(19--).
3

BROWN, John Howard.
A history of the Harvey Grammar School (Folkestone), 1674-1962.
Old Haveians Association. 1962.
1,4,6,7,10,11,12

BRYDONE, James Edward.
Centenary of H.G. Wells, 1866-1966, Spade House, Folkestone, compiled by J.E. Brydone.
Mrs. E.M. May. 1966.
1,2,4,7,11

BUCHANAN, A.G.B.
The parish church, Folkestone: account of Church-wardens, 1487-1590, edited by A.G.B. Buchanan.
n.d.
1

BURROW, Edward J. AND CO. LTD. Publisher.
Folkestone and neighbourhood. ("Borough" guides, 2nd edition).
Burrow. c.1930.
7

CARLILE, John C.
Folkestone during the War (1914-1918), edited by J.C. Carlile.
Folkestone, Parsons. 1920.
1,6,7,11,12,13

CARLILE, John C.
My life's little day.
Blackie. (1935).
7

CASEY, Raymond.
The Ammonite genus Uhligella in the English Albian. (Reprinted from Geological Magazine, Vol. 86, No. 6, 1949).
7

CASEY, Raymond.
The Folkestone beds: aeolian or marine? (Reprinted from South Eastern Naturalist, 1947).
7

CASEY, Raymond.
Junction of the gault and lower greensand in East Sussex and at Folkestone, Kent.
1950.
7

CASEY, Raymond.
A monograph of the ammonoidea of the lower greensand, 6 vols.
Palaeontographical Soceity. 1960-1965.
7

CASEY, Raymond.
Recent additions to the Albian ammonoid faunas of Folkestone. (Extracted from Geological Magazine, Vol. 73, October, 1936).
7

CASEY, Raymond.
Some genera and subgenera...of mesozoic heterodont lamellibranches. (Reprinted from Proceedings of Malacological Society, 1952).
7

CASEY, Raymond.
The stratigraphical palaeontology of the lower greensand. (Reprinted from Palaeontology, Vol. 3, Pt. 4, March, 1961).
7

CASEY, Raymond.
Upper part of the lower greensand around Folkestone.
n.d.
7

CHADWICK, Sir Edwin.
Folkestone as a health resort, by Sir Edwin Chadwick and others.
J. English. 1889.
7

CHAMBERLAIN, Frank.
The first hundred years of Folkestone Methodism.
Folkestone, Grace Hill Methodist Church. (1956).
7

CHAMBERLAIN, POWELL AND SON. Architects.
The Leas, Folkestone, 1965. (Development plan).
(Folkestone Estate). (1965).
7

CHAPMAN, Frederick.
The foraminifera of the gault of Folkestone. (Reprinted from Journal of the Royal Microscopical Society, c.1891).
7

CHARTERED AUCTIONEERS' AND ESTATE AGENTS' INSTITUTE.
Forty-second annual provincial meeting, Folkestone, June, 1951.
7

CHAUVOIS, Louis.
William Harvey.
Hutchinson. 1957.
3,7

CHESTERMAN, C.A.C.
The general rate.
P.T. Publicating. 1954.
12

CHURCH CONGRESS - FOLKESTONE, 1892.
Guide to the Church Congress and...art exhibition...at Folkestone...1892 including a guide to the district.
Multravers. 1892.
7,17

CHURCH CONGRESS - FOLKESTONE, 1892.
The illustrated Church Congress handbook for 1892, by the Rev. Charles Mackeson.
Savoy House. n.d.
3

CHURCH CONGRESS - FOLKESTONE, 1892.
Report of the Church Congress at Folkestone.
1892.
7

CLARK, (John).
Jubilee services at Union Chapel, Uphill, Folkestone...brief history of the Chapel for fifty years.
A. Stace. 1896.
7

CLARKE, R.G.
Altar-tomb of John Pragell in Folkestone Parish Church and Charnel House, Folkestone Parish Church, by R.G. Clarke and V.J. Torr - from Folkestone Parish Church Magazine, 1958-59.
7

(CLOUGH, J.S.).
Folkestone Rotary Club - 1922-1962.
(1963).
7

COLLINS, J.
The Folkestone lift.
Sumner. 1887.
7

COOPER, Francis J.
Accounts of the Wardens of the Parish Church, Folkestone, 1489-1590. (Newspaper cuttings).
Folkestone Herald. 1931.
7

COOPER, G.H.
Folkestone in the last hundred years. (Typescript).
1951.
7

CREED, C. Publisher.
Complete handbook to Folkestone and its neighbourhood, with concise history of town and environs.
Creed. 1869.
7

CREED, C. Publisher.
Creed's almanack for 1873, containing a newly compiled complete directory to Folkestone and neighbourhood.
Creed. (1873).
7

DAVEY, Peter.
Chronicles of the old country theatres of Southern England. (Photostat copies of Folkestone section).
n.d.
7

DAVIS, J. Publisher.
Folkestone illustrated visitor's guide. (Includes Dover, Deal, Sandgate and Hythe, etc.).
J. Davis. n.d.
7(c.1888) 8(c.1908)

DICKENS, Charles.
"Out of town" (Folkestone). In "Household words", No. 288, 29th September, 1855.
7

DOBY, T.
Discoverers of blood circulation. (Includes William Harvey of Folkestone).
Abelard-Schuman. 1963.
12

Dover, Folkestone and Deal local railway guide.
1898.
17

"DOVER CHRONICLE". Publisher.
Dover, Folkestone, Deal and Cinque Ports appendix and almanack for 1870 (containing a short history of Dover).
Dover Chronicle. 1870.
7

"DOVER CHRONICLE". Publisher.
The Dover, Folkestone, Deal guide appendix and almanack - rewritten, revised, corrected and enlarged for 1873.
Dover Chronicle. (1873).
7,17

DUNCAN, Leland Lewis.
Notes from the church and churchyard, Folkestone, Kent.
n.d.
7

DUNK, W.J. Harold.
Dunk, 1666-1963.
1967.
7

ELGAR, W.H.
The ancient buildings of Folkestone district.
Folkestone, Parsons. 1921.
1,6,7,8,11,12

ELGAR, W.H.
Record of a mediaeval house which until 1916 stood on the Bayle, Folkestone.
F.J. Parsons. 1916.
3,7,12

ENGLISH, John. Publisher.
Folkestone fiery serpent and the pantomime based on it.
J. English. 1910.
7

ENGLISH, John. Publisher.
Illustrated penny guide to Folkestone, Sandgate and Hythe.
J. English. 1900 and 1904.
7

ENGLISH, John. Publisher.
Pictorial guide to Folkestone, Hythe and Sandgate and neighbourhood.
J. English. n.d.
10

"FELIX", pseud.
Rambles around Folkestone.
Folkestone, Glanfield. 1913.
6,7,10,11,12,17

FINLASON, W.F.
The judgement of the Judicial Committee in the Folkestone
ritual case.
Stevens. 1877.
7

FISCHER, Michael G.
Saint Peter's Church, Folkestone, 1862-1962: a brief history
...on the occasion of its centenary by, G. Fischer and others.
(1962).
7

FISCHER, Michael G.
A brief history of St. Peter's Church, Folkestone, 1861-
1946. (Typescript).
1960.
7

"FIT".
Pharoah's serpent and the Mayor of Folkestone: a burlesque
opening to the pantomime of Fairy Cinque Ports, Harlequin,
Fish, Flames, Fire and Fury.
Folkestone, English. n.d.
10

Folkestone: its churches, organs etc.
Notebook of Newspaper cuttings. n.d.
3

Folkestone: six views.
Rock Bros. 1851.
11

Folkestone: 18 views.
Creed Library. n.d.
10

FOLKESTONE ADVERTISING COMMITTEE.
Folkestone illustrated: official handbook of the Folkestone
Advertising Committee.
(1909-10).
7

FOLKESTONE AND DISTRICT ELECTRICITY SUPPLY CO. LTD.
Bill to confer further powers upon the Folkestone Electricity
Supply Company Ltd.
1906.
7

FOLKESTONE AND DISTRICT WATER COMPANY.
The undertaking of the Folkestone and District Water Company.
1958.
7

Folkestone and its neighbourhood.
Nelson. 190-?
7,11

FOLKESTONE ART TREASURES EXHIBITION.
English's catalogue of the pictures, prints, statuary and
general contents of the Folkestone Art Treasures Exhibition.
English. (1886).
7

FOLKESTONE ART TREASURES EXHIBITION.
English's pictorial guide to Folkestone and Art Treasures
Exhibition.
English. (1886).
7

FOLKESTONE BAPTIST CHURCH.
A history of the Baptist Church in Folkestone... (Typescript).
(1951).
7

FOLKESTONE BOROUGH COUNCIL.
Common Assembly minute books. (Typescript).
1605-1635, 1670-1715, 1715-1749, 1749-1767, 1767-1812, 1812-
1835.
7

FOLKESTONE BOROUGH COUNCIL.
Corporation minutes, 1894 in progress.
n.d.
7

FOLKESTONE BOROUGH COUNCIL.
Folkestone Sessions Books. (Typescript).
1635-1665, 1765-1779.
7

FOLKESTONE BOROUGH COUNCIL.
Local Government services and administration.
1967.
7

FOLKESTONE BOROUGH COUNCIL.
Minute book of the Folkestone Commissioners of Paving,
1736-1800. (Typescript).
n.d.
7

FOLKESTONE BOROUGH COUNCIL.
Official holiday guide to Folkestone.
1961 etc.
1,7,11,19

FOLKESTONE BOROUGH COUNCIL.
Overseers'accounts and assessments, 1704-1735.
(Typescript).
n.d.
7

FOLKESTONE BOROUGH COUNCIL.
(Folkestone) Overseers' accounts, 1723-1787.
(Typescript).
n.d.
7

FOLKESTONE BOROUGH COUNCIL.
Poor certificates, 1698-1725. (Typescript).
n.d.
7

FOLKESTONE BOROUGH COUNCIL.
Town centre redevelopment report and plans.
1964.
7

FOLKESTONE CHAMBER OF COMMERCE.
Folkestone, the gem of the Kentish coast.
Folkestone Chamber of Commerce. 1933?
7,11,15

FOLKESTONE CHAMBER OF COMMERCE.
Folkestone illustrated, 1921-22.
Folkestone Chamber of Commerce. 1921.
7

Folkestone Dramatic Club, 1902-1920.
n.d.
7

FOLKESTONE HERALD. Publisher.
Front line Folkestone: the story in pictures of
Folkestone's ordeal during five years of war, 1940-45.
Folkestone Herald. (1945).
7

FOLKESTONE NATURAL HISTORY AND GENERAL SCIENCES SOCIETY.
Folkestone and the country around: a popular and
scientific survey of the natural history and archaeology
of the district by members and friends...edited by John
W. Walton.
Folkestone Natural History and General Sciences Society.
1925.
4,17,21

FOLKESTONE NATURAL HISTORY SOCIETY.
Folkestone Natural History Society, 1954 (a special
edition in honour of the Conference of the South Eastern
Union of Scientific Societies, Folkestone, 1955).
Includes natural history of Folkestone.
Folkestone Natural History Society. 1954.
8

FOLKESTONE NATURAL HISTORY SOCIETY.
Some aspects of the natural history of the Folkestone
district. Published to mark the centenary of the
Folkestone Natural History Society, founded 4th April,
1868.
Folkestone Natural History Society. 1968.
3,4,6,8,11,21

Folkestone photographic views.
1897.
11

FOLKESTONE PUBLIC LIBRARY.
Some sources of information on places in Kent.
Folkestone Public Library. 1931.
1,7,8,11,14,15

Folkestone sessions, 1640-62. Typescript transcribed by
Dr. R.E.P. Stuart.
(1969).
7

Folkestone Training College, 1947-1950.
1950.
7,11

Folkestone: visitor's guide.
Folkestone, Earl. n.d.
10

FOX, Elizabeth.
On the Leas: Folkestone, 1939-45.
(1950).
7

FRANKLIN, Kenneth J.
King Charles I and William Harvey. (Reprinted from
Proceedings of Royal Society of Medicine, February, 1961).
7

FRANKLIN, Kenneth J.
William Harvey Englishman, 1578-1657.
MacGibbon. 1961.
3,7

GALER, Henry.
"Cookey": a good old salt, the story of his life and work.
East Folkestone Seamen's Mission. 1886.
7

GARDNER, Leslie J.
Cheriton Baptist Church, Folkestone, Jubilee celebrations,
1901-1951.
(1951).
7

GODWIN, G.N.
Mate's illustrated Folkestone.
Mate. (1900).
7

GREAT BRITAIN: LAWS, etc. (GEO. III).
An Act for altering...an Act...for constructing a pier and
harbour at or near the town of Folkestone...
1818.
7,11

GREAT BRITAIN: LAWS, etc. (GEO. III).
An Act for constructing a pier and harbour at or near the
town of Folkestone.
1807.
7

GREAT BRITAIN: LAWS, etc. (GEO. III).
An Act for paving, repairing and cleansing the highways,
streets, and lanes in the town of Folkestone...
1796.
7

GREAT BRITAIN: LAWS, etc. (GEO. III).
An Act for the more easy and speedy recovery of small debts
within the town and port of Folkestone...
1786.
7,11

GREAT BRITAIN: LAWS, etc. (GEO. III).
An Act for the support and preservation of the Parish Church
of Folkestone and the lower part of the town of Folkestone.
1766.
7

GREAT BRITAIN: LAWS, etc. (GEO. III).
An Act for vesting part of the settled estate of John Baker
Esq., at Folkestone.
1781.
7

GREAT BRITAIN: LAWS, etc. (VIC.).
An Act for confirming certain provisional orders made by the
Board of Trade under the General Pier and Harbour Act, 1861
relating to...Folkestone...
1875.
7

GREAT BRITAIN: LAWS, etc. (VIC.).
An Act for confirming certain provisional orders...
under the Electric Lighting Act, 1882, relating to...
Folkestone, Gravesend...
1883.
9

GREAT BRITAIN: LAWS, etc. (VIC.).
An Act for enclosing Swingfield Minnis, otherwise
Folkestone Common.
1840.
7

GREAT BRITAIN: LAWS, etc. (VIC.).
An Act for granting further powers to the Folkestone
Waterworks Company.
1855.
7

GREAT BRITAIN: LAWS, etc. (VIC.).
An Act for supplying the...Borough of Folkestone with
water.
1848.
7

GREAT BRITAIN: LAWS, etc. (VIC.).
An Act for the construction, maintenance and regulation
of a pier and lift at Folkestone...
1884.
7

GREAT BRITAIN: LAWS, etc. (VIC.).
An Act to amend the existing Acts of the Folkestone
Waterworks Company...(Folkestone Waterworks Acts
Amendment Act, 1864).
1864.
7

GREAT BRITAIN: LAWS, etc. (VIC.).
An Act to authorise the Folkestone Gas and Coke Company
to acquire further lands, to extend their works.
1876.
7

GREAT BRITAIN: LAWS, etc. (VIC.).
An Act to confirm certain provisional orders made by
the Board of Trade under the Electric Lighting Acts,
1882 and 1888 relating to...Folkestone...
1896.
7

GREAT BRITAIN: LAWS, etc. (VIC.).
An Act to confirm certain provisional orders of the
Local Government Board relating to...the Urban
Sanitary District of Folkestone...(Local Government
Board's Provisional Orders Confirmation - Berwick-
upon-Tweed, etc. - Act, 1881).
1881.
7

GREAT BRITAIN: LAWS, etc. (VIC.).
An Act to confirm certain provisional orders of the
Local Government Board relating to...the Urban
Sanitary District of Folkestone...
1887.
7

GREAT BRITAIN: LAWS, etc. (VIC.).
An Act to enable the Folkestone Waterworks Company to
raise further moneys...(Folkestone Waterworks Amendment
Act).
1858.
7

GREAT BRITAIN: LAWS, etc. (VIC.).
An Act to enlarge the powers of the Folkestone Waterworks Company.
1871.
7

GREAT BRITAIN: LAWS, etc. (VIC.).
An Act to extend the limits of the Borough of Folkestone
...(Folkestone Improvement Act).
1855.
7

GREAT BRITAIN: LAWS, etc. (VIC.).
Extracts from the South Eastern Railway Act, 1878 (to
divert a footpath in Folkestone).
1878.
7

GREAT BRITAIN: LAWS, etc. (VIC.).
Folkestone Gas Act.
1865.
7

GREAT BRITAIN: LAWS, etc. (VIC.).
South Eastern Railway Acts, 1893-1900.
n.d.
7

GREAT BRITAIN: LAWS, etc. (EDW. VII).
The Folkestone Corporation Act, 1901.
1901.
7

GREAT BRITAIN: LAWS, etc. (GEO. V).
Folkestone Corporation Act, 1920.
1920.
7

GREAT BRITAIN: LAWS, etc. (GEO. V).
Folkestone Gas Act.
1916.
7

GREAVES, Ralph.
Short histories of Cheltenham, Folkestone, Fontwell Park,
Plumpton....(Race courses of England Series).
Field Sports. 1959.
7

GREEN, E.C.
Some notes on the mosses of the Folkestone district of East
Kent. (Reprinted from The South-Eastern Naturalist and
Antiquary, 1950).
7

Guide to sea angling, Folkestone, Deal, Dover.
Robert McGregor, Angling Association Ltd. 1971.
7

HAINES, George Warden.
Memoirs of the Minter family...
1937.
7

HANNAVY, J.L.
The libraries of Dover and Folkestone.
University Microfilm Ltd. 1968.
7

HARRISON, Eric.
The Folkestone Harbour Branch. (Typescript).
Folkestone, Harrison. 1962.
1,3,4,6,7,8,10,11,12,15

HARRISON, William C.
Dr. William Harvey and the discovery of circulation.
Collier-Macmillan. 1967.
7

HARVEY CHARITY TRUSTEES.
Minutes and accounts, 1674-1817 (and) Harvey Grammar School,
Rendezvous St., notes from title deeds. (Typescript).
(1959).
7

HARVEY CHARITY TRUSTEES.
Sir Eliat Harvey's school foundation, Folkestone: scheme for
the future administration of the foundation and its endowments.
1886.
7

Harvey Tercentenary, 1878, memorial: report of the proceedings
at the public meeting...on September 6th, 1871...
1878.
7

HAWKER, Dennis Gascoyne.
The parish church of St. Mary and St. Eanserythe, Folkestone.
Church Council. (1954).
7

HEYWOOD, ABEL AND SON. Publisher.
A guide to Folkestone ancient and modern.
Heywood. (1886).
7

HEYWOOD, John. Publisher.
Illustrated guide to Folkestone, Hythe and Sandgate.
J. Heywood.
7(1891,1912,1925)
11(1891)

Holbein's visitors' list and court directory for
Folkestone, November 17th, 1886-February 9th, 1887.
n.d.
7

HOLLOWAY, Mark.
William Harvey, 1578-1657.
Tower Publications. 1957.
7

HOWARTH; R.
Folkestone past and present, edited by R. Howarth.
Folkestone, Parsons. n.d.
1,3,7,8,11,12

HUSSEY, Arthur.
Presentments from the parish of Folkestone at the
visitations of the Archdeacons of Canterbury. (MS.).
n.d.
7

Hythe, Sandgate and Folkestone guide...
Hythe, Tiffin. 1816.
7,11

Illustrated handbook to Folkestone and its picturesque
neighbourhood.
Hamilton Adams. n.d.
7(1865) 11(1865) 17(1862)

The Imperial album of Folkestone views.
Newman and Co. n.d.
13

Important sale by auction of the costly and nearly new
appointements of the Officers Mess Quarters of H.M. 6th
Depot Battalion...23rd March, 1870...Messrs Flashman.
(Shorncliff Camp).
Flashman. 1870.
7

JERROLD, Walter.
Folkestone and Dover. (Paintings by G.W. Haselhurst).
Blackie. n.d.
1,6,7,8,11,17

JONES, John. Publisher.
Folkestone and the War.
J. Jones. n.d.
7

JONES, L.R.
The Metropole, Folkestone, the old, the new.
Glanmoor. 1969.
7,11

KEELE, Kenneth D.
William Harvey. (British Men of Science Series).
Nelson. 1965.
7,8

KENT COUNTY COUNCIL - ARCHIVES OFFICE.
Radnor MSS...manorial documents, deeds and papers of the
Barony of Folkestone, 1280-1900.
1955.
7

KENT EDUCATION COMMITTEE.
Eversley College, Folkestone, 1967-68.
1967.
7

KEYNES, Geoffrey.
Bibliography of the writings of Dr. William Harvey, 2nd
edition.
Cambridge University Press. 1953.
7

KEYNES, Geoffrey.
Harvey through John Aubrey's eyes...(The 254 Harveian
Oration...at Royal College of Physicians).
The Lancet. 1958.
7

KEYNES, Geoffrey.
The life of William Harvey.
Oxford University Press. 1966.
7

KEYNES, Geoffrey.
The personality of William Harvey.
Cambridge University Press. 1949.
7

KEYNES, Geoffrey.
The portraiture of William Harvey.
Royal College of Surgeons. 1949.
7

KNAGGS, H. Guard.
A list of macro-lepidoptera occurring in the neighbourhood
of Folkestone.
Folkestone Natural History Society. 1870.
7

KNAGGS, H. Guard.
Variations of butterflies and moths...(Reprinted from
"Folkestone Express").
(J. English). (1895).
7

LANE, GENTRY AND CO. Publishers.
The holiday handbook to Folkestone, Sandgate and district...
Margate, Lane, Gentry and Co. (c.1930?).
7

LARKING, Arthur.
Notes on Folkestone: historical, climatological and
medical...
J. and A. Churchill. 1899.
6,7

LYON, John.
An account of a subsidence of the ground near Folkestone.
In Philosophical Transactions, Vol. LXXVI).
Royal Society. 1786.
7

McDAKIN, S. Gordon.
Geological excursion to the Warren and the Gault Glay.
British Association for the Advancement of Science. 1899.
6,12

McDAKIN, S. Gordon.
Landslip near Folkestone! By which three people lost their
lives...
Association of Natural History Societies of South East
England. 1893.
7

McDOUGAL, C.H.
Folkestone: official holiday guide, (1970), edited by C.H.
McDougal.
Folkestone Corporation Publicity Department. 1969.
11

MACKIE, S.J.
Descriptive and historical account of Folkestone and its
neighbourhood.
J. English.
1(1883)
2(1856,1883,1889)
6(1883)
7(1856)
8(1956)
11(1956,1889)
12(1956,1883)
13(1956,1883)
15(1956)
17(1856)
18(1856)

MACKIE, S.J.
A handbook of Folkestone for visitors. (Many subsequent
editions and from the 6th edition at least, known as "English's
Handbook of Folkestone").
J. English.
7(1856-1895)
12(1856)
17(4th and 12th editions)

MACKIE, S.J.
Outline sketch of the geology of Folkestone...
(Reprinted from The Geologists' Magazine, Nos. 26,27,28,
c.1860).
7

MARSH, Frances.
Romance of old Folkestone.
Fifield. 1906.
6,7,8,11,12

MOLLCY, T. AND CO. Publishers.
Watering places...Folkestone.
T. Molloy and Co. (1863-4).
17

(MORLAND, G.).
The French at Folkestone.
Chelsea, G. Sheild, Printer. 1860?
7

MORLEY, A.M.
Lepidoptera of Folkestone. (Reprinted from The
Proceedings of the South London Entomological and
Natural History Society for 1946-7).
1947.
7

MORLEY, A.M.
List of butterflies and moths (Macro-Lepidoptera)
occurring in the neighbourhood of Folkestone.
Folkestone Natural History Society. 1931.
7

NATIONAL UNION OF TEACHERS.
Folkestone Conference souvenir, 1932.
University of London. 1932.
1,6,7

NEWPORT, W.O.
Concise register of houses to be let and sold
(Folkestone).
1899.
17

"OLD FOLKSTONER", pseud. (ENGLISH, John).
Reminiscences of old Folkestone smugglers and smuggling
days.
F. Graham. 1883 etc.
1,3,4,6,7,10,11,12,17,19

O'NEIL, B.H. St. John.
North Street, Folkestone, Kent.
Antiquaries Journal. 1949.
7,11

OSMAN, C.W.
Landslips of Folkestone Warren...In Proceedings of the
Geologists' Association, Vol. XXVIII, Pt. 2, 1917.
Edward Stanford. 1917.
7

OUR LADY HELP OF CHRISTIANS.
Golden Jubilee of the Church of Our Lady Help of
Christians and of St. Aloysius, Folkestone.
(1939).
7

PARKINSON, James.
Remarks on the fossils...Dover...Folkestone.
W. Phillips. 1819.
6

Parish church of St. Mary and St. Eanswythe, Folkestone.
Folkestone, Kentfield. 1956.
7,11

The parish church of St. Peter on East Cliffe.
1964.
8

(PARKS, W.A.).
The story of a school, Dover Road - 1835-1958: being
No. I, Vol. 3 of "Endeavour".
1958.
7

PARLIAMENTARY PAPERS.
Copy of any (sic) report...to the...Admiralty, on the state
of Folkestone Harbour. (Extract from Parliamentary Papers,
1837-38, Vol. 45).
1838.
7

PARSONS, F.A.
On some Saxon bones from Folkestone. (Reprinted from the
Journal of the Royal Anthropological Institute, Vol. XLI,
1911).
7

Particulars...of sale of...freehold building...land...being
the remaining portions of the Catchpool Estate...comprising
Coolinge Farmhouse, buildings and land...land near Danton's
Farm, the Cheriton brick and tile works...land adjoining the
...Folkestone Waterworks...land and cottages at Broadmead
...(to) be sold by auction...on...25...July, 1901.
Daniel Watney and Sons. 1901.
7

Particulars, plan and certain views of the...freehold
residential, sporting and country seat, known as "Acrise
Place", Folkestone.
Temple Barton and Co. (c.1903).
7

PASCOE, Charles Eyre.
Folkestone of today: an illustrated book for visitors,
season 1889...illustrated by H. Tringham.
Hamilton, Adams and Co. 1889.
7

Pavilionstone: souvenir to commemorate the placing of a
plaque by the Dickens Fellowship on 3 Albion Villas,
Folkestone.
Dickens Fellowship. 1902 and 1963.
3,7

Penfold House, Folkestone County School - hymns with an
index of tunes.
Harrap. n.d.
7

PITT-RIVERS, Augustus H.L.F.
Excavations at Caesar's Camp, Folkestone, conducted in June
and July, 1878. (From The Archaeologia, Vol. XVII).
Society of Antiquaries of London. 1882.
1,7

PLEYDELL-BOUVERIE, Helen.
From a great-grandmother's armchair. (A Folkestone family).
Marshall. (1927?).
7

POWELL, R.C.
History of the Radnor Lodge No. 2,587 (Folkestone), 1895-1955.
Radnor Lodge. (1956).
7

PRICE, F.G. Hilton.
On the lower greensand and gault of Folkestone. In
Proceedings of the Geologists' Association, 1874-5.
7

Property register, Folkestone...1894.
Eiloart and Temple. 1894.
7

Report on the proposed municipal boundary of the Borough of
Folkestone.
Municipal Corporation Commissioners. 1835?
11

RIGDEN, T. Publisher.
True history of...the fiery serpent.
T. Rigden. n.d.
17

ROBERTS, Charles J.
The Warren and its fossils...
F.J. Parsons. (1906).
7

ROBERTSON, William Archibald Scott.
Mediaeval Folkestone. (Reprinted from Archaeologia Cantiana,
Vol. 10).
Mitchell and Hughes. 1876.
8

ROYAL INSTITUTE OF BRITISH ARCHITECTS.
Handbook of the British Architects' Conference,
Canterbury and Folkestone, 10th-13th June, 1953.
W. Heffer. 1953.
3

ROYAL INSTITUTE OF PUBLIC HEALTH.
Guide to Folkestone, Sandgate, Hythe and neighbourhood.
(Royal Institute of Public Health Congress at
Folkestone, 1904).
J. English. 1904.
7

Russell's Folkestone guide and directory.
Russell. 1885.
7

RUTT, F.
Dwellers in our rock pools...
Folkestone, Arthur Stace and Sons. (192-).

SAINSBURY, Frederick G.
Complete guide to Folkestone and neighbourhood. (Four
separate guides bound together, 1880, 1881, 1882, 1883).
Maidstone, W. Cocks and Co.
7

St. Eanswythe of Folkestone.
n.d.
13

ST. MARY AND ST. EANSWYTHE.
Statement of the works and funds, 1901-1914, 1916.
1901-1914, 1916.
7

Sale catalogue of "The Manor House, The Leas, Folkestone,
Hampton and Sons, 5th May, 1914...by direction of the
Rt. Hon. The Earl of Radnor.
Hampton and Sons. 1914.
7

Sandgate, Hythe and Folkestone guide.
Purday. 1823.
11

SHANASY, M.J.
Thorpe and Co's illustrated guide to Folkestone...
Printed by W. and E. Thorpe and Co. c.1897.
7

SHERWOOD, John.
Monthly register of...houses for sale, hire...in
Folkestone.
1889.
17

A short guide to Folkestone Parish Church (St. Mary and
St. Eanswythe).
Norwich, Jarrold. 1927.
11

A short guide to Folkestone Parish Church (St. Mary and
St. Eanswythe).
Skeffington. n.d.
7,10

Sixty-four views of Folkestone and neighbourhood.
Newman and Co. c.1875.
13

SOUTH EASTERN AND CHATHAM RAILWAY.
Completion of the new pier and harbour works at
Folkestone. (Souvenir handbook issued at the laying of
the final stone by the French Ambassador).
South Eastern and Chatham Railway. 1904.
7

SOUTH EASTERN RAILWAY.
Illustrated tourist's guide: views and description
of...Folkestone, Hythe...price, one penny (pages
numbered 297-328 and unnumbered advertisements).
Morton and Co. (c.1871).
7

STACE, R. AND SON. Publishers.
A guide to Sandgate, Shorncliffe, Folkestone, Hythe
and the neighbourhood, with historical, geological and
botanical notes.
R. Stace and Son. c.1860.
7

STACE, R. AND SON. Publishers.
An illustrated guide to Sandgate, Folkestone, Hythe and the
neighbourhood, with historical, typographical (sic),
geological and botanical notices, with six illustrations,
and a map of the walks and rides.
R. Stace and Son. c.1865.
7

STACE, R. AND SON. Publishers.
Sandgate and Shorncliffe illustrated almanack and guide.
R. Stace and Son.
7(1878,1882,1886)

STACE, R. AND SON. Publishers.
Sandgate and Shorncliffe illustrated guide for the year
1873...
R. Stace and Son. 187-?
7

STACE, R. AND SON. Publishers.
Stace's Sandgate, Hythe and Shorncliffe illustrated
historic almanack for 1871 and 1872.
R. Stace and Son. 1871.
7

STOCK, H. Publisher.
Illustrated handbook to Folkestone...description of the
South Eastern Railway...
Folkestone, H. Stock. 1851.
17

STOCK, H. Publisher.
The new illustrated handbook to Folkestone and its
picturesque neighbourhood...
Folkestone, H. Stock. 1848.
1,7,11

SUMNER, D. Publisher.
Sumner's 3d illustrated guide to Folkestone and
neighbourhood, containing map.
Folkestone, D. Sumner. (1889).
7,17

SWAN, Alexander.
Notes on the past and present condition of Folkestone
Harbour.
c.1848.
15

The Temple Lodge No. 558 Centenary Festival, 29th January,
1949 (Folkestone).
Temple Lodge. 1949.
7

Thirty views of Folkestone and neighbourhood.
W. Simpson. n.d.
10,12

THOMPSON, G.M.
Notes on the street names of St. Saviours Parish, Folkestone,
from information supplied by G.M. Cooper. (Extracts from
Parish Magazine, 1968).
7

TOKE, N.E.
The old house behind the Fishmarket, Folkestone. (Reprinted
from Archaeologia Cantiana, Vol. 47).
Ashford, Headley. 1935.
11

THE TONTINE STREET AND HARBOUR TRADER'S ASSOCIATION.
Programme and guide.
Folkestone, F.J. Parsons Ltd. 1923.
3

ULLYETT, H.
Simpson's handbook to Folkestone: giving a description and
history of the ancient and modern portions of the town,
c.1870, c.1872 and c.1887.
W. Simpson.
7

W., H.E.
The ancient buildings of Folkestone and district, 1st series.
Printed by Parsons. 1921.
6

WALTON, John W.
Folkestone and the country around...edited by J.W. Walton.
Folkestone, Parsons. 1925.
1,6,7,8,11,12

WALTON, Marjorie.
Fifteen walks around Folkestone. (Duplicated typescript).
Folkestone, Cross's. (1965).
7

WEBSTER, V.
Methodist Church, Grace Hill, Folkestone. A survey of
the hundred years, 1866-1966.
1966.
7

WILSON, W. Publisher.
Guide to Sandgate, Shorncliffe and Hythe.
Sandgate, W. Wilson. 1889.
7,11

WILSON, W. Publisher.
Wilson's guide to Sandgate and Shorncliffe.
Sandgate, W. Wilson. (1872).
7

WILSON, W. Publisher.
Wilson's illustrated almanack and guide to Sandgate,
Shorncliffe and Hythe, with an account of the walks
and drives of the neighbourhood.
Sandgate, W. Wilson. 1894.
7

WILSON, W. Publisher.
Wilson's Sandgate and Shorncliffe almanack, trades
advertiser and yearbook of useful knowledge for 1871,
contains a short history of Sandgate, Shorncliffe and
the neighbourhood.
Sandgate, W. Wilson. 1871.
7

WINBOLT, Samuel Edward.
Roman Folkestone.
Methuen. 1925.
1,2,4,5,6,7,8,11,12,13,14,15,16,17,18,20,21

WINBOLT, Samuel Edward.
Roman site, East Cliff, Folkestone.
English. 1924 etc.
1,2,3,6,7,11,12,17

"WISE MAN OF THE EAST", pseud.
The Folkestone fiery serpent, together with the
humours of the Dover Mayor, being an ancient ballard
full of mystery and pleasant concert. (1st and 4th
editions).
Dover, T. Rigden.
1(1839)
6(1839)
7(1839,1844,1852,1861)
17(1852)

"WISE MAN OF THE EAST", pseud.
The Folkestone fiery serpent, together with the humours
of the Dover Mayor...5th edition.
Folkestone, W. Simpson. (187-?).
7,10

WOOD, Alan Marshall Muir.
Folkestone Warren landslips: investigations, 1948-50
and Viner-Brady, Noel Edmund - Folkestone Warren landslips, remedial measures, 1948-54.
Institute of Civil Engineers. 1955.
7

WOODWARD, Matthew.
The past and present of the parish church of Folkestone..
Skeffington. 1892 etc.
1,3,4,6,7,8,11,12,17,18

WRIGHT, H. Ray.
General Moore at Shorncliffe.
Sandgate, Sandgate Society. 1965.
4,7,11

FOORD

COOPER, G.H.
Foord Church (1879-1949): a retrospect.
(1949).
7,12

DOWKER, George.
Foord Palace, Reculver, Herne Bay and Herne.
British Association. 1899.
7

FOORD Cont'd

HUSSEY, Arthur.
Foord Manor House and lands in 1647...
Mitchell and Hughes. 1903.
12,17

FOOTPATHS AND COMMONS

BRADDOCK, Joseph.
Footpaths of the Kent- Sussex border.
Chaterson. 1947.
1,3,4,5,6,8,9,11,12,15,18,19,20

CHISLEHURST AND ST. PAUL'S CRAY COMMONS CONSERVATORS.
Chislehurst and St. Paul's Cray commons.
Chislehurst and St. Paul's Cray Commons Conservators. 1970.
3,4,11

COMMONS AND FOOTPATHS PRESERVATION SOCIETY - KENT AND
SURREY COMMITTEE.
Annual Reports.
Commons and Footpaths Preservation Society - Kent and
Surrey Committee.
2(1888-1892, 1899-1900)
9(1898-99, 1904-05)
17(1894,1896-1912)

EVERSLEY, Lord.
Commons, forests and footpaths.
London, Cassell and Co. 1910.
5,12

GRAVESEND SOCIETY AND GRAVESEND AND ROCHESTER DISTRICT
FOOTPATHS COMMITTEE.
Schedules...showing the footpaths in the area.
Gravesend Society and Gravesend and Rochester District
Footpaths Committee. 1939.
9

GREAT BRITAIN: LAWS, etc. (ELIZ. II).
National parks and access to the countryside Act, Pt. IV.
Survey of public rights of way...
1949.
8

MILES, Walker.
Along the Medway...
R.E. Taylor. 1897.
1,11

MILES, Walker.
"Down by the Darent" and series of field path rambles from
Dartford to Westerham.
R.E. Taylor. 1896.
11

MILES, Walker.
Field path rambles (Canterbury and Kent coast series).
R.E. Taylor. 1904.
1,5,7,11,14,17,18

MILES, Walker.
Field path rambles...over the Kentish hills.
Larby. 1906.
11,18

MILES, Walker.
Field path rambles through the Kentish hop-lands.
R.E. Taylor. 1901.
2,11,18

MILES, Walker.
Field path rambles (22nd series) comprising **routes** between
Ramsgate and Margate.
R.E. Taylor. 1901.
3

MILES, Walker.
Field path rambles around Maidstone, Wateringbury etc.
R.E. Taylor. 1900.
2,11,17,18

MILES, Walker.
Field path rambles, comprising **routes** between Margate
and Herne Bay and to Birchington, Reculver...Sarre etc.
R.E. Taylor. 1902.
13

MILES, Walker.
Field path rambles (23rd series) comprising routes between
Ramsgate and Margate.
R.E. Taylor. 1902.
3

MILES, Walker.
Field path rambles (24th series) comprising routes
between Ramsgate and Margate.
R.E. Taylor. 1903.
3

MILES, Walker.
Field path rambles in West Kent: a practical handbook
for pedestrians.
R.E. Taylor. 1893.
2,3(1st series)
1,2,5,11,17,18,19(2nd **and 4th** series)
1,5,11,17,18,19(3rd series)

MILES, Walker.
Field path rambles - routes round West Malling and
over the Kentish hills.
R.E. Taylor. 1906.
11

MILES, Walker.
Field path rambles - Whitstable, Herne Bay, Canterbury.
R.E. Taylor. 1903.
2

"PATHFINDER", pseud.
Wayfaring round London. (See under Bromley).
Warne. 1915.
2,18

WRIGHT, Christopher John.
A guide to the Pilgrims' Way and North Downs Way.
Constable. 1971.
2,3,4,5,7,8,9,21

FOOTS CRAY

BAGENAL, Nicholas Beauchamp.
The French fruit garden at Foots Cray Place.
Royal Horticultural Society. 1947.
11

JOHNSTONE, Rupert.
Church of All Saints, Foots Cray.
Sidcup, D.J. Sharp. 1950.
1,11

The King against the inhabitants of the County of Kent.
n.d.
12

FORDCOMBE

THOMAS, D.F.
Fordcombe School. (Tonbridge School, Local History
Researches).
1961.
11

FORDWICH

DERHAM, Walter.
The Fordwich stone and its legend.
Harrison. 1918.
3,11

EVANS, Sebastian.
The penny guide to the ancient city of Canterbury and
its historic port-Fordwich, 1904,1905,1906,1907,1908,
1909, 10th edition n.d., 1913.
Canterbury, Cross and Jackman.
3,7,11(1907)

FORDWICH AND GROVE FERRY ANGLING CLUB.
Rules, regulations and list of members.
1899.
17

JACQUES , Edward Tyrrell.
The pilgrim from Chicago. (Chapters 3-7 cover Reculver,
Fordwich and Canterbury).
Longmans and Green. 1913.
3

Parish church of Fordwich, St. Mary the Virgin.
Canterbury, Elvy. 193-?
3,11

W., D.
Fordwich Church, St. Mary the Virgin.
1960
1,4,8,11,12

FORDWICH Cont'd

W., J.A. (WILLMORE, J.A.).
Fordwich, the ancient port of Canterbury.
Canterbury, Cross and Jackman.
1(1910).
2(1946)
3(1915)
7(1912,1915,1946)
8(1946)
11(1946)
13(1915)
14(1915)
17(1915)

WOODRUFF, Charles Everleigh.
A history of the town and port of Fordwich...
Canterbury, Cross and Jackman. 1895.
1,3,4,5,6,7,8,11,12,14,15,17

FOREST HILL

BURT, R.K. Publisher.
Sydenham and Forest Hill directory, 1862.
Sydenham, R.K. Burt. 1862.
2

St. James' Methodist Church...Forest Hill...Jubilee souvenir,
1884-1934.
(Pamphlet). 1934.
18

WERNHAM, R.P.
One hundred years: the story of Christ Church, Forest Hill.
(Pamphlet).. 1954.
18

FORESTRY

PARNALL, D.L.
A history of Kentish woodlands. (Copy of original
photostat of article made on 26th July, 1965).
n.d.
3

FRINDSBURY

ARNOLD, A.A.
On Roman remains found at Frindsbury - plates. (Reprinted
from Archaeologia Cantiana, Vol. 18, 1889).
17

ARNOLD, A.A.
Quarry House on Frindsbury Hill.
Mitchell and Hughes. 1887.
12,17

ARNOLD, A.A.
Roman remains and Celt found near Quarry House, Frindsbury -
plates. (Reprinted from Archaeologia Cantiana, Vol. 17,
1887).
17

ORME, William C.
Frindsbury and its parish church.
1959.
15

FRITTENDEN

Little Hungerford Farm etc. - Sale catalogue.
Printed by West. 1866.
12

GAVELKIND

KENT LAW SOCIETY.
An address to the freeholders of the County of Kent on the
subject of gavelkind.
Maidstone, Hall and Son. 1936 etc.
5(1836) 7(1907) 11,17

ROBINSON, Thomas.
The common law of Kent: or, the customs of gavelkind, with
an appendix concerning Borough-English.
Printed by R. and B. Nutt and F. Gosling for F. Cogan. 1741.
5,6,7,8,14

ROBINSON, Thomas.
The common law of Kent: or, the customs of gavelkind,
with an appendix concerning Borough-English, 2nd edition.
Printed for P. Uriel. 1788.
4,6,11

ROBINSON, Thomas.
The common law of Kent: or, the customs of gavelkind,
with an appendix concerning Borough-English, 3rd
edition with notes (etc.).
London, Printed for Butterworth by Strahan. 1822.
1,4,6,15,20

ROBINSON, Thomas.
The common law of Kent: or, the customs of gavelkind.
Ashford, Igglesden. 1858.
3,4,6,12,14,15,17

ROBINSON, Thomas.
Robinson on gavelkind, 5th edition by Charles I. Elton
and Herbert J.H. Mackay.
Butterworth. 1897.
12

SANDYS, Charles.
Consuetudines Kanciae: a history of gavelkind and other
remarkable customs in the County of Kent.
London, John Russell Smith. 1851.
1,2,4,5,6,7,8,11,12,13,14,15,17,21

SOMNER, William.
A treatise of gavelkind, both name and thing...
1660.
4,6,8,11,15

SOMNER, William.
A treatise of gavelkind...2nd edition.
1776.
1,3(1726) 11,12,17(1726)

TAYLOR, Silas.
The history of gavelkind with the etymology thereof.
1663.
1,6,11,12,17

GENEALOGICAL RECORDS

Abstract of the answer and returns...II Geo. IV...
parish register abstract, 1831.
H.M.S.O. 1833.
3

Administrations in the Prerogative Court of Canterbury,
1559-1571, edited by R.M. Glencross.
Pollard. 1912.
12

Allegations for marriage licences issued by the Faculty
Office of the Archbishop of Canterbury, 1543-1886.
Harleian Society. 1886-1892.
1660-1694 edited by G.J. Armytage (4 vols.).
2,5,11,12
1543-1886 edited by G.J. Armytage and J.L. Chester.
11,12

Amherst (family tree).
n.d.
12

ASHFORD, Frederick.
The monuments and gravestones in the churches and
chapels of Deptford, Kent (MSS.)
n.d.
18

ATWATER, Francis.
Atwater: history and genealogy, compiled by F.
Atwater.
1901.
11

Autographs of Justices of the Peace for the County of
Kent, 1805-1880, with woodcuts of the Royal Arms from
1790 to 1880. (Scrapbook).
n.d.
1

Bathurst pedigree and wills. (From " Miscellanea
Geneologica et Heraldica").
1917.
11

BAZELY, Mrs. L.
Pedigree of the family of Bazely of Dover, compiled by
Mrs. L. Bazely.
1909.
11

BEAKESBOURNE - ST. PETER'S CHURCH.
The parish register of St. Peter's, Beakesbourne, Kent,
1558-1812, transcribed by Rev. C.H. Wilkie.
Canterbury, Cross and Jackman. 1896.
3,11,12

BERRY, William.
Pedigrees of the families in the County of Kent.
Sherwood, Gilbert and Piper. 1830.
1,3,4,5,7,11,12,15,16,17,19

BIRCHINGTON- ALL SAINTS' CHURCH.
The parish registers, transcribed by F.A. Crisp.
Privately Printed by Crisp. 1899.
11,13,14

BLOOM, J. Harvey.
Wayman wills and administrations presented in the Prerogative
Court of Canterbury, 1383-1821.
Wallace Gandy. 1922.
3,4,6,11,12

BOUGHTON-UNDER-BLEAN - ST. PETER AND ST. PAUL'S CHURCH.
The registers of Boughton-under-Blean...
    Baptisms   1558-1624
    Marriages 1558-1626
    Burials   1558-1625
Edited by J.A. Boodle.
Parish Register Society. 1903.
3,11

BOWLES, William Henry.
Record of the Bowles family.
1918.
11

BRADE-BIRKS, Stanley Graham.
Table to show the descent of certain properties to Thomas
Knight of Godmersham, Esquire, and his relationship to the
Austen family.
Godmersham, S.G. Brade-Birks. 2nd revised impression, 1941.
3

BRIDGES, Sir. Brook William.
Minutes of evidence given...Sir William Bridges claiming as
of right to be Baron Fitzwalter.
1842.
11

BRIDGMAN, John.
An historical and topographical sketch of Knole in Kent with
a brief genealogy of the Sackville family.
Knole, Lindsell. 1817.
1,2,3,4,6,8,11,14,15,18,19

BRIGG, William.
Genealogical abstracts of wills passed in the Prerogative
Court of Canterbury, edited by W. Brigg.
W. Brigg. 1894-1914.
12

BRIGG, William.
Pedigree of the family of Yardley of Chatham, compiled by
W. Brigg.
Mitchell and Hughes. 1891.
11

BROMLEY, Francis E.
Churchwardens' accounts. (Typescript - some Kentish
examples).
(19--).
3

BROMLEY, Francis E.
Heraldry. (MS. notes of Kentish families and their coats of
arms).
n.d.
3

BROMLEY, Francis E.
Parish registers. (Typescript - some Kent examples).
(19--).
3

BUCKLAND, Walter E.
Parish registers and records in the Diocese of Rochester.
Kent Archaeological Society. 1912.
1,2,3,4,5,7,11,12,15,16,17,18,19

BURKE, Arthur Meredyth.
Key to the ancient parish registers of England and
Wales.
Sackville Press. 1908.
3

C., G.E.
Some notice of various families of the name of Marsh.
Pollard. 1900.
12

Calendar of marriage licences...1632-1714, edited by
G. Cokayne and E.A. Fry.
British Record Society. 1905.
11

Calendar of wills...at Canterbury. Parts 1-4, edited by
H.R. Plomer.
1916-19.
17

CANTERBURY - CATHEDRAL CHURCH OF CHRIST.
Register booke, christenings, marriages and burialls...
edited by R. Hovenden.
Harleian Society. 1878.
1,3,4,11,12,17,19

CANTERBURY - ST. ALPHEGE'S CHURCH.
Regyster booke of chrystenynges, maryages and buryalls
of the parish of St. Alphege in the Cittye of Canterburye
1558-1800, edited by J.M. Cowper.
Canterbury, Cross and Jackman. 1889.
3,8,11,12,17,19

CANTERBURY - ST. DUNSTAN'S CHURCH.
Register book of christenings, marriages and burialls,
1559-1800, edited by J.M. Cowper.
Canterbury, Cross and Jackman. 1887.
1,3,11,12,19

CANTERBURY - ST. GEORGE THE MARTYR'S CHURCH.
The register booke of the parish of St. George the
Martyr...Canterburie of christenings, marriages and
burials, 1538-1800, edited by J.M. Cowper.
Canterbury, Cross and Jackman. n.d.
3,11

CANTERBURY - ST. MARY MAGDELENE'S CHURCH.
The names of them that were crystened, marryed and
buryed in the parish of Saynt Mary Magdelene in
Canterbury, 1559-1800, edited by J.M. Cowper.
Canterbury, Cross and Jackman. 1890.
1,3,11,12,17,19

CANTERBURY - ST. MILDRED'S CHURCH.
St. Mildred's, Canterbury: marriages, 1640-1658,
transcribed by H.R. Plomer. (Reprinted from
"Miscellanea Genealogica et Heraldica", June, 1919).
3

CANTERBURY - CHURCH OF ST. PAULE-WITHOUT-THE-WALLS.
The register book of christenings, marriages (sic)
and burialls in the parish of St. Paule-without-the
walles of the City of Canterbury, 1562-1800, edited
by J.M. Cowper.
Canterbury, Cross and Jackman. 1893.
3,11,12,19

CANTERBURY - ST. PETER'S CHURCH.
A booke of regester of the parish of St. Peter in
Canterbury...1560-1800, edited by J.M. Cowper.
Canterbury, Cross and Jackman. 1888.
3,11,12,17,19

CANTERBURY - THE WALLON CHURCH.
The registers of the Wallon, or Strangers' Church in
Canterbury, edited by Robert Hovenden (3 vols.).
London, Huguenot Society, 1891-8 and Kraus Reprint, 1969.
1(Vol. 1 only) 11,17

CHISLET - ST. MARY'S CHURCH.
The register of all the christenings, marriages and
burials in the parish of St. Mary, Chislet...from...
1538 to 1707, edited by R. Hovenden.
Mitchell and Hughes. 1887.
4,11,12,17(MSS. copy in Latin)

CLARKE, A.W. Hughes.
Kentish wills, edited by A.W.H. Clarke.
Canterbury, Mitchell and Hughes. 1929.
1,11,14,15

COOKE, Robert.
The pedigree of Sir Philip Sidney, compiled by R. Cooke.
Privately Printed. 1869.
1

Copies of wills and other orders in Chancery relating to
William Hatcliffe's charity for the benefit of the poor of
Greenwich, Lee and Lewisham, Kent.
Henry Richardson. 185-?
17

Copy of the inscriptions upon the vaults and tablets erected
to the memory of the Ord family in Bexley Parish Church, Kent.
n.d.
1

COUCHMAN, Conrad.
Couchman: some notes and observations on the antiquity and
origin of the above name.
Coulsden, Surrey, C. Couchman. (1968).
4,9,11

County of Kent and many of its family records.
1896.
1,5,11,12,15,18

COWPER, Joseph Meadows.
Canterbury marriage licences, 6 vols., 1568-1750, compiled by
J.M. Cowper.
Canterbury, Cross and Jackman. 1892-1906.
1(Vol. 1 only) 2(Vol. 2 only) 3,7,11,12,19

CRISP, Frederick Arthur.
Fragmenta genalogica, Vol. 4.   (No. 43 of 50 copies).
Privately Printed. 1899.
13,14

CRISP, Frederick Arthur.
List of parish registers and other genealogical works.
Privately Printed by F.A. Crisp. 1908.
3

CRISP, Frederick Arthur.
Visitation of England and Wales, Vol. 15.
Privately Printed by F.A. Crisp. 1908.
3

CRONK, Anthony.
An uncommon name: a genealogical account of the Cronk
family of West Kent.
West Malling, Privately Published. 1953.
1,11,16

CRUDEN, Robert D.
The Cruden family tree - children and grandchildren of
William Cruden (Gravesend) 1733-1809.
n.d.
9

DARTFORD - INDEPENDENT CHAPEL.
A register of births and baptisms, 1797-1837.   (Photocopy).
London, W. Hardcastle. n.d.
5

DARTFORD - WATERSIDE METHODIST CHAPEL.
Register of births and of baptisms with water, 1811-1837.
(Photocopy).
Methodist Register Office. 1811-1837.
5

DARTFORD - ZION CHAPEL.
Register of baptisms, 1820-33.
Williams. n.d.
5

DOVER - THE FRENCH CHURCH.
Registers, 5th May, 1646-15th November,1726, transcribed by
F.A. Crisp.
Privately Printed. 1888.
7,11,12

DUNCAN, LELAND LEWIS.
A calendar of wills...proved at the Prerogative Court at
Canterbury between 1384 and 1559, edited by L.L. Duncan.
Lewisham Antiquarian Society. 1890.
2,3,5,11,12,17,18

DUNCAN, Leland Lewis.
Extracts from some lost Kentish registers...Pamphlet
Reprinted from Archaeologia Cantiana, 1915, edited by
L.L. Duncan.
18

DUNCAN, Leland Lewis.
Index of wills proved in the Rochester Consistory Court
between 1440-1561, edited by L.L. Duncan.
Kent Archaeological Society - Records Branch. 1924.
2,5,10,11,17

DUNCAN, Leland Lewis.
Testamenta Cantiana: extracts from the wills...proved
in the Prerogative Court of Canterbury, book
"Mellershe",1560.
1894.
18

DUNCAN, Leland Lewis.
Testamenta Cantiana: a series of extracts from 15th
and 16th century wills...
Mitchell, Hughes and Clarke. 1906.
2,3,4,5,6,7,12,17,18,19

DUNCAN, Leland Lewis.
The will of Cardinal Bourgchier, Archbishop of
Canterbury, 1486.   (Pamphlet reprinted from Archaeologia
Cantiana, 1900), edited by L.L. Duncan.
18

DUNCAN, Leland Lewis.
The will of William Courtenay, Archbishop of Canterbury,
1396.   (Pamphlet Reprinted from Archaeologia Cantiana,
1898), edited by L.L. Duncan.
18

DUNLOP, J. Renton.
Pedigrees of the families of Averenches and Crevequer...
Mitchell, Hughes and Clarke. 1927.
11

DUNLOP, J. Renton.
Pedigree of the family of Crioll or Kyriell...
Mitchell, Hughes and Clarke. 1927.
11

DWELLY, Edward.
Parish records, Vol. 3: Kent.
1914.
11,15

EDENBRIDGE - ST. PETER AND ST. PAUL'S CHURCH.
Extracts from the parish registers of Edenbridge,
edited by G. Leveson-Gower.
Mitchell and Hughes. 1895.
11

ELMSTONE - ALL SAINTS' CHURCH.
The parish registers, 1552-1812, transcribed by Rev.
Christopher Hales Wilkie.
Canterbury, Cross and Jackman. 1891.
3,12

FARNBOROUGH - ST. GILES' CHURCH.
The parish registers of Farnborough...Kent from 1538 to
1812, transcribed by H. Wilson.
Henry Wilson. 1904.
2,7,12

Faversham: extracts from wills and other documents
containing benefactions to the town of Faversham.
Faversham, Ratcliffe. 1844.
8,11,14

Fergusson family: genealogical memoranda relating to
the families of Fergusson and Colyer-Fergusson.
Privately Printed. 1897.
11

FOLKESTONE - MILL BAY BAPTIST MEETING HOUSE.
Register of births, 1786-1836.   (Photocopy).
Public Records Office. 1840.
7

FOLKESTONE - ST. MARY AND ST. EANSWYTHE CHURCH.
(Typescript) Churchwardens' accounts, 1487-1590. (7)
Parish registers, transcribed by Dr. E. Pole-Stuart. (7)
Baptisms, Vol. 1, May, 1635-December, 1775. (7)
Baptisms, Vol. 2, 1776-1840. (7)
Burials, 1635-1840. (7)
Marriages, June, 1635-December, 1840. (7)

FOLKESTONE - ZION CHAPEL.
Register of births and baptisms, 1779-1836. (Photocopy).
Public Records Office. 1837.
7

FRANKLYN, Charles A.H.
Short genealogical and heraldic history of the families
of Frankelyn...
Beck. 1932.
11

FRENCH, A.D. Weld.
County records of the surnames of Francus, Franceis, French,
in England, A.D. 1100-1350.
Boston, Privately Printed. 1896.
3

GENERAL REGISTER OFFICE.
List of non-parochial registers and records in the custody
of the Registrar-General. (Kent section only). (Photocopy).
H.M.S.O. 1859.
7

GILLINGHAM - ST. MARY MAGDALENE'S CHURCH.
Parish registers, 1558-1753. Baptisms and burials, 1783-1812
(microfilm).
n.d.
8

GOODHART, Charles E.
Genealogical tree of a section of the Goodhart family...
n.d.
2,11

GREEN, Everard.
Pedigree of James and Grevis-James of Ightham Court, County
of Kent, by E. Green and T.C. Fergusson.
Mitchell, Hughes and Clarke. 1912.
11

GREENSTREET, James.
The "Dering" roll of arms, edited by J. Greenstreet and
Charles Russell. From "The Reliquary", Vol. XVI, 1876.
11

GREENSTREET, James.
Early Kentish wills.
Mitchell and Hughes. 1877.
11

GREENSTREET, James.
Wills and other records relating to the family of Finch,
compiled by J. Greenstreet. (Reprinted from Archaeologia
Cantiana, Vol. XIII, 1875).
3,17

GREENSTREET, James.
Wills and other records relating to the family of Hodsoll.
Mitchell and Hughes. 1881.
11,17

GREENWICH - ST. ALPHEGE'S CHURCH.
The Greenwich parish registers, 1615-1636-7.
Greenwich and Lewisham Antiquarian Society. 1920.
1,11,17

HARBLEDOWN - ST. MICHAEL'S CHURCH.
The christnynges, weddinges and burynges in the parish of
Harballdowne, 1557-1800, edited by J.M. Cowper.
Canterbury, Cross and Jackman. 1907.
3,11,12

HARRIS, Edwin.
Quaint Kentish epitaphs and signs.
Chatham, Harris. 1899.
5,8

HARVEY, William J.
Genealogy of the family of Harvey, of Folkestone...compiled
by W.J. Harvey.
Mitchell and Hughes. 1889.
7

HASLEWOOD, Rev. Francis.
Genealogical memoranda relating to the family of Dearing of
Surrenden-Dearing...Pluckley, edited by F. Haslewood.
Mitchell and Hughes. 1876.
3,11,12

HASLEWOOD, Rev. Francis.
The genealogy of the family of Haslewood.
London, Privately Printed by Mitchell and Hughes. 1881.
3

HIGH HALDEN - ST. MARY'S CHURCH.
Extracts from registers and records...1322-1899.
Privately Printed. 1900.
11

HILL, R.H. Ernest.
Little Mote, Eynsford, with a pedigree of the Sybill
family. In Archaeologia Cantiana, Vol. 26, Vol. 28,
1903,1904,1906.
5(1903) 17

Hodsoll of Loose, County of Kent (pedigree).
n.d.
12

HOLWORTHY, Richard.
New wills...in the Prerogative Court of Canterbury,
edited by R. Holworthy.
Bernau. n.d.
11

HOVENDEN, Robert.
Catalogue of the...library of the late Robert Hovenden.
1900.
11

HOVENDEN, Robert.
(Pedigree of the family of Hovenden)...England,
shewing the descendants in England and U.S.A...compiled
by R. Hovenden.
Privately Printed. 1908.
3,11

HOWARD, Joseph Jackson.
Some pedigrees from the visitation of Kent, 1663-68,
edited by J.J. Howard and R. Hovenden.
Mitchell and Hughes. 1887.
1,2(with extra notes) 3,5,6,11,12,17

HUGHES, W.E.
Register of the Marshams of Kent, by W.E. Hughes and
G.W. Miller.
n.d.
16

HUSSEY, Arthur.
Ash wills - Parts 2 and 3 (only). (Reprinted from
Archaeologia Cantiana, Vols. 36,37, 1923-34).
4

HUSSEY, Arthur.
Ashford wills...1461-1558...from official records...
compiled by A. Hussey.
Ashford, Headley. 1938.
3,5,6,7,10,11,12,13,15

HUSSEY, Arthur.
Eastry wills - 3 parts. (Reprinted from Archaeologia
Cantiana, Vols. 38,39,40, 1926-(30?).
4,10,17

HUSSEY, Arthur.
Folkestone wills: being abstracts of the wills of
residents...A.D. 1461-1558 with index by Dr. E. Pole-
Stuart.
MS. n.d.
7

HUSSEY, Arthur.
Further notes from Kentish wills...(Reprinted from
Archaeologia Cantiana, Vol. 31, 1914).
4

HUSSEY, Arthur.
Herne: abstracts of the wills of parishioners - 2
parts. (Reprinted from Archaeologia Cantiana, 1908-13).
4,10

HUSSEY, Arthur.
Hythe wills.
Ashford, Headley. n.d.
10,17

HUSSEY, Arthur.
Hythe wills (Parts 2 and 3 only, G-M, N-Y). (Reprinted
from Archaeologia Cantiana, Vols. 50,51, 1939-40).
4

HUSSEY, Arthur.
Milton wills (next Sittingbourne) - 4 parts. (Reprinted
from Archaeologia Cantiana, Vols. 44,45,46,47, 1932-35).
4,10,17

HUSSEY, Arthur.
Reculver and Hoath wills.
Mitchell, Hughes and Clarke. 1916.
4,8,10,11

HUSSEY, Arthur.
Sittingbourne wills - 3 parts. (Reprinted from Archaeologia
Cantiana, Vols. 41,42,43, 1929-31).
Ashford, Headley. 1929-31.
4,10,17

HUSSEY, Arthur.
Testamenta Cantiana (...wills relating to church building
in East Kent).
1907.
17,18

Index of administrations in the Prerogative Court of
Canterbury, 5 vols.
British Record Society. 1944-68.
5

Index of administrations in the Prerogative Court of
Canterbury, 1649-1654, edited by J. Ainsworth.
British Record Society. n.d.
5,11

Index of administrations in the Prerogative Court of
Canterbury, Vol. 2, 1655-1660, 2 parts, G-Q, R-Z, edited
by C.H. Ridge.
British Record Society. 1953.
12

Index of administrations in the Prerogative Court of
Canterbury, Vol. 4, 1596-1608, edited by M. Fitch.
British Record Society. 1964.
5

Index of wills and administrations now preserved in the
Probate Registry at Canterbury.
British Record Society. n.d.
3(some) 5,11

Index of wills and administrations now preserved in the
Probate Registry at Canterbury, Vol. 2, edited by C.H.
Ridge.
British Record Society. 1940.
12

Index of wills and administrations now preserved in the
Probate Registry at Canterbury, 1396-1558 and 1640-1650.
(Kent records, Vol. 6), edited by H.R. Plomer.
Kent Archaeological Society. 1920.
1,2,3,4,5,7,8,10,11,12,15,17,18

Index of wills proved in the Prerogative Court of
Canterbury and now preserved...Somerset House. (12 vols.).
British Record Society. 1893 etc.
5,6(some) 11,12(Vols. 1 and 4)

Index of wills proved in the Prerogative Court of
Canterbury, 1671-1675, edited by John Ainsworth.
British Record Society. 1942.
3,5

Index to wills...Canterbury...Vol. X, 1676-1685, edited by
C.H. Ridge.
British Record Society. n.d.
6

Index to wills in the Prerogative Court of Canterbury and now
preserved in the Principal Probate Registry, Somerset House,
London, Vol. 2, 1686-1693, edited by C.H. Ridge.
British Record Society. 1958.
12

Index of wills proved in the Prerogative Court of
Canterbury, Vol. 12, 1694-1700, edited by M. Fitch.
British Record Society. 1960.
5

Index of wills proved in the Prerogative Court of
Canterbury, Vols. 1-4.
Kraus Reprint. 1968.
3

Index of wills proved in the Rochester Consistory
Court between 1440 and 1561...(Kent records Vol. 9).
Kent Archaeological Society. 1924.
4,7,8,10,15,17

JENKINS, Robert Charles.
The Saxon dynasty: pedigree of the Kentish Kings.
J. English. 1867.
1,3,5,6,7,8,9,10,11,12,13,14,15,16,17,19

KEECH, Gertrude Clara.
The history of the Pledge family with the Barrow
ancestry, illustrated by Leslie W. Rowsell.
Research Publishing Co. 1970.
11

Kennett family: the pedigree of the Kennett family.
Mitre. n.d.
7

KENT ARCHAEOLOGICAL SOCIETY.
The parish registers and records of the diocese of
Rochester...(Kent records Vol. 1).
Kent Archaeological Society. 1912.
4,6,8,10,17,18,19

KENT ARCHAEOLOGICAL SOCEITY.
Sede vacante wills: a calendar of wills proved before
the Commissary of the Prior and Chapter of Christ Church,
Canterbury...(Kent records Vol. 3), edited by C.E.
Woodruff.
Canterbury, Cross and Jackman. 1914.
1,2,3,4,5,6,7,8,10,11,12,15,17,18

KINGSTON - ST. GILES' CHURCH.
The parish registers of St. Giles, Kingston, 1558-
1837, transcribed by Rev. C.H. Wilkie.
Brighton Herald. 1893.
3,11,12

Lambarde family: genealogical memoranda relating to
the Lambarde family. Extracted from the Lambarde
diary, copied from the original MS. in the possession
of Multon Lambarde...
Privately Printed. 1869.
4

LAMBARDE, William.
William Lambarde's pedigree notes, with the Lambarde
Cup.
Ashford, Headley. n.d.
12,17

LEE - ST. MARGARET'S CHURCH.
Register of marriages, 1579-1754, edited by L.L. Duncan
and A.O. Barrow.
Lewisham Antiquarian Society. 1888.
1,11,12

LEE - ST. MARGARET'S CHURCH.
Register of marriages, 1621-1754.
Register of christenings, 1579-1800.
Register of burials, 1580-1785.
n.d.
17

LE MAY, Reginald.
Records of the Le May family in England.
Le May. 1958.
12

LEWISHAM - ST. MARY'S CHURCH.
The register of marriages, christenings and burials in
the church of St. Mary, Lewisham from...1588-1750,
edited by L.L. Duncan.
1891.
2,11,12,18

LITTLE CHART - ST. MARY'S CHURCH.
Parish registers, 1538-1813, edited by Rev. C.H. Wilkie.
Canterbury, Cross and Jackman. 1914.
3,11,12

MAIDSTONE - ALL SAINTS' CHURCH.
Marriage registers of the parish church of All Saints',
Maidstone from...1542 to the middle of the 18th century,
transcribed by J. Cave-Browne.
Mitchell and Hughes. 1901.
7,11

MAIDSTONE - ALL SAINTS' CHURCH.
The registers of the parish church of All Saints', Maidstone
from the year 1542 to the middle of the 18th century,
transcribed by J. Cave-Browne.
Mitchell and Hughes. 1890.
7

MARSHAM-TOWNSHEND, Robert.
Chart and narrative pedigree of the Marshams of Kent down
to the end of the year 1902.
Mitchell, Hughes and Clarke. 1908.
11

MATTHEWS, John.
Yearbook of the probates from 1630, edited by J. and G.F.
Matthews.
1903-07.
12

MAYLAM, Percy.
Maylam family records, 1st series.
P. Maylam. 1932.
12

(MILLES, Thomas).
A catalogue of the Earles of Kent, together with their
several armes, wives and issue. (From Catalogue of Honour
and Treasury of True Nobility).
1610.
8

MORRISON, John Harold.
Prerogative Court of Canterbury: register "Scroope" (1630),
edited by J.H. Morrison.
J.H. Morrison. 1934.
2,11,12

MORRISON, John Harold.
Prerogative Court of Canterbury: letters of administration,
1620-1630, edited by J.H. Morrison.
J.H. Morrison. 1935.
2,11

MORRISON, John Harold.
Prerogative Court of Canterbury: wills, sentences and
Probate Acts, 1661-1670 (inclusive).
J.H. Morrison. 1935.
5,12

NAIRNE, Charles.
Pedigree of the Taylor family: a manuscript extract from
"The Old Book of Shadoxhurst", compiled by Charles Nairne.
n.d.
11

NEWENDEN - ST. PETER'S CHURCH.
Register of Newenden, 1559-1813, edited by E. Jermyn.
1897.
3,6,11,12

ORPINGTON - ALL SAINTS' CHURCH.
(List of) parish archives. (Typescript).
1961.
2

ORPINGTON - ALL SAINTS' CHURCH.
Register of the marriages, christenings and burials in the
parish church of All Saints', Orpington...from 1560-1754,
edited by H.C. Kirby.
Lewisham Antiquarian Society. 1895.
2,11,18

Pedigree of Harlakenden: "Harlakenden" in Woodchurch,
Kent and of "Ufton" in Tunstall, same county.
n.d.
11

Pedigree of Jacob of Canterbury and Faversham:
extracted from the records of the College of Arms in
1844.
n.d.
11

PEYRSE, Henry.
Copy of the will of Henry Peyrse of Mylton-nexte-
Gravesend. (Typed transcript of will in possession of
Ightham Parish Council).
1545.
9

PHILIPOT, John.
Pedigrees of the family of Finch Taylor, edited by
J. Philipot.
1872.
12

PHILLIMORE, William P.W.
Kent parish registers: marriages, 2 vols., edited by
W.P.W. Phillimore and R.J. Fynmore.
W.P.W. Phillimore. 1910.
1,3,11,12,18

PHILLIMORE AND CO. LTD. Publishers.
Catalogue of Phillimore's parish register series...
London, Phillimore and Co. 1913.
3

PUTNAM, Eben.
Two early passenger lists, 1635-1637. (Reprinted from
The New England Historical and Genealogical Register,
July, 1921).
3

QUISENBERRY, Anderson Chenault.
Memorials of the Quisenberry family in Germany, England
and America, edited by A.C. Quisenberry.
Washington, Gibson Bros. 1900.
3

Return of deaths - in the sub-districts of East and
West Maidstone during the periods of 1st January, 1879-
31st March, 1879; 16th July, 1879-15th September, 1879.
MSS. 1879.
12

ROCHESTER DIOCESAN CONFERENCE - ECCLESIASTICAL RECORDS
COMMITTEE.
Kent records: the parish registers and records in the
Diocese of Rochester: a summary of information...
Kent Archaeological Society. 1912.
4,5,8,13,19

SABINE, William Henry Waldo.
Sabin(e): the history of an ancient English surname.
New York, Colburn and Tegg. 1953.
3

SENNOCKE, Sir William.
Copies of wills (printed).
Sevenoaks, Clout. 1802.
16

SENNOCKE, Sir William.
Copies of wills (printed).
Sevenoaks, Harrison. 1854.
16

"SMARDONIAN", pseud.
The family names of the Weald of Kent, particularly
Smarden.
Ashford Express. 1901.
1,4,11,12

SOCIETY OF GENEALOGISTS.
Catalogue of the parish registers in the possession of
the Society of Genealogists.
London, Society of Genealogists. 1937.
3

SOCIETY OF GENEALOGISTS, LONDON.
National index of parish register copies, compiled by
K. Bloomfield and H.K. Percy-Smith.
London, Society of Genealogists. 1939.
3

SHIPBOURNE - ST. GILES' CHURCH.
Registers of Shipbourne. (Vol. 1,1560-1658).
1921.
11

SNODLAND - ALL SAINTS' CHURCH.
The register of banns of marriages published in the parish
church of Snodland (1824-81).
(1881).
12

STAPLEHURST - ALL SAINTS' CHURCH.
Parish registers, transcribed by J.S. Chamberlain.
Canterbury, Gibbs. 1907-14.
The old register, 1538-1558 and list of Rectors.
3,11,12,17
The register, 1558-1596. (11)
The register, 1596-1653. (3,11)
The third register, 1653-1695. (3,11,12)

STEPHENSON, Mrs. Theodore.
Pedigree of the Theobalds of Kent.
Mitchell, Hughes and Clarke. 1913.
11

STOCKER, John J.
Pedigree of Smythe of Ostenhanger, of Smythe of Bidborough
and Sutton-at-Hone.
1892.
1,11

STODMARSH - ST. MARY'S CHURCH.
Christenings, 1561-1812; marriages, 1561-1836; burials,
1558-1812; banns of marriages, 1765-1803, transcribed...
by Frank Tyler.
1932.
3

TESTER, M.
Funeral hatchments in Kent. (Reprinted from Archaeologia
Cantiana, Vol. 81, 1966).
Ashford, Headley. 1966.
2

THANET - ST. LAURENCE'S CHURCH.
The register book of St. Laurence in Thanet, from 1560 to
1653, transcribed in part by the late Kenyon Wood Wilkie and
indexed by Christopher Hales Wilkie.
Canterbury, Cross and Jackman. 1902.
3,11,12

THORNTON, Henry John.
Thornton pedigree papers (MS.). - Dover family.
1892.
3

Thornton pedigree. In "Ancestral Tablets"...by William H.
Whitmore.
n.d.
3

The visitations of Kent taken in the years 1530-31, by Thomas
Benolte, Clarenceux, and 1574, Part 1, A-H by Robert Cooke,
Clarenceux, edited by W.B. Bannerman.
Harleian Society. 1923.
1,5,6,11,12,16

The visitation of Kent taken in the years 1574, Part 2, I-Z
and 1592, by Robert Cooke, Clarenceux, edited by W.B.
Bannerman.
Harleian Society. 1924.
5,16

Visitation of arms of Kent, 1594 (i.e. 1574), by R. Griffin.
(Reprinted from Miscellanea Genealogica et Heraldica).
Mitchell, Hughes and Clarke. 1924.
2,11,16

Visitation of Kent taken in the years 1619-1621...by John
Philipott, edited by R. Hovenden.
Harleian Society. 1898.
1,3,4,5,6,7,8,11,12,15,16,17,18

Visitation of the County of Kent taken in the years 1619-21,
by John Philipott, 3 vols., edited by J.J. Howard.
J.E. Taylor. 1863-66.
11,16

Visitation of the County of Kent, begun in 1663, finished in
1668, edited by G.J. Armytage.
Harleian Society. 1906.
12,16

Visitation of the County of Kent, 1663-1668, edited
by Sir E. Bysshe.
Harleian Society. 1906 etc.
1,2,3,5,6,7,11,12,15,16,17,18,19

WATERS, Robert Edmond Chester.
Genealogical memoirs of the families of Chester of
Bristol...also of the families of Astry of London,
Kent, etc.
Reeves and Turner. 1881.
1,11

WATERS, Robert Edmond Chester.
Genealogical memoirs of the kindred families of Thomas
Cranmer, Archbishop of Canterbury, and Thomas Wood,
Bishop of Lichfield.
Robson. 1877.
12

WHITELOCK, Dorothy.
Anglo-Saxon wills.
Cambridge University Press. 1930.
3

WILLIS, Arthur James.
Canterbury licences (general), 1568-1646, compiled by
A.J. Willis.
Phillimore. 1972.
3,11

WILLIS, Arthur James.
Canterbury marriage licences, 1751-1780, compiled by
A.J. Willis.
Folkestone, A.J. Willis. 1967.
1,2,3,6,7,11,12

WILLIS, Arthur James.
Canterbury marriage licences, 1781-1899, compiled by
A.J. Willis.
Folkestone, A.J. Willis. 1969.
6,7,11,12

WILLIS, Arthur James.
Canterbury marriage licences, 1810-1837, compiled by
A.J. Willis.
Phillimore. 1971.
3,11

Wills from Doctors' Commons...from wills...proved in the
Prerogative Court of Canterbury, 1495-1695, edited by
J.G. Nichols and J. Bruce.
Camden Society. 1863.
8

WOMENSWOULD - ST. MARGARET'S CHURCH.
The parish register of Wymyngeweld (Womenswould),
transcribed by Rev. C.H. Wilkie.
n.d.
3,11,12

WOODRUFF, Charles Eveleigh.
An inventory of the parish registers...in the Diocese
of Canterbury, edited by C.E. Woodruff.
Canterbury, Gibbs. 1922.
1,3,7,8,11

WOODRUFF, S.M.
Pedigree of Woodruffe...
Privately Printed. 1878.
11

GEOLOGY

ABBOTT, W.J. Lewis.
The ossiferous fissures in the valley of the Shode,
near Ightham, Kent.
Geological Society. 1894.
17

BAKER, Herbert Arthur.
Evidence...of Chernian Movement in East Kent, etc., on
the unconformity between the Cretaceous and older rocks
in East Kent. (Pamphlet - reprinted).
Geological Magazine. 1917.
17

BAKER, Herbert Arthur.
On the palaeozoic platform beneath the London basin and
adjoining areas. (Typescript).
1964.
5

BAKER, Herbert Arthur.
Quartyite pebbles of the Oldhaven beds of the southern
part of the London Basin. (Extracted from "Geological
Magazine, Vol. LVII, February, 1920).
London, Dulau and Co. 1920.
5

BERRY, F.G.
Longitudinal ripples in the upper Tunbridge Wells delta,
Kent.
Geologists' Association. 1961.
11

BIRD, C.F.
Denudation of the Weald clay vale in West Kent.
Geologists' Association. 1963.
11

DAVIS, A.G.
London clay of Sheppey and location of its fossils. (Reprinted
from Proceedings of the Geologists' Association, Vol. XLVII,
Part 4, 1936, pp. 328-45).
11

DEWEY, Henry.
The geology of the Canterbury district. In Proceedings of
the Geologists' Association, Vol. 36, 1925, by H. Dewey
and others.
3,11

DINES, H.G.
Geology of the country around Chatham, by H.G. Dines and
others.
H.M.S.O. 1971.
1,4,5,6,7,9,11,19

GEOLOGICAL SURVEY AND MUSEUM.
Bulletin of geological research of Great Britain, by W.
Butterwell.
H.M.S.O. 1954.
6

GEOLOGICAL SURVEY AND MUSEUM.
The concealed mesozoic rocks in Kent, by G.W. Lamplugh,
F.L. Kitchin and J. Pringle. (Geological survey - memoirs).
H.M.S.O. 1923.
4,11

GEOLOGICAL SURVEY AND MUSEUM.
Geology of the country around Canterbury and Folkestone.
(Combined memoir in explanation of One-Inch Geological
Sheets, 289,305,306 - new series), by J.G.O. Smart and others.
H.M.S.O. 1966.
1,2,3,4,5,6,7,8,9,10,11,14,15,19

GEOLOGICAL SURVEY AND MUSEUM.
Geology of the country around Chatham.
H.M.S.O. 1954.
1,2,4,5,6,8,9,11,15,19

GEOLOGICAL SURVEY AND MUSEUM.
Geology of the country around Dartford. (Explanation of
sheet 271), by Henry Dewey, C.E.N. Bromehead, C.P. Chatwin
and H.G. Dines.
H.M.S.O. 1924.
1,4,5,8,9,11,19

GEOLOGICAL SURVEY AND MUSEUM.
Geology of the country around Maidstone. (Explanation of
One-Inch Geological Sheet 288 - new series).
H.M.S.O. 1963.
1,3,4,5,6,7,8,11,15,19

GEOLOGICAL SURVEY AND MUSEUM.
Geology of the country around Sevenoaks and Tonbridge, by
H.G. Dines and others.
H.M.S.O. 1969.
4,6,9

GEOLOGICAL SURVEY AND MUSEUM.
Geology of the country between Folkestone and Rye, including
the whole of Romney Marsh.
Longman. 1864.
11

GEOLOGICAL SURVEY AND MUSEUM.
Geology of the country near Hastings and Dungeness.
(Explanation of Sheet Maps 320 and 321).
H.M.S.O. n.d.
7(1928) 11

GEOLOGICAL SURVEY AND MUSEUM.
The geology of the country near Ramsgate and Dover,
by H.J.O. White.
H.M.S.O. 1928.
1,6,7,11,13,14,17

GEOLOGICAL SURVEY AND MUSEUM.
London and the Thames valley, 2nd edition, by R.L.
Sherlock.
H.M.S.O. 1947.
4,9,19

GEOLOGICAL SURVEY AND MUSEUM.
London and the Thames valley, 3rd edition.
H.M.S.O. 1962.
2,5,8

GEOLOGICAL SURVEY AND MUSEUM.
Summary of progress of Geological Survey of Great
Britain, Part 2.
H.M.S.O. 1932.
6

GEOLOGISTS' ASSOCIATION.
The zones of white chalk of the English coast...1,
Kent and Sussex.
Geologists' Association. 1900.
8

HAWKES, L.
Fragments of jet coal in the chalk of Kent. (Reprinted
from Proceedings of the Geologists' Associaton, Vol. LVI,
Part 1, 1945).
3

HUGHES, Thomas McKenny.
Notes on the function of the Thanet sand and the chalk,
and of the Sandgate beds and Kentish rag. (Article from
Quarterly Journal of Geological Society, November, 1866).
3,7

INSTITUTE OF GEOLOGICAL SCIENCES.
Geology of the country around Royal Tunbridge Wells.
(Explanation of One-Inch Geological Sheet 303 - new
series), by C.R. Bristow and R.A. Bazley with
contributions by...(others).
H.M.S.O. 1972.
11

KENWARD, A.S.
The post-pliocene non-marine mollusca of the south of
England by A.S. Kenward and B.B. Woodward.
1901.
5

LAMPLUGH, G.W.
The concealed mesozoic rocks in Kent, by G.W. Lamplugh,
F.L. Kitchin and J. Pringle.
H.M.S.O. 1923.
3,4,6,9,19

LAMPLUGH, G.W.
On the mesozoic rocks in some of the coal explorations
in Kent, by G.W. Lamplugh and F.L. Kitchin.
n.d.
11,19

LAPWORTH, Charles F.
Percolation in the chalk: (part of a hydro-geological
survey of Kent). (Extract from Journal of the Institute
of Water Engineers, Vol. 2, 1948 - photocopy).
4

LAPWORTH, Herbert.
Hydro-geological survey of Kent.
Privately Printed. 1946.
1

MANTELL, Gideon Algernon.
The geology of the South-East of England.
Longman. 1833.
5

MANTELL, Gideon Algernon.
Illustrations of the geology of Sussex.
Relfe. 1827.
12

MANTELL, Gideon Algernon.
The wonders of geology, 2 vols, Vol. 1.
Bohn. 1857.
12

MEYER, C.J.A.
Notes on the correlation of the cretaceous rocks of the
South-East and West of England. In Geological Magazine,
Vol. III, No. XIX, January, 1866).
7

OWEN, H.G.
Lower gault sections in the Northern Weald and the zoning
of the lower gault. (From Proceedings of the Geologists'
Association).
Colchester, Benham. 1958.
11

PHILLIPS, William.
Remarks on the chalk cliffs near Dover.
W. Phillips. 1818.
6

PRESTWICH, Joseph.
Collected papers on some controverted questions of geology.
Macmillan. 1895.
12

PRESTWICH, Joseph.
On some swallows' holes on the chalk hills near Canterbury.
Geological Society. 1854.
7

PRICE, F.G. Hilton.
The Gault, being the substance of a lecture delivered...
before the Geologists' Association, 1879.
Taylor and Francis. 1879.
7

SALTER, A.E.
On the superficial deposits of...Southern England.
1905.
17

SEELEY, H.G.
Handbook of the London Geological Field Class...lectures...
excursions. (Note: includes material on Kent), by H.G.
Seeley and others.
G. Philip. 1892.
2,18

Studies in Kentish chalk, by H.G.H. (Extracted from
"Cornhill Magazine", July, 1880).
3

TOPLEY, William.
Relation of the parish boundaries in the South-East of
England to...physical features.
1873.
17

Well-sections, trial borings, borings etc., Kent etc...
(Details as indicated from made up title. An extract from
an un-named publication, Page 59, starts: Kent).
?18.
17

WHITAKER, William.
Geology of London and of part of the Thames valley.
H.M.S.O. 1889.
1,5

WHITAKER, William.
The geology of the London basin, Part 1: the chalk and the
eocene beds of the southern and western tracks.
Longmans, Green. 1872.
5

WHITAKER, William.
Guide to the geology of London and the neighbourhood.
(Memoirs of the Geological Survey).
H.M.S.O. 1901.
5

WHITAKER, William.
"Lower London tertiaries" of Kent.
Geological Society. 1866.
17

WHITAKER, William.
Report of an excursion to Reculver. (From Proceedings of
the Geologists' Association, Vol. XXIII, Part 4, pp. 247-
49, 1912).
11

WHITAKER, William.
Presidential address..(on underground geology in the
South-East of England).
Geological Society. 1900.
17

WHITAKER, William.
Twelve years of London geology.
1901-2.
17

WHITAKER, William.
Water supply of Kent with records of sinkings and
borings, by W. Whitaker and others.
H.M.S.O. 1908.
1,2,5,7,11,12

WOOD, G.V.
The heavy mineral suites of the Lower Greensand of the
Western Weald. (From Proceedings of the Geologists'
Association).
Colchester, Benham. 1957.
11

WOODWARD, H.B.
The geology of the London district: being the area
included in sheets 1-4 of the special map of London.
H.M.S.O. 1909.
5

WOODWARD, H.B.
A large cirripede of the genus loricula from the chalk
of Kent. (From Geological Magazine, 1908).
London, Dulau and Co. 1908.
5,17

WOOLDRIDGE, Sidney William.
Structure, surface and drainage in South-East England,
by S.W. Wooldridge and D.L. Linton.
G. Philip. 1955.
1,3,5,8,19

WORRALL, G.A.
The mineralogy of some Lower Greensand borehole
samples in Kent. (From Proceedings of the Geologists'
Association).
Colchester, Benham. 1956.
11

GHOSTS

SANDERS, Frederick W.T.
(Physical research in haunted Kent): being an analysis
of the Kentish ghost hunts...carried out from February,
1939 to December, 1940...(Typescript).
1967.
4

GILLINGHAM

ADAMS, William.
Captain Adams' junk sea adventure. Logbook, 1617-19
and 1615. (Microfilm of MS. original).
n.d.
8

ADAMS, William.
History of the English factory of Hirado, 1613-1622.
(Microfilm). (Transactions of the Asiatic Society of
Japan, Vol. XXVI, 1898).
8

ADAMS, William.
Letters, 1614-1617. (Facsimile copies).
n.d.
8

ADAMS, William.
Letters written by and about William Adams, 1614-1620.
(Facsimile copies).
n.d.
8

ADAMS, William.
Logbook of William Adams, 1614-1619. (Microfilm).
(Transactions of the Asiatic Society of Japan, Vol.
XII, Part II, 1915).
8

ADAMS, William.
The original letters of the English pilot William Adams
written from Japan between A.D. 1611 and 1617. (Reprinted
from Hakluyt Society Papers).
n.d.
8

(ADAMS, William).
The William Adams memorial ceremony, April 14th, 1966,
Yokosuka, Japan. (Collection of photographs and order of
service).
n.d.
8

BALDWIN, R.A.
The Jezreelites: the rise and fall of a remarkable
prophetic movement.
Orpington, Lambarde Press. 1962.
4,7,8,11,12,15,17

BALLEINE, G.R.
Past finding out: the tragic story of Joanna Southcott and
her successors.
S.P.C.K. 1956.
8

BATE, J.
William Adams, the pilot-major of Gillingham, by J. Bate and
others.
Gillingham, Mackays. 1934.
4,8,11,12

BELL, Neil.
My brother Charles. (The story is set in Gillingham).
Redman. 1960.
4,8,12

BLAKER, Richard.
The needlewatcher. (Novel about William Adams).
Heinemann. 1932.
8

BLUNDEN, Edmund.
Poem of the commemoration for William Adams at the site of
memorial at Ito.
n.d.
8

BOTZOW, Hermann S.D.
Monorails.
M. Paterson. 1960.
8

BRITISH PETROLEUM CO.
B.P. Kent, News No. 58, 3rd July, 1964. (Contains article
on William Adams).
British Petroleum Co. 1964.
8

BROOKS, F.W.
Masons' marks.
East Yorkshire Local History Society. 1952.
8

BUNT, Cyril George Edward.
The life and work of William James Miller...
1948.
8

COLE, K.R.
Reunion.
Stockwell. n.d.
8

CUTHBERT, H.M.M.
Some notes for a talk on "Civic history in Gillingham"...
1951.
8

DARK, E.J.
A modern tower of Babel. The Jezreel Temple, Chatham.
(Cutting from Strand Magazine, 1903).
4

Fifty great disasters and tragedies that shocked the world.
Odhams. 1937.
8

GRAY, Geoffrey T.
The story of Gillingham Church.
(G.T. Gray). 1968.
11

GILLINGHAM, George Oliver.
The story of Gillingham, compiled by G.O. Gillingham.
Privately Printed in Washington. 1967.
8

GILLINGHAM BOROUGH COUNCIL.
Abstract of accounts: 1963-64, 1964-65, 1965-66,
1966-67.
4

GILLINGHAM BOROUGH COUNCIL.
Byelaws, 1893.
n.d.
8

GILLINGHAM BOROUGH COUNCIL.
Charter of incorporation, 17th August, 1903.
1903.
8

GILLINGHAM BOROUGH COUNCIL.
Conferment of the freedom of the Borough on H.M.S.
Pembroke...1955.
1955.
8

GILLINGHAM BOROUGH COUNCIL.
Festival handbook.
1951.
8

GILLINGHAM BOROUGH COUNCIL.
Gillingham MSS...a catalogue of manorial records,
deeds, etc...1315-1814. (Typescript).
1953.
8

GILLINGHAM BOROUGH COUNCIL.
William Adams memorial: souvenir programme.
1934.
8

GILLINGHAM BOROUGH COUNCIL - PUBLIC LIBRARIES.
Archives collection. (Local History Series 1).
Gillingham Public Libraries. (1971).
2,4,7,8,11

GILLINGHAM BOROUGH COUNCIL - PUBLIC LIBRARIES.
Archives collection, 2nd edition.
Gillingham Public Libraries. (1972).
11

GILLINGHAM BOROUGH COUNCIL - PUBLIC LIBRARIES.
Directory of local societies and organisations, 2nd-
8th editions.
1963 in progress.
4

GILLINGHAM BOROUGH COUNCIL - PUBLIC LIBRARIES.
Forge Lane School: text by A.P. Newton.
Gillingham Public Libraries. 1972.
11

GILLINGHAM BOROUGH COUNCIL - PUBLIC LIBRARIES.
Lecture and an exhibition...William Adams, 1564-1620.
(1964).
4,8

GILLINGHAM BOROUGH COUNCIL - PUBLIC LIBRARIES.
Local history catalogue, 1951.
Kent Education Committee. 1951.
3,7,11

GILLINGHAM BOROUGH COUNCIL - PUBLIC LIBRARIES.
Local history catalogue: 1st supplement.
Gillingham Borough Council. 1951, 1955.
4,7,8,11

GILLINGHAM BOROUGH COUNCIL - PUBLIC LIBRARIES.
McCudden, V.C. (text by R.T. Chadwick).
Gillingham Public Libraries. (1971).
8,11

GILLINGHAM CHURCH OF ST. MARY MAGDALENE.
Vestry minutes, 1763-1808. (Microfilm).
n.d.
8

GILLINGHAM COURT LEET.
Album containing the photographs of the High Constables of
the Manor of Gillingham...
1894-5.
8

GILLINGHAM LOCAL BOARD.
Byelaws made by Gillingham Local Board on 13th day of July,
1876.
James Gale. 1876.
15

Gillingham official guide.
Pyramid Press. 1960 etc.
1,4,5,7(1937) 8,11,19

GREAT BRITAIN: LAWS, etc. (GEO. V).
An Act to confer further powers upon the Mayor...of
Gillingham...
1931.
8

HARKNESS, Ariel Law.
Gillingham parish church, St. Mary Magdalene.
British Publishing Co. 1959.
4,8,12,15

HARRIS, Edwin.
The history of Gillingham. (Eastgate series No. 30).
Chatham, E. Harris. n.d.
8,11,15

HARRIS, Edwin.
The history of Gillingham Church. (Eastgate series No. 31).
Chatham, E. Harris. 1922.
4,11,15

HARRIS, Edwin.
Reminiscences of Gillingham. (Eastgate series No. 32).
Chatham, E. Harris. n.d.
11,15

HARRIS John.
A succinct account of...Mr. William Adams. (Microfilm).
n.d.
8

HOGG, P. Fitzgerald.
Gillingham. (A MS. notebook listing streets as they existed
in 1939; Gillingham, Brompton and Rainham Inns, 1938; and
extinct Gillingham and Brompton Inns), compiled by P.F. Hogg.
n.d.
4

JAPANESE AIR LINES.
Japanese Air Lines Global Courier, Vol. 2, No. 9, September-
October, 1964. (Contains article on William Adams).
8

JEZREEL, James Jershom.
Extracts from the "Flying Roll": being a series of sermons
compiled for the Gentile churches of all sects and
denominations and addressed to the lost tribes of the House
of Israel...1879.
Reprinted by Printway. 1970.
4,8,11

JEZREEL, James Jershom.
Questions et reponses sur la vraie doctrine extraite du
Rouleau Volant. (French text).
1958?
8

JOHNS, William, Earl Byford.
Fighting planes and aces. (Includes chapter about J.B.
McCudden).
J. Hamilton. 1932.
8

KNIGHT, Charles.
Gillingham fort.
1935.
8

KNIGHT, Charles.
The history of Gillingham pier.
1935.
8

KNIGHT, Charles.
Shipbuilding at Gillingham.
1938.
8,15

LANGDON, W.A.
The fireman's wedding tragedy, 11th July, 1929.
Gillingham Public Libraries. 1972.
4

LEEDS, C.S.
Chats about Gillingham...
Gillingham, Parrett and Neves. 1906.
1,2,4,6,8,11,12,15,17,20

Le Grand Magazine: the house magazine of Le Grand,
Sutcliffe and Gell Ltd., 1958-1960.
n.d.
8

LUND, Robert.
Daishi-san (i.e. William Adams of Gillingham): a novel.
Cassell. 1962.
4,8

McCUDDEN, James Thomas Byford.
Documents relating to the presentation of the freedom
of the Borough to Mayor J.T.B. McCudden.
n.d.
8

McCUDDEN, James Thomas Byford.
Five years in the Royal Flying Corps. (Edited by C.G.
Grey).
Chivers' Reprint of Original Edited by "Aeroplane and
General Publishing Co.". (1918, Reprinted 1965).
4,8,15

McCUDDEN, James Thomas Byford.
Flying fury. (Originally published in 1918 as "Five
Years in the Royal Flying Corps.").
London, Aviation Book Club. 1930 Reprinted 1939.
4,8

MANNIN, Ethel.
With William Adams through Japan.
F. Muller Ltd. 1962.
8,15

Memorial to William Adams: Gillingham tribute to its
most famous son.
Gillingham Borough Council. 1930.
8

MONTGOMERY, John.
Abodes of love. (Contains a chapter on the Jezreelites).
Putnam. 1962.
8

MOORE, W.C.
Survey of Gillingham carried out by members of the 5th
and 6th forms of the County Grammar School for Boys,
Gillingham, by W.C. Moore and D.W. Thomas.
1949.
8.

MORGAN, W.L.
A brief history of the Hempstead Congregational Church
(1900-1958).
Hempstead Congregational Church. (1960).
8

MUNRO, William.
A sketch of the symbolism of the armorial bearings
of the Court Leet of Gillingham, Kent.
Brompton, Woolley. 1894.
8

MUNRO, William.
Book of cuttings relating to the life and writings of
William Munro, who lived in Gillingham at the turn of
the century.
n.d.
8

NEW AND LATTER HOUSE OF ISRAEL.
A collection of hymns compiled for use at the public
meetings of the New and Latter House of Israel. (A
new edition, considerably enlarged).
New Brompton, New and Latter House of Israel. 1888.
8

GODMERSHAM Cont'd

WILLS, Charles. 1656-1929.
Reminiscences of my childhood in Godmersham, Kent.
(Typescript).
n.d.
3

GOODNESTON

Badford and Goodneston manor rolls, 1721-1863. (Badford
believed to be Bayford).
n.d.
11

GOODWIN SANDS

BALLANTYNE, R.M.
The floating light of the Goodwin Sands: a tale.
Nisbet. 1870.
11,13

BRENAN, J. Eustace.
The wreck of the "Indian Chief": a tale of the Goodwin Sands.
(London). 1881.
13,14

CARTER, George Goldsmith.
The Goodwin Sands.
Constable. 1953.
1,3,4,6,7,8,11,12,13,14,15

GATTIE, George Byng.
Memorials of the Goodwin Sands...
W.H. Allen. 1890.
1,2,4,6,8,11,12,13,14,17,18,19

GATTIE, George Byng.
Memorials of the Goodwin Sands.
Keliher. 1904.
7,11,14,15

GILMORE, John.
Storm warriors; or, life-boat work on the Goodwin Sands.
Macmillan. 1875 etc.
3,6,8,11,12,13,14,15

HALL, James S.
Sea surgeon. (See Coastal Waters).
Kimber. 1961.
8,12

KING, Edward.
An account of an old piece of ordnance...dragged out of the sea
near Goodwin Sands in 1775...
Society of Antiquaries. 1776.
11

TEGG, T.
Interesting particulars of the loss of the "Admiral Gardner"
and "Britannia" outward bound...and of the "Apollo"...
Goodwin Sands, 1809.
n.d.
11

TREANOR, Thomas Stanley.
The cry from the sea and the answer from the shore.
Religious Tract Society. 1898.
8,11,12,13,14

TREANOR, Thomas Stanley.
Heroes of the Goodwin Sands.
Religious Tract Society. 1904.
1,4,6,7(1893) 11,12,13,14,17

TREANOR, Thomas Stanley.
The log of a Sky Pilot, or work and adventure around the
Goodwin Sands.
Religious Tract Society. 1893 etc.
6(1894) 7,8(1897) 11,12(1894) 13,14

GOTHAM

LIVETT, Grevile Mairis.
Architectural notes on the churches of Northfleet, Shorne and
Gotham.
n.d.
5

GOUDHURST

BURROWS, A.J., WINCH AND SONS.
Gore Court, Goudhurst - catalogue of the antique
furniture, silver, china, pictures, books, bric-a-brac
and effects to be sold by auction...on the premises...
October, 1951.
A.J. Burrows, Winch and Sons. 1951.
3,11

Goudhurst, Black Swan Hall - Sale catalogue, 1967.
12

Goudhurst, "Brandfold" - Sale catalogue.
1926.
11

Goudhurst, Finchurst - Sale catalogue, 1926.
12

Goudhurst, Finchurst - Sale catalogue, 1967.
12

Goudhurst, Larchfield House - Sale catalogue, 1967.
12

Goudhurst official guide.
Croydon, Home Publishing Co. 1961.
4,5,11,12

HILL, R.H. Ernest.
MSS. relating to Goudhurst and neighbourhood. In
Archaeologia Cantiana, Vol. 28, 1909.
17

IGGLESDEN, Sir Charles.
Goudhurst.
Kentish Express. 1924.
18,19

JOHNSTON, Philip Mainwaring.
Church of St. Mary, Goudhurst...
Ashford, Headley. 1933.
11

KENDON, Joseph J.
Work of faith...some account of the Lord's work in
Goudhurst.
Goudhurst, Kendon. 1869.
11

KENDON, Margery.
Ladies' College, Goudhurst...
Bilsington, Kendon. 1963.
11

KENT COUNTY COUNCIL - PLANNING DEPARTMENT.
Goudhurst: village study.
Kent County Council. (1967).
2,3,7,11,12.

LAYTON, Thomas Arthur.
A year at the "Peacock".
Cassell. 1964.
1,8,11,12

RAIKES, W.A.
Eleven hundred years in a Kent parish: records of
Goudhurst.
Tunbridge Wells Courier. 1929.
12

RAIKES, W.A.
Records of Goudhurst.
Tunbridge Wells Courier. 1927.
1,11,12

RAIKES, W.A.
Records of Goudhurst...revised edition.
Tunbridge Wells Courier. 1929.
11,12

TALBOT, Arthur V.
A tour of Goudhurst...
Goudhurst, Talbot. 1962.
1,2,3,4,7,8,11,12,19

TAYLOR, Reginald.
My friend, my enemy. (Smuggling - based at Goudhurst).
Hamilton. 1965.
11

THE BETHANIAN (Special Centenary Edition).
Magazine of Bethany School, Goudhurst.
Vivish and Baker. 1966.
11

The Goudhurst Coronation book: a record of celebrations in
Goudhurst and Kilndown...on May 12, 1937...(Part I Coronation
celebrations, Part II Reminiscences and local lore).
Tunbridge Wells Courier. 1937.
1,3,4,5,8,11,12,15,19

The Goudhurst Jubilee book: a record of celebrations in
Goudhurst and Kilndown on May 6th, 1935...
Tunbridge Wells Courier. 1935.
1,5,6,11,12,19

TOMMOS, Shirley.
The village, with reference to the village of Goudhurst in
the County of Kent, including a short history of the
English village. (Typescript MS.).
1970.
11

GRAVESEND

ALLEN, A.F.
Roman and other remains from chalk near Gravesend. In
Archaeologia Cantiana, Vol. 68, 1954).
17

ARNOLD, George Matthews.
Borough of Gravesend.
Gravesend, Caddel. 1906.
1,9,11,12

ARNOLD, George Matthews.
Catalogue of some of the original charters, deeds and
manuscripts at Milton Hall, Gravesend.
Gilbert and Rivington. 1884.
12

ARNOLD, George Matthews.
A few remarks about Gravesend in olden days. (Written by
request and read at Kent Archaeological Society Annual
Meeting, July, 1876). (Bound with Pocock R. - History of
Gravesend and Milton).
Gravesend, R. Pocock. 1876.
5,17(and in Archaeologia Cantiana, Vol. II, 1877)

ARNOLD, George Matthews.
A few remarks offerred upon the subject of town
improvements at Gravesend.
1889.
9

ARNOLD, George Matthews.
Filborough Farm House, East Chalk, Gravesend, with notes
by Ralph Nevill. (Plate,plan). In Archaeologia Cantiana,
Vol. 21, 1895.
17

ARNOLD, George Matthews.
Gravesend in the very time of olde.
Gravesend, Caddel. 1896.
1,5,7,9,11,15,17

ARNOLD, George Matthews.
Proceedings upon the occasion of unveiling the memorial
stature of Gordon.
1893.
9

ARNOLD, George Matthews.
Robert Pocock: the Gravesend historian, naturalist,
antiquarian, botanist and printer.
Sampson, Low. 1883.
1,5,9,11,12

ARNOLD, George Matthews.
The Roman station of Vagniacae at Springhead, near Gravesend.
(Reprinted from Archaeologia Cantiana).
Mitchell and Hughes. 1889.
9,17

ARNOLD, Wulfhad Leslie Joseph.
Of the tribe of Arnold.
Gravesend, Bryant and Rackstraw. 1907.
8,9,11

BARBER, T.W.
Thames Harbour. Plan and sections, 1903. (Gravesend).
Martin Hood and Larkin. 1903.
9

BAYNES, Godfrey John. Publisher.
A descriptive guide to the panorama of nature seen from
the summit of Windmill Hill...(Gravesend).
Gravesend, G.J. Baynes. 1848.
9,17

BAYNES, Godfrey John. Publisher.
Guide to Gravesend.
Gravesend, G.J. Baynes. 1869.
17

BEATTY, Charles.
His country was the world: a study of Gordon of
Khartoum.
Chatto and Windus. 1954.
12

BERGMAN, George F.J.
Edward Davis: life and death of an Australian bush-
ranger (born in Gravesend). In Australian Jewish
Historical Society, Vol. IV, Part V, 1956).
9

BOULGER, D.C.
The life of Gordon, 2 vols.
Fisher Unwin. 1896.
12

BOUNDARY COMMISSION FOR ENGLAND.
Report with respect to the areas comprised in the
constituencies of Rochester and Chatham; Gravesend.
H.M.S.O. 1963.
4,8,9

BOURNE, William (of Gravesend).
A regiment for the sea and other writings on navigation.
(Hakluyt Society).
Cambridge. 1963.
4,15

BOWEN, Emanuel.
A description of Gravesend. (From "A Complete System of
Geography...of the Known World", Vol. 1).
1747.
9

BOWEN, Frank Charles.
From carrock to clipper.
Halcott and Truscott Smith. 1927.
12

BOWEN, Frank Charles.
Men of the wooden walls.
Staples Press. 1952.
12

BOWEN, Frank Charles.
Ships for all.
Ward Lock. n.d.
12

BOWEN, Frank Charles.
Wooden walls in action.
Halton and Co. 1951.
12

BOWEN, Frank Charles.
William Watkins Ltd., a history: one hundred years of
towage (Gravesend).
1933.
1,5,9

BRABAZON, Elizabeth Jane.
A month at Gravesend.
Simpkin Marshall. 1864.
1,5,6,9,11,12,15,17(1860).

BROWHURST, F.W.
Account book of F.W. Browhurst, 9 High Street, Gravesend,
1884.
9

BUTLER, Sir William Francis.
Charles George Gordon.
Macmillan. 1889.
9,12

CADDEL, John C. Publisher.
Yearbook and directory of Gravesend, Milton, etc.
Gravesend, J.C. Caddel. 1893.
17

CARSON, R.A.G.
Springhead, Gravesend (Kent), Roman imperial treasure trove.
(Reprinted from the "Numismatic Chronicle", 1965).
4

CAVE, A.J.E.
Report on a Saxon skeleton from Pepper Hill, Kent.
(Typescript).
n.d.
9

CLARK, W. Tierney.
Drawing for the further extension of temporary pier
(Gravesend).
W. Tierney Clark. 1833.
9

CLARK, W. Tierney.
Drawings for the proposed alterations to the old town
quays (5 sheets).
W. Tierney Clark. 1832.
9

CLARK, W. Tierney.
Gravesend pier - drawings of design.
Institute of Civil Engineers. 1840.
9

CLIFFORD, J.R.S.
Gravesend and its neighbourhood.
Gravesend, Smither Bros. 1886.
1,9,11,12,17

CRUDEN, Robert Peirce.
Description of three ancient ornamented bricks found at
different periods in London and Gravesend.
1825.
9,15

CRUDEN, Robert Peirce.
The history of the town of Gravesend.
Pickering. 1843.
1,4,5,6,7,8,9,11,12,15,17,18

CULVERWELL, R.J.
Hints to the citizens of London and others in search of
recreation or health on the salubrity of Gravesend.
R.J. Culverwell. 1836.
9

DAVIS, H. AND J. (Auctioneers and Surveyors).
Plan of the land at Blockhouse Fort, Gravesend, Kent to be
sold on 31st March, 1835 by H. and J. Davis.
1835.
9

Diamond Jubilee: a history of the parish church of St. Mary,
Gravesend, 1904-1964.
1964.
12

Enterprise: the monthly journal of the Gravesend and District
Chamber of Trade, No. 41, June-July, 1940.
9

FREEMAN, R. Austin. (Local Author).
As a thief in the night.
Hodder and Stoughton. n.d. (9)

The case of Oscar Brodski and other stories.
Hodder and Stoughton. n.d. (9)

The D'Arblay mystery.
Hodder and Stoughton. n.d. (9)

Dr. Thorndyke's casebook.
Hodder and Stoughton. n.d. (9)

Dr. Thorndyke intervenes.
Hodder and Stoughton. 1933. (9)

The exploits of Danby Croker.
Duckworth and Co. 1916. (9)

The eye of Osiris.
Hodder and Stoughton. n.d. (9)

The great portrait mystery.
Hodder and Stoughton. n.d. (9)

The green check jacket and other stories.
Hodder and Stoughton. n.d. (9)

The magic casket.
Hodder and Stoughton. n.d. (9)

Mr. Pottermack's oversight.
Dodd, Mead and Co. 1930. (9)

The mystery of Angelina Frood.
Hodder and Stoughton. n.d. (9)

The Penrose mystery.
Hodder and Stoughton. 1936. (9)

The puzzle lock.
Hodder and Stoughton. n.d. (9)

The red thumb mark.
Hodder and Stoughton. n.d. (9)

The shadow of the wolf.
Hodder and Stoughton. 1925. (9)

The singing bone.
Hodder and Stoughton. n.d. (9)

The surprising experiences of Mr. Shuttlebury Cobb.
Hodder and Stoughton. n.d. (9)

The unwilling adventurer.
Hodder and Stoughton. n.d. (9)

When rogues fall out.
Hodder and Stoughton. 1932. (9)

FRENCH, E. Gerald.
Gordon Pasha of the Sudan.
n.d.
9

GARNETT, David.
Pocahontas.
Chatto and Windus. 1933.
9,12

General description of the Gravesend Natural History
Exhibition and Museum, 1 High Street...
Printed by William Haslam. 1888.
11

GENERAL REGISTER OFFICE.
Census returns, 1851: Gravesend (photocopy supplied by
Public Record Office).
n.d.
9

"GEORGE ARNOLD" MUSEUM, GRAVESEND.
(Sale) catalogue of library in the...museum.
1912.
17

God's wonders in the Great Deep, recorded in several
wonderful and amazing accounts of sailors...
Gravesend, Reprinted by R. Pocock. 1803.
11

GOELL, Kelmit.
Pocahontas.
Anthony Blond. 1963.
12

Gravesend and the Baronial Halls of Kent: being an
excerpt from Knight's Excursion Companion.
Knight. 1851.
9,13,17

GRAVESEND AND DISTRICT CHAMBER OF TRADE.
Yearbook, 1963 etc.
n.d.
9

GRAVESEND AND DISTRICT SCIENTIFIC AND ARCHAEOLOGICAL
SOCIETY.
Proceedings, presidential address and 1st annual
report, 1924-1925.
Gravesend Borough Library. 1925.
9

GRAVESEND AND DISTRICT SCIENTIFIC AND ARCHAEOLOGICAL
SOCIETY.
Proceedings, 1926-27 and third annual report, 1926-1927,
with presidential address and list of British butterflies and moths taken and further description of ancient
buildings in the locality.
Gravesend Borough Library. 1928.
9

GRAVESEND AND DISTRICT SCIENTIFIC AND ARCHAEOLOGICAL
SOCIETY.
Proceedings, Presidential addresses and reports of Hon.
Secretarys from April, 1927 to March, 1932 and list of
members, at December 31st, 1932.
Gravesend Borough Library. 1933.
9

GRAVESEND AND DISTRICT SCOUT COUNCIL.
Yearbook, 1970 and 1971.
n.d.
9

GRAVESEND AND MILTON MECHANICS INSTITUTION.
1st Annual Report, January 9th, 1839 and 14th Annual Report,
April 14th, 1852.
1839 and 1852.
9

Gravesend and neighbourhood view book.
Gravesend, Caddel. 1900?
11

Gravesend and Northfleet: post-war business and information
guide.
1946.
9

Gravesend, the gateway to the port of London: official
handbook.
1950 in progress.
9

GRAVESEND BOROUGH COUNCIL.
Gravesend redevelopment: draft proposals.
Gravesend Corporation. 1945.
9

GRAVESEND BOROUGH COUNCIL.
Local Government reorganisation. Representations to the
Local Government Boundary Commission for England regarding
the new District Councils.
Gravesend Borough Council. 1971.
9

GRAVESEND BOROUGH COUNCIL.
Official handbooks and guides.
1910 - Corporation guide to Gravesend.
Gravesend Borough Council. (1,4,5,9)

1911 - Corporation guide to Gravesend.
Gravesend Borough Council. (9)

1914 - Official guide to Gravesend (by W. Syms).
Gravesend Borough Council. (1)

1922 - Official guide to Gravesend.
Cheltenham, Burrow. (9)

1924 - Gravesend and neighbourhood.
Cheltenham, Burrow. (4)

1925 - Official guide to Gravesend.
Cheltenham, Burrow. (9)

1927   )
1929   ) Gravesend as a commercial and residential)
1932-1936) centre: official handbook.   ) 9
1938   ) Cheltenham, Burrow.   )
1940   )

1952 etc. - Official handbook.
Cheltenham, Burrow. (4,8,9,11,15,19)

GRAVESEND BOROUGH COUNCIL.
The Woodville Halls, Gravesend: official brochure.
1969.
4

GRAVESEND BOROUGH COUNCIL - PUBLIC LIBRARY.
The Gravesend Borough Library.
1938.
7

GRAVESEND BOROUGH COUNCIL - PUBLIC LIBRARY.
Gravesend Public Library opening ceremony, 1905.
1905.
4,9,11

GRAVESEND BOROUGH COUNCIL - PUBLIC LIBRARY.
Local societies: a list of secretarial addresses, 3rd
edition.
Gravesend Public Library. 1970.
4,9,11

GRAVESEND BOROUGH COUNCIL - PUBLIC LIBRARY.
Local societies: a list of secretaries and addresses,
5th edition, compiled by Peter J. Willis.
Gravesend Public Library and Kent County Library. 1972.
11

GRAVESEND CHURCH UNION.
32nd Annual Report for the year 1870.
1871.
9

Gravesend Gala Week: official programme, 1926, 1927.
n.d.
17

GRAVESEND, MILTON AND NORTHFLEET ELECTRIC LIGHT AND
POWER WORKS.
Electricity in Gravesend.
Gravesend, Milton and Northfleet Electric Light and
Power Works. 1907.
9

GRAVESEND SCHOOL FOR BOYS.
Quill: poems from Gravesend School for Boys.
Gravesend School for Boys. 1968.
11,12

GREAT BRITAIN: LAWS, etc. (GEO. II).
An Act for rebuilding the Parish Church of Gravesend...
1731.
8,9,11

GREAT BRITAIN: LAWS, etc. (GEO. III).
An Act for altering and enlarging the powers of an
Act...for improving...Gravesend and Milton...
1816.
9

GREAT BRITAIN: LAWS, etc. (GEO. III).
An Act for paving, cleansing and lighting...in the town
and parishes of Gravesend and Milton...
1773.
9,11

GREAT BRITAIN: LAWS, etc. (GEO. III).
An Act to explain and amend...an Act...and for better
defending the passage of the River Thames at Gravesend
and Tilbury Port...
1781.
9

GREAT BRITAIN: LAWS, etc. (GEO. IV).
An Act for rebuilding, or for improving, regulating and
maintaining the Town Quay of Gravesend...and the landing
place belonging thereto.
1828.
9

GREAT BRITAIN: LAWS, etc. (GEO. IV).
An Act for the more easy and speedy recovery of small
debts within the town of Gravesend and the Hundreds
of Toltingtrough, Dartford, Wilmington and Oxtane...
1826.
9

GREAT BRITAIN: LAWS, etc. (WILL. IV).
An Act for amending an Act...entitled "An Act for
rebuilding the Town Quay of Gravesend...and the landing
place belonging thereto; and for building a pier or
jetty adjoining thereto".
1833.
9

GREAT BRITAIN: LAWS, etc. (WILL. IV).
An Act for paving, cleansing, lighting, watching and
improving...Gravesend and Milton...
1833.
9

GREAT BRITAIN: LAWS, etc. (WILL. IV).
Minutes of evidence taken before the Lords Committees
to whom was referred the Bill entitled "An Act for
amending an Act...for rebuilding or for improving,
regulating and maintaining the Town Quay of Gravesend...
and the landing place belonging thereto; and for
building a pier or jetty adjoining thereto...".
1832.
9

GREAT BRITAIN: LAWS, etc. (VIC.).
An Act for amending the Acts relating to the Gravesend Town
Quay and Pier.
1842.
9

GREAT BRITAIN: LAWS, etc. (VIC.).
An Act for authorising the sale of Gravesend Terrace Pier...
1875.
9

GREAT BRITAIN: LAWS, etc. (VIC.).
An Act for confirming certain provisional orders...under the
Electric Lighting Act, 1882, relating to Folkestone,
Gravesend...
1883.
9

GREAT BRITAIN: LAWS, etc. (VIC.).
An Act for establishing a general cemetery...Gravesend...
1838.
9

GREAT BRITAIN: LAWS, etc. (VIC.).
An Act for incorporating the Gravesend and Milton Waterworks
Co...
1846.
9

GREAT BRITAIN: LAWS, etc. (VIC.).
An Act for more effectually lighting with gas the parishes of
Gravesend, Milton and Northfleet.
1863.
9

GREAT BRITAIN: LAWS, etc. (VIC.).
An Act for more effectually paving, cleansing, lighting and
otherwise improving...Gravesend...
1856.
9

GREAT BRITAIN: LAWS, etc. (VIC.).
An Act for the sale of Gravesend Town Quay and Pier to the
London, Tilbury and Southend Railway Co...
1884.
9

GREAT BRITAIN: LAWS, etc. (VIC.).
An Act to amend...an Act...for paving, cleansing, lighting,
watching and improving...Gravesend and Milton...
1840.
9

GREAT BRITAIN: LAWS, etc. (VIC.).
An Act to confirm certain provisional orders made by the
Board of Trade under the Electric Lighting Acts, 1882 and
1888 relating to...Chislehurst, Gravesend...
1898.
9

GREAT BRITAIN: LAWS, etc. (VIC.).
An Act to confirm certain provisional orders of the Local
Government Board relating to the districts of...Gravesend...
Sittingbourne...
1874.
9

GREEN, E.R.
Field names of Gravesend. (Typescript).
1971.
9

GUMMER, Selwyn.
St. Andrews Waterside Church, Gravesend: souvenir history.
1965.
9

GUMMER, Selwyn.
When the coloured people come...by S. and J.S. Gummer
(Gravesend).
Oldbourne Press. 1966.
8,9,11,12

GUNKEL, E.C.
A brief history of Gravesend and Northfleet, compiled by
E.C. Gunkel.
Gravesend Public Library and Kent County Library. 1972.
11

GUNKEL, E.C.
The Gravesend chronology, compiled by E.C. Gunkel,
3 vols. (Part I to 1700, Part II 1701-1900, Part III
1900 to date).
Gravesend Public Library. 1971.
11

H., W.T.
A new historical, topographical and descriptive
companion to the visitor of Gravesend, Milton and
their environs, interspersed with curious anecdotes...
in a series of letters from the author to a friend.
W. Holbert. 1843.
1,4,9,17

HALL, T. Publisher.
Catalogue of books in Hall's public library, Gravesend.
Gravesend, T. Hall. 1893.
17

HALL, T. Publisher.
Hall's Gravesend and Milton directory and advertiser,
1853.
Gravesend, T. Hall. n.d.
9

HALL, T. Publisher.
Hall's Gravesend and Northfleet directory and advertiser,
1854-1859.
Gravesend, T. Hall. n.d.
9

HALL, T. Publisher.
Hall's Gravesend, Milton and Northfleet directory and
advertiser, 1861-1889.
Gravesend, T. Hall. n.d.
9,17(1888-9)

HART, W.H.
An enquiry into the tenure of the lands in the parish of
Gravesend...with regard to their gavelkind and non-
gavelkind.
Gravesend, T. Hall. 1873.
9,17

HASTED, Edward.
The Hundred of Toltingtrow (Gravesend area). (Extracted
from the History of Kent).
(1794).
9

HENLEY'S. (Engineering Firm).
One hundred years: the story of Henley's 1837-1937.
(An engineering firm now under G.E.C.) by E. Slater.
Gravesend, Henley's.(1937).
9

HENLEY'S. (Engineering Firm).
The story of Henley's in war-time, 1939-1945.
Gravesend, Henley's. 194-?
9

HEXAM, Henry.
A tongue-combat lately happening between two English
soldiers in the tilt boat of Gravesend.
1623.
9

HIGGINS, John. Publisher.
Gravesend and Northfleet almanac.
Gravesend, J. Higgins. 1891.
9,17(1898)

HISCOCK, Robert Heath.
A history of the parish churches of Gravesend and the
burial place of Pocahontas.
Gloucester, British Publishing Co. 1961.
2,4,5,8,9,11,12,15

History of Royal Air Force, Gravesend and a list of
commanding officers and squadrons, 1940-43. (Typescript).
Air Historical Branch. 1961.
9

HOBCRAFT, John Edward.
The Gravesend guide adapted to the use of the visitors
and inhabitants.
1829.
9,17

HOBCRAFT, John Edward.
The Gravesend guide...to which is added the steamboat
companion to Gravesend.
London, William Mason. 1830.
9,15

HOWELL, George O.
The humour of Gravesend surnames.   (Read at a meeting...
of the Gravesend Wesleyan Institute).
1889.
9,17

ISSAAC, A SON OF ABRAHAM, pseud.
A visit to the Rosherville gardens.
Hart Street School. 1844.
9

JACKSON, Thomas.
Brief records of a useful life: reminiscences of the late Mr.
Jesse Crook of Gravesend.
1868.
17

JENKINS, David William Henry.
St. George's School, Gravesend, 1580-1955.
1955.
1,4,9,11,12

JOHNSON, Isaac Charles.
Autobiography.
Farncombe and Son. 1912.
9

JOHNSTON, James. Publisher.
Addenda to Moore's almanack and Gravesend and Milton
directory with a tide-table for 1841.
Gravesend, James Johnston. n.d.
9

JOHNSTON, James. Publisher.
Appendix to the almanack and Gravesend and Milton directory
with a correct tide-table for 1844 and the same for 1846 and
1847.
Gravesend, J. Johnston. n.d.
9

JOHNSTON, James. Publisher.
A new guide to Gravesend, embracing everything of interest in
Gravesend, Milton and surrounding district.
Gravesend, J. Johnston. 1842.
9,11,17

KEAN, J.S.
Artists of Gravesend up to the end of the 19th century.
Gravesend Historical Society. 1964.
4,9,11

KENT COUNTY COUNCIL - PLANNING DEPARTMENT.
Gravesend town centre map.
Kent County Council. 1967.
9,11

KENT COUNTY COUNCIL - PLANNING DEPARTMENT.
Gravesend town centre map, with revised explanatory notes.
Kent County Council. 1970.
9

KENT COUNTY COUNCIL - PLANNING DEPARTMENT.
Kent development plan (Part B) - Thameside provisional map to
accompany town map, section 2: Borough of Gravesend...
Kent County Council. c.1960.
9

KIDD, William. Publisher.
A trip to Gravesend...a guide to strangers.
London, W. Kidd. c.1850.
9,17

LACEY, A.G.
An account of the burning of the Holy Trinity Schools
(Gravesend) in February 1962 and the subsequent happenings.
(Typescript).
1962.
9

LARGE, James. Publisher.
Gravesend, Milton and Northfleet directory and advertiser
for the year...1849, 1850, 1851.
Gravesend, J. Large. n.d.
9

LEJOINDRE, R. Junior.
Comic history of Gravesend.
Baynes and Irwin. 1872.
9,11,12

LILLEY, W.E.
The life and work of General Gordon at Gravesend.
Kingdom. (1885).
4,9,11

"MAN OF KENT", pseud.
A life's work for the Public Weal, by a Man of Kent.
(Memoirs of Alderman Davis of Gravesend).
Printed by Haycock-Cadle. 1915.
11

MANNIN, Ethel.
England for a change.   (10 pages on Gravesend).
Hutchinson. 1968.
9

MANSFIELD, F.A.
History of Gravesend...
Gravesend and Dartford Reporter. 1922.
4,5,9,11,12

MANSFIELD, F.A.
Wesleyan Methodism in Gravesend: its rise and progress.
(Typescript).
(1904).
9

Mask pulled off; or, the dissection of a Whiggish
Corporation: being the late Curate of Gravesend's
vindication.
J. Baker at the Black Boy in Pater Noster Row, London.
9

MASON. Publisher.
The new steamboat companion and Gravesend guide.
Mason. 1835.
12

MATTEWS, Robert. Auctioneer.
4 Woodville Terrace, Gravesend - catalogue of household furniture and effects; comprising modern and
antique household appointments...and a large collection
of books including scarce and valuable works on Kent
(from the libraries of the late Mr. Charles Cobham and
Mr. George W. Cobham)...which will be sold...on
Wednesday, February 17th, 1909...
Gravesend, Schultz (Printers). 1909.
4

MELVILLE, Henry.
Illustrated guide to the botanical gardens at
Rosherville, near Gravesend.
1843.
9,17

MOREY, Gordon Henry.
When the light was dim.
Epworth. 1965.
9

NATIONAL TELEPHONE COMPANY.
Directory, Southern section, 1901-2, Gravesend and
Northfleet. (3 pages typescript).
n.d.
9

NATIONAL TRUST.
St. John's Jerusalem.
National Trust. 1971.
9

NEWMAN, George.
Links with the past: being recollections of Gravesend
for three score years and more.
1910.
4

NUTTING, Anthony.
Gordon: martyr and misfit.
Constable. 1966.
12

OAKLEY, K.P.
A reconsideration of the Galley Hill skeleton, by K.P. Oakley
and M.F. Ashley Montague. (Bulletin of British Museum
(Natural History), Vol. 1, No. 2, 1949).
9

O'CONNOR, Charles Patrick.
George Newman: "Loegryn", a sketch.
Poplett and Taylor (Printers). (1890).
9

ORR, William S. AND CO. Publishers.
The pictorial guide to Gravesend and its rural vicinity: a
holiday handbook.
Orr. 1845.
9,17

PENNY, W. Publisher.
Gravesend and Milton guide, detailing the principal objects
of interest in the excursion from London.
W. Penny. c.1828.
9

PHILIP, Alexander John.
Gravesend: a survey of its ecclesiastical history. (Typescript).
(190-?).
9

PHILIP, Alexander John.
Gravesend Literary Associations. (2 page typescript).
(1902).
9

PHILIP, Alexander John.
Gravesend: the tercentenary of the Gravesend Mayoralty.
(Cover title: Souvenir Opening of Fort Gardens).
Gravesend Corporation. 1932.
3,4,9,13

PHILIP, Alexander John.
Gravesend, the watergate of London.
Homeland Association. 1906-7.
1,2,4,5,7,9(+ 2nd and 3rd editions) 11,13,15,17,18

PHILIP, Alexander John.
History of Gravesend.
Wraysbury: A.J. Philip. 1954.
1,3,4,5,7,8,9,11,12,15,17,18

PHILIP, Alexander John.
History of Gravesend and its surroundings from pre-historic
times to the opening of the 20th century, Vol. 1 only.
Stanley Paul. 1914.
1,5,9,11,15

PHILIPS, James.
Gravesend present and past, men of mark and local
institutions, Part 1...
(1885).
17

PHILLIPS, Margaret J.
The development of the police force in Gravesend, 1816-1866.
(Thesis: typescript).
1963.
9

PICKERING, R.
Historical and household almanac, Gravesend.
1883 etc.
17

POCOCK, Robert.
A chronology of the most remarkable events...of Gravesend,
Milton and Denton...
1790.
9,11

POCOCK, Robert.
History of the incorporated town and parishes of Gravesend and
Milton...
Gravesend, R. Pocock. 1797.
1,4,5,6,9,11,12,15,17

POCOCK, Robert.
Pocock's Gravesend water companion...between London Bridge and
Gravesend Town...
Gravesend, R. Pocock. 1798.
9,13

POLLARD, Arthur O.
St. Andrew's Waterside Mission Church: souvenir
history.
1952.
9

(PRYCE, Edward Smith).
Sabbath memories of Gravesend.
(1846).
17

REED PAPER GROUP.
Gravesend's paper mill.
Reed Paper Group. 1964.
9

Report from the Committee of Privileges...(Relating to
Gary Allinghan, Gravesend M.P.).
H.M.S.O. 1947.
9

RIDGWAY, A. Publisher.
Ridgway's penny guide to Gravesend and its surroundings.
A. Ridgway. 1891.
9

ROCHARD, J.
A descriptive and historical review of Gravesend and
Northfleet.
Brighton, J. Rochard. 1893.
9,11,17

Rotary Club of Gravesend - Silver Jubilee, May, 1927-
1952.
Rotary Club of Gravesend. 1952.
9

S., F.H.
How Gravesend, Northfleet and district played their
parts in the Great War, edited by F.H.S.
n.d.
9

St. James' National Schools, Gravesend - Magazine.
1902.
17

SAYNOR, Joy.
Gravesend, 1851: some historical notes on Gravesend
and district. (A Census study).
Workers' Educational Association. (1972).
4,8,9,11

SHERWIN, John.
The Gotham swan; or, the rook's flight from Gravesend:
being the remarkable case of Sherwin and his wife
written by himself...
Printed by Mr. Braggs, Princes Street, Drury Lane,
London. 1730.
9

SIMPSON, Joseph. Publisher.
A new historical, topographical and descriptive guide
to Gravesend and its neighbourhood.
J. Simpson. 1858.
9

(SMITH, Cicely Fox).
Making of a seaman: Gravesend and its associations.
n.d.
11

SMITH, V.T.C.
Historical sketch of Gravesend Fort and Milton Chantry.
1965.
11

SMITHER BROTHERS.
Almanack and Gravesend appendix for - 1878, 1882, 1883,
1885, 1886, 1891, 1893, 1894, 1895-1905, 1907, 1908,
1910, 1911, 1912, 1915, 1916. (9)
17(1889-1902, 1908, 1910)

Some historical notes on Gravesend and district.
Workers' Educational Association. 1969.
9

Souvenir programme of "Olde Village Fayre" in aid of
the Gravesend Hospital...April 30th and May 1st, 1913.
Bryant and Rackstraw. 1913.
11

GRAVESEND Cont'd

SPICER, Howard.
Free Church training grounds, Milton Mant College, Gravesend.
(From "The Puritan").
c.1900.
9

SUMSION, Peter.
Festival hymns for the use of the church. (Contains MS. of hymns for St. Aidan's Church, Gravesend).
P. Sumsion. 19--?
4

TALLIS, John. Publisher.
A comprehensive gazetteer of Gravesend with its environs: being a complete guide for visitors on pleasure or business, to which is added a general directory of Gravesend.
J. Tallis, 15 St. John's Lane, Smithfield, London. 1839.
9

THOMAS, Charles A.
Ye true narrative of ye Princess "Pocahontas" (Matoaka).
Smither Bros. 1895.
9

TILLEY, Ernest W.
A short history of Gravesend Historical Society, 1924-1966.
Gravesend Historical Society. 1967.
9,11

Views of Gravesend.
Rock. 1868.
11

"A VISITOR", pseud.
A guide for Gravesend.
1817 - R. Pocock. (9,17)
1819 - Caddel, 2nd edition. (9,15)
1824 - Caddel, 3rd edition. (9)
1929 - Wilkins, 4th edition. (9)
1931 - Chapple, Hays and Herbert, 5th edition condensed. (9)

WALFORD, Edward.
Captain Bedford Pim, R.N. (M.P. for Gravesend).
(c.1874).
17

WILLIS, Peter J.
Gravesend round and about, compiled by P.J. Willis, 3rd edit.
Gravesend Public Libraries. 1970.
4(1972) 11

WILSON, Effingham. Publisher.
A new guide for Gravesend and Milton, also topographical excursions in the environs.
E. Wilson, B. Steill, G. Foster. 1835.
9

Windmill Hill, Gravesend.
n.d.
17

WOODWARD, Grace Steele.
Pocahontas: a life of the Indian Princess.
Bailey Bros. 1969.
9

WORTHAM, H.E.
Gordon: an intimate portrait.
Harrap. 1933.
12

GREAT CHART

Great Chart, Tilmans - Sale catalogue, 1967.
12

GREGORY, J.W.
On a collection of fossils from the Lower Greensand of Great Chart in Kent. (From Geological Magazine, 1895).
11

TUNBRIDGE, J.S.
The church of St. Mary the Virgin, Great Chart: a history and guide.
Blenheim Printing Co. 1964.
11,12

TUNBRIDGE, J.S.
St. Mary-the-Virgin, Great Chart: notes on the brasses.
1968 (Reprint).
11

TUNSTALL, James. Rector of Great Chart.
A vindication of the power of state to prohibit clandestine marriages under the pain of absolute nullity...
Printed for J. and J. Rivington. 1755.
11

WATKINSON, Edward.
An exortation to beneficence. (Sermon by Rector of Great Chart)
York, Ward. 1766.
11

GREAT MONGHAM

STEBBING, W.P.D.
Roman cremation burial at Great Mongham. (Reprinted from Archaeologia Cantiana, Vol. 47, 1935).
11

GREEN STREET GREEN

ALPINE GARDEN SOCIETY.
Catalogue...of the library, edited by K.G. Lazenby.
Green Street Green, Alpine Garden Society. 1955
8

ALPINE GARDEN SOCIETY.
Catalogue of the Alpine Garden Society Library, 4th edition, edited by K.G. Lazenby.
Alpine Garden Society. 1959.
8

CAIGER, John E.L.
An ice house at Green Street Green. (Reprinted from Archaeologia Cantiana, Vol. 80).
Kent Archaeological Society. 1965.
5

COPUS, G.D.
The commons at Green Street Green and Pratts Bottom, Chelsfield. (Typescript).
1955.
2

GREENHITHE

EMPIRE PAPER MILLS.
A story of papermaking.
Greenhithe, Empire Paper Mills. n.d.
9

ORR, W.S. AND CO. Publishers.
Pictorial guide to Erith and Greenhythe.
Orr. 1846.
1,12

PEAKE, W. Brian.
Excavations at a Romano-British occupation site in Stone Wood, Greenhithe.
Dartford and District Antiquarian Society and Well Hall Educational Institute. 1910.
5,17(1919)

PRIEST, Simeon.
Excursion to Greenhithe and Stone.
1919.
5

PRIEST, Simeon.
Report of an excursion to Greenhithe...
Geologists' Association. 1912.
17

PRIEST, SIMEON.
Report of an excursion to Greenhithe and Stone, Saturday, April 25th, 1914. (Reprinted from Geologists' Association, Vol. 26, Part 1).
9

(RICHARDSON, M.).
A short history of the parish and church of Greenhithe.
British Publishing Co. 1951.
9,11

"A SIDESMAN", pseud.
Short history of the parish and church of Greenhith.
British Publishing Co. (1956).
1,5

DE MONTMORENCY, James Edward Geoffrey.
Greenwich records in the Public Record Office.
n.d.
17

DE MONTMORENCY, James Edward Geoffrey.
Weremansacre and the nucleus of Greenwich.
n.d.
17

DUNCAN, Leland Lewis.
Church of St. Alfege, Greenwich from early times to...1710.
Woolwich Antiquarian Society. n.d.
17

DYSON, Sir Frank W.
Report of the Astronomer Royal to the Board of Visitors,
6th June, 1914.
n.d.
17

ELLISTON-ERWOOD, Frank Charles.
Roman remains from Greenwich Park...
Lewisham Antiquarian Society. (1925).
1,11,17,18

FLINN, M.W.
Men of iron. (The Crowleys in the early iron industry).
Edinburgh. 1962.
17

FRASER, Edward.
Greenwich Royal Hospital.
n.d.
1,8,15,17,18

GLENCROSS, Alan.
Grandfather's Greenwich (compiled) by A. Glencross with
photographs from the Spurgeon Collection.
Conway Maritime Press. 1972.
11

GREAT BRITAIN: LAWS, etc. (QUEEN ANNE).
An Act for the better collecting and recovering of the duties
granted for the support of the Royal Hospital at Greenwich...
n.d.
11

GREAT BRITAIN: LAWS, etc. (QUEEN ANNE).
Her Majesty's Commissions for Greenwich Hospital for Seamen.
1704.
17

GREAT BRITAIN: LAWS, etc. (GEO. II).
An Act for securing the payment of such prize...monies as
were appropriated for the use of Greenwich Hospital...
1760.
11

GREAT BRITAIN: LAWS, etc. (GEO. II).
An Act for the benefit of the Royal Hospital at Greenwich.
1749.
17

GREAT BRITAIN: LAWS, etc. (GEO. II).
An Act for the better securing the payment of shares of
prizes taken...to the Royal Hospital at Greenwich...
1747.
11

GREAT BRITAIN: LAWS, etc. (GEO. II).
An Act for the more effectual collection...of the duties
granted for the support of the Royal Hospital at Greenwich.
1729.
8,11

GREAT BRITAIN: LAWS, etc. (GEO. II).
An Act for the more effectual recovering...duties granted
towards the support of the Royal Hospital at Greenwich...
1745.
11

GREAT BRITAIN: LAWS, etc. (GEO. II).
An Act to enable the parishioners of the parish of East
Greenwich...to deposit corpse in the vaults or arches under
the church...
1752.
11

GREAT BRITAIN: LAWS, etc. (GEO. II).
An Act to render valid...all contracts...made by the
Commissioners...of the Royal Hospital for Seamen at
Greenwich...
1752.
11

GREAT BRITAIN: LAWS, etc. (GEO. III).
An Act for enabling His Majesty to grant the Palace
called the King's House...in Greenwich Park...to the...
Royal Naval Asylum...
1807.
11

GREAT BRITAIN: LAWS, etc. (GEO. III).
An Act for improving the funds of the chest at Greenwich
and amending an Act...relating to the said chest.
1806.
11

GREAT BRITAIN: LAWS, etc. (GEO. III).
An Act for the more effectual vesting in the Royal
Hospital at Greenwich forfeited and unclaimed shares.
of naval officers...
1772.
11

GREAT BRITAIN: LAWS, etc. (GEO. III).
An Act for vesting certain estates, now held in trust
for the benefit of the Royal Hospital for Seamen at
Greenwich...
1776.
11

GREAT BRITAIN: LAWS, etc. (GEO. III).
An Act to empower the Commissioners...of the Royal
Hospital for Seamen at Greenwich...to provide for such
seamen.
1763.
11

GREAT BRITAIN: LAWS, etc. (GEO. III).
An Act to empower the Commissioners...of the Royal
Hospital for Seamen at Greenwich...to make certain
allowances...
1806.
11

GREAT BRITAIN: LAWS, etc. (GEO. IV).
An Act for transferring the management of Greenwich
Out Pensions and certain duties in matters of prize
to the Treasurer of the Navy.
1829.
11

GREAT BRITAIN: LAWS, etc. (GEO. IV).
An Act to enable incapacitated persons to convey to
the Commissioners...of the Royal Hospital...certain
premises...in Greenwich...
1826.
11,18

GREAT BRITAIN: LAWS, etc. (GEO. IV).
An Act to provide for the better management of the
affairs of Greenwich Hospital.
1829.
11

GREAT BRITAIN: LAWS, etc. (WILL. IV).
An Act for making and maintaining a pier, wharf and
other works at Greenwich...1836.
1936.
12

GREAT BRITAIN: LAWS, etc. (WILL. IV).
Acts of Parliament relating to Greenwich in the County
of Kent.
1831.
17

GREAT BRITAIN: LAWS, etc. (WILL. IV).
An Act to repeal the laws relating to the contributions
out of merchant seamens' wages towards the support of the
Royal Naval Hospital at Greenwich.
1834.
11

GREAT BRITAIN: LAWS, etc. (VIC.).
Regulations established by the Lords Commissioners of the
Admiralty for the government of Greenwich Hospital.
1853.
17

GREENWICH AND LEWISHAM ANTIQUARIAN SOCIETY.
Greenwich churchyard monumental inscriptions.
n.d.
17

GREENWICH BOARD OF WORKS.
Annual report, 1895.
n.d.
17

GREENWICH HOSPITAL.
Catalogue of the portraits of distinguished naval commanders
... in the naval gallery of Greenwich Hospital.
1841 and 1889.
17

GREENWICH HOSPITAL.
Description of the Royal Hospital for Seamen at Greenwich.
London. n.d.
1(1812 and 1836) 17(1839)

GREENWICH HOSPITAL.
Official papers relating to the operations performed by order
of the Directors of the Royal Hospital for Seamen, Greenwich,
on the several pensioners belonging thereto...for the cure of
various species of cataract and the Egyptian opthalmia.
By Order of the Directors. 1814.
11

GREENWICH HOSPITAL.
Report of the Commissioners to inquire into Greenwich
Hospital with minutes of evidence.
1860.
17

GREENWICH HOSPITAL.
State of facts relative to Greenwich Hospital.
1779.
17

GREENWICH HOSPITAL AND TRAVERS' FOUNDATION.
Accounts (between 1902 and 1915).
n.d.
17

GREENWICH TRACTS.
No. 1 - mysteries of Roan's Schools.
1853.
17

GREENWICH VESTRY.
Schemes relating to the charities in the parish of
Greenwich.
1890.
17

GREENWICH VESTRY.
A statement of facts...with reference to...Greenwich
Hospital.
1831.
17

Greenwich and Blackheath: a handy guide.
Fisher Unwin. n.d.
11,17,18

Greenwich and Blackheath, with rambles in the district.
Marshall Jupp. 1881.
1

Greenwich and its story, illustrated (pamphlet).
1927.
17,18

GREENWICH OFFICIAL GUIDES.
1910-11 - "Borough Guide", published by E.J. Burrow. (17)
c.1946 - Official guide, by J.W. Kirby. (18)
c.1950-58 - Official guide, 6th, 8th and 9th editions,
          published by E.J. Burrow. (17,18)
1972 - Guide to Greenwich, by N. Hamilton. Greenwich
     Book Shop. (11,17)

Greenwich Palace, a history...from earliest times to
1939.
Royal Naval College. 1939.
1,12

Greenwich Park.
1728.
17

GREGG, Pauline.
Free-born John.   (John Lilburne).
Harrap. 1961.
17

HAMILTON, Olive.
Royal Greenwich, by O. and N. Hamilton.
Greenwich Book Shop. 1969.
7,11,17

HANRAHAN, T.W.
History of Greenwich and Deptford.   (Cuttings from
the "Kentish Mercury", 1905-06).
17

HATCHWAY, Lieutenant.
The Greenwich pensioner.
Henry Colburn. 1838.
17

HAWKSMOOR, N.
Remarks on the...buildings...of the Royal Hospital at
Greenwich.
1728.
17

HOWARTH, William.
Greenwich past and present.
Effingham Wilson. (1885).
1,17,18

HOWARTH, William.
Some particulars relating to the ancient and Royal
Borough of Greenwich.
(Greenwich). 1882.
13,18

HUNT, R.W.
Life of Sir Hugh Palliser.   (Royal Hospital, Greenwich).
1844.
18

IRONS, Clarke.
Visit to Greenwich and its park.
1884.
17

JONES, Sir H. Spencer.
The Royal Observatory, Greenwich.
1943.
17(1946) 18

KIMBELL, John.
An account of the legacies, gifts...appertaining to...
St. Alphege, Greenwich.
Greenwich, G. Allen. 1816.
1,11,12,15,17,18

LAMBERT, Brooke.
Sermons and lectures.
Richardson. 1902.
12

LAWFORD, G.L.
The Telcon story, 1850-1950 (Greenwich), by G.L. Lawford
and L.R. Nicholson.
Telegraph Construction and Maintenance Co. 1950.
18

L'ESTRANGE, Alfred Guy K.
The Palace and Hospital; or, Chronicles of Greenwich.
Hurst and Blackett. 1886.
1,4,5,11,12,15,17,18

LINK, Robert.
Goodness and mercy.
Pembrey. 1898.
12

LLOYD, Christopher C.
Greenwich - Palace - Hospital - College.
Royal Naval College. 1969.
4

LOCKER, Edward Hawke.
Memoir of the late William Locker Esq...
1832.
17

LOFTIE, W.J.
Royal Palaces - Eltham and Greenwich.
Art Journal. 1890.
17

Lord Nelson's lying in state at Greenwich, with an account of
his funeral.
1806.
17

MANDY, W.H.
Notes on medieval Greenwich and Lewisham.
n.d.
17

MANNING, F.
Greenwich Hill: a poem.
1697.
17

MARTIN, Alan R.
The Grey Friars of Greenwich. (Reprinted from Archaeological
Journal).
Royal Archaeological Institute. 1923.
1

MATTHEWS, M.C.
Special publication for 1931: notes for visitors to the
Borough of Greenwich.
Greenwich and Lewisham Antiquarian Society. 1931.
17

MAUNDER, E. Walter.
The Royal Observatory, Greenwich: a glance at its history and
work.
Religious Tract Society. 1900.
1,17,18

MEASOM, Sir George Samuel.
Sir George Samuel Measom, J.P., January 1st, 1891. (Press
notices, etc. on his Knighthood).
n.d.
17

MONTAGU, John. 4th Earl of Sandwich.
Speech...14th May, 1779 (at) Committee of Enquiry into
Management of Greenwich Hospital.
Printed for T. Cadell. 1779.
2

NATIONAL MARITIME MUSEUM.
A concise guide.
H.M.S.O. 1960 etc.
1,8,11

ORD, Hubert William.
History of the Greenwich Antiquarian Society.
n.d.
17

ORD, Hubert William.
The story of Greenwich as a port and Blackheath in times of
war, 2nd edition.
Blackheath Press. 1916.
1,17,18

ORR, William S. AND CO. Publishers.
Pictorial guide to Greenwich.
W.S. Orr and Co. 1845.
17

St. Alfege, the parish church of Greenwich. (Pamphlet).
n.d.
18

St. Alfege, the parish church of Greenwich: St. Alfege;
dedication of memorial stone...martyrdom of St. Alfege...1012.
(Pamphlet).
1957.
18

PARRY, Edward.
Memoirs of Rear-Admiral Sir W. Edward Parry,
Lieutenant-Governor of Greenwich Hospital.
1857.
17

PERKINS AND SON. Publishers.
Greenwich and Blackheath souvenir.
Perkins and Son. n.d.
17

POLAND, John.
Records of the Miller Hospital and Royal Kent
Dispensary.
Greenwich, Richardson. 1893.
1,11,12,17,18

Poor old Greenwich Fair (Handbills).
n.d.
17

Report of Committee on the working of the London County
Council Generating Station at Greenwich.
1906.
17

RICHARDSON, Henry.
Greenwich...
Simpkin and Marshall. 1834.
1,11,12,15,17,18

The Royal Hospital for Seamen at Greenwich, 1694-
1728.
The Wren Society, Vol. IV, 1929.
18

SHARP, Arthur D.
Building the Royal Hospital at Greenwich.
n.d.
17

SHOBERL, William.
A summer's day at Greenwich...guide to the Hospital and
Park...
Henry Colburn. 1841.
1,2,17,18(1840)

SHORE, W. Teignmouth.
Trials of Charles Frederick Peace.
1926.
17

SKERRET, Ralph.
The nature and proper evidence of regeneration, or the
new and second birth.
Davis. 1739.
12

SMILES, Samuel.
The Huguenots, their settlements...(References to
Canterbury and Greenwich).
1880.
3

STONE, John M.
Underground passages, caverns, etc., of Greenwich and
Blackheath.
Greenwich Antiquarian Society. 1914.
1,2,17

TIMPSON, Henry C.
The illustrated guide to Greenwich.
Aylott and Jones. 1852.
17,18

WEBSTER, Angus Duncan.
Greenwich Park...
Richardson. 1902.
1,2,11,12,15,17,18

WEBSTER, Angus Duncan.
Greenwich Park: its history and associations.
(Facsimile reprint of 1st edition, Richardson, 1902).
Conway Maritime Press. 1971.
4,11

WITCHELL, W.M.
Greenwich Observatory: a sketch of its history and
functions.
1947.
18

GROOMBRIDGE

Saint John the Evangelist, Groombridge.
1955.
11,19

WEAVER, Sir Lawrence.
Groombridge Place, Kent. (Tuileries brochures).
Ludowici-Celadon Co. 1929.
11

WHITE, Dorothy V.
Groombridge diary.
Oxford University Press. 1914.
19

GUSTON

Short history of the church of St. Bartholomew, Guston.
Extract from Parish Magazine. n.d.
12

GYPSIES

KENT COUNTY COUNCIL - PLANNING DEPARTMENT.
Gypsies and other travellers in Kent, 1951-52, by J.W.R.
Adams.
n.d.
1,3,4,5,6,7,8,9,11,12,14,16,19,20

HACKINGTON

JONES, J.K.
St. Stephen's Church, Hackington.
n.d.
3

SOMERVILLE, P.P.
Short account of the parish of Hackington, alias St. Stephen's,
near Canterbury.
Canterbury, Gibbs. 1915.
3,11

HADLOW

DUMBRECK, William V.
The parish church of St. Mary, Hadlow.
195-?
4,11

DUMBRECK, William V.
A short history of St. Mary's, Hadlow, by W.V. Dumbreck.
Hadlow, Hilton. 1963.
4,11,12

DUMBRECK, William V.
A village folly: being the history of Hadlow Castle.
Hadlow, Hilton. 1964.
1,4,7,8,11,15,19

DUMBRECK, William V.
A village folly: being the history of Hadlow Castle.
Hadlow Local History Society. 1971, 2nd Edition.
9

KENNEDY, Bart.
Golden Green (Hadlow).
Cecil Palmer. 1926.
5,6,8,11,12,17,19

Little Poult House (Hadlow) - Sale catalogue.
1968.
12

HALLING

Church of St. John the Baptist, Halling.
Ramsgate, Church Publications. 1964.
4,8,11,12

COOK, W.H.
On the discovery of a human skeleton in a brick-earth deposit
in the valley of the River Medway at Halling, Kent.
Royal Anthropological Institute. 1912.
7,15

HALLING WOMEN'S INSTITUTE.
Halling: a survey undertaken for "The Countryside in the 70's".
Halling Women's Institute. c.1960.
12

HALSTEAD

An unprecedented case of oppression, with a narrative
of facts showing to what extent a malignant feeling
can be carried, when not checked by those in power...
Halstead.
Printed for the Author. 1838.
11

WARLOW, G.H.
History of Halstead.
Bromley, Kentish Times. 1934.
2,4,5,9,11,16

HAM

HOUGH, James.
The importance of religious knowledge to the soul: a
sermon...
1831.
11

HAM HILL - SEE SNODLAND

HAMPTON

MOUNT, Frank.
My recollections of Hampton.
Printed by Northover and Sons. (1942).
11

HARBLEDOWN

C., C.E.W.
A short history of St. Nicholas Hospital, Harbledown -
(pamphlet)
Canterbury, Eastes. n.d.
7

DUNCOMBE, John.
The history and antiquities of...St. Nicholas at
Harbledown, St. Johns, Northgate and St. Thomas of
Eastbridge...by J. Duncombe and N. Battely.
1785.
1,3,6,11

GARDINER, Mrs. Dorothy.
Hospital of St. Nicholas, Harbledown.
Canterbury, Jennings. 1950.
11

Harbledown, Hall Place - Sale catalogue.
London, Knight, Frank and Rutley. 1919.
3

Harbledown House - Sale catalogue.
Canterbury, Cooper and Wacher. 1924.
3

Harbledown, "Michaels" - Sale catalogue.
Dover, Vernon Shone. 19--?
3

H(USSEY), R(ichard) C.
British settlement in Bigbury Wood, Harbledown. In
Archaeologia Cantiana, Vol. 9, 1874.
17

JESSUP, Ronald Frank.
Objects from Bigberry Camp, Harbledown. (Reprinted
from the Antiquaries Journal, Vol. XVIII, 1938).
3

O'NEILL, Sibyl.
Harbledown, a Kentish village...
Canterbury, Austen. 1910.
1,3

A short history of St. Nicholas Hospital, Harbledown.
Canterbury, Eastes. 1913.
7

HARRIETSHAM

COLEIRE, Richard.
A sermon preached at the Temple Church, January 30th,
1713: being the anniversary of the martyrdom of King
Charles I.
Printed for H. Banks. 1714.
11

Court Lodge Estate, Harrietsham - Sale catalogue, 1966.
12

GOODSALL, Robert Harold.
An illustrated guide to the parish of St. John the Baptist,
Harrietsham.
1956.
4

GOODSALL, Robert Harold.
Stede Hill: the annals of a Kentish home.
Ashford, Headley. 1949.
1,2,3,4,5,7,8,11,12,15,17,18,20

Guide to the parish church of St. John the Baptist,
Harrietsham.
n.d.
12

TAYLOR, John.
The great eater of Kent; or, part of the admirable teeth and
stomach exploits of Nicholas Wood of Harrietsham in the County
of Kent.
Gosson. 1630.
11,12

HARTLEY

BANCKS, Gerald W.
Hartley through the ages.
n.d.
1,3,4,5,6,8,11,12,15,17

Goodwin's Cottage (Hartley Hill) - Sale catalogue, 1966.
12

MARTINDALE, Cyril Charlie.
The romance of a Kentish Mission: Our Lady of Hartley.
Salesian Press. 192-?
11

WILLIAMS, R.A.
About Hartley.
Hartley Publications. n.d.
11

HARTLIP

BALDWIN, R.A.
A history of Hartlip Methodist Chapel: a 150th anniversary
souvenir.
(1971).
11

HARTY

ROBERTSON, William Archibald Scott.
Ancient chest in Harty Church.
Mitchell and Hughes. 1876.
4,11,17

VALLANCE, Aymer.
Harty Church, Sheppey. (Reprinted from Archaeologia Cantiana,
Vol. 37).
Mitchell, Hughes and Clarke. 1924
11,17

HASTINGLEIGH

HARWOOD, Mary W.
Kentish village - Hastingleigh.
Hastingleigh Parochial Church Council. 1952.
1,2,3,7,8,11,21

HATCHAM

St. James', Hatcham, consecrated...1854 - centenary programme.
(Pamphlet).
1954.
18

HAWKENBURY

Hawkenbury Hall - Sale catalogue.
1967.
12

HAWKHURST

CLARK, F.C.
Did the builder of Bodiam Castle also construct Dalyn
Grigg's Bay...
Rye, Adams. 1955.
11

FRIENDLY BROTHERS SOCIETY.
Rules and regulations of the Kent and Sussex Friendly
Brothers Society, established at Hawkhurst, Kent on 5th
day of May, 1823.
Printed by George Waters. 1824.
11

Hall House, (Hawkhurst) - Sale catalogue, 1967.
12

HARRISON, Austin.
Frederic Harrison: thoughts and memories.
Heinemann. 1926.
12

HARRISON, Frederic.
Among my books.
Macmillan. 1912.
12

HARRISON, Frederic.
Autobiographic memoirs.
Macmillan. 1911.
12

Hawkhurst Church. In Bibliographia Topographica
Britannia.
n.d.
11

HUSSEY, Rev. William.
An address to the men of Hawkhurst in Kent...on their
riotous acts and proceedings.
Longman. 1830.
12

JEFFREYS, H.A.
The church of St. Laurence, Hawkhurst: its history and
architecture.
Kent Archaeological Society. 1874.
11,17

JENNINGS, Lady Mary Adelaide.
A Kentish country house...Hall House, Hawkhurst.
Guildford, Billing. 1894.
1,4,11,12,15

LEESE, Arthur Selwyn Mountford.
Parish church of St. Laurence, Hawkhurst.
1957.
4,11,12

24 new photographic views (Hawkhurst).
Hawkhurst, Couchman. 190-?
11

The Risden Estate (Hawkhurst) - Sale catalogue, 1967.
12

Theobalds (Hawkhurst) - Sale catalogue, 1867.
12

WILLIAMS, F.
Visitor's guide to Hawkhurst.
(1889).
17

HAWKINGE

BROWN, John Howard.
A history and description of St. Michael's Church,
Hawkinge. (Typescript).
n.d.
7

Particulars, plan and conditions of sale of...freehold
farms, samll holdings, accomodation, lands and sporting
woodlands, in all about 1,026 acres...to be sold by
auction...on...March 5th, 1920...by direction of the
Right Hon., the Earl of Radnor...(Includes Terlingham
Farm, Coombe Farm, Reinden Wood).
A.T. Burrows. 1920.
7

Album of photographs, prints and extracts on the history
of Hayes Place. (Compiled 1921).
n.d.
2

BURCH, Brian.
Bibliography of printed material relating to Bromley, Hayes
and Keston.
Bromley Public Libraries. 1964.
1,2,3,4,5,7,8,11,12,15,16,17,18

CLINCH, George.
Antiquarian jottings relating to Bromley, Hayes, Keston and
West Wickham.
Edinburgh, Turnbull. 1889.
1,2(and extra illustrated copy) 4,5,7,8,11,12,14,15,
17(1899) 18

COOPER, W.H. Hewlett.
Old Keston.
Strong. 1879.
2,6,17,18

CORNER, George Richard.
An account of excavations on the site of Roman buildings at
Keston...(From The Archaeologia, Vol. XXXVI).
J.B. Nichols (Printer). 1854 and 1855.
1,2,6,17

CRUESS, H.J.
A short history of the 17th Bromley (Keston) Scout Group
by H.J. Cruess and others. (Duplicated typescript).
(1969).
2

CUMMING, Graham LTD. Publishers.
Keston Parish Church.
G. Cumming. 1961 and 1962.
2(1961) 8(1961 and 1962) 12(1961 and 1962)

DAVIES, Susan E. (Later Mrs. McPherson).
A geographical study of Keston, Kent. (Unpublished thesis
photocopy).
1967.
2

DOWLING, D.T.
Keston Common Mill. (Typescript).
1972.
2

FOX, Nancy Piercy.
An interim note on the excavation of Caesar's Camp, Keston.
(Reprinted from Archaeologia Cantiana).
Ashford, Headley. (1957).
2,17

FOX, Nancy Piercy.
Warbank, Keston: a Romano-British site. In Archaeologia
Cantiana, Vol. 69, 1955.
17

GAMMON, Frank Sidney.
Story of Keston in Kent.
Murby. 1931.
2,3,5,11

GENTLEMAN'S MAGAZINE.
Description of some ancient paintings on panel, in Baston
House, Kent (by A.J. Kempe).
Gentlemen's Magazine. 1830.
11,12,17

HAYES PHILHARMONIC SOCIETY.
1945-1970 Jubilee Year commemorative brochure.
Hayes Philharmonic Society. 1970.
2

HOGG, A.H.A.
Earthworks on Hayes and West Wickham Commons, by A.H.A. Hogg
and others. In Archaeologia Cantiana, Vol. 54, 1941.
17

JACKSON, E.D.C.
Excavations at Keston Church, by E.D.C. Jackson and N.P. Fox.
(Reprinted from Archaeologia Cantiana, Vol. 64, 1951).
2,17

JAMES, V.F.
Prehistoric stone implements found at Hayes (Kent).
Oxford, Shakespeare Head. 1934.
11,12

KADWELL, Charles.
History of Hayes. (Photocopy of manuscript).
1833 with notes to 1879.
2

KEMPE, Alfred John.
An account of some recent discoveries at Holwood Hill
in Kent. (From Archaeologia Vol. 22, 1828).
J.B. Nichols. 1829.
1,2,11

KEMPE, Alfred John.
An investigation of the antiquities of Holwood Hill
in the parish of Keston.
n.d.
11

KENT COUNTY COUNCIL - ARCHIVES OFFICE.
Keston parish records.
1964.
2

KESTON CORONATION COMMITTEE.
Keston Coronation souvenir...1953.
2

KESTON FIELD CLUB.
Contribution of climatology to the regional survey of
Keston...(Typescript).
1950.
2

KESTON FIELD CLUB.
Regional survey (1950-1966). (Typescript and photocopies of maps).
n.d.
2

LEE, M.
Keston and Hayes in the nineteenth century. (Typescript
essay).
1966.
2

MUMBY, F.A.
From Sonnenschein to George Allen and Unwin Ltd.
(Note: George Allen started publishing at his house in
Keston), by F.A. Mumby and F.H.S. Stallybrass.
Allen and Unwin. 1955.
2

MUNDY, R.W.
An outer London suburb: Hayes, Kent, case study of the
growth processes of a 20th Century suburb. (Dissertation
from B.Sc. degree - typescript).
1967.
2

MYNOTT, E.
A walk through Keston, compiled by E. Mynott and others.
West Kent Border Archaeological Group. 1969.
2,6,8,11

NORMAN, Philip.
Flint implements found at Keston and note on a pit at
West Wickham Common. (Galley proof from Proceedings of
the Society of Antiquaries, 2nd series, Vol. 17, 1898).
2

PATTULLO HIGGS AND CO. LTD.
60 years with Pattullo Higgs. (Note: manufacturers of
fertilizers - offices at Hayes - formerly produce
merchants at Orpington).
Straker Bros. Printers. (1964).
2

ST. MARY THE VIRGIN'S CHURCH, HAYES.
List of records kept...at (Bromley) Town Hall.
(Typescript).
n.d.
2

SCHAFFER, Gordon.
Light and liberty: 60 years of the Electrical Trades
Union. (Note: Electrical Trades Union Headquarters at
Hayes Court, Hayes, Kent from 1946).
Electrical Trades Union. (1949).
2

STANLEY, Mary Catherine. Countess of Derby.
Memoranda on Keston, Holwood, Hayes Place and Hollydate.
(Mutilated copy - 1½ leaves missing).
Privately Printed. 1887.
2

SUNDAY TIMES MAGAZINE.
The dream of suburbia. (Note: features Keston and West
Wickham).
Times Newspapers. 11th February, 1968.
2

TATE AND LYLE LTD. -- RESEARCH CENTRE.
Sugar. (Note: includes section on research at "Ravensbourne",
Keston).
Tate and Lyle Ltd. (1963?).
2

TATE AND LYLE LTD. - RESEARCH CENTRE.
This is Ravensbourne (Keston).
Tate and Lyle Ltd. (1967).
2

THOMPSON, Henry Percy.
A rhyme of Hayes.
n.d.
2

(THOMPSON, Henry Percy).
We made history: a play in 8 scenes (connecting Hayes with
national history based on material collected by H.P.
Thompson).
1951.
2

THOMPSON, Henry Percy.
History of Hayes...
Lovat Dickson. 1935.
1,2,4,5,7,11,12,15,18

WATTS, M.C.
Catalogue of documents relating to Keston in the Archives
Office, Maidstone. (Typescript).
1965.
2

HEADCORN

ATKINS, Rev. Paul.
Headcorn: its parish, church and people, compiled by Rev. P.
Atkins.
1957.
11,12

COWPER, H.S.
Two Headcorn Cloth Halls.
1915.
12,17

Curteis Farm, Headcorn - Sale catalogue.
1967.
12

Fairmeadow Farm, Headcorn - Sale catalogue.
1967.
12

FURLEY, Robert.
Annals of Headcorn...a lecture.
Ashford, Igglesden. 1878.
1,3,4,6,11,12,15,17

HEADCORN PARISH COUNCIL.
Headcorn, Kent: official guide, compiled by Headcorn Parish
Council.
Croydon, Homeland Publications. 1947.
1,11,12

OYLER, Thomas H.
St. Peter and St. Paul's Church, Headcorn.
S.E. Gazette. 1935.
11

OYLER, Thomas H.
Truth will out (Headcorn).
n.d.
11

Parish church of St. Peter and St. Paul, Headcorn.
"Home Words". 1955.
11,12

St. Peter and St. Paul,(based upon "A History of
Headcorn", by Rev. Paul Atkins).
Ramsgate, G. Cumming. 1959.
4,11

St. Peter and St. Paul, Headcorn (based upon a history
of Headcorn by Rev. Paul Atkins) 3rd edition.
Ramsgate, G. Cumming. 1961.
1,4,8,12

WILKINSON, Edward.
Funeral sermon of the Revq Henry Doyle Sewell, M.A.,
thirty-six years Vicar of Headcorn...
Shaw. 1886.
1

HEALTH AND WELFARE

KENT COUNTY COUNCIL.
Report upon tuberculosis and the administration of
sanatorium benefit, by Kent County Council and Kent
Insurance Committee.
Kent County Council and Kent Insurance Committee.
1914-15.
1(1st and 2nd only)

KENT COUNTY COUNCIL - HEALTH DEPARTMENT.
Annual report of the Medical Officer of Health for the
year 1971.
Kent County Council. (1972).
11

KENT EDUCATION COMMITTEE.
Annual report of the Schools Medical Officer.
Kent County Council. n.d.
1(1912,1913,1924) 6(1945-52) 11(1945-52) 12(1945-52)

KENT EDUCATION COMMITTEE.
Report on the health of the school child for the years
1953 to 1959.
Kent Education Committee. 1954-60.
5(1958-60) 6(1953-65) 11(1953 in progress) 12(1955 in
progress) 19(1963 in progress)

KENT PAEDIATRIC SOCIETY.
A study in the epidemiology of health...schoolchildren
in...Bexley.
1954.
8,19

NATIONAL HEALTH SERVICE - KENT AND CANTERBURY
EXECUTIVE COUNCIL.
Health and allied services in the County of Kent and
the City of Canterbury.
Malcolm Page Ltd. (1960).
4,8,15

NATIONAL HEALTH SERVICE - KENT AND CANTERBURY
EXECUTIVE COUNCIL.
Medical list.
Maidstone, Kent and Canterbury Executive Council. 1962.
3

HENHURST

The family of Master of Henhurst, Kent and Norfolk.
1881.
12

HERALDRY

ELLISTON-ERWOOD, Frank Charles.
The coats of arms from Kent in London. In
Archaeologia Cantiana, Vol. 57, 1944.
17

HERNE BAY Cont'd

Eighteen views of Herne Bay and neighbourhood.
London, Newman and Co. n.d.
3

GOUGH, Harold Eric.
Beyond the Forest of Blean: chapters in the history of
Herne Bay.
Herne Bay Press. 1966.
15

Herne Bay: an invitation to Herne Bay.
Herne Bay Urban District Council. 1949.
3

Herne Bay: picture of the new town, its beauties, history
and the curiosities in its vicinity...
1835.
8,11,13

Herne Bay: 32 views.
Callcut and Beavis. 1900?
11

HERNE BAY PRESS.
The great East Coast storm, 1953: damage at Herne Bay and
Whitstable, Kent.
Herne Bay Press. (1953?).
3,11

HERNE BAY URBAN DISTRICT COUNCIL.
Coronation guide, 1953.
15

HERNE BAY URBAN DISTRICT COUNCIL.
Herne Bay.
Herne Bay, Ridout and Sons. 1928.
3

HERBE BAY URBAN DISTRICT COUNCIL.
Guide, 1957.
4

HEYWOOD, John. Publisher.
Illustrated guide to Herne Bay and neighbourhood.
n.d.
11,17

HIGGINS, William Mullingar.
The restoration of the Herne Bay Pier.
J. Weale. (1844).
11

KENT COAST COLLEGE.
"The Log" of Kent Coast College, No. 1, December, 1887-No. 5,
December, 1890.
Kent Coast College. 1887-1890.
12

KENT COUNTY COUNCIL - PLANNING DEPARTMENT.
Kent development plan (Part A), Herne Bay and Whitstable
town map.
Kent County Council. 1960.
11,12

KENT COUNTY LIBRARY.
A list of books concerning Herne Bay, Herne and Reculver.
Kent County Library. 1951.
7,11

Kidd's picturesque steam boat companion to Herne Bay...
Kidd. 1832.
13,14

KING, Richard S.
Herne Bay, humorously expressed and illustrated (verse).
R.S. King. (190-?).
11,17

"A LADY".
A picture of the new town of Herne Bay by a Lady.
Macrone. 1835.
12,17

MESSENGER AND ADAMS. Architects.
The landbook, November, 1897-1900. A manuscript ledger of a
Herne Bay firm of architects, surveyors and land agents,
relating to property in the town.
n.d.
11

MILLGATE, W.F. Publisher.
Millgate's Herne Bay guide with notes on the surrounding
places of interest. Illustrated by B.C. Dexter.
Herne Bay, W.F. Millgate. 1897.
8

Photographic views (Herne Bay and district).
London, Domestic Bazaar Co. c.1905.
15

RIDOUT AND SONS. Publishers.
Guide to Herne Bay and surrounding neighbourhood.
Herne Bay, Ridout and Sons. 1882.
11,17

Short history of the church of St. Bartholomew, Herne
Bay, produced for the 21st anniversary of the
constitution of the parish, 1957.
Herne Bay, Ridout and Sons. 1957.
12

SMITH, Reginald Anthony.
The wreck on Pudding-Pan Rock: 2nd wreck at Herne Bay.
(From the Proceedings of the Society of Antiquaries
Journal, 2nd series, Vol. XXI, January 17th, 1907).
3

The Standard picture guide to Herne Bay and Canterbury.
London, Standard Picture Guide Co. (1907).
3

Thirty-two views of Herne Bay and neighbourhood.
London, Newman. 1880?
3

Views of Herne Bay.
c.1860.
13

WATKINSON, J.
Herne Bay Congregational Church: history of the church
with biographical notes of its ministers.
1910.
17

WATKINSON, J.
Herne Bay illustrated, edited by J. Watkinson.
Herne Bay Press. 1889.
11,13

WATSON, William.
Visitor's guide to Herne Bay, Canterbury and the most
memorable spots in Kent.
John Dicks. 1855.
11,17

Where you can go and where you can stay in Herne Bay.
1909.
13

WHITEHEAD, C.J.
Herne Bay, 1830 to 1870: a study of the development
of an English seaside resort in the mid 19th century.
(Thesis).
1971.
11

HERNE HILL

JANES, Hurford.
Centenary commemoration of the opening of Hernhill
School, 1872-1972: historical sketch (H. Janes) -
personal memories (K.C. Judges).
Printed by South Litho Printing. (1972).
11

HEVER

ASTOR, Gavin.
Hever Castle and gardens.
Jarrold. 1971.
8

ASTOR, William Waldorf.
Free in a faraway land. (MS. written at Hever Castle,
April 1st, 1546, by Perkin Dethridge...with an
introduction by William Waldorf Astor). (Reprinted
from Pall Mall Magazine, August, 1903).
8

BAILEY, H.C.
The Roman Eagles.
Gill. 1929.
12

BAKER, Alan R.H.
Open fields and partible inheritance on a Kent Manor.
(Reprinted from the Economic History Review, 2nd series,
Vol. XVII, No. 1, 1964).
8

BANNER, Hubert Stewart.
Kentish fire.
Hurst and Blackett. 1944.
1,4,5,9,11,15,19

BASKERVILLE, Geoffrey.
English monks and the suppression of the monasteries.
Cape. 1937.
3

Bibliotheca Topographica Britannica, Vol. 1: antiquities
in Kent and Sussex
John Nichols. 1790.
4

Bibliographica Topographica Britannica, Vol. 1: antiquities
in Kent and Sussex.
New York, Kraus Reprint Company Press. 1968.
11

Biblitheca Topographica Britannia, Vol. 1, No. 1,
containing: 1, queries for the better illustrating the
antiquities and natural history of Great Britain and
Ireland; 2, the history and antiquities of Tunstall in Kent,
by the late Mr. Edward Rowe Mores.
J. Nichols. 1780.
4

Bibliotheca Topographica Britannia, Vol. 1, No. 6, Parts
1 and 2: containing Mr. Thorpe's illustrations of several
antiquities in Kent which have hitherto remained undescribed.
J. Nichols. 1782 and 1783.
3,4,6,11,12,15

Bibliotheca Topographica Britannia (Vol. ?), No. XLII:
St. Radigund's; Thanet Tradesmen's Tokens; The Moat near
Canterbury; Hawkhurst Church; Canterbury Cathedral
(letter from Mr. Essex); Urbo Rutupiae by Mr. Douglas;
Memories of William Lambarde.
Society of Antiquaries. 1787.
8

BOND, Maurice F.
The manuscripts of the House of Lords, Vol. II (new series)
...addenda 1514-1714, edited by Maurice F. Bond.
H.M.S.O. 1962.
3

BRUCE, John.
Proceedings, principally in the County of Kent, in connection
with the Parliament called in 1640, edited by J. Bruce.
Camden Society. n.d.
11

C., E.L.
Queen Bertha of Kent, by E.L.C.
Church Mission Publishing Society. 1899.
11

C., M. (Matthew Carter).
A most true and exact relation of that honourable though
unfortunate Expedition of Kent, Essex and Colchester in
1648, by a loyal actor in that engagement.
1650.
4,6,8,12,17

CHALKLIN, Christopher William.
Seventeenth century Kent.
Longmans. 1965.
1,2,3,4,5,6,7,8,10,11,12,15,17,18,19,20,21

CLAYTON, Joseph.
The true story of Jack Cade, Captain of Kent, 1450.
Palmer. 1909.
11

COLE, William.
History of the Royal Marriage, 1863, together with the
public rejoicings in every town and village in Kent,
edited by W. Cole.
"Kent Times". 1863.
11

COLERIDGE, H.N.
Genuine life of Mr. Francis Swing.
London. 1831.
17

COLLIER, Richard.
Eagle day: the Battle of Britain.
Hodder and Stoughton. 1966.
15

COLOMB, George Hatton.
For King and Kent (1648).
Remington. 1882.
5,8,11,15

COLOMB, George Hatton.
For King and Kent (1648), new edition, 2 vols.
W.H. Allen. 1892.
4

COLOMB, George Hatton.
Royalist rising in Kent, 1648.
n.d.
17

"A COMMONER", pseud.
Kentish men: a satyr occasioned by the late treat at
Mercers Hall, written by a commoner.
Sold by the Booksellers of London and Westminster. 1701.
17

CONGRESS OF ARCHAEOLOGICAL SOCIETIES IN UNION WITH THE
SOCIETY OF ANTIQUARIES OF LONDON.
Report of the Congress: 36th Congress for 1928-29,
37th Congress for 1929-30, 39th Congress for 1931-32,
45th Congress for 1937-38.
3

COOK, Norman.
Roman remains.
Kent Council of Social Service. 1938?
11,12

COOPER, William Durrant.
John Cade's followers in Kent.
1868.
1,11,17

COPLEY, Gordon J.
Archaeology of South-East England.
Phoenix House. 1958.
5,10,12,14

COUNCER, C.R.
Dissolution of the Kentish monasteries. In Archaeologia
Cantiana, Vol. 47, 1935.
17

COUNTRY GENTLEMAN OF KENT, pseud.
A letter to the editor of the Standard...on the
presentation of the Kent Petition to the House of
Peers...
Hatchard. 1829.
12

COWPER, Joseph Meadows.
On some Tudor prices in Kent.
n.d.
11

COX, Thomas.
Magna Britannia et Hibernia, antique et nova, by T.
Cox and A. Hall. (Section dealing with Kent, pp.
1,071-1,270).
London, Strand - Sold by M. Nutt. (1727).
2,3,4,6,7,8,9,11,12,13,17,18,21

COX, Thomas.
A topographical, ecclesiastical and natural history of
Kent. (From Magna Britannia et Hibernia).
London, Strand - Sold by T. Nutt. (1727).
4,5,9,10,11,15,17

(COZENS, Zechariah).
An ecclesiastical, topographical history of Kent...photocopy
of a typescript commentary of this unpublished manuscript by
F.W. Cock of Appledore. Original work c.1793.
c.1943.
11

CRAWFORD, Osbert Guy Stanhope.
Notes on archaeological information incorporated, Part 2,
The long barrows of megaliths in...Kent, Surrey and Sussex.
1924.
11

CROWE, Stanley.
Bygone and historic Kent.
S. Crowe. 1958.
1,11

CULMER, Richard. The Elder.
Lawless tythe-robbers discovered: who maketh tythe-revenue
a mock-mayntenance...
Printed for Thomas Newbery. 1656.
11

A curious chapter in Kentish history. Kentish Estates
Journal, No. 18, 1923.
3

DARBISHIRE, R.D.
On the "Implements from the chalk plateau" in Kent...
Manchester Literary and Philosophical Society. 1901.
11

DARBY, H.C.
The Domesday geography of Southeast England, edited by H.C.
Darby and E.M.J. Campbell.
Cambridge University Press. 1962
1,2,3,5,7,10,11,12,15,17,18,19,20

Dartford Parliamentary Division historical pageant, Hall
Place, Bexley, 1932.
1,5,11,17

DAVIDSON, Hilda R. Ellis.
The ring on the sword. In The Journal of the Arms and Armour
Society, Vol. II, No. 10, June, 1958.
3

A declaration and ordinance of the Lords and Commons...for
the better securing and settling of the peace in the County
of Kent.
Wright. 1643.
12

The Declaration of the Knights, gentry and trained bands of
the County of Kent...
Banks. 1642.
12

A declaration of the Lords and Commons assembled in
Parliament...also three orders...together with an ordinance
of both Houses of Parliament, for the payment of tythes.
Printed for Edward Husband. 1684.
11

A declaration of the several proceedings of both Houses of
Parliament, with those in the County of Kent now in arms
against the authority of Parliament.
E. Husband. 1648.
11,12

DEFOE, Daniel.
History of the Kentish Petition.
1701.
11,17

DERING, Sir Edward.
A declaration by Sir Edward Dering...with his petition...in
Parliament.
Philemon Stephens. 1644.
11

DE VAYNES, Julia Henrietta.
The Kentish garland, edited by J.H. De Vaynes.
Hertford, Stephen Austin. 1881-2.
1,3,4,5,7,8,11,12,13,14,15,16,17,19

DIGGS, Thomas.
England's defence...1588.
Haley. 1680.
12

DITCHFIELD, P.H.
Memorials of old Kent, edited by P.H. Ditchfield and
G. Ginch.
Bemrose. 1907.
1,2,3,4,5,6,7,8,9,10,11,12,13,14,15,16,17,18,19

DOBSON, R.B.
Peasants' revolt of 1381.
Macmillan. 1970.
5

DOMESDAY BOOK.
Domesday: or, an actual survey of South-Britain, by
the Commissioniers of William the Conqueror, completed
in the year 1086...Kent, Sussex and Surrey...illustrated
by S. Henshall and J. Wilkinson.
Bye and Law. 1799.
1,5,6,8,11,12,13,16,17

Domesday Book; or, the great survey of England of
William the Conqueror, A.D. 1086, facsimile of part
relating to Kent.
1863.
2,3,4,5,6,8,11,12,13,17,18

DOMESDAY BOOK.
Domesday Book: section on Kent. (Latin text only).
G. Nichols. 1783.
11

The Domesday Book of Kent: translation, notes and
appendix by Rev. Lambert Blackwell Larking.
J. Toovey. 1869.
1,2,3,4,5,6,7,8,12,14,16,17,18,19

DUDLEY, Donald R.
The Roman conquest of Britain, A.D. 43-57, by D.R. Dudley
and G. Webster.
Batsford. 1965.
12

DUGDALE, Sir William.
Monasticon Anglicanum.
R. Harbin. 1718.
11,15

DUNCAN, Leyland Lewis.
The renunciation of the Papal Authority by the Clergy of
West Kent, 1534. (Reprinted from Archaeologia Cantiana).
n.d.
17(1897) 18(1896)

DUNKIN, Alfred John.
The archaeological mine.
1855.
3,5,11,14,18

DUNKIN, Alfred John.
The chronicles of Kent.
1844.
3,5,6,9,11

DUNKIN. Alfred John.
Corpus Juris Cantici the Dooms, or the Saxon laws of
Kent...edited by A.J. Dunkin.
Privately Printed. n.d.
1,5

DUNKIN, Alfred John.
History of the County of Kent (2 vols.).
1856-8.
1,4(Vol. 2 only) 5,6,7,11,12,14,15,17(Vol. 2 only) 18

DUNKIN, Alfred John.
Prospectus of the history of the County of Kent.
n.d.
2,6,11,17(1853 and 1854)

DUNKIN, John, of Bromley.
The Romans in Britain and the introduction of
Christianity into Kent (2 pamphlets), bound with "Caesar
and the Britons", by H. Barry, edited by J. Dunkin.
1831.
5

DUNNING, G.C.
Roman barrows, by G.C. Dunning and R.F. Jessup.
(Reprinted from "Antiquity", March, 1936).
3

DWELLY, Edward
Parish records, Vol. 3, Kent.
1914
11,15

EADMER, The Monk.
Eadmeri Historia Novorum in Anglia et opuscula duo de vita
Sancti Anselmi et quibusdam miraculis ejus. Edited from
MSS. by M. Rule.
H.M.S.O. 1884. Reprinted Kraus. 1965.
8(1965) 17(1884)

EADMER, The Monk.
Eadmeri Monachi Cantuariensis historiae novorum sive sui
saeculi libri VI res gestas sub Giulielmis I and II et
Henrico I, Angliae regibus ab anno nempe salutis MLXVI ad
MCXXII potissimum complexi.
London, M. and T. Dent. 1623.
17

EADMER, The Monk.
History of recent events in England, translated by G.
Bosanquet from the Latin.
Cresset Press. 1964.
12

ELLIS, William Smith.
Early Kentish armory. In Archaeologia Cantiana, 1883.
6,11,17

ELLIS, William Smith.
Notices of the Ellises of France (from the time of
Charlemagne) and of England (from the Conquest) to the present
day.
London, E. Tucker. n.d.
15

ELLISTON-ERWOOD, Frank Charles.
The adventures of a Kentish spy (Walter Roberts, d. circa
1522). In Archaeologia Cantiana, Vol. 50, 1939.
11,17

ELLISTON-ERWOOD, Frank Charles.
The present state of monastic archaeology in Kent.
1954.
12

ELTON, Charles I.
The tenures of Kent.
Parker. 1867.
1,2,4,8,11,12,14,15,17,18

ELVIRA, pseud.
Kentish yesterdays.
"Kentish Times". (1947).
1,2,5,8,11,15,17

EMMISON, F.G.
County records, by F.G. Emmison and I. Gray.
1948.
8

An enquiry; or, a discourse between a Yeoman of Kent and a
Knight of a Shire, upon the Prorogation of the Parliament to
the second of May, 1693.
n.d.
1

ENTRACT, J.P.
Henry Boswell Bennett, a victim of the last peasants' revolt,
1838. (Reprinted from the Journal of the Society of Army
Historical Research, March, 1966, pp. 14-18).
3,11

EPPS, William.
The genius of Kent; or, County miscellany for November, 1792,
edited by W. Epps.
Canterbury, Printed at Herald Printing Office. 1792.
3

EVANS, John H.
Kentish megalith types. (Reprinted from Archaeologia Cantiana,
Vol. LXIII).
Ashford, Headley. 1952.
4,8,17

EVELYN, John.
A scheme of the posture of the Dutch fleete and action at
Shere-nesse and Chatham, 10th, 11th and 12th June, 1667.
Copy of a map.
n.d.
8

EVERITT, Alan Milner.
An account book of the Committee of Kent, 1646-1647.
Kent Archaeological Society. 1960.
11

EVERITT, Alan Milner.
The community of Kent and the Great Rebellion, 1640-60.
Leicester University Press. 1966.
1,2,3,4,5,6,7,8,10,11,15,17,18,19,21

EVERITT, Alan Milner.
The County Committee of Kent in the Civil War.
Leicester University Press. 1957.
1,2,3,4,5,6,7,8,9,11,12,15,17,18,19,20

EVISON, Vera Ivy.
The fifth-century invasions south of the Thames.
Athlone Press. 1965.
1,3,4,7,11,12,15

Excerpta: consisting of miscellaneous articles taken
from various magazines between 1791-1826...dealing with
various aspects of Kentish history.
15

The Eyre of Kent, A.D. 1313-14, 3 vols.
Vol. I edited by F.W. Maitland and others.
Vol. II edited by F.W. Maitland and W.C. Bolland.
Vol. III edited by W.C. Bolland.
Quaritch and Seldon Society. 1910-13.
1,3,5,11

FAIRFAX, Thomas Fairfax. 3rd Baron.
The Fairfax correspondence, edited by G.W. Johnson, 2
vols.
Richard Bentley. 1848.
12

FAIRFAX, Thomas Fairfax. 3rd Baron.
A letter from His Excellency the Lord Fairfax to the
House of Peers. concerning all the proceedings in Kent...
John Wright. 1648.
11

FAIRFAX, Thomas Fairfax. 3rd Baron.
Memorials of Civil War, edited by R. Bell, 2 vols.
Richard Bentley. 1849.
12

FILMER, Reginald Mead.
A chronicle of Kent, 1250-1760.
London, 12/13 Bow Lane, E.C.4. 1967.
1,2,3,4,5,6,7,8,9,10,11,12,17,18,19,20

FINCH, W.
An historical sketch of the County of Kent, collected
from the celebrated works of Camden, Harris, Seymour,
Phillipot, Hastead, etc...with a directory in 2 parts.
London, Daniel. 1803.
3,6,7,11,13,14,15

FINNY, W.E. St. L.
Lecture on the life of King Athelstan...(Reprinted from
"Local Illustrated News").
Willesden, Lowe and Brydone Ltd. 1924.
3

FLOWER, C.T.
Public works in mediaeval law, Vol. 1, edited by C.T.
Flower.
Selden Society. 1915.
11

FREDETTE, Raymond H.
The first Battle of Britain, 1917-18.
Cassell. 1966.
7

FRERE, Sheppard.
Problems of the Iron Age in Southern Britain.
1961.
3

Furley, Robert.
Sir Thomas Wyatt's rebellion, A.D. 1554.
Maidstone, J. Burgiss-Brown. 1878.
1,6,11

GALBRAITH, V.H.
Making of a Domesday Book.
Oxford, Clarendon Press. 1961.
10

BOISSIER, Rev. G.R.
Hever Castle (MS.).
n.d.
11

EASTMAN, John.
Historic Hever. the church be the Parish Clerk.
1905.
7,11,16

FOSTER, Denis.
Guide to St. Peter's Church, Hever.
1959.
2(1963) 11,12,19

GUNNIS Rupert.
The history of Hever Castle.
1961.
19

GUNNIS, Rupert.
The owners of Hever Castle.
1959.
11

Hever: a study in agricultural geography (MS.).
196-?
11

Hever Castle, Edenbridge.
Times Publishing Co. 195-?
7,11

Hever Castle and gardens.
Times Publishing Co. (1963)
2,11,12,15

Hever parish books: summaries of the contents, compiled by
D.B.L. Foster and others.
1949.
12

HOPKIN, R. Thurston.
Moated houses of England.
"Kent Life". 1935.
5,11,15,18

SERGEANT, Philip W.
Anne Boleyn: a study.
Hutchinson. (Revised Edition 1934).
6(1924) 12

THOMPSON, Stephen.
Old English homes. (Includes Hever Castle).
Sampson Low. 1876.
11,15

HEXTABLE

BALLS, Horace J.
Hextable. (Typescript).
1960.
5

BALLS, Horace J.
Historical notes on Hextable.
1963.
11

HIGH HALDEN

MARTIN, W.W.
The Chequers Inn (High Halden).
Mitre Press. 1929.
3,6,11,12,13

HIGHAM

FIELDING, Cecil Henry.
Handbook of Higham.
Rochester, Wildish. 1882.
1,2,4,6,8,9,11,12,15,17

HARRIS, Edwin.
The history of Higham and its Dickensian and Shakespearian
associations. (Eastgate series No. 29).
Chatham, E. Harris. 1921.
9,15

SPARVEL-BAYLY, J.A.
More Kentish proverbs, Part 2, and Higham Priory.
Walford's Antiquarian and Bibliographical Review. 1887.
5

St. Mary's and St. John's Churches, Higham-with-
Merston.
Ramsgate, Graham Cumming Ltd. (1962?).
4

St. Mary's and St. John's Churches, Higham-with-Merston.
Ramsgate, Church Publishers. 1969.
11

St. Mary's and St. John's Churches, Higham-with-Merston.
Ramsgate, Church Publishers. (197-).
11

St. Mary's and St. John's Churches, Higham-with-
Merston: short history.
Ramsgate, Church Publishers. 1965.
12

TOMS, H.S.
An early bead necklace found at Higham, Kent.
Rochester Naturalist. 1932.
12

HILDENBOROUGH

Church of St. John the Evangelist, Hildenborough,
1844-1944, compiled by Hildenborough Church Parochial
Council.
Tonbridge, Printed by F.M. Bridger. 1944.
11

Hildenborough Air Raid Wardens' pocket-book.
n.d.
11

Orchard Mains, Hildenborough - Sale catalogue.
1968.
12

HINXHILL

Hinxhill Estate - Sale catalogue.
1968.
12

HISTORY AND ARCHAEOLOGY

AIR MINISTRY.
The Battle of Britain...8th August-31st October, 1940.
H.M.S.O. 1941.
2,12

AIRY, George Biddell.
On the place of Caesar's departure from Gaul...and the
place of his landing in Britain...
n.d.
11

AKERMAN, John Yonge.
Remains of Pagan Saxondom.
John Russell Smith. 1855.
3,11

ALLCHIN, J.H.
Glance at the early history of Kent, compiled from
various authorities.
Maidstone, Ruck. 1903.
2,7,11

ALMACK, Richard.
Papers relating to proceedings in the County of Kent,
A.D. 1642-1646, edited by R. Almack.
Camden Society. 1854.
1,3,11,15,17

Ancient monuments in the administrative county of Kent
to 31st December, 1954.
Folkestone, Kent Council of Social Service. 1955.
12

Archaeologia Cantiana.
Kent Archaeological Society. In Progress.
1,2,3,4,5,6,7,8,9,10,11,12,13,14,15,16,17,18,19,20,21

GALE, Samuel.
A dissertation on Julius Caesar's passage over the River
Thames.
1734?
11

GARDINER, Mrs. Dorothy.
Some sources of Kent local history.
Kent County Council. 1937-8.
3,8,11,13

GARDINER, Mrs. Dorothy.
Some travel notes during the Thirty Years War (Thomas Denne).
"History". 1940.
3

GAZE, W.C.
On and along the Thames: James I.
Jarrold. 1913?
11,18

GLANVILLE, John.
Reports of certain cases determined and adjudged by the
Commons...in the 21st and 22nd years...of King James I...
edited by J. Glanville.
Baker and Leigh. 1775.
11

Gravesend and the Baronial Halls of Kent. (From Knight's
Excursion and Companion).
n.d.
17

GREAT BRITAIN: Parliament.
Instructions from...the House of Commons...to the Committee
in Kent...
1642.
11

GREENSTREET, James.
Fragments of the Kent portion of "Kirkby's inquest", temp.
Edward I.
1877.
11

GREENSTREET, James.
Kent fines Edward II, Part 1, Anno 1-6, edited by J. Greenstreet.
Mitchell and Hughes. 1877.
2,4,8,11

GREENSTREET, James.
Jack Cade's rebellion.
n.d.
17

GREENWOOD, C.
An epitome of county history.
1838.
1,2,3,4,5,6,7,8,11,12,14,15,16,17,18,19

GRIFFIN, Ralph.
Calendar, Kent feet of fines, Parts 1 and 2, by R. Griffin
and others.
Ashford, Headley Bros. 1939-1940.
3,12

The Groans of Kent; or, an humble remonstrance...to...Lord
General Fairfax.
1647-9.
17

GROSE, Francis.
The antiquities of England and Wales, Vol. 3, Kent.
Wright. c.1773.
1,2,4,6,7,8,11,17,18

HAMMOND, J.L.
The village labourer, 1760-1832. (Kent references) by J.L.
and B. Hammond.
Longmans. 1927.
18

HAMMOND, W.O.
An address to the freeholders of the County of Kent...
1828.
1

HARRIS, John.
The history of Kent in five parts...Book 1 - an exact
topography...Book 2 - the civil history of Kent. (Bound
in one volume).
D. Midwinter. 1719.
1,3,4,5,6,7,8,9,11,12,13,14,15,16,17,19

HARRISON, Benjamin.
An outline of the history of the eolithic flint
implements.
Ightham, Harrison. 1904.
5,11,16

HART, W.H.
A register of the lands held by Catholics and
Nonjurors in the County of Kent in the reign of King
George I, edited by W.H. Hart.
Smith. 1870.
1,11,17

(HASSELL, John).
Views of noblemen's and gentlemen's seats...in the counties
adjoining London. (Engravings - 5 in Kent).
(1804).
2

HASTED, Edward.
History and topographical survey of the County of Kent...
(1st folio edition).
Simmons and Kirkby. 1778-9.
1,2,3,4,5,6,7,8,10,11,12,13,15,16,17,21

HASTED, Edward.
History and topographical survey of the County of Kent...
illustrations from 1st folio edition, 1778-1798.
(Artificial collection of plates from Hasted).
n.d.
1,3,5,11

HASTED, Edward.
History and topographical survey of the County of Kent...
(1st edition grangerised 1778-1799) 4 vols. in 14 vols.
n.d.
11

HASTED, Edward.
History and topographical survey of the County of Kent.
(2nd edition) 12 vols.
Bristow. 1797-1801.
1,2,3,5,6,7,8,9,11,12,13,14,15,16,17,18(Vol. 1) 19,
20,21

HASTED, Edward.
History and topographical survey of the County of Kent...
(2nd edition - facsimile reprint).
EP Publishing Co. with Kent County Library. 1972.
11

HASTED, Edward.
History...of the County of Kent, Part I: Hundred
of Blackheath.
Mitchell and Hughes. 1886.
1,2(1866) 3,5,7,8,11,12,16,18

HASTED, Edward.
History of Kent, Vol. 2: the Lath of Aylesford
continued...the City and Liberty of Rochester.
n.d.
4,15

HENSHALL, Samuel.
History of South Britain.
1798.
16

HENSHALL, Samuel.
Specimens and parts, containing a history of the County
of Kent...
Rivington. 1798.
1,4,5,6,7,8,11,12,13,15,16,17

HENTZNER, Paul.
Account of England in the year 1598.
n.d.
9

His Majesties declaration to all his loving subjects...
the Kentish petitioners, 1642.
n.d.
6

HOBSBAWM, Eric John.
Captain Swing, by E.J. Hobsbawm and G. Rude. (Note:
includes substantial number of references to incidents in
Kent).
Lawrence, Wishart. 1969.
2,4

HOLMES, T.R.
Ancient Britain and the invasion of Julius Caesar.
Oxford University Press. 1907.
12

HOME, C.M.
The Thanes of Kent.
Catholic Truth Society. 1896.
11,12

HOWARD-FLANDERS, W.
King, Parliament and Army: more particulars relating to...
the unfortunate expedition of Kent, Essex and Colchester in
1648, as narrated by Matthew Carter.
London, Gay and Bird. 1905.
19

HOWELL, George O.
Kentish notebook. (Vols. 1 and 2).
Vol. 1 - Smithers (1891). Vol. 2 - Gray (1894).
2,3,4,5(Vol. 2 only) 6,7,8,9,11,12,14,15,17(1889-92) 18

HUDSON, Elizabeth Harriot.
Bertha: our first Christian Queen and her times.
Tegg. 1868.
3,11

The humble petition and resolution of the Countie of Kent,
August 30th, 1642...
Printed for John Wright. 1642.
3,11

HUNT, R.W.
Studies in medieval history, edited by R. Hunt and others.
Oxford, Clarendon Press. 1948.
3

HUTCHINSON, John.
Men of Kent and Kentish Men.
Canterbury, Cross and Jackman. 1892.
1,2,3,5,6,7,8,11,13,15,17,18

The indictment, arraingment, trial and judgement, at large,
of 29 regicides.
1713.
12

IRELAND, William Henry.
England's topographer; or, a new and complete history of
Kent. (Vols. 1-4).
G. Virtue. 1828-30.
1,2,3,4,5,6,8,9,10,11,12,13,14,15,16(3 vols.) 17,18(Vol. 2)
19,20,21

Is Jack Cade coming? A question considered by "The Age"
newspaper of Sunday, June 10th, 1838.
Thomas Holt. 1838.
3

JAMES, Harold A.
The Dutch in the Medway, 1667.
Chatham Borough Council. 1967.
4,11,19

JENKINS, Frank.
Cult of Dea Nutrix in Kent (autographed copy). (Reprinted
from Archaeologia Cantiana, Vol. LXXI, 1957).
3,17

JENKINS, Frank.
Cult of the "Pseudo-Venus" in Kent. (Reprinted from
Archaeologia Cantiana, Vol. LXXII, 1958).
3,17

JENKINS, Frank.
Men of Kent before the Romans...
Canterbury Archaeological Society. 1962.
1,2,3,4,5,7,8,9,10,11,12,14,15,19

JENKINS, Frank.
Men of Kent in the Dark Ages.
Canterbury Archaeological Society. 1964.
1,2,3,4,5,7,8,10,12,15,19

JENKINS, Frank.
Nameless or Nehalennia. (Reprinted from Archaeologia
Cantiana, Vol. LXX, 1956).
3,17

JENKINS, Frank.
Roman Kent: Cantium in Roman times (A.D. 43 to 449).
Canterbury Archaeological Society. 1966.
1,2,3,4,5,6,7,8,9,10,11,12,15,17,18,19

JENKINS, Frank.
Romano-Gaulish clay figures as indications of the mother
goddess cults in Great Britain. (Reprinted from
Archaeologia Cantiana, Vol. LVIII, 1962).
3

JESSUP, Frank William.
History of Kent.
Finlay and Son. 1958 etc.
1,2,3,5,6,7,8,9,11,12,14,15,17,18,19,20,21

JESSUP, Frank William.
History of Kent: select bibliography, compiled by F.W.
Jessup.
Maidstone, Kent Education Committee. 1966.
1,2,3,4,5,7,8,10,11,12,15,16,18,19,21

JESSUP, Frank William.
Kent history illustrated.
Maidstone, Kent Education Committee. 1966.
1,2,3,4,5,6,7,8,9,10,11,12,14,15,16,17,18,19,20

JESSUP, Ronald Frank.
Anglo-Saxon jewellry.
London, Faber. 1950.
3

JESSUP, Ronald Frank.
Archaeology of Kent.
Methuen. 1930.
1,2,3,4,5,6,7,8,9,11,12,13,14,15,16,17,18,19,20

JESSUP, Ronald Frank.
Barrows and walled cemeteries in Roman Britain. In
British Archaeological Association Journal, 3rd series,
Vol. 22, 1959.
11

JESSUP, Ronald Frank.
Curiosities of British archaeology, compiled by R.F.
Jessup.
1961.
4

JESSUP, Ronald Frank.
Early Bronze Age beakers. (Reprinted from Archaeologia
Cantiana, Vol. 45).
n.d.
4,17

JOLLIFFE, J.E.A.
Pre-feudal England: the Jutes.
Oxford University Press. 1933.
3,5,11,12,15

JOHNSON, Jeremiah.
(Photostat of letter "to His Highness Prince Charles)
1648. (From Kent County Journal, Vol. 8, No. 10).
3

JONES, John Bavington.
Kent at the opening of the 20th century...
Brighton, W.T. Pike. 1904.
1,2,3,4,5,6,7,8,9,11,12,14,15,17,18,19,20

JORDAN, Wilbur Kitchener.
Social institutions in Kent, 1480-1660.
Kent Archaeological Society. 1961.
1,2,3,4,5,7,11,12,15,17,18,19

Jura Populi Anglicani; or, the subjects' right of
petitioning set forth, occasioned by the case of the
Kentish petitioners.
London. 1701.
6,11

KEITH, Sir Arthur.
An autobiography: numerous references to Kent and
Sussex archaeology.
1950.
2,4

(KEMPE, Alfred John).
Curious fragments found in Warbank Field, Kent. (From the
"Gentlemens Magazine", 1829).
11

KENDALL, Harry George O.
The oldest human industry (Stationers Hall).
W.P. Griffith and Sons, Old Bailey Press. n.d.
5

KENT ARCHAEOLOGICAL RESEARCH GROUPS' COUNCIL.
Newsletter, No. 1, April 1965 and No. 2, October 1965.
3

KENT ARCHAEOLOGICAL SOCIETY.
Testamenta Cantiana, 2 vols.
Kent Archaeological Society. 1906.
6,8,11,16

KENT ARCHAEOLOGICAL SOCIETY - RECORDS BRANCH.
Calendar of Kent feet of fines to the end of Henry III's
reign. (Kent records Vol. 15).
Kent Archaeological Society. 1956.
1,4,8,11,17,18

KENT ARCHAEOLOGICAL SOCIETY - RECORDS BRANCH.
Documents illustrative of medieval Kentish Society, edited by
F.R.H. Du Boulay. (Kent records Vol. 18).
Kent Archaeological Society. 1964.
2,3,4,5,7,8,10,11,12,15,17,18

KENT ARCHAEOLOGICAL SOCIETY - RECORDS BRANCH.
East Kent records. A calendar of some unpublished deeds and
court rolls in the library of Lambeth Palace, edited by I.J.
Churchill. (Kent records Vol. 7).
Mitchell, Hughes and Clarke. 1922.
4,8,10,11,17,18

KENT ARCHAEOLOGICAL SOCIETY - RECORDS BRANCH.
A handbook to Kent records: containing a summary account
of the principal classes of historical documents relating to
the county, edited by I.J. Churchill. (Kent records Vol. 2).
Mitchell, Hughes and Clarke. 1914.
4,6,8,10,11,17

KENT ARCHAEOLOGICAL SOCIETY - RECORDS BRANCH.
Kent keepers of the peace, 1316-1317, edited by B.H. Purnam.
(Kent records Vol. 13).
Kent Archaeological Society. 1933.
1,2,3,4,8,11,12,15,17

KENT ARCHAEOLOGICAL SOCIETY - RECORDS BRANCH.
Kent obit and lamp rents, edited by A. Hussey. (Kent records
Vol. 14).
Kent Archaeological Society. 1936.
1,2,3,4,7,8,11,12,15,17,18

KENT ARCHAEOLOGICAL SOCIETY - RECORDS BRANCH.
A Kentish cartulary of the Order of St. John of Jerusalem.
(Kent records Vol. 11).
Kent Archaeological Society. 1930.
4,5,8,10,11,17,18

KENT ARCHAEOLOGICAL SOCIETY - RECORDS BRANCH.
Register of Daniel Rough, Common Clerk of Romney, 1353-1380,
edited by K.M.E. Murray. (Kent records Vol. 16).
Kent Archaeological Society. 1945.
4,8,11,18

KENT ARCHAEOLOGICAL SOCIETY - RECORDS BRANCH.
Registrum Hamonis Hethe: Diocesis Roffensis, edited by
C. Johnson. (Kent records Vol. 4, Part 6).
Kent Archaeological Society. 1935.
11,12

KENT ARCHAEOLOGICAL SOCIETY - RECORDS BRANCH.
17th century miscellany. (Kent records Vol. 17).
Kent Archaeological Society. 1960.
1,2,3,4,5,6,8,9,10,11,12,15,17,18,21

KENT ARCHAEOLOGICAL SOCIETY - RECORDS BRANCH.
The Twysden lieutenancy papers, 1583-1668, edited by G.S.
Thomson. (Kent records Vol. 10).
Kent Archaeological Society. 1926.
1,2,3,4,8,10,11,12,15,17,18

KENT COUNTY COUNCIL.
Economic and social history of Kent.
Kent County Council. 1969.
7

KENT COUNTY COUNCIL - ARCHIVES OFFICE.
Catalogue of the Radnor collection. Part 1, Manorial
documents. (Typescript).
1953.
7

KENT COUNTY COUNCIL - ARCHIVES OFFICE.
English history through Kentish eyes...
Kent County Council. 1955.
1,2,8,11,15,17,20

KENT COUNTY COUNCIL - ARCHIVES OFFICE.
Four centuries of Kentish maps and mapmakers, Bentlif
Gallery, Maidstone Museum, 6th November to 4th December,
1971.
Kent County Council. 1971.
4

KENT COUNTY COUNCIL - ARCHIVES OFFICE.
Guide to the Kent County Archives Office.
Kent County Council. 1958.
2,3,6,11,12,16,17,18

KENT COUNTY COUNCIL - ARCHIVES OFFICE.
Guide to the Kent County Archives Office: First
Supplement, 1957-1968, prepared...by Felix Hull.
Kent County Council. 1971.
4,5,7,8,9,11

KENT COUNTY COUNCIL - ARCHIVES OFFICE.
Handlist of Kent County Council records, 1889-1945,
prepared...by Felix Hull.
Kent County Council. 1972.
4,11

KENT COUNTY COUNCIL - ARCHIVES OFFICE.
Kent Archives Office.
Kent County Council. 1966.
2

KENT COUNTY COUNCIL - ARCHIVES OFFICE.
Kentish estate maps, 1596-1861...work of some local
mapmakers...display held at County Hall, Maidstone.
Kent County Council. 1954.
3,11

KENT COUNTY COUNCIL - ARCHIVES OFFICE.
Report of the County Archivist in respect of the two
years ending 31st December, 1966.
Kent County Council. 1967
4

KENT COUNTY COUNCIL - ARCHIVES OFFICE.
Report of the County Archivist...1969-1971.
Kent County Council. (1972).
3,9,11

KENT COUNTY COUNCIL - ARCHIVES OFFICE.
Twenty-five years: a report on the work of the Kent
County Archives Office.
Kent County Council. 1958.
1,3,4,8,9,11,12,17

"Kent Monthly Messenger", Vol. 1 (1893) and Vol. 2
(1894).
17

Kentish Chronologist. (Photocopied list of important
dates in Kent history, 449-1789. Original of the copy
not known). Last date 1789.
(19---?).
4

Kentish Companion, or useful memorandum and pocket
book.
Canterbury, Simmons and Kirkby.
3(1779)
6(1782,1783,1784)
11(1792)
12(1791)

Kentish Companion...addressed to the inhabitants of the
County of Kent and to the public in general.
Canterbury, Rouse, Kirkby and Laurence.
1(1821)
5(1818)
17(1824)

The Kentish fable of the lion and the foxes, or the honesty
of the Kentish petition made manifest, 1701, bound with:
Authentick memoirs of the wicked life and dying words of the
late John Collington of Throwleigh in Kent, 1750.
6

KENTISH GENTLEMAN.
The apparent danger of an invasion.
Baldwin. 1701.
12

Kentish historical newsletter: monthly notes on topics
relating to Kentish history and archaeology. Edited and
published by P.M.E. Erwood, Nos. 1-3, September-November,
1957.
4,12

Kentish odds and ends. (Scrapbook) 5 vols.
n.d.
11

Kentish (pocket) Companion for the year of our Lord...
H. Ward. n.d.
11(1830)
13(1931)

The Kentish Post, 1750-1752: Kent references.
International Research Publications. (1971).
2,3,4,7,9

Kentish miscellany, Nos. 1,2 and 3.
Canterbury. 1828.
4,11,12,15,17

Kentish register and monthly miscellany, 3 vols.
Canterbury, Simmons. 1793 etc.
1,2,3,4,6,7,8,11(Vol. 1 only) 12,13,16,17,18

The Kentish spy: pamphlet.
1712.
16

The Kentish Petition: the special passages continued from
the 18th to the 24th of July, 1643.
17

Kentish tracts.
London, Robert Barker. 1641.
6

Kentish tracts.
5(1832-39, 1834-42, 1834-59)
17(1834-59)

KERSHAW, S. Wayland.
Kentish annals in Lambeth Library.
1911.
17

KERSHAW, S. Wayland.
Lambeth Palace Library and its Kentish memoranda.
Kent Archaeological Society. 187-?
17

KERSHAW, S. Wayland.
Protestants from France, in their English home.
London, Low, Marston, Searle and Rivington. n.d.
3(1851) 17(1885)

KNIGHT, C.
The Dutch in the Medway...
1939.
4,8,15

KNIGHT, Henry Raleigh.
Loyal to the King: the story of the Kentish Protestant martyrs.
1903?
1,3,4,8,11,12

KNOCKER, Herbert Wheatley.
Kentish manorial incidents.
Manorial Society. 1912.
3,11,16

KNOCKER, Herbert Wheatley.
Kentish register. In Archaeologia Cantiana, Vol. 30.
Kent Archaeological Society. 1914.
11

KNOCKER, Herbert Wheatley.
Special Land Tenure Bill of 1911...
Manorial Society. 1911.
11

LAMBARDE, William.
A perambulation of Kent...written in the yeere 1570...
(various editions).
1(1826)
2(1596,1826)
3(1596)
4(1826)
5(1826)
6(1576,1596,1600,1656,1826)
7(1596,1826)
8(1826)
9(1596,1656,1826)
11(1826)
12(1826)
13(1826)
14(1826)
15(1826)
16(1826)
17(1576,1596,1656,1826)
18(1826)
20(1826)
21(1826)

LAMBARDE, William.
A perambulation of Kent, with an introduction by
Richard Church.
Adams and Dart. 1970.
3,7,11,12,21

LAMBERT, George.
Story of the Field of the Cloth of Gold...as told by
E. Hall (who was present and saw it) Le Sieur B. de
Montfancon, Sir J. Ayloffe and J. Topham. (A paper
read to the British Archaeological Association by
G. Lambert on August 28th, 1883).
17

LAMBERT, R.S.
An aftermath of the last Labourers' Revolt (the Courtenay
Riots). (From "The Highway", Vol. XVII, No. 1, Winter,
1924).
3

LARKBY, J. Russell.
The development of flint implements with special
reference to those of the Ightham district...
Homeland Association. 1907.
12,15

LARKING, Lambert B.
Proceedings, principally in the County of Kent in
connection with the Parliaments called in 1640, and
especially with the Committee of Religion appointed
in that year...from the collections of Sir Edward
Dearing, with a preface by John Bruce.
Camden Society. 1862.
1,7,11,12,15,17

LASLETT, Peter.
The gentry of Kent in 1640. (Cambridgeshire Historical
Journal, 1948).
11

LEEDS, Edward Thurlow.
The archaeology of the Anglo-Saxon settlements.
1913.
5

LEEDS, Edward Thurlow.
The distribution of the Anglo-Saxon saucer brooch in
relation to the Battle of Bedford, A.D. 571.
Society of Antiquaries. 1912.
9

LEEDS, Edward Thurlow.
Early Anglo-Saxon art and archaeology: being the Rhind
lectures...1935, chapters 3-4 - The Kentish Problem.
Oxford, Clarendon Press. 1936, Reprinted 1968.
3,4,8,11

Letter from a gentleman in Kent giving satisfaction to
a friend in London of the beginning, progress and end
of the late great action there.
1648.
11

Letter to a friend in the country, with reflection on the
Petition of the County of Kent.
1701.
3

LEWIN, Thomas.
The invasion of Britain by Julius Caesar.
Longman, Green. 1859.
1,6,8,11,12,17

LEWIN, Thomas.
On the position of the Portus Lemanis.
Nichols. 1867.
11

LEWIN, Thomas.
Replies...upon "The Invasion of Britain by Julius Caesar".
Longmans, Green. 1862.
8,11,17

LINCOLN, Edward Frank.
Heritage of Kent.
Oldbourne. 1966.
1,2,3,4,5,6,7,8,9,11,12,15,19,20

LINDSAY, Jack.
Nine days' hero: Wat Tyler.
Dobson. 1964.
1,5,11,15

LINDSAY, Philip.
The Peasants' Revolt, 1381, by P. Lindsay and R. Groves.
Hutchinson. (1950).
5,12

LITTLEHALES, Henry.
Of Chaucer's Pilgrim's Way from London to Canterbury (with
map).
n.d.
1

LITTLEHALES, Henry.
Some notes on the road from London to Canterbury in the
Middle Ages, edited by H. Littlehales.
Chaucer Society. 1898.
11,12

LODGE, Eleanor Constance.
Account book of a Kentish estate, 1616-1704, edited by E.C.
Lodge.
Oxford University Press. 1927.
1,3,7,11,12,17

LONDON COUNTY COUNCIL.
Court Minutes of the Surrey and Kent Sewer Commission, Vol. 1,
1569-1579.
17

LONG, A.G.
Some things nearly so: the Dutch raid on the River Medway,
June, 1667.
Chatham, H.M. Dockyard, A.G. Long. 1967.
8

Lord Eldon predicting the present crisis. (An attack on
Catholic emancipation).
n.d.
17

LYLE, Helen M.
Rebellion of Jack Cade, 1450.
Historical Association. 1950.
1,5,8

(MACFARLANE, Charles).
The Dutch in the Medway...
Knight. 1845.
8,11,12

MACFARLANE, Charles.
The Dutch in the Medway.
Clarke. 1897.
4,8,11,15

McKEE, J.R.
Dame Elizabeth Barton, O.S.B.: the Holy Maid of Kent.
Burns, Oates and Washbourne. 1925.
11

MADGE, Sidney J.
The Domesday or Crown Lands...(Royal estates under the
Commonwealth).
London, Routledge. 1938.
3

The Maid of Kent.
Robinson. 1778.
12

MATTHEWS, Arnold Gwynne.
Walker revised: being a revision of John Walker's
sufferings of the clergy during the Grand Rebellion,
1642-1660.
Oxford University Press. 1948.
3

MAYER, Joseph.
On the preparations of the County of Kent to resist the
Spanish Armada.
Liverpool, T. Brakell. 1868.
3,11,13,17

(MAYLAM, Percy).
The custom of gavelkind in Kent.
Canterbury, Privately Printed. 1913.
11

MEANEY, Audrey.
A gazetteer of early Anglo-Saxon burial sites.
Allen and Unwin. 1964.
11,15,18

MELLING, Elizabeth.
Kent and the Civil War, edited by E. Melling.
Kent County Council - Archives Office. 1960.
1,2,3,4,5,6,7,8,9,11,12,15,16,18,19,20

MELLING, Elizabeth.
The poor...from original sources in the Kent Archives
Office...edited by E. Melling.
Kent County Council - Archives Office. 1964.
2,3,4,5,6,7,8,9,11,12,14,15,16,17,18,19,20

Men of Kent! come forward boldly (a handbill against
Roman Catholicism).
n.d.
17

MILLER, G. Anderson.
Noble martyrs of Kent.
Marshall, Morgan and Scott. n.d.
1,2,3,4,5,7,8,9,11,12,15,19

MILLER, William.
Jottings of Kent.
Whitaker. 1864 etc.
1,2,3,4,5,6,7,8,9,11,12,13,14,15,16,17

MILNE, F.A.
Topographical history of Kent and Lancashire, edited
by F.A. Milne. (Gentleman's Magazine Library).
Elliot Stock. 1895.
1,7,8,9,11,12,17,20

MONCK, George. 1st Duke of Albemarle.
The Duke of Albemarle's report to the House of Commons
on the Dutch attack in the River Medway.
(1667).
8

MOTHERSOLE, Jessie.
The Saxon shore.
J. Lane. 1924.
1,3,6,7,8,11,12,13,14,15,17,19,20

MYRES, J.N.L.
Three styles of decoration on Anglo-Saxon pottery.
(Reprinted from Antiquaries Journal, Vol. XVII, No.
4, October, 1937).
3

A narrative and declaration of the dangerous design
against the Parliament and Kingdom carried on in the
County of Kent...
1648.
6,11

NATIONAL MARITIME MUSEUM.
The second Dutch War...1665-1667.
H.M.S.O. 1967.
4,8,12,15

NEWMAN, George.
Lirks with the past...in connection with the County of Kent.
n.d.
17

NEWMAN, George.
The Kentish notebook and gleaner, 4 vols. (Press cuttings
mostly from the Gravesend and Dartford Reporter, the
Gravesend Journal and the Maidstone and Kentish Journal).
1886-1895.
9

NICHOLS, John Gough.
The chronicles of Queen Jane, edited by J.G. Nichols.
Camden Society. 1850.
12

NOBLE, Mark.
The history of London and its environs, Part V: Kent.
Stockdale. 1798.
12

NONESUCH AND EWELL ANTIQUARIAN SOCIETY.
Bulletin, series 3, Vol. 1, No. 1, April, 1964, containing
article on "city posts" with a list of city posts in Kent
and Surrey.
2

NORTH, Allan. Publisher.
Kent: historical, biographical and pictorial.
London, Allan North. 1907.
4

Notes mainly on Kent...compiled c.1795-1800, 2 vols, MSS.
(Sections on each parish comparable to Hasted. These 2 vols.
cover N.W. Kent and are probably part of a complete work).
2

OLDFIELD, Thomas Minton Burley.
An entire and complete history, political and personal, of
the boroughs of Great Britain, together with the Cinque Ports
...
Printed for G. Riley...1792.
4(Vol. 3) 10(Vol. 2) 11

OMAN, Charles.
The Great Revolt of 1381.
Oxford University Press. 1969.
5

ORRIDGE, B. Brogden.
Illustrations of Jack Cade's rebellion from researches in the
Guildhall records...
Hotten. 1869.
2,11,12

The parallel; or, a collection of extraordinary cases
relating to concealed births...No. 1. The history of
Richard Plantagenet, son to Richard III...(Photocopy).
Printed for J. Roberts. 1744.
11

PAYNE, George.
Archaeological survey of the County of Kent.
Society of Antiquaries. 1889.
1,9,11,13,15,16,17

PAYNE, George.
Collectanea Cantiana; or archaeological researches in the
neighbourhood of Sittingbourne...
Mitchell and Hughes. 1893.
1,2,3,4,5,6,8,11,12,14,15,17,18,20

PAYNE, George.
Local museums.
Society of Antiquaries. 1893.
3,12

PAYNE, George.
Merry-making in the olden times.
Bunyard. 1891.
12

PAYNE, George.
Report of discoveries in Kent. (Proceedings of the Society
of Antiquaries, December 14th, 1893).
8

PAYNE, George.
Researches and discoveries in Kent, 1905-1907...
(Reprinted from Archaeologia Cantiana, Vol. 28).
London, Mitchell, Hughes and Clark. 1909.
4,17

PAYNE, George.
Romano-British interments.
n.d.
17

PEGGE, Samuel.
An historical account of...the Textus Roffensis.
Nichols. 1784.
12

Petition of the Gentry, Ministers and Commonalty of
the County of Kent.
1648.
3,11

PHILIPOTT, Thomas.
Villare Cantianum.
W. Godbid. 1659 etc.
1,4,6,7,13,14,15,17,21

PHILIPOTT, Thomas.
Villare Cantianum.
Whittingham. 1776.
1,2,3,5,6,8,12,16,17,21

PHILLIPS, Margaret R.
Some Kent children, 1594-1875.
Kent Education Committee. 1972.
9,11

(PINNOCK, William).
The history and topography of the County of Kent...
Pinnock and Maunder. (c.1820).
9,12,17

PLATTS, W.L.
A display of Royal autographs and portraits, great seals
etc. found on documents in the Kent Archives Office,
County Hall, Maidstone.
Alabaster Passmore. 1959.
15

PLOMER, Henry Robert.
The Kentish feast: being notes on the annual meetings
of the Honourable Society of Natives of the County of
Kent, 1657-1701, edited by H.R. Plomer.
Canterbury, Cross and Jackman. 1916.
1,2,3,4,7,9,11,12,13,14,17

POSTE, Beale.
Britannic researches...
Smith. 1853.
12

POWELL, J.R.
Siege of the Downs castles in 1648.
Mariner's Mirror. 1965.
3,7,11

PRESTWICH, Joseph.
On the primitive characters of the flint implements
of the chalk plateau of Kent.
Anthropological Institute. 1892.
17

"A PROTESTANT LAYMAN", pseud.
Animadversions on Lord Bexley's letter to the Freeholders
of Kent, by a Protestant layman.
1829.
4

PUBLIC RECORD OFFICE.
Inquisitions and assessment relating to feudal aids,
Vol. 3, Kent - Norfolk.
H.M.S.O. 1904.
11

PUBLIC RECORD OFFICE.
List of the lands of dissolved religious houses, Kent -
Middlesex.
H.M.S.O. 1964.
7,8

PUBLIC RECORD OFFICE.
List of Court Rolls referring to Kent...No. 6 (MSS.).
n.d.
11

RADCLYFFE, Edward.
Court Baron of Edward Radclyffe, at Hampton, 2nd July,
1650...(parchment).
1651.
17

RAWLINSON, Richard.
The English topographer.
London, Printed for T. Jauncy. 1720.
3

Record of the public and private executions in Kent, from
the year 1798 to the present time.
1888.
17

A remonstrance showing the occasion of the arming of the
County of Kent.
164-?
12

Report from the Select Committee on Malt Tax, 1868.
1868.
12

Report of a conference on the preservation of small towns
and villages.
Folkestone, Kent Council of Social Service. 1965?
11

RICHMOND, Ian.
Roman Britain.
London, Collins. 1947.
21

ROBERTSON, Rev. William Archibald Scott.
Kentish archaeology, 7 vols. (Mostly reprinted from
Archaeologia Cantiana).
London, Mitchell and Hughes. 1876-1886.
3(Vols. 1-7)
1,4,5,15,20(Vol. 1)
5,6(Vol. 2)
5,12,13(Vol. 3)
15,20(Vol. 4)
11,15,20(Vol. 5)

ROGERS, Philip George.
The Dutch in the Medway.
Oxford University Press. 1970.
5,7,8,9,12,19

ROE, D.A.
Gazeteer of British lower and middle palaeolithic sites.
(References to Kent local sites).
Council for British Archaeology. 1968.
5

ROBINSON-MORRIS, Matthew. 2nd Baron Rokeby, 1713-1800.
An address to the County of Kent on their petition to the
King for removing present ministers.
London, Printed for J. Debrett, 1797.
3,6,12,17

ROCHESTER DIOCESAN CONFERENCE - ECCLESIASTICAL RECORDS
COMMITTEE.
Kent records: the parish registers and records in the
Diocese of Rochester, a summary of information...
Kent Archaeological Society. 1912.
4,5,8,13,19

The Royalist and the Republican: a story of the Kentish
insurrection, Vol. 2 only.
Smith Elder. 1852.
12

RUSSELL, W.C.
Betwixt the Forelands.
n.d.
1,7,11,12,13,18

ST. MONSON, Philip.
A new description of Kent.
1596.
17

SALMON, N.
A new survey of England...Part 1, Kent, Sussex and Surrey
J. Roberts. 1728.
1,3

SANDERS, Robert.
The complete English traveller; or, a new survey and
description of England and Wales...by Nathanial Spencer.
London, J. Cooke. 1773.
3

SAUNDERS, H.W.
Extracts relating to local history.
n.d.
12

SAUNDERS, H.W.
History of Kent from the earliest times to 1714.
n.d.
1,5,11,12,14

SAUNDERS, H.W.
History of Kent to 1485.
Murray. (1936).
2,4,15

SCARTH, H.M.
Roman maritime towns in Kent. (From Proceedings of
Royal Archaeological Institute Meeting at Canterbury,
July 27th- 1875).
9,17

SCOTT, B.J.
The Norman Balliols in England, compiled in part from
Mr. Wentworth Huyshe's "Harold and the Balliols".
Scott. 1914.
12

SEARLE, William George.
Onomasticon Anglo-Saxonicum: a list of Anglo-Saxon
proper names from the time of Beda to that of King
John.
Cambridge University Press. 1897.
3

SEYMOUR, C.
New topographical, historical and commercial survey of
the cities, etc. of Kent.
Canterbury, Sold by T. Smith. 1776 etc.
1,2,3,4,5,6,7,8,9,11,12,13,15,16,17

SIMONS, Eric Norman.
Lord of London. (Jack Cade's rebellion, 1450).
Muller. 1963.
5,7,11,12,15

SIMONS, Eric Norman.
The Queen and the rebel: Mary Tudor and Wyatt the
Younger.
Muller. 1904.
11,15

SIMPSON, Samuel.
The agreeable historian; or, the compleat English
traveller...Vol. 11 (Kent section only).
London, C. Walker. 1746.
3

SMITH, Charles Roach.
Collectionia Antiqua: etchings and notices of ancient
remains, 7 vols.
1848-1880.
3,12,15(1-6 only) 20(1-6 only)

SMITH, Reginald Anthony.
Kent. (From Proceedings of the Society of Antiquaries,
February 6th, 1908).
8

SMITH, Reginald Anthony.
Prehistoric man in Kent. (Reprinted from the South
East Naturalist, Vol. 28, 1923).
5

SOMNER, William.
A treatise of the Roman ports and forts in Kent...
Oxford, Sheldon Theatre. 1693.
1,2,3,4,6,7,8,11,12,13,14,15,17,18,21

SPRAT, Thomas.   Bishop of Rochester.
A relation of the late wicked contrivance of Stephen
Blackhead and Robert Young, against the lives of several
persons by forging an association under their hands...
(Note: plot, partly enacted at Bromley Palace).
Savoy, Edward Jones, Printer. 1692.
2

(SPRAT, Thomas). Bishop of Rochester.
The second part of the late wicked contrivance against the
lives of several persons, by forging an association under
their hands: being a further account of the said forgery,
and of the two authors of it...
Savoy, Edward Jones, Printer. 1693.
2,11

SPURRELL, F.C.J.
Deneholes and artificial caves with vertical entrances.
(Reprinted from Archaeological Journal, 1882-3).
5

SPURRELL, F.C.J.
Palaeolithic implements found in West Kent.
Mitchell and Hughes. 1883.
5,17

STEAD, Richard.
Bygone Kent, edited by R. Stead.
Canterbury, Goulden. 1892.
1,2,3,4,5,7,8,9,11,12,13,14,15,17,18,19

STEAD, Richard.
Bygone Kent, edited by Richard Stead.   (Reprint edition).
EP Publishing Co. 1972.
11

STOCKDALE, Frederick Wilton Litchfield.
Etchings from original drawings of antiquities in the County
of Kent.
1810.
1,2,3,4,5,6,8,11,12,13,15,17

Strange Newes, out of Hartford-shire and Kent.
1679.
1

STREATFEILD, Thomas.
Excerpta Cantiana...
William Nicol. 1836?
1,2,3,4,5,7,8,11,12,13,15,17,18

Study of local history.
Kent Council of Social Service. n.d.
17

STUKELEY, William.
Caesar and antiquities - manuscript notes, 1714-1726.
(Photocopy of the Kent extracts).
2

SURTEES, Rev. Scott F.
Julius Caesar, did he cross the Channel?
J.R. Smith. 1866.
11,17

SURTEES, Rev. Scott F.
Julius Caesar, showing beyond reasonable doubt that he
never crossed the Channel...(Reprinted from The Doncaster
Gazette, 1868).
17

SWING, Francis.
Life and history of Swing, the Kent rick-burner, written
by himself.
London. 1830.
8,17

Textus Roffensis.
Oxford, Sheldonian Theatre. 1720.
8,15

Textus Roffensis, edited by P. Sawyer.
1962.
2(Part 1(1957) only) 11,15

Textus Roffensis, Parts I and II, edited by P. Sawyer.
In Early English Manuscripts, Vols. VII and XI, edited by
B. Colgrave.
Copenhagen, Rosenkilde and Bagger. 1957-1962.
11

THANET, Sackville Tufton, 9th Earl of
The whole proceedings upon an information exhibited
ex-officio by the King's Attorney General against the
Right Honourable Sackville, Earl of Thanet...for a riot
and other misdemeanours...April 25th, 1799.
Ogle. 1799.
11

The history of the Kentish petition, 1701.
1701.
6

THORPE, John, Junior.
Custumale Roffense...
John Nichols. 1788.
5,11,12,15

THORPE, John, Senior.
Registrum Roffense.
Richardson for J. Thorpe, Junior. 1769.
1,5,8,11,12,15,16,17

TOLDERVY, William.
England and Wales described in a series of letters,
Vol. 1 (in part) covering Kent.
1762.
17

TYMMS, Samuel.
Compendium of the history of...Kent (etc.).
n.d.
17

VINCENT, William Thomas.
Early men in Kent.
Woolwich Antiquarian Society. 1903-4.
17

VINE, Francis Thomas.
Caesar in Kent.
Edinburgh, Turnbull and Spears. 1886.
1,4,5,7,8,11,12,13,15

VINE, Francis Thomas.
Caesar in Kent...
Elliot Stock. 1887.
1,2,4,5,6,11,12,13,14,15,16,17,21

WADMORE, J.F.
The Knights Hospitallers in Kent.
Mitchell and Hughes. 1896.
11,17

WAINWRIGHT, John.
Julius Caesar: did he cross the Channel?...(Reviewed).
1869.
17

WALPOOLE, G.A.
An historical, biographical, accurate, complete and
comprehensive survey of the County of Kent...
c.1784.
13

WARD, Gordon Reginald.
Dr. Gordon Ward's MS. notebook on the manors of Kent:
extracted by Frank Higenbottam.   (Typescript).
1957.
3

WARD, Gordon Reginald.
The Belgic Britons: men of Kent in B.C. 55.
Sevenoaks, Caxton Press. 1961.
1,2,4,5,6,7,8,11,12,14,15,16,17,19,21

WARD, Gordon Reginald.
Hengist. (Reprinted from Archaeologia Cantiana, Vol.
61).
Ashford, Headley. n.d.
1,8,11,16

WARD, Gordon Reginald.
Hengist...
Anglo-Danish Publishing Co. 1949.
11

WARD, Gordon Reginald.
King Wintred's charter of A.D. 699. In Archaeologia
Cantiana, Vol. 60, 1947.
17

WARD, Gordon Reginald.
A charter of Wintred, King of Kent, A.D. 699.
Kent County Council - Archives Office. 1948.
1,8,11

WEIGALL, Arthur.
Wanderings in Anglo-Saxon Britain.
1927.
13,14

WESTALL, William.
Britannia delineata: comprising views of the antiquities...
of Kent, by W. Westall and others.
Rodwell and Martin. 1822.
6,12,17

WHYMAN, John.
The economic and social history of Kent, 1600-1900.
(University of Kent at Canterbury extra-mural course...),
by J. Whyman and others.
Rutherford College, University of Kent. 1969.
7,11(1968 MSS.).

WHYMAN, John.
A sketch of economic development in Kent, 1600-1900.
Rutherford College, University of Kent. 1969.
3

WILLARD, Barbara.
Augustine came to Kent.
Worlds Work. 1964.
15

WILLIAM, of Byholte.
The chronicle of William of Byholte (1310-1320): an account
of the legal system known as frankpledge, edited by Dom.
Dunstan Prangnel.
Dom. D. Prangnel. 1967.
1,4,7,11,14

WOOD, John Henry.
The martyrs of Kent...
Ashford, Headley. 1885.
11

WORKS, Ministry of.
Illustrated regional guides to ancient monuments, Vol. 2,
Southern England.
H.M.S.O. 1952.
8

WOTTON, Thomas (1521-1586). Sheriff of Kent.
Thomas Wotton's letter-book, 1574-1586, edited by G. Eland.
Oxford University Press. 1960.
11

HITHER GREEN

History of St. Swithun's Church, Hither Green...1880-1957.
(Pamphlet).
(1957).
18

HOATH

HUSSEY, Arthur.
Ford manor house and lands in 1647: from the Parliamentary
survey. (Reprinted from Archaeologia Cantiana, Vol. XXVI).
Printed by Mitchell and Hughes. 1904.
11

PAYNE, J. Lewin.
Reculver Parish Church of St. Mary the Virgin, together
with the Chapelry of the Holy Cross, Hoath, by J.L. Payne
and W.T. Hill.
1931.
13

HOLBOROUGH

EVISON, Vera Ivy.
An Anglo-Saxon cemetery at Holborough, Kent. (Reprinted from
Archaeologia Cantiana, Vol. LXX).
Kent Archaeological Society. 1956.
8,17

HOLLINGBOURNE

CAVE-BROWNE, John.
The story of Hollingbourne.
Maidstone, Dickinson. 1890.
1,3,4,6,8,11,12,15

FREKE, Mrs. Elizabeth.
Mrs. Elizabeth Freke, her diary, 1671-1714.
Guy. 1913.
12

G., E.B.
Hollingbourne, compiled by G.E.B.
Maidstone, British Legion Press. 1963.
11,15

Hollingbourne caves: descriptive guide.
c.1898.
17

Hollingbourne, "The Chestnuts" - Sale catalogue.
1968.
12

MARTIN, Charles Wykeham.
Ancient weapons of wood discovered at Hollingbourne,
Kent.
1858.
17

MARTIN, Charles Wykeham.
On the wooden battleaxe and dagger found at Hollingbourne, Kent.
1863.
12

ORDNANCE SURVEY.
Book of reference to the plan of the parish of
Hollingbourne (Hundred of Eyhorne), in the County of
Kent.
H.M.S.O. 1867.
11

T., L. (Possibly L. Thomas of Eyhorne House).
Hollingbourne.
Maidstone, W.S. Vivish. 1851.
6

Tanyard House, Hollingbourne - Sale catalogue.
1966.
12

THOMAS, Louisa.
Hollingbourne.
Maidstone, W.S. Vivish. 1897.
12

THOMAS, Louisa.
Hollingbourne: lines to Kentish children.
Maidstone, W.S. Vivish. 1906.
15

HOO

GADD, W. Lawrence.
The "Great Expectations" country.
C. Palmer. 1929.
1,4,5,6,8,9,11,13,15,18

GADD, W. Lawrence.
The topography of "Great Expectations", 2 vols.
(Typescript).
1925-26.
15

HAMMOND, F.J.
Hundred of Hoo and the parish of Allhallows, Hoo.
Chatham News. 1914.
4,8,9,11,12,15

HARRIS, Edwin.
The Hundred of Hoo and its Dickensian associations.
(Eastgate series No. 28).
Rochester, Harris. n.d.
15

MAXWELL, Donald.
The Gads Hill country: vignettes from Dicken's last
six books. (Reprinted from "The Treasury").
c.1920.
9

HOO Cont'd

TUTT, James William.
Woodside, burnside, hillside and marsh. (Area bounded by
Rochester, Cobham and the Hoo peninsula).
Swan Sonnenschein. 1894.
11

HOO ST. WERBURGH

ARNOLD, Ralph.
Hundred of Hoo.
Constable. 1947.
1,2,3,4,5,6,7,8,9,11,12,14,15,17,18,20

HARRISON, A.C.
Excavations of a moated site at Abbot's Court, Hoo St.
Werburgh, by A.C. Harrison and E.R. Swain. In
Archaeologia Cantiana, Vol. 78, 1963.
17

MOSELEY, Mary.
Church history of St. Werburgh, Hoo, compiled by M. Moseley.
Ramsgate, Church Publishers. 1962.
11,12
Another edition published in Rochester and printed by
Brewster and Co. 1970.
11

HOP-TOKENS - See COINS AND TOKENS

HORSMONDEN

CRONK, Anthony.
St. Margaret's Church, Horsmonden: an historical and
descriptive account.
A. Cronk. 1967.
4,11

KENDON, Frank.
The smallyears.
Cambridge University Press. 1930 etc.
1,5(1950) 11,12

MAIDSTONE AND DISTRICT EAST KENT BUS CLUB.
Maidstone and district: history of Horsmonden Garage.
1965.
4

HORTICULTURE - See AGRICULTURE

HORTON KIRBY

CRESY, Edward.
Horton Kirby. (Bound typescript).
1857.
5

LATHAM, Charles.
"Franks", a country seat of the sixteenth century,
illustrated in the nineteeth century by C. Latham.
1894.
5

HOSPITALS

AYERS, Gwendoline M.
England's first state hospitalsand the Metropolitan Asylums
Board, 1867-1930.
Wellcome Institute of the History of Medicine. 1971.
5

KENT COUNTY LUNATIC ASYLUMS.
Annual reportsof the Asylums Committee...
Kent County Lunatic Asylums.
1(1909-11, 1913-14)

SOUTH-EAST METROPOLITAN REGIONAL HOSPITAL BOARD.
Directory, July 1971.
South-East Metropolitan Regional Hospital Board. 1971.
9

HOTHFIELD

JACKSON, Nance.
Church of St. Margaret, Hothfield.
1967.
12

KENT COUNTY COUNCIL - EDUCATION DEPARTMENT.
Environmental studies at Hothfield.
Kent County Council. (1972).
11

HOUGHAM

Catalogue of the costly furniture and contents of the
mansion to be sold by auction on Wednesday and Thursday,
7th and 8th September, 1927. (Abbotscliff House,
Hougham).
7

Particulars, plans and conditions of sale of...Little
Farthingale Farm, Hougham...Ford Manor Farm, Hoath...at
Marshside, Chislet, about 50 acres of marshes...three
cottages at Hoath...Chitton's will offer the above for
sale by auction...on...22nd June, 1963.
Cluttons. 1963.
7

HUNTON

The rules and articles of the Bachelors and Widows
Society, held at the house of Mr. William Turner, in
the parish of Hunton.
Printed by D. Chalmers. (1806).
11

HURST

COLLEY, W.W.
Churches of Bonnington, Bilsington and Hurst.
Sellinge, Quick Service Press. 1939.
11

SAMPSON, Aylwin.
The parishes of Bonnington, Bilsington and Hurst.
Kent Messenger. 1957.
1,3,4,7,11,12,15

HYTHE

Album of Folkestone, Sandgate and Hythe.
Charles Reynolds. n.d.
1

BARBER, S.
Hythe crypt.
Elliot Stock. n.d.
7

BEESTON, Frederick.
An archaeological description of Saltwood Castle near
Hythe.
Kent and Co. 1884?
4,7,11,17

BUSK, Hans.
Handbook for Hythe: comprising a familiar explanation
of the laws of projectiles.
Routledge. 1860.
10

Charter of incorporation of the Mayor, jurats and
commonalty of the town and port of Hythe, 4th March,
17 Elizabeth, 1575.
7,10

Correspondence on circumstances arising out of the
contested election for the Borough of Hythe, the 25th
day of July, 1837.
Printed by T. Shrewsbury. 1838.
11

The crypt and human remains at the church of St.
Leonard, Hythe.
Hythe, Paine. 1903.
7

DALE, Herbert Dixon.
Notes on Hythe Church. (Reprinted from Archaeologia
Cantiana, Vol. XXX).
Mitchell, Hughes and Clarke. 1913.
4,17

DALE, Herbert Dixon.
Notes on the crypt and bones of Hythe Church.
Hythe, Paine. 1907 etc.
1,3,7,11,12,17

DALE, Herbert Dixon.
Notes on the parish church of St. Leonard's, Hythe, 2nd edition.
Hythe, Lovick. 1901 etc.
10,11,12,17

DALE, Herbert Dixon.
St. Leonard's Church, Hythe from its foundation, with some account of the life and customs of the town...
Murray. 1931
2,4,6,7,8,10,11,12,13

DAVEY, Peter.
Notes on the theatrical history of Sandgate and Hythe. (Photostat).
n.d.
7

DAVIS, Arthur Randall.
An architectural description of Hythe Church.
1888?
12,13

ENGLISH, John. Publisher.
Illustrated penny guide to Folkestone, Sandgate and Hythe.
J. English. 1900 and 1904. (7)
Pictorial guide to Folkestone, Hythe, Sandgate and neighbourhood.
n.d. (10)

FRAMPTON, Thomas Shipdem.
List of fifty-three vicars of St. Mary, Westhythe. (Bound with Livett, G.M. - The architectural history of the church of St. Leonard, Hythe). Cover title: Hythe and Westhythe Churches.
London, Mitchell, Hughes and Clarke. 1913.
4

GREAT BRITAIN: LAWS, etc. (GEO. III).
An Act for paving, repairing...highways in Hythe...
1798.
11

GREAT BRITAIN: LAWS, etc. (VIC.).
An Act for confirming certain provisional orders made by the Board of Trade under the Gas and Waterworks Facilities Act, 1870 relating to...Hythe and Sandgate Gas...
1876.
7

GREAT BRITAIN: LAWS, etc. (VIC.).
South Eastern and London, Chatham and Dover Railway Companies Act, 1899-1905.
7

GRIFFIN, Ralph.
Kentish items: West Malling, Hythe, Denton, Allington, Elham, Bekesbourne.
n.d.
7

HALL, Thomas Guppy.
Crypt of St. Leonard's Church, Hythe and the human remains contained therein, 2nd edition.
Folkestone, Birch. n.d.
7,10,11,17

HALL, Thomas Guppy.
St. Leonard's Church, Hythe.
Folkestone, Kentfield. n.d.
7(1895) 11(1st edition n.d. and 1895) 17(1895)

HALL, Thomas Guppy.
A short description of St. Leonard's Church, Hythe and of the human remains contained therein. In Kent Miscellanea, Vol. I.
n.d.
11

HEYWOOD, John. Publisher.
Illustrated guide to Folkestone, Hythe and Sandgate.
J. Heywood. c.1891, c.1912, c.1925.
7,11(1891)

HOLMAN-CROFT, Rowena.
Verse Mosaics: illustrated.
n.d.
10

HYTHE BOROUGH COUNCIL.
Catalogue of documents belonging to the Corporation of Hythe, 11th to 20th century...
Hythe Borough Council. n.d.
7,10,12

HYTHE BOROUGH COUNCIL.
Official guide to Hythe.
Health Resorts Association.
11(1922,1923) 12(1922,1923)

HYTHE BOROUGH COUNCIL.
Official guide to Hythe,
Croydon, Abbey.
11(1932) 12(1932) 15(1932) 17(1929)

HYTHE BOROUGH COUNCIL.
Official guide to Hythe. (Hythe, Cinque Port and holiday resort).
Hythe Borough Council and Chamber of Commerce.
11(1971,1972,1973)

HYTHE BOROUGH COUNCIL.
Official guide to Hythe. (Welcome to Hythe).
Hythe Publicity Committee.
3(1969) 11(1964,1969)

Hythe and Sandgate guide, embellished with a new panorama picturesque plan...
n.d.
1,7,11

Hythe, Sandgate and Folkestone guide, containing an account of their ancient and present state...
Hythe, Tiffin. 1816.
7,11

HYTHE SCHOOL OF MUSKETRY.
Four lessons on musketry for the use of officers...
n.d.
17

HYTHE VENETIAN FETE CHARITY SOCIETY.
Hythe Venetian Fete: souvenir programme, 1951.
4

LEE, W. Publisher.
Hythe and Sandgate guide.
W. Lee. (c.1806-10?).
7

LIVETT, Grevile Mains.
Architectural history of the church of St. Leonard, Hythe.
Mitchell, Hughes and Clarke. 1913.
4,7,11,17

LIVETT, G(revile) Mains.
Westhythe Church and the sites of churches formerly existing at Hythe. (Bound with Livett, G.M. - The architectural history of the church of St. Leonard, Hythe).
London, Mitchell, Hughes and Clarke. 1913.
4,17

LOTT, Susannah.
Collection of extracts relating to the crimes...of Susannah Lott and Benjamin Buss, for poisoning Mr. Lott, late of Hythe.
Canterbury, T. Smith. 1769.
1

MACKESON, H.B.
The Fraternity of the Assumption of the Blessed Virgin Mary at Hythe.
Smith. 1873.
1,7,11,17

MACLEAR, George Frederick.
In memoriam, A.J.B. Beresford Hope, M.P.
1887.
17

MILLER, W.S.
The School of Musketry at Hythe.
William Clowes and Sons. 1892.
7,11,15

MORANT, G.M.
The history of the human skeletons preserved in the ossuary of the church of St. Leonard, Hythe.
London, F.J. Parsons. 1934.
3,7

A new guide to Sandgate, Folkestone and Hythe with historical, topographical and botanical notices...
Purday. 1843.
6,11

Old towns by the sea: Hythe and Romney. (Extract from
"All the Year Round, 1878).
17

PAINE, W.S. Publisher.
Paine's new and complete guide to Hythe and its neighbourhood.
W.S. Paine. 1862.
7,17

Parliamentary representation: a report...on the Borough of
Hythe.
1832.
12

PARSONS, F.J. LTD. Publishers.
Illustrated guide to Hythe.
F.J. Parsons Ltd. (191-?).
7

PITTS, Hubert A.
More 19th century fragments of Methodist history in Hythe,
Kent.
(Hythe Methodist Church). 1970.
7,11

Representation for the extension of the Borough of Hythe.
1948.
10

ROYAL INSTITUTE OF PUBLIC HEALTH.
Guide to Folkestone, Sandgate and neighbourhood. Royal
Institute of Public Health Congress at Folkestone, 1904.
J. English. 1904.
7

SOUTH EASTERN RAILWAY.
Illustrated tourist's guide: views and descriptions of...
Folkestone, Hythe...
Morton. c.1871.
7

STACE, R. Publisher.
An illustrated guide to Sandgate, Folkestone, Hythe and the
neighbourhood, with historical, typographical (sic),
geological and botanical notices, with six illustrations and
a map of the walks and rides.
R. Stace. c.1860.
7

STACE, R. Publisher.
Stace's Sandgate, Hythe and Shorncliffe illustrated historic
almanack for 1871, 1872.
R. Stace. 1871 and 1872.
7

Views of Hythe.
1868.
10

Volunteer choruses: sung at Hythe, Tuesday 18th December,
1860.
17

The White Hart, Hythe, 1648-1948. (Published as a
supplement to "The House of Whitbread" by Whitbread and Co.
Ltd. Brewery, London).
London, Whitbread. 1949?
3

WILKS, George.
The early history of Hythe, Part I.
Printed by McCorquodale. 1889.
7

WILSON, W. Publisher.
Guide to Sandgate, Shorncliffe and Hythe.
Sandgate, W. Wilson. n.d.
7(1889 and 1894) 11(1889)

ICKHAM

BROMLEY, Francis E.
The ruined chapel of Well in Ickham. (10 page typescript -
2 page manuscript).
(193-).
3

GOODSALL, Robert Harold.
Diary of Ann Mary Brydes. (From Archaeologia Cantiana, Vol.
LXXVII, 1962).
3

IDE HILL

In memoriam: Rev. A.J. Woodhouse, Vicar of Ide Hill,
1863-1880.
n.d.
7

IFIELD

FFINCH, Kenneth Maule.
The history of Ifield and Singlewell, revised and
edited by Robert Heath Hiscock.
Chatham, Mackay. 1957.
4,9

FFINCH, Kenneth Maule.
Salerna of Ifield: a legend of St. Thomas a Becket,
translated by K.M. Ffinch.
Dartford Antiquarian Society. 1934.
9,11

IGHTHAM

ABBOTT, W.J. Lewis.
The ossiferous fissures in the valley of the Shode,
near Ightham, Kent.
Geological Society. 1894.
17

BENNETT, F.J.
Ightham, by F.J. Bennett and others.
Homeland Association. 1907 and 1917.
1(1907) 2(1907 and 1917) 4,5(1907) 6,7,8,11,12,13,15
16,17(1907) 18,19(1907 and 1917)

BOWRA, Edward.
The Dutch James family of Ightham. (Reprinted from
Archaeologia Cantiana, Vol. 83, 1968).
1969.
16

BOWRA, Edward.
Ightham: some glimpses of local history.
Hilton. 1966.
1,2,11,12,15,16,18

BOWRA, Edward.
Our village church: St. Peter's, Ightham.
Sevenoaks Duplicating Service. (1970).
8,11,12,16

A catalogue of the contents of the famous medieval
moted residence, Ightham Mote, comprising antique and
modern furniture...to be sold by public auction on the
premises by Lofts and Warner on Monday, October 8th,
1951.
Lofts and Warner. 1951.
11

GODWIN, John.
Killers unknown. (Includes murders at Ightham and
Yalding).
Jenkins. 1960.
12

HARRIS, Edwin.
History of Ightham Mote. (Eastgate series No. 8).
Rochester, E. Harris. 1910.
1,2,12,15

HARRISON, Sir Edward R.
The annals of old Ightham: a quest for truth. (MS.).
1957.
11

HARRISON, Sir Edward R.
"Bounds" of Ightham parish (record of 1805).
17

HARRISON, Sir Edward R.
Brief notes on St. Peter's Church, Ightham.
Westerham, Hooker. 195-?
11

HARRISON, Sir Edward R.
Court Rolls and other records of the Manor of Ightham...
Ashford, Headley. 1937?
4,5,11,12,15,17

HARRISON, Sir Edward R.
Harrison of Ightham: a book about Benjamin Harrison of
Ightham, Kent made up principally of extracts from his
notebooks and correspondence.
Oxford University Press. 1928.
1,2,3,4,5,6,7,8,9, 11,12,13,15,16,17,19

HARRISON, Sir Edward R.
History and records of Ightham Church.
Church Army Press. 1932.
1,4,9,11,16

HARRISON, Sir Edward R.
The story of Oldbury Hill...
Sevenoaks, W.H. Smith. 1953.
1,4,8,11,12,15,19

HENBREY, H.G.
West Malling, Wrotham, Ightham and district: residential
attractions...
Abbey Publicity Service. 1928.
17

Holt Hill, Ightham - Sale catalogue.
1968.
12

HOPKINS, R. Thurston.
Moated houses of England.
Country Life. 1935.
5,11,15,18

Ightham and district: official guide.
Kyrle. 192-?
11

Ightham Court - Sale catalogue.
1920?
12

Ightham Mote (descriptive leaflet).
(19--?).
4

(JAMES, Elizabeth).
An Ightham diary of 1750, edited by Sir Edward Harrison.
(Limited edition - private circulation).
Ashford, Headley. 1950.
1,2,11

LARKBY, J. Russell.
The development of flint implements with special reference
to those of the Ightham district...
Homeland Association. 1907.
12,15

LUARD, Charles Edward.
Ightham Mote, Kent.
Wyman. 1893.
7,11

NEWTON, E.T.
Additional notes on the...fauna...at Ightham.
Geological Society. 1899.
17

PRESTWICH, Joseph.
On the occurrence of palaeolithic flint implements in the
neighbourhood of Ightham. (From Quarterly Journal of the
Geological Society, May, 1889).
9,17

SETON, Anya.
Green darkness. (An historical novel partly set in Ightham
Mote).
Hodder and Stoughton. 1972.
11

THOMPSON, Stephen.
Old English homes. (Includes Ightham Mote).
Sampson Low. 1876.
11,15

VALLANCE, Aymer.
Ightham Mote. (Reprinted from Archaeologia Cantiana, Vol.
45).
Ashford, Headley. 1931.
11,17

INDUSTRY AND TRADE

Area survey of Kent and Sussex. In World's Press
News and Advertisers' Review, Vol. 45, No.1,154,
April 27th, 1951.
3

ASSOCIATED PORTLAND CEMENT MANUFACTURERS LTD.
A.P.C.M., 1900-1950: a history.
Associated Portland Cement Manufacturers Ltd. 1950.
5

AVELING-BARFORD LTD.
A hundred years of road rollers: a pictorial record.
1965.
4,8,15

BANBURY, Philip.
Shipbuilders of the Thames and Medway.
David and Charles. 1971.
3,4,5,7,8,9,11,19

BLAW KNOX LTD.
General catalogue...
n.d.
4

BOWATER PAPER CORPORATION.
The Bowater papers, 2 vols.
Bowater Paper Corporation. 1950-51.
12

BOWATER PAPER CORPORATION.
The Bowater papers, No. 3, 1954.
Bowater Paper Corporation. 1954.
12

BOWATER PAPER CORPORATION.
The Bowater papers, No. 4.
Bowater Paper Corporation. 1958.
12

BOWATER PAPER CORPORATION.
Bowaters build a mill in Tennessee.
Bowater Paper Corporation. 1954.
12

BOWATER PAPER CORPORATION.
Bowater in North America, by Robert Sinclair.
Bowater Paper Corporation. 1960.
12

BOWATER PAPER CORPORATION.
Bowaters today.
Keliher, Hudson and Kearns. 1962.
8,12

BOWATER PAPER CORPORATION.
Progress in the world's market places.
Bowater Paper Corporation. 1961.
8

COLBORNE, Barbara T.
The Maidstone paper industry, with special references
to the period between about 1750 to 1850. (A handwritten thesis).
(1972).
11

Craig, D.M.
Development of the paper industry in Dartford and along
the River Darent up to 1933.
1967.
5

Cray Valley Paper Mills.
W. Nash Ltd. (1958).
2

CROMPTON, J.A.
Industrial South-East England, edited by J.A. Crompton.
Burrow. (1956).
7,14

DAVIS, Sir A.C.
A hundred years of Portland cement, 1824-1924.
(Includes several references to Kent).
Concrete Publications. 1924.
9,11

DELANY, Mary Cecilia.
Historical geography of the Wealden iron industry.
Benn. 1921.
1,2,3,5,11,15,19

EYTON, T.C.
A history of the oyster and the oyster fisheries.
London, J. van Ooost. 1858.
15

GARDNER, J.S.
Iron casting in the Weald.
n.d.
11

GREEN, J. Barcham.
One hundred and fifty years of paper-making by hand.
J.B. Green. 1960.
4,7,12,15

GREEN, J. Barcham.
Paper-making by hand in 1953.
Phillips. 1953.
11,12

HOGG, P. Fitzgerald.
Kent blacksmiths. (A scrapbook of newspaper cuttings),
compiled by P.F. Hogg.
c.1940.
4

INDUSTRY, TRADE AND REGIONAL DEVELOPMENT, Department of.
South-East England.
H.M.S.O. 1965.
8

KEMP, Ethelbert Thomas.
A Canterbury apprentice's notebook (MS.).
1835.
3

KENT AND ESSEX SEA FISHERIES COMMITTEE.
Reports. (For details see Thames, River).

KENT COUNTY COUNCIL - PLANNING DEPARTMENT.
Influence of car ownership on shopping habits.
Kent County Council. 1964.
1,11

KENT COUNTY SOCIETY OF INCORPORATED SECRETARIES.
Report and accounts, 1967-8.
9

KENT INSURANCE COMPANY.
Some notes on the early history of the Kent Insurance
Company, 1802-1952.
Newman Neame Ltd. 1952.
3,4,7,21

Kent market data.
Kent Messenger. 1950?
3

Kent's business world '71: a Kent Messenger industrial
supplement, January 29th, 1971.
Kent Messenger. 1971.
4

Kent's distinguished role in British aviation development.
Kent Messenger. May 28th, 1954.
3

Kentish homespuns.
n.d.
9

KENYON, G.H.
Glass industry of the Weald.
Leicester University Press. 1967.
1,2,3,5,6,7,8,21

KIRBY, Harry S.
Sixty years and more of chalk quarrying on the River Thames.
(From Quarry Managers' Journal, September, 1953).
9

Le Grand Magazine: the House Magazine of Le Grand,
Sutcliffe and Gell Ltd. (1958-60).
8

LEWIS, P.W.
Changing factors of location in the paper-making
industry as illustrated by the Maidstone area. (Extract
from "Geography", Vol. 52, Part 3, July 1967, pp. 281-
293 - photocopy).
4,12

LOWE, Jessie.
Tunbridge Ware. In Taylor, Elias "The Lathe and its
Uses".
Trubner. 1871.
19

MARLEY GROUP.
Marley products. Loose-leaf catalogue (196-?).
4

MASON, Harold.
Industrial perspective (5): Kent. (Article in "Transport
Age", Vol. No. 6, July, 1958).
3,8

MELLING, Elizabeth.
Aspects of agriculture and industry, edited by E.
Melling.
Kent County Council - Archives Office. 1961.
1,2,3,4,5,6,7,8,9,11,12,14,15,16,18,19,20,21

MOORE, John.
Whitbread craftsmen, edited by J. Moore.
Whitbread and Co. Ltd. 1948.
3,4

PERCIVAL, Arthur.
The Faversham gunpowder indistry and its development.
Faversham Society. 1967.
1,2,3,4,6,7,8(1969 edition) 9,11(also 1969 edition) 19,20

PINTO, H.
Tonbridge and Scottish souvenir woodware, by H. and E.R.
Pinto.
Bell. 1970.
19

RAND, Duncan.
Industrial review and guide to the Medway, edited by
D. Rand, 1962.
Pyramid Press.
1(1962) 4(1962,1969,1971) 7(1962) 8(1962,1965) 11(1962)
15(1962,1965) 21(1965)

READ, J.G.
Kent clocks and their makers. (Article in "Kent", No.
143, p.13, April, 1959).
3

REED, Albert E. AND CO. LTD.
Reed Paper Group, 1903-1953.
A.E. Reed and Co. Ltd. 1954.
12

REED PAPER GROUP.
Working with "Imperial".
Reed Paper Group. 1964.
9

(ROBERTS, M.).
The woollen industry of Kent from the 13th century.
(Photocopy of a typescript thesis).
(197-?).
11

SCHUBERT, H.R.
History of the British iron and steel industry from
c.450 B.C. to A.D. 1775.
Routledge. 1957.
19

SCOTT, J.D.
Iron from the Weald. (Extract from "Trade Winds",
February, 1962).
4

SHEARS, William Sydney.
William Nash of St. Paul's Cray, papermakers.
Batchworth Press. 1950.
1,2,11

SHELL-MEX AND BRITISH PETROLEUM LTD.
Pride in progress.
Shell-mex and British Petroleum Ltd. 1957.
12

SHORT BROTHERS (ROCHESTER AND BEDFORD) LTD.
Pamphlets describing aircraft and the history of the firm.
c.1920-1945.
4

SHORTER, Alfred H.
Paper mills and paper-making in England, 1495-1800.
Hilversum Paper Publications Society. 1957.
12

Snakeskin industry.
Kent Messenger. 18th June, 1965.
8

SOUTH-EAST ENGLAND DEVELOPMENT BOARD.
Industrial South-East England: the official handbook...
Burrow.
4(1956,1959,1963,1969) 5(1969) 8(1955 etc.) 9(1969)
19(1955 etc.)

SOUTH-EASTERN TRUSTEE SAVINGS BANK.
150 years of public service, 1818-1968.
1968.
19

STRAKER, Ernest.
Iron works and communications in the Weald in Roman times, by
E. Straker and I.D. Margary.
Clowes. 1938.
11

STRAKER, Ernest.
Wealden iron.
Bell. 1931.
1,2,3,4,5,6,7,8,11,12,13,15,19,21

SWEETING, G.S.
Wealden iron ore and the history of its industry.
Geologists' Association. n.d.
19

TAGG, A.C.
Early history of paper-making in Dartford. (Typescript).
1929.
5

TARBUTT, William.
The ancient cloth trade of Cranbrook. (Reprinted from
Archaeologia Cantiana, Vol. IX, 1874).
3

TRADE, Board of.
Report on the census of distribution...1961, Part 7 - London
and South-East Region.
H.M.S.O. 1964.
8

TROWELL, Thomas.
The Kentish farrier.
Printed for R. Wilkin. 1728.
1,11

WHITBREAD AND CO. LTD.
The brewer's art.
London, Whitbread and Co. Ltd. 1948.
3,4

WHITBREAD AND CO. LTD.
Word for word: an encyclopaedia of beer...
London, Whitbread and Co. Ltd. 1953.
3

WHITEWALL (MEDWAY) PORTLAND CEMENT CO. LTD.
Prospectus, 1914.
17

WIGGINS TEAPE.
Dartford Paper Mills: issued to commemorate their opening.
Wiggins Teape. (1958)
1,4,7,8,12,17

INNS

MAYNARD, D.C.
The old inns of Kent.
Allen. 1925.
1,2,3,4,5,6,7,8,9,11,12,13,14,15,16,17,18,19,21

MORGAN, Glyn Howes.
The romance of Thames-side taverns.
n.d.
9

RAINBIRD, G.M.
Inns of Kent.
London, Whitbread and Co. Ltd. 1948.
3,4,5,7,8,11

RAINBIRD, G.M.
Inns of Kent.
London, Whitbread and Co. Ltd. 1949.
4,5,6,8,9,12,15,18

ROPER, Anne.
Kent inns: a distillation, by Anne Roper and H.R.P.
Boorman.
Kent Messenger. 1955.
1,2,3,4,5,6,7,8,9,11,12,13,14,17,18,19,20

SHEPHERD NEAME LTD.
Abbey ale houses in the garden of England.
E.J. Burrow. 1968.
15

TUBBS, Douglas Burnell.
Kent pubs.
Batsford. 1966.
2,3,5,6,7,8,11,12,15,17,19,20

WHITBREAD AND CO. LTD.
Inn crafts and furnishings...
London, Whitbread and Co. Ltd. 1950
4,12

WHITBREAD AND CO. LTD.
Inn-signia.
London, Whitbread and Co. Ltd. 1945.
3,4,12

WHITBREAD AND CO. LTD.
Inns of sport.
London, Whitbread and Co. Ltd. 1949.
3,4

WHITBREAD AND CO. LTD.
Your local.
London, Whitbread and Co. Ltd. 1947.
3

WHITBREAD FREMLINS.
Fifteen inns of character around Kent and other inns
around Kent.
Presswork Publications. 1949.
4

ISLE OF GRAIN

ANGLO-IRANIAN OIL CO. LTD.
The construction of the Kent oil refinery.
Anglo-Iranian Oil Co. Ltd. 1952.
4,14

ANGLO-IRANIAN OIL CO. LTD.
Kent oil refinery: the construction story.
Anglo-Iranian Oil Co. 1954.
1,8

BRITISH PETROLEUM CO.
Annual report and accounts for the year ended 31st
December, 1963.
British Petroleum Co. 1964.
8

BRITISH PETROLEUM CO.
B.P. Kent refinery.
British Petroleum Co. (1958?).
4,8

BRITISH PETROLEUM CO.
B.P. Motor book, 4 vols.
Shell Mex and British Petroleum Co. 1964.
8

BRITISH PETROLEUM CO.
B.P. Tanker Company.
British Petroleum Co. 1964.
8

BRITISH PETROLEUM CO.
Facts and figures from the annual report...1960 and 1961.
British Petroleum Co. 1961 and 1962.
8

BRITISH PETROLEUM CO.
Fifty years in pictures.
British Petroleum Co. 1959.
8

BRITISH PETROLEUM CO.
News in pictures, 1954, 1958-60.
British Petroleum Co. n.d.
8

BRITISH PETROLEUM CO.
Our industry.
British Petroleum Co. 1958.
8

BRITISH PETROLEUM CO.
A technical description of B.P. Kent refinery.
British Petroleum Co. 1957.
4,8

BRITISH PETROLEUM CO.
A visit to Kent oil refinery.
British Petroleum Co. (1955?).
2,4,8,

BURNETT, Charles Buxton.
A history of the Isle-of-Grain, an old-time village in Kent.
Rigg, Allen and Co. 1906.
1,4,9,15

EVANS, John H.
The Rochester Bridge lands in Grain.
Ashford, Headley. n.d.
8,11,17

GORDON, John.
History of the Congregational Churches of...and the Isle-of-
Grain.
(See - under Sheppey).
1898.
1,11,12,16

LONGHURST, Henry.
Adventure in oil: the story of British Petroleum.
1959.
4,8

REX v. James MOUNTAGUE.
Yantlet Creek: Rex v. James Mountague...and others.
Report of the trial...
Corporation of the City of London. 1824.
11

SMALL, E. Milton.
Hundred and Manor of Gillingham and the Isle-of-Grain.
Parrott. 1901.
11

ISLE OF OXNEY

HARDMAN, Frederick William.
Parish and reputed Manor of Oxney, near Dover, by F.W. Hardman
and others. In Archaeologia Cantiana, Vol. 59, 1946.
17

ISLE OF SHEPPEY

BURGESS, M.J.
Dissertation on the changing structure of the manufacturing
industry on the Isle of Sheppey. (Thesis).
1971.
11

BURRILL, William.
A history and topographical survey of the Island of Shepey (sic.).
W. Burrill. 1828.
15

DALY, Augustus A.
The history of the Isle of Sheppey from the Roman occupation to
the reign of...King Edward VII.
Simpkin, Marshall. 1904.
1,2,3,4,6,8,11,12,15,17,18

DAVIS, A.G.
London clay of Sheppey and location of its fossils.
(Proceedings of the Geologists' Association, Vol.
XLVII, Part 4, 1936, pp. 328-45).
11

GORDON, John.
History of the Congregational churches of Sheerness,
Queenborough, Minster and the Isle of Grain, from 1725
to 1898.
Sheerness, John Gordon. 1898.
1,6,11,12

GRASEMAN, C.
English Channel packet boats, by C. Graseman and G.W.P
McLachlan.
Syren. 1939.
6,7,12

HARBOUR, Henry.
Sheerness and the Isle of Sheppey.
Warne. n.d.
1,7,11,15

HARMAN, Reginald Gordon.
Railways in the Isle of Sheppey.
Branch Line Handbooks. 1962.
1,4,7,8,9,11,15

Hogarth's frolic: the five days peregrination around
the Isle of Sheppey of William Hogarth and his fellow
pilgrims, Scott, Tothall, Thornhill and Forrest,
written by E. Forrest and illustrated by William
Hogarth.
J.C. Hotten. 1872.
1,6,8,11,12,17

Hogarth's frolic: the five day peregrination around
the Isle of Sheppey of William Hogarth and his fellow
pilgrims, Scott, Tothall, Thornhill and Forrest,
written by E. Forrest and illustrated by William
Hogarth, 1872. This edition edited by Charles Mitchell
Oxford University Press. 1952.
1,3,4,8

ISLE OF SHEPPEY CHAMBER OF COMMERCE.
Isle of Sheppey and Sheerness-on-Sea official guide.
Croydon, Home Publishing Co. 1952.
11

ISLE OF SHEPPEY AND SHEERNESS-ON-SEA PUBLICITY
COMMITTEE.
Official guide.
Cheltenham, Burrows. 1956.
1(1956) 4(1960) 11(1956) 12(1956) 19(1960)

Isle of Sheppey directory and guide, 1904-1905.
Maidstone, Kent Messenger. 1904.
4

JONES, Percy Thoresby.
Story of the Abbey and Gatehouse, Minster, Isle of
Sheppey, 4th edition.
Canterbury, Gibbs. 196-?
11

KENT COUNTY COUNCIL.
Kingsferry bridge, constructed by Kent County Council
and the British Transport Commission etc. - a programme
of the ceremonial opening by the Duchess of Kent, 20th
April, 1960.
Kent County Council. 1960.
11

KENT COUNTY COUNCIL - PLANNING DEPARTMENT.
The search for a site for a third London airport -
Part 1, background information concerning Sheppey and
Cliffe.
Kent County Council. 1968.
9,11

KENT COUNTY LIBRARY.
The Isle of Sheppey. Part I - libraries in the Isle of
Sheppey. Part II - a select list of books relating to
Sheppey in Kent County Library.
Kent County Library. 1956.
1,2,4,7,8,11,12,15

ISLE OF SHEPPEY

LONDON, CHATHAM AND DOVER RAILWAY CO.
Guide to Sheerness-on-Sea and the Isle of Sheppey.
London, Chatham and Dover Railway Co. 1883.
11

M., A.W.
Guide to Sheerness and the Isle of Sheppey.
Sheerness, Cole. 1870.
11

PARSONS, James.
An account of some fossil fruits, and other bodies, found in
the Island of Sheppey.
1757.
13

SHEERNESS AND DISTRICT ECONOMICAL CO-OPERATIVE SOCIETY.
Rules of the Society.
1935.
11

SHEERNESS URBAN DISTRICT COUNCIL.
Official handbook to Sheerness and Isle of Sheppey.
Sheerness, Cole. 1906.
8

SHEPPEY DEVELOPMENT COMMITTEE.
Sheppey industrial development handbook.
Burrow. 1961.
4,11,12

SHEPPEY RURAL DISTRICT COUNCIL.
Sheppey Rural District: the official guide.
Century Press. (1951) etc.
1,3(2nd edition).

SHRUBSOLE, W.H.
Fossils from the...Isle of Sheppey...
1870.
17

TURMINE, Henry T.A.
Rambles in the Island of Sheppey...
Newman. 1843.
11,12,17

WALLER, John G.
Northwode Brass, Minster Church, Sheppey. (Extract from
Proceedings of the Society of Antiquaries, January 20th, 1881).
2

WOODTHORPE, T.J.
A history of the Isle of Sheppey.
Sheerness, Smith. 1951?
1,2,3,4,8,11,12

ISLE OF THANET

Account of the great storm at Margate, Ramsgate, Westgate-on-
Sea, Broadstairs, Birchington on 29th November, 1897 and the
surf-boat disaster at Margate, 2nd December, 1897.
1898.
13

All about Margate and Herne Bay, including Draper's, St.
Peter's, Salmestone, Chapel Bottom, Hengrove, Twenties and
Nash Court, Kingsgate and its modern antiquities, Garlinge,
Dandelion.
W. Kent and Co.
4(1869) 11(1869) 12(1869) 13 and 14(1864,1866,1867,1869)
17(1867,1886)

ANDREWS, John H.
The Thanet seaports, 1650-1750. In Archaeologia Cantiana,
Vol. 66, 1953.
17

BANKS AND SNELL. Publishers.
A guide to the Isle of Thanet.
Banks and Snell. n.d.
13(1874) 17(1870)

BEAR, J. Publisher.
Bear's new Ramsgate, Margate, Broadstairs, St. Peter's and
Isle of Thanet guide, containing a...account of all places of
interest, combined with the most attractive walks and drives...
J. Bear. 1870.
13,14

BEAR, J. Publisher.
The best and cheapest Margate and Ramsgate guide
including Broadstairs, St. Peter's Minster...
J. Bear. n.d.
13(1871, 1873) 14(1871)

BLACKMANTLE, Bernard.
The merry guide to Margate, Ramsgate and Broadstairs.
1825.
13

BRASIER, W.C. Publisher.
Illustrated guide to Margate, Ramsgate and Broadstairs...
(Also contains "Old Margate Revisited", by Frederick
Stanley).
Margate, W.C. Brasier. 1879.
13

BRASIER, W.C. Publisher.
Illustrated guide to Margate, Ramsgate and Broadstairs...
Margate, W.C. Brasier. 1881.
13

BRASIER, W.C. Publisher.
Margate, Ramsgate and Broadstairs guide...
Margate, W.C. Brasier. 1869.
7,13

BRASIER, W.C. Publisher.
The picturesque companion to the Isle of Thanet, Dover,
Canterbury and parts adjacent.
Margate, W.C. Brasier. c.1860.
7,11,17

BRAYLEY, Edward Wedlake.
The beauties of the Isle of Thanet and the Cinque
Ports, 2 vols.
W. Marshall. 1830.
1,7,11,12,13,14,15

BRAYLEY, Edward Wedlake.
Delineations, historical and topographical of the Isle of
Thanet and the Cinque Ports, illustrated by William
Deeble, 2 vols.
Sherwood, Neely and Jones. 1817.
1,3,4(Vol. 2) 6,7,8,10(Vol. 1) 11,12,13,14,15,16,17

BUBB, Robert.
Thanet.
Hutchins and Crowsley. 1884.
14

BURTON, E.G.
The handbook and companion to Ramsgate, Margate,
Broadstairs, Kingsgate, Minster, etc...
(Ramsgate). c.1865.
13

BURTON, E.G.
The wreck of the "Northern Belle": being a descriptive
poem.
(Ramsgate). 1857.
13

(COLEMAN, Alice).
The case for a University of Thanet in Kent. (Proof
copy).
1959.
2

Collections relating to the history and antiquities of
the Isle of Thanet in the most part intended for the
use of Mr. Boys, Solicitor of Margate, for his proposed
new edition of Lewis's "History of Thanet". MS.
c.1810.
13

COOKE, George Alexander.
A description of (Kent) and of the Isle of Thanet in
particular.
1819.
17

DAVIDSON. Publisher.
Isle of Thanet and Kentish almanack and directory.
Davidson. 1840.
17

Dentdelion Farm near Margate, Kent: a catalogue of
the...auction on...the 18th and 19th December, 1851...
13

A description of the Isle of Thanet and particularly of the town of Margate...
Newbery and Bristow. 1763 etc.
1,11,12,13,14

DIXON, C.D. Publisher.
The visitor's new guide...to the Isle of Thanet...
Margate, C.D. Dixon. 1850 etc.
11,13,14

DOWKER, G.
On the landing place of St. Augustine. (Pamphlet).
Mitchell and Hughes. 1896/7.
7,14,17

DYSON, S.S.
The glories of Thanet and East Kent.
(Dover). 1931.
13

FAIRHOLME, George.
New and conclusive physical demonstrations, both of the fact and period of the Mosaic Deluge...(Isle of Thanet, pp. 220-245).
(London). 1837.
13

FLOWER, Thomas Bruges.
Flora Thanetensis; or, a catalogue of the plants indigenous to the Isle of Thanet.
(Ramsgate). 1847.
11(microfilm) 13,17

FREEMAN, Lucy H.
The Augustine memorial.
1884.
3,11,13,14

FREEMAN, Rowland.
An account of the Huggett copy of Lewis's "History of Thanet" with a narrative of the circumstances which took place between Mr. J. Boys, Solicitor of Margate and R. Freeman of Minster in Thanet relating to that copy. (Copied in MS.).
1809.
11,13

FREEMAN, Rowland.
An answer to the remarks of Mr. Daniel Jarvis of Margate, surgeon.
Canterbury, Privately Printed. 1810.
11,13

Full record of raids in diary form. A concise history of Thanet during the War.
(Ramsgate). 1919.
13,19

GARDNER, J.S.
On the lower eocene section between Reculver and Herne Bay.
Geological Society. 1883.
7

GENTRY, W.C.
The Atlas guide to historical Thanet.
W. Gentry. 1914.
15

GREAT BRITAIN: LAWS, etc. (GEO. III).
An Act for making a harbour and wet dock at or near St. Nicholas Bay...
1811.
3,11,12

GREAT BRITAIN: LAWS, etc. (GEO. IV).
An Act for lighting with gas the towns or villages of Margate, Ramsgate and Broadstairs, and places adjacent in the County of Kent. (Bound in "Gas Acts", Isle of Thanet Gas Co.).
1824.
13

GREAT BRITAIN: LAWS, etc. (VIC.).
An Act for conferring further powers on the Isle of Thanet Gaslight and Coke Company. (Bound in "Gas Acts", Isle of Thanet Gas Co.).
1898.
13

GREAT BRITAIN: LAWS, etc. (VIC.).
An Act to confer further powers upon the Isle of Thanet Gaslight and Coke Company and for other purposes. (Bound in "Gas Acts", Isle of Thanet Gas Co.).
1877.
13

GREAT BRITAIN: LAWS, etc. (GEO. V).
An Act to enable the Isle of Thanet Gaslight and Coke Company to raise additional capital and for other purposes. (Bound in "Gas Acts", Isle of Thanet Gas Co.).
1914.
13

GREAT BRITAIN: LAWS, etc. STATUTORY INSTRUMENTS.
Thanet Water Order, 1968.
H.M.S.O. 1968.
12

GREEN, Emanuel.
The Isle of Ictis and the early tin trade. (Ictis was once thought to be the Isle of Thanet).
Bedford Press. 1906.
11

GREGORY AND CO. Publishers.
Postal directory for Margate, including Ramsgate, St. Lawrence, Broadstairs, Westgate-on-Sea and St. Peter's...
Gregory and Co. 1878.
13

A guide to the Isle of Thanet and souvenir of the Cliftonville Hotel.
Cliftonville Hotel. 1890/1.
1,11,13

HEADLAM, Clinton.
Idylls of Thanet.
n.d.
14

HILLS, William.
Jottings of history relating to the Isle of Thanet.
(Ramsgate). 1886.
13,14

HOUSING AND LOCAL GOVERNMENT, Ministry of.
The Thanet Water Board (Order No. 1). (S.I. 1963, No. 1693).
H.M.S.O. 1963.
4,8

HOUSING AND LOCAL GOVERNMENT, Ministry of.
The Thanet Water Board (Order No. 2) (S.1 1963, No. 1970).
H.M.S.O. 1963.
4

HUDDLESTONE, John.
"Discovering Thanet" in pictures.
H. Marshall. 1954?
1,3,4,6,7,8,11,12,14

HUNTER, Robert Edward.
A short account of the Isle of Thanet...
Burgess. 1815 etc.
11,12,13,14,17

HUNTER, Robert Edward.
Short description of the Isle of Thanet...
Hall or Burgess. 1799 etc.
1,6,13,14

HUNTER, Robert Edward.
The Thanet flora...
Hunter. 1809.
13

HUTCHINGS AND CROWSLEY. Publishers.
Directory and guide to the Isle of Thanet, with map, including articles on the geology and farming of the island, 1883-4.
Hutchings and Crowsley. (1884).
11,13

ISLE OF THANET Cont'd

HUTCHINGS AND CROWSLEY. Publishers.
Thanet: historical and descriptive guide to the Isle of
Thanet.
Hutchings and Crowsley. 1883 etc.
11,13,14

INGOLDSBY, Thomas, pseud. (BARHAM, Richard Harris).
The smuggler's leap: a legend of Thanet by Thomas Ingoldsby,
illustrated by Jane E. Cook.
Autotype Co. 1877.
11

The Isle of Thanet and Canterbury Review, October Vol. 1, No. 3,
Xmas, Vol. 1, No. 5, 1949.
Birchington, Kingsley-Joynes. n.d.
3

ISLE OF THANET GASLIGHT AND COKE CO.
Centenary, 1824-1924.
Isle of Thanet Gaslight and Coke Co. 1924.
13

ISLE OF THANET GAZETTE.
Photographs of gale damage, February, 1953.
3

ISLE OF THANET GEOGRAPHICAL ASSOCIATION.
Panorama: yearbook.
Isle of Thanet Geographical Association.
2(1966) 3(1966) 12(1962 in progress)

Isle of Thanet. (Extract, possibly from "The Land We Live In;
Sketches of the British Empire").
(Orr?). (1883?).
2

The Isle of Thanet as a health and pleasure resort.
1889.
13

Isle of Thanet delineated. Title page missing (binding title:
"The Margate Guide").
n.d.
3

Isle of Thanet guide...
(Ramsgate). 1887.
13(1887 and 1893) 14(1887)

The Isle of Thanet guide...a directory to Ramsgate, Margate
and Broadstairs.
1837.
13

Isle of Thanet illustrated visitor's guide...
(London). 1887.
13,14

Isle of Thanet visitor's guide.
n.d.
3

JACKSON, Alfred Lodington.
A little book of British lyrics.
Ramsgate, W.H. Bligh and Co. n.d.
3

JARVIS, Daniel.
Remarks on such parts of Mr. Rowland Freeman's two
publications relative to the Huggett copy of Lewis's "History
of Thanet"...
(Margate). 1810.
11,13

JONES, Samuel.
A short history of the Strict Baptists in the Isle of Thanet,
from the reign of William III to the present time.
(London). 1877.
13

KEBLE, T.H. Publisher.
Penny guide to Margate, Ramsgate and the Isle of Thanet.
1882 etc.
1,11,14,17

KENNETT, Robert H.
The church of St. Lawrence, Isle of Thanet.
(Ramsgate). n.d.
2,13,14

KENT, W. Publisher.
All about Ramsgate and Broadstairs.
W. Kent. 1864.
11,14

KENT COUNTY COUNCIL.
County services in the Isle of Thanet.
Kent County Council. 1965.
11

KENT EDUCATION COMMITTEE.
A picture of education in Thanet, 1950.
Kent Education Committee. 1950.
11

KERSHAW, S. Wayland.
Thanet in former days...(with "Birchington-on-Sea").
1881.
17

KIDD, William. Publisher.
Kidd's picturesque companion to Margate, Ramsgate and
Broadstairs.
W. Kidd. 1831.
17

Kidd's picturesque companion to the Isle of Thanet and
its environs...carefully revised, corrected and brought
down to the present time, by Rev. James Jones.
Cochrane. c.1840.
4,7,11,12,13,17

Picturesque pocket companion to Margate, Ramsgate,
Broadstairs, etc., illustrated by G.W. Bonner.
W. Kidd. 1831.
1,7,11,12,13(1831 and 1854) 14,15,17

Kidd's picturesque steam-boat companion to Margate,
Ramsgate and Broadstairs...illustrations by G.W. Bonner.
W. Kidd. c.1832.
13

KNIGHT, Charles.
Handbook to Canterbury, Dover, Isle of Thanet...
Nattali and Bond. 1853.
1,13,14

LANE, GENTRY AND CO.
Standard guide to Margate and historical Thanet.
Hastings and Margate, Lane, Gentry and Co. 1906 and 1920.
13

LANE, Leonard G.
Down river to the sea: an historical record of the
Thames pleasure steamers, 1816 to 1934.
1934.
9,13

LEWIS, John.
The history and antiquities, as well ecclesiastical
as civil, of the Isle of Thanet, in Kent, 2nd edition.
London, for J. Ames, etc. 1723 and 1736.
1,4,6,7,11,12,13,14,15,17,21

Margate and historical Thanet.
1921.
13

The Margate, Ramsgate and Broadstairs guide...1853,
1870,1871 and 1873.
13

Margate, Ramsgate and Broadstairs, illustrated by a
series of 19 views with a map of the Island of Thanet.
c.1832.
13

MATHIAS, T.J.
Villae Formianae, apud Portam Regian in Insula Thaneti...
Privately Printed. 1795.
13

Memorials of the family of Tufton, Earls of Thanet.
Gravesend, Pocock. 1800.
6

MOCKETT, John.
A letter to Captain Thomas Garrett, commanding the
Thanet Troop of Volunteer Yeomanry...
1810.
13

MOCKETT, John.
Mockett's journal...
Canterbury, Kentish Observer. 1836.
1,6,11,13,14,17

The new historical guide to the Isle of Thanet...
1848.
13,14

NICHOLLS, Thomas.
Steamboat companion; or, Margate, Isle of Thanet...and River
Thames guide.
Hughes. 1823.
6,11,12,13,14,15

NOEL, Amelia.
Select views of the Isle of Thanet, etched, coloured and
published by Amelia Noel. (5 vols.).
A. Noel. 1797.
13

O'NEILL, Sibyl.
St. Peter the Apostle in the Isle of Thanet - drawn in pen
and ink.
1911.
13

PARKER, John R.A.
In and around lovely Thanet: a book of sketches.
n.d.
13

PEGGE, Samuel.
Examination of the mistaken opinion that Ireland and Thanet
were devoid of serpents.
Society of Antiquaries. 1776.
11

Photographic views of the Isle of Thanet.
c.1900.
13

A physical, poetical and classical account of the Isle of
Thanet, by an eminent writer of the present age.
1781.
13

PITTOCK, George M.
Flora of Thanet: a catalogue of the plants indigenous to the
island with a few rare aliens, by G.M. Pittock and friends.
Margate, Printed by R. Robinson. 1903.
11,12,13,14,17

PRANGNELL, Father Dunstan.
Thanet men and Simon de Montfort (galley proof of article).
n.d.
3

PRIDDEN, John.
Topographical collections for "History of the Isle of Thanet
in Kent". MS. (Note: popular title "Pridden's Papers" - also
on microfilm).
1780-1.
13

"RAMBLER", pseud. (Arthur Montefiore).
The Isle of Thanet with historical and descriptive notes.
1893.
13,14,17

Ramsgate guide, containing a full description of Ramsgate,
Margate and Broadstairs.
n.d.
17

The Ramsgate, Margate and Broadstairs guide...
13(1855,1868,1869 and 1870) 17(n.d.)

The Ramsgate, Margate and Isle of Thanet visitor's guide...
c.1880.
13,14

St. Laurence in Thanet: 900 years, 1062-1962, with centenary
souvenir brochure.
Ramsgate, Cumming. (1962).
1,3,4,12

St. Laurence, Thanet: the church and its story illustrated.
(191-?).
4

St. Peter's in Thanet Church history.
1930.
13

St. Peter's Orphan and Convalescent Homes, Isle of
Thanet - reports 1888-1889.
17

SANGSTER, Alfred.
Historical notes on the parish of St. Peter the
Apostle in Thanet.
A. Sangster. 1904.
13

SAWYER, Minnie.
The story of St. Mildred of Thanet, a Saint of Saxon
times, 2nd edition.
St. Anselm's Society. 1917.
1,11,13,14

The schools of Thanet.
Century Publications. n.d.
3,12

SEDDON, John P.
Ancient examples of domestic architecture in the Isle
of Thanet.
Day. 1872.
1,11,13,14

Select views of Margate, Ramsgate, Broadstairs and
their vicinities.
J. Denne. 1826.
13,14

The shells of Margate, Ramsgate and Broadstairs, with
figures of nearly all species. (Note: also on
microfilm).
Osborne. n.d.
1,11,13

A short description of the Isle of Thanet...
1796.
13

SIMSON, James.
Historic Thanet.
Elliot Stock. 1891.
1,2,3,4,6,8,11,12,13,14,15,17

"SPECTATOR", pseud.
Tourist's complete guide to the Isle of Thanet and
neighbourhood...
Ramsgate, Brooks. (1874).
1,3,11,13,14,17

A summer excursion to the Isle of Thanet, including
descriptions of Margate, Ramsgate, Broadstairs, etc.
c.1845.
13

THE THANET ADVERTISER.
Thanet's raid history: raids, bombs, shells. A
record of the home line of trenches, 3rd edition, maps.
1919.
13,14

THANET CATHOLIC ANNUAL.
Church Publishers for St. Augustine's Abbey.
3(1961,1963,1964,1965,1966,1967,1968,1969)
11(1968)
12(1961,1967)

The Thanet Catholic Review, 2 vols.
1931-3 and 1933-5.
13

THANET COLLEGE.
The Thanetonian, 1892-9.
13

THANET CULTURAL SOCIETIES COUNCIL.
Handbook for 1948-1949.
1948.
13

THANET CULTURAL SOCIETIES COUNCIL.
Season, 1949-1950 and Season, 1950-1951.
13

Thanet Itinerary; or, steam yacht companion, containing a
sketch of the island...
Margate, Bettison Garner and Denne, 1819 etc.
1(1822) 11,13,14

The Thanet Magazine, June-December, 1817.
Margate, Denne, 1817.
11,12,13

THANET WATER BOARD.
Annual reports.
Thanet Water Board.
4(1957-59) 11(1957-1964) 12(1957-1961, 1965 in progress)

Thanet's war-time history. (Excerpts from the East Kent
Times, 18th December, 1918 to 5th March, 1919)
13

TOMSON AND WOTTON LTD.
War zone in England: Thanet, 1914-1918.
Thanet Advertiser. 1919.
13,14

Tour through the Isle of Thanet and some other parts of East
Kent.
Nichols. 1793.
12

TURNER, Peter Theophilus.
The Margate guide: a descriptive poem to which are added
companions to Ramsgate, Broadstairs and their vicinities.
1842.
13,17

W., H.V.
Isle of Thanet personalities: Mr. T.B. White by H.V.W.
Isle of Thanet News. Winter, 1949.
3

WALKER, George. Engraver.
Twenty-four picturesque views in the Isle of Thanet.
Girtin. 1872.
11,13

WALKER, George P.
When Thanet was an Isle: the rehabilitation of Richborough.
The Graphic. 1925.
13

WEIGALL, Rachel.
Lady Rose Weigall.
John Murray. 1923.
14

WILSON, S.R. Publisher.
Isle of Thanet guide...
Ramsgate, S.R. Wilson. (1891).
5,11,17

WITHERDEN, G. Publisher.
The new Margate, Ramsgate and Broadstairs guide...
G. Witherden.
3 (1842)   8 (1809) 11(1842) 12(1842) 13(c.1789, 1801, 1802,
1804, 1805, 1807, 1809, 1816, 1823, 1825, 1842, 1850, 1852, 1861)
14(c.1789) 17(1809)

WYLLIE, W.L.
London to the nore, by W.L. and M.A. Wyllie.
Black. 1905.
1,4,5,8,9,11,12,15

IVYCHURCH

ROPER, Anne.
The church of St. George, Ivychurch.
Privately Printed. 1967.
8,11

St. George's Church, Ivychurch - "The Cathedral of the Marshes".
n.d.
13

IVYHATCH

Coach House, Ivyhatch - Sale catalogue.
1968.
12

IWADE

LOUGH, John.
Sermon preached on 9th March, 1796 in the churches of
Milton and Iwade...
1796.
11

KEARNSEY

Particulars...of the...property known as Kearnsey
Abbey near Dover extending to nearly 28 acres. To
be offered for sale...by Messrs. Knight, Frank and
Rutley...on...12th June, 1930.
Knight, Frank and Rutley. 1930.
7

KEMSING

BOWDEN, V.E.
Guide to the church of St. Mary the Virgin at Kemsing.
Ramsgate, Church Publishers. 1963.
2,4,11

BOWDEN, V.E.
A guide to the church of St. Mary the Virgin at Kemsing.
Ramsgate, Church Publishers. 1969.
11

(BOWDEN, V.E.).
An outline history of Kemsing in Kent.
(V.E. Bowden). (1971).
11

The history of St. Edith of Kemsing and guide to the
church of St. Mary, Kemsing.
Printed by the Caxton and Holmesdale Press. (1955).
11

Kemsing Church and Parish.
(1914).
11

Kemsing tithe apportionment.
1841.
16

The Well: Kemsing Parish Magazine, September 1965-
December, 1969.
11

WILKINSON, J.J.
The Saint Clere Magazine. (4 numbers bound as one).
n.d.
12

KENNINGTON

FURLEY, Robert.
Annals of Kennington in Kent...a lecture...1877.
Kentish Express. 1877.
1,3,4,6,11,12,14,15,17

FURLEY, Robert.
The annals of Kennington in Kent...a lecture...January
29th, 1877. (Reprint edition).
Reprinted by Headley Bros., Ashford. 1972
11

The parish church of St. Mary, Kennington, Ashford.
Church Publishers. 1964.
12

KENT - THE COUNTY OF KENT IN GENERAL

ABELL, Henry Francis.
History of Kent.
Ashford, Kentish Express. 1898.
1,2,3,4,5,6,7,8,10,11,12,13,15,16,17,18,19,20

ABELL, Henry Francis.
Kent and the Great Civil War.
Ashford, Kentish Express. 1901.
1,3,4,5,7,10,11,12,15,17,19

ABELL, Henry Francis.
A short history of Kent for the young.
Ashford, Kentish Express. 1895.
1,2,3,6,8,10,11,14,15,18

An account of travels through Kent, etc. (A collection of letters).
c.1722-3.
17

ADAMS, H.G.
Kentish Coronal.
Simpkin, Marshall. 1841.
1,4,6,7,8,11,12,15,17

AIKEN, John.
The history of the environs of London...within twenty-five miles of the metropolis, by J. Aiken and others.
Stockdale. 1811.
12

ALLEN, Thomas.
The picturesque beauties of Great Britain...Kent.
Virtue. 1833.
1,17

The ambulator; or, a pocket companion in a tour round London, within the circuit of twenty-five miles.
Scatcherd and Letterman.
2(1807) 4(1807) 17(1787) 18(1787)

ANDERSON, John P.
Book of British topography...(Kent pp. 132-150).
1881.
3,11,13

Animadversions on Lord Bexley's letter to the freeholders of Kent.
1829.
14

ARROWSMITH, John.
Hikes in Kent and Sussex.
Besant. 1932.
11,14

ASHLEY, Evelyn.
The life of Henry John Temple, Viscount Palmerston, 2 vols.
Bentley. 1876.
6

ASSOCIATION FOR PLANNING AND REGIONAL RECONSTRUCTION.
Basic survey for planning...the 1947 Town Planning Act.
Association for Planning and Regional Reconstruction. 1949.
11

ASSOCIATION OF MEN OF KENT AND KENTISH MEN.
Kent tells the world.
Association of Men of Kent and Kentish Men. 1933.
19

BADESLADE, Thomas.
Thirty-six different views of noblemen and gentlemen's seats in the County of Kent...
n.d.
1,11

BAGSHAW, Samuel.
Historical gazetteer and directory of the County of Kent, 2 vols.
Sheffield, Ridge. 1847.
1,2,3,4,5,6,7,8,11,12,13,14,15,17,18,19,21

BAKER, J.
Home beauties, as communicated to the author of the Royal Atlas Imperial Guide.
n.d.
11,13

BANKS, F.R.
Kent.
1955.
1,2,3,4,5,6,7,8,11,12,14,15,18,19

BARBER, Edmund.
The counties and shires of Great Britain: Kent. In "Country Life", Vol. LXXI, No. 1,832, 27th February, 1932.
3

BATES, Herbert Ernest.
Kent. In "Country Fair", December 1951 - "Country Fair" supplement No. 6.
3

BAYLY, R.E.
Physical geography of Kent, edited by R.E. Bayly.
Kent Geography Teachers' Association. 1966.
11

BEATTIE, William.
The ports, harbours, watering-places and coast scenery of Great Britain. Illustrated by views taken on the spot by W.H. Bartlett, 2 vols.
1842.
13

BENSTEAD, Charles Richard.
Shallow waters.
Hale. 1958.
11

BETJEMAN, John.
English cities and small towns.
Collins. 1943.
3

BEVAN, G. Phillips.
Handbook to Kent.
Stanford.
1(1887,1891)
2(1876)
4(1876,1885)
6(1876,1887)
7(1876,1880)
8(1876)
9(1882)
11(1876)
12(1876,1887)
13(1880)
15(1876)
16(1882)
17(1876)
18(1876)

BEVAN, G. Phillips.
Tourist's guide to the County of Kent...revised and edited by R.N. Worth.
Stanford. 1891 7th Edition.
3,17

BLACK, ADAM AND CHARLES LTD. Publishers.
Black's guide to Kent.
A. and C. Black Ltd.
1(1862)
2(1872,1928)
3(1874,1886,1890,1928)
4(1861,1874,1878,1886,1890,1901,1905,1928)
5(1890,1901)
6(1860,1879,1890,1928)
7(1862,1872,1882,1893,1901,1928)
8(1879,1886,1890,1893)
9(1860,1893,1915,1928)
11(1860,1862)
12(1870,1882,1901,1923,1925,1928)
13(1878,1879,1881,1893)
14(1872)
15(1862)
16(1928)
17(1886)
18(1867,1886,1928)
19(1886)

BLACK, ADAM AND CHARLES LTD. Publishers.
A guide to the healthiest and most beautiful watering places in the British Islands...
A. and C. Black Ltd. 2nd Edition, 1861. 3rd Edition, 1862.
13

BLANCHARD, Edward Litt. L.
Adam's descriptive guide to the watering places of England...(Dover, Folkestone, Margate, Ramsgate, Gravesend, Herne Bay).
9(1848,1849,1851) 11(1851) 13(1848,1849,1850,1851)

BLIGH, Allan L.
Homes and holidays in the garden of England...handbook to districts served, edited by A.L. Bligh.
South-Eastern and Chatham Railway. 1914.
2

BOGGIS, G. de R.
Sketches in Kent.
c.1870.
13

BOISSIER, Rev. G.R.
The Boissier collection of notes and drawings of places in Kent.
n.d.
16

BONNER, G.W.
Three hundred and twenty picturesque views in Great Britain
(half relate to Kent).
Lacey. n.d.
1,6,11

BOORMAN, Henry Roy Pratt.
Kent, a Royal County.
Kent Messenger. 1966.
1,2,3,4,5,6,7,8,9,10,11,12,14,15,17,19,20

BOORMAN, Henry Roy Pratt.
Kent and the Cinque Ports.
Kent Messenger. 1957.
1,3,4,5,6,7,8,9,10,11,12,14,15,17,18,20

BOORMAN, Henry Roy Pratt.
"Kent Messenger" centenary.
Kent Messenger. 1959.
1,2,3,4,5,6,7,8,9,11,12,14,15,17,18

BOORMAN, Henry Roy Pratt.
Kent, our glorious heritage.
Kent Messenger. 1951.
1,3,4,5,6,7,8,11,12,13,15,17,18,20

BOORMAN, Henry Roy Pratt.
Kent tells the world.
Kent Messenger.
2(1951) 3(1951) 4(1951) 6(1951) 7(1933,1934,1951) 8(1951)
10(1951) 11(1933,1951) 12(1933,1951) 16(1934) 17(1933)

BOORMAN, Henry Roy Pratt.
Kent unconquered.
Kent Messenger. 1951.
1,3,4,5,7,8,9,11,12,13,14,15,17,18,19,20

BOORMAN, Henry Roy Pratt.
Kentish pride.
Kent Messenger. 1952.
1,2,3,4,5,7,8,9,11,12,14,15,17,18

BOORMAN, Henry Roy Pratt.
The spirit of Kent...
Kent Messenger. 1968.
5,6,9,11

BOSWORTH, George F.
Kent. (Cambridge County geographies).
Cambridge University Press. 1909.
1,3,4,5,6,7,8,9,13,14,17,18,21

BOSWORTH, George F.
Kent: past and present.
Phillip.
1(1900)
2(1900)
3(1907,1909)
4(1907,1909)
6(1901)
7(1900,1901,1907,1909)
8(1901,1907)
9(1907)
11(1900)
12(1901,1907,1909)
13(1901)
15(1900)
17(1900)
18(1900)

BRAYLEY, Edward Wedlake.
Beauties of England and Wales. (Kent - part of Vol. 7 and Vol. 8).
Verner, Hood and Sharpe. Vol. 7, 1806 - Vol. 8, 1808.
1(1808)
2(1808)
4(1806,1808)
5(1906,1808)
6(1806,1808)
8(1808)
9(1808)
11(1808)
14(1806,1808)
16(1806,1808)
17(1808)
18(1808)
19(1806,1808)

BRAYLEY, Edward Wedlake.
A topographical and historical description of the County of Kent,
containing an account of its towns, cathedrals, castles...
Sherwood, Neely and Jones. 1810.
6,13,15

BRENINALL, Margaret.
Kent, Surrey and Sussex.
C. Letts and Co. 1971.
8,11

BRINE, James. Publisher.
Kentish appendix and Maidstone manual for 1870.
17

BRITANNIA DELINEATA: comprising views...and picturesque
scenery of Great Britain, Vol. 1 - Kent.
Rodwell and Martin. 1822.
1,11,12

BRITISH CURIOSITIES IN NATURE AND ART.
Section I - curiosities in the County of Kent.
Coningsby. 1713.
13

BROWN, J. Publisher.
Maidstone appendix and Kentish advertiser.
Brown. (1864).
12

BROWN, John Howard.
Bourne flows. (Reprinted from "Geography", June, 1929).
3,7

BRYDGES, Sir Samuel Egerton.
Topographical miscellanies, Vol. 1.
Robson. 1792.
12

BURLINGTON, Charles.
Kent. (Extract from "The Modern Universal British
Traveller"...by C. Burlington and others).
J. Cooke. 1779.
2

BURNAND, F.C.
Z.Z.G. or the zig-zag guide round the bold and beautiful
Kentish coast.
A. and C. Black Ltd. 1897.
1,2,3,6,7,8,11,12,13,14,15,17,18,21

BURROW, EDWARD J. AND CO. LTD. Publishers.
Holidays in South-East England.
Cheltenham, E.J. Burrow. 1924.
17

BURROW, EDWARD J. AND CO. LTD. Publishers.
Kent: a guide to the County. (Kent County Handbook).
Cheltenham, E.J. Burrow.
1(1952,1962)
2(1937,1952,1955,1961,1965,1967)
3(1952,1965)
4(1952,1958,1962,1965)
5(1952,1962)
6(1952,1968)
7(1952 etc.)
8(1952,1958,1962,1971)
9(1962,1965,1971)
10(1952 etc.)
11(1952,1958,1962,1965,1971)
12(1952,1958,1962,1965,1968)
13(1952 etc.)
15(1952 etc.)
17(1952 etc.)
19(1952,1965)

BUSHELL, T.A.
Kent, our County.
Association of Men of Kent and Kentish Men. 1971.
4,5,6,7,8,9,11

CAMDEN, William.
Britannia.
Blaev. 1639.
3,12

CAMDEN, William.
Cantium: being an excerpt from Camden's Britannia, 1610.
(London). 1610.
6,13,14

CAMDEN, William.
Cantium: being an excerpt from Camden's Britannia,
Holland's edition, 1610-1637.
(London). 1637.
13

CAMDEN, William.
Cantium: being an excerpt from Camden's Britannia, Gibson's
edition, 1610-1695.
(London). 1695.
13

CAMDEN, William.
Cantium: being an excerpt from Camden's Britannia, Gibson's
edition, 1610-1722.
(London). 1722.
13,14

CAMDEN, William.
Cantium: being an excerpt from Camden's Britannia, Gough's
edition, 1610-1789.
(London) T. Payne and Son, G. and J. Robinson. 1789.
8,11,13

CAMDEN SOCIETY.
The Camden Miscellany. Vol. 3 containing papers relating to
proceedings in the County of Kent, 1640-46.
Camden Society. 1855.
1,4,6,7,11,12,15,17

CAREY, George Saville.
The Balnea: or, an impartial description of all the popular
watering places in England...
(London). 1799.
13

CATLING, Gordon.
Beauty of Kent.
Jarrold. 1953.
1,4,11,12,18

CHAMBERS, W. AND R. Publishers.
Handy guide to the Kent and Sussex coast - in six routes or
districts...
Edinburgh, Chambers. 1863.
1,6,13,17

CHANDLER, Marjorie E.J.
A new tempskya from Kent.
British Museum (Natural History). 1968.
12

CHAPMAN, Derek.
Kent.
Shell Mex and British Petroleum Ltd. 1963.
11

CHEEM, Aliph.
Lays of the sea-side.
Army and Navy C.U.U.P. Society. 1887.
6,12

CHURCH, Richard.
Kent.
Hale. 1948 etc.
1,2,3,4,5,6,7,8,9,10,11,12,13,14,15,17,18,19, 20

CHURCH, Richard.
The Little Kingdom - a Kentish collection.
Hutchinson. 1964.
1,3,4,5,6,7,8,11,12,15,19,20

CHURCHILL, Irene Josephine.
Calendar of Kent feet of fines to the end of Henry III's reign...
by I.J. Churchill and others.
Kent Archaeological Society. 1956.
1,2,3,4,7,8,11,18

CHURCHILL, Irene Josephine.
Handbook to Kent records.
Kent Archaeological Society. 1914.
1,2,3,4,5,7,8,11,12,15,17

CLAIR, Colin.
A Kentish garner.
Watford, Bruce. 195-?
1,2(1962) 3,4,5,7,8,9(1960) 11,12,14,15,17(1961) 18,19,20

CLARK, F.C.
Kentish fire.
Rye, Adams. 1947.
1,2,3,4,5,6,7,8,9,11,12,14,15,16,17,19,20

CLARK, F.C.
A song of Kent.
Clark. 1953.
12

CLINCH, George.
Handbook of antiquities for the collector and the
student.
L. Upcott Gill. 1905.
3

CLINCH, George.
Kent.
Methuen. 1903.
2,4,8,9,10,11,12,13,15,19

CLINCH, George.
Kent: a concise handbook.
Association of Men of Kent. 1919.
1,3,6,8,11,12,15,18

CLUNN, Harold P.
The face of the Home Counties...2nd edition.
Simpkin, Marshall. 1937.
4

CLUNN, Harold P.
The face of the Home Counties. (pp. 208-315 relate to
Kent).
Spring Book. 1958.
2,5,11,12

CLUNN, Harold P.
Famous South Coast pleasure resorts past and present.
Whittingham. (1929).
7,12,15

COCK, F. William.
Catalogue of...library mainly relating to Kent.
Sotheby. 1944.
7,12

COCK, F. William.
Kentish bibliographical notes.
Ashford, Headley. 1929.
11,17

COGHLAN, Francis.
The steam-packet and coast companion or general guide
to Gravesend, Herne Bay, Canterbury, Margate, Broadsta
Ramsgate, Dover...
Hughes (and others). c.1832 etc.
6,9,12,13,14

COLEMAN, Bryan.
Where to live in Kent: a guide book for the discernin
purchaser of property in the County, compiled by B.
Coleman.
Houses and Estates. (1963?).
1,3,4,5,8,20

COMMISSIONERS OF WORKS.
Illustrated regional guides to ancient monuments...by
the Right Hon. W. Ormsby Gore.
H.M.S.O. 1936.
3

COMMITTEE FOR THE PRESERVATION OF RURAL KENT.
Annual report, 1968-69.
Kent Council of Social Service.
9

COMMITTEE FOR THE PRESERVATION OF RURAL KENT.
Kent today.
Kent Council of Social Service. 1938.
6

COMMITTEE FOR THE PRESERVATION OF RURAL KENT.
Preservation of small towns and villages: report of
a conference held at County Hall...17th March, 1965.
Kent Council of Social Service. 1965.
4

CONSTAPLE, C. AND D. Publishers.
Visitor's guide to Kent.
Constaple. 1971?
9

COOKE, George Alexander.
A topographical and statistical description of the
County of Kent...
Sherwood, Neeley and Jones. 1816.
1,4,6,7,8,9,11,12,13,14,15,17,18,19

(COOKE, George Alexander).
(Topography of Great Britain; or, British traveller's pocket directory...Kent). Title page missing.
Sherwood, Neeley and Jones. c.1838.
3

COOKE, George Alexander.
Walks through Kent.
Sherwood, Neeley and Jones. 1819 etc.
1,5,6,7,11,12,13,17

COOPER, Francis J.
Some sources of information on places in Kent.
Folkestone Herald. 1931.
13

COOPER, Gordon.
A fortnight in Kent.
Marshall. 1950.
1,2,3,4,7,8,9,11,12,15,18

"Country Life" picture-book of Kent.
Country Life. 1962.
1,3,4,5,7,9,11,12 14,15,19

"County" guide to the County of Kent. (Cover title "Come to Kent").
County Associations Ltd.
3(1948) 8(193-?) 11(1950) 12(1950)

The County illustrated - a special Kent number, Vol. II, September, 1922.
3

The County of Kent. (Supplement to "The Draper", March 24th, 1906).
3

COURT, Alexander Norman.
Kent in Colour.
Jarrold. 1958 etc.
1,2,4,5,7,8,11,12

COURTENAY, Ashley R.
Let's halt awhile in and around Kent, Surrey and Sussex, Vol. 1, 2nd edition.
Ashley Courtenay Ltd. 1935.
1,7

COURTENAY, Ashley R.
Let's halt awhile in and around Kent, Surrey and Sussex, Vol. 1, 3rd edition.
Ashley Courtenay Ltd. 1936.
4

COX, John Charles.
Kent,
Methuen. 1920 etc.
1,2,3,4,5,6,7,8,9,11,12,14,15,16,18,19

COX, John Charles.
Ramble in Kent.
Methuen. 1913.
1,2,4,5,6,7,8,9,11,12,13,14,15,16,17,18,19

CRADOCK AND CO. Publishers.
Practical guide to the watering and sea-bathing places on the coasts of Kent, Sussex and Hampshire, including the Isle of Wight etc.
Cradock and Co. 1845.
7

CRESWICK, Paul.
Kent's case for the wounded, by Paul Creswick, G. Stanley Pond and P.H. Ashton.
Hodder and Stoughton. 1915.
1,2,3,7,8,13,17

CROMWELL, Thomas K.
Excursions through the counties of Kent, Surrey and Sussex...
Longman, Hurst, Rees, Orme and Brown.
3(1822) 13(1820)

CROUCH, Marcus.
Detective in the landscape: in South East England.
Longman Young Books. 1972.
9,11

CROUCH, Marcus.
Kent.
Batsford. 1966 etc.
1,2,3,4,5,6,7,8,9,10,11,12,15,16,19,20,21

CRUTTWELL, Clement.
A tour through the whole Island of Great Britain...Vol. 2 (Kent etc.).
G. and J. Robinson. 1801.
8

The curiosities, natural and artificial, of the Island of Great Britain...2 vols. (Kent Vol. 1, pp.337-400, Vol. 2, pp.1-50).
c.1780.
13

DALTON, W.H.
The new and complete English traveller.
Hogg. c.1790.
17

DARTON, Frederick Joseph Harvey.
A parcel of Kent.
Nisbet. 1924.
1,2,3,4,5,6,7,8,9,10,11,12,13,14,15,17,18,19,20

DAVIDSON, G.H.
The Thames and Thanet guide and Kentish tourist.
Reynolds and Son. (c.1843).
7,9,12,13,17

DAVIDSON, J.
A random itinerary.
1894.
18

DAVIES, B.R.
Kent from the Ordnance Survey.
Cassell, Petter and Galpin. n.d.
12

DAVIES, George Macdonald.
Geology of London and South East England.
Murby. 1939.
1,2,4,5,17,18

DAVIS, A.G.
On the geological history of some of our snails, illustrated by some pleistocene and holocene deposits in Kent and Surrey. (Journal of Conchology, Vol. 23, 1953).
5

DEFOE, Daniel.
Tour through England and Wales. Vol. 1 - containing Kent.
Dent. 1948.
3,16

DE KAY, Charles.
Drowsy Kent. (Extract from a periodical of 1890).
3

(DENNE, Samuel and SHRUBSOLE, W.).
The history and antiquities of Rochester..., to which is added a description of the towns, villages (etc.) situated on or near the road from London to Margate, Deal and Dover.
T. Fisher. 1772.
11

DENVIR, Bernard.
William Lambarde and his "Permanulations of Kent".
In The Geographical Magazine, August, 1952).
3

A description of England and Wales, containing particulars of each county...and the lives of the... Vol. 5 (includes Kent).
London, Newbery and Carnan. 1769.
17

DEXTER, Walter.
Days in Dickensland.
Methuen. 1933.
4,8,12,15

DEXTER, Walter.
The Kent of Dickens.
Palmer. 1924.
3,4,5,6,7,8,9,11,12,13, 14,15,17,18,19,20

DIGGES, West.
A poor player: a story of Kent.
Remington. 1888.
3,11

DIXON-SCOTT, J.
Kent coast and countryside: camera pictures of the county, by
J. Dixon-Scott, selected by Prescott Row.
Homeland Association. 1929.
8,11,12

DOBSON, F.R.
The South East: a regional study.
English University Press. 1968.
2

DODSLEY, J. Publisher.
England illustrated (Kent section).
J. Dodsley. 1764.
1,6,17

DUGDALE, James.
The new British traveller; or, modern panorama of England
and Wales...Vol. 3 (Kent).
Dundee. 1819.
11,12

DUNKIN, Alfred John.
The progress of the Princess Alexandra through Kent.
1863.
5,17

ECONOMIC AFFAIRS, Department of, AND CENTRAL OFFICE OF
INFORMATION.
Economic planning in the regions, 2nd edition, 1968.
6

EDMUNDS, F.H.
Geology and water supply in the London district and South-
Eastern England.
Geological Survey and Museum. 1934.
5

EDWARDS, J.
Topographical surveys from London through...Kent.
2nd Edition, 1820.
18

EUPHAN AND KLAXON.
South-country secrets.
Oates and Washbourne. 1935.
12

EVANS, John.
The juvenile tourist; or, excursions into the West of England...
and into the whole County of Kent concluding with an account
of Maidstone and its vicinity...for the rising generation.
Albion Press, 1809. Baldwin, 1818.
1(1809) 12(1809,1818) 13(1809) 15(1809) 17(1809)

EWING, Guy.
Village history. (Contains list of Kent village histories).
Maidstone Rural Community Council. 1927?
3,11,12

Excursions in the County of Kent.
1822 etc.
1,3,5,7,8,9,11,14,15,16,17,18

EYRE BROS. Publishers.
Watering and visiting places of the South and West of England.
Eyre Bros. 1880.
19

FAIRHOLT, F.W.
Proof engravings of buildings and antiquities in Kent, etc.
c.1846.
17

FARNOL, Jeffery.
The broad highway: a novel set in Kent.
Sampson, Low, Marston. (1912).
12

Farther excursions of an observant pedestrian exemplified in a
tour to Margate (4 vols.).
Dutton. 1801.
11,13

FEARON, Henry Bridges. (FIELDFARE, pseud.).
New walks with Fieldfare...(includes 5 in Kent).
London, Associated Newspapers. (1951).
2

FEARON, Henry Bridges.
Twenty walks in Kent.
London, Associated Newspapers. 1955.
2,3,4,13

(FELTHAM, John).
Guide to the watering and sea-bathing places.
1803.
17

FIENNES, Celia.
The journeys of Celia Fiennes, edited by C. Morris.
Cresset Press. 1947.
15,19

FINBERG, J.
Exploring villages. (Kent included).
Routledge and Kegan Paul. 1958.
17,18

FINCH, William Coles.
In Kentish Pilgrim Lane.
London, C.W. Daniel. 1925 etc.
1,2,4,5,6,7,8,9,10,11,12,13,14,15,16,17,18,19,20

FINCH, William Coles.
Life in rural England.
London, C.W. Daniel. (1929).
4,8,12

FINCH, William Coles.
The lure of the countryside.
London, C.W. Daniel. 1927.
4,8,12

FITTER, Richard Sidney Richmond.
Home Counties. (About Britain series No. 3).
Collins. 1951.
4,8,12

FORRESTER, Alfred H.
Summer excursions in the County of Kent, 12 vols.
Orr. 1847.
18

FRY, T. Publisher.
The fashionable guide and directory to the public place
of resort in Great Britain...
T. Fry.
13 (1840) 17 (1831)

GARDINER, Mrs. Dorothy.
Companion into Kent.
Methuen.
1,2(1934,1949) 3,4,5,6,7,8,9,11,12,13,14,15,17,18,20,
21 (1947)

GARDINER, Jane.
An excursion from London to Dover...2 vols.
Longman, Hurst, Rees and Orme. 1806.
1,6,11,13(Vol. 2 only) 17

GARDINER, W.
Rural walks, or walks in Kent.
Derby, Thomas, Richardson. 1837.
15

GARDINER, W.
Walks in Kent.
Cheapside, T. Tegg. Glasgow, R. Griffin. Dublin,
Cumming. 1825.
6

GARDINER, W. Biscombe.
Kent, 2nd edition, by W.B. Gardner and W.T. Shore.
A. and C. Black. 1924.
6

GARDNER, W. Biscombe.
Kent water-colours.
A. and C. Black. 1914, Reprinted 1927 and 1936.
1,2,4,5,6(1936) 8,9,11(and 1936) 12,15,17(1936) 18

Genius of Kent; or, County miscellany. Open to all
parties...biassed by none, for free discussion of
opposite opinions on religion, politics, agriculture,
arts, sciences, manufactures, etc.
Printed for the Editor by William Epps. 1792-95.
1, 3,6,11,17

"A GENTLEMAN", pseud. (DANIEL DEFOE).
A tour through the whole Island of Great Britain...
4 vols., 6th edition.
1762.
18

GEOLOGICAL SURVEY AND MUSEUM.
The water supply of Kent...by William Whitaker...
H.M.S.O. 1908.
3,4,15

GILL, L. Upcott.
Seaside watering places.
Gill. 1898.
7

Gleanings in Kent: cuttings from Kentish newspapers, 1756.
17

GODFREY, Elizabeth.
Our beautiful homeland, by E. Godfrey and others.
Gresham. n.d.
8

GOLDSMITH-CARTER, George.
Forgotten ports of England.
Evans. 1951.
1,7,11,14

GOMME, George Lawrence.
Court Minutes of the Surrey and Kent Sewer Commission, Vol. 1,
edited by G. Lawrence.
1909.
12

GOMME, George Lawrence.
Topographical history of Kent...(Gentleman's Magazine Library).
Elliott Stock. 1895.
1,2,4,5,6,7,8,11,13,14,15,16,18,19

GOODSALL, Robert Harold.
Kentish patchwork.
Constable. 1966.
2,3,4,6,7,8,10,11,12,14,15,16,18,19

GOODSALL, Robert Harold.
A second Kentish patchwork.
Stedehill Publications. 1968.
2,4,5,6,9,11,12,16

GOODSALL, Robert Harold.
A third Kentish patchwork.
Stedehill Publications. 1970.
2,4,5,6,7,9,11,12,16

GOUGH, Richard.
Kent.
1780.
8(1789) 17,18

GRAHAM, G.H.
Kent and Sussex illustrated almanac, 1899, 1903-5.
Graham.
12

GREAVES, Cyril Abdy.
Records of my life.
London, Published for C.A. Greaves. 1912.
3

GROVE, L.R.A.
Kent: list of ruins, moated sites and field antiquities.
(Typescript).
1962.
7

Guides through Kent. (Miscellaneous pamphlets bound in 4 vols.).
n.d.
17

GUPPY, H.B.
The homes of family names in Great Britain.
London, Harrison and Sons. 1890.
5

HALLAM, Jack.
The ghost tour.
Wolfe. 1967.
19

HANNEN, Henry.
An account of a map of Kent dated 1596.
1913.
17,18

HARDY, Sir Edward.
An address...on the transfer of county services under
the National Health Service Act, 1946 and the National
Assistance Act, 1948...
n.d.
11

HARLECH, W.G.A. 4th Baron Harlech.
Southern England.
H.M.S.O.
12(1966) 18(1952)

HARPER, Charles George.
The Autocar road book, Vol. 1: England south of the
Thames.
Methuen, Iliffe. 1910.
12

HARRISON, Lewis.
What's in a name? A Kentish dictionary, Part 1.
Gillingham, Perry and Herring. 1927.
4,5,8,12,15

HASLEHUST, E.W.
Dickens-land.
Blackie and Son Ltd. 1911.
6,11

HEALTH, Ministry of.
Kent Water Survey: summary.
H.M.S.O. 1948.
11

Heritage of Kent. (Special issue of photography,
prepared on behalf of the forces under the care of the
Kent County Welfare Association).
World's Press News Publishing Co. 1943.
3,4

HEYWOOD, ABEL AND SON. Publishers.
Kent and Sussex watering places...
London, Abel Heywood and Son. 1874?
3

HIRST, W.
Rambles in the Home Counties.
Cobden Sanderson. 1927.
18

HISSEY, James John.
A holiday on the road: an artist's wanderings in Kent,
Sussex and Surrey.
Bentley. 1887.
1,4,5,11,12,15,17

HOME PUBLISHING CO. Publisher.
Kent: an illustrated guide to the County. (Spine
title: Kent County Guide).
Croydon, Home Publishing Co.
2(1954,1960)
3(1960)
4(1955,1960)

HOPE, Lady Elizabeth Reid.
English homes and villages - Kent and Sussex. (Early
colour photography).
Sevenoaks, Salmon. 1909.
1,2,3,5,6,7,8,11,12,15,16,17,18,19

HOPE, Sir William Henry St. John.
Inventories of the goods of Henry of Eastry (1331),
Richard of Oxenden (1334) and Robert Hathbrand (1339)...
Harrison. 1896.
1

HOUSING AND LOCAL GOVERNMENT, Ministry of.
The Kent Advisory Water Committee (Dissolution) Order.
H.M.S.O. 1965.
8

HOUSING AND LOCAL GOVERNMENT, Ministry of.
Local government. England and Wales alteration of
areas. The Kent Review (Amendment) Order, 1967.
H.M.S.O. 1967.
5

HOUSING AND LOCAL GOVERNMENT, Ministry of.
Review of the South-East study: County population
forecasts, 1964-81.
H.M.S.O. 1966.
3

HOUSING AND LOCAL GOVERNMENT, Ministry of.
The South-East study, 1961-81.
H.M.S.O. 1964.
1,2,3,5,6,7,8,9,19

HOWARD, William Cecil James. Lord Clonmore.
Shell guide to Kent.
Architectural Press. 1935.
1,7,8,11,13,17,18,19

HUGHES, James Pennethorne.
Shell guide to Kent.
Faber. 1969.
2,5,7,9,11,12

HUGHES, W.R.
Week's tramp in Dickens-land.
Chapman and Hall. 1891 etc.
1,2(1898) 3,4,6,8,9,11,12,14,15,17,18,19,20

HUGHES, William.
The geography of the County of Kent for use in schools.
G. Philip. 1872.
11

HUTTON, Edward.
England of my heart: Spring.
Dent. 1914.
11

IGGLESDEN, Sir. Charles.
Saunter through Kent with pen and pencil, 34 vols.
Ashford, Kentish Express. 1900-1947.
1 (Incomplete)
2 (Vols. 1-18)
3 (Complete)
4 (Complete)
5 (Complete)
6 (Complete)
7 (Complete)
8 (Complete)
11 (Complete)
12 (Complete)
13 (Complete)
15 (Complete)
16 (Vols. 15 and 21)
17 (31 vols.)
18 (Incomplete)
19 (Complete)
20 (Incomplete)
21 (Vols. 1 and 13)

IVIMEY, Alan.
Who slept here? ("A new guide to the romantic south-eastern
counties" - cover).
1961.
4,19

JESSUP, Ronald Frank.
Kent. (Little Guides series - based on the original guide by
J. Charles Cox).
Methuen. 1950.
1,3,4,5,6,7,9,11,15,17

JESSUP, Ronald Frank.
South-East England.
Thames and Hudson. 1970.
2,4,5,7,11,21

JOHNSON, Thomas.
Botanical journeys in Kent and Hampstead: a facsimile reprint
with...translation of his Iter Plantarum, 1629. Descriptio
Itineris Plantarum.
Hunt Botanical Library. 1972.
4

JONES, Sydney Robert.
England south.
Studio. 1948.
3,11,12

Journey-book of England: Kent...
Knight. 1842.
1,2,3,7,8,9,11,12,18

KADWELL, Charles.
Kentish Topography - a series of views illustrative
of the County of Kent, collected and arranged by
Charles Kadwell, 2 vols.
1846.
17

KEATE, George.
Sketches from nature: taken and coloured in a journey
to Margate, 2 vols.
Dodsley.
2nd edition, 1779 (13)
3rd edition, 1782 (11,12,13,15,17)
4th edition, 1790 (13)
5th edition, 1802 (6,8,13)

KENDALL, A.F.
The picture of England and Wales, Vol. 1 (Kent etc.).
Read. 1831.
6,11

Kent: area survey No. 2.
World's Press News and Advertisers Review. 1950.
3

Kent: a reading list.
Dillons University Bookshop. 1971.
7

Kent: a tourist's guide.
St. Albans Photo Precision Ltd. 196-?
3,11

Kent: "The Garden of England".
Maidstone, C.G. Williams Ltd. 196-?
3

Kent and Canterbury illustrated family almanack for 1865.
Canterbury, Jennings. 1865.
3

Kent Argus almanac for the year...1887-8, 1890-1912.
Ramsgate, Kent Argus.
1

KENT COUNCIL OF SOCIAL SERVICE.
Kent today.
Kent Council of Social Service. 1938.
8,11,12,16

KENT COUNTY COUNCIL - PLANNING DEPARTMENT.
Report of the County Planning Officer, 1948-1959.
Kent County Council. 1960.
6

KENT COUNTY COUNCIL - PLANNING DEPARTMENT.
Planning basis for Kent, incorporating reports upon the
County planning survey and the County road plan.
Kent County Council. 1948.
1,2,4,5,6,7,8,9,11,13,15,17,19,21

KENT COUNTY COUNCIL - PLANNING DEPARTMENT.
Preliminary outline County plan: explanatory statement.
Kent County Council. 1949.
3,12

KENT COUNTY LIBRARY.
Catalogue of books on local history.
Kent Education Committee. 1932.
11,13,14

KENT COUNTY LIBRARY.
Kent: a list of books about Kent, 1960 to date.
Maidstone, Kent County Library.
4,6,8,11,12,17,19

KENT COUNTY LIBRARY.
Kent: a select list of references in periodical artic
articles published during 1966 to date.
Maidstone, Kent County Library.
2,3,6,7,11,19

KENT COUNTY LIBRARY.
Local history catalogue, 1939.
Kent Education Committee. 1939.
2(and supplement) 3,4,7,8,11,13,14,17,19

Kent County Magazine, Nos. 1,2.
Ashford, "Kent County Examiner". 1900.
7(No. 2 only) 11

Kent County Yearbook.
Maidstone, Kent Messenger.
1 (1934-5, 1950, 1953)
2 (1934-5, 1950, 1953)
3 (1934-5, 1948, 1950, 1953)
4 (1948, 1950)
5 (1948, 1950, 1953)
6 (1934-5, 1948, 1953)
7 (1934-5, 1950, 1953)
8 (1948, 1950)
9 (1934-5, 1948, 1950, 1953)
11 (1948, 1950)
12 (1934-5, 1948, 1950, 1953)
13 (1948)
17 (1934-5, 1953)
19 (1953)

Kent Illustrated - catalogue...drawings and prints of...Kent
(1760-1860).
For Sale by F.T. Sabin. (1952).
2

KENT MAGAZINE.
(Vol. 1 only issued).
Tower Publishing Co. 1896.
3,5,7,9,11,12,15,17,18,20

Kent Magazine and County Register, Vol. 1
1824.
1,3,6,12

KENT MESSENGER. Publisher.
An introduction to Kent; or, the colour of the County.
Maidstone, Kent Messenger. (1967).
4,5,6,9,21

Kent prints: "being a collection of views of the County", 12
vols.
n.d.
13

Kentish Magazine: a monthly literary miscellany for the
County. Nos. 1-3, May, June, July, 1878.
Maidstone. 1878.
1,4

The Kentish Magazine and companion to the newspaper, edited by
C. MacFarlane.
1850.
17

Kentish Pie. (A magazine mainly about Kent, sold to raise
funds for S.S.A.F.A. and N.A.B.C.), edited by Jean Sewell.
Maidstone, Kent Messenger. 1947.
4

KENTISH SOCIETY.
A concise account of the improvements...made by the gentlemen
of the Kentish Society.
Blake. n.d.
12

Kentish tourist; or, excursions in the County of Kent...
Dowding. n.d.
1,4,8,11,12,17

The Kentish traveller's companion in a descriptive view of the
towns, villages, remarkable buildings, and antiquities,
situated in or near the road from London to Margate, Dover and
Canterbury.
1st edition, 1776. Rochester, T. Fisher.
3,6,8,9,13,14,15,18,20
2nd edition, 1779. Canterbury, Simmons and Kirkby.
1,3,4,5,6,7,8,11,12,21
3rd edition, 1790. Canterbury, Simmons and Kirkby.
6,13,17,18
4th edition, 1794. Canterbury, Simmons and Kirkby.
2,6,13
5th edition, 1799. Canterbury, Simmons and Kirkby.
6,13,14

KIDD, William. Publisher.
Picturesque companion to the watering places of Great Britain.
W. Kidd. 1833.
17

KILBURNE, Richard.
A topographie, or survey of the County of Kent.
H. Atkinson. 1659.
1,3,4,5,6,7,8,11,12,13,14,15,16,16,18,19,20,21

KITTON, Frederick G.
The Dickens country.
Black. 1905 etc.
8,9,12,15,18

KITTON, Frederick G.
The Dickens country, 2nd edition.
Black. 1911.
4,15

KNIGHT, Charles. Publisher.
Journey-book of England: Kent.
C. Knight. 1842 and 1852.
17

KNIGHT, Charles. Publisher.
Excursion companion, 1851-3.
C. Knight.
6

KNIGHT, Charles.
Old England: a pictorial museum...of antiquities
(2 vols.).
Sangster. n.d.
18

KNOCKER, Edward.
The footsteps of the Lord.
Dover, C. Goulden. 1870.
6

Land utilisation survey of Britain: Kent, by L.D.
Stamp.
Geographical Publications for the Survey. 1943.
1,2,3,5,6,7,8,11,12,15

LAWSON, William.
Geography of the County of Kent.
Collins. n.d.
9,11,17

LELAND, John.
The itinerary of John Leland in or about the years
1535-1543, 5 vols.
Centaur Press. 1964.
2,4,5,7,11,15

LEWIS, W. Publisher.
Lewis' new traveller's guide.
Cornhill, London: W. Lewis. 1819.
6

LITTLEBURY AND CO. Publishers.
Kent: a guide to the County. (Kent County Handbook).
Littlebury and Co. (1963).
4,8

LYSONS, Daniel.
Environs of London...Volume the fourth, counties of
Herts., Essex and Kent.
Cadell and Davies. 1796.
1,12(1811) 17,18

MAIR, Gordon.
Kingdom of Kent.
Fawkham, Mair. 1953.
1,9,11,15,18

MAIR, Harold.
The XVth mile stage by Harold Mair, with "The Kingdom of
Kent", by Gordon Mair. (See Dartford).
H. Mair. 1953.
1,2,4,5,8,9,11,12,15,17,18,19,20

MAIS, Stuart Petrie Brodie.
Hills of the South.
1939.
18

MAIS, Stuart Petrie Brodie.
The Home Counties.
Batsford. 1942.
2

MAIS, Stuart Petrie Brodie.
The Home Counties in pictures.
Odhams. n.d.
12

MAIS, Stuart Petrie Brodie.
It isn't far from London.
London, Richards. 1930.
4

MAIS, Stuart Petrie Brodie.
Southern rambles for Londoners.
Southern Railway Co. 1932.
1,2

MAIS, Stuart Petrie Brodie.
Southern rambles - Kent.
British Railways. 1950.
1,3,4,5,7,8,11,15

MAIS, Stuart Petrie Brodie.
Winter walks.
British Railways. 1950.
1,4

MALCOLM, James Peller.
Excursions in the counties of Kent, Gloucester, Hereford,
Monmouth and Somerset in the years 1802, 1803 and 1805 -
illustrated by descriptive sketches of the most interesting
places and buildings, particularly the cathedrals of Canterbury,
Gloucester, Hereford and Bristol, with delineations of
character in different walks of life.
Longman.
1(1814) 6(1805, 1814) 7,8, 12(1805, 1814) 17(1814, 1822)

MALCOLM, James Peller.
First impressions.
John Nicholl, Printer. 1807.
6,15

MANN, E.L.
Unknown warriors and others.
Nelson. 1937.
11

MAXWELL, Donald.
Adventures with a sketchbook.
Lane. 1914.
12

MAXWELL, Donald.
A detective in Kent.
Lane. 1929.
1,3,4,5,6,8,9,11,12,15,16,17,18,19,20

MAXWELL, Donald.
Excursions in colour.
Cassell. 1927.
15

MAXWELL, Donald.
History with a sketchbook.
Lane. 1926.
3,5,9,11,12,14

MAXWELL, Donald.
Unknown Kent.
Lane. 1921
1,2,3,4,5,6,7,8,9,11,12,13,14,15,16,17,18,19(1932) 20

MAXWELL, G.S.
The road to France.
Methuen. 1928.
1,4,5,6,8,11,13,17,18

MEAD, J. Publisher.
Rambles in Kent.
J. Mead. (c.1845).
1,3,4,7,11,12,14,15,17,19

MEE, Arthur.
Kent.
Hodder and Stoughton.
1(1937) 2(1969) 3(1937) 4(1937 and 1969) 5(1937) 6(1937)
7(1936 and 1969) 8(1937 and 1969) 9(1937 and 1969) 11(1937 and
1969) 12(1937) 13(1936) 14(1936) 15(1937) 16(1937) 18(1937)
19(1937) 29(1937)

MELVILLE AND CO. LTD. Publishers.
Directory and gazetteer of Kent...
Melville and Co. 1858.
1,7

MOGG, Edward.
Mogg's South-Eastern or London and Dover railway and
Tunbridge Wells guide.
1843.
19

MOORE, Francis.
Vox Stellarum; or, a loyal almanack for... 1828.
3

MORECROFT, V.W.
50 week-end walks in Berkshire, Surrey, Sussex and
Kent (41 pages on Kent).
Hodder and Stoughton. 1952.
2,12

MORTON, Henry Canova Vollam.
I saw two Englands: record of a journey before the
war, and after the outbreak of war in the year 1939.
(Chapters 1,2,3 relate to Kent - Chapter 3 describes
Canterbury).
London, Methuen. 1942.
3

MOUL, Duncan.
Week-ends in Dickensland: a handbook for the rambler.
Rochester, Goldwin. (190?).
4,6,7,8,9,18

MOUL, Duncan.
Week-ends in hopland.
Homeland Association. n.d.
2,6,7,11,12,17,18

MOUNTJOY, Alan Bertram.
London and South-Eastern England.
London, Educational Publishing Co. 1954.
3

MURBY, Thomas. Publisher.
Murby's county geographies: Kent.
T. Murby. (1873).
17

MURRAY, John. Publisher.
Handbook for travellers in Kent.
J. Murray. 1858 etc.
1,2,3,4,5,7,8,9,11,12,14,15,16,17,18,19

NATIONAL GARDENS SCHEME.
Beautiful Kent gardens.
1948.
17

NATIONAL GARDENS SCHEME.
Gardens of Kent...open to public - 1951, 1952, 1954,
1955 to date.
Tunbridge Wells, Stanford Printing Co.
3

NEALE, John Preston.
Views of the seats of noblemen and gentlemen in England
and Wales, Scotland and Ireland: Kent.
Reid. 1818.
11

New display of the beauties of England, or a description
of the most elegant or magnificent public edifices...
London, R. Goadby. 1776.
3

NEWCOMB, Edward.
Illustrated motor and cycle rides in Kent, Surrey and
Sussex (with map).
Collins, Kew and Co. (190-?).
11,17

NOEL, Amelia.
(Six aquatints of Kent).
A. Noel. 1797.
11

NORTON, Jane E.
Typescript draft of a bibliography of Kent directories,
compiled by J.E. Norton.
1947.
3

NORWOOD, John C.
The glory of Kent.
South-East Gazette. 1930.
2,4,7,11,12,13,19

Nouveau Theatre de la Grande Bretagne (including Kent seats).
n.d.
16

O'CONNOR, H.E.
Kent: an illustrated review of the holiday and industrial
aspects...edited by H.E. O'Connor.
n.d.
8

ORDNANCE SURVEY.
Table of areas of the parishes and extra parochial places in
the County of Kent arranged by divisions, hundreds and
liberties.
Southampton, Ordnance Survey. 1881.
3

The original Kentish appendix and Maidstone and County
annual: being a yearbook...
Maidstone, Burgiss-Brown.
3(1890) 11(1894) 12(1888) 13(1900) 17(1894)

Our outing: where shall we go?
Fremlins. 1953.
12

OVENDEN, Ernest H.
Kent: an illustrated review of the holiday, residential,
sporting and industrial aspects of the county.
Cheltenham, E.J. Burrow. 1938.
15

PAGE, Hugh E.
Rambler's guide to London's countryside: Kent. (3rd edition).
Geographia. c.1930.
2,3,9,11

PAGE, William.
The Victoria history of the County of Kent, 3 vols., edited
by W. Page.
London, St. Catherine Press. 1908-1932.
1,2,3,4,5,6,7,8,9,11,12,13,14,15,16(1 and 2 only) 17,18,19,
20,21

PARKER, Richard.
The sheltering tree.
Gollancz. 1970.
11

PEERS, Bryant.
Kent, Surrey and Sussex. (Letts motor tour guides).
Letts. 1969.
2,12

PENNANT, Thomas.
Journey from London to the Isle of Wight. Vol. 1 - from
London to Dover. Vol. 2 - from Dover to the Isle of Wight.
Oriental Press. 1801.
1,4(Vol. 1) 6,7,8(Vol. 1) 12,13(Vol. 1)

PHILLIPS, G.A.
Southern England calling: historical information and official
local information. Coronation edition, edited by G.A.
Phillips and W.G. Willis.
1952.
4

PHILLIPS, R. Publisher.
A guide to all the watering and sea-bathing places.
R. Phillips. 1803, 1804, 1806, 1810, 1815, c.1818, 1828.
13

PLUMPTRE, H.W.
The Kingdom of Kent. In The Parents' Review, Vol. XXXVI,
January, 1925.
3

POWEL, Sir Nathanael.
Summary relation of the past and present condition of the
Upper Levels lying in the counties of Kent and Sussex.
1662.
11

PUMPHREY, George Henry.
Children's comics. (Local author, Dover)
Epworth. 1955.
6

PUMPHREY, George Henry.
Comics and your children.
1955.
6

PUMPHREY, George Henry.
Conquering the English Channel.
London, Abelard Schuman. 1965.
3,6

PUMPHREY, George Henry.
Juniors.
Livingstone. 1950.
6

RAILWAY CHRONICLE. Publisher.
Travelling charts...passed by the line of railway:
London to Ashford, Folkestone and Dover. (See Railways).
Railway Chronicle. n.d.
1,11

ROBSON, William.
Commercial directory of London and the six Home Counties.
W. Robson. 1838.
14

ROFFE, Robert Cabbell.
My diary of sixty-three days: with memorandums of
occasional trips into Kent. (Privately printed - 50
copies).
Rochester Press. 1858.
6,8,13,15,17

ROUSE, Edward Clive.
The old towns of England.
London, Batsford. 1948.
3

ROWLES, Walter.
The Kentish chronologer and index to the principal
places and objects worthy of observation in the County
of Kent. Comprising a list of the nobility, Lord
Lieutenants (etc.).
Maidstone, Vidion. 1807.
1,2,3,4,12,17

SACKVILLE-WEST, V.
English country houses.
Collins. 1947.
12

SAVORY, H.J.
South-East England. (Geography of the British Isles,
series).
Cambridge University Press. 1972.
4

SCOTT-JOB, Derrick.
County guide to Kent, edited by D. Scott-Job.
Graham Scott. 1958.
1,3,5,7,9,11,12,14,15

SHEARS, William Sidney.
Kent, Surrey and Sussex, edited by W.S. Shears.
Hutchinson. 1939.
9,11

SHELL-MEX AND BRITISH PETROLEUM LTD.
Kent. (Shilling guides series).
Rainbird. 1963.
2,8(1964)

SHELTON, H.
Kentish rambles.
Sidcup, "Kentish District Times". 1939.
1,2,8,11,12,17

SHEPHARD, Michael.
Happy valley.
Museum Press. 1954.
12

SHEPHERD, George.
The picturesque beauties of Great Britain...from an
elaborate survey...Kent, by G. Shepherd, H. Gastineau and
others.
Virtue.
1(1832) 3(1828) 4(1831,1840) 6(1828) 8(1832) 9(1832)
11(1832) 12(1829) 13(1828) 15(1832) 17(1832) 18(1828)
19(1832)

SHEPHERD, George.
A treasury of Kent prints: a series of views from original
drawings by G. Shepherd, H. Gastineau, etc...
Sheerness, A.J. Cassell. (1972).
11

SHORE, W. Teignmouth.
Kent.
Black. 1907 etc.
1,2,4,5,7,8,9,11,13,14,15,17,18,19

SIMPSON, Woolley. (Sometimes known as ROBIN, George).
Professional excursions by an auctioneer - Part I, Kent...
1843.
12,17

SMITH, Alfred Russell.
Catalogue of tracts, pamphlets and prints illustrating the
topography (of Kent).
1878.
17

SMITH, John Russell.
Bibliotheca Cantiana: a bibliographical account of what has
been published on the County of Kent.
J.R. Smith. 1837.
1,2,3,4,5,6,7,8,9,11,12,13,14,15,16,17,18,19,20

SMITH, S. Theobald.
A ramble in rhyme in the country of Cranmer and Ridley: a
Kentish garland.
Chapman and Hall. 1889.
11,13,17

SMITH, W. St. John. Publisher.
Environs of Dover and the watering places of Kent.
W. St. J. Smith. (c.1865-70).
11

SOUTH-EAST ECONOMIC PLANNING COUNCIL.
South-East Kent Study. Recommendations of the South-East
Economic Planning Council, 1969.
South-East Economic Planning Council. 1969.
2,4,6,7,9,11

SOUTH-EAST ECONOMIC PLANNING COUNCIL.
A strategy for the South-East: a first report by the South-
East Economic Planning Council.
H.M.S.O. 1967.
2,6,7,12,14,19

SOUTH-EAST JOINT PLANNING TEAM.
Strategic plan for the South-East.
H.M.S.O. 1970.
6,19

SOUTH-EAST JOINT PLANNING TEAM.
Strategic plan for the South-East. Studies Vols. 1-5, with
general index volume.
H.M.S.O. 1971.
7(Vols. 1,2 and 5) 11

SOUTH-EASTERN AND CHATHAM RAILWAY CO.
Through the garden of England: an illustrated handbook to the
holiday resorts and residential districts in Kent, Sussex-..
South-Eastern and Chatham Railway Co. 1922.
9

SOUTHERN RAILWAY.
Southern homes - Kent.
1939.
6

SPENCER, Nathaniel.
The complete English traveller: a survey and description of
England and Wales. (Kent section only).
1772.
7

STANDING CONFERENCE ON LONDON REGIONAL PLANNING.
The South-East study, 1961-1981.
London, London County Council. April, 1964.
3

"The Star" rambles illustrated. Vol. III - South of the
Thames (Eastern section).
Fleetgate Publishers. c.1930?
1

STAWELL, Mrs. R.
Motoring in Sussex and Kent.
Hodder and Stoughton. 1926 and 1929.
1,2,4,7,8,9,11,12,13,15,18

(STORER, James Sargant).
The antiquarian and topographical cabinet, containing a
series of elegant views (engraved by J.S. Storer and
John Greig)...(section on Kent).
W. Clarke. 1808?
11

STOREY, G.A.
Sketches from memory.
London, Chatto and Windus. 1899.
3

STUKELEY, William.
Itinerarium curiosum; or, an account of the antiquities
and remarkable curiosities in nature or art, observed in
travels through Great Britain.
London, Printed for Messrs. Baker and Leigh. 1776.
3

Summer excursions in the County of Kent.
Orr. 1847.
1,3,4,5,7,8,9,11,12,15,17,18

TAYLOR, Leonard.
London's coast and countryside. (Where shall we go?
No. 1)
Nicholson and Watson. 1950.
8

THOMPSON, Gibson.
Picturesque Kent, by G. Thompson and D. Moul.
F.E. Robinson. 1901.
1,2,3,4,5,7,8,9,11,12,15,17,18,19,20

THORNE, John.
Kent.
Edinburgh, W. and R. Chambers. 1968.
1,2(1949 and 1968) 3(1949 and 1968) 4(1949 and 1968)
5,7,8,9,11,14,15,17,19,20

THORNHILL, J.F.P.
Downs and Weald: a social geography of South-East
England.
Christophers. 1937.
2(1935) 4,11

Tourist's guide: a collection of the railway guides
of the principal main lines in 1883-4, including the
London, Chatham and Dover Railway...
Morton. n.d.
1

Tourist's guide through the County of Kent and part of
Sussex...
Wallis. n.d.
11,17

"A TRAVELLER", pseud.
Kent: the towns, their history etc., the rivers,
ancient customs, etc., by A Traveller.
1760.
9

TRENT, Christopher.
Motoring on regional byways: south of London.
Foulis. 1968.
2,5,7,8,12

TURNER, E.
Handy-book of Kent. (Guide-book).
Turner and Whittaker. 1873.
11,12,17

TURNER, J.M.W.
Picturesque views...including Kent.
London, Arch. 1876.
6

TURNER, J.W.
The Englishman's country, edited by J.W. Turner.
Collins. 1945.
12

TURNOR, Reginald.
Kent.
Elek. 1950?
1,4,5,6,7,8,11,12,13,14,15,16,17,18,21

TURNOR, Reginald.
South-East England: Kent and Sussex, by R. Turner and P.F.
Gaye.
Elek. 1956.
1,3,4,5,8,9,11,12,14,15

TYMMS, Samuel.
The family topographer, Vol. 1.
Nichols. 1832.
11

VAUGHAN, H.S.
The way about Kent.
Iliffe. 1893.
1,2(1892) 3,4,11,12,13,15,17(1892) 18

Views of Kent, 4 vols.
n.d.
19

VOYSEY, Annesley.
An introduction to Kent; or, the colour of the county.
Kent Messenger. 1967.
2,12

WALFORD, Edward.
Holidays in the Home Counties.
Bogue. 1880.
6

WALFORD, Edward.
Pleasant days in pleasant places. (Contains several essays
about places in Kent).
Hardwicke and Bogue. 1879.
6

Walks through Kent...
Sherwood. 1827.
1

WALPOOLE, George Augustus.
The new British traveller.. .(Comprehensive survey of the
County of Kent).
Hogg. 1784.
7,11,17

WARD, LOCK AND CO. Publishers.
Ready guide and tourist's handbook for Kent...
Ward, Lock and Co. (1877).
3

The Watering Places of Great Britain and Fashionable
Directory.
London, I.T. Hinton.
6(1833) 11(1831) 13(1833) 17(1831) 18(1831)

WATTS, R.B.
A topographical description of the principal buildings, towns,
villages, seats, etc., between London and Margate...
1827.
13

WEBB, Montague.
Viewing Kent: an illustrated guide.
Napier Publications. 1971.
8,11

WEBBER, M.
Visitor's guide to the County of Kent, edited by M. Webber.
Constable. (1962).
12

WELLBYE, Reginald.
Road touring in South-East England. (The roadfaring guides).
Phoenix House. 1954.
7,11,12

West Kent Almanack and County Advertiser for 1849.
A.T. Fordham. 1848.
15

WHITBREAD AND CO. Publishers.
Outings in Kent.
Whitbread and Co. c.1935.
15

WILD, Rowland.
Southshire pilgrimage: an unconventional tour from Kent
to Cornwall.
Harrap. 1939.
12

WILLIAMS, C.G. LTD. Publisher.
(Glorious Kent): a plastichrome colour souvenir.
C.G. Williams Ltd. (1963).
4

WILLIS, William.
Pencillings in Kent...photographic reproductions...
printed in platinotype...(process invented by William
Willis Junior).
Bromley, Willis. 1881.
2

WINBOLT, Samuel Edward.
Kent.
Bell. 1930.
1,2,3,5,6,7,8,9,11,12,13,14,15,17,18,19

WINBOLT, Samuel Edward.
Kent, Sussex and Surrey.
Harmondsworth, Penguin. 1939.
1,2,4(1947) 6,7(1947) 8,9,11(1947) 15

WINSCOM, Jane Anne.
Kent.
1861.
13

WOOD, John George.
The County of Kent: a collection of the 36...drawings
and views...of the principal seats of the nobility and
gentry, situate in Kent.
Published in Parts,Atlas Folio. 1785-1800.
11

WOOLDRIDGE, Sidney William.
London's countryside, by S.W. Wooldridge and G.E.
Hutchings.
Collins. 1957.
4

WOOLLARD, T.J.
The geography of the urban and rural districts of the
"garden of England": an unpublished report by a
student of the University of Hull, 1962-3.
6

WYNDHAM, Richard.
South-East England. (Face of Britain series).
Batsford. 1951.
3,8,11,12,18

WYNDHAM, Richard.
South-Eastern survey: a last look round Sussex, Kent
and Surrey.
Batsford. 1940.
1,2,4,8,13,15

KENT, EAST

ABERCROMBIE, Sir Patrick.
The development of East Kent: a paper read before the
Royal Institute of British Architects on Monday, 11th
April, 1927. (Reprinted from Royal Institute of
British Architects Journal, Vol. 34, No. 13, 7th May,
1927).
3

ABERCROMBIE, Sir Patrick.
East Kent Regional Planning Scheme: preliminary survey,
by Sir P. Abercrombie and J. Archibald.
1925.
1,2,3,4,5,6,7,8,11,12,13,14,15,17,19

ABERCROMBIE, Sir Patrick.
East Kent Regional Planning Scheme: final report, by
Sir P. Abercrombie and J. Archibald.
Canterbury, Austens. 1928.
1,2,3,4,5,6,7,11,12,13,14

ASHBEE, P.
Round barrows of East Kent, by P. Ashbee and G.C.
Dunning. In Archaeologia Cantiana, Vol. 74, 1960.
17

BAPTIST CHURCH - EAST KENT ASSOCIATION.
The circular letter from the ministers and messengers of the
several Baptist churches composing the East Kent Association.
Shrewsbury. 1836-53.
7

BAYNTON, Alfred.
Descriptive and pictorial guide to East Kent and Rye,
Winchelsea and Hastings, edited by A. Baynton.
Cheltenham, E.J. Burrow. 1934.
2

BLACK, ADAM AND CHARLES LTD. Publishers.
Black's guide to Canterbury and the watering places of East
Kent.
A. and C. Black.
1(1909, 1915)
3(1921)
4(1909)
5(1909)
7(1904, 1909)
8(1900, 1901, 1909)
11(1901)
12(1900, 1901, 1904)
13(1901)
17(1904)

BLACK, ADAM AND CHARLES LTD. Publishers.
Black's guide to East Kent.
A. and C. Black. 1900.
7(1904) 8(1900) 16(1915)

BOSWORTH, G.H.
Where shall we go this year? An unbiased guide to the East
coast.
1937.
13

BRIDGE-BLEAN RURAL DISTRICT COUNCIL.
Around Canterbury: the Bridge-Blean Rural District guide.
(Rural England series, No. 95).
Century Press.
3(1948) 7(1951) 8(1951)

BRIDGE-BLEAN RURAL DISTRICT COUNCIL.
Bridge-Blean Rural District: the official guide.
Croydon, Home Publishing Co. 1962 and 1965.
1,6,11

A brief history of Dover and Ramsgate Harbours, with a
description of the coast between Dungeness and the Isle of
Thanet, and remarks on the probable construction of a harbour
between the South Foreland and Sandwich Haven.
(London) Brewer. 1837.
6,11,13

CHAMBERLAIN, Neville.
Town planning in East Kent: a speech...delivered at Canterbury,
July 24th, 1926.
11

CHURCHILL, Irene Josephine.
East Kent records, edited by I.J. Churchill.
Kent Archaeological Society. 1922.
1,2,3,4,5,7,8,11,12,15,17,18

COLEMAN, Alice M.
East Kent: a description of the Ordnance Survey, seventh
edition one-inch sheet 173. (British landscape through maps),
by A.M. Coleman and C.T. Lukehurst.
Geographical Association. 1967.
2,4,6

Collection of tracts relating to the City of Canterbury and the
Eastern division of the County of Kent.
Canterbury, Ward. 1836.
3,11,15

COUZENS, S.
A tour through the Isle of Thanet and some other parts of East
Kent, including a particular description of the churches in that
extensive district and copies of the monumental inscriptions etc.
1793.
4

COWELL, M.H.
A floral guide for East Kent, etc.
Faversham, Ratcliffe. 1839.
1,3,5,6,7,9,11,13,15,17

CRAWFORD, Osbert Guy Stanhope.
Field-notes in the Canterbury district. In Archaeologia
Cantiana, Vol. 46, 1934.
17

CROPTON, John.
The road to nowhere.
Hurst and Blackett. 1936.
3,6,11

Deal, Walmer, Kingsdown and Sandwich directory for 1937,
1938 and 1948.
Pain.
11

DE SANDWICH, Peter.
Some East Kent parish history - Elmstone, Stourmouth,
Ash-next-Sandwich, Wingham. In Home Counties Magazine,
1902.
17

Dover, Margate, Broadstairs, Ramsgate, Sandwich and
Deal new and improved itinerary...
1827.
13

Dover, Sandwich and Deal Local History Exhibition
Committee: official catalogue 1935.
6

DOWKER, George.
On the changes which have taken place in East Kent.
n.d.
11

DOWKER, George.
On the junction of the chalk with the tertiary beds in
East Kent. (Extracted from Geological Magazine, Vol. 3,
No. 23, May, 1866).
7

DOWKER, George.
A tabulated list and description of the birds of East
Kent...
n.d.
3,7,11,12,13,17

DUNNING, G.C.
Neolithic occupation sites in East Kent. (Reprinted
from the Antiquaries Journal, Vol. 46, Part 1, 1966).
4

DYSON, S.S.
Glories of Thanet and East Kent.
(Dover). 1931.
13

EAST ASHFORD RURAL DISTRICT COUNCIL.
East Ashford Rural District: official guide.
Century Press. 1954 etc.
1,4,7,11,15

East Kent: sale of brewery premises, maltings, houses,
cottages and land.
Canterbury, Amos and Dawton. 1933.
3

East Kent Annual - Christmas 1880. (Cover title
"The East Kent Christmas Annual").
Herne Bay, East Kent Times. 1880.
3

EAST KENT ROAD CAR COMPANY, CANTERBURY.
Descriptive and pictorial guide to East Kent and Rye,
Winchelsea and Hastings...
Canterbury, East Kent Road Car Company. 1952.
3

EASTRY RURAL DISTRICT COUNCIL.
Building Byelaws made under the Public Health Act, 1936.
1953.
11

EASTRY RURAL DISTRICT COUNCIL.
Eastry Rural District: official guide.
Croydon, Abbey Press. 1931 etc.
4,11,12

HARDMAN, G.W.
East Kent walks.
Deal, Howe. 1936.
5,7,11,13,15

HARPER, Charles George.
The Ingoldsby country.
Black. 1904 etc.
1,2,4,5,6,7,8,10,11,12,13,14,15,17,18

HARPER, Charles George.
The Downs and the sea, by C.G. Harper and J.C. Kershaw.
1923.
1,3,8,11,14

HASLUCK, Eugene Lewis.
Beyond the Forest of Blean...
Herne Bay Press. 1966.
1,2,3,7,11,12,15

Hundred of Bewsborough - The Minutes of the Hundred, 1815-37.
(Original handwritten record).
n.d.
6

INGOLDSBY, Thomas, pseud. (Richard Harris BARHAM).
Ingoldsby legends, 3 vols, edited by Mrs. Bond.
Bentley. 1894.
6,9

JACOB, J.
Wild flowers, grasses and ferns of East Kent.
Dover Express. 1936.
3,6,7,11,13,14

KENNY, Tom.
Angling: reminiscences...giving an account of his experiences...
in East Kent since 1933.
Sittingbourne, Parrett. 1946.
3,11

KERSHAW, S.W.
Foreign refugee settlements in East Kent.
n.d.
11

LABOUR, Ministry of.
Estimated number of insured employees in the areas of Canterbury,
Deal, Dover, Folkestone, Margate and Ramsgate.
H.M.S.O. 1929, 1939 and 1959.
3

LAPWORTH, Herbert.
East Kent water supplies.
Canterbury, Austens. 1930.
11

NATIONAL SOCIETY FOR THE PREVENTION OF CRUELTY TO CHILDREN.
Canterbury and East Mid Kent Branch, 3rd annual report - 1896,
4th annual report - 1897.
17

PACKE, Christopher.
Ancographia sive convallium description. In which are...
expounded the origin, course...extent, elevation and
congruity of all the valleys and hills, brooks and rivers...
of East Kent.
Canterbury. 1743.
1,3,7,8,12,13,17

PACKE, Christopher.
A dissertation upon the surface of the earth, as delineated
in a specimen of a Philosophico-Chorographical Chart of
East Kent.
1737.
13,14

PACKE, Christopher.
A new Philosophico-Chorographical Chart of East Kent, invented
and delineated by Christopher Packe.
1743.
13

PIKE, W.T. AND CO. LTD. Publishers.
Dover, Canterbury, Deal, Walmer and Sandwich by camera and
pen, 1904-5.
Brighton, W.T. Pike. 1905.
6

STAPLETON AND CO. Publishers.
Topographical history and directory of Canterbury,
Faversham, Herne Bay, Sittingbourne and Whitstable.
Stapleton and Co. 1838.
3,8,12,17

The Thompson Estate, East Kent...particulars...of sale
of freehold properties in the parishes of Cheriton,
Burmarsh and St. Leonards, Hythe, comprising a
gentleman's residence (Seabrook Vale)...and...about
321 acres of buildings and rich Romney Marsh pasture
lands...which will be offered for sale...by Messrs.
Cobay Bros...on...13th...September, 1888.
Hythe, Cobay Bros., Auctioneers. 1888.
7

Tour through the Isle of Thanet and some other parts of
East Kent.
Nichols. 1793.
12

WARD LOCK AND CO. LTD. Publishers.
A pictorial and descriptive guide to Margate, Broadstair
Ramsgate, Herne Bay, Canterbury and North-East Kent.
(Various permutations of title from 1899-1965).
Ward Lock and Co. Ltd.
1,2,3,8,11,12,13,14,15,17,18

WARD LOCK AND CO. LTD. Publishers.
Pictorial guide to Deal and Walmer...
Ward Lock and Co. Ltd. 1950 etc.
1,4,11,17,18

WATSON, William.
Visitor's guide to Herne Bay, Canterbury and the most
memorable spots in Kent.
John Dicks. 1855.
11,17

WEST KENT FEDERATION OF WOMEN'S INSTITUTES.
Countryside in the 70's: East and West Kent survey,
1969.
West Kent Federation of Women's Institutes. 1970.
7

KENT, MID

KENT COUNTY COUNCIL - PLANNING DEPARTMENT.
Plan for Maidstone, Snodland, West Malling and related
communities.
Kent County Council. 1954.
11

MAIDSTONE RURAL DISTRICT COUNCIL.
Maidstone Rural District: official guide.
8,11,12 (1952 etc.). Malcolm Page.
4,8,11,12 (1961). Gloucester, British Publishing Co.
12 (n.d.). London, Pyramid Press.

MALLING RURAL DISTRICT COUNCIL.
Annual report on the health of the Malling district.
Malling Rural District Council.
11(1970) 12(1964)

MALLING RURAL DISTRICT COUNCIL.
Byelaws.
Malling Rural District Council. 1905.
12

MALLING RURAL DISTRICT COUNCIL.
Malling Rural District: official guide.
1,11,15 (n.d.). Century Press.
1,4,8,11,12,19 (1957+). Croydon, Home Publishing Co.

MALLING RURAL DISTRICT COUNCIL.
Yearbook.
Malling Rural District Council.
11(1957-8 etc.) 12(1957-8, 1959, 1968-9)

Particulars etc. of sale of valuable freehold agricult-
ural estates about 2,400 acres...in the parishes of
Kingsnorth, Aldington, Ashford, Appledore, Bethersden,
High Malden, Mersham, Newchurch, Orlestone, Ruckinge,
Snave, Tenterden and Woodchurch...which Messrs.
Langridge and Freeman have received instructions from
Sir James H. Danville...to sell by auction...on...
September 10th, 1918.
Langridge and Freeman. 1918.
7

KENT, MID Cont'd

Particulars, plan and conditions of sale of Court Reed Farm and small holdings, Great Chart; accommodation, pastures and arable land at Grafty Green, Boughton Malherbe; cottages, shops and residential property at Charing...which Mr. Alfred J. Burrows...will sell by auction...on 12th April, 1921. (The property was for many years in the ownership of the Streeter family).
A.J. Burrows. 1921.
7

WEST ASHFORD RURAL DISTRICT COUNCIL.
Observation of the Council on the study of Professor Buchanan of the proposal to site a new city in the area of the West Ashford Rural District Council.
Ashford Rural District Council. 1969.
7,11

WEST ASHFORD RURAL DISTRICT COUNCIL.
West Ashford Rural District Council - official guide.
Home Publishing Co.
1(1951) 4(1960) 11(1951) 12(1967) 19(1964)

KENT, NORTH EAST

ADAMS, THOMPSON AND FRY.
North-East Kent Regional Planning Scheme. Report prepared for the North-East Kent Joint Town Planning Committee.
Chatham, Adams, Thompson and Fry. 1930.
4,8,11,12,13,14,15

BLACK, ADAM AND CHARLES LTD. Publishers.
Black's guide to North-East Kent.
A. and C. Black Ltd. 1928.
6

BOYS' BRIGADE - NORTH KENT BATTALION.
Battalion handbook. (Looseleaf).
(1969?).
4

CHELSEA SPELAEOLOGICAL SOCIETY.
Deneholes. (Vol. 4 of the Records of the Society, 1966).
8

DIBLEY, George F.
(The chalk of Rochester district: being a collection of pamphlets relating to the chalk and flint deposits in North-East Kent, 1900-1918) by G.F. Dibley and others.
15

HOLLINGBOURNE RURAL DISTRICT COUNCIL.
Calendar for the year ending 20th May, 1959.
Hollingbourne Rural District Council. 1968.
12

HOLLINGBOURNE RURAL DISTRICT COUNCIL.
Hollingbourne Rural District Council: the official guide.
11(1952) 12(1952)   Burrow.
11(1959+) 12(1959+)   Croydon, Home Publishing Co.
1(1964+) 3(1968) 4(1964+) 11(1964+)   Gloucester, British
                                        Publishing Co.

MASON, L.
Wanderings in North-East Kent.
Herne Bay Press. 1961.
3,4,7,8,11

PEARMAN, Harry.
Deneholes and kindred phenomena, edited by H. Pearman.
Chelsea Spelaeological Society. 1966. (Typescript).
1,2,3,4,5,7,8,9,11,15

PRESTWICH, Joseph.
On the age of some sands and iron-sandstones on the North Downs...with a note on the fossils by S.V. Wood.
Geological Society. 1858.
7

SWALE RURAL DISTRICT COUNCIL.
Swale rural district guide.
Century Press. 193-?
11,12

WARD LOCK AND CO. LTD. Publishers.
Pictorial...guide to Broadstairs...and North-East Kent.
(Various issues 1899-1947 and with varying forms of title).
1,4,8,11,15,17,18,21

KENT, NORTH WEST

ADAMS, W.J.
Pocket descriptive guide to the environs of the Metropolis...thirty miles around London - map of Thames
n.d.
18

ASHDOWN, J.
A survey of industrial monuments of Greater London, by J. Ashdown and others.
(Thames Basin Archaeological Group). n.d.
17

BARTON, N.J.
Lost rivers of London.
Phoenix House. 1962.
17,18

BEADLE, Charles.
Reminiscences of a Victorian.
1924.
5,11

BELL, Mrs. A.G.
The skirts of the Great City.
1907.
18

BELL, Walter G.
When London sleeps: historical journeyings into the suburbs.
1926.
18

BESANT, Walter.
South London.
Chatto and Windus. 1912.
17

BOOTH, Charles.
Life and labour of the people in London, 3rd series: Religious Influences, Vol. 5 - South-East and South-West London, Vol. 6 - Outer South London.
Macmillan. 1902.
17

BOSWELL, J.T.
The Lower Darent region. (Bound typescript thesis).
1965.
5

BRADSHAW. Publisher.
Bradshaw's illustrated handbook for tourists in Great Britain and Ireland: Section I - The Metropolis and environs.
Bradshaw. 1882.
17

BROMHEAD, C.E.N.
Excursions to Sole Street, Holly Hill and West Malling by C.E.N. Bromhead and S. Priest.
n.d.
11

BURTON, John Frederick.
Butterflies of the North-West Kent Marshes. (From "The London Naturalist", 1955).
11, 12

CAIGER, John E.L.
The denehole controversy. (Reprinted from Proceedings of the Croydon Natural History and Scientific Society, 1954).
2,9

CAIGER, John E.L.
Some early chalkwells in North-West Kent. (Reprinted from Archaeologia Cantiana, Vol. 74, 1960).
1,5,9,17

CARNEGIE, Moir.
Church plate in the Hundred of Blackheath.
Blackheath Press. 1939.
1,8,11,18

CARRIER, Elsie Haydon.
The Inner Gate: a regional study of North-West Kent.
Christophers. 1937.
2,5,11,15,17,18,19

CLAYTON, O. Publisher.
Court guide to the environs of London...within the range of the threepenny post...
O. Clayton. 1830.
2

CLINCH, George.
Prehistoric man in the neighbourhood of the Kent and Surrey border: Neolithic age. (Reprinted from Journal of the Anthropological Institute, August and November, 1899).
2

COLLETT, Anthony.
Country rambles round London...
1912.
18

COPPOCK, J.T.
Greater London, edited by J.T. Coppock and H. Prince.
Faber. 1964.
12

COVENEY, P.J.
The North Downs and South Thameside. (Bound typescript thesis).
1963.
5

DARTFORD RURAL DISTRICT COUNCIL.
Dartford Rural District Council - official guide..
Century Press. 1959-1963.
1,4,5,11,15

DARTFORD RURAL DISTRICT COUNCIL.
Dartford Rural District.
Directory Publications. 1965.
1,4(1968) 5,8(1965, 1968) 11(1965, 1968) 12,19

DAVIES, George MacDonald.
Geological excursions round London.
Murby. 1914.
1,5

DEXTER, Walter.
The London of Dickens.
C. Palmer. 1923.
8

DEXTER, Walter.
Mr. Pickwick's pilgrimages.
Chapman and Hall. 1926.
6,8,17,19

DAVIS ,J.F.
The economic geography of Lower Thameside, by J.F. Davis and R.F. Baker. (Reprinted from "Guide to London Excursions", edited by K.M. Clayton, 20th International Geographical Congress, London, 1964).
9

DOCHERTY, J.
Some observations on the dip slope dry valleys of the chalk of North West Kent...(Reprinted from South-East Naturalist and Antiquary, 1967).
Courier Printing Co. (1967).
2

DODSLEY, R. AND J. Publishers.
London and its environs described...(6 vols., Vol. 1, II and IV only).
R. and J. Dodsley. n.d.
18

DUNKIN, Alfred John.
History of the County of Kent: Hundred of Blackheath.
Deptford, J.R. Smith. 1855.
11

EVANS, W.R.
Rustic walking routes in the London vicinity, by W.R. Evans and S. Sharpe.
Philip. n.d.
11,18

FLETCHER, Benton.
Royal homes near London.
1930.
17,18

GEOLOGISTS' ASSOCIATION.
A record of excursions made in North Kent between 1860 and 1908.
Geologists' Association. 1915.
17

A record of excursions made in North Kent between 1860 and 1890, edited by T.V. Holmes and C.D. Sherborn.
London, E. Stanford. 1891.
5

GOSTLING, William.
The Rochester guide...to which is added the traveller's guide from London to the coast.
Rochester, S. Caddell. c.1800.
9

GREAT BRITAIN: LAWS, etc. (GEO. III).
An Act...for the more easy and speedy recovery of small debts within the Hundreds of Blackheath, Bromley, Beckenham...etc.
1766.
1,11

GREENWICH NATURAL HISTORY CLUB - BOTANICAL COMMITTEE.
On the botany of the district lying between the rivers Cray, Ravensbourne and Thames.
Greenwich Natural History Club. 1858.
17

GRINLING, C.H.
A survey and record of Woolwich and West Kent, by C.H. Grinling and others.
South-Eastern Union of Scientific Societies. 1907 etc.
1,2,4,5(1909) 7,9(1909) 11,15,17,18

HALL, Hammond.
Mr. Pickwick's Kent.
Rochester, Mackay. 1899.
1,4,5,6,8,9,11,12,13,15,17

HARPER, Charles George.
Cycle rides round London: ridden, written and illustrated by Charles G. Harper.
Chapman and Hall. 1902.
4,18

HARPER, Charles George.
Motor runs round London (South of the Thames).
E.J. Burrow. n.d.
2,8,18

HART, W.H.
Records of Gravesend, Milton, Denton, Chalk, Northfleet, Southfleet and Ifield - Part 1, edited by W.H. Hart.
Gravesend, Baynes. 1878.

HASTED, Edward.
History of Kent - Vol. I, The Hundred of Blackheath.
Mitchell and Hughes. 1886.
17

HASTED, Edward.
The Hundred of Dartford and Wilmington. (Extracted from "History of the Topographical Survey of the County of Kent"). Vol. 1, folio edition.
1778.
5

HAYES, Rev. J.W.
Deneholes and other chalk excavations: their origin and uses. (Reprinted from "Journal of the Royal Archaeological Institute", January-June, 1909).
9

HAYES, Rev. J.W.
Notes on deneholes. (Reprinted from "Journal of the British Archaeological Association", June, 1908).
9

HOLMES, Edric.
London's countryside.
R. Scott. (1927).
18

HOUSING AND LOCAL GOVERNMENT, Ministry of.
London Government and the London Boroughs Report...
H.M.S.O. 1962.
2

HOWELL, George O.
...Visits to...Gravesend, Rochester, etc., with sketches. (MSS.).
1829-1831.
17

HUGHSON, David.
Walks through London...with the surrounding suburbs...
Sherwood, Neely and Jones. 1817.
18

INGRAM, T.A.
A survey and record of Woolwich and West Kent. (Containing descriptions and records, brought up-to-date, of the geology, botany, zoology, archaeology and industries of the district...
1909.
4

JERROLD, Walter C.
Rambles in Greater London.
Blackie. (1938).
1

KENT, Douglas H.
A hand-list of plants of the London area - Part IV, by D.H. Kent and J.E. Lousley. (Reprinted from "London Naturalist", 1954).
5

KENT COUNTY COUNCIL - PLANNING DEPARTMENT.
Kent development plan (1967 revision). North-West Kent draft town map. Draft explanatory report and written statement (with maps TQ 56NE, 57NE,SE, 66NW,NE, 67NW,SW,SE.
Kent County Council. 1971.
9

KIRBY, Harry S.
Sixty years and more of chalk quarrying on the River Thames. (From "Quarry Managers' Journal", September, 1953).
9

London's country - guide No. 2. By road, stream and field-path - South of the Thames...5th edition.
London's Underground. 192-?
2

MACDONALD, I.H.
Aspects of the problems and development of an area of rural-urban fringe: Dartford Rural District. (Typescript thesis).
1967.
5

MANDY, W.H.
Notes from the Assize Rolls...relating to the Hundred of Blackheath.
n.d.
17

MATTHEWS, Brian.
A history of Strood Rural District.
Strood Rural District Council. 1971.
8,9,11

MAXWELL, G.S.
Just beyond London...
1927.
18

MEDWAY VALLEY SCIENTIFIC RESEARCH SOCIETY - collected papers, 1910-14.
4

MILLWARD, Roy.
South-East England: Thameside and the Weald, by R. Millward and Adrian Robinson.
Macmillan. 1971.
11

MILLWARD, Roy.
The Hoo Peninsula and the Scarplands of Mid-West Kent, by R. Millward and A. Robinson.
Macmillan. 1971.
8,11

MILLWARD, Roy.
Lower Thameside, by R. Millward and A. Robinson.
Macmillan. 1971.
4,8,11

MONTMORENCY, J.E.G. de.
Romano-British defences South-East of London.
n.d.
17

MORGAN, Glyn Howis.
The romance of Thameside taverns.
n.d.
9

NELSON AND CO. Publishers.
Sights near London...Greenwich Hospital, Park and Observatory, Woolwich, Gravesend, the Crystal Palace.
Nelson and Co. n.d.
18

NEVES AND BISCOE. Publishers.
Official guide to the Crystal Palace district, Penge and Anerley.
Neves and Biscoe. (1906).
2

NEWTON, W.M.
On deneholes or drainage pits and their relation to Grime's Graves or first Antler-pick period. In "Man", Vol. XXXVIII, No. 5, 1928.
3,9

ORR, WILLIAM S. AND CO. Publishers.
Pictorial guide to Eltham Palace by way of Charlton and Shooters' Hill...
W.S. Orr and Co. 1845.
2,17

ORR, WILLIAM S. AND CO. Publishers.
Pictorial guide to Erith and Greenhithe, etc.
W.S. Orr and Co. 1846.
17

OWEN, J.A.
Within an hour of London Town, edited by J.A. Owen.
Blackwood. 1892.
12

PAYNE, George.
Notes on rambles with Roach Smith.
Whiting and Co. 1890.
11,12

PAYNE, George.
Walks by the marshes: lecture...
Rochester, Harris. 1901.
1,11,15

PEARMAN, Harry.
Deneholes and kindred phenomena, edited by H. Pearman.
Chelsea Speleological Society. 1966.
1,2,3,4,5,7,8,9,11,15

"A PEDESTRIAN", pseud.
Rambles and remarks on the borders of Surrey and Kent, by A Pedestrian.
Deptford, A. Brown. 1833.
11,13,15

PHILIP, Alexander John.
True deneholes. (Reprinted from the "Journal of the British Archaeological Association", December, 1923).
9

PITCHER, Wallace Spencer.
The London region, by W.S. Pitcher and others. (Guide No. 30, 1958 and Guide No. 30B, 1967).
Geologists' Association. 1958 and 1967.
2(1967)
4(1958, 1967)
9(1967)
11(1967)
12(1958)
17(1958)

PORT OF LONDON SANITARY AUTHORITY.
Report on the main drainage of the Metropolis...
1883.
17

PRESTWICH, Joseph.
Geological enquiry respecting the water, bearing strata of the country around London, with reference especially to the water supply of the Metropolis.
John Van Voorst. 1851.
2

"THE RAMBLER", pseud.
"Star" rambles around London. (Reprinted from "The
Star", (192-?)).
11

ROW, B. Prescott.
Where to live round London (Southern side), edited by B.P.
Row. (Note: includes North-West Kent).
Homeland Association. 1905.
2

SCOTT, W.F.
London and the Thames valley.
W. and R. Chambers Ltd. 1959.
4

SMITH, Charles Roach.
Catalogue of the museum of London, antiquities collected by
him.
C.R. Smith. 1854.
12

SMITH, Charles Roach.
Illustrations of Roman London.
C.R. Smith. 1859.
12

SOCIETY OF THE HUNDRED OF SHAMEL, HOO AND GRAIN.
Resolution of the Society for the protection of persons and
property.
Wildash. 1841.
15

"A SON OF THE MARSHES", pseud.
With the woodlanders and By the tide, edited by J.A. Owen,
2nd edition.
Blackwood. 1893.
8,11,20

"A SON OF THE MARSHES", pseud.
Within an hour of London Town.
Blackwood. 1892.
8

STROOD RURAL DISTRICT COUNCIL.
The Coronation book, 2nd June, 1953.
Strood Rural District Council. 1953.
8

STROOD RURAL DISTRICT COUNCIL.
Strood Rural District - official guide.
Gloucester, British Publishing Co.
3(1957)
4(1949, 1951, 1954, 1958, 1964, 1967)
12(1965)
15(1967)
19(1967)

The suburban homes of London: a residential guide...
Chatto and Windus. 1881.
2,18

THAMESIDE DEVELOPMENT BOARD.
Thameside: Britain's largest workshop.
Thameside Development Board. c.1945.
8,9

THAMES-SIDE JOINT COMMITTEE FOR THE ABATEMENT OF ATMOSPHERIC
POLLUTION.
Report for the period July, 1956 to March, 1958.
Dartford, Thames-side Joint Committee for the Abatement of
Atmospheric Pollution. (1959).
1

THORNE, James.
Handbook to the environs of London, 2 vols.
Murray. 1876.
11,18

THORNE, James.
Handbook to the environs of London. (Originally published in
1876).
Adams and Dart. 1970.
7,11,12

TROTTER, William Edward.
Select illustrated topography of thirty miles round London,
comprising views of various places within this circuit.
The Proprietor, 1 Cloudesly Terrace, Islington. 1839.
11,12

WALFORD, Edward.
Greater London: a narrative of its history, its people
and its places, 2 vols.
Cassell. 1883-4.
1,2,18

WAUGH, Mary.
Suburban growth in North-West Kent, 1861-1961. (Ph. D.
thesis - typescript).
1968.
2

KENT, SOUTH EAST

CHANNEL PUBLISHING CO.
Dover and district local directory, 1943-9.
Dover, Channel Publishing Co.
6

COOK, Raymond A.
Shell-fire corner carries on.
Ashford, Headley. 1943.
3,6,7

DAVIS, John. Publisher.
Folkestone illustrated visitor's guide. (Includes
Dover, Deal, Sandgate, Hythe, etc.).
J. Davis.
7(c.1888) 8(c.1908)

DOVER RURAL DISTRICT COUNCIL.
Dover Rural District - official guide.
Century Publications. (1948-1955).
Croydon, Home Publishing Co. (1963+).
1(1963+)
4(1963+)
6(1955, 1963+)
7(1948, 1955, 1961)
11(1955, 1963+)
12(1955, 1963 +)
15(1955)

EMBRY, Bernard.
The butterflies and moths...found in the Dover and
Deal district of Kent, by B. Embry and G.H. Youden.
Buckland Press. 1949.
6,7,11

FAUSSETT, Bryan.
Inventorium Sepulchrale: an account of some antiquities
dug up at Gilton, Kingston...
Privately Printed. 1856.
1,3,4,5,6,7,8,11,12,13,15,17

GOULDEN, John. Publisher.
Goulden's complete handbook to Folkestone, Sandgate,
Hythe and the neighbourhood.
J. Goulden. (187?).
7

JESSUP, Ronald Frank.
South-East Kent.
Thames and Hudson. 1970.
6

LANE AND GENTRY. Publishers.
Lane and Gentry's standard guide to Folkestone, Hythe,
Sandgate, Ashford, Rye, Winchelsea, Lydd, New Romney,
Dymchurch and the surrounding districts.
Margate, Lane and Gentry. (c.1919).
7

New guide to Sandgate, Folkestone, Hythe, etc.
Sandgate, Purday.
7(1839) 11(1843)

Old Humphrey's country strolls.
Religious Tract Society. (18--?).
6

Particulars...of sale of farms in the parishes of
Postling, Saltwood, Aldington, Sellinge and Lympne, in
all 2,282 acres...being outlying portions of the estates
of William Deedes Esq. (Includes Pent Farm, Court
Lodge Farm, Page Farm and Staple Farm, Postling,
Partridge Farm and Lower Middle and Upper Park Farms,
Aldington.
(A.J. Burrows). 1917.
7

Particulars...of sale of...freehold estates, situate in the
parishes of Saltwood, West Hythe, Lympne and Stanford...
comprising Lympne Castle Farm...Berwick House and Berwick
Farm...Pedlinge Court Farm...Folkeswood...several...building
sites and pieces of accommodation land...quit rents of the
Manor of Redbrooke and Pedlinge.
Messrs. Cooper, Auctioneers. 1869.
7

Particulars, plans and conditions of sale of...Hopton's and
Drellingore Farms...Alkham and Capel-le-Ferne...Grove Farm...
in...Newington and Paddlesworth...Argrove Farm (and wood)...in
...Hawkinge.
(Messrs. Cobb), Auctioneers. 1911.
7

PITTS, Hubert A.
Nineteenth century fragments of Methodist history of Hythe,
Sandgate, Dymchurch, Folkestone, Elham Valley and Sellindge.
Hythe Methodist Church. 1969.
6,7,11,12

REYNOLDS, Donald Hugh Baillie.
Underdraining of the lower chalk of South-East Kent.
(Typescript).
1970.
7

ROYAL AUTOMOBILE CLUB.
Day and half-day tours for motorists around Folkestone, 8th
edition.
Royal Automobile Club. (195-?).
4

WARD LOCK AND CO. LTD. Publisher.
Guide to South-East Kent, Deal, Dover, etc. (Various
permutations of title from 1904-1953).
6(1904, 1910, 1923, 1951 etc.).
11(1951 etc.)
17(1951 etc.)
18(1951 etc.)

WARD LOCK AND CO. LTD. Publisher.
A pictorial and descriptive guide to Folkestone, Sandgate,
Hythe, Dymchurch, New Romney, etc. (Various permutations of
title from 1914-1951).
Ward Lock and Co. Ltd.
2(1914)
6(c.1920)
8(1914)
11(1951 etc.)
15(c.1951)
18(1951)

KENT, SOUTH WEST

ABBEY PUBLICITY SERVICE. Publishers.
Residential and holiday areas of South-West Kent...
Abbey Publicity Service. (193-?).
2

LANE AND GENTRY. Publishers.
Lane and Gentry's standard guide to Folkestone, Hythe, Sandgate,
Ashford, Rye, Winchelsea, Lydd, New Romney, Dymchurch and the
surrounding districts. (See - Kent, South-East).
Margate, Lane and Gentry. c.1919.
7

ROYAL AUTOMOBILE CLUB.
Day and half-day tours for motorists around Tunbridge Wells,
8th edition.
Royal Automobile Club. (195-?).
4

KENT, WEST

BLACK, ADAM AND CHARLES LTD. Publishers.
Black's guide to West Kent.
A. and C. Black Ltd.
1(1901)
4(1901, 1915)
5(1907)
7(1901, 1902)
8(1901, 1909, 1928)
11(1901 etc.)
12(1906)
13(1901 etc.)
15(1901 etc.)
17(1901, 1902)
18(1909)

DAVIDGE, W.R.
Report on the regional planning of West Kent.
North-West Kent and South-West Kent Joint Town Planning
Committee. 1927.
1,7,8,11,12,15,16,17

HOUSING AND LOCAL GOVERNMENT, Ministry of.
The West Kent Main Sewerage Order, 1959.
H.M.S.O. 1959.
12

JOHNSON, M.R.D.
A regional description of the area around Tonbridge and
Tunbridge Wells: being a dissertation submitted in part
fulfilment of the regulation of the Oxford School of
Geography Examination for the Degree of Bachelor of
Arts. (Unpublished MSS.).
1970.
11,19

MILLWARD, Roy.
South-East England: Thameside and the Weald, by R.
Millward and A. Robinson.
Macmillan. 1971.
3,4,5,9,21

RAYNER, R.
The road and you. Proposed Dartford/Croydon sub-
orbital motorway and...Keston Church area. (Typescript)
(1963).
2

SEVENOAKS RURAL DISTRICT COUNCIL.
Sevenoaks Rural District - official guide.
Century Publications. 1952, 1954, 1960.
Directory Publications. 1964.
1(1952, 1954)
4(1952, 1954, 1960, 1964)
11(1952, 1954, 1960 in progress)
19(1952, 1954)

SOUTH EASTERN UNION OF SCIENTIFIC SOCIETIES.
Record and survey of Woolwich and West Kent.
South Eastern Union of Scientific Societies. 1909.
1,5,12,17

TONBRIDGE RURAL DISTRICT COUNCIL.
Tonbridge Rural District - official guide...
Croydon, Home Publishing Co. 1953 etc.
1,4,11,15,19

WEST KENT FEDERATION OF WOMEN'S INSTITUTES.
Countryside in the 70's: East and West Kent survey,
1969.
West Kent Federation of Women's Institutes. 1970.
7

WEST KENT FEDERATION OF WOMEN'S INSTITUTES.
The countryside in the 70's: West Kent survey in 1968.
West Kent Federation of Women's Institutes. 1969.
9,12

KENT ARTISTS

"KENT YEOMAN", pseud.
Sketches by a Kent Yeoman, 1914-18.
A. Melrose. n.d.
8

KENT AUTHORS AND LITERATURE

Aesop at Tonbridge; or, a few select fables in verse.
E. Whitlock. 1698.
11

Aesop returned from Tunbridge Wells; or, Aesop out
of his wits: fables in verse, 1698.
17

ALDEN, John, pseud.
Kentish rhymes; or, Obiter Cantiana.
Canterbury School of Art. 1945.
3,11,12

ALDEN, John, pseud.
Poems in pamphlet, No. 12.
The Hand and Flower Press. 1951.
12

ALFORD, Henry. Dean of Canterbury.
Select poetical works.
1851.
17

Algerine pirate.
Maidstone, West. 1847.
11

APPS, Howard Llewellyn.
Spindle's partner. (Author, Canterbury man - written while in
R.A.F.).
Blackie. (1948).
3

ARCHER, Henry Playsted.
Emmet, the Irish patriot, and other poems.
Canterbury, Colegate. 1832.
3

ARNOLD, Ralph.
The Coronation book...written for the Strood Rural District
Council.
Constable. 1953.
8

Orange Street and Brickhole Lane.
Hart-Davies. 1963.
12

The unhappy Countess and her grandson John Bowes.
Constable. 1957.
12

A very quiet war.
Hart-Davies. 1962.
12

Whiston matter.
Hart-Davies. 1961.
1,3,4,6,7,8,11,12,15

Yeoman of Kent.
Constable. 1949.
1,2,3,4,5,6,7,9,11,12,15,17,18,19

ASHLEY, Sir William.
Commercial education. (Author born in Canterbury).
Williams and Norgate. 1926.
3

BAKER, Sir Herbert.
Architecture and personalities.
Country Life. n.d.
11

BAKER, Loveday Goldie.
Conspiracy at "The Crayfish": a comedy in three acts.
(Chatham resident).
Deane. 1955.
8

BALSTON, Thomas.
Dr. Balston at Eton.
Macmillan. 1952.
11,12

BALSTON, Thomas.
John Martin, 1789-1854, illustrator and pamphleteer.
Bibliographical Society. 1934.
12

BARNSLEY, Alan.
The frog prince and other poems.
Hand and Flower Press. 1952.
12

BARNSLEY, Alan.
Poems in pamphlet, No. 9.
Hand and Flower Press. 1952.
12

BATES, Herbert Ernest.
The country heart.
M. Joseph. 1949.
12

The country of white clover.
M. Joseph. 1952.
1,5,8,12

The day of glory.
M. Joseph. 1945.
12

Down the river.
Gollancz. 1937.
12

Forty years a writer. (Extract from Daily Telegraph
Week-end Supplement).
n.d.
12

In the heart of the country.
Country Life. 1942.
12

O more than happy countryman.
Country Life. 1945.
12

Through the woods.
Gollancz. 1936.
12

The vanished world: an autobiography, Vol. 1.
M. Joseph. 1969.
12

BEAUMONT, Harry.
Old contemptible: a personal narrative. (Author born
at Blean, later lived in Canterbury).
Hutchinson. 1967.
3

BEHN, Athra.
The amours of Philander and Silvia: love letters
between a nobleman and his sister.
1687.
12

BEHRENS, Lilian Boys.
Battle Abbey under thirty-nine kings.
Saint Catherine's Press. 1937.
3

BELL, Authea.
E. Nesbit.
Bodley Head. 1960.
12

BELL, Neil.
My writing life.
Redman. 1955.
8

BENNETT, Charles Frederick.
Donjon, prospect and reflection: a moral, sentimental
and complimentary poem.
Canterbury, Henry Ward. 1835.
3

BERRY, Alfred H.
Light and shade: a small selection of epic, descriptive
and humorous verse.
Canterbury, J.A. Jennings. 1945.
3

BINYON, Laurence.
Akbar.
Davies. 1932.
12

BIRTWHISTLE, John.
Vision of Wat Tyler: original poem by John Birtwhistle -
etchings and calligraphy by Graham Clarke.
Boughton Monchelsea, Ebenezer Press. 1972.
11

BLAKENEY, Edward Henry.
Voices after sunset, and other poems: illustrated
by H. Maurice Page. (Headmaster of Sir Roger Manwood
School, Sandwich).
Gresham Press. 1897.
11

BLOND, William.
The principles of agriculture.
Longmans. 1864.
20

BLIND, Sam.
Wrotham, or Broteham? A venture into the wonderland
of place-names.
Borough Green, Perkins. (1903).
7,12

BOORMAN, Henry Roy Pratt.
Newspaper Society: 125 years of progress.
Kent Messenger. 1961
12,18

BOORMAN, Henry Roy Pratt.
Pictures of Maidstone, the County Town of Kent.
Kent Messenger. 1965.
12

BOORMAN, Henry Roy Pratt.
So this is Russia.
Kent Messenger. 1936.
6

BOSSOM, Alfred Charles. Lord Bossom of Maidstone.
Building to the skies: the romance of the skyscraper.
Studio. 1934.
12

BOYER, P.J. of Barfrestone.
James Boyer. (Headmaster of Christ's Hospital, 1776-99).
Dover, William Giraud. 1936.
6

BOYS, John.
An exposition of the Dominicall epistles and gospels...
Badger. 1638.
12

BOYS, John.
Virgil's Aeneas his descent...
Boys. 1661.
6

BRADDOCK, Joseph.
H.E. Bates - article in "Books and bookmen", Vol. 1, No. 8,
May, 1956.
3

BRADE-BIRKS, S. Graham.
Teach yourself concise encyclopaedia of general knowledge
prepared under the direction of S. Graham Brade-Birks in
association with Frank Higenbottam.
London, English University Press. 1956.
3

BRADLEY, Howard.
Sidelines: a small volume of verse.
Paddock Wood, Turner. 1960.
11

BRANFORD, Violet.
Songs from a Kentish garden.
Oxford, Shakespeare Head Press. 1939.
3

BRENT, John.
Atalanta, Winnee and other poems.
Knight and Co. 1873.
6

BRENT, William.
Sturry and other poems.
Canterbury, Ward. 1826.
11,12,17

BRETON, Nicholas.
Melancholike humours in verses of diverse natures.
London, Richard Bradocke. 1600.
6

BREWER, Derek.
Chaucer.
Longmans Green. 1953.
12

BROCKMAN, William Everett.
The Brockman scrapbook.
n.d.
7

BROCKMAN, William Everett.
Orange County, Virginia, families and their marriages.
Burgess. 1949.
7

BROCKMAN, William Everett.
Orange County, Virginia, families Vol. 4.
Brockman. 1965.
7

BROOKE, Arthur, pseud. (John Chalk CLARIS).
Durovernum, with other poems.
Longman, Hurst, Rees, Orme and Brown. 1818.
3

BROOKE, Jocelyn.
The goose cathedral.
Bodley Head. 1950.
3,7

The military orchid.
Lane. 1948.
7

A mine of serpents.
Bodley Head. 1949.
3,7

Private view.
Barrie. 1954.
7

The scapegoat.
Bodley Head. 1948.
3

The wild orchids of Britain.
Bodley Head. 1950.
3

BROTHERS, M.E.
Just impediment.
Longmans Green. 1934.
6,12

BROWN, Ken.
Poems written in Mote Park.
Stockwell. 1951.
12

BRYANT, Nancy.
Mr. Zells of Tunbridge Wells and other poems.
1962.
11

BRYDGES, Sir Samuel Egerton.
Sonnets and other poems: first published 1785.
London, G. and T. Wilkie. 1789.
6

BRYDGES, Sir Samuel Egerton.
Stemmata illustria.
Paris. 1825.
8

BRYDGES, Sir Samuel Egerton.
The Sylvan wanderer: consisting of a series of moral,
sentimental and critical essays.
Printed at the Private Press of Lee Priory. 1813-1817.
11

BURNELL, Maud M.
Rogation flowers (Poems).
Ashford, Invicta Press. 1928?
11

BURNS, Peter.
Fanfare of hoarded hopes: poems.
1967.
8

CAMDEN, William.
Annals...edited by Thomas Hearne.
Rawlinson. n.d.
12

CAMDEN, William.
Remains concerning Britain.
Smith. 1870.
12

CARNALL, Robert.
Leisure hours employed...
Maidstone, Cutbush. 1822.
11

CARTER, Mrs. Elizabeth.
Poems on several occasions (2nd edition).
Rivington. 1766.
6,11

CARTER, George R.
Poetical works.
Deal, Hayward. n.d.
11

CARTER, George R.
School-boy's reverie.
Dover, Rigden. 1826.
6,11,12,17

CASTLE, Joseph.
Dungeness ballads.
1887.
6,11,12,15

CARTER, Philip.
The great fiction of the times.
Canterbury, S. Prentice. (1844).
3

CAUSTON, Peter.
Tunbrigialia: (A poem).
1709.
11,19

CHARLES, Frank.
Coastguards' view. (Novel set in "Dymstable").
Hale. 1965.
3

CHARLTON, Barbara.
The recollections of a Northumbrian lady, edited by L.E.D.
Charlton.
Cape. 1949.
6

CHARLTON, L.E.O.
Another way to fly. (Under pseud - Sidney OSWALD).
James Barrie. 1950.
6

Deeds that held the Empire by air.
Murray. 1940.
6

The menace of the clouds.
Hodge. 1937.
6

There is still a desert island. (Under pseud - Sidney OSWALD).
London, Children's Books Ltd. 1948.
6

War from the air.
Nelson. 1935.
6

The air defence of Britain, by L.E.O. Charlton, G.T. Garrett
and R. Fletcher.
Penguin. 1938.
6

CHURCH, Richard.
A country window.
Heinemann. 1958.
12

The golden sovereign.
Heinemann. 1957.
12

Over the bridge.
Heinemann. 1955.
12

Prince Albert.
Heinemann. 1963.
15

Small moments.
Hutchinson. 1957.
5,11,12

Speaking aloud.
Heinemann. 1968.
6

A stroll before dark.
Heinemann. 1965.
8

The voyage home.
Heinemann. 1964.
12,15

A window on a hill.
Hale. 1951.
4,5,11,12

CHURCHILL, Charles.
The poetical works.
Oxford University Press. 1956.
6

COLEPEPER, Sir Thomas.
Sir Thomas Colepeper's tracts on usury.
Morphew. 1708.
11

COMPTON, Herbert.
The undertaker's field.
Batchelor and Benedict. 1906.
12

CONWAY, Sir William Martin. 1st Baron Conway of
Allington.
The sport of collecting.
Unwin. 1914.
12

COX, John Charles.
Churchwardens' accounts from the fourteenth century
to the close of the seventeenth century.
Methuen. 1913.
3

The English parish church.
Batsford. 1914.
3

How to write the history of a parish.
Benrose.
3 (3rd edition 1886) 12 (1895)

The parish churches of England.
Batsford. 1935.
3

Pulpits, lecterns and organs in English churches.
Oxford University Press. 1915.
3

CROME, Honor.
The livelihood of man, by H. Crome and G. King.
(Gordon King was born in Dover).
Christophers. 1953.
6

CROUCH, Marcus.
Beatrix Potter.
Bodley Head. 1960.
12

CROUCH, Marcus.
Fingerprints of history.
Longmans Young Books. 1968.
4,12

(CUMMING, Mrs.).
The vicissitudes of life; or, the balloon: a Canterbury
tale for young persons.
Canterbury, Henry Ward. 1845.
3

CURLING, Mary Anne.
Poetical pieces.
Batcheller. 1831.
6

CURTEIS, T.
Eironodia: a poem sacred to peace and the promoting of
human happiness.
Printed for R. Wilkin. 1728.
11

D., L.
Gray's"Elegy in a country churchyard", with a translation
in French verse...with anecdotes of the life of Gray
and some remarks in French by the editor.
Chatham, Kentish Courier. 1806.
4

"A DARTFORDIAN", pseud.
Rough diary of a voyage to the Antipodes.
Dartford, A. Perry. 1885.
5

DAUBENEY, Giles.
History of the Daubeney family.
Privately Printed. 1951.
11

DAVIDSON, Randall Thomas. Archbishop of Canterbury.
The testing of a nation.
Macmillan. 1919.
3

DAY, Leslie.
The gates of Paradise.
Old Royalty Book Publishers. 1927.
6

(DERING, Sir Edward).
A consideration and a resolution: first, concerning the right
of the laity in national councils; secondly, concerning the
power of bishops in affairs secular.
Printed by Thomas Paine. 1641.
11

DERING, Sir Edward.
A discourse of proper sacrifice...
Cambridge, Printed for Francis Englefield. 1644.
6

DERING, Sir Edward.
Speeches.
Printed for F.C. and T.B. 1641.
6

DIBBLE, Lucy Grace.
Return tickets, 2 vols.
Stockwell. 1968.
11

DILNOT, Frank.
The lady Jean.
Brentanos. n.d.
6,12

DOBEL, D.
Primitive Christianity propounded; or, an essay to revive the
antient mode or manner of preaching the Gospel. Humbly
offered to the consideration...but more especially to the
people called Baptists.
Printed for Joseph Edwards. 1755.
11

DOBELL, Leonora Ollive.
Prose and verse.
Faversham, Voile and Roberson. n.d.
1

DOBELL, Leonora Ollive.
Songs of sunshine and night.
Faversham, Voile and Roberson. 1940.
1

DOBELL, Samuel.
A floweret for the wreath of humanity...
Cranbrook, S. Dobell. 1812.
3

DOBELL, Samuel.
Miscellaneous pieces in poetry and prose.
Smallfield. 1840.
11

DODDS, Norman Noel.
Gypsies, didikois and other travellers. (M.P. for Erith and
Crayford).
Johnson Publications. 1966.
1,5

DONKIN, Bryan.
The heat efficiency of steam boilers: land, marine and
locomotive.
Charles Griffin and Co. Ltd. 1898.
5

DORAN, John.
Table traits...
Bentley. 1854.
12

DOWSON, Ernest.
The poems of Ernest Dowson.
Unicorn Press. 1946.
8

DUNNING, George.
Where bleed the many.
Elek Books. 1955.
6

DUPPA, Brian. Bishop.
The correspondence of Bishop Brian Duppa and Sir
Justinian Isham, 1650-1660.
Northamptonshire Record Society. 1955.
12

DUVARD, Primogene.
Flora MacDonald: an historical drama in three acts.
Printed for P. Duvard by H.T. Tidy. 1872.
11

ELLISTON-ERWOOD, Frank C.
De Lana Caprina; or, verses on divers subjects,
mainly Kentish.
Blackheath Press (Printers). 1943.
1,11,12

EVANS, Sebastian.
The high history of the Holy Graal, translated from
the old French...by S. Evans.
London, Dent and Co. 1903.
3

EVANS, Sebastian.
In quest of the Holy Graal: an introduction to the
study of the legend.
London, Dent and Co. 1898.
3

EVANS, Sebastian.
Lady Chillingham's house-party.
London, Dent and Co. 1901.
3

FARRAR, Frederic William. (Dean of Canterbury).
Eric or, little by little: a tale of Roslyn School.
London, A. and C. Black. 1902.
3

FARRAR, Frederic William. (Dean of Canterbury).
Julian Home: a tale of college life.
London, Ward Lock. 1910.
3

FARRAR, Frederic William. (Dean of Canterbury).
St. Winifred's; or, the world of school.
London, Ward Lock. 1910.
3

FEDERATION OF RATEPAYERS' ASSOCIATIONS IN THE COUNTY
OF KENT.
News and views of Kent.
(1956?).
4

FIELDING, G. Hunsley.
On the summer of 1868. (A Tonbridge doctor). (From
Proceedings of the Meteorological Society, 1869).
7

FINCH, William Coles.
Water: its origin and use.
Alston Rivers. 1908.
4,8,12

FISHWICK, V.C.
Good farming in action.
London, English University Press. 1949.
3

FLETCHER, Joseph Smith.
The golden venture.
London, Collins. n.d.
3

FREEMAN, R.
Kentish poets, 2 vols.
Canterbury, Wood. 1821.
1,3,6,8,11,12,15,17

FRIEND, Richard.
A Christmas offering - original poems.
Dover, J. Johnson for R. Friend. 1850.
4,6

FRY, Colin Richard.
Mindsplit: poems.
Magpie Press. 1968.
11

FRY, Colin Richard.
Words from the land of the living: some of the verse of
Colin R. Fry.
Poet and Printer. 1965.
11

GARDINER, Mrs. Dorothy.
Mary in the wood, with other lyric poems.
London, Erskine MacDonald. 1917.
3

GARTSIDE, Vivian Osmond Brock.
Nile additional.
Canterbury, Gibbs and Son. 1947.
6

GERVASE, of Canterbury.
The historical works of Gervase of Canterbury, edited by
William Stubbs, 2 vols.
1879/80.
4(Vol. 2 only) 11,17

(GIBBS, Mrs. Ann).
A selection, in prose and verse...
Cranbrook, S. Waters. 1803.
11

(GLEIG, George Robert).
The chronicles of Waltham. (A novel by the Vicar of Ash-
next-Sandwich).
Paris, A. and W. Galignani. 1835.
11

GLOVER, Richard.
The light of the world. (Holman Hunt's picture in words).
William Mackintosh. 1863.
6

GLOVER, Robert Finlay.
Latin for historians, by R.F. Glover and R.W. Harris. (Harris,
Master of Studies in the King's School, Canterbury).
Oxford, Blackwell. 1954.
3

GOODSALL, Robert Harold.
Home building.
Canterbury, Cross and Jackman. 1924.
3

GOODSALL, Robert Harold.
Palestine memoirs, 1917-1918-1925.
Canterbury, Cross and Jackman. 1925.
3

GOUGH, Benjamin.
Kentish lyrics, edited by B. Gough.
Houlston and Wright. 1867.
1,2,4,5,6,7,8,9,11,12,15,17

GREENWOOD, Alfred.
First report upon tuberculosis and the administration of
sanatorium benefit.
Dickinson. 1914
3,12

GULLIVER, George.
Guilliveriana: an autobiography.
Canterbury, Cross and Jackman. 1881.
3

HALL, John. (1529?-1566?).
The Court of Virtue (1565).
Routledge, Kegan, Paul. 1961.
11

HAM, J.B.
Lyric thoughts: a selection of poems.
Gravesend, Baynes and Carpenter. (1874).
9

HAMILTON, Anthony.
Memoirs of the Court of Charles II, edited by Sir Walter Scott.
Bell. 1891.
19

HAMILTON, Antoine. (i.e. Anthony HAMILTON).
Memoires du Comte de Grammont...nouvelle edition augmentee
par Horace Walpole.
1783.
19

HARDWICK, John Michael and Mollie.
Alfred Deller.
London, Cassell. 1968.
3,6,12

Four Sherlock Holmes plays (one-act) from stories by
Sir Arthur Conan Doyle.
London, Murray- 1964.
3

The man who was Sherlock Holmes.
London, Murray. 1964.
3

The Sherlock Holmes companion.
London, Murray. 1962.
3

Writers' houses.
Phoenix House. 1968.
6,12

HARRISON, Herbert.
The Braganza necklace.
London, S. Low, Marston and Co. Ltd. n.d.
3

HARRISON, Herbert.
A lad of Kent.
New York, Macmillan Co. 1914.
1,3,6 ,11

HAZLITT, W.
Works.
Bohn's Library. 1889-97.
12

HEARNE, Thomas.
Thomae Sprotti...
1719.
17

HICKSON, Stanley.
Evidence of study. (Reprinted from Penrose Annual, Vol.
54, 1960).
3

HIGGS, Richard.
Dreams of the hills.
Simpkin, Marshall, Hamilton. n.d.
6

HIGGS, Richard.
The failure of the Labour movement.
Dover Printing and Publishing Co. n.d.
6

HIGGS, Richard.
Margaret's dream, etc.
Dover Printing and Publishing Co. n.d.
6

HUGH, Philip E.
The mad metropolis.
New York, Ace Books Incorporated. 1966.
3

HUGH, Philip E.
Prodigal sun.
London, Roberts and Vintner Ltd. 1965.
3

HUDSON, John V.P.
The lantern of fate and other poems.
London, A.H. Stockwell Ltd. 1933?
3

Humbug: a satire. (Tracts No. 4).
Ramsgate, Phipps and Bleaden. n.d.
3

HUMPHERY-SMITH, Cecil Raymond.
Pomegranates. (Article in "Coat of Arms", Vol. II, No.
10, April, 1952).
3

HUMPHERY-SMITH, Cecil Raymond.
Up the Beatles family tree, by C.R. Humphery-Smith and
others.
Canterbury,Achievements Ltd. 1966.
3

HYAMS, Edward Solomon.
From the waste land.
London, Turnstile Press. 1950.
1,3,5,8

The grapevine in England.
London, Bodley Head. 1949.
3

Den meget mystiske Barnevogen.
Copenhagen, Grafisk Forlag. 1953.
3

William Medium: en Skal Roman, till Svenska ar Goran Ekblom.
Stockholm, Aktiebolaget Skoglunds Bokforlag.
3

IGGLESDEN, Sir Charles.
Clouds.
John Long. 1912
6

A flutter with fate.
John Long. 1910.
6

Law the wrecker.
John Long. 1914.
6

A mere Englishman in America.
Kentish Express. 1930.
6

Out there.
Johnson. 1916.
6

Strad and other stories.
Simpkin, Marshall, Hamilton. n.d.
6

INGOLDSBY, Thomas. pseud. (Richard Harris BARHAM).
Ingoldsby legends, 3 vols., edited by Mrs. Bond.
Bentley. 1894.
6,9

INGOLDSBY, Thomas. pseud. (Richard Harris BARHAM).
The lay of St. Aloys, by Thomas Ingoldsby.
Eyre and Spottiswoode. n.d.
12

The injur'd lady: contains some particulars of the late elopement of a certain noble Lord with a lady of distinction. (Probably by a local author).
London, Richads and Sympson. c.1700?
9

JENKINS, Robert Charles.
Ancient prayers and devotions, from MSS. and early printed works.
Folkestone, W.P. Birch. n.d.
3,10

Ballads of high and humble life, with some occasional verses.
Folkestone, T. Kentfield. 1893.
10

On church reform in relation to the episcopate.
Folkestone, W.P. Birch. (1890).
3

The parents and kinsfolk of Luther.
Folkestone, Printed by R. Goulden. 1883.
3

A sketch of the life of St. Ethelburga.
Folkestone, W.P. Birch. 1890.
3,7

The title deeds of the Roman Church.
Folkestone, T. Kentfield. n.d.
3

JOHN OF SALISBURY.
Memoirs of the Papal Court.
Nelson. 1956.
12

JOHNSON, Hewlett. Dean of Canterbury.
China's new creative age.
London, Lawrence and Wishart. 1953.
3

Christians and Communism.
London, Putnam. 1956.
3

Eastern Europe in the Socialist world.
London, Lawrence and Wishart. 1955.
3

Searching for light.
London, Joseph. 1968.
3,4

The Socialist sixth of the world.
London, Gollantz. 1939.
3

The Soviet power.
New York, International Publishers. 1941.
3

Soviet strength.
London, Muller. 1945.
3

Soviet success.
London, Hutchinson. 194-?
3

Upsurge of China.
Peking, New World Press. 1961.
3

JONES, John Bavington.
When was it?
n.d.
6

JONES, S.T. (of Dover).
The melange. (Poems and short stories in prose).
Longman, Printed in Dover. 1831.
6

KEABLE, Mrs. Gladys.
Record of the life and worship of St. George the Martyr..
edited by Mrs. G. Keable and J. Lawrence.
Canterbury, Broadwater Press. 1943.
3

KEDDELL, J.S.
A dissertation on the vow of Jephthah...
W.H. Painter. 1840.
11

KENT, Alfred.
Little Lydie.
Dover, Rigden. 1832.
6

KENT AND SUSSEX POETRY SOCIETY.
Poetry folios, 1947 onwards.
Kent and Sussex Poetry Society.
11

KENT COUNTY LIBRARY.
Literary associations of Kent.
Kent Education Committee. 1956.
7

KING, Miss A. ("The Martyr", pseud.).
A Christian martyrdom in the twentieth century.
Canterbury, A. King. 1912.
3

KING, Miss A. ("A Woman", pseud.).
The downfall of Christianity.
Canterbury, A. King. 1914.
3

KINGSFORD, Thomas.
Ellen the revolutionist, 1875.
Canterbury, Caxton. 1875.
6

KINGSFORD, Thomas.
Reminiscences of animals, birds, fishes and meteorology.
Canterbury, Kentish Observer Steam Printing Office. 1877?
3

KINGSFORD, Thomas.
The supernatural and mystical.
Canterbury, Henry J. Goulden. 1874.
3

KNATCHBULL, Sir Norton.
Annotations upon some difficult texts...New Testament, 1693.
Cambridge, Hayes. 1693.
6

KNATCHBULL-HUGESSEN, E.H.   Lord Brabourne.
Crackers for Christmas.
Macmillan. 1870.
6

Ferdinand's adventure.
Routledge. n.d.
6

Friends and foes from fairy land.
Longmans Green. 1886.
11,17

Higgledy-piggledy.
Longmans. 1875.
6

The magic oaktree and Prince Filderkin.
Unwin. 1894.
6

River legends.
Daldy, Isbister. 1875.
6,12

Whispers from fairyland.
Longmans. 1875.
6

"A LADY", pseud.
Past and present times, by A Lady.
Cadell. 1831.
12

LAMBARDE, William.
An alphabetical description of the chief places in England and
Wales.
Fletcher Giles. 1730.
12

LAMBARDE, William.
Apxaionomia sive de priscis Anglorum legibus libri...
Cantabrigiae, Roger Daniel. 1644.
3

LAMBARDE, William.
William Lambarde and Local Government, edited by C. Read.
New York, Cornell University Press. 1962.
1,8,11,12,15

LANGDON, John A.
The "Fireman's Wedding" tragedy, 11th July, 1929.
Gillingham Public Library. (1972).
11

LOUD, Clara.
The early primrose (poems).
Canterbury, Henry Chivers. 1859.
3

LOUD, Clara.
A wreath from the woods.
Dover, Batchellor.   Canterbury, Huggin. 1868.
6

LOVELY, Herbert Clyde.
Hammered ship-shape: a sage of a sailing-ship apprentice, by
Clew Garnet (pseud.).
London, Methuen. 1935.
3

LUTYENS, W.E.
The childrens' crusades.
Salmon. 1911.
12

LYON, Rev. John.
Further proofs that glass is permeable by the electric
Effluvia.
London. 1781.
3

MAGRAW, B.I.
The history at our doors.
London, Bell and Sons. 1939.
3

MAGRAW, B.I.
The thrill of history.
London, Collins. 1950.
3

"MAN OF KENT", pseud.
Kentish fable of the lion and the foxes...debates...
1627 and 1628.
1701.
11

The Man of Kent: poem (broadsheet).
Maidstone, Cutbush. (c.1828).
1

MANN, H.P.
For His Name's Sake.
Canterbury, Jennings. n.d.
3

MARRIOTT, F.S.
The votive offering.   (Poem).
Faithfull. 1866.
11

MAYNE, Frederick.
Poems on various subjects.
Ledger and Pascall, Printers. 1818.
6

MAYNE, William.
A swarm in May...
London, Oxford University Press. 1955.
3

MAYTUM, A.F.
Lone elk and other poems.
Kent Messenger. 1931.
12

MELLOR, John.
The curious particulars relating to King Alfred's
death and burial.
Canterbury, Gibbs. 1871.
3

MIDDLETON, Thomas.
The Mayor of Quinborough: a comedy as it hath been often
acted, with much applause at Black-friars by His
Majesty's servants.
Printed for Henry Herringman. 1661.
11

MILLARD, Louise.
Some palaeoliths from the Bletchley district. (Reprinted
from "Records of Buckinghamshire", Vol. XVII, Part
5, 1965).
3

MITTINS, W.H.
Pattern in England.
Allen and Unwin. 1950.
6

Modern Gilpin; or, the adventures of John Oldstock...
1838.
17

MUMMERY, A.F.
My climbs in the Alps and Caucasus.
Fisher Unwin. 1895.
6

NAIRNE, E.
Kentish tales in verse and other humorous poems.
1824.
1,6,7,8,11,12,13,17

NAIRNE, E.
Poems, miscellaneous and humorous...
1791.
6,11

NEALE, J.M.
Collected hymns, sequences and carols.
London, Hodder and Stoughton. 1914.
12

NEAME, Alan.
The happening at Lourdes.
London, Hodder and Stoughton. 1968.
3

NEAME, Alan.
The heretics: a quadricentenary. (Article in "The
European", November, 1955).
3

NEVILLE, John.
Poems. (Cuttings of poems by J. Neville printed in various publications and bound together).
1857-1876.
9

NEWMAN, George.
Affection's tribute.
Gravesend, Stallworthy. 1863.
9

Other lyrics: an aftermath.
Ashford, "Kent County Examiner". 1900.
1,4,11,12,17

Sketches and glimpses.
Gravesend, Dickering. 1869.
9

Wayside lyrics. 4th edition with additions.
Whittaker. 1891.
1,9,15

White upon black; or, short narratives by a dweller in the region of white chalk of his descents into the region of black coal, 2nd edition.
Gravesend, Printed by T. Hall. 1888.
1,8,9,11,15

O'RHYME, Roderick, pseud.
"Mon journal de huit jours", travesty by Roderick O'Rhyme of Fir Hall...
Maidstone, T. Wickham. 1814.
3

PAINE, Robert.
Academy architecture, 1959. (Mr. Paine is Principal of School of Architecture, Canterbury). (Article in "The Builder", No. 6,058, 8th May, 1959).
3

PARMENTER, John.
Helio-tropes...compiled by J. Parmenter.
Methuen. 1904.
1,11,15

PATER, Walter Horatio.
Emerald Uthwart.
Canterbury, Printed for King's School. 1905.
3

PATER, Walter Horatio.
Marius the Epicurean.
London, Macmillan and Co. 1885.
3

PATTENDEN, T., of Dover.
Voyage sur le Rhin...Dusseldorf (MSS.).
1789.
6

P(EMBERTON), J.E.
Rose of Fainthorpe.
Bermingham, Cornish Bros. 1911.
11

(PENNINGTON, Montague).
Letter to the author of "Hints to the clergy of the established church", etc., by a Kentish Clergyman.
Printed by Rouse, Kirkby and Lawrence. 1814.
11

PERCY, Edward.
Cowferry Isle: novel of Kentish life.
Nicholson and Watson. 1934.
1,6

PETERSON, Alexander Duncan Campbell.
Educating our rulers. (Head of Dover College).
Duckworth. 1957.
6

PILCHER, H.
"The white horses". In Poems of 1962.
Ilfracombe, Stockwell. 1962.
6

PLOMER, Henry Robert.
Edmund Spenser's handwriting. (Reprinted from "Modern Philology", Vol. XXI, No. 2, 1923).
3

PLOMER, Henry Robert.
The 1574 edition of Dr. John Caine's De Antiquitate Cantabriglensis Academiae Libri Duo. (Reprinted from the Transactions of the Bibliographical Society, The Library, 1926)
3

PLOMER, Henry Robert.
The importation of low country and French books into England 1480 and 1502-3. (Reprinted from the Transactions of the Bibliographical Society, The Library, September, 1928).
3

POLAK, H.S.L.
Mahatma Gandhi, by H. Polak and others.
Odhams. 1949.
6

The portfolio, or literary selector.
Faversham, Willoughby. 1832.
1

POST, Thomas.
Selection of verses written by Thomas Post of Wye, aged eighty four and for many years a shepherd.
Ashford, (Kentish Express). 1902.
11,17,21

POTTER, Neil.
Queen Elizabeth II, by N. Potter and J. Frost.
Harrap. 1969.
6

POWELL, H.T. Canon of Rochester Cathedral.
The fall of man, its place in modern thought.
S.P.C.K. 1934.
15

PRATT, Anne, of Dover.
The flowering plants, grasses...Great Britain, 6 vols.
Warne. c.1860.
6

PRENDERGAST, James. "Road Patrol", pseud.
Rhyme and rhythm: a collection of verselets which have appeared from time to time in the pages of the Kentish Gazette and Canterbury Press.
n.d.
3

PRESCOTT-WESTCAR, William V.L.
D-H-A-N-K and the dholes, and other stories, by "Mektomb" (Lt. Col. W. Prescott-Westcar, D.S.O.), illustrated by E.J. Fedarb.
Canterbury, Goulden Ltd. 1932.
3

PUCKLE, John.
The true position of the Church of England.
Simpkin, Marshall, Hamilton. 1840.
6

QUESTED, J.
My leisure-hours (poems).
Canterbury Herald Office. 1825.
3,6

RAMSEY, Arthur Michael. Archbishop of Canterbury.
The authority of the Bible...a reprint of the first article in Peake's Commentary on the Bible, published in 1962.
London, Nelson. 1962.
3

Christ crucified for the world.
London, Mowbray. 1964.
3

Christianity and the supernatural (lecture).
London, Athlone Press. 1963.
3

Constantinople and Canterbury (lecture).
London, S.P.C.K. 1962.
3

The glory of God and the transfiguration of Christ.
London, Darton, Longman and Todd. 1967.
3

The narrative of the Passion.
London, Mowbray. 1962.
3

Problems of Christian belief.
London, B.B.C. 1966.
3

Rome and Canterbury.
London, S.P.C.K. 1967.
3

RANGER, H.W.
Anthology of poems. (MS.).
n.d.
12

REANEY, Mrs. G.S. (Isabel REANEY).
Works. (Mrs. Reaney was a resident of Bromley College).
Nesbit. c.1890.
2

ROBE, William Lamb.
Miscellaneous pieces in verse.
Dover, Batcheller. 1925.
6

ROGERS, George Albert, of Dover.
The valour of faith.
William Mackintosh. 1881.
6

ROOKWOOD, C.M.
Rookery rhymes.
1955.
6

ROOKWOOD, C.M.
The three Desmonds.
Pilgrim Press. n.d.
6

ROSE, Sir Alec.
My "Lively Lady" by Alec Rose. (Author born in Canterbury in 1908).
London, Harrap. 1968.
3

SACKVILLE-WEST, Victoria. (Afterwards Lady Nicolson).
Another world than this...edited by V. Sackville-West and H. Nicolson.
Joseph. 1945.
12

Country notes.
Joseph. 1939.
11,12

Daughter of France.
Joseph. 1959.
12

The eagle and the dove.
Joseph. 1953.
12

Even more for your garden.
Joseph. 1958.
12

In your garden.
Joseph. 1952.
12

The land.
Heinemann. 1926.
5,11,12,16,17,19

Pepita.
Hogarth. 1937.
7,16

SAGE, Margaret.
Down many ways (poems).
Canterbury, Gibbs and Son. 1930?
3

SALOMONS, Sir David Lionel.
Motor traffic: chiefly technical.
Tunbridge Wells Courier. 1897.
19

SALOMONS, Sir David Lionel.
What is the time?
Tunbridge Wells Courier. 1919.
19

SANDERS, Frederick.
The haunting of Old Ben Dogwinkle: a Christmas ghost story. (Extracted from Chatham Observer, 22nd December, 1961).
4

SASSOON, Siegfried.
Siegfried's journey, 1916-1930. (The author lived in Brenchley).
Faber. 1945.
12

SETH, Ronald.
Children against witches.
Hale. 1969.
12

SETH, Ronald.
Stories of great witch trials.
Baker. 1967.
12

SETH, Ronald.
Witches and their craft.
Odhams. 1967.
12

SHEPPARD, Alfred Tresidder.
Here comes an old sailor (6th edition).
London, Hodder and Stoughton. 1933.
3,11(1927)

SHEPPARD, Alfred Tresidder.
Running Horse Inn.
London, Macmillan. 1906.
3

SHIRLEY, John.
Sir Thomas More: an anonymous play of the sixteenth century ascribed in part to Shakespeare, edited in five acts by John Shirley...
Canterbury, H.J. Goulden Ltd. 1938?
3

SHRUBSOLE, William.
Christian memoirs; or, a view of the present state of religion in England.
1807.
12

SIDNEY, Sir Philip.
...Apologie for poetrie: edited with an introduction and notes by J. Churton.
Clarendon Press. 1961.
12

SIMPSON, E.M.
A study of the prose works of John Donne.
Oxford University Press. 1924.
12

SISSON, C.H.
Twenty-one poems.
Sevenoaks, Privately Printed at the Westerham Press. 1960.
4

SKINNER, F.
A sprig of May blossom: a Kentish idyll.
Printed by W. Thomson. n.d.
11

SLADDEN, Dilnot.
The Northmen: a poem in four cantos.
Canterbury, Henry Ward. 1834.
3

SLADDEN, Dilnot.
Woman and other poems, by Tyro (pseudonym of Dilnot Sladden).
Canterbury, Henry Ward. 1831.
3

SMART, Christopher.
Jubilate Agno. (Collected poems).
Hart-Davis. 1954.
12

SMART, Christopher.
Out of Bedlam.
Dublin, Dolman Press. 1956.
11

SMETHAM, Henry.
Sketches, prose and rhyme.
Whiting and Co. 1889.
8,12

SMITH, Charles Roach.
Remarks on Shakespeare, his birth-place etc., suggested by a
visit to Stratford-upon-Avon in the autumn of 1868.
Richards. 2nd Edition, 1874.
12

SMITH, Charles Roach.
Report on excavations made upon the site of the Roman Castrum
at Pevensey...1852.
1858.
15

SMITH, Charles Roach.
The rural life of Shakespeare.
Maidstone and Mid Kent Natural History Society. 1870.
12

SMITH, F.B.
Agriculture in the New World: the record of a visit to the
United States and to Canada...(Published for the Technical
Education Committee of the Kent County Council).
London, Spottiswoode and Co. 1902.
3,9

SMITH, George.
Concise history of English carriages. (The author was a
carriage builder in Tunbridge Wells).
Tunbridge Wells Courier. 1896.
19

SMITH, Horace.
Rejected addresses. (Tunbridge Wells author).
Pickering and Chatto. 1870.
19

SNELL, F.C.
The camera in the fields...a practical guide to nature
photography.
London, T. Fisher Unwin. 1905.
3

SOMERVELL, David Churchill.
The British Empire.
Christophers. 1930.
12

SOMNER, William.
Vocabularium Anglo-Saxonicum...(The author was born in
Canterbury and worked there).
1701.
17

"SON OF THE MARSHES", pseud.
The wild fowl and sea fowl of Great Britain.
Chapman and Hall. 1895.
8

SPARKE, John.
Chimes from north and south.
Deal, Pain. 1918.
6,11

SPARVEL-BAYLY, J.A.
More Kentish proverbs, Part 2, and Higham Priory. (From
Walford's Antiquarian Magazine, March, 1887).
5

SPENDER, J.A.
Weetman Pearson, first Vicount Cowdray, 1856-1927.
Cassell. 1930.
6

SPOUSE, William.
The Sabbath. (Local author).
Dover Standard. n.d.
6

SPROTT, Thomas.
Chronicles. (Monk of St. Augustine's, Canterbury).
Sheldonian Theatre. 1719
12,20 (Reproduction)

STANHOPE, George. Dean of Canterbury, 1660-1728.
Concio ad Clerum, habita, In Ecclesia Cathedrali S. Pauli,
London...
1705.
3

STIRRY, Thomas.
A rot amongst the Bishops. (Poem written when the
Archbishop Lavel was taken to the Tower). 1641.
Fascimile Reprint.
12

STONE, John George Bosworth.
The heyday of Bacchus. (List of publications in
Canterbury, 1860-1955). (Reprinted from "Kentish
Gazette, 4th November, 1955).
3

STUBBS, William.
Theodorus of Tarsus. (Photostat copy of article in Vol
4 of Smith and Wace "Dictionary of Christian Biography"
London, John Murray. 1877-1887).
3

SWINDEN, Tobias. Rector of Cuxton.
An enquiry into the nature and place of Hell. (Local
author).
Printed for Thomas Astley at Dolphin and Crown, London
1727.
6

SWINDEN, Tobias. Rector of Cuxton.
Usefulness of...liturgy.
1713.
6

SYMONS, Arthur.
Notes on Joseph Conrad. (Author lived at Wittersham
at end of his life).
London, Myers and Co. 1925.
3

TALLENTS, Sir Stephen.
Green thoughts. (Author lived near Dartford).
Faber and Faber. 1952.
5

TARRANT, H.P.
Strawberries and cream (verses).
Dover, Wild. n.d.
11

TAYLOR, H.J.
Historical facts relating to music, revised and edited
by Thomas A. Johnson. (Author - Dover Borough organis
and organizer of local pageant).
A. Weekes. 1957.
6

TAYLOR, H.J.
Musical booklets, 1-16 and 17-32.
A. Weekes. n.d.
6

TAYLOR, L.C.
Numbers: 92 poems from Sevenoaks School, edited by
L.C. Taylor and G. Hoare.
Sevenoaks School. 1959.
11

THOMAS, Edward.
Four and twenty blackbirds.
Bodley Head. 1965.
11

THORNDIKE, Russell.
The Slype.
Rich and Cowan. 1936 (1927).
8

THORNDIKE, Russell.
The water witch.
Rich and Cowan. 1936 (1932).
8

THORNTON, Henry John.
Poetical sketches. (Local publication).
Tunbridge Wells, Colbran. 1837.
1,6

THORPE, Michael.
Siegfried Sassoon: a critical study. (Seigfried
Sassoon lived in Brenchley).
Oxford University Press. 1966.
12

TOTTEL, Richard.
Songes and sonnettes, compiled by R. Tottel.
Scolar Press. 1966.
12

TOULMIN, Joshua.
A short essay on Baptism.   (Maidstone author).
Johnson. 1786.
12

TREVORS, Trent, of Dover.
Fugitive poems.
Dover Telegraph. 1861.
6

TWYSDEN, Sir Roger.
Certaine considerations upon the Government of England.
Camden Society. 1849.
12

URRY, William.
Municiple costume.   (Typescript).   (The author was Librarian
of Canterbury Cathedral).
(c.1948).
3

VALLINS, George Henry.
Kent ways: a collection of verse.
Amersham, Morland. 1923.
2,8,11,12

VANE, Sir Henry. (1613-1662).
The retired man's meditations; or, the mysterie and power of
godliness...in which old light is restored and new light
justified...(The author was born at Hadlow).
Brewster. 1655.
12

VAYNES, Julia de.
Kentish garland, 2 vols.   (Ballads about Kentish history and
places).
Stephen Austin. 1881.
3,16,21

Vox 2: a magazine of poetry, drama and speech for schools in
Kent. (Contains poem "East Kent Phonetics", by John Alden,
which, by using rhyme, indicates pronunciation of the names of
Kentish towns and villages).
Kennington, Avice Allchin. 1962.
3

WADDAMS, Canon Herbert Montague.
The church and man's struggle for unity.   (A Canon of Canterbury).
London, Blandford Press. 1968.
3

WADDAMS, Canon Herbert Montague.
Companion to the Book of Common Prayer...(A Canon of Canterbury).
London, Mowbray. 1966.
3

WAKE, William. Archbishop of Canterbury.
The genuine epistles of the apostolic fathers, 6th edition.
Samuel Bagster. 1833.
12

WAKE, William. Archbishop of Canterbury.
Sermons and discourses on several occasions.
Walthoe. 1716.
12

WALKER, Stella Archer.
In praise of Kent...compiled by S.A. Walker.   (Poems and prose
about Kentish places).
Muller. 1952.
1,3,4,5,6,7,8,11,12,15,16,17

WALL, W.
The history of infant baptism. (Local author...at Dover).
Printed for Joseph Downing by Richard Burragh. 1707.
6,16(1705, 1720)

WARLY, Mary.
Letters from Mary Warly to her son Lee Warly (MS.). (Written
from Canterbury).
1739.
3

WARREN, Clarence Henry.
Corn country.
Batsford. 1940.
12

England is a village.
Eyre and Spottiswoode. 1947.
12

English cottages and farm-houses.
Collins. 1948.
12

Footpath through the farm.
Falcon. 1949.
12

Water poetry: a collection of verses written at
several places and most of them never before printed.
Bath, Tunbridge Wells, Margate, Brightelmstone, etc.
Peasch. 1770.
19

WATSON, Thomas.
Annals of the ancient British church.   (The author was
Vicar of East Farleigh).
Wertheim, Macintosh and Hunt. 1862.
11

WATTS, Isaac.
Divine and moral songs for the instruction of children.
(Local publication).
Deal, Hayward. 1847.
11

(WATTS, Thomas).
English cretes and atheistical Christians described and
instanced...(The author was a Vicar of Orpington).
Printed for Joseph Hindmarsh. 1695.
11

WEBB, Harold.
Canterbury bells: a novel of the times of Henry VIII.
Sands. 1938.
3,11

WEEKES, Henry. A.R.A.
The prize treatise on the Fine Arts Section of the Great
Exhibition of 1851, submitted to the Society of Arts in
competition for their medal.   (The author was a
Canterbury sculptor).
London, Vizetelly and Co. 1852.
3

(WEEKES, W.).
The development of a horrible conspiracy.
Printed by G. Wood. 1821.
11

WHARTON, T.
Poems.   (The author was Clerk at Longfield).
Rivington. 1833.
11

WHATMORE, Leonard E.
Blessed Carthusian martyrs: John Houghton, Augustine
Webster and Robert Lawrence.
London, Office of the Vice-Postulation. 196-?
3

WHITE, John Baker.
The big lie. (Author was M.P. for Canterbury division
of Kent, 1945-1953).
London, Evans Bros. 1955.
3

It's gone for good.
Westminster, Vacher and Sons. 1941.
3

The red network.
Canterbury, J.B. White. 1953.
3

The Soviet spy system.
London, Falcon Press. (1948).
3

True blue.
Muller. 1970.
6

WHITE, Thomas Henry.
The marigold windows.
London, Longman. Dover, Batchellor. 1849.
6

WILBERFORCE, Henry William.
Christian unity.   (Author was incumbent of Walmer).
Burns. 1842.
11

WILLCOCKE, James.
The true English Protestant's apology...(The author was a
Vicar of Goudhurst).
Privately Printed. 1642.
11

William de Shoreham.
Religious poems of William de Shoreham.
1849.
11

WILLIAMSON, Catherine Ellis.
The crimson dawn.
London, Merlin Press. 1963.
3,8

WILLIAMSON, G.J.
The ship's career and other poems.   (The author was born in
Rochester).
Judd and Glass. 1860.
12

WILMOT, Edward P.
The Labour Party.
London, Macmillan. 1968.
3

WILSON, John (Boyd).
Public schools and private practice.
London, Allen and Unwin. 1962.
3

WILSON, Thomas.
The aquatic excursion; or, Mrs. Fidget's trip to the Nore:
a local dramatic sketch in one act.   (Descriptive of Thames and
mentions Gravesend).
T. Wilson. 1824.
15

WILSON, Thomas.
David's zeale for Zion: a sermon preached before sundry of
the Honourable House of Commons...April 4th. (Author was a
preacher from Otham).
Printed for John Bartlett. 1641.
11

"WISE MEN OF THE EAST".
The Folkestone fiery serpent, together with the humours of
the Dover Mayor: being an ancient ballad full of mystery and
pleasant concert...
Dover, Thomas Rigden. 1839.
6,7

"WISE MEN OF THE EAST".
The Folkestone fiery serpent, together with the humours of
the Dover Mayor: being an ancient ballad full of mystery and
pleasant concert...second edition.
Dover, Thomas Rigden. 1844.
7

"WISE MEN OF THE EAST".
The Folkestone fiery serpent, together with the humours of
the Dover Mayor: being an ancient ballad full of mystery and
pleasant concert...third edition.
Dover, Thomas Rigden. 1852.
7

"WISE MEN OF THE EAST".
The Folkestone fiery serpent, together with the humours of
the Dover Mayor: being an ancient ballad full of mystery and
pleasant concert...fourth edition.
Dover, Thomas Rigden. 1861.
7

"WISE MEN OF THE EAST".
The Folkestone fiery serpent, together with the humours of
the Dover Mayor: being an ancient ballad full of mystery and
pleasant concert...fifth edition.
W. Simpson, 21 Sandgate Road, Folkestone. (187-?).
7

WOODHEAD, E.W.
The child in the educational system.   (The author was an
Education Officer for Kent).
Gregg. n.d.
12

WOODRUFF, Cumberland H.
Reliquiae literatae; or , verses and essays.
Canterbury, Cross and Jackman. 1907.
3

WOTTON, Sir Henry. (1568-1639).
Reliquiae Wottonianae; or, a collection of lively
letters, poems, with characters of sundry personages and
other incomparable pieces of language and art.   (With
a memoir by Izaak Walton).
Marriott, Bedel and Garthwait. 1654.
11,12,13

WRIGHT, Charles James.
Jesus, the revelation of God; the mission and message
according to St. John.   (C.J. Wright, B.D., Ph.D. -
St. Augustine's College, Canterbury).
London, Hodder and Stoughton. 1950.
3

WRIGHT, Sydney Fowler.
Contemporary Kent and Essex poetry (County Series of
Contemporary Poetry), edited by S.F. Wright.
Merton Press. 1925 etc.
2,3,6,11,17

WYLLIE, James.
Farm management.
Spon. 1955.
12

WYNDHAM, George.
The development of the State.   (The author was an M.P.
for Dover).
Constable. 1904.
6

WYNDHAM, George.
Essays in romantic literature, edited by Charles Whibley.
(The author was an M.P. for Dover).
Macmillan. 1919.
6

"A YOUNG LADY", pseud.
A collection of poems, including some about eminent Kent
people.   Printed at Phoenix Press, Rochester.
Gillman and Etherington. 1792.
15

KENT, SONGS

BUTTERWORTH, Neil.
The dream of a girl at Sevenoaks: unison song.
Chappell. c.1960.
12

CRAMPTON, T.
The Men of Kent.
Graham. n.d.
3,12

EVERSFIELD, William.
The harmonic Ifield woodmen...song.
London, Halliday and Co. 1827.
9

FANSHAWE, David.
Songs of Kent.
Kent Life. (1965).
7

HAIGH, T.
The brave Men of Kent (old ballad, 1719): song with
chorus, words by T.D'Urfey, music by T. Haigh.
Association of Men of Kent and Kentish Men, Thanet and
District Branch. (191-?).
11

KENT, SONGS Cont'd

HOWELLS, H.
Kent Yeoman's wooing song...
Novello. 1953.
11

JOHNSON, Noel.
Ye olde folk songs of the Men of Kent and Kentish Men,
collated by Wilfred Virgo; edited by Douglas Carroll;
music arranged by N. Johnson.
Clifton Bingham Publishing Co. (1921).
1,11,12

"KENT LIFE".
Songs of Kent.
Kent Messenger. 1965.
12

The Kentish songster.
1775.
3(4th edition-Canterbury, Simmons and Kirkby, 1792) 12,17

KING, Harriet Eleanor Hamilton.
Songs of Romney Marsh.
1908.
8

LAKE, Phyllis.
A song of Margate (and) "Invicta" - a song of Kent.
1953.
13

The Men of Kent: an old Kentish song.
Graham and Sons. n.d.
3,12

(Six songs of Kent).
n.d.
11

KESTON - See HAYES AND KESTON

KIDBROOKE

DUNKIN, Edwin Hadlow Wise.
Historical memoranda relating to the liberty of the parish of
Kidbrooke...
Bembrose and Sons. 1874.
1,12,15,17,18

LAW, K.K.
Kidbrooke parish...
1955.
17

KINGSDOWN

ELLISTON-ERWOOD, Frank Charles.
Architectural notes on Kingsdown Church near Sevenoaks
(St. Edmund).
London, Mitchell, Hughes and Clarke. 1921.
5,10,17

KINGSGATE

"The Convent", Kingsgate-on-Sea, to be sold by auction...by
Messrs. Knight, Frank and Rutley...on the 16th...June, 1910.
11

NORTH FORELAND GOLF CLUB.
Official handbook.
North Foreland Golf Club. 1932.
13

The residential attractions of Kingsgate-on-Sea and district.
1931.
13

KIPPINGTON

STANDEN, Hugh Wyatt.
Kippington in Kent: its history and its churches.
Sevenoaks, Standen. 1958.
1,2,3,4,7,8,9,11,12,15,16,17,19

KNOCKHOLT

GREAT BRITAIN - STATUTORY INSTRUMENTS.
London Government. The Greater London, Kent and Surrey Order.
(S.1. 1968, No. 2,020). (Note: transfer of Knockholt from
London Borough of Bromley to Sevenoaks Rural District).
H.M.S.O. 1968.
2

KENT COUNTY COUNCIL - ARCHIVES OFFICE.
Knockholt parish records.
1962.
2

KNOCKHOLT WOMEN'S INSTITUTE.
Scrapbook (photocopy of extracts).
1965.
2

St. Katherine's Church, Knockholt.
Westerham, Hooker Bros., Printers. 196-?
2

WARLOW, G.H.
History of Knockholt, Kent.
Kentish District Times. 1934.
11,16

WARLOW, G.H.
History of Knockholt, new edition. Revised by Norman
Smithers.
Westerham, Hooker Bros., Printers. 1965.
2

KNOCKMILL

CHANDLER, Raymond H.
Excursion to Knockmill (Oaklands) and Cotman's Ash,
13th June, 1908, by R.H. Chandler and A.L. Leach.
(From the Proceedings of the Geologists' Association,
Vol. XX, 1908).
5,17

CHANDLER, Raymond H.
Field meeting at Knockmill, Kent, by R.H. Chandler and
A.L. Leach. (From the Proceedings of the Geologists'
Association, 1936).
17

CHANDLER, Raymond H.
Structure of the eocene outlier near Knockmill, Kent, by
R.H. Chandler and A.L. Leach. (From the Proceedings of
the Geologists' Associaton, 1936).
11,17

LEACH, Arthur L.
Field meeting at Knockmill. (From the Proceedings of the
Geologists' Association, Reprint 1935).
17

KNOLE

BRADY, John H.
Visitor's guide to Knole.
Sevenoaks, Payne. 1839.
1,2,3,4,6,7,8,11,12,15,17

BRADY, John H.
An abridgement of the visitor's guide to Knole.
Sevenoaks, Payne. 1842.
11

BRIDGMAN, John.
An historical and topographical sketch of Knole in
Kent with a brief genealogy of the Sackville family.
Lindsell. 1817.
1,2,3,4,6,8,11,12,14,15,16,17,18,19

BRIDGMAN, John.
An historical and topographical sketch of Knole...
Lindsell. 1821.
12,16,17,18

CAXTON AND HOLMESDALE PRESS. Publishers.
Guide to Knole - new edition.
Caxton and Holmesdale Press. 1948.
2

LAMBERHURST

HOPKINS, R. Thurston.
Moated houses of England.
Country Life. 1935.
5,11,15,18

HUSSEY, Christopher.
Short history of Scotney Castle.
Tunbridge Wells, Stanford Printing Co. 1953.
11

HUSSEY, Edward.
Scotney Castle. In Archaeologia Cantiana, Vol. 17, 1887.
17

Lamberhurst Magazine, September, 1963-July, 1965.
12

MORLAND, William.
The church in Lamberhurst.
W. Morland. 1968.
2,8,11,12,19

LAMBETH PALACE

DUCAREL, Andrew Coltee.
The history and antiquities of the Archiepiscopal Palace of
Lambeth.
Society of Antiquaries. 1785.
3

GARDINER, Mrs. Dorothy.
The story of Lambeth Palace: an historic survey.
London, Constable and Co. 1930.
3

SAYERS, Jane.
Estate documents at Lambeth Palace: a short catalogue.
Leicester University Press. 1965.
1,5,7,11

LAND UTILIZATION

STAMP, Lawrence Dudley.
Kent. (The land of Britain Series).
Land Utilization Survey. 1943.
1,2,3,5,6,7,8,11,12,15

LANGLEY

The Langley Messenger: news and views from church and people.
Langley Messenger. 1964.
12

LARKFIELD

EAST MALLING AND LARKFIELD PARISH COUNCIL.
Official handbook to East Malling and Larkfield.
July, 1962.
11

LAW

GREAT BRITAIN: LAWS, etc. (QUEEN ANNE).
An Act for sale of the Manor of Hampstead and other lands...
Kent and Sussex...
n.d.
11

GREAT BRITAIN: LAWS, etc. (QUEEN ANNE).
An Act for sale of several lands...of William Henden Esq., in
the County of Kent.
n.d.
11

GREAT BRITAIN: LAWS, etc. (GEO. II).
An Act for establishing...an exchange agreed...between William,
Earl Cowper and Sir George Oxenden of certain lands...in Kent.
n.d.
11

GREAT BRITAIN: LAWS, etc. (GEO. III).
An Act for carrying into execution an agreement made
between...Surveyor-General of His Majesty's lands and
the Trustees of Morden College...
1771.
11,12

GREAT BRITAIN: LAWS, etc. (GEO. III).
An Act for empowering the Justices of the Peace for...Kent to
make a...County rate...1807.
H.M.S.O. 1807.
12

GREAT BRITAIN: LAWS, etc. (GEO. III).
An Act for enabling the Justices of the Peace to hold
a General Sessions annually...for levying and applying the
rates...1814.
H.M.S.O. 1814.
12

GREAT BRITAIN: LAWS, etc. (GEO. III).
An Act for re-vesting certain lands...in the former
proprietors thereof, and for other purposes therein
mentioned.
1797.
11

GREAT BRITAIN: LAWS, etc. (GEO. III).
An Act for vesting the estate late of Edmund Hungate
Beaghan...in trustees...
n.d.
11

GREAT BRITAIN: LAWS, etc. (GEO. III-WILLIAM IV).
Some Acts of Parliament relating to Kent.
n.d.
11

GREAT BRITAIN: LAWS, etc. (GEO. IV).
An Act to enable John Cator to grant...building leases
in Kent...and for vesting in trustees, for sale, parts of
the estates.
1825.
2

GREAT BRITAIN: LAWS, etc. (ELIZ. II).
Kent Quarter Sessions Act.
H.M.S.O. 1962.
4,8

GREAT BRITAIN: LAWS, etc. (ELIZ. II).
Kent Quarter Sessions Act, 1966: (an Act to make
provision as to Deputy Chairman of the Court of
Quarter Sessions...).
1966.
1,4,12

LEE

BIRCHENOUGH, Edwyn.
The Manor House, Lee and its associations, by E. and
J. Birchenough.
London, Borough of Lewisham. 1966.
1,12,18

BIRCHENOUGH, Edwyn.
The Manor House, Lee, 2nd edition, by E. and J.
Birchenough.
London Borough of Lewisham. 1971.
2

BIRCHENOUGH, Edwyn.
Two old Lee houses - Dacre House and Lee House, by
E. and J. Birchenough.
London Borough of Lewisham. 1968.
2

BUTTS, Robert.
Historical guide to Lewisham, Ladywell, Lee, Blackheath
and Eltham.
1878.
17,18

CARPENTER, A.B.B.
Sermon preached at Holy Trinity, Lee at the memorial
service for the late Mr. E.W. Bucke, Sunday, January
21st, 1900.
Lee, North. 1900.
12

A descriptive account of Lewisham, Lee, Blackheath and
Catford.
1894.
18

ELLISTON-ERWOOD, Frank Charles.
Making of the New Road at Lee, 1824-1828.
1952.
18

LEE Cont'd

GREGORY, R.R.C.
The story of Lee, by R.R.C. Gregory and F.W. Nunn.
Lewisham Newspaper Co. 1923.
1,2,5,11,17,18

HART, F.H.
History of Lee...
Lee, North. 1882.
1,2,4,7,11,12,17,18

HART, F.H.
History of Lee and its neighbourhood. (New edition).
Conway Maritime Press. 1971.
4,5,11

(LAW, Frederick Henry).
A retrospect, 1873-1896.
Lee, North. 1896.
11

Manuscript book containing poems and articles in Latin and
English. (Some connection with members of the Fairfax family).
n.d.
12

POTTER, W.F.
Lewisham and Lee.
1906.
17

St. Margaret, Lee - the 125th anniversary of the consecration...
1966.
18

SPRAY, Leonard.
The Ravensbourne Club, Eltham Road, Lee.
1914.
17

TARGETT, W.D.
Parish church of St. Margaret, Lee...1839-1939.
Blackheath, Blackheath Press. 1939.
1,18

WOLFFRAM, H.
Thirty years' work (1868-97) in preparing condidates for the
Army at Faraday House, Blackheath and The Manor House, Lee.
1898.
18

WOOD, A.W.
Lee Church of England School. (Pamphlet).
1963.
18

Lee, personalities and places. (Pamphlet).
1965.
18

St. Margaret, Lee...a story and a description...(Pamphlet).
1964.
18

LEE PRIORY

BRYDGES, Sir Samuel Egerton,
List of pictures at the seat of T.B. Brydges Barrett Esq., at
Lee Priory, Kent.
Lee Priory. 1817.
3

GOODSALL, Robert Harold.
Lee Priory and the Brydges circle. (Reprinted from Archaeologia
Cantiana, Vol. LXXVII, 1962).
3,17

LEE PRIORY PRESS.
Catalogue of all the works printed at the private press at
Lee Priory in Kent, 1813-1823.
Lee Priory. 1823.
17

LEEDS

BENNETT, F.J.
(Report on an) excursion to Leeds and the Loose Valley, Kent on
18th June, 1910. (Reprinted from Proceedings of the Geologists'
Association, 6 pages).
n.d.
7

BROWNE, J.C.
Leeds Priory, Kent.
1893?
11

Burgess Hall, Leeds, near Maidstone - catalogue of
the sale of contents on...28th September, 1967.
Printed by Vivish and Baker. 1967.
11

CAVE-BROWNE, John.
In and about Leeds and Bromfield parishes, Kent.
1894.
1,4,11,15

CAVE-BROWNE, John.
Leeds Church, Kent.
1893.
1,4,11,15

CAVE-BROWNE, John.
Leeds Priory, Kent.
1893.
1,4,6,11,12,15

CURRY, John.
The Knight's oath: a story based on the records of
Leeds Castle, Kent. (Typescript).
1923?
11

HARRIS, Edwin.
The seige of Leeds Castle.
Rochester, E. Harris. 1906.
1,4,8,11,12,15,17

HOPKINS, R. Thurston.
Moated houses of England.
Country Life. 1935.
5,11,15,18

MARTIN, Charles Wykeham.
History and description of Leeds Castle.
Nichols. 1869.
1,3,4,6,7,8,11,12,15,17,18,19,20,21

OSBORNE, Thomas. 1st Duke of Leeds.
Copies and extracts of some letters written to and
from the Duke of Leeds.
Nicholson. 1710.
12

ROFFE, Alfred.
Leeds: our Grandfather's native village...in memory
of Robert Cabbell Roffe, engraver, by A. Roffe and
others.
Privately Printed. 1859.
8,11,17

LEGAL CUSTOMS

PRANGNELL, Dom Dunstan.
Chronicle of William of Byholte (1310-1320): an account
of the legal system known as Frankpleage, edited by
Dom D. Prangnell.
Westgate, Prangnell. 1967.
11

LEGENDS

BECKETT, Arthur.
Wonderful Weald and quest of the Crock of Gold.
1924 etc.
1,4(1911) 5,8,11,12,15,19

BRENT, John.
Lays and legends of Kent, 1st edition.
Ball and Arnold. Canterbury, H. Ward. 1840.
3,8,11

BRENT, John.
Lays and legends of Kent, 2nd edition with considerable
additions, edited by J. Brent.
London, Whittaker. Canterbury, H. Ward. 1841.
1,11,12,17

COOMBS, William.
Tonbridge legends.
Tonbridge, Ware. 1866.
8,11,15,17,19

HARRIS, Edwin.
Local legends. (Old Rochester series, No. 12).
Rochester, E. Harris. 1898.
2,8,11

IGGLESDEN, Charles.
Those superstitions.   (Includes some Kentish superstitions).
Jarrolds. 1932.
12,13

NOYES, T.H.
An idyll of the Weald and other lays and legends.
T.H. Noyes. 1868.
12

WINSER, Lilian.
Lays and legends of the Weald of Kent.
Elkin Mathews. 1897.
1,2,16

WINSER, Lilian.
Lays and legends of the Weald of Kent.
Elkin Mathews. 1907.
4,8,9,11,12,15,17,19,20

LEIGH

BARTLETT, P.A.
Poor Law in Leigh, 1731-1766.   (Tonbridge School local history researches).
1961.
11

St. Mary's Church, Leigh.
(1966).
12

LEN, RIVER

GOODSALL, Robert Harold.
Watermills on the River Len.   In Archaeologia Cantiana, Vol. 71, 1957).
17

SPAIN, Robert James.
The Len watermills.   (Typescript MS.).
1966.
11

LENHAM

LENHAM PARISH COUNCIL.
Official guide.
1966.
1,11,12

LESNES ABBEY - See ERITH

LEWISHAM

ANDREWS, D.H.B.
Elementary education in the Lewisham district, 1870-1903.
1965.
18

ASKE'S.
Hatcham School Magazine, Autumn, 1925.   (History of the School to 1925).
1925.
18

BAKER, L.A.J.
Places of worship in the Boroughs of Deptford, Lewisham, Greenwich and Woolwich.
1961.
1,2,5,8,11,12,17,18

BEDWELL, C.E.A.
Lewisham.   (Typescript).
1898.
18

BRABROOK, E.W.
Methodism in Lewisham.
1881.
1

"Burnt Ash Magazine" - 1878.
18

BUTTS, Robert.
Historical guide to Lewisham, Ladywell, Lee, Blackheath and Eltham.
1878.
17,18

A descriptive account of Lewisham, Lee, Blackheath and Catford.
1894.
18

DUNCAN, Leland Lewis.
History of the Borough of Lewisham with an itinerary and with chapters on the geology of the district by W.H. Griffin, and on the local authorities by A.W. Hiscox.
Printed by C. North for the Lewisham Antiquarian Society.
1908.
1,2,7,8,11,12,17,18

DUNCAN, Leland Lewis.
History of the Borough of Lewisham with an itinerary, etc...bound with the Proceedings of the Lewisham Antiquarian Society for 1902-7 - illustrated.
Lewisham Antiquarian Society. 1908.
18

DUNCAN, Leland Lewis.
History of the Borough of Lewisham with an itinerary, etc. (1908) with a supplement - "Odds and Ends of Lewisham History" - and Proceedings of the Lewisham Antiquarian Society, 1908-12.
Lewisham Borough Council. 1963.
2,4,11,17,18

DUNCAN, Leland Lewis.
History of Colfe's Grammar School, Lewisham, with a life of its founder, 1st edition.
For the Worshipful Company of Leathersellers. 1910.
1,2,7,11,12,17,18

DUNCAN, Leland Lewis.
History of Colfe's Grammar School, Lewisham, 1652-1952, with a life of its founder, 2nd edition, edited by H. Beardmore and others.
University of London Press. 1952.
18

DUNCAN, Leland Lewis.
Odds and ends of Lewisham history.   In Proceedings of the Lewisham Antiquarian Society, 1908-1912.
2,18

DUNCAN, Leland Lewis.
Parish church of St. Mary, Lewisham: its building and rebuilding with some account of the Vicars and Curates of Lewisham.
Printed by C. North for the Lewisham Antiquarian Society. 1892.
1,6,11,15,17,18

(DUNCAN, Leland Lewis).
A short history of Colfe's Grammar School, Lewisham.
Printed by C. North for the Lewisham Antiquarian Society. 1902.
11,18

GOLBY, F.W.
History of the Neptune Lodge of Freemasons (1757-1909).
Privately Printed. 1910.
18

GRANT, Mary.
The Manor of Lewisham: a short review of its past history.
n.d.
1

GREAT BRITAIN: LAWS, etc.   (GEO. III).
An Act for inclosing lands in the parish of Lewisham... (Sydenham Common) - Lewisham Inclosure Act, 1810.
18

GREAT BRITAIN: LAWS, etc.   (GEO. III).
An Act for rebuilding the church of the parish of Lewisham...
1774.
11,18

HOLLYBAND, Claudius.
The Elizabethan home, by E. Hollyband and P. Erondell.
(Early Lewisham references).
1949.
18

ISHAM, Giles.
Correspondence of Bishop Brian Duppa (born in Lewisham) with
Sir J. Isham, 1650-60, edited by G. Isham.
Northampton Record Society. 1954.
18

JACKSON, Rev. D.
The parish church of St. Stephen, Lewisham, 1865-1965.
(Pamphlet). 1965.
18

JENNINGS, James.
Ornithologia; or, the birds: a poem. (Refers to Lewisham
and Bromley).
Poole and Edwards. 1828.
2

KIRBY, Herbert Charles.
Monumental inscriptions in the church and churchyard of
St. Mary, Lewisham, edited by H.C. Kirby and L.L. Duncan.
C. North. 1889.
11,17,18

KIRBY, John William.
Lewisham: an historical record.
Lewisham Borough Council. 1950.
1,18

Lewisham: a pamphlet.
c.1790.
17

Lewisham and Blackheath Courier, 1884.
18

LEWISHAM ANTIQUARIAN SOCIETY.
Annual reports and proceedings.
1(1894-6, 1899-1901)
11(9th Annual report, 1894)
17(7th, 12th and 29th annual reports)

LEWISHAM BOROUGH COUNCIL.
Official guide.
Cheltenham, E.J. Burrow.
2(1931, 1948, 1958) 18

Lewisham Grammar School: rules and regulations.
n.d.
17

Lewisham Gunners: a centenary history of 291st (4th London)
Field Regiment, R.A., (T.A.) formerly 2nd Kent R.G.A.
(Volunteers).
1962.
4

MANDY, W.H.
Notes on medieval Greenwich and Lewisham.
n.d.
17

MARTIN, Alan R.
Alien priory of Lewisham.
Greenwich Antiquarian Society. 1927.
17

MARTIN, Alan R.
Old church of St. Mary, Lewisham.
n.d.
17

MORRIS, Leslie Frank.
A history of St. Dunstan's College.
St. Dunstan's College. 1970.
2,11

PEACE, J.W.G.
Lost lands of Lewisham.
n.d.
18

PETERS, George Hertel.
The vanished village.
Blackheath Press. (1955).
1,18

Place House, Lewisham. (One page, probably from a
book).
n.d.
17

Plan and terms of the Grammar School, Lewisham Hill,
founded 1652.
(18--?).
11

POTTER, W.F.
Lewisham and Lee.
1906.
17

ROBERTSON, J.A.B.
Notes on the ancient parish of St. Mary, Lewisham.
1962.
18

ROCQUE, John. (Cartographer).
A plan of the parish of Lewisham...surveyed 1741-1745...
Reprinted by C.F. Kell, 1877.
12

St. John's Hospital, Lewisham: annual report for the
year ended December, 1912.
17

St. Mary, Lewisham - Thousandth Birthday Festival...
list of the Vicars of Lewisham...(pamphlet).
1931.
18

St. Saviour's, Brockley Rise, 1866-1966 - centenary
brochure (pamphlet).
1966.
18

Sixty years at St. Stephen's, Lewisham...1865-1925.
(Pamphlet). 1925.
18

SKEAT, W.W.
On the derivation and meaning of the name "Lewisham".
n.d.
17

STAFFORD, H.
A history of Caterham School. (Originally in Lewisham -
1815-84).
1945.
18

WARD, Gordon Reginald.
The Manor of Lewisham and its Wealden "dens". (Reprinted
from Greenwich and Lewisham Antiquarian Society
Transactions, 19--?).
11

LEYBOURNE

HAWLEY, Sir Joseph.
Leybourne Grange, Malling, Kent: catalogue of the library
of the late Sir Joseph Hawley, Bart...(to be sold by auction
November 22nd, 1905...
3,4,17

KENT COUNTY COUNCIL - PLANNING DEPARTMENT.
Leybourne lakes - proposed country park: a report on
the Leybourne lakes and adjoining areas at Snodland
and New Hythe...
Kent County Council. 1972.
11

LARKING, Lambert Blackwell.
A description of the heart-shrine in Leybourne Church
with some account of Sir Roger de Leyburn...(Reprinted
with notes from Archaeologia Cantiana, Vol. 5, 1863).
15,17

LEYBOURNE Cont'd

LAYBOURN, Robert.
The first English Admiral, Lord William de Leybourne and the
house of Laybourn from 1025-1938.
Copenhagen, Saabye and Christensen. 1939.
3

MCINTOSH, Mary.
Roots and branches: the story...of the Angus and Leybourne
families...
Newcastle, Laybourne. 195-?
11,12

THORNE, H.W.
Short account of Leybourne Church.
West Malling, Stedman.
11(1937, 1956, 1963)

LEYSDOWN-ON-SEA

LEYSDOWN-ON-SEA PARISH COUNCIL.
Official guide.
Burrows. 1952.
1

LIBRARIES

BEXLEY PUBLIC LIBRARIES.
Kent libraries statistics.
4(1962-63) 9(1960-61)

KENT COUNTY LIBRARY.
Catalogue, 1924.
11,17
Seventh annual report, 1928/1929)
3

A letter to Henry Addington on the establishment of parochial
libraries, by a Kentish Clergyman.
Spilsbury. 1802.
12

LOCAL LIBRARY BOOK LABELS.
A collection of mounted book labels of the 18th and 19th
centuries, of circulating libraries in Kent. (Includes 24
labels of libraries in Canterbury).
n.d.
3

LIGHT HOUSES - See COASTAL WATERS

LINGFIELD

COBHAM, F.
A short history of and guide to the antiquities of Lingfield
with some particulars concerning its ancient worthies.
Cassell and Co. 1899.
15

LINSTEAD

EHRMANN, Rev. L.E.A.
The twist of the collar: being memoirs of one abandoning
commerce for the Ministry...by Rev. L.E.A. Ehrmann...twenty
years Vicar of Lynstead, Kent.
Sittingbourne, Rev. L.E.A. Ehrmann. 1949.
3

LINTON

Linton Park...catalogue of the contents...
1961.
11

LITTLE CHART

EAMES, John.
A Roman bath-house at Little Chart, Kent. In Archaeologia
Cantiana, Vol. 71, 1957.
17

FARQHARSON, Victor.
Notes on helmets in Little Chart Church. In Archaeologia
Cantiana, Vol. 36, 1723.
17

GRIFFIN, Ralph.
Inscription in Little Chart Church. In Archaeologia
Cantiana, Vol. 36, 1923.
17

LITTLEBOURNE

ANDREWS, James Chapman.
Lord's men of Littlebourne.
Harrap. 1926 etc.
1,3,6,8,11,12

Littlebourne House - illustrated sale catalogue.
London, Knight, Frank and Rutley. 1935.
3

Particulars and conditions of sale of Littlebourne
Windmill.
Amos and Dowton, Auctioneers. 1972.
3

LITTLESTONE

HODGSON, R.D.
An eye off the ball at Littlestone.
Littlestone Golf Club. 1939.
7

Particulars, plans (2) and conditions of sale of the
Littlestone-on-Sea Estate, comprising important freehold building plots; thirty private residences and
cottages; the Grand Hotel (with vacant possession)...
arable and marsh grazing land and the Greatstone Golf
Links; the whole extending to over 700 acres to be
offered for sale by auction...on...17th September, 1926.
(London, Knight, Frank and Rutley). 1926.
7

LOCAL GOVERNMENT

GREAT BRITAIN: LAWS, etc. (WILL. IV).
Abstract of an Act to provide for the regulation of
Municipal Corporations in England and Wales - (Kent).
1835.
17

GREAT BRITAIN: LAWS, etc. (ELIZ. II).
A Bill to confer further powers on the Kent County
Council and local authorities of the County of Kent in
relation to lands and highways.
H.M.S.O. 1957.
9

GREAT BRITAIN: LAWS, etc. (ELIZ. II).
Kent County Council Act, 1958.
H.M.S.O. 1959.
2,4,6,8,11,12

GREAT BRITAIN: LAWS, etc. (ELIZ. II).
Kent County Council Act, 1970.
H.M.S.O. 1970.
4

GREAT BRITAIN: LAWS, etc. (ELIZ. II).
London Government Bill.
H.M.S.O. 1962.
2

GREAT BRITAIN: LAWS, etc. (ELIZ. II) - STATUTORY
INSTRUMENTS.
Local government...alteration of areas - Kent Review
(Amendment) Order.
H.M.S.O. 1967.
2

GREAT BRITAIN: LAWS, etc. (ELIZ. II) - STATUTORY
INSTRUMENTS.
London government - The Local Law (South-East London
Boroughs) Order, 1965 (S.1 1965, No. 531).
17

HOME OFFICE.
The Kent Police (Amalgamation) Order, 1947.
H.M.S.O. 1947.
8

HOME OFFICE.
The Kent Police (Amalgamation) Order, 1965.
H.M.S.O. 1965.
8

HOPE, Sir William H. St. John.
The corporation plate and insignia of office of the cities
and towns of England and Wales...Vol. 1 - Anglesey to Kent,
edited by Sir W.H. St. J. Hope.
Bemrose. 1895.
8

KENT BOROUGH AND URBAN DISTRICT COUNCILS' ASSOCIATION.
Kent statistics.
4(1951, 1961 in progress)
8(1961 in progress)
15(1946 in progress)
19(1961 in progress)

KENT COUNTY COUNCIL.
An address given by Sir Edward Hardy...on the transfer of
county services under the National Health Service Act, 1946.
Kent County Council. 1948.
11

Byelaws and regulations.
Kent County Council. 1934.
11

County services and your pocket (pamphlet).
Kent County Council. (1961).
4,12

County services: facts and figures.
Kent County Council.
12(1962-3, 1969-70)

Employment byelaws, 19th April, 1951. (Children and Young
Persons Act, 1933).
Kent County Council. 1951.
13

Kent: the county administration in war, 1939-1945.
Kent County Council. 1946.
1,2,3,4,5,6,7,8,10,11,12,14,15,16,17,19

Kent County Council, 1965: a review of events, trends and
problems during 1965.
Kent County Council. 1966.
4,5,11,12

Kent County services.
(1961).
4,19

Local Government Boundary Commission review of County
districts, 1949. Observations of the County Council...
Kent County Council. 1949.
2

Memorandum of evidence on behalf of the Kent County Council
(as presented to the) Royal Commission on London Government.
(1922).
11

Record: No. 1.
Kent County Council. 1889.
17

Report as to the work of the Council, 1946-49.
Kent County Council. 1949.
2,6,11,15

Royal Commission on Local Government. Memorandum of views of
the Kent County Council on local government reform.
1966.
3,4,5,11

Scheme of divisional administration made by the Kent County
Council.
Kent County Council. 1967.
11

Service rendered.
Kent County Council. 1965 etc.
1,3,4,5,8,9,11,12,19

Statistics of County districts and particulars of areas of
County administration...submitted to the Local Government
Boundary Commission.
Kent County Council. 1949.
2

Working for Kent: careers in local government.
Kent County Council. 1968.
12

KENT COUNTY COUNCIL - CHILDREN'S COMMITTEE.
Report on the work of the Children's Committee.
Kent County Council.
1(1948-50, 1958-63)
2(1950-53, 1958-63)
3(1948-50, 1950-53, 1953-58, 1958-63)
4(1953-58, 1958-63)
5(1948-50, 1958-63)
6(1948-50, 1950-53, 1953-58, 1958-63, 1963-70)
8(1953-58, 1958-63, 1963-70)
9(1963-70)
11(1953-58, 1958-63, 1963-70)
12(1948-50, 1950-53, 1953-58, 1958-63)
13(1948-50)
14(1948-50, 1958-63)
15(1953-58)
19(1953-58, 1958-63)

KENT COUNTY COUNCIL - COUNTY ANALYST'S DEPARTMENT.
Annual reports, 1912-1932.
Kent County Council.
12

KENT COUNTY COUNCIL - HEALTH DEPARTMENT.
Annual report of the Medical Officer.
Kent County Council.
1(1910-29)
5(1955-59, 1961-65)
6(1945 in progress)
12(1945-49, 1954 in progress)

KENT COUNTY COUNCIL - HEALTH DEPARTMENT.
Notes on County health services.
Kent County Council. Published at Irregular Intervals.
3

KENT COUNTY COUNCIL - PLANNING DEPARTMENT.
Report on the work of the Planning Department from
1948 to 1959...
Kent County Council. 1959.
1,2,3,4,5,6,8,9,11,12,15,19

KENT COUNTY COUNCIL - PLANNING DEPARTMENT.
Town centre maps: a guide to their preparation in Kent.
Kent County Council. 1964.
1,11

KENT COUNTY COUNCIL - PROBATION COMMITTEE.
Annual report of the Principal Probation Officer for
the year 1963.
Kent County Council. 1963.
12

KENT COUNTY COUNCIL - PROBATION AND AFTER-CARE COMMITTEE
Annual report for the year 1969.
Kent County Council. 1969.
11

KENT COUNTY COUNCIL - PUBLIC ASSISTANCE DEPARTMENT.
Report of the Public Assistance Officer...for the two
years ended 31st March, 1936 and for the two years
ended 31st March, 1938.
Kent County Council. 1936 and 1938.
11

KENT COUNTY COUNCIL - SELECTION AND SPECIAL PURPOSE
COMMITTEE.
Committee's statements of objectives.
Kent County Council. 1970.
11

KENT COUNTY COUNCIL - SURVEYOR'S DEPARTMENT.
Annual report of the County Surveyor.
Kent County Council.
1(1947-1963/4)
5(1952 in progress)
6(1945 in progress)
9(1967/8)
12(1959 in progress)

KENT COUNTY COUNCIL - SURVEYOR'S DEPARTMENT.
Note for the use of Members on matters relating to the
work of the Roads Committee.
Kent County Council. 1970.
5,6,8,9,11

LOCAL GOVERNMENT Cont'd

KENT COUNTY COUNCIL - TREASURER'S DEPARTMENT.
Abstract of the receipts and expenditure...
Kent County Council.
1(1951/2-1961)
3(1951/2-1961)
4(1951/2-1961)
5(1951/2-1961)
6(1951/2-1961)
11(1939)
12(1922, 1923, 1951/2-1961)

KENT COUNTY COUNCIL - TREASURER'S DEPARTMENT.
Budget for the year ending March 31st...
Kent County Council.
1(1964-1966)
4(1964 in progress)
5(1964-1968)
6(1966 in progress)
8(1964 in progress)
9(1965-1969)
12(1964 in progress)

KENT COUNTY COUNCIL - TREASURER'S DEPARTMENT.
Budget, 1971-2 and forecasts, 1972-76.
Kent County Council. 1971.
8,11

Budget, 1972-3 and forecasts, 1973-77.
Kent County Council. 1972.
9

KENT COUNTY COUNCIL - TREASURER'S DEPARTMENT.
County Council finance.
Kent County Council.
3(1952-55)
6(1948-56)
11(1954-55)
12(1953-54, 1954-55, 1955-56)

KENT COUNTY COUNCIL - TREASURER'S DEPARTMENT.
County services.
Kent County Council.
3(1954, 1960, 1968-69)
6(1954)
12(1953-54, 1954-55, 1963-64 in progress)

KENT COUNTY COUNCIL - TREASURER'S DEPARTMENT.
Five years capital plan, 1970-75.
Kent County Council. 1970.
9,11

KENT COUNTY COUNCIL - TREASURER'S DEPARTMENT.
Programme of capital expenditure for the years 1967-70.
Kent County Council. 1967.
5,6,12

KENT COUNTY COUNCIL - WEIGHTS AND MEASURES DEPARTMENT.
Annual reports.
Kent County Council.
1(Some)
2(1958 in progress)
4(1949 in progress)
6(1945 in progress)
7(1969)
8(1945 in progress)
9(Some)
11(1936/7 in progress)
12(1958 in progress)
19(1945 in progress)

KENT FIRE BRIGADE.
Annual report of the Chief Officer.
Kent County Council.
6(1948 in progress)
11(1971/2)

KENT FIRE BRIGADE.
Fire prevention and safety handbook. 1st edition, 1959; 2nd
edition, 1964; 3rd edition, 1971.
Kent County Council.
1(1959)   12(1959, 1964)
3(1964)   14(1959)
4(1959, 1964)
5(1959)
6(1971)
9(1959, 1971)
11(1959, 1964)

LONDON SCHOOL OF ECONOMICS AND POLITICAL SCIENCE -
GREATER LONDON GROUP.
Local government in South-East England.
H.M.S.O. 1968.
3,12

MACKENZIE, Donald.
Mayors and Aldermen of Great Britain...edited by D.
Mackenzie.
London, Causton. 1935.
3

THOMAS, R.L.
Kent Police Centenary...edited by R.L. Thomas.
Maidstone, Kent County Constabulary. 1957.
1,2,3,5,7,8,11,12,14,17

TYRWHITT, Jacqueline.
Basic surveys for planning (conference on planning),
edited by J. Tyrwhitt and W.L. Waide.
W. and J. Mackay. 1949.
11

LONGFIELD

ORDNANCE SURVEY OF ENGLAND.
Book of reference to the plan of the parish of Longfield
(Hundred of Oxton) in the County of Kent.
H.M.S.O. 1868.
9

TRANSPORT, Ministry of.
The London traffic - (prohibition of waiting). (Longfield,
Kent) Regulations, 1964.
H.M.S.O.
8

LOOSE

BENNETT, F.J.
(Report on an) excursion to Leeds and the Loose Valley,
Kent, on the 18th June, 1910. (Reprinted from the
Proceedings of the Geologists' Association).
7

Loose and district illustrated almanac for 1889.
Graham. 1889.
12

Loose Court Estate, Maidstone (brochure).
c.1957.
12

M., L.W.
All Saints Church, Loose.
c.1961.
12

REID, Kenneth C.
Watermills and the landscape. (Includes map of Loose
Valley and its mills).
Society for the Preservation of Ancient Buildings. 1959.
3,11

STATHAM, J.C.B.
The romance of a Tudor house (the Manor House, Loose):
restoration and the discovery of its hidden treasures...
Routledge. 1929.
1,4,8,11,12

LOWER HALSTOW

BURCHELL, J.P.T.
A final account of the investigations carried out at
Lower Halstow, Kent. (Extracted from the Proceedings
of the Prehistoric Society of East Anglia).
1928.
4

(KEABLE, Geoffrey).
Some brief notes on the history of Lower Halstow
parish.
1949.
11

ROBINS, Peter Tyndall.
Lower Halstow.
Canterbury, Gibbs. 1962.
11

WRIGHT, A.K.W.
A guide to St. Margaret's, Lower Halstow.
1943.
8

LUDDESDOWNE WITH DODE

DAVIS, D.H.
A description of the parish church of St. Peter and St. Paul,
Luddesdowne with Dode, and a brief historical survey of the
village and ancient church at Dode.
Peter Ness. 1971.
9,11

PEAKE, W. Brian.
Luddesdowne: the story of a Kentish manor.
Maidstone, South-Eastern Gazette. 1920.
5,9,17

PEAKE, W. Brian.
Luddesdowne Court.
Maidston, South-Eastern Gazette. 1930.
4,5(1928) 8,9,11,12,15,17

LULLINGSTONE

DARENT VALLEY ARCHAEOLOGICAL RESEARCH.
Lullingstone Roman Villa. (Season 1949 to 1950).
1950.
2,4

DYKE, Lady M.Z. Hart.
Lullingstone.
(1953?).
2,7

Lullingstone silk farm, 1932-1947.
1947.
5

Silk farm: the wonderful story of silk...
Westchester. 1948.
15

So spins the silkworm.
Rockliff. 1949?
2,3,4,5,7,8,11,12,15,16,19

EVISON, Vera I(vy).
A bronze mount from the Roman Villa at Lullingstone, Kent.
(Reprinted from the Antiquaries Journal, Vol. 46, Part 1,
1966).
4

MEATES, Geoffrey Wells.
Lullingstone Roman Villa, Kent.
Heinemann. 1955.
1,2,4,5,6,7,8,9,11,12,13,16,17,18,19,20

MEATES, Geoffrey Wells.
Lullingstone Roman Villa, Kent. (Ministry of Works - Ancient
Monuments series).
H.M.S.O. 1958.
4,5,11

MEATES, Geoffrey Wells.
Lullingstone Roman Villa, Kent.
H.M.S.O. 1959.
9,11

MEATES, Geoffrey Wells.
Lullingstone Roman Villa, Kent. (Ministry of Works guide books).
H.M.S.O. 1962.
2,3,5,8,11,12,16,18,19

ROBERTSON, William Archibald Scott.
Church of St. Botolph, Lullingstone.
Day and Son. 1899.
5

LYDD

All Saints Parish Church, Lydd - restoration, 1951-1958,
a brief record of what has been done.
Privately Printed. 1958.
11

All Saints Parish Church, Lydd - restoration, 1951-1961.
Canterbury, Gibbs. (1962).
11

(DUKE, E.M.).
Soldiers home in camp Lydd, Kent.
(1916).
7

DUNCAN, Leland Lewis.
Monumental inscriptions in the churchyard...of All
Saints, Lydd.
Kent Archaeological Society. n.d.
1,3,4,7,8,11,12,15,17

FINN, Arthur.
All Saints Church, Lydd.
Rye, Adams. 1927.
11

FINN, Arthur.
Records of Lydd translated and transcribed by Arthur
Hussey and M.M. Hardy, edited by A. Finn.
Ashford, Kentish Express. 1911.
1,3,4,6,7,8,11,12,15,18,21

GELL, Francis.
Lydd Church...
1882.
17

JACKSON, E. Dudley C.
Excavations at the Lydd Basilica, 1966, by E.D.C.
Jackson and E. Fletcher. (Reprinted from the Journal
of the British Archaeological Association, Vol. 31,
3rd series, 1968).
4

JACKSON, E. Dudley C.
The pre-conquest Basilica at Lydd. (Reprinted from the
Journal of the British Archaeological Association,
Vol. 22, 1959).
12

KENT ARCHAEOLOGICAL SOCIETY.
Monumental inscriptions in the churchyard and church of
All Saints, Lydd...
Ashford, Headley Bros. 1927.
8,17

Lydd Airport: gateway to the garden of England.
Constable. n.d.
1

Lydd Church Restoration Fund.
1950.
12

OYLER, Thomas H.
Lydd and its church.
Ashford, Kentish Express. 1894.
1,3,4,5,6,7,11,12,13,14,15,16,17,18

ROPER, Anne.
Borough of Lydd.
Century Press. 1949 etc.
11

LYDDEN

BUCKINGHAM, Christopher.
Lydden: a parish history.
Thomas Becket Books. 1967.
1,3,4,6,8,11,12

VALLANCE, Aymer.
Lydden Church. (Reprinted from Archaeologia Cantiana,
Vol. 43).
Ashford, Headley. 1929.
11,17

LYMINGE

CHARITY COMMISSION.
In the matter of Bedingfield's charity for the benefit of
the parishes of Lyminge, Dymchurch and Smeeth.
(1924).
7

(CLAYSON, J.J.).
Methodist Church, Lyminge, 1894-1944.
(1944?).
7

DAVIS, Arthur W.
A brief history of the church of St. Mary and St. Ethelburga,
Lyminge, compiled by A.W. Davis.
Canterbury, Gibbs. 1929, 1937.
3,7,11

DAVIS, Arthur W.
A brief history of the parish of Lyminge with Paddlesworth.
Canterbury, Gibbs. 1933.
3,4,7,11

Eastbrook Farm, Lyminge, Kent. Particulars and conditions of
sale of freehold farm and dwelling house, situate at Eastbrook in Lyminge...which will be sold by auction, by Mr. R.
Thompson...on September 6th, 1870...
R. Thompson. 1870.
7

Illustrated particulars, plan and conditions of sale of the
Sibton Park Estate, Lyminge, extending to about 476 acres,
including a Queen Anne style residence...(by direction of
W.R.J. Howard Esq.).
Knight, Frank and Rutley. 1933.

JENKINS, Robert Charles.
Acta in Liminae: the history of the basilical and conventual
church of St. Mary and St. Eadburg in Lyminge...
Riley. n.d.
1,7,17

Burial place of St. Ethelburga...in Lyminge (633-643)...
Folkestone, Birch. n.d.
1,7,11,12

Chartulary of the Monastery of Lyminge...
Folkestone, Goulden. n.d.
1,7,11

Chronological summary of the history of the church...of Lyminge.
(1871).
17

A few observations on the Charter of the Duke Oswulf to the
Monastery of Lyminge.
Folkestone, Printed by T. Kentfield. n.d.
3,7,11

A hand guide to the church of St. Mary and St. Eadburg in
Lyminge.
Folkestone, Printed by T. Kentfield. 1896 and 1954.
3,7

Points of interest in the church of St. Mary and St. Ethelburga,
Lyminge...
Folkestone, Cheriton Press.
3(1954) 11(1948) 12(1948)

St. Dunstan and the church of Lyminge.
1881.
17

A short guide to the church of Lyminge and the adjacent remains.
Lyminge, Printed at Ethelburga Press. n.d.
3,7

Some account of the church of St. Mary and St. Eadburg in
Lyminge.
Folkestone, J. English. 1859.
3

PARSONS, Richard Arthur Felix.
Church of St. Mary and St. Ethelburga, Lyminge.
Canterbury, Elvy Bros. Cross and Jackman, Printers.
n.d.
7,11,12,15

Particulars and conditions of sale of the freehold
residential estate known as "Skeete", Lyminge...about
201½ acres (to be sold by auction by) Messrs. Geering
and Colyer...on...31st July, 1934.
Messrs. Geering and Colyer. 1934.
7

LYMPNE

BATTLEY BROS.
Port Lympne: a descriptive guide to the gardens.
(1934?).
7

BLACK, William Henry.
On the identification of the Roman Portus Lemanis.
"Archaeologia". n.d.
11,17

The church of St. Stephen, Lympne.
Ashford, Headley Bros. n.d.
12

History of Lympne and its castle.
Ashford, Headley Bros. (1970).
11

Illustrated particulars and conditions of sale of...the
French House, Lympne...with the gardens and grounds...
extending to about 2½ acres. To be sold by auction...by
Bernard Thorpe and Partners in conjunction with Burrows
and Co...on...12th October, 1965.
(Burrows and Co.). 1965.
7

Lympne Castle - Sale catalogue.
Trollope. 1914.
12

Lympne Castle, Kent.
Ashford, Headley Bros. (1971).
11

MARGARY, D.
History of Lympne and its castle, by D. and H. Margary.
D. and H. Margary. 1965.
7

Particulars, plan and conditions of sale of...Lympne
Airport...which will be offered for sale by auction...
by Messrs. John D. Wood...on 29th April, 1954.
Messrs. John D. Wood. 1954.
7

Particulars, plan and conditions of sale of Lympne
Castle...together with fine old English pleasure gardens
...cottages...farms...about 333 acres. To be sold by
auction...on...10th October, 1917...Vendors - Stow,
Preston and Lyttleton.
(A.J. Burrows). 1917.
7

Particulars and plan of Lympne Castle...about 316
acres. For sale by private treaty. Agents, Messrs.
Knight, Frank and Rutley.
(Knight, Frank and Rutley). (c.1922).
7

LYMPNE Cont'd

Particulars, plan, views and conditions of sale of the
freehold residential estate, Lympne Castle...including a
farm holding, market gardens, accomodation and building lands,
two small residences and seven cottages...Lympne, extending in
all to about 178 acres. To be offered for sale by auction...
on...12th...May, 1932 (by direction of Henry Beecham Esq.).
(Knight, Frank and Rutley). 1932.
7

SASSOON, Sir Philip.
The third route.
Heinemann. 1929.
12

SMITH, Charles Roach.
Antiquities of Richborough, Reculver and Lympne in Kent.
John Russell Smith. 1850.
1,3,4,5,6,7,8,11,12,13,14,15,17,18

SMITH, Charles Roach.
Report on excavations made on the site of the Roman Casturum
at Lympne in Kent in 1850.
London. 1852.
1,4,5,6,8,11,12,15,17,21

LYMPSFIELD

Lympsfield and its environs...
Westerham, H. George. 1838.
11

LYNSTED

VALLANCE, Aymer.
Anchor House, Lynsted.   (Reprinted from Archaeologia Cantiana,
Vol. 55).
Ashford, Headley Bros. n.d.
11,17

VALLANCE, Aymer.
The Ropers and their monuments in Lynsted Church. (Reprinted
from Archaeologia Cantiana, Vol. 44).
Ashford, Headley Bros. 1930.
11,17

MAIDSTONE

Account of the trial...of six witches at Maidstone...1652, to
which is added the trial...of three witches...at Faversham,
1645.
London. 1837.
11

ADAMS, James Whirler Renwick.
A plan for Maidstone, Snodland and West Malling: report on
preliminary proposals.
Kent County Council. 1954.
12

ALL SAINTS' CHURCH, MAIDSTONE.
All Saints' Church, Maidstone (brochure).
British Publishing Co. 1960.
1,8,11,12

All Saints, Maidstone: a short guide to the church, by J.W.
Bridge.
Kent Messenger. 1969.
2,11,12

A Civic service in the parish church of All Saints', Maidstone
for Mayor's Sunday.
1965, 1966, 1967.
12

Documents relating the the parish of All Saints, Maidstone
and its church.
n.d.
12
Form of service for the Institution...and the Induction...of
the Rev. Colin Charles Guy Tufton, M.A., as Vicar of
Maidstone on Wednesday, 17th May, 1967 at 7.30 p.m.
12

A memorial service for Alfred Charles, Lord Bossom of
Maidstone, 16th October, 1881-4th September, 1965.
12

A memorial service for Samuel James Lyle, Honorary Freeman
of the Borough of Maidstone, 15th November, 1965.
12

Notice and minutes of Vestry Minutes, 1870-1881.
12

The order of service in memory of Robert Jesse
Crispin, Mayor of Maidstone - All Saints' Church,
Maidstone, Friday, 9th April, 1965.
12

Order of service in memory of Alderman William George
Sherman, 13th August, 1968.
12

Resolutions made and agreed to by the Church Wardens
of the parish of Maidstone, 17th July, 1797 and recor
of meetings, 1797-1811. Accounts of the poor paid, 9
March, 1814 and an account of Gills Charity.
12

A service of thanksgiving for the life of Sir Winston
Churchill...3rd February, 1965.
12

A service of thanksgiving for the restoration of All
Saints' Church, 11th January, 1967.
12

Short guide to the ancient collegiate and parish chur
of All Saints, Maidstone, by E.H. Hardcastle.
Maidstone, Vivish and Baker. 1909 etc.
4,7,8,17

Short guide to the ancient collegiate and parish chur
of All Saints, Maidstone, by A.O. Standen.
Maidstone, Vivish and Baker. n.d.
12

ALLINGTON CASTLE, MAIDSTONE - a catalogue of the
antique, English and continental furniture, etc. at
Allington Castle, near Maidstone, Kent to be sold by
Messrs. Knight, Frank and Rutley...April 10th 11th and
12th, 1951.
Knight, Frank and Rutley. 1951.
11

Allington Castle guide.
British Legion Press. 196-?
11

ALLPORT, Douglas.
Maidstone: its geology, history, etc.
Maidstone, Hall and Son. 1842.
1,4,8,11,12,15,17

ALLPORT, Douglas.
Summer wanderings in the neighbourhood of Maidstone,
Kent.
Jacques. 1829.
12,17

The Amici (poetry).
Brown. 1836.
12,17

The Argus Municipal Guide, 1904: a pollbook and a
yearbook combined.
'London Argus' Office. 1904.
12

The Aftifex Lodge, 4,555, Province of Kent: list of
members.
1927.
12

The Artifex Lodge, 4,555, Province of Kent: byelaws.
1927.
12

ASPITEL, Arthur.
Observations on baths and wash-houses (includes
Maidstone) by A. Aspitel and J. Whichcord.
Weale. 1862.
11,12

BAKER, Herschel.
William Hazlitt. (William Hazlitt was born in Maidston
and his father was Minister of the Unitarian Church).
Oxford University Press. 1962.
12

BALDI, Sergio.
Sir Thomas Wyatt. (The Wyatt family lived at Allington
Castle).
Longmans. 1961.
12

BALSTON, Thomas.
The housekeeping book of Susanna Whatman, 1776-1800, edited by
Thomas Balston (Vinters Park).
Bles. 1956.
11,12

BATE, James.
An assize sermon preached at Maidstone in Kent on the 13th
March, 1733-4 before the Lord Chief Baron Reynolds.
Whiston. 1734.
12

BATH AND WEST AND SOUTHERN COUNTIES SOCIETY - Maidstone
meeting, 1925.
Bath, William Lewis and Son. 1925.
1

BAVERSTOCK, J.H.
Some account of Maidstone in Kent.
Nicholls. 1832.
1,8,11,12

BELL, John Any Bird. Defendant.
A narrative of the facts relative to the murder of Richard
Faulkner Taylor...and the trial of John Any Bird Bell for the
murder.
1831.
12

BELL, Robert.
Memorials of the Civil War: comprising the correspondence of
the Fairfax family, 2 vols., edited by R. Bell.
Bentley. 1849.
12

Belvidere Lodge, No. 503 - records and byelaws of the Belvidere
Lodge, No. 503 (Maidstone).
Maidstone, Vivish and Baker. 1935.
12

Benefits of Christian education: a general account...for
educating the children of the poor of the town of Maidstone...
remarks by the Rev. James Reeve.
Austen. 1835.
12

Bibliotheca Topographica Britannica, No. 42.
Society of Antiquaries. 1787.
12

BIRCH, Richard.
Proceedings of a general Court Martial...on seven officers of
the West Kent Regiment of Militia...
1807.
11

BIRRELL, Augustine.
William Hazlitt.
Macmillan. 1902.
12

BLAKE, Robert.
Disraeli. (Disraeli was M.P. for Maidstone).
Eyre and Spottiswoode. 1966.
12

BLOOMFIELD, Paul.
Disraeli.
Longmans, Green. 1961.
12

BOORMAN, Henry Roy Pratt.
Pictures of Maidstone.
Kent Messenger. 1965.
1,2,4,5,7,8,10,11,12,15,19,20

BOTTOMLEY, Horatio.
Convict 13.
Paul. n.d.
12

BOUNDARY COMMISSION.
Report on the Borough of Maidstone, 1831 (with map).
12

BRIDGE, John W.
Maidstone: a short guide for visitors.
n.d.
11,12

BRIDGE, John W.
Maidstone geneva: an old Maidstone industry. In
Archaeologia Cantiana, Vol. 65, 1952.
17

BRIDGE, John W.
Thomas Vicary: a famous Maidstone surgeon. In
Archaeologia Cantiana, Vol. 62, 1949.
17

BRIDGE, John W.
Some historical notes on the Basted paper mills.
1948.
11,12

BROWN, J. Publisher.
Maidstone Appendix and Kentish Advertiser...containing
valuable and useful information appertaining to the
town of Maidstone and County of Kent, 1865.
J. Brown. (1864).
12

BROWN, William K
Three letters to the editor of the Maidstone Gazette,
relative to a free trade in corn in Great Britain...
J. Brown. 1826.
12

BUDE, John.
Trouble a-brewing. (A novel set in Maidstone).
MacDonald. 1946.
12

BULTEEL, John.
Relations of the troubles in the three Foreign Churches
in Kent...
Enderbie. 1645.
12

CANTRILL, M.
Maidstone Grammar School.
n.d.
12

CAVE, AUSTIN AND CO. LTD.
Sixty years of trading...1896-1956. (Greengrocers in
Maidstone).
Cave, Austin and Co. Ltd. (1957).
3,12

CAVE-BROWNE, John.
The Fraternity of Corpus Christi, Maidstone.
British Archaeological Society. 1879.
12

CAVE-BROWNE, Rev. John.
History of the parish church of All Saints', Maidstone.
Maidstone, Bunyard. (1889)
1,2,3,4,5,6,7,8,11,12,14,15,17,18

CAVE-BROWNE, Rev. John.
Penenden Heath.
British Archaeological Association. 1891.
6

CHESHIRE FOUNDATION HOMES FOR THE SICK.
The Cheshire Homes: a pictorial record. (Mote House
is a Cheshire Home).
Le Court. 1963.
12

CHILSTON, Eric Alexander Akers-Douglas. 3rd Viscount.
Chief Whip.
Routledge and Kegan Paul. 1961.
12

"CHRISTIAN FRIEND", pseud.
A serious and affectionate address to the inhabitants
of Maidstone...for the purpose of extending the interests
of the Unitarian Societies.
Wickham and Stanhope. 1815.
12

CIVIL DEFENCE CORPS.- KENT DIVISION.
Defence rally, 21st June, 1964 - Mote Park, Maidstone.
Kent Messenger. 1964.
12

CLARK-KENNEDY, A.E.
Edith Cavell: pioneer and patriot. (Edith Cavell nursed in
Maidstone during the outbreak of typhoid in 1897).
Faber. 1965.
12

COLBORNE, Barbara J.
The Maidstone paper industry, with special reference to the
period between about 1750 and 1850. (A handwritten thesis).
(1972).
11

Concise guide to Maidstone with photographic illustrations.
J. Burgiss-Brown. 1883 etc.
12

CONWAY, Agnes Ethel.
Owners of Allington Castle, Maidstone, 1086-1279. In
Archaeologia Cantiana, Vol. 29, 1911.
17

Cornwallis v Barker - Minutes of proceedings...on the trial of
the Parliamentary Election Petition for the Borough of
Maidstone...1901.
11

DALLY, F.F.
An introductory address...on scientific knowledge...at the
Maidstone Mechanics Institution...1836.
Brown. 1836.
12

DAY, Thomas.
Some considerations on the different ways of removing
confined and infectious air...in Maidstone Gaol.
Day. (1784).
12

DENNE, Samuel.
Remarks on the stalls near the Communion Table in Maidstone
Church.
1788.
11,12

DUFF, A.G.
The life work of Lord Avebury, 1834-1913, edited by A.G. Duff.
(M.P. for Maidstone).
Watts. 1924.
12

EATON, Kenneth J.
Newspapers and politics in Canterbury and Maidstone, 1815-1850.
1972.
3

ELLISTON-ERWOOD, Frank Charles.
Around Maidstone.
St. Catherine's Press. 1947.
1,2,4,8,12,15

"EMPLOYER OF LABOUR", pseud.
Report of an evening institution in Kent, by an Employer of
Labour.
W. West. 1857.
11

ENTRACT, J.P.
"Chlorodyne Browne" - Dr. John Collis Browne, 1819-1884.
(From London Hospital Gazette, October, 1970). (Dr. Browne was
born in Maidstone).
12

Essay on character of Sir W. Courteney, Knight of Malta...with
the recent trial of that remarkable individual at Maidstone on
Thursday, July 25th, 1833.
Canterbury, Henry Ward. n.d.
3,6

Evans v Castlereagh - Maidstone Election Petition trial, May
8th-11th, 1906.
Maidstone and Kentish Journal. (1907).
11

FAMILY PLANNING ASSOCIATION - MAIDSTONE BRANCH.
Annual reports, 1961 in progress.
Family Planning Association. 1961 in progress.
12

Fifty years of the Maidstone Club, 1891-1941 (New York).
East Hampton, Rattray. Maidstone Club. (1941).
12

GARDNER-WATERMAN, W.
The early history of the Clerical Society meeting in
Maidstone.
Burkitt. 1927.
12

GEOLOGICAL SURVEY.
Geology of the country around Maidstone.
H.M.S.O. 1963.
7,11,17

GILBERT, Walter B.
The account of the Corpus Christi Fraternity and pape
relating to the antiquities of Maidstone.
Maidstone, Wescomb and Smith. 1865.
4,8,11,12,15,17

GILBERT, Walter B.
Memorials of the collegiate and parish church of All
Saints...Maidstone...
Maidstone, Wescomb and Smith. 1866.
1,8,11,12,15,17

GOODSALL, Robert Harold.
The Astleys of Maidstone. In Archaeologia Cantiana,
Vol. 72, 1958.
17

GRAHAM AND SONS. Publishers.
Illustrated guide to Maidstone and the neighbourhood.
Graham and Sons. 1884.
17

GRAHAM, G.H. Publisher.
Diamond Jubilee: an illustrated record of Queen
Victoria's reign of 60 years. (Maidstone's celebrati
G.H. Graham. 1897.
12

GRAHAM, G.H. Publisher.
Graham's Maidstone almanack, 1877-1900.
G.H. Graham. (1900).
12

GRAHAM, G.H. Publisher.
Temperance almanack and yearbook for 1899.
G.H. Graham. (1899).
12

GRAHAM, G.H. Publisher.
The Temperance worker and biographical treasury.
G.H. Graham. 1899-1901.
12

GREAT BRITAIN: LAWS, etc. (GEO. II).
An Act to enable the Justices of the Peace...to purch
convenient piece of ground for building a gaol in the
county...
1736.
11,12

GREAT BRITAIN: LAWS, etc. (GEO. III).
An Act for the better government and regulation of th
poor in the town and parish of Maidstone.
1781.
11

GREAT BRITAIN: LAWS, etc. (GEO. III).
An Act for the better government and regulation of th
poor in the town and parish of Maidstone...
n.d.
11

GREAT BRITAIN: LAWS, etc. (GEO. III).
An Act for the better government and regulation of th
poor...of Maidstone...1779.
Eyre and Strahan. 1780.
12

GREAT BRITAIN: LAWS, etc. (GEO. III).
An Act for enabling the Commissioners...an Act for
widening...places within the King's Town of Maidstone
1796.
11

GREAT BRITAIN: LAWS, etc. (GEO. III).
An Act for widening, improving...places within the
King's Town of Maidstone...
1761.
11

GREAT BRITAIN: LAWS, etc. (GEO. III).
An Act to alter and enlarge the powers of an Act...for
the better government...of the poor in the town and
parish of Maidstone.
1805.
11

GREAT BRITAIN: LAWS, etc. (GEO. IV).
An Act for erecting new market places in the town of
Maidstone...1824.
H.M.S.O. 1824.
12

GREAT BRITAIN: LAWS, etc. (ELIZ. II).
Maidstone Corporation Act.
H.M.S.O. 1955.
4,8

GREAT BRITAIN: LAWS, etc. (ELIZ. II).
Maidstone Corporation (Trolley Vehicles) Order Confirmation
Act, 1958.
4

GREAT BRITAIN: LAWS, etc. (ELIZ. II).
Maidstone Corporation (Trolley Vehicles) Provisional Order Bill.
H.M.S.O. 1962.
8

GREAT BRITAIN: LAWS, etc. (ELIZ. II).
Maidstone Corporation (Trolley Vehicles) Order Confirmation
Act.
H.M.S.O. 1962.
4,8

GREAT BRITAIN: LAWS, etc. (ELIZ. II) - STATUTORY INSTRUMENTS.
The Maidstone Corporation (Trolley Vehicles) Order, 1964.
H.M.S.O. 1964.
12

GREAT BRITAIN: LAWS, etc. (ELIZ. II) - STATUTORY INSTRUMENTS.
Maidstone Water Order, 1967.
H.M.S.O. 1967.
12

The Great Brunswick Meeting on Penenden Heath, October 24th,
1828. (See also the Kent County Meeting).
Smith. 1829.
11,17

GREW, B.D.
Prison Governor.
Jenkins. 1958.
12

GRIFFIN, Ralph.
Kentish items: West Malling, Hythe, Denton, Allington, Elham,
Bekesbourne.
n.d.
7

GROOM, J.B.
A Maidstone naturalist's rambles...1903 to March, 1904.
Maidstone, South-Eastern Gazette. 1904.
6,8,11,12,17

GURNEY, Joseph.
The whole genuine proceedings at the Assize...held at
Maidstone, the 11th-14th March, 1766...taken in shorthand by
Joseph Gurney.
W. Nicoll. (1766).
12

The handy directory and guide for Maidstone and the surrounding
villages.
Vivish. 1872.
12

Handy guide to Maidstone and neighbourhood.
Maidstone, Bunyard. n.d.
11

Handy guide to Maidstone and neighbourhood, prefaced by...
Chillington Manor House.
Burgiss-Brown. 1887.
11

HARRISON, Benjamin.
Charges to the clergy of Maidstone, 1883-1886.
17

HARRISON, Benjamin.
Church-rate abolition in its latest form: a charge
delivered...at Maidstone...in May, 1855.
Rivington. 1855.
12

HARRISON, Benjamin.
The remembrance of a departed guide and ruler in the
Church of God: a charge delivered...at Maidstone...in
May, 1848.
Rivington. 1848.
12

HONYWOOD, Lady Frances.
Memorial of the Hon. Lady Honywood. (See Faversham).
Gosnell. 1812.
11

HORNIBROOK, S.
The sale of livings: a paper read at a meeting of the
Maidstone Branch of the Church Defence Association,
2nd edition. (Photocopy).
Maidstone, J.O. Wilkie...1873.
11

HOUSING AND LOCAL GOVERNMENT, Ministry of.
The Maidstone Water (Charges) Order, 1959.
H.M.S.O. 1960.
12

HOWE, P.P.
Life of William Hazlitt.
Hamilton. 1947.
12

(HOWLETT, Rev. John).
Observations on the increased population...of Maidstone.
1782.
11

Indenture between Samuel Cotton and Charles Baker
Senior, Charles Baker Junior and Knowles King, December
4th, 1854.
12

The Index, October 31st, 1889, containing article on
Maidstone as an insurance centre.
Index Publishing Co. 1889.
12

The indictment, arraigment, trial and judgement, at
large, of 29 regicides...
1713.
12

Industries of Maidstone.
Maidstone Standard. 1881.
12

An inventory and valuation of the effects at the Parish
Workhouse, Maidstone, between the Trustees of the
Parish and the Governor, Mr. Sam Sloman, 7th October,
1836. (MSS.).
12

Inventory book of bedding, etc. removed from the
temporary hospitals...
n.d.
12

JACOMB, W.
The King and Kingdom safe...a sermon preached at
Maidstone, November 5th, 1722.
Matthews. 1723.
12

JAMES, William Roberts.
The Charters...relating to...Maidstone...edited by
W.R. James.
Butterworth. 1825.
1,3,8,11,12,15,17

JOHNSON, J.W.
Lamps of the Maidstone Temple...
Leamington, D. Sarney. n.d.
6,8,11,12

JOHNSON, John.
Reasons why vice ought to be punished, but is not, in
a sermon preached at Maidstone...March 17th, 1707-8.
Hive. 1708.
12

JOYCE, J.
Trolleybus trails.
Ian Allen. 1963.
12

KEARTON, Richard.
A naturalist's pilgrimage. (Author connected with Maidstone).
Cassell. 1926.
12

KENT CLUB, MAIDSTONE
Rules and regulations, with list of members.
1881.
17

KENT COUNTY CONSTABULARY.
Programme of centenary parade and exhibitions to be held at
County Police Headquarters at Maidstone.
Maidstone, Kent County Constabulary. 1957.
3

KENT COUNTY COUNCIL - PLANNING DEPARTMENT.
Kent development plan: Maidstone and vicinity with town map.
Kent County Council. 1954.
11,12

Kent County Meeting: a report of the speeches delivered...
on Penenden Heath, 1828. (See also The Great Brunswick Meeting,
October, 24th, 1828).
Ridgway. 1828.
1,3,11,12

KENT COUNTY OPHTHALMIC HOSPITAL.
Annual reports, 1878-1924.
Kent County Ophthalmic Hospital. 1878-1924.
12

Report of the Board of Management at the 7th Annual General
Meeting on March 15th, 1854.
Maidstone, Cutbush. 1854.
11

Report of the Board of Management...: an account of the
receipts and expenditure with the medical report for the year
ending 31st December, 1866.
Kent County Ophthalmic Hospital. 1867.
12

KENT EDUCATION COMMITTEE.
Maidstone College of Art, 1894-1970.
Kent County Council. (1970).
11,12

Maidstone Technical High School for Boys, 1917-1968.
Kent County Council. (1968).
11,12

KENT EDUCATION COMMITTEE - MAIDSTONE DIVISION.
Maidstone Education Week handbook, 1958.
Kent County Council. (1958).
11,12

The Kent Messenger and Maidstone Telegraph popular calendar.
Kent Messenger. 1898.
12

Kentish fragments gleaned from the hustings on Penenden
Heath...
Gravesend, R. Pocock. 1802.
1

The Kentish men: a satire..
1701.
12

KERSHAW, S. Wayland.
On manuscripts and rare books in the Maidstone Museum.
1877.
12

KILLICK, Charles.
A short history of the Kent County Ophthalmic Hospital.
Vivish and Baker. 1913.
12

LABOUR, Ministry of.
Maidstone Employment Exchange: souvenir brochure and
pamphlets.
H.M.S.O. 1966.
12

LAMB, Henry.
Flora of Maidstone.
1889.
17

LAMPREY, Arthur Sidney.
Episodes in the history of Maidstone.
Maidstone, Dickinson. 1910.
11,12

LAMPREY, Arthur Sidney.
Guide to the Borough of Maidstone, edited by A.S.
Lamprey.
Maidstone, Ruck. 1914 etc.
3,5,7,11,12

L(AMPREY), S.C.
Brief historical and descriptive account of Maidstone..
Maidstone, J. Brown. 1834.
1,3,8,11,12,15,17

LANCEFIELD, Arthur P.
Maidstone: past and present.
G.H. Graham. n.d.
12

LARGE, Samuel.
Recovery of lands in the parish of Maidstone, by S.
Large and T. Trebbutt.
1814.
12

The life of William Shipley, 1715-1803, Part XIII -
marriage and Maidstone, 1767-1786. (From Journal of
the Royal Society of Arts, September, 1966).
12

LOADES, D.M.
Two Tudor conspiracies.
Cambridge University Press. 1965.
7,11,15

McCARTHY, Elizabeth.
Apology and retraction. (Appendix to Joshua Waddington
"A plain statement...").
n.d.
11

MACDONALD, W.A.
Ireland as it is: a lecture delivered by W.A. Macdonald
in the Corn Exchange, Maidstone, 1886.
12

MACGIBBON, David.
Elizabeth Woodville (1437-1492): her life and times.
Barker. 1938.
12

MACGILLIVRAM, G.J.
Through the East to Rome.
Oates. 1931.
12

MACLEAN, C.M.
Born under Saturn.
Collins. 1943.
12

MACLEAN, C.M.
Hazlitt: painted by himself.
Temple. 1948.
12

MAIDSTONE AMATEUR PHOTOGRAPHIC SOCIETY.
Minute book, 1891-1896. (MS.).
12

MAIDSTONE AND DISTRICT CHAMBER OF COMMERCE.
Maidstone: the official guide authorised by the
Maidstone Chamber of Commerce.
Burrows. 192-?
12

MAIDSTONE AND DISTRICT CHAMBER OF COMMERCE.
Report by the Planning and Traffic Committee of the
Chamber on the preliminary draft town centre plan.
Maidstone and District Chamber of Commerce. 1968.
12

MAIDSTONE AND DISTRICT COUNCIL OF CHURCHES.
Maidstone: a closer look - a review of social services...
Maidstone and District Council of Churches. 1965.
3,11,12

MAIDSTONE AND DISTRICT COUNCIL OF CHURCHES.
Recommended constitution for a Maidstone Council of
Churches. (Typescript).
n.d.
12

MAIDSTONE AND DISTRICT CREMATORIUM JOINT COMMITTEE.
Vinters Park Crematorium and Garden of Remembrance.
Maidstone and District Crematorium Joint Committee. n.d.
12

MAIDSTONE AND DISTRICT MARRIAGE GUIDANCE COUNCIL.
A report on the work of the Maidstone and District Marriage
Guidance Council, 1960-61.
Maidstone and District Marriage Guidance Council. 1961.
12

MAIDSTONE AND DISTRICT MARRIAGE GUIDANCE COUNCIL.
A short report of the work of the Council.
Maidstone and District Marriage Guidance Council. 1957.
12

MAIDSTONE AND DISTRICT PRODUCTIVITY COMMITTEE.
The 1970's.
British Legion Press. 1966.
12

MAIDSTONE AND DISTRICT YOUTH LEADERS' COUNCIL.
Maidstone and District Youth Festival, May 21st-30th, 1965 -
official programme.
Maidstone and District Youth Leaders' Council. 1965.
12

MAIDSTONE AND KENT COUNTY STANDARD.
Almanack for 1880...
1

MAIDSTONE AREA YOUTH COUNCIL.
Report on the Maidstone Public Library, 1946.
Maidstone Area Youth Council. 1946.
12

MAIDSTONE ART CLUB.
Annual exhibition, 1959. Bentlif Gallery, Maidstone, 29th
September to 31st October: catalogue of exhibits.
(195-?).
12

MAIDSTONE BAND OF HOPE.
Documents relating to Maidstone Band of Hope, 1860. (MS.).
12

MAIDSTONE BOROUGH COUNCIL.
Abstract of accounts, 1903 to date.
12

Analysis of road accidents in 1963.
8

Baths service.
n.d.
12

Borough of Maidstone official guide, 1930.
17

Borough of Maidstone official guide.
Ashford, Redmans. 1950-1959.
5,8,11,12

Borough of Maidstone official guide, by L.R.A. Grove and
Alfred Joyce.
Maidstone Borough Council. 1963-1973.
3,4,8,11,12,19

Catalogue of the Civic Exhibition at the Town Hall, Maidstone,
14th-20th July, 1951.
Maidstone Borough Council. (1951).
12

Catalogue of the fourth centenary exhibition, 2nd-9th July,
1949.
Vivish and Baker. 1949.
11

Census enumerator's book, 1801. (MSS.).
12

Coronation Day, 1902. People's sports and fete -
souvenir programme.
Maidstone Borough Council. 1902.
12

The Coronation of King Edward VII, 1902 - official
programme and posters.
Maidstone Borough Council. 1902.
12

Corporation and Urban District Council, 1900.
Maidstone Borough Council. 1900.
12

Corporation yearbooks, 2 vols. 1901-1902, 1901-1903.
Maidstone Borough Council.
12

Draft town centre map.
Maidstone Borough Council. 1968.
12

Estimates for general district rate of the half year
ending 30th September, 1903 and borough rate for the
year ending 31st March, 1904.
Maidstone Borough Council. 1903.
12

Estimates for general district rate for the half year
ending 30th September, 1906 and borough rate for the
half year ending 31st March, 1907.
Maidstone Borough Council. 1907.
12

Estimates for general district rate for the half year
ending 30th September, 1908 and borough rate for the
year ending 31st March, 1909.
Maidstone Borough Council. 1909.
12

Estimates for general district rate and borough rate for
the year ending 31st March, 1913.
Maidstone Borough Council. 1912.
12

Estimates for general district rate and borough rate for
the year ending 31st March, 1914.
Maidstone Borough Council. 1914.
12

General rate estimates, 1971-72.
Maidstone Borough Council. 1971.
12

Handbook for the use of old people, containing
information of services available in the Borough, 1967.
Maidstone Borough Council. 1967.
12

Illustrated souvenir of the electricity works opened
on Thursday, December 19th, 1901.
Dickinson. 1901.
12

Local War Emergency Committee.
Maidstone Borough Council. 1914.
12

Maidstone (1549-1949) official Charter brochure,
edited by R.V. Hewett.
Maidstone Borough Council. 1949.
1,4,7,8,11,12,15

Maidstone, Kent: an appreciation of the town...by
Ethel Williamson. (The Corporation's official guide).
Homeland Association Ltd. (1909).
4

The Maidstone Municipal Diary, 1949 in progress.
Maidstone Borough Council.
12

Motorists' guide: parking meter scheme, Maidstone.
Maidstone Borough Council. 1964.
12

Municipal tenants' handbook.
British Publishing Co. (1958).
12

Observations on the Medway Gap preliminary draft town
map. (Typescript).
Maidstone Borough Council. n.d.
12

Observations on the preliminary draft town map for
Maidstone and vicinity. (Typescript).
Maidstone Borough Council. n.d.
12

MAIDSTONE BOROUGH COUNCIL.
The opening of the New Bridge, Maidstone. Programme for
Wednesday, August 6th, 1879...
Maidstone Borough Council. 1879.
12

Presentation of the Honorary Freedom of the Borough to the
Right Honourable Lord Cornwallis, K.B.E., M.C., Her Majesty's
Lieutenant for the County of Kent, Wednesday, 14th March, 1962.
12

Presentation of the Honorary Freedom of the Borough to
Alderman Dorothy Mabel Relf at the Town Hall, Maidstone,
Wednesday, 5th April, 1961. Order of Proceedings.
12

Presentation of the Honorary Freedom of the Borough to the
Corps of Royal Engineers at Invicta Park, Maidstone on
Saturday, 8th May, 1965.
12

The Queen's Diamond Jubilee, 1897 - local celebration
(programme).
Maidstone Borough Council. 1897.
12

Records of Maidstone: being selections from documents in the
possession of the Corporation.
Hobbs. 1926.
1,3,4,7,8,11,12

Report on road management and materials...by the Borough
Surveyor, August 18th, 1886.
Vivish. 1886.
12

Report to the Local Board on outbreaks of smallpox in Maidstone,
by Matthew Algernon Adams.
Vivish. 1881.
12

Report upon Thorner's Yard, Upper Stone Street, by Matthew
Algernon Adams.
Dickinson. 1899.
12

Reports on the various officers of the Borough, 1903-5, 1909-13,
7 vols.
Maidstone Borough Council.
12

Swimming baths, Mote Park - plans.
Maidstone Borough Council. 1964.
12

Transfer of the Honorary Freedom of the Borough to the Queen's
Own Buffs, The Royal Kent Regiment, at the Barracks, Maidstone
on Saturday, 20th May, 1962.
12

Well waters: special report upon well supplying 14 and 15
Paradise Row, Maidstone.
Dickinson. n.d.
12

MAIDSTONE BOROUGH COUNCIL - EDUCATION COMMITTEE.
Handbook of the Education Week held in Maidstone from March
14th to 20th, 1926.
Maidstone Borough Council - Education Committee. 1926.
13

Survey of the system of education at present existing in the
Borough of Maidstone, together with a draft scheme in
connection with the Education Act, 1910.
Maidstone Borough Council - Education Committee. 1918.
12

Triennial report for the period ended 30th November, 1906.
Walter Ruck. 1907.
12

MAIDSTONE BOROUGH COUNCIL - HEALTH DEPARTMENT.
Annual Reports of the Medical Officer of Health for 1887, 1890,
1893, 1905, 1911, 1912, 1913, 1957 in progress.
12

MAIDSTONE BOROUGH COUNCIL - MUSEUM AND LIBRARY COMMITTEE.
Estimate for museum and library for the year ending 31st March,
1909 and report of the Museum and Library Committee.
Maidstone Borough Council. 1909.
12

Reports of the Curator and Librarian for the year ending
October 31st, 1901-1908.
Maidstone Borough Council. 1908.
12

Reports of Museum and Library Committee, 1897/8,
1901/10.
Maidstone Borough Council.
12

MAIDSTONE BOROUGH COUNCIL - TRANSPORT COMMITTEE.
Timetable and fare table including all service
alterations up to 19th August, 1963.
Maidstone Corporation. 1963.
12

Timetable and fare table...19th August, 1963 and 16th
April, 1967.
Maidstone Corporation. 1963 and 1967.
12

Timetable and fare table up to 15th October, 1967.
Maidstone Borough Council. 1967.
12

Transport undertaking: abstract of accounts, 1961-62.
Maidstone Borough Council. (1962).
12

MAIDSTONE CHORAL UNION.
Fifty years of singing: a short history of the
Maidstone Choral Union, 1902-1952.
Kent Messenger. 1953.
11,12

MAIDSTONE CHURCH INSTITUTE.
Reports for the years 1884, 1888, 1891, 1895, 1889-97.
Vivish. 1884-97.
12

MAIDSTONE CHURCH INSTITUTE AND Y.M.C.A.
Centenary year, 1854-1954 and winter programme, 1954-5.
Clout and Baker. 1954.
12

Handbook and programme, 1957-58.
Maidstone Church Institute and Y.M.C.A. 1957.
12

Winter programme, 1950-51.
Clout and Baker. 1950.
12

Winter season, 1952-53: programme booklet.
1952.
12

MAIDSTONE CHURCHES.
Church and watch rate books, 1824-1899, 36 vols. (MSS
12

Letters and documents relating to Maidstone churches,
1870.
12

Maidstone church accounts and other manuscripts regard
the churches of Maidstone Parish. (MS.).
1842-49.
12

MAIDSTONE CRICKET WEEK CHARITY COMMITTEE.
Maidstone's Gala Month. Maidstone Cricket Week
Charities programme, July, 1959.
Maidstone Cricket Week Charity Committee. 1959.
12

Maidstone Cricket and Carnival Week programmes, 1951,
1953-1958.
Maidstone Cricket Week Charity Committee. 1953-8.
12

MAIDSTONE DISPENSARY.
First report of the...Maidstone Dispensary for 1830.
1831.
17

MAIDSTONE DIVISION CONSERVATIVE ASSOCIATION.
Year book, 1966-67.
Maidstone Division Conservative Association. 1966.
12

Maidstone election petitions. (For details - See
Elections).

MAIDSTONE FILM SOCIETY.
(Programme) 1961/2, 1962/3, 1965/6 to date.
Maidstone Film Society. 1966.
12

MAIDSTONE FOOTBALL CLUB.
A history of the Maidstone Football Club, R.U. and K.C.R.F.U.,
1880-1954.
Kent and Sussex Advertising Service. 1955.
12

MAIDSTONE GRAMMAR SCHOOLS.
Maidstone Grammar School, 1549-1949.
Alabaster Passmore. 1949?
4,8,11

Maidstone Grammar School, 1549-1965: a record (revised and
enlarged by G.B. Phillips).
Maidstone, The Grammar School. 1965.
8,11,12

Maidstone Grammar School, 1549-1965...edited by G.B. Phillips
and N.W. Newcombe.
Ashford, Headley Bros. 1966.
1,4,11,12

School lists: 1883-1897, 1884-1886, 1889-1900.
Maidstone Grammar School. 1897 and 1900.
12

Maidstone Grammar School Scout Group, 1914-1954, edited by
N.W. Newcombe.
Maidstone Grammar School Scout Group. 1955.
4,8,11,12

Maidstone Grammar School for Girls, 1888-1969.
Maidstone Grammar School for Girls. 1969.
12

MAIDSTONE GRAMOPHONE SOCIETY.
Programmes: September, 1965-January, 1966. 1966/67 to date.
12

Maidstone Journal and Kentish Advertiser, Tuesday, April 11th,
1820.
11

MAIDSTONE LITERARY INSTITUTION.
Rules and regulations...passed at a general meeting of the
subscribers held on the 25th June, 1832.
Maidstone, Henry Ottaway. 1832.
12

MAIDSTONE LOCAL GOVERNMENT BOARD.
Byelaws made by the Local Government Board of the Borough of
Maidstone on the 15th day of January, 1867...
J. Brown. 1867.
12

Maidstone Magazine, Vol. 2, 1916.
1917.
11

MAIDSTONE MUSEUM AND ART GALLERY.
Catalogue of the books in the library of the Maidstone Museum,
Chillington House, compiled by W.J.L.
Vivish. 1875.
12,17

Catalogue of the books in the library of the Maidstone Museum,
Chillington House.
Burgiss-Brown. 1886.
11,12,15

Chillington Manor House: short descriptive guide. (Reprinted
from the South-Eastern Gazette).
1925.
4,12,17

Chillington Manor House, Maidstone and visitor's guide to the
Museum, 1887, by J.H. Allchin.
12

Chronological history of Museum, Public Library and Bentlif
Art Gallery (bound with Kershaw. On manuscripts and rare books
in the museum).
Maidstone Borough Council. n.d.
12

The fishes, amphibians and reptiles of the Maidstone area, by
R. Millichamp and T. Tynan. (Handlist series No. 1).
1956.
4,12

Guide to the collections...with notes on the history of
Chillington Manor House.
Maidstone, W.P. Dickinson. 1909.
11,17

Guide to the collections in the geological and mineral galleries.
Maidstone, W.P. Dickinson. 1909.
5

The guide to the Maidstone Museum prefaced by the
history and antiquities of Chillington Manor House.
Burgiss-Brown. 1879.
3(1887) 7,12

Guide to Maidstone Museum...and history of Chillington
Manor House.
Maidstone Borough Council. 1887.
17

Maidstone Museum and Art Gallery.
Vivish and Baker. n.d.
12

Museum, Public Library and Bentlif Art Gallery: a
brief illustrated description, together with a
catalogue of the Bentlif Collection, 1894 and 1901.
Maidstone Borough Council. 1894 and 1901.
3,12

Museum of carriages at the Archbishop's Stables,
Mill Street. (The Tyrwhitt-Drake Collection).
Kent Messenger. 194-? etc.
7,8,11,12

Museum of carriages at the Archbishop's Stables, Mill
Street, Maidstone - official guide, 3rd edition. (The
Tyrwhitt-Drake Collection).
Maidstone Borough Council. 1966 etc.
12,17

Notes on the history of Chillington Manor House...with
an epitome of the collection.
Maidstone, Hobbs. 1919.
4,11,12,15

Notes on the Kentish collections in the County Room
of Maidstone Museum.
Maidstone Borough Council. 1909.
5,11,17,19

Notes on recent additions to the collections, by the
Curator.
South-Eastern Gazette. 1922.
12

Rules for the management of Museum, Public Library and
Bentlif Art Gallery, 1896.
Maidstone Borough Council. 1896.
12

Rules of Maidstone Museum, 1873.
Maidstone Borough Council.
11,12

Ten lectures on Artizano at the Maidstone Museum, 1881-
1882.
'Standard'. 1882.
12

Visit of the Royal Agricultural Society in 1899 to the
Museum and Art Gallery and a brief guide.
1899.
17

MAIDSTONE PAVEMENT COMMISSIONERS.
Proposed supply of water to the town of Maidstone:
report to the commissioners by Messrs. Whichcord and
Son and Mr. Martin Bulmer.
Wickham and Son. 1852.
12

Proposed supply of water to the town of Maidstone:
report by the Committee to the Maidstone Pavements
Commissioners and the reports of Mr. Hawksley and
Mr. Spencer.
F.W. and H.R. Cutbush. 1855.
12

Proposed supply of water to the town of Maidstone...
Committee of Maidstone Pavements. 1858.
11

MAIDSTONE PERSONAL SERVICE SOCIETY AND CITIZENS'
ADVICE BUREAU.
Annual report, 1952-53, 1958-59, 1960-61.
Maidstone Personal Service Society and Citizens'
Advice Bureau. 1959, 1961.
12

MAIDSTONE PRISON.
Gaol calendar, 1825.
17
Rules and regulations for the government of the gaol
at Maidstone, 1825.
17

MAIDSTONE PUBLIC LIBRARY.
Brief guide to the use of the libraries, with particular reference to the use of the catalogue and classification scheme.
Maidstone Public Library. 1965.
12

Central Library: an introduction to the new building.
Kent Messenger. 1963.
12

Make time to read: books for the home library.
Maidstone Public Library. 1966.
12

Rules and regulations for the public library, 1948.
Maidstone Borough Council. 1948.
12

Rules of Maidstone Public Lending Library, 1890.
Maidstone Borough Council. 1890.
12

Supplements representing additions to stock.
1894-1918.
12

Victoria Library: catalogue of books in the lending department, together with the rules and regulations.
Dickinson. 1893-1896.
12

Victoria Library: catalogue of books, together with the rules and regulations.
Dickinson. 1901.
12

Victoria Library: list of books in the juvenile department, 1910, 1912, 1914 - 3 parts.
Young and Cooper. 1910, 1912 and 1914.
12

MAIDSTONE ROAD SAFETY COMMITTEE.
Borough of Maidstone road safety handbook.
John Morris. 1957.
12

MAIDSTONE SCHOOL OF ART ART AND SCIENCE.
Report, 1890-1891, 2 vols.
Cutbush. 1890-1891.
12

MAIDSTONE SCHOOL BOARD.
Report...of the last three years, 1894.
Dickinson. 1894.
12

MAIDSTONE SUBSCRIPTION BAND.
Programme for grand illuminated Tivoli Promenade Concert at the Corn Exchange and Concert Hall, Maidstone on Wednesday evening, November 30th, 1892 at 7.00 p.m.
Dickinson. 1892.
12

MAIDSTONE THEATRE.
Four playbills for 1817.
12

MAIDSTONE TRADESMENS' £100 PROVIDENT SOCIETY.
Rules and regulations...1842.
Hall and Low. 1845.
11

MAIDSTONE TRUSTEES OF THE POOR.
A list of persons receiving parochial relief in the parish of Maidstone in the County of Kent, November 6th, 1833.
Maidstone Trustees of the Poor. (1833).
12

MAIDSTONE UNION.
Account books, 1816/7, 1823-25, 1825-27.
12

An account of the income and expenditure...of the Maidstone Union during each of the years 1836 to 1845...
J. Smith. 1846.
12

An account of the receipts and expenditure incurred in the maintenance of the poor of the parish of Maidstone (for the year 31st March, 1825 to 31st March, 1826). (Broadsheets).
12

Admittance and discharge register, 1817-20.
12

Cash book, 14th November, 1846-5th August, 1857.
12

Committee book, 1848-63.
12

Half yearly balance sheet, September, 1848-1879. (MS.)
12

House accounts, 1822-36.
12

Labourers employed on Barming Heath, 1818.
12

Labourers employed on Penenden Heath, 1818.
12

Letter books, 1817-34, 1834-60.
12

Loddington county rate receipt and payment book, 1873-
12

Maidstone poor-house sick reports, 1815-28.
12

Maidstone poor rate collecting and deposit book, 1914.
12

Minute books, 1821-25, 1829-36, 1838-82, 1882-1901, 1902-10.
12

Poor law cash book, 1820-54.
12

Poor rate collection book, 1830-36.
12

Provisions ledger, 1816-22.
12

Rate assessment book.
n.d.
12

Rate assessment for the relief of the poor, 1824-27, 1827-8, 1839-40, 1841-42, 1845-6.
12

Rate book, 1909-10.
12

Record book.
n.d.
12

Register of removals, 1764-1819, 1828-31.
12

Relief day books, September, 1822-May, 1826; June, 1826 March, 1829; April, 1833-July, 1834; July, 1834-June, 1839.
12

Ticket books, 1817-18, 1825-30.
12

Valuation of the parish of Maidstone, 1853.
12

MAIDSTONE UNION WORKHOUSE TRUSTEES SUB-COMMITTEE.
Minutes of the Sub-Committee, 7th June, 1824-1st March, 1836.
12

MAIDSTONE URBAN DISTRICT COUNCIL.
Annual statement of receipts and payments, 1895-96, 1896-97, 1899-1900.
Dickinson.
12

Typhoid epidemic accounts, 1897-8.
Young and Cooper. 1898.
12

MAIDSTONE URBAN SANITARY AUTHORITY.
Annual statement of receipts and payments from 1890-91 and 1891-92.
Young and Cooper.
12

A list of mortgages...showing those paid off and those remaining due on 10th November, 1884.
Vivish. 1884.
12

MAIDSTONE WATERWORKS CO.
Account of Hockers Lane pumping station.
1956.
12

MAIDSTONE WATERWORKS CO.
Centenary brochure: 14th June, 1960, compiled by C.H. Harden.
Maidstone Waterworks Co. (1960).
12

Commemorative brochure, compiled by C.H. Harden.
Maidstone Waterworks Co. 1955.
12

Rules, regulations and charges.
Dickinson. 1884.
12

Scale of quarterly charges...
Maidstone, Vale. 1861.
11

Maidstone election petition trial, May 8th to 16th, 1906:
report of proceedings.
Maidstone and Kentish Journal. 1906.
1

Maidstone: features of historical interest and picturesque
views of the borough and neighbourhood.
(c.1902).
12

Maidstone High Street in the Fifties.
Kent Messenger. 1902.
7

Maidstone in 1892, illustrated: its history, manufactures
and trade.
Robinson, Son and Pike. 1892.
12

Maidstone Orders of Afiliation, 1820-34.
12

Maidstone peace souvenir, 1919.
South-Eastern Gazette. 1919.
12

MASLIN, W.
Complaint to the police alleging that Mary Lewis kept a
bawdy house, 1878, by W. Maslin and J. Burridge. (MS.).
1878.
12

MATHEW, Theobald.
Father Mathew, the great apostle of Temperance.
Graham. 1890.
12

MAUPASSANT, George.
His wife, translated by Marjorie Laurie. Designed and
produced in the Department of Printing, Maidstone.
1950.
3

MAUROIS, Andre.
Disraeli: a picture of the Victorian age.
Bodley Head. 1927.
12

Memoir of the Rev. H.H. Dobrey, Maidstone.
1884.
11

MILLS, Benjamin.
An account of a controversy between the Rev. Samuel Weller and
Benjamin Mills...
Oswald. 1741.
11

MILLS, Benjamin.
An examination of the remarks made by a curate of the diocese
of Canterbury on the account of a controversy between the
author of the "Trial of Mr. Whitefield's Spirit" and
Benjamin Mills...
Oswald. 1741.
11,12

MILLS, Benjamin.
The nature, extent and right improvement of Christian
liberty...
Oswald. 1741.
11

"MR. PUNCH".
Benjamin Disraeli, Earl of Beaconsfield, K.G. in
upwards of 100 cartoons from the collections of
"Mr. Punch". (Disraeli was M.P. for Maidstone).
Punch. 1878.
12

MOTE CRICKET CLUB.
Look to your Mote, 1857-1957.
Kent Messenger. 1957.
12

MUGGERIDGE, Sidney John.
A comparative directory of the principal streets of
Maidstone, 1905 and 1965. (Typescript).
1966.
12

MUGGERIDGE, Sidney John.
The postal history of Maidstone and the surrounding
villages, with notes on their postal markings.
Postal History Society. 1972.
3,4,9,11

MUIR, Kenneth.
Life and letters of Sir Thomas Wyatt.
Liverpool University Press. 1963.
12

MUNICIPAL CORPORATION BOUNDARIES (ENGLAND AND WALES).
Report of the proposed municipal boundary and division
into wards of the borough of Maidstone.
(1837).
12

NATIONAL ASSOCIATION OF LOCAL GOVERNMENT OFFICERS.
Book exhibition arranged jointly by Kent County Library
and Maidstone Public Library...29th March-3rd April,
1965: programme. (Typescript).
12

Impact, June, 1963. (Maidstone Branch).
National Association of Local Government Officers -
Maidstone Branch. 1963.
12

Welcome to citizenship, 1967 to date. (Maidstone
Branch).
Pyramid Press.
12

NATIONAL PROVINCIAL BANK LTD.
The Kentish Bank, Maidstone, 1818-1968.
National Provincial Bank Ltd. 1968.
12

National Temperance Hymnal.
Graham. 1904.
12

NEWTON, William.
The history and antiquities of Maidstone.
London. 1741.
1,3,4,5,6,7,8,11,12,17

"NOBODY", pseud.
A word to the wise!!
Printed in Maidstone. n.d.
12

OAKWOOD HOSPITAL.
The history of Oakwood Hospital, Maidstone (pamphlet).
H.F. Reed. 1969.
12

Oakwood Hospital Magazine, Vol. 1, No. 1-Vol. 2, No.
2: March, 1963-December, 1964.
Oakwood Hospital. 1963-64.
12

Observations on the increased population, healthiness,
etc., of the town of Maidstone.
Blake. 1782.
12

OLD BARN ORCHESTRAL SOCIETY.
A history of the Old Barn Orchestral Society (Maidstone),
1927-70.
Old Barn Orchestral Society. (1970).
11

OLD MAIDSTONIAN SOCIETY.
Rule book and list of members.
1930.
12

The original Kentish appendix and Maidstone and County
annual, being a yearbook...
Maidstone, Burgiss-Brown.
3(1890) 11(1894) 12(1888) 13(1900) 17(1894)

OSTEOPATHIC INSTITUTE OF APPLIED TECHNIQUE.
Yearbook, 1960.
Osteopathic Institute of Applied Technique. (1960).
12

PARFITT, A.C.
Maidstone in the 17th century: long history essay. (MS.).
n.d.
12

PAYNE, George.
Catalogue of the Kent Archaeological Society's collection at
Maidstone.
Mitchell and Hughes. 1892.
12,15

PEENE, W.G.
Observations on the subjects of philosophical lectures...read
before the Maidstone Philosophical Society...October 24th, 1834.
Hall. 1834.
12

Population of Maidstone taken in 19th century, 3 vols.
n.d.
12

POSTE, Beale.
Discovery of a Romano-British cemetery at Westborough,
Maidstone.
n.d.
17

POSTE, Beale.
History of the College of All Saints, Maidstone.
Maidstone, Smith. (1848).
1,4,6,8,11,12,17

The Presentment of the Grand Jury for the County of Kent at
the Assizes holden at Maidstone...1682.
Hindmarsh. 1683.
12

READING, John, of Dover.
A sermon delivered at Maidstone in Kent at the Assizes held
there, August 23rd, 1641.
Stafford. 1642.
12

Reports of the trials of Boys v Edmunds, 1815-1817.
Denne. 1816-17.
12

ROBINSON LODGE OF MARK MASTER MASONS NO. 255.
Byelaws and list of members of the Lodge.
Gazette. 1919.
12

ROW, B. Prescott.
Kent's capital: a handbook to Maidstone...and guide to the
district...2nd edition, by B.P. Row and W.S. Martin.
(Homeland Association's handbooks, No. 6).
Maidstone, Ruck. London, Beechings. 1899.
1,2,4,6,7,8,11,12,14,15,17,18

ROWLES, Walter.
A general history of Maidstone...
1809.
3,11,12,17

Royal Star Hotel, Maidstone. (Tariff and an account of
Maidstone).
n.d.
17

RUCK, Walter. Publisher.
Sixteen photographic views of Maidstone (etc.).
W. Ruck. n.d.
17

RUCK, Walter. Publisher.
Street plan of Maidstone, showing the public buildings
of the town.
W. Ruck. (192?).
11

RUSSELL, J.M.
History of Maidstone.
Vivish. 1881.
1,3,4,6,8,11,12,14,15,17,18

RUSSELL, Wilfred.
New lives for old: the story of the Cheshire Homes.
(Includes Mote House, Maidstone).
Gollancz. 1963.
12

St. Luke's Church, Maidstone: a memorial service...
during the funeral of her late Majesty Queen Victoria...
an announcement. (Broadsheet).
1901.
12

St. Martin's Church, Maidstone: consecration of
St. Martin's Church, Maidstone by His Grace, the Lord
Archbishop of Canterbury; the Most Rev. Geoffrey E.
Fisher, P.C., D.D., L.L.D., on Wednesday, October 19th,
1960 at 7.30 p.m.
12

St. Martin's Church, Maidstone: form of service for
the Institution...and the Induction...of the Rev.
William Frank Doe as Vicar of the parish, on Monday,
30th September, 1968.
12

St. Philip's Parish, Maidstone: annual reports,
1874-1883.
Reader. 1874-1883.
12

SCHNEIDER, Elizabeth.
The aesthetics of William Hazlitt.
University of Pennsylvania. 1933.
12

SCHOMBERG, Geoffrey.
British zoos. (Includes Maidstone Zoo).
Wingate. 1957.
12

SCOTNEY, David James Stratton.
The Maidstone trolleybus, 1928-67.
National Trolleybus Association. 1972.
11

SHELTON, John.
Sermons...preached in the parish church of Maidstone.
Blake. 1803.
12

SHILTON, Dorothy O.
High Court of Admiralty examinations, 1637-1638, by
D.O. Shilton and R. Holworthy. (Two trials at Maid-
stone).
Anglo American Records Foundation. 1932.
6,12

(SMITH, Albert W.).
Wesleyan Methodist Church: a short history of the
Maidstone circuit, 1814-1914.
Maidstone, Burkitt. 1923.
11

SMITH, Charles Roach.
On a Roman Villa near Maidstone.
1876.
12

SMITH, Herbert L.
Notes of brasses formerly existing in Dover Castle,
Maidstone and Ashford churches.
n.d.
17

SMITH, J.
Topography of Maidstone and its environs...
Maidstone, J. Smith. 1839.
1,17

SOCIETY FOR MENTALLY HANDICAPPED CHILDREN - MAIDSTONE AND DISTRICT BRANCH.
Yearbook, 1968.
12

SOCIETY OF SCRIBES AND ILLUMINATORS.
The art of writing: an exhibition held at the Maidstone Museum and Art Gallery, 3rd-31st October, 1964.
Kent Messenger. 1964.
12

SOUTH EASTERN GAZETTE.
Old Maidstone: history in pictures. "South Eastern Gazette's" 120th birthday souvenir.
1935.
4,12

SPRINGETT, W.D.
"Our homes". (An address given by a former Rector of Herne Hill Church on December 12th, 1915 in the dedication ceremony of a memorial chapel for Edwin Dames).
12

STANHOPE, George. Dean of Canterbury, 1660-1728.
The duty of witnesses: a sermon preached at the Assizes, August 5th, 1701.
Collins. 1701.
12

STEVENS, John.
Characters I have known; or, who are insane. (In Kent County Lunatic Asylum).
Graham. n.d.
12

STEWART, D.D.
A sermon preached in the parish church of Maidstone against the opening of museums on the Lord's Day, 1878.
Burgiss-Brown. 1878.
12

STREATFIELD, Frank.
An account of the Grammar School in the King's town and parish of Maidstone in Kent.
Oxford, Rogers. 1915.
1,4,8,11,12

SWINNOCK, George.
An account of the life and death of the Rev. Thomas Wilson, M.A., formerly Minister of Maidstone in the County of Kent.
Brown. 1831.
12

SWINTON, W.E.
Gideon Mantell and the Maidstone Iguanodon.
Royal Society. 1951.
12

Topography of Maidstone and its environs...
Maidstone, J. Smith. 1839.
7,11,12

Transactions of the two criminals, George Webb and Richard Russell...tried at the Kent Summer Assizes in 1805.
Crosby. (1805).
1

TRANSPORT, Ministry of.
The London-Folkestone-Dover trunk road - (Maidstone By-pass) (Variation) Order, 1959.
H.M.S.O.
12

The Maidstone By-pass special roads scheme, 1959.
H.M.S.O.
8

Maidstone Corporation (Trolley Vehicles) Order, 1964.
H.M.S.O.
8

Road Traffic: The Parking Places and Controlled Parking Zone (Maidstone) (No. 1) Order, 1964.
H.M.S.O.
8

TRANSPORT AND CIVIL AVIATION, Ministry of. - MARINE SAFETY DIVISION.
Boiler Explosions Act, 1882 and 1890: report of preliminary inquiry (No. 3377) - explosion from a steam trap at Tovil Mill of Reed and Co. Ltd., Maidstone, Kent. (Diagram).
H.M.S.O.
8

Trial of Arthur O'Connor and others for High Treason before Judge Butler at Maidstone.
1798.
17

The trial of Baron Hompesch for a libel which took place at Maidstone on Wednesday, March 16th, 1808.
Empson. 1808.
12

The trial of James O'Coigly, otherwise called James John Fivey, Arthur O'Connor, John Binns, John Allen and Jeremiah Leary for High Treason under a special Commission at Maidstone in Kent...1798. Taken in shorthand by Joseph Gurney.
Gurney. 1798.
1,3,12,13

The trial of Mr. Whitefield's spirit (by Samuel Weller). (Col. Whitefield (1714-1770) was leader of the Calvanistic Methodists). See also MILLS, Benjamin.
T. Gardner. 1740.
11

Two letters on the Test Act signed Hamden, printed in the Gazetteer of January 30th and March 1st...to which is annexed a short account of the late Lord Chatham...
Chalmers. 1790.
12

TYRWHITT-DRAKE, Sir Garrard. (Lived at Cobtree, Maidstone).
Beasts and circuses.
Arrowsmith. 1936.
12

English circus and fairground.
Methuen. 1946.
12

My life with animals and other reminiscences.
Blackie. 1939.
11,12,15

Sir Garrard Tyrwhitt-Drake's Zoo Park: official illustrated guide.
(1938).
12

The Tyrwhitt-Drake scrapbook. Concerning the private collection of animals kept near Maidstone.
n.d.
11

VIDLER, John.
If freedom fail, by J. Vidler and M. Wolfe. (John Vidler was Governor of Maidstone Prison).
Macmillan. 1964.
4,12

WAKE, Rev. W.R.
Letter to Rev. James Reeve, Perpetual, from Rev. W.R. Wake, during four years Stipendiary Curate of Maidstone, stating the real causes which are presumed to have led to his extraordinary dismissal from the Curacy and containing useful hints and cautions to all future curates.
Maidstone, Wickham. (1814).
12

A reply to the remarks on Mr. Wake's letter to Mr. Reeve by the author of the letter.
Maidstone, Wickham. 1814.
12

Mon journal d'huit jours; or, the history of a week's absence from Maidstone and of a visit to France in September, 1814.
Maidstone, Wickham. 1814.
12

Some remarks on the letter of the Rev. W.R. Wake to the Rev. James Reeve upon the subject of Mr. Wake's dismissal from the Stipendiary Curacy of the parish of Maidstone by one of the public.
Maidstone, Wickham. (1814).
12

WELLER, B.R.
The Church of St. Peter, Maidstone.
1961.
12

WEST KENT GENERAL HOSPITAL.
Annual report, 1880.
Burgiss-Brown. 1880.
12

Letter book, 1861-69.
West Kent General Hospital. 1861-69.
12

WHICHCORD, John. Junior.
History and antiquities of the Collegiate Church of All Saints,
Maidstone.
Weale. 1845.
1,6,8,11,12,15,17

WHICHCORD AND SON AND BULMER, Martin.
Proposed water supply to the town of Maidstone.
1852.
12

WHITEHEAD, Bob.
Jesse Ellis: one of the first men in England to produce a
steam motor lorry. In "Old Motor", April, 1967.
12

The whole proceedings upon an information exhibited ex offico
by the King's Attorney-General against the Righ Hon. Sackville,
Earl of Thanet, Robert Fergusson Esq., and others for a riot and
other misdemeanors. Tried at the Bar of the Court of the King's
Bench, April 25th, 1799...(Riot took place at Maidstone).
13

Who's Who in Maidstone.
Pullman. 1960.
1,11,12,15

WILLIAMSON, Ethel.
Maidstone (Kent).
Homeland Association. (1911).
11,12

WINSTEDT, Eric Otto.
The poisoned pudding case. (Concerns the case on 5th October,
1820 of the poisoning of W. Greenstreet and William Hearn in
Maidstone Gaol by a pudding doctored with arsenic delivered
by a gypsy accomplice of Greenstreet). (Included in the Journal
of Gypsy Lore Society, 3rd series, Vol. 33, Pages 1 and 2,
1954).
3

WOOLER, T.J.
Resistance to church rates: report of the case Jeffery v
Pybus, tried at Maidstone, March, 1838.
Jeffery. 1838.
12

MANSTON

AVIATION, Ministry of.
The Civil Aviation Order. (Manston and Biggin Hill).
H.M.S.O. 1964.
8

FRASER, William.
The story of the Royal Air Force, Manston.
R.A.F. 1970.
7,9

FRASER, William.
The story of the Royal Air Force, Manston, 2nd edition.
R.A.F. (1972).
11

MAPLESCOMBE

MARTIN, Ian R.
The ruined church at Maplescombe, Kent.
British Archaeological Association. 1928.
12

MAPS

BAKER, Alan R.H.
Some early Kentish estate maps and a note on their
portrayal of field boundaries. In Archaeologia
Cantiana, Vol. 77, 1962.
17

MARDEN

EVERITT, Mrs. Katherine.
Bricks and flowers.
Constable. 1949.
11

MARDEN PARISH COUNCIL.
Official guide.
Croydon, Home Publishing Co. 1952 etc.
1,11

MARGATE

A., W.H.D.
Descriptive letterpress to "Views of Margate".
c.1870.
13

ABRAHAM, James Johnston.
Lettsom: his life, times, friends and descendants.
(John Lettsom, 1744-1815, co-founded Royal Sea Bathing
Margate).
Heinemann. 1933.
13

An account of a new piece called "Summer Amusement";
or, "An Adventure at Margate", performing at the
Theatre Royal in the Haymarket: being an excerpt from
the Universal Magazine, Vol. LXIV.
1778.
13

The Actor's Regalio...containing "The Celebrated Comic
Song of the Margate Hoy", written and composed by
Mr. Dibden...
London? n.d.
13

ADAM, Adam Fitz.
Landing from the steam boats...a comic recitation...
(Note: bound with Boys and Edmunds Report).
1820.
13

Adam and Eve: a Margate story.
J. and H.L. Hunt. 1824.
13,17

An address to the inhabitants of Margate on the present
state of the town and its civil government as it has bee
of late conducted by the Magistrates, the Commissioners,
the Directors of the Pier and Parish Officers...
Margate. 1831.
13

An address to the inhabitants of Margate on the present
state of the town and its civil government as it has bee
of late conducted...as a preliminary step towards
producing reform...
1831.
13

THE ALEXANDRA PHILANTHROPIC HOME.
An account of the origin of the Society and of the
ceremony of affixing the memorial stone by Mrs. James
Taddy Friend on May 17th, 1866.
Thanet Guardian. 1866.
13

The charity instituted 6th November, 1865 to commemorate
the safe arrival off Margate of Her Royal Highness the
Princess Alexandra.
Alexandra Philanthropic Home. 1866.
13

...for the reception of aged and decayed members and
other inhabitants of the parish of St. John the Baptist,
Margate.
Alexandra Philanthropic Home. 1885.
13

ALEXANDRA PHILANTHROPIC HOME.
Report of annual meeting, 18th November, 1914 and for 1918-19.
Alexandra Philanthropic Home.
13

All about Margate and Herne Bay, including Draper's, St.
Peter's, Salmestone, Chapel Bottom, Hengrove, Twenties and
Nash Court, Kingsgate and its modern antiquities, Garlinge,
Dendelion.
W. Kent and Co.
4(1869) 11(1869) 12(1869) 13 and 14(1864,1866,1867,1869)
17(1867,1886)

ALLOM, E.A.
The seaweed collector...illustrated with natural specimens from
the shores of Margate and Ramsgate. (i.e. actual dried
seaweed not illustrations).
W. Keble. 1841.
13

Amusements at Margate. (Extract from Chamber's Edinburgh
Journal, 1833).
13

ANDERSON, John.
A preliminary introduction to the act of sea-bathing.
1795.
13

ANTHONY, Frank.
The bidden guest: an allegory, produced at the Winter Gardens,
Margate, 10th-16th December, 1928.
Margate, W.J. Parrett. 1931.
11

ARNOLD, Edwin.
Wreck of the Northern Belle.
(Hastings). 1857.
13

The Attic miscellany; or, characteristic mirror of men and
things, 2nd edition, Vol. 1. (Landing at Margate, p.p. 441-
443).
Attic. 1790.
13

B., W.
Ye Yoakley Charity, Drapers Hospital. Almshouses Drapers,
Margate: their origin and endowment.
Leadenhall Press. 1884.
7,11,13(and 1894).

BATEMAN, Josiah.
Address to the parishoners of St. John's, Margate with a report
of various local charities for the year 1866 and for 1867.
1867 and 1868.
13

"BEACHCOMBER", pseud.
That's Margate all over: being an excerpt from the Daily
Express, 13th August, 1929.
13

BEECHAM, Thomas. Publisher.
Photo folio: 24 choice photographic views of Margate and
Herne Bay.
Beecham. 1900.
13

BENHAM, William.
Margate Church restoration: a sermon preached in St. John's
Church, March 26th, 1876...on the first using of the new
pulpit.
Keble. 1876.
13

Parting words: a sermon preached on May 2nd, 1880 in St. John's
Church, Margate with an address on the church restoration.
Keble. 1880.
13

Restoration of the parish church: an address to the
parishoners.
Keble. 1874.
13

The Bijou! A local household almanack for Margate.
Bijou. 1903.
13

BOBBY AND CO. Firm.
Bobbys of Margate...celebrate 50 years of constant
progress.
Bobby and Co. 1937.
13

BONSFIELD. Publisher.
Picture of Margate...
Bonsfield. 1809.
1,12,13

BOWEN, Frank Charles.
London ship types.
1938.
13

BRADEN, J.T.
Photographic views of Margate and neighbourhood.
c.1898.
13

BRADSHAW, Lawrence.
Dreamland, Margate: a sculptural view. (Excerpt from
"Building", June, 1934).
13

BRASIER, W.C. Publisher.
Companion to the Almanacks and General Advertiser,
1859, 1864, 1872, 1878.
W.C. Brasier.
13

BRETHERTON, F.F.
Origin and progress of Methodism in Margate forming a
souvenir of the centenary celebrations held in 1908
to celebrate the formation of the Margate Circuit in
1808.
1908.
13

BRIDGEWATER, Howard.
The Grotto.
Keighley. 1948.
13,14

BUCKLOW, W. Publisher.
Margate and Wesrgate-on-Sea illustrated.
W. Bucklow. 1900.
4,13

BURNBY, John.
Summer amusement; or, miscellaneous poems: inscribed
to the frequenters of Margate, Ramsgate...
1774.
13

CALLCUTT AND BEAVIS. Publishers.
Thirty-two views of Margate and district.
Callcutt and Beavis. c.1895.
13

CHAPLIN, Dorothea.
Matter, myth and spirit. (Margate Grotto).
1935.
13

CHARITY COMMISSION.
In the matter of the charity of John Mickleburgh for the
benefit of the poor of the ancient parish of Margate
in the County of Kent, founded by 1st codicil to will...
25th February, 1870...
1909.
13

The Children's Festival - Her Majesty's Jubilee, 1887.
13

"CHRISTIANUS", pseud.
Remarks on the general sea-bathing infirmary at Westbrook
near Margate.
1820.
11,14,17

CLARK, M. Dudley.
Westgate-on-Sea.
Homeland Association. n.d.
11,13

CLARKE, George Ernest.
Historic Margate.
Margate Public Libraries. 1957 etc.
1,2,3,4,6,7,8,11,12,13,14,15

CLARKE, John S.
Circus parade. (Includes Sanger's Circus).
Batsford. 1936.
13

CLOUD, Yvonne.
Beside the seaside - six variations.
S. Nott. 1934.
13,14

COBB, Mary.
Diary in 5 books, from 22nd February, 1792 to 7th July, 1802.
(MSS.).
13

COBB, W.F.
Memoir of the late Francis Cobb Esq., of Margate...compiled
by W.F. Cobb.
Maidstone, Hall. 1835.
11,12

COBBETT, William.
"Reduction no robbery" - a letter to the freeholders of the
County of Kent on their etition for a reduction of the
interest of the debt. (From Cobbett's "Weekly Register",
Vol. 42, No. 12, 22nd June, 1822).
11

COBBETT, William.
Rural rides in the counties of Surrey, Kent, Sussex...
Cobbett: afterwards Dent. 1853 etc.
6,13,15,16

COGHLAN, Francis.
New guide to Ramsgate, Margate and Dover.
1837.
13,14,17

COMPARATIVE, Dr., Junior, pseud.
Sentimental journey through Margate and Hastings.
Newman. 1819.
3,6,11,12,13,15,17

Congregational Church, Union Crescent, Margate: Centenary,
1845-1945.
13

CORELLI, Marie.
One of the world's wonders.
1885.
13

CORKHILL, W.H.
Avebury, Coldrum and Margate.
c.1953.
3,13

CORNFORD, L. Hope.
A century of sea trading, 1824-1924 - The General Steam
Navigation Company Limited.
A. and C. Black. 1924.
12

Correspondence between James Denne and V. Simmons.
(Margate). 1828.
13

Correspondence relating to a proposed public library, 1911-
1913 (in Margate).
13

Correspondence with Sir Ambrose Heal, relative to Benjamin
Beale.
1933.
13

CORY, Harper.
The Goddess.
Margate Borough Council. 1949.
13

A COUNCIL OF SOCIAL SERVICE.
Suggested scheme for the Borough of Margate.
1927.
13

COZENS, Zechariah.
The Margate Hoy, which was stranded on Sunday morning, 7th
February, 1802: a poem with a sketch of the life of Mr. G.
Bone.
Canterbury, W. Bristow. 1802.
6,11,13,14

CRESY, Edward.
Report to the General Board of Health on a preliminary
inquiry into the sewerage, drainage and supply of water
and the sanitary condition of the inhabitants of the
parish of St. John the Baptist, Margate...
1850.
13

CROOK, H. Evelyn.
Margate as a health resort.
Keble's Gazette. 1893.
13,14

DANE HILL HOUSE: School Magazine, 1881-1892.
13

DANE HILL HOUSE: School songs, No. 2. Cadet corps
song - words and music by P.W. Newton.
n.d.
13

The Dawn of Day: being typewritten transcriptions
from St. John's Parish Magazine...January to July, 1880
and The Vicar's Churchwarden: being as above from
Keble's Gazette, August 25th-September 8th, 1877 and
Contributions toward a history of Margate by W. Benham.
(From Keble's...July 24th-October 9th, 1880).
13

A description of the Isle of Thanet and particularly
of the town of Margate...
Newbery and Bristow. 1763.
1,11,12,13,14

DOWKER, George.
On a cave near Margate.
n.d.
7,11,13

Echoes of Westgate.
Les Oiseaux. 1948.
8

EDWARDS, Joan.
A general valuation of the lands and tenements in the
parish of St. John the Baptist in the Isle of Thanet,
made upon actual survey in the year 1801 with a view
to an equal rate (upon their annual value) for the
relief of the poor. (MS. by Miss Jane Edwards with
notes by A.W. Rowe). (St. John the Baptist, Margate).
1802.
13

"Egerton", No. 2,584. Decree concerning the encroach-
ment of the sea at Margate. (British Museum MSS.).
1621.
13

ELLIS, Stephen.
A detail of all the late proceedings relative to the
General Sea-Bathing Infirmary at Margate...
Axtell and Purser. 1815.
11,12,13

A few days at Margate; or, a guide to persons visiting
the Isle of Thanet...
1828 and 1831.
13

Form and order of consecration of the parish church of
Holy Trinity, Margate...on Friday, June 26th, 1959...
12

FREELING, Arthur.
Picturesque excursions...edited by A. Freeling.
(Includes Margate, Tunbridge Wells and Dover).
Orr. 1840.
2,6,8,11,12,13

FREY, P. AND CO. Publisher.
Margate.
P. Frey and Co. c.1880.
13

FRITH, Francis. Photographer.
Margate and Ramsgate photographed.
F. Frith. 1857.
13

GARNER, William.
Garner's miscellaneous recitations...as recited by William
Garner...of the Marine Library, Margate.
Porter. 1827.
11,13

GASLAKE. Publisher.
Margate: thirty views.
Margate, Gaslake. 1872?
11

GLIDDON, M.A.
A short historical account of Margate in the County of Kent
(MS.).
1846.
13

Going to Margate; or, a water itinerary from London to
Margate. Containing an account of the principal towns,
villages, buildings, seats, etc., observed between those
places, together with extracts from the Margate byelaws of
general utility to readers.
Printed for George Witherden. 1828.
11,13

The Golden Grain Guide to the Al Fresco Fayre and Floral
Fete (on behalf of the Victoria Convalescent Home, Church-
fields, Margate...August, 1889).
13

GREAT BRITAIN: LAWS, etc. (GEO. I).
An Act to enable the Pier-Wardens of the town of Margate...
more effectively to recover the...Droits for the...said pier.
1724.
11,12

GREAT BRITAIN: LAWS, etc. (GEO. II).
An Act for more effectively paving...the town of Margate.
1813.
11,13

GREAT BRITAIN: LAWS, etc. (GEO. III).
An Act for rebuilding the pier of Margate...and for widening,
paving, repairing, cleansing, lighting and watching the
streets...in the town of Margate, 1787.
11

GREAT BRITAIN: LAWS, etc. (GEO. III).
An Act to enable His Majesty to licence a Playhouse within
the town and port of Margate,in the Isle of Thanet,in the
County of Kent,under certain restrictions therein limited.
1786.
11,12

GREAT BRITAIN: LAWS, etc. (GEO. IV).
An Act to amend...several Acts relative to the paving,
lighting, watching and improving...Margate...for erecting
certain defences against the sea for the protection of the
said town and for making further improvements...
1825.
13

GREAT BRITAIN: LAWS, etc. (EDW. VII).
An Act to confer further powers upon the Mayor, Aldermen and
Burgesses of the Borough of Margate with regard to the audit
of accounts and to make further provision with regard to the
health, local government and improvement of the Borough and
for other purposes.
1908.
13

GREAT BRITAIN: LAWS, etc. (EDW. VII).
Margate Corporation Act, 1908.
H.M.S.O. 1908.
13

GREAT BRITAIN: LAWS, etc. (GEO. V).
Margate Corporation Act, 1926.
H.M.S.O. 1926.
13

GREAT BRITAIN: LAWS, etc. (ELIZ. II).
Royal School for Deaf Children, Margate Act.
H.M.S.O. 1958.
8

GUNDRY, Nathaniel.
A short address to the inhabitants of Ramsgate on the
distribution of the Sacrament Money...bound with "Lines from
the Pen of a Young Lady".
1819.
11,13

H., G.N.
The crisis: a plea to the people of Margate and to
the Messrs. Lewis.
1895.
13

HALL, J. Publisher.
Hall's new Margate and Ramsgate guide.
J. Hall. 1779 etc.
14,17

HARRISON, Rev. Thomas.
Diary, 4 vols, January 1st, 1911 to August 26th, 1913.
(M.S.). (Vicar of Margate).
13

HARWOOD, J.
Views of Margate.
1845.
11

HATTON, Joseph.
Deaf-and-dumb-land. (Asylum for Deaf and Dumb,
Margate).
n.d.
17

HEYWOOD, A. Publisher.
A guide to Margate and its principal features of
interest and attraction, 1871, 1872, 1881, 1884, 1887.
A. Heywood.
13

HEYWOOD, John. Publisher.
Illustrated guide to Margate and Westgate.
J. Heywood. 1895.
13,14,17

Holy Trinity Church, Margate, 1829-1959 A.D. - the
years between.
(1960).
12

HOUGHTON, George E.
History of the Fort Road Studios (Margate). (Typewritten by author).
1939.
13

HOUGHTON, George E. Publisher.
Photographic souvenir of Margate and neighbourhood.
G.E. Houghton.
12(1898) 13(1895 and 1898)

Photographic souvenir of the Great Storm, Margate,
November 29th, 1897.
G.E. Houghton. 1898.
13

Souvenir of Margate.
G.E. Houghton. c.1905.
13

32 photographic views of Margate and neighbourhood.
G.E. Houghton. c.1900.
13

HOWE, F.
An exposition of the causes of the present state of
the town of Margate...
1837.
13

The Hydro, Cliftonville...
c.1930.
13

INGOLDSBY, Thomas.
Misadventures at Margate...
Eyre and Spottiswoode. 1880.
12,13

"AN INHABITANT", pseud.
Margate guide: a descriptive poem...also a general
account of Ramsgate, etc.
1797.
11,15,17

Islington-Super-Mare (Margate) from "All the Year
Round", 1878.
17

KAY, A.M.
St. John the Baptist in Thanet (Margate Parish Church).
Parochial Church Council. 1951.
13

KEATE, George.
Sketches from nature: taken and coloured in a journey to
Margate, 2 vols.
Dodsley.
2nd edition, 1779.   (13)
3rd edition, 1782.   (11,12,13,15,17)
4th edition, 1790.   (13)
5th edition, 1802.   (6,8,13)

KEATE, George.
Sketches from nature: taken and coloured in a journey to
Margate...1st American edition, from the 4th London edition.
Dodsley. 1793.
13

KEBLE, T.H.   Publisher.
A week at Margate.
T.H. Keble.
13(1825) 17(1836)

KERSHAW AND SON.   Publishers.
Views of Margate.
Kershaw and Son. c.1870.
13

KNIGHT, J.J.
Margate Monthly, 1906-1920, edited by J.J. Knight.   (Cecil
Square Baptist Church).
13

LADDS, John.
Royal Assembly Rooms and the site of the Royal Hotel, Margate,
Kent.
1884.
17

LAMBERT, George.
Civic and other maces.   (Tenterden, Margate, New Romney).
"The Antiquary", February, 1880
3

LANE.   Publisher.
The Margate guide.
Lane. 1909.
13

LATHAM, Albert.
Report by Captain Douglas Galton on the scheme of drainage,
submitted to the Town Council of the Borough of Margate.
1881.
13

Report on the drainage of Margate, prepared for the Town
Council.
1877.
13

Report on the drainage of Margate, prepared for the Town
Council.
1881.
13

Report on the working of the existing hydraulic sewage pumps.
9th June, 1904.
13

Report prepared for the (Margate) Town Council on the
Electric Lighting Bill.
1882.
17

Report upon the question of the collection of house dust
and refuse in the Borough of Margate. Prepared for Chairman
and Members of the Sanitary Committee of the Town Council of
the Borough of Margate.
1882.
13

LATHAM, Baldwin.
Report on the drainage of Margate, prepared for the Town
Council.
1907.
13

Report upon additional water supply.
1899.
13

Westgate sewerage.
1897.
13

LE BAS, Charles.
A letter addressed to the company who frequent, and to
the inhabitants who reside, in Margate and Ramsgate.
1796.
13

LE BAS, Charles.
A new Margate, Ramsgate and Broadstairs guide...
Margate, J. Warren. 1802.
3

A letter to the visitors of Margate on the suppression
of sacred music.   (Bound up with the Canterbury Weekly
Journal, 1837).
11

Letters relating to Margate clockmakers, addressed to
Dr. Arthur Rowe.
1923.
13

LETTSOM, John Coakley.
Hints for establishing a Sea-Bathing Infirmary at
Margate for the poor of London.
1801.
13

LEWIS, Hardwicke.
An excursion to Margate in the month of June, 1786:
interspersed with a variety of anecdotes, 2nd edition.
Finch. 1787.
11,12,13

The Library Association: programme of the fifty-ninth
Annual Conference to be held at Margate on Monday-
Friday, June 8th-12th, 1936.
Library Association. 1936.
13

LONSDALE, Margaret.
A day at Margate.
March, 1882.
13

M., A.
By the sea-side, No. 5: being an excerpt from the
"Illustrated Times", September 6th, 1856.
13

MANSERGH, James.
Report on the water supply of Margate.
1896 and 1901.
13

MARGATE AMBULANCE CORPS.
Reports for 1913 and 1916.
Margate Ambulance Corps. 1913 and 1916.
13

MARGATE AND DISTRICT GENERAL HOSPITAL.
Annual report and statement of accounts, 1930-39,
10 vols.
Margate and District General Hospital. 1930-40.
13

MARGATE AND DISTRICT NEW HOSPITAL FUND.
Report for the year ending December 31st, 1928.
1929.
13

MARGATE AND THANET PERMANENT BENEFIT BUILDING SOCIETY.
Portfolio of rules, correspondence, etc., 1864-71.
13

MARGATE BOROUGH COUNCIL.
Instructions as to duties of the Officer-in-Charge of
the Police Station and the Constables acting under him,
Constables and Special Constables directing vehicular
and pedestrian traffic leaving the town and Special
Constables acting as motoy cycle messengers, in case of
emergency caused by a threatened or a hostile invasion
of the Isle of Thanet.
Margate Borough Council. 1915.
13

MARGATE BOROUGH COUNCIL.
Instructions as to the duties to be carried out by Constables
and Special Constables in case of emergency caused by a
hostile invasion.
Margate Borough Council. 1915.
13

Margate rating book, 1801.
12

Silver lining campaign: Margate's week.
Margate Borough Council. 1947.
13

Souvenir programme, handbill and photographs of the visit
of H.R.H., The Prince of Wales, on 24th November, 1926 to open
the New Promenade from Palm Bay to Kingsgate and to name it
"The Prince's Walk".
Margate Borough Council. 1926.
13

MARGATE BOROUGH COUNCIL - EDUCATION COMMITTEE.
Margate Education Week handbook. Pavilion and Winter Gardens,
March 16th-20th, 1926.
Margate Borough Council. 1926.
13

MARGATE BOROUGH COUNCIL - ENTERTAINMENTS COMMITTEE.
Margate postal programme.
Margate Borough Council. 1914.
13

MARGATE BOROUGH COUNCIL - PUBLICITY COMMITTEE.
Borough of Margate, including Cliftonville, Westbrook,
Westgate-on-Sea and Birchington - residential guide.
Margate Borough Council. (1958?).
4,12,15

Margate for health.
Margate Borough Council. 1932.
13

Margate official guide.
1(1961 etc.)
3(1958)
5(1961 etc.)
11(1961 etc.)
13(1922 annually except for 1940-45)

MARGATE CHAMBER OF COMMERCE.
Margate, 1901-13 and 1915.
13

Margate arts and crafts exhibition.
1912.
13

Margate at a glance: official guide - Cliftonville,
Westbrook.
1909.
13

Margate: health and pleasure.
1916.
13

Margate: la perle des Plages Anglaises.
Margate Chamber of Commerce. c.1910.
13

Report and balance sheet - list of members, 1905 and 1907-1922.
Rules, 1906, 1907. Annual banquet, 1907, 1909-1911, 1913, 1914.
13

Review, July, 1953. Special items include "The Town Sergeant",
by R.F. Walbourne and "Old House, King Street".
1953.
13

MARGATE CHURCH INSTITUTE.
Minutes. Vol. 1 - 30th November, 1866-31st October, 1890.
Vol. 2 - 6th January, 1891-31st July, 1895.
13

MARGATE COLLEGE.
Prospectus, 1904.
17

MARGATE COTTAGE HOSPITAL.
Balance sheets for 1893, 1894 and 1896.
Margate Cottage Hospital. 1897.
13

Minute book of the Sub-Committee appointed to carry out the
scheme of enlarging the Margate Cottage Hospital - Queen
Victoria's Diamond Jubilee, 1897. (MS.).
13

Reports for the years 1895, 1898, 1907, 1908, 1909,
1910, 1913, 1914, 1915, 1916, 1917, 1918, 1919, 1920
and 1927.
13

Reports for the years 1882, 1883 and 1884.
Margate Cottage Hospital. 1885.
13

Report for the year ending 31st December, 1928, with
report of Special Appeal Committee for 1928.
Margate Cottage Hospital. 1928.
13

Rules and regulations for the management of the
hospital.
Margate Cottage Hospital. 1897.
13

MARGATE CRICKET CLUB.
Rules and regulations.
1864.
13

THE MARGATE FREE PRESS.
Clippings and correspondence. Exchange and advertising
medium. (Nos. 1-71, March 23rd, 1878 to July 26th,
1879).
13

MARGATE HOTEL, BOARDING AND APARTMENT HOUSE ASSOCIATION.
Guide.
1938.
13

MARGATE MARINERS' SOCIETY.
Rules and orders...
1846.
13

MARGATE MICROSCOPIAL CLUB.
Being a transcription of the various proceedings
extracted from newspapers. (MS.).
1871-79.
13

MARGATE PROSECUTION SOCIETY.
Rules and regulations - established 1803.
1863.
13

MARGATE PUBLIC LIBRARY.
Catalogue of books, pamphlets and excerpts dealing with
Margate...in the local collection of the Borough of
Margate Public Library, compiled by A.J. Gritten.
Margate Library Committee. 1934.
1,3,7,11,13

Catalogue of prints, drawings and maps of old Margate
on view at Hartsdown House.
Margate, Cooper. 1930.
3

Opening of the Public Library, Victoria Road by...
Mayor...2nd June, 1932.
Clarke and Knapp.
3

MARGATE SAVINGS BANK.
Rules and regulations, 1876.
13

MARGATE, THANET AND EAST KENT PERMANENT BENEFIT
BUILDING SOCIETY.
Rules, 1854.
13

MARGATE TOTAL ABSTINENCE ASSOCIATION.
Treasurer's accounts, November, 1894-12th February,
1904. (MS.).
13

MARGATE TRADE PROTECTION SOCIETY.
Rules - established, 1853.
1859.
13

MARGATE WESLEYAN CHURCH.
Wesleyan £20 Burial Society for the Margate circuit.
1867.
13

Margate and historical Thanet.
1921.
13

Margate and Westgate with Birchington.
1903-4.
13

The Margate Bellman...the steam packets, their time of
starting, public gardens and other places of amusement...
13(1st edition, n.d. New edition, 1849) **17**(1849)

Margate, Birchington, Westgate-on-Sea.
1936.
13

Margate carnival and regatta, June 17th-25th, 1950 - official
programme.
13

The Margate Coronation Exhibition, 10th-20th February, 1937.
13

Margate Delineated...
12(1829)
13(1826, 1829, 1831, 1832, 1834, 1837, 1841)
17(1820)

Margate drainage: extracts from newspapers from August, 1866 to
November, 1890.
13

Margate drainage controversy: the transmission of hydraulic
versus compressed air power and hydraulic pressure pumps for
pumping sewage versus the Shone Hydro-Pneumatic Sewerage
System for drainage and sewerage purposes.
1888.
13

Margate fete programmes, 1899-1902.
13

The Margate "Front" in the Great War, 1914-1919 - illustrated
peace souvenir.
1919.
13

Margate Gala Week in aid of the Margate Cottage Hospital and
Alexandra Homes, 13th-18th August, 1923.
1923.
13

Margate grievances and remedies: a collection of home truths...
n.d.
11,13

The Margate Grotto.
1929.
13,14

The Margate guide.
11(1770 and 1780) 13(1770, 1775, 1780, 1785)

Margate: a guide arranged for quick and easy reference.
1920.
13

Margate: a humorous poem by the author of "Brighton".
Kidd. 1831.
12,17

Margate: illustrated and historical, its attractions as a
sea-side and holiday resort.
c.1900.
13

Margate Jetty extension: report to accompany the design marked
"Dolphin, Westminster".
1870.
13

Margate postal souvenir.
1913.
13,17

Margate surf-boat disaster, 2nd December, 1897. List of
suscribers to the fund.
1898.
13

MAYHEW, Athol.
The chronicles of Westgate-on-Sea.
Canterbury, Kent County News. n.d.
11,13,17

Memoirs of the Margate Special Constabulary, 1914-1918.
13

MERCER, William John AND ROWE, Arthur Walton. Printers.
Margate printers, 1795-1919: being manuscript notes.
13

MITCHELL, E.C.
The story of Margate Grotto.
n.d.
17

"MOMUS", pseud.
Letters of Momus from Margate, describing the most
distinguished characters there and the virtues, vices
and follies to which they gave occasion in what was
called the season of the year 1777.
1778.
13

MORLEY, Malcolm.
Margate and its theatres, 1730 to 1965.
Museum Press. 1966.
1,3,4,6,7,11,15,19

MORRIS, T.E.
St. John the Baptist (Margate Parish Church): a
diagramatic history of the church, its brasses and
monuments. (Photostat copy).
1953.
13

MOTTLEY, Edward.
A report on the sanitary condition of the town of
Margate...1837-1862...the numbers dying and the cause
of death of inhabitants, visitors and inmates of the
infirmaries.
1863.
13

Statistical examination of the Margate death-rate for
the five years, 1863-1867.
1868.
13

The vital statistics of the town of Margate.
1849.
13

The vital statistics of the town of Margate for twelve
years, ending June, 1849, compiled from records at the
Registry Office, for the purpose of ascertaining the
sanitary condition of the town.
1850.
13

Narrative of the loss of the "Hindostan"...wrecked
off Margate, January 11th, 1803...
13

NATIONAL ASSOCIATION OF LOCAL GOVERNMENT OFFICERS.
Annual Conference at Margate, Whitsuntide, 1937.
National Association of Local Government Officers. 1937
13

NATIONAL UNION OF CONSERVATIVE AND UNIONIST ASSOCIATION
Sixty-third Annual Conference, Margate. 1st and 2nd
October, 1936: programme of proceedings, report of the
Council...
National Union of Conservative and Unionist
Associations. 1936.
13

NATIONAL UNION OF TEACHERS.
Conference souvenir (at Margate).
Parrett. 1927. (1,3,8,11,13)
National Union of Teachers. 1938. (3,13)

NEC TIMET IRATUM MARE.
Report on the proposed extension of the jetty at
Margate in the County of Kent, October, 1870.
13

A new catalogue of Silver's Circulating Library
(formerly under) now removed opposite the Assembly
Rooms, Margate.
c.1787.
13

NEWMAN, J. AND CO. Publishers.
The Imperial Album of Margate and neighbourhood.
J. Newman and Co. c.1880.
13

Six coloured views of Margate.
J. Newman and Co. c.1874.
13

Six tinted views in Margate.
J. Newman and Co. c.1870.
13

Thirty views of Margate and neighbourhood.
J. Newman and Co. 1871-78.
13

Thirty-two views of Margate and neighbourhood.
J. Newman and Co. 1871-79.
13

Thirty-two views of Margate and neighbourhood.
J. Newman and Co. 1873-79.
13,14

Thirty-two views of Margate and neighbourhood.
J. Newman and Co. 1873-80.
13

Twenty-four views of Margate and neighbourhood.
J. Newman and Co. 1870-75.
13

Nineteen photographs of the official opening of the Public
Library, Victoria Road on 2nd June, 1932 and the visit of the
Railway Queen (Miss Patricia Clark) on the same day.
1932.
13

Observations on...proceedings relative to the Grand Sea-Bathing
Infirmary at Margate, 1816.
17

Official programme of the arrangements for the public reception
of H.R.H. Princess Louise (Marchioness of Lorne)...1st July,
1892 for the purpose of opening the new Victoria Convalescent
Home.
13

One hundred and thirteen views of Margate and district.
c.1900.
13

OSBORNE, R.C.
New Margate guide; or, Steam Packet Companion...
13(1832, 1833, 1834) 14(1833)

OULTON, W.C.
Picture of Margate and its vicinity.
Baldwin, Cradock and Joy. 1820.
1,6,7,11,12,13,14,15,17

PACKE, Christopher.
A reply to Dr. Gray's "Three Answers to a Written Paper",
entitled "Mr. Worger's Case".
1727.
13

PADGET, Frank W.
Margate Water Works: a brief survey, 1857-1936. (With 10
photographs inserted).
1936.
13

PAGE, David.
Report to the Local Government Board on the general sanitary
condition of Margate in relation to the continued existence of
typhoid fever in the Borough.
1887.
13

PARKYN, Walter A.
The Britannia Comprehensive Guide to Margate.
1898.
13

PERRY, W. Publisher.
Six views in Margate.
W. Perry. 1854-57.
13

Photographic views of Margate and neighbourhood.
c.1895.
13

Photographic views of Margate and neighbourhood.
(Printed in Bavaria).
n.d.
13

Photographs of the Great Storm, Margate, November 29th,
1897.
13

PICKETT, W.
Six views of Margate and its environs.
1st July, 1797.
13

A pictorial guide to Margate amusements: The Lido,
Cliftonville; Dreamland, Margate; The Greyhound
Racing Track, Ramsgate.
1938.
13

PILKINGTON, Mrs. Mary.
Margate...
Harris. 1813.
6,11,13

Plan and regulations of the Sea-Bathing Infirmary at
Margate, opened August 1st, 1796, with a list of
subscribers to that Institution.
1801.
13

Plan of the General Sea-Bathing Infirmary for the relief
of the diseased poor, including purposes of the
Institution, laws and lists of the officers and
governors.
1815.
13

POCOCK, Robert. Publisher.
Margate water companion...
R. Pocock. 1802.
9,12

PUBLIC RECORD OFFICE.
(Domestic Series) Treasury books - records relating to
Margate, 1580-1745.
13

The Quiver Lifeboats: being an extract from "The
Quiver"...Vol. 2, 1867.
13

Rate book of the lands and tenements in the parish of
St. John the Baptist, Margate in the Isle of Thanet,
made upon actual surveys in the year 1835, with a view
to an equal rate for the relief of the poor, together
with the old rate of 1802 progressively to 1835.
1836.
13

The Ratepayers' Journal...(Nos. 12-66, November 12th,
1881 to November 25th, 1882).
13

REEVE, Robert Dalby.
"Naboth's Vineyard": being a short account of an
ancient footpath in the parish of St. John the Baptist,
Margate...
1934.
13

RENDEL, James M.
Report to the Trustees of Margate Harbour, by J.M.
Rendel and R. Stephenson.
1845.
13

Report on the fire at the Assembly Rooms, Cecil Square,
October 27th, 1882, by H.E. Davis, Chief Officer of
the Margate Fire Brigade. (MS.).
13

The residential attractions of Margate...
1912.
13

REYNOLDS, Charles AND CO. Publisher.
The album of Margate views.
C. Reynolds and Co. c.1878.
13,14

REYNOLDS, Charles AND CO. Publisher.
Westgate-on-Sea and Margate.
C. Reynolds and Co. c.1880.
13

ROBINSON, W.
A trip to Margate with a description of its environs,
written in the year 1805.
6,11,13

ROCK AND CO. Publishers.
The Royal Cabinet Album of Margate, 1861-78 and 1862-75.
Rock and Co.
13

Thirty views of Margate.
Rock and Co. 1861-69.
13

Views and scenery of Margate.
Rock and Co. 1861-67.
13

ROGERS, James R.
The loss of nine gallant lives. Written on the capsizing of
the surf-boat "Friend of All Nations", off Margate on
Thursday, December 2nd, 1897.
1897.
13

The romance of the Grotto...
1903.
13

ROSS, Charles H.
Margate and Ramsgate.
"Judy" Office. (1880).
12,13,14,17

Rotary International Annual Conference, Margate, October 9th to
11th, 1936.
13

ROWE, Arthur Walton.
Abstract of deeds - MS. (From numerous addresses in Margate).
n.d.
13

The accounts of the Poor House from 1716-1729. (MS.).
13

Amusements at Margate in the olden days. (MS.).
n.d.
13

Archaeological notes, 1923-25.
13

Bathing at Margate from 1870. (MS.).
n.d.
13

Century houses: houses occupied by the same profession or
trade for 100 consecutive years. (MS.).
n.d.
13

The early Margate steam packets. (MS.).
n.d.
13

Early references (1322-1776) - MS.
13

The early stage-coaches. (MS.).
n.d.
13

Extract from Register for Briefs, St. John's Church,
Margate, 1678-1844. (MS.).
13

Extracts from the "Accounts of the Poor House" in our rate
books, from 1666 to 1716. (MS.).
13

Extracts from the Kentish Companion, 1797 and 1817. (MS.).
13

Fountain Inn. (From the Kentish Gazette) - MS.
13

George Inn. (From the Kentish Gazette) - MS.
13

Hamlets, street and buildings. (Extracts from the Kentish
Gazette) - MS.
n.d.
13

Holdens' Directory, Margate, 1811. List of professions
and trades - alphabetical index. (MS.).
13

An index to streets and buildings. (MS.).
n.d.
13

Kentish Register, Margate. Official names only -
alphabetical index, 1814. Kentish Companion, 1819.
(MS.).
13

The libraries in the rate books. (MS.).
n.d.
13

(Local) Acts of Parliament. (MS.).
n.d.
13

Margate chronolgy. (MS.).
n.d.
13

Margate's famous storms. (MS.).
n.d.
13

Margate hotels, inns, taverns, up to 1878. (MS.).
13

Margate streets named after personal names. (MS.).
n.d.
13

Margate theatres from 1762. (M.S.).
n.d.
13

The marsupites-chalk of Margate.
1906.
13

Mercer's notes on Margate guides. (MS.).
n.d.
13

The mills in the rate books. (MS.).
n.d.
13

The old academies and schools of Margate - from guides
and directories. (MS.).
n.d.
13

Old luggers and their builders. (MS.).
n.d.
13

The old Margate Hoys. (MS.).
n.d.
13

The origin and decadence of the creek and the brooks -
MS. (Typescript).
n.d.
13

Other local references. (MS.).
n.d.
13

Personal names. (MS.).
n.d.
13

Personal names, chiefly before 1800. (MS.).
n.d.
13

Re-naming of streets and re-numbering of houses,
March 7th, 1868. (MS.).
13

Robins' Watering Places and Fashionable Directory,
1833: abstract and summary of trades. (MS.).
13

The sequence of the libraries: 1766 to 1838. (MS.).
13

Smuggling at Margate and in Thanet. (MS.).
n.d.
13

Streets and buildings. (MS.).
n.d.
13

Streets, etc., in 1811 and 1823 Directory. Streets
and houses in 1834-39. (MS.).
13

ROWE, Arthur Walton.
The streets of Margate in 1800: a summary from the 1801
valuation book and a retrospect. (MS.).
13

A summary of the general valuation of the lands and tenements
in the parish of St. John the Baptist...(MS.).
n.d.
13

Summary of public buildings, streets and houses. Maps of
1821, 1835 and 1852 (Margate). (MS.).
13

Summary relating to the Boulevard, Jolly's French Bazaar,
London Bazaar (Margate). (MS.).
n.d.
13

Universal British Directory of Trade: a summary of local trades,
old names and the civil life of the town. (MS.).
n.d.
13

Varia. Kentish Gazette, 1768 to 1866. (MS.).
13

Varia. Local references. (MS.).
n.d.
13

Varia. Margate. (MS.).
n.d.
13

William Rowe's Church Book, 1770, 1771, 1772. (MS.).
13

Williams' South-Eastern Coast Directory, 1849. Transcribed
in extenso. Abstract of trades. (MS.).
13

ROWE, William.
Church Book, 1770, 1771, 1772. (MS.).
13

The houses account, 1763. (MS.).
13

ROYAL NATIONAL HOSPITAL, MARGATE.
...for patients afflicted with Scrofula...rules and regulations
to be observed in the Medical and Household Departments of
the Hospital.
1861.
13

ROYAL NATIONAL LIFEBOAT INSTITUTION - MARGATE BRANCH.
Naming ceremony of the motor lifeboat "North Foreland" on 17th
May, 1951 - programme.
13

ROYAL SCHOOL FOR DEAF AND DUMB CHILDREN, MARGATE.
A short history of the school (being the) Special Historical
Number of "The Royal School Magazine", Summer, 1938.
13

THE ROYAL SEA-BATHING HOSPITAL.
An album of photographs.
c.1900.
13

THE ROYAL SEA-BATHING HOSPITAL.
Report, list of governors, etc., for the years 1906, 1908, 1909,
1910, 1913, 1914, 1915, 1916, 1918, 1919 and 1921.
13

St. John's Burial Board, Margate: rules and regulations, 1914-15.
13

ST. JOHN THE BAPTIST'S CHURCH, MARGATE.
Register for Briefs, 1678-1844 (MS.).
Statement of Parish Receipts and expenditure for the years,
1885-94.
13

St. John's in the Isle of Thanet. (St. John the Baptist,
Margate - MS.).
1757.
13

St. Peter's Church, Westgate-on-Sea - souvenir brochure.
Ramsgate, Church Publishers. (1965).
3

SANDERS, John AND CO. Publishers.
Six views near Margate.
J. Sanders and Co. July, 1790.
13

Thirty views of Margate.
J. Sanders and Co. c.1860-70.
13

Twenty-four views of Margate.
J. Sanders and Co. c.1860-70.
13

SANGER, Lord George.
Seventy years a showman.
1926.
13

Scheme for removing civil population of Margate to a
place of safety in the event of it being found necessary
to do so in consequence of an unexpected raid or
invasion of the Isle of Thanet by Germans. (Typewritten)
1915.
13

SCOTT, Clement W.
Round about the Island. (pp. 100-133 deal with Ramsgate
and Margate).
1874.
13

The sea-side; or, Margate: a poem in four cantos.
1781.
13

SELECT COMMITTEE ON RAMSGATE AND MARGATE HARBOURS.
Report, 1850. (See Ramsgate).
13,14

SENIOR, W.S.
A faithful minister: a brief memoir of the late Rev.
Walter Senior, M.A., by his son, W.S.S., together with
some of the sermons preached by him in Holy Trinity
Church, Margate during his vicariate, 1887-1902.
1904.
13

A series of letters to the inhabitants of Margate on the
subject of existing differences!!!
1819.
13

Service arranged by the Mayor of Margate (Alderman W.
Booth Reeve, J.P.), for special Intercession for the
help of God in the present war...August 4th, 1915.
13

SEYMOUR, Robert.
A trip to Margate by Paul Pry, Esq.
1820-25.
13

SHAW, Conan.
The secret language of the Shell Temple of Margate,
by C. and N.I. Shaw.
(Petts Wood, Shaw). (1955).
2,3,12

The Shell Temple of Margate: an archaic masterpiece,
by C. and N.I. Shaw.
1954.
13,14

The Shell Temple of Margate: new light on its antiquity
through the translation of its hidden language, by C.
and N.I. Shaw.
(Petts Wood, Shaw). (1958).
3,12

SHEA, Francis M.
The old house, King Street (Margate): its historical
background with a description of the restoration work
(4 photographs), by F.M. Shea and A.M. Kay.
n.d.
13

The Shell Temple of Margate, known as the Grotto.
n.d.
13

SHEPHERD, T.L.
A short history of Cecil Square Baptist Church (formerly
known as Ebenezer Baptist Chapel), Margate, 1762-1912.
Compiled from the church records and other sources.
1912.
13

SHONE, Isaac.
A criticism of Mr. Baldwin Latham's proposed scheme for
the drainage of Margate, addressed to the Chairman of
the Vigilance Committee (Margate), T. Smith Rowe, Esq.,
V.D.
1889.
13

SHONE, Isaac.
The Shone system as applicable to the drainage of Margate.
1888.
13

SKELSMERGH HOUSE SCHOOL, MARGATE.
Record, I-LXXXI, 4 vols. (At LII, 1911, the name of the school
changes to Laleham).
Skelsmergh House School. 1894-1920.
13

SKETCHLEY, Arthur, pseud.
Mrs. Brown at Margate.
1874.
13

SNELLING, H.
A few wheezes about Margate by a one-eyed man.
1911.
13

Souvenir and programme of the Tenth Annual Margate Exhibition
and Civic Festival, 1931. Eleventh Annual Exhibition, 1932.
Fourteenth Annual Exhibition, 1935.
13

Souvenir of Margate.
1900.
13

Souvenir of Pettman's up-to-date bathing.
1911.
13

Souvenir of the opening of the new Dreamland Cinema, Margate.
1935.
13

Souvenir of the opening of the Thanet School of Art and Crafts,
Margate.
1931.
13

Souvenir programme of the laying of the foundation stone of the
Margate and District General Hospital, St. Peter's Road,
Margate by the Lord Mayor of London, September 25th, 1928.
13

Souvenir programme of the opening of the Astoria (Cinema),
Cliftonville, August 4th, 1934.
13

Souvenir programme of the opening of the Regal Cinema, Margate,
21st December, 1934.
13

Souvenir programme to commemorate the official opening (of)
Margate and District General Hospital...by Their Royal Highnesses,
Prince and Princess Arthur of Connaught on July 3rd, 1930.
13

Souvenir to commemorate the opening of the new Post Office,
Margate, July 19th, 1910. (Incomplete).
13

SPRY, John Hume.
A sermon preached before His Grace, the Lord Archbishop of
Canterbury...at Trinity Chapel, in Margate, September 24th, 1830.
13

STANLEY, Frederick.
Old Margate revisited. (Contained in BRASIER, W.C. -
"Illustrated guide to Margate", etc.).
Margate; Brasier. 1879.
13

STANLEY, Frederick.
A short history of Margate Parish Church (St. John the Baptist,
Thanet).
1921.
13

STAREY, W.H.
Notes on Margate: numerous and humerous. In prose and verse.
1874.
13

Statement of the proceedings of two meetings, held at
the Royal Hotel, Margate, for the purpose of considering
the propriety of establishing an asylum for the treatment of Cancer and Scrofula under the care of Mr.
Charles Whitlaw.
1822.
13

Suppression of sacred music in Margate...a correct
report of the important trial for libel...at Maidstone,
1817. (Included in Boys, S.S. and Chancellor,
defendants, in a trial for libel).
J. Denne. 1817.
11

THORNE, E. Publisher.
Thirty views of Margate.
E. Thorne. n.d.
3

THORNTON, A.
The storm; or, a winter at Margate. (A poem about
an actual storm).
1809.
13

Tivioli Gardens, Margate: programme of re-opening and
costume fete, representing the gardens in the year
1775. August 16th and 18th, 1898.
13

TOMPSETT, B.P.
The making of a new garden: Crittenden House,
Matfield, Kent.
Ballantyne and Co. 1960.
15

TRADES UNION CONGRESS.
Souvenir of the Trades Union Congress, Margate, 1935,
edited by H. Tracey.
13

A true rehearsall and survey of all the barques and
vessells belonginge to the peere or harbour at Margate
in the parishe (of Sct. John's Thanett) with their
severall burthens, and also the names of all such
masters, pilotts and seamen belonging to the said
parishe. Transcribed from Calender of State Papers,
Domestic, 1584, Public Record Office, by R.A. Coates.
1939.
13

TURPIN, H.
New Margate and Ramsgate guide in letters to a friend.
n.d.
17

Twenty-four views of Margate. (Reproduced from
engravings).
n.d.
11

The Vortigern smuggler's caves and ancient deneholes,
Margate.
Clark and Knapp. 1912.
6,13

W., J. AND CO. LTD. Publisher.
Souvenir of Margate.
J.W. and Co. Ltd. c.1900.
13

WADDINGTON, Joshua.
The addresses, last words and more last words!, at the
Town Hall (Margate). (J. Waddington was slandered in
conncection with acts of vandalism committed by his
uncle Dr. Jarvis).
1836.
13

WADDINGTON, Joshua.
A plain statement illustrative of a late base conspiracy.
1837.
13

WALTON, Hugh Merscy.
The history of the Margate Ambulance Corps. (Typewritten).
1935.
13

WALTON, Hugh Merscy.
A short history of Holy Trinity Church, Margate, 1825-1932.
Margate, Simpson and Turner. 1932.
3,12,13

WATERHOUSE, F. Aelred.
Notes for a guide to Salmestone Grange.
1936.
13,14

WATERHOUSE, F. Aelred.
Short history of Salmestone Grange.
Cooper.
13(1948) 14(1939)

"WAYFARER", pseud.
From Leeds to Margate...
Yorkshire Weekly Post. 1923.
13

A week's journal at Margate.
"The Mirror". 1823.
13

Westbrook improvements. Particulars, plan and conditions of
sale of 45 plots of choice freehold land...26th August, 1913.
13

The Westgate Chronicle and Birchington News. (Nos. 1 to 13,
August 21st, 1880-November 6th, 1880).
1880.
13

WESTGATE-ON-SEA CHAMBER OF COMMERCE.
Sunshine, health, happiness: Westgate-on-Sea, Kent - the ideal
holiday resort.
1947.
13

WESTGATE-ON-SEA CHAMBER OF COMMERCE.
Westgate-on-Sea, Thanet: official guide.
1(1954 etc.) 4(1956) 12(1936 and 1954) 13(1935-1939)

Westgate-on-Sea.
I. Venis. c.1900?
8

WHITTEN, Wilfred. (John o' London, pseud.).
The sea-side past and present.
T.P's Magazine. 1911.
13

WHITTEN, Wilfred. (John o' London, pseud.).
Why I like Margate.
John o' London's Weekly. 1938.
13

WOOD, J.G.
Along Margate sands.
1866.
13

WOODRUFF, Cumberland H.
The making of Margate.
Home Counties Magazine. 1902.
13,14,17

MARKBEECH

Markbeech Holy Trinity Church: report of speeches...by the
Bishop of Rochester and the Rev. Canon Hunt at Dedication
Festival, 1902.
Spottiswoode. 1903.
7

MARLOWE, CHRISTOPHER

BAKELESS, John Edwin.
Christopher Marlowe.
Cape. 1938.
3

Christopher Marlowe and the newsbooks. (Reprinted from the
"Journalism Quarterly", March, 1937).
3

The tragicall history of Christopher Marlowe, 2 vols.
Harvard University Press. 1942.
3

BOAS, Frederick S.
Marlowe and his circle.
Oxford University Press. 1929.
3

BROOKE, C.F. Tucker.
The life of Marlowe and the Tragedy of Dido, Queen of
Carthage.
Methuen. 1930.
12

CAWSTON, Edward P.
Plight and flight of Christopher Marlowe: an
Elizabethan drama.
St. Leonards, Silverhill Academic Enterprises. n.d.
3

ELLIS, Havelock.
Christopher Marlowe...(biographical introduction...
and text of works).
Benn. 1951.
18

HALL, E. Vine.
Instrumentary papers III, Marlowe's death at
Deptford...
1937.
18

HEILBRONER, R.L.
The murder of the man who was Shakespeare (Marlowe).
(Pamphlet).
"Esquire". 1954.
18

HENDERSON, Philip.
And morning in his eyes...Christopher Marlowe.
London, Boriswood. 1937.
3,18

HENDERSON, Philip.
Christopher Marlowe.
British Council. Longmans Green. 1956.
3,18(1952)

HOFFMAN, Calvin.
The man who was Shakespeare.
London, Parrish. 1956.
3

HOFFMAN, Calvin.
The Shakespeare murder mystery. (Article in "Coronet",
July, 1955).
3

HOTSON, J. Leslie.
The death of Christopher Marlowe.
Nonesuch Press. 1925.
18

INGRAM, John H.
Christopher Marlowe and his associates.
London, G. Richards. 1904.
3

LEVIN, Harry.
The overreacher: a study of Christopher Marlowe.
1954.
4

LEWIS, J.G.
Christopher Marlowe: his life and works. (Lecture
delivered in Canterbury, 8th May, 1890 in aid of the
Marlowe Memorial Fund).
Canterbury, N.E. Goulden. 1890.
1,3,11

LEWIS, J.G.
Christopher Marlowe: outlines of his life and works.
London, W.W. Gibbings. 1891.
3

MARLOWE, Christopher.
Marlowe's Doctor Faustus, 1604-166-. Parallel texts
edited by W.W. Greg.
Oxford University Press. 1950.
3

MARLOWE, Christopher.
The works of Christopher Marlowe...by the Rev.
Alexander Dyce.
Routledge, Warne, Routledge. 1862.
3

GREAT BRITAIN: LAWS, etc. (GEO. II).
An Act to revive ...an Act...for making the River of Medway navigable...
1740.
8,11

GREAT BRITAIN: LAWS, etc. (GEO. II).
An Act for the more effectual preservation and improvement of the spawn and fry of the fish of the River Thames and waters of the Medway...
Printed by Thomas Baskett. 1757.
11

GREAT BRITAIN: LAWS, etc. (GEO. III).
An Act for improving the navigation of the River Medway.
1792.
8

GREAT BRITAIN: LAWS, etc. (WILL. IV).
Minutes of evidence on Medway Navigation Bill (fragment).
1836.
11

GREAT BRITAIN: LAWS, etc. (VIC.).
Medway Conservancy Act.
1881.
8

GREAT BRITAIN: LAWS, etc. (GEO. V).
Medway Conservancy Act.
1919.
8

GREAT BRITAIN: LAWS, etc. (GEO. V).
Medway Conservancy Act.
1926.
8

GREAT BRITAIN: LAWS, etc. (GEO. V).
Upper Medway Navigation and Conservancy Act, 1911. (Photocopy).
Printed by Eyre and Spottiswoode. 1911.
11

GREAT BRITAIN: LAWS, etc. (GEO. VI).
Medway Conservancy Act.
1939.
8

GREAT BRITAIN: LAWS, etc. (ELIZ. II).
Medway Conservancy Act.
H.M.S.O. 1963.
4,8

GREAT BRITAIN: LAWS, etc. (ELIZ. II).
Pier and Harbour Order (Medway Lower Navigation) Confirmation Act.
H.M.S.O. 1959.
4,8,12

GREAT BRITAIN: LAWS, etc. (ELIZ. II) - STATUTORY INSTRUMENTS.
The Medway Ports Reorganisation Scheme, 1968 Confirmation Order, 1969. Made, 12th May, 1969. Coming into operation, 21st July, 1969. (S.1, 1969 No. 1,045).
H.M.S.O. (1969).
2,4,8

GREAT BRITAIN, Parliament.
Thames and Medway Conservancy Bill.
1857.
8

HANCOCK, E.W.
Excursion to Penshurst and the Medway Valley. (From Proceedings of the Geologists' Association, Part 7, 1908).
17

HARRIS, Edwin.
Notable visits to the Navie Royall lying in the Medway.
Rochester, E. Harris. 1913.
1,15

The riverside: an itinerary of the Medway within the City of Rochester and the memories it recalls. Limited edition.
Rochester, Mackays. (1930).
8,11,12,15

A trip down the Medway. (Old Rochester series, No. 5).
Rochester, E. Harris. 1897.
11

A trip up the River Medway...(Old Rochester series, No. 6).
Rochester, E. Harris. 1897.
8,11

HARRISON, Jeffery Graham.
Breeding birds of the Medway Estuary, by J. Harrison, J.N. Humphreys and Geoffrey Graves.
Kent Ornithological Society and W.A.G.B.I. 1972.
11

HARRISON, Jeffery Graham.
Peril in perspective: an account of the Medway Estuary oil pollution of September, 1966, by J.G. Harrison and W.F.A. Buck.
Kent Ornithological Society. 1967.
12

HIRE CRUISERS (MAIDSTONE) LTD.
Holidays afloat on the River Medway.
Hire Cruisers (Maidstone) Ltd. 1963.
12

HOUSING AND LOCAL GOVERNMENT, Ministry of.
The Medway Water (No. 1) Order, 1957. (S.1, 1957 No. 1,772).
H.M.S.O. 1957.
4

The Medway Water (No. 2) Order, 1957. (S.1, 1957 No. 2,022).
H.M.S.O. 1957.
4

The Medway Water Order, 1959.
H.M.S.O. (1959).
12

The Medway Water Order, 1966. (S.1, 1966 No. 556).
H.M.S.O. 1966.
4

The Medway Water (No. 2) Order, 1966. (S.1, 1966 No. 557).
H.M.S.O. 1966.
4

HUTCHINGS, G.E.
River deposits of the Lower Medway Basin. (From Proceedings of the Geologists' Association, 1925).
11,15,17

INLAND WATERWAYS ASSOCIATION - LONDON AND SOUTH-EASTERN. BRANCH.
The River Medway, Allington to Tonbridge: a handbook of useful information for river users, with a detailed description of the navigation, diagrams of locks and map, edited by D.C.N. Salmon.
Inland Waterways Association. 1972.
11

IRELAND, Samuel.
Picturesque views on the River Medway...
Egerton. 1793.
1,3,4,5,6,8,11,12,15

JESSUP, Ronald Frank.
Bronze Age antiquities from the Lower Medway. (Reprinted from Archaeologia Cantiana, Vol. 45, (1933)).
4,17

JOHNSTON, G.D.
The Medway Scrapbooks, compiled by G.D. Johnston, 7 vols. (MSS.).
n.d.
11

JONES, H. Lewis.
Swin, Swale and Swatchway; or, cruises down the Thames, the Medway and the Essex rivers, by H.L. Jones and C.B. Lockwood.
Waterlow. 1892.
1,8

KENT COUNTY COUNCIL.
The Medway could make a maritime industrial development area...(notes for News Conference at County Hall). (Typescript).
May, 1970.
4

KENT COUNTY COUNCIL - PLANNING DEPARTMENT.
Potential of the Medway Estuary as a maritime industrial development area: a discussion of the economic factors and an appraisal of its impact on Mid and North Kent.
Kent County Council. 1970.
2,3,4,8,11

KENT RIVER BOARD.
River Medway through Maidstone...
Kent River Board. 1959.
1,11,12

KERENSKY, Oleg A.
Medway Bridge: design, by O.A. Kerensky and G. Little.
In Proceedings of the Institute of Civil Engineers, Vol. 29,
September, 1964.
2

KNIGHT, R.J.B.
Medway navigation. (Tonbridge School Local History Researches).
1961.
11

McCULLOCH, Joseph.
Medway adventure.
M. Joseph. 1946.
1,5,8,12,17

MACKAY, Charles.
The Thames and its tributaries; or, rambles among rivers,
Vol. 2.
Richard Bentley. 1840.
11

MARCH, Edgar James.
Spritsail barges of the Thames and Medway. (See Ships and
Shipping).
Marshall. 1948.
1,3,4,5,8,11,12,13,14,15,17

MARSH, Ronald J.
The conservancy of the River Medway, 1881-1969.
Medway Conservancy Board. 1971.
4,5,6,7,8,9,11,19

MEDWAY LOWER NAVIGATION.
Share certificate for £100, No. 1,547.
Blake. 1802.
12

Medway papers by Medway people, Nos. 1-3, April-December,
1923, 3 vols.
4,8,11,12

MEDWAY PORTS AUTHORITY.
Boating on the River Medway and the Swale.
Medway Ports Authority. 1969 and 1970.
8

A handbook to the Medway Ports Authority.
(Duncan Rand). (1971).
11

River Medway.
Medway Ports Authority. 1971.
4,8

THE MEDWAY PRESERVATION SOCIETY.
The effects of a M.I.D.A. on the Medway Estuary.
The Medway Preservation Society. 1971.
8

Minutes of evidence taken before the Committee on the Medway
Navigation Bill, 1836.
Taylor. 1836.
12

MUNRO, William.
The early defences of the Medway. (Reprinted from the "United
Services Magazine", September, 1910).
8

NICKLIN, J.A.
Dickens land.
Blackie. 1911.
1,3,4,5,7,8,9,11,12,15,18

NORIE, J.W.
Sailing directions for the River Thames from London to the
Nore and Sheerness...Rochester...
C. Wilson. 1855.
15

(ORDNANCE, Board of).
(Plan of the River Medway from Rochester to Sheerness showing
the depth of water at low water at spring tides, the positions
of the forts and the dispositions of the guns. Surveyed by
G. Collins, 1688). (Photograph of tracing of original,
expanded so that 2.4 inches = 1 mile).
1688.
4

ORR, William S. Publisher.
Summer excursions in the County of Kent, along the banks
of the Rivers Thames and Medway.
1847.
2,4,15,17

PARLIAMENT: BILLS - (ELIZ. II).
Pier and Harbour Provisional Order (Medway Lower
Navigation)...
H.M.S.O. 1959.
4

PROSSER, Arthur.
Medway history.
Evening Post. (1970).
4

PURDY, John.
The new piloting directory for the different channels
of the Thames and Medway.
R.H. Laurie. 1846.
12

River Medway. (Extracted from "Precision", January,
1967).
4

River Medway Dutch Week: souvenir programme, 10th to
17th June, 1967.
Chatham Borough Council. 1967.
11

SHAW, Terence David.
A study of the bridges over the River Medway.
(Photocopy of a typescript thesis).
1970.
11

TOMBLESON, W.
Eighty picturesque views on the Thames and Medway...
the descriptions by W.G. Fearnside.
W. Tombleson. n.d.
4,7

TOMBLESON, W.
...Panoramic map of the Thames and Medway, new edition.
(c.1850).
4,8

TURNER, Sydney K. of Luton.
Story of early man in the Medway Valley. (Typescript).
1945-52.
4,8,15

USHERWARD, P.L.
Nineteenth century monopoly in question. (Tonbridge
School Local History Researches).
1963.
11

VOYSEY, Annesley.
The Medway Valley. (Film strip and lecture notes).
Common Ground Ltd. 1961.
8

WATERS, Brian.
Thirteen rivers to the Thames.
Dent. 1964.
1,4,5,11,12,15

WATSON, P.B.
Navigation of the River Medway, 1600-1842. (Typescript
MS.).
1964.
11

WILSON, Charles. Publisher.
Sailing directions for the Rivers Thames and Medway.
C. Wilson. 1881.
15

WILSON, Effingham. Publisher.
A new steamboat companion in an excursion to
Greenhithe, Northfleet, Gravesend, the Nore and Herne
Bay with a trip up the Medway to Rochester Bridge.
E. Wilson, B. Stead and W. Strange. c.1835.
1,9,11,17

WOODHOUSE, P.S.
Leisure on the Medway, edited by P.S. Woodhouse.
Rochester, Ampersand Publications. 1963.
4,11

WOODTHORPE, T.J.
The Tudor navy and the Medway...(Typescript).
n.d.
11

YOUNG, M.G.
A new navigation enterprise and its problems. (Tonbridge
School Local History Researches).
Tonbridge School. 1963.
11

MEDWAY TOWNS

Borough pocket guide to Rochester, Chatham and Gillingham.
c.1910.
8

BOUNDARY COMMISSION FOR ENGLAND.
Report with respect to the areas comprised in the constituencies
of Rochester and Chatham, Gravesend...
H.M.S.O. 1963.
4,8,9

BRAIN, Richard F.
The by-pass road: the problem of traffic relief for the
Medway Towns. (Reprinted from "Chatham News", 3rd·August,
1934 and 18th January, 1935).
8

CATHOLIC MARRIAGE ADVISORY COUNCIL - MEDWAY TOWNS CENTRE.
Annual reports, 1967-1968, 1969.
4

CHATHAM AND DISTRICT HISTORICAL SOCIETY.
List of the books on the Medway Towns and district in the
public libraries of Chatham, Gillingham and Rochester.
c.1950.
4

CHATHAM NEWS.
Almanack and yearbook.
Parrett and Neves.
4(1898, 1899, 1906)
8(1893-97, 1898-1902, 1903, 1907, 1908-12, 1913-17)
17(1899, 1907, 1908)

CHATHAM, ROCHESTER, STROOD AND BROMPTON MECHANICS INSTITUTION -
Established, 1836.
Rules.
Reynolds. 1837.
4

Chatham, Rochester, Strood and Brompton illustrated almanac
and local guide.
Mackay. 1898.
8

COULSON, Barbara May.
The Medway Towns: growth of the Medway Towns since the
Second World War (1945 onwards). Bibliography. (Typescript).
1967.
4

COXWELL, Henry.
My life and balloon experiences. (Extract relating to his
early life in the Medway Towns), 2nd edition. (A photocopy).
W.H. Allen. 1889.
4,11

DICKSON, George.
The local democrat, 1925-45.
1945.
8

FAYNE, Eric.
Tramways of the Medway Towns. (In "Trams", No. 19, October,
1965).
4

GILLINGHAM PUBLIC LIBRARY.
The Medway Towns and district: a list of books...
n.d.
8

GREAT BRITAIN: LAWS, etc. (VIC.).
Brompton, Chatham, Gillingham and Rochester Water Bill,
Monday, 2nd May, 1898.
15

HARRIS, Edwin.
The Eastgate series. (35 pamphlets concerning the history and
description of the Medway Towns...).
Rochester, E. Harris and Sons. 1909-22.
4,8,11,12,15

HARRIS, Edwin.
Short excursions...
Mackays Ltd. 1928.
12

HOGG, P. Fitzgerald.
Chatham, Rochester and Gillingham, etc. (A scrapbook
of press cuttings and other items of local interest,
mainly of the period c.1945-50), compiled by P.F.
Hogg.
4

HOUSING AND LOCAL GOVERNMENT, Ministry of.
Rochester, Chatham and Gillingham Joint Sewerage Order.
H.M.S.O. 1963.
8

JONES, John Gale.
Sketch of a political tour through Rochester, Chatham,
etc. Part 1.
1796.
17

KENT COUNTY COUNCIL - PLANNING DEPARTMENT.
Kent development plan, 1967 revision. Medway Towns
map (1970 revision); report on the survey and analysis.
Kent County Council. 1970.
2,7,8

KENT COUNTY COUNCIL - PLANNING DEPARTMENT.
Kent development plan (1967 revision). Medway Towns
map (1970 revision) amendment to written statement.
Kent County Council. 1970.
7

KENT COUNTY COUNCIL - PLANNING DEPARTMENT.
Kent development plan...Medway Towns, town map (1970
revision) written statement.
Kent County Council. 1970.
2,8

KENT EDUCATION COMMITTEE.
The arts in the Medway Towns, 1951-52.
Kent Education Committee. (1953).
4

Development plan for education in the Medway Towns.
Kent County Council. 1947.
15

Medway youth organisations.
Parrett Ltd. c.1950.
8,15

KENT EDUCATION COMMITTEE - MEDWAY DIVISIONAL EXECUTIVE.
Medway Division, Kent.
(1972).
4

MACKAY, W. AND J. AND CO. Publishers.
Illustrated tourist guide to Rochester, Chatham and
neighbourhood.
W. and J. Mackay and Co. (c.1895).
2,7,11,15

MASS RADIOGRAPHY CAMPAIGN JOINT COMMITTEE.
X-ray campaign, Medway Towns, June, 1959.
1960.
8

MEDWAY AMATEUR RECEIVING AND TRANSMITTING SOCIETY.
M.A.R.T.S. newsletter. Nos. 1-5, November, 1963-
March, 1964. Nos. 9-10, July-August, 1964.
4

MEDWAY AMATEUR SWIMMING ASSOCIATION.
Handbook, 1961, edited by G.R.T. Capeling.
Medway Amateur Swimming Association. 1961.
8

MEDWAY AMATEUR SWIMMING ASSOCIATION.
Handbook, 1962, edited by P. O'Connell.
Rochester, Brewster. 1962.
8

MEDWAY AREA SUNDAY FOOTBALL LEAGUE.
Official handbook, season 1971-72.
4

MEDWAY ARTS COUNCIL.
Medway Arts Festival, 18th June-4th July, 1966:
souvenir programme.
4,8

MEDWAY CAMERA CLUB.
View: the magazine of the Medwa- Camera Club, No. 7, May, 1963.
4

MEDWAY CIVIL DEFENCE COMMITTEE.
(Minutes), 13th January, 1959 in progress.
4

MEDWAY CREMATORIUM COMMITTEE.
Medway Crematorium.
(1960).
4

MEDWAY CREMATORIUM COMMITTEE.
Minutes of meetings, 16th December, 1958 in progress.
4

MEDWAY GROUP CONTROL.
(Secret) "Blitzmerg" Medway Towns, No. 208.
Medway Group Control. 11th January, 1941.
7

MEDWAY INDUSTRIES EXHIBITION, 1949.
Souvenir guide to Medway Industries Exhibition, May 21st-28th, 1949.
Kent Art Printers. 1949.
4,8,11,15

MEDWAY POSTGRADUATE MEDICAL SOCIETY.
Medway Postgraduate Medical Centre.
(1972).
4

MEDWAY PRODUCTIVITY ASSOCIATION.
Report and accounts, 1970-71.
4

MEDWAY TOWNS METHODIST CHURCHES.
Circuit plan and directory, March, 1970. (In progress - 4 per year).
4

MEDWAY TOWNS SPORTS ADVISORY COUNCIL.
Medway Festival of Sport, 1969. (Programme).
4

MEDWAY YOUTH EMPLOYMENT COMMITTEE.
Annual report for the year ended 30th September.
4(1957, 1959-64)   8(1956-57, 1959-61)

New Voice, No. 1, Autumn, 1962. (Editors: Colin R. Fry and Howard Inchbold). (Ceased publication).
Rochester. 1962.
4

OMNIBUS SOCIETY.
Short historical notes and itinerary in connection with Medway Towns study tour, Saturday, 20th May, 1967. (Duplicated).
4

PHIPPEN, James.
Descriptive sketches of Rochester, Chatham and their vicinities.
Rochester, Phippen. 1862.
1,4,5,8,11,12,15

A pictorial guide to Rochester (and Strood), Chatham and New Brompton (Gillingham).
n.d.
12

PRESNAIL, James.
Life in the Medway Valley and beyond. (Cuttings from the Rochester, Chatham and Gillingham News), 3 folio vols.
4

REES, Henry.
The Medway Towns - their settlement, growth and economic development: thesis...photocopy. (Typescript).
1954.
4,8

RAND, D.
Industrial review and guide to the Medway, edited by D. Rand.
1(1962)
4(1962, 1969, 1971)
7(1962)
8(1962, 1965)
11(1962)
15(1962, 1965)
21(1965)

ROCHARD, J.
Chatham, Rochester and Strood, Old and New Brompton... a concise and comprehensive account...
(Chatham, Stafford). (1894).
4,15

ROCHESTER AND CHATHAM HOME SAFETY COMMITTEE.
Rochester and Chatham home safety handbook.
(1964).
4

Rochester, Chatham and Gillingham as an industrial centre and as a residential neighbourhood.
(19--?).
4

ROCHESTER, CHATHAM AND GILLINGHAM JOINT SEWERAGE BOARD.
Guide to the purification works of the Joint Sewerage Board at Motney Hill, Rainham, Kent.
(1961).
8

(Minutes), 1924-25 in progress. (From 1924-34 the Board was the Rochester and Chatham Joint Sewerage Board).
4,8(1965 in progress)

Trunk sewer and extensions to Motney Hill Sewage Disposal Works: estimated expenditure, 1962-71.
(1961).
4

ROCK AND CO. Publishers.
Royal album: Rochester, Chatham and neighbourhood.
Rock and Co. c.1890.
15

ROWE, Mrs. Mercy Elizabeth.
John Tetley Rowe and his work: a brief record of his life and work in London, Chatham and Rochester by his wife.
Chatham, Parrett and Neves. 1915.
4,8,12,15

RYE, William Brenchley.
Visits to Rochester and Chatham made by royal, noble and distinguished personages English and foreign, 1300-1783. (From Archaeologia Cantiana, Vol. 6, 1866).
1,4,8,11,12,15,17

SPASTICS SOCIETY - MEDWAY TOWNS BRANCH.
Yearbook, 1965.
4,8

STARKIE, D.N.H.
Traffic and industry...
London School of Economics. 1967.
3,5,11,15

View album of New Brompton, Chatham and Rochester.
(c.1899).
1

WHITTA, Terry.
Art and entertainment in the Medway Towns: a report produced from the findings of Breakaway Arts.
September, 1964.
4,8

WRIGHT, I.G. Publisher.
Topography of Rochester, Chatham, Strood, Brompton, etc...
Chatham, I.G. Wright. 1838.
1,4,8,11,15,17

YOUNG, Percy.
The Tide Mill secret: a novel (set in the Medway Towns).
Stockwell. 1908.
4

MEOPHAM

CARLEY, James.
The lost roads of Meopham and nearby parishes.
Meopham Publications Committee. 1971.
4,9,11

CARLEY, James.
The story of Meopham Mill.
Meopham Publications Committee. 1972.
2,9,11

MEOPHAM Cont'd

GOLDING-BIRD, Cuthbert Hilton.
The history of Meopham.
Williams and Norgate. 1934.
1,2,4,5,6,9,11,12,13,14,15,17,18,19

Short account of Meopham and its church.
Chatham, Parrett. n.d.
5,11

The story of old Meopham.
1918.
4,5,8,9,11,12,15

GUNNING, George.
Documents of the Gunning family, edited by G. Gunning.
Privately Printed. 1834.
11

MEOPHAM PARISH COUNCIL.
The Meopham book.
Meopham Parish Council. c.1963 and 1970.
9

MEOPHAM SOCIETY.
Broadwalk: report on the A227 through Meopham.
Meopham Society. 1970.
4,8,9,11

NORTON, L.M.
A short history of Meopham Parish Church.
Peter Ness. 1957.
12

MEREWORTH

BRENTNALL, Margaret.
Mereworth Castle. (Taken from "Coming Events in Britain",
1957).
11

HILTON, John Anthony.
Mereworth: a village history.
Hadlow, Hilton. 1964.
1,4,7,8,11,12,15,19

MASTER, James. (of Yotes Court, Mereworth).
Expense-book of James Master, Esq., from A.D. 1646 to A.D.
1676, edited by Mrs. Dalison.
Mitchell and Hughes. 1883.
4(Parts 1 and 2 only, 1646-1657)   12

Mereworth Castle...(Reprinted from "The Antique Collector",
October, 1954).
2

WARREN, Clarence Henry.
Boy in Kent.
Bles. 1937.
1,3(1947) 4,5,8,9,11,12,15,17,18

MERSHAM

EDINGER, J.H.
The parish church of St. John the Baptist, Mersham.
Dover Express. 1955.
4,11,12

LEWIS, Hilda.
Deprived children: the Mersham experiment.
Oxford University Press. 1954.
12

RENDEL, Sheila.
The Caldecott Community.
Mersham-le-Hatch, Caldecott Community. 1960.
2,4,7,8,11,12

MERSHAM HATCH

RODERICK, Colin.
John Knatchbull, from quarterdeck to gallows.
Angus and Robertson. 1963.
7

MERSTON

ALLEN, A.F.
The lost village of Merston. In Archaeologia Cantiana, Vol. 71,
1957.
17

MILITARY AND NAVAL HISTORY

ABELL, Francis.
Prisoners of war in Britain, 1756 to 1815: a record of
their lives, their romance and their sufferings.
H. Milford. 1914.
4

ADAMS, C.
Notes on the history of The Queen's Own Royal West
Kent Regiment (MSS.).
1916.
11

ADMIRALTY.
The Royal Marines: the Admiralty account of their
achievement, 1939-43.
H.M.S.O. 1944.
4

ATKINSON, Christopher Thomas.
Queen's Own Royal West Kent Regiment, 1914-19.
Simpkin Marshall etc. 1924.
1,2,3,4,5,6,7,8,9,11,12,14,15,16,17,18

BACKHOUSE, J.B.
With "The Buffs" in South Africa.
Aldershot, Gale and Polden. 1903.
11

BAILEY, Captain H.
"Playboys" - an unofficial history of B. Squadron,
141st Regiment R.A.C. (The Buffs), 1944-45. (Late
7th Regiment).
Leeds, J.H. Davenport and Sons, Printers. n.d.
12

BAKER, Bernard Granville.
Old cavalry stations.
Heath Cranton. 1934.
3

BIRCH, Richard.
Proceedings of a general Court Martial...on seven
officers of the West Kent Regiment of Militia...
1807.
11

BLAXLAND, Gregory.
The Buffs: Royal East Kent Regiment, the 3rd Regiment
of Foot.
L. Cooper. 1972.
4,5,9,11

The farewell years: the final historical records of
The Buffs, Royal East Kent Regiment (3rd foot)...
1948-67.
Canterbury, Queen's Own Buffs Office. 1967.
1,2,3,4,5,6,9,11,12

A guide to The Queen's Regiment.
Canterbury, Privately Printed. 1970.
1,2,3,6

Home Counties Brigade.
Canterbury, Gibbs. 196-?
3,6,11(with duplicated amendments, 1962 and 1963)
14

Story of The Queen's Own Buffs, The Royal Kent
Regiment.
Canterbury, Gibbs. 1963.
1,2,3,4,5,6,7,8,9,11,12,15,19

BLOMEFIELD, Thomas.
(Surveys of the English coast, 1779-1793). (From
records of reports made by the Inspector of Royal
Artillery on the coast defences of England...extracts).
n.d.
4

BLUMBERG, Sir. H.E.
Britain's sea soldiers: a record of the Royal Marines
during the War, 1914-1919.
Devonport, Swiss and Co. 1927.
4

BONHOTE, John.
Historical records of the West Kent Militia: with
some account of the earlier defensive levies in Kent.
Printed by Hudson-Kearns. 1909.
1,2,4,5,8,9,11,12,15,17,18

BRANCH-JOHNSON, William.
Wolves of the channel (1681-1856).
London, Wishart and Co. 1931.
6

Brief history of the 297th (Kent Yeomanry) L.A.A. Regiment, R.A.
(T.A.).
  Aldershot, Gale and Polden. (c.1946).
2

THE BUFFS (ROYAL EAST KENT REGIMENT).
Pamphlet.
H.M.S.O. n.d.
3
Recruiting brochure.
Malcolm Page. 1954.
3,4,20
Roll of officers and men of The Buffs who fell in the Great
War, 1914-18.
Medici Society. n.d.
3

THE BUFFS (ROYAL EAST KENT REGIMENT) PAST AND PRESENT ASSOCIATION.
Veteri frondescit honore, 1572-1924: handbook of the...
Association.
The Buffs (Royal East Kent Regiment) Past and Present
Association. 1924.
3

BUSK, Hans.
Handbook for Hythe: comprising a familiar explanation of the
laws of projectiles.
Routledge. 1860.
10

(CANNON, Richard).
Historical record of the Third Regiment of Foot, or The Buffs
...from its origin in the reign of Queen Elizabeth...to 1838.
Longman, Orme and Co. 1839.
3,7

CAPPER, Douglas Parode.
Moat defensive: a history of the waters of the Nore Command,
55 B.C. to 1961.
Barker. 1963.
4,8,12,15

CHAPLIN, Howard Douglas.
The Queen's Own Royal West Kent Regiment, 1881-1914.
Maidstone, Regimental History Committee. 1959.
1,2,3,4,5,7,8,9,11,12,15,16,17,19

The Queen's Own Royal West Kent Regiment, 1920-50.
Michael Joseph. 1954.
1,2,3,4,5,6,8,9,11,12,15,17,19

The Queen's Own Royal West Kent Regiment, 1951-61.
Maidstone, Regimental Museum Committee. 1964.
1,2,3,4,5,8,9,15,19

The Queen's Own Royal West Kent Regiment, 1954-64.
Michael Joseph. 1964.
2

The Queen's Own Royal West Kent Regiment: a short account of
its origins, service and campaigns, 1756-1956.
Kent Messenger. 1956.
1,5,11,12

CLARKE, Edward Bryan Stanley.
From Kent to Kohima: being the history of the 4th Battalion,
The Queen's Own West Kent Regiment (T.A.), 1939-47, by E.B.S.
Clarke and A.T. Tillott.
Aldershot, Gale and Polden. 1951.
1,3,4,5,8,11,12,15,16

COMMONWEALTB WAR GRAVES COMMISSION.
The War dead of the Commonwealth: register of names, 1939-
45 War...of those buried in...the County of Kent.
1960-61.
2,7

DUGAN, James.
The Great Mutiny.
Deutsch. 1966.
15

DUNCAN, Francis.
History of the Royal Regiment of Artillery, compiled from the
original records by Captain F. Duncan, 2 vols.
London, John Murray. 1872-73.
17

East Kent Regiment of Militia standing orders, 1812.
17

The East Kent Yeoman: War Number, August, 1914-
September, 1915.
East Kent Yeomanry. (1915).
11

EDMEADES, J.F.
Some historical records of the West Kent (Queen's
Own) Yeomanry, 1794-1909.
London, A. Melrose. 1909.
1,2,4,5,6,8,9,11,12,13,15,17,18

EDYE, Major L.
The historical records of the Royal Marines, including
the Duke of York and Albany's Maritime Regiment of
Foot...Vol. 1, 1664-1701, edited by Major L. Edye.
London, Harrison and Sons. 1893.
4

EHRMAN, John.
The Navy in the war of William III, 1689-97: its
state and direction.
Cambridge University Press. 1953.
4,15

FARMER, Henry George.
History of the Royal Artillery Band, 1762-1953.
Royal Artillery Institution. 1954.
17

FAZAN, E.A.C.
Cinque Ports Battalion: the story of the 5th (Cinque
Ports) Battalion, the Royal Sussex Regiment (T.A.),
formerly 1st Cinque Ports Rifle Volunteer Corps: its
antecendents, traditions and uniforms.
Royal Sussex Regimental Association. 1971.
3,7,11

FAZAN, E.A.C.
The New Romney Fencible Cavalry (Duke of York's Own),
1794-1800. (Reprinted from Archaeologia Cantiana,
Vol. LXII, 1949).
Ashford, Headley Bros. 1950.
11,17

(FELTON, L.).
Number 8 Sub-Section "D" Troop - 71st Company of London
(Home Guard) Heavy A.A. Battery, 1942-44. Thornett
Wood. (Bickley).
(1944).
2

1st Kent Artillery Volunteer Corps - Gravesend
Detachment: annual report and statement of accounts,
1886-87.
9

1st Kent Volunteer Rifles: rules, 1859.
12

FLEMING, Peter.
Invasion, 1940.
Hart-Davis. 1957.
7

FYLER, Arthur Evelyn.
History of the 50th, or (The Queen's Own) Regiment
from the earliest date to 1881.
Chapman and Hall. 1895.
1,7,11,17

GILL, Conrad.
The naval mutinies of 1797.
1913.
4

GOULD, J.A.
Short history of the 19th County of Kent (S.S. Gas
Company) British Home Guard (and full typescript from
which the printed text was abbreviated).
South Suburban Gas Co. (1945).
2

GREAT BRITAIN: LAWS, etc. (GEO. III).
An Act for the encouragement...of Petty Officers,
Seamen and Royal Marines, for long and faithful
service...
1814.
11

The Greenwich Volunteers: records, 1859-1900.
17

H.M.S. Kent: a short history, 1653-1928.
Sampson Low. 1928.
4,16

H.M.S. Kent, 1934-36. (8th H.M.S. Kent). (Flagship on China
Station).
Hong Kong, Ye Olde Printerie. 1936.
12

HANGER, George. Baron Coleraine.
Reflections on the menaced invasion and the means of protecting
the capital by preventing the enemy from landing in any part
contiguous to it...and a correct military description of Essex
and Kent.
Stockdale. 1804.
1,8

HANGER, George. Baron Coleraine.
Reflections on the menaced invasion and the means of protecting
the capital by preventing the enemy from landing in any part
contiguous to it. (Facsimile reprint).
E. and W. Books. 1970. Paul P.B. Minet. 1972.
7(1970) 11(1970 and 1972)

HARRIS, George Robert Canning. 4th Baron.
Century of Yeoman Service: records of the Royal East Kent
Mounted Rifles (The East Kent Yeomanry).
Ashford, Kentish Express. 1899.
1,3,6,7,8,11,12,14,15,17,19

HENNIKER, A.M.
The military archaeology of Kent.
Royal Engineers Institute. 1912.
12

HEWITT, T.
From dark to dawn in the King's Navy: the Nelson influence.
A study of life between decks throughout naval history.
1930.
4

HIRST, H.D.
The 3rd Battalion,"The Buffs" in South Africa.
Canterbury, H.J. Goulden. 1908.
3,6,7

Historical records of The Buffs (Royal East Kent Regiment),
5 vols.
Vol 1. Knight, Henry Raleigh. 1572-1704. Gale and Polden.
1905. Medici Society. 1923.
1(1923) 4(1923) 7(1905) 8(1923) 9(1905)
11(1905, 1923) 14(1923)

Vol. 2. Knight, Charles Henry Bruere. 1704-1814.
Medici Society. 1935.
1,3,5,7,8,9,11

Vol. 3. Knight, Charles Henry Bruere 1814-1914.
Medici Society. 1935.
1,3,5,7,8,9,11,14

Vol. 4. Moody, R.H.S. 1914-19. Medici Society. 1922.
1,3,4,5,6,7,9,11,12,13,14,15,17

Vol. 5. Knight, Charles Henry Bruere. 1919-48.
Medici Society. 1951.
1,3,4,5,6,7,8,9,11,12,13,14

History of the Corps of Royal Engineers, 9 vols, 1889-1958.
Vol. 1. Porter, Whitworth. Longmans,Green and Co. 1889
(Reprinted, 1951)
8,15

Vol. 2. Porter, Whitworth. Longmans, Green and Co. 1889
(Reprinted, 1951)
8,15

Vol. 3. Watson, Sir Charles M. Chatham, Royal Engineers
Institute. 1915.
8,15

Vol. 4. Brown, W. and Baker. Chatham, Institution of Royal
Engineers. 1952. (Reprinted, 1954).
8

Vol. 5. The Home Front, France, Flanders and Italy in the First
World War. Chatham, Institution of Royal Engineers. 1952.
8

Vol. 6. Gallipoli, Macedonia, Egypt and Palestine. 1914-18.
Chatham, Institute of Royal Engineers. 1952.
8.

Vol. 7. Campaigns in Mesopotamia and East Africa and the Inter-
War Period. 1919-38. Chatham Institution of Royal
Engineers. 1952.
8

Vol. 8. Pakenham-Walsh, R.P. 1938-48. Campaigns in
France and Belgium. 1939-40. Norway, Middle
East, etc. Chatham, Institution of Royal
Engineers. n.d.
8

Vol. 9. Pakenham-Walsh, R.P. 1938-48. Campaigns in
Sicily and Italy, the war against Japan, North
West Europe. 1944-45 etc. Post-war, 1945-48.
Chatham, Institution of Royal Engineers. n.d.
8

History of the mutiny at Spithead and the Nore, with
an enquiry into its origin and treatment and suggestions
for the prevention of future discontent in the Royal
Navy.
London, Thomas Tegg. 1842.
4

HOWARD, Keble, pseud. (J. Keble BELL).
The glory of Zeebrugge and the "Vindictive".
Chatto and Windus. 1918.
6

HUNT, Leslie.
From hind to hunter: a short history of No. 2 (B)
Group R.A.F.
L. Hunt. 1969.
12

HYTHE SCHOOL OF MUSKETRY.
Four lessons on musketry for the use of officers...
n.d.
17

IGGLESDEN, Sir Charles.
History of the East Kent Volunteers.
Ashford, Kentish Express. 1899.
1,3,4,6,7,8,11,12,14,15,17

IKIN, C.W.
Lewisham Gunners, by C.W. Ikin and others.
Privately Printed. 1962.
1,18

HALL, Eric Foster.
Short history of The Buffs, East Kent Regiment (3rd
Foot).
Medici Society. 2nd Edition. 1950.
1,2,3,7,8,11,14

IVES, J.C.
Six years with the colours: The Buffs, East Kent
Regiment.
Canterbury, Milton Small. 1891.
3

Kent Fencible: the organ of the Kent Volunteer
Fencibles, November, 1915-July, 1918.
Bexleyheath, T.W. Jenkins. 1915-18.
1

Kent National Reserve: register of No. 20 Company,
1911-15.
5

Kent National Reserve: rules and organisation.
Kent County Territorial Force Association. 1912.
5

KENT TERRITORIAL AND AUXILIARY FORCES ASSOCIATION.
A short history of the units administered by the Kent
Territorial and Auxiliary Forces Association.
London, Reid-Hamilton. 1951.
3,5,6,7,8,19

Kent Zone Home Guard.
1941.
5

KEYES, Sir Roger.
Naval memoirs, Vol. 2 - Scapa Flow to Dover Straits,
1916-18.
Thornton, Butterworth. 1935.
6

KNIGHT, Henry Raleigh.
Brief digest of the services of The Buffs (East Kent
Regiment) for the occasion of the Presentation of the
Colours to the 1st Battalion, by the Lord Mayor of
London on 16th May, 1906.
Aldershot, Gale and Polden. 1906.
6,20

(KNIGHT, Richard Lake).
A brief history of the Sittingbourne Volunteers.
Parrett. 1884.
15,20

(LAMBERT, H.J.).
1st Cadet Battalion, Queen's Own Royal West Kent Regiment...
30 years of cadet training...1913-43.
A. Smith and Co., Printers. (1944).
2

LUSHINGTON, Franklin.
Yeoman service: short history of the Kent Yeomanry, 1939-45.
Medici Society. 1947.
2,3,5,8,11,12,15

MANWARING, G.E.
The floating republic: an account of the mutinies at Spithead
and the Nore in 1797, by G.E. Manwaring and B. Dobree.
1935.
4,8,15

(MARSH, Catherine M.).
Memorials of Captain Hedley Vicars, 97th Regiment.
Nisbet. 1856.
2,11

MAUDE, F.F.
Standing orders of the Third (The Buffs) Regiment of Infantry,
compiled by F.F.Maude.
Dublin, Frazer. 1848.
11

MAURICE-JONES, K.W.
The history of the Coast Artillery in the British Army.
Royal Artillery Institution. 1959.
8

A memorial of the late George White Martin...containing a
brief sketch of his life and two funeral sermons, preached in
the parish church of St. Nicholas, Rochester.
London,Clowes. (186-?).
4,8

MILLER, W.S.
School of Musketry at Hythe.
London,Clowes. 1892.
7,11,15

MOLONY, C.V.
"Invicta": with the 1st Battalion, The Queen's Own Royal
West Kent Regiment.
London, Nisbit and Co. 1923.
1,4,5,6,7,8,9,11,12,17

MORGAN, Captain W.A.
The Thames National Training College, "H.M.S. Worcester",
1862-1919.
London, Charles Griffin. 1929.
5

NEALE, Johnson.
The munity at the Nore and the mutiny at Spithead.
n.d.
15

Order of service at the unveiling and dedication of the
memorial tablet in memory of all the ranks of the Kent
Yeomanry who gave their lives...1939-45.
1952.
12

OVENDEN, Ernest H.
Kent Yeomanry Campaigners.
Canterbury,Kentish Gazette. 1920?
3

O'WERT, John.
Rampart of steel...permanent coast, Milton and army reserve.
1825.
17

PARKER, Richard. Defendant.
The whole trial and defence of Richard Parker for mutiny
at the Nore, May, 1797.
Thompson.1797.
12

PONSONBY, Charles.
West Kent (Queen's Own) Yeomanry and 10th (Yeomanry) Battalion,
The Buffs, 1914-19.
A. Melrose. 1920.
1,5,6,7,11,12

PORTER, Samuel.
A favorite bugle horn troop, composed and compiled
for the West Kent Militia...
Printed for Goulding, Phipps and D'Almaine. (1798).
11

Presentation of the Colours to the 2nd Battalion of
The Queen's Own Royal West Kent Regiment, by H.R.H.
Duke of Gloucester at Blenheim Barracks, Aldershot.
Aldershot,Gale and Polden. 1931.
3

The Queen's Own Gazette, No. 462, January, 1914 to
No.533,December, 1919, Vol. 33-Vol. 38.
Maidstone, Queen's Own Royal West Kent Regiment.
1914-19.
3

Queen's Own (Royal West Kent Regiment), 2nd Volunteer
Regiment: rules, 1892.
5

"Rapid fire"..."D" (Machine Gun) Co., 55 Kent Battalion
Home Guard, 1940-44. (Duplicated Typescript).
1946.
2

RITCHIE, A.T.
Lord Amherst and the British advance eastwards to
Burma, by A.T. Ritchie and R. Evans.
Oxford University Press. 1894.
12

ROBSON, Walter.
Letters from a soldier.
Faber. 1960.
12

Royal Air Force, Biggin Hill, 1917-54.
Royal Air Force, Biggin Hill. 1954.
1

ROYAL NAVAL VOLUNTEER RESERVE.
Anti-aircraft Corps, Royal Naval Volunteer Reserve:
member's manual.
W.E. Giraud, Printer. 1916.
6

RUSSELL, R.O.
The history of the 11th (Lewisham) Battalion, The
Queen's Own Royal West Kent Regiment.
Lewisham Newspaper Co. 1934.
11,18

SANDEMAN, Aernold Eric Noble.
Notes on the military history of Chatham. (Two
photocopies of notes intended for eventual publication).
c.196-?
4

SANDES, E.W.C.
The Royal Engineers in Egypt and the Sudan.
Chatham, Institution of Royal Engineers. 1937.
12

SCOTT, Sir Arthur B.
History of the 12th (Eastern) Division in the Great
War, 1914-18, edited by Major-General, Sir Arthur
B. Scott and P.M. Brumwell.
London, Nisbet and Co. 1923.
3

The Searchlight: being a chronicle of No. 2 Coy.
London Electrical Engineers, Thames and Medway
Defence, Vols. 2,3,4, Nos. 7-24.
October, 1915-March, 1917.
9

A short history of The Queen's Own (Royal West Kent
Regiment).
Aldershot, Gale and Polden. 1920.
2

A short history of The Queen's Own, Royal West
Kent Regiment.
Maidstone, Kent Messenger. 1930.
2,11

Special illustrated yeomanry souvenir - Wednesday, July
24th, 1901.
Kent Messenger. 1901.
12

TERRITORIAL AND AUXILIARY FORCES ASSOCIATION OF THE COUNTY
OF KENT.
Short history of the units...
1950.
1,2,11

12th KENT RIFLE VOLUNTEERS (DARTFORD).
Minute book, 3rd December, 1859-21st February, 1878 (MSS.).
5

12th KENT RIFLE VOLUNTEERS (DARTFORD).
Order books, 1st February, 1864-1st June, 1873 (MSS.).
November, 1874-24th July, 1884.
5

WENYON, H.J.
The history of the Eighth Battalion, The Queen's Own Royal
West Kent Regiment, 1914-1919 (by) H.J. Wenyon and H.S.
Brown.
London, Hazell, Watson and Viney. 1921.
1,3,4,8,11,12

WILCOX, Leslie Arthur.
Mr. Pepy's navy.
Bell. 1966.
8

WOOD, Frederick J.
The 1st Home Counties Field Ambulance and the Great War,
1914-1919.
Kent Messenger. 1923.
11,12

WOOD, Frederick J.
The history of the Maidstone Companies, Royal Army Medical
Corps (Volunteers).
Kent Messenger. 1907.
1,11,12

WOODTHORPE, T.J.
The Tudor Navy and the Medway...(Typewritten script).
n.d.
11

WILSON, James.
A view of the volunteer army of Great Britain in the year
1806...(photocopy of the part relating to Kent).
Journal of the Society of Army Historical Research. 1953.
4

The work of the Royal Engineers in the European War, 1914-
1919.
Chatham, Institution of Royal Engineers. 1921-27.
8

MILTON-NEXT-GRAVESEND

Christ Church, Milton-next-Gravesend, 1856-1956 - centenary
souvenir.
Graham Cumming Ltd. 1956.
9

GRAVESEND AND MILTON MECHANICS INSTITUTION.
1st annual report, January 9th, 1839 and 14th annual report,
April 14th, 1852.
9

GREAT BRITAIN: LAWS, etc. (GEO. III).
An Act for paving, cleansing and lighting...in the town and
parishes of Gravesend and Milton...
1773.
9,11

GREAT BRITAIN: LAWS, etc. (VIC.).
An Act for more effectually lighting with gas the parishes of
Gravesend, Milton and Northfleet.
1863.
9

GREAT BRITAIN: LAWS, etc. (VIC.).
An Act to amend...an Act...for paving, cleansing, lighting,
watching and improving Gravesend and Milton...
1840.
9

H., W.T.
New historical, topographical and descriptive companion to
the visitor of Gravesend, Milton and their environs.
1843.
9

HALL, T. Publisher.
Hall's Gravesend and Milton directory and advertiser,
1853.
Gravesend, T. Hall.
9

HALL, T. Publisher.
Hall's Gravesend, Milton and Northfleet directory and
advertiser, 1861-89.
Gravesend, T. Hall.
9,17(1888-89)

HARWOOD, Hilda.
History of Milton Mount College.
Independent Press. 1959.
9,11,12

HISCOCK, Robert Heath.
The story of Milton Parish Church, St. Peter and St.
Paul.
Gloucester, British Publishing Co. 1955.
8,9,11

LARGE, James. Publisher.
Gravesend, Milton and Northfleet directory and advertiser
for the years, 1849, 1850 and 1851.
Gravesend, J. Large.
9

POCOCK, Robert.
A chronology of the most remarkable events...of
Gravesend, Milton and Denton...
1790.
9,11

SMITH, V.T.C.
Historical sketch of Gravesend Fort and Milton
Chantry.
1965.
11

MILTON REGIS

Draft of a petition of the free dredgermen and oyster
fishermen of Milton in the County of Kent. (MSS.).
c.1825.
15

FAVRESFELD, Charles.
Milton Regis and its legend. (Reprinted from
"Invicta", 1910).
20

GRAYLING, Francis.
Churches of Sittingbourne and Milton.
11

HAWKES, Sonia Chadwick.
Finds from a 7th century Anglo-Saxon cemetery at Milton
Regis, by S.C. Hawkes and L.R.A. Grove. (From
Archaeologia Cantiana, Vol. 78, 1963).
12,17

JONES, J. Bedworth.
History of Paradise Chapel, Milton, Kent.
Sittingbourne, Parrett. 1910.
11,12,20

LOUGH, John.
Sermon preached on 9th March, 1796 in the churches of
Milton and Iwade...
1796.
11

MILTON IMPROVEMENTS COMMISSIONERS.
Byelaws made by the Improvement Commissioners for the
district of Milton.
1879.
20

PARSONS, Richard Arthur Felix.
The church of the Holy Trinity, Milton Regis.
Parsons. 1951.
8,11,12

PAYNE, George.
Roman coffins of lead from Bex Hill, Milton-next-
Sittingbourne. (From Archaeologia Cantiana, Vol. 9,
1874).
11,17

(RICHMOND, Paul E.).
The church of the Holy Trinity, Milton Regis.
1956.
8

"A SON OF THE MARSHES", pseud.   (J.A. OWEN and D. JORDAN).
Annals of a fishing village.
Blackwood. 1891.
11,15,20

Annals of a fishing village.
Chivers (Reprint). 1969.
7,11

Drift from longshore.
Hutchinson. 1898.
8,11,12

Forest ties.
Smith, Elder and Co. 1893.
8

From spring to fall.
Blackwood. 1894.
8

In the green leaf and the sere.
Kegan Paul. 1896.
8

Woodland, moor and stream.
Smith, Elder and Co. 1890.
8

VALLANCE, Aymer.
Old chimney-piece from Back's House, Milton-by-Sittingbourne.
(Reprinted from Archaeologia Cantiana, Vol. 28).
Mitchell, Hughes and Clarke. 1909.
11,17

MINSTER-IN-SHEPPEY

BISH, Gregory.
Minster Abbey, 670-1947.
Minster Abbey.
11(1947) 13(1951)

BRAMSTON, William.
History of the Abbey Church of Minster, Isle of Sheppey.
Hazell, Watson and Viney. 1896.
1,4,7,8,11,12,13,14

FRAMPTON, Thomas Shipden.
St. Mary's Church, Minster: list of vicars.
Mitchell and Hughes. 1902.
8

HALL, Mary.
The Abbey Church of Minster, Sheppey.
Canterbury, Gibbs. 195-?
11

JONES, P.T.
Story of the Abbey Church and Gate House...
Gloucester, British Publishing Co. 1950.
11

Minster Abbey.
1928.
12

NORWOOD, John C.
With the dead at Minster.
1910.
3,11

WITHERS, Hartley.
Canterbury and Rochester with Minster-in-Sheppey, by H. Withers
and others.
Bell. 1929.
6

MINSTER-IN-THANET

ALDRED, Henry W.
The Manor of Minster and other estates.
1889.
1,3,7,8,11,12,13,14,15

"BEARRA BERRE", pseud. (R.A. CAIRD).
A guide to an souvenir of Minster-in-Thanet.
Printed by Vacher and Sons. (1932).
3

BUBB, Robert.
Bells of Minster Tower.
1886.
11,13,17

GELL, Francis.
The Minster of Minster-in-Thanet.
Ramsgate, Pullen. 1879 etc.
1,2(1907) 7,11,13,14,17

HERD, S.
Guide to Minster Parish Church.
Chevens. 1895 etc.
11,13

A LAY-TERTIARY OF ST. FRANCIS.
Life of St. Mildred, Abbess of Minster-in-Thanet.
Washbourne. 1884.
11,13

Minster Church: a pamphlet and a print.
n.d.
13

MINSTER-IN-THANET PARISH COUNCIL.
Official guide (by L.E. Pike).
Gloucester, Home Publishing Co. 1956 etc.
1,3,4,6,8(1960) 11(1956 and 1960) 12,14

St. Mary's Church, Minster-in-Thanet.
Ramsgate, Bligh. 192-?
11

WHEELER, Rev. (Vicar of Minster-in-Thanet).
Sermon on the occasion of consecration by the Bishop of
Sierra Leone.
1862.
6

MONKS HORTON

Particulars and conditions of sale of the...XIV
century manor house, Kite Manor or Old Kite House,
Monks Horton (to be sold by) Messrs. Geering and
Colyer...on...16th July, 1929.
(Geering and Colyer). 1929.
7

Particulars, plans and conditions of sale of the
residential and agricultural estate known as Monks
Horton...(to be sold by) Messrs. Knight, Frank and
Rutley...on 4th October, 1912.
(Knight, Frank and Rutley). 1912.
7

MONUMENTAL INSCRIPTIONS

ARCHIBALD, John.
English churchyard memorials through the centuries.
Mineral Publications Ltd. 1939.
3,13

BELCHER, W.D.
Kentish brasses, 2 vols.
Sprague. Vol. I, 1885. Vol. II, 1905.
1,3,5,7,8,11,12,15,17,18

FYNMORE, A.H.W.
Memorial stones in churchyard of Paddlesworth,
compiled by A.H.W. Fynmore.
1915.
3

FYNMORE, A.H.W.
Monumental inscriptions. Baptist burial ground at
Brabourne, Kent, compiled by A.H.W. Fynmore.
n.d.
3

GRIFFIN, Ralph.
Kentish items. (From Transactions of Monumental
Brass Society, Vol. 6).
London, John Bale, Sons and Danielsson Ltd. (1913).
3,7,8(Manuscript index to illustrations included)
11

List of monumental brasses remaining in the County of
Kent, by R. Griffin and M. Stephenson.
Ashford, Headley. 1922.
1,2,3,4,5,6,8,11,12,15,17,19

Monumental brasses in Kent. (From Transactions of
the Monumental Brass Society, Vol. 7).
Ashford, Headley. 1938.
11,17

GRIFFIN, Ralph.
Some illustrations of monumental brasses and indents in Kent.
Ashford, Headley for Monumental Brass Society. 1946.
2,8,11,12

Some indents of lost brasses in Kent.
London, John Bale, Sons and Danielsson Ltd. 1914.
2,3,7,11

GUNNIS, Rupert.
Signed monuments in Kentish churches. (Reprinted from
Archaeologia Cantiana, Vol. LXII, 1949).
19

(HAINES, Herbert).
Manual of monumental brasses - Kent. (Portion of Vol. 2).
1862.
17

HARRIS, Edwin.
Quaint Kentish epitaphs and signs.
Rochester, E. Harris. 1899.
11

OYLER, Thomas H.
Epitaphs and inscriptions from the churches of Kent, edited
by T.H. Oyler.
Kentish Express. 1912.
1,2,3,4,5,6,7,8,11,12,15,16,17

SMITH, Charles Roach.
Inventorium Sepulchrale...
Privately Printed. 1856.
8

STEPHENSON, Mill.
List of palimpsest brasses...Kent to Leicestershire.
(Reprinted from Transactions of the Monumental Brass Society).
London, John Bale, Sons and Danielsson Ltd. 1903?
2

THORPE, John.
Index to the monumental inscriptions in the "Registrum
Roffense".
Privately Printed by Frederick A. Crisp. 1885.
11,12

VINCENT, William Thomas.
In search of gravestones old and curious.
Mitchell and Hughes. 1896.
5,11,15,17

WEEVER, John.
Ancient funeral monuments...of Great Britain. (Dioceses of
Canterbury and of Rochester).
Thomas Harper. 1631.
3,12

MOTTINGHAM

CHISLEHURST AND MOTTINGHAM CHAMBER OF COMMERCE.
Brochure, 1948-49. (Includes brief histories of Chislehurst
and Mottingham).
1948.
2

GRACE, W.G.
Cricket. (Note: includes autobiographical information. Grace
was resident in Mottingham and Sydenham).
J.W. Arrowsmith and Simpkin Marshall. 1891.
2

KENNETT, W.R.
Some notes on the history of Mottingham. (Photocopy of
typescript).
(195-?).
2

MURSTON

ANDREWS, George.
Memories of Murston.
Sittingbourne, Parrett. 1930.
1,4,11,12,20

LUMAN, June.
Short history of All Saints Parish Church, Murston.
1962.
11

MUSEUMS

AREA MUSEUMS SERVICE FOR SOUTH-EASTERN ENGLAND.
Annual report, 1966-67.
Area Museums Service for South-Eastern England. 1967.
12

ARMSTRONG, J.R.
Weald and Downland Open Air Museum, edited by J.R.
Armstrong.
Phillimore. (1971).
11

MUSIC

KENT COUNTY MUSIC COMMITTEE.
Kent Fellowship of Music: 50th bulletin.
Kent County Music Committee. 1956.
11

NATURAL HISTORY

ALLOM, Elizabeth Anne.
The seaweed collector: an introduction to the study
of the marine algae...(on microfilm).
Margate, T.H. Keble. 1841.
11

ASSOCIATED NATURAL HISTORY SOCIETIES OF THE SOUTH-EAST
OF ENGLAND.
The South-Eastern Naturalist. Vol. 1, Part I-V.
Vol. II, Part I-II.
Canterbury, Printed by Gibbs. 1896-99.
3

BALSTON, Richard James.
Notes on the birds of Kent, by R.J. Balston, C.W.
Shepherd and E. Bartlett.
London, Porter. 1907.
1,2,3,4,5,6,7,8,11,12,14,15,17,18,19,21

BOND, John Arthington Walpole.
Birds of Bromley(Kent) and its neighbourhood.
Bromley, S. Bush. 1901.
1,2

BRADE-BIRKS, Hilda K.
Luminous Chilopoda, by H.K. and S.G. Brade-Birks,
(with some reference to those found in Kent).
Dartford Naturalists' Club. 1920.
5,11

BRADE-BIRKS, Hilda K.
Notes on Myriapoda - XIII: some Kent records, with
special reference to luminous forms, by H.K. and S.G.
Brade-Birks. (Reprinted from Lancashire and Cheshire
Naturalist, 1918).
5

BROOKE, B.J.
Notes on the occurrence of Orchis Simia Lamarck in
Kent. (Extract from Journal of Botany, 1938).
7

BURNESS, Gordon.
The white badger, by G. Burness and G. Cliffe. (Note:
badgers in the woods around Orpington).
Harrap. 1970.
2

BURTON, John Frederick.
Butterflies of the North-West Kent Marshes. (From
"The London Naturalist", 1955).
11,12

BURTON, John Frederick.
Bird-watching in Kent, by J.F. Burton and D. Owen.
Royal Society for the Protection of Birds. 1955.
3,4,8,11,12

CHALMERS-HUNT, J.M.
The butterflies and moths of Kent.
Arbroath, Buncle. 1960.
6,7,11,15

CHANDLER, Marjorie Elizabeth Jane.
A new Tempskya from Kent.
British Museum (Natural History). 1968.
11

COOPER, D.
Flora metropolitana; or botanical rambles within 30
miles of London.
1837.
17

COOPER, J.E.
The mollusca of Chislet Marshes.
n.d.
11

DAVIS, William J.
The birds of Kent.
W.J. Davis. 1907.
1,4,5,9,11,12

DAVIS, William J.
The Naturalist's Quarterly Review, edited by W.J. Davis.
2 vols., 1906-07.
W.J. Davis.
5

DOWKER, George.
A tabulated list and description of the birds of East Kent.
n.d.
3,7,11,12,13,17

DUNGENESS BIRD OBSERVATORY.
Annual reports, 1957 (onwards).
3,7(1961-62) 11,15

DUNGENESS BIRD OBSERVATORY.
Dungeness Bird Observatory.
1964.
7

EAST KENT NATURAL HISTORY SOCIETY.
Catalogue of the library...laws and regulations.
Canterbury, Kentish Gazette and Canterbury Press Office. 1895.
3

President's address, 1864.
17

Report of first meeting.
Printed by J. Ward. 1858.
3,17

Report of third meeting.
Printed by J. Ward. 1859.
3,17

Reports.
Canterbury.
3(1860-99) 6(1866) 17(1860-93)

Rules and regulations.
Canterbury, Cross and Jackman. 1886.
3,17

Transactions...Nos. 1,2,3 and 4.
Canterbury, Gibbs and Sons. 1885-89.
3,6(No. 1) 17

EAST KENT SCIENTIFIC AND NATURAL HISTORY SOCIETY WITH WHICH IS
INCORPORATED THE CANTERBURY PHOTOGRAPHIC SOCIETY.
Reports and transactions for years ending September 30th, 1901,
1902, 1903, 1904, 1905, 1906, 1907, 1908, 1909, 1910, 1911,
1912-13, Series II, Vols. 2-13.
East Kent Scientific and Natural History Society With Which Is
Incorporated The Canterbury Photographic Society.
3

Reports, 1872, 1878, 1901-04, 1907-09.
7

EMBRY, Bernard.
Butterflies and moths...found in the Dover and Deal district of
Kent, by B. Embry and G.H. Youden.
Buckland Association. 1949.
6,7,11

FITTER, Richard Sidney Richmond.
Check-list of the birds of the London area: 20 miles of St.
Paul's Cathedral, 1924-43, by R.S.R. Fitter and E.R. Parrinder.
London Natural History Society. 1944.
1

Check-list of the mammals, reptiles and amphibia of the London
area, 1900-49.
London Natural History Society. 1949.
1

Contributions to the bibliography of the natural history of the
London area. No. 2, A subject index of the Society's journals,
1914-51.
London Natural History Society. 1953.
5

GILLHAM, Eric Howard.
The birds of the North Kent marshes, by E.H. Gillham and R.C.
Holmes.
Collins. 1950.
1,2,3,4,5,7,8,9,11,12,14,15,17,18

GILLHAM, Eric Howard.
Census of the breeding birds of the Medway Islands,
June 3rd-5th, 1955, edited by E.H. Gillham and others.
1,2,4,8,11

GILMOUR, John.
Wild flowers of the chalk. (King Penguin books).
Penguin. 1947.
4

GREENWICH NATURAL HISTORY CLUB.
The fauna of Blackheath and its vicinity, Part 1.
Clowes. 1859.
11

HANBURY, Frederick Janson.
Flora of Kent: being an account of the flowering
plants, ferns, etc., with notes on the topography,
geology and meteorology, and a history of the botanical
investigation of the County...by F.J. Hanbury and
E.S. Marshall.
1899.
1,2,3,4,5,6,7,8,9,11,12,13,15,16,21

HARRISON, James Maurice.
Birds of Kent, 2 vols.
Witherby. 1953.
1,2,3,4,5,6,7,8,9,11,14,15,16,19

Bristow and the Hastings rarities affair.
Printed by A.H. Butler Ltd., 33-35 Western Road, St.
Leonards, Sussex. 1968.
11

Hand-list of the birds of the Sevenoaks or Western
district of Kent.
Witherby. 1942.
1,2,4,7,8,11,12,15,16

HARRISON, Jeffery Graham.
Breeding birds of the Medway Estuary, by J.G. Harrison,
J.N. Humphreys and Geoffrey Graves.
Kent Ornithological Society and W.A.G.B.I. 1972.
11

The nesting birds of Chetney marsh.
Kent Ornithological Society. 1970.
2,7,12

Wildfowl of the North Kent Marshes, illustrated by
Pamela Harrison and foreword by George Atkinson-Willes.
Wildfowlers' Association of Great Britain and Ireland.
(1972).
11

HAYDON, Walter T.
Catalogue of the flowering plants found in Dover and
its neighbourhood.
1890.
6,7

JACOB, J.
Wild flowers, grasses and ferns of East Kent.
Dover Express. 1936.
3,6,7,11,13,14

JOHNSON, Thomas.
Botanical journeys in Kent and Hampstead: a facsimile
reprint with introduction and translations of his
"Iter Plantarum", 1629 (and) "Descriptio Itineris
Plantarum", 1632...
Hunt Botanical Library. 1972.
11

JOURDAIN, F.C.R.
The Dartford warbler...and its allies. (Extract from
North Staffordshire Field Club Annual Report, 1903-04).
5

KENT AND SURREY NATURALISTS FIELD CLUB.
Transactions...1877. (Photocopy). Thought to be the
only issue of this publication.
Stansfield, Peckham. 1877.
2

KENT FIELD CLUB.
An atlas of Bryophytes found in Kent (by A.G. Side).
1970.
7,8,9,11

Officers, aims, meetings, etc., 1957.
3

Transactions, Vol. 1, 1957-63.
2,3,4,8,11

Transactions, Vol. 2, 1964.
4,11

KENT NATURALISTS' TRUST. (Afterwards - Kent Trust for Nature Conservation).
The first five years.
London, Solicitors' Law Stationery Society. 1963.
3,8

Memorandum and articles of association.
London, Solicitors' Law Stationery Society. (1959).
11

Newsletter, September, 1961.
4

Typescript and handbill on the formation and first Annual General Meeting...December, 1958-January, 1959.
3

KENT ORNITHOLOGICAL SOCIETY.
Kent bird report, in progress.
1(1952 in progress)
2(1952 in progress)
3(1952-63)
4(1954 in progress)
6(1952 in progress)
7(1952 in progress)
8(1952 in progress)
9(1967-70)
11(1952 in progress)
12(1952-65)
14(1952 in progress)
15(1952 in progress)

KENT TRUST FOR NATURE CONSERVATION. (Formerly Kent Naturalists' Trust).
Annual report, 1971.
Kent Trust for Nature Conservation. (1972).
11

The first ten years, 1958-68.
(1968).
4,9

Newsletter. No. 11, September, 1966.
4

Newsletter. No. 14, September, 1967.
4

Progress report, 1965-66.
1966.
4,19

LEWISHAM NATURAL HISTORY SOCIETY.
Darenthis. Nos. 2 and 3.
Lewisham Natural History Society. 1962 and 1965.
5

List of the rare plants found in the neighbourhood of Tunbridge Wells.
Printed by W. Thorne. (17--?).
19

A list of wild flowers collected in Kent during four years, with the dates when they were in flower.
Wickham. 1870.
11

LONDON NATURAL HISTORY SOCIETY.
Birds of the London area (revised edition).
Hart-Davis. 1964.
2

LOUSLEY, Job Edward.
Wild flowers of chalk and limestone.
London, Collins. 1950.
3

LOUSLEY, Job Edward.
Wild flowers of chalk and limestone, 2nd edition. (The New Naturalist).
London, Collins. 1969.
3

M., L.V.
On a Kentish butterfly farm. (From "Daily Chronicle", 1905).
17

MAIDSTONE AND MID-KENT NATURAL HISTORY AND PHILOSOPHICAL SOCIETY.
Annual report, 1890.
Bunyard. 1891.
12

MARRIOTT, St. John.
British woodlands as illustrated by Lesness Abbey Woods. (Typescript).
1925.
5,12

(MARTIN, B.).
Natural history of Kent.
1(1759) 9(1759) 11(1759) 12(1756 and 1762)

MILLICHAMP, R.
The fishes...of the Maidstone area, by R. Millichamp and T. Tynan.
12

MILNE, Colin.
Indigenous botany; or, habitations of English plants, containing the result of several botanical excursions chiefly in Kent, Middlesex and the adjacent counties in 1790, 1791 and 1792, Vol. 1, by C. Milne and A. Gordon.
W. Lowndes. 1793.
8

NATURE CONSERVANCY - SOUTH-EAST REGION.
Wild-life conservation in the North Kent Marshes: a report of a Working Party.
Nature Conservancy - South-East Region. 1971.
4,9,11

NEWMAN, Leonard Hugh.
Create a butterfly garden, by L.H. Newman and M. Savonius. (See - Westerham).
J. Baker. 1967.
2

OWEN, D.F.
Ecology and distribution of the Satydidae in West Kent.
London Natural History Society. 1953.
5,11

PITTOCK, George M.
Flora of Thanet: a catalogue of the plants indigenous to the island, with a few rare aliens, by G.M. Pittock and friends.
Margate, Printed by R. Robinson. 1903.
11,12,13,14,17

POCOCK, Robert.
Observations and memoranda in botany. (MS.).
1821.
9

PRATT, H.M.
Flowering plants observed in the Dartford area of Kent in the years 1947-54. (Typescript).
(1955).
5

PRENTIS, W.
Notes on the birds of Rainham.
Gurney and Jackson. 1894.
1,3,4,5,6,8,11,12,15,17,20

RIGDEN, T. Publisher.
The wild flowers of Dover and its neighbourhood...
T. Rigden. c.1855.
7,11

RUTT, F.
Dwellers in our rockpools...
Folkestone, Arthur Stace and Sons. (192-?).
7

SCOLEY.
The Rochester Naturalist, 1924.
15

SCOTT, E.
List of butterflies and moths (Macro Lepidoptera) occurring in the neighbourhood of Ashford.
Ashford, Headley. 1936 and 1950.
4(1950) 7,8,11,15

SIDCUP NATURAL HISTORY SOCIETY.
Annual reports, 1957-63.
Sidcup Natural History Society. 1958-64.
5

SMITH, Gerard Edwards.
Catalogue of rare or remarkable phaenogamous plants collected in South Kent.
Longman. 1829.
1,6,7,11,12,15,17,19

SOUTH-EASTERN UNION OF SCIENTIFIC SOCIETIES.
Botanical Section - reports for 1928-29, 1933-34, 1934-35.
17

SOUTH-EASTERN UNION OF SCIENTIFIC SOCIETIES.
South-Eastern bird report: being an account of bird-life in
Hampshire, Kent, Surrey and Sussex.
3(1938 and 1939) 4(1936, 1937, 1938, 1939, 1946 and 1947)
7(1943) 11(1939, 1942, 1943, 1945 and 1947)

The South-Eastern Naturalist: being the Transcations of the
South-Eastern Union of Scientific Societies...1912.
11

The South-Eastern Naturalist: being the 30th vol. of
Transactions of the South-Eastern Union of Scientific Societies
...1925.
11

SOUTH-EASTERN UNION OF SCIENTIFIC SOCIETIES - See also ORNITHOLOGY.

SOUTH LONDON FIELD STUDIES SOCIETY.
Journal, 1963-65.
South London Field Studies Society. 1964.
5

TICEHURST, Norman F.
History of the birds of Kent.
Witherby. 1909.
1,2,3,4,5,6,7,8,11,12,15,17,18,20

On certain birds, other species of birds and their former
status in Kent.
Witherby. 1909.
12

On certain other species of birds and their former status in
Kent. (Reprinted from "British Birds", Vol. XIV, No. 4,
September 1st, 1920).
3

On the former abundance of the Kite, Buzzard and Raven in Kent.
(Reprinted from "British Birds", Vol. XIV, No. 2, July 1st,
1920).
3

TURNER, Dawson.
The botanist's guide through England and Wales. (Vol. 1
includes Kent), by D. Turner and L.W. Dillwyn.
London, Phillips and Farden. 1805.
3

WATSON, Joan.
A revision of English Wealden flora...Vol. 1 - Charales-Gink-
goales.
British Museum. 1969.
3,19

WEBSTER, A.D.
Flora of Kent.
Bromley, Strong. c.1910.
1,2,17,18

WEST KENT NATURAL HISTORY, MICROSCOPICAL AND PHOTOGRAPHIC
SOCIETY.
President's address, papers and reports, 1891-92, with rules,
list of members and catalogue of the library.
Greenwich, Berryman. 1892.
2

Transactions, 1907-09.
17

NETTLESTEAD

HILTON, John Anthony.
Nettlestead: a village history.
Hadlow, Hilton. 1964.
1,2,4,7,8,11,15,19

NEW ASH GREEN

SPAN KENT LTD.
New Ash Green.
c.1967.
9

THOMAS, Denis.
A village in Kent: the historic and cultural heritage of
New Ash Green, edited by D. Thomas.
Quadrangle Books. (1967).
1,2,3,4,5,6,7,8,9,11,12,15,18

NEW BROMPTON

Short history of St. Luke's Church, New Brompton
(Gillingham), 1959.
12

NEW CROSS

BRITTON, O.M.H.
New Cross Turnpike Trust. (Tonbridge School Local
History Researches).
1963.
11

"These many years" - Zion Baptist Chapel, New Cross...
1849-1949. (Pamphlet).
1949.
18

TUCK, Oswald.
The old Telegraph - article in "The Fighting Forces",
Vol. 1, No. 3. (References to New Cross Telegraph
Station).
Aldershot, Gale and Polden. 1924.
18

NEW HYTHE

BATES, H.E.
Pastoral on paper.
Medway Paper Co. 1955?
1,2,3,4,5,6,7,8,10,11,12,14,17,18

NEW ROMNEY

FORSETT, John.
The custumal of New Romney.
Kent Archaeological Society. 1945.
8,11,12,15

GRIFFIN, R.
Note on the brass of William Holyngbroke...New Romney.
London, John Bale, Sons and Danielsson Ltd. 1911.
2

HOLWORTHY, Richard.
Records of New Romney: a paper read before the
Society of Genealogists, 25th January, 1928. (From
"Genealogists' Magazine", (1928)).
4,11,12

JACKSON, N.G.
Southlands, 1610-1960.
Nottingham, Bell. 1960.
1,4,7,8,11,12

JESSUP, Frank William.
A New Romney mayoral dispute. In Archaeologia
Cantiana, Vol. LXII, 1949.
11,17

LAMBERT, George.
Civic and other maces. (Tenterden, Margate, New
Romney). (From "Antiquary", Vol. 1, No. 2, pp. 66-
71, February, 1880).
3

LIVETT, Grevile Mauis.
Church of St. Nicholas, New Romney...with additional
notes by the Rev. A.W. McMichael...Vicar of New
Romney.
Ashford, Geering. 1930.
1,3,7,14

MARTON, Mrs. M.E.
The church of St. Nicholas, New Romney.
Ashford, Geering. 1927.
11,12

MOORE, Doris Langley.
E. Nesbit.
Cassell. 1951.
12

MURRAY, K.M. Elizabeth.
Register of Daniel Rough, Common Clerk of Romney,
1353-1380, edited by K.M.E. Murray.
Kent Archaeological Society (Records Branch). 1945.
1,2,3,7,11,12,15,17,18

NEW ROMNEY BOROUGH COUNCIL.
New Romney official guide.
New Romney Borough Council. 1959 etc.
1,4,6,7,8,11,12,17

Old towns by the sea: Hythe and Romney. (Extract from "All
the Year Round", 1878).
17

SALISBURY, Edward.
Mr. Salisbury's report on the records of New Romney.
(Reprinted from Archaeologia Cantiana, 1887).
Mitchell and Hughes. 1887.
11,17

TEICHMAN-DERVILLE, Max.
The annals of the town and port of New Romney...
Ashford, Headley. 1929.
7,11,17

NEWCHURCH

DONALDSON, Christopher.
Newchurch...parish church of St. Peter and St. Paul.
Derby Publishing Co. 195-?
11

Particulars and conditions of sale of...excellent and rich
Romney pasture land in the parishes of Newchurch and Bilsington,
Romney Marsh...for sale by auction...on Tuesday, July 14th, 1885
...by order of the Trustees...of the late Thomas Kingsnorth Esq.
(Messrs. Cobb). 1885.
7

NEWENDEN

CLARK, F.C.
Articles relating to Sandhurst and Newenden appearing in the
Sandhurst with Newenden Monthly Magazine,1956-57.
3

ROPER, Anne.
The church of Saint Peter, Newenden.
Printed by Thanet Printing Works. 1972.
11

NEWINGTON-NEXT-SITTINGBOURNE

DRAKE-BROCKMAN, D.H.
Record of the Brockman and Drake-Brockman family.
Privately Printed by C. Clarke. 1936.
3,7

HEWETT, G.W.
Lesnes Abbey and Newington-next-Sittingbourne...
Woolwich, Pryce. 1911.
4,11,17

Particulars, plan and conditions of sale of...The Beachborough
Estate, Newington.
Burrows. 1971.
7

PAYNE, George.
Newington. (From the Proceedings of the Society of Antiquaries,
June 21st, 1883).
8

RAMELL, F.M. Photographer.
Views of St. Mary's, Newington.
Wright and Hoggard. 1920?
4

A short guide to the parish church of St. Mary the Virgin,
Newington.
(1962).
4

NEWSPAPERS

EAST KENT GAZETTE.
A brief history of the East Kent Gazette.
East Kent Gazette. 1934.
13

EAST KENT NEWSPAPER AND PRINTING COMPANY.
Leaflet showing first issue of shares and names of provisional
directors and officers of the Company.
Canterbury, Printed by S. Hyde. n.d.
3

Introducing Invicta Films.
Maidstone, Invicta Films. 1961.
3

KENT MESSENGER.
Centenary edition.
Kent Messenger. 2nd January, 1959.
3

A County newspaper is born.
Kent Messenger. 1960.
3

Exhibition of pictures...catalogue.
Kent Messenger. 1965.
3

Supplement (75th birthday).
Kent Messenger. 30th December, 1933.
3

KENTISH EXPRESS AND ASHFORD NEWS.
Jubilee of the Kentish Express, 14th July, 1855-
15th July, 1905...
Kentish Express. 1905.
7,11,17

KENTISH GAZETTE.
Bridging three centuries: the story of the Kentish
Gazette.
Canterbury, Kentish Gazette. 1929.
3

KENTISH GAZETTE.
Style book.
Canterbury, Kentish Gazette. n.d.
3

Key Note: a monthly musical journal for the County
of Kent, Vol. 1.
Maidstone, "Key Note". 1893-94.
11,12

MACFARLANE, Charles.
The Kentish Magazine and Companion to the Newspaper,
edited by C. MacFarlane.
1850.
17

North Kent Florist and Fancier's Gazette.
1898-99.
17

SMITH, C.G.
"The Reporter", 1856-1966.
Gravesend and Dartford Reporter. 1966.
5,9,11

NONINGTON

ABBOTT, William.
Gleanings from Nonington. (Duplicated typescript).
1970.
3

GRIFFIN, Ralph.
Brass at Nonington, Kent. In Archaeologia Cantiana,
Vol. 48, 1936).
17

Nonington book of quotations with brief notes of its
church and history.
Canterbury, Gibbs. 1912.
1

Notes on the church of St. Mary the Virgin, Nonington.
1938.
11

NORTH KENT MARSHES

HARRISON, Jeffery Graham.
Wildfowl of the North Kent Marshes, illustrated by
Pamela Harrison, foreword by George Atkinson-Willes.
Wildfowlers' Association of Great Britain and Ireland.
(1972).
11

NATURE CONSERVANCY - SOUTH-EAST REGION.
Wild-life conservation in the North Kent Marshes: a
report of a Working Party.
Nature Conservancy - South-East Region. 1971.
4,9,11

NORTHBOURNE

HONE, Joseph.
The life of Henry Tonks.
Heinemann. 1939.
11

ARNOLD, George M.
On the Old Rectory at Northfleet. (Reprinted from
Archaeologia Cantiana).
Mitchell and Hughes. 1892.
9,17

BROWN, Henry.
A true narrative...of...an accident...at the Cement Works...
of Northfleet.
Dartford, Perry. 1862.
11

CHINERY, John R.
St. Bototph's Parish Church School, Northfleet.
Ramsgate, Church Publishing Co. 1962.
1,4,8,9,11,12

COBHAM, Eleanor M.
Battle of Northfleet Bridge, June 1st, 1648.
Smither Bros. 1895.
9,17

COOKE, Stanley Horace.
History of Northfleet and its parish church.
Ashford, Headley. 1942.
2,5,7,8,9,11,12,13,15,17

COURT, Capel.
"Wet and Dry"; or, the Docks of London: being an inquiry
concerning the proposed Northfleet Docks.
Baily Bros. 1859.
9

CROLY, George.
A sermon preached in pursuance of the King's letter in the
parish church at Northfleet, Kent on...November 27th, 1831, in
aid of the funds of the above institution, with a brief
memoir of the Society.
Printed for J. Duncan. 1831.
11

DUNDAS, Henry. 1st Viscount Melville.
Letter from the Right Honourable Lord Viscount Melville to
the Right Honourable Spencer Percival.
Printed for Samuel Bagster. 1810.
11

Gravesend and Northfleet: post-war business and information
guide.
1946.
9

GRAVESEND BOROUGH COUNCIL - PUBLIC LIBRARY.
A brief history of Gravesend and Northfleet, compiled by E.C.
Gunkel.
Gravesend Public Library and Kent County Library. 1972.
9,11

GREAT BRITAIN: LAWS, etc. (VIC.).
An Act for more effectually lighting with gas the parishes of
Gravesend, Milton and Northfleet.
1863.
9

GRIFFIN, R.
Monumental brasses in Kent: St. James, Dover and Northfleet.
Mitchell, Hughes and Clarke. 1916.
2,12

HALL, T. Publisher.
Hall's Gravesend and Northfleet directory and advertiser,
1854-59.
Gravesend, T. Hall.
9

HALL, T. Publisher.
Northfleet directory and advertiser, 1861-89.
Gravesend, T. Hall.
9,17(1888-89)

HIGGINS, John. Publisher.
Gravesend and Northfleet almanac.
Gravesend, J. Higgins. 1891.
9,17(1898)

HUGGENS COLLEGE, NORTHFLEET.
The College Quarterly, November, 1936; February, May, August,
November, 1937; February, May, August, November, 1947.
9

LARGE, James. Publisher.
Gravesend, Milton and Northfleet directory and advertiser for
the years, 1849, 1850 and 1851.
Gravesend, J. Large.
9

LIVETT, Grevile Mairis.
Architectural notes on the churches of Northfleet,
Shorne and Gotham.
n.d.
5

NATIONAL TELEPHONE COMPANY.
Directory - Southern Section, 1901-02. Gravesend and
Northfleet. (3 pages - typescript).
9

Naval considerations upon the letters of Lord Melville
and Mr. Rose relative to the construction of...arsenal
at Northfleet.
1810.
11,15

NORTHFLEET CONGREGATIONAL CHURCH.
Magazine, 1895-96.
9

NORTHFLEET URBAN DISTRICT COUNCIL.
Official guide.
1959 etc.
1,4,5,8,9,11,12,19

NORTHFLEET URBAN DISTRICT COUNCIL.
Tenant's handbook.
Northfleet Urban District Council. British Publishing
Co. 1960.
9

Opening of the new vestry extension at St. Botolph's
Church, Northfleet. (Order of Service), May 21st,
1966.
4

ORDNANCE SURVEY.
Book of reference to the plan of the parish of Northfleet. (Hundred of Toltingtrough).
n.d.
9

ROCHARD, J.
Descriptive and historical review of Gravesend and
Northfleet.
Brighton, Rochard. 1893.
9,11,17

ROSE, George.
A letter to the Right Honourable Lord Viscount
Melville on the subject of His Lordship's letter to
the Right Honourable Spencer Percival...(Concerns
Naval Arsenal at Northfleet).
1810.
9,11

ROSHERVILLE GARDENS CO. LTD.
Particulars...of the Rosherville Gardens, Northfleet.
1900.
17

St. Botolph's Church, Northfleet: a short guide and
history.
British Publishing Co. 1960.
4

SMITH, Reginald A.
A palaeolithic industry at Northfleet, Kent. (A
paper read on 4th May, 1911).
9

STEADMAN, W.H.
Excavations on a Roman site at Northfleet.
Dartford District Antiquarian Society. 1913.
1,4,5,9,11,17

TABBERNER, John Loude.
The proposed Northfleet Docks. "Something short" in
reply to "Capel Court Esq." on "Wet and dry", shewing
the advantage which the Northfleet Docks will possess
over the wet and dry docks of London.
Effingham Wilson, Royal Exchange. 1859.
9

NURSTEAD

C., E.I.
Nursted Court, Kent. (From the "Gentleman's Magazine",
1837).
11

NURSTEAD Cont'd

CAIGER, John E.L.
Plans of a Chalkwell at Nurstead.
October, 1958.
9

LANDON, John.
An answer to the dissenting gentleman's third letter to the
Rev. Mr. White.
Robinson. 1758.
12

OFFHAM

STAGG, Frank Noel.
Some historical notes concerning the parish of Offham in Kent.
(Typescript).
1950.
11,12

OLD ROMNEY

ROPER, Anne.
Church of St. Clement, Old Romney.
Ashford, Geering. 1938 etc.
1,8,11

WARD, Gordon Reginald.
The Saxon history of the town and port of Romney. (From
Archaeologia Cantiana, Vol. 65, 1952).
11,17

OLD SOAR -- See PLAXTOL

OLDBURY

GRIGSON, Geoffrey.
An inland Gibraltar. (Article on Oldbury, Kent from "Country
Life", No. 3,066, 20th October, 1955).
3

PAYNE, George.
Oldbury and its surroundings.
1888.
11,14

PERKINS, J.B. Ward.
Excavations on Oldbury Hill, Ightham, 1938.
Kent Archaeological Society. 1940.
12,17

ORGANISATIONS

ASSOCIATION OF THE MEN OF KENT AND KENTISH MEN.
Annual reports: 3rd-5th, 7th, 8th, 9th-13th, 16th and 17th.
17

Roll of members and rules.
1922.
3

Roll of members and rules.
1950.
2

Year books.
1(1906, 1913, 1916, 1917, 1918)
2(1897 etc.)
3(1913-14)
6(1913-14)
7(1913-14, 1916-17)
14(1902, 1904-05, 1905-06, 1906-07, 1907-08)

BENEVOLENT MEDICAL SOCIETY.
Laws and regulations of the Benevolent Medical Society (1787)...
in the County of Kent.
William Burrill. 1833.
15

BOY SCOUTS. 5th BROMLEY (ST. LUKE'S) GROUP.
50 years of scouting.
5th Bromley (St. Luke's) Group Boy Scouts. 1962.
2

BOYS' BRIGADE - NORTH-WEST KENT BATTALION.
Battalion handbook.

BRITISH RED CROSS - KENT BRANCH.
Annual report, statement of accounts and directory.
4(1965-66, 1966-67, 1968-69, 1969-70, 1970-71)
8(1965-66)

Year book.
4(1972)

CAMPBELL, Marjorie A.
The story of Guiding in Kent, 1910-60, compiled by
M.A. Campbell.
1961.
4,8

CANTERBURY AND DISTRICT ANGLING ASSOCIATION.
Handbook, 1960.
3

EAST KENT AND CANTERBURY CONSERVATIVE CLUB.
Rules and regulations.
Canterbury, Kentish Observer Steam Printing Office.
1884?
3

EAST KENT CHAMBER OF AGRICULTURE.
Laws and constitution, annual reports, etc., 1884-5,
1886-7.
17

EAST KENT DISCHARGED PRISONERS AID SOCIETY.
Sixteenth annual report...for the year 1910.
J.A. Jennings. 1911.
11

EAST KENT LIBERAL REGISTRATION ASSOCIATION.
Second annual report, 1862 and annual reports for
1881 and 1884.
17

FEDERATION OF RATEPAYERS' ASSOCIATIONS IN THE COUNTY
OF KENT.
Minutes. Vol. 1 - 1930-35 (handwritten). Vol. 2 -
1935-11th December, 1937 (typescript).
5

Freemasons' Manual and Official Directory for the
Province of Kent.
Maidstone, Provincial Grand Lodge.
2(1958) 12(1894-1945)

JENKINS, Sidney A.
A Masonic Jubilee, 1895-1944: being the story of the
first 50 years of the North Kent Lodge, No. 2,499.
T.W. Jenkins. 1949.
7,8

KENT AND CANTERBURY PERMANENT BENEFIT BUILDING SOCIETY.
Rules, tables and forms.
1875.
17

Kent and Sussex Temperance Advocate, 1883.
Baldwin. 1883.
12

KENT ARCHAEOLOGICAL SOCIETY.
Descriptive catalogue of the documents belonging to
the Kent Archaeological Society.
Mitchell and Hughes. 1902.
11

Folder on the history and aims of the Society.
Kent Archaeological Society. 1957.
3

KENT ARCHAEOLOGICAL SOCIETY - RECORDS BRANCH.
Prospectus of a Records Branch.
1913.
3

Accounts for 1919.
17

Balance sheet for 1922.
3

Reports.
3(1922) 17(1892, 1919, 1920, 1921)

KENT ASSOCIATION FOR THE BLIND.
Annual report, 1867-68.
(1968).
4

KENT ASSOCIATION OF BOYS' CLUBS.
Annual report, 1964-65.
Kent Association of Boys' Clubs. 1966.
12

KENT ASSOCIATION OF YOUTH CLUBS.
Official Youth handbook.
Pyramid Press. 1964 etc.
4,11,12,19

KENT COUNCIL OF SOCIAL SERVICE.
Annual reports.
3(1946-95)
4(1951 in progress)
7(1954 in progress)
9(1966 in progress)
11(1971 in progress)
12(1939 in progress, with some gaps)

Thirty years of voluntary social service in the County of Kent...
1923-53.
Kent Council of Social Service. 1954.
7,12

Voluntary social service in Kent: 10th anniversary report.
Kent Council of Social Service. 1934.
6,12

Kent County Cancer Appeal Fund, 1933-39...
Oxford University Press. n.d.
3,11

Kent County Scout handbook.
9(1970) 11(1971, 1972)

KENT COUNTY TEMPERANCE FEDERATION.
Temperance Congress programmes, 1897-1903.
12

KENT COUNTY WAR SAVINGS COMMITTEE.
Report, 1st-31st January, 1918. July, 1918.
Maidstone, W.P. Dickinson. 1918.
3

KENT EDUCATION COMMITTEE.
Medway youth organisations.
Parrett Ltd. c.1950.
8,15

KENT FIRE INSURANCE INSTITUTION.
Copy deed of constitution...7th December, 1802...and of
resolutions which have been passed since...and of the
Solicitor's report dated 10th June, 1846.
Shaw and Sons and Kent Fire Insurance Institution. n.d.
1

KENT INSURANCE COMMITTEE.
Report for two years ended 14th July, 1914 and for the year
ended 14th July, 1915.
1915.
4

KENT RURAL COMMUNITY COUNCIL.
Annual reports.
1(1927-28)
3(1926-27)
12(1927-28)

Review. No. 1, April, 1930.
3

KENT STANDING CONFERENCE OF NATIONAL VOLUNTARY YOUTH
ORGANISATIONS.
Handbook of Kent Youth Organisations.
3(1959) 8(1959) 12(1957, 1959, 1967)

KENTISH PRESIDENT'S ASSOCIATION: GAZETTE.
Beckenham, Federation of President's Associations in County of
Kent. 1960.
3

KENTISH SOCIETY.
A concise account of the improvements which have been made by
the gentlemen of the Kentish Society...
Maidstone, J. Blake. (1793).
1

LEWIS, J.D.
Womens' Voluntary Service in Kent, 1939-45.
Maidstone, Kent Messenger. 1946?
3,4,11,12,13,14

NATIONAL UNION OF TOWNSWOMEN'S GUILDS - KENT COUNTY BRANCH.
Yearbook and annual report.
3(1962-65)
7(1961, 1962, 1963, 1964, 1965, 1967)
10(1963)

THE NORTH KENT PERMANENT BENEFIT BUILDING SOCIETY.
Official handbook.
E.J. Burrow. 1959.
9

ORDER OF ST. JOHN OF JERUSALEM: COUNCIL FOR KENT.
Yearbook and directory.
4(1955, 1965-66, 1967)
8(1964)
12(1964, 1965, 1967)

POPE, Sidney.
The growth of freemasonry in England and Wales since
1717.
Tunbridge Wells, Hepworth and Co. 196-?
3

ROYAL BRITISH LEGION.
The official handbook.
4(1969)
9(1968, 1971)
11(1971, 1972)

ROYAL LIFE SAVING SOCIETY - KENT BRANCH.
Kent life saver's handbook, 1972.
Royal Life Saving Society - Kent Branch. 1972.
9

ROYAL SOCIETY FOR THE PREVENTION OF CRUELTY TO
ANIMALS - EAST KENT BRANCH.
Annual reports, 1881, 1883, 1884.
17

ROYAL SOCIETY FOR THE PREVENTION OF CRUELTY TO
ANIMALS - MID KENT BRANCH.
Annual report, 1960 in progress.
12

ST. JOHN AMBULANCE BRIGADE - KENT BRANCH.
Yearbook...and directory.
3(1967) 5(1967) 6(1968) 11(1964 in progress)

SOCIETY OF ANTIQUARIES.
Report of Kent Branch, 1893.
11

SOUTH-EASTERN UNION OF SCIENTIFIC SOCIETIES.
Bulletin Nos. 2,3 and 4, 1913-14.
17

Bulletin No. 6, December, 1914.
4

Catalogue of the library, 1912.
17

Catalogue of the library, now incorporated in the
Science Library, 1939.
17

Rules of the Society.
n.d.
17

WEST KENT AND TUNBRIDGE WELLS MARRIAGE GUIDANCE
COUNCIL.
Annual report, 1966-67.
19

WEST KENT FEDERATION OF WOMEN'S INSTITUTES.
Borough Green scrapbook, 1965. (MS. copy).
11

WEST KENT FEDERATION OF WOMEN'S INSTITUTES.
County handbook.
4(1967 in progress)
8(1970)
9(1968, 1971)
12(1966)
19(1970)

WEST KENT MEDICO-CHIRURGICAL SOCIETY.
The centenary handbook.
1956.
18

ORLESTONE

WILKINSON, Edward.
Memorials of the Rev. Charles Rolfe, Rector of
Shadoxhurst and Orlestone.
Nisbet. 1879.
11,15

ORPINGTON

AUSTIN, Francis W.
Guide to Orpington.
Cheltenham, E.J. Burrow. 1910.
2,11

(BOWEN, M.).
Illustrated guide to the parish church of All Saints,
Orpington, by M. Bowen and L.B. Timmis.
Orpington Press, Printers. 1969.
2,17

BURNESS, Gordon.
The white badger. (Note: badgers in the woods around
Orpington), by G. Burness and G. Cliffe.
Harrap. 1970.
2

CARRINGTON, R.C.
Two schools: a history of the St. Olave's and St. Saviour's
Grammar School Foundation. (Note: the Boy's school moved
to Orpington in 1968).
The Governors. 1971.
2

The church of Orpington - All Saints. (Copy of an article
from "The Builder", April 16th, 1904).
2

DRINKWATER, Florence E.
Place names, Kent. (Photocopy of MSS. - placenames of
Orpington and district).
1926.
2

GREAT BRITAIN: LAWS, etc. (ELIZ. II).
Orpington Urban District Council Act.
H.M.S.O. 1962.
8

GREAT BRITAIN, Parliament.
A Bill to confer further powers on the Urban District Council
of Orpington...1953.
H.M.S.O. 1953.
2

HARRILD, Frederick.
Views and points of interest in connection with Orpington
churchyard.
191-?
2,11

History of Orpington. (Typescript: a 12 page synopsis).
1958.
2

HOUSING AND LOCAL GOVERNMENT, Ministry of.
Greater London. (Out-building at the Priory...Orpington)
Building Preservation Order...Proof of evidence (given by).,.
P.R. Whitbourn. (Photocopy of typescript).
1967.
2

KENT COUNTY COUNCIL - ARCHIVES OFFICE.
Parish index to documents, Orpington district. (Typescript
extracts from index).
1967.
2

KENT PUBLISHING CO. Publishers.
Buying a house in Orpington.
Kent Publishing Co. 1968.
2

MARCHAM, Patricia.
Aspects of the history of the parishes of Orpington and St.
Mary Cray. (Photocopy of study for Diploma of Education).
1967.
2

MULLOCK, A.F.
Notes on All Saints Church, Orpington. (Typescript).
1957 (Revised 1967).
2

ORPINGTON PUBLIC LIBRARIES.
(Local collection) books, pamphlets, reports, etc., in
Orpington stock...(Typescript).
(1956).
2

Harlow bequest collection. Author list of books dealing...
with Kent. (Typescript).
(1960).
2

List of some material in Orpington Reference Library which is of
use for local historical and geographical studies. (Typescript).
1965.
2

ORPINGTON URBAN DISTRICT COUNCIL.
Official guide.
1(1961 etc.)
2(1938, 1951 etc.)
5(1963 etc.)
8(1959 etc.)
12(1959 etc.)
19(1959 etc.)

ORPINGTON URBAN DISTRICT COUNCIL.
The Priory and Central Library.
Orpington Urban District Council. 1961.
2,11,12

ORPINGTON WORKERS' EDUCATIONAL ASSOCIATION.
History of Orpington. (Duplicated typescript).
1967.
2

ORPINGTON WORKERS' EDUCATIONAL ASSOCIATION.
Orpington from Saxon times to the Great War.
Kentish District Times. 1919.
1,2,6,11,12,18

The Orpington cookery book, compiled by members of
All Saints' Church, Orpington and others.
Dumfries, Robert Dinwiddie, Printer. n.d.
2

O'SULLIVAN, Maureen.
The parishes of Orpington and St. Mary Cray...
population and educational facilities. (Photocopy,
thesis for Technical Teacher's Training Certificate).
1966.
2

The parish church of All Saints, Orpington: a short
guide and history.
(1962).
1,4,8,12

PARKES, M.B.
The Orpington Psalter. (Typescript).
(196-?).
2

PATULLO HIGGS AND CO. LTD.
60 years with Patullo Higgs. (See Hayes and Keston).
Straker Bros., Printers. (1964).
2

REDWOOD, William Arthur Hugh.
Bristol fashion (autobiography). (Author resident in
Orpington from about 1939).
Latimer House. (1948).
2

REDWOOD, William Arthur Hugh.
Residue of days: a confession of faith (autobiography).
Hodder. 1958.
2

RISPIN, F.
Orpington: a study. (Typescript, a geography thesis).
1963.
2

ST. OLAVE'S AND ST. SAVIOUR'S GRAMMAR SCHOOL,
ORPINGTON.
(Opening and dedication - includes description of
the buildings).
Cambridge, R.I. Severs, Printers. 1968.
2

SMITH, E.
The motor car in an affluent society. (Unpublished
thesis based on research in Orpington).
1963.
2

SMITH, E.
The motor car today. (Unpublished thesis based on
research in Orpington).
1967.
2

TENNENT, A.C.
Orpington Village. (Geography survey, typescript
essay).
1966.
2

ORPINGTON Cont'd

TRENCH, F. Chenevix.
Story of Orpington.
Bromley, Bush. 1898.
1,2,4,6,11,16,17

WATKINS, D.J. AND CO.
Report on facilities for leisure in the Orpington Urban
District Council area, February, 1965.   (Typescript).
2

OSPRINGE

Catalogue of the Roman relics in the Maison Dieu Museum,
Ospringe and 2nd supplement.
Maison Dieu Museum. 1925 etc.
3,12

DRAKE, Charles H.
The hospital of St. Mary of Ospringe, commonly called Maison
Dieu.
Kent Archaeological Society. 1913.
7,11,17

Parish church of St. Peter and St. Paul, Ospringe.
Faversham, Voile and Robertson. 1935.
1

RIGOLD, S.E.
The medieval hospital at Ospringe.   (Minsitry of Works Ancient
Monuments Series).
H.M.S.O. n.d.
1,5,8,11,15

RIGOLD, S.E.
Maison Dieu, Ospringe, Kent.   (Ministry of Works Ancient
Monuments Series), by S.E. Rigold and G.C. Dunning.
H.M.S.O.
5(1962) 8(1958) 11(1958) 12(1958)

Roman discoveries at Ospringe.   (Reprinted from the Faversham
and North East Kent News for April 14th, 21st, 28th, 1923.
3

WHITING, William.
Report on the excavation of the Roman cemetery at Ospringe,
by W. Whiting and others.
London, Society of Antiquaries. 1931.
1,4,5,7,8,11,12,15,17,20

WHITING, William.
When the Romans were at Ospringe.
Faversham, Austen. 1922.
11

OTFORD

Becket's Well, Otford: report on excavations.
n.d.
16

BENNETT, R.G.
The Kentish Polhills: an account of an old Kentish family...
Private Circulation. 1958.
16,17,18

BOX, Ernest George.
Pre-Conquest Otford. (MSS.).
1929.
16

BOX, Ernest George.
Saxon Otford.
Kent Archaeological Society. 1931.
16,17

CHANDLER, Raymond H.
Excursion of the Geologists' Association to Otford and the
Darent Valley (Reprint), by R.H. Chandler and A.L. Leach.
1909.
17

CLARK, F.L.
Beginnings and growth of Methodism in Otford.
n.d.
16

CLARKE, Reginald Dennis.
An outline history of Otford (pamphlet).
(Otford and District Historical Society). 1967.
2,4

ELDER, D.G.
Otford past and present.
(1950).
2

HESKETH, C.
History and antiquities of Otford.
Sevenoaks, Reliance Press. 1909 etc.
1,5,11,12,16,17

HESKETH, C.
Manor House and Great Park of the Archbishop of
Canterbury at Otford.   In Archaeologia Cantiana,
Vol. 31, 1915.
17

HUNT, The Rev. Dr.
Old Otford (pamphlet).
n.d.
13,16

OTFORD AND DISTRICT HISTORICAL SOCIETY AND OTFORD
PARISH COUNCIL.
Otford, Kent: the official guide.
1(1953, 1956, 1958 etc.)
5(1958, 1960, 1964)
8(1956 etc.)
11(1956 etc.)
12(1958 etc.)
19(1958 etc.)

OTHAM

CAVE-BROWNE, J.
Otham Church and Parish - a paper read on 6th March,
1895.   (Extract from the Journal of the Kentish
Archaeological Association, June, 1895).
3

CONWAY, William Martin.   1st Baron Conway of Allington.
Stoneacre, Otham, Kent.
Country Life. 1930.
11

SPURLING, Cuthbert Terence.
Guide to St. Nicholas' Church, Otham, 2nd edition.
Otham, Spurling. 1953.
1,12

Stoneacre, Otham, Kent.
National Trust. n.d.
11

VALLANCE, L.A.   (Mrs. Aymer VALLANCE).
A brief account of Stoneacre, Otham and its restoration.
1928.
11,12

OTTERDEN

RACKETT, Thomas.
A description of Otterden Place and Church and of the
Archiepiscopal Palace at Charing...
Nichols. 1832.
1,11,12

OXENHOATH

WADMORE, J.F.
The Manor of Old Sore and the Colepeper family at
Oxenhoath.   (Reprinted from Archaeologia Cantiana).
Mitchell and Hughes. 1896.
1,11,17

PADDLESWORTH - See also LYMINGE

(To be sold by auction on 17th August, 1918)...The
Arpinge Estate...in the parishes of Newington-next-
Hythe and Paddlesworth...comprising the home and
lower farms...about 269 acres.
(Honeyball and Finn). 1918.
7

DAVIS, Arthur W.
A brief history of the church of St. Oswald,
Paddlesworth, compiled by A.W. Davis.
Folkestone, Sumner. 1929.
3,7

Particulars...of sale of...residential and farm property at
Arpinge, containing about 262 acres...with...the home farm...
which will be sold by auction...on...25th August, 1904.
(Banks and Son). 1904.
7

PADDOCK WOOD

JOSEPH, Kenneth I.
Suggested satellite for Paddock Wood, Kent.
1947.
19

NIGHTINGALE, G.W.
St. Andrew's Church, Paddock Wood, by G.W. Nightingale and others.
O.V. Turner. n.d.
12

PARISH RECORDS - See GENEOLOGICAL RECORDS

PATRIXBOURNE

BOWTELL, J.
A sermon preached at Patrixbourne, near Canterbury...
Knaplock. 1711.
12

PEGWELL BAY

CLARKE, Harold George.
The Pot Lid Recorder, No. 3. (Contains Pegwell Bay Series).
Courier Press. 1952.
14

HEYWOOD, John. Publisher.
Illustrated guide to Ramsgate and Pegwell Bay.
Manchester, J. Heywood. 1897.
11,15

PEMBURY

BETTS, Maria.
The Dickensons; or, God's work in Pembury.
Baldwin. 1888.
19

JENNINGS, Letitia.
Margery Polley: the Pembury Martyr.
Protestant Reformation Society. 1910.
11,19

PEARCE, Luke.
Historical associations of Pembury.
Pearce. 1912.
19

STANDEN, E.J.
Just one village, 1910-60.
Privately Printed. (1962).
11

The parish church of St. Peter in Pembury. (Duplicated typescript).
1970.
11

The story of the Upper Church of St. Peter, Pembury. (Duplicated
typescript).
1962.
11,12

STANDEN, Mary Eileen.
History of the parish of Pembury, edited by M.E. Standen.
1947.
11,12,19

STORRS, W. Townsend.
The church of St. Peter at Pembury.
Mitchell and Hughes. 1909.
11,12,17

PENGE

BRIDLE, William.
Penge Public Library. Supplemental catalogue...compiled by
the Librarian.
(Penge) Public Library Commissioners. 1895.
2

The call to higher service of Mrs. Commissioner Carleton
(Salvationist, Penge).
Salvation Army Printing Works, Printers. (1915).
2

CLARKE, Samuel J.
Penge Public Library...catalogue and supplement,
compiled by S.J. Clarke.
J. Nichols, Printers. 1901-11.
2

CROYDON NATURAL HISTORY AND SCIENTIFIC SOCIETY.
Regional survey atlas of Croydon and district
(includes Beckenham, Penge, Shortlands, West Wickham).
Croydon Natural History and Scientific Society.
1936 in progress.
2

GWYER, Joseph.
Sketches of the life...poems...ramble round the
neighbourhood and glimpses of departed days,
Penge...
Privately Printed. 1875, 1877.
2

HODGSON, Sidney.
Brief notes on the history of the Hamlet of Penge...
Riddle, Smith and Duffus. 1927.
1,2,11,18

JENKINS, Elizabeth.
Harriet. (Historical novel on the murder of Mrs.
Louis Staunton of Cudham, who died at Penge).
Gollancz. 1934 (1949 impression).
2

KENT COUNTY COUNCIL - ARCHIVES OFFICE.
Parish records of Penge St. John.
Kent County Council. 1966.
2

MUNCY, G.N.
Penge Public Library: a history, 1891-1965. (Note:
student's project essay).
1971.
2

PAGET, C.G.
A boundary dispute - Croydon and Penge boundary.
(Extract from "By-ways in the history of Croydon..."
by C.G. Paget).
Croydon Library. 1929.
2

Penge Congregational Church, 1908-58. Golden Jubilee
...programme and historical notes.
Penge Congregational Church. 1958.
2

PENGE PUBLIC LIBRARY COMMISSIONERS.
Report(s) of the Commissioners of the Penge Public
Library, 1895-1901.
J. Nichols, Printer. 1895-1901.
2

PENGE URBAN DISTRICT COUNCIL.
Penge: official guide.
2(1922, 1939 etc.) 4(1963) 8(1959) 19(1961)

SPENCER, Frank.
Come dancing, by Frank and Peggy Spencer. (Note:
Royston Hall Ballroom, Penge).
W.H. Allen. 1968.
2

Trial of the Stauntons, edited by J.B. Atlay...
(murder of Mrs. Louis Staunton of Cudham, who died
at Penge).
Hodge. New Edition, 1952.
2

PENSHURST

ADDLESHAW, Percy.
Sir Philip Sidney.
Methuen. 1909.
11,12

BALDWIN, C. Publisher.
Parish church of St. John the Baptist, Penshurst.
C. Baldwin. 1960.
4,11,12

BALDWIN, C. Publisher.
Penshurst Place: a short account.
C. Baldwin. n.d.
12

ZOUCH, Thomas.
Memoirs of the life and writings of Sir Philip Sidney.
Wilson. 1808.
12

PEPYS, SAMUEL

BRYANT, Arthur.
Samuel Pepys: the saviour of the navy.
Collins. 1949.
18

Samuel Pepys: the man in the making.
Cambridge. 1933.
18

Samuel Pepys: the years of peril.
Collins. 1948.
18

EMDEN, Cecil Stuart.
Pepys himself.
Oxford University Press. 1963.
18

HEATH, Helen Truesdell.
The letters of Samuel Pepys...edited by H.I. Heath.
Oxford, Clarendon Press. 1955.
18

HUNT, Percival.
Samuel Pepys in the Diary.
Oxford University Press. 1959.
18

PETHAM

BRADSHAW, Cecil F.
Notes on Petham, Kent (village and church). (Typescript).
1949.
3

COUNCER, C.R.
Ancient glass from Petham Church, now in Canterbury Cathedral.
In Archaeologia Cantiana, Vol. 65, 1952.
17

PETHAM FRIENDLY SOCIETY.
Rules.
1868.
17

Wadden Hall Farm. Particulars...of sale with plan of the
desirable freehold agricultural and sporting estate known as
"Wadden Hall"...a total area of 495 acres...comprising Wadden
Hall Farm...244 acres...Eindery Field...containing 93 acres...
an excellent sporting property consisting of Castlefield,
Wadden Hall and Stubbs Woods, part Dunlies and Brockhanger
Woods...758 acres, to be sold by auction...on...June 13th,
1925...(in Petham and Waltham).
A. Marchant. (1925).
7

PETTS WOOD

CHADWICK, Mrs. E.
An ecological study of part of Petts Wood, Kent...1970-71.
(Typescript).
1971.
2

PETTS WOOD CONGREGATIONAL CHURCH.
Yearbook, 1964-65.
Ramsgate, Church Publishers. 1964.
12

RAVEN, Susan.
Our guest and sometime friend...General de Gaulle...in England.
(Article in Sunday Times Magazine, 5th May, 1968: De Gaulle
in Petts Wood, 1940).
2

PEDIGREES - See GENEALOGICAL RECORDS

PILGRIMS' WAY

AVERIES, F.
Books and pamphlets on the Pilgrims'Way to Canterbury read at
the Brandy House, Sarre, May 27th, 1959. (Tavern Pamphlets
No. 1). (Typescript).
3

BELLOC, Hilaire.
The Old Road.
Constable. 1904 etc.
1,3,4,5,6,7,8,11,12,13,18,19,21

CALDER, W.
Canterbury pilgrimage.
William Blackwood and Sons. 1842.
12

CAPPER, Douglas Parode.
On the Pilgrims' Way.
Methuen. 1928.
1,3,6,8,9,11,12,13,15,17,18

CARTWRIGHT, Julia. (Mrs. Henry ADY).
Pilgrims' Way from Winchester to Canterbury.
1893 etc.
1,2,3,4,5,6,7,8,10,11,12,15,19,21

ELLISTON-ERWOOD, Frank Charles.
The pilgrims' road: a practical guide for the
pedestrian...
Warne. 1910.
2

The pilgrims' road: a practical guide for the
pedestrian...
Homeland Association. 1923 etc.
1,3,5,6,8,10,11,12,13,17,18

The "Pilgrims' Way": its antiquity and its alleged
medieval use. (Reprinted from Archaeologia Cantiana,
Vol. 37).
Mitchell, Hughes and Clarke. 1924.
11,17

FEARON, Henry Bridges.
Pilgrimage to Canterbury.
1956.
5,7,8,10,11,12

GOODSALL, Robert Harold.
The ancient road to Canterbury: a progress through
Kent.
Ashford, Headley. 1959.
1,3,4,5,6,7,8,9,10,11,12,14,15,17,20, 21

HART, Edwin.
The Pilgrims' Way in Kent. (Typescript MS.).
1927.
11

HEATH, Sidney.
In the steps of the pilgrims.
London, Rich and Cowan. 195-?
3,6

HOLLYMAN, Jean.
The road to Canterbury...by J. and T. Hollyman.
(Article in "Holiday", October, 1948).
3

HOOPER, Wilfred.
The Pilgrims' Way and its supposed pilgrim use.
Surrey Archaeological Collections. 1936.
11

JAMES, E. Renouard.
The Pilgrims' Way: a lecture.
Elliot Stock. (1900).
11

JENNETT, Sean.
The Pilgrims' Way from Winchester to Canterbury.
Cassell. 1971.
3,4,7,8,11,19,21

KIRKHAM, Nellie.
The Pilgrims' Way...
Muller. 1948.
1,3,4,8,9,11,15,18

LAKE, W.E. Photographer.
The Pilgrims' Way, a series of camera studies with
descriptive text by Nellie Kirkham.
Muller. 1948.
8,12,15

LASHAM, Frank.
Notes on the antiquity of the Pilgrims' Way: a
lecture.
Elliot Stock. (1900).
11

MAXWELL, Donald.
The Pilgrims' Way in Kent (1st edition).
Kent Messenger. 1932.
6,11

MAXWELL, Donald.
Pilgrims' Way in Kent.
Kent Messenger. 1934.
1,3,4,5,7,8,9,11,12,13,14,15,16,17,18,20

PALMER, P.G.
To the shrine of St. Thomas of Canterbury: a modern pilgrimage.
Elliot Stock. (1900).
11

PARR, H.
New wheels in old ruts: a pilgrimage to Canterbury via the
ancient Pilgrims' Way.
Fisher Unwin. 1896.
3,4,8,11,12,15,17,18

PENNELL, Joseph.
A Canterbury pilgrimage, by J. and E.R. Pennell.
Seeley. 1885.
1,4,5,6,8,9,11,12,14,15,17,18

WARD, H. Snowden.
The Canterbury pilgrimages. (See Canterbury Cathedral).
Black. 1904 etc.
1,3,4,5,6,7,8,9,11,12,13,15,17,19

WILSON, S. Gordon.
With the pilgrims to Canterbury and the history of the hospital
of Saint Thomas.
S.P.C.K. 1934.
3,6,11,12,14

WATT, F.
Canterbury pilgrims and their ways.
1917.
1,3,4,5,6,7,8,11,12,18

WRIGHT, Christopher John.
A guide to the Pilgrims' Way and North Downs Way.
Constable. 1971.
2,3,4,5,7,8,9,21

PITT, WILLIAM

(ALMON, John).
Anecdotes of the life of...William Pitt...with his speeches in
Parliament...1736-78, 6th edition.
Seeley. 1797.
2

LEVER, Sir Tresham.
The house of Pitt, a family chronicle.
Murray. 1947.
2

PITT, William. (1759-1806).
Letters relating to the love episode of William Pitt...(and)
an account of his health by his physician, by W. Pitt and W.
Eden, 1st Baron Auckland. (Pitt resident at Holwood, Keston).
Private Circulation. 1900.
2

SHERRARD, O.A.
Lord Chatham, 3 vols.
Bodley Head. 1952-58.
2

STANHOPE, P.H. 5th Earl.
Life of...William Pitt, 4 vols. (Note: lived at Holwood, Keston).
Murray. 1861-62.
2(Vols. 2,3 and 4) 6(4 vols.)

WALFORD, Edward.
William Pitt: a biography.
Chatto and Windus. 1890.
2

PLACE-NAMES AND SURNAMES

BROMLEY, Francis E.
Kentish place-names. (MS.).
n.d.
3

HARDMAN, Frederick William.
The Danes in Kent: a survey of Kentish place-names of
Scandinavian origin. (A lecture given at Walmer on 7th February,
1927).
1,3,4,6,11,12

History in local place-names.
T.F. Pain. 1926.
13

The pronunciation of Kent place-names.
1933.
1,2,3,4,7,8,11,12,13

HORSLEY, John William.
Place-names in Kent.
Maidstone, South-Eastern Gazette. 1921.
1,2,4,5,6,8,10,11,12,14,15,16,18,19

"AN IGNORANT STUDENT", pseud.
Origins in place-names.
London, Chiswick Press. 1923.
3

IRWIN, John.
Place-names of Edenbridge.
Edenbridge Historical Society. 1964.
1,2,3,4,7,8,11,12,15,19

Kentish family names in manuscript.
n.d.
12

WALLENBERG, J.K.
Kentish place-names...
Uppsala. 1931.
1,2,3,4,5,7,8,11,12,13,17,18,19,20,21

WALLENBERG, J.K.
Place-names of Kent.
Uppsala. 1934.
1,2,3,4,5,7,8,9,11,12,13,14,15,17,18,19,20,21

PLAISTOW

MACFARLANE, William Angus.
St. Mary's first hundred years, 1863-1963: a history
of Plaistow Parish Church.
Bookprint Ltd. 1963.
2,12

PLAXTOL

LEWIS, Mary.
Plaxtol.
Hadlow, Hilton Press. 1965.
1,2,4,7,8,11,15,19

PERRY, John Tavenor.
Plaxtol: a Kentish Borough.
Batsford. 1895.
1,12

Plaxtol: a Kentish Village, compiled by the members
of Plaxtol Women's Institute.
Plaxtol Women's Institute. 1957.
4,11

STAGG, Frank Noel.
Notes on the local history of...Plaxtol. (Typescript).
1948.
11

WILLCOCK, John.
Life of Sir Henry Vane, The Younger...1613-1662.
St. Catherine's Press. 1913.
11

WOOD, Margaret.
Old Soar, Plaxtol.
H.M.S.O. 1950 etc.
1,2,8,11,12

PLUCKLEY

A catalogue of the contents of the Mansion, Surrenden
Dering, Pluckley, near Ashford, Kent...to be sold by
auction...on...8th October, 1928...
J. Davy. (1928).
11

COLLINSON, Patrick.
A mirror of Elizabethan Puritanism: the life and
letters of "Godly Master Dering".
Dr. William's Trust. 1964.
1,12

DERING, Sir. E.
The most excellent Maria...
Published by R. Roberts for the Author. 1701.
11

GRIFFIN, Ralph.
Kentish items: Aylesford, Pluckley, Stourmouth, Faversham,
Sittingbourne, Wouldham, Chatham.
n.d.
7

HAMMOND, W.O.
Posthumous trial of Sir. E.C. Dering, Bart.
Canterbury, H. Ward. Kentish Gazette Office. 1852.
3

HASLEWOOD, Francis.
The parish of Pluckley, Kent.
1899.
1,3,12,15

Kentish Industries, No. 12 - Pluckley Brick and Tile Works.
1892.
17

OXENDEN, Ashton.
The home beyond; or, a happy old age.
William MacIntosh. 1863.
11

SANDERS, Frederick.
The natural history of Mundy Bois. (Typescript).
1937.
4

PLUMSTEAD

BAKER, Herbert Arthur.
Excursion to East Wickham and Plumstead, by H.A. Baker and
S. Priest. (Proceedings of the Geologists' Association,
Vol. XXX, 1919).
5

ELLISTON-ERWOOD, Frank C.
The architectural history of the church of St. Nicholas,
Plumstead and its chapel...of St. Michael, East Wickham.
Proceedings of the Woolwich Antiquarian Society. 1913.
7

The church of St. Nicholas, Plumstead. In Archaeologia
Cantiana, Vol. 72, 1958).
17

The history of the church, manor and parish of Plumstead with
East Wickham in Kent in the Middle Ages, by F.C. Ellison-Erwood
and W.H. Mandy.
Ascham Press. 1937.
11,18

MANDY, W.H.
The Manor of Plumstead in the XIIIth and XIVth centuries.
Woolwich Antiquarian Society. 1912.
7

PRIEST, Simeon.
An excursion to Plumstead and Bostall Heath and an excursion
to Cobham and Strood.
1924.
5

WALPOLE, J.K.
Historical sketch of Plumstead, Kent...
Woolwich, Pryce. 1860.
1,11,18

POLICE

KENT COUNTY CONSTABULARY.
Annual report of the Chief Constable for 1951.
6(1945-59) 11(1970 etc.) 12(1951)

The Kent Police Centenary: recollections of a hundred years,
1857-1957.
1957.
4,7,9,13,14,19

Programme of centenary parade and exhibitions to be held at
County Police Headquarters at Maidstone.
Maidstone, Kent County Constabulary. 1957.
3

POLL BOOKS - See ELECTIONS

POOR LAW

Five letters on the state of the poor in the County of Kent, as
first printed in the year 1770, to which is added a short
introduction containing a few additional observations on the
same subject in the year 1808.
Printed by Rouse, Kirkby and Lawrence. 1808.
11

REX vs. MARTEN, John.
The King on the prosecution of the inhabitants of the
parish of Wrotham..., against John Marten, one of the
overseers of the poor of the said parish for the
years 1806, 1807 and 1808.
Printed by T. Clout. 1809.
11

ROCH, Thomas.
Proceedings of the Guardians of the Poor of the City
of Canterbury against John Cantio, brewer, landlord
and Alderman Rolfe and Mr. Thomas Giles, tenant, for
the recovery of a barn and some land given by Queen
Elizabeth for the maintenance of the poor Bluecoat
Boys of that city.
Canterbury, Sold by T. Smith and Son and W. Flackton.
1778.
3

PORT VICTORIA

ROYAL CORINTHIAN YACHT CLUB.
One hundred years of amateur yachting, 1872-1972.
(The Royal Corinthian Yacht Club had a clubhouse at
Port Victoria, Isle-of-Grain for 15 years).
Royal Corinthian Yacht Club. (1972).
4

PORTUS LEMANIS - See LYMPNE

POSTAL HISTORY

Remarks on the conveyance of the mails between London
and Paris showing the advantages that would result by
adopting the shortest route, by Folkestone and Boulogne.
Effingham Wilson, 11 Royal Exchange. 1850.
7

SANKEY, Marjorie.
"Care of Mr. Waghorn": a biography...
Postal History Society. 1964.
4,8,15

SIDEBOTTOM, John K.
The overland mail: a postal historical study of the
mail route to India. (Special reference to Thomas
Fletcher Waghorn).
Postal History Society. 1948.
4,8,15

POSTLING

Illustrated particulars, plan and conditions of sale
of...Postling Court Estate...delightful Tudor period
residence...five cottages...a pair of attractive
houses...about 68 acres...by order of Mrs. N. Kahn.
Finn, Kelsey and Ashenden. 1955.
7

VALLANCE, Aymer.
Postling Church, by A. Vallance and G.M. Livett.
(Reprinted from Archaeologia Cantiana, Vol. 30).
Mitchell, Hughes and Clarke. 1913.
11,17

PRATTS BOTTOM

COPUS, G.D.
The commons of Green Street Green and Pratts Bottom,
Chelsfield. (Typescript).
1955.
2

HOOK, Judith Ann.
Pratts Bottom: an English village.
Norman-Stahli Publishing Co. 1972.
11

PRESTON (NR. WINGHAM)

A brief memoir of Mrs. Ann Elgar Toomer of Preston
Court, near Wingham.
1829.
11

DOWKER, George.
On Romano-British fictile vessels from Preston, near
Wingham.
Mitchell and Hughes. 1892.
7,11,14

SPURLING, C. Terence.
Historical notes: St. Mildred's, Preston by Wingham.
Martell Press. 1967.
4,12

PRESTON-NEXT-FAVERSHAM

GRIFFIN, Ralph.
Kentish items: Elham, Preston-next-Faversham, Addington.
n.d.
7

ROBERTSON, William Archibald Scott.
Preston Church, next Faversham, with memoirs of the rectors
and vicars from 1283-1894. (Reprinted from Archaeologia
Cantiana, Vol. XXI).
Printed by Mitchell and Hughes. 1895.
11

PUBLIC UTILITIES

GREAT BRITAIN: LAWS, etc. (VIC.).
An Act for consolidating in one Act certain provisions usually
inserted in Acts with respect to the constitution of companies
incorporated for carrying on undertakings of a public nature.
(Bound in "Gas Acts", Isle of Thanet Gas Co.).
1845.
13

GREAT BRITAIN: LAWS, etc. (VIC.).
An Act for consolidating in one Act certain provisions usually
contained in Acts authorising the making of Gasworks for
supplying towns with gas. (Bound in "Gas Acts", Isle of Thanet
Gas Co.).
1847.
13

GREAT BRITAIN: LAWS, etc. (VIC.).
An Act for consolidating in one Act certain provisions
frequently inserted in Acts relating to the constitution and
management of companies incorporated for carrying on undertakings of a public nature. (Bound in "Gas Acts", Isle of
Thanet Gas Co.).
1863.
13

GREAT BRITAIN: LAWS, etc. (VIC.).
An Act for regulating measures used in sales of gas. (Bound
in "Gas Acts", Isle of Thanet Gas Co.).
1859.
13

GREAT BRITAIN: LAWS, etc. (VIC.).
An Act to amend the Act for regulating measures used in sales
of Gas. (Bound in "Gas Acts", Isle of Thanet Gas Co.).
1860.
13

GREAT BRITAIN: LAWS, etc. (VIC.).
An Act to amend the Gasworks Clauses Act, 1847. (Bound in
"Gas Acts", Isle of Thanet Gas Co.).
1871.
13

GREAT BRITAIN: LAWS, etc. (VIC.).
The North Kent Waterworks Act, 1860.
Printed by W. Clowes and Sons. 1860.
11

GREAT BRITAIN: LAWS, etc. (EDW. VII).
Electric Lighting Orders Confirmation (No. 4) Act.
1902.
8

GREAT BRITAIN: LAWS, etc. (EDW. VII).
Kent Electric Power Act.
1902.
8

GREAT BRITAIN: LAWS, etc. (EDW. VII).
Kent Electric Power Act.
1906.
8

GREAT BRITAIN: LAWS, etc. (GEO. V).
Kent Electric Power Act, 1913.
8

GREAT BRITAIN: LAWS, etc. (GEO. V).
South Suburban Gas Bill (8 and 9 George V).
1918.
5

GREAT BRITAIN: LAWS, etc. (ELIZ. II).
An Act to apply to the Canterbury and District Water Co. certain
provisions of the third schedule to the Water Act, 1945.
H.M.S.O. (1960).
12

GREAT BRITAIN: LAWS, etc. (ELIZ. II).
Canterbury and District Water Act.
H.M.S.O. 1960.
8

GREAT BRITAIN: LAWS, etc. (ELIZ. II).
Kent Water Act, 1955.
H.M.S.O. 1955.
4,8,11,12

GREAT BRITAIN: LAWS, etc. (ELIZ. II).
Ministry of Housing and Local Government Provisional
Order Confirmation (West Kent Main Sewerage District)
Act, 1966.
H.M.S.O. 1966.
12

GREAT BRITAIN: LAWS, etc. (ELIZ. II) - STATUTORY
INSTRUMENTS.
Mid Kent (New Sources) Order, 1968.
H.M.S.O. 1968.
12

GREAT BRITAIN, Parliament.
Special report...on the Kent Water Bill.
H.M.S.O. 1955.
8

GREAT BRITAIN, Parliament - House of Lords.
Special report from the Select Committee of the House
of Lords on the Kent Water Bill.
H.M.S.O. 1955.
4

HOUSING AND LOCAL GOVERNMENT, Ministry of.
The Sevenoaks and Tonbridge and Mid Kent (Variation of
Limits) Water Order, 1959.
H.M.S.O. (1959).
12

The Sevenoaks and Tonbridge Water Order, 1959.
H.M.S.O. 1960.
12

The Sevenoaks and Tonbridge Water Order.
H.M.S.O. 1964.
4,8

LAYTON, T.W.
Early years of the South Metropolitan Gas Co., 1833-71.
1920.
18

MEDWAY WATER BOARD.
Report upon the operation of the undertaking for the
period...
4(1960-61, 1961-62) 8(1959-60)

METROPOLITAN WATER BOARD.
A brief description of the undertaking. (Note:
includes section on Kent area).
Metropolitan Water Board. 1969.
2

MID KENT WATER CO.
Share prospectus.
1907.
17

SOUTH-EASTERN ELECTRICITY BOARD.
Annual report and accounts.
3(1956, 1963-64)
6(1957 in progress)
8(1949 in progress)
9(1955 in progress)
12(1951 in progress)

SOUTH-EASTERN GAS BOARD.
Annual report and accounts, 1957 in progress.
12

SOUTH-EASTERN GAS BOARD.
Reconstruction of manufacturing plant at Dover Works.
1955.
6

SOUTH-EASTERN GAS CONSULTATIVE COUNCIL.
Annual report.
3(1955)
4(1963-64)
6(1960 in progress)
8(1949 in progress)
9(1956 and 1957)
19(1969)

PUBLIC UTILITIES Cont'd

SOUTH METROPOLITAN GAS CO.
A century of gas in South London.
1924.
17

THE UNDERGROUND WATER PRESERVATION ASSOCIATION.
On the underground water supply of the Country...(Note:
includes reports on Kent Water Co. area (West Kent)).
The Underground Water Preservation Association. (1902).
2

WATER RESOURCES BOARD.
Water supplies in South-East England.
H.M.S.O. 1966.
3,6,12

QUEENBOROUGH

CASTLE, Joseph.
Queenborough and its church.
Sheerness, Rigg. 1907.
11

Copy of the Charter of the Borough of Queenborough.
Printed by Ellerton and Henderson. n.d.
1,11

GARRINGTON, D.S.
An answer to the address of Mr. T.Y. Greet to the Freemen of
Queenborough, bearing the date June, 1824...
Printed by C. Hodson. 1824.
11

KOGAN, Herman.
The long white line.
U.S.A., New York, Random House. 1963.
12

PUCKLE, J.
Copy of the Charter of Charles I of the Borough of Quinborowe.
London, Beckford. n.d.
4,11,12

Queenborough-in-Sheppey Industrial Development Handbook.
E.J. Burrows. (1969).
11

SETTLE, SPEAKMAN AND CO. LTD.
History of the Queenborough undertaking.
Queenborough, S. Settle and Co. Ltd. 1957.
11

"To all people...". (The original deedpoll concerning oyster
fisheries in 1750). A broadsheet.
n.d.
11

RAILWAYS

ABC of British Railways locomotives. Part 2 - Southern Region.
I. Allan. 1957 and 1958.
8

THE ABC of Southern electric trains.
I. Allan. 1950?
4

ACWORTH, W.M.
The railways of England...Chatham and Dover, South-Eastern.
Murray. 1900.
14

AHRONS, E.L.
Locomotive and train working in the latter part of the nineteenth
century. Vol. 5 - South-Eastern Railway - London, Chatham and
Dover Railway etc.
Heffer. 1953.
2,5,6,8,12

ALLEN, Cecil John.
ABC of British express trains. No. 2 - Southern Region.
I. Allan. 1960.
8

ALLEN, G. Freeman.
The line that Jack built: the Romney, Hythe and Dymchurch Railway.
I. Allan. 1950.
1,6,7,8(1954) 11,12

ASSOCIATION OF REGULAR KENT COASTERS.
The Kent Coaster: "Official bulletin of the Association of
Regular Kent Coasters", i.e. regular travellers by train from the
North Kent coast to and from London - season ticket holders.
1919-20.
13

AUSTIN, Thomas.
Speech of Mr. Austin on behalf of the South-Eastern
and North Kent lines...in the House of Commons, 1846.
Rowarth. 1846.
8,11

BEHREND, George.
Grand European Express.
Allen and Unwin. 1962.
6

BENNETT, Alfred Rosling.
The first railway in London: being the story of the
London and Greenwich Railway from 1832 to 1878.
Locomotive Publishing Co. 1926.
17,18

BENNETT, Alfred Rosling.
The first railway in London: being the story of the
London and Greenwich Railway from 1832 to 1878
(reprint edition).
Conway Maritime Press. 1971.
11

BODY, Geoffrey.
Ramsgate Tunnel Railway, by G. Body and R. Eastleigh.
Trans-Rail Publications. 1966.
7,12

The Bowater Railway, 1906-69.
Locomotive Club of Great Britain. 1969.
2,4,11

The Bowater Railway in pictures, 1906-70, compiled by
...the Sittingbourne and Kemsley Light Railway,
Publicity Department, produced by R.L. Ratcliffe.
Locomotive Club of Great Britain. (1971).
11

BRADLEY, Donald Laurence.
The locomotives of the London, Chatham and Dover
Railway.
Railway Correspondence and Travel Society. 1960.
1,2,3,4,6,7,8,9,11,12,15

The locomotives of the South-Eastern and Chatham
Railway.
Railway Correspondence and Travel Society. 1961.
1,2,3,4,6,7,8,9,11,12,15

The locomotives of the South-Eastern Railway.
Railway Correspondence and Travel Society. 1953 and 1963.
4,7,8,9(1963) 15

BRITISH RAILWAYS - SOUTHERN REGION.
Extension of electrification from Gillingham to
Sheerness-on-Sea, Ramsgate and Dover.
British Railways. 1959.
1

Locomotives - Eastern section, revised (drawings).
British Railways. 1959.
4

South-East report, Vol. 1, February, 1959 in progress.
British Railways.
8

South-East report (on the electrification of the
South-East Division) Nos. 1-5.
British Railways. n.d.
4

South-East report (on the electrification of the
South-East Division) June, 1960, June, 1961.
British Railways.
4,8(June, 1961)

Southern traveller's handbook.
British Railways.
2(1967) 7(1967) 8(1965-66)

BRUTON, J.F.
Some industrial steam locomotives and railways.
(Typescript).
Newcomen Society. 1956.
8

BUCKNALL, Rixon.
Boat trains and channel packets: the English short
sea routes.
Vincent Stuart. 1957.
1,3,4,5,6,7,8,9,12,14,15

BURTT, Frank.
L.B. and S.C.R. locomotives: an up-to-date survey
to 1870.
I. Allan. 1946.
12

BURTT, Frank.
S.E. and C.R. locomotives: a survey...1874-1923.
I. Allan. 1947.
4,6,7,9,11

C., H.R.
The Canterbury and Whitstable Railway. (Article in Southern
Railway Magazine, Vol. VIII, No. 90, June, 1930).
3

Canterbury and Whitstable Railway - The Railway Companion:
utility and advantages of the Canterbury and Whitstable
Railway. In Pamphlets Relating to Canterbury, Vol. 7, 1836.
17

CASSERLEY, Henry Cyril.
Locomotives at the grouping: Southern Railway, by H.C.
Casserley and S.W. Johnston.
I. Allan. 1965.
7

CASSERLEY, Henry Cyril.
Locomotives of British Railways...Southern Group, by H.C.
Casserley and L.L. Asher.
Dakers. 1956 etc.
8,12,15

CATT, Andrew Robert.
The East Kent Railway.
Oakwood Press. 1970.
2,4,7,12

CAWSTON, Rev. A.C.
A railway photographer's diary.
Town and Country Press. 1972.
3

Centenary of the opening of the South-Eastern Railway to
Maidstone from Paddock Wood, September 25th, 1844.
Southern Railway. 1944.
11

CLARK, R.H.
A Southern Region record.
Oakwood Press. 1964.
3,4,6,7,8

CLAYTON, Howard.
The atmospheric railways (including London and Croydon Railway).
Privately Printed. 1966.
2

COLE, D.
Kent and East Sussex Railway.
Union Publications. 1963.
1,3,4,11,12,19

COLLARD, William.
Proposed London and Paris Railway.
Clowes. 1928.
1,4,6,7,8,11,12

COURSE, Edwin A.
The Bexley Heath Railway, 1883-1900...(Proceedings of the
Woolwich and District Antiquarian Society, Vol. XXX, 1954).
1,4,5,8,11,12

COURSE, Edwin A.
The evolution of the railway network of South-East England.
1958.
17

CROMBLEHOLME, Roger.
The Hawkhurst Railway.
Narrow Gauge and Light Railway Society. 1961.
4,15

CROMBLEHOLME, Roger.
Kent and Sussex Railway stockbook.
Union Publications. 1965.
2,3,4,8,11

DARTFORD DISTRICT LIGHT RAILWAYS - See DARTFORD.

DARWIN, Bernard.
War on the line: the story of the Southern Railway in war-time.
Southern Railway. 1946.
4,5,6,7,8,12,15

DAWSON, Philip.
The electrification of...the suburban system of the London,
Brighton and South Coast Railway.
Institute of Civil Engineers. 1911.
12

DIXON, Alan G.
Kent and East Sussex Railway stockbook, 1970.
Farmer's Line Publications. 1970.
11

Dover, Folkestone and Deal local railway guide.
1898.
17

DUNK, J.L.
History of Kent railways.
1950.
7

ELLIS, Hamilton.
The London, Brighton and South Coast Railway.
I. Allan. (1960).
12

ELLISTON-ERWOOD, P.M.
The railway enthusiast's guide to railway societies
and clubs...compiled by P.M. Elliston-Erwood.
Sidcup, Lambarde Press. 1962.
12

EMERSON, George Rose.
Guide to the South-Eastern Railway, including the
Hastings, North Kent and Guildford and Reading
Branches.
c.1850.
11,17

ENGLISH, John. Publisher.
English's abridged time-table of the South-Eastern,
London and Chatham Railways; steam packet service between
Folkestone and Boulogne...
J. English. 1869.
7

ENVIRONMENT, Department of the.
Railway accident: report of the accident that occurred
on 15th July, 1970 at Shalmsford Street Occupation
Level Crossing, near Canterbury in the Southern
Region, British Railways.
H.M.S.O. 1971.
11

ENVIRONMENT, Department of the.
Report of the collision that occurred on 12th November,
1970 at Bexley Station.
H.M.S.O. 1972.
8

Episode in the history of the Canterbury and
Whitstable Railway.
Canterbury College of Art. 1960.
3

FELLOWS, Reginald B.
History of the Canterbury and Whitstable Railway.
Canterbury, Jennings. 1930.
1,2,3,4,6,7,8,11,12,15,17,19

FINCH, M. Lawson.
The Rother Valley, later the Kent and East Sussex
Railway, 1896-1948.
Dunton Green, M.L. Finch. 1949.
1,7,11,12,13,15,16

GARRETT, S.R.
The Kent and East Sussex Railway.
Oakwood Press. 1972.
2,11

GREAT BRITAIN: LAWS, etc. (GEO. IV).
An Act for making and maintaining a railway...from...
Whitstable...to...Canterbury. (George IV, Cap. LXX -
10th June, 1825).
3

GREAT BRITAIN: LAWS, etc. (GEO. IV).
An Act for enlarging and amending the powers and
provisions of the Acts passed for the making and
maintaining a railway...from...Whitstable...to...
Canterbury. (Royal assent, 21st July, 1825).
3

GREAT BRITAIN: LAWS, etc. (WILL. IV).
An Act for making a railway from the London and
Croydon Railway to Dover, to be called the South-
Eastern Railway.
1836.
7

GREAT BRITAIN: LAWS, etc. (VIC.).
An Act to alter and divert the line of the South-Eastern
Railway...
1839.
7

GREAT BRITAIN: LAWS, etc. (VIC.).
An Act to alter and divert a portion of the (South-Eastern
Railway) line...
1840.
7

GREAT BRITAIN: LAWS, etc. (VIC.).
An Act...to make a branch railway to...Maidstone.
1843.
7

GREAT BRITAIN: LAWS, etc. (VIC.).
An Act...to make a railway...to Swan Street...in the Old Kent
Road...
1843.
7

GREAT BRITAIN: LAWS, etc. (VIC.).
An Act...to make a railway from...Ashford to...Canterbury...
1844.
7

GREAT BRITAIN: LAWS, etc. (VIC.).
An Act...to maintain a branch railway...to the Harbour of
Folkestone...
1844.
7

GREAT BRITAIN: LAWS, etc. (VIC.).
An Act to enable the company of proprietors of the Thames and
Medway Canal to raise a further sum of money...to...maintain a
railway from Gravesend to Rochester.
1845.
9

GREAT BRITAIN: LAWS, etc. (VIC.).
An Act to authorise the purchase of the Gravesend and Rochester
Railway and Canal by the South-Eastern Railway Company.
1846.
9

GREAT BRITAIN: LAWS, etc. (VIC.).
An Act for dissolving the Canterbury and Whitstable Railway
Company and for vesting in the South-Eastern Railway Company
the undertaking of the South-Eastern and Continental Steam
Packet Company...(The South-Eastern Railway (Canterbury and
Whitstable, and Steam Packets) Act).
1853.
7

GREAT BRITAIN: LAWS, etc. (VIC.).
An Act for authorising the South-Eastern Railway Company to make
and maintain extensions of their railway to Cranbrook, Hythe and
Sandgate, respectively, and to raise further monies.
1864.
7

GREAT BRITAIN: LAWS, etc. (VIC.).
An Act to authorise the London, Chatham and Dover Railway
Company to make a short connecting railway at Beckenham...
1865.
7

GREAT BRITAIN: LAWS, etc. (VIC.).
An Act for empowering the South-Eastern Railway to abandon
certain authorised lines...
1870.
7

GREAT BRITAIN: LAWS, etc. (VIC.).
An Act to amend and enlarge some of the powers and provisions
of the Acts relating to the South-Eastern Railway Company.
1873.
7

GREAT BRITAIN: LAWS, etc. (VIC.).
An Act to confer upon the South-Eastern Railway Company further
powers with respect to their own undertaking and the undertakings
of certain other companies.
1875.
7

GREAT BRITAIN: LAWS, etc. (VIC.).
An Act to authorise the South-Eastern Railway Company to extend
the Hythe and Sandgate Branch Railway to Folkestone...
1876.
7

GREAT BRITAIN: LAWS, etc. (VIC.).
An Act for extending the time for completion of works
at Bermondsey and for the purchase of lands for...
the Rye and Denge-ness Railway and Pier (South-
Eastern Railway Act, 1877).
7

GREAT BRITAIN: LAWS, etc. (VIC.).
A Bill to enable the South-Eastern Railway Company to
make a railway from the North Kent line of the South-
Eastern Railway at Lewisham, to Tunbridge, with branches
to Dartford, Sevenoaks, Maidstone and Paddock Wood.
Roworth and Sons. 1847.
11

GREAT BRITAIN: LAWS, etc. (VIC.).
Bexley Heath Railway Act, 1883...An Act for authorising
the construction of a railway...to be called the
Bexley Heath Railway...
4

GREAT BRITAIN: LAWS, etc. (VIC.).
Folkestone, Sandgate and Hythe Tramway Acts, 1884-
92. South-Eastern Railway Acts, 1893-1900. S.E.
and L.C.D. Railway Companies Acts, 1899-1905.
7

GREAT BRITAIN: LAWS, etc. (VIC.).
Herne Bay and Faversham Railway: an Act to enable the
...Railway Company to extend their railway to Margate.
1859.
8

GREAT BRITAIN: LAWS, etc. (VIC.).
London, Chatham and Dover Railway (Metropolitan
Extensions) Act, 1860...
4

GREAT BRITAIN: LAWS, etc. (VIC.).
London, Chatham and Dover Railway (Arrangement) Act,
1867. An Act to authorise the...Railway Company to
raise a sum of money for the satisfaction of certain
claims...
4

GREAT BRITAIN: LAWS, etc. (VIC.).
London, Chatham and Dover Railway Act, 1874. (37
and 38 Victoria).
8

GREAT BRITAIN: LAWS, etc. (VIC.).
London, Chatham and Dover Railway (Further Powers)
Bill. Minutes of Proceedings of Select Committee on
Railway Bills.
1884.
7

GREAT BRITAIN: LAWS, etc. (VIC.).
London, Chatham and Dover Railway Act, 1886. An Act
to confer further powers...
4

GREAT BRITAIN: LAWS, etc. (VIC.).
London, Chatham and Dover Railway Act, 1892. An Act
to enable the...Railway Company to make agreement with
the Dover Harbour Board...
4

GREAT BRITAIN: LAWS, etc. (VIC.).
London, Chatham and Dover Railway Act, 1898. An Act
to authorise the...Railway Company to widen certain
bridges, to stop up certain level crossings...(etc.).
4

GREAT BRITAIN: LAWS, etc. (VIC.).
South-Eastern Railway Act, 1881.
7

GREAT BRITAIN: LAWS, etc. (VIC.).
South-Eastern Railway (New Lines and Widenings) Act,
1882.
4

GREAT BRITAIN: LAWS, etc. (VIC.).
The South-Eastern Railway (Various Powers) Act, 1882.
7

GREAT BRITAIN: LAWS, etc. (VIC.).
The South-Eastern Railway (Various Powers) Act, 1884.
7

GREAT BRITAIN: LAWS, etc. (VIC.).
The South-Eastern Railway (Various Powers) Act, 1885.
7

GREAT BRITAIN: LAWS, etc. (VIC.).
The South-Eastern Railway Act, 1887.
7

GREAT BRITAIN: LAWS, etc. (VIC.).
The South-Eastern Railway (Various Powers) Act, 1888.
7

GREAT BRITAIN: LAWS, etc. (VIC.).
The South-Eastern Railway Act, 1889.
7

GREAT BRITAIN: LAWS, etc. (VIC.).
South-Eastern Railway Act, 1891. An Act for conferring
further powers on the South-Eastern Railway Company and upon the
Cranbrook and Paddock Wood Railway Company...
4,7

GREAT BRITAIN: LAWS, etc. (VIC.).
South-Eastern Railway Company (Rates and Charges) Order
Confirmation Act, 1891.
4

GREAT BRITAIN: LAWS, etc. (VIC.).
South-Eastern Railway Act, 1892. An Act for conferring further
powers on the South-Eastern Railway Company and upon the
Cranbrook and Paddock Wood Railway Company...
4,7

GREAT BRITAIN: LAWS, etc. (VIC.).
The South-Eastern Railway Act, 1893.
7

GREAT BRITAIN: LAWS, etc. (VIC.).
South-Eastern Railway Act, 1895. An Act to confer further
powers on the South-Eastern Railway Company in reference to
their own undertaking...
4

GREAT BRITAIN: LAWS, etc. (VIC.).
South-Eastern Railway Act, 1896. An Act for conferring
further powers on the South-Eastern Railway Company and to make
further provision with respect to their own undertaking...
4

GREAT BRITAIN: LAWS, etc. (VIC.).
South-Eastern Railway Act, 1897. An Act for conferring
further powers...
4

GREAT BRITAIN: LAWS, etc. (VIC.).
The South-Eastern Railway (Confirmation of Cator Agreement)
Act, 1897.
7

GREAT BRITAIN: LAWS, etc. (VIC.).
South-Eastern Railway Act, 1898. An Act for conferring
further powers...
4

GREAT BRITAIN: LAWS, etc. (VIC.).
South-Eastern Railway Act, 1899. An Act for conferring
further powers...
4,7

GREAT BRITAIN: LAWS, etc. (VIC.).
South-Eastern Railway Act, 1900. An Act for conferring
further powers...
4

GREAT BRITAIN: LAWS, etc. (VIC.).
South-Eastern and London, Chatham and Dover Railway Companies
Act, 1899. An Act to provide for the working union of the...
Companies and for other purposes.
2,4,7

GREAT BRITAIN: LAWS, etc. (VIC.).
South-Eastern and London, Chatham and Dover Railway Companies
(New Lines etc.) Act, 1899. An Act for conferring further
powers...
4

GREAT BRITAIN: LAWS, etc. (VIC.).
South-Eastern and London, Chatham and Dover Railway Companies
Act, 1900. An Act to enable the South-Eastern Railway
Company to make new railways...
4

GREAT BRITAIN: LAWS, etc. (VIC.).
West London and Crystal Palace Railway (Extension to
Bromley and Farnborough) Act...1854.
2

GREAT BRITAIN: LAWS, etc. (VIC.).
West Wickham and Hayes Railway Act, 1880.
2

GREAT BRITAIN: LAWS, etc. (EDW. VII).
South-Eastern and London, Chatham and Dover Railways
Act, 1901. An Act to enable the South-Eastern Railway
Company to make new works, to acquire additional lands...
(etc.).
4,7

GREAT BRITAIN: LAWS, etc. (EDW. VII).
South-Eastern and London, Chatham and Dover Railways Act,
1902. An Act to enable the South-Eastern Railway Company
to make a new railway and widenings...
4,7

GREAT BRITAIN: LAWS, etc. (EDW. VII).
The South-Eastern and London, Chatham and Dover Railways
Act, 1903.
7

GREAT BRITAIN: LAWS, etc. (EDW. VII).
South Eastern and London, Chatham and Dover Railways Act,
1906. An Act to confer further powers...
4

GREAT BRITAIN: LAWS, etc. (EDW. VII).
South-Eastern and London, Chatham and Dover Railways Act,
1909. An Act to extend the time for compulsory purchase
of lands...(etc.).
4,7

GREAT BRITAIN: LAWS, etc. (GEO. V).
London, Chatham and Dover Railway Act, 1915. An Act to enable
the...Railway Company to raise further capital and for other
purposes.
4

GREAT BRITAIN, Parliament.
Minutes of evidence taken before the Committee on the
London and Dover (South-Eastern) Railway Bill, 1836.
Hansard. 1836.
15

GREAT BRITAIN, Parliament.
...Minutes of evidence given before the Select
Committee on Railway Bills (Group A) on the North Kent
lines, by the South-Eastern, North Kent (Vignoles) and
London and Croydon Railway Companies.
London, Printed by C. Roworth. 1845.
2,3,9

GREAT BRITAIN, Parliament.
Digest of the evidence offered before the Parliamentary
Committee by the South-Eastern Railway Company.
1847.
17

HARMAN, Reginald Gordon.
Railways in the Isle of Sheppey.
Branch Line Handbooks. 1962.
1,4,7,8,9,11,15

HARVEY, John (pseud.).
Early railway historical news...extracts from early
books and journals, 1832-53.
R.H. Clark. n.d.
7

HASENSON, A.
The Golden Arrow.
H. Baker. 1970.
6,7

HILTON, H.F.
The White Horse of Kent.(locomotive) on Croydon and
Dover Railway. (Article in "The Locomotive...Review",
Vol. L, No. 620, April 15th, 1944).
3

HILTON, John. Publisher.
The Canterbury and Whitstable Railway.
Hadlow, J. Hilton. 1966.
1,2,3,4,8,9,11,15

The illustrated guide to the London and Dover Railway,
accompanied by the Tourist's and Traveller's Directory.
Mead. 1844.
8,13,17

Illustrated ramble book of the London and Dover Railway.
Mead. 1845.
2,6,18

KENT COAST RAILWAY COMPANY.
List of proprietors, 1866.
12

KENT MESSENGER. Publisher.
Complete road and rail timetable, Gravesend and district,
August, 1938.
Kent Messenger.
9

KIDNER, Roger Wakeley.
The Colonel Stephens Railways (Light Railway Handbook No. 1).
Oakwood Press. 1948.
6

The Dartford loop line, 1866 to 1966.
Oakwood Press. 1966.
1,2,5,8,11,17,18

The London, Chatham and Dover Railway.
Oakwood Press. 1952.
1,2,3,4,5,6,7,8,9,11,12,13,15,17,18

The Romney, Hythe and Dymchurch Railway.
Oakwood Press. 1967.
1,2,3,4,5,6,7,8,11,12,14

The South-Eastern and Chatham Railway.
Oakwood Press. 1963.
4,5,7

South-Eastern Railway.
Oakwood Press. 1953.
1,3,4,5,6,7,8,11,12,13,14,15,18,19

The Southern Railway.
Oakwood Press. 1958.
3,4,5,7,9,12,14,15

KLAPPER, Charles.
The East Kent Light Railways, by C. Klapper and H.F.G. Dalston.
In Railway Magazine, March, 1937 (photostat copy).
6

LEWIN, H.G.
Early British railways...1801-1844. (London-Greenwich via
Deptford, etc.).
18

LONDON AND GREENWICH RAILWAY.
Guide.
1836.
17

LONDON, CHATHAM AND DOVER RAILWAY.
Continental timetables and merchandise and parcels service.
London, Chatham and Dover Railway. 1873.
6

LYNE, R.M.
The Gravesend Branch Railway.
Privately Printed. 1972.
9

MACK, Lawrence Albert.
Southern electric service stock.
Loughton, Electric Railway Society. 1958.
1

Map of the proposed Kent railway.
Canterbury Journal. 1847.
12

MARSHALL, C.F. Dendy.
A history of the Southern Railway.
London, Southern Railway Co. 1936.
3,4,5,7,8,12,14,15,18

MARSHALL, C.F. Dendy.
A history of the Southern Railway, 2nd enlarged edition in two
volumes. Revised by R.W. Kidner.
I. Allan. 1963.
5,7,8,11,12,14,15,18,19

MAXTED, Ivan.
The Canterbury and Whitstable Railway.
Oakwood Press. 1970.
11

(MEASOM, George).
New guide to the South-Eastern Railway system and the
official illustrated guide to the Northern Railway of
France.
1863?
8

MEASOM, George.
The official illustrated guide to the South-Eastern
and the North and Mid Kent Railways, and all their
branches, with descriptions of the most important
manufactures in the towns...
London, Griffin. 1863.
1,2,4,8,9,11,15,17

The official illustrated guide to the South-Eastern
Railway and its branches, including the North Kent
and Greenwich lines.
W.H. Smith and Son and Arthur Hall, Virtue and Co.
1858.
9,17

The official illustrated guide to the South-Eastern
Railway and its branches...
E. and W. Books. 1970, Facsimile of 1858 edition.
5,6,7,8,12,14,15,17,18

MITTON, Geraldine Edith.
The South-Eastern and Chatham and London, Brighton and
South Coast Railways. (Peeps at Great Railways Series).
A. and C. Black. 1912.
1,8,11,12

MITTON, Geraldine Edith.
The Southern Railway, 2nd edition.
A. and C. Black. 1925.
12

Modern locomotives and electric traction of the
Southern Railway.
Locomotive Publishing Co. Ltd. (1939).
4,8

MOODY, G.T.
Southern electric.
I. Allan. 1957 etc.
2,3,4,5,6,7,8,12,14,15

MORRIS, O.J.
Railways before the grouping. No. 1 - L.B. and S.C.R.
(i.e. London, Brighton and South Coast Railway)...
I. Allan. (1952).
4

MORRIS, O.J.
The world's smallest public railway: (birth,
progress and majority of the Romney, Hythe and
Dymchurch Railway).
1946.
4,7,12(1949)

NOCK, Oswald Stevens.
The locomotives of R.E.L. Maunsell.
Everard. 1954.
12

South-Eastern and Chatham Railway.
I. Allan. 1961 and 1971.
1,2,3,4,5,6,7,8,9,11,12,14,15

Southern steam.
David and Charles. 1966.
2,3,7,12

NOKES, pseud. (G.A. SEKON).
The history of the South-Eastern Railway.
Railway Press. 1895.
2,7,8

Opening of South-Eastern Railway to Canterbury.
(Article in Illustrated London News, February 14th,
1846).
3

ORFORD, V.W.
The Bromley Direct Branch, Southern Railway. (Extract
from Railway Magazine, Vol. 65, No. 385, July, 1929).
2

Our iron roads. (A bound collection of guides issued
by the various railway companies).
(1879).
4

PERKINS, W. Turner.
South-Eastern and Chatham Railway: popular coast guide.
McCorquodale.
7(1905) 8(1903) 11(1907) 17(1903)

PHILP, Robert Kemp.
The South-Eastern Railway panoramic guide: a description of
the principal objects of historic interest...over the main
lines and chief branches of the South-Eastern Railway, edited
by R.K. Philp.
South-Eastern Railway. 1877.
11,13

The railway companion...utility and advantages of Canterbury
and Whitstable Railway clearly demonstrated, with a glance at
the St. Nicholas Bay and Stour navigation schemes...
Canterbury, R. Colegate for J. Wrightson. (1836).
3

RAILWAY MAGAZINE.
Canterbury and Whitstable Railway (with an engraving).
(Extract from Railway Magazine, No. 6, October, 1835).
3

RAILWAY MAGAZINE.
The Canterbury and Whitstable Railway and the Greenwich
Railway. (Extracts from the Railway Magazine, May, 1835 to
February, 1836).
Effingham Wilson. (1836).
2

RANSOME-WALLIS, Patrick.
Southern album.
I. Allan. 1968.
5,6

RANSOME-WALLIS, Patrick.
The world's smallest public railway: the Romney, Hythe and
Dymchurch.
I. Allan. 1957 etc.
1,2,3,5,6,7,8,11,12,14,15

READ, Thomas C.
Memoirs of Richard Trevithick and his inventions.
Dartford, T.C. Read. n.d.
5

Reply to the statement put forth by the Directors of the South-
Eastern Railway Company.
Effingham Wilson. 1846.
8

ROLT, L.T.C.
The Cornish giant: the story of Richard Trevithick, father of
the steam locomotive.
Lutterworth Press. 1960.
5

Romney, Hythe and Dymchurch Railway.
Locomotive Publishing Co. 1926?
7,11

ROMNEY, HYTHE AND DYMCHURCH RAILWAY.
Official time-table and guide.
Hythe, Romney, Hythe and Dymchurch Railway Co.
1(1932) 3(1968) 8(1951)

SANDERSON, Geoffrey F.
A short history of the Chatham and District Light Railway
Company, 1899 A.D.-1930 A.D. (Typescript).
1955.
4

SAVILL, Raymond Arthur.
The Southern Railway, 1923-47.
Oakwood Press. 1950.
1,4,5,6,7,8,12

SCHULTZ AND SON. Publishers.
Schultz's pocket timetable, December, 1926; January, 1937;
June, 1939.
Gravesend, Schultz and Son.
9

SCIENCE MUSEUM, SOUTH KENSINGTON.
Catalogue of the collections in the Science Museum, South
Kensington: land transport - railway centenary supplement...
London, H.M.S.O. 1925.
3

SIMMS, F.W.
Practical tunnelling: explaining in detail...the work as
exemplified by...Blechingly and Saltwood tunnels.
Troughton and Simms. 1844.
7,11

SITTINGBOURNE AND MAIDSTONE RAILWAY.
Plan, section and book of reference showing the line
of the above railway...through...Hollingbourne.
1876.
12

Smallest public railway in the world! (Romney, Hythe
and Dymchurch Railway).
Folkestone, "Day-by-Day". 1936.
7

SMITH, John L.
Rails to Tenterden.
Sutton (Surrey) Lens of Sutton. 1967.
1,2,3,4,6,7,8,11,12,15,19

SOUTH-EASTERN AND CHATHAM RAILWAY COMPANY.
Appendix to the working time-table books...May, 1922.
11

Code to be used in despatching telegraph messages
upon railway companies' business, 1st January, 1914.
4

Control of railway by H.M. Government in emergency -
poster 37 x 25½ cm. - issued by Francis H. Dent,
General Manager from London Bridge Station on 4th
August, 1914.
3

Coronation souvenir, 1911.
17

Instructions for train signalling by block telegraph
and lock and block system on double and single lines of
railway, 1913.
8

Notice of special traffic working arrangements in
connection with the funeral of His Late Majesty,
King Edward VII, 1910.
8

The official guide to the South-Eastern and Chatham
Railways, The Royal Mail express routes to the Kent
coast and to the continent.
Cassell.
1(1912) 7(1913) 17(1902)

Rules and regulations for the guidance of the officers
and men in the service of the...Company.
1st May, 1905.
8

Time-tables.
South-Eastern and Chatham Railways. 1899.
1

Time-tables of the journeys of the Royal Special Trains,
Monday, June 19th, 1911.
South-Eastern and Chatham Railways. 1911.
8

SOUTH-EASTERN AND HASTINGS RAILWAY COMPANY.
Statement of facts in opposition to the Bill.
n.d.
1

SOUTH-EASTERN RAILWAY COMPANY.
Abridged and popular edition of the official guide to
the South-Eastern Railway.
1896.
17

Cheap pleasure excursions, 1st June, 1850.
17

Extension of railway from Sandgate to Folkestone
Harbour: report of proceedings at public meeting,
held at Town Hall, Folkestone on Wednesday, February
2nd, 1876.
South-Eastern Railway Co. 1876.
7

General statement of the position and projects of
the Company, 1845-46.
1,2,4,8,9,11,12,17

Official guide to the South-Eastern Railway and the
Royal Mail route to Paris, India and the colonies.
Cassell. 1889.
7,9,17

Official guide to the South-Eastern Railway and the
Royal Mail route to Paris, India and the colonies.
Cassell. 1891.
2

Official guide to the South-Eastern Railway...
Cassell. 1896.
17

RAILWAYS Cont'd

SOUTH-EASTERN RAILWAY COMPANY.
Reply to the statement put forth by the Directors of the
South-Eastern Railway Company.
1846.
11

Report and accounts for 1909 and for 1917.
11

Report of proceedings at the Seventieth Half-Year General
and Special Meeting of Proprietors...on Thursday, 20th July,
1871.
South-Eastern Railway Co. (1871).
7

Report of the proceedings at the Seventy-first Half-Yearly
General Meeting and Extraordinary Meeting of the Proprietors...
on Thursday, 25th January, 1872.
South-Eastern Railway Co. 1872.
7

South-Eastern Railway, illustrated tourist guide.
4(1879) 17(1889)

The South-Eastern Railway Manual: describing the cities, towns
and villages, the principal seats...the scenery in the most
picturesque districts and the bathing and watering places on or
near the line.
Smith, Elder and Co. c.1850.
1,2,6,7,13

The South-Eastern Railway Manual for Travellers, No. 1 –
main line to the coast and continent...(by William Jerdan).
1854.
13

Timetables for the North Kent and the London, Chatham and Dover
Railway. (Lines to Gravesend only, includes London, Tilbury,
and Southend Steam Ferry – cover missing).
April, 1888.
9

Timetables of the South-Eastern Railway and Steam Packets.
South-Eastern Railway Co.
1(1868, 1873, 1882)

SOUTHERN RAILWAY COMPANY.
Another South-Eastern Railway Centenary – Gravesend to Strood.
(Typescript).
1945.
3,4,9

Centenary of the opening of the London and Dover (via Tonbridge)
Railway, South-Eastern Railway, February 7th, 1844.
Southern Railway Co. 1944.
1,3,4,8,19

Centenary of the opening of the London and Dover (via Tonbridge)
Railway: catalogue of exhibition held at Maison Dieu, Dover,
February 7th to February 12th, 1944.
Southern Railway Co.
6

Centenary of the opening of the South-Eastern Railway from
Tonbridge to Tunbridge Wells.
1945.
19

Centenary of the opening of the South-Eastern Railway to
Maidstone from Paddock Wood, September 25th, 1844: (catalogue
of) exhibition held at Maidstone Museum, Monday, September 25th-
October 8th, 1944.
3

The Dover Railway Centenary: celebration of the opening, on
February 7th, 1844, of the last section of the South-Eastern
Railway main line to Dover. (Reprinted from the Railway
Gazette, 1944).
11

General and Central-Eastern appendices to the working time-tables,
26th March, 1934 until further notice (with supplement No. 5).
1934.
4

Instructions to Station Masters, Inspectors, Drivers, Motormen,
Guards, Signalmen, Crossing Keepers, permanent way staff and all
others concerned as to a Royal Special Trail – Victoria to
Selling and Canterbury West to Victoria on Thursday, 11th July,
1946.
London, Printed by McCorquodale and Co. Ltd. 1946.
3

Locomotives of the Southern Railway.
Southern Railway Co. 1925.
8

Locomotives of the Southern Railway, 2nd edition.
Southern Railway Co. 1929.
7,8

London (East) and Southern Divisions – notice of
special traffic from Saturday, October 20th to Friday,
October 26th, 1928 inclusive.
4

London (East) and Southern Divisions – notice of
special traffic from Saturday, April 20th to Friday,
April 26th, 1929 inclusive.
4

Southern Railway electrification extension; Rochester,
Chatham, Gillingham and Maidstone. (Electric Railway
Traction Supplement to the Railway Gazette, June 30th,
1939).
4

Speed-up on the Southern (Railway): an Evening
Standard survey, June 9th, 1959.
4

SYMES, Rodney.
Railway architecture of the South-East, by R. Symes
and D. Cole.
Osprey. 1972.
9

TAYLOR, Michael Minter.
The Davington Light Railway. (Locomotive Papers,
No. 40).
Oakwood Press. 1968.
3,8,11

THOMAS, Ronald H.G.
London's first railway – the London and Greenwich.
Batsford. 1972.
11

TILLING, W.G.
Locomotives of the Southern Railway (Central Section).
W.G. Tilling. 1935.
1,8

Locomotives of the Southern Railway (Eastern Section).
W.G. Tilling. 1934.
1,7,8

Locomotives of the Southern Region of British Railways.
W.G. Tilling. 1948.
1,8

TRADE, Board of. – RAILWAY DEPARTMENT.
Report of the Railway Department of the Board of Trade
on the Kentish and South-Eastern Railway schemes.
Printed by Order of the House of Commons. 1845.
11

TRANSPORT, Ministry of.
Railway accident: report on derailment, 10th September,
1963 between Longfield and Farningham Road, Southern
Region of British Railways.
H.M.S.O. 1963.
8

Railway accident: report on the collision that
occurred on 4th January, 1969 between Paddock Wood
and Marden...
H.M.S.O. 1969.
4

Railway accident: report on the collision which
occurred on 17th February, 1959 between Slade Green
and Dartford.
H.M.S.O. 1959.
1

Travelling charts...passed by the line of railway:
London to Ashford, Folkestone and Dover.
Railway Chronicle. n.d.
1,11

TUCK, Henry.
The Railway Shareholder's Manual...(photocopy of
sections relating to South-Eastern and London,
Brighton and South Coast Railways only).
Effingham Wilson. 1847.
2

VALLANCE, H.H.
The Canterbury and Whitstable Railway. (Reprinted
from "Edgar Allen News", September and October,
1927).
3

WAKEMAN, Norman.
The South-Eastern and Chatham Railway locomotive list,
1842-1952...compiled by N. Wakeman.
Oakwood Press. 1953.
1,3,4,6,8,11,15

WALLIS, P. Ransome.
Southern album.
I. Allan. 1968.
7

WELLS, Arthur G.
Bowaters' Sittingbourne Railway.
Narrow Gauge Railway Society. 1962.
1,2,4,8,9,11,12,15,20

WHETMATH, C.F.D.
Hundred of Hoo (Branch Line), by C.F.D. Whetmath and E.J.S.
Gadsden.
Teddington Branch Line Handbooks. 1962.
2,4,8,11,12,14,15,17

WHISHAW, Francis.
Analysis of railways: consisting of a series of reports...
(photocopy of sections on Kent, London and Penge and London,
Rochester and Chatham Railways only).
J. Weale. 1838.
2

WHITE, H.P.
Southern England. (Regional History of the Railways of Great
Britain, Vol. 2).
Phoenix House. 1961.
4,6,19

WHITE, H.P.
Southern England. (Regional History of the Railways of Great
Britain, Vol. 2).
David and Charles. 1970.
7

WIKELEY, Nigel.
Railway Stations, Southern Region, by N. Wikeley and J.
Middleton.
Peco. 1971.
4,7,9

WOODCOCK, George.
Minor railways of England and their locomotives, 1900-39.
Goose and Son. 1970.
6

RAINHAM

BELL. Police Constable.
The parish of Rainham. (Unfinished typescript, commenced 1st
April, 1958 by P.C. Bell of Chatham Police, who emigrated to
Australia, c.1963).
4

COLE, George. (Curate of Rainham).
The story of a barren fig tree.
1852.
8

COOK, Norman.
Pit dwelling of the early Iron Age at Rainham, Kent. In
Archaeologia Cantiana, Vol. 49, 1937).
17

GILLINGHAM BOROUGH COUNCIL.
A plan for Rainham Village.
Gillingham Borough Council. 1965.
8

GILLINGHAM BOROUGH COUNCIL.
Rainham: district centre plan, 1970.
Gillingham Borough Council.
8

GILLINGHAM PUBLIC LIBRARY.
Opening of Rainham Branch Library, Birling Avenue, by Russell
Thorndike, Wednesday, 29th March, 1961.
4

HARRIS, Edwin.
The history of Rainham, Kent. (Eastgate series, No. 27).
Rochester, E. Harris. n.d.
8,15

NOEL, Gerard T. Vicar of Rainham.
A letter to the Right Honourable Lord Teignmonth, President
of the British and Foreign Bible Society, on the present character
of the Institution.
1831.
8

A sermon preached at the parish church of Christ's
Church, Newgate Street on Thursday, May 5th, 1814
before the Prayer Book and Homily Society.
Published for the Society by Taylor and Hessey. 1814.
8

(Sermons), 1812-31.
8

PEARMAN, Augustus John.
Rainham Church. (Reprinted from Archaeologia
Cantiana, 1886).
8,17

PRENTIS, W.
Notes on the birds of Rainham...
Gurney and Jackson. 1894.
1,3,4,5,6,8,11,12,15,17,20

RAINHAM METHODIST CHURCH, STATION ROAD.
Jubilee souvenir handbook.
1950.
8

RAINHAM PARISH CHURCH MAGAZINE: (St. Margaret's),
January-November, 1931; January-December, 1932
(except for June); January, 1935-October, 1942.
8

S., J.C.
Historical account of Rainham Church, Kent, by J.C.S.
(From "Gentleman's Magazine", 1813).
4

SMITH, R. Allington.
A new guide to Rainham Parish Church.
R.A. Smith. 1969.
11

RAMSGATE

ALLOM, E.A.
The seaweed collector...illustrated with natural
specimens from the shores of Margate and Ramsgate.
(i.e. actual dried seaweed not illustrations).
W. Keble. 1841.
13

ANSON, Peter F.
British sea fishermen.
Collins. 1944.
14

AUSTEN, Charles A.F.
H.M. Patrols, Ramsgate: a short naval history of the
Port, 1914-19.
Addington Publicity Bureau. 1919.
14

AUSTEN, Charles A.F.
Ramsgate raid records: a war history of England's
most bombed town.
Addington Publicity Bureau. 1919.
14

The badger's plot; or, unlimited smash: a parable
from nature.
Ramsgate, Printed by S.R. Wilson (18--?).
11

BARNARD, Howard Clive.
Records (1909-22) of the Ramsgate County School for
Boys, 2nd edition, by H.C. Barnard and F.N. Taylor.
Ramsgate, Chatham House School. 1923.
11,13,14

BEAR, J. Publisher.
The New Ramsgate Guide...
J. Bear. 1867.
13,14

BODY, Geoffrey.
The Ramsgate Tunnel Railway, by G. Body and
R. Eastleigh.
Trans-Rail Publications. 1966.
7,12

BRITTON, Percy W.
The Ramsgate Marine Drive.
Leeds, Bernard. 1879.
11,12

BROWNING, Robert H.K.
St. Augustine's Golf Club.
Golf Clubs Association. 1929.
14

BURNBY, John.
Summer amusement; or, miscellaneous poems: inscribed to the
frequenters of Margate, Ramsgate...
1774.
13

CARDOZO, D.A.
Think and thank: the Montefiore Synagogue and College,
Ramsgate, by D.A. Cardozo and P. Goodman.
Oxford University Press. 1933.
11,12,14

CHARLES, REYNOLDS AND CO. Publishers.
Souvenir album of Ramsgate.
Charles, Reynolds and Co. c.1880.
13,14

Chatham House, Ramsgate: a short history, 1797-1914.
Ramsgate, Chatham House School. 1914.
14

COGHLAN, Francis.
A new guide to Ramsgate, Margate and Dover...
1837.
13,14,17

CURLING, Richard, and others: Defendants.
The trial of Richard Curling, Thomas Moss, John Forwood, John
Sanders and Thomas Read, boatmen of Ramsgate...
Causton, Henry Kent. 1807.
11

DANIEL, H. Kenyon.
Particulars of the family of Daniel of Ramsgate.
1954.
14

DAVIS, Israel.
Sir Moses Montefiore: a biographical study.
Jewish Chronicle. 1883.
11

DOWKER, George.
Roman remains at Walmer and Ramsgate.
n.d.
11,14

FAGG, Brian R.
A history of St. George's Church, Ramsgate, 1827-1947.
Canterbury, Gibbs. 1948.
14

A few days at Ramsgate; or, a guide to persons visiting the
Isle-of-Thanet...3rd edition.
1830.
13

FINN, R.
Romansgate in Thanet.
Ramsgate, W.E. White. 1969.
2,4,7,8,11

FRITH, Francis. Photographer.
Margate and Ramsgate photographed.
F. Frith. 1857.
13

GREAT BRITAIN: LAWS, etc. (GEO. II).
An Act for enlarging and maintaining the Harbour of Ramsgate...
and preserving the Haven of Sandwich.
1749.
11,14

GREAT BRITAIN: LAWS, etc. (GEO. III).
An Act for better paving...and watching highways...in the vill of
Ramsgate...1785.
11

HALL, J. Publisher.
Hall's new Margate and Ramsgate guide.
J. Hall. 1779 etc.
14,17

HARWOOD, J.
Views of Ramsgate.
1848,
11

HEYWOOD, ABEL AND SON. Publishers.
A guide to Ramsgate...
A. Heywood and Son. (1878).
17

HEYWOOD, John. Publisher.
Illustrated guide to Ramsgate and Pegwell Bay.
Manchester, J. Heywood. 1897.
11,15

HICKS, Robert.
Roman remains found at Ramsgate. In Archaeologia
Cantiana, Vol. 12, 1878.
17

HILLIER, James T.
British village at Ramsgate. In Archaeologia
Cantiana, Vol. 18, 1889.
17

HOARE, Edward.
Civil and religious liberty: a lecture by the Rev.
Edward Hoare, incumbent of Christ Church, Ramsgate,
delivered...January 20th, 1851.
12

HUDDLESTONE, John.
Four hundred facts and curiosities of Ramsgate.
Ramsgate, Thanet Publishing Service. 1937.
1,14

"Old Ramsgate": cartoons.
Ramsgate, Thanet Publishing Service. 1936.
14

"Recollections": 155 curious things not generally
known about Ramsgate.
Ramsgate, Thanet Publishing Service. 1932.
12

Tales of Old Ramsgate, by J. Huddlestone and I.
Dancyger.
Ramsgate, Thanet Publishing Service. 1938.
1,14

"AN INHABITANT", pseud.
Margate guide: a descriptive poem...also a general
account of Ramsgate, etc.
1797.
11,15,17

J.S. AND CO. AND KERSHAW AND SON. Publishers.
Thirty views of Ramsgate.
J.S. and Co. and Kershaw and Son. 1870-1880.
13,14

KEMPE, A.B.C.
Midst bands and bombs.
Kent Messenger. 1946.
3,4,6,8,11,13,14

KENT, W. AND CO. Publishers.
All about Ramsgate and Broadstairs...
W. Kent and Co. 1864 and 1870.
13,14

LE BAS, Charles.
A letter addressed to the company who frequent, and
to the inhabitants who reside, in Margate and Ramsgate.
1796.
13

LEWIS, G.W.
Farewell sermon, delivered by the Rev. G.W. Lewis, M.A.,
in the Chapel of Ease, Ramsgate, on Sunday morning,
October 20th, 1839.
Hatchard. 1839.
12

MOSES, H.
Picturesque views of Ramsgate.
H. Moses. 1817.
1,6,11,12,13,14,15

"A NAVAL OFFICER", pseud.
A brief history of Dover and Ramsgate Harbours.
Ramsgate, Brewer. 1837.
1

NEWMAN AND CO. Publishers.
Thirty views of Ramsgate.
Newman and Co.
13(1851-68, 1870-78) 14(1870-78)

NEWMAN AND CO. Publishers.
Twelve views of Ramsgate.
Newman and Co. c.1870.
13,14

Nine hundred years, 1062-1962: St. Laurence-in-Thanet ninth
century souvenir brochure.
Ramsgate, Church Publications. (1962).
4,6

OSBORNE, R.C.
New Ramsgate guide; or, Isle-of-Thanet directory...
c.1830.
13

PARRY, David.
Monastic century: St. Augustine's Abbey, Ramsgate, 1861-1961.
Tenbury Wells, Fowler Wright. 1965.
8,11

PARRY, David.
Scholastic century: St. Augustine's Abbey School, Ramsgate,
(1865-1965)
Tenbury Wells, Fowler Wright. 1965.
1,6,8,11

A pictorial guide to Margate amusements: The Lido, Cliftonville;
Dreamland, Margate; The Greyhound Racing Track, Ramsgate.
1938.
13

Picture of Ramsgate in Thanet.
Ramsgate, J. Knott. 1838.
6

Picture of Ramsgate: a guide to various amusements...of that
celebrated watering place...
Ramsgate, Sackett. 1833.
11,14

RAMSGATE BOROUGH COUNCIL.
Official guide.
Ramsgate Borough Council. 1955 etc.
4,8

Ramsgate, the sun-spot of the South.
Ramsgate Publicity Committee. (1925).
11

Ramsgate Historical Pageant and Charter Jubilee Celebrations,
1934.
14

RAMSGATE BOROUGH COUNCIL - ADVERTISING COMMITTEE.
Ramsgate guide.
1914 etc.
13,17

RAMSGATE HARBOUR TRUST.
Extracts from the byelaws.
H.M.S.O. 1922.
11

RAMSGATE HARBOUR TRUST.
Harbour Board of Ramsgate Trust: accounts...
1852.
17

RAMSGATE HISTORICAL PAGEANT COMMITTEE.
Ramsgate Historical Pageant, produced by Nugent Monck (in aid of
Ramsgate General Hospital)...1934.
Ramsgate, Bligh, Printers.
3,6

RAMSGATE LOCAL BOARD.
Report of the Ramsgate Local Board upon the proposed transfer
of the Royal Harbour of Ramsgate to the town.
Printed by Order of the Local Board. 1869.
11

RAMSGATE SCIENTIFIC ASSOCIATION.
Scrapbook of the Ramsgate Scientific Association covering the
years 1880-84.
14

RAMSGATE SMACKOWNERS.
The policy register of the former Ramsgate Smackowners' Mutual
Insurance Society Ltd., 1904-17.
14

RAMSGATE WATERWORKS COMPANY.
Minutes of meetings held from 1855-72.
14

Ramsgate: photographic views.
Domestic Bazaar. n.d.
12

Ramsgate: typewritten articles on the history...
n.d.
12

Ramsgate during the Great War, 1914-18...
1919.
13,14

Ramsgate Life Boat rescuing the crew of the Spanish
Brig "Samanitano"...(From "Macmillan's Magazine",
1860).
11,14

Ramsgate penny guide.
Ramsgate, S.R. Wilson. n.d.
3

Register of St. Lawrence College, Ramsgate, 1897-1911.
1912.
13

RICHARDSON, Christopher Thomas.
Fragments of history pertaining to the vill, or wille,
or liberty of Ramsgate, edited by C.T. Richardson.
Ramsgate, Fuller. 1885.
1,6,7,11,12,13,14,15,17

ROCK AND CO. Publishers.
30 views of Ramsgate, engraved between 1851 and 1878.
Rock and Co.
1,11,13,14

Twenty-four views of Ramsgate.
Rock and Co. 1851-68.
13

Views and scenery of Ramsgate.
Rock and Co. 1851-68.
11,13

ROSS, Charles H.
Margate and Ramsgate.
"Judy" Office. (1880).
12,13,14,17

ROYAL BRITISH LEGION - RAMSGATE BRANCH.
Ramsgate British Legion: a record of ten years,
1921-31.
1932.
14

The Royal Cabinet Album of Ramsgate.
1868.
17

ST. AUGUSTINE'S ABBEY, RAMSGATE.
The book of saints.
Black. 1966.
12

SCOTT, Clement W.
Round about the island; or, sunny spots near home.
(pp. 100-133 deal with Ramsgate and Margate).
1874.
13

SELECT COMMITTEE ON RAMSGATE AND MARGATE HARBOURS.
Report from the Select Committee on Ramsgate and
Margate Harbours, together with the Proceedings of the
Committee, Minutes of Evidence, Appendix and Index.
1850.
13,14

Short account of facts relative to Ramsgate Pier and
Harbour...
Ramsgate, Burgess. 1815.
1

SIBTHORP, Mary L.
The sea-side: a poem on Ramsgate...
London, Longman. London, Bell. 1798.
6

SLENDERWIT, Simkin, pseud.
The sea-side: a poem in a series of familiar epistles
from...summerising at Ramsgate to his dear mother in
town.
Ramsgate, Printed for Mr. Burgess. 1797.
11,14

PAYNE, J. Lewin.
Reculver Parish Church of St. Mary the Virgin, together with
the Chapelry of the Holy Cross, Hoath, by J.L. Payne and
W.T. Hill.
Herne Bay, Ridout and Sons. 1931.
3, 13

PHILP, Brian J.
The Roman Fort at Reculver.
Reculver Excavation Group.
2(1969)
7(1969)
8(1966, 1969)
9(1969)
11(1963, 1969)
12(1963 etc.)
14(1963 etc.)

The Reculver; or, the two sisters of Thanet.
Herne Bay, Ridout and Sons. 1855.
11,13,14,17,19

St. Mary the Virgin, Reculver.
Reculver Parochial Church Council. 1969.
11

St. Mary the Virgin, Reculver Church.
Townsend. n.d.
12

SMITH, Charles Roach.
Antiquities of Richborough, Reculver and Lympne in Kent.
J.R. Smith. 1850.
1,3,4,5,6,7,8,11,12,13,14,15,17,18

TAYLOR, H.M.
Reculver reconsidered. (Reprinted from the Archaeological
Journal, 1969).
4

VAUGHAN, Eliza, pseud.
The Cloister and the Beacon: an historical romance founded on
the legend of the Reculver Towers.
City of London Publishing Co. 1886.
1,13

WHITAKER, W.
Report of an excursion to Reculver. (Proceedings of the
Geologists' Association, Vol. XXIII, Part 4, 1912, pp. 247-49).
11

WICKHAM, W.
The two sisters: a tale of Reculver.
n.d.
13,14

WORKS, Ministry of.
Reculver, Kent.
H.M.S.O.
2(1947) 3(1951) 4(1947 and 1951) 8(1947) 11(1947) 12(1947)

RELIGIOUS DENOMINATIONS

BIBLIOTHECA TOPOGRAPHICA BRITANNICA, No. XXVIII.
Some account of Suffragen Bishops in England, by J. Lewis.
London, J. Nichols. 1785.
3

BUFFARD, Frank.
Kent and Sussex Baptist Association.
Faversham, Mrs. E. Vinson. (1963).
1,2,3,4,5,7,8,9,11,15

The call to higher service of Mrs. Commissioner Carleton.
(Salvationist, Penge).
Salvation Army Printing Works, Printers. (1915).
2

Called home: being tributes...concerning Mrs. W.J. Gibbs
(Miss Ada Rox) with memorial service. (Note: W.J. Gibbs was
Superintendent of Farwig Wesleyan Mission, Bromley).
Robert Culley. 1905.
2

A caring church: the report of a Working Party...to consider
"the responsibilities of the Church to society in West Kent..."
(Rochester, Diocese of Rochester). 1968.
11,12

CHAMBERS, Ralph Frederick.
The strict Baptist Chapels of England: Vol. 3, Kent.
R.F. Chambers. 1955.
1,3,7,12

CHARITY COMMISSION.
Scheduled charities in connection with the Strict and
Particular Baptist Society.
Charity Commission. (1961).
12

COTTON, Charles.
A Kentish cartulary of the Order of St. John of
Jerusalem.
Kent Archaeological Society. 1930.
1,2,3,5,6,7,8,11,12,15,17,18

EAST KENT CHURCH MISSIONARY ASSOCIATION.
Forty-ninth annual report, 1882.
17

Ecclesiastical census: census of Great Britain, 1851.
(Places of worship in...Charlton, Deptford, etc...).
Public Record Office. n.d.
18

EMBRY, John.
The Catholic Movement and Society of the Holy Cross.
Faith Press. 1931.
6

GENERAL BAPTIST CHURCHES.
Proceedings of the messengers, elders and representatives
...
1791-1828 and 1830.
3

Hints on ecclesiastical discipline...
1814.
17

KENT EDUCATION COMMITTEE.
Christians in Kent. Prepared for the Kent Council of
Religious Education.
Kent County Council. 1972.
11

KENT EDUCATION COMMITTEE.
Story of Christianity in Kent...
Kent Education Committee. 1961.
1,2,3,6,7,11,12,15

KNIGHTON, G.L.
Three hundred years of religious freedom, 1662-1962.
Maidstone Unitarian Church. 1962.
11,12

LE NEVE, John.
Fasti Ecclesiae Anglicanae...
Oxford University Press. 1854.
3

McCALL, Sir Robert A.
The Huguenots in Kent. (Proceedings of the Huguenot
Society of London, Vol. XIII, No. 1, 1924).
3

MACKESON, Charles.
Illustrated Church Congress handbook for 1892.
17

MARTIN, J.A.
Christian firmness of the Huguenots.
Canterbury, Gibbs. 1881.
3,7,11,12

"Departure of the Huguenots...", (translated by J.A.
Martin).
(1887).
17

PAUL, Sydney F.
Further history of the Gospel Standard Baptists, Vol. 5 -
Some Surrey and Kent churches.
S.F. Paul. 1966.
1

Pearman, Augustus John.
Rochester -(Diocesan history).
S.P.C.K. 1897.
1,4,5,8,11,12,15,17,18

PITTS, Hubert A.
Nineteenth century fragments of Methodist history of
Hythe, Sandgate, Dymchurch, Folkestone, Elham Valley
and Sellindge.
Hythe Methodist Church. 1969.
6,7,11,12

Provision for public worship in the County of Kent...
Bemrose. 1878.
3,11,17

PURFIELD, N.K.
Indexes to "The book of sufferings of Friends in the County of
Kent" (names of peoples and places), compiled by N.K. Purfield.
(Typescript).
(1956).
7

RIDSDEL, W.
The Salvation Army, Third Kent.
n.d.
17

SALVATION ARMY.
Third Kent and Sussex Review...1887-88.
17

SHOWLER, Karl.
A review of the history of the Society of Friends in Kent, 1655-
1966.
Canterbury Preparative Meeting of the Society of Friends. 1970.
2,3,4,9,11

SOCIETY OF CIRPLANOLOGISTS.
A register of Methodist circuit plans, 1777-1860 (for the whole
country, including Kent).
Supplements: 1st - 1777-1860 (1963)
              2nd - 1777-1860 (1965)
              3rd - 1777-1860 (1970)
6

SOUTH-EASTERN CLERICAL AND LAY CHURCH ALLIANCE.
Fourteenth annual report, 1885 and nineteenth annual report, 1890.
17

TIMPSON, Thomas.
Church history of Kent...(Non-conformist).
Ward. 1859.
1,3,4,5,6,7,8,11,12,13,15,17,19

TOASE, William.
The Wesleyan Mission in France, with an account of the labours of
Wesleyan ministers among the French prisoners during the late war.
Printed for W. Toase. 1835.
11

RICHBOROUGH

BAKER, Oscar.
History of the antiquities of Sandwich and Richborough Castles
in Kent.
Savill and Edwards. 1848.
6,7,11,12,13,16,17

BATTELY, John.
Antiquitates Rutupiae.
Oxford, Sheldonian Theatre. 1711 and 1745.
1,3,4,5,6,7,8,11,13,14,15,17

BATTELY, John.
Antiquities of Richborough and Reculver, abridged from the Latin.
Printed for J. Johnson. 1774.
1,8,11,12,13,14,15,17

BEST, Halstead.
The mystery port, Richborough.
Printed by Blackpool Gazette and Herald. 1929.
11

BIBLIOTHECA TOPOGRAPHICA BRITANNICA, Vol. 1.
Dissertation on the Urbs Rutupiae of Ptolemy, by Mr. James
Douglas.
Kraus Reprint. 1968.
1,8,11

BOYS, William.
Collections for an history of Sandwich...and of Richborough.
Canterbury. 1792.
3,6,7,8,11,12,13,14,15,17

D., W. (W. DENNE).
Short account of the records of Richborough.
Margate, Keble's Gazette Office. 1903.
1,3,7,13,17

DENNE, W.
Richborough: the ancient Rutupiae, records and modern developments.
(Antiquarian pamphlets).
1919.
11,13

DOWKER, George.
Excavations at Richborough in 1887 (pamphlet).
Mitchell and Hughes. 1888.
7,11,13,17

Handbook to Richborough Castle.
Dover and County Chronicle. 1899.
12

Richborough Castle (pamphlet).
British Association. 1899.
7,14

DU FRESNE, Charles. Seigneur du Cange.
Dissertatio de Porto Iccio.
1694.
17

ELGAR, W.H.
Cross and platform at Richborough. In Archaeologia
Cantiana, Vol. 41, 1929.
17

HENDERSON, Aileen M.
Richborough Castle: guide to the museum. (Typescript).
n.d.
3

History of Sandwich and Richborough Castle.
Sandwich, H. Baker. n.d.
1,11

JOHNSON, J.S.
The date of construction of the Saxon shore fort at
Richborough. (Reprinted from "Britannia", Vol. 1,
1970).
6

LEWIS, John.
Dissertation on the antiquities of Richborough and
Sandwich.
Royal Society of Antiquities. 1744.
11

LEWIS, John.
A little dissertation on...Richborough and Sandwich...
Bell. 1851.
11

LEWIS, T. Hayter.
Archaeological notes on Sandown, Sandgate and
Richborough Castles, St. Margaret-at-Cliffe, etc.,
by T.H. Lewis and others.
c.1883.
6

MATTINGLY, Harold.
The Richborough hoard of "radiates", 1931, by H.
Mattingly and W.P.D. Stebbing.
New York, American Numismatic Society. 1938.
11

MATTINGLY, Harold.
Site-finds from Richborough, by A. Mattingly and
W.P.D. Stebbing.
Numismatic Chronicle. 1939.
11

Reports on the excavation of the Roman Fort at
Richborough.
Society of Antiquaries. 1926-68.
First report, by J.P. Bushe-Fox, 1926.
1,2,3,4,5,6,7,8,11,12,13,14,15,17,18

Second report, by J.P. Bushe-Fox, 1928.
1,2,3,4,5,6,7,8,11,12,13,14,15,17,18

Third report, by J.P. Bushe-Fox, 1932.
1,2,3,4,5,6,7,8,11,12,13,14,15,17

Fourth report, by J.P. Bushe-Fox, 1949.
1,2,4,5,6,7,11

Fifth report, by B.W. Cunliffe, 1968.
4,6,7,8,11

ROCHE, H.P.
Damien; or, the Centurion of Rutupiae.
1905.
14

SHANDEL, Lewis.
Romance of Richborough. (Antiquarian pamphlets).
Ramsgate, Thanet Advertiser. 1921.
1,2,3,11,13

SMITH, Charles Roach.
Antiquities of Richborough, Reculver and Lympne in Kent.
John Russell Smith. 1850.
1,3,4,5,6,7,8,11,12,13,14,15,17,18

WESTON, Rev. Stephen.
Description of a bronze figure found at Richborough, 1811.
Royal Society of Antiquaries. n.d.
11

WORKS, Ministry of.
Richborough Castle, by J.P. Bushe-Fox.
H.M.S.O.
1922(1,3,5,6,7,8,10,11,13,14,15)
1924(11,17)
1930(17)
1955(2,4,8,12,21)

RIDLEY

HOUSING AND LOCAL GOVERNMENT, Ministry of.
Mid Kent Water (Ridley) Orders, various, 1955-1965.
H.M.S.O.
8

STAGG, Frank Noel.
Some historical notes concerning the parish of Ridley in
Kent. (Typescript).
1948.
11

RINGWOLD

EELES, F.C.
Ringwold Church: a report in March, 1925. In Archaeologia
Cantiana, Vol. 40, 1928.
17

RIPLE

FRENCH, E. Gerald.
The life of Field Marshal, Sir John French.
Cassell. 1931.
6

RIVERS

AUSTIN, A.B.
Rivers of the South: a series of camera pictures by J.
Dixon-Scott, with text by A.B. Austin.
Muller. 1938.
4

BOSWELL, J.T.
The Lower Darent region. (Bound typescript thesis).
1965.
5

HOUSING AND LOCAL GOVERNMENT, Ministry of.
The Kent River Authority (Seaward Boundaries of Area) Order.
H.M.S.O. 1964.
4,8

Kent rivers-hydrological survey.
H.M.S.O. 1964.
1,2,3,4,5,6,7,8,11,12,17,19

HOUSING AND LOCAL GOVERNMENT, Ministry of. and AGRICULTURE,
FISHERIES AND FOOD, Ministry of.
Kent River Authority Constitution Order.
H.M.S.O. 1964.
4

KENT COUNTY COUNCIL - ROADS DEPARTMENT.
Report of the County Surveyor on the problems of flooding.
(See Roads).
Kent County Council. 1969 .
4,5,9,11

KENT RIVER AUTHORITY.
Annual report, 1965-66 in progress.
Kent River Authority.
1(1965-66) 9(1967-68) 12(1966-67)

KENT RIVER AUTHORITY.
First periodical survey of water resources, 1970.
Kent River Authority.
11

KENT RIVER BOARD.
Annual reports.
Kent River Board.
1(1958-59 and 1959-60) 8(1960-61 and 1964-65) 11(1950-51 and
1964-65) 12(1959-65)

Byelaws and licence duties.
Kent River Board. 1952.
1

Recreational navigation on waterways in the River
Board area.
Kent River Board. 1963.
1

MITCHELL, John.
Kentish waters.
Peterborough, E.M. Art. 1965.
1,2,3,4,5,6,7,8,11,19,20

RODGERS, John.
English rivers...
Batsford. 1947-48.
4

SNELL, F.C.
Collection of manuscript and miscellaneous material
relating to the Nailbourne Streams - photographs,
correspondence re Nailbourne. (Transactions of the
South-Eastern Union of Scientific Studies).
n.d.
3

SNELL, F.C.
The intermittent (or Nailbourne) Streams of East Kent.
Canterbury, Hunt. 1937?
3,4,6,7,11,17

SPURRELL, F.C.J.
A sketch of the history of the rivers and denudation
of West Kent, etc...
West Kent Natural History Society. n.d.
17

ROAD TRANSPORT

CARLEY, James.
Public transport timetables, 1838, Part 1 - Kent and
East Sussex, compiled by J. Carley.
Fourteen Petham Road Ltd. 1971.
2,9,11

East Kent Omnibus, Vol. XV, March-April, 1962, No. 3-4.
Canterbury, East Kent Road Car Co. Ltd. 1962.
3

EAST KENT ROAD CAR CO. LTD.
East Kent: a brief history of the Company's
development (1916-66).
East Kent Road Car Co. Ltd. 1966.
7

FULFORD, Roger.
The sixth decade, 1946-56.
London, British Electric Traction Co. Ltd. 1956.
3

GREAT BRITAIN: LAWS, etc. (VIC.).
Folkestone, Sandgate and Hythe Tramway Acts, 1884-1906.
7

GREAT BRITAIN: LAWS, etc. (ELIZ. II).
Chatham and District Traction Act.
H.M.S.O. 1955.
4,8

HARVIE, K.B.
South-East London Tramways, 1849-1949 (pamphlet).
17

"INVICTA", pseud.
The tramways of Kent, by "Invicta", edited by G.E.
Baddeley - Vol. 1, West Kent.
Light Railway Transport League. 1971.
11

KENT MESSENGER. Publishers.
Complete road and rail timetable - Gravesend and
district, August, 1938.
Kent Messenger.
9

KIDNER, Roger Wakely.
The London tramcar, 1861-1951.
Oakwood Press. 1951.
5

KLAPPER, Charles.
The golden age of tramways.
Routledge and Kegan Paul. 1961.
5

MAIDSTONE AND DISTRICT MOTOR SERVICES LTD.
ABC of the Maidstone and District Motor Services Ltd.
London, Allan Ltd. 1950.
12

Comprehensive timetables, 1961 and 1964.
12

A descriptive and pictorial guide to those areas of Kent and
East Sussex served by the Maidstone and District Motor Services
Ltd.
Regal Publicity Service. 1953.
12

"50 years of service". (Golden Jubilee issue of "Inside Only",
staff magazine, Vol. 15, No. 6, October, 1961).
8,9

Mid Kent timetable, 9th July, 1967.
12

Share prospectus, November, 1924.
17

MARSHALL, P.J.
ABC of British bus fleets.
1 - South-Eastern area, compiled by P.J. Marshall.
4(1958, 1960, 1961)
8(1956,1961)
12(1961)
15(1958)

OMNIBUS SOCIETY.
Short historical notes and itinerary in connection with Medway
Towns study tour, Saturday, 20th May, 1967. (Duplicated).
4

POOLE, S.L.
The ABC of East Kent buses and coaches.
London, Allan Ltd. 1949 and 1950.
3,7,13

PUBLIC SERVICE VEHICLE CIRCLE.
A detailed history of the fleet of Southdown Motor Services
Ltd., from the early days to the present time.
1957.
4

SOUTHDOWN MOTOR SERVICES LTD.
The Southdown story: a history...
1965.
4,19

"SOUTHEASTERN", pseud.
The tramways of Woolwich and South-East London.
Light Railway Transport League. 1963.
5,8,12

WAGSTAFF, J.S.
The London country bus.
Oakwood Press. 1968.
2

ROADS

BOX, Ernest George.
Kent in early road books of the 17th century.
1932.
12,16,17

Notes on some West Kent roads.
n.d.
16,17

Two sixteenth century maps of Kent with further notes on early
road-books (illustrated). In Archaeologia Cantiana, Vol. 45,
1933.
17

BRADY, John H.
Dover road sketch book.
Canterbury, Ward. 1837.
1,6,7,8,11,12,15,17,18

BRITISH ROAD FEDERATION.
Road needs in Kent.
British Road Federation. 1971.
2

BRITTON, O.M.H.
New Cross Turnpike Trust.
n.d.
11

CARLEY, James.
The lost roads of Meopham and nearby parishes.
Meopham Publications Committee. 1971.
4,9,11

CASTELLS, Francis de Paula.
The old Roman road in West Kent. (Reprinted from
the Dartford Chronicle).
Dartford Antiquarian Society. n.d.
5

CODRINGTON, Thomas.
Roman roads in Britain.
S.P.C.K. 1903.
15

DAVIS, B.F.
Roman road from West Wickham to London. In Surrey
Archaeological Collections, Vol. 43.
2

ELLISTON-ERWOOD, Frank Charles.
Biddenden and Boundgate Turnpike Roads, 1766-1883
(pamphlet). (From Archaeologia Cantiana, Vol. LXXI,
1957).
4,17,18

Miscellaneous notes on some Kent roads and allied
matters...
Ashford, Headley Bros. n.d.
12,17,18

More notes on Kentish roads.
Kent Archaeological Society. 1960.
5,17

Reprinted papers on Kent roads.
Ashford, Headley Bros. n.d.
12

The Turnpike Roads between Greenwich and Woolwich.
(Reprinted from the Proceedings of the Woolwich and
District Antiquarian Society, Vol. XXX).
Independent Printing Works. 1954.
8,15,18

GALE, T.
Antonini inter Britanniarum. (Latin text: Roman
road network in Britain, including Kent).
London, M. Atkins. 1709.
15

GREAT BRITAIN: LAWS, etc. (GEO. I).
An Act for enlarging the term granted by an Act...
for repairing the highways...near Blackheath and to
Lewisham Church...
1720.
11

GREAT BRITAIN: LAWS, etc. (GEO. I).
An Act for enlarging the term granted by an Act...
for amending and maintaining the road between
Northfleet, Gravesend and Rochester...
1724.
4,9,11

GREAT BRITAIN: LAWS, etc. (GEO. I).
An Act for enlarging the term granted by an Act...
for repairing...the highways leading from Sevenoaks...
Tunbridge Wells...
1724.
11

GREAT BRITAIN: LAWS, etc. (GEO. II).
An Act for repairing...the road leading from the...
Sign of the Bells...in Rochester to Maidstone...
1728.
8,11,12

GREAT BRITAIN: LAWS, etc. (GEO. II).
An Act for repairing...the road from...Chatham...to
St. Dunstan's Cross...Canterbury...
1730.
8,11

GREAT BRITAIN: LAWS, etc. (GEO. II).
An Act for repairing...the road leading from
St. Dunstan's Cross...to the waterside at Whitstable...
1736.
11

GREAT BRITAIN: LAWS, etc. (GEO. II).
An Act to explain and amend an Act...for repairing
and enlarging the road leading from the house called
The Sign of the Bells...to Maidstone...
1736.
11,12

GREAT BRITAIN: LAWS, etc. (GEO. II).
Acts for amending and maintaining the road from Dartford to
Northfleet, etc.
1738.
5

GREAT BRITAIN: LAWS, etc. (GEO. II).
An Act for enlarging the terms...by an Act...for enlarging,
amending and maintaining the road between Northfleet...
1738.
9,11

GREAT BRITAIN: LAWS, etc. (GEO. II).
An Act for enlarging the terms and powers granted by two
Acts...of...George I, for repairing the road from Stones End...
Southwark...(leading to the Lime Kilns in East Greenwich), to
the first Mill Pond at South End in the Parish of Lewisham...
Printed by John Baskett. 1738.
11

GREAT BRITAIN: LAWS, etc. (GEO. II).
An Act enlarging the terms...granted by two Acts of Parliament
for repairing the roads leading from Seven Oaks...to
Tunbridge Wells...
1740.
11

GREAT BRITAIN: LAWS, etc. (GEO. II).
An Act for enlarging the terms and powers granted...for
repairing...the road...that part of Chatham which lies next
to the City of Rochester.
1743.
4,11

GREAT BRITAIN: LAWS, etc. (GEO. II).
An Act for repairing...the road leading from the Well at the
North West end...of Farnborough to...Riverhill in the Parish
of Sevenoaks.
1748.
11

GREAT BRITAIN: LAWS, etc. (GEO. II).
An Act...for repairing and enlarging the road leading from a
house called The Sign of the Bells...Rochester to...Maidstone
...1749.
4,12

GREAT BRITAIN: LAWS, etc. (GEO. II).
An Act for amending...several Acts for amending the roads
from the City of London to East Grinstead...and for more
effectually repairing the road from Newington through
Camberwell...to New Cross in the County of Kent.
Printed by Thomas Baskett. 1752.
11

GREAT BRITAIN: LAWS, etc. (GEO. II).
An Act for repairing the road leading from the Royal Oak on
Wrotham Heath to the town of Wrotham...
1752.
11

GREAT BRITAIN: LAWS, etc. (GEO. II).
An Act...for enlarging...road from Dartford to Northfleet and
Gravesend...
1754.
5,9

GREAT BRITAIN: LAWS, etc. (GEO. III).
An Act for rendering more effectual several Acts...for
enlarging, amending and maintaining the road from Dartford
to Northfleet, Gravesend, Chalk, etc.
1761.
9

GREAT BRITAIN: LAWS, etc. (GEO. III).
Collection of all the Acts of Parliament relating to New Cross
Turnpike, etc., in the counties of Kent and Surrey from 1714 to
1765.
1765.
17

GREAT BRITAIN: LAWS, etc. (GEO. III).
An Act for amending and widening the road from...Biddenden
...through Smarden and Charing to join the Turnpike Road at...
Bound Gate, 1766.
12

GREAT BRITAIN: LAWS, etc. (GEO. III).
An Act for repairing and widening the road from Maidstone
through Detling to Key Street...1769.
Printed by (Thomas) Baskett. 1769.
12

GREAT BRITAIN: LAWS, etc. (GEO. III).
An Act...for repairing...the road from Tonbridge
to Maidstone...1769.
12

GREAT BRITAIN: LAWS, etc. (GEO. III).
An Act to amend an Act...for repairing and widening
the road from Tonbridge to Maidstone...1769.
12

GREAT BRITAIN: LAWS, etc. (GEO. III).
An Act for continuing the term and altering the
powers of an Act...for amending the road from Dartford
to Northfleet...
1782.
5,9

GREAT BRITAIN: LAWS, etc. (GEO. III).
An Act for continuing an Act...for amending and
widening the road from Biddenden...through...Smarden
and Charing to join the Turnpike Road at...Bound Gate.
1785.
12

GREAT BRITAIN: LAWS, etc. (GEO. III).
An Act...for lighting and watching certain parts of...
the Turnpike Road leading from...New Street in
Southwark to Deptford.
Eyre and Strahan. 1785.
12

GREAT BRITAIN: LAWS, etc. (GEO. III).
An Act for repairing and widening the road leading
out of the Turnpike Road from Dover through Folkestone
to Hythe...
1792.
7

GREAT BRITAIN: LAWS, etc. (GEO. III).
An Act for altering, widening and repairing the road
leading from the town and port of Dover to...
Sandwich...1801.
12

GREAT BRITAIN: LAWS, etc. (GEO. III).
An Act for continuing the term and altering the powers
of two several Acts...for amending and maintaining
the road from Dartford to Northfleet...
1801.
5,9

GREAT BRITAIN: LAWS, etc. (GEO. III).
An Act for amending and improving the road from the
North end of...Tonbridge to...Ightham and two other
roads...1809.
12

GREAT BRITAIN: LAWS, etc. (GEO. III).
An Act for continuing and amending two Acts...for
repairing the roads from Golford Green...to the
Turnpike Road in...Sandhurst...1811.
12

GREAT BRITAIN: LAWS, etc. (GEO. III).
An Act to continue the term...for repairing the
road from Wrotham Heath to Foot's Cray...
1817.
11

GREAT BRITAIN: LAWS, etc. (GEO. III).
An Act for repairing...the lower road leading from
...Greenwich to...Woolwich.
1818.
11

GREAT BRITAIN: LAWS, etc. (GEO. III).
An Act to continue the term and alter...an Act...
for repairing the road from Dover...to Sandwich...
1818.
11

GREAT BRITAIN: LAWS, etc. (GEO. IV).
An Act for widening and improving the road leading
from the Turnpike Road in...Tenterden...1820.
12

GREAT BRITAIN: LAWS, etc. (GEO. IV).
An Act for repairing, widening and maintaining the
road...from Dartford to...Strood.
1822.
9

GREAT BRITAIN: LAWS, etc. (GEO. IV).
An Act for making and maintaining a Turnpike Road from...
Gravesend to...Borough Green...
1825.
9

GREAT BRITAIN: LAWS, etc. (GEO. IV).
An Act for more effectually repairing the roads from
Haselden's Wood...to Appledore Heath...1829.
12

GREAT BRITAIN: LAWS, etc. (GEO. IV).
An Act for repairing the road from Stocker's Head...to
Bagham's Cross in...Chilham...1829.
12

GREAT BRITAIN: LAWS, etc. (GEO. IV).
New Cross Roads. An Act to improve the road through the town
of Bromley...(Royal assent, 29th May, 1830).
1830.
2

GREAT BRITAIN: LAWS, etc. (VIC.).
An Act to amend and extend the provisions of an Act for
widening and improving the road leading from the Turnpike
Road in Tenterden...1851.
12

GREAT BRITAIN: LAWS, etc. (VIC.).
An Act for more effectually repairing the road from Gravesend...
to Borough Green...
1853.
9

GREAT BRITAIN: LAWS, etc. (VIC.).
An Act to continue the Biddenden Turnpike Trust...1861.
12

GREAT BRITAIN: LAWS, etc. (VIC.).
An Act for extending the term and amending the provisions of
the Acts relating to the Folkestone to Banham Downs Turnpike
Road...
1862.
7

GREAT BRITAIN: LAWS, etc. (ELIZ. II) - STATUTORY INSTRUMENTS.
The South of Aylesford-East of Wrotham Special Road Scheme, 1966.
H.M.S.O.
12

HARDMAN, Frank William.
The roads of South-East Kent.
Deal, Pain. 1919.
11,12,19

HARPER, Charles George.
The Dover Road: annals of an ancient Turnpike.
Chapman and Hall. 1895 etc.
1,3,4,5,6,7,8,9,11,12,13,14,15,17,18,20

The Dover Road: annals of an ancient Turnpike, 2nd edition.
London, Cecil Palmer. 1922.
21

The Hastings Road and the "Happy Springs of Tunbridge".
Chapman and Hall. 1906.
1,5,7,11,12,15,19

HARRIS, Rendal.
Watling Street. (Woodbrooke Essays, No. 17).
Cambridge, W. Heffer and Sons. n.d.
5

HISCOCK, Robert Heath.
The road between Dartford, Gravesend and Strood. (Reprinted
from Archaeologia Cantiana, Vol. 83, 1968).
11

HUGHES, George Martin.
Roman roads in South-East Britain: romance and tragedy.
Allen and Unwin. 1936.
1,2,4,8,9,11,12

INSTITUTION OF MUNICIPAL ENGINEERS.
Proceedings, Vol. 78, 1951-52. (Containing articles on Bromley
and road development in Kent).
2

JERROLD, Walter.
Highways and byways in Kent.
Macmillan. 1907, etc.
1,2,3,5,6(1908) 7,8,9(1907 and 1924) 10,11,12,13,14,15,16,17,18,
19,20

KENT COUNTY CONSTABULARY.
Analysis of road traffic and accidents.
3(1959)
5(1965, 1971)
6(1945-56)
8(1958)
9(1963, 1964, 1965, 1967, 1970, 1971)
12(1959, 1969, 1970)
15(1958)
19(1958)

KENT COUNTY CONSTABULARY.
Road accidents in...: supplement to the annual
reports of the Chief Constable.
3(not dated)
4(1954 in progress)
6(not dated)
12(1950-57 with 1952 and 1955 missing)

KENT COUNTY COUNCIL - ARCHIVES OFFICE.
Some roads and bridges...edited by Elizabeth Melling.
(Kentish Sources, No. 1).
Kent County Council. 1959.
1,2,3,4,5,6,7,8,9,11,12,14,15,16,18,19,20

KENT COUNTY COUNCIL - ROADS DEPARTMENT.
Annual report of the County Surveyor for...1971-72.
Kent County Council. (1972).
11

County road plan report, adopted by the Roads Committee
on 25th October, 1945.
Kent County Council. (1945).
5,11,15

Report of the County Surveyor on the problems of
flooding.
Kent County Council. 1969.
4,5,9,11

KNOX, Cecil.
St. Margaret's Bay and the Roman roads from Richborough
to Dover and Canterbury. (Reprinted from Archaeologia
Cantiana, Vol. LIV, 1943).
3,17

MARGARY, Ivan Donald.
The new Roman road to the coast (pamphlet).
n.d.
16

MARGARY, Ivan Donald.
Roman roads in Britain.
London, Baker. 1967.
3

MAXWELL, Donald.
The enchanted road.
Methuen. 1927.
1,3,4,5,6,7,8,11,12,13,17,18,19

Milestone guides: Book I, from London Bridge...
Book II, Southern Crossroads.
n.d.
17

NOLAN, Michael.
Substance of the speech of M. Nolan Esq., before a
Committee of the House of Commons upon a Bill...
for repairing and maintaining the road from Eynsford
to Shoreham.
1811.
11

OGILBY, John.
The Traveller's Pocket Book: being the 2nd edition
of Mr. Ogilby's and Mr. Morgan's Book of the Roads...
by J. Ogilby and W. Morgan.
J. Brotherton. 1761.
18

The Traveller's Pocket Book: being the 4th edition of
Mr. Ogilby's and Mr. Morgan's Book of the Roads...
by J. Ogilby and W. Morgan.
J. Brotherton. 1766.
18

OWENS, W.H.
Famous highways of Britain - the Folkestone Road.
American and Commonwealth Visitor. 1949.
12

ROADS Cont'd

PATERSON, Daniel.
A...description of all the...roads in England and Wales, 11th edition and 18th edition.
1796.
18

PATERSON, Daniel.
Paterson's roads, edited by E. Mogg.
1826.
16

PHIPPEW, James.
The road guide from London to Tunbridge Wells through Lewisham, Bromley, etc.
Joseph Thomas. 1836.
11

RAYNER, R.
The road and you: proposed Dartford/Croydon sub-orbital motorway and...Keston Church area...(Typescript).
(1963).
2

RODEN, M.H.
Finances of a Turnpike Company. (Tonbridge School Local History Researches, 1961).
11

Sevenoaks By-pass. (Article from the Kent Messenger, 4th June, 1965).
8

Survey of the road from London to Hith in Kent.
n.d.
12

TRANSPORT, Ministry of.
London Traffic. Regulations of Traffic. Regulations, 1963.
H.M.S.O. 1963.
8

The London Traffic (Prohibition of Waiting) Regulations.
H.M.S.O. 1964.
8

Rights of Way: The Stopping up of Highways (County of Kent) Orders, 2,3,5,7,8,9,10,11,12,13,14,15,16,17,18,19,20,21. 1959.

and Revocation of Order, No. 1, 1957. (1959).
H.M.S.O. 1959.
12

Rights of Way: The Stopping up of Highways (County of Kent) Orders, 1,2,3,10,11,21,22. 1962.
H.M.S.O. 1962.
8

Rights of Way: The Stopping up of Highways (County of Kent) Order, 1963. Order 1 - in progress.
H.M.S.O.
8

TRISTRAM, W. Outram.
Coaching days and coaching ways.
Macmillan.
6(1903) 9(1894) 12(1914)

VALLIS, E.W.H.
Road development in Kent. In Proceedings of Institute of Municipal Engineers, Vol. 78, 1951-52.
2

WHITAKER, E.J.
The M2: the Medway Towns By-pass. (Duplicated).
Chatham Technical High School for Boys. 1964.
4

WOOLWICH AND DISTRICT ANTIQUARIAN SOCIETY.
Road works at Shorters Hill, Kent, 1816.
Woolwich and District Antiquarian Society. 1947.
8

ROCHESTER

ADAMS, H.G.
An historical and descriptive account of Rochester Bridge.
J.E. Macaulay. 1856.
1,8,11,17

An alphabetical list of the Freemen of the City of Rochester distinguishing the date of their admission.
Rochester, W. Epps. 1807.
15

AMICABLE SOCIETY OF FRIENDS AND NEIGHBOURS, ROCHESTER.
Articles made and fully agreed on the 17th April, 1832 by an Amicable Society of Friends...
1834.
15

ARNOLD, A.A.
The earliest Rochester Bridge.
Mitchell, Hughes and Clarke. 1921.
12,17

A fourteenth-century Court Roll of the Manor of Ambree, Rochester. In Kent Miscellanea, Vol. 4, 1911.
7,11,17

The Poll Tax in Rochester, September, 1660. (Reprinted from Archaeologia Cantiana).
Mitchell, Hughes and Clarke. 1912.
7,17

An authentic copy of the Charter and byelaws, etc., of the City of Rochester...
J. Hughes. 1749.
1
Rochester, W. Epps. 1816.
4,11,15

AVELING, S.T.
Rochester Inns. (From Archaeologia Cantiana, Vol. 21, 1895).
17

BARNABY, H.
Historic notes of Chatham and Rochester in bygone days.
1899.
4,15,17

BARTLETT, Philip H.
The City of Rochester Charters.
Rochester City Council. 1961.
1,2,4,8,11,12,15

BECKER, M. Janet.
Rochester Bridge, 1387-1856.
Constable. 1930.
1,2,3,4,5,8,9,11,12,15,17,18,19

BELL, G. AND SON. Publishers.
Canterbury and Rochester with Minster-in-Sheppey.
1929.
17

BELL, L.H.
Where travellers rest: the story of Richard Watt's Charity, Rochester.
Rochester Printing Co. 1926.
1,3,4,8,11,12,13,15

BELL, Neil.
Crocus: (novel with a Rochester setting).
Collins. 1936.
15

BENNETT, A.S.
"June" of Rochester.
Arnold. 1939.
4,8,9,11,12,15

BIRD, Charles.
Sir Joseph Williamson, Kt., the founder of the Rochester Mathematical School.
Rochester, Parrett and Neves. 1894.
7,15

BLACK, ADAM AND CHARLES LTD. Publishers.
Black's guide to Canterbury and Rochester.
A. and C. Black Ltd. 1893.
7

BLENCOWE, Robert Willis.
Rochester records, 1578-80: an account of the expenditure of the Corporation of Mayoralty, Richard Harlow.
n.d.
15,17

BRIDGE, Sir Frederick.
A Westminster pilgrim.
Novelle. 1918.
12

BRIDGE, Joseph C.
Two Cheshire soldiers of fortune in the XIV century. (Includes
Sir Robert Knolles).
G.R. Griffith. 1907.
15

BROWN, Reginald Allen.
Rochester Castle, Kent.
H.M.S.O.
2(1969) 4(1964 and 1969) 7(1969(8(1964) 9(1969) 11(1969)
15(1964)

The castle of Rochester. (Article from "Castles and Abbeys of
England").
1842.
3

CAVE AND WILLIAMS.
Rochester election petition, report of the enquiry.
Rochester, Parrett and Neves. 1892.
12

CHARLES, REYNOLDS AND CO. Publishers.
The album of Chatham and Rochester views.
Charles, Reynolds and Co. n.d.
12

Charter celebrations, 1961...Souvenir programme of events,
24th June-10th July, 1961.
4,8,15

The church of Saint Nicholas with Saint Clement, Rochester.
n.d.
12

CLARK, G.T.
Tracts concerning places in Kent and Sussex - Rochester
Castle, by G.T. Clark and others.
n.d.
15

CLAYTON, Charles.
Parochial sermons preached at Chatham and Rochester.
J. Jackson. 1846.
15

A collection of Statutes concerning Rochester Bridge, with a
list of the contributory lands etc.
W. Burrill. 1832.
15

COOK, W.H.
On the discovery of a flint-working site of palaeolithic date
in the Medway Valle at Rochester, Kent..., by W.H. Cook and
J.R. Killick. (Extracts from Proceedings of the Prehistoric
Society of East Anglia, 1924).
4,8

COOKE, James Herbert.
The shipwreck of Sir Cloudesley Shovell on the Scilly Islands
in 1707: from original and contemporary documents...
John Bellows. 1883.
15

CROFT-COOKE, Rupert.
The last of spring.
Putnam. 1964.
8

CROFT-COOKE, Rupert.
The purple streak.
W.H. Allen. 1966.
8

DADSON, W.
Sketches of the picturesque in Rochester and its vicinity.
Chatham, W. Dadson. 1824-25.
11

(DENNE, Samuel and SHRUBSOLE, W.).
The history and antiquities of Rochester and its environs: to
which is added a description of the towns, villages (etc.)
situate on or near the road from London to Margate, Deal and
Dover.
Rochester, T. Fisher. 1772.
1,2,3,4,7,8,11,12,13,14,15,17,18

The history and antiquities of Rochester and its
environs...2nd edition, with considerable additions
and improvements. (Edited by W. Wildash).
Rochester, W. Wildash. 1817.
1,4,5,15

The history and antiquities of Rochester and its
environs...
Rochester, W. Wildash. 1833.
4,11,15

The history and antiquities of Rochester and its
environs...
Rochester, W. Wildash. 1838.
17

The history and antiquities of Rochester and its
environs...
Rochester, W. Wildash. 1890.
15,20

Dickens Festival Pageant...Rochester, 1951: souvenir
programme.
4,11,15

ESSEX, Mr.
A description and plan of the ancient timber bridge
at Rochester...,
1785.
12,17

Fabric Roll of Rochester Castle (in the time of
Edward III, 1367-69).
n.d.
15

FIELDING, Cecil Henry.
The records of Rochester.
Dartford, Snowden. 1910.
1,2,3,4,5,6,8,9,11,12,14,15,16,17,18,19

Fifteen views of Chatham, Rochester and neighbourhood.
(Drawings).
(Iver) Lowe. c.1861-84.
4

FINCH, William Coles.
The Foords of Rochester.
Rochester, Parrett and Neves. 1917.
1,5

FLOWER, David Edwin Laurence.
Short history of Sir Joseph Williamson's Mathematical
School, edited by D.E.L. Flower.
Privately Printed. 1951.
3,8,11,15

FORT PITT CENTRAL MILITARY HOSPITAL.
Comforts for the wounded in our hospitals.
Rochester, W. and J. Mackay. 1915.
15

GOLDWIN, J.H. Publisher.
The visitor's guide to Rochester, 2nd edition.
Rochester, Goldwin. 1885.
8(1885) 11(6th edition, n.d.) 15(1885)

GOMME, George Lawrence.
Boley Hill, Rochester. In Archaeologia Cantiana,
Vol. 17, 1887.
17

GOSTLING, William.
The Rochester guide...to which is added the traveller's
guide from London to the coast.
Rochester, S. Caddel. c.1800. ·
9

GREAT BRITAIN: LAWS, etc. (GEO. III).
An Act for the more easy and speedy recovery of small
debts within the City of Rochester...
n.d.
11

GREAT BRITAIN: LAWS, etc. (GEO. III).
An Act for paving, cleansing...the High Streets...
in the Parish of St. Nicholas within the City of
Rochester...
1769.
11,12

GREAT BRITAIN: LAWS, etc. (GEO. IV).
An Act to enable His Majesty to defray the charge of a certain
Barrack by the grant of an annuity on the consolidated fund.
(Builders involved were from Rochester).
Printed by Eyre and Strahan. 1820.
11

GREAT BRITAIN: LAWS, etc. (ELIZ. II).
Rochester Corporation Act.
H.M.S.O. 1952.
4,8

GREAT BRITAIN: LAWS, etc. (ELIZ. II).
Rochester Bridge Act, 1965.
H.M.S.O.
4

GREAT BRITAIN, Parliament.
Proceedings of a Select Committee of the House of Commons,
on the petition against the return of James Barnett Esq...
City of Rochester.
Rochester, W. Epps. 1808.
3,15

GREAT BRITAIN, Parliament.
Report of the Select Committee on the present state of
Rochester Bridge, etc.
House of Commons. 1820.
1

GREENWOOD, E.J.
The hospital of St. Bartholomew, Rochester.
E.J. Greenwood. 1962.
4,15

HARRIS, Edwin.
The Bull Hotel, Rochester and its Dickens associations.
(Old Rochester Series, No. 22).
Rochester, E. Harris. 1908.
1,4,8,11

Civic Rochester. (Old Rochester Series, No. 10).
Rochester, E. Harris. 1898.
1,8,11

Durobrivae; or, Roman Rochester.
Rochester, E. Harris. 1909.
1,4,8,9,11,12,15,17

The guide to Rochester, 4th edition. (Old Rochester Series,
No. 25).
Rochester, W. and J. Mackay. (1914).
11

The Guildhall, Rochester. (Old Rochester Series, No. 15).
Rochester, E. Harris. 1900.
1,8,11

Gundulf the Good; or, Saxon Rochester.
Rochester, E. Harris. 1910.
4,8,9,12,15,17

Historic houses of Old Rochester. (Old Rochester Series,
No. 7).
Rochester, E. Harris. n.d.
1,5,8,11,15

The history and will of Sir Joseph Williamson. (Eastgate
Series, No. 9).
Rochester, E. Harris. n.d.
15

History of Richard Watt's Charity. (Old Rochester Series,
No. 20).
Rochester, E. Harris. 1924.
11,15

History of Rochester Bridge. (Old Rochester Series, No. 23).
Rochester, E. Harris. 1909.
1,8,11

The history of Rochester Castle. (Old Rochester Series,
No. 2).
Rochester, E. Harris.
1(1897 etc.) 3(1897 etc.) 4(1902) 7(1908) 8(1897 etc.)
9(1897 etc.) 11(1897 etc.)

Illustrated guide to Dickensian Rochester (with plan).
(Old Rochester Series, No. 18).
Rochester, E. Harris. 1904.
4(1904) 5(1904) 8(1918 and 1921) 12(1918 and 1921)

Illustrated guide to the interesting and historical places
within easy distance of the City of Rochester.
Rochester, E. Harris. 1917.
1,15

Odo; or, the siege of Rochester Castle.
Rochester, E. Harris. 1900.
1,4,8,11,12,14,15,17

Old churches of Rochester. (Old Rochester Series,
No. 11).
Rochester, E. Harris. 1898.
8,11

Old Rochester. (Collected volume of Old Rochester
Series).
Rochester, E. Harris. n.d.
4,8,11,15,17

Pen and ink sketches of bygone Rochester inns.
(Old Rochester Series, No. 16).
Rochester, E. Harris. 1902.
8,11

Picturesque Rochester and vicinity: illustrations
(only). (Old Rochester Series, No. 21).
Rochester, E. Harris.
1(1911) 4(1908) 8(1911) 11(1908) 12(1911)

The Priory of Rochester. (Old Rochester Series,
No. 9).
Rochester, E. Harris. 1897.
4,8,11

Reminiscences of Old Rochester. (Old Rochester
Series, No. 1).
Rochester, E. Harris. n.d.
4,8,11,12

Restoration House.
Rochester, E. Harris. 1904.
1,4,8,11,12,15,17

Richard Watts; or, Rochester in the time of the
Tudors.
Rochester, E. Harris. n.d.
1,4,8,11,12,14,15,17

Richard Watt's Charity. (Old Rochester Series,
No. 20).
Rochester, E. Harris. 1906.
4

Rochester. (Collected volume of the Eastgate Series).
Rochester, E. Harris. 1909.
11,17

Rochester inns and signs. (Old Rochester Series,
No. 19).
Rochester, E. Harris. 1905 etc.
8,11,12

The Rochester of "Edwin Drood". (Old Rochester
Series, No. 6).
Rochester, W. and J. Mackay. (1929).
11

A short history of the Druids. (Eastgate Series,
No. 1).
Rochester, E. Harris. 1909.
4,15

Simon de Montfort; or, the third seige of Rochester
Castle.
Rochester, E. Harris. 1902.
1,4,8,11,12,15,17

Sir Robert Knowles: the founder of Rochester Bridge.
Rochester, E. Harris. 1911.
1,4,8,11,12,15,17

Story of Ye Olde Curiosity Shop, Eastgate,
Rochester. (Old Rochester Series, No. 24).
Rochester, Harris and Sons. 1921.
8,12

William D'Albini; or, the second seige of Rochester
Castle.
Rochester, E. Harris. 1901.
1,4,8,11,12,15,17

HEARNDEN, Isaac.
The lady of Rochester Castle: a romance in rhyme.
Gravesend, Munday. 1891.
1,11,15,17

HEPWORTH, J.
Rochester and district: a sketch-book to its geology,
flora and fauna, compiled by J. Hepworth.
Rochester, Parrett and Neves. 1913.
4,5,8,11,12,15

The history and antiquities of Rochester, its cathedral,
castle, etc.
Joseph E. Macaulay. (1858).
4

HOGG, P. Fitzgerald.
Rochester, compiled by P.F. Hogg. (An MS. notebook listing
streets as they existed in 1938; inns and signs, 1938; Strood
inns and signs, 1938; Frindsbury etc., inns and extinct inns
of Rochester, etc.).
n.d.
4

HOPE, <u>Sir</u> William Henry St. John.
On the seal and counterseal of the City of Rochester.
1886.
15

HUTCHINGS, G.E.
Vegetation of the Rochester district...
South-Eastern Union of Scientific Societies. 1928.
11

JENKINS, Thomas John.
Conrad d'Alleyne: a romance of Rochester and Magne Charta.
n.d.
1,17

JESSUP, Ronald Frank.
Rochester. (Information Sheet, No. 40 in the Travel Association
Series).
Travel Association. 1946.
4

JOHNSON, Frank.
Sir Francis Belsey, a knight-errant of love.
Sunday School Union. (1916).
11

JOHNSTONE, Rupert.
Rochester Cathedral Choir School: a short history.
Printed by S.G. Mason. 1959.
11

JONAS, Alfred Charles.
Rochester, its castle and bridges.
1902.
17

Jubilee - souvenir of the Gundulph Lodge, No. 1,050,
Rochester, consecrated March 22nd, 1865.
J. Morton: Printed by Longley (1916).
4

KERSHAW, S. Wayland.
Ancient bridge chapels, chiefly described for Rochester.
Wyman. 1882.
7

KIMBALL, Katharine.
Rochester.
A. and C. Black. 1912.
1,4,7,8,11,12,15,18

KING'S SCHOOL, ROCHESTER.
The Roffensian, Vol. 25, No. 76-Vol. 28, No. 86, 1919-22.
12

KING'S SCHOOL, ROCHESTER.
Roffensian Register containing the names of all the members
of the school...
From 1842-1904 - Rochester, Parrett and Neves. 1904.
11
From 1835-1920 - Maidstone, Hobbs. 1920.
8,11
From 1835-1936 - Rochester, W. and J. Mackay. 1937.
8,11,15

LANGTON, Robert.
Charles Dickens and Rochester. (An essay read to the Manchester
Literary Club, 1880).
Chapman and Hall. 1880
1,4,8,9,15,18

LANGTON, Robert.
Charles Dickens and Rochester, 4th edition.
T. Oldroyd. 1888.
6,7,11,12,13

LARKIN, Charles.
Truth unmasked; or, a true delineation of circumstances
attending the late extraordinary contest for the
representation of the City of Rochester...
Rochester, W. Epps. 1806.
15

LONDON AND MIDDLESEX ARCHAEOLOGICAL SOCIETY.
Visit of the...Society to Rochester and Strood on
Thursday, 26th June, 1884.
Nichols and Sons. 1884.
1,8,15,17

MARSH, Ronald J.
The expanding City of Rochester: twenty-three Royal
Charters since Richard The Lionheart. (Extract from
"The Municipal Review", April, 1965).
4

(MARSHALL, Jane).
Tour of Cnaterbury and Rochester.
Oxford University Press. 1954.
3,11

MAXWELL, Donald.
Rochester.
Rochester City Council. 1935.
4,8,11,13,15

A memorial of the late George White Martin...containing
a brief sketch of his life and two funeral sermons,
preached in the parish church of St. Nicholas,
Rochester.
London, Clowes. (186-?).
4,8

MURRAY, J(ohn) O(liver).
Some aspects of the martial, medical and social history
of the Port of Rochester.
Rochester City Council. (1952).
4,8

A narrative of the facts relative to the murder of
Richard Faulkner Taylor...between Rochester and
Maidstone...1831...
Rochester, S. Caddel. (1831).
1

ORR, William S. AND CO. <u>Publishers</u>.
Pictorial guide to Rochester.
W.S. Orr and Co. 1846.
8,11,17

PALMER, William Stern.
A narrative of the distressing accident which occurred
at Rochester Bridge...13th September, 1816...
Romsey, W. Sharp. 1817.
4,8,11,12,15

PARKER, W.
Camren Roffense: poem.
n.d.
12

Pastoral address, with a statement of the parochial
schools, charities...of the parish of St. Nicholas,
Rochester, 1869.
Rochester, S. Caddel. 1870.
11

PHILLIPS, <u>Rev</u>. H.F.
A sermon preached in the parish church of St. Margaret-
next-Rochester on the 10th April, 1859.
Wildash. 1860.
15

PHIPPEN, James.
The boundaries of St. Margaret's Parish, Rochester...
Rochester, J.E. Macaulay. 1857.
11,15

PORTER, <u>Mrs</u>. Adrian.
Life and letters of Sir John Henniker Heaton Bt.,
by his daughter.
London, John Lane. 1916.
3

PRESNAIL, James.
The history of Rochester. (62 instalments from the
Chatham News, in loose-leaf folder).
Rochester, Chatham and Gillingham News. n.d.
4

The reconstruction of Rochester Bridge, 1911-14.
(Series of 37 photographs).
S.E. Willis. 1914.
15

Reflections on a paper, intituled "His Majesty's reasons for withdrawing himself from Rochester".
John Staikey and Richard Chiswell. 1689.
15

RENN, Derek Frank.
Norman castles in Britain.
Baker. 1968.
6

Report on the demolition of a portion of old Rochester Bridge by the Royal Engineers in the winter of 1856-57...
1857.
15

Reports and documents relating to Rochester Bridge, printed at the request of the Commonalty.
1832.
12,15

The Restoration House at Rochester.
n.d.
13

RICHARD WATT'S CHARITY.
The scheme for the management of the Charity and for the application of the income thereof...
Richard Watt's Charity. 1934.
8

RICHARD WATT'S CHARITY.
A terrier or rental of the estates of Watt's Charity, Rochester, 1859...
1860.
11

ROBINS, F.W.
The story of the Bridge (contains references to bridges in Rochester and Kent).
n.d.
15

ROCHESTER BRIDGE TRUST.
Rochester Bridge: copy of the inscriptions on the tablets in the Bridge Chamber, with some notes thereon.
4(1921) 8(1921) 15(1937)

The bridges of Rochester.
J. and W. Mackay. 1970.
4,11,12

Rochester Bridge Trust: presented by the Wardens and Officers of the Rochester Bridge Trust to commemorate the occasion of the opening of their new bridge...on the 15th day of April, 1970.
8

ROCHESTER CITY COUNCIL.
Abstracts of...accounts for the year ended 31st March, 1963, 1964, 1965, 1966.
4,15

The City and Borough of Rochester: official guide, 2nd edition.
G.W. May Ltd. (1958).
1,4,5,8,15

The City of Rochester, Kent: the official guide.
British Publishing Co.
4(1962)
6(1968)
8(1962, 1965, 1968)
11(1965, 1967)
12(1968)
15(1962)
19(1962)

Coronation of Their Majesties King George VI and Queen Elizabeth: official programme of the celebrations within the City of Rochester, 1937.
4

A guide to Rochester. ("Borough" Guides, No. 90).
Cheltenham, E.J. Burrow. n.d.
4

Official guide to Rochester with notes on Chatham, Strood and Gillingham.
Cheltenham, E.J. Burrow. n.d.
4,11,15,17

Report of the Librarian, for the year ending 31st March, 1909.
17

Rochester City records, 1225-1894. Catalogued at the Kent Archives Office by Hugh Hanley, May-July, 1963. (Typescript).
15

A terrier or account of the estates belonging to the Mayor, Aldermen and Citizens of the City of Rochester.
Rochester City Council. 1877.
11,15

A terrier or account of the estates belonging to the Mayor, Aldermen and Citizens of the City of Rochester.
Rochester City Council. 1890.
11,15

ROCHESTER - CONSISTORY COURT.
Index of wills proved in the Rochester Consistory Court, 1440 and 1561, compiled by the late Leland L. Duncan. (Kent Archaeological Society Records Branch, Vol. IX).
Canterbury, Printed by Gibbs and Sons. 1924.
3

ROCHESTER CORN EXCHANGE.
Catalogue of brass rubbings (exhibition 1886) interleaved with MS. notes.
Rochester, Printed by W.T. Wildash. (1886).
2

ROCHESTER GRAMMAR SCHOOL FOR GIRLS.
Grammar School echoes, Nos. 1,10,21 and 26. (1896, 1901, 1910, 1913).
Rochester Grammar School for Girls. 1896-1913.
12

ROCHESTER GRAMMAR SCHOOL FOR GIRLS.
Scheme.
Rochester, W. and J. Mackay. 1886.
15

ROCHESTER HISTORICAL PAGEANT COMMITTEE.
Rochester historical pageant: presented during Civic Week in the Castle gardens, June 22nd-27th, 1931. (Book of the words).
Rochester Historical Pageant Committee. 1931.
3,4,11,13,15

ROCHESTER HISTORICAL PAGEANT COMMITTEE.
Rochester historical pageant...June, 1931. Historical, industrial and trades exhibition...
Rochester Historical Pageant Committee. 1931.
4

ROCHESTER MUSEUM COMMITTEE.
Eastgate House Museum, Rochester, compiled by J.C. Taylor.
Rochester Museum Committee. 1953.
8

ROCHESTER SOCIETY.
Rochester: a walk around the City (illustrated folder).
1968.
4

Rochester, Kent. (From an unidentified work, Vol. IV, No. 54).
1792.
3

ST. ANDREW'S HIGH SCHOOL, ROCHESTER.
The Andrean, Summer, 1968.
4

ST. ANDREW'S HIGH SCHOOL, ROCHESTER.
Prospectus, 1963.
8

ST. BARTHOLOMEW'S HOSPITAL.
Historical account, extracts from scheme and rules and orders for the internal regulation...of St. Bartholomew's Hospital at Chatham.
Rochester, W.T. Wildash. 1863.
15

The scheme for the management and regulation of St. Bartholomew's Hospital...1858.
C. Roworth and Sons. 1858.
15

A terrier or rental of the charity estates, as let at Lady Day, 1908.
n.d.
8

CHAVASSE, Christopher M. Bishop of Rochester.
The meaning of the psalms.
S.P.C.K. 1951.
8

CHAVASSE, Christopher M. Bishop of Rochester.
This is our faith...
S.P.C.K. 1959.
15

A collection of anthems, used in the Cathedral Church of
Rochester...
Rochester, W.T. Wildash. 1817.
15

Collection of anthems used in the Cathedral Church of Rochester.
J. Sampson. 1871.
15

COLLINGS, T.
The history and antiquities of the Cathedral Church of
Rochester, edited by T. Collings.
Chatham, Collings. 1848.
11,15,17

COOPER, Harold George.
Choristers of Rochester Cathedral: a chronological list...
from 1679 to the end of 1955...compiled by H.G. Cooper.
Chatham, Rochester Cathedral Old Choristers' Association. 1956.
2,11

COTTINGHAM, L.N.
Some account of an ancient tomb, etc., discovered at Rochester
Cathedral, 1825.
J. Taylor. c.1826.
15

Diocese of Rochester, Church Chronicle, Vol. 1.
William Poole. 1882.
4

DOWSE, I.R.
The pilgrim shrines of England. (Canterbury and Rochester
Cathedrals).
The Faith Press. 1963.
15

(DUFFIELD, F.H.).
A sketch of the history of the Diocese of Rochester with a short
account of the Cathedral and precincts: a souvenir of the
Thanksgiving Anniversary, by F.H. Duffield and H.T. Knight.
Chatham, Diocesan Chronicle. 1926.
2,3,5,8,11,12,15

DUGDALE, Henry Geast.
The life and character of Edmund Geste, S.T.P...the first
Protestant Bishop of Rochester.
W. Pickering. 1840.
15

FAIRBAIRNS, Arnold.
Portfolio of English cathedrals, with historical and
architectural notes, No. 19 - Rochester.
T.W. Dennis. n.d.
15

FAIRBAIRNS, W.H.
Rochester. (Notes on the Cathedral Series).
S.P.C.K. 1920.
15

FAIRWEATHER, F.H.
Gundulf's Cathedral and Priory Church of St. Andrew,
Rochester...by F.H. Fairweather. (Reprinted from the
Archaeological Journal, Vol. 86, 2nd series, Vol. 36).
Royal Archaeological Institute. 1930.
8

FRIENDS OF ROCHESTER CATHEDRAL.
Annales Amicorum Cathedralis Roffensis: being the...annual
reports of The Friends...
Friends of Rochester Cathedral.
1(1936-54) 8,12(1936-37) 15

FRIENDS OF ROCHESTER CATHEDRAL.
Festival of The Friends of Rochester Cathedral. The Medway
Theatre Guild presents "The mystery of the finding of the Cross",
by Henri Gheon...programme.
Rochester, Printed by W. and J. Mackay. (1956).
4

GRIFFIN, R.
Rochester Cathedral: some indents of lost brasses.
London, John Bale, Sons and Danielsson Ltd. 1913.
2,7,11,15

GUMMER, Selwyn.
The Chavasse twins.
Hodder. 1963.
1,4,8,9

HAMO, of Hythe. Bishop of Rochester.
Diocesis Roffensis: Registrum Hamonis Hethe.
Pars prima.
Canterbury and York Society.
1(1948) 2(1948) 7(1914) 8(1948) 11(1948) 12(1914
and 1948) 17(1948) 18(1948)

HARRIS, Edwin.
Bishops of Rochester, A.D. 601-1897. (Rochester
Series, No. 4).
Rochester, E. Harris. 1897.
1,8,11

The guide to Rochester Cathedral, 4th edition. (Old
Rochester Series, No. 17).
Rochester, E. Harris. 1925.
11

The life of Bishop Gundulf. (Rochester Series, No. 8).
Rochester, E. Harris. 1897.
8,11

Rochester Cathedral. (Old Rochester Series, No. 3).
Rochester, E. Harris. 1902.
4,11

HEATH, Sidney.
Our Homeland Cathedrals, Vol. 11. The cathedrals of
the South, East and West of England, by S. Heath and
P. Row.
Homeland Association. n.d.
8

HER MAJESTY'S COMMISSIONERS FOR INQUIRING INTO THE
CONDITION OF CATHEDRAL CHURCHES IN ENGLAND AND WALES.
Report...upon the Cathedral Church of Rochester.
Eyre and Spottiswoode for H.M.S.O. 1883.
8

HOLE, Samuel Reynolds. Dean of Rochester.
The letters of Samuel Reynolds Hole.
George Allen. 1907.
4,8,11

The memories of Dean Hole.
E. Arnold. 1894.
4,8

Memories of Dean Hole.
Nelson. 1908.
8

Then and now.
Hutchinson. 1902.
19

HOPE, Sir William Henry St. John.
Architectural history of the Cathedral Church and
Monastery of St. Andrew at Rochester.
Mitchell and Hughes. 1900.
1,2,4,8,11,12,15,17

Notes on the architectural history of Rochester Cathedral
1886.
15

Rochester Cathedral Church: conjectural plan of
Gundulf's work.
Kell and Son. n.d.
8

HUGO, Thomas.
Memoir of Gundulf, Bishop of Rochester, 1077-1108...
Richards. 1853.
1,4,11,15,17

Inventories of the goods of Cardinal Fisher, Bishop of
Rochester. (Proceedings of the Society of Antiquaries,
April 11th, 1872).
8

JOHNSTONE, R.
Rochester Cathedral Choir School: a short history.
Rochester, R. Johnstone. 1959.
15

KENT COUNTY COUNCIL - ARCHIVES OFFICE.
Records of the Diocese of Rochester, 1436-1900.
Kent County Council. 1959.
15

KING, Richard John.
Handbook to the cathedrals of England. Southern Division,
Parts I and II - Canterbury, Rochester, etc.
J. Murray. 1876.
1,8,12(1861)

LAW, John. Archdeacon of Rochester.
A charge delivered to the clergy of the Archdeaconry of
Rochester, in the year 1779.
Rochester, T. Fisher. 1780.
1

A charge delivered to the clergy of the Diocese of Rochester
in June, 1811.
J. M'creery. 1811.
15

A charge delivered to the clergy of the Arch deaconry of
Rochester in May, 1817.
W. Wildash. 1817.
15

A charge delivered to the clergy of the Diocese of Rochester
in June, 1820.
T. Wildash. 1820.
15

A sermon preached at the anniversary meeting of the sons of
the clergy in the Cathedral Church of St. Paul on Thursday,
May 11th, 1780...
C. Bathurst. 1780.
15

LEE-WARNER, E.H.
Bishops of Rochester. (Series of lectures - Oxford extra-
mural and W.E.A., No. 6 only: Warner). (Typescript).
1966.
2

LEE-WARNER, Edward.
The life of John Warner, Bishop of Rochester, 1637-1666...
London, Mitchell and Hughes. 1901.
2,3

LEWIS, John.
The life of Dr. John Fisher, Bishop of Rochester, 2 vols.
Joseph Lilly. (Reprinted from MSS. n.d.). 1855.
15

LIVETT, Grevile Mairis.
Brief notes on Rochester Cathedral Church.
n.d.
7

MACKEAN, William Herbert. Canon of Rochester Cathedral.
The eucharistic doctrine of the Oxford Movement: a critical
survey.
Putnam. 1933.
15

MACKEAN, William Herbert. Canon of Rochester Cathedral.
Rochester Cathedral Library.
Rochester, Staples. 1953.
1,4,8,9,11,15

MACKLEM, Michael.
God have mercy: the life of John Fisher of Rochester.
1967.
4,12,15

Memoir of John Warner, Bishop of Rochester. (Founder of
Bromley College). In Church Magazine, Vol. 3, No. 35,
November, 1841.
2

MURRAY, George. Bishop of Rochester.
Charge...to the clergy of his Diocese at the triennial
visitation, October, 1843.
17

Observations on the circumstances which occasioned the death
of Fisher, Bishop of Rochester.
J.B. Nichols for The Society of Antiquaries. 1833.
8

O'GORMAN, Richard A.
Haymo of Hythe, Bishop of Rochester...
Washbourne. 1895.
1,2,8,11,12,17

PALMER, George Hendy.
The Cathedral Church of Rochester.
Bell. 1899.
1,2(1897) 4,5,6,7,8(1897) 11,12,15,17,18(1897).

PEARCE, Zachary. Bishop of Rochester.
A sermon on self-murder, 3rd edition.
John Rivington. 1773.
15

PENTREATH, Arthur Godolphin Guy Carleton.
The pictorial history of Rochester Cathedral.
Pitkin. 1962.
1,4,8,9,11(1971) 12,15

"PHILALETHES", pseud.
Memoirs of the life and conduct of Dr. Francis
Atterbury, late Bishop of Rochester, from his birth
to his banishment.
1723.
15

PHIPPS, Sir Constantine.
The defence of Francis, late Lord Bishop of Rochester
at the Bar of the House of Lords...
J. Bowyer. 1723.
15

RAWLINSON, Rev. Richard.
The history and antiquities of the Cathedral Church
of Rochester.
E. Curll.
1(1717) 4(1723) 5(1723) 8(1723) 11(1717) 15(1717) 17(1717)

REYNOLDS, Ernest Edwin.
Saint John Fisher (Bishop of Rochester).
Burns and Oates. 1955.
12,15

ROBINSON, C.E.R.
A sermon preached at Rochester Cathedral on St. Peter's
Day, 1873.
Gravesend, St. Andrew's Waterside Mission.
9

Rochester. (Notes on the Cathedrals Series).
Photocrom Co. n.d.
11

ROCHESTER CATHEDRAL.
Church Register, 1657-1837...edited by T. Shuidler.
Canterbury, Cross and Jackman. 1892.
3,8,9,11,12,15

Rochester Cathedral: a souvenir of the festival of
commemoration of the 800th anniversary.
Diocesan Chronicle Office. 1930.
4,8,15

ROCHESTER CATHEDRAL LIBRARY.
A catalogue of the books in the Cathedral Library of
the Dean and Chapter of Rochester.
Caddel and Son. 1860.
15

ROCHESTER DIOCESE.
Operation projectile.
Diocese of Rochester. 1966.
9

ROCHESTER DIOCESE.
Your Diocese, Rochester, 27th Jubilee.
Rochester, Jubilee Executive Committee. 1954.
1,9

SEDGWICK, Thomas E.
Indents of the despoiled brasses in Rochester Cathedral.
(From "Home Counties Magazine", Vol. VI, pp.311-2).
(MSS. copy).
8

SEDGWICK, Thomas E.
Rochester Cathedral: some indents of lost brasses...
London, John Bale, Sons and Danielsson Ltd. 1913.
1

The See of Rochester (past and present) with a plea
for the restoration of her ancient inheritance.
Rochester, Parrett and Neves. 1905.
7

Sketch of the history of the Diocese of Rochester.
Chatham, Diocesan Chronicle. 1926.
11,19

SMITH, Richard L.
Saint John Fisher.
London, Catholic Truth Society. 1964.
3

SPRAT, Thomas. Bishop of Rochester.
A collection of sermons by Thomas Sprat and other Kentish
clergymen, 1678-1713.
15

A discourse...to the clergy of his Diocese, 1695.
Edward Jones. 1696.
6,15

A letter from the Bishop of Rochester to the Right Honourable,
the Earl of Dorset and Middlesex...
Edward Jones. 1688.
15

STORER, J.
History and antiquities of the Cathedral Church and See of
Rochester, A.D. 600-1816.
c.1818.
15

SURTZ, Edward.
The works and days of John Fisher...(1469-1535), Bishop of
Rochester.
Oxford University Press. 1967.
15

UNDERHILL, Francis.
The story of Rochester Cathedral.
British Publishing Co.
1(11th edition, n.d.)
2(13th edition, 1960 - 14th edition, 1962)
4(8th edition, n.d.)
8(11th edition, n.d.).
9(Revised edition, 1969)
11(14th edition, 1962 - Revised edition, 1969)

A walk through Rochester Cathedral.
Limbird. 1840.
12,15

WARD,LOCK AND CO. LTD. Publishers.
Ward and Lock's illustrated historical handbook to Rochester
Cathedral...
Ward, Lock and Co. Ltd. 1890.
15

WHEATLEY, Sydney William.
Our monumental brasses: a sad story.
Rochester, Parrett and Neves. n.d.
3

Rochester Cathedral: notes on some of its monuments.
Chatham, Parrett and Neves. n.d.
3,8,11,15

Rochester Cathedral: notes on some of its wall paintings and
other coloured decorations.
Chatham, Parrett and Neves. n.d.
3,11,15

Rochester Cathedral and its Priory...
Chatham, Parrett and Neves. n.d.
3,11

St. Justus, first Bishop of Rochester, died 627.
Diocesan Chronicle Office. 1927.
3,11,15

St. William of Perth: his story.
Rochester, Parrett and Neves. n.d.
3,11

WHISTON, Robert.
Cathedral trusts and their fulfilment.
Olivier. 1849.
3,8,9,11,13,15,17

Copy of letters and protest, 1849. (Typescript).
15

Whiston and Rochester. (Typescript).
n.d.
15

WINKLES, H.
Cathedral Churches, by H. and B. Winkles. (Extract relating
to Rochester Cathedral).
8(1885) 12(1836)

ROLVENDEN

BOWEN, Harold Townshend.
Rolvenden.
Ashford, Headley Bros. 1939.
1,3,4,11,12

BOWEN, Harold Townshend.
St. Mary the Virgin, Rolvenden.
Ashford, Headley Bros. n.d.
12

GREAT BRITAIN: LAWS, etc. (ELIZ. II) - STATUTORY
INSTRUMENTS.
Mid Kent Water (Rolvenden) Order, 1968.
H.M.S.O.
12

HELYER, P.J.
St. Mary the Virgin, Rolvenden.
Ashford, Headley Bros. 1963.
11

ROMNEY MARSH

AGRICULTURAL LANDS COMMISSION.
Romney Marsh investigation report.
H.M.S.O. 1949.
1,4,7,8,11,21

APPACH, F.H.
Caius Julius Caesar's British expeditions, from
Boulogne to the Bay of Apuldore, and the subsequent
formation geologically of Romney Marsh.
London, J. Russell Smith. 1868.
1,3,6,7,11,12,17,21

BARRY, J. Wolfe.
Romney Marsh Level: Dymchurch Wall, joint report by
J.W. Barry and Messrs. Coode, Son and Matthews, 22nd
February, 1894.
Ashford, Printed by Igglesden. 1894.
11

BRADLEY, Arthur Granville.
An old gate of England: Rye, Romney Marsh and the
Western Cinque Ports.
Scott.
1,2,3,4(1917,1925) 5(1925) 6,7,8,9,10,11,12,13,14,
15,17(1935) 18,19,21(1917)

BRENDON, J.P.
Walland Marsh Commissioners of Sewers, by J.P.
Brendon and S.E.H. Lovegrove. (Tonbridge School
Local History Researches).
1963.
11

BRENTNALL, Margaret.
The Cinque Ports and Romney Marsh.
Gifford. 1972.
11

BURROWS, Alfred J.
Romney Marsh. (An article taken from The Journal of the
Royal Institution of Chartered Surveyors, Vol. XXI,
Part I, July, 1951).
10,11

BURROWS, A.J.
Romney Marsh past and present: a sketch of the
reclamation of this and adjoining marshes. (From
"Transactions of the Surveyors' Institution",
Vol. XVII, Part X, 1884-85).
3,7,11

CARTER, George Goldsmith.
Forgotten ports of England. (Including Sandwich,
Reculver and Romney Marsh).
Evans. (1951).
3,4,6,8,12,15

CASE, Edward.
Dymchurch wall and reclamation of Romney Marsh.
H. Underdown. 1899.
10,11

CHAMPNEYS, Basil.
A quiet corner of England...Winchelsea, Rye and
Romney Marsh.
Seeley, Jackson and Halliday. 1875.
1,3,4,6,7,11,12,15,16

The Charter and several ordinances concerning Romney Marsh.
Printed by Isaac Parsons. n.d.
11

The Charter of Romney Marsh.
London, Printed by John Wolfe. 1597.
21

The Charter of Romney Marsh, 1597.
Dover, "The Chronicle". 1854.
4,6,11,17

DE BATH, Henry.
The Charter of Romney Marsh.
Keble. 1686.
6,11,12

DOWKER, George.
On Romney Marsh (pamphlet).
Geologists' Association. 1898.
7,14

DREW, Frederic.
The geology of the country between Folkestone and Rye, including
the whole of Romney Marsh.
London, Longman, Green, Longman, Roberts and Green. 1864.
11

FURLEY, Robert.
An outline history of Romney Marsh, Kent.
Mitchell and Hughes. 1879.
11

ELLISTON-ERWOOD, Frank Charles.
Note on the churches of Romney Marsh.
Hughes and Clarke. 1925.
10,17

GARRAD, G.H.
The Romney Marsh problem.
Maidstone, Kent Education Committee. 1936.
11,21

GILBERT, C.J.
The evolution of Romney Marsh.
Ashford, Headley Bros. 1933.
11,17

GREEN, R.D.
Soils of Romney Marsh.
Rothamsted Experimental Station. 1968.
2,4,7,8,12,19,21

HOLLOWAY, William.
History of Romney Marsh from its earliest formation to 1837.
Smith. 1849.
1,3,4,6,7,11,12,17,21

JACOBS, Elsie M.
Across the Marshes.
Adams. 1949.
11

JACOBS, Elsie M.
Across the Marshes, 2nd edition.
Adams. 1959.
11

JONES, Daniel.
Sheep farming in Romney Marsh in the 18th century: transcipt
of a letter written in 1786...
Wye College. 1956.
3,11

KAYE-SMITH, Sheila.
Joanna Godden. Uniform edition. (Novel set in Romney Marsh).
Cassell. 1923.
11

KENTISH EXPRESS.
Guide and directory to Ashford, Romney Marsh, Tenterden and
district...
Ashford, Kentish Express. 1911.
1

KING, Harriet Eleanor Hamilton.
Songs of Romney Marsh.
1908.
8

KLASEN, Jurgen.
Vergleichende Landschaftskunde der Englischen
Marschen (pages 30-129 - Romney Marsh). (Kolner
geographischen arbeiten, 19).
Cologne University. 1967.
21

Laws and customs of Romney Marsh...
Routledge. 1840.
1,12

Laws of sewers...to which are added the laws relating
to Romney Marsh.
Printed by E. and R. Nott. 1726, Revised edition 1732.
11(and 2nd edition) 12

MURRAY, Walter John Campbell.
Romney Marsh.
Hale. 1953.
1,2,3,4,5,6,7,8,11(1953 and 1970) 12,18,21

MURRAY, Walter John Campbell.
Romney Marsh, 2nd edition.
Hale. 1972.
11

PARKES, Mrs. Hadden.
Ermengarde: a story of Romney Marsh.
Elliott Stock. 1893.
1,3,6,7,11

Particulars...of a portion of the Carter Estate,
including Jacques Court, Lydd; Brookland Court Lodge;
Horton Green Farm; Old House Land and Woodlands;
Orlestone and Ruckinge and various...parcels of...
land...in...Romney Marsh.
(A.J. Burrows). 1907.
7

Particulars...of sale of...freehold property situate in
the parishes of Eastbridge, Orgarswick, Bornington and
Kingsnorth, comprising four excellent farms, building
land and...a modern residence near Dymchurch, the whole
embracing an area of about 635 acres...to sell by auction
...on...22nd June, 1926...(by direction of J.W.
Pickering Esq.).
W. and B. Hobbs. 1926.
7

Particulars...of sale of the Romney Marsh and uplands
estate of 2,630 acres, comprising in Romney Marsh, 1,400
...in the parishes of West Hythe, Burmarsh, Dymchurch,
St. Mary's, Ivychurch, Snave, Brenzett, Brookland and
Newchurch. The Manor of Aldington. The upland estate
of 700 acres containing in 7...farms and holdings in
Hawkinge, Newington, Lyminge and Elham, 105 acres
in Sellinge, 405 acres...in Stowting and Elmstead.
12 acres in Ashford and valuable cottage property in
...Ashford and Lyminge.
(H.F. Finn-Kelcey). 1928.
7

PIPER, John.
Romney Marsh.
Penguin Books. 1950.
1,2,3,4,7,8,11,12,15,18,19,20,21

ROMNEY MARSH RURAL DISTRICT COUNCIL.
Official guide to Romney Marsh (by Anne Roper).
London, Century Press.
1(1948 etc.)
3(1954)
4(1959 etc.)
6(1954, 1963, 1967)
7(1948)
8(1954 etc.)
11(1948 etc.)
12(1948 etc.)
19(1962)

ROPER, Anne.
Gift of the sea: a guide to Romney Marsh.
Ashford, Redmans. 1952?
1,2,4,7,11

A guide to Romney Marsh, 8th edition.
Ashford, Redmans. 1970.
11

Little guide to the church of St. Mary-in-the-Marsh.
Ashford, Geering. 1934.
11

St, Mary-in-the-Marsh.
Privately Printed. 1929.
7,11

SMITH, R.D.
Poems on Romney Marsh.
Printed by Lydd Printing Co. 1972.
11

TEICHMAN-DERVILLE, Max.
The level and the liberty of Romney Marsh in the County of Kent.
Ashford, Headley Bros. 1936.
1,2,3,4,6,7,8,10,11,12,13,15,17,18,21

THORNDIKE, Russell.
Children of the garter: (Novel set in Romney Marsh).
Rich and Cowan. 1937.
12

TOWN AND COUNTRY PLANNING, Ministry of.
Social survey of Romney Marsh.
H.M.S.O. 1948.
12

ROTHER, RIVER

A description of the ancient vessel recently found under an old branch of the River Rother in Kent.
Mason. 1823.
3,11,12,17

GOODSALL, Robert Harold.
Arun and the Western Rother.
Constable. 1962.
3,8,10,12

GOODSALL, Robert Harold.
The Eastern Rother.
Constable. 1961.
1,3,4,5,7,8,10,11,12,15,17,19

Headley's guide to the Rother Valley.
Ashford, Headley Bros. 1911.
1

RICE, William McPherson.
An account of an ancient vessel recently found under an old bed of the River Rother in Kent: in a letter from W.M.R... addressed to Henry Ellis, F.R.S., Secretary. (Appears to be from the Transactions of the Royal Society, 1822).
11,12

ROTHERHITHE

WALKER, Eric Henry.
A short history of the parishes of St. Katharine and St. Barnabas, Rotherhithe.
Church Publishers. 1962.
12

ROUGH COMMON

ROUGH COMMON WOMEN'S INSTITUTE.
Rough Common Village Scrapbook.
1965.
3

RUCKINGE

MURIEL, E.M.
Ruckinge Church. (Reprinted from Archaeologia Cantiana, Vol. 13, 1880).
Mitchell and Hughes. 1880.
1,11,17

RUSTHALL

An abstract of Manor of Rusthall.
Strange. 1809.
19

Rusthall Manor (map) with names of freehold tenants.
1833.
19

Rusthall Parish Magazine, January 1919-December, 1923.
19

St. Paul's Church, Rusthall - centenary, 1850-1950.
19

SMITH, Rev. B.F.
Addresses...on his leaving St. Paul's, Rusthall.
Tunbridge Wells, Stidolph. 1874.
19

SMITH, Rev. B.F.
Farewell sermons addressed to the congregation of St. Paul's, Rusthall...1874.
Tunbridge Wells, Stidolph. 1874.
19

RUXLEY

ELLISTON-ERWOOD, Frank Charles.
History of the parish church of St. Botolph, Ruxley, Kent.
1916.
17

TRADE AND INDUSTRY, Department of. - ACCIDENTS INVESTIGATION BRANCH.
Piper PA28 Cherokee...Report on the accident at Ruxley, Kent - 30th August, 1970.
H.M.S.O. 1971.
2

RYARSH

HODGSON, J.
A sermon preached at Ryarsh Church, 8th October, 1832...
Sittingbourne, Coulter. n.d.
11

ST. CLERE'S

IRELAND, William Henry.
Extracts from "The history of the County of Kent - Yaldham, St. Clere's and Shipbourne".
1886?
11

ST. LAURENCE-IN-THANET

C., C.C.
The story of St. Laurence Church in the Isle of Thanet.
(Margate). n.d.
13

COTTON, Charles.
The history and antiquities of the church and parish of St. Laurence, Thanet.
Simpkin Marshall. 1895.
1,3,4,11,12,13,14,15,17

ST. MARGARET'S-AT-CLIFFE

ELLIOTT, J.G.
The story of the church of St. Margaret-at-Cliffe, compiled by J.G. Elliott and others.
Dover, Giraud. 1960.
11

JONES, John Bavington.
St. Margaret's-at-Cliffe visitor's guide.
n.d.
11

LEWIS, T. Hayter.
Archaeological notes on Sandown, Sandgate and Richborough Castle, St. Margaret's-at-Cliffe... etc., by T.H. Lewis and others.
c.1883.
6

LUCEY, Rev. E.C.
St. Margaret's-at-Cliffe, Kent. (From the Proceedings of the British Archaeological Association, 1884).
7

ST. MARGARET'S BAY

KNOX, Cecil.
St. Margaret's Bay and the Roman roads from Richborough to Dover and Canterbury. (Reprinted from Archaeologia Cantiana, Vol. LIV, 1943).
3,17

STONE, J. Harris.
The Piccadilly of the sea: St. Margaret's Bay.
Central Publishing Co. 1910.
6,7,11,13

STONE, J. Harris.
The Piccadilly of the sea: St. Margaret's Bay.
(Reprinted edition).
Dover, Printed by D. Weaver. (197-?).
6,11

ST. MARY CRAY

COOTE, Jeanne.
History of...St. Mary Cray (unpublished thesis).
(1957).
2

GALER, Ralph Fry. (Also known as GALER, Ray F.).
Fantasies of St. Mary Cray.
Bromley, Kentish District Times. 1946.
1,2,11

Historical sketches of St. Mary Cray.
Bromley, Kentish District Times. 1948.
1

Romances of St. Mary Cray.
Bromley, Kentish District Times. 1947.
1,2,11

Traveller's joy in St. Mary Cray.
Bromley, Kentish District Times. 1950.
1,2

KENT COUNTY COUNCIL - ARCHIVES OFFICE.
St. Mary Cray parish records.
Kent County Council. 1966.
2

MARCHAM, Patricia.
Aspects of the history of the parishes of Orpington and
St. Mary Cray. (Photocopy of study for Diploma of
Education).
1967.
2

O'SULLIVAN, Maureen.
The parishes of Orpington and St. Mary Cray...population
and educational facilities. (Photocopy of thesis for
Technical Teacher's Training Certificate).
1966.
2

TESTER, M.
St. Mary Cray survey - High Street, The Rookery. (Typescript).
1965.
2

WILLOUGHBY, W.F.
Historical notes of St. Mary Cray and St. Paulinus Cray
churches and parishes.
Church Publishers. (1964).
2

ST. MARY'S BAY

DYMCHURCH AND DISTRICT CHAMBER OF TRADE.
Dymchurch and St. Mary's Bay.
Adams. 1954.
15

ST. NICHOLAS-AT-WADE

CLARKE, Joseph.
The church of St. Nicholas-at-Wade.
Mitchell and Hughes. 1878.
11

Exhibition of Great Grandmama's Home: a catalogue.
Printed by the St. Nicholas-at-Wade Parish Church Magazine
Committee. (196-?).
11

GRANT, R. Parkin.
A short account of the rise and progress of Wesleyan
Methodism in the village of St. Nicholas, forming a souvenir
of centenary celebrations, 1822-1922.
Canterbury, Printed by J. Goulden. 1922.
11,13

PARKER, Richard.
The schools of St. Nicholas-at-Wade, 1640-1957.
Canterbury, Gibbs and Sons. 1957.
3,6,7,11

St. Nicholas Church: a pilgrim's guide to the parish church
of St. Nicholas-at-Wade with Sarre...
1957.
11

A short guide to the parish church of St. Nicholas-at-Wade,
Thanet.
1932.
13

ST. PAUL'S CRAY

CHISLEHURST AND ST. PAUL'S CRAY COMMONS CONSERVATORS.
Chislehurst and St. Paul's Cray Commons.
Chislehurst and St. Paul's Cray Commons Conservators.
1970.
2,4,11

GREAT BRITAIN: LAWS, etc. (VIC.).
Metropolitan Commons (Chislehurst and St. Paul's Cray)
Supplementary Act, 1888.
2

HEALES, Alfred.
St. Paul's Cray Church. In Archaeologia Cantiana,
Vol. 18, 1889.
17

KENT COUNTY COUNCIL - ARCHIVES OFFICE.
St. Paul's Cray parish records.
Kent County Council. (196-?).
2

SHEARS, William Sydney.
William Nash of St. Paul's Cray - papermakers.
Batchworth Press. 1950.
1,2,11

(WILLOUGHBY, W.F.).
Historical notes of St. Mary Cray and St. Paulinus
Cray Churches and Parishes.
Church Publishers. (1964).
2

ST. THOMAS A BECKETT

ABBOTT, Edwin A.
St. Thomas of Canterbury (2 vols.).
Black. 1898.
1,3,11,12,17

SALTWOOD

Brockhill Park...a catalogue of the contents of the
residence...which will be sold by auction by Messrs.
Cobay Bros...on October 14th, 1903 and the following
day...by direction of the executors of the late
W. Tournay Tournay.
Cobay Bros. 1903.
7

Brockhill Park...a catalogue of about 2,000 volumes of
books which will be sold by auction by Messrs.
Cobay Bros...on the premises, on Thursday, October
15th, 1903 (by direction of the executors of the late
W. Tournay Tournay).
Cobay Bros. 1903.
7

DALE, Herbert Dixon.
History of the parish church of St. Peter and St. Paul,
Saltwood, Hythe, Revised edition. In Saltwood Parish
Church Historical Notes.
Kent Messenger. 1962.
3,7,11

ENTERPRISE, Harvy.
Historical traces of Saltwood Castle.
Boulogne, LeRoy-Mabille. 1840.
10

MURRAY, A.H. Hallam.
Saltwood Castle...
Privately Printed. 1913.
7,10

PAINE, W.S. Publisher.
History of Saltwood Castle and surrounding district:
from Anglo-Saxon times to the present day.
Hythe, W.S. Paine. c.1910.
7,11

Particulars, with plan, views and conditions of sale
of the freehold residential property known as Saltwood
Castle near Hythe...to be offered for sale by auction
by Messrs. Knight, Frank and Rutley...on Thursday,
23rd July, 1925.
Knight, Frank and Rutley. 1925.
7

Saltwood Castle: from notes supplied by a member of
the Deedes family.
1913.
13

Saltwood Castle near Hythe, Kent. Catalogue of the
valuable contents comprising furniture and furnishings of
the 16th, 17th and 18th centuries...which will be sold by
auction by Messrs. Hatch and Waterman...on Tuesday, 8th
October (1953) and three following days.
Hatch and Waterman. 1953.
7

SLYTHE, Margaret.
The library of Saltwood Castle, included in "Kent News Letter",
Vol. 13, No. 6, December, 1962.
3

VILLIERS, Oliver G.
Further historical facts on the parish church of St. Peter
and St. Paul, Saltwood, Hythe, Kent, compiled by O.G.
Villiers. In Saltwood Parish Church Historical Notes.
Kent Messenger. 1962.
7,11

(VILLIERS, Oliver G.).
Saltwood Parish Church: historical notes, with illustrations.
Kent Messenger. 1962.
1,2,3,4,6,8,11,12

VILLIERS, Oliver G.
Saltwood Parish Church: one thousand years of history, edited
by O.G. Villiers.
Kent Messenger. 1966.
7

WILLCOCKS, F.
Saltwood...some notes of its history, edited by F. Willcocks.
Hythe, Lovick. 1906.
1,7,11,17

SANDGATE

Album of Folkestone, Sandgate and Hythe views.
Charles, Reynolds. n.d.
1

BENNETT-GOLDNEY, Francis.
The first arrivals of wounded at Folkestone Pier and the
early importance and development of the Bevan Military
Hospital at Sandgate.
Bevan Military Hospital. 1917?
3,7

BLACKWELL, Thomas E.
Report...on the drainage and water supply of Sandgate, in
connection with the late outbreak of cholera in that town.
Hansard. 1855.
7

BLAKE, J.F.
The landslip at Sandgate. In "Nature", 16th March, 1893.
7

CHAPLIN, Winifred M.
Sandgate.
Sandgate Society. 1920.
4,6,7(1965).

DAVEY, Peter.
Notes on the theatrical history of Sandgate and Hythe.
(Photostat of 26 sheets).
n.d.
7

ENGLISH, John. Publisher.
Illustrated penny guide to Folkestone, Sandgate and Hythe.
J. English. 1900.
7

Illustrated penny guide to Folkestone, Sandgate and Hythe.
J. English. 1904.
7

Pictorial guide to Folkestone, Hythe and Sandgate and
neighbourhood.
J. English. n.d.
10

F(YNMORE), P.J.
Sandgate Castle, 1539-1950.
(1951).
7

GANE, Francis A.
Sandgate illustrated, compiled by F.A. Gane.
1911.
7

GIBSON, A.H.
The parish church of St. Paul, Sandgate.
Sandgate Parish Magazine. 1969.
12

HEYWOOD, John. Publisher.
Illustrated guide to Folkestone, Hythe and
Sandgate.
J. Heywood.
7(1891, 1912, 1925) 11(1891)

Hythe and Sandgate guide, embellished with a new
panorama picturesque plan...
n.d.
1,7,11

Hythe, Sandgate and Folkestone guide, containing an
account of their ancient and present state...
Hythe, Tiffin. 1816.
7,11

The inhabitants, ratepayers of Sandgate, are requested
to attend at the National School on Friday, 20th
August, 1841...to consider the capability of lighting
the village with gas (Broadsheet).
Hythe, Tiffin. 1841.
11

LANE, GENTRY AND CO. Publishers.
The holiday handbook to Folkestone, Sandgate and
district...
Margate, Lane, Gentry and Co. c.1930.
7

LEE, W. Publisher.
Hythe and Sandgate guide.
W. Lee. c.1806-10.
7

LEWIS, T. Hayter.
Archaeological notes on Sandown, Sandgate and
Richborough Castle, St. Margaret's-at-Cliffe, etc.,
by T.H. Lewis and others.
c.1883.
6

MOSELEY, George.
Sandgate as a residence for invalids.
Sandgate, Purday. 1853.
6,7,11

Particulars and conditions of sale of the Alfred
Bevan Memorial Convalescent House...which will be
sold by auction...on...28th July, 1908.
Farebrother, Ellis and Co. 1908.
7

Particulars...of sale of a...freehold marine property
called Encombe, Sandgate...which will be offered for
sale by auction...on 9th August, 1883. (By order of
the executors of James Morris, Esq., deceased).
Farebrother, Ellis, Clark and Co. 1883.
7

Particulars...of sale of a number of valuable
residential, building, accommodation and house
properties, comprising the...Mansion known as Enbrook
...and Shorncliffe Lodge...the whole estate...82 acres.
Messrs Walton and Lee will offer...for sale...on 27th
September, 1912.
Messrs. Walton and Lee. 1912.
7

Particulars...of sale of the...modern residence
"Castle Close" including in its grounds Sandgate
Castle...for sale by auction by Messrs. Knight, Frank
and Rutley on 18th June, 1936.
Messrs. Knight, Frank and Rutley. 1936.
7

Particulars...of sale of the modern detached freehold
marine residence "Castle Close" and including Sandgate
Castle. To be offered for sale...by Messrs. Temple
Barton Ltd., on 10th November, 1954.
Messrs. Temple Barton. 1954.
7

ROYAL INSTITUTE OF PUBLIC HEALTH.
Guide to Folkestone, Sandgate, Hythe and neighbourhood.
Royal Institute of Public Health, Congress at Folkestone,
1904.
J. English. 1904.
7

RUTTON, W.L.
Sandgate Castle, 1539-1894.
1894.
1,3,6,7,11,13,17

SANDGATE URBAN DISTRICT COUNCIL vs KENT COUNTY COUNCIL.
In the House of Lords, an appeal from Her Majesty's Court
of Appeal (England), between the Urban District Council of
Sandgate, appellants, and the County Council of Kent,
respondents.
Matthews, Drew. (1898).
12

Sandgate: a new guide to Sandgate, Folkestone and Hythe.
n.d.
11

Sandgate: a poem.
Edward Churton, Holles Street, London. 1847.
7,12,13,17

Sandgate, Hythe and Folkestone guide.
Hythe, Tiffen. Folkestone, Boxer. Sandgate, Purday and Son.
1823.
6

STACE, R. Publisher.
A guide to Sandgate, Shorncliffe, Folkestone and the
neighbourhood, with historical, geological and botanical notes.
R. Stace. c.1860.
7

An illustrated guide to Sandgate, Folkestone, Hythe and the
neighbourhood, with historical, typographical (sic),
geological and botanical notices, with six illustrations,
a map of the walks and rides.
R. Stace. c.1865.
7

Stace's Sandgate, Hythe and Shorncliffe illustrated historical
almanack for 1871 and 1872.
R. Stace.
7

Sandgate and Shorncliffe illustrated almanack and guide for
1878, 1882 and 1886.
R. Stace.
7

Sandgate and Shorncliffe illustrated guide for the year 1873...
R. Stace.
7

WILSON, W. Publisher.
Guide to Sandgate, Shorncliffe and Hythe.
Sandgate, Wilson. 1889.
7,11

WILSON, W. Publisher.
Wilson's illustrated almanack and guide to Sandgate, Shorncliffe
and Hythe, with an account of the walks and drives of the
neighbourhood.
W. Wilson. 1894.
7

SANDHURST

The circular letter from the Elders, Ministers and Messengers
of the Baptist Churches assembled at Sandhurst in Kent...1784.
11

CLARK, F.C.
Articles relating to Sandhurst and Newenden appearing in the
Sandhurst with Newenden Monthly Magazine, 1956-57.
3

Parish Church of St. Nicholas, Sandhurst.
n.d.
11

SANDOWN

LEWIS, T. Hayter.
Archaeological notes on Sandown, Sandgate and Richborough
Castles, St. Margaret's-at-Cliffe...etc...,by T.H. Lewis
and others.
c.1883.
6

REDMAN, J.B.
Report on Sandown Castle.
War Office. 1857.
11

SANDWICH

ANDERSON, Arthur Henry.
Sandwich.
Homeland Association. 1907.
7,11,13,15

ANDERSON, Mason.
Self-defence: a letter to the Rev. William Wodsworth
occasioned by his late attack on Dissenters.
Sandwich, Cocking. 1820.
11

AUSTEN, B.
Gates of the Cinque Port and Borough of Sandwich, past
and present.
1892?
3,6,11,12,14

BAKER, Oscar.
History of the antiquities of Sandwich and Richborough
Castles in Kent.
Savill and Edwards. 1848.
6,7,11,12,13,16,17

BENTWICH, Hel
History of Sa   ch in Kent.
T.F. Pain. 197 .
3,8,11

BENTWICH, Helen C.
History of Sandwich in Kent, 2nd edition.
T.F. Pain. 1972.
4

BOUNDARY COMMISSION.
Report on the town and port of Sandwich.
H.M.S.O. 1831.
12

BOYS, Edward.
Remarks, etc., on the practicability and advantages
of a Sandwich or Downs Harbour.
Sandwich, Giraud. 1832.
7,11,13

BOYS, William.
Collections for an history of Sandwich...and of
Richborough.
Canterbury. 1792.
3,6,7,8,11,12,13,14,15,17

BOYS, William.
Collection of the minute and rare shells lately
discovered...near Sandwich.
c.1790.
6,11,13

BRITISH ARCHAEOLOGICAL ASSOCIATION.
92nd congress to be held in East Kent, 24th June-
29th June, 1935 at Sandwich (programme).
6

BULMER, Thomas Ivor.
St. Mary's, Sandwich in the Middle Ages. In
Transactions of the Ancient Monuments Society,
New Series, Vol. 7, 1959.
2,3,4,11

BULTEEL, John.
A relation of the troubles of the three forraign
churches in Kent caused by the injunction of William
Laud, Archbishop of Canterbury. (Wallons
in Canterbury, Dutch in Sandwich and Maidstone).
Enderbie. 1645.
12

CARTER, George Goldsmith.
Forgotten ports of England. (Including Sandwich,
Reculver and Romney Marsh).
Evans. (1951).
3,4,6,8,12,15

CAVELL, John.
History of Sir Roger Manwood's School, Sandwich,
1563-1963, by J. Cavell and B. Kennett.
Cory, Adams and Mackay. 1963.
3,6,7,8,11,15

DAY, B.W.
A short history of St. Peter's, Sandwich.
T.F. Pain. n.d.
1,3

Deal, Walmer and Sandwich: their attractions as sea-side and holiday resorts.
n.d.
11

Deal, Walmer and Sandwich illustrated.
Gravesend, Rochard. n.d.
11

DE GOLS, Gerard.
Consolations against the fears of death: sermon preached on Sunday, November 4th, 1711 at St. Peter's, Sandwich.
11

DE GOLS, Gerard.
The terrors of God's judgments: a sermon preached at St. Peter's at Sandwich on 21st February, 1713.
R. Smith. 1714.
11

DEVIS, James.
The principles of the Church of Rome exploded...(sermon).
Silver. 1756.
11

Dover, Canterbury, Deal, Walmer and Sandwich by camera and pen, 1904-05.
Brighton, W.T. Pike.
6

Dover, Deal, Canterbury, Sandwich and Walmer.
Brighton, W.T. Pike. n.d.
11

EDWARDS, David Lawrence.
F.J. Shirley: an extraordinary headmaster.
S.P.C.K. 1969.
6

EMMERSON, Richard. Junior.
A few observations on the impropriety of admitting the non-resident seamen of Sandwich to have a vote...
1816.
11

GARDINER, Mrs. Dorothy.
Historic Haven: the story of Sandwich.
Derby, Pilgrim Press. 1952.
1,2,3,4,6,7,8,11,12,13,14,17,18,20

GORDON, W.J.
Sandwich and round about it.
Botolph Printing Works. n.d.
1,7,11,12,13

GORDON, Major William.
Trial of Major William Gordon of 2nd, or Queen's Regiment, of Dragoon Guards...at Guildhall, Sandwich on Friday, April 15th, 1814.
Canterbury, Rouse, Kirby and Lawrence. n.d.
3

GRAY, George.
Sandwich.
Homeland Association. 1907.
1,2,7,8,11,12,13,14,15,17,18

GREAT BRITAIN: LAWS, etc. (GEO. II).
An Act for enlarging and maintaining the Harbour of Ramsgate... and preserving the Haven of Sandwich.
1749.
11,14

GREAT BRITAIN: LAWS, etc. (GEO. III).
An Act for the better repairing...the highways...in the town and port of Sandwich...1787.
11

HAMILTON, J. Vesey.
A sermon preached on August 24th, 1833 at St. Bartholomew's Hospital, Sandwich.
Sandwich, Giraud. 1833.
11

HATTON, James.
The old house at Sandwich.
New York, Phoenix. 1892.
11

HEWITT, J.
Knightly effigies at Sandwich and Ash. (From Archaeological Journal, 1851).
12

History of Sandwich and Richborough Castles.
Sandwich, H. Baker. n.d.
1,11

HUTT, Charles H.
Church of St. Mary, Sandwich: a short guide.
Sandwich, Chapman. n.d.
1,3,13

LEWIS, John.
Dissertation on the antiquities of Richborough and Sandwich.
Royal Society of Antiquaries. 1744.
11

LEWIS, John.
A little dissertation on...Richborough and Sandwich.
Bell. 1851.
11

Lists of inhabitants and autographs of Town Clerks, Mayors and incumbents of Sandwich.
n.d.
12

LOVERING, J. Publisher.
The Guildhall, Sandwich.
n.d.
11

LOVERING, J. Publisher.
A souvenir of Sandwich.
London, Lovering and Co. (1907).
3,6

MACMEIKAN, John A.
Sandwich and the Old House.
Snowden Bros. n.d.
3,12

Minerva Railway Guide and Visitor's Handbook for Deal, Walmer, Sandwich and district.
1906.
17

New handbook to the Downs neighbourhood...Deal, Walmer, Sandwich...
Deal, Hayward. 18--?
1,11,14

PAYNE, Orlebar D. Bruce.
Church of St. Clement, Sandwich.
Sandwich, T.F. Pain. 1925.
1,3,7,8,11,13

PEMBLE, Henry.
Letter to the Rev. Dr. Wiseman in reply to his Roman Catholic lectures.
Rivington. 1836.
11

PETTMAN, William Robert.
Considerations on the right of admitting the non-resident seamen...of Sandwich to have a vote...
1817.
11

PETTMAN, William Robert.
Letter addressed to the freemen of the town and port of Sandwich...relative to an intended application to Parliament for the purpose of reducing the tolls of Sandwich Bridge.
1807.
11,17

The Port of Sandwich.
1920.
6,13

Report of the trial which took place at the General Sessions of the town and port of Sandwich, held on the 28th day of August...1817.
Ramsgate, Wood. 1817.
11

SANDWICH Cont'd

RIGOLD, S.E.
Two Kentish Carmelite houses - Aylesford and Sandwich.
Ashford, Headley Bros. 1965.
11

ROBINSON, A.W.H.
Coastal evolution in Sandwich Bay. (From Proceedings of the
Geologists' Association, Vol. 64, Part 2, 27th June, 1953).
Benham. 1953.
11

ROGER, John Lewis.
Sketches of Deal, Walmer and Sandwich.
Longmans. 1911.
1,3,4,6,11,12,15,17,18

St. Peter's Church. (Printed extracts from Sandwich, St. Peter's
Parish Magazine). Transcribed by the late H.N. Nowell M.A.,
Rector of Sandwich, 1933.
3,13

SANDWICH BOROUGH COUNCIL.
The ancient town and port of Sandwich: official guide.
Sandwich Borough Council.
1(1954)
3(1927)
4(1954)
6(1927)
7(1927, 1937)
11(1927, 1937, 1954, 1955)
13(1927, 1948)
14(1927)

SANDWICH GRAMMAR SCHOOL.
Sir Roger Manwood's endowment. (Typescript).
(1929).
12

Sandwich: the case of the inhabitants and Corporation...touching
a Bill to enable the Commissioners of Sewers...
Canterbury, Simmons and Kirkby. n.d.
11

Sandwich: a descriptive and historical guide.
n.d.
3,13

Sandwich: a descriptive and historical sketch.
Sandwich, Griffin. n.d.
1,11

Sandwich, Kent. (From unidentified directory, Vol. IV, No. 55).
n.d.
3

SCROGGS, Edith S.
A classified list of the records lodged in the Guildhall of the
town and port of Sandwich.
Printed by T.F. Pain and Sons for Sandwich Corporation. 1932.
3,6,7,13

Short guide to the church of St. Clement's, Sandwich.
Church Publishers. 1964.
1,3,8,11

Sonnets and stangas: from a correspondent's headquarters in
the Strand, Sandwich, Kent.
Deal, Giraud. 1872.
11

STEBBING, W.P.D.
House of the White Friars, Sandwich, A.D. 1272. (Reprinted from
Archaeologia Cantiana, Vol. 48, 1937).
Ashford, Headley Bros. n.d.
1,11

THOMASON, D.R.
Self vindication: an address...
Sandwich, Cocking. 1828?
11

SARRE

BRENT, John. *Junior*.
Account of the (Kent Archaeological) Society's researches
in the Anglo-Saxon cemetery at Sarre. In Archaeologia
Cantiana, Vols. 5,6 and 7, 1862-68.
17

LEAVER, E.B.
Sarre and the Wantsum Channel.
1939.
3

SARRE, A.C.
Sarre: Thanet, Kent/Channel Islands - a treatise on
the name and the place. (Typescript).
1956.
3

SEAL

BROWNLOW, Margaret Eileen.
The delights of herb-growing.
Seal, Herb Farm. 1965.
1,4,11,12,19

BROWNLOW, Margaret Eileen.
Herbs and the fragrant garden.
Seal, Herb Farm. 1957.
12,15,16

Historic notes of St. Peter's and St. Paul's Church,
Seal.
n.d.
12

STAGG, Frank Noel.
Parish of St. Lawrence, Seal: historical notes.
(Typescript).
1946.
11

STAGG, Frank Noel.
Some historical notes on the present ecclesiastical
parish of Seal. (Typescript).
1947.
11,16

SEASALTER

GOODSALL, Robert Harold.
Whitstable, Seasalter and Swalecliffe.
Canterbury, Cross and Jackman. 1938.
1,2,3,4,5,6,8,11,12,13,15,20

LUGARD, Cecil E.
Communicants at Seasalter, Kent, 1615-1710, edited by
C.E. Lugard.
Ashover, Derbyshire; Lugard. 1929.
3,11,12

Seasalter: borough, manor and parish, edited by C.E.
Lugard.
Whitstable, Elvy. n.d.
11

The sess of Seasalter, 1653-1678, with index; 1704-1745,
with index and 1821, compiled by C.E. Lugard.
Ashover, Derbyshire; Lugard. 1930.
3,11

Old Seasalter Church: a pamphlet and a print.
n.d.
13

SELLINDGE

PETTY, Ronald.
History of the church of St. Mary-the-Virgin, Sellindge.
Canterbury, Cross and Jackman. 1951.
11

Short history of the parish church of St. Mary.
Sellindge. 1935.
11

ABBOTT, W.J. Lewis.
Three papers: The Hastings Kitchen Middens - notes on a
remarkable barrow at Sevenoaks; notes on some specialized
and diminutive forms of flint implements from Hastings
Kitchen Midden and Sevenoaks.
London, Harrison and Sons. 1895.
5

BAKER, F.A.
Story of Sundridge Old Hall (Sevenoaks).
Tinsley. n.d.
11,12

BALD, R.C.
Donne and the Drurys.
Cambridge University Press. 1959.
12

BENNETT, George Charles Warner.
Guide and handbook to Sevenoaks and district.
Sevenoaks, Caxton Press. 1948.
1,2,5,11,16

BIBLIOTHECA TOPOGRAPHICA BRITANNICA.
Memoirs of William Lambarde, Esq...(Extracted from Nichols'
Bibliotheca Topographica Britannica, 1787?). Reputed to have
been written by John Randolph, Bishop of London.
1,4,8,11,12,16

BOX, Ernest George.
Sevenoaks and district archaeological notes. (MSS.).
n.d.
16

BOX, Ernest George.
Sevenoaks and the neighbouring parishes. (MSS.).
n.d.
16

BUCHANAN, Colin and Partners.
Traffic in Sevenoaks: a report to Sevenoaks Urban District
Council.
Sevenoaks Urban District Council. 1968.
2,11,12,16

"CHRISTIAN FRIEND", pseud.
A serious and affectionate address to the inhabitants of
Maidstone, Sevenoaks...occasioned by the Kent and Sussex
Unitarian Association held...7th June, 1815...
Wickham and Cutbush. 1815.
12

CLARKE, Reginald Dennis.
A brief history and guide to the church of St. John-the-Baptist,
Sevenoaks, Kent.
Printed by Longmore Press. 1970.
11,16

CLARKE, Reginald Dennis.
The medieval hospital of St. John the Baptist, Sevenoaks.
Sevenoaks Society. 1971.
16

COFFIN, Charles Monroe.
John Donne and the new philosophy. (Rector of Sevenoaks).
Routledge and Kegan Paul. 1958.
12

CORKE, C. Essenhigh.
The Sevenoaks view book.
Sevenoaks, Salmon. n.d.
11

CORKE, C. Essenhigh.
Views of Sevenoaks and neighbourhood.
Sevenoaks, Salmon. n.d.
11

CROFT-COOKE, Rupert.
The gardens of Camelot.
Putnam. 1958.
12

DINES, H.G.
Geology of the country around Sevenoaks and Tunbridge, by
H.G. Dines and others.
H.M.S.O. 1969.
7,16

DUNKEL, Wilbur.
William Lambarde, Elizabethan jurist, 1536-1601.
Rutgers University Press. 1965.
11

DUNLOP, Sir John Kinninmont.
The pleasant town of Sevenoaks.
Sevenoaks, Dunlop. 1964.
1,2,3,4,5,7,8,10,11,12,15,16,18,19

DURTNELL, C.S.
Durtnell family, 1496-1946.
12,16

History of the Durtnells. (MSS.).
n.d.
16

Sevenoaks: local notes. (MSS.).
n.d.
16

EDWARDS, Jane. (1792-1869).
Recollections and conversations of Old Sevenoaks
between Mary and her Aunt. (MSS.).
1863.
16

Endowed charities in the Sevenoaks division of Kent.
1895.
16

FENTON, Elijah.
Life of Elijah Fenton, sometime Master of Sevenoaks
School.
n.d.
16

FISHER, Joseph.
Married life: a sermon.
1695.
16

HARRISON. Publisher.
Guide to Sevenoaks and the neighbourhood.
Sevenoaks, Harrison.
11(1864 and 1873) 16(1864)

HARRISON, Jeffery G.
A gravel pit wildfowl reserve. (Bradbourne Pit,
Sevenoaks).
Wildfowlers Association. 1972.
2,16

HICKMOTT, Arthur.
Walks round Sevenoaks.
n.d.
16

HOLLAND, J.G.
The story of Sevenoaks.
Warne. 1876.
12

HOW AND SONS, SEVENOAKS.
Undertakers' note books of the firm of How and Sons,
Sevenoaks, 1837-1851.
16

HUNT, W.
Old Sennocke: pamphlet.
1885.
16

JUDD, Walter D.
The Record of Wesleyan Methodism in the Sevenoaks
Circuit, 1746-1932, compiled by W.D. Judd.
Bedford, Rush. 1932.
1,2,11,16

Kentish Polhills. (MSS.).
n.d.
16

KNIGHT, C.T.
Old Sevenoaks. (MSS.).
n.d.
16

LEAVETT, Alan.
Historic Sevenoaks: a picture book, compiled by Alan
Leavett.
Sevenoaks Society. (197-?).
11,16

LENNOX, J.T.
Sevenoaks School and its founder, 1432-1932.
Sevenoaks, Caxton Press. 1932.
1,11,12,16(Sevenoaks has MSS. and proofs also) 19

LOCK, Max.
Sevenoaks takes public into confidence on urban renewal.
(Extract from Municipal Journal, 14th August, 1959).
4

MEYERSTEIN, Edward Harry William.
Ratscastle (a Kentish interlude).
Sevenoaks, Caxton Press. 1924.
5,11

MILBOURNE, R.A.
The Gault at Greatness Lane, Sevenoaks. (From Proceedings of
the Geologists' Association).
Colchester, Benham. 1956.
11

Militia Book of Sevenoaks, 1795.
16

MUELLER, William R.
John Donne: preacher.
Princeton University Press. 1962.
12

PEAL, A.
Six days near Sevenoaks: a narrative of a balloon ascent.
1825.
16

PHILLIPS, Charles J.
The Phillips manuscripts: chronicles of Sevenoaks and district,
15 vols.
n.d.
16

PIKE, Elsie.
Story of Walthamstow Hall (Sevenoaks).
Carey Press. 1938.
11,16

The pursuit of fashion: a satire, 4th edition.
Ebers. 1812.
12

R., E.A.
The Carterets; or, country pleasures.   (A novel set near
Sevenoaks).
Ward Lock. 1862.
11

RANDS, William Brightly.
The dream of a girl at Sevenoaks.
Chappell. c.1960.
12

Reasons against large unions of parishes and the erection of
central workhouses, particularly in the neighbourhood of
Sevenoaks.
1835.
17

RICHARDS, F.
Old Sevenoaks.
Sevenoaks Chronicle. 1901.
1,2,3,4,5,6,7,8,11,12,15,16

ROOKER, John.
Notes on the parish church of St. Nicholas, Sevenoaks.
Sevenoaks, Salmon. 1910.
1,2,4,7,11,12,15,16

ROOKER, John.
Sevenoaks and the Great War.
1919.
16

RUDGE, Charles.
William Jeffery, the Puritan Apostle of Kent. (Author was once
Baptist Minister of Sevenoaks).
(190-?).
11,16

St. Nicholas Church, Sevenoaks: parish registers and register
of memorials (copies).
n.d.
16

SALMON, Joseph. Publisher.
Guide to Sevenoaks.
J. Salmon.
2(1897)
5(1905)
11(1854)
12(1897)
13(1930)
15(1897)
16(1884 and 1897)
17(1897)

SALMON, Joseph. Publisher.
Sevenoaks: sixteen views in sepia phototone.
Sevenoaks, Salmon. n.d.
1

SEALE, Florence E.
Reminiscences of Sevenoaks. (MSS.).
1930.
16

Sevenoaks almanac, 1841.
Sevenoaks, Payne.
16

SEVENOAKS AMICABLE SOCIETY.
Minute book, 1770-1844. (MSS.).
16

SEVENOAKS BOROUGH COUNCIL.
Minute book, 1576-1719. (MSS.).
16

SEVENOAKS CIVIC SOCIETY.
Sevenoaks Rural District, with district map and 16
photographs...
Century Press. 1957.
11,15

SEVENOAKS LAND TAX.
List of persons charged to Land Tax and the Militia,
1702-1705.
16

SEVENOAKS LOCAL BOARD.
Letter books, 1871-1877. (MSS.).
16

SEVENOAKS PARISH.
Income Tax and Inhabited Duties, Collector's Duplicate
of First Assessments, 1908-1910.
16

Minute book of the Parish Officers, 1820-1823.
16

Overseers' accounts, 1878-1918.
16

SEVENOAKS SCHOOL.
Ward collection of manuscripts.
n.d.
16

SEVENOAKS SOCIETY.
The historic heart of Sevenoaks.
Sevenoaks Society. 1967.
2

SEVENOAKS URBAN DISTRICT COUNCIL.
Medical Officer of Health's reports.
1906 to date.
16

SEVENOAKS URBAN DISTRICT COUNCIL.
A plan for Sevenoaks: draft town centre map.
Sevenoaks Urban District Council. 1971.
16

SMART, Kenneth John.
Sevenoaks and Vine cricket, 1731-1959.
Sevenoaks and Vine Cricket Club. (1959).
1,4,11,12,15,16

SOUTH-EASTERN RAILWAY CO.
Illustrated tourist guide...Chislehurst, Sevenoaks,
Tunbridge Wells...
Morton. n.d.
11

STYLES, E.A.
1st Sevenoaks (Hicks Own) Group Boy Scouts: the first 50
years, 1909-1959, by E.A. Styles and others.
1959.
16

TAYLOR, L.C.
Experiments in education at Sevenoaks School, by L.C. Taylor
and others.
Constable. 1965.
8,11

TRANSPORT, Ministry of.
London Traffic (Prescribed Routes) (Sevenoaks) Regulations,
1964, Nos. 1 and 2.
H.M.S.O.
8

VERHOEVEN, Jack.
Emblems of Sevenoaks: a guide to the coat-of-arms badge and
flags of the Sevenoaks Urban District Council.
Sevenoaks Urban District Council. 1971.
16

WARD, Dr. Gordon Reginald.
Bibliographia Sennockiana. (MS.).
n.d.
16

Notebooks on Sevenoaks and district. (MSS.).
n.d.
16

Sevenoaks essays.
Metcalfe and Cooper. 1931.
1,3,4,5,8,11,12,13,15,16,17,19

Short history of Suffolk House in the High Street, Sevenoaks,
from 1624-1935...(Christmas card, 1935).
11,16

WESTMINSTER BANK LTD.
The Westminster Bank, Sevenoaks: some historical notes. (MSS.).
1971.
16

SEVINGTON

The parish church of St. Mary, Sevington, welcomes you.
Peregrine Press. 1965.
12

SHADOXHURST

MILES, Harold.
The Chequers of East Kent: a typescript manuscript of a
lecture.
1961.
11

MILES, Harold.
The old book of Shadoxhurst: a brief account of the parish
of Shadoxhurst in the County of Kent, compiled by Harold
Miles. (Typescript MS.).
1960.
11

NAIRNE, Charles.
A brief account of the parish of Shadoxhurst.
1836.
11

WILKINSON, Edward.
Memorials of the Rev. Charles Rolfe, Rector of Shadoxhurst
and Orlestone.
Nisbet. 1879.
11,15

SHEERNESS

Account of the disastrous storm and flood which visited
Sheerness and the Isle of Sheppey on November 29th, 1897.
Sheerness Times. 1897.
11

ADMIRALTY.
Navy (trial of coal)...for the return of all experiments made
by the Admiralty on coal and patent fuel...(Contains reports
from Chatham and Sheerness Dockyards).
H.M.S.O. 1877.
8

ATKINSON, David A.
The explosive cargo of the USS "Richard Montgomery"...
Southend-on-Sea and District Chamber of Trade and
Industry. (1972).
11

COPLAND, John.
The taking of Sheerness by the Dutch, edited by
J. Copland.
Sheerness, Cole. 1895.
4,11

ENVIRONMENT, Department of the.
Railway accident: report on the accident that
occurred on 26th February, 1971 at Sheerness-on-Sea
in the Southern Region, British Railways.
H.M.S.O. 1972.
9

GREAT BRITAIN: LAWS, etc. (GEO. III).
An Act for making compensation...for better securing
His Majesty's docks, ships and stores at Plymouth and
Sheerness...1782.
12

GREAT BRITAIN: LAWS, etc. (GEO. III).
An Act for the purchase of certain lands...at Sheerness
and Chatham...for the use of the Navy.
1816.
4,11

GREAT BRITAIN: PARLIAMENT, BILLS.
Pier and Harbour Order (Sheerness) Confirmation Bill
(as amended by the Committee on Unopposed Bills).
H.M.S.O. 1958.
4

Guide to Sheerness-on-Sea and the Isle of Sheppey.
London, Chatham and Dover Railway Co. 1883.
11

HARBOUR, Henry.
Sheerness and the Isle of Sheppey.
Warne. n.d.
1,7,11,15

HOBBES, Robert George.
Reminiscences and notes of seventy years' life...
Stock. 1893-95.
4,11

JERROLD, Blanchard.
Life and remains of Douglas Jerrold.(First three chapters
describe Sheerness in the early 19th century).
1859.
11

LITTLE, Bryan Desmond G.
A relic from the age of sail: the Dockyard at
Sheerness.
"Country Life". 1958.
11

M., A.W.
Guide to Sheerness and the Isle of Sheppey.
Sheerness, Cole. 1870.
11

(ORDNANCE, Board of).
Plan of the present state of Sheerness with the proposed
works marked in yellow. Scale: 1 inch = 200 feet.
(Photograph of original, slightly reduced).
1780.
4

POTTER, John.
Plan of Sheerness at the mouth of the River Medway,
1725. Scale: 1 inch = 400 feet. (Photograph of
original, slightly reduced).
1725.
4

SEARS, Alfred.
James Prankard, Minister of the Bethel Independent
Chapel, Sheerness from 19th February, 1811 to 11th
January, 1838.
Sheerness, Sears. 1962.
7,11

SHEERNESS URBAN DISTRICT COUNCIL.
Official handbook to Sheerness and Isle of Sheppey.
Sheerness, S. Cole. 1906.
8

MARCH, Edgar James.
Sailing trawlers.
David and Charles. 1970.
14

Spritsail barges of Thames and Medway.
Marshall. 1948.
1,3,4,5,8,11,12,13,14,15,17

Spritsail barges of Thames and Medway, new edition.
David and Charles. 1970.
2,4,11,12

MATHEWS, R.G.
Sailing craft.
Eyre and Spottiswoode. n.d.
12

MAXWELL, Henry.
The "Canterbury" remembered.
Eyre and Spottiswoode. 1970.
6,7,11

NATIONAL MARITIME MUSEUM.
Royal yachts, compiled by G.P.B. Naish.
H.M.S.O. 1953.
4

New Channel Ferry Service - a new service inaugurated by the
Southern Railway and Chemin de Fer du Nord. (From "Railway
Gazette", 1936).
6

The New Margate Packet "Royal Sovereign". Copy of a letter from
"The Times", Thursday, June 22nd, 1815.
13

PAIN, E.C.
The last of our luggers and the men who sailed them.
Deal, T.F. Pain. 1929.
4,6,7,11,13,15

PERKS, R.H.
A history of Faversham sailing barges.
Society for Spritsail Barge Research. 1967.
2,3,4,7(1968) 8,9,11,12,18,19,20

POLLARD, Arthur O.
Ships of London River.
Model and Allied Publications. 1969.
9

ROCHE, T.W.E.
Ships of Dover, Folkestone, Deal and Thanet...
Southampton, Coles. 1959.
1,3,4,6,7,11,12,15

SOUTH-EASTERN RAILWAY CO.
Minutes of the proceedings at the christening and launch of the
"Albert Victor" steel paddle wheel steamer...
(Sainuda Bros.). 1880.
7

SOUTHERN RAILWAY.
Over the points, No. 31. (Dover-Dunkerque ferry service).
1936.
6

The splendid and romantic history of the Kent barge...
(From "Kent Messenger", 31st December, 1954).
3

THORNTON, Edward Charles Bexley.
South coast pleasure steamers.
Stephenson and Sons. 1962.
12,19(1969)

THORNTON, Edward Charles Bexley.
Thames coast pleasure steamers.
Stephenson and Sons. 1972.
9

THURSTON, Gavin.
The great Thames disaster. (The sinking of the "Princess Alice").
Allen and Unwin. 1965.
1,5

WILSON, Maurice.
Coastal craft.
Noel Carrington. 1947.
4

WOOD, Walter.
Fishing boats and barges from the Thames to Land's
End.
Bodley Head. 1922.
4

SHOLDEN

LAWREY, John.
Notes on the history of the parish of Sholden...
Deal, T.F. Pain. 1946.
3,6,7,11

STEBBING, W.P.D.
A sketch of the history of the parish of Sholden,
Kent...
Deal, Manor Press. 1951.
1,7,11

SHOOTER'S HILL

ADAMS, J.W.
Sevendroog Castle (pamphlet).
n.d.
17

ADDISON, William.
English spas.
Batsford. 1951.
3

ELLISTON-ERWOOD, Frank Charles.
Discoveries on the line of Watling Street at Shooter's
Hill.
n.d.
17

ELLISTON-ERWOOD, Frank Charles.
Road works at Shooter's Hill, Kent, 1816.
Woodwich Antiquarian Society. 1947.
1,8,11,12,18

Fifty years of the parish of Shooter's Hill, 1856-1906.
7

Shooter's Hill Castle...the capture, A.D. 1755 of
Sevendroog...by Commodore James...resident at Eltham
in Kent...
1849.
18

SHOREHAM

Assessment to a subsidy granted to Charles I, 1628.
n.d.
16

DENCE, Thomas.
Reminiscences of a septuagenarian.
Causton. 1911.
12

DUNCAN, Leland Lewis.
Ecclesio-logical notes respecting the Deanery of
Shoreham, Kent. In Archaeologia Cantiana, Vol. 23,
1898.
17,18

DUNSANY, Edward J.M.D.P.
Patches of sunlight.
Heinemann. 1938.
8

GLIDDON, Paul.
St. Peter and St. Paul, Shoreham, Kent.
Sevenoaks, Caxton Press. n.d.
2,11,12

LISTER, Raymond.
Samuel Palmer and his etchings.
Faber. 1969.
12

PAYNE, Augustus.
A history of the parish church of St. Peter and
St. Paul, Shoreham.
A. Payne. 1930.
2,5,12,16

PEACOCK, Carlos.
Samuel Palmer: Shoreham and after.
John Baker. 1968.
12

STOYEL, A.D.
Discoveries at the parish church of St. Peter and St. Paul, Shoreham. (MS.).
n.d.
16

Tithe Apportionment, 1843 (original).
16

Valuation list of Shoreham, 1835.
16

SHORNE

ARNOLD, George A.
The ruined chapel of St. Katherine at Shorne, Kent. (Reprinted from Archaeologia Cantiana).
Kent Archaeological Society. 1892.
9,17

Church of St. Peter and St. Paul, Shorne.
Shorne History Group. 195-?
11,12

LIVETT, Grevile Maius.
Architectural notes on the churches of Northfleet, Shorne and Gotham.
n.d.
5

SHORTLANDS

DUFFIELD, F.H.
The story of St. Mary's, Shortlands, by F.H. Duffield and H.T. Knight.
Bromley, Kent District Times. 1926.
2,4,6,11,18

CROYDON NATURAL HISTORY AND SCIENTIFIC SOCIETY.
Regional survey atlas of Croydon and district. (Survey area includes Beckenham, Penge, Shortlands, West Wickham).
Croydon Natural History and Scientifwc Society. 1936 in progress.
2

The parish church of St. Mary, Shortlands, Kent: a short history.
1965.
2,4,12

SUGDEN, A.N.B.
The parish church of St. Mary, Shortlands, Kent: a short history, revised edition.
1967.
4

SIBERTSWOLD (SHEPHERDS WELL)

MORECROFT, Mrs. E.G.
A guide to St. Adnrew's Church, Sibertswold.
Shepherdswell Parish Council. 1964.
1,4,6,7,8,11

SIDCUP

CHISLEHURST URBAN DISTRICT COUNCIL.
Chislehurst and Sidcup: official guide.
Cheltenham, E.J. Burrows. 1954 etc.
1,2(1951-59) 4,5,11

DUNKIN, Alfred John.
Account of St. John's Church, Sidcup. (Taken from J. Dunkin's "History of Dartford").
n.d.
1,11

SINGLEWELL

FFINCH, Kenneth Maule.
The history of Ifield and Singlewell, revised and edited by Robert Heath Hiscock.
Chatham, Mackay. 1957.
4,9

SISSINGHURST

BAKER, Frank Vidler.
Notes on the life of Sir John Baker of Sissinghurst, compiled by F.V. Baker.
Mitchell, Hughes and Clarke. 1926.
11,17

NICOLSON, Sir Harold.
Diaries and letters, 1939-45, edited by Nigel Nicolson.
Collins. 1967-68.
12

(NICOLSON, Nigel).
Sissinghurst Castle: an illustrated guide.
Sidney Press, Printers. 1964.
2,4,11,19

NICOLSON, Nigel.
Sissinghurst Castle: an illustrated history.
Printed by Headley Bros., Ashford for Sissinghurst Castle. 1964.
11

PILE, Cecil Charles Relf.
The parish farm at Sissinghurst Castle.
Cranbrook Local History Society. 1952.
1,4,7,8,11,19

SACKVILLE-WEST, Victoria.
Sissinghurst.
Hogarth Press. 1933.
11,12

Short account of Sissinghurst Castle.
Tunbridge Wells, Stanford. 1959.
7,11,12,17

Sissinghurst Castle.
Edinburgh, R. and R. Clarke. n.d.
3

SITTINGBOURNE

BENNETTS, Rev. H.J.T.
Moll of Sittingbourne: a story of the days of Richard Rolle, the Saintly hermit of Hampole.
London, Faith Press. (19--?).
4

BOROUGH DIRECTORIES LTD.
Business and residential directory for Faversham and Sittingbourne.
Borough Directories Ltd.
1963(4,7,8)
1965(20)
1966(4,8,12,19)

Coulter's country miscellany and literary selector, January, February, April-July, 1832.
Sittingbourne, J.E. Coulter.
11

ELAND, G.
Shardeloes papers of the 17th and 18th centuries, edited by G. Eland. (The documents are owned by, and concern, the Drake family, who owned an estate near Sittingbourne in the 18th century).
Cumberledge. 1947.
4,18

GRAYLING, Francis.
Story of Sittingbourne Parish Church (St. Michael the Archangel).
Gloucester, British Publishing Co. (1950).
11

GREAT BRITAIN: LAWS, etc. (VIC.).
An Act to confirm certain provisional orders of the Local Government Board relating to the district of ...Gravesend...Sittingbourne...
1874.
9

GRIFFIN, Ralph.
Kentish items: Aylesford, Pluckley, Stourmouth, Faversham, Sittingbourne, Wouldham, Chatham.
n.d.
7

PARRETT, W.J. LTD. Publishers.
Parish church of St. Michael, Sittingbourne.
W.J. Parrett Ltd. 1920.
20

PAYNE, George.
Antiquities of the Sittingbourne district.
Sittingbourne, W.J. Parrett Ltd. 1896.
11

PAYNE, George.
Catalogue of the museum of local antiquities (Sittingbourne).
1882.
11,17

Remains of Roman interments from East Hall near Sittingbourne.
n.d.
17

Sittingbourne. In the Proceedings of the Society of
Antiquaries, April 7th, 1881.
8

ROBERTSON, William Archibald Scott.
Sittingbourne and the names of land and houses in or near it...
Parrett. 1879.
11,17,20

ROBERTSON, William Archibald Scott.
Sittingbourne during the Middle Ages.
n.d.
20

Roman lead coffin...discovered near Sittingbourne.
c.1880.
17

SIMS-WILLIAMS, Michael.
Ickthuse Club. (St. John's Boy's Secondary Modern School,
Sittingbourne).
British Council of Churches. 1963.
1

SITTINGBOURNE AND DISTRICT CONSUMER GROUP.
The Sittingbourne Consumer, Nos. 1-7, 1965-69.
20

SITTINGBOURNE FRIENDLY SOCIETY.
Rules of the Friendly Society established at Sittingbourne...
1830.
13

"URBAN RUS", pseud.
Old faces in odd places. (Account of people in Sittingbourne
area with fictitious names)
Wyman. 1882.
20

SMALLHYTHE

CAMPBELL, Barry.
The Ellen Terry Memorial: written and compiled by Barry
Campbell. Transmission - Wednesday, 21st November, 1962.
(Broadcasting script).
3

CRAIG, E.G.
Ellen Terry and her secret self.
Sampson Low. n.d.
12

Ellen Terry Memorial, Smallhythe Place, Kent.
Country Life for the National Trust.
2(1960) 11(1948)

HASLEWOOD, Francis.
Smallhythe Church. In Archaeologia Cantiana, Vol. 14, 1882.
17

MANVELL, Roger.
Ellen Terry.
Heinemann. 1968.
12

An outline guide to Smallhythe Church and Parish.
n.d.
12

TAYLOR, A.H.
The Chapel of St. John the Baptist, Smallhythe.
Mitchell, Hughes and Clarke. 1913.
12

SMARDEN

EVANS, Leonard.
The church of St. Michael the Archangel, Smarden.
Printed by W. Bear. n.d.
11

HASLEWOOD, Francis.
Antiquities of Smarden.
Privately Printed. 1866.
1,6,11,12,15

Memorials of Smarden, Kent.
Privately Printed. 1886.
1,3,4,5,6,11,12,14,15,17,19

Smarden Church. In Archaeologia Cantiana, Vol. 14,
1882.
17

MILLS, Halford L.
Smarden, particularly the parish church.
(Tenterden), Thomson. 1931.
11

SMEETH

CHARITY COMMISSION.
In the matter of Bedingfield's Charity for the
benefit of the parishes of Lyminge, Dymchurch and
Smeeth.
(1924).
7

SCOTT, James Renat.
Memorials of the family of Scott, of Scot's Hall,
in the County of Kent. With an appendix of illustrative
documents.
1876.
3,4,11,15,17

SMUGGLING

BANKS, John.
Reminiscences of smugglers and smuggling.
E. Graham. 1966.
1,6,7,10,11,12,19

BEHRENS, Lilian Boys.
Love, smugglers and naval heroes.
Palmer. 1929.
7,11,13

BISHOP, George.
Remarks and means to prevent smuggling, humbly
submitted to the consideration of the Right Honorable,
the House of Peers and the Honorable House of Commons.
Maidstone, Bishop, 1783. A report by Frank Graham,
1968.
Bishop, 1783. Facsimile Reprint, F. Graham, 1968.
3(1968) 11(1783) 12(1783, 1968)

FINN, Ralph.
Kent coast blockade: "The story of the days when
Kentish smugglers battled with the men of the Royal
Navy".
Ramsgate, W.E. White. 1971.
3,4,8,11

GRAHAM, Frank.
Famous smugglers' inns.
Newcastle, F. Graham. 1966.
6

GRAHAM, Frank.
More smuggling inns.
Newcastle, F. Graham. 1969.
6

GREAT BRITAIN: LAWS, etc. (GEO. III).
An Act for the more effectually preventing the
pernicious practices of smuggling in this Kingdom and
for indemnifying persons who have been guilty of
offences against the laws of Customs and Excise.
Printed by Eyre and Strahan. 1779.
11

HARPER, Charles George.
The smugglers.
Chapman and Hall. 1909 etc.
3,6,7,10,11,12,19

JAMES, G.P.R.
The smugglers, 3 vols.
Smith, Elder. 1845.
1,7,11

LAPTHORNE, William H.
Smuggler's Broadstairs: an historical guide to the
smuggling annals of the ancient town of Bradstow,
illustrated with old views, 2nd edition revised.
Thanet Antiquarian Book Club. 1971.
11

MACKINNON, Donald D.
History of Speldhurst.
Tunbridge Wells, Groves. 1902.
1,8

Speldhurst Parish Magazine, Vols. 1-16, 1870-1937.
11

STEBBING, W.P.D.
Four miscellaneous notes: Hearth Tax for Speldhurst in 1663;
Court Leet and Court Baron record for the Manor of Deal
Prebend in 1708; the response of the parish of Ash and its
neighbours to the fear of a French invasion in 1798 and Howbury
Moated Manor House, Crayford. (Reprinted from Archaeologia
Cantiana, Vol. 48, 1936).
Ashford, Headley.
11

STEBBING, W.P.D.
An inventory of an innkeeper's possessions in 1685. (Reprinted
from Archaeologia Cantiana, Vol. 46, 1934).
Ashford, Headley.
11

SPORT

BARNES, Greville F.
The rail and the rod - the Tourist's and Angler's guide to
waters and quarters on the South Eastern Railway.
London, Horace Cox. 1869.
6

BLAXLAND, Gregory.
Tom Glasse and the East Kent Hunt.
G. Blaxland. 1958.
3,7,11

BROWNING, Robert H.K.
Golf in Kent.
Golf Clubs Association. 1953.
1,5,6,8,11

CANTERBURY AND DISTRICT BAT AND TRAP LEAGUE.
Laws of the Kent Bat and Trap Association and Canterbury and
District Bat and Trap League rules.
1959.
4

CENTRAL COUNCIL OF PHYSICAL RECREATION.
Regional sport (London and South-East Region).
1968.
4

DAY, James Wentworth.
Inns of sport.
Naldrett. 1949.
15

EELES, Henry Swanston.
The Eridge Hunt.
Tunbridge Wells Courier. 1936.
1

FAIRFAX-BLAKEBOROUGH, John.
The hunting and sporting reminiscences of H.W. Selby Lowndes.
P. Allen. 1926.
3,7,11

FAIRFAX-BLAKEBOROUGH, John.
Some Kent Hunts: the East Kent, the West Kent, the Ashford
Valley, the Eridge and the Mid-Kent Staghounds.
Dundee, Simmath. 193-?
11

FRANCIS, Lionel.
Seventy-five years of Southern league football.
Pelham. 1969.
5,12

GREATER LONDON AND SOUTH-EAST SPORTS COUNCIL.
Sports facilities - initial appraisal, Vol. 2. Water
recreation, May, 1969.
Greater London and South-East Sports Council. 1969.
12

GREATER LONDON AND SOUTH-EAST SPORTS COUNCIL.
Water recreation strategy.
Greater London and South-East Sports Council. 1971.
8

GREAVES, Ralph.
Foxhunting in Kent.
Field Sports Publications. 1958.
1,2,4,11,12,15

GREAVES, Ralph.
The West Kent Hunt.
Reid-Hamilton. 1951.
6

HEATH, Ernest Gerald.
Archery associations of Canterbury. (From Journal of
the Society of Archer-Antiquaries, Vol. 6, 1963).
3

The Canterbury archers, 1955-60.
Canterbury, Canterbury Archers' Society. 1960.
3

Canterbury archers, 1955-65.
Canterbury, Canterbury Archers' Society. 1965.
3

Notes for a talk on archery in Kent.
Canterbury Archaeological Society. 1961.
3

(JORDAN, J.P.).
History of Kent rugby football.
1949.
1,2

KENNY, Tom.
Angling: reminiscences...giving an account of his
experiences...in East Kent since 1933.
Sittingbourne, Parrett. 1946.
3,11

KENT COUNTY AMATEUR SWIMMING ASSOCIATION.
Handbook, 1959.
Sevenoaks News.
11

KENT COUNTY FOOTBALL ASSOCIATION.
Handbook, 1967-68.
Canterbury, Kent County Football Association. n.d.
8

KENT COUNTY FOOTBALL ASSOCIATION.
Kent League Football Manual, 1956-57.
Canterbury, Kent County Football Association. 1956.
3

KENT COUNTY LAWN TENNIS ASSOCIATION.
Annual handbook, 1955 in progress.
1,4,6,8,11,12

KENT COUNTY PLAYING FIELDS ASSOCIATION.
Annual reports.
3(1966)
4(1966, 1967)
7(1967)
8(1960-63)
9(n.d.)
11(1970)
12(n.d.)
19(1960-63, 1967)

KENT COUNTY RIFLE ASSOCIATION.
45th annual report for 1905.
Maidstone, Dickinson. 1906?
11

KENT RIVER AUTHORITY.
Fishery byelaws.
Kent River Authority. 1970.
8

KENT RIVER AUTHORITY.
Fishing available...
Kent River Authority.
1(1967) 11(1965)

KENT TABLE TENNIS MAGAZINE.
Vols. 1 and 2, 1949 (odd numbers).
3

KENT WOMEN'S HOCKEY ASSOCIATION.
Record of the Kent Women's Hockey Association...
1898-1923.
11

Kentish angler; or, the young fisherman's instructor...
1804.
17

KENTISH DISTRICT TIMES.
District Times sketches: local athletes, 1894-95. (Bromley).
Kentish District Times. 1896.
2

LONDON UNIVERSITY, WYE COLLEGE - DEPARTMENT OF AGRICULTURAL
ECONOMICS.
Outdoor recreation enterprises in problem rural areas.
Wye College. 1967.
12

MINTER, Derek.
Racing all my life.
London, Barker. 1965.
3

NORTH KENT COURSING CLUB.
Meeting...1883.
17

PYATT, Edward Charles.
Climbing and walking in South-East England.
David and Charles. 1970.
6,7

PYATT, Edward Charles.
South-East England. (Climbers' Club Guides).
Climbers' Club. 1969.
19

Riding in Kent.
Addison Press. 1954.
1,3,5,6,12

SCARTH-DIXON, William.
The Tickham Hunt.
Hunts Association. 1927.
12

STOKER, Hugh.
Sea fishing in Kent.
Peterborough, E. Mart. 1965.
1,2,4,5,6,7,8,11,12,15

TEICHMAN, Oskar.
Black horse Nemo and other memories. (West Kent point-to-point).
Davies. 1957.
7

VENABLES, Bernard.
Guide to angling waters. (South-East England).
Daily Mirror. 1954.
12

WAKEFIELD, W.W.
Rugger, by W.W. Wakefield and H.P. Marshall. (Kent rugby).
Longmans. 1930.
12

WALKER, J.
Fox hunting map of Kent, by J. and C. Walker.
n.d.
1,11

SPRINGHEAD

DUNKIN, Alfred John.
Memoranda of Springhead and its neighbourhood during the
Primeval Period.
1848.
1,4,5,6,8,9,11,12,15,17

DUNKIN, Alfred John.
Twelve pennyworth of refreshment for the visitors to
Springhead.
(Gravesend), Newman. n.d.
9,11

GRAVESEND HISTORICAL SOCIETY.
Excavations of Roman settlement at Springhead, 1950-51,
1951-52 - (Excavations Report, No. 1). 1952-53 - (Excavations
Report, No. 2).
9

JENKINS, Frank.
Romano British settlement at Springhead. (Reprinted from
Archaeologia Cantiana, Vol. LXXIII, 1959).
3,4

PENN, William S.
History of the Springhead Pleasure Garden and water-cress
plantation (c.1805-1936). (Reprinted from Archaeologia
Cantiana, Vol. 81, 1966).
11

PENN, William S.
Possible evidence from Springhead for the Great Plague
of A.D. 166. (Reprinted from Archaeologia Cantiana,
Vol. 82, 1967).
Ashford, Headley Bros. 1967.
11

The Roman town at Springhead.
Gravesend Historical Society. c.1966.
2,4,9,11

Springhead: Temples 11 and V. (Reprinted from
Archaeologia Cantiana, Vol. 77, 1962).
11

Springhead: Temple VI - gateway (with a note on the
coin hoard). (Reprinted from Archaeologia Cantiana,
Vol. 82, 1967).
11

Springhead: the temple ditch site. (Reprinted from
Archaeologia Cantiana, Vol. 79, 1964).
1

SMITH, Charles Roach.
Discovery of a hoard of Roman coins at Springhead.
(Reprinted from Numismatic Chronicle, Vol. VII, 3rd
Series, pp. 312-315, 1887).
9

STAPLE

REGIS, B.
A sermon preached on the fast-day, the 18th December,
1745 at Adisham and at Staple the 22nd.
Canterbury, J. Abree. 1746.
3

STAPLEHURST

BALLEY, E.
Struggle for conscience; or, Religious annals of
Staplehurst: a memorial.
Jackson, Walford and Hodder. 1862.
11

COWPER, H.S.
Loddenden and the Usbornes of Loddenden.
Ashford, Kentish Express. 1914.
1,4,6,11,12

(GRIFFIN, Ralph).
A brass once at Staplehurst in Kent.
Monumental Brass Society. 1939.
11

KEECH, Gertrude Clara.
Staplehurst and the Weald of Kent.
Research Publishing Co. 1965.
1,2,4,7,8,11,19

"OCTOGENARIAN", pseud.
Interesting recollections of Staplehurst, by an
Octogenarian. (Reprinted from the Kent County Examiner
and Ashford Chronicle, August 12th, 1898.
12

THATCHER, Thomas.
A brief history of the Staplehurst Independent or
Congregational Church and its ministers, from 1662 to
1888...
11

WORSSAM, B.C.
Eight centuries in stone: an account of the building
of All Saints' Church, Staplehurst.
Cranbrook, Eagle Printing Co. n.d.
11

STATISTICS AND SURVEYS

BRITISH INSTITUTE OF PUBLIC OPINION, SOCIAL SURVEYS
(GALLUP POLL), LTD.
Market survey of Kent. Conducted for the Kent
Newspaper Proprietors' Association by the Institute.
British Institute of Public Opinion. 1956.
3

BRITISH MARKET RESEARCH BUREAU LTD.
Shopping in suburbia...reaction to supermarket shopping.
(Note: Bromley, Kent one of 7 areas surveyed).
J. Walter Thompson Co. 1963.
2

STEEPLETON

Steepleton; or, High Church and Low Church, being the present tendencies of parties in the Church.
Longmans. 1847.
12

STOCKBURY

PUGH, Christine.
Stockbury: a regional study in North-East Kent, by C. Pugh and G.E. Hutchings.
Stockbury, The Hill Farm. 1928.
2,3,4,5,7,8,11,12,15,21

STODMARSH

NEWTON, William.
A sermon preached at Wingham and Stodmarsh in Kent, 1720.
Childe. 1720.
12

STONAR

BADEN-POWELL, D.
Report on erratics from Stonar, Kent. In Archaeologia Cantiana, Vol. 55, 1942.
17

HARDMAN, Frederick William.
Stonar and the Wantsum Channel, by F.W. Hardman and W. Stebbing.
Ashford, Headley Bros. c.1940.
11,17

JACOBS, J.A.
Short account of the ancient town of Stonar.
J. Heywood. n.d.
3,7,11,13,14,19

STONE (Near Dartford)

BALLS, H.J.
St. Mary's, Stone.
Privately Printed. 1970.
5

BARRE, Leonora.
Historical notes of the parish church of St. Mary, Stone, edited by L. Barre.
Ramsgate, Cummings. 1958.
4,5,11

BARRE, Leonora.
Historical notes of the parish church of St. Mary, Stone, 2nd edition.
Church Publishers. 1959.
2,4

CASTELLS, Francis de Paula.
The village of Stone and its Druidical Circle in prehistoric times. (Reprinted from "West Kent Advertiser", 1915-16).
5,17

COTTON, M.A.
A Belgic cremation site at Stone, Kent, by M.A. Cotton and K.M. Richardson. (Reprinted from the Proceedings of the Prehistoric Society, 1941).
5

CRESY, Edward.
Illustrations of Stone Church.
Hooper. 1840.
1,5,11,12,15,17

DUNKIN, John of Bromley.
Account of Stone Church. (From J. Dunkin's "History of Dartford").
n.d.
9

N., H. pseud.
Thirty-two years in a house of mercy (St. Mary's Home, Stone).
1895.
5,17

PRIEST, Simeon.
Excursion to Greenhithe and Stone.
1919.
5

STREET, George Edmund.
Some account of the church of St. Mary, Stone. (Reprinted from Archaeologia Cantiana, Vol. 3, 1861).
1,11,15

STREET, George Edmund.
Some account of the church of St. Mary, Stone, near Dartford.
Swan and Sonnenschein. 1896.
5,6,9,11,12,17

STONE-BY-FAVERSHAM

FLETCHER, Sir Eric.
The ruined church of Stone-by-Faversham, by Sir E. Fletcher and G.W. Meates. (Reprinted from the Antiquaries Journal, 1969).
4

STONE-IN-OXNEY

(SAMPSON, Aylwin).
St. Mary's Church, Stone-in-Oxney, Kent.
Tenterden, Parochial Church Council. 1966.
1,4,8,11,12

WEALD OF KENT PRESERVATION SOCIETY.
Stone-in-Oxney, Kent: a village study.
Weald of Kent Preservation Society. 1970.
2,4,6,8,11

YEANDLE, W.H.
Historical notes on the church of Stone-in-Oxney.
Oxford, Church Army Press. 1935.
1,3,7,13,19

STOUR, RIVER

CABLE, Ernest.
The River Stour: a lecture...(Typescript).
1944.
3

CANTERBURY AND SANDWICH COMMITTEE.
Prospectus of an intended navigation from the City of Canterbury to the town and port of Sandwich and... navigating the River Stour.
1823 and 1824.
17

CANTERBURY NAVIGATION AND SANDWICH HARBOUR COMPANY.
A short exposition.
Giraud. 1826.
11

CANTERBURY TECHNICAL HIGH SCHOOL FOR GIRLS.
The pastoral Stour.
Barton Court Technical High School for Girls. 1967.
11

GEDNEY, Charles William.
Angling holidays in pursuit of salmon, trout and pike. (Includes sections on Rivers Darenth and Stour).
Bromley Telegraph. 1896.
2

GOODSALL, Robert Harold.
The Kentish Stour.
London, Cassell. 1952 etc.
1,3,4,5,6,7,8,9,10,11,12,13,14,15,17,18,19,20,21

HOUSING AND LOCAL GOVERNMENT, Ministry of.
Essex Rivers and Stour: hydrological survey.
Hydrometric areas 36 and 37.
1961.
4

Plan and estimates for improving and extending the navigation of the River Stour...
c.1820.
17

Practicability...of navigating the River Stour through Canterbury...
1823.
17

The Railway Companion - utility and advantages of Canterbury and Whitstable Railway clearly demonstrated, with a glance at the St. Nicholas Bay and Stour navigation schemes.
Canterbury, R. Colegate for J. Wrightson. (1836).
3

RIVER STOUR GROUP.
River Stour: a draft appraisal.
Canterbury, River Stour Group. 1967.
3

STOUR NAVIGATION AND SANDWICH HARBOUR.
Prospectus, sketch of the plan, report of the engineer...
Canterbury, Wood. 1824.
1

TELFORD, T.
Report of Mr. T. Telford, engineer, on the Stour navigation –
Sandwich Harbour (pamphlet).
1824.
17

YEOMAN, Thomas.
Mr. Yeoman's strictures and observations on the M'Kenzie's
report, etc. (River Stour).
Privately Printed. 1775.
11,12

STOURMOUTH

COLLINS, A.H.
Stourmouth Church. In Archaeologia Cantiana, Vol. 42, 1930.
17

GRIFFIN, Ralph.
Kentish items: Aylesford, Pluckley, Stourmouth, Faversham,
Sittingbourne, Wouldham, Chatham.
n.d.
7

JOHNSON, John.
Case of a rector (Stourmouth)...
1721.
17

SPURLING, Cuthbert Terence.
Stourmouth Church.
C.T. Spurling. 1966.
4,6,11

STOWTING

BRENT, John.
An account of researches in an Anglo-Saxon cemetery at
Stowting, 1866.
Society of Antiquaries. 1866.
11

SMITH, Charles Roach.
Anglo-Saxon remains discovered at Stowting, Kent.
1846.
17

WRENCH, Frederick.
A brief account of the parish of Stowting in the County of
Kent...
Smith. 1845.
1,3,4,7,11,12,17

STROOD

ALLEN, Rev. John Ward.
A sermon preached on May 6th, 1787 before the Mayor and
Corporation of the City of Rochester, at the parish church
of Strood...
8,15

AVELING-BARFORD LTD.
A hundred years of road rollers: a pictorial record.
1965.
4,8,15

BURREN, M.J.
Strood Parish Church of St. Nicholas. (Articles taken from
the Parish Magazine).
1965.
12

HEINZ, H.J. AND CO. LTD.
Research for quality.
H.J. Heinz and Co. Ltd. 1967.
12

KENT ARCHAEOLOGICAL SOCIETY - RECORDS BRANCH.
Churchwardens' accounts of St. Nicholas', Strood, 1555-1662,
transcribed by H.R. Plomer. (Kent Records, Vol. 5).
Kent Archaeological Society. 1927.
1,2,4,8,10,11,12,15,17,18

LONDON AND MIDDLESEX ARCHAEOLOGICAL SOCIETY.
Visit of the...Society to Rochester and Strood on
Thursday, 26th June, 1884.
Nichols and Sons. 1884.
1,8,15,17

MERCER, Francis R.
Churchwardens' accounts at Betrysden, 1515-1573.
Kent Archaeological Society. n.d.
3,11,12,18

PAYNE, George.
In memoriam: Charles Roach Smith. (Reprinted from the
Journal of the British Archaeological Association, 1891).
Note: C.R. Smith was an archaeologist and lived in
Strood.
12

PRIEST, Simeon.
An excursion to Plumstead and Bostall Heath and an
excursion to Cobham and Strood.
1924.
5

ROBERTSON, William Archibald Scott.
Strood in the olden time: a lecture delivered in
St. Nicholas' School, Strood, April 26th, 1877.
(Typescript copy).
8

ST. NICHOLAS' CHURCH, Strood.
Parish Magazine, 1869.
London, Wells Gardner. 1869.
4

SMETHAM, Henry.
C.R.S. and his friends. (Recollections of Charles
Roach Smith).
C.W. Daniel. 1929.
3,4,9,12,15,17

History of Strood.
Chatham, Parrett. 1899.
1,2,3,4,5,6,7,8,9,11,12,15,17

Personal recollections of the late Charles Roach
Smith, F.S.A.
C.W. Daniel. n.d.
12

SMITH, Charles Roach.
Retrospections, social and archaeological.
London, Bell and Sons. 1883-1891.
3(Vol. 11)
4(Vols. 1 and 11).
8,9,12,17

STROOD BURIAL BOARD.
Table of Board charges and rules and regulations.
Sweet and Sons. (1883).
12

STROOD WATER WORKS COMPANY.
The charges and regulations of the Strood Water Works
Company.
Sweet and Sons. 1850.
15

TEMPLE SECONDARY SCHOOL, STROOD.
International Exhibition of Child Art, November 28th
to December 3rd, 1955.
4

WORKS, Ministry of.
Temple Manor, Strood, by S.E. Rigold.
H.M.S.O. 1962.
1,2(1970) 4,8,11,12,15

STURRY

BRENT, William.
Sturry and other poems.
Canterbury, Ward. 1826.
11,12,17

BUTLER, Derek R.
100 years of Sturry cricket: the official history of
the Sturry Cricket Club.
Canterbury, Printed by Kentish Gazette. 1963.
3,7

STURRY Cont'd

BUTTON, R.
The bells of St. Nicholas' Church, Sturry.
Canterbury, Gibbs. (1965).
3

Guide to the parish church of St. Nicholas, Sturry, with a
short history of the village.
(1969).
11

JESSUP, Ronald Frank.
A Bronze Age hoard from Sturry. (Reprinted from the Antiquaries
Journal, Vol. 23, 1943).
3

MCINTOSH, K.H.
Sturry: the changing scene, edited by K.H. McIntosh and others.
Sturry, K.H. McIntosh. 1972.
4,11

STURRY CHURCH OF ENGLAND SCHOOL.
The Centenary Magazine...1851-1951.
Canterbury, Elvy Bros. 1951.
3

SUNDRIDGE

DARWIN, Bernard.
The Sundridge Park Golf Club. (Includes history of the Club).
Golf Clubs Association. 1927.
2

FLETCHER, W.G.D.
The family of Hyde of Bore Place and Sundridge. (Reprinted from
Archaeologia Cantiana).
Mitchell and Hughes. 1896.
8,17

KNOCKER, Herbert W.
Evolution of the Holmesdale: No. 3 - Manor of Sundridge.
(Reprinted from Archaeologia Cantiana, Vol. 44, 1933).
Ashford, Headley Bros. n.d.
11

Sundridge charities, 1583-1946.
16

VALLANCE, Aymer.
An old timber house at Sundridge. (Reprinted from Archaeologia
Cantiana, Vol. 37).
Mitchell, Hughes and Clarke. 1925.
11,17

SUTTON-AT-HONE

(BALLS, Horace).
The parish church of St. John the Baptist, Sutton-at-Hone.
n.d.
12

BALLS, Horace J.
Sutton-at-Hone Church and its worshippers.
Dartford, Ellis. 1953.
1,2,4,5,9,11,12,17

Parish of Sutton-at-Hone, Kent (and) guide to Swanley and
district...
Croydon, Home Publishing Co. (1951).
1,5

STEWART, Cecil.
The village surveyed.
Edward Arnold. 1948.
1,2,5,9,11,15

SUTTON-BY-DOVER

HOBDAY, R.H.
Notes on the church of St. Peter and St. Paul, Sutton-by-Dover,
compiled by R.H. Hobday.
"Southern Post". n.d.
7,11,12

TAYLOR, A.E.
A short guide to the ancient parish church: St. Peter and
St. Paul, Sutton-by-Dover.
1937.
3,11,12

SUTTON VALENCE

ANGEL, Charles Frederick.
St. Mary's Town Sutton, or Sutton Valence.
Adlard. 1874.
1,11,12,17

BLATCHLEY-HENNAH, Frank Tregory Wolfe.
Short history of Sutton Valence School.
Kent Messenger. 1952.
1,11,12

CAVE-BROWNE, John.
Sutton Valence and East Sutton.
Maidstone, Dickinson. 1898.
1,6,10,11,12,15,17

FLEMING, Abraham.
Some account of William Lambe, citizen and cloth
worker, 1568...
J.E. Adlard. 1875.
11

Sutton Valence School Magazine, 1902-08.
11

SWALECLIFFE

GOODSALL, Robert Harold.
Whitstable, Seasalter and Swalecliffe.
Canterbury, Cross and Jackman. 1938.
1,2,3,4,5,6,8,11,12,13,15,20

JOHNSON, Isaac.
A sermon preached at the parish churches of Swalecliffe and St. Paul's, Canterbury.
Canterbury, Printed by J. Abree. 1739.
3

WORSFOLD, F.H.
An examination of the contents of the brick-earths
and gravels of Tankerton Bay, Swalecliffe, Kent.
(Reprinted from the Proceedings of the Geologists'
Association, Vol. XXXVII, 1926).
3

WORSFOLD, F.H.
Observations on the provenance of the Thames Valley
pick, Swalecliffe, Kent...November 2nd, 1926.
(Reprinted from the Proceedings of the Prehistoric
Society for East Anglia, Vol. 5, No. 2, (1926)).
3

SWANLEY

ARNETT, Kathleen.
St. Paul's School, Swanley, 1862-1962.
St. Paul's School, Swanley. 1963.
1,2,5,11

DRURY, M.
A socio/economic study of Swanley Junction, 1865-
1965. (Bound typescript for Teacher's Certificate).
1966.
5,11

METROPOLITAN ASYLUMS BOARD.
Programme of the opening of White Oak School, Swanley
Junction, 23rd May, 1903.
17

Parish of Sutton-at-Hone, Kent (and) guide to Swanley
and district...
Croydon, Home Publishing Co. (1951).
1,5

TRANSPORT, Ministry of.
London Traffic, Prohibition of Waiting, (Swanley, Kent)
Regulations, 1964.
H.M.S.O.
8

SWANSCOMBE

BROWN, E.E.S.
Watling Street, sections through Swanscombe Hill,
with reports of excursions, by E.E.S. Brown and
S. Priest.
Geologists' Association. 1924.
17

CHANDLER, Raymond H.
On the Clactonian industry of Swanscombe. (Prehistoric
Society for East Anglia).
1928-29.
17

The church of St. Peter and St. Paul, Swanscombe.
Church Publishers. 1963.
4,8,11,12

SWANSCOMBE Cont'd

DURKIN, M.K.
Field meeting at Abbey Wood and Swanscombe, Kent, by M.K. Durkin and S.A. Baldwin. (Reprinted from the Proceedings of the Geologists' Association, Vol. 79, Part 2, 1968).
5

ELLISTON-ERWOOD, Frank Charles.
Architectural notes on the church of St. Peter and St. Paul, Swanscombe.
Archaeologia Cantiana. n.d.
11,17

HOGG, A.H.A.
Sweyn's camp, Swanscombe. (Typescript).
1935.
5,17

RALPH, E.L.
Swanscombe through the ages. ..
Ramsgate, Church Publishers. 1964 and 1965.
1,4,5,11

ROYAL ANTHROPOLOGICAL INSTITUTE: SWANSCOMBE COMMITTEE.
Report on the Swanscombe skull. (Reprinted from the Royal Anthropological Journal, January-June, 1938).
8

The Swanscombe skull, edited by C.D. Ovey.
Royal Anthropological Institute. 1964.
1,4,5,9,11,15

SPARVEL-BAYLY, J.A.
A history of Swanscombe, edited by J.A. Sparvel-Bayly.
Gravesend, Caddell. 1875.
1,5,9,11,12

STAMP, L. Dudley.
The geology of the Swanscombe eocene outlier, Kent, and report of an excursion...by L.Dudley Stamp and S. Priest.
1920.
5

SWANSCOMBE URBAN DISTRICT COUNCIL.
Sexennial report on certain matters concerning public health, 1958-63.
Swanscombe Urban District Council. 1966.
5

SWARLING

BUSHE-FOX, Jocelyn Plunkett.
Excavation of the Late-Celtic urn-field at Swarling, Kent.
Society of Antiquaries. 1925.
1,3,4,5,6,7,11,12,17

SWINGFIELD

BROWN, John Howard.
A brief history and description of St. Peter's Church, Swingfield, by J.H. Brown and A.W. Crewe.
Kentfield, Taylor and Co. 1958.
12

A history and description of St. Peter's Church, Swingfield. (Typescript).
(1950).
7

A history and description of the preceptory of the Knights of St. John, Swingfield. (Typescript).
(1950).
7

A history of Swingfield. (MS.).
1957.
7

GREAT BRITAIN: LAWS, etc. (QUEEN ANNE).
A Bill for sale for the manors of North Court and Baynton in the parish of Swingfield.
n.d.
11

LAMBERT, George.
Swingfield: and what little is known about it...result of a visit to Swingfield, Tuesday, August 22nd, 1893.
London, T. Brettell and Co. (1893).
3,11

Particulars, plans and conditions of sale of freehold building land...which H.F. Finn-Kelcey...will sell...on...October 10th, 1922.
H.F. Finn-Kelcey. 1922.
7

SWINGFIELD MINNIS

Swingfield Minnis inclosure...to be sold by auction... at the Guildhall in Folkestone on Wednesday, September 22nd, 1841...141 acres of freehold common land, part of Swingfield Minnis.
Printed by Elliot and Son, Ashford. (1841).
7

SYDENHAM

An account of the memorial of Rev. Thomas Bowdler... in the church of St. Bartholomew...Sydenham...Kent... etc. (Pamphlet).
1858.
18

ADAMS, Mayow Wynell.
Sydenham (...private circulation, 1878). Bound with: Some notes on Sydenham, by C. Edgar Thomas.
"The Antiquary", November, 1913.
18

ADDISON, William.
English spas.
Batsford. 1951.
3

CAMPBELL, Thomas.
Life and letters, 3 vols. (Resident of Sydenham).
Virtue and Co. 1850.
2

CHAMBERS, W. AND R. Publishers.
Thomas Campbell (Papers for the People Series). Note: Campbell a resident of Sydenham.
Chambers. 1850-51?
2

COURTNEY LEWIS, C.T.
George Baxter, the picture printer.
n.d.
18

GRACE, W.G.
Cricket. (Note: includes autobiographical information. Grace was resident in Mottingham and Sydenham).
J.W. Arrowsmith and Simpkin Marshall. 1891.
2

MADDOCK, Alfred Beaumont.
On Sydenham, its climate and palace...the efficacy of pure air...in the prevention and treatment of disease.
Simpkin Marshall. 1860.
2,17,18

SMITH, Sydney W.
History of St. Bartholomew's Church and School, Sydenham. (Pamphlet).
1939.
18

SUNDERLAND, S.
Old London's spas, baths and wells. (References to Sydenham).
n.d.
18

Sydenham, Dulwich and Norwood: handy guide to rambles...
T. Fisher Unwin. (188-?).
2

Sydenham High School, 1887-1967.
2

TANKERTON

COLLAR, A.
Whitstable, Tankerton and district.
1939.
7

GOODSALL, Robert Harold.
Home building. (Illustrations, mostly in Tankerton).
Canterbury, Cross and Jackman. 1924.
3

Whitstable and Tankerton-on-Sea: official guide.
E.J. Burrow. 1955 etc.
1,4,11,15

ADDISON, William.
Thames Estuary.
Hale. 1954.
1,4,5,8,9,11,12,14

ALLDERIDGE, Brian.
State barges on the Thames, illustrated by Brian Allderidge,
with notes...by Anne Petrides.
H. Evelyn. 1959.
4

ARMSTRONG, Walter.
The Thames from its rise to the Nore (2 vols. in 1).
Virtue. (1887).
4

BATES, L.M.
The Londoner's river.
F. Muller. 1949.
8

BELLOC, Hilaire.
The historic Thames.
Dent. 1914.
11

BELLOC, Hilaire.
The river of London.
Foulis. 1912.
4

BOWEN, Frank Charles.
Collection of some of the Articles "Gravesend to the Sea",
1934-35.
9

BOWEN, Frank Charles.
Sailing ships of the London River.
Sampson Low, Marston and Co. n.d.
12

BRANCH-JOHNSON, William.
The English prison hulks, revised edition.
Phillimore. 1970.
11

BRERETON, Austin.
Daily sea trips: the official guide to the New Palace
Steamers, giving the history of the Thames from London Bridge
to the Nore, Southend, Margate, Ramsgate...
1903.
13

BRYANT, Arthur.
Liquid history: to commemorate fifty years of the Port of
London Authority, 1909-1956.
1960.
9,17

CASE AND CUNNINGHAM.
Dartford and Crayford creeks: a report to Dartford and
Crayford Navigation Commissioners...by Case and Cunningham.
Dartford and Crayford Navigation Commission. 1928.
5

COOPER, Frederick Stephen.
Racing sailormen.
Marshall. 1963.
4,11,12,15

CRACKNELL, Basil E.
Portrait of London River.
Hale. 1968.
9

DAGENHAM PUBLIC LIBRARIES.
London River: catalogue of an exhibition at Valence House.
1960.
17

DAVIS, Dennis J.
Thames sailing barge, her gear and rigging.
David and Charles. 1970.
4,8

DICKENS, Charles.
Dickens' dictionary of the Thames...
Macmillan. 1888.
17

DODD, R.
Reports with plans, sections, etc., of the proposed
dry tunnel, or passage, from Gravesend in Kent, to
Tilbury in Essex.
Printed for J. Taylor, Architectural Library, High
Holborn, London. 1798.
1,8,11,17

EVANS, H. Muir.
Short history of the Thames Estuary.
Imray Laurie. c.1934.
1,9,14,15

FEARNSIDE, W.G.
Eighty picturesque views on the Thames and Medway.
c.1830.
1,12,15

FINDLAY, Alexander George.
A handbook for the navigation of the different
channels of the Thames and the Medway.
R. Holmes Laurie. 1877.
1,11,12

(GALE, Samuel).
A dissertation on Julius Caesar's passage over the
River Thames.
Society of Antiquaries. 1734?
11

GENERAL STEAM NAVIGATION CO. LTD.
The way of the Eagles: an illustrated guide of the
river trip from Greenwich to Ramsgate.
Gale and Polden. c.1923.
9

Going to Margate; or, a water itinerary from London
to Margate. Containing an account of the principal
towns, villages, buildings, seats, etc., observed
between those places, together with extracts from the
Margate byelaws of general utility to readers.
Printed for George Witherden. 1828.
11,13

GOODSALL, Robert Harold.
The widening Thames.
Constable. 1965.
1,3,4,5,7,10,12,15,17

GREAT BRITAIN: LAWS, etc. (QUEEN ANNE).
An Act for the better ordering and governing the watermen and lightermen upon the River of Thames.
1705.
9

GREAT BRITAIN: LAWS, etc. (QUEEN ANNE).
An Act for the better preservation and improvement of
the fishery within the River Thames...
1711.
11

GREAT BRITAIN: LAWS, etc. (GEO. II).
An Act for making more effectual several Acts passed
relating to watermen...rowing on the River Thames...
1729.
9,11

GREAT BRITAIN: LAWS, etc. (GEO. II).
An Act to explain...an Act...for making more effectual
several Acts relating to watermen, wherrymen and
lightermen, rowing on the River Thames...ferryboats
and flat-bottomed boats.
1731.
9

GREAT BRITAIN: LAWS, etc. (GEO. II).
An Act for regulating the Company of Watermen...rowing
on the River Thames.
1737.
11

GREAT BRITAIN: LAWS, etc. (GEO. II).
An Act...for the better regulation of Lastage and
Ballastage in the River Thames.
1745.
11

GREAT BRITAIN: LAWS, etc. (GEO. II).
An Act for the more effectual preservation and
improvement of the spawn and fry of the fish of the
River Thames and waters of the Medway...
Printed by Thomas Baskett. 1757.
11

GREAT BRITAIN: LAWS, etc. (GEO. III).
An Act...and for better defending the passage of the River
Thames at Gravesend and Tilbury Fort.
1780.
9

GREAT BRITAIN: LAWS, etc. (GEO. III).
An Act for the better regulation and government of pilots
licensed by the Corporation of Trinity of Deptford Strand...
and to prevent mischiefs and annoyances on the River of
Thames below London Bridge.
1788.
12

GREAT BRITAIN: LAWS, etc. (GEO. III).
An Act for better regulating...the watermen, wherrymen and
lightermen upon the River of Thames between Gravesend and
Windsor.
1794.
9,11

GREAT BRITAIN: LAWS, etc. (GEO. III).
An Act for making and maintaining a tunnel or road under the
River Thames from, or near, to the town of Gravesend...to...
Tilbury Fort in the County of Essex.
1799.
9,17

GREAT BRITAIN, Parliament.
Thames and Medway Conservancy Bill...
1857.
8

GREAT BRITAIN, Parliament.
Thames Barrier and Flood Prevention Bill...
H.M.S.O. 1971.
4

GREATER LONDON COUNCIL.
Taming the Thames. Protecting London from flooding: Greater
London Council's first report of studies.
Greater London Council. December, 1969?
4,9

HAILL, C.R.
Memoirs of life on a River Thames tug.
1896.
9

HALL, Mr. and Mrs. S.C.
Book of the Thames.
London, Virtue and Co. n.d.
18

HASTINGS, Warren.
The Monarch of the Thames.
Privately Printed. 1955.
4,8

HIGGINS, Walter.
Father Thames, Part 1.
Wells, Gardner and Darton. n.d.
1

HOUSING AND LOCAL GOVERNMENT, Ministry of.
Technical possibilities of a Thames flood barrier.
H.M.S.O. 1960.
1,5

HOUSING AND LOCAL GOVERNMENT, Ministry of - DEPARTMENTAL
COMMITTEE ON THE EFFECTS OF HEATED AND OTHER EFFLUENTS AND
DISCHARGES ON THE CONDITION OF THE TIDAL REACHES OF THE RIVER
THAMES.
Pollution of the tidal Thames: report.
H.M.S.O. 1961.
1,5,12

IRVING, John.
Rivers and creeks of the Thames Estuary.
Sunday Review. 1927.
1,11

JONES, H. Lewis.
Swin, Swale and Swatchway; or, cruises down the Thames,
the Medway and the Essex rivers, by H.L. Jones and C.B. Lockwood.
Waterlow. 1892.
1,8

JONES, L.L. Rodwell.
The geography of London River.
Dial Press. 1932.
9

JONES, Norman.
When commuters went by steamer. (From "Country
Life", 22nd December, 1960).
9

KENT AND ESSEX SEA FISHERIES COMMITTEE.
Annual reports.
4(1961-2, 1969-70, 1971)
7(1959 etc., 1968)

KENT AND ESSEX SEA FISHERIES COMMITTEE.
Report on the sea fisheries and fishing industries
of the Thames Estuary...Part 1, prepared by Dr. James
Murie. (Part 1 only printed).
Waterlow and Layton. 1903.
1,2,4,9,11,14

LAMPE, David.
The Tunnel. (Brunel's Thames Tunnel).
Harrap. 1963.
12

LEE, John.
A tour from Northamptonshire to London, down the River
Thames to the Isle of Thanet, from thence to Dover and
the coast of France...
1827.
13

LEESE, Leonard Ernest Selwyn.
Thames trip from the Pool to the Nore.
G. Phillip. 1954.
1,8

LESLIE, George D.
Our river.
Bradbury. 1881.
1

LIMNELIUS, George, pseud. (Lewis ROBINSON).
Medbury Fort murder.
E. Benn. 1929.
9

LONDON AND INDIA DOCKS COMPANY.
The proposed Thames Barrage.
London and India Docks Company. 1905.
9

MARCH, Edgar James.
Spritsail barges of Thames and Medway.
Marshall. 1948 and 1970.
1948 (1,3,4,5,8,11,12,13,14,15,17)   1970 (2,4,11,12)

MAXWELL, Donald.
A pilgrimage of the Thames.
Centenary Press. 1932.
1,5,9,12,15

MAXWELL, W.B.
Tales of the Thames.
Simpkin Marshall. 1892.
1

MORGAN, Captain W.A.
The Thames Nautical Training College. "H.M.S.
Worcester", 1862-1919.
London, Charles Griffin. 1929.
5

The new steamboat companion and Gravesend guide.
Mason. 1835.
12

NICHOLLS, Thomas.
Steamboat companion; or, Margate, Isle of Thanet...
and River Thames guide.
Hughes. 1823.
6,11,12,13,14,15

NOBLE, Edward.
Fisherman's gat: a story of the Thames Estuary.
Blackwood. 1906.
9,11,15

NOBLE, Edward.
Shadows from the Thames.
C.A. Pearson. 1900.
9

NORIE, J.W.
Sailing directions for the River Thames from London to the
Nore and Sheerness...Rochester...
C. Wilson. 1855.
15

ORR, William S. Publisher.
Summer excursions in the County of Kent, along the banks of the
rivers Thames and Medway.
W.S. Orr. 1847.
2,4,15,17

PENNEY, Stephen.
Concise navigating directions for the River Thames.
Patter. 1896.
1

Pilot's guide for the River Thames...
Imray Laurie. 1920.
1

The Pilot's guide to the Thames Estuary for yachtsmen, revised
by Commander H.L. Wheeler.
1960.
4

POCOCK, Robert. Publisher.
Pocock's Gravesend Water Companion...between London Bridge and
Gravesend Town...
Gravesend, R. Pocock. 1798.
9,13

POLLARD, Arthur O.
Ships of London River.
Model and Allied Publishers. 1969.
9

PORT OF LONDON AUTHORITY.
Handbook of tide tables, particulars of docks, etc., 1971.
Port of London Authority.
9

PORT OF LONDON AUTHORITY.
Thames navigation service.
Port of London Authority. c.1959.
9

PURDY, John.
The new piloting directory for the different channels of the
Thames and Medway...
R.H. Laurie. 1846.
12

ROLT, L.T.C.
The Thames from mouth to source.
1951.
18

The Royal River: the Thames from source to sea - descriptive,
historical, pictorial.
Cassell. 1885.
3(1901) 4,15

SHERWOOD, GILBERT AND PIPER. Publishers.
Steamboat companion from London to Gravesend (etc.).
Sherwood, Gilbert and Piper. 1830.
17

SIMPICH, Frederick.
Time and tide on the Thames. (From National Geographic
Magazine, February, 1939).
9

SMITH, Allen.
Balancing Foulness: transesturial communications, by A. Smith
and A.M. Wood.
1972.
9

SMITH, Cicely Fox.
Thames-side yesterdays, by C. Fox Smith, illustrated by E.A.
Cox.
London, F. Lewis. 1945.
3

Steamboat guide to Greenwich, Woolwich and Gravesend...
Clarke. 1862.
11

STOREY, A.J.
Pilots (on River Thames). (From "The Strand Magazine, c.1910).
9

THAMES SURVEY COMMITTEE.
Effects of polluting discharges on the Thames Estuary:
the reports of the Thames Survey Committee and of the
Water Pollution Research Laboratory.(Water Pollution
Paper No. 12).
H.M.S.O. 1964.
4,5

(THAMES TUNNEL CO.).
An explanation of the works of the tunnel under the
Thames from Rotherhithe to Wapping.
Warrington. 1842.
12

The Thames and its story: from the Cotswolds to the
Nore.
Cassell. 1906.
4,9

The Thames book, 1967, 1969, 1970.
G. Dibb Ltd.
9

THOMPSON, A.G.
The romance of London River.
Bradley and Son. 1934.
9

THOMPSON, A.G.
The Thames from Tower to Tilbury.
Bradley and Son. 1939.
9

THURSTON, Gavin.
The great Thames disaster. (Sinking of the Princess
Alice).
Allen and Unwin. 1965.
1,5

TOMBLESON, W.
Eighty picturesque views on the Thames and Medway...
the descriptions by W.G. Fearnside.
n.d.
4,7

TOMBLESON, W.
Panoramic map of the Thames and Medway, new edition.
c.1850.
4,8

Trip to Greenhithe, Northfleet and Gravesend...by sea -
the things one sees from the steamer.
C. Wilson. c.1835.
1,9,17

WILSON, Charles. Publisher.
Sailing directions for the rivers Thames and Medway...
C. Wilson. 1881.
15

WILSON, Effingham. Publisher.
A new steamboat companion in an excursion to Greenhithe, Northfleet, Gravesend, the Nore and Herne Bay
with a trip up the River Medway to Rochester Bridge.
E. Wilson, B. Stead and W. Strange. c.1835.
1,9,11,17

WILSON, J.D.
Later nineteenth century defences of the Thames,
including Grain Fort. (Extracted from the Journal
of the Society for Army Historical Research, 2 parts,
1962).
4,9

WYLLIE, W.L.
The tidal Thames.
Cassell. c.1880.
1,9

THAMESMEAD

GREATER LONDON COUNCIL.
Thamesmead: a riverside development.
Greater London Council. 1967.
9

THANINGTON

FRY, Miss E.T.B.
Notes on Tonford Manor, near Canterbury, by Miss E.T.B. Fry and
Rev. L.E. Whatmore.
1949 and 195-?
3

HANCOCK, Jardins.
Tonford Manor.
London, Fisher and Unwin. 1903.
3

WILSON, S. Gordon.
A short history of Thanington Church.
Canterbury, Jennings. n.d.
3,11

THEATRE

BROWNE, Mrs. Hengie.
Pilgrim story: the Pilgrim Players, 1939-1943.
Muller. 1945.
3,11,12

DAWSON, Giles E.
Records of plays and players in Kent, 1450-1642. (VOL. 7 of the
Malone Society Collections).
Malone Society. 1965.
7,11

DE SALVO, Brian.
Bromley Repertory Company...anecdote and opinion to celebrate
the thirteenth birthday of the New Theatre, Bromley...edited by
B. De Salvo.
(1960).
2

HODGSON, Norma.
Sarah Baker (1736/7-1816): Governess-general of the Kentish
Drama. (Reprinted from Studies in English Theatre History).
Society for Theatrical Research. 1922.
3,7,11,19

MORLEY, Malcolm.
Margate and its theatres, 1730-1965.
Museum Press. 1966.
1,3,4,6,7,11,15,19

ROSENFELD, Sybil Marion.
Strolling players and drama in the provinces, 1660-1765.
(The Kentish Circuit, 1723-1765, Chapters XI and XII).
Cambridge University Press. 1939.
3,7

THROWLEY

Authentick memoirs of the wicked life and dying words of the
late John Collington of Throwleigh in Kent, 1750. (Contained
in "The Kentish Fable").
n.d.
6

THURNHAM

The parish church of St. Mary the Virgin, Thurnham.
Maidstone, Young and Cooper. 1968.
11

TILMANSTONE

BUTTERWELL, W.
Bulletin of the Geological Survey of Great Britain. (Contains
gravimeter survey of Tilmanstone), compiled by W. Butterwell.
Department of Scientific and Industrial Research. 1954.
6

FRAMPTON, Thomas Shipden.
List of 45 vicars of Tilmanstone, compiled by T.S. Frampton.
Mitchell and Hughes. 1892.
1

TONBRIDGE

ANDREWS, S.M.
Jane Austen...her Tonbridge connections.
Tonbridge Free Press. 1949.
11,12,19

BAILEY, Lorna.
History of non-conformity in Tunbridge Wells, Tonbridge and
Southborough. (Typescript).
c.1970.
19

BEVAN, Patricia.
The 1st Tonbridge (B.P.) Scout Group, 1908 to 1968.
J.S. Bevan, 13 Parkway, Tonbridge. 1968.
11,12

BOORMAN, Henry Roy Pratt.
Tonbridge Free Press Centenary.
Tonbridge Free Press. 1969.
4,8,11

BRIDGER, W. Publisher.
Handbook of Tonbridge and neighbourhood.
W. Bridger. 18--?
11

CHALKLIN, Christopher William.
A Kentish wealden parish (Tonbridge), 1550-1750.
(Photocopy of a typescript MS.).
1960.
11

COOMBS, William.
Tonbridge legends.
1866.
8,17

CORNWALLIS, H.
A sermon on hospitality preached at Tunbridge, in Kent.
Hills. 1708.
12

Correspondence...with respect to the neglect and
spiritual destitution of the parish of Tonbridge.
Spottiswoode. 1875.
11

CROFT-COOKE, Rupert.
The altar in the loft.
Putnam. 1960.
8

DUKE, Neville.
Test pilot.
Wingate. 1953.
12

ELLIOTT, Douglas.
Tonbridge Parish Church.
British Publishing Co. 196-?
12

FLEMING, I. Plant.
Tonbridge Castle to the year 1322..
Longmans, Green. 1865.
1,11,12

FORSTER, T.F.
Flora Tonbrigensis.
Tunbridge Wells, Clifford. 1816 and 1842.
1(1842) 6(1816) 11(1842) 15(1842) 19(1842)

GARDNER, Henry.
Penny guide to Tunbridge Wells, Southborough and
Tonbridge.
n.d.
19

GREAT BRITAIN: LAWS, etc. (GEO. III).
An Act to enable certain persons therein named to
continue to work a Pestle Mill...at Old Forge Farm
in the parish of Tonbridge...
1773.
11

HARDINGE, Sir Charles.
A practical exposition of the election of Grace in four
sermons.
Printed by W. Bridger. 1847.
11

HARRIS, Edwin.
The history of Tonbridge Castle. (Eastgate Series,
No. 11).
Rochester, E. Harris. 1911.
15

(HODGE, Sydney).
The Methodist Church, East Street, Tonbridge, 1872-1972.
Printed by the Wood Press. (1972).
11

INLAND WATERWAYS ASSOCIATION - LONDON AND HOME COUNTIES
BRANCH.
Spring rally of boats at Tonbridge on the River Medway...
May, 1967...
Inland Waterways Association. 1967.
11

JAMES, Thomas.
The scriptural constitution of Christian Churches: being the
substance of a discourse delivered on November 13th, 1834...
Congregational Church, Tunbridge, Kent.
Westley and Davis...1835.
11

JEFFERSON, T.
Two sermons, on the reasonableness and salutary effects of
fearing God as governor and judge of the world...
Tonbridge, Printed by Maunder and Holmes. 1808.
11

KENT COUNTY COUNCIL - PLANNING DEPARTMENT.
Tonbridge: a plan for the town centre.
Kent County Council. 1966.
11

KNOCKER, Herbert W.
Lowy of Tonbridge...
Manorial Society. 1929.
11,16

KNOX, Thomas.
An exhortation to the poor: a sermon preached in the parish
church of Tunbridge on Sunday, 20th November, 1831, 2nd
edition.
B. Fellowes. 1831.
11

LE FLEMING, John.
Tonbridge Castle: (an) historical sketch.
n.d.
11,19

LONGLEY, P.H.
The town lands, 1571-1633. (Tonbridge School Local History
Researches, 1961).
2,11

LOWE, Jessie.
Tunbridge Ware. In Taylor, Elias, "The lathe and its uses".
Trubner. 1871.
19

MARTIN, W. Stanley.
Tonbridge for the resident...by W.S. Martin and B.P. Row.
Tonbridge, Flemons. 1896.
1,7,8,11,12,15,17,18,19

(MOULE, A.W.H.).
(History of Mabledon, Tonbridge). A photocopy of some
typescript notes.
(197-?).
11

MURRAY, Anne.
The story of Fosse Bank School, by the Sixth Form of 1969-70,
edited by Anne Murray.
Tonbridge, Fosse Bank School. 1970.
11

NEVE, Arthur Henry.
Mate's illustrated Tonbridge, written by A.H. Neve.
W. Mate. 1906.
11,17

NEVE, Arthur Henry.
Tonbridge of yesterday.
Tonbridge Free Press. 1933 and 1934.
1,3,4,5,7,11,12,13,17,18(1934) 19

NEVE, Walter N.
Tonbridge and Tonbridge School. (A "Borough" Guide).
Cheltenham, E.J. Burrow. n.d.
11,19

OLBY, G.C.
The Tonbridge Union Poor Laws. (Tonbridge School Local
History Researches, 1963).
11

RIVINGTON, Septimus.
History of Tonbridge School...from 1553 to the present
date.
London, Rivingtons. Four editions, 1869. 1898, 1910
and 1925.
1(1898)
2(1869, 1898, 1925)
4(1925)
6(1898)
7(1898)
11(1869, 1910)
12(1869)
15(1869)
17(1910)
19(1898)
21(1898)

SABINE, James.
A sermon delivered on...February 8th, 1809 in the
Protestant Dissenting Church, Tunbridge.
Printed by Townsend, Powell and Co. 1809.
11

St. Eanswythe's Mission, Tonbridge: a short history.
Tonbridge Free Press. 1948.
1

SIMPSON, W.D.
Tonbridge Castle (photocopy). (Reprinted from the
Journal of the British Archaeological Association,
1940).
11

SMITH, George Mabberley.
Essay on the life of Sir Andrew Judde, Knight, founder
of the Free Grammar School at Tonbridge.
Tonbridge, Governors of Tonbridge School. 1849.
1

SOMERVELL, David Churchill.
History of Tonbridge School.
Faber. 1947.
1,2,4,6,8,11,12,15,17,18

STAGG, Frank Noel.
A few historical notes concerning certain parishes in
the neighbourhood of Tonbridge.
1948.
11

Statement...concerning a proposed new church at
Tonbridge.
Spottiswoode. 1875.
11

TONBRIDGE FREE LIBRARY.
Catalogue of the books in the Free Public Library.
Blair and Twort. 1892.
15

Tonbridge legends, etc.
Tonbridge, Ware. 1866.
11,15,17,19

TONBRIDGE RURAL DISTRICT COUNCIL.
Tonbridge Rural District - official guide.
Home Publishing Co.
11(1953, 1955, 1957, 1969)

TONBRIDGE SCHOOL.
Historical sketches, 1968. (By the boys of Tonbridge
School).
Tonbridge School. 1968.
12

Local history research studies. (By the boys of
Tonbridge School). (Typescript - duplicated).
1958-1963.
11

Tonbridge: a progress report written by the boys.
Kenneth Mason Publications. 1964.
1,2,11,12,15,17,19

Tonbridge School and the Great War, edited by
H.R. Stokoe.
Tonbridge, Whitefriars Press. 1923.
4,7,8,11,12,19

Tonbridge School, July 30th, 1884: end of term
markings and miscellaneous school information.
1

TONBRIDGE SCHOOL REGISTERS.
The old school lists of Tonbridge School, by W.G. Hart.
Allen and Unwin. 1933.
11,17

Registers, 1553-1820, edited by W.G. Hart.
London, Rivingtons. 1935.
11,19

Registers, 1820-1886, edited by W.O. Hughes-Hughes.
Reading, Beecroft. 1886.
1,2,11,16,17

Registers, 1820-1893, edited by W.O. Hughes-Hughes.
London, Bentley. 1893.
4,11,12,18

Registers, 1826-1910, edited by H.E. Steed.
London, Rivingtons. 1911.
11,12,16,19

Registers, 1847-1926, edited by H.E. Steed.
London, Rivingtons. 1927.
2,11,12,19

Registers, 1861-1945, edited by H.D. Furley.
London, Rivingtons. 1951.
2,8,11,12

Registers, 1900-1965, edited by C.H. Knott.
Tonbridge School. 1966.
1,2,11,12,15,17

Tonbridge School song book.
Oxford University Press. 1927.
12

TONBRIDGE URBAN DISTRICT COUNCIL.
Tonbridge, Kent - official guide.
E.J. Burrow (1924)
Sussex Courier. 1937
Century Press. 1946
Caxton and Holmesdale Press. 1950
Pyramid Press. 1960 and 1971
5(1924)
11(1924, 1937, 1946, 1950, 1960, 1971)

Tonbridge ware. (An extract from Chambers' Edinburgh Journal,
1st December, 1894).
17

Tonbridgian, Vols. 5 and 6, 1873-1876; Vol. 9, No. 13;
Vol. 10, No. 2, 1890-1894.
12

VALLANCE, Aymer.
An old view of Tonbridge. (Reprinted from Archaeologia
Cantiana, Vol. 44).
Ashford, Headley Bros. 1932.
11

VERE-HODGE, Hugh Sydenham.
Sir Andrew Judde, Lord Mayor of London, 1550-51...
Tonbridge School. 1953.
1,8,11,12

WADMORE, Beauchamp.
Some details on the history of the parish of Tonbridge...
Tonbridge, M. Stonestreet. 1906?
1,11,12,17,19

WADMORE, J.F.
The Priory of St. Mary Magdalene at Tonbridge...(Reprinted
from Archaeologia Cantiana).
Mitchell and Hughes. 1881.
11

WADMORE, J.F.
Tonbridge Castle and its Lords. (Reprinted from Archaeologia
Cantiana).
Mitchell and Hughes. 1885.
1,3,17

WARNER, Rev. G.B. Lee.
"Faith's victory over death": a sermon on the death of the Very
Rev. Henry Alford...
Kentish Gazette. n.d.
3

WILMOT, Edward P.
Tonbridge Parish, 1600-1750.
Tonbridge Free Press. 1953.
11,19

WOOD, M.B.
Petty Sessions in the 18th century. (Tonbridge School Local
History Researches).
1961.
11

WORSHIPFUL COMPANY OF SKINNERS.
Statutes and regulations of the Free Grammar School
at Tunbridge, Kent...1533.
1826-7 and 1844.
11,17

TONGE

HOGG, A.H.A.
Tonge Castle. In Archaeologia Cantiana, Vol. 44, 1932.
17

WOOD, Walter F.
A chapter of the ancient history of Tonge, compiled by
W.F. Wood.
Parrett. 1937?
11

TRADE - See INDUSTRY AND TRADE

TRANSPORT

KENT COUNTY COUNCIL - ARCHIVES OFFICE.
Transport in Kent: catalogue of documents from the
Kent Archives Office displayed at the Museum...
Maidstone...1959.
Kent County Council. (1959).
4,7,11,12

TRIALS

Account of the trial...of six witches at Maidstone...
1652, to which is added the trial...of three witches...
at Faversham, 1645.
London. 1837.
11

BELL, John Any Bird. Defendant.
A narrative of the facts relative to the murder of
Richard Faulkner Taylor...and the trial of John Any
Bird Bell for the murder.
1831.
12

BIRCH, Richard.
Proceedings of a general Court Martial...on seven
officers of the West Kent Regiment of Militia...
1807.
11

BOYS vs EDMUNDS.
Reports of the trials of the Boys v Edmunds, 1815-17.
Denne. 1816-17.
12

BOYS, J.J. and CHANCELLOR, S.S. vs THE KING.
Correct report of the important trial for libel, the
King v Boys and Chancellor...
Margate. 1817.
11

CANTERBURY PREROGATIVE COURT.
The judgement of the Right Honourable, Sir John
Nicholl, Knight, in the cause of Kinteside against
Harrison...
Brooke. 1818.
12

Copies of all the minutes and proceedings taken
at and upon the several tryals of Captain George
Burrish (and others) respectively; before the Court
Martial lately held at Chatham...
1746.
4

CURLING, Richard AND OTHERS, Defendants.
The trial of Richard Curling, Thomas Moss, John
Forwood, John Sanders and Thomas Read, boatmen of
Ramsgate...
Henry Kent Causton. 1807.
11

DEARN, Thomas Downes Wilmot.
Edmeads vs Charles Lewis...before a special jury at
Croydon in the County of Surrey on 28th July, 1815.
Wickham and Cutbush. 1815.
8

TRIALS, Cont'd

EMANUEL, Manley.
Full report of the trial of Mrs. Levi Manley Emanuel, Mary
Emanuel and Benjamin Wanstall. (Contained in brief memoir
of the life of Benjamin Wanstall...(See Canterbury).
Henry Ward. 1831.
3

GORDON, Major William.
Trial of Major William Gordon of the 2nd, or Queen's, Regiment
of Dragoon Guards...at Guildhall, Sandwich on Friday, April 15th,
1814.
Canterbury, Rouse, Kirby, Lawrence. n.d.
3

MODERS, Mary, alias STEDMAN, Defendant.
Trial of Mary Moders, alias Stedman styled the German Princess,
at the Old Bailey for bigamy. 15 Charles II, A.D. 1663.
(Extracted from Cobbett's (Howell's) State Trials, 1810).
(She was alledged to be from parish of St. Mildred's,
Canterbury).
3

REX vs John MARTEN.
The King on the prosecution of the inhabitants of the parish of
Wrotham...against John Marten, one of the Overseers of the Poor
of the said parish for the years 1806, 1807 and 1808...
Printed by T. Clout. 1809.
11

REX vs James MOUNTAGUE AND OTHERS.
Yantlet Creek: Rex v James Mountague...and others: report of
the trial...
Corporation of the City of London. 1824.
11

Rules...for the Assizes.
1816.
17

SACKVILLE, Lord George.
Trial, 1760?
16

STAHLSCHMIDT v WALFORD.
An account of the proceedings in the late case of Stahlschmidt
versus Walford...
Waterlow. 1878?
2,11

STAPLETON, T. 2nd Baron Le Despencer and Others.
Stapleton v Eveleigh, W.: report of the proceedings of the trial.
n.d.
8,11

Transactions of the two ciminals, George Webb and Richard
Russell - tried at the Kent Summer Assizes in 1805.
Crosby. (1805).
1

Trial of Arthur O'Connor and others for High Treason before
Judge Butler at Maidstone, 1798.
17

Trial of James O'Coigly, otherwise called James Quigley, otherwise
...James John Fivey, Arthur O'Connor, Esq., John Binns, John Allen
and Jeremiah Leary, for High Treason under a special Commission
at Maidstone in Kent...May, 1798. (Taken in shorthand by
Joseph Gurney).
Gurney. 1798.
3

TUFTON, Sackville. 9th Earl of Thanet.
The whole proceedings upon an information exhibited, ex officio,
by the King's Attorney-General, against the Right Honourable
Sackville, Earl of Thanet, Robert Fergusson, Esquire and others,
for a riot and other misdemeanours: tried at the Bar of the
Court of King's Bench, April 25th, 1799; taken in shorthand by
William Ramsey...the evidence compared with the notes of two
other shorthand writers, to which are added some observations by
Robert Fergusson on his own case and on the points of law
arising upon the information.
Printed for R. Ogle. 1799.
11

WOOLER, T.J.
Resistance to church rates: report of the case of Jeffery v
Pybus, tried at Maidstone, March, 1838.
Jeffery. 1838.
12

TROTTISCLIFFE

Church of St. Peter and St. Paul, Trottiscliffe
(788 A.D.-1955 A.D.).
Privately Printed. 1955?
11

TUNBRIDGE WELLS

An account of the towns of Dover and Tunbridge Wells
in 1804.
19

ADDISON, William.
English spas.
Batsford. 1951.
3

AMSINCK, Paul.
Tunbridge Wells and its neighbourhood.
Miller and Lloyd. 1810.
1,3,4,6,8,11,12,15,17,18,19

An analysis of the medicinal waters of Tunbridge Wells.
J. Murray. 1792.
19

ARCHER, John.
The kingdom turned about: a sermon preached at
Tunbridge Wells, August 8th, 1714...
Burleigh. 1714.
19

ARCHER, John.
A sermon preached at the opening of the New Chappal
at Tunbridge Wells, August 1st, 1720.
Richard Ford. 1720.
19

BAILEY, Lorna.
A history of non-conformity in Tunbridge Wells,
Tonbridge and Southborough. (Typescript).
c.1970.
19

BAKER, Thomas.
Tunbridge walks...
1703 etc.
1,11,17,19

BALDOCK, William.
Catalogue of Baldock's circulating library at Tunbridge
Wells.
1804.
19

BARTON, (G.H.).
Cook's illustrated guide to Tunbridge Wells.
1948.
19

BARTON, Margaret.
Tunbridge Wells.
Faber. 1937.
1,3,4,5,6,8,11,12,13,14,15,17,18,19,20

BONNER, G.W.
Kidd's picturesque pocket companion to Tunbridge Wells.
W. Kidd. 1838.
17

BOWRA, John.
A survey of Tunbridge Wells...
1738.
19

BRACKETT, Arthur William.
The Spa Hotel and Tunbridge Wells through the
centuries.
Printed by Tunbridge Wells Courier. (195-?).
11

Tunbridge Wells and its old prints. In Print
Collector's Quarterly, January, 1933.
19

Tunbridge Wells through the centuries.
(1928).
1,2,3,4,8,11,12,19

BRACKETT AND CO.
Centenary and three generations, with a short history of
Tunbridge Wells.
Tunbridge Wells, Brackett and Co. 1928.
1,11,12,19

BRACKETT AND SONS. Auctioneers.
Sale catalogues, 1872-1900.
19

BRITTON, John.
Descriptive sketches of Tunbridge Wells...
London, J. Britton. 1832.
1,2,4,6,8,11,12,15,17,19

Broomhill, Kent, 1898: a souvenir.
Courier Printing Co. 1898.
11

BROWNE, Dr.
An account of the wonderful cures performed by the cold baths...
at Tunbridge...
1707.
19

BURGHOPE AND STRANGE. Publishers.
Handy guide to Tunbridge Wells, etc.
Burghope and Strange. 1877.
17

BURR, Thomas Benge.
The history of Tunbridge Wells.
1766.
1,4,6,7,8,11,12,17,19

CAUSTON, Peter.
Tunbrigialia: (a poem).
1709.
11,19

CLEMENTS, Robert H.M.
Mate's illustrated Tunbridge Wells.
W. Mate and Sons.
11(1906) 12(1905) 17(1905) 19(1905, 1906 and 1907)

CLEMENTS, Robert H.M.
A peep into the past: the Jubilee of...Tunbridge Wells, 1889-
1939.
19

CLIFFORD, John. Publisher.
The Tunbridge Wells guide.
Tunbridge Wells, J. Clifford.
1(1817)
4(1817)
5(1817)
8(1834, 1836)
11(1817)
12(1817)
15(1817, 1823)
17(1829, 1840)
19(1817, 1818, 1821, 1822, 1823, 1828, 1832, 1834, 1840, 1843)

CLIFFORD, John. Publisher.
Visitor's guide to Tunbridge Wells and its environs...
Tunbridge Wells, Printed and Published by J. Clifford.
3(3rd edition, n.d.) 11(1833, 1855) 19(1817-43)

COGHLAN, Francis.
Guide to Tunbridge Wells.
(Trubner). 1840 and 1863.
17

COLBRAN, John. Publisher.
Colbran's new guide for Tunbridge Wells, edited by J. Stephens.
Tunbridge Wells, J. Colbran. London, A.H. Bailey. 1840.
8,11,12,15,17,19

Colbran's new guide for Tunbridge Wells, 2nd edition, 1844,
edited by J. Phippen.
Tunbridge Wells, J. Colbran. London, A.H. Bailey. 1844.
1,2,6,7,11,12

Handbook and directory for Tunbridge Wells.
Tunbridge Wells, J. Colbran. 1847, 1850.
19

Rocks of Tunbridge Wells...
Tunbridge Wells, J. Colbran. 1857.
17

COLBRAN, St. John. Publisher.
St. John Colbran's guide and visitor's handbook to
Tunbridge Wells and neighbourhood.
Tunbridge Wells, St. John Colbran. 1881, 1884.
19

CONNELY, Willard.
Beau Nash: Monarch of Bath and Tunbridge Wells.
Werner Laurie. 1955.
12,19

THE COUNTESS OF HUNTINGDON'S CONNEXION.
A short history of Emmanual Church, Tunbridge Wells.
1941.
19

(COWAN, L. Gibson).
A descriptive guide and souvenir of the High Rocks,
Tunbridge Wells.
Stanford Press. 1964.
19

DEAKIN, Richard.
The flowering plants of Tunbridge Wells and
neighbourhood.
Tunbridge Wells, Stidolph and Bellamy. 1871.
6,11,15,17,19

DINES, H.G.
Geology of the country around Sevenoaks and Tunbridge,
by H.G. Dines and others.
H.M.S.O. 1969.
7,16

DORRINGTON, Theophilus.
The regulations of play...: a sermon preached at the
Chapel of Tunbridge Wells, August 19th, 1706.
M. Jenour. 1706.
19

DOWDING, Air Chief Marshal, Lord.
Service of memorial and burial of Air Chief Marshal,
the Lord Dowding, on Thursday, 12th March, 1970 at
Westminster Abbey (pamphlet).
12

DUDENEY AND PILCHER. Auctioneers.
Tunbridge Wells and district.
n.d.
19

ELERS, F. Wadham.
The Tunbridge Wells General Hospital: a diary...from
its foundation in 1828 to the present time, compiled
by E.F. Elers.
Pelton. 1910.
19

ELWIG, Henry.
A biographical dictionary of notable people at Tunbridge
Wells, 17th-20th centuries. Also a list of local
place-names.
1941.
19

ELWIG, Henry.
Holy Trinity Church (Tunbridge Wells): a centenary
history.
Courier Printing Co. 1929.
19

EVANS, John.
An excursion to Brighton, with...a visit to
Tunbridge Wells...
Whittingham. 1823.
19

EVANS, John.
A visit to Tunbridge Wells, July, 1820: two letters
to a friend. In The European Magazine and London
Review, July-December, 1820.
19

EVEREST, D.
30 views of Tunbridge Wells.
n.d.
19

FISHER UNWIN. Publisher.
Round Tunbridge Wells: a handy guide to rambles in
the district.
Fisher Unwin. n.d.
11,15

FREELING, Arthur.
Picturesque excursions...edited by A. Freeling. (Includes
Margate, Tunbridge Wells and Dover).
Orr. 1840.
2,6,8,11,12,13

GARDNER, Henry.
Penny guide to Tunbridge Wells, Southborough and Tonbridge.
n.d.
19

GASPEY, William.
Brackett's descriptive handguide to Tunbridge Wells and
neighbourhood...
Brackett. 1863.
12,17(1866-68) 19

A general account of Tunbridge Wells and its environs:
historical and descriptive.
Pearch. 1771.
11,19

GIVEN, J.C.M.
Royal Tunbridge Wells, past and present, edited by J.C.M. Given.
Tunbridge Wells, Courier Printing Co. 1946.
1,2,4,8,11,12,18,19

GOULDEN AND NYE. Publishers.
Guide to Tunbridge Wells: with a list of walks and drives in
the neighbourhood.
Goulden and Nye.
1(1900) 17(1889)

GOWER, Sir Robert Vaughan.
Scrapbooks of newscuttings relating to the family, 1918-45.
19

GRANVILLE, Augustus Bozzi.
The spas of England...
Colburn. 1841.
11

GREAT BRITAIN: LAWS, etc. (VIC.).
Rusthall Manor Act, 1839.
19

GREAT BRITAIN: LAWS, etc. (VIC.).
Rusthall Manor Act, 1863.
19

GREAT BRITAIN: LAWS, etc. (VIC.).
Tunbridge Wells Improvement Act, 1846.
19

GREAT BRITAIN: LAWS, etc. (VIC.).
Tunbridge Wells Improvement Act, 1890.
19

GUNNIS, Rupert.
The Church of King Charles the Martyr: the story of the clock.
(1961).
19

GUNNIS, Rupert.
Pictures in the Ashton Bequest.
Tunbridge Wells Public Library. 1952.
11

HAMPSON, John (1760-1817?).
A blow at the root of pretended Calvinism; or, real
Antinomianism.
Tunbridge Wells, J. Sprange. 1788.
11

HARPER, Charles George.
The Hastings Road and the "Happy Springs of Tunbridge".
Chapman and Hall. 1906.
1,5,7,11,12,15,19

HARRINGTONS OF TUNBRIDGE WELLS.
Our Diamond Jubilee Year.
1964.
19

HARTNELL, H.C.
A reverie upon the Pantiles. (Bound with "The armed strength
of the Pantiles").
1878.
19

HEPWORTH, Martyn.
Son et Lumiere: the story of the town (Tunbridge
Wells) from 1606 until the present day.
Tunbridge Wells Borough Council. 1969.
4,8,9,11

HEPWORTH, Martyn.
The story of the Pantiles, Tunbridge Wells.
Tunbridge Wells, Pantiles Association. 1962.
2,4,11,19

HEPWORTH, Printers.
Hepworth's annual, 1902.
19

HOARE, Edward.
Multiplied blessings: eighteen short readings.
S.P.C.K. 1907.
19

HOLLAND, J.D.
The Rev. Thomas Bayes, F.R.S. (1702-61). (Reprinted
from the Journal of the Royal Statistical Society,
Vol. 125, Part 3, 1962).
19

HOPE, Lady Elizabeth Reid.
Tunbridge Wells and its neighbourhood...
Sevenoaks, Salmon. 1909.
1,4,11,12,13

HOPKINS, R. Thurston.
Moated houses of England.
"Country Life". 1935.
5,11,15,18

An Illustrated guide to the residential attractions
and amenities of Royal Tunbridge Wells, Kent.
Croydon, Home Publishing Co. 1952.
11

JARVIS, JOHN LTD. Publishers.
Souvenir of the new Kent and Sussex Hospital, Mount
Ephraim, Tunbridge Wells, July, 1934.
John Jarvis Ltd.
19

JENNER, Edward.
A flora of Tunbridge Wells...
Tunbridge Wells, Colbran. 1845.
1,6,11,12,17,19

JONES, Edgar Yoxall.
A prospect of Tunbridge Wells and adjacent countryside.
Lambarde Press. 1964.
1,2,4,8,10,11,15,19

JOWITT, (R.L.P.).
Discovering spas.
Shire Publications. 1971.
19

KENT AND SUSSEX HOSPITAL, TUNBRIDGE WELLS.
Annual report, 1947. (Last voluntary report).
19

KENT COUNTY COUNCIL - ARCHIVES OFFICE.
Catalogue of Rusthall Estate. (MSS.).
1966.
19

KNIPE, Henry R.
Tunbridge Wells and neighbourhood...1608 to 1915...
edited by H.R. Knipe.
Tunbridge Wells, Pelton. 1916.
1,2,6,8,11,12,14,15,17,19

LEE, Edwin.
Tunbridge Wells. (Reprinted from..."Baths and
Watering Places of England").
Tunbridge Wells, Colbran. 1849.
19

Life and death of John Carpenter, alias Hell-fire
Dick.
Crosby. 1805.
12

LINDON, D.W.
Tunbridge Wells in Kent and their chalybeate waters.
1748.
17

List of the rare plants found in the neighbourhood of Tunbridge
Wells.
W. Thorne, Printer. n.d.
19

Map of Tunbridge Wells with the improvements on the
Calverley Estate.
1838.
11,19

MARSHALL, Emma.
Up and down the Pantiles.
Seeley. 1890.
11,12,17,19

MARSHALL, JAPP AND CO. Publishers.
Round Tunbridge Wells...
Marshall, Japp and Co. 1881.
17

MARTIN, W. Stanley.
Tunbridge Wells of today, by W.S. Martin and B.P. Row.
Tunbridge Wells, Clements. 1897.
1,2,8,11,12,17,18,19

MARTIN, W. Stanley.
Tunbridge Wells of today, with its surroundings. An illustrated
handbook for the town and district, 2nd edition, by W.S. Martin
and B.P. Row.
Homeland Association Ltd. 1906.
4,7,15,19

MELVILLE, Lewis.
Society at Royal Tunbridge Wells in the 18th century and after.
Nash. 1912.
1,4,5,6,7,8,11,12,15,18,19

"METELLUS", pseud.
Metellus, his dialogues. The first part containing a relation
of a journey to Tunbridge Wells...
1693.
19

The Mirror, August 1st, 1829 and October 1st, 1831, containing
articles on Tunbridge Wells.
19

MONEY, J.H.
Excavations at High Rocks, Tunbridge Wells, 1954-56.
Sussex Archaeological Society. n.d.
5,11,12

MONEY, J.H.
Excavations in the Iron Age Hill For at High Rocks near
Tunbridge Wells, 1957-61. (Reprinted from Sussex Archaeological
Society Proceedings, Vol. 106, 1968).
4

MUDFORD, William.
Life of Richard Cumberland.
Neely and Jones. 1812.
19

NASH, Richard.
The life of Richard Nash Esq.
J. Newberry. 1762.
12,19

NATIONAL COUNCIL OF WOMEN.
Some war work in Tunbridge Wells, May, 1915-April, 1919.
Baldwin. (1920).
19

NEWMAN, A. Publisher.
Tunbridge Wells: twelve views.
A. Newman. 1868.
19

NICHOLS, William.
God's blessing on the use of mineral waters: a sermon preached
at the Chapel of Tunbridge Wells, September 6th, 1702.
Thomas Bennet. 1702.
19

NOYES, J. Publisher.
Tunbridge Wells: 30 views.
Tunbridge Wells, J. Noyes. n.d.
11,19

PANTILES ASSOCIATION.
Romance of the Pantiles (Tunbridge Wells).
Pearce. n.d.
19

The Pantiles Lodge, No. 2,200: souvenir of the
Jubilee Festival, April 29th, 1937, Pump Room,
Tunbridge Wells.
Pantiles Lodge. 1937.
7

The Pantiles Papers, Vol. 1.
Allen. 1878.
19

PEARCE, Luke.
Historical association of the free churches of Tunbridge
Wells...1642-1904.
Tunbridge Wells, Pearce. 1904?
11

PEARCE, Luke.
Historical associations of Royal Tunbridge Wells from
1606 to 1909.
Tunbridge Wells, Pearce. 1912.
11,19

PELTON, Aubrey John. Publisher.
Illustrated guide to Royal Tunbridge Wells.
Tunbridge Wells, A.J. Pelton. n.d.
7,13,19

PELTON, Richard.
Pelton's illustrated guide to Tunbridge Wells.
R. Pelton.
1(1893 etc.) 8(1905) 11(1891) 15(1891) 17(1871)
19(1874, 1875, 1881, 1883, 1888, 1891, 1893 1896, 1905)

PELTON, Richard.
Pelton's illustrated guide to Tunbridge Wells and the
neighbouring seats, towns and villages, (9th edition,
1881). Reprinted with a new introduction by Jean
Mauldon).
S.R. Publishers. 1970.
3,4,8,11,19

PHIPPEN, James.
An account of the planting of the Royal Victoria
Grove at Tunbridge Wells.
Brighton, Levy E. Cohen. 1835.
11

Pictorial history of Tunbridge Wells and district.
1892.
4

Pictorial record of H.R.H., the Prince of Wale's visit,
25th July, 1928.
19

PILCHER, Donald E.
"Early nineteenth century architecture at Tunbridge
Wells". In Journal of the British Architectural
Association, September, 1934.
19

PINTO, H.
Tunbridge and Scottish souvenir woodware, by H. and
E.R. Pinto.
Bell. 1970.
19

Plans of Tunbridge Wells Civic Centre competition.
In "The Builder", November 16th, 1934.
19

POPE, W.L.
A word about "The Grove".
Tunbridge Wells, Nash. 1868.
19

POWELL, Robert Hutchinson.
Guide to the mineral waters of Tunbridge Wells.
1847.
17

A medical topography of Tunbridge Wells...
Tunbridge Wells, Colbran. 1846.
1,6,11,12,171,9

The mineral spring of Tunbridge Wells.
Tunbridge Wells, Colbran. 1861.
19

QUINTON, A.R.
Tunbridge Wells and neighbourhood from the original
watercolour paintings.
J. Salmon. 189-?
11

REED, Margaret S.E.
Henry Reed: an eventful life devoted to God and man.
Morgan and Scott. 1906.
19

REYNOLDS, CHARLES AND CO. Publishers.
The album of Tunbridge Wells views.
n.d.
11,19

RHODES, S.
Map of Tunbridge Wells...showing the position of the new
church...
Neele. 1828.
11,17

ROBERTS, Fred.
The High Rocks Hotel and Pleasure Gardens.
n.d.
17,19

ROBERTS, Fred.
The walks and drives guide to Tunbridge Wells, 2nd edition
revised.
1899.
17,19

ROBINSON. Publisher.
Guide to Tunbridge Wells and district.
Brighton, Robinson. 1908.
19

ROBINSON. Publisher.
Who's who and where: the illustrated year book of Tunbridge
Wells and district.
Brighton, Robinson. 1908.
1,19

ROUSE, Lewis.
Tunbridge Wells; or, a directory for the drinking of those
waters.
Roberts. 1725.
12

ROWZEE, Lodwick.
The Queen's Wells.
Robert Boulter. 1671.
19

ROYAL TUNBRIDGE WELLS BOROUGH COUNCIL.
Central area plan: report upon the survey and analysis.
1964.
19

Certified copy of the Charter of Incorporation.
1889.
19

Chalybeate springs, Pantiles.
Advertiser Co. 1906.
11

Golden Jubilee Year, 1959.
Baldwin. (1959).
19

Municipal offices, 1846-1936.
19

A plan for the town centre.
1966.
3,12,19

Royal Tunbridge Wells: Diamond Jubilee, 1969.
19

Royal Tunbridge Wells: the official guide.
C.J. Burrow. n.d.
1,5,7,11,12

Royal Tunbridge Wells: the official guide.
Tunbridge Wells Borough Council.
1(1961) 4(1963) 11(1961) 17(1911, 1961) 19(1902 in progress)

A welcome to Royal Tunbridge Wells.
Clarke and Sherwell. 19---?
11

ROYAL TUNBRIDGE WELLS BOROUGH COUNCIL - PUBLICITY AND
ENTERTAINMENTS COMMITTEE.
A warm welcome to Royal Tunbridge Wells.
Royal Tunbridge Wells Borough Council - Publicity and
Entertainments Committee. (1954).
11

ROYAL TUNBRIDGE WELLS PUBLIC LIBRARY.
Local history catalogue, 1966.
Royal Tunbridge Wells Public Library.
2,3,4,5,7,8,9,11,12,19

Royal Tunbridge Wells: the chalybeate spring that
brought court patronage and civic development.
(Municipal Review, November, 1962).
4

St. John's Church, Tunbridge Wells, 1858-1958.
19

St. Luke's Church, Tunbridge Wells, the first forty
years, 1910-1950.
19

SAUNDERS. Publisher.
Royal Tunbridge Wells: guide and handbook of useful
information.
Saunders. 1920.
19

SAVIDGE, Alan.
The story of the church of King Charles-the-Martyr,
Royal Tunbridge Wells.
British Publishing Co. 1969.
4,8,11,19

Scenic attractions of Tunbridge Wells and environs.
Tunbridge Wells Borough Improvement Association.
1896.
11,19

SCUDAMORE, Charles.
Analysis of the mineral water of Tunbridge Wells...
1816.
17

SHAW, John.
Travels in England: a ramble with the city and town
missionaries. (Chapter on Tunbridge Wells).
Johnson. 1861.
19

SMITH, William.
Memoir of William Smith, for twenty-six years Pastor
of Rehobath Baptist Chapel, Tunbridge Wells.
Farncombe. 1904.
1,19

SOCIETY FOR PROMOTING CHRISTIAN KNOWLEDGE.
The watering places of England. (Tunbridge Wells and
others).
1853.
19

SOUTH-EASTERN RAILWAY CO.
Illustrated tourist guide...Chislehurst, Sevenoaks,
Tunbridge Wells...
Morton. n.d.
11

SOUTH-EASTERN UNION OF SCIENTIFIC SOCIETIES.
Tunbridge Wells and neighbourhood.
South-Eastern Union of Scientific Societies. 1916.
1,17

SPALDING, Helen.
Tunbridge Wells: a report presented at the request
of the Borough Council by the Tunbridge Wells Civic
Association, 1945, edited by H. Spalding.
Courier Printing and Publishing Co. 1945.
8,12,17

SPIERS, R.E.A.
A history of Christ Church, Tunbridge Wells, 1835-
1946.
19

SPRANGE, J. Publisher.
Tunbridge Wells guide.
Tunbridge Wells, J. Sprange.

1(1797)	11(1780, 1808, 1819, 1834)
2(1811)	12(1780, 1817)
4(1801)	15(1784)
5(1801, 1806)	16(1801)
6(1780)	17(1811)
7(1780)	18(1780)
8(1780)	19(1780-1817)

SPRANGE, J. Publisher.
Visitor's guide to the watering places. (Tunbridge Wells -
Pages 80-126).
Tunbridge Wells, J. Sprange. 1841.
19

SQUIRRELL, F.C.
Civil defence: a history of civil defence in the Borough of
Royal Tunbridge Wells, 1939-1945.
Printed by Tunbridge Wells Courier. 1945.
11,19

STACE, R.A.
Country walks around Tunbridge Wells, compiled by R.A. Stace.
Tunbridge Wells, Clements. 1946.
11,19

STAPLEY, William. Publisher.
Stapley's Tunbridge Wells visitor's guide.
W. Stapley. 1847.
19

STRANGE, Charles Hilbert.
The Jubilee of Tunbridge Wells as an Incorporated Borough.
Tunbridge Wells Borough Council. 1939.
19

Mount Pleasant Congregational Church, Tunbridge Wells...
1830-1930.
Tunbridge Wells, Pelton. n.d.
11,19

Non-conformity in Tunbridge Wells.
Courier Printing Co. 1949.
11,19

The Stranges of Tunbridge Wells.
n.d.
19

Summer excursion to Tunbridge Wells and its neighbourhood.
E. Marks. 1847.
19

(THOMSON, J. Radford).
Brief memorial of the ministry of the Rev. J. Radford Thomson
...Tunbridge Wells.
Tunbridge Wells Gazette. 1882.
11

TOWNSEND, Rev. J.H.
Edward Hoare, M.A.: a record of his life...edited by Rev. J.H.
Townsend.
Hodder and Stoughton. 1896.
19

TOWNSEND, Rev. J.H.
Where old and new meet: a brief record of the church and
parish of Broadwater Down (Tunbridge Wells).
Tunbridge Wells, Pelton. n.d.
19

TRIMNELL, Charles. Bishop of Norwich.
A sermon preached at Tunbridge Wells in Kent on Sunday,
September 18th, 1715.
D. Midwinter. 1715.
12

The Tunbridge Miscellany...poems...
E. Curll. 1711.
19

TUNBRIDGE WELLS ADVERTISER.
The Jubilee of Incorporation...
n.d.
19

Tunbridge Wells and County Magazine, Vol. 1, No. i, 1923.
19

TUNBRIDGE WELLS AND DISTRICT COUNCIL OF SOCIAL SERVICE.
Annual report, 1968-69.
19

TUNBRIDGE WELLS CIVIC ASSOCIATION.
Tunbridge Wells...1945.
Tunbridge Wells Courier. 1945.
2,8,11,12,15,19

TUNBRIDGE WELLS LITERARY SOCIETY.
Early reports.
Clifford. 1839 etc.
19

TUNBRIDGE WELLS NATURAL HISTORY AND PHILOSOPHICAL
SOCIETY.
Annual reports, 1897, 1899, 1900 and 1906.
17

TUNBRIDGE WELLS OPERA HOUSE.
Programme of the foundation stone laying ceremony,
1901.
19

TUNBRIDGE WELLS TRADEMENS' ASSOCIATION.
Prize essays on the best way to increase the
attractiveness of Tunbridge Wells...
Tunbridge Wells Advertiser. 1887.
19

Tunbridge Wells. (Extract from unknown book).
(1803).
17

Tunbridge Wells. (A folder of views).
n.d.
17

Tunbridge Wells hailstorm, 25th May, 1922: reports
and photographs.
19

Tunbridge Wells views.
1866.
11,19

Tunbrigialia; or, Tunbridge miscellany for the years
1709, 1730, 1737, 1738, 1739 and 1740.
11(1730) 19(1709, 1730, 1737, 1738, 1739 and 1740)

WALLINGER, W.
A sermon preached in...Tunbridge Wells, June 18th,
1840.
Tunbridge Wells, Colbran. 1840.
12

WALTERS, John.
Splendour and scandal: the reign of Beau Nash.
Jarrolds. 1968.
19

War memorial unveiling.
(1920).
19

WARING, Col. L.H.
The story of the church of King Charles the Martyr.
Hepworth. 1936.
19

WILSON, Thomas.
The Diaries, 1731-37, 1750.
S.P.C.K. 1964.
19

YOUNGHUSBAND, Ethel.
Mansions, men and Tunbridge Ware.
Slough, Windsor Press. 1949.
1,2,4,5,7,8,11,12,15,19

TUNSTALL

Bibliotheca Topographica Britannica, No. 1, containing
1..., 2 - The history and antiquities of Tunstall in
Kent, by the late Mr. Edward Rowe Mores. (See HISTORY
AND ARCHAEOLOGY).
J. Nichols. 1780.
1,4,5,6,8,11,12,15,17

MIDWINTER, Arthur.
The church and village of Tunstall, Kent.
Sittingbourne, Parrett. 1957.
3,4,8,11,12,15,20

ULCOMBE

BREDIN, E.R.
A short history of the parish church of All Saints,
Ulcombe.
Maidstone, Burkitt, Printer. (1931).
3,7

HILTON, John Anthony.
Joseph Hatch: the Ulcombe bellfounder.
Hilton. 1965.
3,7,8,19

UPCHURCH

HUME, I. Noel.
Ritual burials in the Upchurch Marshes. In Archaeologia
Cantiana, Vol. 70, 1956.
17

HUME, I. Noel.
Romano-British potteries on the Upchurch Marshes. In
Archaeologia Cantiana, Vol. 68, 1954.
17

JAMES, Harold A.
The church of St. Mary the Virgin, Upchurch.
Church Publishers. 1965.
1,2,4,8,11

WOODRUFF, Cumberland H.
The antiquities of Upchurch.
1889.
11

UPNOR

ANDREWS, Charles William.
On a specimen of elephas antiquus from Upnor by the late
C.W. Andrews.
British Museum. 1928.
4

The "Arethusa": a unique home and school.
(196-?).
4

EVANS, S.
Upnor: some notes on the Castle and other things.
Privately Printed. c.1951.
4,8,15

HARRIS, Edwin.
The history of Upnor Castle. (Eastgate Series, No. 10).
Rochester, E. Harris. 1911.
15

SAUNDERS, A.D.
Upnor Castle, Kent. (Ministry of Public Building and Works,
Ancient Monuments and Historical Buildings).
H.M.S.O. 1967.
1,2,3,4,6,7,8,11,12,15,19

TURNER, Sydney K. of Luton.
(Poems) Ode to the Upnor Elephant. The Upnor Elephant.
(Typescript).
1940.
4,8,15

TURNER, Sydney K. of Luton.
The story of Upnor. (Typescript).
c.1940.
4,8,15

VISITATIONS - See GENEALOGICAL RECORDS

WALDERSLADE

KENT COUNTY COUNCIL - PLANNING DEPARTMENT.
Walderslade: informal action area plan.
Kent County Council. 1972.
11

WALDERSHARE

LUCAS, Reginald.
Lord North, 1732-92, 2 vols.
Humphreys. 1913.
6

WALMER - See Also DEAL

BRASSEY, Sybil. Countess.
Episodes and reflections.
Murray. 1923.
12

BRASSEY, Thomas. Earl. (Lord Warden of the Cinque Ports -
c.1889).
The Sunbeam, R.Y.S. voyages.
Murray. 1918.
6

BRIDGES, Robert.
The testament of beauty.
Oxford University Press. 1930.
3,12

BRIDGES, Robert.
Three friends...
Oxford University Press. 1938.
12

BULWER, Sir Henry Lytton.
Life of Henry John Temple, Viscount Palmerston (Lord
Warden of the Cinque Ports, 1861), 2 vols.
Richard Bentley. 1870.
6

CURZON, George Nathaniel. 1st Marquess Curzon of
Kedleston.
The personal history of Walmer Castle and its Lord
Wardens, edited by S. Gwynn.
Macmillan. 1927.
1,4,6,7,8,11,12,13,14,15,18

DOWKER, George.
Roman remains at Walmer and Ramsgate. In "Kent
Miscellanea", Vol. 4.
n.d.
11,14

ELVIN, Charles R.S.
History of Walmer and Walmer Castle.
Privately Printed. 1887 etc.
1,3,4,6,7,8,11,12,15,17

ELVIN, Charles R.S.
Records of Walmer...
Henry Gray. 1890.
1,3,4,6,7,11,12,14,15,17

Inventory and valuation of furniture, the property of
the Most Honourable, the Marchioness of Willingdon...
June, 1938. (Daughter of Thomas, Earl Brassey).
11

LAW, Ernest.
Walmer Castle illustrated: a popular guide to the
Castle...
H. Rees. 1906.
7,13

LEE-WARNER, Sir William.
The life of the Marquis of Dalhousie, 2 vols. (Lord
Warden of the Cinque Ports, 1853).
Macmillan. 1904.
6

LYALL, Sir Alfred.
The life of the Marquis of Dufferin and Ava, 2 vols.
(Lord Warden of the Cinque Ports, 1891-5).
John Murray. 1905.
6

MAXWELL, Sir Herbert.
Life and times of the Right Honourable William Henry
Smith, 2 vols. (Lord Warden of the Cinque Ports,
1891).
Blackwood. 1893.
6

MAXWELL, Sir Herbert.
The life of Wellington, 2 vols. (Lord Warden of the
Cinque Ports, 1829).
Slow, Marston, etc. 1899.
6

Minerva Railway guide and visitor's handbook for Deal,
Walmer, Sandwich and district.
1906.
17

O'NEIL, Bryan Hugh St. John.
Walmer Castle, Kent.
H.M.S.O. 1950.
1,4,6,8,11,12,13

ROGER, John Lewis.
Sketches of Deal, Walmer and Sandwich.
Longmans. 1911.
1,3,4,6,11,12,15,17,18

RONALDSHAY, Earl of.
Life of Lord Curzon, 3 vols. (Lord Warden of the
Cinque Ports, 1904-5).
Benn. 1928.
6

CRANBROOK RURAL DISTRICT COUNCIL.
Cranbrook Rural District, Kent: official guide.
Croydon, Home Publishing Co. 1952 and various editions.
1,2,4,7,11,12,15

CRANBROOK RURAL DISTRICT COUNCIL.
Cranbrook Rural District, Kent: official guide.
Cheltenham, Burrow. 1963 etc.
1,7,11,12,19

DAVISON, Ian.
When night comes.
Jenkins. 1936.
1,4,11,12,19

DAVISON, Ian.
Where smugglers walked.
Jenkins. 1935.
1,7,8,11,12,17,19

DEARN, Thomas Downes Wilmot.
An historical, topographical and descriptive account of the
Weald of Kent.
Cranbrook, Waters. 1814.
1,3,4,5,6,8,11,12,15,17,18,19

DELANY, Mary Cecilia.
The historical geography of the Wealden Iron Industry.
Benn. 1921.
1,2,3,5,11,15,19

Famous old inns of Mid Kent.
Hamilton-Fisher. n.d.
11

FAWCETT, William.
Report of the Weald series of excursions of the Geologists'
Association of London...
Geologists' Association. 1879.
1

FURLEY, Robert.
History of the Weald of Kent, 2 vols.
Ashford, Igglesden. 1871-74.
1,2,3,4,5,6,7,8,9,11,12,13,14,15,16,17,19,20,21

GARDNER, J. Starkie.
Iron casting in the Weald.
Nichols. 1898.
11

GEOLOGICAL SURVEY AND MUSEUM.
Geology of the country around Tenterden, edited by E.R. Shephard-
Thom and others.
H.M.S.O. 1966.
1,4,5,7,8,11,15,19

The geology of the Weald.
Longman. 1875.
1,7,8,11,15

The Wealden district, by F.H. Edmunds. (British Regional
Geology Series).
H.M.S.O.
1st edition, 1935 (1,2,4,7,8,11,17)
2nd edition, 1948 (1,3,4,5,6,7,9,11,13,15,19,20)
3rd edition, 1954 (17)
4th edition, 1965 (by R.W. Gallois, based on the previous editions
by the late F.H. Edmunds).
2,3,4,5,6,7,8,9,10,11,15,19

KAYE-SMITH, Sheila.
Weald of Kent and Sussex.
Hale. 1953.
1,2,3,4,5,7,8,10,11,12,15,18,19,21

KEECH, Gertrude Clara.
Staplehurst and the Weald of Kent.
Research Publishing Co. 1965.
1,2,4,7,8,11,19

KENYON, G.H.
Glass industry of the Weald.
Leicester University Press. 1967.
1,2,3,5,6,7,8,21

KIRKALDY, J.F.
Geology of the Weald. (Geologists' Association Guides, No. 29).
Colchester, Benham and Co. 1958 and 1967.

1(1958)	8(1958)
2(1967)	9(1958)
3(1958)	11(1958)
4(1958)	12(1958)
5(1958)	15(1958)
6(1967)	17(1958)
7(1958)	

LANE AND GENTRY. Publishers.
Lane and Gentry's standard guide to the Weald of
Kent, including Tenterden, Hawkhurst, Cranbrook and the
Rother Valley.
Margate, Lane and Gentry. (1921 etc.).
7

MARGARY, I.D.
Roman ways in the Weald.
Pheonix House. 1948 and 1965. (Baker, 3rd
edition, 1973).
1,2(1965) 3,4,5,7,8,9,11(1948, 1973) 12,15,17,18,19
21

MARKHAM, Gervase.
Farewel to husbandry...Bound with, The inrichment of
the Weald of Kent.
1684.
4,19

MARKHAM, Fervase.
The inrichment of the Weald of Kent; or, a direction
to the husbandman for the true ordering, manuring and
inriching of all the grounds within the Wealds of
Kent and Sussex.
1625. Printed by G.P. for Roger Jackson.
11,21

1631. Printed for G. Oakes for John Harison.
11

1636. Printed by A. Griffin for John Harison.
5,11,15,21

1649. Printed by B.A. for John Harison.
7

1656/7. Printed by W. Wilson for E. Brewster and
G. Sawbridge.
6

1660. No publisher or printer given.
1

1664. Printed by W. Wilson for G. Sawbridge.
11

1668. Printed by J. Streater for G. Sawbridge.
8

1683. Printed for G. Sawbridge.
1,4,17

1973. Facsimile reprint. De Capo Press.
11,19

MASON, R.T.
Framed buildings of the Weald.
Hand-Cross, Mason. 1964. Coach Publishing House. 1969.
1,3,4,5,6,7(1969) 8(1964, 1969) 9(1969) 11(1964 and 1969)
12,17,19(1969)

MILLS, Halford L.
The River Beult and ponds of the Weald.
South-Eastern Gazette. 1930.
11

MILLWARD, Roy.
The High Weald, by R. Millward and A. Robinson.
Macmillan. 1971.
4,8,11

MILLWARD, Roy.
South-East England: Thameside and the Weald, by
R. Millward and A. Robinson.
Macmillan. 1971.
3,4,5,9,11,21

The Mirror; or, Weald of Kent repository of literature,
amusement and instruction.
1824.
17

MOORE, John S.
Laughton: a study in the evolution of the Wealden
landscape.
1965.
4,15,21

NEWMAN, John.
West Kent and the Weald. (From "The Building of England,
edited by Nikolaus Pevsner, Vol. 38).
Penguin. 1969.
2,4,7,9,19,21

NOYES, T.H.
An idyll of the Weald and other lays and legends.
T.H. Noyes. 1868.
12

REEVES, J.W.
Field meetings in the Cretaceous of the Western part of the
Weald, by J.W. Reeves and J.F. Kirkaldy. (Proceedings of the
Geologists' Association, Vol. 69, 1958).
Reprinted by Benham, Colchester, 1959.
11

SANDERS, Frederick.
Kentish (Wealden) churchyards. (Typescript).
1936.
4

SANDERS, Frederick.
Kentish (Wealden) dialect. First issued, 1935. This copy
(4), 1966. (Typescript).
1935.
4

SCOTT, J.D.
Iron from the Weald. (Extract from "Trade Winds", February,
1962).
4

SHINDLER, Robert.
Mission work among the hop-pickers in the Weald of Kent.
Morgan and Scott. 1893.
11,12,13,17

SIMMONS, W.T. Publisher.
Cranbrook almanac; or Weald of Kent compendium for 1904-5.
Cranbrook, W.T. Simmons.
1

STRAKER, Ernest.
Wealden Iron.
Bell. 1931.
1,2(and 1967) 3,4,5,6,7,8,11,12,13,15,19,21

STRAKER, Ernest.
Ironworks and communications in the Weald in Roman times, by
E. Straker and I.D. Margary.
Clowes. 1938.
11

(SUTHERLAND, Alexander).
Reports...of proposed canal through the Weald of Kent intended
to form a junction of the rivers Medway and Rother...
London, Printed by R.B. Scott. 1802.
3

SWEETING, G.S.
Wealden iron ore and the history of its industry. (Proceedings
of the Geologists' Association, Vol. 1, 1944).
19

TENTERDEN BOROUGH COUNCIL.
Borough and Rural District of Tenterden.
Gloucester, British Publishing Co. 1956 etc.
1,4,8,11,15,19

TENTERDEN CHAMBER OF TRADE.
Tenterden and district guide (1936 edition).
Thomson.
11

TICEHURST, John.
The first ten years, 1960-70: the record of an amenity society.
Weald of Kent Preservation Society. 1970.
4,6,11

WARD, Gordon Reginald.
Manor of Lewisham and its Wealden "dens". (Reprinted from
Greenwich and Lewisham Antiquarian Society Transactions, 191-?).
11

WATSON, Joan.
A revision of English Wealden flora...Vol. 1 - Charales -
Ginkgoales.
London, British Museum. 1969.
3,19

Weald of Kent News Almanac for 1883.
Hawkhurst, Williams. 1882.
1

Will she bear it? A tale of the Weald, 3 vols.
London, S. Tinsley. 1872.
17

WINSER, Lilian.
Lays and legends of the Weald of Kent.
Elkin Matthews. 1897 and 1907.
1(1897) 2(1897) 4(1907) 8(1907) 9(1907) 11(1907) 12(1907)
15(1907) 16(1897) 17(1907) 19(1907) 20(1907)

WOOD, G.V.
The heavy mineral suites of the Lower Greensand of the
Western Weald. (From Proceedings of the Geologists'
Association).
Colchester, Benham. 1957.
11

WOOLDRIDGE, Sidney William.
The Weald, by S.W. Wooldridge and F. Goldring.
Collins. 1953 etc.
1,2,3,4,5(1953, 1962, 1966) 7,8,9,11,12,15,17,19

WYE COLLEGE.
The small farm on heavy land: a study of the problems
of farming in the Wealden area of South-East England...
by Ian G. Reid.
Wye College. 1958.
12

WELLING

CASTELLS, Francis de Paula.
Bexley Heath and Welling.
Bexley Heath, Jenkins. 1910.
1,2,5,8,11,12,17,18

The church of St. Michael, Welling.
Church Publishers. 1964.
8

Plan and conditions of sale of the Danson Estate.
Daniel Smith, Oakley and Garrard. 1922.
17

THOMAS, John.
A Welsh shepherd boy and his descendants. (Last one
lived in Welling).
1876.
17

WELLS, H.G.

BELGION, Montgomery.
H.G. Wells.
Longmans. 1953.
12

BERGONZI, Bernard.
The early H.G. Wells.
Manchester University Press. (1961).
12

BROME, Vincent.
H.G. Wells: a biography.
Longmans, Green. 1951.
2,12

BRYDONE, James Edward.
Centenary of H.G. Wells, 1866-1966: Spade House,
Folkestone, compiled by J.E. Brydone.
Mrs. E.M. May. 1966.
1,2,4,7,11

DICKSON, Lovat.
H.G. Wells: his turbulent life and times.
Macmillan. 1969.
12

DOUGHTY, F.H.
H.G. Wells, educationist.
Cape. 1926.
12

NICHOLSON, Norman.
H.G. Wells.
Barker. 1950.
12

WAGAR, W. Warren.
H.G. Wells and the world state.
Yale University Press. 1961.
12

WILSON, Harris.
Arnold Bennett and H.G. Wells, edited by H. Wilson.
Hart-Davis. 1960.
12

WEST FARLEIGH

All Saints' Church, West Farleigh, 25th anniversary of
the Battle of Britain: order of commemoration service...
September 19th, 1965.
12

DANBY, J. Collinson.
Graphic pen and ink sketches of old portions of West Wickham,
Kent, 1882-84. (Cyclostyle facsimiles).
J.C. Danby for Private Circulation. (1885?).
2

DENNY, Sir Henry L.L.
History of West Wickham, Kent.
Printed by Plaistow Press. 1928.
2

FARNABY, Sir Charles F.
A farewell sermon preached at the parish church of West Wickham.
Gilbert and Rivington. 1848.
2

GREENHILL, F.A.
An incised slab at West Wickham. (Reprinted from Archaeologia
Cantiana, Vol. 61, 1949).
2,17

HEWITT, George.
Memorials of the Rev. William Taynton.
Robinson. 1892.
2

HEWITT, George.
Story of Emmanuel, 1886-1964 - Congregational Church, West
Wickham. (Duplicated typescript).
1964.
2

HILL, D. Ingrade.
Ancient heraldic glass at Wickham Court, West Wickham, by
D.I. Hill and C.R. Councer. (Photocopy of account in Journal
of the British Society of Master Glass Painters, Vol. 11, No. 2,
1952-3).
2

HOGG, A.H.A.
Earthworks on Hayes and West Wickham Commons, by A.H.A. Hogg
and others. In Archaeologia Cantiana, Vol. 54, 1941.
17

MARY GREGORY, Mother.
The purchase of Wickham Court by the Lennards. (Reprinted from
Archaeologia Cantiana, Vol. 79).
Ashford, Headley Bros. 1964.
2

MARY GREGORY, Mother.
Wickham Court and the Heydons. (Reprinted from Archaeologia
Cantiana, Vol. 78).
Ashford, Headley Bros. 1963.
2

MILLS, A.R.
The Halls of Ravenswood (West Wickham). More pages from the
Journal of Emily and Ellen Hall.
Muller. 1967.
2

MILLS, A.R.
Two Victorian ladies. More pages from the Journal of Emily and
Ellen Hall. (Note: residents of West Wickham from 1842).
Muller. 1969.
2

NORMAN, Philip.
Flint implements found at Keston and note on a pit at West
Wickham Common. (Galley proof from the Proceedings of the
Society of Antiquaries, 2nd Series, Vol. 17, 1898).
2

PALMER, Harold.
Souvenir of Wickham Hall, 1897. (Photographs, no text).
2

RAVENSWOOD (WEST WICKHAM) WOMEN'S INSTITUTE.
Ravenswood (West Wickham) Village Scrapbook. (Photocopy).
(1955).
2

SHERRARD, O.A.
Two Victorian girls with extracts from the Hall Diaries.
(Halls of West Wickham, Kent).
Muller. 1966.
2

SUNDAY TIMES MAGAZINE.
The dream of suburbia. (Note: features Keston and
West Wickham).
Times Newspapers Ltd. February 11th, 1968.
2

WALKER, Joyce E.
British Red Cross Society, 1870-1970: an account of
the British Red Cross Society in West Wickham (Kent).
(Formed in 1913 - duplicated typescript).
1970.
2

WALKER, Joyce E.
A Wickham hotpot. (West Wickham historical miscellany
and reminiscences, 1872-1972 - typescript).
1972.
2

WALLER, John G.
(Figures in painted glass in West Wickham Church...).
Photocopy from Proceedings of the Society of
Antiquaries, 2nd Series, Vol. 15, 1894.
2

WALLER, John G.
Painted or stained glass from West Wickham Church,
Kent. (Extract from the Quarterly Papers on
Architecture, edited by J. Weale, Vol. 2, 1844).
2

WATSON, Ida L.
History of West Wickham, Kent.
Sidcup, Erwood. 1959.
1,2,8,19

WATSON, Ida L.
I remember... (photocopies of a series of articles in the
Parish News from St. Francis (West Wickham)).
1967-68.
2

WEST WICKHAM CHAMBER OF COMMERCE.
Shops and businesses in and around West Wickham.
West Wickham Chamber of Commerce. (1970).
2

WEST WICKHAM COMMUNITY COUNCIL.
Programme of activities in celebration of the Coronation
...1953.
West Wickham Community Council.
2

WEST WICKHAM FESTIVAL WEEK.
Brochure and programme. (Includes outline history of
West Wickham).
Coney Hall Toc H. 1951.
2

WEST WICKHAM WOMEN'S INSTITUTE.
Scrapbook of Glebe House, West Wickham, 1634-1964.
(Photocopy).
1964.
2

WEST WICKHAM WOMEN'S INSTITUTE.
West Wickham Scrapbook (photocopy).
1955.
2

Wickham Court 500 year anniversary...open day...21st
May, 1969. (Includes short history).
2

Wickham Court, Kent: the seat of Sir Henry Lennard
Bart. (Extract from "Gardens Old and New..." Country
Life Library Series).
Country Life. (19--?).
2

Wickham Court (Hotel), West Wickham... (Brochure with
illustrations).
c.1933.
2

WRIGHT, Aubrey K.W.
A brief sketch in black and white of the parish church
of St. John the Baptist, West Wickham. (Reprinted from
"Parish Life", August, 1971).
2

WESTBERE

BROMLEY, Francis E.
Our old church (Westbere) in the olden times. (MS.).
1931.
3

JESSUP, Ronald Frank.
An Anglo-Saxon cemetery at Westbere. (Reprinted from The
Antiquaries Journal, Vol. XXVI, 1946).
1,3

Restoration of the ancient church of All Saints, Westbere.
1883.
3

WESTENHANGER

CLINCH, George.
Notes on the remains of Westenhanger House, Kent.
Mitchell and Hughes. 1915.
7,17

WADMORE, J.F.
Thomas Smythe of Westenhanger...(Reprinted from Archaeologia
Cantiana).
Mitchell and Hughes. 1887.
1,11,17

WESTERHAM

AMERICAN HERITAGE MAGAZINE AND UNITED PRESS INTERNATIONAL.
Churchill: the life triumphant, the historical record of
ninety years.
American Heritage Publishing Co. 1965.
12

ARTHUR, Sir George.
Concerning Winston Spencer Churchill.
Heinemann. 1940.
12

AYLWARD. A.E. Wolfe.
Pictorial life of Wolfe.
Plymouth, Mayflower Press. 1924.
11,12

BLACK, G.T.
Westerham Valley.
1962.
1,2,4,6,8,11,12,15,17

BONE, David.
The bees of Westerham.
Beckenham, Bone. 1952.
11,12

BRADLEY, Arthur Granville.
Wolfe.
Macmillan. 1904.
12

BROAD, Lewis.
The adventures of Sir Winston.
Hutchinson. 1957.
12

BROAD, Lewis.
Winston Churchill, 1874-1952.
Hutchinson. 1952.
12

BURBRIDGE, William F.
The Right Honourable Winston Leonard Spencer Churcill.
John Crowther. 1943.
12

CARTER, Violet Bonham.
Winston Churchill as I knew him.
Eyre and Spottiswoode and Collins. 1965.
12

CASTLE, J.A.
Parish Church of St. Mary the Virgin, Westerham.
1951.
11

CHAPMAN, John.
A most true report of the myraculous moving and sinking
of a plot of ground about nine acres, at Westram in
Kent which began the 18th of December and so continued
'till the 29th of the same month, 1596. (Photocopy).
Thomas Creed. 1596.
12

Chartwell: a commemorative booklet.
Illustrated London News. 1970.
12

Chartwell: a guide to Winston Churchill's home, now
owned by the National Trust.
Westerham Press. (1970?).
4

Chartwell: the home of Sir Winston Churchill.
(National Trust).
Illustrated London News. 1967.
19

Chartwell, Westerham.
Nicholson. (1966).
11

CHURCHILL, Randolph Spencer.
Winston S. Churchill, Vol. 1 and companion volumes.
Heinemann. 1966-69.
12

CHURCHILL, Randolph Spencer.
Churchill: his life in photographs, edited by R.S.
Churchill and H. Gernsheim.
Weidenfeld and Nicolson. 1955.
12

COOTE, C.R.
Churchill: a self portrait, edited by C.R. Coote.
Eyre and Spottiswoode. 1954.
12

DAVENPORT, John.
The lives of Winston Churchill, by J. Davenport and
C.J.V. Murphy.
Charles Scribners and Sons. 1945.
12

FEDDEN, Robin.
Churchill and Chartwell.
Pergamon Press: National Trust. 1968.
11

FEDDEN, Robin.
Churchill at Chartwell.
Pergamon Press. 1969.
11,12

A guide to Westerham.
Home Publishing Co. c.1930.
2

HAMPTON, J.S.
An exposure of chalk rock near Westerham, Kent.
"London Naturalist". 1955.
11

Hosey School, Westerham: brief history.
n.d.
16

JONES, Percy Thoresby.
The parish church of St. Mary-the-Virgin, Westerham.
Hooker Bros. 1948 etc.
2(1951) 11,12,19

KENT COUNTY COUNCIL - ROADS DEPARTMENT.
Westerham traffic study, 1971.
Kent County Council. (1972).
11

KENT EDUCATION COMMITTEE.
Westerham, Kent.
1966.
19

SMILES, Oswald D.
Monumental inscriptions in the churchyard and church of
St. Michaels, Wilmington, Kent.
1929.
5

WINDMILLS AND WATERMILLS

ADAMS, James Whirter Renwick.
Windmills in Kent.
Kent County Council. 1955.
1,2,3,4,5,6,7,8,9,11,12,13,14,19,20

BATTEN, M.I.
English windmills, Vol. 1...mills in Kent, Surrey and Sussex.
Architectural Press. 1930.
1,2,4,5,6,7,8,9,12,13,15

FINCH, William Coles.
Watermills and windmills...as portrayed by Kent.
Daniel. 1933.
1,2,4,5,7,8,9,11,12,13,15,17,18,19

HOPKINS, R. Thurston.
In search of English windmills, by R.T. Hopkins and S. Freese.
1931.
4

HOPKINS, R. Thurston.
Old watermills and windmills.
P. Allan. 1930.
13

MAIS, Stuart Petrie Brodie.
England of the windmills.
1931.
13

MANNERING, John.
Vanishing landmarks of the hills.
Country Life. 1961.
3

MEYER, G.H.
Early watermills in relation to changes in the rainfall of
East Kent.
Royal Meteorological Society. 1927.
3,11

PADDON, J.B.
Windmills in Kent. In "Kent Miscellanea", Vol. 3, 1926.
5,7,8,11,12,13,14,15

PILE, Cecil Charles Reef.
Watermills and windmills of Cranbrook.
Cranbrook Local History Society. 1954.
1,4,7,8,11,12,19

PRESTON, Hayter.
Windmills.
1923.
13

REID, Kenneth C.
Watermills and the landscape. (Includes map of Loose Valley and
its mills).
Society for the Preservation of Ancient Buildings. 1959.
3,11

SMITH, Donald.
English windmills, Vol. 2. (Bromley, Blackheath, Gravesend,
Plumstead, Woolwich).
Architectural Press. 1932.
12

Tidemills in England and Wales. (Photocopy of an extract dealing
with those in Kent). From the Transactions of the Newcomen
Society, Vol. 20, n.d.
8

WAILES, Rex.
The English windmill.
1954.
13

WAILES, Rex.
Windmills in Kent, by R. Wailes and J. Russell. (Excerpt from
the Transactions of the Newcomen Society, 1958).
1,5,8,11,12

WINGHAM

A brief memoir of the late Mrs. Ann Elgar Toomer, of
Preston Court, near Wingham, Kent.
Privately Printed by J.B.G. Vogel. 1829.
3

DOWKER, George.
A Roman Villa at Wingham.
Mitchell and Hughes. 1881.
7,11,12,14,17

HUSSEY, Arthur.
Chronicles of Wingham...
Canterbury, Jennings. 1896.
1,3,4,6,7,8,11,12,13,14,15,17

(HUSSEY, Arthur).
Some accounts of the parish of Wingham (MS.) - printed
extracts.
n.d.
3

KENT COUNTY COUNCIL - PLANNING DEPARTMENT.
Wingham (Village Study).
Kent County Council. 1967.
2,3,7,11,12

NEWTON, William.
A sermon preached at Wingham and Stodmarsh in Kent,
1720.
Childe. 1720.
12

WITCHLING

CLARK, Arthur.
Some remarks on the boundaries of the parish of Witchling
taken on the 12th of May, 1763. (Thermofax copy of
typescript).
3

WITHYAM

SUTTON, C.N.
Historical notes of Withyam, Hartfield and Ashdown
Forest, together with the history of the Sackville
family.
Baldwin. 1902.
12

WOODCHURCH

BOUGHEN, Edward.
A sermon concerning decencie and order in the Church.
Preached at Woodchurch...April 30th, 1637.
Printed by I. Raworth for I. Cooper. 1638.
11

BOURNE, W.H.
Church of All Saints, Woodchurch.
Bear. 1938.
11

MANSELL, M.H.
The parish church of All Saints, Woodchurch, Kent.
Rye, Printed by Adams. 1972.
11

RICHARDSON, Jessie Winifred Packham.
A history of Woodchurch.
Ashford, J.W.P Richardson. 1968.
4,7,8,11,12,14

WYNBURNE, Victor Barry.
Woodchurch, near Ashford, Kent.
Rye, Printed by Adams. 1957.
2,4,11,12

WOODNESBOROUGH

DAVIDSON, Hilda R. Ellis.
The Anglo-Saxon burial at Coombe (Woodnesborough),
Kent, by H.R.E. Davidson and L. Webster. (Reprinted
from "Medieval Archaeology", Vol. XI, 1967).
4

ASPLIN, Samuel.
A sermon preached in the parish church of St. Mary, Woolwich,
in Kent, on Sunday, May 29th, 1715...
Printed by G. James for G. Sawbridge. 1715.
11

BADDELEY, G.E.
The tramways of Woolwich and South-East London, edited by
G.E. Baddeley.
Light Railway Transport League. 1963.
11

BAKER, L.A.J.
List of places of worship in the Boroughs of Deptford, Lewisham,
Greenwich and Woolwich.
1961.
1,2,5,8,11,12,17,18

BAREFOOT, William.
Twenty-five years' history of the Woolwich Labour Party, 1903-
1928. Election addresses and pamphlets (with others), 1909,
1912, 1922 and 1925.
17

BELCHER, C.A.
Woolwich and its ferries.
Port of London Authority Monthly. October, 1966.
18

BROOKS, William Collin.
An educational adventure: a history of Woolwich Polytechnic.
Woolwich Polytechnic. 1955.
1,5,8,17

BROOKS, William Colin.
The first hundred years of the Woolwich Equitable Building
Society.
Privately Printed. 1947.
1,17,18

BURNE, Alfred Higgins.
Royal Artillery Mess, Woolwich and its surroundings.
Woolwich,Royal Artillery Institution. 1935.
17

CLAYTON, F.S.
John Wilson of Woolwich: a Baptist Pastorate of 50 years.
Kingsgate Press. 1927.
1

COMMITTEE OF ENQUIRY INTO THE ROYAL ORDNANCE FACTORIES,
WOOLWICH.
Reports to the Ministry of Munitions.
1919.
17

CONNOLLY, Jane.
Old days and old ways.
Arnold. 1912.
11

Copywright index directory for Woolwich...
1885.
18

DAVIS, Walter T.
The history of the Royal Arsenal Co-operative Society Ltd.,
1868-1918...
Woolwich, Pioneer Press. (1921).
1,17,18

Ecclesiastical taxes of Pope Nicholas IV, granted to Edward I
in 1288 and covering the churches of Woolwich, etc.
n.d.
17

ELLISTON-ERWOOD, Frank Charles.
Affairs of the Corporation of the Woolwich Ferry Co., 1811-44.
(Pamphlet).
1953.
17

New records of the Woolwich district, edited by F.C.
Elliston-Erwood.
1937-38.
17

Woolwich and District Antiquarian Society, Occasional Papers,
No. 2, 1934, edited by F.C. Elliston-Erwood.
K.I. Printing Works for Woolwich and District Antiquarian
Society. 1935.
11

ELLISTON-ERWOOD, Peter M.
Woolwich in 1846: an early Victorian guidebook
(i.e., The pictorial guide to Woolwich: a handbook
for residents and visitors), edited...by P.E. Elliston-
Erwood.
Sidcup, Lambarde Press. 1963.
1,2,4,8,11,17,18

FERGUSON, Ruby.
Children at "The Shop".
Hodder and Stoughton. 1967.
1,5

FULLER, F.M. (London County Council Chief Engineer).
Woolwich and its ferries.
1963.
17

GRAHAM, C.A.L.
The story of the Royal Regiment of Artillery, 6th
edition.
Woolwich, Royal Artillery Institution. 1962.
4,17

GREAT BRITAIN: LAWS, etc. (GEO. II).
An Act for rebuilding the parish church of Woolwich...
1732.
11

GREAT BRITAIN: LAWS, etc. (GEO. II).
An Act for applying a sum of money given by the will of
Daniel Wiseman...for finishing the new church at
Woolwich...
1739.
11

GREAT BRITAIN: LAWS, etc. (GEO. III).
An Act to enable John Bowater, Esq., to grant leases in
possession...of a dockyard with land at Woolwich...
1781.
11

GREAT BRITAIN: LAWS, etc. (GEO. III).
An Act for vesting certain lands...in trustees, for
further promoting the service of H.M. Ordnance at
Woolwich.
1803.
11

GREAT BRITAIN: LAWS, etc. (GEO. III).
An Act for making compensation to the proprietors of
certain lands...situate in Woolwich and Charlton...
1804.
11

GREAT BRITAIN: LAWS, etc. (GEO. III).
An Act to vest certain messuages...in trustees for
better securing His Majesty's docks...at Chatham...
and Woolwich.
1804.
4,11

GREAT BRITAIN: LAWS, etc. (WILL. IV).
An Act to enable the Commissioners for Executing the
Office of Lord High Admiral...to acquire certain lands
at Woolwich...
1833.
11,18

GRINLING, C.H.
Fifty years of pioneer work in Woolwich.
Woolwich, Pioneer Press. 1922.
5,17

GRINLING, C.H.
A survey and record of Woolwich and West Kent.
(Containing descriptions and records,brought up-to-
date, of the geology, botany, zoology, archaeology
and industries of the district to commemorate the 12th
Annual Congress..., edited by C.H. Grinling, T.A.
Ingram and B.C. Polkinghorne.
South-Eastern Union of Scientific Societies. 1909.
1,2,4,5,7,9,11,12,15,17,18

GUGGISBERG, F.G.
"The Shop": the story of the Royal Military Academy
(Woolwich).
Cassell. 1900.
1,2,6(1902) 11,17,18

HOGG, Brigadier Oliver Frederick Gillilan.
The Royal Arsenal: its background, origin and subsequent
history, 2 vols.
Oxford Unviersity Press. 1963.
1,4,7,17,18

HOGG, Brigadier Oliver Frederick Gillilan.
The Woolwich Mess: an abridgement and revision of "The Royal
Artillery Mess, Woolwich and its surroundings", by the late
Col. A.H. Burne.
Royal Artillery Institution. 1971.
4,11

JACKSON, Richard J.
"Borough" guide to Woolwich.
Cheltenham, E.J. Burrow. 1910.
17

JEFFERSON, E.F.E.
The Woolwich story, 1890-1965.
Woolwich and District Antiquarian Society. 1970.
2,11,17

KAESTLIN, J.P.
Catalogue of the Museum of Artillery in the Rotunda at
Woolwich, Parts 1 and 2, compiled by J.P. Kaestlin.
1963.
17

KNELL, Henry.
Guide to the British Arsenal with an historical sketch of
Woolwich and its environs.
1865.
17

ORR, William S. AND CO. Publishers.
Pictorial guide to Woolwich.
W.S. Orr and Co. 1846.
17

PRYCE, H. AND SON. Publishers.
Views of Woolwich and neighbourhood.
Woolwich, H. Pryce and Son. n.d.
1

REEVES, Sim.
His life and recollections.
Simpkin Marshall. 1888.
12

ROYAL MILITARY ACADEMY, WOOLWICH.
Records...1741-1840.
Woolwich, Royal Artillery Institution. 1851.
8

RUEGG, Richard.
Summer's evening rambles round Woolwich.
Woolwich, Boddy. 1847.
1,17,18

RUEGG, Richard.
Woolwich and its environs.
1st edition - Woolwich, Cock. 1837.
2nd edition - Woolwich(?), R. Rixon. 1852.
1(1837) 18(1837 and 1852)

VINCENT, William Thomas.
Handbook of the twenty-eighth annual Co-operative Congress of
1896 at Woolwich, with a history and description of Woolwich
and its environs.
Co-operative Printing Society. 1896.
1

The records of Woolwich District, 2 vols.
Woolwich, Jackson. 1888.
1,2,4,5,7,8(Vol. 2) 11,12,17,18

A selection of local pictures from the W.T. Vincent collection
now reproduced...
Woolwich, Molyneux. 1930.
1(Part 1 only)

The story of Severndroog...(Reprinted from the "Records of
Woolwich").
Woolwich, Molyneux. 1928.
1

Walks and talks about Woolwich.
Woolwich, Kentish Independent. 1901.
1

Warlike Woolwich.
Woolwich, Jackson. (1875).
1,18

WHITE, R.E.
Recollections of Woolwich.
Kegan Paul. 1885.
1

WILLIAMS, Marguerite.
John Wilson of Woolwich.
Marshall, Morgan and Scott. 1937.
1

WOOLWICH AND DISTRICT ANTIQUARIAN SOCIETY.
Annual reports, lists of officers and members,
abstract of proceedings, papers, etc.
Woolwich and District Antiquarian Society. 1895 etc.
1,5

WOOLWICH AND DISTRICT ANTIQUARIAN SOCIETY.
Annual reports and balance sheets, 1910, 1912-15,
1945-57, 1963-66.
8

WOOLWICH BOROUGH COUNCIL.
Official guide.
Woolwich Borough Council. 1962.
1

WOOLWICH COUNCIL OF SOCIAL SERVICE.
The Woolwich and District Provident Dispensary: a
brief history, 1894-1948.
Woolwich Council of Social Service. 1950.
1

WOOTTON

Wootton Court: particulars and conditions of sale...of
Wootton Court..and several farms and small holdings,
the whole embracing an area of 600 acres situate in the
parishes of Wootton, Barham, Swingfield and Lydden, also
the advowson of Wootton Rectory, which will be sold by
auction...on...24th...July, 1920.
Worsfold and Hayward. 1920.
7

WORLD WAR I

CONRAD, Joseph.
The Dover Patrol; a tribute.
Canterbury, Printed by Goulden. 1922.
11

Full record of raids in diary form. A concise history
of Thanet during the War.
Ramsgate. 1919.
13,19

IGGLESDEN, Charles.
Crimson glow (2nd edition).
Ashford, Kentish Express. (1940).
4,6

KENT VOLUNTARY AID DETACHMENT.
Report of hospitals and detachments, 1914-19.
1920.
7

KENT VOLUNTARY AID GAZETTE.
July to December, 1917, January to July, 1918.
16

MARGATE BOROUGH COUNCIL.
Instructions as to duties of the Officer-in-Charge of
the Police Station and the Constables acting under him,
Constables and Special Constables directing vehicular
and pedestrian traffic leaving the town and Special
Constables acting as motor cycle messengers, in case
of emergency caused by a threatened or a hostile
invasion of the Isle of Thanet.
Margate Borough Council. 1915.
13

MARGATE BOROUGH COUNCIL.
Instructions as to the duties to be carried out by
Constables and Special Constables in case of emergency
caused by a hostile invasion.
Margate Borough Council. 1915.
13

MORRIS, Joseph.
The German air raids on Great Britain, 1914-18.
1925.
13

Thanet's raid history: raids, bombs, shells - a record of
the home line of trenches, 3rd edition with maps.
Thanet Advertiser. 1919.
13,14

TOMSON AND WOTTON LTD.
Warzone in England: Thanet, 1914-18.
Thanet Advertiser. 1919.
13,14

WORLD WAR II

ADMIRALTY AND AIR MINISTRY.
Report of the Board of Enquiry...the Scharnhorst and Gneisenau,
etc...
H.M.S.O. 1942.
6

BOORMAN, Henry Roy Pratt.
Hell's corner, 1940.
Kent Messenger. 1942 etc.
1,2,3,4,5,6,7,8,9,11,12,15,17,19

BOORMAN, Henry Roy Pratt.
Recalling the Battle of Britain...by H.R.P. Boorman and
H.R. Long.
Kent Messenger. 1965.
1,3,5,8,9,15

History of the Royal Air Force, Gravesend,and a list of Commanding
Officers and Squadrons, 1940-43. (Typescript).
Air Historical Branch. 1961.
9

IGGLESDEN, Charles.
Downs Valley Farm.
Ashford, Kentish Express. 1941.
3,4,11

ILLINGWORTH, Frank.
Britain under shellfire.
Hutchinson. n.d.
6

LAMPE, David.
The last ditch.
Cassell. 1968.
4,7

MOSLEY, Leonard.
The Battle of Britain: the making of a film.
Weidenfeld and Nicolson. 1969.
4

MOUCHOTTE, Rene.
Diaries. (Pilot based at Biggin Hill and Manston).
Staples Press. 1956.
11

PAIN, E.C.
Deal and the Downs in the War of Liberation, 1939-45.
Deal, T.F. Pain. 1948.
1,8,11,14

RICHARDSON, Anthony.
Wingless victory.
Odhams. 1950.
6

ROBERTSON, Terence.
Channel clash.
Evan Bros. 1958.
6

SCOTT, Peter.
The battle of the narrow seas...1939-45.
Country Life. 1946.
6

WOOD, Derek.
The narrow margin, by D. Wood and D. Dempster. (The Battle of
Britain).
Hutchinson. 1961.
6

WRIGHT, Robert.
Dowding and the Battle of Britain.
Macdonald. 1969.
12

WORMSHILL

GROVE, L.R.A.
A chest of 13th century type from Wormshill.
Ashford, Headley Bros. (1958).
12,17

(MAGINN, C.A.).
Wormshill...
Parrett. 1922.
1

WOULDHAM

GODFREY, Rev. R.B.
Wouldham and its church, 1058-1959.
Printed by the Brewster Printing Co. 1967-
9,11

GRIFFIN, Ralph.
Kentish items: Aylesford, Pluckley, Stourmouth,
Faversham, Sittingbourne, Wouldham, Chatham.
n.d.
7

PEARL, A.
Wouldham and its church, 1058-1959, edited by
A. Pearl.
(1959).
15

WRECKS - See LOCATION AND SHIPS AND SHIPPING

WROTHAM

BAILEY v HOPPERTON AND OTHERS.
Claim to rents and services by the Lord of the Manor
of Wrotham...given at Sevenoaks County Court, 1913 in
the presence of Judge Edward Abbott Parry.
Sherratt and Hughes. 1913.
1,11,12

EWING, J.W.
Some materials for a flora of Wrotham...1882-1883.
West Malling, Chamberlain. 1883.
11,16

FLOWER, Sir Newman.
Battle of Wrotham Hill (pamphlet).
1917.
16

FRAMPTON, Thomas Shipden.
A glance at the Hundred of Wrotham, edited by
T.S. Frampton.
Simpkin Marshall. 1881.
1,3,5,9,11,12,14,15,17

FRESHFIELD, Frances Heath.
The Wrothams of Wrotham Court.
Cassell. 1897.
11,12

GRIFFIN, Ralph.
Kentish items: Wrotham.
London, John Bale, Sons and Danielsson Ltd. 1915.
3,7

Guide to the church of St. George, Wrotham.
Privately Printed. n.d.
8

HENBREY, H.G.
West Malling, Wrotham, Ightham and district: residential
attractions.
Abbey Publicity Service. 1928.
17

KIDDELL, A.J.B.
Wrotham slipware and the Wrotham Brickyard: a paper
read...on 24th March, 1949. (From the Transactions of
the English Ceramic Society, 1949).
11

PASCOE, A.P.
Old ways and days at Wrotham.
Kent Messenger. 1926.
11

REX v John MARTEN.
The King on the prosecution of the inhabitants of the parish
of Wrotham...against John Marten, one of the overseers of the
poor of the said parish for the years 1806, 1807 and 1808...
Printed by T. Clout. 1809.
11

STAGG, Frank Noel.
Some notes on the local history of the present ecclesiastical
parish of Wrotham. (Typescript).
1948.
11

TERRY, John.
Sport extraordinary and The reminiscences of an old city
"Free Trader". (John Terry lived at Platt Grange).
J. Terry. 1888.
1,11

THURLOW, A.W.
Wrotham pottery.
Maidstone College of Art. 1952.
11

WINTLE, Alfred Daniel.
The last Englishman: an autobiography.
Joseph. 1968.
12

WROTHAM PARISH COUNCIL.
Official guide to Wrotham, Borough Green and district.
Croydon, Home Publishing Co. 1952 etc.
1(1952 etc.) 4(1961) 5(1952 etc.) 19(1965)

WYE

BECKWITH, Muriel C.
Catharine Macaulay. In the Proceedings of the South Carolina
Historical Association, 1958.
3

BRADE-BIRKS, Stanley Graham.
A series of historical articles on Wye - In the Parish Magazine
of St. Gregory and St. Martin, Wye, September, 1953-February, 1955.
3

BRADE-BIRKS, Stanley Graham.
Wye Church: its history and principal features, by S.G Brade-Birks
and G.E. Husband.
Ramsgate, Cumming. 1950 and 1960.
1,3,4,8,11,12,21

BRENT, John, Junior.
On glass beads with a chevron pattern. (From "Archaeologia",
Vol. XLV).
1879.
3

Church of St. Gregory and St. Martin, Wye.
Ashford, Headley Bros. 1949 etc.
4,11

DALE, Harold Edward.
Daniel Hall, pioneer in scientific agriculture. (1st Principal
of Wye College).
London, John Murray. 1956.
3,21

FRAMPTON, Thomas Shipden.
The vicars, masters or provosts and perpetual curates of the
church of St. Gregory and St. Martin, Wye.
Mitchell, Hughes and Clarke. 1909.
8

HAHN, Emily.
Aphra Behn.
London, Cape. 1951.
3

HITCHIN-KEMP, Fred.
A general history of the Kemp and Kempe families of Great
Britain and her colonies.
London, Leadenhall Press. 1902.
21

H(OOPER), E(vangeline) L.
Short history of Wye.
Ashford, Headley Bros. 1921.
1,3,13

HUBBARD, Gilbert Ernest.
The Old Book of Wye: being a record of a Kentish
country parish from the time of Henry the Eighth to
that of Charles the Second.
Derby, Pilgrim Press. 1951.
3,6,7,10,11,12,14,21

Memorial service (to) Basil Sidney Furneaux on
Monday, 3rd February, 1969 at Wye Church.
3

MOORE, E.W.
A short history of Wye.
Wye Historical Society. 1957 and 1967 (Revised Edition).
11(1967) 12,21

MORRIS, W.S.
History and topography of Wye.
Canterbury, Chivers. 1842.
1,3,6,7,8,11,12,13,14,15,17,21

MUHLFELD, Helen Elizabeth.
A survey of the Manor of Wye, edited by H.E. Muhlfeld.
New York, Columbia University Press. 1933.
1,3,11

ORWIN, C.S.
A history of Wye Church and Wye College, compiled from
various sources by C.S. Orwin and S. Williams.
Ashford, Kentish Express. 1913.
1,3,7,8,11,12,15,21

SACKVILLE-WEST, Victoria.
Aphra Behn.
Howe. (1927).
3,12

St. Gregory and St. Martin, Wye - Parish Magazine,
January, 1958.
3

Stour music - programmes.
Ashford, Headley Bros.
3(1964, 1965, 1966, 1968, 1969) 8(1966)

WOODCOCK, George.
The incomparable Aphra.
Boardman. 1948.
12

WYE COLLEGE.
(Coloured facsimile) from the statutes of Wye College
(15th century) (Christmas card).
1946.
3

WYE COLLEGE.
Prospectus, 1953-54.
Ashford, Headley Bros. 1953.
3

Wye College, 1447-1947: the commemoration of the
foundation of the College of St. Gregory and St. Martin
at Wye.
1947.
3,11

WYE COLLEGE ARCHAEOLOGICAL SOCIETY.
Exhibition of antique silver, June 26th-29th, 1948
(by) Dorothy Smith and Michael Nightingale.
3,21

WYE HISTORICAL SOCIETY.
Report for 1956. (Typescript).
3

WYE HISTORICAL SOCIETY.
Wye and the Norman Conquest. Exhibition at Wye College
...3rd to 5th September, 1966.
Wye Historical Society. 1966.
3

Wye poor rate litigation and costs, 1885.
11

YALDHAM

IRELAND, William Henry.
Extracts from the History of the County of Kent –
Yaldham, St. Clere's and Shipbourne.
1886?
11

YALDING

COHEN, C.R.F.
The Cleaves School, Yalding. (Tonbridge School Local History
Researches, 1963).
11

GODWIN, John.
Killers unknown.   (Includes murders at Ightham and Yalding).
Jenkins. 1960.
12

HILTON, John Anthony.
Yalding: a village history.
Hadlow, J.A. Hilton. 1965.
1,7,8,11,15,19

KENT COUNTY COUNCIL – PLANNING DEPARTMENT.
Yalding (Village Study).
Kent County Council. 1968.
2,7,11,12

TAYLOR, Francis.
The danger of vowes neglected and the necessity of
reformation; or, a sermon preached before the House of
Lords, May 27th, 1646
12

ALEXANDER, John: Addington

ALEXANDER, Joseph J.: West Malling

ALEXANDER, M.B.: Dulwich

ALEXANDRA PHILANTHROPIC HOME: Margate

ALFORD, Henry: Canterbury Cathedral, Kent Authors and
      Literature

"ALFRED CROWQUILL", pseud. - See SEYMOUR, Robert:
      Dickens, Charles; Margate

ALGERINE PIRATE: Kent Authors and Literature

"ALIQUIS", pseud.: Canterbury

ALL ABOUT MARGATE AND HERNE BAY, ETC.: Herne Bay, Margate,
      Isle-of-Thanet

ALL ABOUT RAMSGATE AND BROADSTAIRS: Broadstairs, Ramsgate

"ALL THE YEAR ROUND": Canterbury Cathedral, Hythe, Margate,
      New Romney

ALLAN, B.M.: Gravesend

ALLAN, D.G.C.: Biography

ALLAN, Mea: Biography

ALLANSON, G.: Agriculture

ALLBUT, Robert: Dickens, Charles

ALLCHIN, J.H.: History and Archaeology, Maidstone

ALLDER, J.T.: Catford

ALLDERIDGE, Brian: Thames, River

ALLEN, A.F.: Gravesend, Merston

ALLEN, Charles H.: Biography

ALLEN, C.J.: Railways

ALLEN, Derek F.: Canterbury

ALLEN, G.F.: Railways

ALLEN, Grant: Biography

ALLEN, Joseph Stanley: Deal

ALLEN, Rev. J.W.: Strood

ALLEN, P.: Geology, Weald

ALLEN, Terry: Conrad, Joseph

ALLEN, Thomas: Kent

ALLOM, E.A.: Margate, Natural History, Ramsgate

ALLPORT, Douglas: Aylesford, Maidstone
See Also - "Round About Kits Coty": Aylesford

ALLPORT, H.M.: Herne Bay

ALMACK, Richard: History and Archaeology

ALMENDINGEN, Edith Martha: Biography

ALMON, John: Pitt, William

ALPINE GARDEN SOCIETY: Green Street Green

AMATEUR ANGLER: Folkestone

"AMBULATOR", pseud.: Kent

AMERICAL HERITAGE MAGAZINE: Westerham

AMES, Leslie: Cricket

AMHERST: Genealogical Records

AMICABLE SOCIETY OF FRIENDS AND NEIGHBOURS, ROCHESTER:
      Rochester

AMICI (TE): Maidstone

AMOS, E.G.J.: Dover

AMOS, J. - See POINTER, A.H. Publisher:
      Dover

AMOS AND DAWTON, Auctioneers: Kent, East;
      Littlebourne

AMSINK, P.: Tunbridge Wells

ANCIENT FREEMAN: Dover

ANCIENT ORDER OF FORESTERS: Canterbury, Chatham

AN ANCIENT PROPHECY...: Canterbury

ANDERSON, A.: West Malling

ANDERSON, A.E.: Deal

ANDERSON, Arthur H.: Sandwich

ANDERSON, E.: Eltham

ANDERSON, H.J.: Aylesford

ANDERSON, J.: Margate

ANDERSON, John P.: Kent

ANDERSON, M.: Sandwich

ANDREW, DOUGLAS LTD.: Canterbury

ANDREWS, C.W.: Upnor

ANDREWS, D.H.B.: Lewisham

ANDREWS, G.: Murston

ANDREWS, J.C.: Littlebourne

ANDREWS, J.H.: Faversham, Isle-of-Thanet

ANDREWS, S.M.: Tonbridge

ANDREWS, Rev. Thomas: Bredhurst

ANGEL, C.F.: Sutton Valance

ANGLO IRANIAN OIL CO.: Isle-of-Grain

ANIMADVERSIONS ON LORD BEXLEY'S LETTER TO THE
FREEHOLDERS OF KENT: Kent

"ANOTHER OLD PAST MASTER", pseud.: Erith

ANSON, Peter F.: Ramsgate

ANSTRUTHER, Robert: Canterbury

ANTHONY, Frank: Margate

ANTHONY, Jane: Biggin Hill

ANTIQUARIES JOURNAL: Deal

ANTIQUITIES IN KENT
See Also - THORPE, John: History and Archaeology

APPACH, F.H.: Romney Marsh

APPLETON, G.: Deal

APPS, Howard Llewellyn: Kent Authors and Literature

APSE, L.: Kent Authors and Literature

ARBER, E.A. Newell: Coal

ARCHAEOLOGIA CANTIANA: History and Archaeology

ARCH DEACON, Publisher: Greenwich, Woolwich

ARCHER, H.P.: Kent Authors and Literature

ARCHER, J.: Tunbridge Wells

ARCHER, Thomas: Dickens, Charles

B Cont'd

BARHAM WOMEN'S INSTITUTE: Barham

BARKER, Matthew Henry: Greenwich

BARLOW, J.M.: Ashford

BARLOW, L.: Folkestone

BARLOW, P.W.: Broadstairs

BARNABY, H.: Chatham, Rochester

BARNARD, Alfred: Farnborough

BARNARD, Howard Clive: Ramsgate

BARNES, A.W.: Dickens, Charles

BARNES, C.H.: Borstal

BARNES, Ernest: Canterbury

BARNES, Greville F.: Sport

BARNETT, Corelli - See SLATER, Humphrey: Channel Tunnel

BARNETT, James: Elections, Rochester

BARNSLEY, Alan: Kent Authors and Literature

BARRE, Leonora: Stone (Nr. Dartford)

BARRETT, C.R.B.: Deptford

BARRETT, J.P.: Birchington

BARRIE, E.A.: Canterbury

BARRINGTON, C.A. - See Forestry Commission: Weald

BARRON, Arthur Oswald - See DUNCAN, Leland Lewis: Genealogical Records, Greenwich, Lewisham

BARROW, J.: Deptford

BARRY, H. - See DUNKIN, John: History and Archaeology

BARRY, John Wolfe: Chatham, Romney Marsh

BARTH, Karl: Canterbury Cathedral, Archbishops

BARTLETT, P.A.: Leigh

BARTLETT, Philip H.: Rochester

BARTLETT, Thomas: Canterbury Cathedral

BARTLETT, W.V.: Greenwich

BARTON, G.H.: Tunbridge Wells

BARTON, L.R. - See COOKE, H.B.S.: Birchington

BARTON, Margaret: Tunbridge Wells

BARTON, N.J.: Kent, North West

BARWICK, John: Canterbury

BASKCOMB, G.H.: Bromley

BASKERVILLE, Geoffrey: History and Archaeology

BASSETT, Herbert H.: Eynsford

BATCHELLER, W.: Dover

BATE, J.: Gillingham

BATE, James: Maidstone

BATE, P.H.: West Malling

BATEMAN, John Frederic: Channel Tunnel

BATEMAN, Josiah: Margate

BATES, Herbert Ernest: Kent, Kent Authors and Literature, New Hythe

BATES, L.M.: Thames, River

BATH AND WESTERN, SOUTHERN COUNTIES SOCIETY: Maidstone

BATHURST FAMILY (PEDIGREES AND WILLS): Genealogical Records

BATTELEY BROS.: Lympne

BATTELY, John: Reculver, Richborough

BATTELY, Nicholas - See DUNCOMBE, John: Canterbury, Harbledown

BATTEN, M.I.: Windmills and Watermills

BAVERSTOCK, J.H.: Maidstone

BAVINGTON-JONES, T.: Biography

BAX, Arthur Newsham: Biography

BAX, Clifford: Cricket

BAXTER, Dudley: Canterbury, Canterbury Cathedral, Archbishops

BAXTER, W.E.: Domesday Book

BAXTER, William: Bromley

BAYFORD...MANORIAL ROLLS: Bayford, Genealogical Records, Goodnestone

BAYLEY, George Bethel: Coastal Waters

BAYLY, J.A. Sparvel - See SPARVEL-BAYLY, J.A.: Customs, Dartford, Higham, Kent Authors and Literature, Swanscombe

BAYLY, R.E.: Kent

BAYNES, Godfred John. Publisher: Gravesend

BAYNTON, Alfred: Canterbury, Kent, East

BAZELY, Mrs. L.: Genealogical Records

"BEACHCOMBER", pseud.: Margate

BEADLE, Charles: Kent, North West

BEALE, Benjamin - See HEAL Sir Ambrose: Margate

BEAN, Charles: Ashford

BEAN, James: Beckenham

BEAR, J.: Isle-of-Thanet, Ramsgate

BEARDMORE, H. - See DUNCAN, Leland Lewis: Lewisham

"BEARRA BERRE", pseud.: Minster-in-Thanet

BEATTIE, William: Architecture, Kent

BEATTY, Charles: Gravesend

BEAUMONT, Harry: Kent Authors and Literature

BEAVER, Patrick: Crystal Palace

BEAZLEY, M.: Canterbury Cathedral

BECCATELLI, Lodovico: Canterbury Cathedral

BECK, P.M.: Dartford

BECKENHAM PUBLIC LIBRARY: Beckenham

BECKENHAM URBAN DISTRICT COUNCIL: Beckenham

BECKER, Charles Norris: Dover

BECKER, M. Janet: Rochester

BECKER, May Lamberton: Dickens, Charles

BECKET, Thomas: Canterbury Cathedral, Archbishops

BECKETT, Arthur: Legends, Weald

BECKLEY, William. Publisher: Bromley

BECKWITH, Muriel C.: Wye

BEDWELL AND CO. Publishers: Canterbury

BEDWELL, C.E.A.: Lewisham

BEEBY, Walter Thomas: Bromley

BEECHAM, Thomas. Publisher: Canterbury, Deal, Herne Bay,
    Margate

BEESTON, Frederick: Hythe

BEETENSON, G.H.: Herne Bay

BEHN, Aphra: Kent Authors and Literature

BEHREND, George: Railways

BEHRENS, Lilian Boys: Biography, Bromley, Kent Authors and
    Literature, Smuggling

BELCHER, C.A.: Woolwich

BELCHER, W.D.: Monumental Inscriptions

BELGION, Montgomery: Wells, Herbert George

BELL, Police Constable: Rainham

BELL, Mrs. A.G.: Kent, North West

BELL, Anthea: Kent Authors and Literature

BELL, G. AND SONS. Publishers: Canterbury, Canterbury
    Cathedral, Minster-in-Sheppey, Rochester

BELL, G.K.A. Bishop of Chichester: Canterbury Cathedral,
    Archbishops

BELL, John Any Bird. Defendant: Chatham, Maidstone, Trials

BELL, L.H.: Rochester

BELL, Neil: Gillingham, Kent Authors and Literature,·
    Rochester

BELL, Robert: Maidstone

BELL, Walter G.: Kent, North West

BELL, William: Cranbrook

BELLOC, Hilaire: Canterbury Cathedral, Archbishops;
    Pilgrims Way, Thames, River

BELSEY, F.F.: Chatham

BELSON, S.H.: Whitstable

BELVIDERE LODGE, 503: Maidstone

BENEDICT, Abbot of Peterborough: Canterbury Cathedral,
    Archbishops

BENEFITS OF CHRISTIAN EDUCATION: Maidstone

BENEVOLENT MEDICAL SOCIETY OF KENT: Organisations

BENHAM, D.: Bromley

BENHAM, Harvey: Coastal Waters

BENHAM, William: Canterbury Cathedral, Archbishops;
    Margate, Rochester Cathedral

See Also - DAVIDSON, Randall Thomas: Canterbury Cathedral,
    Archbishops

BENJAMIN, J.: Bromley

BENNETT, A.R.: Railways

BENNETT, Arnold: Wells, Herbert George

BENNETT, A.S.: Medway, River; Rochester

BENNETT, Charles Frederick: Kent Authors and Literature

BENNETT, F.J.: Aylesford, Ightham, Leeds, Loose

BENNETT, George Charles Warner: Sevenoaks

BENNETT, J.J.: Dover

BENNETT, R.G.: Otford

BENNETT-GOLDNEY, Francis: Canterbury

See Also - EVANS, Sebastian: Canterbury, Dover,
    Sandgate

BENNETTS, Rev. H.J.T.: Sittingbourne

BENNEY, M.: Greenwich

BENOLTE, T.: Genealogical Records

BENSON, Arthur Christopher: Canterbury Cathedral,
    Archbishops

BENSON, G.: Chatham

BENSON, Robert Hugh: Canterbury Cathedral,
    Archbishops

BENSTEAD, Charles Richard: Kent

BENSTED, Hubert: Aylesford

See Also - "Round About Kit's Coty": Aylesford

BENTWICH, Helen C.: Sandwich

BENTWICH, Norman: Canterbury

BERBIERS, John L.: Canterbury

BERESFORD-JONES, A.B.: Canterbury

BERGMAN, George F.J.: Gravesend

BERGONZI, Bernard: Wells, Herbert George

BERKELEY, George: Canterbury Cathedral

BERLYN, P.: Crystal Palace

BERNEY, Thomas: Channel Tunnel

BERRY, Alfred H.: Kent Authors and Literature

BERRY, F.G.: Geology

BERRY, William: Genealogical Records

BERRY, W.T.: Dartford

BESANT, Walter: Kent, North West

BEST, Halstead: Richborough

BEST, Robin Hewitson: Agriculture

BETHANIAN, THE: Goudhurst

BETJEMAN, John: Kent

See Also - Rediffusion Television Ltd.: Canterbury

BETTANY, G.T.: Darwin, Charles

BETTERIDGE, V.I.: Dartford

BETTS, Maria: Pembury

BEVAN, Gladys Mary: Canterbury Cathedral, Archbishops

BEVAN, G. Phillips: Kent

BEVAN, Patricia: Tonbridge

BEWSBOROUGH HUNDRED: Kent

BEXLEY BOROUGH COUNCIL: Bexley

BEXLEY, LONDON BOROUGH OF: Bexley

BEXLEY PUBLIC LIBRARIES: Bexley, Libraries

BEYNON, V.C.: Beckenham

BIBLIOTHECA TOPOGRAPHICA BRITANNICA: Canterbury
    Cathedral, Herne, History and Archaeology,
    Maidstone, Reculver, Religious Denominations,
    Richborough, Sevenoaks, Tunstall

BICKERSTETH, Samuel: Biography

BIDDEN, J.: Darenth

BIDDENDEN LOCAL HISTORY SOCIETY: Biddenden

BIJOU, THE: Margate

BILL, A.H.: Penshurst

BILLINGS, B.R.: Folkestone

BINFIELD, E.J.: Dover

BING, F.G.: Canterbury

BING, Harold F.: Canterbury Cathedral, Archbishops
See Also - TESTER, P.J.: Cheriton

BINGHAM, Frederick: Blackheath

BINNIE, K.S.: Greenwich

BINYON, Laurence: Canterbury Cathedral, Kent Authors and
    Literature

BIRCH, Richard: Maidstone, Military and Naval History,
    Trials

BIRCHENOUGH, Edwyn J.: Lee

BIRCHINGTON PUBLICITY COMMITTEE: Birchington

BIRD, Charles: Rochester

BIRD, E.C.F.: Geology, Medway, River; Weald

BIRRELL, Augustine: Maidstone

BIRTWHISTLE, John:. Kent Authors and Literature

BIRTWHISTLE, N.A.: Bromley

BISH, Gregory: Minister-in-Sheppey

BISHOP, C.M.: Dickens, Charles

BISHOP, George: Smuggling

BISHOP, Terence Alan Martyn: Canterbury Cathedral

BISMIRE, A.S.: Bromley

BLACK, ADAM AND CHARLES LTD. Publishers: Canterbury, Kent,
    Kent, East; Kent, North East; Kent, West; Rochester

BLACK, G.T.: Westerham

BLACK, William Henry: Lympne

BLACK, William H.J.: Cinque Ports

BLACKBURNE, Heidee F.: Ashford

BLACKDEN, Paul: Kent, Weald

BLACKHEATH RUGBY FOOTBALL CLUB: Blackheath

BLACKMANTLE, Bernard: Isle-of-Thanet

BLACKWELL, Thomas E.: Sandgate

BLADES, William: Biography

BLAKE, J.F.: Sandgate

BLAKE, N.F.: Biography

BLAKE, Philip Haslewood: Canterbury Cathedral

BLAKE, Robert: Maidstone

BLAKENEY, Edward Henry: Kent Authors and Literature

BLAKER, Richard: Gillingham

BLANCHARD, Edward Litt. L.: Kent

BLAND, William: Kent Authors and Literature

BLANDFORD, J. Harland: Farnborough

BLANDFORD, Percy William: Coastal Waters

BLATCHLEY-HENNAH, Frank Tregory Wolfe: Sutton Valence

BLAW KNOX LTD.: Borstal, Industry and Trade

BLAXLAND, Gregory: Military and Naval History,
    Sport

BLEAN UNION AND RURAL DISTRICT COUNCIL: Blean

BLEAN WOMEN'S INSTITUTE: Blean

BLENCOWE, Robert Willis: Rochester

BLIGH, Allan L.: Kent

BLIND, Sam: Kent Authors and Literature

BLOMEFIELD, Thomas: Military and Naval History

BLOMFIELD, Kathleen: Genealogical Records

BLOOM, J. Harvey: Genealogical Records

BLOOM, Ursula: Biography

BLOOMFIELD, Paul: Maidstone

BLORE, W.P.: Canterbury Cathedral

BLUMBERG, Sir H.E.: Military and Naval History

BLUNDEN, Edmund: Gillingham

BOARD OF EDUCATION: Education

BOARD OF TRADE: Dover

BOAS, Frederick S.: Marlowe, Christopher; Penshurst

BOBBY AND CO.: Margate

BODDINGTON, M.A.B.: Agriculture

BODSWORTH, George F.: Kent

BODY, Geoffrey: Railways, Ramsgate

BOGER, Mrs. E.: Southward

BOGGIS, G. de R.: Kent

BOGGIS, Robert James Edmund: Canterbury

BOISSIER, Rev. G.R.: Hever, Kent

BOLLAND, W.C.: History and Archaeology

BOLTON, Arthur Thomas: Chilham

BOLTON, Herbert: Coal

BOND, John Arthington Walpole: Bromley, Natural
    History

BOND, M.F.: Farnborough

BOND, Maurice F. - See House of Lords: History and
    Archaeology

BONE, David: Westerham

BONHOTE, John: Military and Naval History

BONNER, G.W.: Isle-of-Thanet, Kent, Tunbridge Wells

BONNER, Stephen: Barfreston

BONYTHON, William: Dover

BOODLE, John Adolphus: Boughton-under-Blean,
    Genealogical Records

BOOK OF THE CHRONICLES...: Canterbury

BOOKE OF LOST BEAUTY: Canterbury

BOORMAN, B.P. Publisher: Ashford

BOORMAN, Henry Roy Pratt: Churches, Kent, Kent Authors
    and Literature, Maidstone, Tonbridge, World War II

See Also - ROPER, Anne: Inns

BOOTH, Charles: Kent, North West

BOREMAN, Robert: Biography, Maidstone

BORENIUS, Tancred: Canterbury Cathedral

BOROUGH DIRECTORIES LTD.: Deal, Faversham, Greenwich,
    Medway Towns, Sittingbourne, Tonbridge

BOROUGH GREEN PARISH COUNCIL - See Wrotham Parish Council:
    Borough Green, Wrotham

BOROUGH GREEN WOMEN'S INSTITUTE: Borough Green,
    Organisations

BORROWMAN, Robert: Beckenham

BOSSOM, Alfred Charles. (Lord Bossom of Maidstone):
    Kent Authors and Literature

BOSTOCK, Joan: Tenterden

BOSWELL, J.T.: Kent, North West; Rivers

BOSWORTH, George F.: Kent

BOSWORTH, G.H.: Kent, East

BOTTEN, Arthur H.: Dartford

BOTTOMLEY, Horatio: Maidstone

BOTZOW, Hermann S.D.: Gillingham

BOUGHEN, Edward: Woodchurch

BOULGER, D.C.: Gravesend

BOULTER, L.D.: Chatham Dockyard

BOUNDARY COMMISSION FOR ENGLAND: Dover, Gravesend, Hythe,
    Maidstone, Medway Towns, Sandwich

BOUQUET, Michael: Coastal Waters, Ships and Shipping

BOURGCHIER, Thomas. Cardinal Archbishop of Canterbury:
    Canterbury Cathedral, Archbishops

BOURNE, H.R. Fox: Penshurst

BOURNE, W.H.: Woodchurch

BOURNE, William, OF GRAVESEND: Gravesend

BOWATER PAPER CORPORATION: Industry and Trade

BOWDEN, B.E.: Kemsing

BOWDLER, Henry: Channel Tunnel

BOWEN, Emanuel: Gravesend

BOWEN, Frank Charles: Coastal Waters, Gravesend, Margate,
    Thames, River

BOWEN, Harold Townshend: Rolvenden

BOWEN, J.P.: Coastal Waters

BOWEN, M.: Orpington

BOWEN, William Henry: Dickens, Charles

BOWEN-ROWLANDS, Ernest: Dover

BOWERS, R.W.: Southwark

BOWLER, E.: Canterbury

BOWLES, William Henry: Genealogical Records

BOWMAN, W.: Canterbury

BOWRA, Edward: Ightham, Tunbridge Wells

BOWRA, John: Tunbridge Wells

BOWTELL, J.: Patrixbourne

BOX, Ernest George: Canterbury Cathedral, Otford,
    Roads, Sevenoaks

BOX, E.S.: Ashford

BOY SCOUTS: Bromley, Organisations

BOYCE, Charles: Biography, Canterbury Cathedral,
    Archbishops

BOYER, P.J.: Barfreston, Kent Authors and Literature

BOYLE, John: Canterbury

BOYNE, D.A.C. - See CHILDS, Rigby: Canterbury

BOYNE, William: Coins and Tokens

BOYS' BRIGADE: Kent, North West; Organisations

BOYS, Edward: Biography, Sandwich

BOYS, J.: Agriculture

BOYS, John: Kent Authors and Literature

BOYS, (J.J.) AND CHANCELLOR v REX: Trials

BOYS v EDMUNDS: Maidstone, Trials

BOYS, William: Aylesford, Richborough, Sandwich

BOYSON, V.F. - See SOMMERS-COCKS, Henry L.:
    Edenbridge

BRABAZON, E.: Gravesend

BRABY, B.E.: Beckenham

BRACKETT AND CO.: Tunbridge Wells

BRACKETT AND SONS. Auctioneers: Tunbridge Wells

BRACKETT, Arthur W.: Tunbridge Wells

BRADDOCK, Joseph: Footpaths and Commons, Kent Authors
    and Literature

BRADE-BIRKS, Helda K.: Natural History

BRADE-BIRKS, Stanley Graham: Agriculture,
    Architecture, Brook, Canterbury, Chilham,
    Genealogical Records, Godmersham, Kent Authors
    and Literature, Wye

See Also - HUBBARD, Gilbert Ernest: Wye

BRADEN, J.T.: Margate

BRADFORD, C.A.: Greenwich

BRADFORD, Ernle: Coastal Waters

BRADLEY, Arthur Granville: Cinque Ports, Romney
    Marsh, Westerham

BRADLEY, Donald Laurence: Railways

BRADLEY, Howard: Kent Authors and Literature

BRADLOUGH, Charles: Channel Tunnel

BRADSHAW, Publisher: Kent, North West

BRADSHAW, Cecil F.: Petham, Waltham

BRADSHAW, Lawrence: Margate

BRADY, Francis: Coal, Dover

BRADY, John H.: Knole, Roads

BRAIN, M.: Bickley

BRAIN, Richard F.: Medway, River; Medway Towns

BRAITHWAITE, Lewis: Canterbury, Dover

BRAMSTONE, William: Minster-in-Sheppey

BRAMWELL, Frederick J. - See BARRY, John Wolfe:
    Chatham

BRANCH-JOHNSON, W.: Medway, River; Military and Naval History, Thames, River

BRAND, C.W.: Wickhambreux

BRANFORD, Violet: Kent Authors and Literature

BRASIER, W.C.: Isle-of-Thanet, Margate

BRASSEY, Sybil. Countess: Walmer

BRASSEY, Thomas. Earl: Walmer

BRAYBROOK, E.W.: Lewisham

BRAYLEY, Edward Wedlake: Cinque Ports, Isle-of-Thanet, Kent
See Also - BRITTON, John: Kent

BREDIN, E.R.: Ulcombe

BRENAN, J. Eustace: Goodwin Sands

BRENDON, J.P.: Romney Marsh

BRENT, Cecil: Canterbury, Wye

BRENT, John: Canterbury, Kent Authors and Literature, Legends, Stowting
See Also - SUMMERLY, Felix: Canterbury

BRENT, John. Junior: Bekesbourne, Canterbury, Sarre, Wye

BRENT, William: Kent Authors and Literature, Sturry

BRENTNALL, Margaret: Cinque Ports, Kent, Mereworth, Romney Marsh

BRERETON, Austin: Thames, River

BRETHERTON, F.F.: Margate

BRETHERTON, Ralph Harold: Canterbury

BRETON, Nicholas: Kent Authors and Literature

BRETT, Thomas: Betteshanger, Cranbrook

BRETT v SAWRIDGE AND OTHERS: Bexley

BRETTON, Frederick: Cinque Ports

BREWER, Derek: Kent Authors and Literature

BREWSTER, G.B.: Coastal Waters

BRIDDLE, William: Penge

BRIDGE, Sir Frederick: Rochester

BRIDGE, John W.: Maidstone

BRIDGE, Joseph C.: Rochester

BRIDGE, W.E.: Maidstone

BRIDGE-BLEAN RURAL DISTRICT COUNCIL: Kent, East

BRIDGER. Publisher: Tonbridge

BRIDGES, Sir Brook William: Genealogical Records

BRIDGES, Joseph S.: Dartford

BRIDGES, Robert: Walmer

BRIDGETT, T.E.: Rochester Cathedral

BRIDGEWATER, Howard: Margate

BRIDGMAN, John: Genealogical Records, Knole

BRIDLE, William: Penge

BRIGG, William: Genealogical Records

BRIGGS, Alice Jane: Biography

BRIGGS, Enid Semple: Broadstairs

BRIGHT, William: Canterbury Cathedral

BRIGSTOCKE, J. - See ROBERTSON, James Craigie: Canterbury Cathedral, Archbishops

BRINE, James. Publisher: Kent

BRINTON, Thomas: Rochester Cathedral

BRISTOL UNIVERSITY, DEPARTMENT OF ECONOMICS: Agriculture

BRITANNIA DELINEATA: Kent

BRITISH ARCHAEOLOGICAL ASSOCIATION: Canterbury Dover, History and Archaeology, Sandwich

BRITISH ASSOCIATION FOR THE ADVANCEMENT OF SCIENCE: Canterbury, Darwin, Charles; Dover, Folkestone

BRITISH ASTRONOMICAL ASSOCIATION: Greenwich

BRITISH INSTITUTE OF PUBLIC OPINION - SOCIAL SURVEYS (GALLUP POLL) LTD.: Statistics and Surveys

BRITISH LEGION: Ashford, Ditton, Dover, Organisations, Ramsgate

BRITISH MARKET RESEARCH BUREAU: Bromley, Statistics and Surveys

BRITISH MUSEUM (MSS.): Margate

BRITISH MUSEUM (NATURAL HISTORY) - DEPARTMENT OF GEOLOGY: Weald

BRITISH NUMISMATIC SOCIETY: Coins and Tokens

BRITISH PETROLEUM CO.: Gillingham, Isle-of-Grain

BRITISH RAIL (SOUTHERN REGION): Railways

BRITISH RECORD SOCIETY: Canterbury Cathedral, Genealogical Records

BRITISH RED CROSS SOCIETY: Organisations

BRITISH ROAD FEDERATION: Roads

BRITISH TRAVEL ASSOCIATION: Folkestone

BRITISH TRAVEL AND HOLIDAY ASSOCIATION: Dover

BRITISH VETERINARY ASSOCIATION: Folkestone

"BRITISH WORKMAN", pseud.: Canterbury

BRITTAIN, F.: Dover

BRITTON, John: Canterbury Cathedral, Kent, Tunbridge Wells

BRITTON, O.M.H.: New Cross, Roads

BRITTON, Percy W.: Ramsgate

BROAD, Lewis: Westerham

BROADLEY, A.M. - See ROSE, J. Holland: Coastal Defences

BROCK, E.P. Loftus: Canterbury, Whitfield

BROCKINGTON, C. Fraser: Canterbury

BROCKMAN, William Everett: Kent Authors and Literature

BROME, Vincent: Wells, Herbert George

BROMHEAD, C.E.N.: Kent, North West

BROMILEY, G.W.: Canterbury Cathedral, Archbishops

BROMLEY, Francis E.: Aylesford, Canterbury, Canterbury Cathedral, Customs, Folkestone, Genealogical Records, Ickham, Place Names, Reculver, Westbere

BROMLEY, John: Bromley

BROMLEY AND DISTRICT CONSUMERS' GROUP: Bromley

BROMLEY AND WEST KENT TELEGRAPH: Bromley

BROMLEY BOROUGH COUNCIL: Bromley

BROMLEY CENTRAL HALL: Bromley

BROMLEY CHAMBER OF COMMERCE: Bromley

BROMLEY COLLEGE: Bromley

BROOK, Cyril A.: Dartford

BROOK, G.L.: Dickens, Charles

BROOK, Roy: Eltham

BROOK, Victor John Knight: Canterbury Cathedral, Archbishops

BROOKE, Arthur, pseud.: Kent Authors and Literature

BROOKE, B.J.: Natural History

BROOKE, C.F. Tucker: Marlowe, Christopher

BROOKE, F.C.: Cobham

BROOKE, Jocelyn: Biography, Kent Authors and Literature

BROOKE, W.F.: Greenwich

BROOKS, Charles S.: Canterbury

BROOKS, Collin - See BROOKS, William Collin: Woolwich

BROOKS, F.W.: Cinque Ports, Gillingham

BROOKS, William Collin: Woolwich

BROTHERS, M.E.: Kent Authors and Literature

BROU, Father: Canterbury Cathedral, Archbishops

BROUGHAM, Henry Peter. Baron Brougham and Vaux: Dover

BROWHURST, F.W.: Gravesend

BROWN, A.G.: Channel Tunnel

BROWN, E.E.S.: Bromley, Geology, Herne Bay, Reculver, Swanscombe

BROWN, Henry: Northfleet

BROWN, H.S.J. - See WENYON, H.J.: Military and Naval History

BROWN, Ivor: Dickens, Charles

BROWN, J. Publisher: Kent, Maidstone

BROWN, J.C.: Leeds

BROWN, John: Canterbury

BROWN, John Howard: Acrise, Folkestone, Hawkinge, Kent Swingfield, Whitfield

BROWN, Kevin: Kent Authors and Literature

BROWN, Malcolm Denis: Southborough

BROWN, R. Allen: Rochester
See Also - Public Buildings and Works, Ministry of: Dover

BROWN, Theodore: Chelsfield

BROWN, W. Baker - See History of the Corps of Royal Engineers: Military and Naval History

BROWN, William Keer: Maidstone

BROWNE, A.L.: Rochester

BROWNE, Andrew R. Gore: Chartham

BROWNE, Dr.: Tunbridge Wells

BROWNE, Mrs. Heugie: Theatres

BROWNE, J.C.: Leeds

BROWNE, R.P.: Greenwich

BROWNING, Robert H.K.: Ramsgate, Sport

BROWNLOW, Margaret Eileen: Agriculture, Seal

BRUCE, C.R.: Canterbury

BRUCE, John: Rochester Cathedral

BRUCE, John: History and Archaeology
See Also - MANNINGHAM, John: Bradbourne

BRUICE, John - See NICHOLS, John Gough: Genealogical Records

BRUMWELL, P. Middleton - See SCOTT, Sir Arthur B.: Military and Naval History

BRUNSWICK MEETING: Maidstone

BRUTON, J.F.: Railways

BRYANT, Arthur: Dover, Pepys, Samuel; Thames, River

BRYANT, Nancy: Kent Authors and Literature

BRYANT, T.: Medway, River

BRYDGES, Ann Mary: Canterbury

BRYDGES, Sir Samuel Egerton: Biography, Kent, Kent Authors and Literature, Lee Priory

BRYDONE, James Edward: Folkestone, Wells, Herbert George

BUBB, Robert: Isle-of-Thanet, Minster-in-Thanet

BUCHANAN, A.G.B.: Folkestone

BUCHANAN, COLIN AND PARTNERS: Ashford, Canterbury, Sevenoaks

BUCHANAN, James Robert: Herne

BUCK, Nathaniel - See BUCK, Samuel: Architecture

BUCK, Samuel: Architecture

BUCK, W.F.A. - See HARRISON, Jeffery G.: Chetney, Medway, River; Natural History, North Kent Marshes, Sevenoaks

BUCKINGHAM, Christopher: Dover, Lydden

BUCKLAND, Frank: Bexley

BUCKLAND, G.: Agriculture

BUCKLAND, Walter E.: East Malling, Genealogical Records

BUCKLER, John Chessell: Eltham

BUCKLOW, W.: Margate

BUCKNALL, Rixon: Railways, Ships and Shipping

BUDD, G.L. Culver: Greenwich

BUDE, John: Maidstone

BUDGEN, T.: All Hallows

BUFFARD, Frank: Religious Denominations

THE BUFFS: Canterbury, Military and Naval History

BUGLER, Arthur: Chatham Dockyard

THE BUILDER: Tunbridge Wells

BULLARD, I. Vincent: Flamstead

BULMER, Martin - See Whichcord and Son: Maidstone

BULMER-THOMAS, Ivor: Sandwich

BULTEEL, John: Canterbury, Maidstone, Sandwich

BULWER, Sir Henry Lytton: Walmer

BUMPUS, Thomas Francis: Canterbury Cathedral

BUNCE, Cyprian Rondeau: Canterbury

BUNT, Cyril George Edward: Gillingham

BUNYARD, GEORGE AND CO. LTD.: Agriculture

"CALLED HOME": Bromley, Religious Denominations

CALLENDER, <u>Sir</u> Geoffrey: Chatham, Greenwich

CALLENDER'S CABLE AND CONSTRUCTION CO. LTD.: Belvedere

CALVER, Edward Killwick: Dover

CAMDEN, William: Genealogical Records, Kent, Kent Authors
    and Literature

CAMDEN SOCIETY: Genealogical Records, Kent

CAMMIDGE, John: Canterbury

CAMPBELL, Barry: Canterbury, Cricket, Smallhythe

CAMPBELL, E.M.J. - <u>See</u> DARBY, H.C.: History and
    Archaeology

CAMPBELL, J.C.: Ships and Shipping

CAMPBELL, Marjorie A.: Organisations

CAMPBELL, R.R.: Dover

CAMPBELL, Thomas: Sydenham

CANNON, Richard: Military and Naval History

CANON FROM THE LESNES ABBEY MISSAL: Erith

CANTACUZINO, Sherban: Canterbury

CANDID REMARKS ON A SERMON...PREACHED AT CHATHAM: Chatham

"CANTEBURIENSIS", <u>pseud.</u>: Canterbury

CANTERBURY AND DISTRICT ANGLING ASSOCIATION: Organisations

CANTERBURY AND DISTRICT BAT AND TRAP LEAGUE: Sport

CANTERBURY AND SANDWICH COMMITTEE: Stour, River

CANTERBURY AND WHITSTABLE RAILWAY: Canterbury, Railways,
    Whitstable

CANTERBURY AND YORK SOCIETY: Canterbury Cathedral,
    Archbishops

CANTERBURY ARCHAEOLOGICAL SOCIETY: Canterbury

CANTERBURY BENEVOLENT AND STRANGER'S FRIEND SOCIETY:
    Canterbury

CANTERBURY BENEVOLENT SOCIETY: Canterbury

CANTERBURY BICYCLE CLUB: Canterbury

CANTERBURY BURIAL SOCIETY: Canterbury

CANTERBURY CATCH CLUB: Canterbury

CANTERBURY CHAMBER OF TRADE: Canterbury

CANTERBURY CHURCH OF ENGLAND YOUNG MEN'S LITERARY
SOCIETY: Canterbury

CANTERBURY CITY COUNCIL: Canterbury

CANTERBURY CLUB: Canterbury

CANTERBURY CRICKET WEEK: Canterbury, Cricket

CANTERBURY DIOCESAN BOARD OF EDUCATION: Education

CANTERBURY DIOCESAN REGISTRY: Genealogical Records

CANTERBURY EXCAVATION COMMITTEE: Canterbury

CANTERBURY FESTIVAL COMMITTEE: Canterbury

CANTERBURY FRIENDLY SOCIETY: Canterbury

CANTERBURY GUARDIANS OF THE POOR: Canterbury

CANTERBURY "HANDWEAVER AND SPINNER": Canterbury

CANTERBURY HOUSE OF COMMONS: Canterbury

CANTERBURY JOURNAL. Publishers: Railways

CANTERBURY NAVIGATION AND SANDWICH HARBOUR CO. - AN
EXPOSITION: Stour, River

CANTERBURY PHILOSOPHICAL AND LITERARY INSTITUTION:
    Canterbury

CANTERBURY PHOTOGRAPHIC SOCIETY - <u>See</u> East Kent
Scientific and Natural History Society: Natural
History

CANTERBURY PREROGATIVE COURT: Genealogical Records,
    Trials

CANTERBURY PRESS - <u>See</u> Kentish Gazette: Canterbury,
    Canterbury Cathedral

CANTERBURY PSALTER: Canterbury Cathedral

CANTERBURY RAGGED SCHOOLS: Canterbury, Education

CANTERBURY RHYMES: Canterbury Cathedral

CANTERBURY SOCIETY: Canterbury

CANTERBUTY TECHNICAL HIGH SCHOOL FOR GIRLS:
    Stour, River

CANTERBURY TIMES - <u>See</u> Kentish Observer:
    Canterbury

CANTRILL, M.: Maidstone

CAPE, H.J. - <u>See</u> WOODRUFF, Charles Everleigh:
    Canterbury

CAPPER, B.P.: Herne Bay

CAPPER, Douglas Parode: Cinque Ports, Coastal Waters.
    Military and Naval History, Pilgrims Way,
    Ships and Shipping

CAPPER, Henry D.: Chatham Dockyard

CARDEN, Percy T.: Dickens, Charles

CARDOZO, D.A.: Ramsgate

CARDWELL, E.: Deal

CAREY, George Saville: Kent

CAREY, Susan Jane: Ashford

A CARING CHURCH: Religious Denominations

CARLETON, Mary: Canterbury
<u>See Also</u> - Mary Carleton: Canterbury

CARLEY, James: Meopham, Roads

CARLILE, John C.: Folkestone

CARLISLE, J.A.: Religious Denominations

CARLISLE, Nicholas: Education

CARLTON, William J.: Dickens, Charles

CARNALL, Robert: Kent Authors and Literature

CARNEGIE, Moir: Kent, North West

CARNEGIE UNITED KINGDOM TRUST: Education

CARNELL, George F.: Sevenoaks

CAROE, William Douglas: Canterbury Cathedral,
    Cranbrook

CARPENTER, A.B.B.: Lee

CARPENTER, Edward: Canterbury Cathedral, Archbishops

CARPENTER, R. Herbert: Canterbury

CARR, Frank George Griffith: Greenwich, Ships and
    Shipping

CARR, T.A.: Cranbrook

CARR, Thomas William: Southborough

CARR, William: Crayford

CARRE, Meyrick H.: Barham

CARRECK, J.N.: Darwin, Charles; Hayes and Keston

CARRIER, Elsie Hayden: Kent, North West

CARRINGTON, R.C.: Orpington

CARROLL, Douglas: Kent Songs

CARRUTHERS, W.: Herne Bay

CARSON, Katherine: Herne Bay

CARSON, R.A.G.: Coins and Tokens, Gravesend

CARTER, Mrs. Elizabeth: Biography, Deal, Kent Authors and
    Literature

CARTER, George Goldsmith: Goodwin Sands, Kent, Reculver,
    Romney Marsh, Sandwich

CARTER, George R.: Kent Authors and Literature

CARTER, Matthew: History and Archaeology

CARTER, Nicholas: Deal

CARTER, Violet Bonham: Westerham

CARTWRIGHT, Julia: Penshurst, Pilgrims Way

CARWELL, George F.: Sevenoaks

CASE AND CUNNINGHAM: Thames, River

CASE, Edward: Romney Marsh

CASEY, Raymond: Folkestone

CASSERLEY, Henry Cecil: Railways

CASTELLS, Francis de Paula: Bexleyheath, Roads,
    Stone (Nr. Dartford), Welling

CASTLE, Alice: Bishopsbourne

CASTLE, J.A.: Westerham

CASTLE, Joseph: Kent Authors and Literature, Queenborough

CASTLE, Roger A.B.: Weald

CASWALL, Henry: Canterbury

CATALOGUE OF MR. LEE WARLY'S LIBRARY: Elham

CATER, Philip: Kent Authors and Literature

CATHEDRAL RHYMES: Canterbury

CATHOLIC MARRIAGE ADVISORY COUNCIL: Medway Towns

CATHOLIC RECORD SOCIETY: Genealogical Records

CATLING, Gordon: Kent

CATT, Andrew Robert: Railways

CAUSTON, Peter: Kent Authors and Literature, Tunbridge Wells

CAVE, A.J.E.: Gravesend

CAVE, C.J.P.: Canterbury Cathedral

CAVE AND WILLIAMS: Rochester

CAVE, AUSTIN AND CO. LTD. Publishers: Maidstone

CAVE-BROWNE, John: Boxley, Brasted, Bromfield, Canterbury
    Cathedral, Archbishops; Cranbrook, Detling, East
    Sutton, Elections, Genealogical Records, Hollingbourne,
    Leeds, Maidstone, Minster-in-Sheppey, Otham, Sutton
    Valence

CAVELL, John: Sandwich

CAVENAGH, W.O.: Boughton Malherbe

CAWLEY, A.C.: Chaucer, Geoffrey

CAWSTON, Rev. A.C.: Railways

CAWSTON, Edward P.: Marlowe, Christopher

CAXTON AND HOLMESDALE PRESS. Publishers: Knole
    Sevenoaks

CAZENEUVE, John and WITHERIDGE, William. Protagonists:
    Chatham

CEMENT AND CONCRETE ASSOCIATION. Publishers: Medway,
    River

CENTRAL BROMLEY COUNCIL OF YOUTH: Bromley

CENTRAL COUNCIL OF PHYSICAL RECREATION: Sport

CENTRAL ELECTRICITY GENERATING BOARD: Dungeness

CHADWICK, Mrs. E.: Petts Wood

CHADWICK, Sir Edwin: Folkestone

CHADWICK, Howard: West Wickham

CHALKLIN, Christopher William: Canterbury Cathedral,
    History and Archaeology, Medway, River;
    Rochester Cathedral, Tonbridge

CHALMERS, James: Channel Tunnel

CHALMERS-HUNT, J.M.: Natural History

CHAMBERLAIN, Frank: Folkestone

CHAMBERLAIN, J.S.: Genealogical Records

CHAMBERLAIN, Neville: Kent, East

CHAMBERLIN, POWELL AND BON. Architects: Folkestone

CHAMBERS' EDINBURGH JOURNAL: Religious Denominations

CHAMBERS, F., OF MARGATE: Biography

CHAMBERS, Ralph Frederick: Religious Denominations

CHAMBERS, W. AND R. Publishers: Kent, Sydenham

CHAMPION, G.H.J. - See Swale Footpaths Group:
    Faversham

CHAMPION, Sir Reginald: Chilham

CHAMPNEYS, Basil: Romney Marsh

CHANDLER, Marjorie E.J.: Natural History

CHANDLER, Raymond H.: Cobham, Cray, River; Crayford,
    Darent, River; Dartford, Erith, Kent, North
    West; Knockmill, Shorne, Swanscombe

CHANNEL BRIDGE AND RAILWAY CO. LTD.: Channel Tunnel

CHANNEL PUBLISHING CO.: Dover, Kent, South East

CHANNEL TUNNEL ASSOCIATION: Channel Tunnel

CHANNEL TUNNEL CO. LTD.: Channel Tunnel

CHANNEL TUNNEL STUDY GROUP: Channel Tunnel

CHAPLAS, Pierre - See BISHOP, Terence Alan Martyn:
    Canterbury Cathedral

CHAPLIN, Dorothea: Margate

CHAPLIN, Howard Douglas: Military and Naval History

CHAPLIN, Winifred M.: Sandgate

CHAPMAN AND HALL LTD. Publishers: Dickens, Charles

CHAPMAN, Derek: Kent

CHAPMAN, Frederick: Folkestone

CHAPMAN, Henry Stephen: Deal

CHAPMAN, Herbert Turlay: Biography

CHAPMAN, Hester W.: Chislehurst

CHAPMAN, John: Westerham

CHAPPELOW, Eric Barry Wilfred: Canterbury Cathedral

CLARK, Frank J.: Beckenham

CLARK, G.T.: Dover, Rochester

CLARK, John: Folkestone

CLARK, M. Dudley: Birchington, Margate

CLARK, R.H.: Railways

CLARK, Ronald William: Dover

CLARK, Thomas: Canterbury

CLARK, W.M. Publisher: Crystal Palace

CLARK, W. Tierney: Gravesend

CLARK-KENNEDY, A.E.: Maidstone

CLARKE, A.W. Hughes: Genealogical Records

CLARKE, Amanda: Bromley

CLARKE, Charles: Barfreston, Chalk

CLARKE, Edward Brian Stanley: Military and Naval History

CLARKE, Frank: Erith

CLARKE, George Ernest: Margate

CLARKE, Harold George: Pegwell Bay, Souvenirs

CLARKE, John S.: Margate

CLARKE, Joseph: St. Nicholas-at-Wade

CLARKE, R.G.: Folkestone

CLARKE, Reginald Dennis: Otford, Sevenoaks

CLARKE, Samuel J.: Penge

CLARK'S GUIDE AND HISTORY OF RYE: Cinque Ports

CLASSIFIED TRADES DIRECTORY: Industry and Trade

CLAY, Rotha Mary: Canterbury, Canterbury Cathedral

CLAYSON, J.J.: Lyminge

CLAYTON, A. - See KING, David: Eltham

CLAYTON, Charles: Chatham, Rochester

CLAYTON, F.S.: Woolwich

CLAYTON, Howard: Railways

CLAYTON, Joseph: History and Archaeology

CLAYTON, O.: Kent, North West

CLEAVE-WARNE, T.J. - See King's School, Rochester: Rochester

CLEAVER, Arthur H. - See HATTON, Thomas: Dickens, Charles

CLEEVES, Janet D.: Aylesford

CLEGG, W. Paul: Ships and Shipping

CLEMENTS, Robert H.M.: Tonbridge Wells

CLIFFE, Gary - See BURNESS, Gordon: Orpington, Natural History

CLIFFORD, Lady Anne: Knole

CLIFFORD, Henry: Canterbury

CLIFFORD, John: Tunbridge Wells

CLIFFORD, J.R.S.: Gravesend

CLINCH, George: Agriculture, Bromley, Coastal Defences, Hayes and Kestone, Kent, Kent, North West; Kent Authors and Literature, Westernhanger, West Wickham

See Also - DITCHFIELD, P.H.: History and Archaeology

CLINCH, V.: Ditton

CLOET, R.L. - See ROBINSON, Adrian H.W.: Coastline

CLOUD, Yvonne: Margate

CLOUGH, J.S.: Folkestone

CLUETT, Leslie Gordon: Isle-of-Sheppey

CLUNN, Harold P.: Kent

CLUTTON, Margaret M.: Chislehurst

COAD, J.G.: Chatham

COBB, Mary: Margate

COBB, W.F.: Margate

COBBETT, William: Kent, Margate

COBHAM, Charles: Gravesend

COBHAM, Eleanor M.: Cooling, Northfleet

COBHAM, F.: Lingfield

COBHAM, George W. - See COBHAM, Charles: Gravesend

COCK, F. William: Agriculture, Appledore, Biography, Canterbury, Kent, Newspapers

See Also - COZENS, Zechariah: History and Archaeology

COCKRANE, Carola: Charing

COCKS, Thomas: Canterbury Cathedral

COCKSHUT, A.O.J.: Dickens, Charles

CODRINGTON, Thomas: Roads

COFFIN, Charles Monroe: Sevenoaks

COGHLAN, Francis: Dover, Kent, Margate, Ramsgate, Tunbridge Wells

COHEN, C.R.F.: Yalding

COKAYNE, George E. - See British Record Society: Genealogical Records

COLBOURNE, A.F. Photographer: Canterbury Cathedral

COLBORNE, Barbara J.: Industry and Trade, Maidstone

COLBRAN, John. Publisher: Tunbridge Wells

COLBRAN, St. John. Publisher: Tunbridge Wells

COLE, D. - See SYMES, Rodney: Railways

COLE, George: Rainham

COLE, Helen Margaret: Agriculture

COLE, Sir Henry - See "DENARIUS", pseud.: Crystal Palace

COLE, Herbert: Eynsford

COLE, James: Canterbury Cathedral

COLE, K.R.: Gillingham

COLE, W.J.: Isle-of-Sheppey

COLE, William: History and Archaeology

COLEBROOK, J. - See Royal Tunbridge Wells Borough Council: Tunbridge Wells

COLEIRE, Richard: Harrietsham

COLEMAN, Alice M.: Isle-of-Thanet: Kent, East

COLEMAN, Bryan: Kent

COLEMAN, Donald Cuthbert: Aylesford

COLEPEPER, Sir Thomas: Kent Authors and Literature

COLERIDGE, H.N.: History and Archaeology

COOPER, Thomas Sidney: Canterbury

COOPER, William Durrant: Cinque Ports, History and Archaeology

COOPER, W.H. Hewlett: Hayes and Keston

COOTE, C.R.: Westerham

COOTE, Jeanne: St. Mary Cray

COPELAND, H. Robert: Beckenham

COPLAND, John: Sheerness

COPLEY, Gordon J.: History and Archaeology

COPPERTHWAITE, William Charles: Greenwich

COPPOCK, J.T.: Kent, North West

COPUS, G.D.: Green Street Green, Pratts Bottom

COPY OF THE INSCRIPTIONS...ORD FAMILY: Bexley, Genealogical Records, Monumental Inscriptions

CORELLI, Marie: Margate

CORKE, C.E.: Sevenoaks

CORKHILL, W.H.: Margate

CORLEY, T.A.B.: Chislehurst

CORNER, George Richard: Hayes and Keston

CORNER, John: Canterbury Cathedral

CORNFORD, L. Hope: Margate

CORNHILL MAGAZINE: Biography

CORNWALLIS, Charles. 1st Marquess: Biography

CORNWALLIS, H.: Tonbridge

CORNWALLIS, James. Dean of Canterbury: Canterbury Cathedral

CORNWALLIS v BARKER: Maidstone

CORRESPONDENCE ON CIRCUMSTANCES ARISING...HYTHE: Hythe

CORRESPONDENCE...PROPOSED PUBLIC LIBRARY: Margate

CORRESPONDENCE...SPIRITUAL DESTITUTION OF THE PARISH OF TONBRIDGE: Tonbridge

CORY, Harper: Margate

CORYN, M.: Canterbury Cathedral

COTTERELL, Howard Herschel: Canterbury

COTTINGHAM, L.N.: Rochester Cathedral

COTTON, Charles: Canterbury, Canterbury Cathedral, Margate, Religious Denominations, St. Laurence-in-Thanet

COTTON, Joseph: Deptford

COTTON, M.A.: Stone-next-Dartford

COTTRELL, Leonard: Coastal Defences

COUCHMAN, Conrad: Genealogical Records

COULSON, Barbara May: Medway Towns

COULTER, J.E. Publisher. Sittingbourne

COUNCER, C.R.: Boughton Aluph, Churches, History and Archaeology, Petham, Reculver, Teynham
See Also - HILL, Derek Ingram: West Wickham

COUNCIL FOR THE ORDER OF ST. JOHN - FOR KENT: Organisations

COUNCIL OF SOCIAL SERVICE: Margate

COUNTESS OF HUNTINGDON'S CONNEXION: Tunbridge Wells

"COUNTRY GENTLEMAN OF KENT", pseud.: History and Archaeology

"COUNTRY LIFE": Kent

COUNTY GUIDE TO THE COUNTY OF KENT: Kent

COUNTY ILLUSTRATED: Kent

COUNTY OF KENT...FAMILY RECORDS: Genealogical Records

COUNTY PUBLICITY CO. Publishers: Industry and Trade

COURSE, Edwin A.: Eltham, Railways

COURT, Alexander Norman: Kent

COURT, Capel: Northfleet

COURTAULD, S.L.: Eltham

COURTENAY, Ashley R.: Kent

COURTENAY, Sir William: Canterbury, Maidstone

COURTENEY, Sir William: Biography

COURTFIELD PRESS. Publishers: Kent, Industry and Trade

COURTNEY-LEWIS, C.T.: Sydenham

COURTS OF BROTHERHOOD AND GUESTLING: Dover

COUZENS, S.: Kent, East; Margate

COVENEY, P.J.: Kent, North West

(COWAN, L. Gibson): Tunbridge Wells

COWDREY, Michael Colin: Cricket

COWELL, M.H.: Kent, East

COWLES, Frederick: Canterbury, Canterbury Cathedral, Pilgrims Way

COWPER, Frank: Coastal Waters

COWPER, H.S.: Architecture, Headcorn, Staplehurst

COWPER, Joseph Meadows: Canterbury, Canterbury Cathedral, Elections, Faversham, Genealogical Records, History and Archaeology, Monumental Inscriptions

COWTAN, Robert: Biography

COX, E.W.: Bromley

COX, H.: Elections

COX, Horace: Biography

COX, John Charles: Canterbury, Kent, Kent Authors and Literature

COX, R.C.W.: West Wickham

COX, Thomas: History and Archaeology

COX, W.J.: Whitstable

COXALL, J.N.: Bromley

COXERE, Edward: Dover

COXON, S.W.: Dover

COXWELL, Henry: Medway Towns

COZENS, Walter: Canterbury

COZENS, Zechariah: History and Archaeology, Isle-of-Thanet, Margate, Thames, River

CRACE, Admiral Sir John Gregory: Chatham Dockyard

CRACKNELL, Basil E.: Thames, River

CRADOCK AND CO. Publishers: Kent

CRAFTSMEN OF KENT EXHIBITION, 1963: Canterbury

CRAIG, D.M.: Darent, River; Dartford, Industry and Trade

CRAIG, E.G.: Smallhythe

CRAIG, Henry: Canterbury

CRAIK, Mrs. pseud.: Dover

CRAMPTON, T.: Kent Songs

CRAN, Marion: Benenden

CRANBROOK RURAL DISTRICT COUNCIL: Weald

CRANBROOK AND SISSINGHURST LOCAL HISTORY SOCIETY:
    Cranbrook, Sissinghurst
See Also - PILE, C.R.R.: Cranbrook

CRANE, Maurice A.: Bexley

CRASK, C.W.: Blackheath

CRAWFORD, Deborah: Greenwich

CRAWFORD, Osbert Guy Stanhope: History and Archaeology,
    Kent, East

CRAWSHAW, J.D.: Chatham Dockyard

CRAWSHAY, De Barri: South Ash

CRAY VALLEY PAPER MILLS: Cray, River; Industry and Trade

CRAYFORD URBAN DISTRICT COUNCIL: Crayford

CREED, C.: Folkestone

CREEVEY, Thomas: Greenwich

CRELLIN, J.K.: Darwin, Charles

CRESWELL, D'Arcy: Bromley

CRESWICK, Paul: Kent

CRESY, Edward: Horton Kirby, Margate, Stone (Nr. Dartford)

CREWE, A.W. - See BROWN, John Howard: Swingfield

CRISP, Frederick Arthur: Birchington, Genealogical Records,
    Monumental Inscriptions

CROCKALL, R.: Coal

CROFT, Sir John: Doddington

CROFT-COOKE, Rupert: Edenbridge, Rochester, Sevenoaks,
    Tonbridge

CROGGAN, Lucy E.: Penshurst

CROLY, George: Northfleet

CROMBLEHOLME, Roger: Railways

CROME, Honor: Kent Authors and Literature

CROMPTON, J.A.: Industry and Trade

CROMWELL, Archibald: Dover

CROMWELL, Thomas Kitson: Kent

CRONK, Anthony: Agriculture, Genealogical Records, Horsmonden,
    West Malling

CROOK, H. Evelyn: Margate

CROPTON, John: Kent, East

CROSLAND, Newton: Eltham

CROSS, Francis W.: Canterbury

CROSS, H.J.: Hayes and Keston

CROSS AND JACKMAN. Publishers: Canterbury

CROTCH, W. Walter: Dickens, Charles

CROUCH, Marcus S.: Canterbury, Kent, Kent Authors and
    Literature

CROW, Martin Michael: Chaucer, Geoffrey

CROWE, Stanley: History and Archaeology

CROWLEY, George: Northfleet

CROYDON NATURAL HISTORY AND SCIENTIFIC SOCIETY:
    Beckenham, Penge, Shortlands, West Wickham

CRUDEN, Robert Peirce: Genealogical Records,
    Gravesend

CRUESS, H.J.: Hayes and Keston

CRUIKSHANK, P.: Crystal Palace

CRUIKSHANK, R.J.: Dickens, Charles

C(RUM), J.M.C.: Canterbury Cathedral

CRUTTWELL, Clement: Kent

CUFF BROTHERS. Publishers: Dover

CULL, Frederick: Chatham, Chatham Dockyard

CULLEN, Gordon - See McManus, Frederick and Partners
    Tenterden

CULMER, George G.: Architecture, Churches,
    Davington, Faversham

CULMER, Richard. The Elder: Canterbury Cathedral,
    History and Archaeology

CULMER, Richard. The Younger: Canterbury Cathedral

CULVERWELL, R.J.: Gravesend

CUMBERLAND, George: Bromley

CUMING, H. Syer: Dover

CUMMING, Mrs.: Kent Authors and Literature

CUMMING, GRAHAM LTD. Publishers: Hayes and Keston

CUNDILL, J.: Chatham

CUNLIFFE, B.W. - See Reports on the Excavation of th
Roman Fort at Richborough: Richborough

CUNNINGTON, Susan: Tenterden

CURIOSITIES IN THE COUNTY OF KENT...: Kent

CURLE, Richard: Conrad, Joseph

CURLING, Mary Anne: Kent Authors and Literature

CURLING, Richard AND OTHERS. Defendants: Ramsgate,
    Trials

CURNOW, W.I.: Eynsford

CURRY, John: Leeds

CURTEIS, Mrs. R.: Pembury

CURTEIS, T.: Kent Authors and Literature

CURTIS, Lillian Pitt: Chilham

CURZON, George Nathaniel. 1st Marquess Curzon of
Kedleston: Walmer

CUST, Lionel: Faversham

CUTHBERT, H.M.M.: Gillingham

CUTTS, Edward L.: Canterbury

CUXTON WOMEN'S INSTITUTE: Cuxton

"CYGNUS", pseud.: Crystal Palace

D

D., G.: Kent

D., L.: Kent Authors and Literature

D., W. - See DENNE, W.: Richborough

D Cont'd

DAVIS ESTATE RATEPAYERS' ASSOCIATION: Chatham

DAVIS, H. AND J. Auctioneers and Surveyors: Gravesend

DAVIS, H.E.: Isle-of-Sheppey

DAVIS, Israel: Ramsgate

DAVIS, J. Publisher: Deal, Dover, Folkestone, Kent, South East

DAVIS, J.F.: Kent, North West

DAVIS, Walter Goodwin: Canterbury

DAVIS, Walter T.: Woolwich

DAVIS, William J.: Dartford, Natural History

DAVISON, G.H.: Kent

DAVISON, Ian: Cranbrook, Weald

DAWBER, E. Guy: Architecture

DAWKINS, W. Boyd: Coal

DAWLEY, Powel Mills: Canterbury Cathedral, Archbishops

THE DAWN OF DAYS: Margate

DAWSON, Charles: Cinque Ports

DAWSON, Giles F.: Theatre

DAWSON, Philip: Railways

DAWSON, Ralph: Canterbury

DAY, B.W.: Sandwich

DAY, James Wentworth: Biography, Sport

DAY, Leslie: Kent Authors and Literature

DAY, Thomas: Maidstone

DAY ACCOUNT...: Birchington

DEACON, J.L.: Cinque Ports

DEAKIN, Richard: Tunbridge Wells

DEAL BOROUGH COUNCIL: Deal

DEAL AND DISTRICT LOCAL HISTORY AND RESEARCH SOCIETY: Deal

DEAL AND WALMER LOCAL HISTORY SOCIETY: Deal

DEANESLY, Margaret: Canterbury

DEARN, Thomas Downes Wilmot: Trials, Weald

DEBATE ON THE MEDWAY RIVER NAVIGATION...: Medway, River

DEBATH, Henry: Romney Marsh

DEBENHAM, Betty: Chelsfield

DECLARATION AND ORDINANCE OF THE LORDS AND COMMONS...: History and Archaeology

DECLARATION OF MANY THOUSANDS...: Canterbury

DECLARATION OF THE KNIGHTS...: History and Archaeology

DECLARATION OF THE SEVERAL PROCEEDINGS...: History and Archaeology

DEEBLE, William: Cinque Ports, Isle-of-Thanet

DEEDES FAMILY: Saltwood

DEFOE, Daniel: Canterbury, Chislehurst, History and Archaeology, Kent
See Also - "A Gentleman": Kent

DE GOLS, Gerard: Sandwich

DE KAY, Charles: Kent

DE LA CHAPELLE, Alfred Comte: Chislehurst

DELANY, Mary Cecelia: Industry and Trade, Weald

D'ELBOUX, R.H.: History and Archaeology

DE L'ISLE and DUDLEY, Lord: Penshurst

DELL, John, OF DOVER: Dover

DELSIGNORE, J.: Bromley

DE MONTMORENCY, James Ewart Geoffrey: Greenwich

DEMPSTER, Derek: Dover
See Also - WOOD, Derek: History and Archaeology

"DENARIUS", pseud. (Sir Henry COLE): Crystal Palace

DENCE, Thomas: Shoreham

DENKINGER, E.M.: Penshurst

DENMAN, John L.: Canterbury Cathedral

DENNE, James: Margate

DENNE, Samuel: Aylesford, Chatham Dockyard, Churches, Kent, Maidstone, Rochester

DENNE, William: Richborough
See Also - SHRUBSOLE, William: Rochester

DENNY, Sir Henry L.L.: West Wickham

DENT, H.C.: Dickens, Charles

DENVIR, Bernard: Kent

DE PARAVICINI, Frances: Canterbury Cathedral, Archbishops

DEPTFORD BOROUGH COUNCIL: Charities, Deptford

DERHAM, Walter: Fordwich

DERING, Sir Edward: Canterbury Cathedral, Archbishops, History and Archaeology, Kent Authors and Literature, Pluckley

DE RODSKOWSKI, Ernest: Ships and Shipping

DE SALVO, Brian: Bromley, Theatre

DE SANDWICH, Peter: Kent, East

DESBOROUGH, V.F.: Kent, West

DESCRIPTION OF THE ANCIENT VESSEL RECENTLY FOUND...: Rother, River

A DESCRIPTION OF ENGLAND AND WALES, VOL. 5: Kent

A DESCRIPTION OF THE ISLE-OF-THANET...: Isle-of-Thanet, Margate

DESCRIPTION OF THE MOAT...: Canterbury

DESSIOU, Joseph: Coastal Waters

DE VAYNES, Julia Henrietta: History and Archaeology

DE VERE, Aubrey Thomas: Canterbury Cathedral, Archbishops

DEVIS, James: Sandwich

DEVLIN, Christopher: Shipbourne

DEVLIN, Mary Aquinas: Rochester Cathedral

DEWEY, Henry: Dartford

DEWS, Nathan: Deptford

DEXTER, B.C.: Herne, Herne Bay, Reculver

DEXTER, Walter: Kent, Kent, North West

DIBBLE, Lucy Grace: Kent Authors and Literature

D Cont'd

DIBDEN, Thomas Frognall: Dover, Tenterden

DIBLEY, George F.: Kent, North East

DICK AND SAL...(POEM): Dover

DICKENS, Charles: Dickens, Charles; Folkestone, Thames, River

DICKENS FESTIVAL PAGEANT: Dickens, Charles; Rochester

DICKENS, Marnie: Dickens, Charles

THE DICKENSIAN: Broadstairs

DICKINSON, Patric: Canterbury Cathedral

DICKSON, George: Medway Towns

DICKSON, Lovat: Wells, Herbert George

DIGGES, Thomas: Dover

DIGGES, West: Kent

DIGGS, Thomas: History and Archaeology

DILLENIUS, John James: Eltham

DILLWYN, L.W. - See TURNER, Dawson: Natural History

DILNOT, Frank: Ash-next-Sandwich, Canterbury, Kent Authors and Literature

DINES, H.G.: Coal, Geology, Sevenoaks, Tunbridge Wells

DITCHFIELD, P.H.: History and Archaeology

DITTON LABORATORY: Ditton

DIVING, A.D.: Dover

DIXON, Alan G.: Railways

DIXON, Willmott: Kent Authors and Literature, Sheldwich

DIXON-SCOTT, J.: Kent

DIXSON, Owen: Blackheath

DOBEL, D.: Kent Authors and Literature, Religious Denominations

DOBELL, Leonora Ollive: Kent Authors and Literature

DOBELL, Samuel: Kent Authors and Literature

DOBREE, Bonamy - See MANWARING, G.E.: Military and Naval History

DOBREY, H.H.: Maidstone

DOBSON, F.R.: Kent

DOBSON, R.B.: History and Archaeology

DOBY, T.: Folkestone

DOCHERTY, J.: Darent, River; Kent, North West

DODD, C.E.: Faversham

DODD, R.: Chatham Dockyard, Medway, River; Thames, River

DODDS, Norman Noel: Kent Authors and Literature

DODSLEY, J.: Kent, Kent, North West

DODWELL, Charles Reginald: Canterbury

DOLBY, George: Dickens, Charles

DOLLEY, R.H. Michael: Coins and Tokens

DOMESDAY BOOK: History and Archaeology

DOMESDAY BOOK - PORTION OF A RETURN OF OWNERS...1873: Census

DOMESDAY BOOK FOR THE COUNTY OF KENT: History and Archaeology

DONALDSON, Christopher: Canterbury, Newchurch

DONKIN, Bryan: Kent Authors and Literature

DONKIN, J.: Canterbury Cathedral

DONNE, Charles E.: Faversham
See Also - GIRAUD, Francis F.: Faversham

DONOVAN, Frank: Dickens, Charles

DORAN, Dr. John: Kent Authors and Literature

DORLING, M.J.: Agriculture

DORMAN, Thomas: Sandwich

DORRICOTT, Rev. I.: Dover

DORRINGTON, Theophilus: Tunbridge Wells

DOUGHTY, F.H.: Wells, Herbert George

DOUGLAS, Mr.: Richborough

DOUGLAS, David C.: Canterbury Cathedral

DOUGLAS, James - See BIBLIOTHECA TOPOGRAPHICA BRITANNICA, VOL. I: Richborough

DOUIE, D.L.: Canterbury Cathedral, Archbishops

DOVE, Ronald Hammerton: Churches

DOVER AND COUNTY CHRONICLE. Publisher: Dover

DOVER BOROUGH COUNCIL: Dover

DOVER CHAMBER OF COMMERCE: Dover

DOVER CHRONICLE: Cinque Ports, Deal, Dover, Folkestone

DOVER COLLEGE: Dover

DOVER EXPRESS AND EAST KENT NEWS: Dover

DOVER HARBOUR BOARD: Dover

DOVER HOSPITAL: Dover

DOVER PUBLIC LIBRARY: Dover

DOVER RAILWAY CENTENARY: Dover, Railways

DOVER RURAL DISTRICT COUNCIL: Kent, South East

DOVER, SANDWICH AND DEAL LOCAL HISTORY EXHIBITION COMMITTEES: Kent, East

DOVER STANDARD: Canterbury, Coal, Deal, Dover

DOWDING, Hugh Caswal Tremenhere: Tunbridge Wells

DOWIE, Robin: Ashford

DOWKER, George: Canterbury, Coastline, Deal, Foord, Herne, Herne Bay, Isle-of-Thanet, Kent, East; Margate, Natural History, Preston, Ramsgate, Reculver, Richborough, Romney Marsh, Walmer, Wickhambreux, Wingham

DOWLING, D.T.: Hayes and Keston

DOWN, H. - See MINTON, R.: Chiddingstone

DOWNIE, S.C.: Cray, River; Darent, River

DOWNTON, H.M.: Canterbury

DOWRICK, C.E.J.: Blackheath

DOWSE, A.W.E.: Barfreston

DOWSE, I.R.: Canterbury Cathedral, Rochester Cathedral

DOWSON, Ernest: Kent Authors and Literature

DRAFT OF A PETITION...OYSTER FISHERMAN OF MILTON...: Milton Regis

DRAKE, Charles H.: Ospringe

DRAKE, H.H. - See HASTED, Edward: Kent, North West

DRAKE-BROCKMAN, D.H.: Newington-next-Sittingbourne

"THE DRAPER": Kent

DREW, Bernard: Cricket, Farningham

DREW, Frederic: Romney Marsh

DRINKWATER, Florence E.: Orpington

DRUCE, George C.: Brookland, Eynsford

DRURY, M.: Swanley

DUBLES, Charles: Canterbury

DUBOULAY, Francis Robin Houssemayne: Bexley, Canterbury, Canterbury Cathedral, Archbishops; History and Archaeology, Knole, Otford

DUCANN, Charles Garfield Lott: Dickens, Charles

DUCAREL, Andrew Coltee: Churches, Lambeth Palace

DUCK, Arthur: Canterbury Cathedral, Archbishops

DUCKETT, Eleanor Shipley: Canterbury

DUDENEY AND PILCHER. Auctioneers: Tunbridge Wells

DUDLEY, Ronald R.: History and Archaeology

DUFF, A.G.: Maidstone

DUFF, David: Biography

DUFFIELD, F.H.: Rochester Cathedral, Shortlands

DUFRESNE, Carelius: Richborough

DUGAN, James: Military and Naval History

DUGARD, Donald: Bromley

DUGDALE, Henry Geast: Rochester Cathedral

DUGDALE, James: Kent

DUGDALE, Sir William: Coastline, History and Archaeology

DUGGAN, Alfred: Canterbury, Canterbury Cathedral, Archbishops

DUKE, E.M.: Lydd

DUKE, Neville: Tonbridge

DULLEY, A.T.F.: Medway Towns

DULWICH MILLENNIUM CELEBRATIONS COMMITTEE: Dulwich

DUMBRECK, William V.: East Peckham, Hadlow, Tonbridge

DUNCAN, Francis: Military and Naval History

DUNCAN, Mrs. Isabella: Crystal Palace

DUNCAN, Leland Lewis: All Hallows, Chislehurst, Churches, Cowden, Cranbrook, Folkestone, History and Archaeology, Lydd, Shoreham, Tenterden
See Also - KIRBY, Herbert Charles: Genealogical Records, Greenwich, Lewisham, Monumental Inscriptions

DUNCAN-JONES, A.S.: Canterbury Cathedral, Archbishops

DUNCOMBE, John: Canterbury, Canterbury Cathedral, Harbledown, Herne, Reculver

DUNDAS, Henry. 1st Viscount Melville: Northfleet

DUNGENESS BIRD OBSERVATORY: Dungeness, Natural History

DUNGEY, Henry: Chatham

DUNK, J.L.: Railways

DUNK, W.J. Harold: Folkestone

DUNKEL, Wilbur: Sevenoaks

DUNKIN, Alfred John: Bromley, Canterbury, Canterbury Cathedral, Dartford, Deptford, Erith, Eynsford, History and Archaeology, Kent, Kent, North West; Sidcup, Springhead

DUNKIN, Edwin Hadlow Wise: Canterbury Cathedral, Archbishops; Kidbrooke

DUNKIN, John, OF BROMLEY: Bromley, Dartford, History and Archaeology, Sidcup, Stone (Nr. Dartford)

DUNLOP, J. Renton: Genealogical Records

DUNLOP, Sir John Kinninmoul: Sevenoaks

DUNN-PATTISON, R.P.: Canterbury

DUNNAGE, H.: Eltham

DUNNING, G.C.: Brookland, History and Archaeology, Kent, East
See Also - RIGOLD, S.E.: Ospringe

DUNNING, George: Kent Authors and Literature

DUNSANY, Edward J.M.D.P.: Shoreham

DUNSTALL, W. - See BELSEY, F.F.: Chatham

DUNTON GREEN PARISH COUNCIL: Dunton Green

DU-PLAT-TAYLOR, M.: Coastline

DUPPA, Brian. Bishop: Kent Authors and Literature

DURKIN, M.K.: Abbey Wood, Swanscombe

DURNFORD, A.W.: Chatham

DURTNELL, C.S.: Sevenoaks

DUTCH IN THE MEDWAY: History and Archaeology

DUVARD, Primogene: Kent Authors and Literature

DWELLY, Edward: Genealogical Records

DWYER, J.J.: Canterbury Cathedral, Archbishops

DYKE, Lady Zoe Hart: Lullingstone

DYMCHURCH AND DISTRICT CHAMBER OF TRADE: Dymchurch, St. Mary's Bay

DYMOND, Thomas Southall: Cinque Ports

DYSON, Sir Frank W.: Greenwich

DYSON, S.S.: Isle-of-Thanet, Kent, East

E

E., S.: Canterbury Cathedral

E., W.H., pseud. - See ELGAR, W.H.

EADMER: Canterbury Cathedral, Archbishops; History and Archaeology

EAMES, Geoffrey Leonard: Bromley

EAMES, John: Little Chart

EARLE. Publisher: Bromley

EARLY HISTORY OF THE ROBERTS FAMILY...: Cranbrook

EAST ASHFORD RURAL DISTRICT COUNCIL: Kent, East

EAST KENT AGRICULTURAL SOCIETY: Canterbury

EAST KENT AND CANTERBURY CONSERVATION CLUB: Organisations

EAST KENT ART SOCIETY: Canterbury

EAST KENT CHAMBER OF AGRICULTURE: Agriculture, Organisations

EAST KENT CHRISTMAS ANNUAL: Kent, East

EAST KENT CHURCH MISSIONARY ASSOCIATION: Religious Denominations

EAST KENT CLUB: Canterbury

EAST KENT DISCHARGED PRISONERS' AID SOCIETY: Organisations

EAST KENT FEDERATION OF WOMEN'S INSTITUTES: Recipes

EAST KENT GAZETTE: Newspapers

EAST KENT LIBERAL REGISTRATION ASSOCIATION: Organisations

EAST KENT NATURAL HISTORY SOCIETY: Natural History, Organisations

EAST KENT NEWSPAPER AND PRINTING CO.: Newspapers

EAST KENT OMNIBUS: Road Transport

EAST KENT REGIMENT OF MILITIA: Military and Naval History

EAST KENT ROADCAR CO.: Kent, East; Road Transport

EAST KENT SCIENTIFIC AND NATURAL HISTORY SOCIETY: Natural History, Organisations

EAST KENT TIMES: Biography, Isle-of-Thanet

EAST KENT YEOMAN: Military and Naval History

EAST MALLING AND LARKFIELD PARISH COUNCIL: East Malling, Larkfield

EAST MALLING RESEARCH STATION: Agriculture

EAST PEACKHAM CORONATION COMMITTEE: East Peckham

EAST YORKSHIRE LOCAL HISTORY SOCIETY - See BROOKS, F.W.: Cinque Ports, Gillingham

EASTLEIGH, Robert - See BODY, Geoffrey: Ramsgate

EASTRY RURAL DISTRICT COUNCIL: Kent, East

EASTMAN, John: Hever

EATON, Kenneth J.: Canterbury, Maidstone

EBENEZER CONGREGATIONAL CHURCH: Chatham

ECCLESIASTICAL CENSUS: Census, Religious Denominations

ECCLESIASTICAL TAXES OF POPE NICHOLAS IV...: Woolwich

ECONOMIC AFFAIRS, DEPARTMENT OF: Kent

ECTON, John: Churches

EDEN, William. 1st Baron Auckland - See PITT, William (1759-1806): Hayes and Keston

EDENBRIDGE PARISH COUNCIL: Edenbridge

EDINGER, J.H.: Dymchurch, Mersham

EDMEADES, J.F.: Military and Naval History

EDMUNDS, F.A. - See BROWN, E.E.S.: Bromley

EDMUNDS, F.H. - See Geological Survey and Museum: Geology, Weald

EDUCATIONAL FACILITIES IN THE COUNTY OF KENT: Education

EDWARDS, Anthony J.: Canterbury

EDWARDS, David Lawrence: Canterbury, Sandwich

EDWARDS, Frank: Barham

EDWARDS, J.: Kent

EDWARDS, Jane: Isle-of-Thanet, Sevenoaks

EDWARDS, J.W.F.: Boxley

EDYE, Major L.: Military and Naval History

EELES, F.C.: Ringwould

EELES, Henry Swanton: Biography, Sport

EHRMAN, John: Military and Naval History

EHRMAN, Rev. L.E.A.: Lynstead

ELAM, Charles C.: Canterbury Cathedral

ELAND, G.: Sittingbourne
See Also - WOTTON Thomas: Boughton Malherbe

ELDER, D.G.: Otford

ELERS, F. Wadham: Tunbridge Wells

ELEY, W.: Agriculture

ELGAR, W.H.: Folkestone, Richborough

ELIOT, Thomas Stearns: Canterbury Cathedral Archbishops

ELIZABETH I, QUEEN OF ENGLAND: Eltham

ELLEY, Richard: Dover

ELLIOTT, Douglas: Tonbridge

ELLIOTT, J.G.: St. Margaret-at-Cliffe

ELLIS, Aytoun: Ships and Shipping

ELLIS. Bookseller: Evelyn, John

ELLIS, Clarence: Biography

ELLIS, Hamilton: Railways

ELLIS, Havelock: Marlowe, Christopher

ELLIS, Sir Henry: Deptford

ELLIS, S.J.: Canterbury

ELLIS, S.M.: Canterbury

ELLIS, Stephen: Margate

ELLIS, William Smith: Biography, History and Archaeology

ELLIS-MACE, J.: Tenterden

ELLISON, Grace: Biography

ELLISTON-ERWOOD: Frank Charles: Aldington, Charlton, Churches, Darenth, Eltham, Erith, Greenwich, Heraldry, History and Archaeology, Kent Authors and Literature, Kingsdown, Lee, Maidstone, Pilgrims Way, Plumstead, Roads, Romney Marsh, Ruxley, Shooters Hill, Swanscombe, Teynham, West Malling, Woolwich

ELLISTON-ERWOOD, Peter M.: Railways, Woolwich

ELSNA, Hebe, pseud. (D.P. ANSLE): Dickens, Charles

ELTHAM SOCIETY: Eltham

ELTON, Charles I.: History and Archaeology

ELVIN, Charles R.S.: Walmer

ELVIN, S.W.G.: Dover

ELVIRA, pseud.: History and Archaeology

ELWIG, Henry: Tunbridge Wells

ELY, John: Chatham

EMANUEL, Manly: Canterbury, Trials

EMBRY, Sir Basil: Dover

EMBRY, Bernard: Kent, South East; Natural History

EMBRY, John: Religious Denominations

EMDEN, Alfred Brotherston: Canterbury

EMDEN, Cecil Stuart: Pepys, Samuel

FAIRBAIRNS, Arnold: Canterbury Cathedral, Rochester
   Cathedral

FAIRBAIRNS, W.H.: Canterbury Cathedral, Rochester
   Cathedral

FAIRFAX, Thomas Fairfax. 3rd Baron: History and
   Archaeology

FAIRFAX-BLAKEBOROUGH, J.: Sport

FAIRHOLME, George: Isle-of-Thanet

FAIRHOLT, F.W.: Kent

FAMILY NAMES OF THE WEALD OF KENT: Genealogical Records

FAMILY PLANNING ASSOCIATION: Maidstone

FAMOUS OLD INNS OF MID-KENT: Weald

FANSHAWE, David: Kent Songs

FARLEY, James George Wilson: Agriculture

FARMER, Henry George: Military and Naval History

"FARMER IN KENT", pseud.: Agriculture

FARMERS' HOUSEHOLD ACCOUNTS BOOK: Agriculture

FARNABY, Sir Charles F.: West Wickham

FARNINGHAM, Marianne: Farningham

FARNOL, Jeffery: Kent

FARQUHARSON, Victor: Little Chart

FARQUHARSON AND MILLARD. Auctioneers: Canterbury

FARRAR, Frederic William: Canterbury, Canterbury Cathedral
   Kent Authors and Literature

FARRAR, Reginald: Canterbury Cathedral

FARTHER EXCURSIONS OF AN OBSERVANT PEDESTRIAN...: Kent

FASHIONABLE GUIDE AND DIRECTORY...: Kent

FAUSSETT, T.G. Godfrey - See GODFREY-FAUSETT, T.G.: Canterbury

FAUSSETT, Bryan: Kent, South East

FAVERSHAM BOOK SOCIETY: Faversham

FAVERSHAM BOROUGH COUNCIL: Faversham

FAVERSHAM AND DISTRICT CHAMBER OF COMMERCE: Faversham

FAVERSHAM AND DISTRICT NATIONAL SCHOOL: Faversham

FAVERSHAM INSTITUTE: Faversham

FAVERSHAM SOCIETY: Faversham

FAVRESFELD, Charles: Milton Regis

FAWCETT, F. Dubrez: Dickens, Charles

FAWCETT, William: Weald

FAYNE, Eric: Medway Towns

FAZAN, E.A.C.: Military and Naval History

FEAR, Herbert: Cricket

FEAR, William H.: Brenchley

FEARNSIDE, W.G.: Medway, River; Thames, River
   See Also - TOMBLESON, W.: Thames, River

FEARON, Henry: Canterbury, Kent, Pilgrims Way

FEATHERSTONES, 1901-1951: Canterbury

FEDDEN, Robin: Westerham

FEDERATION OF RATEPAYERS' ASSOCIATIONS IN THE COUNTY OF KENT:
   Kent, Kent Authors and Literature, Organisations

FEDERATION OF WOMEN'S INSTITUTES: Kent, Kent Authors
   and Literature

"FELIX", pseud.: Folkestone

FELIX ON THE BAT: Cricket

FELLOWES, H. Le M.: Tenterden

FELLOWS, Edward: Canterbury Cathedral

FELLOWS, Reginald B.: Railways

FELLS, J.M.: Deal

FELTHAM, John: Kent

FELTOE, Charles Lett: Canterbury

FELTON, Herbert: Canterbury Cathedral

FELTON, L.: Military and Naval History

FELTONS, CATTLEY AND CO.: Agriculture

FENTON, Elijah: Sevenoaks

FENWICK, Kenneth: Chatham Dockyard

FERGUSON, Ruby: Woolwich

FERGUSSON FAMILY: Genealogical Records

FERGUSSON, Robert - See TUFTON, Sackville. 9th Earl
of Thanet: Trials

FERGUSSON, Thomas Colyer - See GREEN, Everard:
   Genealogical Records

FESTIVAL AT DOVER...: Cinque Ports

FFINCH, Kenneth Maule: Ifield, Singlewell

FIDO, Martin: Dickens, Charles

FIELD, C.: Chatham Dockyard

FIELD, E.J.: Chartham

FIELD, Thomas: Canterbury, Canterbury Cathedral

FIELDFARE, pseud. (Henry Bridges FEARON): Kent

FIELDING, Cecil Henry: Higham, Rochester, West
   Malling

FIELDING, Edwina: Aylesford

FIELDING, G. Hunsley: Kent Authors and Literature

FIELDING, K.J.: Dickens, Charles

FIENNES, Celia: Kent

FIFTY GREAT DISASTERS AND TRAGEDIES THAT SHOCKED THE
WORLD: Gillingham

FILMER, Reginald Mead: History and Archaeology

FILMER, Sir Robert: East Sutton

FINBERG, J.: Kent

FINCH, M. Lawson: Railways

FINCH, W.: History and Archaeology

FINCH, William Coles: Kent, Kent Authors and
   Literature, Medway, River; Rochester, Windmills
   and Watermills

FINDLAY, Alexander George: Medway, River; Thames,
   River

FINESTEIN, Israel: Dover

FINLASON, W.F.: Folkestone

FINN, Arthur: Agriculture, Lydd, Smuggling

FINN, R.: Ramsgate, Smuggling

F Cont'd

FINNY, W.E. St. L.: History and Archaeology

FIRESIDE FACTS FROM THE GREAT EXHIBITION: Crystal Palace

FIRST DAY COVERS: Canterbury Cathedral, Archbishops

1ST KENT ARTILLERY VOLUNTEER CORPS (GRAVESEND): Military
and Naval History

FIRTH, Sir Charles H.: Canterbury, Deptford

FIRTH, John B.: Dover

FISCHER, Michael: Folkestone

FISHER, Geoffrey. Archbishop of Canterbury: Canterbury
Cathedral, Archbishops

FISHER, Joseph: Sevenoaks

FISHER, T.: Kent

FISHER, Thomas: Churches

FISHER UNWIN. Publisher: Tunbridge Wells

FISHWICK, V.C.: Kent Authors and Literature

"FIT", pseud.: Folkestone

FITCH, Marc: Genealogical Records

FITTER, Richard Sidney Richmond: Kent, Natural History

FITZGERALD, Percy: Dickens, Charles

FITZGERALD, S.J. Adair: Dickens, Charles

FITZMAURICE, Edmond: Biography

FITZSTEPHEN, William: Canterbury Cathedral, Archbishops

FIVE LETTERS ON THE STATE OF THE POOR, 1770...: Poor
Law

FLAHERTY, W.E.: History and Archaeology

FLASHMAN, W.E.: Dover

FLEMING, Abraham: Sutton Valence

FLEMING, G.C. - See RIX, M.M.: Dover

FLEMING, I. Plant: Tonbridge

FLEMING, Peter: Military and Naval History

FLETCHER, Benton: Kent, North West

FLETCHER, Sir Eric: Churches, Stone-by-Faversham

FLETCHER, Eric G.M. - See JACKSON, E. Dudley C.: Lydd

FLETCHER, Geoffrey: Dickens, Charles

FLETCHER, Joseph Smith: Kent Authors and Literature

FLETCHER, R. - See CHARLTON, L.E.O.: Kent Authors and
Literature

FLETCHER, W.G.D.: Sundridge

FLINN, M.W.: Greenwich

FLOWER, C.T.: History and Archaeology

FLOWER, David Edwin Laurence: Rochester

FLOWER, Sir Newman: Wrotham

FLOWER, Thomas Bruges: Isle-of-Thanet

FLOYDD, W.: Dover

FOLEY, R.R.W.: Agriculture

FOLKESTONE ADVERTISING COMMITTEE: Folkestone

FOLKESTONE AND DISTRICT ELECTRICITY SUPPLY CO. LTD.:
Folkestone

FOLKESTONE AND DISTRICT WATER CO.: Folkestone

FOLKESTONE BOROUGH COUNCIL: Elections, Folkestone

FOLKESTONE CHAMBER OF COMMERCE: Folkestone

FOLKESTONE FIERY SERPENT - See ENGLISH, John.
Publisher: Folkestone

FOLKESTONE HERALD: Folkestone

FOLKESTONE NATURAL HISTORY SOCIETY: Folkestone

FOLKESTONE PUBLIC LIBRARY: Folkestone, Kent

FOLLEY, Roger Roland Westwell: Agriculture

See Also - DORLING, M.J.: Agriculture
HUNT, A.R.: Agriculture

FORAN, E.A.: Canterbury

FORD, Ford Madox: Cinque Ports

FORESTRY COMMISSION: Bedgebury, Weald

See Also - BARRINGTON, C.A.: Weald

FOREVILLE, Raymonde: Canterbury Cathedral, Archbishops

FORREST, Ebenezer: Isle-of-Sheppey

FORRESTER, Alfred H.: Kent

FORSETT, John: New Romney

FORSTER, John: Dickens, Charles

FORSTER, R.H. - See FORSTER, T.E.: Chislehurst

FORSTER, T.E.: Chislehurst

FORSTER, T.F.: Tonbridge

FORT PITT CENTRAL MILITARY HOSPITAL: Rochester

FOSS, Edward: History and Archaeology

FOSTER, C. Le Neve: Medway, River

FOSTER, Denis: Cricket, Hever

FOSTER, Joseph: Churches

FOSTER, Reginald: Dover

FOTHERINGHAM, David Ross: Charing

FOUR TELEGRAMS FROM THE SECRETARY OF THE ADMIRALTY,
ETC.: Canterbury

FOWLER, C. - See BERLYN, P.: Crystal Palace

FOWLER, Frank: Canterbury, Dover

FOWLER, Montagu: Canterbury Cathedral, Archbishops

FOX, Elizabeth: Folkestone

FOX, Sir Francis: Channel Tunnel

FOX, George: Coastal Defences

FOX, John: Canterbury Cathedral

FOX, Nancy Piercy: Hayes and Keston

See Also - JACKSON, E. Dudley C.: Hayes and Keston

FRAMPTON, Thomas Shipden: Churches, Hythe,
Minster-in-Sheppey, Tilmanstone, Wrotham, Wye

FRANCE, Walter Frederick: Canterbury

FRANCIS, Lionel: Sport

FRANCIS ILES GALLERIES: Chatham

FRANKLIN, Kenneth J.: Folkestone

FRANKLIN, W.H. Publisher: Deal

FRANKLYN, Charles A.H.: Genealogical Records

FRASER, Alan C.: Deptford

FRASER, Edward: Greenwich

FRASER, William: Manston

GARNETT, Mrs. Robert Singleton: Smuggling

GARNIER, Rev. A.J.: Canterbury

GARRAD, G.H.: Agriculture, Romney Marsh

GARRETT, G.T. - See CHARLTON, L.E.O.: Kent Authors and
    Literature

GARRETT, Richard: Coastal Waters

GARRETT, S.R.: Railways

GARRINGTON, D.S.: Queenborough

GARROW, D.W.: Canterbury Cathedral, Archbishops

GARSTANG, John: Richborough

GARTSIDE, Vivian Osmond Brock: Kent Authors and Literature

GARY, Geoffrey T.: Gillingham

GASPEY, William: Tunbridge Wells

GASQUET, A. Cardinal: Canterbury

GASSON, H.M.: Agriculture

GASSON, R.M. - See BEST, R.H.: Agriculture

GASSON, Ruth: Agriculture

GASTINEAU, H. - See SHEPHERD, G.: Kent

GATES, Henry: Canterbury

GATHORNE-HARDY, Alfred E.: Biography

GATHORNE-HARDY, Gathorne. 1st Earl of Cranbrook: Benenden

GATTIE, George Byng: Goodwin Sands

GATTY, Charles T.: Dover

GAUSDEN, John: Rochester

GAYE, Phoebe Fenwick - See TURNER, Reginald: Kent

GAZE, W.C.: History and Archaeology

GEARY: West Peckham

GEDGE, T.E. Publisher: Deal

GEDNEY, Charles William: Darent, River; Stour, River

GEISS, P. - See BENNEY, M: Greenwich

GELIG, George Robert: Ash-next-Sandwich

GELL, Francis: Dungeness, Lydd, Minster-in-Thanet

GEM, R.D.H.: Canterbury Cathedral

GENERAL BAPTIST CHURCHES: Religious Denominations

"GENERAL BAPTIST AND LOVER OF PEACE", pseud.: Dover

GENERAL POST OFFICE: Bromley

GENERAL REGISTER OFFICE: Census, Genealogical Records,
    Gravesend (For census publications since 1971 - See
Office of Population, Censuses and Surveys)

GENERAL STEAM NAVIGATION CO. LTD.: Coastal Waters, Thames,
    River

GENIUS OF KENT: Kent

"A GENTLEMAN", pseud.: Kent

GENTLEMAN'S JOURNAL: Canterbury

GENTLEMAN'S MAGAZINE: Hayes and Keston

GENTRY, W.C.: Isle of Thanet

GEOLOGICAL SURVEY AND MUSEUM: Bromley, Canterbury,
    Coal, Dartford, Dover, Folkestone, Geology,
    Kent, Kent, East; Kent, Mid; Kent, North West,
    Maidstone, Ramsgate, Sevenoaks, Tenterden,
    Tonbridge, Weald

GEOLOGISTS' ASSOCIATION: Kent, North West

See Also - ABBOTT, George: Eridge, Geology,
    Tunbridge Wells, Weald
        ALLEN, P.: Geology, Weald
        FAWCETT, William: Geology, Weald
        KIRKALDY, J.F.: Geology, Weald
        REEVES, J.W.: Geology Weald
        ROBINSON, A.W.H.: Sandwich
        SWEETING, G.S.: Geology, Industry and
            Trade, Weald
        WOOD, G.V.: Geology, Weald

"GEORGE ARNOLD" MUSEUM: Gravesend

GERALD, Sydney: Deal

GERNSHEIM, Helmut - See CHURCHILL, Randolph Spencer:
    Westerham

GERUASE OF CANTERBURY: Canterbury Cathedral,
    Kent Authors and Literature

GEYELIN, George Kennedy: Agriculture

GIBB, George D.: Bromley

GIBBONS, Gavin: Channel Tunnel

GIBBS, Mrs. Ann: Kent Authors and Literature

GIBBS, W.: Deal

GIBBS-SMITH, C.H.: Crystal Palace

GIBSON, A.H.: Sandgate

GILBERT, C.J.: Romney Marsh

GILBERT, E.C.: Canterbury Cathedral

GILBERT, George: Canterbury

GILBERT, R.G.: Canterbury

GILBERT, W.G.L.: Cinque Ports

GILBERT, Walter B.: Maidstone

GILES, J.A.: Canterbury Cathedral, Archbishops

GILES, John: Eythorne

GILES, Musgrave G. - See WOODGATE, Gordon: Biography

GILL, Conrad: Military and Naval History

GILL, D.M.C. - See COLLINS I.: Boughton-under-Blean

GILL, L. Upcott: Kent

GILL, Walter: Alkham; Dour, River

GILLETTE CUP FINAL, 1971: Cricket

GILLHAM, Christopher: Dartford

GILLHAM, Eric Howard: Medway, River; Natural
    History

GILLINGHAM, George Oliver: Gillingham

GILLINGHAM BOROUGH COUNCIL: Elections, Gillingham,
    Rainham

GILLINGHAM COUNTY GRAMMAR SCHOOL FOR BOYS - See
MOORE, W.C.: Gillingham

GILLINGHAM LOCAL BOARD: Gillingham

GILLINGHAM PUBLIC LIBRARIES: Biography, Gillingham
    Kent Authors and Literature, Medway, River;
    Medway Towns, Rainham

GILLMAN, Webster: Elections

GILMORE, John: Goodwin Sands

GILMOUR, John: Natural History

GILPIN, William: Coastline

GINDER. Publisher: Canterbury

GIRAUD, Francis F.: Faversham, Genealogical Records, History and Archaeology

GIROUARD, Mark: Bexleyheath, Crystal Palace

GISSING, George: Dickens, Charles

GITTINGS, Robert: Canterbury Cathedral

GIVEN, J.C.M.: Tunbridge Wells

GLANVILLE, John: History and Archaeology

GLANVILLE, W.G.: Folkestone

GLEANINGS IN KENT: Kent

GLEIG, G.R.: Ash-next-Sandwich, Kent Authors and Literature, Waltham

GLENCROSS, Alan: Greenwich

GLENCROSS, R.M.: Genealogical Records

GLIDDON, M.A.: Margate

GLIDDON, Paul: Shoreham

GLOVER, Frederick Robert Augustus: Dover

GLOVER, Rev. Richard: Kent Authors and Literature

GLOVER, Robert Finlay: Kent Authors and Literature

GLUNTZ, J.W.: Dartford

GLYNNE, Sir Stephen R.: Churches

GODINTON PARK: Ashford

GODFREY, Elizabeth: Kent

GODFREY-FAUSSETT, T.D.: Canterbury
See Also - Memorials of...: Canterbury

GODFREY, Rev. R.B.: Wouldham

GODFREY, Walter Hines: Architecture, Eltham

GOD'S WONDERS IN THE GREAT DEEP: Gravesend

GODWIN, G.N.: Folkestone

GODWIN, J.H.: Rochester

GODWIN, John: Ightham, Yalding

GOELL, Kermit: Gravesend

GOING TO MARGATE!: Margate, Thames, River

GOLBY, F.W.: Lewisham

GOLDEN GRAIN GUIDE...: Margate

GOLDING-BIRD, Cuthbert Hilton: Meopham

GOLDRING, Douglas: Deal

GOLDRING, Frederick - See WOOLDRIDGE, Sidney William: Weald

GOLDSMITH-CARTER, George - See CARTER, George Coldsmith: Goodwin Sands, Kent, Reculver, Romney Marsh, Sandwich

GOLDWYN, J.H.: Rochester

GOMME, C.L.: Kent, Rochester

GOODHART, Charles E.: Genealogical Records

GOODMAN, Paul - See CARDOZO, D.A.: Ramsgate

GOODMAN, W.L.: Sarre

GOODRICH, Alec T.: Aylesford

GOODRICH, Harold S.: Canterbury

GOODSALL, Robert Harold: Ash-next-Sandwich, Barfreston, Canterbury, Harrietsham, History and Archaeology, Ickham, Kent, Kent Authors and Literature, Lee, Len, River; Maidstone, Medway, River; Pilgrims Way, Roads, Rother, River; Seasalter, Stour, River; Swalecliffe, Tankerton, Thames, River; Whitstable

GORDON, Alexander - See MILNE, Colin: Natural History

GORDON, Sir Home - See Kent County Cricket Club: Cricket

GORDON, John: Isle-of-Grain, Isle-of-Sheppey

GORDON, R.A. - See TURNER, J.W.: Bromley

GORDON, W.J.: Sandwich

GORDON, Major William: Sandwich, Trials

GORST, Sir John: Chatham Dockyard

GOSTLING, William: Canterbury, Kent, North West; Rochester

GOUGH, Benjamin: Kent Authors and Literature

GOUGH, G.H.: Alkham

GOUGH, Harold Eric: Herne, Herne Bay

GOUGH, John Ballantine: Biography

GOUGH, Richard: Kent

GOULD, J.A.: Military and Naval History

GOULDEN, A.T.: Canterbury

GOULDEN, C. Publisher: Canterbury, Deal, Dover, Folkestone

GOULDEN, H.J. LTD. Publisher: Canterbury

GOULDEN, John: Kent, South East

GOULDEN AND NYE. Publishers: Tunbridge Wells

GOULDER, Laurance: Canterbury

GOULSTONE, John: Cricket

GOWER, Sir Robert Vaughan: Tunbridge Wells

GRACE, J.G.: Chatham Dockyard

GRACE, W.G.: Mottingham, Sydenham

GRAHAM, C.A.L.: Woolwich

GRAHAM, Frank: Smuggling

GRAHAM, G.H. Publisher: Kent, Maidstone

GRAHAM, John: Cobham

GRAHAM, Rose: Canterbury Cathedral, Archbishops; Dover, Maidstone, Reculver

GRAHAM, Stephen: Deptford

GRANT. Publisher: Isle-of-Thanet

GRANT, L.: Cinque Ports

GRANT, Mary: Deptford, Lewisham

GRANT, R. Parkin: St. Nicholas-at-Wade

GRANVILLE, Augustus: Deptford

GRANVILLE, Augustus Bozzi: Tunbridge Wells

GRANVILLE, Wilfred: Ships and Shipping

GRANVILLE-BAKER B.: Canterbury

GRASEMAN, C.: Isle-of-Sheppey, Ships and Shipping

GRAVER, Lawrence: Conrad, Joseph

GRAVES, Charles: Dickens, Charles

GRAVESEND AND THE BARONIAL HALLS OF KENT: Gravesend, History and Archaeology

GRAVESEND AND DISTRICT CHAMBER OF TRADE: Gravesend

GRAVESEND AND DISTRICT SCIENTIFIC AND ARCHAEOLOGICAL SOCIETY: Gravesend

GRAVESEND AND DISTRICT SCOUT COUNCIL: Gravesend

GRAVESEND AND MILTON MECHANICS INSTITUTE: Gravesend, Milton-next-Gravesend

GRAVESEND BOROUGH COUNCIL: Gravesend

GRAVESEND, CHATHAM, MARGATE, RAMSGATE AND NORTHFLEET DISTRICT TRADES DIRECTORY: Kent

GRAVESEND CHURCH UNION: Gravesend

GRAVESEND CONGREGATIONAL MAGAZINE: Gravesend

GRAVESEND HISTORICAL SOCIETY: Gravesend, Milton-next-Gravesend, Springhead

GRAVESEND, MILTON AND NORTHFLEET ELECTRIC LIGHT AND POWER WORKS: Gravesend

GRAVESEND PUBLIC LIBRARY: Gravesend, Northfleet

GRAVESEND SCHOOL FOR BOYS: Gravesend

GRAVESEND SOCIETY AND GRAVESEND AND ROCHESTER DISTRICT FOOTPATHS SOCIETY: Footpaths and Commons

GRAVESEND WORKERS' EDUCATION ASSOCIATION: Gravesend

GRAVETT, Kenneth: Architecture

GRAY, George: Sandwich

GRAY, Irvine - See EMMISON, F.G.: History and Archaeology

GRAYLING, Francis: Churches, Milton Regis

GREAT BRITAIN: LAWS, STATUTES, ETC. (HENRY VIII): Eltham

GREAT BRITAIN: LAWS, STATUTES, ETC. (CHARLES II): Dover, Medway, River

GREAT BRITAIN: LAWS, STATUTES, ETC. (WILLIAM III): Dover

GREAT BRITAIN: LAWS, STATUTES, ETC. (ANNE): Bexley, Greenwich, Law, Swingfield, Thames, River

GREAT BRITAIN: LAWS, STATUTES, ETC. (GEORGE I): Canterbury, Coastal Waters, Dover, Margate, Roads

GREAT BRITAIN: LAWS, STATUTES, ETC. (GEORGE II): Canterbury, Chatham, Coastal Waters, Deal, Deptford, Dover, Gravesend, Greenwich, Law, Maidstone, Medway, River; Ramsgate, Roads, Sandwich, Thames, River; Woolwich

GREAT BRITAIN: LAWS, STATUTES, ETC. (GEORGE III): Bexley, Blackheath, Broadstairs, Bromley, Canals, Canterbury, Charlton, Chatham, Chatham Dockyard, Chetney, Coastal Defences, Coastal Waters, Coxheath, Dartford, Deal, Dover, Drainage, Faversham, Folkestone, Gravesend, Greenwich, Hythe, Isle-of-Thanet, Kent, North West; Law, Lewisham, Maidstone, Margate, Medway, River; Military and Naval History, Milton-next-Gravesend, Northfleet, Ramsgate, Roads, Rochester, Sandwich, Sheerness, Smuggling, Thames, River; Tonbridge, Whitstable, Woolwich

GREAT BRITAIN: LAWS, STATUTES, ETC. (GEORGE IV): Bromley, Cinque Ports, Coastal Waters, Deptford, Gravesend, Greenwich, Isle-of-Thanet, Law, Maidstone, Margate, Railways, Roads, Rochester

GREAT BRITAIN: LAWS, STATUTES, ETC. (WILLIAM IV): Blackheath, Deptford, Dover, Gravesend, Greenwich, Law, Local Government, Medway, River; Milton-next-Gravesend, Railways, Woolwich

GREAT BRITAIN: LAWS, STATUTES, ETC. (VICTORIA): Canals, Chislehurst, Deal Dover, Elections, Folkestone, Gravesend, Greenwich, History and Archaeology, Hythe, Isle-of-Thanet, Medway, River; Medway Towns, Milton-next-Gravesend, Northfleet, Public Utilities, Railways, Roads, Road Transport, St. Paul's Cray, Ships and Shipping, Sittingbourne, Tunbridge Wells

GREAT BRITAIN: LAWS, STATUTES, ETC. (EDWARD VII): Dartford, Dover, Folkestone, Gravesend, Margate, Northfleet, Public Utilities, Railways, Road Transport

GREAT BRITAIN: LAWS, STATUTES, ETC. (GEORGE V): Crystal Palace, Dartford Tunnel, Dover, Folkestone, Gillingham, Isle-of-Thanet, Margate, Medway, River; Public Utilities, Railways

GREAT BRITAIN: LAWS, STATUTES, ETC. (GEORGE VI): Crystal Palace, Dartford Tunnel, Dover, Medway, River

GREAT BRITAIN: LAWS, STATUTES, ETC. (ELIZABETH II): Bromley, Charities, Chatham Dockyard, Chevening, Dartford Tunnel, Dover, Footpaths and Commons, Law, Local Government, Maidstone, Margate, Medway, River; Orpington, Public Utilities, Ravensbourne, River; Road Transport, Rochester

GREAT BRITAIN: LAWS, STATUTES, ETC. - STATUTORY INSTRUMENTS: Bedgebury, Canterbury, Chatham Dockyard, Dartford, Drainage, Elections, Isle-of-Thanet, Knockholt, Local Government, Maidstone, Medway, River; Public Utilities, Roads, Rolvenden

GREAT BRITAIN - PARLIAMENT: Agriculture, Bromley, Channel Tunnel, Charities, Chevening, Cinque Ports, Dover, History and Archaeology, Medway, River; Orpington, Public Utilities, Railways, Rochester, Thames, River

GREAT BRITAIN - PARLIAMENT: SELECT COMMITTEE ON THE HOP INDUSTRY: Agriculture

GREAT BRITAIN - PRIVY COUNCIL: Chatham Dockyard

GREAT EXHIBITION OF 1851: Crystal Palace

GREATER LONDON COUNCIL: Erith, Sport, Thames, River; Thamesmead

GREATER LONDON COUNCIL - RESEARCH AND INTELLIGENCE UNIT: Bromley, Census

GREATER LONDON AND SOUTH-EAST SPORTS COUNCIL: Sport

GREAVES, Cyril Abdy: Kent, Kent Authors and Literature

GREAVES, Ralph: Folkestone, Sport

GREEN, E.C.: Folkestone

GREEN, E.R.: Gravesend

GREEN, Emanuel: Isle-of-Thanet

GREEN, Everard: Genealogical Records

GREEN, Frank: Dickens, Charles

GREEN, I.W.: Whitstable

GREEN, J. Barcham: Industry and Trade

GREEN, R.D.: Romney Marsh

GREEN, T. Frank: Blackheath

GREENAWAY, George: Canterbury Cathedral, Archbishops

GREENAWAY, M.: Wilmington

GREENFIELD, Ernest: Darent, River; Wingham

GREENFIELD, Lilian: Canterbury

GREENHILL, F.A.: West Wickham

GREENSTED, Frances: Faversham

GREENSTREET, James: Genealogical Records, History and
    Archaeology

GREENWICH AND LEWISHAM ANTIQUARIAN SOCIETY: Blackheath,
    Genealogical Records, Greenwich

GREENWICH BOARD OF WORKS: Greenwich

GREENWICH BOROUGH COUNCIL: Greenwich

GREENWICH HOSPITAL: Greenwich

GREENWICH NATURAL HISTORY CLUB: Blackheath, Kent, North
    West; Natural History

GREENWICH PARK (POEM): Kent Authors and Literature

GREENWICH TRACTS: Greenwich

GREENWICH VESTRY: Charities, Greenwich

GREENWICH VOLUNTEERS: Military and Naval History

GREENWOOD, Alfred: Kent Authors and Literature

GREENWOOD, C.: History and Archaeology

GREENWOOD, E.J.: Rochester

GREGG, Pauline: Greenwich

GREGOR, Arthur S.: Darwin, Charles

GREGORY, C.W.: Canterbury

GREGORY, J.W.: Great Chart

GREGORY, Olianthus: Deptford

GREGORY, R.R.C.: Eltham, Lee

GREGORY AND CO. Publishers: Isle-of-Thanet

GREW, B.D.: Maidstone

GREY, Ian: Deptford

GRIERSON, Elizabeth: Canterbury

GRIFFIN, Frederick: Crystal Palace

GRIFFIN, Ralph: Addington, Allington, Aylesford, Barham,
    Bekesbourne, Canterbury Cathedral, Chatham, Churches,
    Denton, Dover, Elham, Faversham, Genealogical Records,
    Heraldry, History and Archaeology, Hythe, Little Chart,
    Maidstone, Mersham, Minster-in-Sheppey, Monumental
    Inscriptions, New Romney, Nonington, Northfleet, Pluckley,
    Preston-next-Faversham, Rochester Cathedral, Sittingbourne,
    Staplehurst, Stourmouth, West Malling, Wouldham, Wrotham

GRIFFIN, W.H. - See DUNCAN, Leland Lewis: Lewisham

GRIFFITH, Dudley David: Chaucer, Geoffrey

GRIGG, G.W. AND SON. Publisher: Dover

GRIGSON, Geoffrey: Oldbury

GRIMSHAW, Geoffrey: Ships and Shipping

GRINLING, C.H.: Kent, North West; Tunbridge Wells, Woolwich

"GRIP", pseud.: Channel Tunnel

GRITTEN, Archibald John: Margate

GROANS OF KENT...: History and Archaeology

GROOM, J.B.: Maidstone

GROOMBRIDGE, Garth: Donnington

GROSE, Francis: Dialects, History and Archaeology

GROSS, John: Dickens, Charles

GROSSJEAN, Paul - See DEANESLY, Margaret: Canterbury

GROSVENOR, Joan: Deptford

GROTE, Mrs. Harriet: Beckenham

GROVE, L.R.A.: Kent, Maidstone, Natural History,
    Wormshill

See Also - HAWKES, Sonia Chadwick: Milton Regis

GROVES, Reg - See LINDSAY, Philip: History and
    Archaeology

GUENTHER, John: Dartford

GUEST, Ivor: Chislehurst

GUGGISBERG, F.G.: Woolwich

GULLIVER, Diogenes, pseud.: Channel Tunnel

GULLIVER, George: Kent Authors and Literature

GUMMER, John Selwyn - See GUMMER, Selwyn: Gravesend

GUMMER, Selwyn: Brompton, Gravesend, Rochester
    Cathedral

GUNDRY, Nathaniel: Margate, Ramsgate

GUNKEL, E.C.: Gravesend

GUNNING, George: Meopham

GUNNIS, Erhart: Canterbury

GUNNIS, Rupert: Chiddingstone, Hever, Monumental
    Inscriptions, Tunbridge Wells

GUPPY, H.B.: Kent

GURNEY, James: Maidstone, Trials

GURNEY, Joseph: Maidstone

GWINNETT, Ambrose: Deal

GWYER, Joseph: Penge

GWYNN, Stephen: Walmer

H

H., C. - See H(ARDY), C(harles Frederick): Chilham

H., G.N.: Margate

H., J.C.: Ashford

H., M.: Dover

"H.M.S. Kent": Military and Naval History

H., W.T.: Gravesend, Milton-next-Gravesend

HACKETT, Benedict: Canterbury

HADFIELD, Charles: Canals, Canterbury Cathedral

HADLOW LOCAL HISTORY SOCIETY: Hadlow

HADWELL, Charles: Hayes and Keston, Kent

HAGGAR, R.J.: Agriculture

HAHN, Emily: Wye

HAIGH, F.H.: Cricket

HAIGH, T.: Kent Songs

HAILES, W.L.: Tenterden

HAILL, C.R.: Thames, River

HAINES, Charles Reginald: Dover

HAINES, George Warden: Folkestone

HAINES, Herbert: Monumental Inscriptions

HALL, Sir Alfred Daniel: Agriculture

HALL, Anthony - See COX, Thomas: History and
    Archaeology

HARRINGTONS OF TUNBRIDGE WELLS: Tunbridge Wells

HARRIS, C.W.J.: Beckenham, Bromley

HARRIS, Edwin: Brompton, Chatham, Chatham Dockyard,
    Cliffe-at-Hoo, Cobham, Cooling, Customs, Dickens,
    Charles; Genealogical Records, Gillingham, Higham,
    Hoo, Ightham, Leeds, Legends, Medway, River; Medway
    Towns; Monumental Inscriptions, Rainham, Rochester,
    Rochester Cathedral, Tonbridge, Upnor

HARRIS, George: Dover

HARRIS, George Robert Canning. 4th Baron: Cricket,
    Military and Naval History

HARRIS, John: Erith, Gillingham, History and Archaeology

HARRIS, Rendal: Roads

HARRIS, Ronald Walter - See GLOVER, Robert Finlay: Kent
    Authors and Literature

HARRIS, Sarah E.: Rochester

HARRISON. Archdeacon: Canterbury Cathedral, Archbishops

HARRISON, A.C.: Hoo St. Werburgh

HARRISON, Austin: Hawkhurst

HARRISON, Benjamin: Canterbury Cathedral, History and
    Archaeology, Maidstone

HARRISON, Sir Edward R.: Ightham

HARRISON, Eric: Folkestone

HARRISON, Frederic: Hawkhurst

HARRISON, Herbert: Kent Authors and Literature

HARRISON, James Maurice: Natural History

HARRISON, Jeffery Graham: Chetney, Medway, River; Natural
    History, North Kent Marshes, Sevenoaks

HARRISON, Lewis: Kent, Kent Authors and Literature

HARRISON, Michael: Dickens, Charles

HARRISON, Norman: Coal

HARRISON, Rev. Thomas: Margate

HARRISON, W.J.: Coal

HARRISON, William C.: Folkestone

HARROD, J.G. AND CO. Publishers: Kent

HART, Edwin: Pilgrims Way

HART, F.H.: Lee

HART, Henry: Canterbury

HART, W.G. - See Tonbridge School Registers: Tonbridge

HART, W.H.: Gravesend, History and Archaeology; Kent, North
    West

HARTHOORN, P.A.: Canterbury

HARTNELL, H.C.: Tunbridge Wells

HARTSHORN, Albert: Dover

HARVEY, A.E. Martin: Blackheath

HARVEY, C.: Eynsford

HARVEY, John, pseud.: Railways

HARVEY, John H.: Architecture

HARVEY, Sidney W.: Canterbury Cathedral

HARVEY, Thomas: Dover

HARVEY, Wallace: Canterbury, Whitstable

HARVEY, William J.: Genealogical Records

HARVEY AND HEMMIN. Publishers: Dover

HARVEY CHARITY TRUSTEES: Folkestone

HARVIE, K.B.: Road Transport

HARWOOD, Hilda: Milton-next-Gravesend

HARWOOD, J.: Dover, Margate, Ramsgate

HARWOOD, Mary W.: Hastingleigh

HARWOOD'S SCENERY OF THE SOUTHERN COAST: Coastline

HASELOFF, G.: Bekesbourne

HASENSON, A.: Railways

HASLEHURST, E.W.: Kent

HASLEHURST, G.W. - See JERROLD, W.: Dover, Folkestone

HASLEWOOD, Rev. Francis: Benenden, Chislet,
    Genealogical Records, Pluckley, Smallhythe,
    Smarden

HASLUCK, Eugene Lewis: Kent, East

HASSALL, J.M.: Darent, River

HASSALL, W.O.: History and Archaeology

HASSARD-SHORT, F.W.: Bromley

HASSELL, Christopher: Canterbury, Canterbury
    Cathedral

HASSELL, John: History and Archaeology, Kent

HASTED, Edward: Biography, Canterbury, Faversham,
    Gravesend, History and Archaeology, Kent,
    North West; Maidstone

HASTINGS AND THANET BUILDING SOCIETY: Canterbury

HASTINGS BOROUGH COUNCIL: Cinque Ports

HASTINGS, T.: Canterbury

HASTINGS, Warren: Thames, River

HATCHWAY. Lieutenant: Greenwich

HATTON, James: Sandwich

HATTON, Joseph: Margate

HATTON, Ronald G.: East Malling

HATTON, Thomas: Dickens, Charles

HAWKER, Dennis Gascoyne: Folkestone

HAWKES, Sonia Chadwick: Milton Regis

HAWKES, L.: Geology

HAWKSMOOR, N.: Greenwich

HAWLEY, Sir Joseph: Leybourne

HAY, David: Coastal Waters

HAYDON, Walter T.: Dover, Natural History

HAYES, Dagmar: Canterbury Cathedral

HAYES, John: Bromley

HAYES, Rev. J.W.: Kent, North West

HAYES PHILHARMONIC SOCIETY: Hayes and Keston

HAYNES, Alfred Henry: Dover

HAYNES, R.C.: Dover

HAYWARD, Arthur L.: Dickens, Charles

HAZAEL, Patricia H.: Bexley

HAZLITT, William: Kent Authors and Literature

HEAD, Sir John: Boughton Monchelsea

HEADINGTON, DOMINICAN NUNS OF: Dartford

HEADLAM, Clinton: Isle-of-Thanet

HEADLEY BROS. Publishers: Ashford, Canterbury; Rother, River

"HEADLIGHT" - SCHOOL MAGAZINE: Canterbury

HEAL, Sir Ambrose: Margate

HEALES, Alfred: St. Paul's Cray

HEALTH, CENTRAL BOARD OF: Dartford, Whitstable

HEALTH, MINISTRY OF: Bromley, Kent

HEARNDEN, Isaac: Chatham, Rochester

HEARNE, Thomas: Kent Authors and Literature

HEARTH TAX REGISTER: Chatham

HEATH, Arthur George: Bromley

HEATH, Ernest George: Sport

HEATH, Ernest Gerald: Canterbury, Sport

HEATH, Helen Irnesdell: Pepys, Samuel

HEATH, Sidney: Canterbury Cathedral, Charities, Pilgrims
     Way, Rochester Cathedral

HEATH, William: Dover

HEATHER, William: Coastal Waters

HEDLEY, John Cuthbert: Canterbury

HEILBRONER, R.L.: Marlowe, Christopher

HEINZ, H.J. AND CO. LTD.: Strood

HELLICAR, Arthur Gresley: Bromley

HELYER, P.J.: Rolvenden

HENBREY, H.G.: Ightham, West Malling, Wrotham

HENDERSON, Aileen M. - See Public Buildings and Works,
Ministry of: Richborough

HENDERSON, Arthur E.: Canterbury Cathedral

HENDERSON, Philip: Marlowe, Christopher

HENDY, John F.: Ships and Shipping

HENFREY, Henry W.: Canterbury, Coins and Tokens

HENLEYS (ENGINEERING FIRM): Gravesend

HENNELL, Thomas: Agriculture, Ash-cum-Ridley

HENNIKER, A.M.: Military and Naval History

HENRY VIII, KING OF ENGLAND: Eltham

HENSHALL, Samuel - See Domesday Book: History and Archaeology

HENTZNER, Paul: History and Archaeology

HEPWORTH, J.: Rochester

HEPWORTH, Martyn: Tunbridge Wells

HER MAJESTY'S COMMISSIONER FOR INQUIRING INTO THE CONDITION
OF CATHEDRAL CHURCHES...: Canterbury Cathedral, Rochester
     Cathedral

HER MAJESTY'S DOCKYARD MANAGEMENT TRAINING CENTRE:
     Chatham Dockyard

HERBERT, Charles: Canterbury Cathedral, Archbishops

HERD, S.: Minster-in-Thanet

HERMIT OF DUMPTON CAVE...: Dumpton

HERNE BAY PRESS: Herne Bay, Whitstable

HERNE BAY URBAN DISTRICT COUNCIL: Herne Bay

HERRING, T.S.: Dover

HERSSENS, Leon: Deal

HESELTINE, W.: Canterbury Cathedral

HESKETH, C.: Otford

HESKETH, Everard: Dartford

HEWETT, G.W.: Erith, Newington-next-Sittingbourne

HEWETT, Raymond V.: Maidstone

HEWITT, George: West Wickham

HEWITT, Herbert James: Edward, the Black Prince

HEWITT, J.: Ash-next-Sandwich , Sandwich

HEWITT, T.: Military and Naval History

HEXAM, Henry: Gravesend

HEYLYN, P.: Canterbury Cathedral, Archbishops

HEYWOOD, ABEL AND JOHN. Publishers: Broadstairs, Folkestone, Herne
     Bay, Hythe, Kent, Margate, Pegwell Bay, Ramsgate, Sandgate

HIBBERT, Christopher: Dickens, Charles

HICKINGBOTHAM, W.R. - See FLOYDD, W.: Dover

HICKMOTT, Arthur: Sevenoaks

HICKS, Sir Henry: Elections

HICKS, Robert: Ramsgate

HICKSON, Stanley: Kent Authors and Literature

HIGENBOTTAM, Frank: Brabourne, Canterbury, Canterbury Cathedral
See Also - BRADE-BIRKS, S.G.: Kent Authors and Literature

HIGGENS, William Mullinger: Herne Bay

HIGGINS, John: Gravesend, Northfleet

HIGGINS, Walter: Thames, River

HIGGS, Lionel F.: Bexleyheath

HIGGS, Richard: Kent Authors and Literature

HIGGS, William Miller: Biography

HIGH, Philip: Kent Authors and Literature

HILDYARD, J. Publisher: Canterbury Cathedral

HILL, Derek Ingram: Buckland, Canterbury, Canterbury Cathedral,
     West Wickham

HILL, J.M.: Bromley

HILL, R.H. Ernest: Eynsford, Genealogical Records, Goudhurst

HILL, Walter T. - See PAYNE, J. Lewin: Hoath, Reculver

HILLIER, James T.: Ramsgate

HILLS, Peter J.: Broadstairs

HILLS, William: Isle-of-Thanet

HILLS, William H.: Faversham

HILTON, H.F.: Railways

HILTON, John Anthony: Hadlow, Mereworth, Nettlestead,
     Railways, Shipbourne, Ulcombe, Wateringbury, Yalding

HIND, H.: Erith

HINGELEY, John: Evelyn, John

HINSCLIFF, M.W.: Canterbury

HINTON, D.R.: Coastal Defences

HINTS ON ECCLESIASTICAL DISCIPLINE...: Religious Denominations

HINXHILL ESTATE: Maidstone

HIRE CRUISERS (MAIDSTONE) LTD.: Medway, River

HIRST, H.D.: Military and Naval History

HIRST, W.: Kent

HIS MAJESTIE'S DECLARATION TO ALL HIS LOVING SUBJECTS...: History and Archaeology

HISCOCK, Robert Heath: Milton-next-Gravesend, Roads

See Also - FFINCH, Kenneth Maule: Gravesend

HISCOCK, W.G.: Evelyn, John

HISCOX, A.W. - See DUNCAN, Leland Lewis: Lewisham

HISSEY, James John: Kent

HISTORICAL MANUSCRIPTS COMMISSION: Canterbury, Knole, Penshurst

See Also - HULL, Felix: Cinque Ports

HISTORY OF BETTY BOLAINE...: Canterbury

HISTORY OF THE KENTISH PETITION, 1701: History and Archaeology, Kent

HISTORY OF THE MUTINY AT SPITHEAD AND THE NORE...: Military and Naval History

HISTORY OF PARLIAMENT - POLL BOOKS...: Elections

HISTORY OF THE ROYAL AIR FORCE (GRAVESEND): Gravesend, World War II

HITCHIN-KEMP, Fred: Wye

HOARE, Edward: Brenchley, Ramsgate, Tunbridge Wells

HOARE, Geoffrey - See TAYLOR, L.C.: Kent Authors and Literature

HOBBES, Robert George: Chatham Dockyard, Sheerness

HOBCRAFT, John Edward: Gravesend

HOBDAY, R.H.: Sutton-by-Dover

HOBHOUSE, Christopher: Crystal Palace

HOBSBAWM, Eric John: History and Archaeology

HOBSON, John Morrison: Canterbury, Canterbury Cathedral, Archbishops

HODGE, Sydney: Tonbridge

HODGKIN, L.V.: Dover

HODGSON, Sir Gerald: Bromley

HODGSON, J.: Ryarsh

HODGSON, Norma: Theatre

HODGSON, R.D.: Littlestone

HODGSON, Sidney: Penge

HOFFMAN, Calvin: Marlowe, Christopher

HOGARTH, William: Isle-of-Sheppey

HOGG, A.H.A.: Bexley, Hayes and Keston, Swanscombe, Tonge, West Wickham

HOGG, Oliver Frederick Gillilan: Woolwich

HOGG, P. Fitzgerald: Chatham, Gillingham, Industry and Trade, Medway Towns, Rochester

HOGG, Warrington: Architecture

HOLBEIN'S VISITOR'S LIST AND COURT DIRECTORY: Folkestone

HOLBERT, W. Publisher: Gravesend

"HOLCOMBEIAN" - MAGAZINE OF CHATHAM TECHNICAL SCHOOL FOR BOYS: Chatham

HOLDEN. Publisher: Kent

HOLDSWORTH, Mrs. John - See HODGKIN, L.V.: Dover

HOLE, Christina: Canterbury Cathedral

HOLE, Samuel Reynolds: Rochester Cathedral

HOLLAND, Clive: Coastline

HOLLAND, Edward Lancelot: Canterbury

HOLLAND, J.D.: Tunbridge Wells

HOLLAND, J.G.: Sevenoaks

HOLLAND, Mary Sibylla: Canterbury

HOLLIDAY, A.C.: Dickens, Charles

HOLLINGBOURNE RURAL DISTRICT COUNCIL: Kent, Mid

HOLLIS, Gertrude: Dover

HOLLOWAY, John: Bromley

HOLLOWAY, Mark: Folkestone

HOLLOWAY, William: Cinque Ports, Romney Marsh

HOLLYBAND, Claudius: Lewisham

HOLLYMAN, Jean: Pilgrims Way

HOLLYMAN, Tom - See HOLLYMAN, Jean: Pilgrims Way

HOLMAN-CROFT: Rowena: Hythe

HOLME, C.: Architecture

HOLMES, Eric: Kent, North West

HOLMES, Richard C. - See GILLHAM, Eric Howard: Natural History

HOLMES, Thomas Vincent - See Geologists' Association: Kent, North West

HOLMES, T.R.: History and Archaeology

HOLMES, W. - See HAGGAR, R.J.: Agriculture

HOLT, Anita: Faversham

HOLWORTHY, Richard: Bromley, Genealogical Records, New Romney

HOLWORTHY, Rochard - See SHILTON, Dorothy O.: Maidstone

HOLYOAK, Walter: Dover

HOMAN-CROFT, Rowena: Hythe

HOME, C.M.: History and Archaeology

HOME, Gordon: Canterbury

"HOMECRAFTS" NATIONAL HANDWEAVING EXHIBITION: Canterbury

HOME OFFICE: Local Government

HOME PUBLISHING CO. Publishers: Kent

HOME WORDS FOR HEART AND HEARTH: Chatham

HOMERSHAM, Samuel Collett: Ashford

HOMEWOOD SCHOOL PAGEANT: Tenterden

HOMPESCH. Baron: Maidstone

HONE, Joseph: Northbourne

HONYWOOD, Lady Frances: Faversham, Maidstone

HOOK, Judith A.: Pratts Bottom

HOOK, Walter Farquhar: Canterbury Cathedral, Archbishops

"HOOKER HERALD": Canterbury

HOOKER SCHOOL: Canterbury

HOOPER, Evangeline L.: Wye

HOOPER, Wilfred: Pilgrims Way

HOP PLANTER'S ASSISTANT: Agriculture

HOP TRADE: Agriculture

HOPE, Lady Elizabeth Reid: Kent, Tunbridge Wells

HOPE, Sir William Henry St. John: Canterbury,
    Canterbury Cathedral, Edward, the Black Prince;
    Kent, Local Government, Rochester, Rochester
    Cathedral

See Also - LEGG, J. Wickham: Canterbury Cathedral

HOPKINS, Albert A.: Dickens, Charles

HOPKINS, R. Thurston: Allington, Architecture,
    Eltham, Hever, Ightham, Lamberhurst, Leeds,
    Tunbridge Wells, Windmills and Watermills

HOPS MARKETING SCHEME: Agriculture

HORN, J. Publisher: Deal, Dover

HORN, John Vivian: Dover

HORNE, Dr. George: Canterbury Cathedral

HORNIBROOK, S.: Maidstone

HORNSEY PUBLIC LIBRARY: Conrad, Joseph

HORSBOROUGH, E.L.S.: Bromley

HORSLEY, John William: Place Names

HORSLEY, M.: Dover

HORSLEY, Victor: Coastal Defences

HOSEASON, John Cochrane: Dover

HOTSON, J. Leslie: Marlowe, Christopher

HOTTEN, John Camden: Dickens, Charles

HOUGH, James: Ham

HOUGHTON, Charles: Crayford

HOUGHTON, G.E.: Margate

HOUSE, Humphrey: Dickens, Charles

HOUSE OF COMMONS: Railways, Rochester

HOUSE OF LORDS: History and Archaeology, Public
    Utilities

HOUSEHOLD WORDS: Dickens, Charles

HOUSING AND LOCAL GOVERNMENT, MINISTRY OF: Beckenham,
    Bromley, Chatham, Dartford, Deal, Isle-of-Thanet,
    Kent, Kent, Mid; Kent, North West; Kent, West;
    Maidstone, Medway, River; Medway Towns,
    Orpington, Public Utilities, Ridley, Rivers,
    Sevenoaks, Stour, River; Thames, River;
    Tonbridge

HOVENDEN, Robert: Genealogical Records

See Also - HOWARD, Joseph Jackson: Genealogical
    Records

HOW AND SONS. Undertakers: Sevenoaks

HOW, Harry: Canterbury

HOWARD, Joseph Jackson: Genealogical Records

HOWARD, Keble, pseud. (J. Keble BELL): Military and
    Naval History

HOWARD, Luke: Dover

HOWARD, William Cecil James. Lord Clonmore: Kent

HOWARD, WILLIAM AND SON LTD.: Chatham

HOWARD-FLANDERS, W.: History and Archaeology

HOWARTH, Eleanor K. - See HOWARTH, O.J.R.: Downe

HOWARTH, O.J.R.: Downe

HOWARTH, R.: Folkestone

HOWARTH, William: Greenwich

HOWE, F.: Margate

HOWE, P.P.: Maidstone

HOWELL, George D. - See NEMAN, George: History and Archaeology

HOWELL, George O.: Cobham, Gravesend, History and Archaeology,
    Kent, North West

HOWELLS, H.: Kent Songs

HOWLETT, Rev. John: Maidstone

HOWORTH, Sir Henry H.: Canterbury

HOWSON, H.A. - See ABBE, Truman: Biography

HOYS, Frank Dudley (L.D.V., pseud.): Bromley

HUBBARD, Gilbert Ernest: Wye

HUDD, A.G.: Erith

HUDDLESTONE, John: Cinque Ports, Isle-of-Thanet, Ramsgate

HUDSON, Alfred W.: Cranbrook

HUDSON, Elizabeth Harriot: History and Archaeology

HUDSON, John V.P.: Kent Authors and Literature

HUDSON, R.H.: Weald

HUDSON, Ronald Loftus: Dartford

HUEFFER, Ford Madox - See FORD, Ford Madox: Cinque
    Ports

HUGGENS COLLEGE: Northfleet

"HUGHENDEN" SALE CATALOGUE: Dover

HUGHES, George Martin: Roads

HUGHES, James Pennethorne: Kent

HUGHES, M.: Bromley

HUGHES, Thomas McKenny: Geology

HUGHES, W.E.: Blackheath, Genealogical Records

HUGHES, William: Kent

HUGHES, W.R.: Kent

HUGHES-HUGHES, Walter Oldham - See Tonbridge School Registers:
    Tonbridge

HUGHSON, D., pseud.: Aldington; Kent, North West

HUGO, Thomas: Rochester Cathedral

HULL, Dr. Felix - See Kent County Council, Archives Office:
    Cinque Ports, History and Archaeology

A HUMBLE PETITION...AUGUST 30th, 1642: History and Archaeology

HUMBUG - A SATIRE BY THE AUTHOR: Kent Authors and Literature

HUME, I. Noel: Upchurch

HUMPAGE, E. Caroline: Cobham

HUMPHERY-SMITH, Cecil Raymond: Canterbury Cathedral, Kent
    Authors and Literature

HUMPHRY, G.W. - See COCK, F. William: Appledore

HUNDLEY, V.A.: Dover

HUNT, Rev. Dr.: Otford

HUNT, A.R.: Agriculture

HUNT, Cecil: Customs

HUNT, Leslie: Military and Naval History

HUNT, Percival: Pepys, Samuel

H Cont'd

HUNT, R.W.: Greenwich, History and Archaeology

HUNT, T.J.: Dartford

HUNT, W.: Sevenoaks

HUNT, Wray: Cinque Ports

HUNTER ("RUSTICUS", pseud.): Canterbury

HUNTER, D.M.: Edenbridge

HUNTER, Robert Edward: Isle-of-Thanet

HURD, Sir Archibald S.: Dover

HURD, Howard: Broadstairs

HUSSEY, Arthur: Canterbury, Charities, Churches,
    Folkestone, Foord, Genealogical Records,
    History and Archaeology, Hoath, Lydd, Wingham

HUSSEY, Christopher: Architecture, Blackheath,
    Chilham, Lamberhurst, West Farleigh

HUSSEY, Edward: Lamberhurst

HUSSEY, Maurice: Chaucer, Geoffrey

HUSSEY, Richard C.: Barfreston, Harbledown,
    Kent, South

HUSSEY, Rev. William: Chislehurst, Hawkhurst

HUTCHINGS, G.E.: Medway, River; Rochester

HUTCHINGS, Geoffrey E. - See PUGH, Christine:
    Stockbury - WOOLDRIDGE, Sidney William:
    Kent

HUTCHINGS, Richard J.: Dickens, Charles

HUTCHINSON, Horace Gordon: Farnborough

HUTCHINSON, John: History and Archaeology

HUTT, Charles H.: Sandwich

HUTTON, Edward: Kent

HUTTON, William Holden: Canterbury Cathedral,
    Archbishops

HUXLEY, Sir Julian: Darwin, Charles

HUXLEY, T. Scott: Canterbury

HYAMS, Edward Solomon: Kent Authors and Literature

HYAMSON, Albert M.: Southborough

HYANES, Alfred Henry: Dover

HYDE, S. Publisher: Canterbury

HYDER, William Augustus. Defendant: Whitstable

HYTHE BOROUGH COUNCIL: Hythe

HYTHE SCHOOL OF MUSKETRY: Hythe, Military and
    Naval History

HYTHE VENETIAN FETE CHARITY SOCIETY: Hythe

I

I ZINGARI...: Cricket

I'ANSON, Bryan: Eastwell

IGGLESDEN, Sir Charles: Ashford, Cricket, Goudhurst,
    Kent, Kent Authors and Literature, Legends,
    Military and Naval History, World War I,
    World War II

"AN IGNORANT STUDENT", pseud.: Place Names

IKIN, C.W.: Military and Naval History

ILLINGWORTH, Frank: World War II

THE ILLUSTRATED EXHIBITOR...: Crystal Palace

ILLUSTRATED GUIDE TO LONDON AND DOVER RAILWAYS: Railways

ILLUSTRATED LONDON NEWS: Westerham

ILLUSTRATED VIEWS OF THE METROPOLITAN CATHEDRAL CHURCH OF
CANTERBURY: Canterbury Cathedral

ILOT, Charles Henry: Canterbury

IMPERIAL WAR GRAVES COMMISSION: Bromley, Chatham

INDENTURE BETWEEN EDWIN WYATT, ETC.: Boxley

INDENTURE BETWEEN SAMUEL COTTON, ETC.: Maidstone

INDEPENDENT CHAPEL, DARTFORD: Genealogical Records

INDEPENDENT ORDER OF ANCIENT DRUIDS: Canterbury

INDEPENDENT SCHOOLS OF KENT: Education

INDERWICK, F.A.: Agriculture

"THE INDEX": Maidstone

INDEXES TO THE GREAT WHITE BOOK...: Cinque Ports

INDICTMENT, ARRAIGNMENT...OF 29 REGICIDES: Maidstone, History and
    Archaeology

INDUSTRIAL DISPUTES TRIBUNAL: Chatham

INDUSTRIAL REVIEW AND GUIDE TO THE MEDWAY: Industry and Trade,
    Medway Towns

INDUSTRY ILLUSTRATED...: Eltham

INDUSTRY, TRADE AND REGIONAL DEVELOPMENT, DEPARTMENT OF:
    Industry and Trade

INGLE, Joy: Ditton

INGLIS, K.S.: Canterbury

INGOLDSBY, Thomas, pseud. (R.H.D. BARHAM): Isle-of-Thanet,
    Kent Authors and Literature, Kent, East; Margate
See Also - BARHAM, Richard Harris Dalton: Canterbury

INGRAM, John H.: Marlowe, Christopher

INGRAM, T.A.: Kent, North West; Woolwich
See Also - GRINLING, C.H.: Tunbridge Wells

INGRAMS, William Harold: Ash-next-Sandwich

"AN INHABITANT", pseud.: Canterbury, Cinque Ports, Margate,
    Ramsgate

THE INJURED LADY: Kent Authors and Literature

INLAND WATERWAYS ASSOCIATION - LONDON AND SOUTH-EASTERN BRANCH:
    Medway, River; Tonbridge

IN MEMORIAM, THE REV. A.J. WOODHOUSE: Ide Hill

IN MEMORIAM, WALTER CHARLES, LORD NORTHBOURNE: Betteshanger

INSTALLATION OF THE LORD WARDEN OF THE CINQUE PORTS: Cinque
    Ports

INSTITUTE OF CIVIL ENGINEERS: Medway, River

INSTITUTE OF GEOLOGICAL SCIENCES: Channel Tunnel, Geology

INSTITUTE OF HANDICRAFT TEACHERS...: Education

INSTITUTE OF MUNICIPAL ENGINEERS: Bromley, Roads

INSTITUTION OF ROYAL ENGINEERS: Brompton, Military and Naval
    History, Rochester

INTERNATIONAL COMPUTERS AND TABULATORS: Bromley, Education

INTRODUCING INVICTA FILMS: Newspapers

INVENTORY AND VALUATION OF FURNITURE OF THE MARCHIONESS OF
WILLINGDON: Walmer

JOWITT, R.L.P.: Tunbridge Wells

JOYCE, Alfred - See GROVE, L.R.A.: Maidstone

JOYCE, J.: Maidstone

JOYCE, L.: Maidstone

JUDD, Walter D.: Sevenoaks

JURA POPULI ANGLICANI: History and Archaeology

K

KADWELL, Charles: Hayes and Keston, Kent

KAEHLER, Richard D.: Canterbury

KAESTLIN, J.P.: Woolwich

KAMM, Josephine: Crystal Palace

KATSCHER, Ludwig: Channel Tunnel

KAY, Alan M. - See SHEA, Francis M.: Margate

KAYE-SMITH, Sheila: Romney Marsh, Weald

KEABLE, Geoffrey: Lower Halstow

KEABLE, Mrs. Gladys: Kent Authors and Literature

KEAN, J.S.: Gravesend

KEARSEY, E. Maslin: Kent

KEARTON, Richard: Maidstone

KEATE, George: Kent, Margate

KEBLE, T.H. Publisher: Isle-of-Thanet, Margate

KEDDELL, J.S.: Kent Authors and Literature

KEECH, Gertrude Clara: Genealogical Records, Southborough, Staplehurst, Weald

KEELE, Kenneth D.: Folkestone

KEESEY, Walter M.: Canterbury

KEITH, Sir Arthur: Dartford, History and Archaeology

KELLY, Rear Admiral Edward: Chatham Dockyard

KELLY, Robin A. - See GRANVILLE, Wilfred: Ships and Shipping

KEMP, E.W.: Canterbury Cathedral, Archbishops

KEMP, Ethelbert Thomas: Canterbury, Industry and Trade

KEMP, John: Biddenden

KEMPE, A.B.C.: Ramsgate

KEMPE, Alfred John: Hayes and Keston, History and Archaeology

KENDALL, A.F.: Kent

KENDALL, Henry George Ommanney: History and Archaeology

KENDALL, S.C.: Kent

KENDALL'S GUIDE TO DOVER CASTLE: Dover

KENDON, Frank: Horsmonden

KENDON, Joseph J.: Goudhurst

KENDON, Margery: Goudhurst

KENNEDY, Bart: Hadlow

KENNETT, Brian - See CAVELL, John: Sandwich

KENNETT FAMILY: Genealogical Records

KENNETT, Robert H.: Isle-of-Thanet

KENNETT, W.R.: Mottingham

KENNETT, White - See SOMNER, William: Coastal Defences, History and Archaeology

KENNY, Tom: Kent, East; Sport

KENT, Alfred: Dover, Kent Authors and Literature

KENT, Douglas H.: Canterbury, Kent, North West

KENT, W. Publisher: Isle-of-Thanet

KENT, W. Herman: Tunbridge Wells

KENT ALLOTMENTS AND GARDENS COUNCIL: Agriculture

KENT AND CANTERBURY HOSPITAL: Canterbury

KENT AND CANTERBURY ILLUSTRATED FAMILY ALMANACK: Canterbury, Kent

KENT AND CANTERBURY INSTITUTE FOR TRAINED NURSES: Organisations

KENT AND CANTERBURY PERMANENT BENEFIT BUILDING SOCIETY: Organisations

KENT AND ESSEX SEA FISHERIES COMMITTEE: Industry and Trade, Thames, River

KENT AND ROMNEY MARSH SHEEP BREEDERS' ASSOCIATION: Agriculture

KENT AND SURREY COMMITTEE OF THE COMMONS AND FOOTPATHS PRESERVATION SOCIETY - See Commons and Footpaths Preservation Society, Kent and Surrey Committee: Footpaths and Commons

KENT AND SURREY NATURALISTS' FIELD CLUB: Natural History

KENT AND SUSSEX HOSPITAL: Tunbridge Wells

KENT AND SUSSEX POETRY COMPILER: Kent Authors and Literature

KENT AND SUSSEX TEMPERANCE ADVOCATE: Organisations

KENT ARCHAEOLOGICAL SOCIETY: Canterbury, Canterbury Cathedral, Cinque Ports, Genealogical Records, History and Archaeology, Kent, East; Lydd, Monumental Inscriptions, New Romney, Organisations, Strood, Tenterden

KENT ARCHAEOLOGICAL RESEARCH GROUP'S COUNCIL: History and Archaeology

KENT ARGUS: Kent

KENT ASSOCIATION FOR THE BLIND: Organisations

KENT ASSOCIATION OF BOYS' CLUBS: Organisations

KENT ASSOCIATION OF TEACHERS OR RURAL SCIENCE: Education

KENT ASSOCIATION OF YOUTH CLUBS: Organisations

KENT BEE-KEEPERS' ASSOCIATION: Agriculture

KENT BOROUGH AND URBAN DISTRICT COUNCILS' ASSOCIATION: Local Government

KENT CLUB, MAIDSTONE: Maidstone

KENT COAL CONCESSIONS...: Coal

KENT COAST COLLEGE: Herne Bay

KENT COAST RAILWAY CO.: Railways

KENT COLLEGE: Canterbury

KENT COUNCIL OF SOCIAL SERVICE: Customs, History and Archaeology, Kent, Organisations

KENT COUNTY AGRICULTURAL SOCIETY: Agriculture

KENT COUNTY ALLOTMENTS AND GARDENS COUNCIL: Agriculture

KENT COUNTY AMATEUR SWIMMING ASSOCIATION: Sport

KENT COUNTY ASSOCIATION OF CHANGE RINGERS: Churches

KENT COUNTY ASSOCIATION OF TEACHERS: Education

KENT COUNTY CANCER APPEAL FUND: Organisations

KENT COUNTY CONSTABULARY: Crime, Maidstone, Police, Roads

KENT COUNTY COUNCIL: Ashford, Channel Tunnel, Cliffe, Elections, History and Archaeology, Isle-of-Sheppey, Isle-of-Thanet, Local Government, Maidstone, Medway River; Ravensbourne River, Trials, Windmills and Watermills

KENT COUNTY COUNCIL AND KENT INSURANCE COMMITTEE: Health and Welfare

KENT COUNTY COUNCIL - ANALYST'S DEPARTMENT: Local Government

KENT COUNTY COUNCIL - ARCHITECT'S DEPARTMENT: Architecture

KENT COUNTY COUNCIL - ARCHIVES OFFICE: Agriculture, Bickley, Bromley, Chelsfield, Crime, Dartford, Downe, Education, Folkestone, Hayes and Keston, Heraldry, History and Archaeology, Knockholt, Orpington, Penge, Roads, Rochester, Rochester Cathedral, St. Mary Cray, St. Paul's Cray, Transport, Tunbridge Wells

KENT COUNTY COUNCIL - CHILDRENS' COMMITTEE: Local Government

KENT COUNTY COUNCIL - KENT EDUCATION COMMITTEE: Agriculture, Bromley, Education, Folkestone, Gillingham, Godmersham, Health and Welfare, History and Archaeology, Hothfield, Isle-of-Thanet, Maidstone, Medway Towns, Organisations, Religious Denominations, Westerham

KENT COUNTY COUNCIL - HEALTH DEPARTMENT: Health and Welfare, Local Government

KENT COUNTY COUNCIL - MALLING DIVISION EMERGENCY COMMITTEE: West Malling

KENT COUNTY COUNCIL - PLANNING DEPARTMENT: Architecture, Ashford, Aylesford, Biddenden, Biggin Hill, Brenchley, Canterbury, Channel Tunnel, Cliffe-at-Hoo, Cobham, Deal, Dover, Edenbridge, Farningham, Faversham, Goudhurst, Gravesend, Gypsies, Herne Bay, Industry and Trade, Isle-of-Sheppey, Kent, Kent, Mid; Kent, North West; Leybourne, Local Government, Maidstone, Medway, River; Medway Towns, Penshurst, Roads, St. Margaret's Bay, Snodland, Tenterden, Tonbridge, Waldershare, Whitstable, Windmills and Watermills, Wingham, Yalding

KENT COUNTY COUNCIL - PROBATION COMMITTEE: Local Government

KENT COUNTY COUNCIL - PUBLIC ASSISTANCE DEPARTMENT: Local Government

KENT COUNTY COUNCIL - ROADS DEPARTMENT: Coastline, Local Government, Rivers, Roads, Westerham

KENT COUNTY COUNCIL - SELECTION AND SPECIAL PURPOSES COMMITTEE: Local Government

KENT COUNTY COUNCIL - SURVEYOR'S DEPARTMENT: Local Government, Rivers, Roads

KENT COUNTY COUNCIL - TECHNICAL EDUCATION COMMITTEE COMMITTEE: Agriculture, Education

KENT COUNTY COUNCIL - TREASURER'S DEPARTMENT: Local Government

KENT COUNTY COUNCIL - WEIGHTS AND MEASURES DEPARTMENT: Local Government

KENT COUNTY CREMATORIUM LTD.: Barham, Charing

KENT COUNTY CRICKET CLUB: Cricket

KENT COUNTY FOOTBALL ASSOCIATION: Sport

KENT COUNTY LAWN TENNIS ASSOCIATION: Sport

KENT COUNTY LIBRARY: Cinque Ports, Herne, Herne Bay, Isle-of-Sheppey, Kent, Kent Authors and Literature, Libraries, Reculver

KENT COUNTY LUNATIC ASYLUMS: Hospitals

KENT COUNTY MUSIC COMMITTEE: Music

KENT COUNTY OPHTHALMIC HOSPITAL: Maidstone

KENT COUNTY PHOTOGRAPHIC ASSOCIATION: Canterbury

KENT COUNTY PLAYING FIELDS ASSOCIATION: Sport

KENT COUNTY RIFLE ASSOCIATION: Sport

KENT COUNTY SCOUT HANDBOOK: Organisations

KENT COUNTY SOCIETY OF INCORPORATED SECRETARIES: Industry and Trade

KENT COUNTY TEMPERANCE FEDERATION: Organisations

KENT COUNTY TOWNSWOMEN'S GUILDS: Organisations

KENT COUNTY WAR SAVINGS COMMITTEE: Organisations

"KENT CUTTER", pseud.: Coal

KENT FEDERATION OF HEAD TEACHERS' ASSOCIATIONS: Education

KENT FENCIBLE: Military and Naval History

KENT FIELD CLUB: Natural History

KENT FIRE BRIGADE: Local Government

KENT FIRE INSURANCE INSTITUTION: Organisations

KENT - HISTORICAL, BIOGRAPHICAL AND PICTORIAL: Biography

KENT INCORPORATED SOCIETY FOR PROMOTING EXPERIMENTS IN HORTICULTURE - See East Malling Research Station: Agriculture

KENT INSURANCE COMMITTEE: Organisations

KENT INSURANCE CO.: Industry and Trade

KENT LAW SOCIETY: Gavelkind

KENT LIBRARIES' STATISTICS: Local Government

KENT LIFE: Kent Songs

KENT MAGAZINE (VOL. 1 ONLY): Kent

KENT MAGAZINE AND COUNTY REGISTER: Kent

KENT MESSENGER: Ashford, Biography, Canterbury, Customs, Dartford Tunnel, History and Archaeology, Industry and Trade, Kent, Maidstone, Military and Naval History, Newspapers, Railways, Road Transport, Ships and Shipping

KENT MILK RECORDING SOCIETY: Agriculture

KENT MONTHLY MESSENGER: History and Archaeology

KENT MUSIC SCHOOL: Education

KENT NATIONAL RESERVE: Military and Naval History

KENT NATURALISTS' TRUST: Natural History
See Also - Kent Trust for Nature Conservation: Natural History

KENT NUMISMATIC SOCIETY: Coins and Tokens

KENT OR ROMNEY MARSH SHEEP BREEDERS' ASSOCIATION (1951-1967): Agriculture, Romney Marsh

KENT ORNITHOLOGICAL SOCIETY: Natural History, Organisations

KENT PAEDRIATIC SOCIETY: Bexley, Health and Welfare

KENT PRE-SCHOOL PLAYGROUPS ASSOCIATION: Education

KENT PUBLISHING CO. Publishers: Beckenham, Bromley, Orpington

KENT RIVER AUTHORITY (FORMERLY KENT RIVER BOARD): Medway, River; Rivers, Sport

KENT RIVER BOARD - See Kent River Authority: Medway, River; Rivers, Sport

KENT RURAL COMMUNITY COUNCIL: Organisations

KENT SERVICE LTD. Publishers: Deal

KENT SOCIETY FOR THE ENCOURAGEMENT OF AGRICULTURE AND INDUSTRY: Canterbury

KENT STANDING CONFERENCE OF NATIONAL VOLUNTARY
YOUTH ORGANISATIONS: Organisations

KENT TABLE TENNIS MAGAZINE: Sport

KENT TERRITORIAL AND AUXILIARY FORCES ASSOCIATION:
Military and Naval History

KENT TRACTS: History and Archaeology

KENT TRUST FOR NATURE CONSERVATION: Natural History

KENT VISITATIONS: Genealogical Records

KENT VOLUNTARY AID DETACHMENTS: World War I

KENT VOLUNTARY AID GAZETTE: World War I

KENT, W. AND CO. Publishers: Herne Bay, Margate

KENT WOMEN'S HOCKEY ASSOCIATION: Sport

"KENT YEOMAN", pseud.: Kent Artists

KENT ZONE HOME GUARD: Military and Naval History

KENTISH ANGLER...: Sport

KENTISH CHRONOLOGIST: History and Archaeology

KENTISH COMPANION: History and Archaeology

KENTISH CONSPIRACY, 1645: Dover

KENTISH DISTRICT TIMES: Sport

KENTISH ESTATES JOURNAL: History and Archaeology

KENTISH EXPRESS: Ashford, Heraldry, Romney Marsh,
Tenterden

KENTISH EXPRESS AND ASHFORD NEWS: Newspapers

KENTISH FABLE OF THE LION AND THE FOXES...: History
and Archaeology

KENTISH FAMILY NAMES: Place Names and Surnames

KENTISH FRAGMENTS: Maidstone

KENTISH GAZETTE: Canterbury, Canterbury Cathedral,
Canterbury Cathedral, Archbishops; Newspapers

"KENTISH GENTLEMAN", pseud.: History and
Archaeology

KENTISH HISTORICAL NEWSLETTER: History and
Archaeology

KENTISH HOMESPUNS: Industry and Trade

KENTISH INDUSTRIES, NO. 12: Pluckley

KENTISH MEN - A SATIRE: Maidstone

KENTISH MISCELLANY: History and Archaeology

KENTISH OBSERVER: Canterbury

KENTISH ODDS AND ENDS: History and Archaeology

KENTISH PETITION, 1643: History and Archaeology

KENTISH PIE: Kent

KENTISH POLHILLS (FAMILY): Sevenoaks

KENTISH POST: History and Archaeology

KENTISH PRESIDENT'S ASSOCIATION GAZETTE:
Organisations

KENTISH REGISTER AND MONTHLY MISCELLANY: History
and Archaeology

KENTISH SOCIETY: Kent, Organisations

"KENTISH SONGSTER", pseud.: Kent Songs

KENTISH SPY: History and Archaeology

KENT'S NEW COLLEGE OF TECHNOLOGY: Dartford

KENWARD, A.S.: Geology

KENWARD, James: Architecture

KENYON, G.H.: Industry and Trade, Weald

KERENSKY, Oleg A.: Medway, River

KERNEY, J.N. - See CARRECK, J.N.: Downe, Hayes and Keston

KERNEY, M.P.: Brook, Wateringbury
See Also - CARRECK, J.N.: Darwin, Charles

KERSHAW AND SON AND J.S. AND CO. Publishers - See J.S. and
Co. and Kershaw and Son: Ramsgate

KERSHAW, Alister: Dover

KERSHAW, J.C. - See HARPER, Charles George: Kent

KERSHAW, S. Wayland: Architecture, Canterbury, Canterbury
Cathedral, Canterbury Cathedral, Archbishops; Coins and
Tokens, History and Archaeology, Isle-of-Thanet, Kent,
East; Maidstone, Rochester

KESTON CORONATION COMMITTEE: Hayes and Keston

KESTON FIELD CLUB: Hayes and Keston

KETTLE, L.D.: Canterbury

KETTLEWELL, H.B.D. - See HUXLEY, Sir Julian: Darwin, Charles

KEY NOTE: Newspapers

KEYES, Sir Roger: Dover, Military and Naval History

KEYES, Sidney Kilworth: Dartford

KEYNES, Geoffrey: Evelyn, John; Folkestone

KEYS, Robert P.: Dover

KIDD, E.R.: Eynsford

KIDD, William. Publisher: Gravesend, Herne Bay, Isle-of-Thanet,
Kent
See Also - BONNER, G.W.: Tunbridge Wells

KIDDELL, A.J.B.: Wrotham

KIDNER, Roger Wakely: Railways, Road Transport

KILBURNE, Richard: History and Archaeology, Kent

KILEY, A.V.: Dartford

KILLICK, Charles: Maidstone

KILLICK, J.R. - See COOK, W.H.: Rochester

KIMBALL, Katharine: Rochester

KIMBELL, John: Greenwich

KIMBERLEY-CLARK LTD.: Aylesford

KING, Miss A. (Pseuds. - "A Martyr", "A Woman"): Kent Authors
and Literature

KING, David: Eltham

KING, Edward: Architecture, Goodwin Sands

KING, Gordon - See CROME, Honor: Kent Authors and Literature

KING, Harriet Eleanor Hamilton: Kent Songs, Romney Marsh

KING, Richard John: Canterbury Cathedral, Rochester Cathedral

KING, Richard S.: Herne Bay

KING, Stella: Biography

THE KING AGAINST THE INHABITANTS OF KENT: Footscray

KING GEORGE V SILVER JUBILEE CELEBRATIONS: Canterbury

KING JOHN AND THE ABBOT OF CANTERBURY (POEM): Canterbury

KING'S SCHOOL, CANTERBURY: Canterbury

KINGSFORD, Felix: Canterbury

KINGSFORD, Thomas: Canterbury, Kent Authors and Literature

KIRBY, Harry S.: Industry and Trade, Kent, North West

KIRBY, Herbert Charles: Genealogical Records, Lewisham, Monumental Inscriptions

KIRBY, John William: Blackheath, Dartford, Greenwich, Lewisham

KIRKALDY, J.F.: Weald
See Also - REEVES, J.W.: Weald

KIRKHAM, Nellie: Pilgrims Way
See Also - LAKE, W.E.: Pilgrims Way

KITCHIN, F.L. - See LAMPLUGH, G.W.: Geology, Geological Survey and Museum

KITTON, Frederick G.: Biography, Dickens, Charles; Kent

KLAPPER, Charles: Railways, Road Transport

KLASEN, Jurgen: Romney Marsh

KNAGGS, H. Guard: Folkestone

KNATCHBULL, Sir Norton: Kent Authors and Literature

KNATCHBULL-HUGESSEN, E.H. Lord Brabourne: Kent Authors and Literature

KNATCHBULL-HUGESSEN, Sir Hughe: Biography

KNELL, Henry: Woolwich

KNIGHT, A. Charles: Deptford

KNIGHT, C.: History and Archaeology

KNIGHT, C.T.: Sevenoaks

KNIGHT, Charles: Canterbury, Dover, Gillingham, Isle-of-Thanet, Kent

KNIGHT, Charles. Publisher: Kent

KNIGHT, Charles J.: Agriculture

KNIGHT, Charles Henry Bruere - See Historical Records of the Buffs: Military and Naval History

KNIGHT, Henry Raleigh: History and Archaeology, Military and Naval History
See Also - Historical Records of the Buffs: Military and Naval History

KNIGHT, H.T. - See DUFFIELD, F.H.: Rochester Cathedral, Shortlands

KNIGHT, J.J.: Margate

KNIGHT, J.Y.: Agriculture

KNIGHT, R.J.B.: Medway, River

KNIGHT, Richard Lake: Military and Naval History

KNIGHT, Roy: Dartford

KNIGHTON, G.L.: Religious Denominations

KNIGHT'S PICTORIAL GALLERY OF ARTS...: Crystal Palace

KNIPE, Henry R.: Tunbridge Wells

KNOCKER, Edward: Cinque Ports, Dover, Kent, Kent Authors and Literature

KNOCKER, Sir E. Wollaston: Cinque Ports, Dover

KNOCKER, Frederic: Dover

KNOCKER, Herbert Wheatley: History and Archaeology, Sundridge, Tonbridge

KNOLLYS, E.E.: Folkestone

KNOOP, D.: Cobham

KNOTT, Alan: Cricket

KNOTT, C.H. - See Tonbridge School Registers: Tonbridge

KNOWLES, Dom David: Canterbury Cathedral, Archbishops

KNOWLES, James: Channel Tunnel

KNOX, Cecil W.: Roads, St. Margaret's Bay

KNOX, Thomas: Tonbridge

KNOX, Vicesimus: Education

KOGAN, Herman: Queenborough

KRAUS, Rene: Churchill, Winston S.

KROPOTKIN, Prince Peter: Bromley

L

L., S.C. (LAMPREYS, S.C.): Maidstone

L., W.J.: Maidstone

LABARGE, Margaret Wade: Dover

LABOUR, MINISTRY OF: Kent, East; Maidstone

LACAILLE, A.D.: Dartford

LACEY, A.G.: Gravesend

LA CHARD, Theresa: Bromley

LACY, Joseph Melville: Coastline

LADD, G.P. Publisher: Canterbury

LADDS, John: Margate

"A LADY", pseud.: Herne Bay, Kent Authors and Literature

LAIRD, A. Bonnet: Agriculture

LAITHWAITE, Michael: Faversham

LAKE, Phyllis: Kent Songs

LAKE, W.E.: Pilgrims Way

LAKER, John: Deal

LAMB, Charles: Ships and Shipping

LAMB, Henry: Maidstone

LAMB, John William: Canterbury Cathedral, Archbishops

LAMBARDE FAMILY: Genealogical Records

LAMBARDE, Fane F.: Ash-by-Wrotham, Faversham, Genealogical Records, Reculver, Wickhambreux

LAMBARDE, William: History and Archaeology, Kent Authors and Literature, Sevenoaks
See Also - Bibliotheca Topographica Britannica: Sevenoaks

LAMBERT, Audrey: Dover

LAMBERT, Brooke: Greenwich

LAMBERT, George: History and Archaeology, Margate, New Romney, Swingfield, Tenterden

LAMBERT, H.J.: Military and Naval History

LAMBERT, Jeffrey Maurice: Chatham

LAMBERT, R.S.: History and Archaeology

LEE, John: Coastline, Thames, River

LEE, Judith M.: Hayes and Keston

LEE, Laurie: Canterbury Cathedral

LEE PRIORY PRESS: Lee Priory

LEE, Sophia: Canterbury

LEE, W. Publisher: Hythe, Sandgate

LEE, W.S.: Dover

LEE-WARNER, Edward H.: Rochester Cathedral

LEE-WARNER, Sir William: Walmer

LEEDS, C.S.: Gillingham

LEEDS, Edward Thurlow: History and Archaeology

LEEMING, J.R.: Canterbury Cathedral, Archbishops

LEESE, Arthur Selwyn Mountford: Hawkhurst

LEESE, Leonard Ernest Selwyn: Thames, River

LEFEVRE, William LTD.: Canterbury

LE FLEMING, John: Tonbridge

LE FRANCQ, Paul: Chatham Dockyard

LEFTWICH, B.R.: Deptford

LE GRAND MAGAZINE: Gillingham, Industry and Trade

LEGEND OF BAB'S OAK: Canterbury

LEGG, J. Wickham: Canterbury Cathedral

LEGG, Michael Arthur: Cranbrook

LE JOINDRE, R. Junior: Gravesend

LELAND, John: Kent

LE MAY, Reginald: Genealogical Records

LEMPRIERE, C.: Chatham Dockyard

LE NEVE, John: Religious Denominations

LENNARD, T.B.: Knole

LENNOX, J.T.: Sevenoaks

LEROI, David: Channel Tunnel

LESLIE, George D.: Thames, River

LESLIE, Shane: Borstal

LESTER, H.F.: Dover

L'ESTRANGE, Alfred Guy K.: Greenwich

LETTER II: Kent

LETTER FROM A GENTLEMAN IN KENT...: History and Archaeology

LETTER TO A FRIEND IN THE COUNTRY...: History and Archaeology

LETTER TO A NOBLE LORD...: Smuggling

LETTER TO THE VISITORS OF MARGATE: Margate

LETTERS PATENT, ELIZABETH I: Eltham

LETTER TO HENRY ADDINGTON...: Libraries

LETTSOM, John Coakley: Margate

LEVER, Sir Tresham: Hayes and Keston; Pitt, William

LEVESON-GOWER, Granville William Gresham: Westerham

LEVIN, Harry: Marlowe, Christopher

LEVY, L.A.: Bexley

LEVY, L.M. - See LEVY, L.A.: Bexley

LEVY, Mary L.S.: Agriculture

LEWIN, H.G.: Railways

LEWIN, Thomas: History and Archaeology

LEWIS, Arthur D.: Coastline

LEWIS, Bernard: Dickens, Charles

LEWIS, Rev. G.W.: Ramsgate

LEWIS, Hardwicke: Margate

LEWIS, Hilda: Mersham

LEWIS, J. - See Bibliotheca Topographica Britannica:
     Religious Denominations

LEWIS, J.D.: Organisations

LEWIS, J.G.: Marlowe, Christopher

LEWIS, J.H.: Dover

LEWIS, John: Faversham, Isle-of-Thanet, Religious
     Denominations, Richborough, Rochester Cathedral,
     Sandwich
See Also - Collections Relating To...: Isle-of-Thanet

LEWIS, Mary: Plaxtol

See Also - West Kent Federation of Women's Institutes:
     Agriculture

LEWIS, P.W.: Industry and Trade

LEWIS, T. Hayter: Richborough, St. Margaret's-at-Cliffe,
     Sandgate, Sandown

LEWIS, W. Publisher: Kent

LEWISHAM ANTIQUARIAN SOCIETY: Genealogical Records, Lewisham

LEWISHAM NATURAL HISTORY SOCIETY: Natural History

LEY, J.W.T.: Dickens, Charles

LIBRARY ASSOCIATION: Margate

LIBRARY ASSOCIATION - KENT SUB-BRANCH: Bibliography

LICHFIELD, Nathaniel: Ashford

LIFE AND DEATH OF JOHN CARPENTER...: Tunbridge Wells

LIFE MAGAZINE: Churchill, Winston S.

LIFE OF SIR WILLIAM COURTENAY: Canterbury

LIFE OF SISTER MILDRED...: Minster-in-Thanet

LIFE OF WILLIAM SHIPLEY, 1715-1803...: Maidstone

LIFE THROUGH YOUNG EYES...: Betteshanger

LIGHT, W.E.: Dover

LIGHT THROUGH A CENTURY: Dover

LIGHTWOOD, James T.: Dickens, Charles

LILLEY, W.E.: Gravesend

LILLO, George: Faversham

LILLYWHITE, Nigel Gordon

LIMNELIUS, George, pseud. (Lewis ROBINSON): Thames,
     River

LINCOLN, Edward Frank: Canterbury, History and
     Archaeology

LINCOLN, Victoria: Dickens, Charles

LINDON, D.W.: Tunbridge Wells

LINDSAY, Jack: Dickens, Charles; History and
     Archaeology

L Cont'd

LYALL, Sir Alfred: Walmer

LYALL, William Rowe: Canterbury Cathedral

LYLE, Helen M.: History and Archaeology

LYLE, Laurence: Canterbury

LYNE, R.M.: Railways

LYNN, Rev. James: Chatham

LYON, John: Dover, Folkestone

LYON, Rev. John: Kent Authors and Literature

LYSONS, Daniel: Kent

M

M., A.: Margate

M., A.W.: Isle-of-Sheppey, Sheerness

M., G.: Dover

M., L.V.: Natural History

M., L.W.: Loose

MACAULAY, Joseph E. Publisher: Rochester

M'BEAN, James: Canterbury

McCALL, Sir Robert A.: Religious Denominations

McCALL, Dorothy: Chislehurst

McCARTHY, Elizabeth: Maidstone

McCARTHY, M.J. - See COOK, Norman: West Wickham

McCLEMENT, Rev. F.: Canterbury

McCLINTOCK, Marjorie K: Chilham
See Also - BROWNE, Andrew R. Gore: Chartham

McCRERIE, Alan: Aylesford

McCUDDEN, James Thomas Byford: Gillingham

McCULLOCH, Joseph: Medway, River

McCULLOCH, William: Canterbury

McDAKIN, Captain S. Gordon: Dover, Folkestone

McDERMOTT, Edward: Crystal Palace

MACDONALD, I.H.: Kent, North West

MACDONALD, W.A.: Maidstone

McDOUGAL, G.H.: Folkestone

MACDOUGALL, Mrs. Sylvia (Paul WAINMAN, pseud.) - See WAINMAN, Paul: Faversham

MACE, J. Ellis - See ELLIS-MACE, J.: Tenterden

MACECHERN, A.A.: Knole

MACFARLANE, Charles: History and Archaeology, Newspapers

MACFARLANE, William Angus: Plaistow

MACGIBBON, David: Maidstone

MACGILLIVRAY, G.J.: Maidstone

McHUGH, Stuart: Dickens, Charles

MACINTOSH, K.H.: Sturry

McINTOSH, Mary: Leybourne

MACK, Lawrence Albert: Railways

MACKAIL, J.W.: Biography

MACKAY, Charles: Medway, River

MACKAY, W. AND J. AND CO. LTD. Publishers: Chatham, Medway Towns

MACKAYE, Percy - See TATLOCK, John S.P.: Chaucer, Geoffrey

MACKEAN, William Herbert: Rochester Cathedral

McKEE, J.R.: History and Archaeology

MACKENZIE, Donald: Local Government

MACKENZIE, Norman: Canterbury

MACKENZIE, P.A.: Canterbury

McKENZIE-SMITH, A.: Organisations

MACKESON, Charles: Religious Denominations

MACKESON, Rev. Charles: Folkestone

MACKESON, H.B.: Hythe

MACKIE, S.J.: Dover, Folkestone, Knole

McKILLIAM, A.E.: Canterbury Cathedral, Archbishops

MACKINNON, Donald D.: Speldhurst

MACKLEM, Michael: Rochester Cathedral

McLACHLAN, G.W.P. - See GRASEMAN, C.: Isle-of-Sheppey, Ships and Shipping

MACLEAN, C.M.: Maidstone

MACLEAR, George Frederick: Canterbury, Canterbury Cathedral, Hythe

MACMANUS, FREDERICK AND PARTNERS: Tenterden

MACQUEEN, John: Dover

MACKMEIKAN, John A.: Sandwich

McMILLAN, Margaret: Bromley

MADDAN, James Gracie: Addington

MADDOCK, Alfred Beaumont: Sydenham

MADGE, Sidney J.: History and Archaeology

MAGINN, C.A.: Wormshill

MAGRAW, B.I.: Kent Authors and Literature

THE MAID OF KENT: History and Archaeology

MAIDSTONE AMATEUR PHOTOGRAPHIC SOCIETY: Maidstone

MAIDSTONE AND DISTRICT CHAMBER OF COMMERCE: Maidstone

MAIDSTONE AND DISTRICT COUNCIL OF CHURCHES: Maidstone

MAIDSTONE AND DISTRICT CREMATORIUM JOINT COMMITTEE: Maidstone

MAIDSTONE AND DISTRICT EAST KENT BUS CLUB: Horsmonden

MAIDSTONE AND DISTRICT MARRIAGE GUIDANCE COUNCIL: Maidstone

MAIDSTONE AND DISTRICT MOTOR SERVICES LTD.: Road Transport

MAIDSTONE AND DISTRICT PRODUCTIVITY COMMITTEE: Maidstone

MAIDSTONE AND DISTRICT YOUTH LEADERS' COUNCIL: Maidstone

MAIDSTONE AND KENT COUNTY STANDARD: Maidstone

MAIDSTONE AND KENTISH JOURNAL: Maidstone

MAIDSTONE AND MID KENT NATURAL HISTORY AND PHILOSPHICAL SOCIETY: Natural History, Organisations

MAIDSTONE AREA YOUTH COUNCIL: Maidstone

MAIDSTONE ART CLUB: Maidstone

MAIDSTONE BAND OF HOPE: Maidstone

MAIDSTONE BOROUGH COUNCIL - TRANSPORT COMMITTEE: Maidstone

MAIDSTONE CHORAL UNION: Maidstone

MAIDSTONE CHURCH INSTITUTE AND Y.M.C.A.: Organisations

MAIDSTONE CRICKET WEEK (CHARITY) COMMITTEE: Maidstone

MAIDSTONE DISPENSARY: Maidstone

MAIDSTONE DIVISION CONSERVATIVE ASSOCIATION: Maidstone

MAIDSTONE EDUCATION COMMITTEE: Maidstone

MAIDSTONE ELECTION PETITION: Elections, Maidstone

MAIDSTONE FILM SOCIETY: Maidstone

MAIDSTONE FOOTBALL CLUB: Maidstone

MAIDSTONE GRAMMAR SCHOOL: Maidstone

MAIDSTONE GRAMOPHONE SOCIETY: Maidstone

MAIDSTONE JOURNAL AND KENTISH ADVERTISER: Maidstone

MAIDSTONE LITERARY INSTITUTION: Maidstone

MAIDSTONE MUSEUM: Maidstone

MAIDSTONE MUSEUM OF CARRIAGES: Maidstone, Transport

MAIDSTONE PERSONAL SERVICE SOCIETY AND CITIZENS' ADVICE BUREAU:
    Maidstone

MAIDSTONE PUBLIC LIBRARY: Maidstone

MAIDSTONE ROAD SAFETY COMMITTEE: Maidstone

MAIDSTONE RURAL DISTRICT COUNCIL: Kent, Mid

MAIDSTONE SCHOOL BOARD: Maidstone

MAIDSTONE SCHOOL OF ART AND SCIENCE: Maidstone

MAIDSTONE SESSIONS: Maidstone

MAIDSTONE SUBSCRIPTION BAND: Maidstone

MAIDSTONE THEATRE: Maidstone

MAIDSTONE TRADESMENS' £100 PROVIDENT SOCIETY: Maidstone

MAIDSTONE TRUSTEES OF THE POOR: Maidstone

MAIDSTONE UNION: Maidstone

MAIDSTONE URBAN DISTRICT COUNCIL: Maidstone

MAIDSTONE URBAN SANITARY AUTHORITY: Maidstone

MAIDSTONE WATERWORKS CO.: Maidstone

MAIR, Gordon: Kent

MAIR, Harold: Dartford, Kent

MAIS, Stuart Petrie Brodie: Cinque Ports, Kent, Windmills and
    Watermills

MAISON DIEU MUSEUM, OSPRINGE: Ospringe

MAITLAND, Frederic William: History and Archaeology

MAJOR, Kathleen: Canterbury Cathedral, Archbishops

MAJOR, M.B.: Canterbury

MALCOLM, James: Agriculture

MALCOLM, James Peller: Kent

MALIM, Mary Charlotte: Blackheath

MALLING RURAL DISTRICT COUNCIL: Kent, Mid

MALLORIE, Rev. W.T.: Barham

MALONE SOCIETY - See DAWSON, Giles E.: Theatre

"MAN OF KENT", pseud.: Gravesend, Kent Authors and
    Literature
See Also - COWTAN, Robert: Biography

MAN WHO SLEW KIT MARLOWE...: Deptford, Marlowe,
    Christopher

MANDY, William H.: Greenwich
See Also - ELLISTON-ERWOOD, Frank Charles: East
    Wickham, Greenwich, Kent, North West;
    Lewisham, Plumstead

MANN, E.L.: Kent

MANN, H.P.: Kent Authors and Literature

MANN, Sir James: Canterbury Cathedral

MANN, Sidney L.:. Bromley

MANNERING, John: Dover, Windmills and Watermills

MANNIN, Ethel: Gillingham, Gravesend

MANNING, Anne: Eltham

MANNING, F.: Greenwich

MANNING, John: Dickens, Charles

MANNINGHAM, John: Bradbourne

MANNOCK, Edward: Canterbury

MANSBRIDGE, Albert: Bromley

MANSELL, M.H.: Woodchurch

MANSERGH, James: Margate

MANSFIELD, F.A.: Gravesend

MANTELL, Gideon Algernon: Geology

MANTELL, Sir Thomas: Cinque Ports

MANUSCRIPT BOOK...: Lee

MANUELL, Roger: Smallhythe

MANWARING, G.E.: Military and Naval History

MANWARING, H.M.: Agriculture

MAP OF THE PROPOSED KENT RAILWAY - See Canterbury
Journal. Publisher: Railways

MARCEL, Jean Marie: Canterbury Cathedral,
    Archbishops

MARCH, Edgar James: Medway, River; Ships and
    Shipping, Thames, River

MARCHAM, Patricia: Orpington, St. Mary Cray

MARGARY, D. AND H. Publishers: Lympne

MARGARY, Ivan D. - See STRAKER, Ernest: Industry
    and Trade, Roads, Weald

MARGATE, W.D.: Richborough

MARGATE AMBULANCE CORPS: Margate

MARGATE AND DISTRICT GENERAL HOSPITAL: Margate

MARGATE AND HISTORICAL THANET: Isle-of-Thanet,
    Margate

MARGATE AND THANET PERMANENT BENEFIT BUILDING
SOCIETY: Margate

MARGATE AND WESTGATE WITH BIRCHINGTON: Birchington,
    Margate

MARGATE BOROUGH COUNCIL: Margate

MARGATE BOROUGH COUNCIL - EDUCATION COMMITTEE:
    Margate

M Cont'd

MARGATE BOROUGH COUNCIL - ENTERTAINMENTS COMMITTEE: Margate

MARGATE BOROUGH COUNCIL - PUBLICITY COMMITTEE: Margate

MARGATE, BROADSTAIRS...AND NORTH EAST KENT PICTORIAL AND DESCRIPTIVE GUIDE: Kent, East

MARGATE CHAMBER OF COMMERCE: Margate

MARGATE CHURCH INSTITUTE: Margate

MARGATE CORPORATION - See Margate Borough Council: Isle-of-Thanet, World War I

MARGATE COTTAGE HOSPITAL: Margate

MARGATE CRICKET CLUB: Margate

MARGATE FREE PRESS: Margate

MARGATE HOTEL, BOARDING AND APPARTMENT HOUSE ASSOCIATION: Margate

MARGATE MARINERS' SOCIETY: Margate

MARGATE MICROSCOPICAL CLUB: Margate

MARGATE PIER AND HARBOUR CO. AND COMMISSIONERS OF PAVEMENTS: Coastline

MARGATE PROSECUTION SOCIETY: Margate

MARGATE PUBLIC LIBRARY: Margate

MARGATE, RAMSGATE AND BROADSTAIRS GUIDE: Broadstairs, Isle-of-Thanet, Ramsgate

MARGATE SAVINGS BANK: Margate

MARGATE TOTAL ABSTINENCE ASSOCIATION: Margate

MARGATE TRADE PROTECTION SOCIETY: Margate

MARKHAM, Gervase: Agriculture, Weald

MARKHAM, Violet R.: Crystal Palace

MARLEY GROUP: Industry and Trade

MARLOWE SOCIETY. Publishers: Marlowe, Christopher

MARRIOTT, Charles Stowel: Cricket

MARRIOTT, F.S.: Kent Authors and Literature

MARRIOTT, J.W.: Chislehurst

MARRIOTT, St. John: Erith, Natural History

MARSH, Catherine (M.): Crystal Palace, Military and Naval History

MARSH, Frances: Folkestone

MARSH, John B.: Agriculture

MARSH, Ronald J.: Medway, River; Rochester

MARSH, T.: Blackheath

MARSHALL, C.F. Dendy: Railways

MARSHALL, Edward Shearburn - See HANBURY, Frederick Janson: Natural History

MARSHALL, Emma: Canterbury, Penshurst, Tunbridge Wells

MARSHALL, H.P. - See WAKEFIELD, W.W.: Sport

MARSHALL, HORACE AND SON. Publishers: Channel Tunnel

MARSHALL, Jane: Canterbury, Rochester

MARSHALL, M.A.N.: Cinque Ports, Dover, Folkestone, Ships and Shipping

MARSHALL, P.J.: Road Transport

MARSHALL, TAPP AND CO. Publishers: Tunbridge Wells

MARSHALL, W.: Agriculture

MARSHAM-TOWNSHEND, Robert: Genealogical Records

MARSTON, John: Canterbury

MARTIN, Alan R.: Burham, Canterbury, Charlton, Cliffe-at-Hoo, Greenwich, Lewisham, Maplescombe

MARTIN, B.: Natural History

MARTIN, Charles Wykeham: Hollingbourne, Leeds

MARTIN, J.A.: Religious Denominations

MARTIN, Kenneth Beacham: Cinque Ports, Coastline

MARTIN, Norah Baldwin: Canterbury

MARTIN, Sidney: Dartford

MARTIN, W. Stanley: Cranbrook

See Also - ROW, B. Prescott: Maidstone, Tonbridge, Tunbridge Wells

MARTIN, W.W.: High Halden

MARTINDALE, Cyril Charlie: Hartley

MARTINDALE, T.D.: Bromley

MARTON, Mrs. M.E.: New Romney

MARY GREGORY, Mother: West Wickham

MARZIALS, Frank T.: Dickens, Charles

MASLIN, W.: Maidstone

MASON, Arthur James: Canterbury, Canterbury Cathedral, Canterbury Cathedral, Archbishops

MASON, Harold: Industry and Trade

MASON, L.: Kent, North East

MASON, R.T.: Architecture, Weald

MASS RADIOGRAPHY CAMPAIGN JOINT COMMITTEE: Medway Towns

MASSEE, A.M.: Agriculture

MASTER, Alfred: Henhurst

MASTER, James: Mereworth

MASTER OF HOUNDS...HARRY BUCKLAND: Ashford

MASTERS, John Neve: Biography

MASTERS, W.: Dover

MATE, W. AND SONS. Publishers - See CLEMENTS, Robert H.M.: Tunbridge Wells

MATHEW, George: Dartford

MATHEW, Theobald: Maidstone

MATHEWS, R.G.: Ships and Shipping

MATHIAS, T.J.: Isle-of-Thanet

MATTHEW, Sir Tobie: Biography

MATTHEWS, Arnold Gwynne: History and Archaeology

MATTHEWS, Brian: Kent, North West

MATTHEWS, G.F. - See MATTHEWS, John: Genealogical Records

MATTHEWS, John: Genealogical Records

MATTHEWS, Pat: Bromley

MATTHEWS, Robert. Auctioneer: Gravesend

MATTINGLY, Harold: Richborough

MATZ, B.W.: Dickens, Charles; Kent, North West

MAUDE, F.F.: Military and Naval History

MERCER, Richard C.H.: East Malling

MERCER, William John: Canterbury, Margate

MERRIOTT, Jack: Canterbury

MESSENGER, A.W.B.: Canterbury Cathedral

MESSENGER AND ADAMS. Architects: Herne Bay

"METELLUS", pseud.: Tunbridge Wells

METROPOLITAN ASYLUMS BOARD: Darenth, Swanley

METROPOLITAN WATER BOARD: Public Utilities

MEYER, C.J.A.: Geology

MEYER, G.H.: Windmills and Watermills

MEYERSTEIN, Edward Harry William: Sevenoaks

MICHEL, Dan: Dialects

MIDDLETON, John - See WIKELEY, Nigel: Railways

MIDDLETON, Thomas: Kent Authors and Literature

MIDFIELD JUNIOR SCHOOL: Cray, River

MID KENT WATER CO.: Godmersham, Public Utilities

MIDWINTER, Arthur: Tunstall

MILBOURNE, R.A.: Sevenoaks

MILES, Harold: Shadoxhurst

"MILES, Walker", pseud.: Footpaths and Commons

MILESTONE GUIDES: Roads

MILITARY HANDBOOK OF DOVER GARRISON: Dover

"MILITARY RAILWAY EXPERT", pseud.: Channel Tunnel

MILLAR, Christine Flora: Cheriton, Elham

MILLARD, Louise: Kent Authors and Literature

MILLER, A.C.: Eythorne

MILLER, Alice Duer: Dover

MILLER, Amos: Canterbury

MILLER, E.A.: Canterbury

MILLER, G. Anderson: History and Archaeology

MILLER, G.W. - See HUGHES, W.E.: Genealogical Records

MILLER, R.R.: Bexleyheath

MILLER, William: History and Archaeology

MILLER, W.S.: Hythe, Military and Naval History

MILLES, Thomas: Genealogical Records

MILLGATE, W.F. Publisher: Herne Bay, Reculver, Whitstable

MILLICHAMP, R.: Maidstone, Natural History

MILLS, A.R.: West Wickham

MILLS, Benjamin: Maidstone

MILLS, Dorothy: Canterbury Cathedral, Canterbury Cathedral, Archbishops, Edward, the Black Prince

MILLS, Halford L.: Beult, River; Smarden, Weald

MILLS, Mark: Ashford

MILLS, Mary C.S.: Biography

MILLWARD, Roy: Kent, West; Weald

MILNE, A.G.: Eltham

MILNE, Colin: Natural History

MILNE, F.A.: History and Archaeology

MILTON, Ernest: Marlowe, Christopher

MILTON IMPROVEMENT COMMISSIONERS: Milton Regis

MILTOUN, Francis: Dickens, Charles

MINERVA RAILWAY GUIDE: Deal, Sandwich

MINET, James: Dover

MINET, William: Dover

MINNOWS FROM BRENCHLEY BROOK: Brenchley

MINTER, Derek: Sport

MINTON, R.: Chiddingstone

MINUTES OF EVIDENCE TAKEN BEFORE THE COMMITTEE...: Medway, River

MINUTES OF THE SELECT COMMITTEE...: Elections

"THE MIRROR"...: Tunbridge Wells, Weald

MISCELLANEA GEOLOGICA ET HERALDICA: Bromley, Genealogical Records, Monumental Inscriptions

"MR. PUNCH" (CARTOONS OF BENJAMIN DISRAELI): Maidstone

MITCHELL, Alan Fyson: Bedgebury

MITCHELL, Charles: Isle-of-Sheppey

MITCHELL, E.C.: Margate

MITCHELL, Elizabeth Harcourt: Dover

MOORE, E.W.: Wye

MITCHELL, John: Rivers

MITCHINSON, John: Canterbury Cathedral

MITTINS, W.H.: Kent Authors and Literature

MITTON, G.E.: Railways

MOCKETT, John: Broadstairs, Isle-of-Thanet

MODERN GILPIN...: Kent Authors and Literature

MODERN LOCOMOTIVES...OF SOUTHERN RAILWAY: Railways

MODERS, Mary - Alias STEDMAN. Defendant: Canterbury, Trials

MOGG, Edward: Kent Roads

MOLESWORTH, Sir Guilford Lindsey: Canterbury

MOLESWORTH, J.E.N.: Canterbury Cathedral
See Also - Penny Sunday Reader: Canterbury

MOLLOY, T. AND CO. Publishers: Folkestone

MOLONY, C.V.: Military and Naval History

MOLONY, Eileen: Canterbury

"MOMUS", pseud.: Margate

MONCK, George. 1st Duke of Albemorle: History and Archaeology

MONCRIEFF, A.R. Hope - See A. AND C. BLACK. Publishers: Kent, West

MONEY, J.H.: Tunbridge Wells

MONK, Captain: Canterbury

MONTAGU, John. 4th Earl of Sandwich: Greenwich

MONTAGUE, Mrs. - See CARTER, Mrs. Elizabeth: Biography

MONTAGUE, M.F. Ashley - See OAKLEY, K.P.: Gravesend

MONTEFIORE, Arthur - See "RAMBLER", pseud.: Isle-of-Thanet
    Kent, North West

MONTEFIORE, Eade: Dickens, Charles

MONTGOMERY, John: Gillingham

MONTMORENCY, J.E.G. de: Greenwich, Kent, North West

MONUMENTA ANGLICANA: Dartford

MONUMENTAL BRASS SOCIETY: Monumental Inscriptions

MOODY, G.T.: Railways

MOODY, John. Photographer - See CORNER, John: Canterbury
    Cathedral

MOODY, R.S. - See Historical Records of the Buffs: Military
    and Naval History

MOORE, C.: Boxley

MOORE, Doris Langley: New Romney

MOORE, E.N.: Eynsford

MOORE, Francis: Kent

MOORE, John: Industry and Trade

MOORE, John S.: Weald

MOORE, Ruth: Darwin, Charles

MOORE, W.C.: Gillingham

MOORE, Walter: Bickley, Bromley

MOOREHEAD, Alan: Darwin, Charles

MORAN, James: Westerham

MORANT, G.M.: Hythe

MORDEN COLLEGE - A BRIEF GUIDE AND HANDBOOK: Blackheath

MORE, Margaret: Eltham

MORECROFT, Mrs. E.G.: Sibertswold

MORECROFT, V.W.: Kent

MORELAND, Arthur: Dickens, Charles

MORES, Edward Rowe - See Bibliotheca Topographica Britannica:
    Tunstall

MOREY, George: Coastal Waters

MOREY, Gordon Henry: Gravesend

MORGAN, D.R.: Education

MORGAN, Glyn Howis: Inns, Kent, North West

MORGAN, Captain W.A.: Military and Naval History, Thames, River

MORGAN, William - See OGILBY, John: Roads

MORGAN, W.L.: Gillingham

MORLAND, G.: Folkestone

MORLAND, William: Lamberhurst

MORLEY, A.M.: Folkestone

MORLEY, Malcolm: Margate, Theatre

MORLEY, M.M.: Dartford

MORRAH, Patrick: Cricket

MORRIS, Henry A.: Dover

MORRIS, J.E.: Kent

MORRIS, John: Canterbury, Canterbury Cathedral, Canterbury
    Cathedral, Archbishops

MORRIS, Joseph: World War I

MORRIS, Joyce M.: Education

MORRIS, Leslie Frank: Lewisham

MORRIS, O.J.: Railways

MORRIS, P.E.: Bexley

MORRIS, Richard: Dialects

MORRIS, T.E.: Margate

MORRIS, W.S.: Wye

MORRIS-JONES, K.W.: Military and Naval History

MORRISON, John Harold: Genealogical Records

MORTON, Henry Canova Vollan: Canterbury, Kent

MOSELEY, George: Sandgate

MOSELEY, Mary: Hoo St. Werburgh

MOSER, Thomas: Conrad, Joseph

MOSES, H.: Ramsgate

MOSLEY, Leonard: World War II

MOTE CRICKET CLUB: Maidstone

MOTHERSOLE, Jessie: History and Archaeology

MOTTLEY, Edward: Margate

MOUCHEL, L.G. AND CO. Publishers: Dover

MOUCHOTTE, Rene: World War II

MOUL, Duncan: Kent

MOULD, Daphne Desiree Charlotte Pochin: Aylesford

MOULE, A.W.H.: Tonbridge

MOULE, Thomas: Canterbury Cathedral

MOULTON, W.R.: Aldington, Court-at-Street, Lympne,
    Studfall, West Hythe

MOUNT, Frank: Hampton

MOUNTJOY, Alan Bertram: Kent

MOWLL, John H.: Dover

MUDDOCK, J.E. Preston: Crystal Palace

MUDFORD, William: Tunbridge Wells

MUELLER, William R.: Sevenoaks

MUGGERIDGE, Sidney J.: Maidstone

MUHLFELD, Helen Elizabeth: Wye

MUIR, Kenneth: Maidstone, Penshurst

MUIRHEAD, Litellus Russell: Kent

MULLER, N.J.: Ash-by-Wrotham

MULLOCK, A.F.: Orpington

MULOCK, Dinah M. - See CRAIK, Mrs. pseud.: Dover

MUMBY, F.A.: Hayes and Keston

MUMMERY, A.F.: Kent Authors and Literature

MUNCY, G.N.: Penge

MUNDEN, Alan Frederick: Faversham

MUNDY, R.W.: Hayes and Keston

MUNFORD, William A.: Dover

MUNICIPAL CORPORATION BOUNDARIES: Maidstone

MUNICIPAL CORPORATION COMMISSIONERS: Cinque Ports

MUNICIPAL JOURNAL: Canterbury

MUNRO, A.G.: Chatham, Rochester

MUNRO, William: Gillingham, Medway, River

MURBY, Thomas. Publisher: Kent

MURIE, Dr. James - See Kent and Essex Sea Fisheries Committee:
    Thames, River

MURIEL, E.M.: Ruckinge

MURPHY, Charles J.V. - See DAVENPORT, John: Westerham

MURPHY, Leonard: Canterbury

MURRAY, A.H. Hallam: Saltwood

MURRAY, Anne: Tonbridge

MURRAY, Charles J.V. - See DAVENPORT, John: Westerham

MURRAY, F.H.: Chislehurst

MURRAY, George: Bromley, Rochester Cathedral

MURRAY, John. Publisher: Kent

MURRAY, J.O. - See Rochester City Council: Rochester

MURRAY, K.M. Elizabeth: Cinque Ports, Faversham, New Romney

MURRAY, Walter John Campbell: Romney Marsh

MUSEUMS ASSOCIATION: Canterbury

MYDANS, Sheila: Canterbury Cathedral, Archbishops

MYNARD, D.C.: Dover

MYNOTTE, E.: Hayes and Keston

MYRES, J.N.L.: History and Archaeology

N

N., H.: Stone (Nr. Dartford)

NAIRN, Ian: Canterbury

NAIRNE, Charles: Genealogical Records, Shadoxhurst

NAIRNE, E.: Kent Authors and Literature

NARES, Edward: Danbury

A NARRATIVE AND DECLARATION...: History and Archaeology

NARRATIVE OF THE FACTS RELATIVE TO THE MURDER OF RICHARD
FAULKNER TAYLOR: Rochester

NARRATIVE OF THE LOSS OF THE "HINDOSTAN": Margate

NARRATIVE OF THE PROCEEDINGS AGAINST G. WILSON: Blackheath

NASH, Richard: Tunbridge Wells

NASONS (CANTERBURY) LTD.: Canterbury

NATIONAL ASSOCIATION OF LOCAL GOVERNMENT OFFICERS: Maidstone,
    Margate

NATIONAL COUNCIL OF WOMEN: Tunbridge Wells

NATIONAL GARDEN SCHEME: Kent

NATIONAL HEALTH SERVICE - KENT AND CANTERBURY EXECUTIVE COUNCIL:
    Health and Welfare

NATIONAL MARITIME MUSEUM: Greenwich, History and Archaeology,
    Ships and Shipping

NATIONAL PARKS COMMISSION: Coastline

NATIONAL PROVINCIAL BANK LTD.: Maidstone

NATIONAL SOCIETY FOR THE PREVENTION OF CRUELTY TO CHILDREN:
    Canterbury, Kent, East

NATIONAL TELEPHONE CO.: Gravesend, Northfleet

NATIONAL TEMPERANCE HYMNAL: Maidstone

NATIONAL TRUST: Gravesend, Smallhythe, Westerham

NATIONAL UNION OF CONSERVATIVE AND UNIONIST
ASSOCIATIONS: Margate

NATIONAL UNION OF TEACHERS: Bromley, Folkestone,
    Margate

NATIONAL UNION OF TOWNSWOMEN'S GUILDS: Organisations

"A NATIVE", pseud. - See DALE, E.: Dickens, Charles

NATURE CONSERVANCY - SOUTH-EAST REGION: Natural
    History, North Kent Marshes

NAVAL CONSIDERATIONS...: Northfleet

"A NAVAL OFFICER", pseud.: Dover, Ramsgate

NAYES, Robert: Cranbrook

NEALE, C.M.: Dickens, Charles

NEALE, J.M.: Blackheath, Kent Authors and Literature

NEALE, John Preston: Kent

NEALE, Johnson: Military and Naval History

NEAME, Alan: Aldington, Kent Authors and Literature

NEAME, George: Elections

NEAME, Sir Philip: Biography

NEC TIMET IRATUM MARE: Margate

NEIL, B.H. St. J.O.: Folkestone

NEILL, Robert: Dover

NEILSON, C.P. - See Sandwich Borough Council:
    Sandwich

NEILSON, N.: Bilsington

NELSON AND CO. Publishers: Kent, North West

NELSON, T. AND SONS. Publishers: Dover

"NEMO", pseud. - See ADAMS, Henry Gardiner: Kent,
    Kent Authors and Literature

NEVE, Arthur H.: Tonbridge

NEVE, Walter N.: Tonbridge

NEVES AND BISCOE. Publishers: Kent, North West

NEVILLE, John: Kent Authors and Literature

NEW AND LATTER HOUSE OF ISRAEL: Gillingham

NEW CATALOGUE OF SILVER'S CIRCULATING LIBRARY...:
    Margate

NEW CHANNEL FERRY SERVICE: Ships and Shipping

NEW DISPLAY OF THE BEAUTIES OF ENGLAND: Architecture,
    Kent

NEW DOVER GROUP: Channel Tunnel, Dover

A NEW HISTORICAL, TOPOGRAPHICAL AND DESCRIPTIVE
COMPANION...: Gravesend

THE NEW MARGATE PACKET...: Ships and Shipping

A NEW PICTORIAL AND DESCRIPTIVE GUIDE...: Kent,
    East

A NEW PICTURESQUE STEAM-BOAT COMPANION: Medway,
    River; Thames, River

NEW ROMNEY BOROUGH COUNCIL: New Romney

A NEW STEAMBOAT COMPANION...: Gravesend, Thames,
    River

NEW, Vincent: Bromley

NEW VOICE: Medway Towns

NEWMAN, George: History and Archaeology, Kent, Kent Authors
    and Literature

NEWBERRY AND CARNAN. Publishers - See A Description of England
and Wales: Kent

NEWCOMB, E.: Kent

NEWCOMBE, N.W. - See PHILLIPS, Geoffrey Broomfield: Maidstone

NEWCOMEN SOCIETY: Windmills and Watermills

NEWMAN, A. Publisher: Tunbridge Wells

NEWMAN, Aubrey: Chevening

NEWMAN, George: Gravesend, History and Archaeology, Kent
    Authors and Literature, Wateringbury

NEWMAN, John: Architecture, Weald

NEWMAN, J.S.: Chatham

NEWMAN, Leonard Hugh: Bexley, Natural History, Westerham

NEWPORT, W.O.: Folkestone

NEWTON, A.P.: Knole

See Also - Gillingham Public Libraries: Gillingham

NEWTON, E.T.: Ightham

NEWTON, William: Maidstone, Stodmarsh, Wingham

NEWTON, W.M.: Kent, North West

NICHOLAS, Frieda - See HALL, Hubert: Canterbury

NICHOLLS, Thomas: Isle-of-Thanet; Thames, River

NICHOLS, Beverley: Canterbury Cathedral

NICHOLS, John. Publisher - See Bibliotheca Topographica
Britannica: Biography, Herne, History and Archaeology,
    Reculver, Tunstall

NICHOLS, John Gough: Genealogical Records, History and
    Archaeology

NICHOLS, W.J.: Beckenham, Chislehurst

NICHOLS, William: Tunbridge Wells

NICHOLSON, L.R. - See LAWFORD, G.L.: Greenwich

NICHOLSON, Norman: Wells, Herbert George

NICKLIN, J.A.: Medway, River

NICOLL, Sir William Robertson: Dickens, Charles

NICOLSON, Lady Harold - See SACKVILLE-WEST, Victoria:
    Agriculture, Kent, Kent Authors and Literature, Knole,
    Sissinghurst, Wye

NICOLSON, Sir Harold: Sissinghurst

NICOLSON, Nigel: Sissinghurst

NIGHTINGALE, G.W.: Paddock Wood

NISBETT, Marjorie: Canterbury Cathedral

NISBETT, Nehemiah: Ash-next-Sandwich

NOBLE, Edward: Thames, River

NOBLE, Mark: History and Archaeology

NOBLE, T.: Blackheath

"NOBODY", pseud.: Maidstone

NOCK, Oswald Stevens: Railways

NOEL, Amelia: Isle-of-Thanet, Kent

NOEL, Charles: Teston

NOEL, Rev. Gerard T.: Rainham

NOKES, pseud. (Also known as G.A. Sekon): Railways

NOLAN, Michael: Roads

NONESUCH PRESS: Dickens, Charles

NONSUCH AND EWELL ANTIQUARIAN SOCIETY: History
    and Archaeology

NORE COMMAND AND CHATHAM AREA OFFICIAL DIRECTORY:
    Coastal Waters

NORIE, J.W.: Medway, River; Thames, River

NORMAN, Charles: Marlowe, Christopher

NORMAN, G.W.: Bromley

NORMAN, Philip: Bromley, Cricket, Hayes and Keston,
    West Wickham

NORTH, Allan. Publisher: Biography, History and
    Archaeology

NORTH, George: Coins and Tokens

NORTH, Roger: Dover

NORTH-EAST KENT JOINT TOWN PLANNING COMMITTEE:
    Kent, North East

NORTHFLEET URBAN DISTRICT COUNCIL: Northfleet

NORTH FORELAND GOLF CLUB: Kingsgate

NORTH KENT COURSING CLUB: Sport

NORTH KENT FLORIST AND FANCIERS GAZETTE: Newspapers

NORTH KENT PERMANENT BENEFIT BUILDING SOCIETY:
    Organisations

NORTH-WEST AND SOUTH-WEST KENT JOINT REGIONAL TOWN
PLANNING COMMITTEE: Kent, West

NORTON, Jane E.: Kent

NORTON, L.M.: Meopham

NORWOOD, John C.: Kent, Minster-in-Sheppey

NOTES MAINLY ON KENT, 1795-1800: History and
    Archaeology

NOTESTEIN, Wallace: Knole

NOUVEAU THEATRE DE LA GRANDE BRETAGNE: Kent

NOWELL, Hugh Noel: Sandwich

NOYES, Alfred: Bexleyheath

NOYES, J. Publisher: Tunbridge Wells

NOYES, Robert: Cranbrook

NOYES, T.H.: Legends, Weald

NUNN, F.W.: Blackheath

See Also - GREGORY, R.R.C.: Lee

NUTTING, Anthony: Gravesend

O

OAKELEY, Edward Murray: Dover

OAKLEY, K.P.: Gravesend

OAKWOOD HOSPITAL: Maidstone

O'BEIRNE, T.P.: Chislehurst

OBSERVATIONS ON THE CIRCUMSTANCES...DEATH OF FISHER,
BISHOP OF ROCHESTER: Rochester Cathedral

O'COIGLY, James. Defendant - See Trial of James O'Coigly:
Maidstone, Trials

O'CONNOR, Arthur: Maidstone, Trials
See Also - Trial of James O'Coigly: Maidstone, Trials

O'CONNOR, Charles Patrick: Gravesend

O'CONNOR, H.E.: Kent

"OCTOGENARIAN", pseud.: Staplehurst

"THE ODD FARMWIFE", pseud.: Kynaston

OFFICE OF POPULATION, CENSUSES AND SURVEYS: Census

OFFICIAL ARCHITECTURE AND PLANNING: Canterbury

OFFORD, A.G.: Bromley

OGILBY, John: Roads

O'GORMAN, Richard A.: Rochester Cathedral

OLBY, G.C.: Tonbridge

OLD BARN ORCHESTRAL SOCIETY: Maidstone

OLDCASTLE, Geoffrey: Canterbury

"OLD FOLKESTONER", pseud.: Folkestone, Smuggling

OLD HUMPHREY'S COUNTRY STROLLS: Kent, South East

"AN OLD INHABITANT", pseud.: Canterbury

OLD MAIDSTONIAN SOCIETY: Maidstone

OLSON, Clair Colby - See CROW, Martin Michael: Chaucer, Geoffrey

OMAN, Carola: Dover

OMAN, Charles: History and Archaeology

OMNIBUS SOCIETY: Medway Towns, Road Transport

O'NEIL, Bryan Hugh St. John - See Public Building and Works,
Ministry of: Deal, Walmer

O'NEILL, Sibyl: Canterbury, Harbledown, Isle-of-Thanet

ORAM, E. - See THOMAS, Edward: Canterbury

ORCZY, Baroness Emuska: Bearsted

ORD FAMILY - See Copy of the Inscription...: Bexley, Genealogical
Records, Monumental Inscriptions

ORD, Hubert William: Blackheath, Greenwich

ORDER OF ST. JOHN OF JERUSALEM - COUNCIL FOR KENT: Organisations

ORDISH, George: Ashwell

ORDNANCE, BOARD OF: Brompton, Chatham, Chatham Dockyard; Medway,
River, Sheerness

ORDNANCE SURVEY: Bromley, Hollingbourne, Kent, Longfield,
Northfleet

ORFORD, V.W.: Railways

ORGER, E.R.: Canterbury

O'RHYME, Roderick, pseud.: Kent Authors and Literature

ORIGINAL AND WHIMSICAL POETICAL FANCIES...: Canterbury

ORIGINAL KENTISH APPENDIX: Kent, Maidstone

ORME, William C.: Frindsbury

O'RORKE, L.E.: Crystal Palace

ORPINGTON DEANERY SYNOD: Churches

ORPINGTON PUBLIC LIBRARIES: Orpington

ORPINGTON RURAL DEANERY: Churches

ORPINGTON URBAN DISTRICT COUNCIL: Orpington

ORPINGTON WORKERS' EDUCATION ASSOCIATION:
Orpington

ORR, WILLIAM S. AND CO. Publishers: Chatham,
Cobham, Eltham, Erith, Gravesend, Greenhythe,
Greenwich, Kent, North West; Medway, River;
Rochester, Thames, River; Woolwich

ORRIDGE, B. Brogden: History and Archaeology

ORTON, Harold: Dialects

ORWELL, George: Agriculture

ORWIN, C.S.: Wye

OSBORNE, E. Allen: Dickens, Charles

OSBORNE, R.C.: Margate, Ramsgate

OSBORNE, Thomas. 1st Duke of Leeds: Leeds

OSMAN, C.W.: Folkestone

OSTEOPATHIC INSTITUTE OF APPLIED TECHNIQUE: Maidstone

O'SULLIVAN, Maureen: Orpington, St. Mary Cray

OSWALD, Allan: Chilham

OSWALD, Arthur: Architecture, Cinque Ports

OSWALD, Sidney - See CHARLTON, L.E.O.: Kent
Authors and Literature

OTFORD AND DISTRICT HISTORICAL SOCIETY: Otford

OTFORD PARISH COUNCIL: Otford

OUGHTON, Frederick: Canterbury

OUGHTON, W.C.: Isle-of-Thanet, Margate

OUR IRON ROADS: Railways

OUR OUTING - WHERE SHALL WE GO?: Kent

"OUT PATIENT", pseud.: Canterbury

OUTLINE, Oliver: Canterbury

OVENDEN, Ernest H.: Kent, Military and Naval
History

OVERS, John: Dickens, Charles

OVEY, Cameron Darrell - See Royal Anthropological
Institute - Swanscombe Committee: Swanscombe

OWEN, Denis - See BURTON, John Frederick: Natural
History

OWEN, D.M.: Canterbury Cathedral, Archbishops

OWEN, D.P.: Natural History

OWEN, H.G.: Geology

OWEN, J.A.: Kent, North West
See Also - "SON OF THE MARSHES", pseud.: Kent, North
Kent Authors and Literature, Milton Regis

OWEN, Mrs. Julia: Bromley

OWEN, Walter Tallant: Canterbury Cathedral

OWENS, W.H.: Roads

O'WERT, John: Coastal Defences, Military and Naval
History

OXENDEN, Ashton: Pluckley

OXENDEN, Sir Henry: Barham

OXINDEN PORTRAITS...: Canterbury

OYLER, Thomas H.: Churches, East Sutton, Headcorn,
Lydd, Monumental Inscriptions

P

PACKE, Christopher: Kent, East; Margate

PADDON, J.B.: Windmills and Watermills

PADGET, Frank W.: Margate

PAGE, David: Margate

PAGE, Hugh E.: Kent

PAGE, Sir Thomas Hyde: Dover

PAGE, William: History and Archaeology, Kent

PAGET, C.G.: Penge

PAIN, E.C.: Deal, Ships and Shipping, World War II

PAIN, Harold W.: Deal

PAIN, Nesta: Canterbury Cathedral, Archbishops

PAIN, T.F. Publisher: Deal

PAINE, Norman: Dartford

PAINE, Robert: Kent Authors and Literature

PAINE, William James: Biggin Hill

PAINE, W.S. Publisher: Hythe, Saltwood

PAINTER, Kenneth S.: Canterbury

PAKENHAM-WALSH, R.P. - See History of the Corps of Royal
Engineers: Military and Naval History

PALMER, C.F.R.: Dartford

PALMER, George Henry: Rochester Cathedral

PALMER, Harold: West Wickham

PALMER, Henry R.: Coastline

PALMER, James L.: Canterbury

PALMER, P.G.: Pilgrims Way

PALMER, Sutton - See GARDNER, W. Biscombe: Kent

PALMER, William Stern: Rochester

PANTILES ASSOCIATION: Tunbridge Wells

PANTILES PAPERS: Tunbridge Wells

THE PANTILES LODGE, NO. 2200: Tunbridge Wells

PAPILLON, A.F.W.: Dover

THE PARALLEL...: History and Archaeology

PARFITT, A.C.: Maidstone

PARISH, William Douglas: Dialects

THE PARISH CHURCH OF ST. PETER...: Broadstairs

PARKER, E.N.: Chislehurst

PARKER, Hubert H.: Agriculture

PARKER, John R.A.: Isle-of-Thanet

PARKER, K. Bewsher: Canterbury Cathedral

PARKER, Louis N.: Dover

PARKER, Matthew: Canterbury Cathedral

PARKER, Michael St. John: Canterbury

PARKER, Richard: Kent, St. Nicholas-at-Wade

PARKER, Richard. Defendant: Military and Naval History

PARKER, W.: Rochester Cathedral

PARKER GALLERY: Dover

PARKES, Mrs. Hadden: Romney Marsh

PARKES, James: Broomhill

PARKES, M.B.: Canterbury Cathedral, Orpington

PARKIN, E.W.: Eastwell, Elham

PARKINSON, James: Dover, Folkestone

PARKS, W.A.: Folkestone

PARKYN, Walter A.: Margate

PARLIAMENT - BILLS: Medway, River; Sheerness, Thames,
River

PARLIAMENTARY PAPERS, 1837-38: Folkestone

PARMENTER, John: Kent Authors and Literature

PARNALL, D.L.: Forestry, Natural History

PARR, H.: Pilgrims Way

PARRETT, W.J. LTD. Publishers: Sittingbourne

PARRINDER, Eric Reginald - See FITTER, Richard
Sidney Richmond: Kent, Natural History

PARRY, David: Ramsgate

PARRY, Edward: Greenwich

PARRY, Judge Edward Abbott - See BAILEY v HOPPERTON
AND OTHERS: Wrotham

PARSONS, Charles, OF DOVER: Dover

PARSONS, F.A.: Folkestone

PARSONS, F.J. Publisher: Hythe

PARSONS, James: Isle-of-Sheppey

PARSONS, Philip: Churches

PARSONS, Richard Arthur Felix: Lyminge, Milton Regis

PASCOE, A.P.: Wrotham

PASCOE, Charles Eyre: Dickens, Charles; Folkestone

PASKE, Dr.: Canterbury Cathedral

PASKE, C.T.: Dover

PASKE-SMITH, M.: Gillingham

PASTORAL ADDRESS...: Rochester

PATCH, Rev. John D.H.: Canterbury Cathedral,
Archbishops

PATER, Walter: Kent Authors and Literature

PATERSON, Daniel: Roads

PATERSON, J.D.: Dover

"PATHFINDER", pseud.: Bromley, Footpaths and Commons

PATTENDEN, Ann: Agriculture

PATTENDEN, T., OF DOVER: Kent Authors and Literature

PATULLO HIGGS AND CO. LTD.: Hayes and Keston,
Orpington

PAUL, Leslie: Biography, Eltham

PAUL, Sydney F.: Religious Denominations

"PAUL PRY", pseud. - See SEYMOUR, Robert: Margate

PAYNE, Augustus: Shoreham

PAYNE, Edward F.: Dickens, Charles

PAYNE, George: Boxted, Burham, Darenth, History and
Archaeology, Kent, North West; Maidstone, Milton
Regis, Newington-next-Sittingbourne, Oldbury,
Sittingbourne, Strood

PAYNE, J. Lewin: Hoath, Reculver

PAYNE, Nicholas, OF DOVER: Dover

PAYNE, Orlebar D. Bruce: Sandwich

PAYTON, George: Edenbridge

PEACE, J.W.G.: Lewisham

PEACHELL, J.W.: Gillingham

PEACOCK, Carlos: Shoreham

PEAKE, W. Brian: Aylesford, Greenhithe, Luddesdown

PEAL, A.: Sevenoaks

PEARCE, Rev. E.H.: Canterbury

PEARCE, Luke: Pembury, Tunbridge Wells

PEARCE, Zachary. Bishop of Rochester: Rochester Cathedral

PEARE, Catherine Owens: Dickens, Charles

PEARL, A.: Wouldham

PEARMAN, A.I.: Religious Denominations

PEARMAN, Augustus John: Ashford, Bethersden, Rainham, Religious Denominations

PEARMAN, Henry: Kent, North East; Kent, North West

PEARMAN, R.G.: Cudham

PEARS, Charles: Coastal Waters

PEARSON, G. - See GROSS, John: Dickens, Charles

PEARSON, Hesketh: Dickens, Charles

PECK, F.: Coastal Defences, Dover

"A PEDESTRIAN", pseud.: Kent, North West

PEDIGREE OF HARLAKENDEN...: Genealogical Records

PEDRICK, Gale: Heraldry

PEEBLES, Ian: Cricket

PEENE, W.G.: Maidstone

PEERS, Bryant: Kent

PEGGE, Samuel: Coins and Tokens, Dialects, History and Archaeology, Isle-of-Thanet

PEILE, Diana: Bromley

PELLEW, Rev. George: Canterbury Cathedral

PELTON, Aubrey John. Publisher: Tunbridge Wells

PELTON, Richard: Tunbridge Wells

PEMBERTON, J.E.: Kent Authors and Literature

PEMBERTON, T. Edgar: Dickens, Charles

PEMBLE, Henry: Sandwich

PENGE PUBLIC LIBRARY COMMISSIONERS: Public Services

PENGE URBAN DISTRICT COUNCIL: Penge

PENN, William S.: Springhead

PENNANT, Thomas: Kent

PENNELL, Elizabeth Robins: Canterbury

PENNELL, Joseph: Pilgrims Way

PENNEY, Stephen: Thames, River

PENNINGTON, Montagu: Deal, Kent Authors and Literature
See Also - CARTER, Mrs. Elizabeth: Deal

PENNY, W. Publisher: Gravesend

PENNY MAGAZINE: Canterbury

PENNY SUNDAY READER: Canterbury

PENSHURST PARISH COUNCIL: Penshurst

PENTREATH, Arthur Godolphin Guy Carleton: Rochester Cathedral

PEQUIGNOT, C.A.: Channel Tunnel

PERCIVAL, Arthur: Faversham, Industry and Trade

PERCY, Edward: Canterbury, Kent Authors and Literature

PERCY-SMITH, H.T. - See BLOMFIELD, Kathleen: Genealogical Records

PERKINS, E.J. - See United Kingdom Atomic Energy Authority: Whitstable

PERKINS, Frederick: Chipstead

PERKINS, J.B. Ward: Crayford, Oldbury

PERKINS, Rev. Malcolm B.: Chalk

PERKINS, W. Turner: Channel Tunnel, Railways

PERKINS AND SON. Publishers: Greenwich

PERKS, R.H.: Faversham, Ships and Shipping

PERRAULT, Charles: Canterbury

PERRONET, Edward: Canterbury

PERRY, John: Dover

PERRY, John Tavenor: Dover, Plaxtol

PERTWEE, Guy: Dickens, Charles

PETERS, George Hertel: Lewisham

PETERSON, Alexander Duncan Campbell: Kent Authors and Literature

PETHAM FRIENDLY SOCIETY: Petham

PETITION OF THE GENTRY, MINISTERS AND COMMONALTY OF THE COUNTY OF KENT: History and Archaeology

PETLEY, J.L. Ward: Penshurst

PETTIT, W.J., OF DOVER: Dover

PETTMAN, William Robert: Agriculture, Sandwich

PETTY, Ronald: Sellindge

PEVERLEY, J.R.: Dover

PEVSNER, Nikolaus: Crystal Palace

PEYRSE, Henry: Genealogical Records

PEYTON, H.N.: Charities

"PHILALETHES", pseud.: Rochester Cathedral

PHILIP, Alexander John: Dickens, Charles; Gravesend, Hoo, Kent, North West

PHILIPOT, John: Cinque Ports, Dover

PHILIPOTT, John: Genealogical Records

PHILIPOTT, Thomas: History and Archaeology

PHILLIMORE AND CO. LTD. Publishers: Genealogical Records

PHILLIMORE, William P.W.: Genealogical Records

PHILLIPPS, Sir Thomas: Chilham

PHILLIPS, Charles J.: Architecture, Bradbourne, History and Archaeology, Knole, Sevenoaks

PHILLIPS, Charles Stanley: Canterbury Cathedral

PHILLIPS, Frederick Wallace: Faversham

PHILLIPS, G.A.: Kent

PHILLIPS, Geoffrey Brownfield: Maidstone

PHILLIPS, Rev. H.F.: Rochester

PHILLIPS, James: Gravesend

PHILLIPS, Margaret J.: Gravesend

PHILLIPS, Margaret R.: History and Archaeology

PHILLIPS, Samuel: Crystal Palace

PHILLIPS, William: Dover, Geology

PHILOMATH, James Almond: Chatham

PHILP, Brian J.: Faversham, Reculver

PHILP, Robert Kemp: Railways

PHILPOTT, D.R.E.: Dover

PHIPPEN, James: Deal, Medway Towns, Roads, Rochester, Sandwich, Tunbridge Wells
See Also - COLBRAN, John. Publisher: Tunbridge Wells

PHIPPS, Sir Constantine: Rochester Cathedral

PHOTOGRAPHIC ALLIANCE: Canterbury

"PHOTOGRAPHY": Kent

THE PHOTOMINIATURE, VOL. 1, No. 7: Bromley

PICCADILLY FOUNTAIN PRESS: Dickens, Charles

PICKERING, P. - See WHEATLEY, Sydney William: Rochester

PICKERING, R.: Gravesend

PICKETT, W.: Margate

PICKFORD, Clifford: Westerham

PICTORIAL AND DESCRIPTIVE GUIDE TO HERNE BAY...: Kent, East

A PICTORIAL AND DESCRIPTIVE GUIDE TO MARGATE...: Kent, East

PICTORIAL GUIDE TO MARGATE AMUSEMENTS: Margate, Ramsgate

PICTURESQUE BEAUTIES OF GREAT BRITAIN...: Kent

THE PICTURESQUE POCKET COMPANION TO MARGATE...: Isle-of-Thanet

PIERCE, Gilbert A.: Dickens, Charles

PIGGOTT, Stuart: Chislehurst

PIKE, Elsie: Sevenoaks

PIKE, Leslie Elgar: Edenbridge, Minster-in-Thanet, Otford

PIKE, W.T. AND CO. LTD. Publishers: Biography, Kent, East
See Also - BAVINGTON-JONES, T.: Biography

PILBROW, James: Canterbury

PILCHER, Donald E.: Tunbridge Wells

PILCHER, Dorothy: Kent

PILCHER, H.: Kent Authors and Literature

PILCHER, James William: Elections

PILCHER, William H.: Kent Authors and Literature

PILE, Cecil Charles R.: Cranbrook
See Also - Cranbrook and Sissinghurst Local History Society: Cranbrook, Sissinghurst, Windmills and Watermills

PILKINGTON, Mrs. Mary: Margate

PILOT'S GUIDE...: Thames, River

PINHORN, Malcolm: Bridge

PINN, W.: Chatham

PINNOCK, K.A.T.: Canterbury Cathedral

PINNOCK, Kenneth: Canterbury

PINNOCK, William: History and Archaeology

PINTO, H.: Industry and Trade, Tunbridge Wells

PIPER, John: Romney Marsh

PITCHER, Wallace Spencer: Kent, North West

PITT, Barrie: Dover

PITT, William (1759-1806): Hayes and Keston, Pitt, William

PITT-RIVERS, Augustus H.L.F.: Folkestone

PITTOCK, G.M.: Isle-of-Thanet, Natural History

PITTS, Hubert A.: Hythe, Kent, South East; Religious Denominations

PLANCHE, J.R.: Ash-next-Sandwich

PLANT PROTECTION LTD.: Agriculture

PLATT, Bryan: Agriculture

PLATT, J. Printer: Crystal Palace

PLATTS, W.L.: History and Archaeology

PLAXTOL WOMEN'S INSTITUTE: Plaxtol

PLAYBOYS: Military and Naval History

PLEYDELL-BOUVERIE, Helen: Folkestone

PLOMER, Henry Robert: Canterbury, Canterbury Cathedral, Genealogical Records, History and Archaeology, Kent Authors and Literature, Tenterden
See Also - Kent Archaeological Society - Records Branch: Strood

PLOWMAN, Allan W.: Canterbury

PLUMPTRE, H.W.: Kent

PLUMTRE, F.C.: Dover

PLUNKETT, G.T.: Dover

"POCOCK": Gravesend, Thames, River

POCOCK, D.C.D.: Agriculture

POCOCK, Robert. Printer: Biography, Denton, Gravesend, Margate, Milton-next-Gravesend, Natural History
See Also - Memoirs of the Families of Sir Edward Knatchbull...: Biography

POINTER, A.H. Publisher: Dover

POIRIER, Michel: Marlowe, Christopher

POLAK, H.S.L.: Kent Authors and Literature

POLAND, John: Greenwich

POLKINGHORNE, B.E. - See GRINLING, C.H.: Tunbridge Wells

POLLAND, W.C.: History and Archaeology

POLLARD, Arthur O.: Gravesend, Ships and Shipping, Thames, River

POLLEN, John Hungerford: Canterbury Cathedral

PONSONBY, Charles: Military and Naval History

POOLE, S.L.: Road Transport

POOLMAN, Kenneth: Borstal

POPE, Sydney: Canterbury, Organisations

POPE, Thomas Tolbutt: Elections

POPE, W.L.: Tunbridge Wells

POPE-HENNESSY, Una: Dickens, Charles

PORT OF LONDON AUTHORITY: Thames, River

PORT OF LONDON SANITARY AUTHORITY: Kent, North West

PORTEOUS, G.H.: Dartford

PORTER, Mrs. Adrian: Rochester

PORTER, Samuel: Military and Naval History

PORTER, Whitworth - See History of the Corps of Royal Engineers:
    Military and Naval History

THE PORTFOLIO, OR LITERARY SELECTOR: Kent Authors and
    Literature

POST, Thomas: Kent Authors and Literature

POSTE, Beale: Deal, History and Archaeology, Maidstone

POTTER, John: Sheerness

POTTER, Neil: Kent Authors and Literature

POTTER, W.F.: Lee, Lewisham

POTTS, R.V.: Canterbury

POULTER, Molly - See Kent Pre-School Play Groups Association:
    Education

POWEL, Sir Nathaniel: Kent

POWELL, A.H.: Canterbury

POWELL, F.R.: History and Archaeology

POWELL, H.T.: Kent Authors and Literature

POWELL, J.R.: History and Archaeology

POWELL, L.H.: Bromley

POWELL, R.C.: Folkestone

POWELL, Robert Hutchinson: Tunbridge Wells

POWELL-COTTON MUSEUM: Birchington

POWICKE, F.M.: Canterbury Cathedral, Archbishops

A PRACTICAL GUIDE TO THE WATERING AND SEA-BATHING PLACES...:
    Coastline

PRANGNELL, Dunstan: Canterbury, Isle-of-Thanet, Legal Customs

PRATT, Anne, OF DOVER: Kent Authors and Literature

PRATT, H.M.: Dartford, Natural History

PRENDERGAST, James: Kent Authors and Literature

PRENTICE. Publisher: Canterbury

PRENTIS, W.: Natural History, Rainham

PRESCOTT-WESTCAR, V.: Kent Authors and Literature

PRESENTMENT OF THE GRAND JURY...1682: Maidstone

PRESNAIL, James: Chatham, Medway Towns, Rochester

PRESTON, Hayter: Windmills and Watermills

PRESTWICH, Joseph: Canterbury, Channel Tunnel, Darent, River;
    Geology, History and Archaeology, Ightham, Kent, Mid;
    Kent, North West

PRICE, Bernard: Wilmington

PRICE, Daniel: Agriculture, Romney Marsh

PRICE, F.G. Hilton: Folkestone, Geology

PRICE, Martin - See LEBON, Cicely: Benenden

PRIDDEN, John: Isle-of-Thanet

PRIEST, Simeon: Bostall Heath, Cobham, Crockenheath,
    Dartford, Greenhithe, Plumstead, Stone (Nr.
    Dartford), Strood
See Also - BAKER, Herbert Arthur: East Wickham
          BROOK, Cyril A.: Dartford
          BROWN, E.E.S.: Swanscombe
          EPPS, F.J.: Abbey Wood

PRIESTFIELD PRESS: Gillingham

PRIESTLEY, John Boynton: Dickens, Charles

PRINCE, Hugh - See COPPOCK, J.T.: Kent, North West

PRINGLE, J.: Geology

PRINGLE, M.L. Kellmer: Education

PRITCHARD, H.L.: Military and Naval History

PRITCHARD, Stephen: Deal

PROBY, Mrs. Charles J.: Dent de Lion

PROCEEDINGS OF THE CLAIM OF MR. LEDGER...: Dover

PROCTOR, Richard A.: Dickens, Charles

PROFESSIONAL EXCURSIONS BY AN AUCTIONEER: Kent

"PROFESSOR PROTEUS", pseud.: Chatham

PROSSER, Arthur: Medway, River

"PROTESTANT LAYMAN", pseud.: History and Archaeology

PROTESTANT REFORMATION SOCIETY: Pembury

PROTHERO, Rowland E.: Canterbury Cathedral

PROUDFOOT, W.F.: Fawkham

PROVIDENT INSTITUTION: Canterbury

PROVISION FOR PUBLIC WORSHIP IN THE COUNTY OF KENT:
    Religious Denominations

PROVISIONAL PROPOSALS FOR A MEASURE OF POOR LAW
REFORM...: Canterbury

PRYCE, Edward Smith: Gravesend

PRYCE, H. AND SON. Publishers: Woolwich

PUBLIC BUILDINGS AND WORKS, MINISTRY OF: Deal,
    Dover, Richborough, Walmer

PUBLIC CHARACTERS OF 1805: Biography

PUBLIC RECORD OFFICE: History and Archaeology,
    Margate

PUBLIC SERVICE VEHICLE CIRCLE: Road Transport

PUCKLE, John: Canterbury, Dover, Kent Authors and
    Literature, Queenborough

PUGH, Christine: Stockbury

PUGH, Edwin: Dickens, Charles

PULLE, John: Canterbury

PUMPHREY, George Henry: Kent

PUNTON-SMITH, S.P.: Dover

PURCELL, William Ernest: Canterbury Cathedral,
    Archbishops

PURDIE, A.B.: Canterbury

PURDY, John: Coastal Waters, Medway, River; Thames,
    River

PUREY-CUST, Arthur Percival: Cobham

PURFIELD, N.K.: Canterbury Cathedral, Religious
    Denominations

R Cont'd

REDIFFUSION TELEVISION LTD.: Canterbury

REDMAN, J.B.: Sandown

REDSHAW, Charles J.: Dartford, Kent

REDWOOD, William Arthur Hugh: Orpington

REED, ALBERT E. AND CO. LTD.: Aylesford, Gravesend,
    Industry and Trade

REED, H.F.: Industry and Trade

REED, Margaret S.E.: Tunbridge Wells

REED PAPER GROUP: Aylesford, Gravesend, Industry and Trade

REES, Henry: Medway Towns

REEVE, James - See Benefits of Christian Education:
    Maidstone

REEVE, Robert Belby: Margate

REEVE, W. Booth: Margate

REEVES, J.W.: Weald

REEVES, Sim: Woolwich

REFLECTIONS ON A PAPER...: Rochester

REGAL PUBLICITY SERVICE LTD.: Canterbury

REGIS, B.: Adisham, Staple

REGISTRAR OF DEATHS: Genealogical Records

REID, D.A.G.: Bickley, Cricket

REID, Ian G.: Agriculture

REID, Kenneth C.: Loose, Windmills and Watermills

REID, Percy G.: Westerham

REID-HAMILTON. Publishers: Military and Naval History

REINHARDT, E.A.: Chislehurst

THE RELIGION OF A LAWYER, A CRAZY TALE...: Brookland

REMARKS ON THE CONVEYANCE OF MAIL...: Postal History

REMARKS ON THE INCIDENTAL AMBIGUITIES...: Canterbury

"REMINISCOR", pseud.: Whitstable

A REMONSTRANCE...: History and Archaeology

RENDEL, James M.: Margate

RENDEL, Leila: Mersham

RENN, Derek Frank: Dover, Rochester

RENNELL: Deal

RENSSELAER, M.G. Van: Canterbury Cathedral

REPORT FROM THE COMMITTEE OF PRIVILEGES...: Gravesend

REPORT ON THE PROPOSED DIVISION OF THE COUNTY OF KENT, 1831:
    Elections

REPORT OF THE TRIALS, AUGUST 28th, 1817: Sandwich

REPORTS OF THE TRIALS OF THE BOYS v EDMUNDS, 1815-1817:
    Maidstone, Trials

RETURN OF OWNERS OF LAND - See Domesday Book for the County of
Kent: Census

"THE REVIEW": Canterbury

REVY, Julian John - See BATEMAN, John Frederick: Channel
    Tunnel

REX v JAMES MONTAGUE: Isle-of-Grain, Trials

REX v JOHN MARTEN: Poor Law, Trials, Wrotham

REYNOLDS, CHARLES AND CO. Publishers - See CHARLES
REYNOLDS AND CO. Publishers: Tunbridge Wells

REYNOLDS, Donald Hugh Baillie: Kent, South East;
    Dour, River

REYNOLDS, Ernest Edwin: Eltham, Rochester Cathedra

REYNOLDS, George W.M.: Dickens, Charles

REYNOLDS, Thomas: Bromley

RHIND, Neil: Blackheath

RHOADES, James: Dover

RHODES, Alfred: Crayford, Deptford

RHODES, S.: Tunbridge Wells

RHODES: Canterbury

RICE, John: Ashford

RICE, William McPherson: Rother, River

RICHARD WATTS' CHARITY: Rochester

RICHARDS, F.: Sevenoaks

RICHARDS, Frederick J.: Boxley

RICHARDSON, Anthony: World War II

RICHARDSON, Christopher Thomas: Ramsgate

RICHARDSON, Henry S.: Greenwich

RICHARDSON, Jessie Winifred Packham: Woodchurch

RICHARDSON, K.M. - See COTTON, M.A.: Stone (Nr.
    Dartford)

RICHARDSON, M.: Greenhithe

RICHARDSON, Olive: Canterbury

RICHMOND, Ian: History and Archaeology

RICHMOND, Paul E.: Milton Regis

"THE RICKBURNERS": Agriculture

RIDEAL, Charles F.: Dickens, Charles

RIDGE, C. Harold: Genealogical Records

RIDGEWAY, W.: Canterbury

RIDGWAY, A. Publisher: Gravesend

RIDLER, Anne: Downe

RIDLEY, Jasper: Canterbury Cathedral, Archbishops

RIDOUT. Publisher: Herne Bay

RIDSEL, W.: Religious Denominations

RIDSPACE, Charles Joseph: Folkestone

RIGDEN, Brian: Canterbury

RIGDEN, George: Canterbury

RIGDEN, T. Publisher: Dover, Folkestone, Natural
    History
See Also - BATCHELLER, W.: Dover

RIGG, J.M.: Canterbury

RIGG, Ronald E. - See Rochester Historical Pageant
Committee: Rochester

RIGOLD, S.E.: Architecture, Aylesford, Dover,
    Eynsford, Ospringe, Sandwich
See Also - Public Building and Works, Ministry of:
    Strood

RILEY, Peter: Canterbury

RONALDSHAY, Earl of: Walmer

ROOKER, John: Sevenoaks

ROOKWOOD, C.M.: Buckland, Kent Authors and Literature

ROPER, Anne: Brookland, Burmarsh, Inns, Ivychurch, Lydd,
Newenden, Old Romney, Romney Marsh
See Also - Romney Marsh Rural District Council: Romney Marsh

ROPER, F.M. Hodgess: Southfleet

ROSE, Sir Alec: Kent Authors and Literature

ROSE, George: Northfleet

ROSE, J. Holland: Coastal Defences

ROSENFELD, Sybil Marion: Canterbury, Theatre

ROSEVEARE, Helen: Bromley

ROSHERVILLE GARDENS CO. LTD.: Northfleet

ROSS, Charles H.: Margate, Ramsgate
See Also - CORNWALLIS, Charles. 1st Marquess: Biography

ROTARY CLUBS: Gravesend, Margate

ROTH, Cecil: Canterbury

ROUGH COMMON WOMEN'S INSTITUTE: Rough Common

ROUGH, Daniel: New Romney

ROUSE, Edward Clive: Kent

ROUSE, Lewis: Tunbridge Wells

ROUTLEDGE, Charles Francis: Canterbury, Canterbury Cathedral,
Canterbury Cathedral, Archbishops
See Also - FIELD, Thomas: Canterbury Cathedral

ROUTLEDGE, GEORGE AND CO. Publishers: Crystal Palace

ROUTLEDGE, J.M.: Canterbury Cathedral, Archbishops

ROW, B. Prescott: Kent, North West; Maidstone
See Also - MARTIN, W. Stanley: Tonbridge, Tunbridge Wells

ROW, John: Blackheath

ROWE, Mrs.: Medway Towns

ROWE, Arthur Walton: Coastline
See Also - MERCER, William John: Margate

ROWE, John Tetley: Chatham

ROWE, William: Margate

ROWLAND, J.: Broadstairs

ROWLES, Walter: Kent, Maidstone

ROWSE, Jane - See General Valuation...: Isle-of-Thanet

ROWSELL, T. Norman: Canterbury

ROWZEE, Lodwick: Tunbridge Wells

ROYAL AIR FORCE, BIGGIN HILL: Biggin Hill, Military and Naval
History

ROYAL ANTHROPOLOGICAL INSTITUTE: Swanscombe

ROYAL ARCHAEOLOGICAL INSTITUTE OF GREAT BRITAIN AND IRELAND:
Canterbury, Dartford, Rochester Cathedral

ROYAL AUTOMOBILE CLUB: Canterbury, Kent, South East; Kent,
South West

ROYAL BRITISH LEGION: Organisations

ROYAL COLLEGE OF SURGEONS OF ENGLAND: Darwin, Charles

ROYAL COMMISSION ON AGRICULTURE: Agriculture

ROYAL COMMISSION ON HISTORICAL MANUSCRIPTS: Canterbury
Knole, Penshurst
See Also - Historical Manuscripts Commission:
Knole, Penshurst

ROYAL CORINTHIAN YACHT CLUB: Port Victoria

ROYAL EAST KENT REGIMENT (THE BUFFS): Canterbury
Cathedral

ROYAL INSTITUTE OF BRITISH ARCHITECTS: Canterbury,
Folkestone

ROYAL INSTITUTE OF PUBLIC HEALTH: Folkestone, Hythe,
Sandgate

ROYAL LIFE SAVING SOCIETY - KENT BRANCH:
Organisations

ROYAL MILITARY ACADEMY, WOOLWICH: Woolwich

ROYAL NATIONAL HOSPITAL: Margate

ROYAL NATIONAL LIFEBOAT INSTITUTION: Margate

ROYAL NAVAL BENEVOLENT TRUST: Chatham, Gillingham

ROYAL NAVAL VOLUNTEER RESERVE: Dover, Military and
Naval History

ROYAL SCHOOL FOR DEAF AND DUMB CHILDREN: Margate

ROYAL SEA BATHING HOSPITAL: Margate

ROYAL SOCIETY FOR THE PREVENTION OF CRUELTY TO
ANIMALS: Chatham, Kent, East; Kent, Mid;
Organisations

ROYAL SOCIETY OF LONDON: Darwin, Charles

ROYAL UNITED SERVICE INSTITUTION: Channel Tunnel

ROYAL VICTORIA HOSPITAL: Dover

THE ROYALIST AND THE REPUBLICAN: History and
Archaeology

RUCK, Walter: Maidstone

RUDD, Lewis C.: Dover

RUDE, G. - See HOBSBAWM, E.J.: History and Archaeology

RUDGE, Charles: Sevenoaks

RUDKIN, Mabel S.: Dover

RUEGG, R.: Woolwich

RULE, Martin: Canterbury, Canterbury Cathedral
See Also - EADMER, The Monk: History and
Archaeology

RULES AND ARTICLES OF THE BACHELORS' AND WIDOWS'
SOCIETY: Hunton

RULES FOR ASSIZES: Trials

RUSKIN, John: Coastline

RUSSELL, Sir Edward John - See HALL, Sir Alfred
Daniel: Agriculture

RUSSELL, James: Cinque Ports

RUSSELL, J.M.: Maidstone

RUSSELL, John - See WAILES, Rex: Windmills and
Watermills

RUSSELL, R.O.: Military and Naval History

RUSSELL, Spencer C. - See COOKE, Richard: Detling

RUSSELL, W.C.: History and Archaeology

RUSSELL, Wilfred: Maidstone

RUSSELL, RUSSEL AND WILLMOTT: Agriculture

"RUSTICUS", pseud. - See HUNTER: Canterbury

RUTT, F.: Folkestone, Natural History

RUTTON, W.L.: Sandgate

RUXTON, Matthias, OF BOUGHTON MONCHELSEA - See HAMMON, George: Biddenden

RYE, Alan: Kent, North West

RYE, William Brenchley: Medway Towns

RYE MUSEUM: Cinque Ports

S

S., E.: Canterbury Cathedral

S., F.H.: Gravesend

S., G.: Canterbury Cathedral

S., J.C.: Rainham

SABIN, F.T. (Sale) - See Kent Illustrated: Kent

SABINE, James: Tonbridge

SABINE, William Henry Wald : Genealogical Records

SACKVILLE, Lord George: Knole, Trials

SACKVILLE-WEST, Lionel: Knole

SACKVILLE-WEST, Victoria (Afterwards Lady Nicolson): Agriculture, Kent, Kent Authors and Literature, Knole, Sissinghurst, Wye

SADLER, Elizabeth A.: Chevening

SAGE, Margaret: Kent Authors and Literature

SAINSBURY, Frederick G.: Folkestone

SAINT ANDREW'S COLLEGE: Bexley

ST. AUGUSTINE'S COLLEGE: Canterbury

ST. AUGUSTINE'S GAOL: Canterbury

ST. AUGUSTINE'S MISSIONARY STUDENTSHIP ASSOCIATION: Canterbury

SAINT CLERE MAGAZINE - See WILKINSON, J.J.: Kemsing

ST. EDMUND'S SCHOOL: Canterbury

ST. JAMES' NATIONAL SCHOOL: Gravesend

ST. JOHN'S AMBULANCE BRIGADE: Organisations

ST. JOHN OF JERUSALEM, ORDER OF - COUNCIL FOR KENT: Organisations

ST. JOHN FISHER R.C. COUNTY SECONDARY SCHOOL: Chatham

ST. JOSEPH'S CONVENT SCHOOL: Chatham

ST. MARTIN AND ST. PAUL'S PARISH GUILD: Canterbury

ST. MARY'S COLLEGE: Canterbury

ST. MONSON, Philip: History and Archaeology

ST. PAUL'S ECCLESIOLOGICAL SOCIETY: Churches

ST. STEPHEN'S COMMUNITY ASSOCIATION: Canterbury

SALA, George Augustus: Dickens, Charles

SALISBURY, Edward: New Romney

SALMON, E.S.: Agriculture

SALMON, Joseph. Publisher: Knole, Sevenoaks

SALMON, N.: History and Archaeology

SALOMONS, Sir David Lionel: Kent Authors and Literature, Southborough

SALTER, A.E.: Geology

SALTER, Emma Gurney: Canterbury

SALTER, H.E. - See TURNER, G.J.: Canterbury

SALTMAN, Aurom: Canterbury Cathedral, Archbishops

SALVATION ARMY: Penge, Religious Denominations

SAMPSON, Aylwin: Aldington, Bilsington, Bonnington, Brabourne, Hurst, Stone-in-Oxney

SANCROFT, William. Archbishop of Canterbury, Defendant: Canterbury Cathedral

SANDEMAN, Aernold Eric Noble: Chatham, Military and Naval History

SANDERS, Frederick: Chatham Dockyard, Churches, Dialects, Kent Authors and Literature, Pluckley Weald

SANDERS, Frederick W.T.: Chatham, Ghosts

SANDERS, John: Margate

SANDERS, Robert: History and Archaeology

SANDERSON, Geoffrey F.: Railways

SANDES, E.W.C.: Military and Naval History

SANDFORD, E.G.: Canterbury Cathedral, Archbishops

SANDGATE URBAN DISTRICT COUNCIL v KENT COUNTY COUNCIL: Sandgate

SANDWICH BOROUGH COUNCIL AND CHAMBER OF COMMERCE: Sandwich

SANDYS, Charles: Canterbury, Canterbury Cathedral, Gavelkind

SANGER, "Lord" George: Margate

SANGSTER, Alfred: Isle-of-Thanet

SANKEY, Marjorie: Postal History

SANTER, J.R.:. Bromley

SARGENT, Miles: Agriculture

SARRE, A.C.: Sarre

SASSOON, Sir Philip: Lympne

SASSOON, Siegfried: Biography, Kent Authors and Literature

SATURDAY MAGAZINE, 1834: Canals, Chatham Dockyard, Cinque Ports, Dover, Reculver

SAUNDERS. Publisher: Tunbridge Wells

SAUNDERS, A.D. - See Public Buildings and Works, Ministry of: Deal, Upnor, Walmer

SAUNDERS, H.W.: Education, History and Archaeology

SAUNDERS, Montagu: Dickens, Charles

SAUNDERS, Sibert: Whitstable

SAVIDGE, Alan: Tunbridge Wells

SAVILL, Raymond Arthur: Railways

SAVOIE-CARIGNAN, C.E. de. Count de Soissons: Chislehurst

SAVONIUS, Moira - See NEWMAN, Leonard Hugh: Natural History, Westerham

SAVORY, H.J.: Kent

SAWYER, Charles J.: Dickens, Charles

SAWYER, Minnie: Isle-of-Thanet

SAWYER, Peter: History and Archaeology

SAYERS, Dorothy Leigh: Canterbury Cathedral

SIDNEY, Robert. 1st Earl of Leicester: Penshurst

SIDNEY, William Philip. 1st Viscount de L'Isle: Penshurst

SIDNEY COOPER SCHOOL OF SCIENCE AND ART: Canterbury

SIMMONS, V. - See DENNE, James: Margate

SIMMONS, W.T. Publisher: Cranbrook, Weald

SIMMS, F.W.: Railways

SIMON LANGTON HIGH SCHOOL FOR GIRLS: Canterbury

SIMONS, Eric Norman: History and Archaeology

SIMPICH, Frederick: Thames, River

SIMPKINSON, C.H.: Canterbury Cathedral, Archbishops

SIMPSON. Publisher: Folkestone

SIMPSON, Dorothy: Dartford

SIMPSON, E.M.: Kent Authors and Literature

SIMPSON, James B.: Canterbury Cathedral, Archbishops

SIMPSON, Janet: Bromley

SIMPSON, Joseph: Gravesend

SIMPSON, Samuel: History and Archaeology

SIMPSON, W.D.: Tonbridge

SIMPSON, W. Sparrow: Canterbury Cathedral, Archbishops

SIMPSON, Woolley (Also Known as George ROBIN): Kent

SIMS, Victor: Churchill, Winston S.

SIMSON, James: Biography, Isle-of-Thanet

SIMS-WILLIAMS, Michael: Sittingbourne

SINCLAIR, W.B.: Blackheath

SINDALL, H.W.: Bromley

SISSON, C.H.: Kent Authors and Literature

SITTINGBOURNE AND DISTRICT CONSUMER GROUP: Sittingbourne

SITTINGBOURNE FRIENDLY SOCIETY: Sittingbourne

SIX SONGS OF KENT: Kent Songs

SKEAT, Walter W.: Dialects, Lewisham

SKELSMERGH HOUSE SCHOOL: Margate

SKERRET, Ralph: Greenwich

A SKETCH OF THE LIFE OF GEORGE WILSON: Blackheath

SKETCHLEY, Arthur, pseud. (George ROSE): Crystal Palace, Margate

SKINNER, F.: Kent Authors and Literature

SKINNER, Frederick A.: Bidborough

SLADDEN, Dilnot: Kent Authors and Literature

SLATER, Ernest: Gravesend

SLATER, Humphrey: Channel Tunnel

SLATER, Michael: Dickens, Charles

SLATTERIE, Joseph: Rochester

SLENDERWIT, Simpkin, pseud.: Ramsgate

SLEVIN, Bernard: Bickley

SLYTHE, Margaret: Saltwood

SMALL, E. Milton: Canterbury, Gillingham, Isle-of-Grain

SMALL, H.J. - See LOUGHBOROUGH, George W.: Canterbury

"SMARDONIAN", pseud.: Genealogical Records

SMART, Christopher: Kent Authors and Literature

SMART, J.G.O. - See Geological Survey and Museum: Geology

SMART, Kenneth John: Sevenoaks

SMEATON, John: Dover, Ramsgate

SMETHAM, Henry: Churches, Kent Authors and Literature, Strood

SMILES, John F.: Ramsgate

SMILES, Oswald D.: Wilmington

SMILES, Samuel: Canterbury, Greenwich

SMITH, Albert W.: Maidstone

SMITH, Alfred Russell: Kent

SMITH, Allen: Thames, River

SMITH, Rev. B.F.: Rusthall

SMITH, Baker Peter: Coastline

SMITH, Basil H.: Rochester

SMITH, C.G.: Newspapers

SMITH, Charles John: Erith

SMITH, Charles Roach: Broadstairs, Canterbury, Davington, Deal, Faversham, History and Archaeology, Kent Authors and Literature, Kent, North West; Lympne, Maidstone, Monumental Inscriptions, Reculver, Richborough, Rochester, Springhead, Stowting, Strood

SMITH, Cicely Fox: Gravesend, Thames, River

SMITH, Danvers McCall: Ash-next-Sandwich

SMITH, Donald: Windmills and Watermills

SMITH, E.: Orpington

SMITH, F.B.: Kent Authors and Literature

SMITH, F. Hopkinson: Dickens, Charles

SMITH, Frederick Francis: Rochester

SMITH, G.: Canterbury Cathedral

SMITH, George: Kent Authors and Literature

SMITH, George Mabberly: Tonbridge

SMITH, G.W.: Bromley

SMITH, George Walter: Agriculture

SMITH, Gerard Edwards: Natural History

SMITH, Gilbert Arthur: Biggin Hill

SMITH, Gill: Biography

SMITH, Herbert L.: Ashford, Dover, Maidstone

SMITH, Horace: Kent Authors and Literature

SMITH, J.: Maidstone

SMITH, J.J.: Cliffe-at-Hoo

SMITH, John L.: Railways

SMITH, John Russell: Bibliography, Kent

SMITH, Logan Pearsall: Biography

SMITH, Percy: Dover

SMITH, R. Allington: Rainham

S Cont'd

SMITH, R.D.: Romney Marsh

SMITH, Reginald Anthony Lendon: Canterbury, Canterbury
Cathedral, Herne Bay, History and Archaeology, Northfleet,
Thames, River

See Also – RIDGEWAY, W.: Canterbury

SMITH, Richard L.: Rochester Cathedral

SMITH, S. Theobald: Kent

SMITH, Sydney W.: Sydenham

SMITH, Thomas: Biography

SMITH, V.T.C.: Gravesend, Milton-next-Gravesend

SMITH, W.: Coastline

SMITH, W.H.: Blackheath

SMITH, W.H. AND SON. Publishers: Dover

SMITH, W. St. John: Dover, Kent

SMITH, William: Tunbridge Wells

SMITH, Sir William Sidney: Biography

SMITHER BROTHERS: Gravesend

SMYTH, Vernon – See OUGHTON, Frederick: Canterbury

SNAITH, Frank William: Farningham

SNAKESKIN INDUSTRY: Industry and Trade

SNELL, F.C.: Rivers

SNELL, F.J.: Canterbury Cathedral, Archbishops; Kent Authors
and Literature

SNELLING, H.: Margate

SNOWDEN. Publishers: Dartford

SOCIETY FOR THE MENTALLY HANDICAPPED: Maidstone

SOCIETY FOR PROMOTING CHRISTIAN KNOWLEDGE: Tunbridge Wells

SOCIETY FOR THE PROTECTION OF ANCIENT BUILDINGS – See
BATTEN, M.I.: Windmills and Watermills

SOCIETY OF ANTIQUARIES: Newington-next-Sittingbourne,
Organisations, Rochester Cathedral, Sittingbourne

See Also – ELLISTON-ERWOOD, Frank Charles: West Malling

SOCIETY OF CIRPLANOLOGISTS: Religious Denominations

SOCIETY OF GENEALOGISTS: Genealogical Records

SOCIETY OF THE HUNDRED OF SHAMEL, HOO AND GRAIN: Kent, North
West

SOCIETY OF SCRIBES, ILLUMINATORS: Maidstone

SOIL SURVEY OF GREAT BRITAIN: Romney Marsh

SOME NOTES ON THE WRITINGS...: Dickens, Charles

SOMERS-COCKS, Henry L.: Edenbridge

SOMERVELL, David Churchill: Kent Authors and Literature,
Tonbridge

SOMERVILLE, P.P.: Hackington

SOMNER, William: Canterbury, Chartham, Coastal Defences,
Gavelkind, History and Archaeology, Kent Authors and
Literature

"SON OF THE MARSHES", pseud.: Milton Regis, Kent Authors and
Literature, Kent, North West

SONGS OF THE TEMPLE: Gillingham

SONNETS AND STANZAS...: Sandwich

SORRELL, Alan: Canterbury

SOTHEBY AND CO. Auctioneers: Appledore

SOUTH, Robert: Rochester Cathedral

SOUTH-EAST DEVELOPMENT BOARD: Industry and Trade

SOUTH-EAST ECONOMIC PLANNING COUNCIL: Kent

SOUTH-EAST ENGLAND DEVELOPMENT BOARD: Industry and
Trade

SOUTH-EAST JOINT PLANNING TEAM: Kent

SOUTH-EAST METROPOLITAN REGIONAL HOSPITAL BOARD:
Hospitals

"SOUTH-EASTERN", pseud.: Road Transport

SOUTH-EASTERN AND CHATHAM RAILWAY CO.: Chatham,
Folkestone, Kent, Railways

SOUTH-EASTERN AND HASTINGS RAILWAY: Railways

SOUTH-EASTERN BIRD REPORT: Natural History

SOUTH-EASTERN CLERICAL AND LAY CHURCH ALLIANCE:
Religious Denominations

SOUTH-EASTERN COLLEGE MAGAZINE: Ramsgate

SOUTH-EASTERN ELECTRICITY BOARD: Public Utilities

SOUTH-EASTERN ELECTRICITY COUNCIL: Public Utilities

SOUTH-EASTERN GAS BOARD: Public Utilities

SOUTH-EASTERN GAS CONSULTATIVE COUNCIL: Public
Utilities

SOUTH-EASTERN GAZETTE: Maidstone

THE SOUTH-EASTERN NATURALIST: Natural History

SOUTH-EASTERN RAILWAY: Channel Tunnel, Chislehurst,
Folkestone, Hythe, Railways, Sevenoaks,
Ships and Shipping, Tunbridge Wells

SOUTH-EASTERN SOCIETY OF ARCHITECTS: Architecture

SOUTH-EASTERN TRUSTEE SAVINGS BANK: Industry and
Trade

SOUTH-EASTERN UNION OF SCIENTIFIC SOCIETIES:
Folkestone, Kent, Kent, North West; Kent, West;
Natural History, Organisations, Rochester, Woolwich

See Also – GRINLING, C.H.: Tunbridge Wells

SOUTH LONDON FIELD STUDIES JOURNAL: Natural History

SOUTH METROPOLITAN GAS CO.: Public Utilities

SOUTHBOROUGH URBAN DISTRICT COUNCIL: Southborough

SOUTHCOTT, E.J.: Catford

SOUTHDOWN MOTOR SERVICES LTD: Road Transport

SOUTHERN, J.A.: Bromley

SOUTHERN, L.W.: Cinque Ports, Colne, River

SOUTHERN, Richard William: Canterbury Cathedral,
Archbishops

THE SOUTHERN COAST OF ENGLAND: Coastline

SOUTHERN RAILWAY: Ashford, Dover, Kent, Railways,
Ships and Shipping

SOUTHEY, H.J.: Dover

SOUTHOUSE, Thomas: Faversham

SPAIN, Robert James: Len, River

SPALDING, Helen: Tunbridge Wells

SPAN KENT LTD.: New Ash Green

SPARKE, John: Deal, Kent Authors and Literature

SPARVEL-BAYLY, J.A.: Customs, Dartford, Higham, Kent
  Authors and Literature, Swanscombe

SPASTICS SOCIETY: Medway Towns

SPEAIGHT, Robert: Canterbury Cathedral, Archbishops

"SPECTATOR", pseud.: Isle-of-Thanet

SPEECHES DELIVERED AT THE KENT COUNTY MEETING, 1828:
  Maidstone

SPEIRS, John: Chaucer, Geoffrey

SPENCE, G.M.: Bromley

SPENCE, Graeme: Coastal Waters

SPENCER, Frank: Penge

SPENCER, Nathaniel: Kent

SPENCER, Peggy - See SPENCER, Frank: Penge

SPENDER, J.A.: Kent Authors and Literature

SPICER, Howard: Gravesend

SPIERS, R.E.A.: Tunbridge Wells

SPILKA, Mark: Dickens, Charles

SPILLETT, H.C.: Canterbury

SPILLETT, P.J.: Canterbury

SPOUSE, William: Kent Authors and Literature

SPRANGE, J.: Tunbridge Wells

SPRAT, Thomas: History and Archaeology, Rochester Cathedral

SPRAY, Leonard: Lee

SPRIGGE, Elizabeth: Biography

SPRINGETT, W.D.: Maidstone

SPROAT, Iain - See SYKES, Adam: Churchill, Winston S.

SPROTT, Thomas: Kent Authors and Literature

SPRY, John Hume: Margate

SPURLING, Cuthbert Terrence: Elmstone, Otham, Preston-by-
  Wingham, Stourmouth

SPURRELL, F.C.J.: Crayford, Dartford, Erith, History and
  Archaeology, Rivers

SQUERRYES COURT: Westerham

SQUIRES, A.W.: Erith

SQUIRRELL, F.C.: Tunbridge Wells

STACE, R.A.: Folkestone, Hythe, Sandgate, Tunbridge Wells

STAFFORD, Ann: Aylesford

STAFFORD, Frederick H.: Greenhithe

STAFFORD, H.: Lewisham

STAGG, Frank Noel: Ash-by-Wrotham, Chiddingstone, Offham,
  Penshurst, Plaxtol, Ridley, Seal, Shipbourne, Tonbridge,
  West Malling, Wrotham

STAHLSCHMIDT, J.C.L.: Churches

STAHLSCHMIDT v WALFORD: Trials

STANLEY, Vernon: Canterbury Cathedral, Archbishops

STALLYBRASS, F.H.S. - See MUMBY, F.A.: Hayes and Keston

STAMP, Lawrence Dudley - See Land Utilisation Survey
of Britain: Kent

STANDEN, A.O.: Maidstone

STANDEN, E.J.: Pembury

STANDEN, Hugh Wyatt: Kippington

STANDEN, Mary Eileen: Pembury

STANDING CONFERENCE ON LONDON REGIONAL PLANNING:
  Kent

STANHOPE, George. Dean of Canterbury: Kent Authors
  and Literature, Maidstone

STANHOPE, James Richard. 7th Earl: Chevening

STANHOPE, Philip Henry: Hayes and Keston, Pitt,
  William; Walmer

STANLEY, Arthur Penrhyn: Canterbury, Canterbury
  Cathedral

STANLEY, Frederick: Margate

STANLEY, Mary Catherine. Countess of Derby: Hayes
  and Keston

STANLEY-WRENCH, Margaret: Chaucer, Geoffrey

STANTON, Frederick W.S.: Coastline

STANTON, William: Coastal Waters, Deal

STAPLES, Leslie C.: Dickens, Charles

STAPLETON AND CO.: Kent, East

STAPLETON, T. 2nd Baron Le Despencer: Trials

STAPLEY, William: Tunbridge Wells

"STAR": Kent

STAREY, W.H.: Margate

STARKIE, D.N.H.: Medway Towns

STATHAM, J.C.B.: Loose

STATHAM, Samuel Percy Hammond: Dover

STATUARY OF THE CRYSTAL PALACE: Crystal Palace

STATUTES OF THE CATHEDRAL...: Canterbury Cathedral

STAUNTON FAMILY: Penge

STAWELL, Mrs. R.: Kent

STEAD, Richard: History and Archaeology

STEAD, W.T.: Crystal Palace

STEADMAN, W.H.: Northfleet

STEAM PACKET COMPANION: Coastline

STEAMBOAT COMPANION: Coastline

STEAMBOAT GUIDE TO GREENWICH, WOOLWICH AND GRAVESEND
...: Thames, River

STEANE, J.B.: Marlowe, Christopher

STEBBING, W.P.D.: Ash-next-Sandwich, Crayford,
  Deal, Finglesham, Great Mongham, Sandwich,
  Sholden, Speldhurst

See Also - HARDMAN, F.W.: Stonar
            MATTINGLY, Harold: Richborough

STEED, H.E. - See Tonbridge School Registers:
  Tonbridge

STEED, Wickham: Coal

STEELE, E.: Erith

STEELE, Gordon: Greenhithe

STEER, Francis W.: Bromley

STEERS, James Alfred: Coastline

STEINMAN, G. Steinman: Cudham

STEPHENS, J.A.: Chatham

STEPHENS, James: Tunbridge Wells
See Also - COLBRAN, John. Publisher: Tunbridge Wells

STEPHENSON, Mill - See GRIFFIN, Ralph: Monumental Inscriptions

STEPHENSON, Robert - See RENDEL, James M.: Margate

STEPHENSON, Mrs. Theodore: Genealogical Records

STEVENS AND SON. Publishers: Canterbury Cathedral

STEVENS, John: Maidstone

STEVENSON, R. Scott: Chislehurst, Darwin, Charles

STEWART, Cecil: Sutton-at-Hone

STEWART, D.D.: Maidstone

STEWART, H.L: Churchill, Winston S.

STIRRY, Thomas: Kent Authors and Literature

STOCK, H.: Folkestone

STOCKDALE, Frederick Wilton Litchfield: History and Archaeology

STOCKER, John J.: Genealogical Records

STODDART, Anna M.: Penshurst

STOKER, Hugh: Sport

STOKES, H.G.: Coastline

STOKOE, H.R.: Tonbridge

STONACH, George W.: Gillingham

STONE, J. Harris: St. Margaret's Bay, St. Mary's Bay

STONARD, John: East Malling

STONE, John George Bosworth: Kent Authors and Literature

STONE, John M.: Blackheath, Greenwich

STONE, Phyllis: Dickens, Charles

STONEACRE, Otham: Otham

STONEHOUSE, J.H.: Dickens, Charles

STONER, J.: Canterbury Cathedral, Rochester Cathedral

STORER, James Sergeant: Kent

STOREY, A.J.: Thames, River

STOREY, G.A.: Kent

STOREY, Gladys: Dickens, Charles

STORR, Francis: Canterbury

STORRS, W. Townsend: Pembury

STORY OF HENLEYS: Gravesend

STOUR MUSIC: Wye

STOYEL, A.D.: Shoreham

STRACHAN, C. Gordon: Dickens, Charles

STRAHAN, A.: Coal, Ebbsfleet, Ramsgate

STRAKER, Ernest: Industry and Trade, Weald

STRANGE, Charles Hilbert: Tunbridge Wells

STRANGE, Edward: Bromley

STRANGE NEWES...: History and Archaeology

STRANGERS' AND VISITORS' COMPANION...: Canterbury

STRANGEWAYS, J.G.V.: Boughton Monchelsea

STRATTON, John Young: Agriculture

STRAUS, Ralph: Dickens, Charles

STREATFIELD, Frank: Maidstone

STREATFIELD, J. Fremlyn: Architecture
See Also - GRAVETT, Kenneth: Agriculture

STREATFIELD, Thomas: History and Archaeology

STREET, George Edward: Stone (Nr. Dartford)

STRONG, D.E.: Eltham

STRONG, Edward: Bromley

STROOD BURIAL BOARD: Strood

STROOD RURAL DISTRICT COUNCIL: Kent, North West

STROOD WATER WORKS CO.: Strood

STRUTT, Elizabeth: Ramsgate

STRYPE, John: Canterbury Cathedral, Archbishops

STUBBLEFIELD, C.J.: Coal

STUBBS. Publishers - See Town and County Trades Directories Ltd.: Industry and Trade

STUBBS, William: Canterbury Cathedral, Archbishops; Kent Authors and Literature

STUDIES IN KENTISH CHALK: Geology

STUKELEY, William: History and Archaeology, Kent

STURDEE, Thankful: Deptford

STYLES, E.A.: Sevenoaks

STYRING, John S. - See CLEGG, W. Paul: Ships and Shipping

SUBURBAN HOMES OF LONDON: Kent, North West

SUCKLING, Florence Horatio: Biography

SUGDEN, A.N.B.: Cricket, Shortlands

SUMMER EXCURSIONS...: Isle-of-Thanet, Kent, Tunbridge Wells

SUMMERLY, Felix: Canterbury, Cobham, Erith, Rochester

SUMMERS, D.L.: Chatham

SUMMERSON, J. - See LEFTWICH, B.R.: Deptford

SUMNER, O.: Folkestone

SUMSION, Peter: Gravesend

SUNDAY TIMES: Hayes and Keston, West Wickham

SUNDERLAND, Oliver: Bexleyheath

SUNDERLAND, S.: Sydenham

SUPPLEMENT TO THE POLL BOOK: Elections

SUPPRESSION OF SACRED MUSIC: Margate

SURREY AND KENT SEWER COMMISSION: Drainage

SURRIDGE, R.G.: Bromley

SURTEES, Rev. Scott F: History and Archaeology

SURTZ, Edward: Rochester Cathedral

SURVEY OF THE ROAD...: Roads

TIFFEN, William: Folkestone, Hythe

TIFFIN, Alfred W.: Goudhurst

TILDEN, Philip: Allington, Lympne, Saltwood, Westerham

TILLEY, Ernest W.: Gravesend

TILLING, W.G.: Railways

TILLOTSON, John. Archbishop of Canterbury, 1630-94: Canterbury Cathedral, Archbishops

TILLOTT, Alan Theodore - See CLARKE, Edward Brian Stanley: Military and Naval History

TIMBS, John: Architecture

"TIMES": Churchill, Winston S.

TIMMIS, L.B. - See BOWEN, M.: Orpington

TIMPSON, Henry C.: Greenwich

TIMPSON, Thomas: Religious Denominations

TIPPING, H. Avray: Chevening

TISDALL, E.E.D.: Chislehurst

TIVIOLI GARDENS: Margate

TOASE, William: Religious Denominations

TOC H - CANTERBURY BRANCH: Canterbury

TODD, H.I.: Canterbury Cathedral

TODD, Henry John: Canterbury Cathedral

TOKE, N.E.: Folkestone

TOLDERVY, William: History and Archaeology

TOM, John Nichols - See COURTENAY, Sir William P.H.: Canterbury

TOMBLESON, W.: Medway, River; Thames, River

TOMLIN, E.W.F.: Dickens, Charles

TOMLINSON, Charles: Crystal Palace

TOMLINSON, F.W.: Canterbury Cathedral
See Also - Sandwich Borough Council: Sandwich

TOMLINSON, Norman: Gillingham

TOMMOS, Shirley: Goudhurst

TOMPSETT, B.P.: Matfield

TOMS, H.S.: Higham

TOMSON AND WOTTON LTD.: Isle-of-Thanet, World War I

TONBRIDGE FREE LIBRARY: Rochester, Tonbridge

TONBRIDGE LEGENDS: Legends, Tonbridge

TONBRIDGE PUBLICITY COMMITTEE: Tonbridge

TONBRIDGE RURAL DISTRICT COUNCIL: Kent, West

TONBRIDGE URBAN DISTRICT COUNCIL: Tonbridge

TONKS, Rev. Charles Frederick: Canterbury, Walmer

TONNET, Pierre: Chislehurst

TOOKEY, G.W.: Beckenham

TOOMER, Mrs. Ann Elger: Preston (Nr. Wingham)

TOOTH FAMILY HISTORY: Cranbrook

TOPHAM, John: Dover

TOPLEY, William - See FOSTER, C. le Neve: Medway, River

TOPLEY, William: Agriculture, Coastal Waters, Geology, Hythe, Weald

"TOPOGRAPHER": Kent

TOPOGRAPHICAL ASSOCIATION OF GREAT BRITAIN: Deal

TOPOGRAPHICAL MISCELLANIES: Canterbury, Nonington

TOPOGRAPHICAL QUARTERLY: Genealogical Records, History and Archaeology

TOPOGRAPHICAL SCENES: Dover

TOPOGRAPHY OF MAIDSTONE: Maidstone

TORR, V.J. - See CLARKE, R.G.: Folkestone

TORRENS, R.: Rochester

TORRINGTON. Viscount: Agriculture

TOTTEL, Richard: Kent Authors and Literature

TOUCHEFEU-MEYNIER, Odette: Canterbury

TOULMIN, Joshua: Kent Authors and Literature

TOUR THROUGH THE ISLE-OF-THANET...: Isle-of-Thanet, Kent, East

TOURIST'S GUIDE...: Kent

TOUT, Thomas Frederick: Canterbury Cathedral, Archbishops

TOWER HAMLETS LIBRARIES: Dickens, Charles

TOWN, John Nichols - See COURTENAY, Sir W.P.H., pseud.: Biography, Maidstone, Trials

TOWN AND COUNTRY PLANNING, MINISTRY OF: Bromley, Romney Marsh

TOWN AND COUNTRY TRADES DIRECTORIES LTD. Publishers: Industry and Trade

TOWN PLANNING INSTITUTE: Canterbury

TOWNSEND, George: Canterbury, Ramsgate

TOWNSEND, J.H.: Tunbridge Wells

TOWNSEND, William: Canterbury
See Also - MOLONY, Eileen: Canterbury

TOWNSHEND, R.M.: Genealogical Records

TOY, Sidney: Architecture

TRACEY, Herbert: Margate

TRADE AND INDUSTRY, DEPARTMENT OF - ACCIDENTS INVESTIGATION BRANCH: Ruxley

TRADE, BOARD OF: Industry and Trade

TRADE, BOARD OF - RAILWAY DEPARTMENT: Railways

TRADESMEN'S TOKENS...: Cinque Ports, Coins and Tokens, Isle-of-Thanet

TRAILL, Joan - See TRAILL, John: Canterbury

TRAILL, John: Canterbury

TRANSACTIONS OF THE TWO CRIMINALS...: Maidstone, Trials

TRANSPORT, MINISTRY OF: Channel Tunnel, Dartford, Dover, Folkestone, Gillingham, Greenhithe, Longfield, Maidstone, Railways, Roads, Sevenoaks, Swanley, Westerham

TRANSPORT, MINISTRY OF - COMMITTEE ON ROAD SAFETY: Gillingham

TRANSPORT AND CIVIL AVIATION, MINISTRY OF - MARINE SAFETY DIVISION: Maidstone

"A TRAVELLER", pseud.: Kent

TRAVELLERS' MAGAZINE: Gravesend, Herne Bay, Sheerness

T Cont'd

TRAVELLER'S MISCELLANY: Dover

TRAVIS, Anthony Stewart: Channel Tunnel

TREANOR, Thomas Stanley: Goodwin Sands

TRENCH, F. Chenevix: Orpington

TRENT, Christopher: Kent

TREVOR-ROPER, Hugh Redwald: Canterbury Cathedral, Archbishops

TREVORS, Trent: Kent Authors and Literature

TREWIN, J.C.: Biography

TRIAL AND SENTENCE OF THE KNIGHT OF MALTA: Canterbury, Trials

TRIAL OF...ARTHUR O'CONNOR: Maidstone, Trials

TRIAL OF JAMES O'COIGLY: Maidstone, Trials

TRIAL OF MR. SAVILL: Dover

TRIMNELL, Charles. Bishop of Norwich: Tunbridge Wells

TRINITY HOUSE: Coastal Waters, Deptford

TRIP TO GREENHITHE...: Thames, River

TRIPP, H. Alker ("Leigh Hoe", pseud.): Coastal Waters

TRISTRAM, Ernest William: Brook, Canterbury Cathedral, Churches

TRISTRAM, W. Outram: Cinque Ports, Roads

TRITTON, Joseph Herbert: Biography

TROLLOPE, Constance A.N.: Beckenham

TROTTER, William Edward: Kent, North West

TROWELL, Thomas: Industry and Trade

TRUE HISTORY OF A KENTISH LAWYER: Biography

A TRUE REHEARSALL AND SURVEY OF ALL THE BARQUES AND VESSELLS...
AT MARGATE: Margate, Ships and Shipping

TRUE STATE OF FACTS...: Ramsgate

TRUMBLE, Alfred: Dickens, Charles

TUBBS, Douglas Burnell: Inns

TUCK, Henry: Railways

TUCK, Oswald: New Cross

TUCKER, Alfred G.: Canterbury

TUFTON, Sackville. 9th Earl of Thanet: Trials

See Also - THANET, Sackville Tufton, 9th Earl of: History and
    Archaeology

TUKER, Sir Francis: Dover

TUNBRIDGE, J.S.: Great Chart

TUNBRIDGE MISCELLANY: Tunbridge Wells

TUNBRIDGE WELLS ADVERTISER: Tunbridge Wells

TUNBRIDGE WELLS AND DISTRICT COUNCIL OF SOCIAL SERVICE:
    Tunbridge Wells

TUNBRIDGE WELLS BOROUGH COUNCIL: Tunbridge Wells

TUNBRIDGE WELLS LITERACY SOCIETY: Tunbridge Wells

TUNBRIDGE WELLS NATURAL HISTORY AND PHILOSOPHICAL SOCIETY:
    Tunbridge Wells

TUNBRIDGE WELLS OPERA HOUSE: Tunbridge Wells

TUNBRIDGE WELLS PUBLIC LIBRARY: Tunbridge Wells

TUNBRIDGE WELLS TRADESMEN'S ASSOCIATION: Tunbridge Wells

TUNBRIGIALIA: Tunbridge Wells

TUNSTALL, James: Great Chart

TUPLEY, William: Geology

TURMINE, Henry T.D.: Isle-of-Sheppey

TURNER, B.V.: Dover

TURNER, C.F.: Cranbrook

TURNER, Dawson: Natural History

TURNER, E.: Kent

TURNER, G.J.: Canterbury

TURNER, Hawes - See STORR, Francis: Canterbury

TURNER, John: Chatham

TURNER, J.M.W.: Bromley, Kent

TURNER, J.W.: Kent

TURNER, Peter Theophilus: Isle-of-Thanet

TURNER, Sydney K.: Chatham, Medway, River; Upnor

TURNER, Thomas: East Hoathly

TURNOR, Reginald: Kent

See Also - GATE, Phoebe Fenwick: Kent

TURPIN, H.: Margate, Ramsgate

TUTT, James William: Hoo Peninsula

12th KENT RIFLE VOLUNTEERS (DARTFORD): Military
    and Naval History

TWELVE PENNYWORTH OF REFRESHMENT...: Springhead

TWISDEN, Sir John Ramskill: East Malling

TWYMAN, Frank: Biography

TWYSDEN, Sir Roger: History and Archaeology,
    Kent Authors and Literature

TYLER HILL HOUSE: Blean

TYMMS, Samuel: History and Archaeology, Kent

"TYRO", pseud. - See SLADDEN, Dilnot: Kent Authors
    and Literature

TYRO, Carmine, pseud.: Cranbrook

TYRWHITT, Jacqueline: Local Government

TYRWHITT-DRAKE, Sir Garrard: Maidstone

TYRWHITT-DRAKE MUSEUM OF CARRIAGES: Maidstone

TYRWHITT-DRAKE SCRAPBOOK: Maidstone

U

UFTON FAMILY OF TUNSTAL - See Pedigree of
Harlakenden: Genealogical Records

ULLYETT, H.: Folkestone, Natural History

UNDERHILL, Francis: Rochester Cathedral

UNDERGROUND WATER PRESERVATION ASSOCIATION: Public
    Utilities

UNITED KENTISH BRITONS FRIENDLY SOCIETY: Canterbury

UNITED KINGDOM ATOMIC ENERGY AUTHORITY - PRODUCTION
GROUP: Whitstable

UNIVERSITY OF KENT: Canterbury

AN UNPRECEDENTED CASE OF OPPRESSION: Halstead

UNSWORTH, Walter: Dover

UNWIN, T. Fisher. Publisher: Blackheath, Bromley,
    Greenwich, Hayes and Keston

UPCOTT, William: Bibliography

THE UPPER TEN THOUSAND FOR 1877: Biography

"URBAN RUS", pseud.: Sittingbourne

U Cont'd

URQUHART, Fred: Churchill, Winston S.

URRY, Dr. William: Canterbury, Canterbury Cathedral, Canterbury
    Cathedral, Archbishops; Kent Authors and Literature

See Also - Congres International Du IXem Centenaire De L'Arrivee
D'Anselme Au Bec: Canterbury Cathedral, Archbishops

USHERWOOD, P.L.: Medway, River

V

VALENTINE AND SONS LTD. Publishers: Canterbury

"A VALETUDINARIAN", pseud.: Coastline

VALLANCE, Aymer: Biography, Canterbury Cathedral, Cobham,
    Faversham, Harty, Ightham, Lydden, Lynsted, Milton Regis,
    Monumental Inscriptions, Postling, Sundridge, Tonbridge

VALLANCE, L.A.: Otham, Railways

VALLINS, George Henry: Kent Authors and Literature

VALLIS, E.W.H.: Roads

VANE, Sir Henry: Kent Authors and Literature

VANE-TEMPEST, Stewart Charles Stuart Henry. 7th Marquess of
Londonderry: Elections

VAUGHAN, Eliza, pseud.: Reculver

VAUGHAN, H.S.: Kent

VAYNES, Julia de: Kent Authors and Literature

VEALE, Ernest William Partington: Coastal Waters

VENABLES, Bernard: Sport

VERE-HODGE, Hugh Sydenham: Tonbridge

VERHOEVEN, Jack: Sevenoaks

VESEY, Mrs. - See CARTER, Mrs. Elizabeth: Biography

VICKERS, John A.: Canterbury

VICKERSON, Edmund: Westerham

VICTORIA AND ALBERT MUSEUM: Crystal Palace

VICTORIA CORONATION FESTIVAL: Canterbury

VIDLER, John: Maidstone

VIDLER, Leopold Amon: Cinque Ports

VIEW ALBUM OF NEW BROMPTON, ETC.: Medway Towns

VILLIERS, Oliver G.: Saltwood

VINCENT, William Thomas: Erith, History and Archaeology,
    Monumental Inscriptions, Woolwich

VINE, Francis Thomas: Canals, History and Archaeology

VINE, Paul Ashley Laurence: Canals

VINER-BRADY, Noel Edmund - See WOOD, Alan Marshall Muir:
    Folkestone

VIPOND, W.: Deal

"A VISITOR", pseud.: Gravesend

VISITOR'S GUIDE TO THE WATERING PLACES...: Tunbridge Wells

VITA ET PROCESSUS ST. THOMAE: Canterbury Cathedral, Archbishops

"VOICE FROM KENT" pseud.: Agriculture

VOLUNTARY SOCIAL SERVICE IN KENT: Organisations

VOLUNTEER CHORUSES: Hythe

THE VORTIGERN SMUGGLERS' CAVES: Margate

VOX 2 - A MAGAZINE OF POETRY...: Kent Authors and Literature

VOYSEY, Annesley: Kent, Medway, River

W

W., B.: Margate

W., D.: Fordwich

W., F.A.: Margate

W., H.E.: Folkestone

W., H.V.: Isle-of-Thanet

W., J.A. - See WILLMORE, J.A.: Fordwich

WACHER, Harold: Canterbury

WADDAMS, Herbert Montague: Canterbury, Kent
    Authors and Literature

WADDINGTON, Joshua: Margate

WADMORE, Beauchamp: Tonbridge

WADMORE, J.F.: History and Archaeology, Oxenhope,
    Tonbridge, Westenhanger

WAGAR, W. Warren: Wells, Herbert George

WAGENKNECHT, Edward: Dickens, Charles

WAGHORN, H.T.: Cricket

WAGHORN, Thomas: Rochester

WAGSTAFF, J.S.: Road Transport

WAIDE, W.L. - See TYRWHITT, Jacqueline: Local
    Government

WAILES, Rex: Windmills and Watermills

WAINMAN, Paul, pseud. (Mrs. Sylvia MACDOUGALL):
    Faversham

WAINWRIGHT, John: History and Archaeology

WAKE, W.R.: Maidstone

WAKE, William. Archbishop of Canterbury: Kent
    Authors and Literature

WAKEFIELD, W.W.: Sport

WAKELIN, Martin F. - See ORTON, Harold: Dialects

WAKEMAN, Norman: Railways

WALCOTT, Mackenzie E.C.: Canterbury, Churches,
    Coastline, Rochester

WALFORD, Edward: Gravesend, Hayes and Kestone,
    Kent, Kent, North West; Pitt, William

WALISZEWSKI, K.: Deptford

WALKER, Alfred T.: Birchington

WALKER, Colin W.: Canterbury Cathedral

WALKER, Eric Henry: Rotherhithe

WALKER, George: Isle-of-Thanet

WALKER, George P.: Isle-of-Thanet, Richborough

WALKER, J. AND C. Publishers: Sport

WALKER, James: Dover

WALKER, Joyce E.: West Wickham

WALKER, Stella Archer: Kent Authors and Literature

WALKS...: Kent

WALL, Charles de Rochfort: Snodland

WALL, J. Charles: Canterbury

WEBB, A.E.: Harrietsham

WEBB, David B.: Farnborough

WEBB, Edward Alfred: Chislehurst

WEBB, Harold: Kent Authors and Literature

WEBB, Montague: Kent

WEBB MEMORIAL FUND COMMITTEE: Dover

WEBBER, M.: Kent

WEBSTER, Angus Duncan: Greenwich, Natural History

WEBSTER, Graham: Canterbury
See Also - DUDLEY, Donald R.: History and Archaeology

WEBSTER, Leslie - See DAVIDSON, Hilda R. Ellis: Woodnesborough

WEBSTER, V.: Folkestone

WEEKES, Brian: Dartford

WEEKES, Henry: Kent Authors and Literature

WEEKES, W.: Kent Authors and Literature

WEEVER, John: Monumental Inscriptions, Rochester

WEIGALL, Arthur: History and Archaeology

WEIGALL, Rachel: Isle-of-Thanet

WEIR, W.R.: Cricket

WELBY, Mrs.: Canterbury

WELL, Walter G.: Kent, North West

WELL SECTIONS...: Geology

WELLBYE, Reginald: Roads

WELLER, B.R.: Maidstone

WELLER, Samuel: Maidstone

WELLINGTON BANQUET...: Dover

WELLS, Arthur G.: Railways

WELLS, George: Dickens, Charles

WELLS, Herbert George: Folkestone, Wells, Herbert George

WELSBY, Paul Anthony: Canterbury Cathedral, Archbishops

WENYON, H.J.: Military and Naval History

WERNHAM, R.P.: Forest Hill

WEST ASHFORD RURAL DISTRICT COUNCIL: Kent, Mid

WEST, Rebecca: Canterbury

WEST, Richard: Canterbury

WEST KENT ADVERTISER: Dartford

WEST KENT ALMANACK: Kent

WEST KENT BORDER ARCHAEOLOGICAL GROUP: Hayes and Keston

WEST KENT FEDERATION OF WOMEN'S INSTITUTES: Agriculture, Kent, East; Kent, West; Organisations, Recipes

WEST KENT GENERAL HOSPITAL: Maidstone

WEST KENT MEDICO-CHIRURGICAL SOCIETY: Organisations

WEST KENT NATURAL HISTORY, MICROSCOPICAL AND PHOTOGRAPHIC SOCIETY: Natural History, Organisations

WEST KENT AND TUNBRIDGE WELLS MARRIAGE GUIDANCE COUNCIL: Organisations

WEST MALLING AND DISTRICT CO-OPERATIVE LAND HOLDINGS ASSOCIATION LTD.: Organisations, West Malling

WEST WICKHAM CHAMBER OF COMMERCE: West Wickham

WEST WICKHAM COMMUNITY COUNCIL: West Wickham

WEST WICKHAM FESTIVAL WEEK: West Wickham

WEST WICKHAM WOMEN'S INSTITUTE: West Wickham

WESTALL, William: History and Archaeology

WESTBROOK IMPROVEMENTS: Margate

WESTERHAM PARISH COUNCIL: Westerham

WESTERN MOTOR WORKS: Chislehurst, Industry and Trade

WESTGATE-ON-SEA CHAMBER OF COMMERCE: Margate

WESTGATE PRISON: Canterbury

WESTMINSTER BANK LTD.: Sevenoaks

WESTON, Stephen: Richborough

WETHERELT, Alexander: Canterbury, Canterbury Cathedral

WHARTON, T.: Kent Authors and Literature

WHATMAN, Susannah: Maidstone

WHATMORE, Leonard E.: Bobbing, Canterbury, Canterbury Cathedral, Kent Authors and Literature
See Also - FRY, E.T.B.: Thanington
          SHARP, W.: Genealogical Records

WHEATLEY, Sydney William: Rochester, Rochester Cathedral

WHEELER, Clifford: Canterbury

WHEELER, R.E.M.: Dover
See Also - AMOS, E.G.J.: Dover

WHEELER, Rev.: Minster-in-Sheppey

WHEELER, W.H.: Coastline

WHEELER-BENNETT, Sir John: Churchill, Winston S.

WHETMATH, C.F.D.: Railways

WHETMORE, S.A.M.: Biography

WHICHORD, John. Junior: Maidstone

WHICHORD AND SON: Maidstone

THE WHIM: Canterbury

WHISHAW, Francis: Railways

WHISTON, R.: Rochester Cathedral

WHITAKER, E.J.: Roads

WHITAKER, Joseph: Deer Parks

WHITAKER, W.: Geology, Reculver

WHITBREAD AND CO.: Beltring, Industry and Trade, Inns, Kent, Recipes

WHITE, A.C.: Ashurst

WHITEY, Dorothy V.: Groombridge

WHITE, Gleeson: Canterbury Cathedral

WHITE, H.J.O. - See Geological Survey and Museum: Kent, East

WHITE, H.P.: Railways

WHITE, John Baker: Kent Authors and Literature

WHITE, R.E.: Woolwich

WHITE, Thomas Henry: Kent Authors and Literature

WHITEBROOK, J.C.: Canterbury Cathedral, Archbishops

WHITEFIELD, George: Blackheath

WHITEHEAD, Bob: Maidstone

WHITEHEAD, C.J.: Herne Bay

WHITEHEAD, Sir Charles: Agriculture

WHITEHOUSE, Arch.: Gillingham

WHITELOCK, Dorothy: Genealogical Records

WHITESIDE, Thomas: Channel Tunnel

WHITEWALL (MEDWAY) PORTLAND CEMENT CO. LTD.: Industry and Trade

WHITFIELD, O.G.: Bromley

WHITAKER, William: Coal, Geology, Rochester, Wickhambourne, River

WHITING, William: Canterbury, Ospringe

WHITLOCK, Ralph: Natural History

WHITNEY, John: Darent, River; Medway, River

WHITSTABLE CIVIC SOCIETY: Whitstable

WHITSTABLE OYSTER CO. v GANN, Thomas: Whitstable

WHITSTABLE URBAN DISTRICT COUNCIL: Whitstable

WHITTA, Terry: Medway Towns

WHITTEN, Wilfred: Margate

WHO WAS CAXTON?: Tenterden

WHO'S WHO AND WHERE: Tunbridge Wells

WHO'S WHO IN KENT: Biography

WHO'S WHO IN MAIDSTONE: Maidstone

WHORMBY, J.: Deptford

WHYMAN, Herbert Francis: Chatham

WHYMAN, John: History and Archaeology

WIBBERLEY, G.P.: Agriculture
See Also - SYKES, Joseph Donald: Agriculture

WICKHAM, Humphrey: Chatham

WICKHAM, W.: Reculver

"WIDE AWAKE DARTFORD": Dartford

WIGAN, RICHARDSON AND CO.: Agriculture

WIGGINS TEAPE GROUP: Dartford, Industry and Trade

WIKELEY, Nigel: Railways

WILBERFORCE, Henry William: Kent Authors and Literature

WILCOCK, F.: Saltwood

WILCOCKE, James: Kent Authors and Literature

WILCOX, Leslie Arthur: Military and Naval History

WILD, Charles: Canterbury Cathedral

WILD, Rowland: Kent

WILD FLOWERS AT DOVER: Dover, Natural History

WILDISH, W.T.: Rochester, Rochester Cathedral

WILKIE, C.T.: Genealogical Records

WILKIE, Christopher Hales: Genealogical Records

WILKIN, W.H.: Chilham

WILKINS, William Clyde: Dickens, Charles

WILKINSON, Edward: Biography, Headcorn, Orlestone, Shadoxhurst

WILKINSON, Gladys J.: Whitstable

WILKINSON, J.J.: Kemsing

WILKINSON, John - See Domesday Book: History and Archaeology

WILKINSON, John Eric: Canterbury

WILKINSON, John J.: Erith

WILKS, George: Cinque Ports, Hythe

WILL SHE BEAR IT?: Weald

WILLARD, Barbara: History and Archaeology, Penshurst

WILLCOCK, John: Plaxtol

WILLCOCKS, F.: Saltwood

WILLEMENT, Thomas: Canterbury Cathedral, Davington

WILLETT, Charles: Canterbury, Canterbury Cathedral

WILLIAM ADAMS...: Gillingham

WILLIAM OF BYHOLTE: History and Archaeology

WILLIAM OF MALMESBURY: Canterbury

WILLIAM OF POICTOU: Dover

WILLIAMS, Audrey: Canterbury

WILLIAMS, C.G. LTD.: Kent

WILLIAMS, Charles: Canterbury Cathedral, Archbishops

WILLIAM DE SHOREHAM: Kent Authors and Literature

WILLIAMS, Emily: Canterbury Cathedral

WILLIAMS, F.: Hawkhurst

WILLIAMS, Geoffrey: Cinque Ports

WILLIAMS, Harry: Westerham

WILLIAMS, Irene: Dialects

WILLIAMS, J. Publisher: Dartford

WILLIAMS, Marguerite: Woolwich

WILLIAMS, Neville: Smuggling

WILLIAMS, R.A.: Hartley

WILLIAMS, R.H. Isaac: Elham

WILLIAMS, S. - See ORWIN, C.S.: Wye

WILLIAMSON, Catherine Ellis: Canterbury, Kent Authors and Literature

WILLIAMSON, Ethel: Maidstone

WILLIAMSON, G.C.: West Malling

WILLIAMSON, G.J.: Kent Authors and Literature

WILLIAMSON, Hugh Ross: Canterbury Cathedral, Canterbury Cathedral, Archbishops

WILLIAMSON, J.A.: Coastal Waters

WILLIAMSON, Sir Joseph: Rochester

WILLIFORD, Jean: Faversham

WILLIS, Arthur James: Genealogical Records

WILLIS, Browne: Churches

WILLIS, Peter J.: Gravesend

WILLIS, Robert: Canterbury Cathedral

WILLIS, W.G. - See PHILLIPS, G.A.: Kent

WILLIS, William: Kent

WILLMORE, J.A. (W., J.A.): Fordwich

WILLOUGHBY, W.F.: St. Mary Cray, St. Paul Cray

WILLS, Charles: Godmersham

WILLS, F.G.B.: Rochester

WILLS, W. David: Bromley

WILLS, William: Dover

WILMOT, Edward P.: Kent Authors and Literature, Tonbridge

WILSON, Charles. Publisher: Medway, River; Thames, River

WILSON, Effingham. Publisher: Gravesend, Medway, River;
    Thames, River

WILSON, F.P.: Marlowe, Christopher

WILSON, Harris: Wells, Herbert George

WILSON, Henry: Genealogical Records

WILSON, J.D.: Coastal Defences; Thames, River

WILSON, James: Military and Naval History

WILSON, John: Kent Authors and Literature

WILSON, Maurice: Ships and Shipping

WILSON, Mona: Penshurst

WILSON, S. Gordon: Canterbury, Dickens, Charles; Pilgrims Way,
    Thanington

WILSON, S.R. Publisher: Isle-of-Thanet

WILSON, Sydney: Faversham

WILSON, Thomas: Bromley, Kent Authors and Literature, Tunbridge
    Wells

WILSON, W. Publisher: Folkestone, Hythe, Sandgate

WILSON, William Eric: Coastal Waters

WILSON, W.T. - See WILSON, William Eric: Coastal Waters

WILTON, Eric: Bromley

WILTSHIRE, F.A.R.: Kent, North West

WINBOLT, Samuel Edward: Folkestone, Kent

WINFIELD, J.E.: Gillingham

WING, George: Dickens, Charles

WINGFIELD-STRATFORD, Esme: Biography, Churchill, Winston S.;
    Cobham

WINKLES, H. AND B.: Rochester Cathedral

WINNIFRITH, Alfred: Biography

WINSCOM, Jane Anne: Kent

WINSER, Lilian: Legends, Weald

WINSTEDT, Eric Otto: Maidstone

WINSTON, Richard: Canterbury Cathedral, Archbishops

WINTER, William: Canterbury

WINTLE, Alfred Daniel: Biography

"WISE MAN OF THE EASE" pseud.: Dover, Folkestone, Kent Authors and
    Literature

WITCHELL, W.M.: Greenwich

WITHERDEN, G.: Isle-of-Thanet

WITHERS, Hartley - See BELL, G. AND SONS. Publishers:
    Canterbury, Rochester, Minister-in-Sheppey

WITTING, Clifford: Eltham

WOLFE, Barry J.: Romney Marsh

WOLFE-AYLWARD, A.E.: Westerham

WOLFF, Michael - See VIDLER, John: Maidstone

WOLFFRAM, H.: Blackheath, Lee

WOLLARD, T.J.: Kent

WOLLASTON, Francis: Chislehurst

WOLLASTON, Sir Gerald Woods: Deal

WOLS (Alfred Otto Wolfgang Schulze): Gillingham

WOMEN'S INSTITUTE: Borough Green, Farnborough,
    Farningham, Halling, Organisations, West Wickham

WOOD, A.C.: Canterbury Cathedral, Archbishops

WOOD, A.W.: Lee

WOOD, Alan Marshall Muir: Channel Tunnel, Folkestone

WOOD, Derek: World War II
    See Also - DEMPSTER, Derek: Dover

WOOD, Elizabeth: Canterbury

WOOD, Frederick J.: Military and Naval History

WOOD, G.V.: Geology, Weald

WOOD, J.G.: Margate

WOOD, John George: Kent

WOOD, John Henry: History and Archaeology

WOOD, Margaret: Plaxtol

WOOD, M.B.: Tonbridge

WOOD, Susan: Canterbury

WOOD, Walter: Ships and Shipping

WOOD, Walter F.: Tonge

WOODCOCK, Audrey M.: Canterbury

WOODCOCK, Brian Lindsay: Canterbury Cathedral

WOODCOCK, George: Railways, Wye

WOODGATE, Gordon: Biography

WOODGATE, Mildred Violet: Canterbury Cathedral,
    Archbishops

WOODHEAD, E.W.: Kent Authors and Literature

WOODHOUSE, P.S.: Medway, River

WOODHOUSE, Reginald Illingworth: Canterbury Cathedral,
    Archbishops

WOODMAN, George: Whitstable

WOODMAN, Greta - See WOODMAN, George: Whitstable

WOODRUFF, Charles Eveleigh: Blean, Canterbury,
    Canterbury Cathedral, Churches, Fordwich,
    Genealogical Records

WOODRUFF, Cumberland H.: Kent Authors and Literature,
    Margate, Upchurch, Walmer

WOODRUFFE, S.M.: Genealogical Records

WOODS, Frederick: Churchill, Winston S.

WOODTHORPE, T.J.: Isle-of-Sheppey, Medway, River; Military and Naval History

WOODWARD, B.B. - See KENWARD, A.S.: Geology

WOODWARD, Grace Steele: Gravesend

WOODWARD, H.B.: Geology

WOODWARD, Matthew: Folkestone

WOOLDRIDGE, Sidney William: Geology, Kent, Weald

WOOLER, T.J.: Maidstone, Trials

WOOLLARD, T.J.: Kent

WOOLLEY, Frank: Cricket

WOOLLEY, R.M.: Canterbury Cathedral

WOOLMER, Samuel: Sheerness

WOOLNER, Anne: Biddenden

WOOLNOTH, William: Canterbury Cathedral

WOOLWICH AND DISTRICT ANTIQUARIAN SOCIETY: Bromley, Erith, Railways, Roads, Woolwich

See Also - ELLISTON;ERWOOD, Frank Charles: Woolwich

WOOLWICH ANTIQUARIAN SOCIETY: Erith

WOOLWICH BOROUGH COUNCIL: Woolwich

WOOLWICH COUNCIL OF SOCIAL SERVICE: Woolwich

WOOLWICH POLYTECHNIC: Woolwich

WORD-FOR-WORD - AN ENCYCLOPEDIA OF BEER: Industry and Trade

WORDSWORTH ROAD SCHOOL, STOKE NEWINGTON: Whitstable

WORKERS' EDUCATIONAL ASSOCIATION: Gravesend, Orpington

WORKS, MINISTRY OF - Guides - See Under Individual Places and Public Buildings and Works, Ministry of

WORLD'S PRESS NEWS AND ADVERTISERS' REVIEW: Industry and Trade

WORMALD, H.: Agriculture

WORRALL, G.A.: Geology

WORSFOLD, Frederick Henry: Barfrestone, Birchington, Swalecliffe

WORSFOLDE, E.M.: Dover

WORSHIPFUL COMPANY OF SKINNERS: Tonbridge

WORSSAM, B.C.: Staplehurst

WORTHAM, H.E.: Gravesend

WORTHINGTON, B.: Dover

WOTTON, Sir Henry: Canterbury, Kent Authors and Literature

WOTTON, Thomas: Boughton Malherbe, History and Archaeology

WRAIGHT, A.D.: Marlowe, Christopher

WREN SOCIETY: Greenwich

WRENCH, Frederick: Stowting

WRIGHT, Aubrey K.W.: Lower Halstow, West Wickham

WRIGHT, Charles James: Kent Authors and Literature

WRIGHT, Christopher John: Footpaths and Commons, Pilgrims Way

WRIGHT, H. Roy: Folkestone

WRIGHT, I.G. Publisher: Medway Towns

WRIGHT, John - See Humble Petition: History and Archaeology

WRIGHT, Robert: World War II

WRIGHT, Sydney Fowler: Kent Authors and Literature

WRIGHT, Thomas: Aylesford, Canterbury

WROTHAM PARISH COUNCIL: Borough Green, Wrotham

WURTEMBERG STUFFED ANIMALS CO. LTD.: Crystal Palace

WYATT, M. Digby: Crystal Palace

WYATT, Sir Stanley Charles: Allington, Chilham

WYE COLLEGE ARCHAEOLOGICAL SOCIETY: Wye

WYE COLLEGE: Wye

See Also - London University, Wye College: Agriculture, Weald

WYE HISTORICAL SOCIETY: Wye

WYLLIE, James: Agriculture, Kent Authors and Literature

WYLLIE, M.A. - See WYLLIE, W.L.: Coastline, Thames, River

WYLLIE, W.L.: Coastline, Isle-of-Thanet, Thames, River

WYNBURNE, Victor Barry: Woodchurch

WYNDHAM, George: Kent Authors and Literature

WYNDHAM, Guy - See MACKAIL, J.W.: Biography

WYNDHAM, Richard: Kent

Y

YATES, Elizabeth: Chilham

YATES, K.C. - See FOLLEY, Roger Roland Westwell: Agriculture

YEANDLE, W.H.: Stone-in-Oxney

YEOMAN, Thomas: Stour, River

YGLESIAS, J.R.C.: Crystal Palace

YOAKLEY CHARITY: Margate

YOKOSUKE CITY COUNCIL: Gillingham

YONGE, Charlotte: Dover

YORKE, Philip C.: Dover

YORKSHIRE GEOLOGICAL SOCIETY: Chatham

YOUDEN, George H. - See EMBRY, Bernard: Kent, South East

YOUNG, Kenneth: Churchill, Winston S.

YOUNG, M.G.: Tonbridge

YOUNG, Percy: Medway Towns

YOUNG ENTERPRISE, CHATHAM: Chatham

"A YOUNG LADY", pseud.: Kent Authors and Literature, Ramsgate

YOUNG WOMEN'S CHRISTIAN ASSOCIATION: Canterbury

YOUNGHUSBAND, Ethel: Tunbridge Wells

YOUNGMAN, E.: Canterbury

Z

ZION CHAPEL: Genealogical Records

ZOUCH, Thomas: Penshurst